Rick Steves'
FRANCE
2008

P9-ELG-570

Rick Steves & Steve Smith

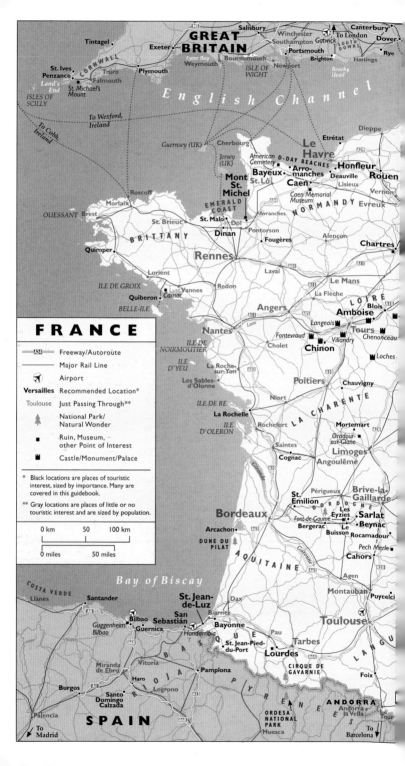

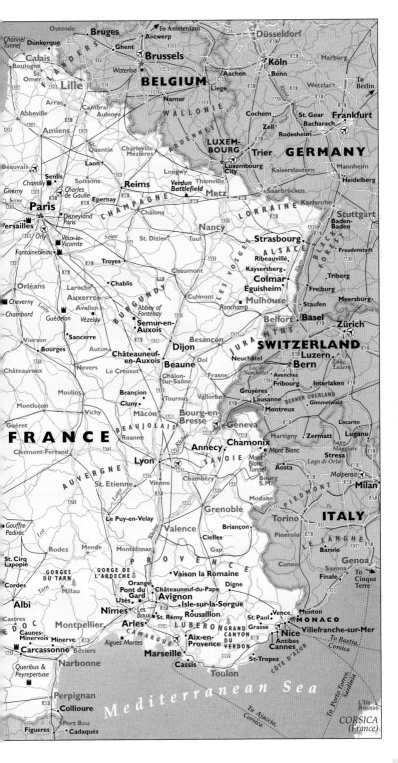

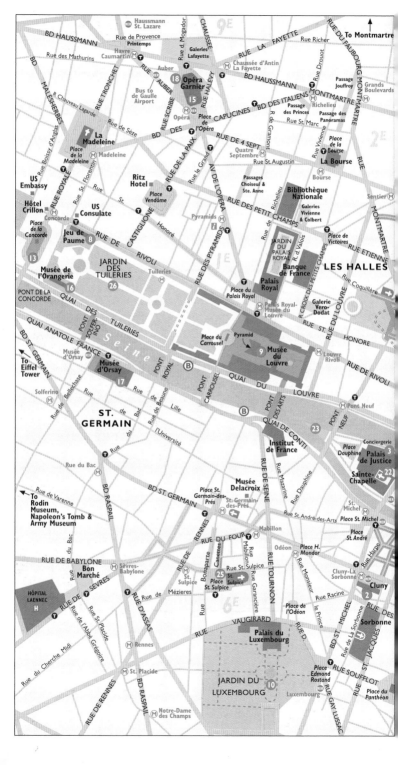

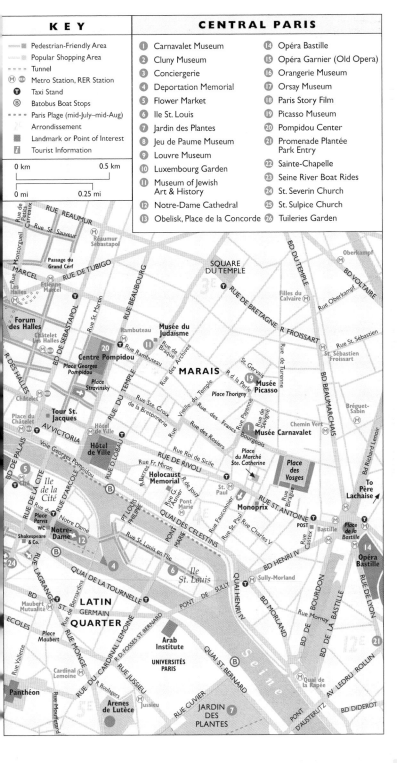

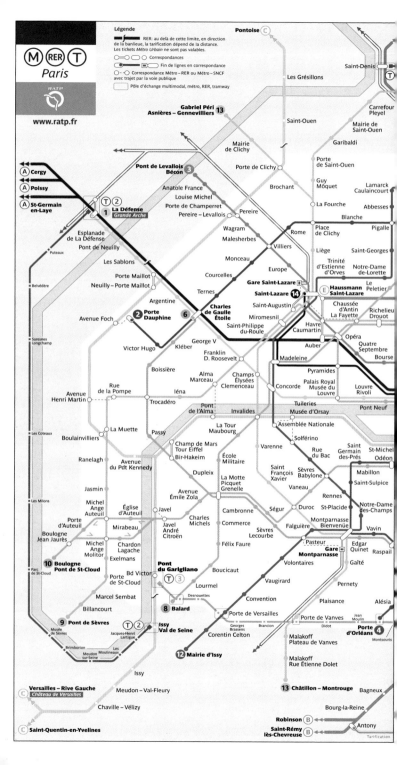

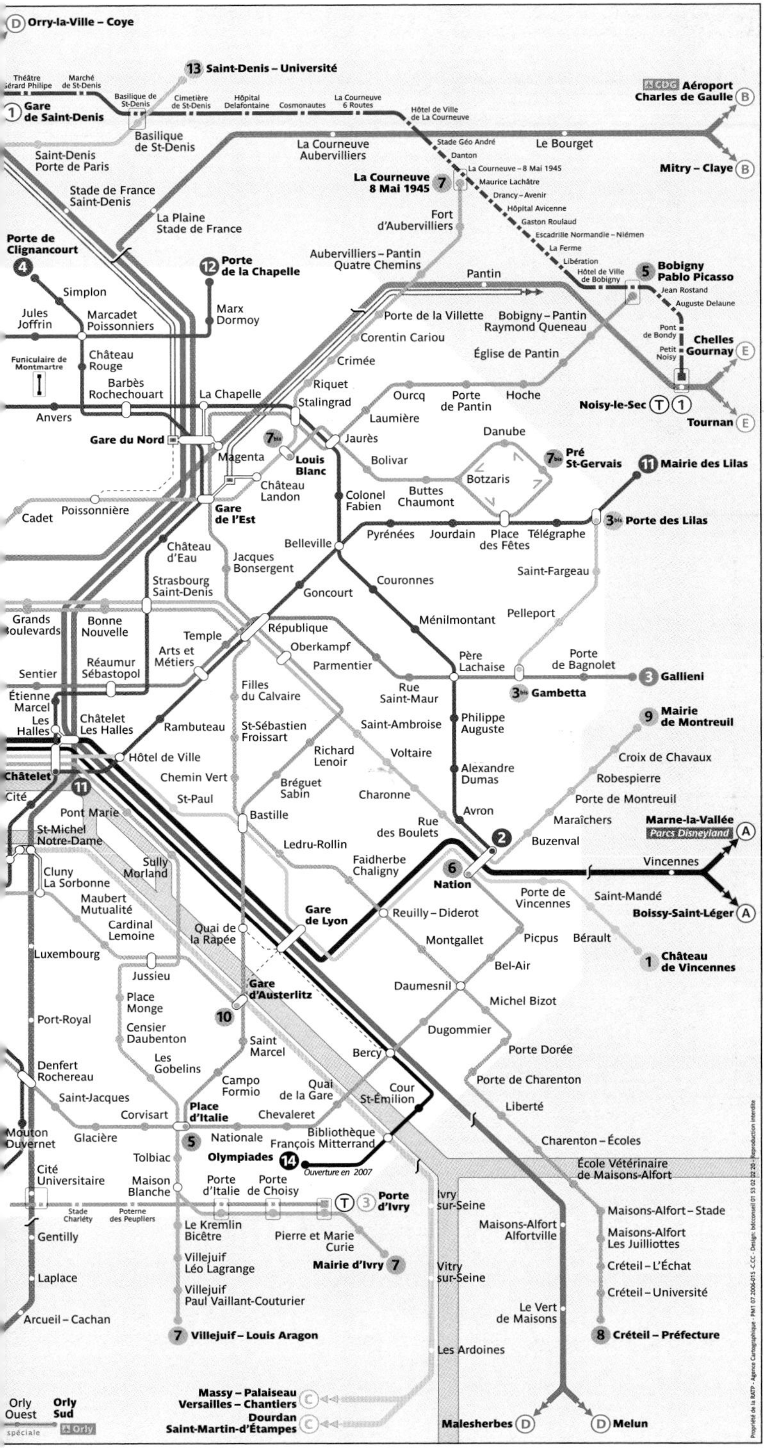
D Orry-la-Ville – Coye
13 Saint-Denis – Université
Théâtre Gérard Philipe
Marché de St-Denis
Basilique de St-Denis
Cimetière de St-Denis
Hôpital Delafontaine
Cosmonautes
La Courneuve 6 Routes
Hôtel de Ville de La Courneuve
1 Gare de Saint-Denis
Basilique de St-Denis
CDG Aéroport Charles de Gaulle B
Saint-Denis Porte de Paris
La Courneuve Aubervilliers
Stade Géo André
Le Bourget
Danton
Mitry – Claye B
La Courneuve 8 Mai 1945 7
La Courneuve – 8 Mai 1945
Maurice Lachâtre
Drancy – Avenir
Stade de France Saint-Denis
Hôpital Avicenne
Gaston Roulaud
La Plaine Stade de France
Fort d'Aubervilliers
Escadrille Normandie – Niémen
La Ferme
Porte de Clignancourt
4
Aubervilliers – Pantin Quatre Chemins
Libération
Hôtel de Ville de Bobigny
5 Bobigny Pablo Picasso
12 Porte de la Chapelle
Pantin
Jean Rostand
Simplon
Auguste Delaune
Jules Joffrin
Marcadet Poissonniers
Marx Dormoy
Porte de la Villette
Bobigny – Pantin Raymond Queneau
Pont de Bondy
Corentin Cariou
Chelles Gournay E
Petit Noisy
Funiculaire de Montmartre
Château Rouge
Église de Pantin
Crimée
Barbès Rochechouart
Riquet
Ourcq
Porte de Pantin
Hoche
La Chapelle
Stalingrad
Noisy-le-Sec T 1
Anvers
Laumière
Tournan E
Gare du Nord
Jaurès
Danube
7bis
Magenta
Louis Blanc
Bolivar
7bis Pré St-Gervais
11 Mairie des Lilas
Botzaris
Château Landon
Colonel Fabien
Buttes Chaumont
Cadet
Poissonnière
Gare de l'Est
Pyrénées
Jourdain
Place des Fêtes
Télégraphe
3bis Porte des Lilas
Belleville
Château d'Eau
Jacques Bonsergent
Saint-Fargeau
Strasbourg Saint-Denis
Couronnes
Goncourt
Grands Boulevards
Bonne Nouvelle
Ménilmontant
Pelleport
Temple
République
Oberkampf
Arts et Métiers
Parmentier
Père Lachaise
Porte de Bagnolet
Réaumur Sébastopol
Sentier
3 Gallieni
Étienne Marcel
Filles du Calvaire
Rue Saint-Maur
3bis Gambetta
Les Halles
Châtelet Les Halles
Rambuteau
St-Sébastien Froissart
Saint-Ambroise
Philippe Auguste
9 Mairie de Montreuil
Hôtel de Ville
Richard Lenoir
Voltaire
Croix de Chavaux
Châtelet
Chemin Vert
Alexandre Dumas
Robespierre
11
Bréguet Sabin
Charonne
Porte de Montreuil
Cité
St-Paul
Pont Marie
Bastille
Avron
Maraîchers
Marne-la-Vallée
Parcs Disneyland A
St-Michel Notre-Dame
Rue des Boulets
2
Buzenval
Ledru-Rollin
Sully Morland
Faidherbe Chaligny
6 Nation
Vincennes
Cluny La Sorbonne
Porte de Vincennes
Saint-Mandé
Maubert Mutualité
Gare de Lyon
Reuilly – Diderot
Boissy-Saint-Léger A
Cardinal Lemoine
Quai de la Rapée
Montgallet
Picpus
Bérault
Luxembourg
1 Château de Vincennes
Jussieu
Bel-Air
Gare d'Austerlitz
Daumesnil
Place Monge
Michel Bizot
Port-Royal
10
Censier Daubenton
Dugommier
Saint Marcel
Bercy
Porte Dorée
Denfert Rochereau
Les Gobelins
Campo Formio
Quai de la Gare
Cour St-Émilion
Porte de Charenton
Saint-Jacques
Corvisart
Place d'Italie
Chevaleret
Liberté
Mouton Duvernet
Glacière
5
Nationale
Bibliothèque François Mitterrand
Tolbiac
Olympiades 14
Ouverture en 2007
Charenton – Écoles
Cité Universitaire
Maison Blanche
Porte d'Italie
Porte de Choisy
École Vétérinaire de Maisons-Alfort
Stade Charléty
Poterne des Peupliers
T 3 Porte d'Ivry
Ivry sur-Seine
Maisons-Alfort – Stade
Gentilly
Le Kremlin Bicêtre
Pierre et Marie Curie
Maisons-Alfort Alfortville
Maisons-Alfort Les Juilliottes
Villejuif Léo Lagrange
Mairie d'Ivry 7
Laplace
Vitry sur-Seine
Créteil – L'Échat
Villejuif Paul Vaillant-Couturier
Créteil – Université
Arcueil – Cachan
Le Vert de Maisons
7 Villejuif – Louis Aragon
8 Créteil – Préfecture
Les Ardoines
Massy – Palaiseau
Versailles – Chantiers C
Orly Ouest
Orly Sud
Dourdan
Saint-Martin-d'Étampes C
Malesherbes D
D Melun
spéciale
Orly

Rick Steves'

FRANCE

2008

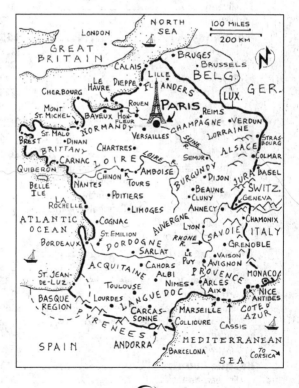

AVALON
TRAVEL

CONTENTS

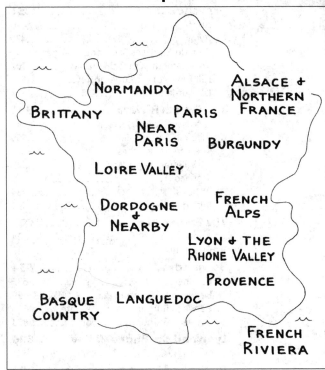

INTRODUCTION

Bienvenue! You've chosen well. France is Europe's most diverse, tasty, and, in many ways, exciting country to explore. It's a multi-faceted cultural fondue.

France is nearly as big as Texas, with 61 million people and more than 400 different cheeses. *Diversité* is a French forte. This country features three impressive mountain ranges (the Alps, the Pyrénées, and the Massif Central), two coastlines that are as different as night and day (Atlantic and Mediterranean), cosmopolitan cities (such as Paris, Lyon, Strasbourg, and Nice—all featured in this book), and countless sleepy villages. From the Swiss-like Alps to the *molto* Italian Riviera, and from the Spanish Pyrénées to *das* German Alsace, you can stay in France and feel like you've sampled much of Europe—and never be more than a short stroll from a *bon vin rouge*.

We've covered the predictable must-sees while mixing in a healthy dose of Back Door intimacy. Along with seeing the Eiffel Tower, Mont St. Michel, and the French Riviera, you'll take a minivan tour of the D-Day beaches with our favorite guides, pedal your way from village to vineyard in the Alsace, marvel at 15,000-year-old cave paintings, and paddle a canoe down the lazy Dordogne River. You'll find a *magnifique* hill-town perch to catch a Provençal sunset, ride Europe's highest mountain lift over the Alps, and touch the quiet Romanesque soul of Burgundian abbeys and villages. You'll learn about each region's key monuments and cities with our walking tours and thoughtfully presented background information. Just as important, you'll meet the intriguing people who run your hotel, bed-and-breakfast, or restaurant. We've also listed our favorite local guides, all well worth the time and money, to help you gain a better understanding of this marvelous country's past and present.

The destinations covered in this book are balanced to include the most interesting cities and intimate villages, from jet-setting beach resorts to the traditional heartland. We've been selective, including only the most exciting sights and romantic villages. For example, there are hundreds of beautiful châteaux in the Loire region—but we cover just the best. And while there are dozens of Loire towns where you could base yourself, we recommend only the top two: Amboise and Chinon.

The best is, of course, only our opinion. But after spending half of our adult lives travel writing, lecturing, guiding tours, and gaining an appreciation for all things French, we've developed a sixth sense for what touches the traveler's imagination.

About This Book

Rick Steves' France 2008 is a personal tour guide in your pocket. Better yet, it's actually two tour guides in your pocket: The coauthor of this book is Steve Smith. Steve has been traveling to France—as a guide, researcher, home owner, and devout Francophile—every year for the last 20 years. He has restored an old farmhouse in Burgundy and today keeps one foot on each side of the Atlantic. Together, Steve and I keep this book up-to-date and accurate (though for simplicity, from this point "we" will shed our respective egos and become "I").

This book is organized by destination. Each of these destinations is a mini-vacation on its own, filled with exciting sights, strollable towns, homey affordable places to stay, and memorable places to eat. In the following chapters, you'll find these sections:

Planning Your Time offers ideas on how best to use your limited time in each destination.

Orientation includes tourist information, specifics on city transportation, and easy-to-read maps designed to make the text clear and your arrival smooth.

Sights, described in detail, are rated:

▲▲▲—Don't miss.

▲▲—Try hard to see.

▲—Worthwhile if you can make it.

No rating—Worth knowing about.

Self-Guided Walks take you through interesting neighborhoods, with a personal tour guide in hand.

Sleeping is a guide to my favorite hotels, from unbeatable deals to cushy splurges.

Eating offers good-value restaurants ranging from inexpensive cafeterias to romantic bistros.

Transportation Connections has information on linking destinations by train and bus, plus route tips for drivers.

French History and Contemporary Politics gives you a quick overview of France from the past to the present.

The **appendix** is a traveler's tool kit, with a handy packing checklist, recommended books and films, instructions on how to use the telephone, useful phone numbers, and the procedure for dealing with lost credit cards. The detailed information on trains and driving includes a day-by-day description of my favorite three-week trip by car (page 796) or by train and bus (page 786). You'll also find a climate chart, festival list, hotel reservation form, pronunciation guide for French place names, French survival phrases, and lots more.

Browse through this book and choose your favorite sights. Then have a *fantastique* trip! Traveling like a temporary local, you'll get the absolute most out of every mile, minute, and euro. As you visit places I know and love, I'm happy you'll be meeting my favorite French people.

PLANNING

Trip Costs

Five components make up your total trip cost: airfare, surface transportation, room and board, sightseeing and entertainment, and shopping and miscellany.

Airfare: A basic round-trip US-to-Paris flight costs from $800 to $1,600, depending on where you fly from and when (cheaper in winter). You can find cheaper round-trip flights from the US to London or Amsterdam, but the cost of train tickets (to get you back to London or Amsterdam for your flight home) eliminate most of your savings. Smaller budget airlines provide bargain service from several European capitals to many French cities (see "Cheap Flights" on page 802 for details). Within France, these inexpensive flights can get you between Paris and other major cities (such as Nice, Marseille, Strasbourg, Toulouse, Lyon, and Bordeaux), often at less cost than by train.

Always consider saving time and money in Europe by flying "open jaw"—into one city and out of another. Flying into Nice and out of Paris costs roughly the same as flying round-trip to Paris. (Many find the relaxed, Mediterranean city of Nice far easier than Paris as a starting point for their trip.)

Surface Transportation: For a three-week whirlwind trip of my recommended destinations, allow $650 per person for public transportation (trains and buses) or $800 per person (based on 2 people sharing) for a three-week car rental, tolls, gas, and insurance (figure about $200 per week for gas and tolls). Car rental is cheapest if arranged from the US. Train passes are normally available only outside of Europe. You may save money by simply buying tickets as you go (see "Transportation," page 784, for more details on car rental, rail trips, and bus travel).

Room and Board: You can easily manage in France on $120 a day per person for room and board (allow $140 a day for Paris). A $120-a-day budget allows $10 for breakfast, $15 for lunch, $40 for dinner with drinks, and $55 for lodging (based on 2 people splitting the cost of a $100 double room). That's definitely doable. Students and tightwads do it on $50 a day ($25 per bed, $25 for meals and snacks).

Sightseeing and Entertainment: In cities, figure about $6–12 per major sight, $3 for minor ones (climbing church towers), $15 for guided walks, and $35 for bus tours and splurge experiences (concerts in Paris' Sainte-Chapelle or a ride on the Chamonix gondola).

Many major sights rent audioguides for about $7 (often including them for free). While the information in this book is generally enough (and more interesting), eager students can supplement it with an audioguide and learn even more (to save money, bring along extra headphones and a Y-jack for the second person).

An overall average of $15 a day for sightseeing and entertainment works for most. Don't skimp here. After all, this category is the driving force behind your trip—you came to sightsee, enjoy, and experience France.

Shopping and Miscellany: Figure $4 per ice cream cone, coffee, or soft drink. Shopping can vary in cost from nearly nothing to a small fortune. Good budget travelers find that this category has little to do with assembling a trip full of lifelong and wonderful memories.

Sightseeing Priorities

Depending on the length of your trip, here are my recommended priorities:

3 days:	Paris and maybe Versailles
5 days, add:	Normandy
7 days, add:	Loire
10 days, add:	Dordogne, Carcassonne
15 days, add:	Provence, the Riviera
18 days, add:	Burgundy, Chamonix
21 days, add:	Alsace, northern France
23 days, add:	Basque Country

For a day-by-day itinerary of a three-week trip, see the plans for drivers (page 796 of appendix) and for people using trains and buses (page 786).

For a more focused 10- to 14-day trip that highlights Paris, Provence, and the Riviera, fly into Paris and out of Nice, take the TGV train from Paris to Avignon, rent a car there and drop it in Nice (or use trains, buses, and minivan tours to get around). This

Major Holidays and Weekends

Popular places are even busier on weekends...and inundated on three-day weekends. Holiday weekends can make towns, trains, roads, and hotels more crowded than in summer. The French are masters at the long weekend, and you're no match for them when it comes to driving and finding hotels during these peak periods. Book your accommodations well in advance.

In 2008, be ready for unusually big crowds during these holiday periods: Easter weekend and the two weeks following it (March 21–April 6); Labor Day and Ascension weekend (May 1–4); Pentecost weekend (May 9–12); Bastille Day and the week after (July 14–20); Assumption weekend (Aug 15–19); and the winter holidays (Dec 20–Jan 4; note that Christmas week is quieter than the week of New Year's). These last two holidays are usually quiet, but holidays nonetheless: All Saints' Day (Nov 1), and Armistice Day weekend (Nov 7–10).

For information on festivals, see page 803 of the appendix.

trip also works in reverse.

For travelers with a little more time, Burgundy and the Alps are about halfway between Paris and Provence and are easy to explore by car or train. If all you have is a week and it's your first trip to France, do Paris, Normandy, and the Loire.

When to Go

Late spring and fall are best, with generally good weather and lighter crowds, though summer brings festivals, reliable weather, and long opening hours at sights. Book ahead for the holidays that occur throughout the year (see "Major Holidays and Weekends," above).

Europeans vacation in July and August, jamming the Riviera and the Alps (worst July 15–Aug 20), but leaving the rest of the country reasonably tranquil. And while many French businesses close in August, the traveler hardly notices. Winter travel is fine for Paris, Nice, and Lyon, but you'll find smaller cities and villages buttoned up tight. Winter weather is gray, noticeably milder in the south (unless the wind is blowing), and colder and wetter in the north. Sights and tourist information offices keep shorter hours, and some tourist activities (such as English-language castle tours) vanish altogether. On the other hand, winter travel allows you to see cities though the lens of a local, as hotels, restaurants and sights are wonderfully tourist-free. To get the latest weather forecast in English, dial 08 99 70 11 11, then press 1. Also see the climate chart in the appendix on page 805.

France Almanac

Official Name: It's officially the *République Française*, but locals just call it France.

Population: France has 61 million people (nearly twice the population of California). They're a mix of Celtic, Latin, and Teutonic DNA, plus many recent immigrants from around the globe—especially North Africa. Four of five French are (at least nominally) Roman Catholic. Every French citizen is expected to speak French.

Area: At 215,000 square miles, it's Western Europe's largest nation. (But Texas is still 20 percent bigger.)

Latitude and Longitude: 46°N and 2°E (similar latitude to the states of Washington, North Dakota, and Maine).

Geography: The terrain consists of rolling plains in the north and mountains in the southwest (Pyrénées), southeast (Alps), and south-central (Massif Central). Capping the country on both ends are 1,400 miles of coastline (Mediterranean and Atlantic). The Seine River flows east–west through Paris, the Rhône rumbles north–south 500 miles from the Alps to the Mediterranean, and the Loire travels east–west, roughly dividing the country into north and south. Mont Blanc (15,771 feet) is Western Europe's highest point.

Major Cities: Nearly one in five French lives in greater Paris (11.3 million in the metropolitan area, 2.2 million in the city). Marseille on the Mediterranean coast has 800,000, and Lyon has 450,000.

Economy: France's gross domestic product is $1.66 trillion (same as California); the GDP per capita is $28,000 (America's is $40,000). Money-makers include tourism, pharmaceuticals, and Airbus planes. Though the French produce nearly a quarter of the world's wine, they drink much of it themselves. France's free market economy is tempered by the

Thanks to France's relatively mild climate, fields of flowers greet the traveler much of the year:

April–May: Crops of brilliant yellow colza bloom, mostly in the north (best in Burgundy). Wild red poppies *(coquelicots)* begin sprouting in the south.

June: Red poppies pop up throughout the country. Late in June, lavender blooms begin covering the hills of Provence.

July: Lavender is in full swing in Provence, and sunflowers are awakening. Cities, towns, and villages everywhere overflow with carefully tended flowers.

August–September: Sunflowers flourish north and south.

October: In the latter half of the month, the countryside

government: high taxes (one of Europe's highest rates at 44 percent of GDP), government investment in industry, and social spending (to narrow the income gap between rich and poor). Hoping to jumpstart its economy, which is suffering from slow growth and 10 percent unemployment, France has recently upped its trademark 35-hour work week to 39 hours for many workers. Despite the three-hour lunch stereotypes, the French work as much as their EU neighbors—that is, 20 percent less than Americans (but with greater per-hour productivity).

Government: President Nicolas Sarkozy, elected by popular vote in 2007, heads a conservative government (but by conservative Americans' standards, it's leftist) along with the president-appointed Prime Minister, François Fillon. The upper-house Senate (321 seats) is elected by an electoral college; the National Assembly (577 seats) is chosen by popular vote. While France is a cornerstone of the European Union, in 2005 French voters gave a resounding *non* to a proposed EU constitution that would expand the EU's powers.

Flag: The Revolution produced the well-known *tricolore,* whose three colors are vertical bands of blue, white, and red.

The Average Jean: The average French person is 38 years old and will live almost 80 years. This person eats lunch in 38 minutes (twice as fast as 25 years ago), and consumes a glass-and-a-half of wine and a pound of fat a day. The average French pops a bottle of champagne about every four months. The typical French woman is 5' 4", weighs 140 pounds, and wears a size 8–10 dress. The average worker enjoys five weeks of holiday and vacation a year. A dog is a part of one in three French households; cats are animals *non grata.*

glistens with fall colors, as most trees are deciduous. Vineyards go for the gold.

Travel Smart

Your trip to France is like a complex play—easier to follow and really appreciate on a second viewing. While no one does the same trip twice to gain that advantage, reading this book in its entirety before your trip accomplishes much the same thing.

Design an itinerary that enables you to visit museums and festivals on the right days. Note the days when sights are closed. Sundays have the same pros and cons as they do for travelers in the US: Special events and weekly markets pop up, sightseeing

Know Before You Go

Your trip is more likely to go smoothly if you plan ahead.

Since **airline carry-on restrictions** are always changing, visit the Transportation Security Administration's website (www.tsa.gov/travelers) for an up-to-date list of what you can bring on the plane with you...and what you have to check. Remember to arrive with plenty of time to get through security.

Call your **debit- and credit-card companies** to let them know the countries you'll be visiting, so that they'll accept (and not deny) your international charges. Confirm what your daily withdrawal limit is; consider asking to have it raised so you can take out more cash at each ATM stop.

Be sure that your **passport** is valid at least six months after your ticketed date of return to the US. If you need to get or renew a passport, it can take up to three months (for more on passports, see www.travel.state.gov).

Book your rooms well in advance if you'll be traveling during any major **holidays** (see "Major Holidays and Weekends," page 5).

If you'll be **traveling with children**, read the sidebar on page 22.

If you plan to hire a **local guide,** it's smart to reserve ahead by email. Popular guides can get booked up in peak season.

If you're taking an **overnight train** (especially to international destinations such as Rome), and you need a *couchette* (overnight bunk) or sleeper—and you *must* leave on a certain day—consider booking it in advance, even though it may cost more. All high-speed trains in France require a seat reservation, but it's usually possible to make arrangements in France just a few days ahead unless it's a holiday weekend. (For more on train travel, see page 784.)

If you're planning on **renting a car** in France, it's recommended—but not required—that you carry an International Driver's Permit (available at your local AAA office for $15 plus two passport photos; www.aaa.com).

attractions are generally open, shops and banks are closed, public transportation options are fewer, and there's no rush hour. Saturdays are virtually weekdays (without the rush hour).

If you're using public transportation, read up on the tips for trains and buses (see pages 791 and 792). If you're driving, peruse my driving tips and study the examples of road signs (see page 800).

Be sure to mix intense and relaxed periods in your itinerary.

Every trip (and every traveler) needs at least a few slack days. Pace yourself. Assume you will return.

Reread this book as you travel, and visit local tourist information offices. Upon arrival in a new town, lay the groundwork for a smooth departure; write down the schedule for the train or bus you'll take when you depart.

Plan ahead for laundry, picnics, and Internet stops. Get online at Internet cafés or your hotel to research transportation connections, confirm events, check the weather, and get directions to your next hotel. Buy a phone card and use it for reservations, reconfirmations, and double-checking hours.

Enjoy the friendliness of the local people. Slow down and ask questions—most locals are eager to point you in their idea of the right direction. Keep a notepad in your pocket for organizing your thoughts. Wear your money belt, and learn the local currency and how to estimate prices in dollars. Those who expect to travel smart, do.

PRACTICALITIES

Red Tape: You need a passport—but no visa or shots—to travel in France. Your passport must be valid for at least six months beyond the time you leave France. Pack a photocopy of your passport in your luggage in case the original is lost or stolen. You are required to have proof of identity on you at all times in France.

Time: In France—and in this book—you'll use the 24-hour clock. It's the same through 12:00 noon, then keep going: 13:00, 14:00, and so on. For anything later than 12, subtract 12 and add p.m. (14:00 is 2:00 p.m.).

France, like most of continental Europe, is generally six/nine hours ahead of the East/West Coasts of the US. The exceptions are the beginning and end of Daylight Saving Time: Europe "springs forward" the last Sunday in March (two weeks after most of North America), and "falls back" the last Sunday in October (one week before North America). For a handy online time converter, try www.timeanddate.com/worldclock.

Business Hours: In France, most shops are open Monday through Saturday (10:00–19:00) and closed Sunday, though many small markets, *boulangeries* (bakeries), and street markets are open Sunday mornings until noon. On Mondays, some businesses are closed until 14:00, and possibly all day. Saturdays are like weekdays (but most banks are closed).

Shopping: For details on clothing-size conversions, customs regulations, and VAT refunds (the tax refunded on large purchases made by non-EU residents), see the appendix.

Just the FAQs, Please

Whom do I call in case of emergency?
Dial 17 for police help. In a medical emergency, call 15.

What if my credit card is stolen?
Act immediately. See "Damage Control for Lost Cards," page 771, for instructions.

How do I make a phone call to, within, and from Europe?
For detailed dialing instructions, refer to page 774.

How can I get tourist information about my destination?
France has a national tourist information office in the US, as well as a network of local offices (see page 765 for specifics on both). Note that Tourist Information is abbreviated **TI** in this book.

What's the best way to pack?
Light. For a recommended packing list, see page 807.

Does Rick have other materials that will help me?
Thanks for asking. For more on Rick's guidebooks, public television series, free audio tours, public radio show, guided tours, travel bags, accessories, and railpasses, see page 766.

Are there any updates to this guidebook?
Check www.ricksteves.com/update for changes to the most recent edition of this book.

Can you recommend any good books or movies for my trip?
Sure. For suggestions, see page 769.

Watt's Up? Europe's electrical system is different from North America's in two different ways: the shape of the plug (two round prongs) and the voltage of the current (220 volts instead of 110 volts). For your North American plug to work in Europe, you'll need an adapter, sold inexpensively at travel stores in the US. As for the voltage, most newer electronics or travel appliances (such as hair dryers, laptops, and battery chargers) automatically convert the voltage—if you see a range of voltages printed on the item or its plug (such as "110–220"), it'll work in Europe. Otherwise, you can buy a converter separately in the US (about $20).

News: Americans keep in touch via the *International Herald Tribune* (published almost daily via satellite throughout Europe). Every Tuesday, the European editions of *Time* and *Newsweek* hit

Do I need to speak some French?

Many French people—especially those in the tourist trade, and in big cities—speak English. Still, you'll get better treatment if you learn and use the French pleasantries. For background information on the language barrier, see page 782. For a list of survival phrases, see page 815.

Do you have information on driving, train travel, and flights?

Absolutely. See "Transportation" on page 784.

How much do I tip?

Relatively little. For tips on tipping, see page 772.

Will I get a student or senior discount?

While discounts aren't listed in this book, seniors (age 60 and over), students with International Student Identification Cards, teachers with proper identification, and youths under 18 or even 26 often get discounts—but you have to ask. If you want a teacher or student ID card, visit www.statravel.com or www.isic.org.

How can I get a VAT refund on major purchases?

See the details on page 773.

How do I calculate metric amounts?

Europe uses the metric system. A liter is about a quart, four to a gallon. A kilometer is six-tenths of a mile. I figure kilometers to miles by cutting them in half and adding back 10 percent of the original (120 km: 60 + 12 = 72 miles, 300 km: 150 + 30 = 180 miles). For more metric conversions, see page 805.

the stands with articles of particular interest to European travelers. Sports addicts can get their daily fix online or from *USA Today*. Good websites include www.europeantimes.com and http://news.bbc.co.uk.

MONEY

Banking

Throughout Europe, cash machines (ATMs) are the standard way for travelers to get local currency. Bring plastic—credit and/or debit cards—along with several hundred dollars in hard cash as an emergency backup. It's smart to bring two cards, in case one gets demagnetized or eaten by a temperamental machine. Traveler's

Exchange Rate

1 euro (€) = about $1.30

To convert prices in euros to dollars, add about 30 percent: €20 = about $26, €50 = about $65. Just like the dollar, the euro is broken down into 100 cents. You'll find coins ranging from 1 cent to 2 euros, and bills from 5 euros to 500 euros.

checks are a waste of time (long waits at slow banks) and a waste of money (in fees).

Cash from ATMs

To use a cash machine to withdraw money from your account, you'll need a debit card (ideally with a Visa or MasterCard logo for maximum usability), plus a PIN code. Know your PIN code in numbers; there are only numbers—no letters—on European keypads.

Before you go, verify with your bank that your card will work overseas, and alert them that you'll be making withdrawals in Europe; otherwise, the bank may not approve transactions if it perceives unusual spending patterns.

French cash machines are labeled *point d'argent* or *distributeur des billets* (the French call them *D.A.B.*—day-ah-bay). You'll find these cash machines all over France—they're always open and provide quick transactions.

Try to take out large sums of money to reduce your per-transaction bank fees. If the machine refuses your request, try again and select a smaller amount; some cash machines won't let you take out more than about €150 (don't take it personally).

To keep your cash safe, use a money belt—a pouch with a strap that you buckle around your waist like a belt, and wear under your clothes. Thieves target tourists. A money belt provides peace of mind, allowing you to carry lots of cash safely. Don't waste time every few days tracking down a cash machine—withdraw a week's worth of money, stuff it in your money belt, and travel!

Credit and Debit Cards

For purchases, Visa and MasterCard are more commonly accepted than American Express. Just like at home, credit or debit cards work easily at larger hotels, restaurants, and shops, but smaller businesses prefer payment in local currency (in small bills—break large bills at a bank or larger store). Your US credit and debit cards will not work in train- or Métro-ticket machines or at self-service gas pumps.

Credit and debit cards—whether used for purchases or ATM withdrawals—often come with additional, tacked-on "international transaction" fees of up to 3 percent, plus $5 per transaction. To avoid unpleasant surprises, call your bank or credit-card company before your trip to ask about these fees.

If your cards are lost or stolen, see page 771 for advice on what to do.

SIGHTSEEING

Sightseeing can be hard work. Use these tips to make your visits to France's finest sights meaningful, fun, fast, and painless.

Plan Ahead

Set up an itinerary that allows you to fit in all your must-see sights. For a one-stop look at opening hours, see the "At a Glance" sidebars for the bigger cities. Most sights keep stable hours, but you can easily confirm the latest by calling the local TI.

Don't put off visiting a must-see sight—you never know when a place will close unexpectedly for a holiday, strike, or restoration. If you'll be visiting during a holiday, find out if a particular sight will be open by phoning ahead or visiting its website.

When possible, visit key museums first thing (when your energy is best) and save other activities for the afternoon. Hit the highlights first, then go back to other things if you have the stamina and time.

Depending on the sight, there are ways to avoid crowds. This book offers tips on specific sights. For example, Paris' Louvre, Orsay, and Orangerie museums are open selected evenings, while the Pompidou Center is always open late. Evening visits are usually peaceful with fewer crowds. At Mont St. Michel or Carcassonne, it's best to arrive at about 17:00, spend the night, and go exploring in the morning before the crowds descend. Finally, do your best to visit these sights first thing or late: Château de Chenonceau, Les Baux, and the Pont du Gard.

Read ahead. To get the most out of the self-guided tours and sight descriptions in this book, read them before you visit. Several cities offer sightseeing passes that are worthwhile values for serious sightseers; plan ahead.

At the Sights

All sights have rules, and if you know about these in advance, they're no big deal.

Some important sights have metal detectors or conduct bag searches that will slow your entry.

At churches—which generally offer interesting art (usually

free) and a cool, welcome seat—a modest dress code (no bare shoulders or shorts) is encouraged.

Most museums require you to check daypacks and coats. They'll be kept safely. If you have something you can't bear to part with, stash it in a pocket or purse. If you don't want to check a small backpack, carry it (at least as you enter) under your arm like a purse...and hope the guards don't notice.

If you check a bag, the attendant may ask you (in French) if it contains anything of value—camera, phone, money, passport—since these cannot be checked.

Cameras are normally allowed, but not flashes or tripods (without special permission). Flashes damage oil paintings and distract others in the room. Even without a flash, a handheld camera will take a decent picture (or buy postcards or posters at the museum bookstore). Video cameras are usually allowed.

Some museums have special exhibits in addition to their permanent collection. Some exhibits are included in the entry price, while others come at an extra cost. Occasionally you have to pay even if you don't want to see the exhibit.

Many sights rent audioguides, which offer dry-but-useful recorded descriptions in English (about €5). For 2008 I have produced free audioguides for the major sites in Paris (see page 768). If you bring along your own pair of headphones and a Y-jack, two people can share one audioguide and save money. Guided tours in English (usually €6 and widely ranging in quality) are most likely to occur during peak season.

Expect changes—paintings can be on tour, on loan, out sick, or shifted at the whim of the curator. To adapt, pick up any available free floor plans as you enter, and ask museum staff if you can't find a particular painting. Say the title or artist's name, or point to the photograph in this book, and ask, *"Où est?"* (oo ay; meaning, "Where is?").

Most important sights have an on-site café or cafeteria (usually a good place to rest and have a snack or light meal). The WCs at many sights are free and generally clean.

Museums have bookstores selling postcards and souvenirs. Before you leave, scan the postcards and thumb through the biggest guidebook (or skim its index) to be sure you haven't overlooked something that you'd like to see.

Most sights stop admitting people 30–60 minutes before closing time, and some rooms close early (generally about 45 minutes before the actual closing time). Guards usher people out, so don't save the best for last.

Every sight or museum offers more than what is covered in this book. Use this information as an introduction—not the final word.

SLEEPING

Accommodations in France are a good value and easy to find. Choose from one- to three-star hotels (two stars is my mainstay), bed-and-breakfasts *(chambres d'hôte)*, hostels, campgrounds, and even homes *(gîtes,* rented by the week).

I like hotels and B&Bs that are clean, small, central, traditional, friendly, and a good value. Most places I list have at least four of these six virtues.

Hotels

In this book, the price for a double room ranges from €40 (very simple, toilet and shower down the hall) to €300-plus (maximum plumbing and more), with most clustering at about €75.

The French have a simple hotel-rating system based on amenities (zero through four stars, indicated in this book by * through ****). One star is modest, two has most of the comforts, and three is generally a two-star with a fancier lobby and more elaborately designed rooms. Four stars offer more luxury than you usually have time to appreciate. Two- and three-star hotels are required to have an English-speaking staff, though virtually all hotels I recommend have someone who speaks English (unless I note otherwise in the listing).

Generally, the number of stars does not reflect room size or guarantee quality. Some two-star hotels are better than many three-star hotels. One- and two-star hotels are inexpensive, but some three-star (and even a few four-star) hotels offer good value, justifying the extra cost. Unclassified hotels (no stars) can be bargains or depressing dumps.

Most hotels have lots of doubles and a few singles, triples, and quads. Traveling alone can be expensive, as singles (except for the rare closet-type rooms that fit only one twin bed) are simply doubles used by one person—so they cost about the same as a double. Room prices vary within each hotel depending on size, and whether the room has a bath or shower, and twin beds or a double bed (tubs and twins cost more than showers and double beds). A triple and a double are often the same room, with a double or queen-size bed plus a sliver-size single. Quad rooms usually have two double beds. Hotels cannot legally allow more in the room than what's shown on their price list. Modern hotels generally

Sleep Code

(€1 = about $1.30, country code: 33)
To help you sort easily through these listings, I've divided the rooms into three categories based on the price for a standard double room with bath:

$$$ **Higher Priced**
$$ **Moderately Priced**
$ **Lower Priced**

To give maximum information in a minimum of space, I use the following code to describe the accommodations. Prices listed are per room, not per person. Unless otherwise noted, English is spoken and breakfast is not included (but is usually optional). You can assume a hotel takes credit cards unless you see "cash only" in the listing.

S = Single room (or price for one person in a double).
D = Double or Twin.
T = Triple (generally a double bed with a single).
Q = Quad (usually two double beds).
b = Private bathroom with toilet and shower or tub.
s = Private shower or tub only (the toilet is down the hall).
* = French hotel rating system, ranging from zero to four stars.

According to this code, a couple staying at a "Db-€140" hotel would pay a total of €140 (about $180) for a double room with a private bathroom. The staff speaks English and credit cards are accepted.

have a few family-friendly rooms that open to each other *(chambres communiquantes)*.

You can save as much as €20–25 by finding the rare room without a private shower or toilet. A room with a bathtub costs about €10–15 more than a room with a shower and is generally larger. Hotels often have more rooms with tubs than showers, and are inclined to give you a room with a tub (which the French prefer).

A double bed is usually €5–10 cheaper than twins, though rooms with twin beds tend to be larger, and French double beds are smaller than American double beds. Many hotels have queen-size beds (a bed that's 63 inches wide—most doubles are 55 inches). To find out if a hotel has queen-size beds, ask, *"Avez-vous des lits de cent-soixante?"* (ah-vay-voo day lee duh sahn-swah-sahnt). Some hotels push two twins together under king-size sheets and blankets (king-size beds are 70 inches wide).

Types of Rooms

Study the price list on the hotel's website or posted at the desk, so you know your options. Receptionists often don't mention the cheaper rooms (they assume you want a private bathroom or a bigger room). Here are the types of rooms and beds:

une chambre sans douche et WC	room without a private shower or toilet (uncommon these days)
une chambre avec cabinet de toilette	room with a toilet but no shower (some hotels charge for down-the-hall showers)
une chambre avec bain et WC	room with private bathtub and toilet
une chambre avec douche et WC	room with private shower and toilet
chambres communiquantes	connecting rooms (ideal for families)
un grand lit	double bed (55 inches wide)
deux petits lits	twin beds (30–36 inches wide)
deux lits séparés	two beds separated
un lit de cent-soixante	queen-size bed (literally, 160 centimeters, or 63 inches, wide)
un lit dépliant	folding bed
un berceau	baby crib
un lit d'enfant	child's bed

If you prefer a double bed (instead of twins) and a shower (instead of a tub), you need to ask for it—and you can save €10–20. If you'll take either twins or a double, ask generically for *une chambre pour deux* (room for two) to avoid being needlessly turned away.

You'll almost always have the option of breakfast at your hotel, which is pleasant and convenient, but it's more than the price of breakfast at the corner café, and with less ambience (though you get more coffee at your hotel). Some hotels offer only the classic continental breakfast for about €6–8, but others offer buffet breakfasts for about €10–15 (cereal, yogurt, fruit, cheese, croissants, juice, and sometimes hard-boiled eggs)—which I usually spring for. (The price of breakfast usually correlates with the price of the room: The more expensive the room, the more expensive the breakfast. This can add up, particularly for families—so beware.) While hotels hope you'll buy their breakfast, it's optional unless otherwise noted.

Some hotels, especially in coastal resort towns, strongly encourage their peak-season guests to take *demi-pension* (half-pension)—that is, breakfast and either lunch or dinner. By law, they can't require you to take half-pension unless you are staying three or more nights, but, in practice, many do during summer. While the food is usually good, it limits your ability to shop around. I've indicated where I think *demi-pension* is a good value.

Hotels in France must charge a daily tax *(taxe du séjour)* of about €1 per person per day. While some hotels include it in the price list, most add it to your bill.

Rooms are safe. Still, keep cameras and money out of sight. Towels aren't always replaced every day; drip-dry and conserve. If that French Lincoln Log pillow isn't your idea of comfort, American-style pillows (and extra blankets) are sometimes in the closet or available on request. To get a pillow, ask for "*Un oreiller, s'il vous plaît*" (uhn oar-ray-yay, see voo play).

If you're planning to visit France in the summer, the expense of an air-conditioned room can be money well spent, particularly in the south. Most hotel rooms with air-conditioners come with a control stick (like a TV remote) that generally has the same symbols and features: fan icon (click to toggle through wind power, from light to gale); louver icon (choose steady airflow or waves); snowflake and sunshine icons (cold air or heat, depending on season); clock ("O" setting: run X hours before turning off; "I" setting: wait X hours to start); and the temperature control (20 or 21 degrees Celsius is comfortable; also see the thermometer diagram on page 806).

Some hoteliers will ask you to sign their *Livre d'Or* (literally, "Golden Book," for client comments). They take this seriously and enjoy reading your remarks.

France is littered with sterile, ultramodern hotels, usually located on cheap land just outside of town, providing drivers with low-stress accommodations. The antiseptically clean and cheap Formule 1 and ETAP chains (about €35–50 per room for up to 3 people), the more attractive Ibis hotels (€65–85 for a double), and the cushier Mercure and Novotels hotels (€110–160 for a double) are all run by the same company, Accor (www.accorhotels.com). While far from quaint, these can be a good value (particularly if you find deals on their website) and some are centrally located. A smaller, up-and-coming chain, Kyriad, has its act together, offering good prices and quality (Kyriad Prestige offers a bit more comfort; France tel. 08 25 00 30 03, from overseas tel. 33 1 64 62 46 46—push 1 to make a reservation, www.kyriad.com; these telephone numbers also work for eight affiliated chains, including Clarine, Climat de France, and Campanile). For a long listing of

> ### Smoke Free? We'll See.
>
> Smoking is now supposed to be off-limits in all of France's public places. While this new law is favored by 78 percent of the French public, the devil is in the details. For example, what's considered public and private space in a hotel is unclear; many consider individual hotel rooms to be private. In hotels, you'll find that lobbies, halls, and elevators are non-smoking, but smoking in individual rooms may be up to the hotelier's discretion. Some hoteliers proudly advertise their hotels as "100 percent non-smoking," while others might designate certain floors as non-smoking. If you detect the stale odor of smoke in your room, ask to be moved. In all the hotel rooms I inspect every year, I seldom notice smoke.

various hotels throughout France, see www.france.com, and for more personality, check www.charming-french-hotels.com.

Phoning

To make an international call to France, you'll need to know its country code: 33. To call France from the US or Canada, dial 011-33-local number (drop the initial 0 of the local number). If calling France from another European country, dial 00-33-local number (without the initial 0).

Making Reservations

Given the quality of the gems I've found for this book, I'd recommend that you reserve your rooms in advance, particularly during peak season and for Paris any time of year. Book several weeks ahead, or as soon as you've pinned down your travel dates. Note that some national holidays jam things up and merit your making reservations far in advance (see "Major Holidays and Weekends," page 5). To make a reservation, contact hotels directly by email, phone, or fax.

Some travelers make reservations as they travel, calling hotels a few days to a week before their visit. If you prefer the flexibility of traveling without any reservations at all, you'll have greater success snaring rooms if you arrive at your destination early in the day. When you anticipate crowds, call hotels at about 9:00 on the day you plan to arrive, when the hotel clerk knows who'll be checking out and just which rooms will be available. (If you encounter a language barrier, ask the fluent receptionist at your current hotel to call for you.)

Most recommended hotels are accustomed to English-only travelers. Email is the clearest and most economical way to make a reservation. If phoning from the US, be mindful of time zones (see page 9). To ensure you have all the information you need for your reservation, use the form in this book's appendix (also at www .ricksteves.com/reservation). If you don't get a reply to your fax, it usually means the hotel is already fully booked. But if you don't get a response to your email right away, call to follow up.

When you request a room for a certain time period, use the European style for writing dates: day/month/year. Hoteliers need to know your arrival and departure dates. For example, a two-night stay in July would be "2 nights, 16/07/08 to 18/07/08." Consider carefully how long you'll stay; don't assume you can add days at the last minute.

If the response from the hotel gives its room availability and rates, it's not a confirmation. You must tell them that you want that room at the given rate.

The hotelier will sometimes request your credit-card number for a one-night deposit. While you can email your credit-card information (I do), it's safer to share that personal info via phone call, fax, or secure online reservation form (if the hotel has one on its website). Don't give your credit-card number as a deposit unless you're absolutely sure you want to stay at the hotel and are clear that they have a room available. If you don't show up, you can be billed for one night.

If you must cancel your reservation, it's courteous to do so with as much advance notice as possible (simply make a quick phone call or send an email). Hotels, which are often family-run, lose money if they turn away customers while holding a room for someone who doesn't show up.

Be warned that some hotels have strict cancellation policies. For example, you might lose a deposit if you cancel within one week of your reserved stay, or you might be billed for the entire visit if you leave early. Ask about cancellation policies before you book.

Always reconfirm your room reservation a few days in advance from the road. If you'll be arriving after 17:00, let them know. Don't have the tourist office reconfirm rooms for you; they'll take a commission.

On the small chance that a hotel loses track of your reservation, bring along a hard copy of their emailed or faxed confirmation.

Bed-and-Breakfasts (Chambres d'Hôte)

B&Bs (*chambres d'hôte*, abbreviated CH in this book)—a great deal—are generally found in smaller towns and rural areas. They offer double the cultural intimacy for a good deal less than most hotel rooms, and help compensate for the low value of the dollar.

While you may lose some hotel conveniences—such as public lounges, in-room phones, daily bed-sheet changes, and credit-card payments—I happily make the tradeoff for the extra charm. This book and local tourist offices list B&Bs, often by the owner's family name. While some CHs post small green *Chambres* or *Chambres d'hôte* signs in their front windows, many are found only through the local tourist office.

I recommend reliable CHs that offer a good value and/or unique experience (such as CHs in renovated mills, châteaux, and wine *domaines*). While *chambres d'hôte* have their own star-rating system, it doesn't quite correspond to the hotels' rating system. So, to avoid confusion, I haven't listed these stars for CHs. But most of my recommended CHs have private bathrooms in all rooms, and some have common rooms with refrigerators. Doubles with breakfast generally cost €50–70 (breakfast may or may not be included—ask). *Tables d'hôte* are CHs that offer an optional, reasonably priced, home-cooked dinner (usually a fine value, must be requested in advance). While your hosts may not speak English, they will almost always be enthusiastic and pleasant.

Hostels (Auberges de Jeunesse)

You'll pay about €18 per bed to stay at a hostel *(auberge de jeunesse)*. Travelers of any age are welcome if they don't mind dorm-style accommodations (usually in rooms of four to eight beds) or meeting other travelers. Cheap meals are sometimes available, and kitchen facilities are usually provided for do-it-yourselfers. Expect youth groups in spring, crowds in the summer, snoring, and incredible variability in quality from one hostel to the next. Family and private rooms are sometimes available on request, but it's basically boys' dorms and girls' dorms. You usually can't check in before 17:00 and must be out by 10:00. There is often a 23:00 curfew. Official hostels are marked with a triangular sign that shows a house and a tree. Some hostels only accept reservations by email. If you'll be staying for several days in an official hostel, consider buying a membership card before you go (www.hihostels.com).

Camping

In Europe, camping is more of a social than an environmental experience. It's a great way for American travelers to make European friends. Camping costs about €15–20 per campsite per night, and almost every destination recommended in this book has a campground within a reasonable walk or bus ride from the town center and train station. A tent and sleeping bag are all you need. Many campgrounds have small grocery stores and washing machines, and some even come with discos and miniature golf. Hot showers are better at campgrounds than at many hotels. Local

Traveling with Kids

France is kid-friendly for young children, partly because so much of it is rural. (Teenagers, on the other hand, tend to prefer cities.) Both of this book's authors have kids (from 6 to 20 years old), and we've used our substantial experience traveling with children to improve this book. Our kids have greatly enriched our travels, and we hope the same will be true for you.

My kids' favorite places have been Mont St. Michel, the Alps, the Loire châteaux, Carcassonne, and Paris (especially the Eiffel Tower and Seine River boat ride)—and any hotel with a pool. To make your trip fun for everyone in the family, mix heavy-duty sights with kids' activities (playing miniature golf, renting bikes, and riding the little tourist trains popular in many towns). While Disneyland Paris is the predictable draw, my kids had more fun for half the expense simply by enjoying the rides in the Tuileries Garden in downtown Paris. If you're in France near Bastille Day, remember that firecracker stands pop up everywhere on the days leading up to July 14. Putting on their own fireworks show can be a highlight for teenagers.

Minimize hotel changes by planning three-day stops. Aim for hotels with restaurants, so the kids can go back to the room and play while you finish a pleasant dinner.

I've listed public pools in many places (especially the south), but be warned: Public pools in France commonly require a small, Speedo-like bathing suit for boys and men (American-style swim trunks won't do)—though they usually have these little suits to loan. At hotel pools, either kind of suit will do.

For breakfast, croissants are a hit. For lunch and dinner, I've developed a knack for finding *créperies* with plenty of kid-friendly stuffings for both savory crêpes and sweet dessert crêpes. It's easy to find fast-food places and restaurants with kids' menus, but for food emergencies, I travel with a plastic container of peanut butter brought from home and smuggle small jars of jam from breakfast.

Swap babysitting duties with your partner if one of you wants to take in an extra sight. Kids homesick for friends can

TIs have camping information. You'll find more detailed information in the annually updated *Michelin Camping France*, available in the US ($16) and at most French bookstores.

Gîtes and Apartments

Gîtes (zheet) are country homes (usually urbanites' second homes) that the government rents out to visitors who want a week in the countryside. The original objective of the *gîte* program was to save characteristic rural homes from abandonment and to make it

keep in easy touch with cheap international phone cards (a dollar buys 10 min of time for catching up) and through Internet cafés.

For memories that will last long after the trip, keep a family journal. Pack a small diary and a glue stick. While relaxing at a café over a *citron pressé* (lemonade, needs sugar), take turns writing down the day's events, and include mementos such as ticket stubs from museums, postcards, or stalks of lavender.

What to Bring: Children's books are scarce and expensive in France. My children read more when traveling in Europe than while at home in the US, so don't skimp here. Bring peanut butter (hard to find in France)...or help your kids acquire a taste for Nutella, the tasty hazelnut-chocolate spread available everywhere. Choose items that are small and convenient for use on planes, trains, and in your hotel room: compact travel games, a deck of cards, a handheld video game, and drawing and coloring supplies. Bring your own drawing paper (it's expensive in Europe). For younger kids, Legos are easily packed and practical (it's also fun to purchase kits overseas, as Legos are sometimes different in Europe from those in the US). Budding fashionistas might enjoy traveling with—and buying new outfits for—a Corelle doll or another 16-inch doll. The French have wonderful doll clothes, with a much wider selection than what's typically found in the US.

Benadryl works miracles in keeping ears and noses open during flights—with the added benefit of sleepiness for most children. I give my kids Benadryl before bed for the first two nights in Europe, and they rarely have serious jet-lag issues. For traveling with infants, car-rental agencies usually have car seats for a small price, though you must reserve one ahead of time. And while most hotels have some sort of crib, I brought a portable crib and did not regret it. Cameras (even disposable ones) are a great investment to get your kids involved. For longer drives, books on tape or CD can be fun for the whole family (if carefully chosen). I recommend Peter Mayle's *A Year in Provence,* available on both cassette tape and CD (or put it on your MP3 player).

easy and affordable for families to reacquaint themselves with the French countryside. The government offers subsidies to renovate such homes, then coordinates rentals to make it financially feasible for the owner. Today, France has more than 8,000 *gîtes.* One of your authors restored a farmhouse a few hours north of Provence, and even though he and his wife are 100 percent American, they received the same assistance French owners do.

Gîtes are best for drivers (they're usually rural, with little public-transport access) and ideal for families and small groups (since they can sleep many for the same price). Homes range in comfort from simple cottages and farmhouses to restored châteaux. Most have at least two bedrooms, a kitchen, a living room, a bathroom or two, and no sheets or linens (though you can usually rent them for extra). Like hotels, all *gîtes* are rated for comfort from one to four (using ears of corn—*épis*—rather than stars). Two or three *épis* are generally sufficient quality, but I'd lean toward three for more comfort. Prices generally range €350–1,300 per week, depending on house size and amenities, such as pools. For more information on *gîtes*, visit www.gites-de-france.fr/eng or www.gite.com. My readers also report finding long lists of non-*gîte* homes for rent through TIs and on the Internet, though these are usually more expensive than staying in a *gîte* (try www.villeetvillage.com).

While less common than *gîtes*, **apartments** can be rented by the week in some cities where tourist demand is high (such as the Riviera or in the Alps). Tourist offices have lists.

EATING

The French eat long and well. Relaxed lunches, three-hour dinners, and endless hours sitting in outdoor cafés are the norm. Here, chefs are as famous as great athletes, and mamas hope their babies grow up to be great cooks. Local cafés, cuisine, and wines should become a highlight of any French adventure. It's sightseeing for your palate. Even if the rest of you is sleeping in cheap hotels, let your taste buds travel first class in France. (They can go coach in England.)

You can eat well without going broke—but choose carefully: You're just as likely to blow a small fortune on a mediocre meal as you are to dine wonderfully for €20. Carefully read the information below, consider my restaurant suggestions in this book, and you'll do fine. For advice on tipping, see page 772.

Eating well in France is a pleasure that will get even better in 2008 for non-smokers. This is the year that a full ban on smoking inside restaurants and cafés goes into effect. Smoking indoors is now only allowed inside expensive sealed chambers—so nearly all restaurants and cafés are opting to go smoke-free. You'll still see people smoking at outdoor tables along the sidewalk.

Breakfast

Petit déjeuner (puh-tee day-zhu-nay) is traditionally *café au lait*, hot chocolate, or tea; a roll with butter and marmalade; and a croissant—though many hotels now provide breakfast buffets with fruit, cereal, yogurt, and cheese (usually for a few extra euros and well worth it). Breakfast, which costs about €6–15 at your hotel, is cheaper at corner cafés, but you won't get coffee refills (see also "Café Culture," on page 27). It's fine to buy a croissant or roll at a bakery and eat it with your cup of coffee at a café. Better still, some bakeries offer worthwhile breakfast deals with juice, croissant, and coffee or tea for about €4–5. If you crave eggs for breakfast, drop into a café and order *une omelette* or *œufs sur le plat* (fried eggs). You could also buy (or bring from home) plastic bowls and spoons, buy a box of cereal and a small box of milk, and eat in your room before heading out for coffee.

Picnics

For many lunches—*déjeuner* (day-zhuh-nay)—I picnic, munch a take-away sandwich from a *boulangerie* (bakery), or get a crêpe from a *crêperie*.

Picnics can be first-class affairs and adventures in high cuisine. Be daring. Try the smelly cheeses, ugly pâtés, sissy quiches, and minuscule (usually drinkable) yogurts. Local shopkeepers are accustomed to selling small quantities of produce. Try the tasty salads-to-go and ask for a plastic fork *(une fourchette en plastique)*. A small container is *une barquette*.

Gather supplies early for a picnic lunch; you'll probably visit several small stores to assemble a complete meal, and many close at noon for their lunch break. Look for a *boulangerie* (bakery), a *crémerie* or *fromagerie* (cheeses), a charcuterie (deli items, meats, salads, and pâtés), an *épicerie* or *magasin d'alimentation* (small grocery with veggies, drinks, and so on), and a *pâtisserie* (delicious pastries). While wine is taboo in public places in the US, it's *pas de problème* in France.

Open-air markets *(marchés)* are fun and photogenic and close at about 13:00 (many are listed in this book; local TIs have complete lists). Local *supermarchés* offer less color and cost, more efficiency, and adequate quality. Department stores often have supermarkets in the basement. On the outskirts of cities, you'll find the monster *hypermarchés*. Drop in for a glimpse of hyper-France in action.

In stores, unrefrigerated soft drinks, bottled water, and beer are one-third the price of cold drinks. Milk, bottled water, and boxed fruit juice are the cheapest drinks. Avoid buying drinks to-go at streetside stands; you'll find them far cheaper in a shop. Try to keep a water bottle with you. Water quenches your thirst better and cheaper than anything you'll find in a store or café. I drink tap water throughout France, filling my bottle in hotel rooms as I go.

Sandwiches, Quiche, and Pizza

Throughout France, you'll find bakeries and small stands selling baguette sandwiches, quiche, and pizza-like items to go for €3–5. Usually filling and tasty, they also streamline the picnic process.

Market Day (Jour du Marché)

Try to buy at least one of your picnics at an open-air market. Market days are a big deal throughout France. They have been a central feature of life in rural areas since the Middle Ages. No single event better symbolizes the French preoccupation with fresh products and their strong ties to the small farmer than the weekly market. It's said that locals mark their calendars with the arrival of fresh produce. Notice the signs as you enter towns indicating the *jours du marché* (essential information to any civilized soul, and a reminder to non-locals not to park on the streets the night before).

Most *marchés* take place once a week in the town's main square and, if large enough, spill into nearby streets. Markets combine fresh produce; tastings of wine and other locally produced beverages (such as brandies and ciders); and a smattering of nonperishable items, such as knives, berets, kitchen goods, and cheap clothing. The bigger the market, the greater the overall selection—particularly for nonperishable goods. Bigger towns (such as Beaune and Arles) may have two weekly markets. The biggest market days are usually on weekends, so that everyone can go.

Providing far more than fresh produce, market day is a weekly chance to resume friendships and get current on gossip. Friends catch up on Henri's barn renovation, see photos of Jacqueline's new grandchild, and relax over *un café*. Dogs are tethered to café tables while friends exchange kisses. Tether yourself to a café table, and observe: generally three cheek-kisses for good friends (left–right–left; but only two kisses in Paris) plus an extra kiss for friends you haven't seen in a while. You should never be in a hurry on market day. Allow the crowd to set your pace. Watch the interaction between vendor and client, then think of your home supermarket routine.

All perishable items are sold directly from the producers—no middlemen, no Visa cards, just really fresh produce. Most vendors follow a weekly circuit of markets they feel work best for them, and most show up every market day, year in and year out. Notice how much fun they have chatting up their customers and each other. Many speak enough English to allow you to learn about their product. Space rental is cheap (about €5–10, depending on the size). Markets end by 13:00—in time for lunch, allowing the town to reclaim its streets and squares.

(If you don't want your sandwich drenched in mayonnaise, ask for it *sans mayonnaise;* sahn my-oh-nehz). Here are some sandwiches you'll see:

Jambon beurre (zhahn-bohn bur): Ham and butter (boring for most).

Fromage beurre (froh-mahzh bur): Cheese and butter (white on white on beige).

Poulet crudités (poo-lay krew-dee-tay): Chicken with tomatoes, lettuce, carrots, and cucumbers.

Thon crudités (tohn krew-dee-tay): Tuna with tomatoes, lettuce, carrots, and cucumbers.

Jambon crudités (zhahn-bohn krew-dee-tay): Ham with tomatoes, lettuce, carrots, and cucumbers.

Jambon or **poulet à la provençal** (zhahn-bohn/poo-lay ah lah proh-vehn-sahl): Ham or chicken, usually with marinated peppers, tomatoes, and eggplant. I love these.

Look also for grilled *panini* sandwiches *à la italienne.*

Café Culture

French cafés (or brasseries) provide budget-friendly meals and a refuge from museum and church overload. They are carefully positioned places from which to watch the river of local life flow by. Feel free to order only a bowl of soup or a salad or *plat* (main course) for lunch or dinner at a café.

Cafés generally open by 7:00, but closing hours vary. Unlike restaurants, which open only for lunch and dinner and close in between, most cafés serve meals throughout the day—making them the best option for a late lunch or early dinner. Note, though, that smaller cafés close their kitchens from about 14:00 until 18:00.

If you're a novice, it's easier to sit and feel comfortable when you know the system. Check the price list first, which by law must be posted prominently. You'll see two sets of prices: you'll pay more for the same drink if you're seated at a table *(salle)* than if you're seated at the bar or counter *(comptoir).*

Your waiter probably won't overwhelm you with friendliness. Notice how hard they work. They almost never stop. Cozying up to clients (French or foreign) is probably the last thing on their minds. To get a waiter's attention, say, "*S'il vous plaît.*"

Standard Menu Items: *Croque monsieur* (grilled ham-and-cheese sandwich) and *croque madame* (*monsieur* with a fried egg on top) are generally served day and night. Sandwiches are least expensive but plain. (They're much better at the *boulangerie*—bakery.) To get more than a piece of ham *(jambon)* on a baguette, order a sandwich *jambon crudité,* which means garnished with veggies. Omelets come lonely on a plate with a basket of bread. The daily special—*plat du jour* (plah dew zhoor), or just *plat*—is your fast, hearty, and garnished hot plate for €10–15. At most cafés, feel free to order only entrées (which in French means the first course); many find these lighter and more interesting than a main course. A vegetarian can enjoy a tasty, filling meal by ordering two entrées. Regardless of what you order, bread is free; to get more, just hold up your bread basket and ask, "*Encore, s'il vous plaît.*"

Salads: They're typically large—one is perfect for lunch or a light dinner, or split between two people as a first course. Among the classics are *salade niçoise* (nee-swaz), a specialty from Nice that usually consists of a green salad topped with green beans, boiled potatoes, tomatoes, anchovies, olives, hard-boiled eggs, and lots of tuna; *salade au chèvre chaud,* a mixed green salad topped with warm goat cheese and toasted bread croutons; and *salade composée,* "composed" of any number of ingredients, such as *lardons* (bacon), *comte* (a Swiss-style cheese), Roquefort (bleu cheese), *œuf* (egg), *noix* (walnuts), *jambon* (ham, generally thinly sliced), *saumon fumé* (smoked salmon), and the highly suspect *gesiers* (chicken livers). The filling *salade compagnarde* usually includes a base of lettuce and potatoes; most will also toss in *lardons* (bacon bits) or smoked duck, and some will add eggs and olives. To get salad dressing on the side, order *la sauce à part* (lah sohs ah par).

For tips on beverages, see page 32.

Restaurants

Choose restaurants filled with locals. Consider my suggestions and your hotelier's opinion, but trust your instinct. If a restaurant doesn't post its prices outside, move along. Refer to my restaurant recommendations to get a sense of what a reasonable meal should cost.

French restaurants open for dinner at 19:00 and are typically most crowded about 20:30 (the early bird gets the table). Last seating is usually about 21:00 or 22:00 in cities (even later in Paris and on the Riviera), and earlier in small villages during the off-season.

If a restaurant serves lunch, it generally begins at 11:30 and goes until 14:00, with last orders taken at about 13:30. In contrast, most cafés serve food all day. Go to a café if you're hungry when restaurants are closed (late afternoon), or anytime you want just a soup or salad.

If you ask for the *menu* (muh-noo) at a restaurant, you won't get a list of dishes; you'll get a fixed-price meal. *Menus,* which include three or four courses, are generally a good value if you're hungry: You'll get your choice of soup, appetizer, or salad; your choice of three or four main courses with vegetables; plus a cheese course and/or a choice of desserts. Service is included (*service compris* or *prix net*), but wine and other drinks are generally extra.

Coffee and Tea Lingo

By law, the waiter must give you a glass of tap water with your coffee or tea if you request it; ask for *"Un verre d'eau, s'il vous plaît"* (uhn vayr doh, see voo play).

Coffee

French	Pronounced	English
un express	uh nex-press	shot of espresso
une noisette	oon nwah-zeht	espresso with a shot of milk
café au lait	kah-fay oh lay	coffee with lots of steamed milk (closest to an American latte)
un grand crème	uhn grahn krehm	big café au lait
un petit crème	uhn puh-tee krehm	small café au lait
un grand café noir	uhn grahn kah-fay nwahr	cup of black coffee, closest to American-style
un décaffiné	uhn day-kah-fee-nay	decaf—available for any of the above drinks

Tea

French	Pronounced	English
un thé nature	uhn tay nah-tour	plain tea
un thé au lait	uhn tay oh lay	tea with milk
un thé citron	uhn tay see-trohn	tea with lemon
une infusion	oon an-few-see-yohn	herbal tea

Restaurants that offer a *menu* for lunch often charge about €5 more for the same *menu* at dinner.

Many restaurants offer cheaper versions of their *menu*, with a choice of two rather than three or four courses. These pared-down *menus* are commonly called *formules* and feature an *entrée et plat* (first course and main dish), or *plat et dessert* (main dish and dessert). Most restaurants offer a *menu–enfant* (kids' menu).

Ask for *la carte* (lah kart) if you want to see a menu and order à la carte, like the locals do. Request the waiter's help in deciphering the French. Go with his or her recommendations and anything *de la maison* (of the house), as long as it's not an organ meat *(tripes, rognons,* and *andouillette)*. Galloping gourmets should bring a menu translator; the *Marling Menu-Master* is good. The *Rick Steves'*

French Wine-Tasting 101

France is peppered with opportunities to taste wines. Look for vineyards posted with *Dégustation Gratuite* signs, which mean you're welcome to stop in for a free tasting. Some towns have *cave coopératives,* providing an excellent opportunity to taste wines from a number of local vintners in a single, less-intimidating setting (sometimes for a nominal price).

The American wine-tasting experience (I'm thinking Napa Valley) is generally informal, chatty, and entrepreneurial (baseball caps and golf shirts festooned with logos). Throughout France, wine-tasting is a more serious, wine-focused experience.

Vintners are happy to work with you—if they can figure out what you want. When you enter a winery, it helps to know what you like (drier or sweeter, lighter or full-bodied, fruity or more tannic, and so on). The people serving you may know those words in English, but you're better off knowing and using the key words in French (see the next page).

For reds, you'll be asked if you want to taste younger wines that still need maturing, or older wines, ready to drink now. (Whites and rosés are always ready to drink.) The French like to sample younger wines and determine how they will taste in a few years, which allows them to buy at cheaper prices and stash the bottles in their cellars. Americans want it now—for today's picnic. While many Americans like a big, full-bodied wine, most French tend to prefer more subtle flavors. They judge a wine by virtue of what food it would go well with—and a big, oaky wine would overwhelm most French cuisine (yes, even cheese courses).

Remember that the vintner is hoping that you'll buy at least a bottle or two. If you don't buy, you may be asked to pay a minimal fee for the tasting. They know that Americans can't take much wine with them, and they don't expect to make a big sale, but they do hope you'll look for their wines in the US. Some of the places I list will ship your purchase home—ask.

French Phrase Book, with a menu decoder, works well for most travelers. Wines are often listed on a separate *carte des vins*.

Remember that in France an entrée is the first course, and *le plat* or *le plat du jour* is the main course with vegetables. At restaurants, it's common to order *une entrée* and *un plat,* or *un plat* and *un dessert,* or just *un plat* from *la carte.* Because small-size dinner salads are rare, I often split a big salad (of which several are usually available) with my companion, and get my own *plat principal* (this also works well for other starter courses). Note that at finer

French Wine Lingo

Here are the steps you should follow when entering any wine-tasting:

1. Greetings, Sir/Madam: *Bonjour, Monsieur/Madame.*
2. We would like to taste a few wines.
   Nous voudrions déguster quelques vins
   (noo voo-dree-ohn day-goo-stay kehl-kuh van).
3. We want a wine that is _____ and _____.
   Nous voudrions un vin _____ et _____.
   (noo voo-dree-ohn uhn van _____ ay _____).
   Fill in the blanks with your favorites from this list:

English	French	Pronounced
wine	*vin*	van
red	*rouge*	roozh
white	*blanc*	blahn
rosé	*rosé*	roh-zay
light	*léger*	lay-zhay
full-bodied, heavy	*robuste*	roh-boost
fruity	*fruité*	frwee-tay
sweet	*doux*	doo
tannic	*tannique*	tah-neek
jammy	*confituré*	koh-fee-tuh-ray
fine	*fin, avec finesse*	fahn, ah-vehk fee-nehs
ready to drink (mature)	*prêt à boire*	preh ah bwar
not ready to drink	*fermé*	fair-may
oaky	*goût de la chêne*	goo duh lah sheh-nuh
from old vines	*de vieille vignes*	duh vee-yay-ee veen-yah
sparkling	*pétillant*	pay-tee-yahn

restaurants, it's not considered appropriate for two diners to share one main course.

To get a waiter's attention, simply say, *"S'il vous plaît"* (see voo play)—"Please." At the end of your meal, your server is likely to ask, *"Ça y était?"* (sah ee ay-tay, "Was it good?"), then, *"Desirez-vous autre chose?"* (day-zee-ray voo oh-truh shohz, "Would you like anything else?").

Restaurants are almost always a better value in the country-side than in Paris. If you're driving, look for red-and-blue Relais

Routier decals on main roads outside cities, indicating that the place is recommended by the truckers' union. These truck-stop cafés offer inexpensive and hearty fare.

The local beer, which costs about €4 at a restaurant, is cheaper on tap (*une pression;* oon pres-yohn) than in the bottle (*bouteille;* boo-teh-ee). France's best beer is Alsatian; try Kronenbourg or the heavier Pelfort. *Une panaché* (oon pah-nah-shay) is a refreshing French shandy (beer and 7-Up).

Regional Specialty Drinks: For a refreshing before-dinner drink, order a *kir* (pronounced keer): a thumb's level of *crème de cassis* (black currant liqueur) topped with white wine. If you like brandy, try a *marc* (regional brandy, e.g., *marc de Bourgogne*) or an Armagnac, cognac's cheaper twin brother. *Pastis,* the standard southern France aperitif, is a sweet anise (licorice) drink that comes on the rocks with a glass of water. Cut it to taste with lots of water.

Beverages at Cafés and Restaurants

Water: The French are willing to pay for bottled water with their meal (*eau minérale;* oh mee-nay-rahl) because they prefer the taste over tap water. Badoit is my favorite carbonated water (*l'eau gazeuse;* loh gah-zuhz). If you prefer a free pitcher of tap water, ask for *une carafe d'eau* (oon kah-rahf doh). Otherwise, you may unwittingly buy bottled water.

Coffee and Tea: See "Coffee and Tea Lingo" on page 29.

Wine and Beer: House wine at the bar is generally cheap and good (about €3 per glass at modestly priced places). At a restaurant, a bottle or carafe of house wine costs €8–15. To get inexpensive wine, order regional table wine (*un vin du pays;* uhn van duh pay) in a pitcher (*un pichet;* uhn pee-shay), rather than a bottle. Note though, that finer restaurants usually offer only bottles of wine.

If all you want is a glass of wine, ask for *un verre de vin rouge* for red wine or *blanc* for white wine (uhn vehr duh van roozh/blahn). A half-carafe of wine is *un demi-pichet* (uhn duh-mee pee-shay); a quarter-carafe (ideal for one) is *un quart* (uhn kar).

Soft Drinks: These cost about €4 in restaurants. Kids love the local lemonade; ask for *citron pressé* (see-trohn preh-say) and add sugar. If you order a *lemonade,* you'll get 7-Up or Sprite. The flavored syrups mixed with bottled water (*sirops à l'eau;* see-roh ah loh) are kid- and adult-friendly. Be adventurous and try *un diablo menthe* (uhn dee-ah-bloh mahnt; 7-Up with mint syrup) or *un diablo pêche* (pehsh; 7-Up with peach syrup). The ice cubes have melted since the last Yankee tour group left.

French Cuisine

The following listing of items found commonly throughout France should help you navigate a typical French menu. For dishes specific to each region, see the "Cuisine Scene" section in every chapter but Paris (which borrows cuisines from all regions).

First Course *(Entrée)*

Salades: With the exception of a *salade mixte* (simple green salad, often difficult to find), the French get creative with their *salades*. (See "Café Culture," above, for good salad suggestions.)

Crudités: Made of raw and lightly cooked fresh vegetables, this mix usually includes grated carrots, celery root, tomatoes, and beets, often with a hefty dose of vinaigrette dressing. Remember that you can get the dressing on the side by requesting *la sauce à part* (lah sohs ah par).

Escargots: The snails of this famous French dish are usually cooked in parsley-garlic butter. You don't even have to like the snail itself. Just dipping your bread in garlic butter is more than satisfying. Prepared a variety of ways, the classic is *à la bourguignonne* (served in their shells).

Huîtres: Oysters, served raw any month, are particularly popular at Christmas and on New Year's Eve.

Pâtés and *Terrines:* Slowly cooked, ground meat (usually pork, though chicken and rabbit are also common) is highly seasoned and served in slices with mustard and *cornichons* (little pickles). Pâtés are smoother than the similarly prepared but chunkier *terrines*.

Foie Gras: Rich, buttery in consistency, and pricey, foie gras is made from the swollen livers of force-fed geese *(foie gras d'oie)* or ducks *(foie gras de canard)*. Spread it on toast with your knife, and never add mustard. For a real French experience, try this dish with some sweet white wine (often offered by the glass for an additional cost). For more on foie gras, see the sidebar on page 344.

Main Course *(Plat Principal)*

Duck, lamb, and rabbit are popular in France, and each is prepared in a variety of ways. You'll also encounter various stew-like dishes that vary by region. The most common regional specialties are available almost everywhere and are described below.

Coq au vin: Native to Burgundy, this dish consists of chicken marinated ever so slowly in red wine, then cooked until it melts in your mouth. It's served (often family-style) with vegetables.

Bœuf bourguignon: Another Burgundian specialty, this classy beef stew is cooked slowly in red wine, with onions, potatoes, and mushrooms.

Gigot d'agneau: A specialty of Provence, a leg of lamb often grilled and served with white beans.

Confit de canard: A Southwest favorite from the Dordogne region is duck that has been preserved and cooked, and often served, in the same fat with potatoes (which have also been cooked

Introduction

in the fat). Not for dieters.

Steak: Referred to as *pavé, bavette,* or *entrecôte,* French steak is usually thinner than American steak and is always served with sauces (*au poivre* is a pepper sauce; *une sauce roquefort* is a bleu-cheese sauce). You will also see *steak haché,* which is a lean, gourmet hamburger patty served *sans* bun. By American standards, the French undercook meats: rare, or *saignant* (seh-nyahn), is close to raw; medium, or *à point* (ah pwan), is rare; and well-done, or *bien cuit* (bee-yehn kwee), is medium.

Steak tartare: This wonderfully French dish is for adventurous types only. It's very lean, raw hamburger served with spices (usually Tabasco, onions, salt, and pepper on the side) and topped with a raw egg.

Saumon and *truite:* You'll see salmon dishes served in various styles. Like steak, salmon always comes with sauce, most commonly a sorrel *(oiselle)* sauce. Trout *(truite)* is also fairly routine on menus.

Daube: Generally made with beef but sometimes lamb, this is a long and slowly simmered dish, typically paired with noodles or other pasta.

Cheese Course *(Le Fromage)*

In France, the cheese course is served just before (or instead of) dessert. It not only helps with digestion, it gives you a great opportunity to sample the tasty regional cheeses. There are more than 400 different French cheeses to try. Many restaurants will offer a cheese platter from which you select a few different cheeses. A good cheese plate has four cheeses: a hard cheese (such as Emmentaler—a.k.a., "Swiss cheese"), a flowery cheese (like Brie or Camembert), a bleu or Roquefort cheese, and a goat cheese. Those most commonly served are *brie de Meaux* (mild and creamy, from just outside Paris), Camembert (semi-creamy and pungent, from Normandy), *chèvre* (goat cheese with a sharp taste, usually from the Loire), and Roquefort (strong and blue-veined, from south-central France). If you'd like a little of several types of cheese from the cheese plate, say: *"Un assortiment, s'il vous plaît"* (uhn ah-sor-tee-mahn, see voo play). If you serve yourself from the cheese plate, observe French etiquette and keep the shape of the cheese. It's best to politely shave off a slice from the side or cut small wedges.

Dessert *(Le Dessert)*

Here are typical desserts you'll find on many menus:

Crème brûlée: A rich, creamy, dense, and caramelized custard.

Tarte tatin: This is apple pie like grandma never made, with caramelized apples cooked upside down, but served upright.

Mousse au chocolat: Chocolate mousse.

How Was Your Trip?

Were your travels fun, smooth, and meaningful? If you'd like to share your tips, concerns, and discoveries, please fill out the survey at www.ricksteves.com/feedback. I value your feedback. Thanks in advance—it helps a lot.

Ile flottante: This lighter dessert consists of islands of meringue floating on a pond of custard sauce.

Profiteroles: Cream puffs filled with vanilla ice cream, smothered in warm chocolate sauce.

Tartes: Narrow strips of fresh fruit, baked in a crust and served in thin slices (without ice cream).

Sorbets: Known to us as sherbets, these light, flavorful, and fruity ices are sometimes laced with brandy. *Citron* (lemon) and *citron-vert* (lime) are particularly popular and refreshing.

Glaces: Ice cream, typically vanilla, chocolate, or strawberry *(fraise).*

Coffee (Café)

If you order espresso at a restaurant, it will always come after dessert. To have coffee with dessert, ask for *"café avec le dessert"* (kah-fay ah-vehk luh day-sayr). For more on tea and coffee, see page 29.

TRAVELING AS A TEMPORARY LOCAL

We travel all the way to Europe to enjoy differences—to become temporary locals. You'll experience frustrations. Certain truths that we find "God-given" or "self-evident," such as cold beer, ice in drinks, bottomless cups of coffee, hot showers, and bigger being better, are suddenly not so true. One of the benefits of travel is the eye-opening realization that there are logical, civil, and even better alternatives.

France is an understandably proud country. To enjoy its people, you need to celebrate the differences. A willingness to go local ensures that you'll enjoy a full dose of French hospitality.

If there is a negative aspect to the image the French have of Americans (apart from our foreign policy), it's that we are big, loud, aggressive, impolite, rich, superficially friendly, and a bit naive.

Americans tend to be noisy in public places, such as restaurants and trains. My French friends place a high value on speaking quietly in these same places. Listen while on the bus or in a restaurant—the place can be packed, but the decibel level is low. Try to remember this nuance, and soften your speaking voice as a way of respecting their culture.

Given our reluctance to work with the world on climate change issues, Europeans don't respond well to Americans complaining about being too hot or too cold. Bring a sweater in winter, and in summer, be prepared to sweat a little like everyone else.

While the French look bemusedly at some of our Yankee excesses—and worriedly at others—they nearly always afford us individual travelers all the warmth we deserve. Judging from all the happy feedback I receive from travelers who have used this book, it's safe to assume you'll enjoy a great, affordable vacation—with the finesse of an independent, experienced traveler.

Thanks, and *bon voyage!*

BACK DOOR TRAVEL PHILOSOPHY
From *Rick Steves' Europe Through the Back Door*

Travel is intensified living—maximum thrills per minute and one of the last great sources of legal adventure. Travel is freedom. It's recess, and we need it.

Experiencing the real Europe requires catching it by surprise, going casual..."Through the Back Door."

Affording travel is a matter of priorities. (Make do with the old car.) You can travel—simply, safely, and comfortably—nearly anywhere in Europe for $100 a day plus transportation costs. In many ways, spending more money only builds a thicker wall between you and what you came to see. Europe is a cultural carnival, and, time after time, you'll find that its best acts are free and the best seats are the cheap ones.

A tight budget forces you to travel close to the ground, meeting and communicating with the people, not relying on service with a purchased smile. Never sacrifice sleep, nutrition, safety, or cleanliness in the name of budget. Simply enjoy the local-style alternatives to expensive hotels and restaurants.

Extroverts have more fun. If your trip is low on magic moments, kick yourself and make things happen. If you don't enjoy a place, maybe you don't know enough about it. Seek the truth. Recognize tourist traps. Give a culture the benefit of your open mind. See things as different but not better or worse. Any culture has much to share.

Of course, travel, like the world, is a series of hills and valleys. Be fanatically positive and militantly optimistic. If something's not to your liking, change your liking. Travel is addictive. It can make you a happier American as well as a citizen of the world. Our Earth is home to six and a half billion equally important people. It's humbling to travel and find that people don't envy Americans. Europeans like us, but, with all due respect, they wouldn't trade passports.

Globe-trotting destroys ethnocentricity. It helps you understand and appreciate different cultures. Regrettably, there are forces in our society that want you dumbed down for their convenience. Don't let it happen. Thoughtful travel engages you with the world—more important than ever these days. Travel changes people. It broadens perspectives and teaches new ways to measure quality of life. Rather than fear the diversity on this planet, travelers celebrate it. Many travelers toss aside their hometown blinders. Their prized souvenirs are the strands of different cultures they decide to knit into their own character. The world is a cultural yarn shop, and Back Door travelers are weaving the ultimate tapestry. Join in!

PARIS

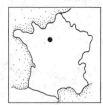

Paris—the City of Light—has been a beacon of culture for centuries. As a world capital of art, fashion, food, literature, and ideas, it stands as a symbol of all the fine things that human civilization can offer. Come prepared to celebrate, rather than judge, the cultural differences, and you'll capture the romance and joie de vivre that Paris exudes.

Paris offers sweeping boulevards, chatty crêpe stands, chic boutiques, and world-class art galleries. Sip decaf with deconstructionists at a sidewalk café, then step into an Impressionist painting in a tree-lined park. Climb Notre-Dame and rub shoulders with the gargoyles. Cruise the Seine, zip up the Eiffel Tower, and saunter down the avenue des Champs-Elysées. Master the Louvre and Orsay museums. Save some after-dark energy for one of the world's most romantic cities.

Planning Your Time

For three very busy but doable days in Paris, I've listed sights in descending order of importance in the planning sections below. Therefore, if you have only one day, just do Day 1; for two days, add Day 2; and so on. When planning where to plug in Versailles (see next chapter), remember that the palace is closed on Mondays and especially crowded on Sundays and Tuesdays—try to avoid these days if possible. For other itinerary considerations on a day-by-day basis, check the "Daily Reminder" on page 43.

Day 1
Morning: Follow this book's Historic Paris Walk, featuring Ile de la Cité, Notre-Dame, the Latin Quarter, and Sainte-Chapelle.

Afternoon: Tour the Louvre.

Evening: Cruise the Seine River or take the Paris Illumination nighttime bus tour (see page 103 in the Nightlife section).

Day 2

Morning: Wander the Champs-Elysées from the Arc de Triomphe down the grand avenue des Champs-Elysées to Tuileries Garden.

Midday: Cross the pedestrian bridge from the Tuileries Garden, then visit the Orsay Museum.

Afternoon: Tour the Rodin Museum or the Army Museum and Napoleon's Tomb, or visit Versailles (take the RER suburban train direct from Orsay).

Evening: Enjoy the Trocadéro scene and a twilight ride up the Eiffel Tower.

Day 3

Morning: Explore the Marais, starting at place des Vosges, and tour your choice of sights: the Jewish Quarter (located along rue des Rosiers), the Picasso, Carnavalet, Pompidou Center, or Jewish Art and History museums.

Afternoon: Stay in the Marais and continue to tour your choice of sights. (Or visit Versailles, if you haven't already.)

Evening: Visit Montmartre and the Sacré-Cœur basilica.

ORIENTATION

Paris (population of city center: 2,200,000) is split in half by the Seine River, divided into 20 arrondissements (proud and independent governmental jurisdictions), circled by a ring-road freeway (the *périphérique*), and speckled with Métro stations. You'll find Paris easier to navigate if you know which side of the river you're on, which arrondissement you're in, and which Métro stop you're closest to. If you're north of the river (the top half of any city map), you're on the Right Bank (Rive Droite). If you're south of it, you're on the Left Bank (Rive Gauche). The bull's-eye of your Paris map is Notre-Dame, which sits on an island in the middle of the Seine. Most of your sightseeing will take place within five blocks of the river.

Arrondissements are numbered, starting at the

Paris Arrondissements

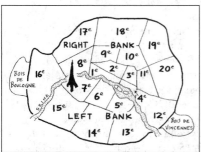

Louvre and moving in a clockwise spiral out to the ring road. The last two digits in a Parisian zip code are the arrondissement number. The abbreviation for "Métro stop" is "Mo." In Parisian jargon, the Eiffel Tower is on *la Rive Gauche* (the Left Bank) in the *7ème* (7th arrondissement), zip code 75007, Mo: Trocadéro.

Paris Métro stops are used as a standard aid in giving directions, even for those not using the Métro. As you're tracking down addresses, these words and pronunciations will help: Métro (may-troh), *place* (plahs—square), *rue* (roo—road), *avenue* (ah-vuh-noo), *boulevard* (boo-luh-var), and *pont* (pohn—bridge).

Tourist Information

Paris tourist offices (abbreviated as **TI** in this book) have long lines, offer little information, and may charge for maps. But all you really need are this book and one of the freebie maps available at any hotel (or in the front of this book). Paris' TIs share a single phone number: 08 92 68 30 00 (from the US, dial 011 33 8 92 68 30 00).

If you must visit a TI, there are several locations, including: **Pyramides** (daily 9:00–19:00, at Pyramides Métro stop between the Louvre and Opéra); **Gare de Lyon** and **Gare du Nord** (both Mon–Sat 8:00–18:00, closed Sun); and **Montmartre** (daily 10:00–19:00, place du Tertre). The official website for Paris' TIs is www.parisinfo.com. Both **airports** have handy information offices (called ADP) with long hours and short lines (see "Airports," page 156).

Pariscope: The weekly €0.40 *Pariscope* magazine (or one of its clones, available at any newsstand) lists museum hours, art exhibits, concerts, festivals, plays, movies, and nightclubs. Smart tour guides and sightseers rely on this for the latest listings.

Other Publications: Look for the *Paris Times*, which provides similar coverage but with fresh insights into living in Paris, available at any English-language bookstore, French-American establishment, the American Church, and online at www.theparistimes.com. The *Paris Voice*, which has snappy reviews of concerts, plays, and current events is available only online at www.parisvoice.com. For a complete schedule of museum hours and English-language museum tours, get the free *Musées, Monuments Historiques, et Expositions* booklet at any museum.

American Church and Franco-American Center: This interdenominational church—in the rue Cler neighborhood, facing the river between the Eiffel Tower and Orsay Museum—is a nerve center for the American émigré community. Worship services are at 9:00 and 11:00 on Sunday; the coffee hour after church, and the free Sunday concerts (generally Sept–June at 17:00—but not every week) are a great way to make some friends and get a taste of émigré life in Paris (reception open Mon–Sat 9:00–12:00 & 13:00–22:00, Sun 14:30–19:00, 65 quai d'Orsay, Mo: Invalides, tel. 01 40 62 05 00, www.acparis.org). It's also a good place to pick up a free copy of *France–USA Contacts* (an advertisement paper with info on housing and employment for the 30,000 Americans living in Paris, www.fusac.fr).

Arrival in Paris
For a comprehensive rundown of Paris' train stations and airports, see "Transportation Connections," page 150.

Helpful Hints
Heightened Security *(Plan Vigipirate):* You may notice an abundance of police at monuments, on streets, and on the Métro, as well as security cameras everywhere. You'll go through quick and reassuring airport-like security checks at many major attractions. This is all part of Paris' anti-terror plan. The police are helpful, the security lines move quickly, and there are fewer pickpocket problems than usual on the Métro.

Theft Alert: Although the greater police presence has scared off some, troublesome thieves still thrive near famous monuments and on Métro and RER lines that serve high-profile tourist sights. Wear a money belt, put your wallet in your front pocket, loop your day bag over your shoulders, and keep a tight grip on your purse or shopping bag. Muggings are rare, but do occur. If you're out late, avoid the dark riverfront embankments and any place where the lighting is dim and pedestrian activity is minimal.

Tourist Scams: Be aware of the latest scams, including these current favorites. The "found ring" scam is when an innocent-looking person picks up a ring on the ground, and asks if you dropped it. When you say no, the person examines the ring more closely, then shows you a mark "proving" that it's pure gold. He offers to sell it to you for a good price—several times more than he paid for it before dropping it on the sidewalk.

In the "friendship bracelet" scam, a vendor approaches you and asks if you'll help him with a demonstration. He proceeds to make a friendship bracelet right on your arm. When finished, he asks you to pay for the bracelet he created just for you. And since you can't easily take it off on the spot, he counts on your feeling obliged to pay up.

Distractions by "salesmen" can also function as a smoke-screen for theft—an accomplice picks your pocket as you try to wriggle away from a pushy vendor.

Street Safety: Parisian drivers are notorious for ignoring pedestrians. Look both ways (many streets are one-way) and be careful of seemingly quiet bus/taxi lanes. Don't assume you have the right of way, even in a crosswalk. When crossing a street, keep your pace constant and don't stop suddenly. By law, drivers must miss pedestrians by only one meter—a little more than three feet (1.5 meters in the countryside). Drivers carefully calculate your speed and won't hit you, provided you don't alter your route or pace.

Paris' new bike program, which offers short-term rentals to the French, means that more bikes than ever are on the roads. When crossing streets, beware of this silent transportation.

Paris Museum Pass: This worthwhile pass, covering most sights in Paris, is sold at TIs and museums. For detailed information, see page 64.

Museum Strategy: When possible, visit key museums first thing (when your energy is best) and save other activities for the afternoon. Remember, most museums require you to check daypacks and coats, and important museums have metal detectors that will slow your entry. The Louvre, Orsay, and Pompidou are open on selected nights (see "Paris at a Glance," page 62), making for peaceful visits with fewer crowds.

Bookstores: There are many English-language bookstores in Paris, where you can pick up guidebooks (at nearly double their American prices). Most carry this book. My favorite is the friendly **Red Wheelbarrow Bookstore** in the Marais neighborhood, run by charming Penelope and Abigail (Mon–Sat 10:00–19:00, Sun 14:00–18:00, 22 rue St. Paul, Mo: St. Paul, tel. 01 48 04 75 08). Others include **Shakespeare and Company** (some used travel books, daily 12:00–24:00, 37 rue de la Bûcherie, across the river from Notre-Dame, Mo: St. Michel, tel. 01 43 26 96 50; see page 55 in Historic Paris Walk), **W.H. Smith** (Mon–Sat 10:00–19:00, closed Sun, 248 rue de Rivoli, Mo: Concorde, tel. 01 44 77 88 99), **Brentanos** (Mon–Sat 10:00–19:00, closed Sun, 37 avenue de l'Opéra, Mo: Opéra, tel. 01 42 61 52 50), and **Village Voice** (Mon 14:00–19:30, Tue–Sat 10:00–19:30, Sun 13:00–18:00, near St. Sulpice Church at 6 rue Princesse, tel. 01 46 33 36 47).

Public WCs: Public toilets are free (though leaving a small tip if there's an attendant is appreciated). Modern, sanitary street-booth toilets provide both relief and a memory (don't leave small children inside unattended). The restrooms in museums are free and the best you'll find. Or walk into any sidewalk café like you own the place, and find the toilet in the back. Keep toilet paper or tissues with you, as some toilets are poorly supplied.

Bike Rental: Fat Tire Bike Tours runs tours (see page 52) and also rents bikes (€2/hr, €15/24 hrs, includes helmets and locks, credit-card imprint required for deposit, ask for their suggested bike-route map, daily 9:00–19:00, south of Eiffel

Daily Reminder

Monday: These sights are closed today: Orsay, Rodin, Marmottan, Catacombs, Petit Palais, Carnavalet, Victor Hugo's House, Montmartre Museum, Quai Branly, and Paris Archaeological Crypt. Giverny and the Château at Versailles are also closed; the Louvre and Eiffel Tower are more crowded because of these closings. The Army Museum (and Napoleon's Tomb) is closed the first Monday of each month in winter (Oct–May). Some small stores don't open until 14:00. Street markets such as rue Cler and rue Mouffetard are dead today. Some banks are closed. It's discount night at most cinemas.

Tuesday: Many museums are closed today, including the Louvre, Orangerie, National Maritime, Cluny, Pompidou, and Picasso. The Eiffel Tower, Orsay, Versailles, and Giverny are particularly busy today.

Wednesday: All sights are open (Louvre until 21:45). The weekly *Pariscope* magazine comes out today. Most schools are closed, so many kids' sights are busy. Some cinemas offer discounts.

Thursday: All sights are open except the Sewer Tour. The Orsay is open until 21:45. Department stores are open late.

Friday: All sights are open (Louvre until 21:45 and Orangerie until 21:00) except the Sewer Tour. Afternoon trains and roads leaving Paris are crowded; TGV train reservation fees are higher.

Saturday: All sights are open except the Jewish Art and History Museum and the Holocaust Memorial. The fountains run at Versailles (April–Sept). Department stores are jammed. The Jewish Quarter is quiet.

Sunday: Many sights are free the first Sunday of the month, including the Louvre, Orsay, Rodin, Cluny, Picasso, and Pompidou Center museums. These free days attract hordes of visitors.

Versailles is more crowded than usual on Sunday, but the garden's fountains are running (April–Sept). Most of Paris' stores are closed on Sunday, but shoppers will find relief in the Marais neighborhood's lively Jewish Quarter and in Bercy Village, where many stores are open. Look for organ concerts at St. Sulpice and possibly other churches. The American Church often hosts a free evening concert (generally Sept–June at 17:00—but not every week). Many recommended restaurants in the rue Cler neighborhood are closed for dinner.

Tower at 24 rue Edgar Faure, Mo: Dupleix, tel. 01 56 58 10 54, www.fattirebiketoursparis.com).

Parking: Most of the time, drivers must pay to park curbside (buy parking card at tobacco shops), but not at night (19:00–9:00), all day Sunday, or anytime in August, when many Parisians are on vacation. There are parking garages under Ecole Militaire, St. Sulpice Church, Les Invalides, the Bastille, and the Panthéon for about €20–25 per day (it's cheaper the longer you stay). Some hotels offer parking for less—ask.

Tobacco Stands *(Tabacs)*: These little kiosks—usually just a counter inside a café—sell cards for parking meters, public-transit tickets (usually), postage stamps, and...oh yeah, cigarettes. To find one anywhere in Paris, just look for a *Tabac* sign and the red, cylinder-shaped symbol above some (but not all) cafés.

Getting Around Paris

For such a sprawling city, Paris is easy to navigate. Your basic choices are Métro (in-city subway), RER (suburban rail tied into the Métro system), public bus, and taxi. (Also consider the hop-on, hop-off bus and boat tours, described under "Tours" on page 50.) You can buy tickets and passes at most *tabacs* (tobacco stand—described above) and at most Métro stations. While the majority of Métro stations have staffed ticket windows, smaller stations might discontinue this service as the Métro system converts to automated machines.

Public-Transit Tickets: The Métro, RER, and buses all work on the same tickets. (Note that you can transfer between the Métro and RER on a single ticket, but combining a Métro or RER trip with a bus ride takes two tickets.) A **single ticket** costs €1.40. To save 30 percent, buy a *carnet* (kar-nay) of 10 tickets for €10.90 (that's €1.09 per ticket—€0.31 cheaper than single tickets). It's less expensive for kids (ages 4–10 pay €5.40 for a *carnet*). Big Métro stations have staffed ticket windows, but at smaller stations you need to buy tickets at machines (using coins).

If you're staying in Paris for even just a few days, consider the rechargeable **Carte Navigo**, which pays for itself in 15 rides. For about €16, you get free run of the bus and Métro system for one week, starting Monday and ending Sunday. Ask for the Carte Navigo *hebdomadaire* (ehb-doh-mah-dair) and supply a passport-size photo. Larger Métro stations have photo booths. The month-long version costs about €54—request a Carte Navigo *mensuelle* (mahn-soo-ehl, good from the first day of the month to the last, also requires photo). These passes cover only central Paris. You can pay more for passes covering regional destinations (such as Versailles), but for most visitors, this is a bad value (instead, buy individual tickets for longer-distance destinations). Despite what

Paris Neighborhoods

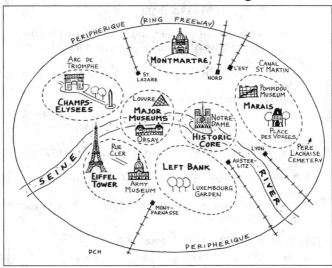

some Métro agents say, Carte Navigo passes are definitely not limited to residents; if you're refused, simply go to another station or a *tabac* to buy your pass. There's a one time €5 fee.

The overpriced **Paris Visite** passes were designed for tourists and offer minor reductions at minor sights (1 day/€9, 2 days/€14, 3 days/€19, 5 days/€28), but you'll get a better value with a cheaper *carnet* of 10 tickets or a Carte Navigo.

By Métro
In Paris, you're never more than a 10-minute walk from a Métro station. Europe's best subway allows you to hop from sight to sight quickly and cheaply (runs daily 5:30–24:30 in the morning). Learn to use it. Begin by studying the color Métro map (at the beginning of this book, free at Métro stations, and included on freebie Paris maps at your hotel).

Pickpockets: Thieves dig the Métro. Be on guard. For example, if your pocket is picked as you pass through a turnstile, you end up stuck on the wrong side (after the turnstile bar has closed behind you) while the thief gets away. Stand away from Métro doors to avoid being a target for a theft-and-run just before the doors close. Any jostling or commotion—especially when boarding or leaving trains—is likely the sign of a thief or a team of thieves in action. Make any fare inspector show proof of identity (ask locals for help if you're not certain). Never show anyone your wallet.

How the Métro Works: To get to your destination, determine the closest "Mo" stop and which line or lines will get you

Métro Basics

- The same tickets are good on the Métro, RER (within the city), and city buses (but not to transfer between Métro/RER and bus).
- Save money by buying a *carnet* of tickets or a Carte Navigo.
- Find your train by its end-of-the-line stops.
- Insert your ticket into the turnstile (brown stripe down), retrieve it, and keep it until the end of your journey.
- Beware of pickpockets.
- Transfers *(correspondance)* within the Métro or RER system are free.
- At the end of your trip, choose the right exit *(sortie)* to avoid extra walking.
- Dispose of used tickets after your ride to avoid confusing them with fresh ones.

Key Words for the Métro and RER

French	Pronounced	English
direction	dee-rek-see-ohn	direction
ligne	leen-yuh	line
correspondance	kor-res-pohn-dahns	transfer
sortie	sor-tee	exit
carnet	kar-nay	cheap set of 10 tickets
Pardon, madame/monsieur.	par-dohn, mah-dahm/ mes-yur	Excuse me, lady/ bud.
Je descends.	juh day-sahn	I'm getting off.
Donnez-moi mon porte-monnaie!	duh-nay-mwah mohn port-moh-nay	Give me back my wallet!

Etiquette

- When waiting at the platform, get out of the way of those exiting the train. Board only once everyone is off.
- Avoid using the hinged seats near the doors of some trains when the car is jammed; they take up valuable standing space.
- In a crowded train, try not to block the exit. If you're blocking the door when the train stops, step out of the car and to the side, let others off, then get back on.
- Talk softly in the cars. Listen to how quietly Parisians communicate and follow their lead.
- On escalators, stand on the right and pass on the left.

there. The lines have numbers, but they're best known by their end-of-the-line stops. (For example, the La Défense/Château de Vincennes line, also known as line 1, runs between La Défense in the west and Vincennes in the east.) Once in the Métro station, you'll see blue-and-white signs directing you to the train going in your direction (e.g., *direction: La Défense*). Insert your ticket in the automatic turnstile, pass through, reclaim your ticket, and keep it until you exit the system (some stations require you to pass your ticket through a turnstile to exit). *Fare inspectors regularly check for cheaters and accept absolutely no excuses, so keep that ticket!*

Transfers are free and can be made wherever lines cross. When you transfer, look for the orange *correspondance* (connections) signs when you exit your first train, then follow the proper direction sign.

Even though the Métro whisks you quickly from one point to another, be prepared to walk sig-

nificant distances within stations to reach your platform (most notice-able when you transfer). Escalators are common, but they're often out of order. To limit excessive walk-ing, avoid transferring at these sprawling stations: Montparnasse–Bienvenüe, Chatelet–Les Halles, Charles de Gaulle–Etoile, Gare du Nord, and Bastille.

Before taking the *sortie* (exit) to leave the Métro, check the helpful *plan du quartier* (map of the neighborhood) to get your bearings, locate your destination, and decide which *sortie* you want. At stops with several *sorties*, you can save lots of walking by choosing the best exit.

After you exit the system, toss or tear your used ticket so you don't confuse it with your unused ticket—they look virtually identical.

By RER

The RER (Réseau Express Régionale; air-ay-air) is the suburban arm of the Métro, serving outlying destinations (such as Versailles, Disneyland Paris, and the airports). These routes are indicated by thick lines on your subway map and identified by the letters A, B, C, and so on. Some routes are operated by France's railroad (SNCF) and are called **Transilien;** they function the same way and use the same tickets as the RER, but they also accept rail-passes (show pass at ticket window to get a free turnstile ticket). For all of these trains, you need your ticket to exit the system.

Within the city center, the RER works like the Métro, but

Key Buses for Tourists

Of Paris' many bus routes, these are some of the most scenic. They provide a great, cheap, and convenient introduction to the city.

Bus #69 runs east–west between the Eiffel Tower and Père Lachaise Cemetery by way of rue Cler (recommended hotels), quai d'Orsay, the Louvre, and the Marais (recommended hotels).

Bus #87 also links the Marais and rue Cler areas, but stays mostly on the Left Bank, connecting the Eiffel Tower, St. Sulpice, Luxembourg Garden (more recommended hotels and restaurants), St. Germain-des-Prés, the Latin Quarter, the Bastille, and Gare de Lyon.

Bus #24 runs east–west along the Seine riverbank from Gare St. Lazare to Madeleine, Place de la Concorde, Orsay Museum, the Louvre, St. Michel, Notre-Dame, and Jardin des Plantes, all the way to trendy Bercy Village (cafés and shops).

Bus #63 is another good east–west route, connecting the Marmottan Museum, Trocadéro (Eiffel Tower), pont de l'Alma, Orsay Museum, St. Sulpice, Luxembourg Garden, Latin Quarter/Panthéon, and Gare de Lyon.

can be speedier (if it serves your destination directly) because it makes fewer stops. Métro tickets are good on the RER when traveling in the city center. (You can transfer between the Métro and RER systems with the same ticket.) But to travel outside the city (to Versailles or the airport, for example), you'll need to buy a separate, more expensive ticket at the station window before boarding. You need to insert your ticket in a turnstile to exit the RER lines. Also, unlike the Métro, not every train stops at every station along the way; check the sign over the platform to see if your destination is listed as a stop ("*toutes les gares*" means it makes all stops along the way), or confirm with a local before you board.

By City Bus

Paris' excellent bus system is worth figuring out. Remember, even though buses use the same tickets as the Métro and RER, you can't use a single ticket to transfer between the systems—or even to transfer from one bus to another. One ticket buys you a bus ride anywhere in central Paris—but if you leave the city center (shown as zone 1 on the diagram on board the bus) or transfer to another bus, you must validate a second ticket.

Buses don't seem as romantic as the famous Métro and are subject to traffic jams, but savvy travelers know that buses can have you swinging through the city like Tarzan in an urban jungle.

Anywhere you are, you can generally see a bus stop, each complete with all the information you need: a good city bus map, route maps showing exactly where each bus that uses this stop goes, a frequency chart and schedule, a *plan du quartier* map of the immediate neighborhood, and a *soirées* map explaining night service, if available. While the Métro shuts down at about 24:30 in the morning, some buses continue much later (called *Noctilien* lines, www.noctilien.fr).

Enter buses through the front door. Punch your ticket in the machine behind the driver, or pay the higher cash fare. When you reach your destination, push the red button to signal you want a stop, then exit through the rear door. Even if you're not certain you've figured out the system, do some joyriding (outside of rush hour: Mon–Fri 8:00–9:30 & 17:30–19:30). Be warned: Not all city buses are air-conditioned, so they can become rolling greenhouses on summer days. For information on some of Paris' most scenic and convenient routes, see the sidebar. Handy bus-system maps *(plan des autobus)* are available in any Métro station (and in the €7 *Paris Pratique* map book sold at newsstands). Major stops are displayed on the side of each bus. The handiest bus routes are listed for each recommended hotel neighborhood (see "Sleeping," page 104).

By Taxi

Parisian taxis are reasonable, especially for couples and families. The meters are tamper-proof. Fares and supplements (described in English on the rear windows) are straightforward. There's a €5.20 minimum. A 10-minute ride (e.g., Bastille to Eiffel Tower) costs about €10 (versus €1.09 to get anywhere in town using a *carnet* ticket on the Métro or bus).

Higher rates are charged at night (19:00–7:00), all day Sunday, and to either airport. There's a €1 charge for each piece of baggage and for train station pickups. To tip, round up to the next euro (minimum €0.50).

You can try waving down a taxi, but it's often easier to ask for the nearest taxi stand (*"Où est une station de taxi?"*; oo ay oon stah-see-ohn duh taxi). Taxi stands are indicated by a circled *T* on good city maps, and on many maps in this book. A taxi can fit three people comfortably, and cabbies are legally required to take up to four for a small extra fee (though some might resist). Groups of up to five can use a *grand taxi*, which must be booked in advance—ask your hotel to call. If a taxi is summoned by phone, the meter starts as soon as the call is received, adding €3–6 to the bill.

Taxis are tough to find when it's raining and on Friday and Saturday nights, especially after the Métro closes (about 24:30 in the morning). If you need to catch a train or flight early in the morning, book a taxi the day before.

TOURS

By Bus

Bus Tours—**Paris Vision** offers bus tours of Paris, day and night (advertised in hotel lobbies). I'd take a Paris Vision tour only at night (for more on the Paris Illumination tour, see page 103 of the Nightlife section). During the day, the hop-on, hop-off bus tours (listed immediately below) and the Batobus (see "By Boat," below)—which both provide transportation between sights as well as commentary—are a better value.

Hop-on, Hop-off Bus Tours—Double-decker buses connect Paris' main sights while providing a basic running commentary, allowing you to hop on and hop off along the way. You get a disposable set of ear plugs (dial English and listen to the so-so narration). You can get off at any stop, tour a sight, then catch a later bus. These are best in good weather, when you can sit up top. There are two companies: L'Open Tours and Les Cars Rouges; pick up their brochures showing routes and stops from any TI or on their buses. You can start either tour at just about any of the major sights, such as the Eiffel Tower, where both companies stop on avenue Joseph Bouvard.

L'Open Tours uses bright yellow buses and provides more extensive coverage (and slightly better commentary) on four different routes, rolling by most of the important sights in Paris. Their Paris Grand Tour (the green route) offers the best introduction. The same ticket gets you on any of their routes within the validity period. Buy your tickets from the driver (1 day-€25, 2 days-€28, kids 4–11 pay €12 for 1 or 2 days, allow 2 hours per tour). Two or three buses depart hourly from about 10:00 to 18:00; expect to wait 10–20 minutes at each stop (stops can be tricky to find—look for yellow signs; tel. 01 42 66 56 56, www.paris-opentour.com). A combo-ticket covers both the Batobus boats (described in "By Boat" below) and L'Open Tours buses (€40, kids under 12 pay €17, valid 3 days).

Les Cars Rouges' bright red buses offer largely the same service, with only one route and just nine stops, for a bit less money (adult-€22, kids 4–12 pay €11, good for 2 days, tel. 01 53 95 39 53, www.carsrouges.com).

By Boat

Seine Cruises—Several companies run one-hour boat cruises on the Seine (by far best at night).

Two companies are convenient to the rue Cler hotels: **Bateaux-Mouches** departs from pont de l'Alma's right bank and has the biggest open-top, double-decker boats. But this company often has too many tour groups, causing these boats to get packed (€9, kids 4–12 pay €5, tel. 01 40 76 99 99, www.bateaux-mouches.com).

Bateaux Parisiens has smaller covered boats with hand-held audioguides, fewer crowds, and only one deck (€10, kids 4–11 pay €5, discounted half-price if you have a valid France or France–Switzerland railpass—does not use up a day of a flexipass, leaves from right in front of the Eiffel Tower, tel. 08 25 01 01 01, www.bateauxparisiens.com). Both companies run daily year-round (April–Oct 10:00–22:30, 2–3/hr; Nov–March shorter hours, runs hourly).

The still smaller and more intimate **Vedettes du Pont Neuf** are closer to the Marais- and Luxembourg-area hotels. During the day, they depart once an hour from the center of pont Neuf (2/hr after dark), but they come with a live guide who gives explanations in French and English (€11, kids 4–12 pay €5, tip requested, tel. 01 46 33 98 38).

Hop-on, Hop-Off Boat Tour—**Batobus** allows you to get on and off as often you like at any of eight popular stops along the Seine: Eiffel Tower, Champs-Elysées, Orsay/place de la Concorde, the Louvre, Notre-Dame, St. Germain-des-Prés, Hôtel de Ville, and Jardin des Plantes. Safety-conscious glass enclosures turn the boats into virtual ovens on hot days (1 day-€13, 2 days-€15, boats run June–Aug 10:00–21:30, mid-March–May and Sept–Oct 10:00–19:00, Nov–early Jan and Feb–mid-March 10:30–16:30, no boat last three weeks in Jan, every 15–20 minutes, 45 min one-way, 90 min round-trip, worthless narration). If you use this for getting around—sort of a scenic, floating alternative to the Métro—this can be worthwhile. But if you just want a guided boat tour, Batobus is not as good a value as the regular tour boats described above. A special combo-ticket covers L'Open Tour buses (described above) and Batobus boats (€40, kids under 12 pay €17, valid 3 days, www .batobus.com).

Low-Key Cruise on a Tranquil Canal—**Canauxrama** runs a lazy 2.5-hour cruise on a peaceful canal, without the Seine in sight. Tours start from place de la Bastille and end at Bassin de la Villette (near Mo: Stalingrad). During the first segment of your trip, you'll pass through a long tunnel (built at the order of Napoleon in the early 19th century, when canal boats were vital for industrial transport). Once outside, you glide—not much faster than you can walk—through sleepy Parisian neighborhoods and slowly climb through four double locks as a guide narrates the trip in French and English (€16, departs at 9:45 and 14:30 across from Opéra Bastille, just below boulevard de la Bastille, opposite #50—where the canal meets place de la Bastille, tel. 01 42 39 15 00). The same tour also goes in the opposite direction (from Bassin de la Villette to place de la Bastille). It's okay to bring a picnic on board.

By Foot

Paris Walks—This company offers a variety of excellent two-hour walks, led by British or American guides. Tours are thoughtfully prepared, relaxing, and humorous. Don't hesitate to stand close to the guide to hear (€10, generally 2/day, private tours available, recorded English schedule tel. 01 48 09 21 40, www.paris-walks .com). Tours focus on the Marais (4/week), Montmartre (3/week), medieval Latin Quarter (Mon), Ile de la Cité/Notre-Dame (Mon), the "Two Islands" (Ile de la Cité and Ile St. Louis, Wed), *Da Vinci Code* sights (Wed), and Hemingway's Paris (Fri). Ask about their family-friendly tours. Call a day or two ahead to learn their schedule and starting point. Most tours don't require reservations, but specialty tours (such as the *Da Vinci Code* tour) require advance reservations and prepayment with credit card (not refundable if you cancel fewer than two days in advance).

Context Paris—These "intellectual by design" walking tours are led by docents (historians, architects, and academics) and cover both museums and neighborhoods, often with a fascinating theme (explained on their website). Try to book in advance, since groups are small and can fill up (limited to 6 participants, generally 3 hours long and €55 per person plus admissions, tel. 06 13 09 67 11, US tel. 1-888-467-1986, www.contextparis.com). They also offer private tours.

Private Guides—For many, Paris merits hiring a Parisian as a personal guide. **Arnaud Servignat** is an excellent licensed local guide (€155/half-day, €260/day, also does car tours of the countryside around Paris for a little more, tel. 06 68 80 29 05, www .arnaud-servignat.com, arnotour@mac.com). **Elizabeth Van Hest** is another highly likeable and capable guide (€170 maximum/half-day, €260/day, tel. 01 43 41 47 31, e.van.hest@erenis.fr). **Paris Walks** or **Context Paris** can also set you up with one of their guides; some Paris Walks guides are trained to work with families (both companies described above).

By Bike and Segway

Although Paris has a new, inexpensive, city-wide bike-rental system (you may notice scads of white and green bikes at various locations), it's unavailable to tourists, since you must have a French-issued credit card. Instead, consider renting a bike through this company:

Fat Tire Bike Tours—Hit the road with a younger crowd for frolicking four-hour guided rides in English through Paris. Daytime tours feature more history (€24, daily from mid-Feb–Jan at 11:00, April–Oct also at 15:00), while nighttime tours are more lively and fun (€28, April–Oct nightly at 19:00). For all tours, meet at the south pillar of the Eiffel Tower, then go to the Fat Tire office to pick up bikes (cash only, up to 26 people per group, no bikes or reservations needed, helmets available upon request at no extra charge, office at 24 rue Edgar Faure, Mo: Dupleix, tel. 01 56 58 10 54, www.fattirebiketoursparis.com).

They also rents bikes *sans* tour for independent types (€2/hr, €15/24 hrs, includes helmets and locks, credit-card imprint required for deposit, ask for their suggested bike-route map, daily 9:00–19:00, same address as above).

Fat Tire's pricey **Segway Tours**—on futuristic, stand-up motorized scooters—are novel in that you learn to ride a Segway while exploring Paris (€70, up to 8 per group, daily from mid-Feb–Jan at 9:30 and at 18:30 from April–Oct, plan on spending nearly an hour getting used to the machine, reservations required for this tour, www.parissegwaytours.com).

Excursions from Paris

Many companies offer bus tours to regional sights, including all of the day trips described in this book. **Paris Vision** offers mass-produced, full-size bus and minivan tours to several popular regional destinations, including the Loire Valley, Champagne region, D-Day beaches, and Mont St. Michel. Minivan tours are more expensive but more personal, given in English, and offer convenient pickup at your hotel (€130–200/person). Their full-size bus tours are multilingual and cost about half the price of a minivan tour—worthwhile for some travelers simply for the ease of transportation to the sights (about €60, destinations include Versailles and Giverny). Paris Vision's full-size buses depart from 214 rue de Rivoli (Mo: Tuileries, tel. 01 42 60 30 01, www.parisvision.com).

SELF-GUIDED WALK

Historic Core of Paris Walk

(This information is distilled from the Historic Paris Walk chapter in *Rick Steves' Paris,* by Rick Steves, Steve Smith, and Gene Openshaw.)

Allow four hours to do justice to this three-mile walk. Start where the city did—on the Île de la Cité. Face Notre-Dame and follow the gray line on the "Historic Core of Paris" map (see page 54).

• *To get to Notre-Dame, ride the Métro to Cité, Hôtel de Ville, or St. Michel and walk to the big square facing toward the cathedral. View it from the bronze plaque on the ground (30 yards from the central doorway) marked "Point Zero." You're standing at the center of France, the point from which all distances are measured...*

Historic Core of Paris

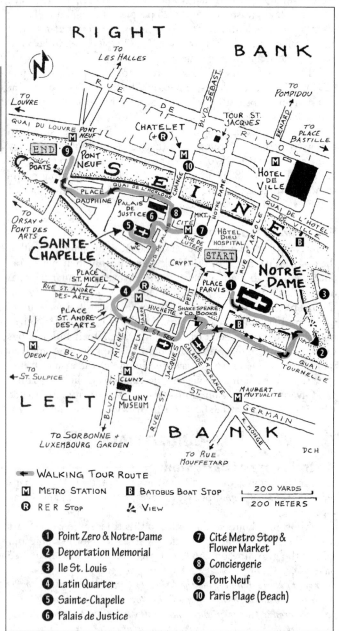

WALKING TOUR ROUTE

M METRO STATION   **B** BATOBUS BOAT STOP

R RER STOP   **View**

200 YARDS
200 METERS

1. Point Zero & Notre-Dame
2. Deportation Memorial
3. Ile St. Louis
4. Latin Quarter
5. Sainte-Chapelle
6. Palais de Justice
7. Cité Metro Stop & Flower Market
8. Conciergerie
9. Pont Neuf
10. Paris Plage (Beach)

▲▲Notre-Dame Cathedral

This 700-year-old cathedral is packed with history and tourists. Study its sculpture and windows, take in a Mass, eavesdrop on guides, and walk all around the outside.

The **cathedral facade** is worth a close look. The church is dedicated to "Our Lady" (Notre-Dame). Mary is center stage—cradling Jesus, surrounded by the halo of the rose window. Adam is on the left and Eve is on the right.

Below Mary and above the arches is a row of 28 statues known as the Kings of Judah. During the French Revolution, these biblical kings were mistaken for the hated French kings. The citizens stormed the church, crying, "Off with their heads!" All were decapitated, but have since been recapitated.

Speaking of decapitation, look at the carving above the doorway on the left. The man with his head in his hands is St. Denis. Back when there was a Roman temple on this spot, Christianity began making converts. The fourth-century bishop of Roman Paris, Denis, was beheaded. But these early Christians were hard to keep down. The man who would become St. Denis got up, tucked his head under his arm, and headed north until he found just the right place to meet his maker: Montmartre. (Although the name "Montmartre" comes from the Roman "Mount of Mars," later generations—thinking of their beheaded patron, St. Denis— preferred a less pagan version, "Mount of Martyrs.") The Parisians were convinced of this miracle, Christianity gained ground, and a church soon replaced the pagan temple.

Medieval art was OK if it embellished the house of God and told biblical stories. For a fine example, move to the base of the central column (at the foot of Mary, about where the head of St. Denis could spit if he were really good). Working around from the left, find God telling a barely created Eve, "Have fun, but no apples." Next, the sexiest serpent I've ever seen makes apples à la mode. Finally, Adam and Eve, now ashamed of their nakedness, are expelled by an angel. This is a tiny example in a church covered with meaning.

Now move to the right and study the carving above the **central portal.** It's the end of the world, and Christ sits on the throne of Judgment (just under the arches, holding his hands up). Below him an angel and a demon weigh souls in the balance. The "good" stand to the left, looking up to heaven. The "bad" ones to the right are chained up and led off to a six-hour tour of the Louvre on a hot day. The "ugly" ones must be the crazy, sculpted demons to the right, at the base of the arch.

Wander through the interior. You'll be routed around the ambulatory, much as medieval pilgrims would have been. Don't miss the rose windows filling each of the transepts. Back outside, walk around the church through the park on the riverside for a close look at the flying buttresses.

The neo-Gothic, 300-foot **spire** is a product of the 1860 reconstruction. Around its base are apostles and evangelists (the green men) as well as Eugène-Emmanuel Viollet-le-Duc, the architect in charge of the work. Notice how the apostles look outward, blessing the city, while the architect (at top, seen from behind the church) looks up, admiring his spire.

The **archaeological crypt** is a worthwhile 15-minute stop if you have a Paris Museum Pass (€3.50, covered by Museum Pass—described on page 64, Tue–Sun 10:00–18:00, closed Mon, enter 100 yards in front of cathedral). You'll see Roman ruins, trace the street plan of the medieval village, and see diagrams of how the earliest Paris grew and grew, all thoughtfully explained in English.

Cost, Hours, Location: Free, cathedral open daily 7:45–19:00; Treasury–€3, not covered by Museum Pass, Treasury open daily 9:30–17:30; audioguide–€5, ask about free English tours, normally Wed and Thu at 12:00, Sat at 14:30; Mo: Cité, Hôtel de Ville, or St. Michel; tel. 01 42 34 56 10, www.cathedraledeparis.com.

Tower: You can climb to the top of the facade between the towers, and then to the top of the south tower, 400 steps total, for a grand view (€7.50, covered by Museum Pass but no bypass line for passholders, daily April–Sept 10:00–18:30—also June–Aug Sat–Sun until 23:00, Oct–March 10:00–17:30, last entry 45 min before closing, arrive before 10:00 or after 17:00 to avoid long lines).

• Behind Notre-Dame, squeeze through the tourist buses, cross the street, and enter the iron gate into the park at the tip of the island. Look for the stairs and head down to reach the...

▲Deportation Memorial

This memorial (Mémorial de la Déportation) to the 200,000 French victims of the Nazi concentration camps draws you into their experience. As you descend the steps, the city around you disappears. Surrounded by walls, you have become a prisoner. Your only freedom is your view of the sky and the tantalizing glimpse of the river below.

Enter the single-file chamber ahead. Inside, the circular plaque in the floor reads, "They went to the end of the earth and

Ile St. Louis

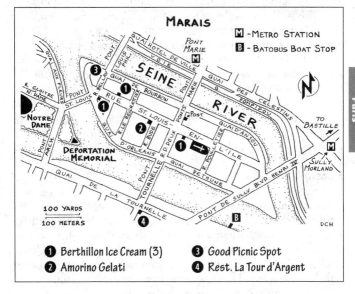

MARAIS

M – METRO STATION
B – BATOBUS BOAT STOP

SEINE RIVER

TO BASTILLE

NOTRE DAME

DEPORTATION MEMORIAL

SULLY MORLAND

100 YARDS
100 METERS

DCH

❶ Berthillon Ice Cream (3)   ❸ Good Picnic Spot
❷ Amorino Gelati   ❹ Rest. La Tour d'Argent

did not return." A hallway stretches in front of you, lined with 200,000 lighted crystals, one for each French citizen who died. Flickering at the far end is the eternal flame of hope. The tomb of the unknown deportee lies at your feet. Above, the inscription reads, "Dedicated to the living memory of the 200,000 French deportees sleeping in the night and the fog, exterminated in the Nazi concentration camps."

Above the exit as you leave is the message you'll find at all Holocaust sights: "Forgive, but never forget." (Free, daily April–Sept 10:00–12:00 & 14:00–19:00, Oct–March 10:00–12:00 & 14:00–17:00, at the east tip of the island named Ile de la Cité, behind Notre-Dame and near Ile St. Louis, Mo: Cité, tel. 01 49 74 34 00.)

• Look across the river to the...

Ile St. Louis

If the Ile de la Cité is a tug laden with the history of Paris, it's towing this classy little residential dinghy laden only with boutiques, famous sorbet shops, and restaurants (see "Eating," page 131). This island wasn't developed until much later (18th century). What was a swampy mess is now harmonious Parisian architecture. The pedestrian bridge, pont St. Louis, connects the two islands, leading right to rue St. Louis-en-l'Ile. This spine of the island is lined with interesting shops. A short stroll takes you to the famous Berthillon ice cream parlor (#31). Loop back to the pedestrian bridge along the parklike quays (walk north to the river and turn left). This walk is about as peaceful and romantic as Paris gets.

Before walking to the opposite end of the Ile de la Cité, loop through the Latin Quarter (as indicated on the map on page 54).

• *From the Deportation Memorial, cross the bridge onto the Left Bank and enjoy the riverside view of Notre-Dame, window-shopping among the green book stalls and browsing through used books, vintage posters, and souvenirs. At the little park and church (over the bridge from the front of Notre-Dame), venture inland a few blocks, basically arcing through the Latin Quarter and returning to the island two bridges down at place St. Michel.*

▲Latin Quarter

The touristic fame of this neighborhood relates to its intriguing artsy, bohemian character. This was perhaps Europe's leading university district in the Middle Ages—home, since the 13th century, to the prestigious Sorbonne University. Back then, Latin was the language of higher education. And, since students here came from all over Europe, Latin served as their linguistic common denominator. Locals referred to the quarter by its language: Latin.

The neighborhood's main boulevards (St. Michel and St. Germain) are lined with far-out bookshops, street singers, and jazz clubs. While still youthful and artsy, the area has become a tourist ghetto filled with cheap North African eateries. The cafés that were once the haunts of great poets and philosophers are now the hangout of tired tourists. For colorful wandering or café sitting, afternoons and evenings are best (Mo: St. Michel).

Walking along rue St. Séverin, you can still see the shadow of the medieval sewer system (the street slopes into a central channel of bricks). In the days before plumbing and toilets, when people still went to the river or neighborhood wells for their water, "flushing" meant throwing it out the window. Certain times of day were flushing times. Maids on the fourth floor would holler, *"Garde de l'eau!"* ("Watch out for the water!") and heave it into the streets, where it would eventually be washed down into the Seine.

Consider a visit to the Cluny Museum for its medieval art and unicorn tapestries (see page 81).

Place St. Michel (facing the St. Michel bridge) is the traditional core of the Left Bank's artsy, liberal, hippie district of poets, philosophers, winos, and tourists. In less commercial times, place St. Michel was a gathering point for the city's malcontents and misfits. Here, in 1871, the citizens took the streets from government troops, set up barricades *Les Mis*–style, and established the Paris Commune. During World War II, the locals rose up against their Nazi oppressors (read the plaques by St. Michel fountain). And in the spring of 1968, a time of social upheaval all over the

Sainte-Chapelle

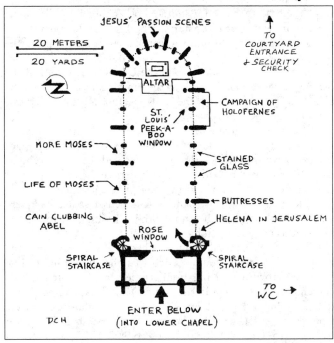

world, young students—battling riot batons and tear gas—took over the square and demanded change.

• *From place St. Michel, look across the river and find the spire of Sainte-Chapelle church and its weathervane angel (below). Cross the river on pont St. Michel and continue along boulevard du Palais. On your left, you'll see the high-security doorway to Sainte-Chapelle. You'll need to pass through a metal detector to get into Sainte-Chapelle complex. (There are tentative plans for Sainte-Chapelle to have a shared entrance with the Conciergerie, listed below, but it's not likely in 2008, if at all.) Once past security, restrooms are ahead on the left. The line into the church may be long. (Museum Pass–holders can bypass this line; pick up an English info flier.) Enter the humble ground floor of...*

▲▲▲Sainte-Chapelle

This triumph of Gothic church architecture is a cathedral of glass like no other. It was speedily built between 1242 and 1248 for Louis IX (the only French king who is now a saint) to house the supposed Crown of Thorns. Its architectural harmony is due to the fact that it was completed under the direction of one architect in only six years—unheard of in Gothic times. (Notre-Dame took more than 200 years to build.)

The design clearly shows an Old Regime approach to worship. The basement was for staff and other common folk. Royal Christians worshipped upstairs. The ground-floor paint job, a 19th-century restoration, is a reasonably accurate copy of the original.

Climb the spiral staircase to the **Chapelle Haute.** Fill the place with choral music, crank up the sunshine, face the top of the altar, and really believe that the Crown of Thorns is there, and this becomes one awesome space.

"Let there be light." In the Bible, it's clear: Light is divine. Light shining through stained glass was a symbol of God's grace shining down to earth. Gothic architects used their new technology to turn dark stone buildings into lanterns of light. The glory of Gothic shines brighter here than in any other church.

There are 15 separate panels of stained glass (6,500 square feet—two-thirds of it 13th-century original), with more than 1,100 different scenes, mostly from the Bible.

The altar was raised up high to better display the relic—the Crown of Thorns—around which this chapel was built. The supposed crown cost King Louis three times as much as this church. Today, it is kept in the Notre-Dame Treasury and shown only on Fridays during Lent (€7.50, €11.50 combo-ticket covers Conciergerie—see next page, both covered by Museum Pass; open daily March–Oct 9:30–18:00, Nov–Feb 9:00–17:00, last entry 30 min before closing, Mo: Cité).

• *Head back outside.*

Palais de Justice

As you walk around the church exterior, look down and notice how much Paris has risen in the 800 years since Sainte-Chapelle was built. You're in a huge complex of buildings that has housed the local government since ancient Roman times. It was the site of the original Gothic palace of the early kings of France. The only surviving medieval parts are the Sainte-Chapelle church and the Conciergerie prison.

Most of the site is now covered by the giant Palais de Justice, home of France's supreme court (built in 1776). "*Liberté, Egalité, Fraternité,*" emblazoned over the doors, is a reminder that this was also the headquarters of the Revolutionary government.

• *Now pass through the big iron gate to the noisy boulevard du Palais. Cross the street to the wide pedestrian-only rue de Lutèce and walk about halfway down.*

Cité "Métropolitain" Stop and Flower Market

Of the 141 original early-20th-century subway entrances, this is one of only a few survivors—now preserved as a national art treasure.

The curvy, plantlike ironwork is a textbook example of Art Nouveau, the style that rebelled against the erector-set squareness of the Industrial Age (e.g., Mr. Eiffel's tower).

The flower and plant market on place Louis Lépine is a pleasant detour. On Sundays, this square is all aflutter with a busy bird market. And across the way is the Prefecture de Police, where Inspector Clouseau of *Pink Panther* fame used to work, and where the local resistance fighters took the first building from the Nazis in August of 1944, leading to the Allied liberation of Paris a week later.

• *Pause here to admire the view. Sainte-Chapelle is a pearl in an ugly architectural oyster. We'll double back to the Palais de Justice, turn right and enter the...*

▲Conciergerie

Though barren inside, this former prison echoes with history. It's a gloomy place. Kings used it to torture and execute failed assassins. The leaders of the Revolution put it to similar good use. A tower along the river, called "the babbler," was named for the painful sounds that leaked from it.

Marie-Antoinette was imprisoned here. During a busy eight-month period in the Revolution, she was one of 2,600 prisoners kept here on the way to the guillotine. You can see Marie-Antoinette's cell, which houses a collection of her mementos. In another room, a list of those made "a foot shorter at the top" by the "national razor" includes ex-King Louis XVI, Charlotte Corday (who murdered Jean-Paul Marat in his bathtub), and the chief revolutionary who got a taste of his own medicine, Maximilien de Robespierre (€7.50, €11.50 combo-ticket covers Sainte-Chapelle, both covered by Museum Pass, daily April–Sept 9:30–18:00, Oct–March 10:00–17:00, last entry 30 min before closing, 4 boulevard du Palais, Mo: Cité, tel. 01 53 40 60 80, www.monuments-nationaux.fr).

Back outside, turn left on boulevard du Palais and head toward the river (north). On the corner is the city's oldest public clock. The mechanism of the present clock is from 1334, and even though the case is Baroque, it keeps on ticking.

• *Turn left onto quai de l'Horloge and walk west along the river, past the round medieval tower called "the babbler." The bridge up ahead is the pont Neuf, where we'll end this walk. At the first corner, veer left into a sleepy triangular square called place Dauphine. Marvel at how such quaintness could be lodged in the midst of such greatness as you walk through the park to the end of the island (the departure point for Seine river cruises offered by Vedettes du Pont-Neuf; see page 51). At the equestrian statue of Henry IV, turn right onto the bridge and take refuge in one of the nooks on the Eiffel Tower side.*

Paris at a Glance

▲▲▲**Louvre** Europe's oldest and greatest museum, starring *Mona Lisa* and *Venus de Milo*. **Hours:** Wed–Mon 9:00–18:00, closed Tue. Most wings open Wed and Fri until 21:45. See page 67.

▲▲▲**Orsay Museum** Nineteenth-century art, including Europe's greatest Impressionist collection. **Hours:** Tue–Sun 9:30–18:00, Thu until 21:45, closed Mon. See page 73.

▲▲▲**Sainte-Chapelle** Gothic cathedral with peerless stained glass. **Hours:** Daily March–Oct 9:30–18:00, Nov–Feb 9:00–17:00. See page 59.

▲▲▲**Eiffel Tower** Paris' soaring exclamation point. **Hours:** Daily mid-June–Aug 9:00–24:45 in the morning, Sept–mid-June 9:30–23:45. See page 75.

▲▲▲**Arc de Triomphe** Arch with viewpoint, marking start of Champs-Elysées. **Hours:** Outside always open; inside open daily April–Sept 10:00–23:00, Oct–March 10:00–22:00. See page 87.

▲▲▲**Versailles** The ultimate royal palace (Château), with Hall of Mirrors, vast gardens, a grand canal, plus queen's playground (Domaine de Marie-Antoinette). **Hours:** Château—April–Oct Tue–Sun 9:00–18:30, Nov–March Tue–Sun 9:00–17:30, closed Mon. Domaine—Daily April–Oct 12:00–19:30, Nov–March 9:00–17:00. Gardens open daily 9:00 until sunset. See page 163.

▲▲**Orangerie Museum** Monet's water lilies, plus art by Cézanne, Renoir, Matisse, and Picasso in a lovely setting. **Hours:** Wed–Mon 12:30–19:00, Fri until 21:00, closed Tue. See page 72.

▲▲**Notre-Dame Cathedral** Paris' most beloved church, with towers and gargoyles. **Hours:** Cathedral open daily 7:45–19:00; Tower open daily April–Sept 10:00–18:30—also June–Aug Sat–Sun until 23:00, Oct–March 10:00–17:30; Treasury open daily 9:30–17:30. See page 55.

▲▲**Army Museum and Napoleon's Tomb** The emperor's imposing tomb, flanked by army museums. **Hours:** Daily April–Sept 10:00–18:00—mid-June–mid-Sept tomb stays open until 19:00, Oct–March 10:00–17:00, Oct–May closed first Mon of every month. See page 79.

▲▲**Marmottan Museum** Untouristy art museum focusing on Monet. **Hours:** Tue–Sun 10:00–18:00, closed Mon. See page 80.

▲▲**Rodin Museum** Works by the greatest sculptor since Michelangelo, with many sculptures in a peaceful garden. **Hours:** April–Sept Tue–Sun 9:30–17:45, Oct–March Tue–Sun 9:30–16:45, closed Mon. See page 80.

▲▲**Cluny Museum** Medieval art with unicorn tapestries. **Hours:** Wed–Mon 9:15–17:45, closed Tue. See page 81.

▲▲**Champs-Elysées** Paris' grand boulevard. **Hours:** Always open. See page 85.

▲▲**Jacquemart-André Museum** Art-strewn mansion. **Hours:** Daily 10:00–18:00. See page 89.

▲▲**Pompidou Center** Modern art in colorful building with city views. **Hours:** Wed–Mon 11:00–21:00, closed Tue. See page 91.

▲▲**Jewish Art and History Museum** Displays history of Judaism in Europe. **Hours:** Mon–Fri 11:00–18:00, Sun 10:00–18:00, closed Sat. See page 92.

▲▲**Picasso Museum** World's largest collection of Picasso's works. **Hours:** April–Sept Wed–Mon 9:30–18:00, Oct–March Wed–Mon 9:30–17:30, closed Tue. See page 94.

▲▲**Carnavalet Museum** Paris' history wrapped up in a 16th-century mansion. **Hours:** Tue–Sun 10:00–18:00, closed Mon. See page 95.

▲▲**Sacré-Cœur** White basilica atop Montmartre with spectacular views. **Hours:** Daily 7:00–23:00. See page 96.

▲**Conciergerie** Historic prison for Marie-Antoinette and others on their way to the chopping block. **Hours:** Daily April–Sept 9:30–18:00, Oct–March 10:00–17:00. See page 61.

▲**Panthéon** Neoclassical monument to French notables. **Hours:** Daily 10:00–18:30 in summer, until 18:00 in winter. See page 83.

▲**Opéra Garnier** Grand belle époque theater with a modern ceiling by Chagall. **Hours:** Daily 10:00–16:30, July–Aug until 18:00. See page 87.

▲**Père Lachaise Cemetery** Final resting place for Paris' illustrious dead. **Hours:** Mon–Sat 8:00–18:00, Sun 9:00–18:00. See page 95.

Pont Neuf

This "new bridge" is now Paris' oldest. Built during Henry IV's reign (about 1600), its 12 arches span the widest part of the river. The fine view includes the park on the tip of the island (note Seine tour boats), the Orsay Museum, and the Louvre. These turrets were originally for vendors and street entertainers. In the days of Henry IV, who originated the promise of "a chicken in every pot," this would have been a lively scene.

• *As for now, you can tour the Seine by boat, continue to the Louvre, or head to the...*

Paris *Plage* (Beach)

The Riviera it's not, but this newly developed faux beach—assembled in summer along a two-mile stretch of the Seine on the Right Bank—is a fun place to stroll, play, and people-watch on a sunny day. Each summer since 2002, the Paris city government has shut down the embankment's highway and trucked in potted palm trees, hammocks, lounge chairs, and 2,000 tons of sand to create a colorful urban beach. You'll also find climbing walls, a swimming pool, trampolines, *boules*, a library, beach volleyball, badminton, and Frisbee areas in three zones: sandy, grassy, and wood-tiled. As you take in the playful atmosphere, imagine how much has changed here since the Middle Ages when this was a grimy fishing community (free, mid-July–mid-Aug daily 7:00–24:00, no beach off-season; on the Right Bank of the Seine, just north of the Ile de la Cité, between pont des Arts and pont de Sully).

SIGHTS

Paris Museum Pass

In Paris, there are two classes of sight-seers—those with a Paris Museum Pass, and those who stand in line. Serious sight-seers save time and money by getting this pass.

Buying the Pass

The pass pays for itself with four admissions in two days, and lets you skip the ticket line at most sights (2 days/€30, 4 days/€45, 6 days/€60, no youth or senior discount). It's sold at the participating museums, monuments, and TIs (even at airports). Try to avoid buying the pass at a major museum (such as the Louvre), where the supply can be spotty and lines long. For more info, call 01 44 61 96 60 or visit www.parismuseumpass.com.

Paris Sights

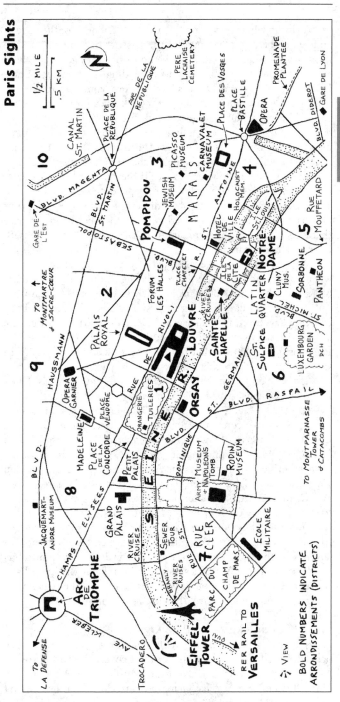

Tally up what you want to see from the list on opposite page—and remember, an advantage of the pass is that you skip to the front of most lines, which can save hours of waiting, especially in summer. Note that at a few sights (including the Louvre, Sainte-Chapelle, and Notre-Dame's Tower), everyone has to shuffle through the slow-moving baggage-check lines for security—but you still save time by avoiding the ticket line.

The pass isn't worth buying for children and teens, as most museums are free or discounted for those under 18 (teenagers may need to show ID as proof of age). Of the few museums that charge for children, some allow kids in free if their parent has a Museum Pass, while others charge admission, depending on age (the cutoff age varies from 5 to 18). The free directory that comes with your pass lists the current hours of sights, phone numbers, and the price that kids pay. If a sight is free for kids, they can skip the line with their passholder parents.

Think ahead to make the most of your pass. Validate it only when you're ready to tackle the covered sights on consecutive days. Make sure the sights you want to visit will be open (Mondays and Tuesdays are big days for museums to be closed). While the Paris Museum Pass covers the Château and Domaine de Marie-Antionette at Versailles, this major sight is best covered with Versailles' Le Passeport pass. On days that you don't have pass coverage, visit free sights, as well as sights that aren't covered by passes.

If you're on a tight budget and have four days in Paris, here's a plan to best use the Paris Museum Pass and Versailles' Le Passeport pass. Get a two-day Paris Museum Pass and visit these key sights in two consecutive days: the Louvre, Sainte-Chapelle, Cluny Museum, and Panthéon on one day, and the Orsay, Rodin Museum, Orangerie, and maybe the Army Museum on the other. Remember that sights such as the Arc de Triomphe and Pompidou Center are open later in the evening, and that the Louvre, Orsay, and Orangerie are open later on selected evenings, allowing you to stretch the day for your Paris Museum Pass. On a separate day, see Versailles (buy your Le Passeport pass in Paris to cover the round-trip train ride to Versailles). On another day, see sights not covered by the pass, such as the Eiffel Tower. If you plan to buy Le Passeport to see Versailles, don't do it on a day that your Paris Museum Pass is active—but if you must visit Versailles when your Paris Museum Pass is active, then use it for Versailles.

What the Paris Museum Pass Covers

Most of the sights listed in this chapter are covered by the pass (see list below). The pass does not cover: the Eiffel Tower, Montparnasse Tower, Marmottan Museum, Opéra Garnier, Notre-Dame Treasury, Jacquemart-André Museum, Jewish Art and History Museum, Grand Palais, La Défense and La Grande Arche, Catacombs, *Paris Story* film, Montmartre Museum, Sacré-Cœur's dome, Dalí Museum, Museum of Erotic Art, and the ladies of Pigalle.

Here's a list of included sights and their admission prices without the pass:

Louvre (€9)	Notre-Dame Tower (€7.50)
Orsay Museum (€7.50)	Paris Archaeological Crypt (€3.50)
Orangerie Museum (€6.50)	Picasso Museum (€7.70)
Sainte-Chapelle (€7.50)	Cluny Museum (€6.50)
Arc de Triomphe (€8)	Pompidou Center (€10)
Rodin Museum (€6)	National Maritime Museum (€9)
Conciergerie (€7.50)	Panthéon (€7.50)
Sewer Tour (€4)	Army Museum and Napoleon's Tomb (€8)

Versailles (Château–€13.50, Domaine de Marie-Antoinette–€9)

Activating and Using the Pass

The pass isn't activated until the first time you use it (write the starting date on the pass). To use your pass at sights, boldly walk to the front of the ticket line, hold up your pass, and ask the ticket-taker: *"Entrez, pass?"* (ahn-tray pahs). You'll either be allowed to enter at that point or you'll be directed to a special entrance. For major sights, such as the Louvre and Orsay museums, we've identified passholder entrances on the maps in this book.

With the pass, you'll pop freely into sights that you're walking by (even for a few minutes) that otherwise might not be worth the expense (e.g., the Conciergerie or Paris Archaeological Crypt).

Major Museums Neighborhood

Paris' grandest park, the Tuileries Garden, was once the private property of kings and queens. Today, it links the museums of the Louvre, Orangerie, and the Orsay. And across from the Louvre are the tranquil, historic courtyards of the Palais Royal.

▲▲▲**Louvre (Musée du Louvre)**— This is Europe's oldest, biggest, greatest, and second-most-crowded museum (after the Vatican). Housed in a U-shaped, 16th-century palace (accentuated by a 20th-century glass pyramid), the Louvre is Paris' top museum and one of its key landmarks. It's home to the *Mona Lisa, Venus de Milo,* and hall after hall of Greek and Roman masterpieces, medieval jewels, Michelangelo statues,

Major Museums Neighborhood

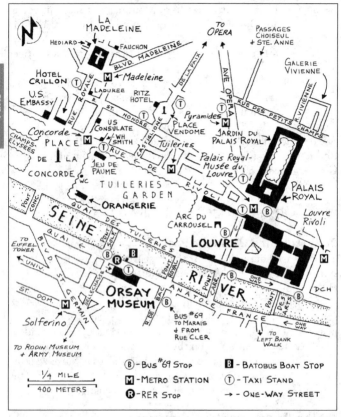

and paintings by the greatest artists from the Renaissance to the Romantics (mid-1800s).

Touring the Louvre can be overwhelming, so be selective. The **Denon Wing** (south, along the river) holds Greek sculptures, Italian paintings (by Raphael and da Vinci), and—of course—French paintings (Neoclassical and Romantic). The adjoining **Sully Wing** contains the *Venus de Milo*, Egyptian artifacts, and more French paintings. For extra credit, tackle the **Richelieu Wing** (north, away from the river), with works from ancient Mesopotamia (today's Iraq), as well as French, Dutch, and Northern art.

Expect changes—the sprawling Louvre is constantly in flux. Rooms are periodically closed for renovation, and their paintings and sculpture are moved to a new place within the museum. In 2008, for example, don't be surprised if *Venus de Milo* and a few other Greek pieces have been moved. To find the piece you're looking for, check with the nearest guard for its new location: Say the title or point to a photo and ask, *"Où est, s'il vous plaît?"* (oo ay see voo play)

Cost: €9, €6 after 18:00 on Wed and Fri, free on first Sun of month, covered by Museum Pass. Tickets good all day and reentry allowed. Optional additional charges apply for temporary exhibits.

Hours: Wed–Mon 9:00–18:00, closed Tue. Most wings open Wed and Fri until 21:45. Galleries start closing 30 minutes early. The last entry is 45 minutes before closing. Crowds are worst on Sun, Mon, Wed, and mornings. Tel. 01 40 20 53 17, recorded info tel. 01 40 20 51 51, www.louvre.fr.

Location: At Palais Royal–Musée du Louvre Métro stop. (The old Louvre Métro stop, called Louvre-Rivoli, is farther from the entrance.)

Buying Tickets: The *tabac* in the underground mall at the Louvre sells tickets to the Louvre, Orsay, and Versailles, plus Paris Museum passes, for the same prices as elsewhere but without the lines. Under the pyramid, self-serve ticket machines are faster than the ticket windows (they accept euro notes, coins, and Visa cards, but not MasterCard).

Crowd-Beating Tips: There is no grander entry than through the pyramid, but metal detectors (not ticket-buying lines) create a long line at times. There are several ways to avoid the line. Museum Pass–holders can use the group entrance in the pedestrian passage-way between the pyramid and rue de Rivoli (under the arches, a few steps north of the pyramid, find the uniformed guard at the entrance, with the escalator down). Otherwise, you can enter the Louvre from its (usually less-crowded) underground entrance, accessed through the "Carrousel du Louvre" shopping mall. Enter the mall at 99 rue de Rivoli (the door with the red awning, daily 8:30–23:00) or directly from the Métro stop Palais Royal–Musée du Louvre (stepping off the train, exit at the end of the platform, following signs that read *Musée du Louvre–Le Carrousel du Louvre*).

Tours: The 90-minute English-language tours leave three times daily except Sun (normally at 11:00, 14:00, and 15:45, €6.50 plus your entry ticket, tour tel. 01 40 20 52 63). Sign up for tours at the *Accueil des Groupes* area. Digital audioguides give eager students a directory of about 130 masterpieces, allowing you to dial a commentary on included works as you stumble upon them (€5, available at entries to the three wings, at the top of the escalators). I prefer the self-guided tour described below, which is also available as a free audiotour for users of iPods and MP3 players (download from www.ricksteves.com or iTunes).

❷ Self-Guided Tour: Start in the Denon Wing and visit the highlights, in the following order (thanks to Gene Openshaw for his help with this).

Wander through the **ancient Greek and Roman works** to see

The Louvre

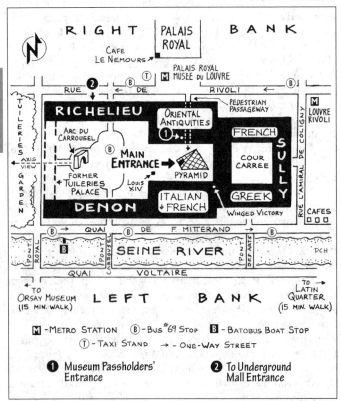

the Parthenon frieze, Pompeii mosaics, Etruscan sarcophagi, and Roman portrait busts. Pop into the adjoining Sully Wing to see the lovely *Venus de Milo (Aphrodite)*. This goddess of love (c. 100 B.C., from the Greek island of Melos) created a sensation when she was discovered in 1820. Most "Greek" statues are actually later Roman copies, but Venus is a rare Greek original. She, like Golden Age Greeks, epitomizes stability, beauty, and balance. Later Greek art was Hellenistic, adding motion and drama. For a good example, see the exciting *Winged Victory of Samothrace* (*Victoire de Samothrace*, on the landing). This statue of a woman with wings, poised on the prow of a ship, once stood on a hilltop to commemorate a great naval victory. This is the *Venus de Milo* gone Hellenistic.

The **Italian collection** is on the other side of the *Winged Victory*. The key to Renaissance painting was realism, and for the Italians "realism" was spelled "3-D." Painters were inspired by the realism and balanced beauty of Greek sculpture. Painting a 3-D world on a 2-D surface is tough, and after a millennium of Dark

Ages, artists were rusty. Living in a religious age, they painted mostly altarpieces full of saints, angels, Madonnas-and-bambinos, and crucifixes floating in an ethereal gold-leaf heaven. Gradually, though, they brought these otherworldly scenes down to earth. (The Italian collection—including the *Mona Lisa*—are scattered throughout the rooms of the long Grand Gallery.)

Two masters of the Italian High Renaissance (1500–1600) were Raphael (see his *La Belle Jardinière,* showing the Madonna, Child, and John the Baptist) and Leonardo da Vinci. The Louvre has the greatest collection of Leonardos in the world—five of them, including the exquisite *Virgin, Child, and St. Anne,* the neighboring *Madonna of the Rocks,* and the androgynous *John the Baptist.* His most famous, of course, is the *Mona Lisa.*

The **Mona Lisa** *(La Joconde)* is in the Salle des Etats, midway down the Grand Gallery, on the right. After a €5 million renovation, Mona is behind glass on her own false wall.

Leonardo was already an old man when François I invited him to France. Determined to pack light, he took only a few paintings. One was a portrait of Lisa del Giocondo, the wife of a wealthy Florentine merchant. When Leonardo arrived, François I immediately fell in love with the painting and made it the centerpiece of the small collection of Italian masterpieces that would, in three centuries, become the Louvre museum. He called it *La Gioconda.* We know it as a contraction of the Italian for "my lady Lisa"—*Mona Lisa.* Warning: François I was impressed, but *Mona* may disappoint you. She's smaller and darker than you'd expect, located in a huge room, behind a glaring pane of glass.

Mona's overall mood is one of balance and serenity, but there's also an element of mystery. Her smile and long-distance beauty are subtle and elusive, tempting but always just out of reach, like strands of a street singer's melody drifting through the Métro tunnel. *Mona* doesn't knock your socks off, but she winks at the patient viewer.

Now for something **Neoclassical.** Notice the fine work, such as *The Coronation of Napoleon* by Jacques-Louis David, near *Mona* in the Salle Daru. Neoclassicism, once the rage in France (1780–1850), usually features Greek subjects, patriotic sentiment, and a clean, simple style. After Napoleon quickly conquered most of Europe, he insisted on being made emperor (not merely king) of this "New Rome." He staged an elaborate coronation ceremony in Paris, and rather than let the pope crown him, he crowned himself. The setting is the Notre-Dame Cathedral, with Greek columns and Roman arches thrown in for effect. Napoleon's mom was also added, since she couldn't make it to the ceremony. A key on the frame describes who's who in the picture.

The **Romantic** collection, in an adjacent room (Salle Mollien), has works by Théodore Géricault *(The Raft of the Medusa)* and Eugène Delacroix *(Liberty Leading the People)*. Romanticism, with an emphasis on motion and emotion, is the complete flip side of Neoclassicism, though they both flourished in the early 1800s. Delacroix's *Liberty*, commemorating the stirrings of democracy in France, is also a fitting tribute to the Louvre, the first museum opened to the common rabble of humanity. The good things in life don't belong only to a small wealthy part of society, but to all. The motto of France is *"Liberté, Egalité, Fraternité"*—liberty, equality, and brotherhood.

Exit the room at the far end (past the café) and go downstairs, where you'll bump into the bum of a large, twisting male nude who looks like he's just waking up after a thousand-year nap. The two *Slaves* (1513–1515) by Michelangelo are a fitting end to this museum—works that bridge the ancient and modern worlds. Michelangelo, like his fellow Renaissance artists, learned from the Greeks. The perfect anatomy, twisting poses, and idealized faces look like they could have been done 2,000 years earlier. Michelangelo said that his purpose was to carve away the marble to reveal the figures God had put inside. The *Rebellious Slave*, fighting against his bondage, shows the agony of that process and the ecstasy of the result.

Palais Royal Courtyards—Across from the Louvre on rue de Rivoli are the pleasant courtyards of the stately Palais Royal. Although the palace is closed to the public, the courtyards are open. As you enter, you'll pass through a whimsical courtyard filled with stubby, striped columns and playful fountains (with fun, reflective metal balls) into another, curiously peaceful courtyard. This is where in-the-know Parisians come to take a quiet break, walk their poodle, or enjoy a rendezvous—surrounded by a serene arcade and a handful of historic restaurants.

Exiting the courtyard at the side facing away from the Seine brings you to the galeries Colbert and Vivienne, good examples of shopping arcades from the early 1900s (courtyards free, always open).

▲▲Orangerie Museum (Musée de l'Orangerie)—This Impressionist museum, lovely as a water lily, has recently reopened

after years of renovation. Step out of the tree-lined, sun-dappled Impressionist painting that is the Tuileries Garden and into the Orangerie (oh-rahn-zheh-ree). You'll start with the museum's claim to fame:

Claude Monet's water lilies. Then head downstairs to enjoy a little *bijou* of select works by Maurice Utrillo, Paul Cézanne, Pierre-Auguste Renoir, Henri Matisse, and Pablo Picasso.

Cost, Hours, Location: €6.50, under 18 free, covered by Museum Pass, audioguide-€5, Wed–Mon 12:30–19:00, Fri until 21:00, closed Tue, located in Tuileries Garden near place de la Concorde, Mo: Concorde, tel. 01 44 77 80 07, www.musee -orangerie.fr.

▲▲▲Orsay Museum (Musée d'Orsay)—The Musée d'Orsay (mew-zay dor-say) houses French art of the 1800s (specifically, art from 1848 to 1914), picking up where the Louvre leaves off. For us, that means Impressionism. The Orsay houses the best general collection anywhere of Edouard Manet, Monet, Renoir, Edgar Degas, Vincent van Gogh, Paul Cézanne, and Paul Gauguin.

The museum shows art that is also both old and new, conservative and revolutionary. You'll start on the ground floor with the Conservatives and the early rebels who paved the way for the Impressionists, then head upstairs to see how a few visionary young artists bucked the system, revolutionized the art world, and paved the way for the 20th century.

Cost: €7.50, €5.60 after 16:15 and on Sun, free at exactly 17:00 (Thu at 21:00) and on first Sun of month, covered by Museum Pass.

Free Entry near Closing: Right when the ticket booth stops selling tickets (Tue–Wed and Fri–Sun at 17:00, Thu at 21:00), you're welcome to scoot in free of charge. (They won't let you in much after that, however.) You'll have the art mostly to yourself before the museum closes. The Impressionist galleries upstairs start shutting down first, so go there right away.

Hours: Tue–Sun 9:30–18:00, Thu until 21:45, last entry one hour before closing (45 min before on Thu), Impressionist galleries start closing at 17:15, closed Mon. Note that the Orsay is crowded on Tuesday, when the Louvre is closed.

Location: Above the RER-C stop called Musée d'Orsay; the nearest Métro stop is Solférino, three blocks southeast of the Orsay.

Bus #69 from the Marais neighborhood stops at the museum on the river side (quai Anatole France); from the rue Cler area, it stops behind the museum on the rue du Bac. From the Louvre, catch bus #69 along rue de Rivoli; otherwise, it's a lovely 15-minute walk through the Tuileries Garden and across the river on

Orsay Museum—Ground Floor

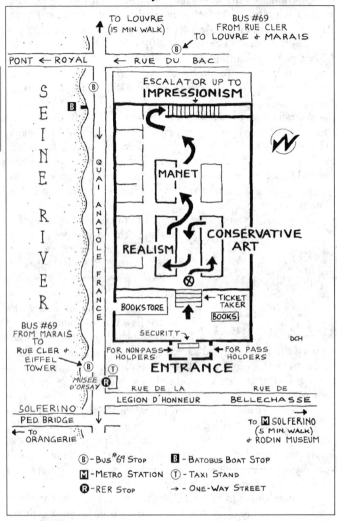

the pedestrian bridge to the Orsay. The museum is at 1 rue de la Légion d'Honneur (tel. 01 40 49 48 14, www.musee-orsay.fr). A taxi stand is in front of the entrance on quai Anatole France.

Information: The booth inside the entrance gives free floor plans in English. Tel. 01 40 49 48 14, www.musee-orsay.fr.

Tours: Audioguides are €5. English-language tours usually run at 11:30 daily (except Sun), cost €6, and take 90 minutes. Tours in English focusing on the Impressionists are held on Tue at 14:30 (€6, sometimes also on other days).

Paris

Cuisine Art: There's a pricey but *très* elegant restaurant on the second floor, with affordable tea and coffee served 15:00–17:30. A simple fifth-floor café is sandwiched between the Impressionists; above it is an easy self-service place with sandwiches and drinks.

Ƽ Self-Guided Tour: For most visitors, the most important part of the museum is the Impressionist collection upstairs. Here, you can study many pictures you've probably seen in books, such as Manet's *Luncheon on the Grass*, Renoir's *Dance at the Moulin de la Galette*, Monet's *Cathedral of Rouen*, James Abbott McNeill Whistler's *Portrait of the Artist's Mother*, Van Gogh's *The Church at Auvers-sur-Oise*, and Cézanne's *The Card Players*. As you approach these beautiful, easy-to-enjoy paintings, remember that there is more to this art than meets the eye.

Here's a primer on Impressionism: After the camera was invented, it threatened to make artists obsolete. A painter's original function was to record reality faithfully, like a journalist. Now a machine could capture a better likeness faster than you could say Etch-A-Sketch.

But true art is more than just painted reality. It gives us reality from the artist's point of view, putting a personal stamp on the work. It records not only a scene—a camera can do that—but the artist's impressions of that scene. Impressions are often fleeting, so the artist has to work quickly.

The Impressionist painters rejected camera-like detail for a quick style more suited to capturing the passing moment. Feeling stifled by the rigid rules and stuffy atmosphere of the Academy, the Impressionists took as their motto, "Out of the studio, into the open air." They grabbed their berets and scarves and took excursions to the country, where they set up their easels on riverbanks and hillsides, or sketched in cafés and dance halls. Gods, goddesses, nymphs, and fantasy scenes were out; common people and rural landscapes were in.

The quick style and simple subjects were ridiculed and called childish by the "experts." Rejected by the Salon, the Impressionists staged their own exhibition in 1874. They brashly took their name from an insult thrown at them by a critic, who laughed at one of Monet's impressions of a sunrise. During the next decade, they exhibited their own work independently. The public, opposed at first, was slowly drawn in by the simplicity, color, and vibrancy of Impressionist art.

Eiffel Tower and Nearby

▲▲▲**Eiffel Tower (La Tour Eiffel)**—It's crowded and expensive, but this 1,000-foot-tall ornament is worth the trouble. Visitors to Paris may find *Mona Lisa* to be less than expected, but the Eiffel Tower rarely disappoints, even in an era of skyscrapers.

Built a hundred years after the French Revolution (and in the midst of an industrial one), the tower served no function but to impress. Bridge-builder Gustave Eiffel won the contest for the 1889 Centennial World's Fair by beating out such rival proposals as a giant guillotine. To a generation hooked on technology, the tower was the marvel of the age, a symbol of progress and human ingenuity. Indeed, despite its 7,000 tons of metal and 50 tons of paint, the tower is so well-engineered that it weighs no more per square inch at its base than a  linebacker on tiptoes. Not all were so impressed, however; many found it a monstrosity. The writer Guy de Maupassant routinely ate lunch in the tower just so he wouldn't have to look at it.

Delicate and graceful when seen from afar, the Eiffel Tower is massive—even a bit scary—from close up. You don't appreciate the size until you walk toward it; like a mountain, it seems so close but takes forever to reach. There are three observation platforms, at 200, 400, and 900 feet; the higher you go, the more you pay. One elevator will take you to the first or second level (just stay on after first stop), but the third level has a separate elevator and line. Plan on at least 90 minutes if you want to go to the top and back. While being on the windy top of the Eiffel Tower is a thrill you'll never forget, the view is actually better from the second level.

The stairs—yes, you can walk up to the second level—are next to the Jules Verne restaurant entrance (allow $300 per person for the restaurant, reserve three months in advance). As you ascend through the metal beams, imagine being a worker, perched high above nothing, riveting this giant erector set together.

The top level, called *le sommet* (900 feet), is tiny. (It can close temporarily without warning when it reaches capacity.) All you'll find here are wind and grand, sweeping views. The city lies before you, with a panoramic guide. On a good day, you can see for 40 miles.

The second level (400 feet) has the best views because you're closer to the sights (walk up stairway to get above netting). There's also a cafeteria and WCs. While you'll save no money, consider taking the elevator up and the stairs down (five minutes from second level to first, five minutes more to ground) for good exercise and views.

The first level (200 feet) has exhibits, a post office (daily 10:00–19:00, cancellation stamp will read Eiffel Tower), a snack bar, WCs, and souvenirs. Read the informative signs (in English)

Eiffel Tower and Nearby

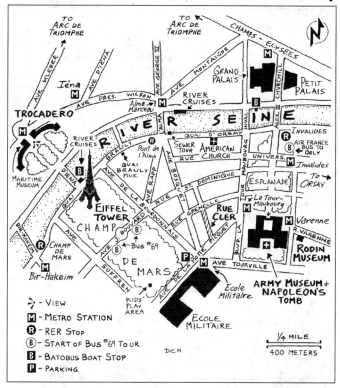

describing the major monuments, see the entertaining free movie on the history of the tower, and don't miss a century of fireworks—including the entire millennium blast—on video. Then consider a drink or a sandwich overlooking all of Paris at the snack café (outdoor tables in summer) or at the city's best view bar/restaurant, **Altitude 95** (see page 135).

Seeing It All: If you don't want to miss a single level, here's a plan for getting the most out of your visit. Ride the lift to second level, then immediately line up and catch the next lift to the top. Enjoy the views on top, then ride back down to the second level. Frolic there for a while and take in some more views. When you're ready, hike down the stairs (no line) or line up for the lift to the first level. Explore the shops and exhibits on this level, have a snack, and take the stairs or lift back to earth.

Cost, Hours, Location: It costs €4.50 to go to the first level, €7.80 to the second, and €11.50 to go to the top (not covered by Museum Pass). You can skip the elevator line and climb the stairs to the first or second level for €4.50, or €3 if you're under 25. The elevators and stairs are both free going down (daily mid-June–Aug 9:00–24:45 in the morning, last ascent to top at 23:00 and to lower levels at 24:00; Sept–mid-June 9:30–23:45, last ascent to top at 22:30 and to lower levels via elevator at 23:00 or by stairs at 18:00; Mo: Bir-Hakeim or Trocadéro, RER: Champ de Mars–Tour Eiffel, tel. 01 44 11 23 23, www.tour-eiffel.fr).

If you climb the stairs, or buy a ticket only to one of the lower levels, you can buy your way up once you're in the Tower—ticket machines on the first and second levels sell supplements to go higher with no penalty.

Tips: To avoid most crowds, go early (get in line by 8:45, before it opens) or late in the day (after 20:00 May–Aug, after 18:00 in off-season—see above for last ascent times); weekends and holidays are worst. Weekdays off-season are not as crowded. Ideally, you should arrive with some light and stay as it gets dark. At the top of the hour, a lighting display features thousands of sparkling lights (this is best viewed from the ground).

To pass the time in line, pick up whatever free reading material is available at the tourist stands at ground level. I like the wonderful *Eiffel Tower Gazette,* a free newspaper featuring a century of Eiffel Tower headlines.

Before or after your tower visit, you can catch the Bateaux Parisiens boat for a Seine cruise (near the base of Eiffel Tower, see page 51 for details).

Best Views: The best place to view the tower is from Trocadéro Square to the north. It's a 10-minute walk across the river, a happening scene at night, and especially fun for kids. Consider arriving at the Trocadéro Métro stop for the view, then walking toward the tower. Another delightful viewpoint is the long, grassy field, le parc du Champ de Mars, to the south (great for dinner picnics). However impressive it may be by day, the tower is an awesome thing to see at twilight, when it becomes engorged with light, and virile Paris lies back and lets night be on top. When darkness fully envelops the city, the tower seems to climax—with a spectacular light show—at the top of each hour... for 10 minutes.

Quai Branly Museum (Museé du Quai Branly)—You probably aren't visiting Paris to see so-called Primitive Art from Africa, Polynesia, Asia, and America, but if you are, this is a world-class collection. This new museum is popular with locals and is often crowded. Masks, statuettes, musical instruments, clothes, voodoo dolls, and a variety of temporary exhibits and activities are presented in a modern building that's a sight in itself. It's a 10-minute walk east (upriver) of the Eiffel Tower, along the river (€8.50, more for some temporary exhibits, covered by Museum Pass, Tue–Sun 10:00–18:30, Thu until 21:30, closed Mon, 37 quai Branly, RER:

Champ de Mars–Tour Eiffel or Pont de l'Alma, tel. 01 56 61 70 00, www.quaibranly.fr).

National Maritime Museum (Musée National de la Marine)— This extensive museum houses an amazing collection of ship models, submarines, torpedoes, cannonballs, *beaucoup* bowsprits, and naval you-name-it—including a small boat made for Napoleon. You'll find limited English information on the walls, but kids like the museum anyway (adults-€9, kids-€7, covered by Museum Pass, Wed–Mon 10:00–18:00, closed Tue, on left side of Trocadéro Square with your back to Eiffel Tower, tel. 01 53 65 69 53, www.musee-marine.fr).

▲**Paris Sewer Tour (Les Egouts de Paris)**—This quick and easy visit takes you along a few hundred yards of underground water tunnel lined with interesting displays, well-described in English, that explain the evolution of the world's longest sewer system. (If you straightened out Paris' sewers, they would reach beyond Istanbul.) Don't miss the slide show, the fine WCs just beyond the gift shop, and the occasional tour in English (€4, covered by Museum Pass, May–Sept Sat–Wed 11:00–17:00, Oct–April Sat–Wed 11:00–16:00, closed Thu–Fri, located where pont de l'Alma greets the Left Bank, Mo: Alma–Marceau, RER: Pont de l'Alma, tel. 01 53 68 27 81).

▲▲**Army Museum and Napoleon's Tomb (Musée de l'Armée)**— The emperor lies majestically dead inside several coffins under a

grand dome glittering with 26 pounds of gold—a goose-bumping pilgrimage for historians. Napoleon is surrounded by the tombs of other French war heroes and fine military museums in the Hôtel des Invalides. Follow signs to the "crypt" to find Roman Empire–style reliefs that list the accomplishments of Napoleon's administration. Check out the interesting World War II wing. The Army Museum's new WWI exhibit is well presented in English and complements the WWII rooms, while the East Wing (which focuses on Napoleonic history) will likely be closed during your 2008 visit for renovation.

Cost, Hours, Location: €8, ticket includes both Army Museum and Napoleon's Tomb, covered by Museum Pass, free for all military personnel with ID, includes audioguide for tomb, daily April–Sept 10:00–18:00, mid-June–mid-Sept tomb stays open until 19:00, Oct–March until 17:00, last entry 30 minutes before closing, Oct–May closed first Mon of every month, at Hôtel des Invalides at 129 rue de Grenelle; Mo: La Tour-Maubourg, Varenne, or Invalides; tel. 01 44 42 37 72, www.invalides.org.

▲▲Rodin Museum (Musée Rodin)—This user-friendly museum is filled with passionate works by the greatest sculptor since  Michelangelo. The entire museum is being gradually renovated over the next few years; pick up the essential museum map to guide you. Auguste Rodin (1840–1917) sculpted human figures on an epic scale, revealing through the body their deepest thoughts and feelings. Rodin's statues rise from the raw stone around them, driven by the life force. With missing limbs and scarred skin, these are prefab classics, making ugliness noble. Rodin's people are always moving restlessly. Even the famous *Thinker* is moving. Rodin worked with many materials—he chiseled marble (though not often), modeled clay, cast bronze, worked plaster, painted, and sketched. He often created different versions of the same subject in different media.

Rodin lived and worked in this mansion, renting rooms alongside Henri Matisse, the poet Rainer Maria Rilke (Rodin's secretary), and the dancer Isadora Duncan. Well-displayed in the mansion where the sculptor lived and worked, exhibits trace Rodin's artistic development, explain how his bronze statues were cast, and show some of the studies he created to work up to his masterpiece (the unfinished *Gates of Hell*). Learn about Rodin's tumultuous relationship with his apprentice and lover, Camille Claudel. Mull over what makes his sculptures some of the most evocative since the Renaissance. For many, the gardens are the highlight of this museum. Here you'll find several of his greatest works, such as the *Thinker, Balzac,* the *Burghers of Calais,* and the *Gates of Hell.* The gardens are ideal for artistic reflection.

Cost, Hours, Location: €6, €4 on Sun, free on the first Sun of the month, covered by Museum Pass. You'll pay €1 to get into the gardens only—which may be Paris' best deal, as many works are on display there (also covered by Museum Pass). Audioguides are €4, and baggage check is mandatory. Open April–Sept Tue–Sun 9:30–17:45, gardens close 18:45; Oct–March Tue–Sun 9:30–16:45, gardens close 17:00, last entry 30 minutes before closing, closed Mon. It's near the Army Museum and Napoleon's Tomb, 79 rue de Varenne, Mo: Varenne, tel. 01 44 18 61 10, www.musee-rodin.fr.

▲▲Marmottan Museum (Musée Marmottan Monet)—In this private, intimate, untouristy museum, you'll find the best collection anywhere of works by Impressionist headliner Claude Monet. Follow Monet's life through more than a hundred works, from simple sketches to the *Impression: Sunrise* painting that gave his artistic movement its start—and a name. You'll also enjoy classic Monet canvases featuring the water lilies from his garden at Giverny (see next chapter).

Cost, Hours, Location: €8, not covered by Museum Pass, Tue–Sun 10:00–18:00, last entry at 17:30, closed Mon, 2 rue Louis Boilly, Mo: La Muette, tel. 01 44 96 50 33, www.marmottan.com. To get to the museum from the Métro stop, follow the brown museum signs six blocks down chaussée de la Muette through the park; pause to watch kids play on the old time, crank-powered carousel.

Left Bank

This Left Bank neighborhood, just opposite Notre-Dame, is the Latin Quarter. (For more information and a walking tour, see the "Historic Core of Paris Walk," page 53.)

▲▲Cluny Museum (Musée National du Moyen Age)—This treasure trove of Middle Age (Moyen Age) art fills old Roman baths, offering close-up looks at stained glass, Notre-Dame carvings, fine goldsmithing and jewelry, and rooms of tapestries. The star here is the exquisite *Lady and the Unicorn* tapestry series: In five panels, a delicate, as-medieval-as-can-be noble lady introduces a delighted unicorn to the senses of taste, hearing, sight, smell, and touch.

Cost, Hours, Location: Free Jan–June, then €6.50 and free on first Sun of month, covered by Museum Pass, Wed–Mon 9:15–17:45, closed Tue, near corner of boulevards St. Michel and St. Germain at 6 place Paul Painlevé; Mo: Cluny–La Sorbonne, St. Michel, or Odéon; tel. 01 53 73 78 16, www.musee-moyenage.fr.

St. Germain-des-Prés—A church was first built on this site in A.D. 452. The church you see today was constructed in 1163 and is all that's left of a once sprawling and influential monastery. The colorful interior reminds us that medieval churches were originally painted in bright colors. The surrounding area hops at night with venerable cafés, fire-eaters, mimes, and scads of artists (free, daily 8:00–20:00, Mo: St. Germain-des-Prés).

▲St. Sulpice Church and Organ Concert—Since it was featured in *The Da Vinci Code,* this grand church has become a trendy stop for the book's many fans. But the real reason to visit is to see and

to hear its intimately accessible organ. For pipe-organ enthusiasts, this is one of Europe's great musical treats. The Grand Orgue at St. Sulpice Church has a rich history, with a succession of 12 world-class organists—including Charles-Marie Widor and Marcel Dupré—that goes back 300 years. Widor started the tradition of opening

Left Bank

the loft to visitors after the 10:30 service on Sundays. Organist Daniel Roth continues to welcome guests in three languages while playing five keyboards. (See www.danielrothsaintsulpice.org for his exact dates and concert plans.)

The 10:30–11:30 Sunday Mass is followed by a high-powered 25-minute recital. Then, just after noon, the small, unmarked door is opened (left of entry as you face the rear). Visitors scamper like sixteenth notes up spiral stairs, past the 19th-century StairMasters that five men once pumped to fill the bellows, into a world of 7,000 pipes. You can see the organ and visit with Daniel. You'll generally have 30 minutes to kill (there's a plush lounge) before you can watch the master play during the next Mass; you can leave at any time. If you're late or rushed, show up at about 12:30 and wait at the little door. As someone leaves, you can slip in, climb up, and catch the rest of the performance (church open daily 7:30–19:30, Mo: St. Sulpice or Mabillon).

Tempting boutiques surround the church (see "Shopping," page 98), and nearby is the...

▲**Luxembourg Garden (Jardin du Luxembourg)**—Paris' most beautiful, interesting, and enjoyable garden/park/recreational area is a great place to watch Parisians at rest and play (open daily until dusk, Mo: Odéon, RER: Luxembourg). It's ideal for families. These private gardens are property of the French Senate (housed in the château) and have special rules governing their use (e.g., where cards can be played, where dogs can be walked, where joggers can run, when and where music can be played). The brilliant flower beds are completely changed three times a year, and the boxed trees are brought out of the orangery in May. Challenge the card and chess players to a game (near the tennis courts), rent a toy sailboat, or find a free chair near the main pond and take a breather.

The grand, Neoclassical-domed Panthéon, now a mausoleum housing the tombs of several great Frenchmen, is a block away and only worth entering if you have a Museum Pass.

If you enjoy the Luxembourg Garden and want to see more green spaces, you could visit the more elegant **Parc Monceau** (Mo: Monceau), the colorful **Jardin des Plantes** (Mo: Jussieu or Gare d'Austerlitz, RER: Gare d'Austerlitz), or the hilly and bigger **Parc des Buttes-Chaumont** (Mo: Buttes-Chaumont).

▲**Panthéon**—This dramatic Neoclassical monument celebrates France's illustrious history and people, balances Foucault's pen-

dulum, and is the final home to many French VIPs. Step inside the vast building (360' by 280' by 270'), and you'll see an altar to liberty—the **Monument to the National Convention** (the political body that opposed the monarchy during the Revolution), inscribed with the familiar motto, "Live free or die." Working clock-

wise around the church-like space, you'll trace the celebrated struggles of the French people: a martyred St. Denis picking up his head, St. Genevieve saving Paris from the Franks, St. Louis as king and crusader, Joan of Arc and her exploits, and so on.

Foucault's pendulum swings gracefully at the end of a 220-foot cable suspended from the towering dome. It was here in 1851 that the scientist Léon Foucault first demonstrated the rotation of the Earth. Stand a few minutes and watch the pendulum's arc (appear to) shift as you and the earth rotate beneath it.

Stairs in the back lead down to the **crypt** where a pantheon of greats are buried, including famous French writers Victor Hugo *(Les Misérables, The Hunchback of Notre-Dame)*, Alexandre Dumas *(The Three Musketeers, The Count of Monte Cristo)* and Emile Zola *(Les Rougon-Macquart, Nana)*. You'll also find the discoverers of radium, Polish-born Marie Curie and her French husband, Pierre, along with many others. An **exhibit** explores the building's fasci-nating history (good English descriptions). And you can climb 206 steps to the **dome gallery** for fine views of the interior as well as the city (accessible only with an escort who leaves about every hour until 17:15—see schedule as you enter).

Cost, Hours, Location: €7.50, covered by Museum Pass, daily 10:00–18:30 in summer, until 18:00 in winter, last entry 45 minutes before closing (Mo: Cardinal Lemoine). Ask about occasional English tours or call ahead for schedule (tel. 01 44 32 18 00).

Montparnasse Tower (La Tour Montparnasse)—This 59-story superscraper is cheaper and easier to ascend than the Eiffel

Tower, with the added bonus of one of Paris' best views. (The Eiffel Tower is in sight, and Montparnasse Tower isn't.) Buy the €3 photo guide to the city, then go to the rooftop and orient yourself. As you zip up 56 floors in 38 seconds, watch the altitude meter above the door. At the top, scan the city with the wind in your hair, noticing the lush courtyards hiding behind grand street fronts. Back inside and downstairs, you'll find a small, overpriced café, fascinating historic black-and-white photos, and a plush little theater playing *Paris Like Never Seen* (free, 12 min, shows continuously). You'll float past unseen visual delights, spiraling down the Eiffel Tower as the French narration explains, "Paris is radiant and confident, like a lover who finally took her blouse off."

Cost, Hours, Location: €9, not covered by Museum Pass, daily April–Sept daily 9:30–23:30; Oct–March Sun-Thu 9:30–23:30, Fri–Sat 9:30–23:30; last entry 30 minutes before closing, disappointing after dark, entrance on rue de l'Arrivée, Mo: Montparnasse–Bienvenüe, tel. 01 45 38 52 56, www.tourmontparnasse56.com. The tower is an efficient stop when combined with a day trip to Chartres (see next chapter), which begins at the Montparnasse train station.

▲**Catacombs**—Reopening in Spring 2008, these underground tunnels contain the anonymous bones of six million permanent Parisians. In 1786, the Revolutionary Government of Paris decided to relieve congestion and improve sanitary conditions by emptying the city cemeteries (which traditionally surrounded churches) into an official ossuary. The perfect locale was the many miles of underground tunnels from limestone quarries, which were, at that time, just outside the city. For decades, priests led ceremonial processions of black-veiled, bone-laden carts into the quarries, where the bones were stacked into piles five feet high and as much as 80 feet deep behind neat walls of skull-studded tibiae. Each transfer was completed with the placement of a plaque indicating the church and district from which that stack of bones came and the date they arrived. Note to wannabe Hamlets: An attendant checks your bag at the exit for stolen souvenirs. A flashlight is handy. Being shorter than 6'2" is helpful.

Cost, Hours, Location: Closed through Spring 2008, €7, not covered by Museum Pass, Tue–Sun 10:00–17:00, ticket booth closes at 16:00, closed Mon, 1 place Denfert-Rochereau, tel. 01 43 22 47 63. Take the Métro to Denfert-Rochereau, then find the lion in the big traffic circle; if he looked left rather than right, he'd stare right at the green entrance to the Catacombs. You'll exit at 36 rue Remy Dumoncel, far from where you started. If you walk to the right, to avenue du Général Leclerc, you'll be equidistant from Métro stops Alésia (walk left) and Mouton Duvernet (walk right).

Champs-Elysées and Nearby

▲▲Place de la Concorde and the Champs-Elysées—This famous boulevard is Paris' backbone, and has the greatest concentration of traffic. All of France seems to converge on the place de la Concorde, the city's largest square. The Tour de France bicycle race ends here, as do all parades (French or foe) of any significance. While the Champs-Elysées has become as international as it is local, a walk here is still a must.

In 1667, Louis XIV opened the first section of the street as a short extension of the Tuileries Garden. This date is considered the birth of Paris as a grand city. The Champs-Elysées soon became *the* place to cruise in your carriage. (It still is today—traffic can be jammed up even at midnight.) One hundred years later, the café scene arrived. It was here that the guillotine took the lives of thousands—including King Louis XVI and Marie-Antoinette. Back then it was called the place de la Révolution.

From the 1920s until the 1960s, this boulevard was pure elegance. Locals actually dressed up to come here. It was mainly residences, rich hotels, and cafés. Then, in 1963, the government pumped up the neighborhood's commercial metabolism by bringing in the RER (commuter underground). Suburbanites had easy access, and bam—there went the neighborhood.

The *nouveau* Champs-Elysées, revitalized in 1994, has new benches and lamps, broader sidewalks, and a fleet of green-suited workers armed with high-tech pooper-scoopers. Blink away the modern elements, and it's not hard to imagine the boulevard pre-1963, with only the finest structures lining both sides all the way to the palace gardens.

To saunter down the Champs-Elysées, take the Métro to the Arc de Triomphe, described below (Mo: Charles de Gaulle–Etoile; Métro stops every few blocks: Franklin D. Roosevelt, George V, and Charles de Gaulle–Etoile).

Paris

Champs-Elysées and Nearby

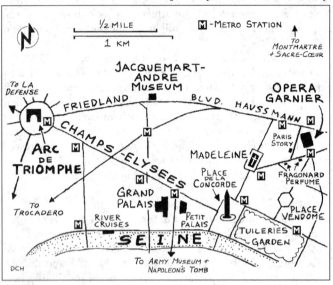

Inspect the fancy car dealerships—**Peugeot** at #136 (showing off its futuristic concept cars next to the classic models) and **Mercedes-Benz,** a block down at #118 (like an English-language car show). In the 19th century, this was an area for horse stables; today, it's the district of garages, limo companies, and car dealerships.

Next to Mercedes is the famous **Lido,** Paris' largest cabaret (and a multiplex cinema). Check out the perky photos, R-rated videos, and shocking prices. Paris still offers the kind of burlesque-type spectacles combining music, comedy, and scantily clad women that have been performed here since the 19th century. Movie-going on the Champs-Elysées is also popular, at theaters that show the very latest releases. Check to see if there are films you recognize, then look for the showings *(séances)*. A "v.o." *(version originale)* next to the time indicates the film will be in its original language.

Fouquet's café-restaurant (#99), under the red awning, is a popular spot among French celebrities and charges accordingly (€4.90 for espresso). Opened in 1899 as a coachman's bistro, Fouquet's gained fame as the hangout of France's WWI biplane fighter pilots—those who weren't shot down by Germany's infamous "Red Baron." It also served as James Joyce's dining room. Since the early 1900s, Fouquet's has been a favorite of French actors and actresses. The golden plaques by the entrance honor winners of France's Oscar-like film awards, the Césars—see plaques for Gérard Depardieu, Catherine Deneuve, and more.

Ladurée (two blocks downhill at #75, with green and purple awning) is a classic 19th-century tea salon/restaurant/*pâtisserie*. Its interior is right out of the 1860s. Wander in...even peeking into the cozy rooms upstairs. A coffee here is *très élégant* (only €3.30). The bakery sells traditional macaroons, cute little cakes, and gift-wrapped finger sandwiches to go (your choice of four mini-macaroons for €6).

▲▲▲**Arc de Triomphe**—Napoleon had the magnificent Arc de Triomphe commissioned to commemorate his victory at the battle of

Austerlitz. There's no triumphal arch bigger (165 feet high, 130 feet wide). And, with 12 converging boulevards, there's no traffic circle more thrilling to experience—either from behind the wheel or on foot (take the underpass).

The foot of the arch is a stage on which the last two centuries of Parisian history have played out—from the funeral of Napoleon, to the goose-stepping arrival of the Nazis, to the triumphant return of Charles de Gaulle after the Allied liberation. Ponder the Tomb of the Unknown Soldier (from World War I, at base of arch), where the flame is rekindled daily at 18:30. Find François Rude's famous relief, "La Marseillaise" (on the right pillar), showing a shouting Lady Liberty rallying weary troops.

The 284 steps lead to a cute museum about the arch, sweeping skyline panoramas, and a mesmerizing view down onto the traffic that swirls around the arch.

Cost, Hours, Location: Outside—free, always open. Interior—€8, free for kids under 18, free on first Sun of month Oct–March, covered by Museum Pass, daily April–Sept 10:00–23:00, Oct–March 10:00–22:00, last entry 30 minutes before closing, place Charles de Gaulle, use underpass to reach arch, Mo: Charles de Gaulle–Etoile, tel. 01 55 37 73 77, www.monuments-nationaux.fr.

▲**Opéra Garnier**—This grand theater of the belle époque was built for Napoleon III and finished in 1875. While the building is huge, the actual auditorium seats only 2,000. The real show was before and after the performance, when the elite of Paris—out to see and be seen—strutted their elegant stuff in the extravagant lobbies. Think of the grand marble stairway as a theater itself. As you wander the halls and gawk at the decor, imagine the place filled with the beautiful people of its day. The massive foundations straddle an underground lake (inspiring the mysterious world of *The Phantom of the Opera*). Visitors can peek from two boxes into the actual red-velvet performance hall to view Marc Chagall's colorful ceiling (1964) playfully dancing around the eight-ton chandelier (guided tours take you into the performance hall). Note the box seats next to the stage—the most expensive in the house, with an obstructed view of the stage...but just right if you're here only to be seen.

The elitism of this place prompted a people's opera house, built in the 1980s, symbolically on place de la Bastille, where the French Revolution started in 1789. This left the Opéra Garnier home only to ballet and occasional concerts (see below).

Cost, Hours, Location: €8, not covered by Museum Pass, daily 10:00–16:30, July–Aug until 18:00, closed during performances, 8 rue Scribe, Mo: Opéra, RER: Auber.

Tours: Ask about English tours of the building during summer and off-season weekends (€12, includes entry, 90 min, call for schedule, tel. 01 40 01 17 89).

Ballet and Concert Tickets: Check the performance schedule at the information booth (inside entry), in *Pariscope* magazine (see page 40), or on the website to see the upcoming schedule (www.opera-de-paris.fr). To buy tickets by phone, call 08 92 89 90 90 (toll call, office closed Sun). There are usually no performances mid-July–mid-Sept.

Nearby: The *Paris Story* film and Fragonard Perfume Museum (see below) are on the left side of the Opéra, and the venerable Galeries Lafayette department store (top-floor café with marvelous views, see page 98) is just behind. Across the street, the illustrious Café de la Paix has been a meeting spot for the local glitterati for generations. If you can afford the coffee, this spot offers a delightful break.

Paris Story **Film**—This entertaining film offers a painless overview of the city's turbulent and brilliant past, covering 2,000 years in 45 fast-moving minutes. The theater's wide-screen projection and cushy chairs provide a break from bad weather and sore feet, and the movie's a fun activity with kids. It makes a good first-day orientation, but don't go out of your way to get here.

Cost, Hours, Location: €10, kids-€6, family of four-€26, not covered by Museum Pass. Individuals get a 20 percent discount with this book in 2008 (no discount on family rate). The film shows on the hour daily 10:00–18:00. Next to Opéra Garnier at 11 rue Scribe, Mo: Opéra, tel. 01 42 66 62 06.

Fragonard Perfume Museum—Near Opéra Garnier, two perfume shops masquerade as museums. Either location will teach you a little about how perfume is made (ask for the English handout), but the one on rue Scribe smells even sweeter—and it's in a beautiful 19th-century mansion (both free, daily 9:00–18:00, at 9 rue Scribe and 30 rue des Capucines, tel. 01 47 42 04 56, www.fragonard.com).

▲▲Jacquemart-André Museum (Musée Jacquemart-André)—This thoroughly enjoyable museum showcases the lavish home of a wealthy, art-loving, 19th-century Parisian couple. After wandering the grand boulevards, get inside for an intimate look at the lifestyles of the Parisian rich and fabulous. Edouard André and his wife Nélie Jacquemart—who had no children—spent their lives and fortunes designing, building, and then decorating this sumptuous mansion. What makes the visit so rewarding is the excellent audioguide tour (in English, free with admission, plan on spending an hour with the audioguide). The place is strewn with paintings by Rembrandt, Botticelli, Uccello, Mantegna, Bellini, Boucher, and Fragonard—enough to make a painting gallery famous.

Cost, Hours, Location: €9.50, not covered by Museum Pass, daily 10:00–18:00, at 158 boulevard Haussmann, Mo: Miromesnil or Saint-Philippe de Roule, bus #80 makes a convenient connection to Ecole Militaire, tel. 01 45 62 11 59, www.musee-jacquemart-andre.com.

After Your Visit: Consider a break in the sumptuous museum tearoom, with delicious cakes and tea (daily 11:45–17:45). From here, walk north on rue de Courcelles to see Paris' most beautiful park, Parc Monceau.

Petit Palais (and its Musée des Beaux-Arts)—In this free museum, renovated and reopened in 2006, you'll find a broad collection of paintings and sculpture from the 1600s to the 1900s. To some, it feels like a museum of second-choice art, as the more famous museums in Paris have better collections from the same periods. Some even find the beautifully restored building more interesting than its art collection. Others find a few diamonds in the rough from Monet, Renoir, Boudin, and other Impressionists; some interesting Art Nouveau pieces; and a smattering of works from Dutch, Italian, and Flemish Renaissance artists (Wed–Sun 10:00–18:00, Tue 10:00–20:00 for temporary exhibits, closed Mon, across from Grand Palais on avenue Winston Churchill, just west of place de la Concorde, tel. 01 53 43 40 00, www.petitpalais.paris.fr).

Grand Palais—This grand exhibition hall, built for the 1900 World's Fair, is busy with generally worthwhile temporary exhibits. Get details on the current schedule from the TIs, in *Pariscope,* or from www.rmn.fr (usually €10, not covered by Museum Pass, Mon and Thu–Sun 10:00–20:00, Wed 10:00–22:00, last entry 45 min before closing, closed Tue and between exhibitions, avenue Winston Churchill, Mo: Rond-Point or Champs-Elysées, tel. 01 44 13 17 17, www.rmn.fr).

▲La Défense and La Grande Arche—On the outskirts of Paris, the centerpiece of Paris' ambitious skyscraper complex (La Défense) is the Grande Arche. Inaugurated in 1989 on the 200th anniversary of the French Revolution, it was dedicated to human rights and brotherhood. The place is big—38 floors holding offices for 30,000 people on more than 200 acres. Notre-Dame Cathedral could fit under its arch. The complex at La Défense is an interesting study in 1960s land-use planning. More than 150,000 workers commute here daily, directing lots of business and development away from downtown and allowing central Paris to retain

its more elegant feel. This makes sense to most Parisians, regardless of whatever else they feel about this controversial complex.

For an interesting visit, take the Métro to the La Défense stop, explore La Grande Arche (take the elevator to the top for great city views and displays on the arch's construction), then stroll among the glass buildings to the Esplanade de la Défense Métro station, and return home from there. After enjoying the elegance of downtown Paris' historic, glorious monuments, it's clear that man can build bigger, but not more beautiful.

Cost, Hours, Location: La Grande Arche elevator-€7.50, kids-€6, family deals, not covered by Museum Pass, daily April–Sept 10:00–20:00, Oct–May until 19:00, RER or Mo: La Défense, follow signs reading *La Grande Arche*, tel. 01 49 07 27 57, www.grandearche.com. The entry price includes art exhibits and a film on the arch's construction.

Marais Neighborhood and Nearby

The Marais neighborhood extends along the Right Bank of the Seine from the Pompidou Center to the Bastille. It contains more pre-revolutionary lanes and buildings than anywhere else in town and is more atmospheric than touristy. It's medieval Paris. This is how much of the city looked until, in the mid-1800s, Napoleon III had Baron Haussmann blast out the narrow streets to construct broad boulevards (wide enough for the guns and ranks of the army, too wide for revolutionary barricades), thus creating modern Paris. Originally a swamp *(marais)* during the reign of Henry IV, this area became the hometown of the French aristocracy. In the 17th century, big shots built their private mansions *(hôtels)* close to Henry IV's place des Vosges. When strolling the Marais, stick to the west–east axis formed by rue Sainte-Croix de la Bretonnerie, rue des Rosiers (heart of Paris' Jewish community), and rue St. Antoine. On Sunday afternoons, this trendy area pulses with shoppers and café crowds.

▲**Place des Vosges**—Study the architecture in this grand square: nine pavilions per side. Some of the brickwork is real, some is fake.

Marais Neighborhood and Nearby

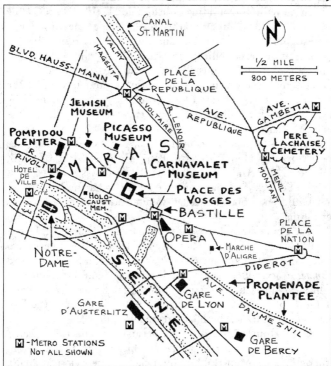

Walk to the center, where Louis XIII sits on a horse surrounded by locals enjoying their community park. Children frolic in the sand-box, lovers warm benches, and pigeons guard their fountains while trees shade this retreat from the glare of the big city. Henry IV built this centerpiece of the Marais in 1605. As hoped, this turned the Marais into Paris' most exclusive neighborhood. As the nobility flocked to Versailles in a later age, this too was a magnet for the rich and powerful of France. With the Revolution, the aristocratic elegance of this quarter became working-class, filled with gritty shops, artisans, immigrants, and Jews. **Victor Hugo** lived at #6, and you can visit his house (free, Tue–Sun 10:00–18:00, last entry at 17:40, closed Mon, 6 place des Vosges, tel. 01 42 72 10 16). Leave the place des Vosges through the doorway at the southwest corner of the square (near the three-star Michelin restaurant, l'Ambroisie) and pass through the elegant **Hôtel de Sully** (great example of a Marais mansion, grand courtyard open until 19:00, fine bookstore inside) to rue St. Antoine.

▲▲**Pompidou Center (Centre Pompidou)**—Europe's greatest collection of far-out modern art is housed in the Musée National d'Art Moderne, on the fourth and fifth floors of this colorful exhibition hall. The building is "exoskeletal" (like Notre-Dame or a crab), with its functional parts—the pipes, heating ducts, and escalator—on the outside, and the meaty art inside. It's the epitome of modern architecture, where "form follows function." Once ahead of its time, the 20th-century art displayed in this museum has been waiting for the world to catch up with it. The 20th century—accelerated by technology and fragmented by war—was exciting and chaotic, and this art reflects the turbulence of that century of change. In this free-flowing and airy museum (with great views over Paris), you'll come face to face with works by Henri Matisse, Pablo Picasso, Marc Chagall, Salvador Dalí, Andy Warhol, Wassily Kandinsky, Max Ernst, Jackson Pollock, and many more. And after so many Madonnas-and-Children, a piano smashed to bits and glued to the wall is refreshing.

The Pompidou Center and its square are lively, with lots of people, street theater, and activity inside and out—a perpetual street fair. Kids of any age enjoy the fun, colorful fountain called *Homage to Stravinsky*, next to the Pompidou Center. If you need a light meal or snack, try the places lining the Stravinsky fountain: Dame Tartine and Crêperie Beaubourg (to the right as you face the museum entrance; both have reasonable prices).

Cost, Hours, Location: €10, permanent collection covered by Museum Pass (but not special exhibitions), free on first Sun of month, Wed–Mon 11:00–21:00, ticket counters close at 20:00, closed Tue, Mo: Rambuteau or farther-away Hôtel de Ville, tel. 01 44 78 12 33, www.centrepompidou.fr.

▲▲**Jewish Art and History Museum (Musée d'Art et Histoire du Judaïsme)**—This fascinating museum, located in a beautifully restored Marais mansion, tells the story of Judaism throughout Europe, from the Roman destruction of Jerusalem to the theft of famous artworks during World War II. Displays illustrate the cultural unity maintained by this continually dispersed population. You'll learn about the history of Jewish traditions from bar mitzvahs to menorahs, and see the exquisite traditional costumes and objects central to daily life. Don't miss the explanation of "the Dreyfus affair," a major event in early 1900s French politics. You'll also see photographs of and paintings by famous Jewish artists, including Marc Chagall, Amedeo Modigliani, and Chaim Soutine. A small but moving section is devoted to the deportation of Jews from Paris during World War II.

Helpful audioguides and many English explanations make this an enjoyable history lesson (red numbers on small signs indicate the number you should press on your audioguide). Move along at your own speed.

The Marais Neighborhood

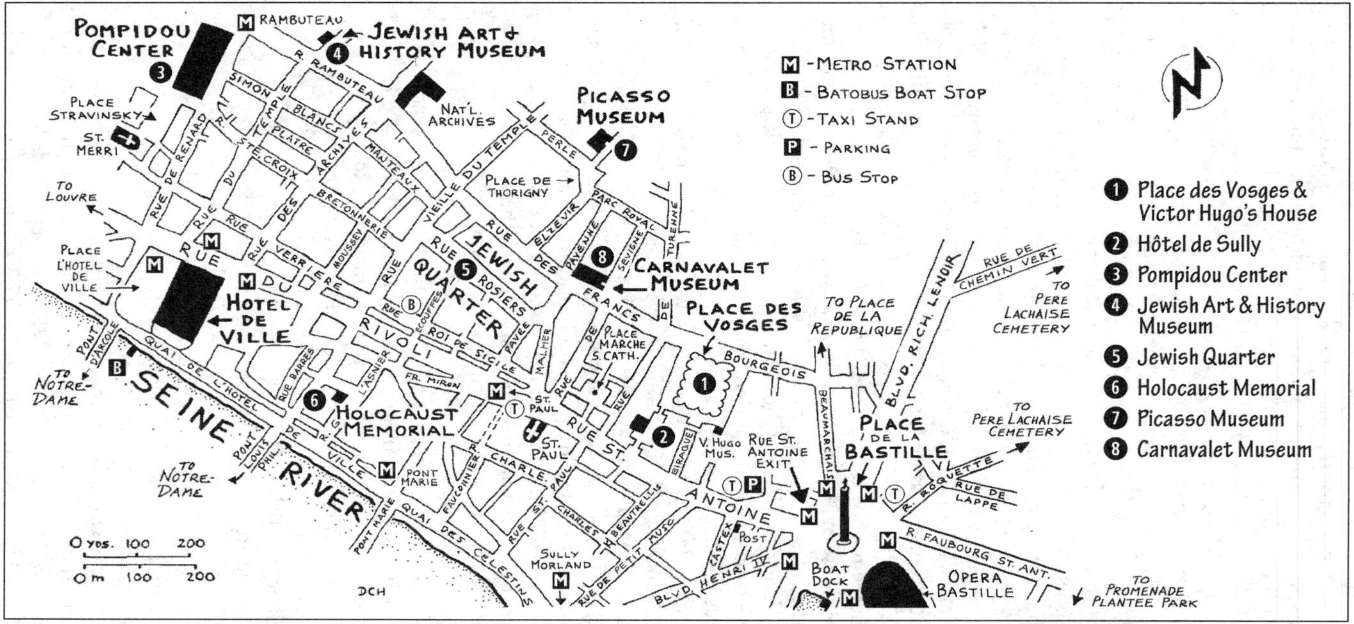

M - Metro Station
B - Batobus Boat Stop
T - Taxi Stand
P - Parking
B - Bus Stop
1 Place des Vosges & Victor Hugo's House
2 Hôtel de Sully
3 Pompidou Center
4 Jewish Art & History Museum
5 Jewish Quarter
6 Holocaust Memorial
7 Picasso Museum
8 Carnavalet Museum
Pompidou Center
Jewish Art & History Museum
Picasso Museum
Carnavalet Museum
Place des Vosges
Jewish Quarter
Hotel de Ville
Holocaust Memorial
Place de la Bastille
Opera Bastille
Seine River
Nat'l. Archives
Place Stravinsky
St. Merri
Place de Thorigny
Place l'Hotel de Ville
To Louvre
To Notre-Dame
To Place de la Republique
To Pere Lachaise Cemetery
To Promenade Plantee Park
Rambuteau
Rue St. Antoine Exit
V. Hugo Mus.
Boat Dock
Sully Morland
Pont Marie
St. Paul
0 yds. 100 200
0 m 100 200
DCH

Cost, Hours, Location: €6.80 but more during special exhibits, includes audioguide, not covered by Museum Pass, Mon–Fri 11:00–18:00, Sun 10:00–18:00, last entry 1 hour before closing, closed Sat, 71 rue du Temple, Mo: Rambuteau or Hôtel de Ville a few blocks farther away, tel. 01 53 01 86 60, www.mahj.org.

Jewish Quarter—Located along rue des Rosiers, the tiny yet colorful Jewish district of the Marais was once considered the largest in Western Europe. Today, while rue des Rosiers is lined with colorful Jewish shops and kosher eateries, the district is being squeezed by the trendy boutiques of modern Paris (visit any day but Saturday, when most businesses are closed—best on Sunday). If you're visiting at lunch time, you'll be tempted by kosher pizza and plenty of €4-falafel-to-go joints (*emporter* means "to-go"). The best falafel is at L'As du Falafel, with a bustling New York–deli atmosphere (at #34, sit-down or to go). The Sacha Finkelsztajn Yiddish bakery (at #27) is also good. The Jewish Quarter is also home to the Holocaust Memorial (see below).

Holocaust Memorial (Mémorial de la Shoah)—Commemorating the lives of the more than 76,000 Jews deported from France in World War II, this memorial's focal point is underground, where victims' ashes are buried, and a corridor contains original police records of arrests and deportations (free, Sun–Fri 10:00–21:00, Thu until 22:00, closed Sat and certain Jewish holidays, 17 rue Geoffroy l'Asnier, tel. 01 42 77 44 72, www.memorialdelashoah.org).

▲▲Picasso Museum (Musée Picasso)—Tucked into a corner of the Marais and worth ▲▲▲ if you're a Picasso fan, this museum contains the world's largest collection of Picasso's paintings, sculptures, sketches, and ceramics, and includes his small collection of Impressionist art. The art is well-displayed in a fine old mansion with a peaceful garden café. The room-by-room English introductions help make sense of Picasso's work—from the Toulouse-Lautrec-like portraits at the beginning of his career to his gray-brown Cubist period to his return-to-childhood, Salvador Dalí–like finish. The well-done English guidebook helps Picasso-philes appreciate the context of his art and learn more about his interesting life. Most will be happy reading the posted English explanations while moving at a steady pace through the museum—the ground and first floors satisfied my curiosity.

Cost, Hours, Location: €7.70, covered by Museum Pass, additional fees for temporary exhibits, free on first Sun of month and for kids under 18 with ID, April–Sept Wed–Mon 9:30–18:00, Oct–March Wed–Mon 9:30–17:30, last entry 45 min before closing, closed Tue, 5 rue de Thorigny, Mo: St. Paul or Chemin Vert, tel. 01 42 71 25 21, www.musee-picasso.fr.

▲▲**Carnavalet Museum (Musée Carnavalet)**—The tumultuous history of Paris is well-portrayed in this hard-to-navigate museum, offering a good overview of everything from Louis XIV period rooms, to Napoleon, to the belle époque. The Carnavalet, which opened in 1880, is housed in two Marais mansions connected by a corridor. The first half of the museum (pre-Revolution) dates from a period when people generally accepted the notion that some were born to rule, and most were born to be ruled. This section is difficult to follow (rooms numbered out of order, no English descriptions, and sections closed due to understaffing) so see it quickly, then concentrate your energy on the Revolution and beyond.

The Revolution is the museum's highlight. Fascinating exhibits cover this bloody period of French history, when atrocious acts were committed in the name of government "by, for, and of the people." The exhibits take you from events that led up to the Revolution, to the storming of the 100-foot-high walls of the Bastille, to the royal beheadings, and through the reigns of terror that followed. They then trace the rise and fall of Napoleon and end with the Paris Commune uprisings. While explanations are in French only, many displays are fairly self-explanatory.

Cost, Hours, Location: Free, Tue–Sun 10:00–18:00, closed Mon; avoid lunchtime (12:00–14:00), when many rooms close; 23 rue de Sévigné, Mo: St. Paul, tel. 01 44 59 58 58, www.carnavalet .paris.fr.

▲**Promenade Plantée Park**—This two-mile-long, narrow garden walk on a viaduct was once used for train tracks and is now a joy. Part of the park is elevated. At times, you'll walk along the street until you pick up the next segment. The shops below the viaduct's arches (a creative use of once-wasted urban space) make for entertaining window-shopping.

Cost, Hours, Location: Free, opens Mon–Fri at 8:00, Sat–Sun at 9:00, closes at sunset. It runs from place de la Bastille (Mo: Bastille) along avenue Daumesnil to Saint-Mandé (Mo: Michel Bizot). From place de la Bastille (follow signs reading *Sortie Opéra* or *Sortie rue de Lyon* from Bastille Métro station), walk down rue de Lyon with the Opéra immediately on your left. Find the steps up the redbrick wall a block after the Opéra.

▲**Père Lachaise Cemetery (Cimetière du Père Lachaise)**— Littered with the tombstones of many of the city's most illustrious dead, this is your best one-stop look at Paris' fascinating, romantic past residents. The tree-lined cemetery is enclosed by a massive wall with peaceful, car-free lanes that encourage parklike meandering. Named for Father *(Père)* La Chaise, whose job was listening to Louis XIV's sins, the cemetery is relatively new, having opened in

1804 to accommodate Paris' expansion. Today, this city of the dead (pop. 70,000) still accepts new residents, but real estate prices are very high.

The 100-acre cemetery is big and confusing, with thousands of graves and tombs crammed every which way, and only a few pathways to navigate by. The helpful €2 map (sold at the flower stores located near either entry) will direct you to the graves of Frédéric Chopin, Molière, Edith Piaf, Oscar Wilde, Gertrude Stein, Jim Morrison, Héloïse and Abélard, and many more.

Cost, Hours, Location: Free, Mon–Sat 8:00–18:00, Sun 9:00–18:00, actually closes at dusk. It's down avenue du Père Lachaise from Mo: Gambetta (also across the street from the less convenient Père Lachaise Métro stop and reachable via bus #69). Tel. 01 55 25 82 10.

Montmartre

▲▲**Sacré-Cœur and Montmartre**—Stroll along Paris' highest hilltop (420 feet) for a different perspective on the City of Light. Walk in the footsteps of the people who've lived here—monks stomping grapes (1200s), farmers grinding grain in windmills (1600s), dust-coated gypsum miners (1700s), Parisian liberals (1800s), modernist painters (1900s), and all the struggling artists, poets, dreamers, and drunkards who came here for cheap rent, untaxed booze, rustic landscapes, and cabaret nightlife. With vineyards, wheat fields, windmills, animals, and a village tempo of life, it was the perfect escape from grimy Paris.

The five-domed, Roman-Byzantine basilica of **Sacré-Cœur** took 44 years to build (1875–1919). It stands on a foundation of 83 pillars sunk 130 feet deep, necessary because the ground beneath was honeycombed with gypsum mines. The exterior is laced with gypsum, which whitens with age.

For an unobstructed panoramic view of Paris, climb 260 feet up the tight and claustrophobic spiral stairs to the top of the **dome** (church free, open daily 7:00–23:00; €5 to climb dome, ticket machine requires coins or Visa card, not covered by Museum Pass, daily June–Sept 9:00–19:00, Oct–May 10:00–18:00).

One block from the church, the **place du Tertre** was the haunt of Henri de Toulouse-Lautrec and the original bohemians. Today, it's mobbed with tourists and unoriginal bohemians, but it's still fun (go early in the morning to beat the crowds).

To get to Montmartre, take the Métro to the Anvers stop (one more Métro ticket buys your way up the funicular and avoids the stairs, but the funicular may be closed for repairs) or the closer but less scenic Abbesses stop. A taxi to the top of the hill saves time and avoids sweat (costs about €10, €20 at night). For restaurant recommendations, see "Eating," page 148.

Dalí Museum (L'Espace Dalí)—This beautifully lit black gallery (well-described in English) offers a walk through statues, etchings, and paintings by the master of surrealism. Don't miss the printed interview on the exit stairs (€10, not covered by Museum Pass, daily 10:00–18:30, 11 rue Poulbot, tel. 01 42 64 40 10, www .daliparis.com).

Montmartre Museum—This 17th-century home recreates Montmartre's traditional cancan and cabaret scene, with paintings, posters, photos, music, and memorabilia (€7, not covered by Museum Pass, Tue–Sun 11:00–18:00, closed Mon, 12 rue Cortot, tel. 01 46 06 61 11, www.museedemontmartre.fr).

Pigalle—Paris' red light district, the infamous "Pig Alley," is at the foot of butte Montmartre. *Ooh la la.* It's more shocking than dangerous. Walk from place Pigalle to place Blanche, teasing desperate barkers and fast-talking temptresses. In bars, a €150 bottle of cheap champagne comes with a friend. Stick to the bigger streets, hang onto your wallet, and exercise good judgment. Cancan can cost a fortune, as can con artists in topless bars. After dark, countless tour buses line the streets, reminding us that tour guides make big bucks by bringing their groups to touristy nightclubs like the famous Moulin Rouge (Mo: Pigalle or Abbesses).

Museum of Erotic Art (Musée de l'Erotisme)—Paris' sexy museum has five floors of risqué displays—mostly paintings and drawings—ranging from artistic to erotic to disgusting, with a few circa-1920 porn videos and a fascinating history of local brothels tossed in. It's in the center of the Pigalle red light district (€8, no... it's not covered by Museum Pass, daily 10:00–2:00 in the morning, 72 boulevard de Clichy, Mo: Blanche, tel. 01 42 58 28 73, www .musee-erotisme.com).

Disappointments de Paris
Here are a few negatives to help you manage your limited time:

La Madeleine is a big, Neoclassical church with a postcard facade and a postbox interior but it's surrounded by fine shops and hosts occasional concerts.

The Bastille is Paris' most famous non-sight. The square is there, but confused tourists look everywhere and can't find the prison of Revolution fame. The building's gone, and the square is good only for its nightlife as a jumping-off point if you're going to the Marais district (see page 138) or Promenade Plantée Park (see page 95).

The Latin Quarter is mostly a frail shadow of its once bohemian self. The blocks nearest the river (across from Notre-Dame) are more Tunisian, Greek, and Woolworth's than old-time Paris. The neighborhood merits a wander (kids love it), but you're better off focusing on the area around boulevard St. Germain and rue de Buci, and on the streets around the Maubert-Mutualité Métro stop.

SHOPPING

Even staunch anti-shoppers may be tempted to partake in chic Paris. Wandering among the elegant and outrageous boutiques provides a break from the heavy halls of the Louvre, and, if you approach it right, a little cultural enlightenment.

Here are some tips for avoiding *faux pas* and making the most of the experience.

French Etiquette: Before you enter a Parisian store, remember the following points.

- In small stores, always say, *"Bonjour, Madame/Mademoiselle/ Monsieur"* when entering and *"Au revoir, Madame/Mademoiselle/Monsieur"* when leaving.
- The customer is not always right. In fact, figure the clerk is doing you a favor by waiting on you.
- Except in department stores, it's not normal for the customer to handle clothing. Ask first before you pick up an item.
- For clothing-size comparisons between the US and France, see page 772.
- Forget returns (and don't count on exchanges).
- Saturdays are busiest.
- Observe French shoppers. Then imitate.
- Don't feel obliged to buy. The expression for "window-shopping" in French is *faire du lèche-vitrines* ("window-licking").

Department Stores *(Les Grands Magasins)*: Like cafés, department stores were invented here (surprisingly, not in America). Parisian department stores, monuments to a more relaxed and elegant era, begin with their spectacular perfume sections. Helpful information desks are usually nearby (pick up the handy store floor plan in English). Most stores have a good selection of souvenirs and toys at fair prices and reasonable restaurants; some have great view terraces. Choose from these great Parisian department stores: Galeries Lafayette (behind old Opéra Garnier, Mo: Opéra), Printemps (next-door to Galeries Lafayette), and Bon Marché (Mo: Sèvres-Babylone).

Boutiques: I enjoy window-shopping, pausing at cafés, and observing the rhythm of neighborhood life. While the shops are more intimate, sales clerks are more formal—mind your manners.

Here are four very different areas to explore:

- A stroll from Sèvres-Babylone to St. Sulpice allows you to sample smart, classic clothing boutiques while enjoying one of Paris' prettier neighborhoods—for sustenance along the way, there's La Maison du Chocolat at 19 rue de Sèvres, selling handmade chocolates in exquisitely wrapped boxes.

• The ritzy streets connecting place de la Madeleine and place Vendôme form a miracle mile of gourmet food shops, jewelry stores, four-star hotels, perfumeries, and exclusive clothing boutiques. Fauchon, on place de la Madeleine, is a bastion of over-the-top food products, hawking €7,000 bottles of Cognac (who buys this stuff?). Hédiard, at #21, across the square from Fauchon, is an older, more appealing, and accessible gourmet food shop. Next door, La Maison des Truffes sells black mushrooms for up to €1,000 a pound, and white truffles from Italy for €2,500 a pound.

• For more eclectic, avant-garde stores, peruse the artsy shops between the Pompidou Center and place des Vosges in the Marais (along rue Ste. Croix de la Bretonnerie and rue des Rosiers).

• For a contemporary, more casual, and less frenetic shopping experience, and to see Paris' latest urban renewal project, take the Métro to Bercy Village, a once-thriving wine-warehouse district that has been transformed into an outdoor shopping mall (Mo: Cour St. Emilion).

Flea Markets: Paris hosts several sprawling weekend flea markets (*marché aux puces,* mar-shay oh poos; literally translated, since *puce* is French for flea). These oversized garage sales date back to the Middle Ages, when middlemen would sell old, flea-infested clothes and discarded possessions of the wealthy at bargain prices to eager peasants. Today, some travelers find them claustrophobic, crowded, monster versions of those back home, though others find their French diamonds-in-the-rough and return happy.

The Puces St. Ouen (poos sahn-wahn) is the biggest and oldest of them all, with more than 2,000 vendors selling mostly antiques. Gritty and seamy, this market could be overwhelming for inexperienced travelers (Sat 9:00–18:00, Sun 10:00–18:00, Mon 11:00–17:00, closed Tue–Fri, pretty dead the first 2 weeks of Aug, tel. 01 58 61 22 90, www.st-ouen-tourisme.com and www.parispuces.com).

Street Markets: Several traffic-free street markets overflow with flowers, produce, fish vendors, and butchers, illustrating how most Parisians shopped before there were supermarkets and department stores. Good market streets include the rue Cler (Mo: Ecole Militaire), rue Montorgueil (Mo: Etienne Marcel), rue Mouffetard (Mo: Censier-Daubenton), and rue Daguerre (Mo: Denfert-Rochereau). Browse these markets to collect a classy picnic (open daily except Sun afternoons and Mon, also closed for lunch 13:00–15:00).

Souvenir Shops: Avoid souvenir carts in front of famous monuments. Prices and selection are better in shops and department stores. The riverfront stalls near Notre-Dame sell a variety of used books, magazines, and tourist paraphernalia in the most romantic setting.

Whether you indulge in a new wardrobe, an artsy poster, or just one luscious pastry, you'll find that a shopping excursion provides a priceless slice of Parisian life.

NIGHTLIFE

Paris is brilliant after dark. Save energy from your day's sightseeing and get out at night. Whether it's a concert at Sainte-Chapelle, an elevator ride up the Arc de Triomphe, or a late-night café, experience the City of Light when it's lit up. If a **Seine River cruise** sounds appealing, check out "Tours," on page 50.

The *Pariscope* magazine (€0.40 at any newsstand, in French) offers a complete weekly listing of music, cinema, theater, opera, and other special events. The *Paris Voice* website in English has a helpful monthly review of Paris entertainment (www.parisvoice.com).

Music

Jazz Clubs—With a lively mix of American, French, and international musicians, Paris has been an internationally acclaimed jazz capital since World War II. Unfortunately, many clubs are smoky, some wedge too many customers in at too few tables, others are downright expensive, and some are guilty of all of the above. You'll pay €12–25 to enter a jazz club (one drink may be included; if not, expect to pay €5–10 per drink; beer is cheapest). For specifics, see *Pariscope* magazine (look under "Musique"), visit www.parisvoice.com, or drop by the clubs to check out the calendars posted on their front doors. Music starts after 21:00 in most clubs. Some offer dinner concerts from about 20:30 on. Here are several good bets:

Caveau de la Huchette, a characteristic old jazz club, fills an ancient Latin Quarter cellar with live jazz and frenzied dancing every night (admission about €11 on weekdays, €13 on weekends, €6 drinks, Tue–Sun 21:30–2:30 in the morning or later, closed Mon, 5 rue de la Huchette, Mo: St. Michel, recorded info tel. 01 43 26 65 05, www.caveaudelahuchette.fr).

For a hotbed of late-night activity and jazz, go to the two-block-long rue des Lombards, at boulevard Sébastopol, midway between the river and the Pompidou Center (Mo: Châtelet). **Au Duc des Lombards,** right at the corner, is one of the most popular and respected jazz clubs in Paris, with concerts generally at 21:00 (42 rue des Lombards, tel. 01 42 33 22 88). **Le Sunside** offers more traditional jazz—Dixieland and big band—and fewer crowds, with concerts generally at 21:00 (60 rue des Lombards, tel. 01 40 26 21 25, www.sunset-sunside.com).

At the more down-to-earth and mellow **La Cave du Franc Pinot,** you can enjoy a glass of chardonnay at the main-floor wine bar, then drop downstairs for a cool jazz scene. They have good dinner-and-jazz values as well—allow about €50 per person (closed Sun–Mon, located on Ile St. Louis where pont Marie meets the island, 1 quai de Bourbon, Mo: Pont Marie, tel. 01 46 33 60 64, www.franc-pinot.com).

Old-Time Parisian Cabaret on Montmartre: Au Lapin Agile— This historic cabaret maintains the atmosphere of the heady days when bohemians would gather here to enjoy wine, song, and sexy jokes. For €24, you gather with about 25 French people in a dark room for a drink and as many as 10 different performers—mostly singers with a piano. Performers range from sweet and innocent Amélie types to naughty Maurice Chevalier types. While tourists are welcome, it's exclusively French, with no accommodation for English-speakers (and non-French-speakers will be lost). You sit at carved wooden tables in a dimly lit room, taste the traditional drink (brandy with cherries), and are immersed in a true Parisian ambience. The soirée covers traditional French standards, love ballads, sea chanteys, and more. The crowd sings along, as it has here for a century (Tue–Sun 21:00–2:00 in the morning, closed Mon, best to reserve ahead, 22 rue des Saules, tel. 01 46 06 85 87, www.au-lapin-agile.com).

A Modern Cabaret near Canal St. Martin: Chez Raymonde— This club proves that the art of dinner cabaret is still alive in Paris. Your evening begins with a good three-course dinner (including apéritif, wine, a half-bottle of champagne, and coffee) in an intimate dining room, where you get to know your neighbors. At about 22:00, the maître d'hôtel and the chef himself kick off the performance with a waltz together. Then it's feather boas, song, and dance—audience participation is encouraged (€85–100/person, Fri–Sun evenings only, dinner starts at 20:00 and performance usually finishes about 23:00, reservations necessary, 119 avenue Parmentier, Mo: Goncourt, Parmentier, or République, tel. 01 43 55 26 27, www.chez-raymonde.com). On Sunday afternoons, you can also attend a performance over lunch (€70–85, starts at 12:30).

Classical Concerts—For classical music on any night, consult *Pariscope* magazine (check "Concerts Classiques" under "Musique" for listings of fee and free events) and look for posters at tourist-oriented churches. From March through November, these churches regularly host concerts: St. Sulpice, St. Germain-des-Prés, Ste. Madeleine, St. Eustache, St. Julien-le-Pauvre, and Sainte-Chapelle. It's well worth the €25 entry for the pleasure of hearing Mozart or Vivaldi while surrounded by the stained glass of the tiny **Sainte-Chapelle** (unheated—bring a sweater). Pick up concert schedules and tickets during the day at the small ticket booth to the left of the chapel entrance. Or call 01 42 77 65 65 to reserve ahead; you can leave your message in English (just speak clearly and spell your name). Seats are unassigned, so arrive 30 minutes early to snare a good view. There are often two concerts per evening at 19:00 and 20:30; specify which one you want when you buy or reserve your ticket. Look also for daytime concerts in parks, such as the Luxembourg Garden. Even the Galeries Lafayette department store offers concerts. Many concerts are free *(entrée libre),* such as the Sunday atelier concert sponsored by the American Church (Sept–May at 17:00 or 18:00 but not every week, 65 quai d'Orsay, Mo: Invalides, RER: Pont de l'Alma, tel. 01 40 62 05 00).

Opera—Paris is home to two well-respected opera venues. The **Opéra Bastille** is the massive modern opera house that dominates place de la Bastille. Come here for state-of-the-art special effects and modern interpretations of classic ballets and operas. In the spirit of this everyman's opera, unsold seats are available at a big discount to seniors and students 15 minutes before the show. Standing-room-only tickets for €15 are also sold for some performances (Mo: Bastille, tel. 01 43 43 96 96). The **Opéra Garnier,** Paris' first opera house, hosts opera and ballet performances. Come here for less-expensive tickets and grand belle époque decor (Mo: Opéra, tel. 01 44 73 13 99). To get tickets for either opera house, call 01 44 73 13 00, or easier, reserve online at www.opera-de-paris.fr. You can also go directly to each opera house's ticket office (open 11:00–18:00).

Night Walks

Go for an evening walk to best appreciate the City of Light. Break for ice cream, pause at a café, and enjoy the sidewalk entertainers as you join the post-dinner Parisian parade. Consider these suggestions:

Champs-Elysées and the Arc de Triomphe—The avenue des Champs-Elysées glows after dark. Start at the Arc de Triomphe (inside open daily April–Sept 10:00–23:00, Oct–March 10:00–22:00), then stroll down Paris' lively grand promenade. A right turn on avenue George V leads to the Bateaux-Mouches river cruises.

Trocadéro and Eiffel Tower—This is one of Paris' most spectacular views at night. Take the Métro to the Trocadéro stop and join the party on place du Trocadéro for a magnificent view of the glowing Eiffel Tower. Pass the fountains and cross the river to the base of the tower, worth the effort even if you don't go up (daily mid-June–Aug 9:00–24:45 in the morning, Sept–mid-June 9:30–23:45). See "Eiffel Tower," page 75.

From the Eiffel Tower, you can stroll through parc du Champ de Mars, past Frisbees, soccer balls, and romantic couples, and take the Métro home (Ecole Militaire stop, across avenue de la Motte-Picquet from far southeast corner of park).

Ile St. Louis and Notre-Dame—This stroll features floodlit views of Notre-Dame and a taste of the Latin Quarter. Take the Métro (line 7) to the Pont Marie stop, then cross to Ile St. Louis. Turn right up rue St. Louis-en-l'Ile, stopping for dinner (or at least a Berthillon ice cream at #31 or Amorino Gelati at #47). Then cross to Ile de la Cité, with a great view of Notre-Dame. Wander to the Left Bank on quai de l'Archevêché, and drop down to the river to the right for the best floodlit views. From May through September, you'll find fun bar-barges (daily until 2:00 in the morning, closed Oct–April, live music often Thu–Sun from 21:00). End your walk trolling pedestrian streets in the Latin Quarter.

After-Dark Bus Tour

Several companies offer evening tours of Paris. I've described the company offering the most tours below. These trips are sold through your hotel (brochures in lobby) or directly at the office listed below. You save no money by buying direct.

Paris Illumination Tours, run by Paris Vision, connect all the great illuminated sights of Paris with a 100-minute bus tour in 12 languages. The double-decker buses have huge windows, but the most desirable front seats are sometimes reserved for customers who have bought tickets for the overrated Moulin Rouge. Left-side seats are better. Visibility is fine in the rain.

Warning: These tours are not for everyone. You'll stampede on with a United Nations of tourists, get a set of headphones, dial up your language, and listen to a tape-recorded spiel (which is interesting, but includes an annoyingly bright TV screen and a pitch for the other, more-expensive excursions). Uninspired as it is, the ride provides an entertaining first-night overview of the city at its floodlit and scenic best. Bring your city map to stay oriented as you go. You're always on the bus, but the driver slows for photos at viewpoints (adults-€24, kids under 12 ride free, 1.5 hours, departures 19:00–22:00 depending on time of year, usually April–Oct only, reserve 1 day in advance, arrive 30 min early to wait in line for best seats, departs from Paris Vision office at 214 rue de Rivoli, across the street from Mo: Tuileries, tel. 01 42 60 30 01, fax 01 42 86 95 36, www.parisvision.com). Skip their pricier minivan night tours.

SLEEPING

I've focused most of my recommendations on four safe, handy, and colorful neighborhoods: the village-like rue Cler (near the Eiffel Tower), the artsy and trendy Marais (near place de la Bastille), the lively and Latin yet classy Luxembourg (on the Left Bank), and a less central but up-and-coming neighborhood near Canal St. Martin (just north of the Marais). Before reserving, read the descriptions of the neighborhoods. Each offers different pros and cons, and your neighborhood is as important as your hotel for the success of your trip.

Reserve ahead for Paris—the sooner, the better. Conventions clog Paris in September (worst), October, May, and June (very tough). There's unusually large crowds during holiday periods (see "Major Holidays and Weekends" on page 5), so book your accommodations well in advance. In August, when Paris is quiet, some hotels offer lower rates to fill their rooms (if you're planning to visit Paris in the summer, the extra expense of an air-conditioned room can be money well spent). For advice on booking rooms, see "Making Reservations" on page 19.

Old, characteristic, budget Parisian hotels have always been cramped. Retrofitted with elevators, toilets, and private showers (as most are today), they are even more cramped. Even three-star hotel rooms are small and often not worth the extra expense in Paris. Some hotels include the hotel tax (*taxe du séjour*, about €1 per person per day), though most will add this to your bill.

Recommended hotels have an elevator unless otherwise noted. Quad rooms usually have two double beds. Because rooms with double beds and showers are cheaper than rooms with twin beds and baths, room prices vary within each hotel.

Continental breakfasts run about €8–10, buffet breakfasts (baked goods, cereal, yogurt, and fruit) cost about €10–15. Café or picnic breakfasts are cheaper, but hotels usually give unlimited coffee.

Get advice from your hotel for safe parking (consider long-term parking at either airport—Orly is closer—and a taxi in). Garages are plentiful (€20–25/day, with special rates through some hotels). Curb parking is free at night (19:00–9:00), all day Sunday, and throughout the month of August. Self-serve launderettes are common; ask your hotelier for the nearest one (*"Où est un laverie automatique?"* ooh ay uh lah-vay-ree auto-mah-teek).

Rue Cler

Lined with open-air produce stands six days a week, rue Cler is a safe, tidy, village-like pedestrian street. It's so French that when I step out of my hotel in the morning, I feel like I must have been a

Sleep Code

(€1 = about $1.30, country code: 33)
S = Single, **D** = Double/Twin, **T** = Triple, **Q** = Quad, **b** = bathroom,
s = shower only, * = French hotel rating system (0–4 stars).
Unless otherwise noted, credit cards are accepted and English
is spoken.

To help you easily sort through these listings, I've divided
the rooms into three categories based on the price for a standard double room with bath:

$$$ **Higher Priced:** Most rooms €150 or more.
$$ **Moderately Priced:** Most rooms between €100–150.
$ **Lower Priced:** Most rooms €100 or less.

poodle in a previous life. How such coziness lodged itself between the high-powered government district and the wealthy Eiffel Tower and Invalides areas, I'll never know. This is a neighborhood of wide, tree-lined boulevards, stately apartment buildings, and lots of Americans. The American Church, American Library, American University, and many of my readers call this area home. Hotels here are relatively spacious and a good value, considering the elegance of the neighborhood and the higher prices of the more cramped hotels in other central areas. And for sightseeing, you're within walking distance of the Eiffel Tower, Army Museum and Napoleon's Tomb, the Seine River, and the Orsay and Rodin museums.

Become a local at a rue Cler café for breakfast, or join the afternoon crowd for *une bière pression* (a draft beer). On rue Cler, you can eat and browse your way through a street full of pastry shops, delis, cheese shops, and colorful outdoor produce stalls. Afternoon *boules* (outdoor bowling) on the Esplanade des Invalides is a relaxing spectator sport (look for the dirt area to the upper right as you face Les Invalides; for more on *boules,* see page  771). The manicured gardens behind the golden dome of the Army Museum and Napoleon's Tomb are free, peaceful, and filled with flowers (at southwest corner of grounds, closes at about 19:00).

While hardly a happening nightlife spot, rue Cler offers many low-impact after-dark activities. Take an evening stroll above the river through the parkway between pont de l'Alma and pont des Invalides. For an after-dinner cruise on the Seine, it's a 15-minute walk to the river and the Bateaux-Mouches (see page 149). For a post-dinner cruise on foot, saunter into parc du Champ de Mars to admire the glowing Eiffel Tower. For more ideas on Paris after hours, see "Nightlife" on page 100.

American Church: The American Church and Franco-American Center is the community center for Americans living in Paris. They offer interdenominational worship services (every Sun at 9:00 and 11:00) and occasional concerts (most Sun at 17:00 Sept–June—but not every week), and distribute the useful *France–USA Contacts* (reception open Mon–Sat 9:00–12:00 & 13:00–22:00, Sun 14:30–19:00, 65 quai d'Orsay, Mo: Invalides, tel. 01 40 62 05 00, www.acparis.org). See page 40 for more info.

Services: There's a large post office at the end of rue Cler on avenue de la Motte-Picquet, and a handy SNCF train office at 78 rue St. Dominique (Mon–Sat 8:30–19:30, closed Sun). At both of these offices, take a ticket with a number and wait your turn. A smaller post office is closer to the Eiffel Tower on avenue Rapp, one block past rue St. Dominique towards the river.

Markets: Cross parc du Champ de Mars to mix it up with bargain-hunters at the twice-weekly open-air market, Marché Boulevard de Grenelle, under the Métro a few blocks southwest of parc du Champ de Mars (Wed and Sun until 12:30, between Mo: Dupleix and Mo: La Motte-Picquet–Grenelle). The Epicerie de la Tour grocery is open until midnight (197 rue de Grenelle). Rue St. Dominique is the area's boutique-browsing street.

Internet Access: Two Internet cafés compete in this neighborhood: Com Avenue is best (about €5/hr, shareable and multiuse accounts, Mon–Sat 10:00–20:00, closed Sun, 24 rue du Champ de Mars, tel. 01 45 55 00 07); Cyber World Café is more expensive but open later (about €7/hr, Mon–Sat 12:00–22:00, Sun 12:00–20:00, 20 rue de l'Exposition, tel. 01 53 59 96 54). For laptop users, Caffè Vergnano offers 30 minutes of free Wi-Fi for the price of a cup of coffee (40 rue Cler, across from Café du Marché, tel. 01 47 05 00 53).

Laundry: Launderettes are omnipresent; ask your hotel for the nearest. Here are three handy locations: on rue Auguer (between rue St. Dominique and rue de Grenelle), on rue Amélie (between rue St. Dominique and rue de Grenelle), and at the southeast corner of rue Valadon and rue de Grenelle.

Métro Connections: Key Métro stops are Ecole Militaire, La Tour-Maubourg, and Invalides. The RER-C line runs from the pont de l'Alma and Invalides stations, serving Versailles to the west; Auvers-sur-Oise to the north; and the Orsay Museum, Latin Quarter (St. Michel stop), and Austerlitz train station to the east.

Bus Routes: Smart travelers take advantage of these helpful bus routes (see map on page 108 for stop locations): Line #69 runs east–west along rue St. Dominique and serves Les Invalides, Orsay, Louvre, Marais, and Père Lachaise Cemetery (Mon–Sat only—no

Sun service; see sidebar, page 48). Line #63 runs along the river (the quai d'Orsay), serving the Latin Quarter along boulevard St. Germain to the east (ending at Gare de Lyon), and Trocadéro and the Marmottan Museum to the west. Line #92 runs along avenue Bosquet, north to the Champs-Elysées and Arc de Triomphe (far better than the Métro) and south to the Montparnasse Tower. Line #87 runs on avenue de la Bourdonnais and serves St. Sulpice, Luxembourg Garden, the Sèvres-Babylone shopping area, and Gare de Lyon (also more convenient than Métro for these destinations). Line #28 runs on boulevard de la Tour-Maubourg and serves Gare St. Lazare.

Paris

Sleeping in the Rue Cler Neighborhood
(7th arrondissement, Mo: Ecole Militaire, La Tour-Maubourg, or Invalides)
Rue Cler is the glue that holds this handsome neighborhood together. From here you can walk to the Eiffel Tower, Army Museum and Napoleon's Tomb, the Seine River, and the Orsay and Rodin museums.

In the Heart of Rue Cler
Many of my readers stay in the rue Cler neighborhood. If you want to disappear into Paris, choose a hotel elsewhere. The first five hotels listed below are within Camembert-smelling distance of rue Cler; the others are within a five- to 10-minute stroll.

$$$ **Hôtel Relais Bosquet***** is modern, spacious, and a bit upscale, with snazzy electric darkness blinds. The staff are politely formal, and offer free breakfast to anyone booking direct with this book in 2008 (standard Db-€170, bigger Db-€190, check website for special discounts, extra bed-€25, Internet access and Wi-Fi, parking-€20, 19 rue du Champ de Mars, tel. 01 47 05 25 45, fax 01 45 55 08 24, www.relaisbosquet.com, hotel@relaisbosquet.com).

$$$ **Hôtel du Cadran***** is perfectly located, with a smart lobby and tight, slender, and pricey rooms that become a fair value with the 10 percent discount and free breakfast that you'll get with this book in 2008 (Db-€165–190, discount not valid for promotional rates on website; bathtubs, air-con, Internet access and Wi-Fi, 10 rue du Champ de Mars, tel. 01 40 62 67 00, fax 01 40 62 67 13, www.hotelducadran.com, info@cadranhotel.com).

$$ **Hôtel Beaugency*****, a particularly good value on a quieter street a short block off rue Cler, has 30 small but good rooms, a helpful staff, and a lobby you can stretch out in (Sb-€110, Db-€130–140, Tb-€168, these special rates promised in 2008 with this book—mention when you reserve, air-con, Internet access, 21 rue Duvivier, tel. 01 47 05 01 63, fax 01 45 51 04 96, www.hotel-beaugency.com, infos@hotel-beaugency.com, Christelle).

Rue Cler Hotels

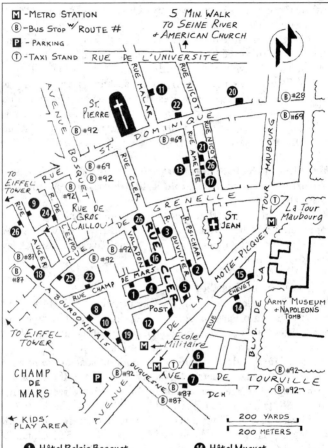

Ⓜ – Metro Station
Ⓑ – Bus Stop w/ Route #
Ⓟ – Parking
Ⓣ – Taxi Stand

5 Min. Walk
To Seine River
& American Church

❶ Hôtel Relais Bosquet
❷ Hôtel Beaugency
❸ Grand Hôtel Lévêque
❹ Hôtel du Champ de Mars
❺ Hôtel de la Motte Picquet
❻ Hôtels le Tourville & de Turenne
❼ Hôtel Splendid
❽ Hôtel La Bourdonnais
❾ Hôtel de Londres Eiffel
❿ Hôtel Eber Mars
⓫ Hôtel de la Tulipe
⓬ Hôtel Royal Phare
⓭ Hôtel Les Jardins d'Eiffel

⓮ Hôtel Muguet
⓯ Hôtel de l'Empereur
⓰ Hôtel du Cadran
⓱ Best Western Eiffel Park
⓲ Hôtel Kensington
⓳ Hôtel Prince
⓴ Hôtel Le Pavillon
㉑ Hôtel Amélie
㉒ SNCF Office
㉓ Com Avenue Internet Café
㉔ Cyber World Internet Café
㉕ Epicerie de la Tour Grocery
㉖ Launderettes (3)

Warning: The next two hotels are super values, but very busy with my readers (reserve long in advance).

$$ Grand Hôtel Lévêque** is ideally located, with a singing maid and a slim, slow-dance elevator. This well-designed hotel has all the comforts, including air-conditioning (S-€67, Db-€97–130 depending on views and beds, Tb-€140 for two adults and one child only, first breakfast free with this book in 2008, €9 all-you-can-eat breakfast buffet, adding Internet access and Wi-Fi in 2008, 29 rue Cler, tel. 01 47 05 49 15, fax 01 45 50 49 36, www.hotel-leveque .com, info@hotel-leveque.com, helpful Christophe).

$ Hôtel du Champ de Mars**, with adorable pastel rooms and serious owners Françoise and Stephane, is a cozy rue Cler option. This plush little hotel has a Provence-style, small-town feel from top to bottom. Rooms are little but comfortable, and an excellent value. Single rooms can work as tiny doubles (Sb-€78, Db-€86–90, Tb-€107, laptop available for guests, Wi-Fi, 30 yards off rue Cler at 7 rue du Champ de Mars, tel. 01 45 51 52 30, fax 01 45 51 64 36, www.hotelduchampdemars.com, reservation @hotelduchampdemars.com). This popular hotel receives an overwhelming amount of reservations, so please be patient.

Near Rue Cler, Close to Ecole Militaire Métro Stop

The following listings are a five-minute walk from rue Cler, near Métro stop Ecole Militaire or RER: Pont de l'Alma.

$$$ Hôtel le Tourville**** is the classiest and most expensive of my rue Cler listings. It's surprisingly intimate for its four stars—from its handsome lobby and vaulted breakfast area to its pretty but small pastel rooms (small standard Db-€190, superior Db-€250, Db with private terrace-€290, junior suite for 3–4 people-€420, air-con, 16 avenue de Tourville, tel. 01 47 05 62 62, fax 01 47 05 43 90, www.hoteltourville.com, hotel@tourville .com).

$$$ Hôtel La Bourdonnais*** is a *très* Parisian place, mixing an Old World feel with comfortable and generous public spaces. Its mostly spacious rooms are traditionally decorated (Sb-€140, Db-€175, Tb-€195, Qb-€220, Sophie promises a 10 percent discount with this book through 2008, air-con, Internet access, 111 avenue de la Bourdonnais, tel. 01 47 05 45 42, fax 01 45 55 75 54, www.hotellabourdonnais.fr, hlb@hotellabourdonnais.fr).

$$ Hôtel Prince**, across from the Ecole Militaire Métro stop, has a spartan lobby and acceptable rooms at reasonable rates (Sb-€83, Db with shower-€105, Db with tub-€120, Tb-€130, air-con, 66 avenue Bosquet, tel. 01 47 05 40 90, fax 01 47 53 06 62, www.hotel-paris-prince.com, paris@hotelprince.com).

$$ Hôtel Eber Mars** has larger-than-most rooms with weathered furnishings. The hotel features oak-paneled public spaces and a beam-me-up-Jacques, coffin-size elevator. There's no air-conditioning and absolutely no eating in your room (Sb-€94, Db-€112–132, Tb-€164, Qb-€186, 20 percent cheaper Nov–March and July–Aug, first breakfast free with this book in 2008, 117 avenue de la Bourdonnais, tel. 01 47 05 42 30, fax 01 47 05 45 91, www.hotelebermars.com, reservation@hotelebermars.com, manager Mr. Eber is a wealth of information for travelers).

$ Hôtel de Turenne** is simple and well-located, with the cheapest air-conditioned rooms I found. While the halls are frumpy and the rooms are modest, the price is right. The bright, open lobby has a pleasant bar and sitting area. There are five truly single rooms and several connecting rooms good for families (Sb-€67, Db-€77–90, Tb-€110, extra bed-€10, 20 avenue de Tourville, tel. 01 47 05 99 92, fax 01 45 56 06 04, hotel.turenne.paris7 @wanadoo.fr).

Near Rue Cler, Closer to Rue St. Dominique (and the Seine)

$$ Hôtel de Londres Eiffel*** is my closest listing to the Eiffel Tower and parc du Champ de Mars. A particularly good value, it offers immaculate, warmly decorated rooms, cozy public spaces, and air-conditioning. The helpful staff takes good care of their guests. It's less convenient to the Métro (10-min walk) but handy to bus #69 and RER-C: Pont de l'Alma (Sb-€99–135, Db-€110–165, deluxe Db-€175, Tb-€165–195, check website for special discounts, Internet access and Wi-Fi, 1 rue Augerau, tel. 01 45 51 63 02, fax 01 47 05 28 96, www.londres-eiffel.com, info@londres-eiffel.com). Show them this book in 2008 for a free Seine cruise (inquire upon arrival).

$$ Hôtel de la Tulipe***, three blocks from rue Cler toward the river, is unique. The 20 smallish but artistically decorated rooms—each one different—come with little, stylish bathrooms and surround a seductive, wood-beamed lounge and a peaceful, leafy courtyard (Db-€145, Tb-€165, two-room suite for up to five people-€270, no elevator or air-con, friendly staff, 33 rue Malar, tel. 01 45 51 67 21, fax 01 47 53 96 37, www.paris-hotel-tulipe.com, hoteldelatulipe@wanadoo.fr).

$ Hôtel Kensington** has tight and worn rooms, but is a fair value (Sb-€58, Db-€75, big Db on back side-€90, extra bed-€12, Eiffel Tower views for those who ask, 79 avenue de la Bourdonnais, tel. 01 47 05 74 00, fax 01 47 05 25 81, www.hotel-kensington.com, hk@hotel-kensington.com, run by elegant Daniele).

Near La Tour-Maubourg Métro Stop

The next three listings are within two blocks of the intersection of avenue de la Motte-Picquet and boulevard de la Tour-Maubourg.

$$$ Hôtel Les Jardins d'Eiffel***, on a quiet street, feels like the modern motel it is, with professional service, its own parking garage (€24/day), and a spacious lobby. The 81 rooms are all designed for double occupancy (Sb/Db–€155–175, 15 percent Rick Steves discount when you book direct through 2008 or check website for special discounts; air-con, Internet access and Wi-Fi, 8 rue Amélie, tel. 01 47 05 46 21, fax 01 45 55 28 08, www.hoteljardinseiffel .com, paris@hoteljardinseiffel.com).

$$ Hôtel Muguet**, a peaceful, stylish, and immaculate refuge, gives you three-star comfort for a two-star price. This delightful place offers 43 tasteful, air-conditioned rooms, a greenhouse lounge, and a small garden courtyard. The hands-on owner, Catherine, gives her guests a restful and secure home in Paris (Sb–€105, Db with one big bed–€125, twin Db–€135, small Db with view–€150, big Db with view and balcony–€185, Tb–€180, Wi-Fi, 11 rue Chevert, tel. 01 47 05 05 93, fax 01 45 50 25 37, www .hotelmuguet.com, muguet@wanadoo.fr, gentle Jacqueline runs reception).

$ Hôtel de l'Empereur** lacks intimacy, but it's roomy and a fair value. Its 38 pleasant rooms come with real wood furniture and all the comforts. Streetside rooms have views, but some noise; fifth-floor rooms have small balconies and Napoleonic views (Db–€102, Tb–€125, Qb–€145, air-con, Internet access and Wi-Fi, 2 rue Chevert, tel. 01 45 55 88 02, fax 01 45 51 88 54, www .hotelempereur.com, contact@hotelempereur.com).

Lesser Values in the Rue Cler Area

Given how fine this area is, these are acceptable last choices.

$$$ Hôtel de la Motte Picquet***, at the end of rue Cler, is elaborately decorated with a feminine flair. Most of its 18 tiny, adorable, and spendy rooms face a busy street and don't have air-conditioning; rooms with twins are on the quieter side (Sb–€130–140, standard Db–€160, bigger Db with air-con–€190, 30 avenue de la Motte-Picquet, tel. 01 47 05 09 57, fax 01 47 05 74 36, www .hotelmottepicquetparis.com, book@hotelmottepicquetparis.com).

$$$ Hôtel Splendid*** is Art Deco–modern, professional, and pricey, considering there's no air-conditioning and the rooms are small. This hotel plays up its Eiffel Tower views: All rooms are streetside; sixth-floor rooms have small balconies with sideways tower views; and three small "suites" directly face the tower. They offer free breakfasts with this book in 2008 (Db–€200, Db suite–€300, check online for promotional rates, 29 avenue de Tourville, tel. 01 45 51 24 77, fax 01 44 18 94 60, www.hotel-splendid-paris .com, reservation@hotel-splendid-paris.com).

$$$ Best Western Eiffel Park*** is a dead quiet, concrete business hotel with all the comforts, a relaxing lobby, 36 pleasant if unexceptional rooms, and a rooftop terrace (Db-€215, bigger "luxe" Db-€240, check online for promotional rates, air-con, Wi-Fi, friendly staff, 17 bis rue Amélie, tel. 01 45 55 10 01, fax 01 47 05 28 68, www.eiffelpark.com, reservation@eiffelpark.com).

$$ Hôtel Amélie, a modest place in a skinny building, has no lobby or elevator, but it is undergoing a total facelift in 2008. The hotel will remain open throughout (Sb-€90, Db-€100–135, 5 rue Amélie, tel. 01 45 51 74 75, fax 01 45 56 93 55, www.hotelamelie -paris.com, contact@hotelamelie-paris.com).

$ Hôtel Le Pavillon, a former convent, is quiet, with 18 no-frills rooms, creaky floors, no elevator, and cramped halls in a charming location. The owner promises shiny new bathrooms for 2008 (Sb-€80, Db-€115, large Tb/Qb-€160, 54 rue St. Dominique, tel. 01 45 51 42 87, fax 01 45 51 32 79, www.hotel-lepavillon.com, contact@hotel-lepavillon.com).

$ Hôtel Royal Phare is a humble place—ideal for back-packers—facing the busy Ecole Militaire Métro stop. The 34 basic, pink-pastel rooms are overpriced and unimaginative with claustro-phobic hallways, but are comfortable enough. Rooms on the court-yard are quietest, with peek-a-boo views of the Eiffel Tower from the fifth floor up (Sb-€73, Db with shower-€80–95, Db with tub-€100, Tb-€105, fridges in rooms, 40 avenue de la Motte-Picquet, tel. 01 47 05 57 30, fax 01 45 51 64 41, www.hotel-royalphare-paris .com, royalphare-hotel@wanadoo.fr).

Marais

Those interested in a more SoHo/Greenwich Village locale should make the Marais their Parisian home. Not long ago, it was a for-gotten Parisian backwater, but now the Marais is one of Paris' most popular residential, tour-ist, and shopping areas. This is jumbled, medieval Paris at its finest, where classy stone man-sions sit alongside trendy bars, antique shops, and fashion-con-scious boutiques. The streets are a fascinating parade of artists,  students, tourists, immigrants, and babies in strollers munching baguettes. The Marais is also known as a hub of the Parisian gay and lesbian scene. This area is *sans doute* livelier (and louder) than the rue Cler area.

In the Marais, you have these sights close at hand: Picasso Museum, Carnavalet Museum, Victor Hugo's House, the Jewish Art and History Museum, and the Pompidou Center. You're also a manageable walk from Paris' two islands (Ile St. Louis and Ile de la

Cité), home to Notre-Dame and the Sainte-Chapelle. The Opéra Bastille, Promenade Plantée Park, place des Vosges (Paris' oldest square), Jewish Quarter (rue des Rosiers), and nightlife-packed rue de Lappe are also walkable. (For sight descriptions, see page 90; for the Opéra, see page 102.)

Most of my recommended hotels are located a few blocks north of the Marais' main east–west drag, the rue St. Antoine/rue de Rivoli.

Tourist Information: The nearest TI is in Gare de Lyon (Mon–Sat 8:00–18:00, closed Sun, all-Paris TI tel. 08 92 68 30 00).

Services: Most banks and other services are on the main street, rue de Rivoli, which becomes rue St. Antoine. Marais **post offices** are on rue Castex and at the corner of rue Pavée and rue des Francs Bourgeois. There's an **SNCF Boutique** where you can take care of all train needs on rue St. Antoine at rue de Turenne (Mon–Sat 8:30–20:30, closed Sun). A quieter SNCF Boutique is nearer Gare de Lyon at 5 rue de Lyon (Mon–Sat 8:30–18:00, closed Sun).

Markets: The Marais has two good open-air markets: the sprawling **Marché de la Bastille,** around place de la Bastille (Thu and Sun until 12:30); and the more intimate, untouristy **Marché de la place d'Aligre** (Tue–Sun 9:00–12:00, closed Mon, cross place de la Bastille and walk about 10 blocks down rue du Faubourg St. Antoine, turn right at rue de Cotte to place d'Aligre; or, easier, take Métro line 8 from Bastille toward Créteil-Préfecture to the Ledru-Rollin stop and walk a few blocks southeast). A small **grocery shop** is open until 23:00 on rue St. Antoine (near intersection with rue Castex). To shop at a Parisian Sears, find the **BHV** next to Hôtel de Ville.

Bookstore: The Marais is home to the friendliest English-language bookstore in Paris, **Red Wheelbarrow** (Mon–Sat 10:00–19:00, Sun 14:00–18:00, 22 rue St. Paul, Mo: St. Paul, tel. 01 48 04 75 08). Abigail and Penelope sell most of my guidebooks and carry a great collection of other books about Paris and France for both adults and children.

Internet Access: Try **@aron** (3 rue des Ecouffes, Mo: St. Paul, tel. 01 42 71 05 07), **Paris CY** (8 rue de Jouy, Mo: St. Paul, tel. 01 42 71 37 37), or **Cyber Cube** (12 rue Daval, Mo: Bastille, tel. 01 49 29 67 67).

Laundry: While there are many launderettes, here are three you can count on: on impasse Guéménée (north of rue St. Antoine), on rue du Platre (just west of rue du Temple), and on rue Daval (near Cyber Cube).

Métro Connections: Key Métro stops in the Marais are, from east to west: Bastille, St. Paul, and Hôtel de Ville (Sully-Morland, Pont Marie, and Rambuteau stops are also handy). Métro service to the Marais neighborhood is excellent, with direct service to the Louvre, Champs-Elysées, Arc de Triomphe, and La Défense (all on line 1); the rue Cler area and Opéra Garnier (line 8 from Bastille stop); and four major train stations: Gare de Lyon, Gare du Nord, Gare de l'Est, and Gare d'Austerlitz (all accessible from Bastille stop).

Bus Routes: Line #69 on rue St. Antoine takes you eastbound to Père Lachaise Cemetery and westbound to the Louvre, Orsay, and Rodin Museums, plus the Army Museum and Napoleon's Tomb, ending at the Eiffel Tower (Mon–Sat only—no Sun service). Line #86 runs down boulevard Henri IV, crossing Ile St. Louis and serving the Latin Quarter along boulevard St. Germain. Line #87 follows a similar route, but also serves Gare de Lyon to the east and the Eiffel Tower and rue Cler neighborhood to the west. Line #96 runs on rues Turenne and François Miron and serves the Louvre and boulevard St. Germain (near Luxembourg Garden), ending at the Gare Montparnasse. Line #65 runs from Gare de Lyon up rue de Lyon, around place de la Bastille, and then up boulevard Beaumarchais to the Gare de l'Est and Gare du Nord.

Taxis: You'll find taxi stands on place de la Bastille (where boulevard Richard Lenoir meets the square), on the south side of rue St. Antoine (in front of St. Paul Church), and a quieter one on the north side of rue St. Antoine (where it meets rue Castex).

Sleeping in the Marais Neighborhood
(4th arrondissement, Mo: Bastille, St. Paul, and Hôtel de Ville)
The Marais runs from the Pompidou Center to the Bastille (a 15-min walk), with most hotels located a few blocks north of the main east–west drag, the rue de Rivoli/rue St. Antoine. It's about 15 minutes on foot from any hotel in this area to Notre-Dame, Ile St. Louis, and the Latin Quarter. Strolling home (day or night) from Notre-Dame along the Ile St. Louis is marvelous.

Near Place des Vosges
$$ Hôtel Castex*,** a well-managed place with tiled floors and dark wood accents, is well-situated on a quiet street near place de la Bastille. A clever system of connecting rooms allows families total privacy between two rooms, each with its own bathroom. The 30 rooms are narrow but tasteful and air-conditioned, and the elevator is big by Parisian standards. It's a good value year-round. Your fourth night is free in August and from November through February, except around New Year's (Sb-€95–120, Db-€120–150, Tb-€190–220, 5 percent discount and free buffet breakfast with this book through 2008, Wi-Fi, just off place de la Bastille and rue St. Antoine at 5 rue Castex, Mo: Bastille, tel. 01 42 72 31 52, fax 01 42 72 57 91, www.castexhotel.com, info@castexhotel.com).

Marais Hotels

1. Hôtel Castex
2. Hôtel Bastille Spéria
3. Hôtel Daval
4. Hôtel des Chevaliers
5. Hôtel Saint-Louis Marais
6. Grand Hôtel Jeanne d'Arc
7. Hôtel Lyon-Mulhouse
8. Hôtel Sévigné
9. Hôtel du 7ème Art
10. Hôtel du Sully
11. MIJE Hostels (3)
12. Hôtel de la Bretonnerie
13. Hôtel Caron de Beaumarchais
14. Hôtel du Vieux Marais
15. Hôtel Beaubourg
16. Hôtel de Nice
17. Hôtel du Loiret
18. BHV Department Store
19. Red Wheelbarrow Books
20. SNCF Boutique (Train Tickets)
21. @aron Internet Café
22. Cyber Cube Internet Café
23. Paris CY Internet Café & Launderette
24. Launderettes (2)

M – METRO STATION
T – TAXI STAND
P – PARKING
B – BUS STOP w/ ROUTE #

$$ Hôtel Bastille Spéria***, a short block off place de la Bastille, offers business-type service. The 42 well-configured rooms are modern and comfortable, with big beds and air-conditioning. Walls are thin, and the elevator operates at glacial speed, but it's English-language-friendly, from the *International Herald Tribune*s in the lobby to the history of the Bastille posted in the elevator (Sb-€105–115, Db-€135–172, child's bed-€20, excellent buffet breakfast-€13, 1 rue de la Bastille, Mo: Bastille, tel. 01 42 72 04 01, fax 01 42 72 56 38, www.hotel-bastille-speria.com, info @hotel-bastille-speria.com).

$$ Hôtel Saint-Louis Marais**, tiny and welcoming, is tucked on a quiet residential street between the river and rue St. Antoine. The lobby is inviting, and the 19 rooms are cozy, but there's no air-conditioning and the bathrooms are worn (small Sb-€59, standard Sb-€99, small Db-€115, standard Db-€140, Tb-€140, no elevator but only three floors, ask about newer street-level annex rooms, bargain-priced parking-€12, 1 rue Charles V, Mo: Sully Morland, tel. 01 48 87 87 04, fax 01 48 87 33 26, www.saint-louismarais.com, slmarais@noos.fr).

$$ Hôtel des Chevaliers***, a pretty little hotel with a hand-some lobby one block northwest of place des Vosges, offers small, sharp, and pricey rooms with air-conditioning. Four of its 24 rooms are off the street and quiet—worth requesting (Sb-€140–160, Db-€150–165, 30 rue de Turenne, Mo: St. Paul, tel. 01 42 72 73 47, fax 01 42 72 54 10, www.chevaliers-paris-hotel.com, info @hoteldeschevaliers.com).

$ Hôtel de 7ème Art**, two blocks south of rue St. Antoine toward the river, is a funky, Hollywood-nostalgia place. It has a full-service café-bar and Charlie Chaplin murals, but no elevator. Its 23 good-value rooms have brown 1970s decor, but are com-fortable enough. The large rooms are American-spacious (small Db-€80, standard Db-€100, large Db-€115–145, Tb-€135–165, extra bed-€20, air-con, 20 rue St. Paul, Mo: St. Paul, tel. 01 44 54 85 00, fax 01 42 77 69 10, www.paris-hotel-7art.com, hotel7art @wanadoo.fr).

$ Grand Hôtel Jeanne d'Arc**, a lovely little hotel with thoughtfully appointed rooms, is ideally located for (and very pop-ular with) connoisseurs of the Marais. It's a fine value and worth booking way ahead (three months in advance, if possible). Sixth-floor rooms have views, and corner rooms are wonderfully bright in the City of Light, though no rooms are air-conditioned. Rooms on the street can be noisy until the bars close (Sb-€60–86, Db-€86, larger twin Db-€100, Tb-€120, good Qb-€150, 3 rue de Jarente, Mo: St. Paul, tel. 01 48 87 62 11, fax 01 48 87 37 31, information @hoteljeannedarc.com).

$ Hôtel Lyon-Mulhouse** is located on a busy street barely off place de la Bastille. While less intimate than some, it is a solid deal, with pleasant, relatively large rooms (Sb-€65, Db-€90, Tb-€120, Qb-€140, air-con, 8 boulevard Beaumarchais, Mo: Bastille, tel. 01 47 00 91 50, fax 01 47 00 06 31, www.1-hotel-paris.com, hotelyonmulhouse@wanadoo.fr, Nathalia).

$ Hôtel Daval**, an unassuming place with good rates on the lively side of place de la Bastille, is ideal for night owls. Ask for a quieter room on the courtyard side (Sb-€72, Db-€79, Tb-101, Qb-€112, air-con, Wi-Fi, 21 rue Daval, Mo: Bastille, tel. 01 47 00 51 23, fax 01 40 21 80 26, www.hoteldaval.com, hoteldaval @wanadoo.fr, Didier).

$ Hôtel Sévigné**, a snappy little hotel, has lavender halls and 30 tidy, comfortable rooms at good prices, but a one-night, no-refund policy for any cancellation (Sb-€66, Db-€79–90, Tb-€102, air-con, 2 rue Malher, Mo: St. Paul, tel. 01 42 72 76 17, fax 01 42 78 68 26, www.le-sevigne.com, contact@le-sevigne.com, straight-faced owner Monsieur Mercier).

$ Hôtel du Sully, sitting right on rue St. Antoine, is nothing fancy, but it is cheap. The entry is long and narrow, and the rooms are dimly lit but sleepable (Db-€55, Tb-€72, no elevator, 48 rue St. Antoine, Mo: St. Paul, tel. 01 42 78 49 32, fax 01 44 61 76 50, sullyhotel@orange.fr, run by friendly Monsieur Zeroual).

$ *MIJE Youth Hostels:* The Maison Internationale de la Jeunesse et des Etudiants (MIJE) runs three classy old residences clustered a few blocks south of rue St. Antoine. Each is well-maintained, with simple, clean, single-sex, one- to four-bed rooms for travelers of any age. None has an elevator or double beds, all rooms have showers, and each has Internet access. Rates favor single travelers—two people can find a double in a very simple hotel for a comparable price (all prices per person: Sb-€46, Db-€34, Tb-€30, Qb-€29, cash only, includes breakfast but not towels; required membership card-€2.50 extra/person; 7-day maximum stay, rooms locked 12:00–15:00, curfew at 1:00 in the morning). The hostels are **MIJE Fourcy** (€11 dinners available with a membership card, 6 rue de Fourcy, just south of rue de Rivoli), **MIJE Fauconnier** (11 rue du Fauconnier), and the best, **MIJE Maubisson** (12 rue des Barres). They all share the same contact information (tel. 01 42 74 23 45, fax 01 40 27 81 64, www.mije.com, info@mije.com) and Métro stop (St. Paul). Reservations are accepted (six weeks ahead online), though you must show up by noon or call the morning of arrival to confirm a later arrival time.

Near the Pompidou Center

These hotels are farther west, closer to the Pompidou Center than to place de la Bastille. The Hôtel de Ville Métro stop works well for all of these hotels, unless a closer stop is noted.

$$$ Hôtel Caron de Beaumarchais*** feels like a folk museum run by an eccentric owner. It has 20 sweet little rooms and a lobby cluttered with bits from an elegant 18th-century Marais house. Short antique collectors should sleep here (small Db in back-€142, larger Db facing the front-€162, breakfast served until noon, air-con, Wi-Fi, 12 rue Vieille du Temple, tel. 01 42 72 34 12, fax 01 42 72 34 63, www.carondebeaumarchais.com, hotel @carondebeaumarchais.com).

$$ Hôtel de la Bretonnerie***, three blocks from the Hôtel de Ville, makes a fine Marais home. It has a warm, welcoming lobby, classy decor, and 29 tastefully appointed rooms with an antique, open-beam warmth (perfectly good standard "classic" Db-€120, bigger "charming" Db-€155, Db suite-€180, Tb/Qb-€180, Tb/Qb suite-€205, no air-con, free Internet access and Wi-Fi, between rue Vieille du Temple and rue des Archives at 22 rue Ste. Croix de la Bretonnerie, tel. 01 48 87 77 63, fax 01 42 77 26 78, www .bretonnerie.com, hotel@bretonnerie.com).

$$ Hôtel du Vieux Marais**, with a quirky owner and modern rooms, is tucked away on a quiet street two blocks east of the Pompidou Center. Say *bonjour* to friendly bulldog Leelou who runs the small lobby (Sb-€95–110, Db-€115–150, extra bed-€23, air-con, Wi-Fi, just off rue des Archives at 8 rue du Plâtre, Mo: Rambuteau or Hôtel de Ville, tel. 01 42 78 47 22, fax 01 42 78 34 32, www .vieuxmarais.com, hotel@vieuxmarais.com).

$$ Hôtel Beaubourg*** is a fine three-star value on a quiet street in the shadow of the Pompidou Center. The lounge is inviting and the 28 rooms are wood-beam comfy and air-conditioned (standard Db-€118, bigger twin Db-€148, Internet access and Wi-Fi, 11 rue Simon Le Franc, Mo: Rambuteau, tel. 01 42 74 34 24, fax 01 42 78 68 11, www.hotelbeaubourg.com, htlbeaubourg @hotellerie.net).

$$ Hôtel de Nice**, on the Marais' busy main drag, is a turquoise-and-fuschia, "Marie-Antoinette does tie-dye" place. Its narrow halls are littered with paintings and covered with carpets, and its 23 air-conditioned rooms are filled with thoughtful touches and include tight bathrooms. Twin rooms, which cost the same as doubles, are larger and on the street side—but have effective double-paned windows (Sb-€80, Db-€110, Tb-€135, Qb-€150, extra bed-€20, reception on second floor, 42 bis rue de Rivoli, tel. 01 42 78 55 29, fax 01 42 78 36 07, www.hoteldenice.com, contact @hoteldenice.com, laissez-faire management).

$ Hôtel du Loiret** is a centrally located backpacker hotel, though the rooms are better than you might think (S-€45, WC across hall, Sb-€60–70, Db-€60–80, Tb-€95, 8 rue des Mauvais

Hotels and Restaurants on Ile St. Louis

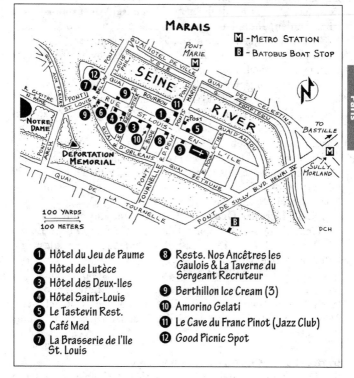

❶ Hôtel du Jeu de Paume
❷ Hôtel de Lutèce
❸ Hôtel des Deux-Iles
❹ Hôtel Saint-Louis
❺ Le Tastevin Rest.
❻ Café Med
❼ La Brasserie de l'Ile St. Louis

❽ Rests. Nos Ancêtres les Gaulois & La Taverne du Sergeant Recruteur
❾ Berthillon Ice Cream (3)
❿ Amorino Gelati
⓫ Le Cave du Franc Pinot (Jazz Club)
⓬ Good Picnic Spot

Garçons, tel. 01 48 87 77 00, fax 01 48 04 96 56, www.hotel-loiret
.fr, hotelduloiret@hotmail.com).

In the Historic Core, on Ile St. Louis

The peaceful, residential character of this river-wrapped island, its brilliant location, and homemade ice cream have drawn Americans for decades, allowing hotels to charge dearly for their rooms. There are no budget values here, but the island's coziness and proximity to the Marais, Notre-Dame, and the Latin Quarter help compensate for higher rates. All are on the island's main drag, the rue St. Louis-en-l'Ile, where I list several restaurants (see page 143). Use Mo: Pont Marie or Sully-Morland.

$$$ Hôtel du Jeu de Paume**,** located in a 17th-century tennis center, is the most expensive hotel I list in Paris. When you enter its magnificent lobby, you'll understand why. Greet Scoop, the hotel dog, then ride the glass elevator for a half-timbered-treehouse experience, and marvel at the cozy lounges. The 30 quite comfortable rooms are carefully designed and *très* tasteful, though small for the price (you're paying for the location and public spaces—check for deals on their website). Most rooms face a small garden, and all are pin-drop peaceful (standard Db-€260, larger Db-€310, deluxe Db-€370, 54 rue St. Louis-en-l'Ile, tel. 01 43 26 14 18, fax 01 40 46 02 76, www.jeudepaumehotel.com, info @jeudepaumehotel.com).

The following two hotels are owned by the same person. For both, if you must cancel, do so a week in advance or pay fees:

$$$ Hôtel de Lutèce*** charges top euro for its island address but comes with a sit-a-while, wood-paneled lobby, a fireplace, and warmly designed rooms. Twin rooms are larger and the same price as double rooms (Db-€190, Tb-€210, air-con, Internet access and Wi-Fi, 65 rue St. Louis-en-l'Ile, tel. 01 43 26 23 52, fax 01 43 29 60 25, www.hotel-ile-saintlouis.com, lutece@hotel-ile-saintlouis .com, friendly Nathalie and Thierry).

$$$ Hôtel des Deux Iles*** is brighter and more colorful, with marginally smaller rooms (Db-€180, Wi-Fi, 59 rue St. Louis-en-l'Ile, tel. 01 43 26 13 35, fax 01 43 29 60 25, www.2iles.com, hotel.2iles@free.fr).

$$$ Hôtel Saint Louis*** has less personality but good rooms with parquet floors, air-conditioning, and comparatively good rates (Db-€142–160, extra bed-€50, 75 rue St. Louis-en-l'Ile, tel. 01 46 34 04 80, fax 01 46 34 02 13, www.hotel-saint-louis.com, slouis @noos.fr).

In the Historic Core, on Ile de la Cité

$$ Hôtel Dieu Hospitel Paris is the only Paris hotel with an Ile de la Cité address. It's located in the oldest city hospital of Paris, on the square in front of Notre-Dame (find the hospital on the map on page 54.) Originally intended to receive families of patients, it now offers rooms for tourists, too. To get a spot in this prime location in front of Notre-Dame with only 14 rooms, you'll need to book well in advance. You'll be surprised by the modern, comfortable decor and may even forget you're in a hospital (Sb-€104, Db-€115, some rooms have peek-a-boo views of Notre-Dame, air-con, Wi-Fi, 1 place du Parvis, tel. 01 44 32 01 00, www.hotel-hospitel.fr, hospitelhoteldieu@wanadoo.fr). Enter the hotel's main entrance, turn right, follow signs to wing B2, and take the elevator to the sixth floor.

Luxembourg Garden

This neighborhood revolves around Paris' loveliest park and offers quick access to the city's best shopping streets and grandest café-hopping. Sleeping in the Luxembourg area offers a true Left Bank experience without a hint of the low-end commotion of the nearby

Latin Quarter tourist ghetto. The Luxembourg Garden, boulevard St. Germain, Cluny Museum, and Latin Quarter are all at your doorstep. Here you get the best of both worlds: youthful Left Bank energy and the classy trappings that surround the monumental Panthéon and St. Sulpice Church. Hotels in this central area are generally more expensive than in other areas I list.

Having the Luxembourg Garden at your back door allows strolls through meticulously cared-for flowers, a great kids' play area, and a purifying escape from city traffic. Place St. Sulpice offers an elegant, pedestrian-friendly square and some of Paris' best boutiques (see "Shopping," page 98). Sleeping in the Luxembourg area also puts several movie theaters at your fingertips (Mo: Odéon), as well as lively cafés on the boulevard St. Germain, rue de Buci, rue des Canettes, place de la Sorbonne, and place de la Contrescarpe, all of which buzz with action until late.

Tourist Information: The nearest TI is across the river in Gare de Lyon (Mon–Sat 8:00–18:00, closed Sun, all-Paris TI tel. 08 92 68 30 00).

Markets: The colorful **street market** at the south end of rue Mouffetard is a worthwhile 10- to 15-minute walk down from these hotels (Tue–Sat 8:00–12:00 & 15:30–19:00, Sun 8:00–12:00, closed Mon, five blocks south of place de la Contrescarpe, Mo: Place Monge).

Bookstore: The **Village Voice** bookstore carries a full selection of English-language books (including mine) and is near St. Sulpice (Mon 14:00–19:30, Tue–Sat 10:00–19:30, Sun 13:00–18:00, 6 rue Princesse, tel. 01 46 33 36 47, www.villagevoicebookshop .com).

Internet Access: You'll find it at **Le Milklub** (always open, between the Luxembourg Garden and Panthéon at 17 rue Soufflot).

Métro Connections: Métro lines 10 and 4 serve this area (10 connects to the Austerlitz train station, and 4 goes to the Montparnasse, Est, and Nord train stations). Neighborhood stops are Cluny–La Sorbonne, Mabillon, Odéon, and St. Sulpice. RER-B (Luxembourg station is handiest) provides direct service to Charles de Gaulle Airport and Gare du Nord trains, and access to Orly Airport via the Orlybus (transfer at Denfert-Rochereau).

Bus Routes: Buses #63, #86, and #87 run eastbound through this area on boulevard St. Germain, and westbound along rue des Ecoles, stopping on place St. Sulpice. Lines #63 and #87 provide direct connections to the rue Cler area. Line #63 also serves the Orsay, Army, Rodin, and Marmottan museums and Gare de Lyon. Lines #86 and #87 run to the Marais, and #87 continues east to Gare de Lyon.

Sleeping in the Luxembourg Garden Area

(5th and 6th arrondissements, Mo: St. Sulpice, Mabillon, Odéon, and Cluny-La Sorbonne; RER: Luxembourg)

While it takes only 15 minutes to walk from one end of this neighborhood to the other, I've located the hotels by the key monument they are close to (St. Sulpice Church, the Odéon Theater, and the Panthéon). No hotel is further than a five-minute walk from the Luxembourg Garden.

Hotels near St. Sulpice Church

These hotels are all within a block of St. Sulpice Church, and two blocks from the famous boulevard St. Germain. This is nirvana for boutique-minded shoppers—and you'll pay extra for the location. Métro stops St. Sulpice and Mabillon are equally close.

$$$ Hôtel de l'Abbaye**,** which lies hidden on a quiet street just west of Luxembourg Garden, is a find for well-heeled connoisseurs of this area. This four-star luxury refuge offers refined lounges inside and out, and 44 plush rooms with every amenity (Db-€220, bigger Db-€335, suites and apartments available for €390–425, includes breakfast, 10 rue Cassette, tel. 01 45 44 38 11, fax 01 45 48 07 86, www.hotel-abbaye.com, hotel.abbaye @wanadoo.fr, well-run by manager Lionel and his helpful team).

$$$ Hôtel Relais St. Sulpice*,** on the small street just behind St. Sulpice Church, is a boutique hotel with a cozy lounge and 26 pricey yet carefully designed rooms, most surrounding a leafy glass atrium. Top-floor rooms get more light (Db-€180–215 depending on size, most Db-€185–200, air-con, sauna free for guests, 3 rue Garancière, tel. 01 46 33 99 00, fax 01 46 33 00 10, www.relais-saint-sulpice.com, relaisstsulpice@wanadoo.fr).

$$$ Hôtel la Perle*** is a spendy pearl in the thick of the lively rue des Canettes, a block off place St. Sulpice. At this snappy, modern, business-class hotel, sliding glass doors open onto the traffic-free street, and you're greeted by a fun lobby built around a central bar and atrium (standard Db-€175, bigger Db-€195, luxury Db-€235, air-con, Internet access and Wi-Fi, check website or call for last-minute deals within five days of your stay, 14 rue des Canettes, tel. 01 43 29 10 10, fax 01 46 34 51 04, www.hotellaperle .com, booking@hotellaperle.com).

$$ Hôtel Bonaparte*** is an unpretentious place wedged between boutiques, a few steps from place St. Sulpice on the smart rue Bonaparte. While the 29 Old World rooms don't live up to the handsome entry, they're adequately comfortable and generally spacious, with big bathrooms and molded ceilings (Sb-€98–117, Db-€124–147, big Db-€162, Tb-€170, includes breakfast, air-con, Wi-Fi, 61 rue Bonaparte, tel. 01 43 26 97 37, fax 01 46 33 57 67, www.hotelbonaparte.fr, reservation@hotelbonaparte.fr,

Hotels and Restaurants near St. Sulpice and the Odéon Theater

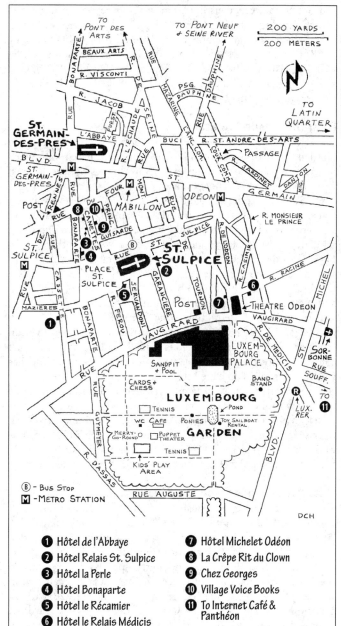

Paris

① Hôtel de l'Abbaye

② Hôtel Relais St. Sulpice

③ Hôtel la Perle

④ Hôtel Bonaparte

⑤ Hôtel le Récamier

⑥ Hôtel le Relais Médicis

⑦ Hôtel Michelet Odéon

⑧ La Crêpe Rit du Clown

⑨ Chez Georges

⑩ Village Voice Books

⑪ To Internet Café & Panthéon

helpful Frédéric at reception).

$$ Hôtel le Récamier**, romantically tucked in the corner of place St. Sulpice, feels like grandma's house—but it has a new owner with big plans. For now, it's marked by flowery wallpaper, dark halls, and clean, simple rooms, but all this could change by 2008. Regardless, the location is ideal (pre-renovation rates: S-€90, Sb-€110, D-€90, Db-€110, bigger Db-€130, Tb-€155, Qb-€190, 3 bis place St. Sulpice, tel. 01 43 26 04 89, fax 01 46 33 27 73, hotelrecamier@wanadoo.fr).

Near the Odéon Theater

These hotels are between the Odéon Métro stop and Luxembourg Garden (five blocks east of St. Sulpice), and may have rooms when others don't. In addition to the Odéon Métro stop, the RER-B Luxembourg stop is a short walk away.

$$$ Hôtel le Relais Médicis*** is perfect in every way—if you've always wanted to live in a Monet painting and can afford it. Its 16 rooms surround a fragrant little garden courtyard and fountain, giving you a countryside break fit for a Medici in the heart of Paris. This delightful place is tastefully decorated with floral Old World charm, and is permeated with thoughtfulness (Sb-€172, Db-€200–228, deluxe Db-€258, Tb-€298, €30 cheaper mid-July–Aug and Nov–March, sumptuous €10 continental breakfast required, Wi-Fi, faces the Odéon Theater at 23 rue Racine, tel. 01 43 26 00 60, fax 01 40 46 83 39, www.relaismedicis.com, reservation @relaismedicis.com, eager-to-help Isabelle runs reception). Don't confuse it with the similarly named but far less swanky Hôtel des Médicis, described on page 126.

$$ Hôtel Michelet Odéon** sits shyly in a corner of place de l'Odéon with big windows on the world. It's a good value in this pricey area, with 24 spacious and simple rooms with modern decor, tiger-striped carpeting, and views of the square (Db-€100–125, Tb-€155, Qb-€175, 6 place de l'Odéon, tel. 01 53 10 05 60, fax 01 46 34 55 35, www.hotelmicheletodeon.com, hotel@micheletodeon.com).

Near the Panthéon and Rue Mouffetard

The last three listings are cheap dives, but in a great area.

$$ Hôtel des Grandes Ecoles*** is idyllic. A private cobbled lane leads to three buildings that protect a flower-filled garden courtyard, preserving a sense of tranquility rare in this city. Its 51 rooms are French-countryside pretty, spotless, and reasonably spacious. This romantic spot is deservedly popular, so call well in advance (Db-€115–140 depending on size, extra bed-€20, parking garage-€30, Wi-Fi, 75 rue du Cardinal Lemoine, Mo: Cardinal Lemoine, tel. 01 43 26 79 23, fax 01 43 25 28 15, www.hotel -grandes-ecoles.com, hotel.grandes.ecoles@wanadoo.fr, mellow

Hotels and Restaurants near the Panthéon

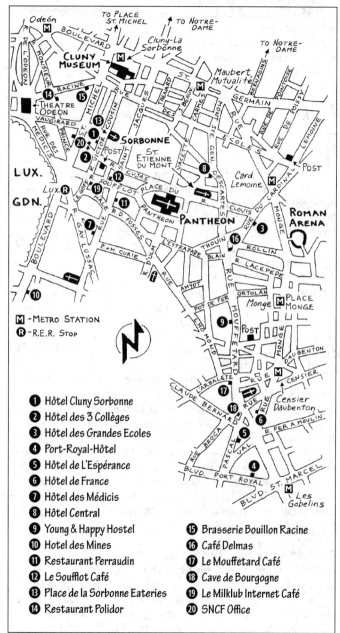

M - METRO STATION
R - R.E.R. STOP

1 Hôtel Cluny Sorbonne
2 Hôtel des 3 Collèges
3 Hôtel des Grandes Ecoles
4 Port-Royal-Hôtel
5 Hôtel de L'Espérance
6 Hôtel de France
7 Hôtel des Médicis
8 Hôtel Central
9 Young & Happy Hostel
10 Hotel des Mines
11 Restaurant Perraudin
12 Le Soufflot Café
13 Place de la Sorbonne Eateries
14 Restaurant Polidor

15 Brasserie Bouillon Racine
16 Café Delmas
17 Le Mouffetard Café
18 Cave de Bourgogne
19 Le Milklub Internet Café
20 SNCF Office

Marie speaks English, Mama does not).

$$ Hôtel des 3 Collèges** is bright and efficient, with generous public spaces, claustrophobic hallways, and tight yet comfy rooms (small Sb-€77, Db-€100–107, bigger Db-€122–145, Tb-€132–165, 16 rue Cujas, tel. 01 43 54 67 30, fax 01 46 34 02 99, www.3colleges.com, hotel@3colleges.com).

$ Hôtel Cluny Sorbonne** is a welcoming place that's also a good deal. Located in the thick of things across from the famous university, it's just below the Panthéon. Rooms are clean and comfortable, with wood furnishings (standard Db-€95, really big Db-€155, Wi-Fi, 8 rue Victor Cousin, tel. 01 43 54 66 66, fax 01 43 29 68 07, www.hotel-cluny.fr, cluny@club-internet.fr).

$ Hôtel des Médicis is a cheap, stripped-down, soiled-linoleum dive flanked by Chinese takeouts. Request Jim Morrison's old room, if you dare (dirt—and I mean dirt—cheap: Jim's S-€16–20 but rarely available; S-€28–30, D-€31–35, Ds-€45, 214 rue St. Jacques, Mo: Cluny–La Sorbonne or RER-B Luxembourg, tel. 01 43 54 14 66, hotelmedicis@aol.com, gentle Denis owns the place).

$ Hôtel Central*, wedged between two cafés, has a smoky, dingy reception, a steep and slippery stairway, dumpy beds, and mildewed rooms. Bottom line: It's youth-hostel cheap, but with a charm only romantic hobos will appreciate. All rooms have showers, but toilets are down the hall (Ss-€32–37, Ds-€45–50, cash only, no elevator, 6 rue Descartes, Mo: Cardinal Lemoine, tel. 01 46 33 57 93). Do your best to get a smile out of Madame Pilar, who doesn't speak English.

$ Young & Happy Hostel is easygoing, well-run, and English-speaking, with Internet access, kitchen facilities, and acceptable hostel conditions. It sits dead center in the rue Mouffetard bar, café, and people action...which can be good or bad (beds in 4- to 10-bed rooms-€23, beds in double rooms-€26, includes breakfast, sheets-€2.50, no lockers but safety box at reception, rooms closed 11:00–16:00 but reception stays open, no curfew, secure reservations with credit card but pay in cash, 80 rue Mouffetard, Mo: Place Monge, tel. 01 47 07 47 07, fax 01 47 07 22 24, www.youngandhappy.fr, smile@youngandhappy.fr). They have 10 doubles and are open to "anyone with an open mind."

Farther Away from the Seine, at the Bottom of Rue Mouffetard

These hotels, away from the Seine and other tourists in an appealing workaday area, offer more room for your euro. They require a longer walk or Métro ride to sights, but often have rooms when other accommodations are booked up. Rue Mouffetard is the bohemian soul of this area, running south from its heart—place de la Contrescarpe—to rue de Bazeilles. Two thousand years ago, it was the principal Roman road south to Italy. Today, this small, meandering street has a split personality. The lower half thrives in the daytime as a pedestrian shopping street. The upper half sleeps during the day but comes alive after dark, teeming with bars, restaurants, and nightlife. Use Métro stops Censier-Daubenton or Les Gobelins.

$$ Hôtel de France, on a busy street, is a modest place with comfortable rooms. The best and quietest rooms are *sur la cour* (on the courtyard), though streetside rooms are okay (Sb-€90, Db-€95–110, Tb-€135, 108 rue Monge, Mo: Censier-Daubenton, tel. 01 47 07 19 04, fax 01 43 36 62 34, www.hotelfrancequartierlatin .com, hotel.de.fce@wanadoo.fr).

$ Port-Royal-Hôtel* has only one star, but don't let that fool you. Its 46 rooms are polished top to bottom, and have been well-run by the same proud family for 67 years. You could eat off the floors of its spotless, comfy rooms. Ask for a room away from the street (S-€41–55, D-€55, Db-€79–89 depending on size, big shower down the hall-€3, cash only, nonrefundable cash deposit required, on busy boulevard de Port-Royal at #8, Mo: Les Gobelins, tel. 01 43 31 70 06, fax 01 43 31 33 67, www.hotelportroyal.fr, portroyalhotel @wanadoo.fr).

$ Hôtel de l'Espérance** is a solid two-star value. It's quiet, pink, fluffy, and comfortable, with thoughtfully appointed rooms and canopy beds (Sb-€72–80, Db-€80–88, Tb-€107, 15 rue Pascal, Mo: Censier-Daubenton, tel. 01 47 07 10 99, fax 01 43 37 56 19, www.hoteldelesperance.fr, hotel.esperance@wanadoo.fr).

On the South Side of the Luxembourg Gardens

$$ Hotel des Mines** is less central, but well worth the walk. Its 50 well-appointed rooms are a great value and come with updated bathrooms and a comfortable lobby (standard Db-€90, bigger Db-€96–110, Tb-€130, Qb-€160, check for website deals, air-con, between Luxembourg and Port-Royal stations on the RER-B line, a 10-min walk from Panthéon, one block past the Luxembourg Gardens at 125 boulevard St. Michel; tel. 01 43 54 32 78, fax 01 46 33 72 52, www.hoteldesminesparis.com, hotel @hoteldesminesparis.com).

Near Canal St. Martin

This up-and-coming neighborhood is just north of the Marais, between place de la République and Canal St. Martin. It feels blue-collar and unspoiled. This area is the least touristy and most international (read "melting pot") of those I list, and its hotels and restaurants tend to be great values (for restaurant suggestions, see page 147; for nighttime fun, head over to rue Oberkampf and join the young crowd). This neighborhood is less polished and more remote—but if you can put up with some rough edges and don't mind using the Métro and buses for all of your sightseeing, you'll save plenty (hotels are €20–40 less for comparable rooms than in other areas I list).

The murky canal and its tree-lined boulevard form the central feature of this unpretentious area, with pleasing walkways, arching footbridges, and occasional boats plying its water. A flowery parkway covers the canal where it goes underground toward place de la Bastille. When the weather agrees, the entire neighborhood seems to descend on the canal in late afternoon, filling the cafés, parkway, and benches.

Market: The parkway plays host to an open-air market on Tuesdays and Fridays until 14:00.

Métro Connections: The hotels listed are easily accessed from the République and Oberkampf Métro stations. Both stations are on line 5, which serves the Est and Nord train stations, the Bastille, and many recommended restaurants (see page 147). République is an important Métro hub that serves six different train lines, including the Marais (Mo: Hôtel de Ville) and Pompidou Center (Mo: Rambuteau, both line 11); rue Cler (Mo: Ecole Militaire, line 8); the Opéra Garnier (Mo: Opéra, line 8); the Champs-Elysées (Mo: F. Roosevelt) and the Eiffel Tower (Mo: Trocadéro, both line 9); the Bastille (Mo: Bastille, line 5); Père Lachaise Cemetery (Mo: Gambetta, line 3); and the Austerlitz, Est, and Nord train stations (all three on line 10).

Internet Access: Cyber Malte is convenient (Mon–Sat 10:30–22:00, closed Sun, across from Hôtel de Nevers at 38 rue de Malte).

Bus Routes: Bus #65 connects place de la République with the Marais and Gare de Lyon via the rue du Temple, and the Nord and Est train stations along boulevard de Magenta.

Sleeping near Canal St. Martin
(10th and 11th arrondissements, Mo: République, Oberkampf)
This neighborhood is convenient to the Nord and Est train stations (about 15 minutes by foot to either) and is also a 15-minute walk from the Pompidou Center and the place des Vosges in the Marais.

Near Oberkampf Métro Station
These hotels cluster near each other. The best budget values are on rue Malte between avenue de la République and boulevard Voltaire. The Oberkampf Métro station is a bit closer than the République one.

$$ Hôtel Saint-Louis Bastille* is an attractive hotel with a welcoming, wood-beamed lobby, light stone floors, good firm beds, carefully selected furnishings, and air-conditioning. It's situated

Hotels and Restaurants near Canal St. Martin

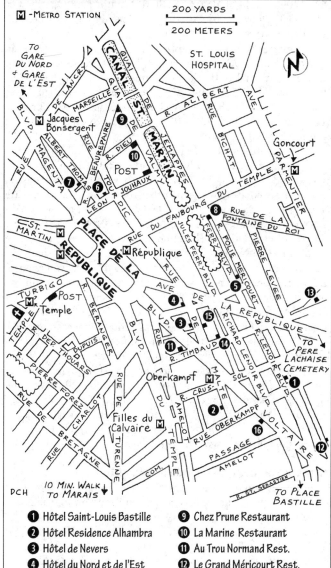

Hotels and Restaurants near Canal St. Martin map. Labels on the map include: Metro Station, 200 Yards / 200 Meters scale, To Gare du Nord & Gare de l'Est, St. Louis Hospital, Canal St. Martin, Quai de Lancry, R. de Marseille, Blvd. Magenta, Albert Thomas, Jacques Bonsergent, R. Beaurepaire, R. Dieu, Quai de Valmy, Quai de Jemmapes, R. Albert, R. Bichat, Ave., Goncourt, Parmentier, Post, R. Léon Jouhaux, Rue du Faubourg du Temple, Rue de la Fontaine du Roi, St. Martin, Place de la République, République, Rue Jules Ferry Blvd., R. Folle Méricourt, Pierre Levée, Turbigo, Post, Temple, R. Beranger, Ave. de la République, R. Richard Lenoir, To Père Lachaise Cemetery, Dep. Thouars, R. Dupuis, Pierre Foren, Blvd. du Temple, R. Charlot, Oberkampf, R. Crussol, R. Sol., Blvd. Voltaire, Rue de Bretagne, Rue de Turenne, Filles du Calvaire, R. Amelot, Rue Oberkampf, Passage Amelot, R. Com., R. St. Sébastien, To Place Bastille, 10 Min. Walk to Marais, DCH.

❶	Hôtel Saint-Louis Bastille	❾	Chez Prune Restaurant
❷	Hôtel Residence Alhambra	❿	La Marine Restaurant
❸	Hôtel de Nevers	⓫	Au Trou Normand Rest.
❹	Hôtel du Nord et de l'Est	⓬	Le Grand Méricourt Rest.
❺	Auberge de Jeunesse Jules Ferry (Hostel)	⓭	Les Tables de la Fontaine
❻	Hôtel Ibis	⓮	Chez Imogene
❼	République Hôtel	⓯	Cyber Malte Internet Café
❽	Hostel Absolute Paris	⓰	Launderette

across from the canal parkway (Sb-€99–109, "superior" Sb-€110, Db-€120–140, 114 boulevard Richard Lenoir, Mo: Oberkampf, tel. 01 43 38 29 29, fax 01 43 38 03 18, www.saintlouisbastille.com, slbastille@noos.fr).

$ Hôtel Residence Alhambra** is a good value and well-run by two friendly brothers, with a big (by Paris standards) flowery courtyard with tables. The 58 rooms are simple and plain (Sb-€69, Db-€77–86, Tb-€93–115, Qb-€128, free breakfasts for Rick Steves readers July–Aug 2008, no air-con, free Internet access, 13 rue de Malte, tel. 01 47 00 35 52, fax 01 43 57 98 75, www.hotelalhambra .fr, info@hotelalhambra.fr).

$ Hôtel du Nord et de l'Est** makes me feel good when I enter—and even better when I see the rates. About half of its spotless and renovated 45 rooms are sharp, with plush carpet, firm beds, and air-conditioning. The other rooms—€10 cheaper—are older, with no air-conditioning (Db-€79–90, extra bed-€20, Wi-Fi, 49 rue de Malte, tel. 01 47 00 71 70, fax 01 43 57 51 16, www .hotel-nord-est.com, info@hotel-nord-est.com).

$ Hôtel de Nevers* might be the best budget deal in Paris, and reminds me of how all hotels I listed used to be. It's a vintage, Old World, one-star place with an historic elevator and smiling owner Sophie and her cats, Misty and Lea, ready to take care of you (S-€40, Sb-€54, D-€38–48, Db-€55, Tb-€75, Qb-€84, shower down the hall-€4, dim room lighting, Internet access and Wi-Fi, 53 rue de Malte, tel. 01 47 00 56 18, fax 01 43 57 77 39, www .hoteldenevers.com, reservation@hoteldenevers.com).

$ Auberge de Jeunesse Jules Ferry is a fun-loving, relaxed youth hostel right on the parkway. Arrive before 10:00 or book online to be assured a room (€22 per bunk in sink-equipped 2-, 4-, or 6-bed rooms; more for nonmembers, small lockers available, rooms closed 10:00–14:00, 8 boulevard Jules Ferry, tel. 01 43 57 55 60, fax 01 43 14 82 09, www.hihostels.com).

Near the Canal and Place de la République

To find these hotels from place de la République, walk toward boulevard de Magenta and turn right on rue Léon Jouhaux. Use the République Métro stop.

$ Hôtel Ibis**, cheery though not personal, is in a grand old building. Barely off the place de la République toward the canal, it offers air-conditioning, white rooms, and a good value (Db-€90, €76 Fri–Sun, extra bed-€10, 9 rue Léon Jouhaux, tel. 01 42 40 40 50, fax 01 42 40 11 12, www.ibishotel.com, h0751@accor.com).

$ République Hôtel **, a block toward the canal from the place de la République, is well-run. Rooms are sufficiently comfortable, with good natural light, showers instead of baths, and small balconies on the fifth floor (Sb-€61–69, Db-€71–79, Tb-€90–99,

Qb–€110–125, Wi-Fi, 31 rue Albert Thomas, Mo: République, tel. 01 42 39 19 03, fax 01 42 39 22 66, www.republiquehotel.com, info@republiquehotel.com).

$ Hostel Absolute Paris is part two-star hotel, part four-beds-per-room hostel. It's in the thick of this lively area, facing the canal and filled with backpackers. The rooms are industrial-strength clean and adequate—only worth considering for dorm-style accommodations (€24 each in 4-bed room with private bathroom, Db–€85, Tb–€100, includes breakfast, 1 rue de la Fontaine du Roi, tel. 01 47 00 47 00, fax 01 47 00 47 02, www .absolute-paris.com, bonjour@absolute-paris.com).

EATING

The Parisian eating scene is kept at a rolling boil. Entire books (and lives) are dedicated to the subject. Paris is France's wine-and-cuisine melting pot. While it lacks a style of its own (only French onion soup is truly Parisian), it draws from the best of France. Paris could hold a gourmets' Olympics and import nothing.

Cafés are happy to serve a *plat du jour* (garnished plate of the day, about €10–16) or a chef-like salad (about €9) day or night, while restaurants expect you to enjoy a full dinner. Restaurants open for dinner at about 19:00, and small local favorites get crowded after 21:00. Most of the restaurants listed below accept credit cards.

To save money, review the budget eating tips in this book's Introduction. Go to bakeries for quick take-out lunches, or stop at a café for a lunch salad or *plat du jour,* but linger longer over dinner. To save even more, consider picnics (tasty take-out dishes available at *charcuteries*).

Good Picnic Spots: For great people-watching, try the Pompidou Center (by the *Homage to Stravinsky* fountains), the elegant place des Vosges (closes at dusk), the gardens behind Les Invalides and surrounding the Rodin Museum, and the Tuileries and Luxembourg gardens. The Palais Royal (across place du Palais Royal from the Louvre) is a good spot for a peaceful, royal picnic, as is the little triangular Henry IV park on the west tip of Ile de la Cité. The pedestrian pont des Arts, across from the Louvre, has great views and plentiful benches, as does the parc du Champ de Mars below the Eiffel Tower.

> ## Restaurant Price Code
>
> To help you choose among these listings, I've divided the res-
> taurants into three categories, based on the price for a typical
> meal without wine.
>
> $$$ **Higher Priced**—Most meals €35 or more.
> $$ **Moderately Priced**—Most meals between €20–35.
> $ **Lower Priced**—Most meals less than €20.

Restaurants

My recommendations are centered around the same great neighborhoods for which I list accommodations (above); you can come
home exhausted after a busy day of sightseeing and have a good
selection of restaurants right around the corner. And evening is a
fine time to explore any of these delightful neighborhoods, even
if you're sleeping elsewhere. Most restaurants I've listed in these
areas have set-price *menus* between €15 and €30. In most cases, the
few extra euros you pay are well-spent, and open up a variety of
better choices. You decide.

If you are traveling outside of Paris, save your splurges for the
countryside, where you'll enjoy regional cooking for less money.
Many Parisian department stores have huge supermarkets hiding
in the basement and top-floor cafeterias that offer affordable, low-
risk, low-stress, what-you-see-is-what-you-get meals.

Rue Cler Neighborhood

The rue Cler neighborhood caters to its residents. Its eateries, while
not destination places, have an intimate charm. I've provided a full
range of choices from cozy ma-and-pa diners, to small and trendy
boutique restaurants, to classic, big bistros. You'll generally find
great dinner *menus* for €20–30 and *plats du jour* for about €14–18.
Eat early with tourists or late with locals. For all restaurants listed
in this area, use the Ecole Militaire Métro stop (unless another
station is listed).

Close to Ecole Militaire, Between Rue de
la Motte-Picquet and Rue de Grenelle

$$$ **Café de l'Esplanade** is your opportunity to be surrounded
by chic and sophisticated Parisians enjoying top-notch traditional
cuisine as foreplay. It has a sprawling floor plan: Half its tables fill
a plush, living-room-like interior, and the other half are lined up
outside under its elegant awning facing the grand Esplanade des
Invalides in front of Napoleon's Tomb. Notice the cannons that
decorate the walls and the cannonballs used for chandeliers. Dress

Rue Cler Restaurants

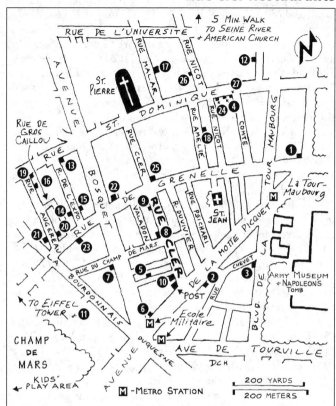

1. Café de l'Esplanade
2. Le Florimond
3. Restaurant Pasco
4. Thoumieux Brasserie
5. La Litote
6. La Terrasse du 7ème
7. Café le Bosquet
8. Café du Marché & Tribeca Rest.
9. Ulysée en Gaule
10. Petite Brasserie PTT
11. To Altitude 95 Rest. & Jules Verne Restaurant
12. Au Petit Tonneau
13. La Fontaine de Mars
14. Le P'tit Troquet
15. Billebaude Bistro
16. Chez Agnès
17. L'Ami Jean
18. Chez Pierrot
19. Café Constant
20. La Varangue
21. La Gourmandise Pizzeria
22. Real McCoy
23. Late-Night Groceries
24. Julien's Bakery
25. Café la Roussillon
26. Pourjauran Bakery
27. O'Brien's Pub

competitively, as this is *the* place to be seen in the 7th arrondissement; and consider a stylish drink, if not dinner (€25 *plats du jour,*
€55 plus wine for dinner, open daily, reserve ahead—especially if
you want a curbside table, 52 rue Fabert, Mo: La Tour-Maubourg,
tel. 01 47 05 38 80). This is the only actual business on the entire
esplanade that stretches all the way to the Champs-Elysées.

$$$ Le Florimond is good for a special occasion. The ambi-
ence, while spacious and quiet, is also intimate and welcoming.
Locals come for classic French cuisine with elegant indoor or
breezy streetside seating. Friendly English-speaking Laurent—
with his playful ties changing daily—will take good care of you
(€35 *menu*, closed Sun, good and affordable wine selection and
explosively tasty stuffed cabbage, reservations smart, 19 avenue de
la Motte-Picquet, tel. 01 45 55 40 38).

$$ Restaurant Pasco is perched elegantly overlooking Les
Invalides. The owner, Pasco Vignes, attracts a local clientele with
his modern Mediterranean cuisine, generously endowed with olive
oil (€12–20 *plats*, €20–26 *menus*, closed Mon, 74 boulevard de la
Tour-Maubourg, Mo: La Tour-Maubourg, tel. 01 44 18 33 26).

$$ Thoumieux, the neighborhood's classy, traditional
Parisian brasserie, is a popular local institution. It's big and white-
tablecloth dressy, with formal, no-nonsense waiters. The owner is
from southwest France, and much of the menu is as well (3-course
€30 dinner *menu*, open daily, 79 rue St. Dominique, Mo: La Tour-
Maubourg, tel. 01 47 05 49 75). They open at 18:30, and head waiter
Pascal advises making a reservation if you're arriving after 20:00.

$$ La Litote is the new kid on the block. It's discreetly located
on tiny rue Bosquet (not the avenue), and is making a splash with
its trendy decor and beautifully presented, well-prepared dishes.
Book ahead—it's small (good choices from French classics, €19
plats, 3-course €36 *menu*, closed Mon, try the chef's rum *digestif,*
24 rue Bosquet, tel. 01 45 51 78 82).

$$ La Terrasse du 7ème is a sprawling, happening café with
grand outdoor seating and a living-room-like interior with comfy
love seats. Located on a corner, it overlooks a busy intersection
with a constant parade of people. A meal here is like dinner the-
ater—and the show is slice-of-life Paris (no fixed-price *menu*, good
salade niçoise, open daily until at least 24:00 and sometimes until
2:00 in the morning; try the 4-item starter with salmon *tartare*,
green beans, rabbit *terrine*, and tomato with mozzarella; at Ecole
Militaire Métro stop, tel. 01 45 55 00 02).

$$ Café le Bosquet is a modern, chic Parisian brasserie with
dressy waiters and your choice of the mod-elegant interior or
sidewalk tables on a busy street. Come here for a bowl of French
onion soup, or a full three-course *menu* with good fish and meat
choices, and say *bonsoir* to owner Jean-François (closed Sun, many

choices—including vegetarian options—from a fun menu, escargots are great here, the house red wine is plenty good, reservations smart Fri–Sat, corner of rue du Champ de Mars and avenue Bosquet, 46 avenue Bosquet, tel. 01 45 51 38 13).

$ **Café du Marché** boasts the best seats, coffee, and prices on rue Cler. The owner's philosophy: Brasserie on speed—crank out great food at great prices to trendy locals and savvy tourists. It's high-energy, with waiters who barely have time to smile...*très* Parisian. This place is ideal if you want a light lunch or dinner (good, hearty €12 salads) or a more substantial but simple meal (filling €12 *plats du jour,* listed on chalkboard; open Mon–Sat 11:00–23:00, Sun 11:00–17:00, arrive before 19:30 for dinner—it's packed at 21:00, and service can be slow, at the corner of rue Cler and rue du Champ de Mars, at 38 rue Cler, tel. 01 47 05 51 27). Their **Tribeca Restaurant,** next door, offers similar (if not even better) value and more space, a calmer ambience, more patient service, and a menu focusing on pizza and Italian cuisine.

$ **Ulysée en Gaule,** in a prime location right on rue Cler, offers good, cheap, front-row seats for the people-watching fun. The Ulysée family—Stephanos, Chrysa, and their English-speaking son, Vassilis—seem to make friends with all who drop by for a bite. The family loves to serve Greek dishes, and their excellent crêpes (to go, or sit down for €2 extra) are your cheapest rue Cler hot meal (open daily, 28 rue Cler, tel. 01 47 05 61 82).

$ **Petite Brasserie PTT** is a classic time warp, popular with postal workers and offering traditional café fare at reasonable prices next to the PTT (post office) on rue Cler. They offer a great *deux pour douze* breakfast deal for Rick Steves readers: two American breakfasts (normally €8 each) for €12 total (closed Sun, opposite 53 rue Cler).

Between Rue de Grenelle and the River

$$$ **Altitude 95** is in the Eiffel Tower, 95 meters (about 300 feet) above the ground. Reserve a month in advance for a view table (€21–31 lunches, €50 dinners, daily 12:00–21:45, dinner seatings nightly at about 19:00 and 21:00, bar open until 23:00; before you ascend to dine, drop by the booth between the north/*nord* and east/*est* pillars to buy your Eiffel Tower ticket and pick up a pass that enables you to skip the line; Mo: Bir-Hakeim or Trocadéro, RER: Champ de Mars–Tour Eiffel, tel. 01 45 55 20 04, fax 01 47 05 94 40). Also in the Eiffel Tower is the even more-expensive **Jules Verne Restaurant,** described on page 76.

$$$ **Au Petit Tonneau** is a souvenir of old Paris. Fun-loving owner-chef Madame Boyer prepares everything herself, wearing her tall chef's hat like a crown as she rules from her family-style kitchen. The small, plain dining room doesn't look like it's changed

in the 25 years she's been in charge. Her steaks and lamb are excellent (allow €30 for 2-course *menu*, open daily, 20 rue Surcouf, Mo: La Tour-Maubourg, tel. 01 47 05 09 01).

$$$ La Fontaine de Mars is a longtime favorite for locals, charmingly situated on a classic, tiny Parisian street and jumbled square. It's a happening scene, with tables jammed together for the serious business of good eating. Reserve in advance for a table on the ground floor (or in summer on the square), or eat upstairs without the fun street-level ambience (€25–30 *plats*, superb foie gras, open nightly, where rue de l'Exposition and rue St. Dominique meet, 129 rue St. Dominique, tel. 01 47 05 46 44).

$$ Le P'tit Troquet, a petite eatery taking you back to the Paris of the 1920s, is gracefully and earnestly run by Dominique. She's particularly proud of her foie gras and lamb. The delicious, three-course €32 *menu* comes with traditional choices. Its delicate charm and gourmet flair make this restaurant a favorite of connoisseurs (closed Sun, reservations smart, 28 rue de l'Exposition, tel. 01 47 05 80 39).

$$ Billebaude, run by patient Pascal, is an authentic Parisian bistro where the focus is on what's fresh and meats from the hunt. New in the area, it's become popular overnight (€29 *menu*, closed Sun–Mon, 29 rue de l'Exposition, tel. 01 45 55 20 96).

$$ Chez Agnès, the smallest of my recommended Paris restaurants, is not for everyone. It's tiny, flowery, family-style, and filled with kisses on the cheek. Eccentric but sincere Agnès (a French-Tahitian Rosie O'Donnell) does it all—cooking in her minuscule kitchen and serving, too. Agnès, who cooks "French with an exotic twist" and clearly loves her work, makes children feel right at home. Don't come for a quick dinner (€23 *menu*, closed Mon, 1 rue Augereau, tel. 01 45 51 06 04).

$$ L'Ami Jean offers excellent Basque specialties at fair prices. The chef has made his reputation on the quality of his cuisine. Arrive by 19:30 or call ahead—by 20:00, there's a line out the door of people waiting to join the shared tables and lively commotion of happy eaters (€33 *menu*, closed Sun–Mon, 27 rue Malar, Mo: La Tour-Maubourg, tel. 01 47 05 86 89).

$$ Chez Pierrot is a warm, welcoming bistro serving large portions of traditional fare and big salads—all at reasonable prices (count on €30–40 with wine, closed Mon, 9 rue Amélie, tel. 01 45 51 50 08).

$ Café Constant is a tiny, cool two-level place that feels more like a small bistro–wine bar than a café. They serve delicious and affordably priced dishes (€14 *plats*) in a fun setting to a well-established clientele (closed Sun–Mon, corner of rue Augereau and rue St. Dominique, next to recommended Hôtel de Londres Eiffel).

$ La Varangue is an entertaining one-man show featuring English-speaking Philippe, who ran a French catering shop in Pennsylvania for three years. He lives upstairs, and has found his niche serving a mostly American clientele, who are all on a first-name basis. The food is cheap and basic (don't come here for high cuisine), the tables are few, and he opens early (at 17:30). Norman Rockwell would dig his tiny dining room. Try his snails and chocolate cake...but not together (€11 *plats*, €17 *menu*, always a vegetarian option, closed Sun, 27 rue Augereau, tel. 01 47 05 51 22).

$ La Gourmandise is a tiny, friendly pizzeria across the street from La Varangue. Its good, cheap pizza is ideal for kids (closed Sun, eat-in or take-out, 28 rue Augereau, tel. 01 45 55 45 16).

Picnicking in Rue Cler

Rue Cler is a moveable feast that gives "fast food" a good name. The entire street is clogged with connoisseurs of good eating. Only the health-food store goes unnoticed. A festival of food, the street is lined with people whose lives seem to be devoted to their specialty: polished produce, rotisserie chicken, crêpes, or cheese.

For a magical picnic dinner at the Eiffel Tower, assemble it in no fewer than five shops on rue Cler. Then lounge on the best grass in Paris, with the dogs, Frisbees, a floodlit tower, and a cool breeze in the parc du Champ de Mars.

Asian delis (generically called *Traiteur Asie*) provide tasty, low-stress, low-price take-out treats (€6 dinner plates, the one on rue Cler near rue du Champ de Mars has tables). **Ulysée en Gaule,** the Greek restaurant on rue Cler across from Grand Hôtel Lévêque, sells take-away crêpes (described above). **Real McCoy** is a little shop selling American food and sandwiches (closed Sun, 194 rue de Grenelle). There's a small **late-night grocery** at 197 rue de Grenelle (open daily until midnight). For excellent baguettes and sandwiches, try **Julien**'s bakery at 85 rue St. Dominique.

Breakfast in Rue Cler

Hotel breakfasts, while convenient, are generally not a good value. For a great rue Cler start to your day, drop by the **Petite Brasserie PTT** (a two-minute walk from most area hotels, described above), where managers Jerome and Eric promise Rick Steves readers a *deux pour douze* breakfast special (2 "American" breakfasts—juice, coffee, croissant, ham, and eggs—for €12). **Café la Roussillon** serves a good American-style breakfast (open daily, at corner of rue de Grenelle and rue Cler, tel. 01 45 51 47 53). To eat breakfast while watching Paris go to work, stop by **La Terrasse du 7ème** (described above). The **Pourjauran** bakery, offering great baguettes, hasn't changed in 70 years (closed Sun–Mon, 20 rue Jean Nicot).

Nightlife in Rue Cler

This sleepy neighborhood is not ideal for night owls, but there are a few notable exceptions. **Café du Marché** and **La Terrasse du 7ème** (both listed above) are busy with a Franco-American crowd until at least midnight, as is the flashier **Café la Roussillon** (nightly, corner of rue de Grenelle and rue Cler). **O'Brien's Pub** is a relaxed Parisian rendition of an Irish pub, full of Anglophones (77 avenue St. Dominique, Mo: La Tour-Maubourg).

In the Marais Neighborhood

The trendy Marais is filled with locals enjoying good food in color-ful and atmospheric eateries. The scene is competitive and changes all the time. I've listed an assortment of eateries—all handy to rec-ommended hotels—that offer good food at reasonable prices, plus a memorable experience.

Dining on Romantic Place des Vosges

On this square, which offers Old World Marais elegance, you'll find several different eateries. Enjoy a square stroll around the entire arcade—fun art galleries alternate with enticing restaurants. Choose the restaurant that best fits your mood and budget; each one has perfect arcade seating and provides big space heaters to make outdoor dining during colder months an option. Also con-sider a drink or dessert on the square at Café Hugo or Nectarine after eating elsewhere.

$$$ Ma Bourgogne is a classic old eatery where you'll sit under arcades in a whirlpool of Frenchness, as bow-tied and black-aproned waiters serve you traditional Burgundian specialties: steak, *coq au vin,* lots of French fries, escargot, and great red wine. Service comes with food, but few smiles (€35 *menu,* open daily, dinner reservations smart, cash only, at northwest corner at #19, tel. 01 42 78 44 64).

$ Nectarine is small and demure—with a wicker, pastel, and feminine ambience. This peaceful teahouse serves healthy €10 sal-ads, quiches, and €12–14 *plats du jour* day and night. Its menu lets you mix and match omelets and crêpes, and the huge desserts are splittable (open daily, at #16, tel. 01 42 77 23 78).

$ Café Hugo, named for the square's most famous resident, is best for drinks only, as the cuisine does not live up to its setting (open daily, at #22).

Near the Bastille

The nearest Métro stop to the following restaurants is Bastille.

$$ Brasserie Bofinger, an institution for over a century, is famous for fish and traditional cuisine with Alsatian flair. You're surrounded by brisk, black-and-white-attired waiters. The

Marais Restaurants

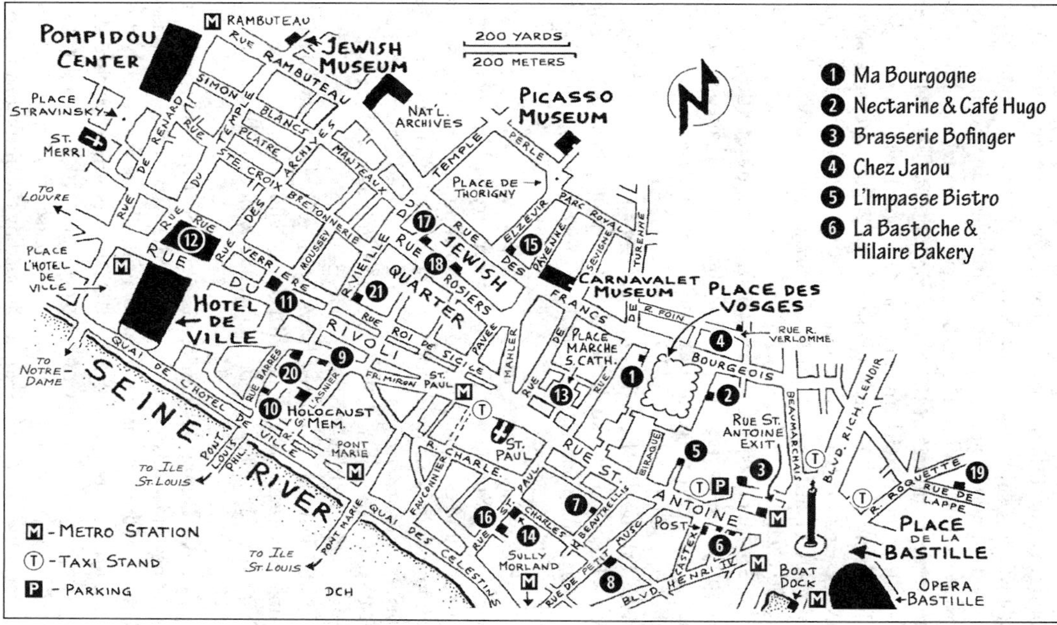

1. Ma Bourgogne
2. Nectarine & Café Hugo
3. Brasserie Bofinger
4. Chez Janou
5. L'Impasse Bistro
6. La Bastoche & Hilaire Bakery
7. Vins des Pyrénées
8. Au Temps des Cerises
9. Au Bourguignon du Marais
10. L'Ebouillanté
11. Restaurante Sant Antonio
12. BHV Cafeteria
13. Place du Marché Ste. Catherine Eateries
14. L'Enoteca Wine Bar
15. Camille Brasserie
16. Le Rouge Gorge
17. Chez Marianne
18. L'As du Falafel
19. Bistrot les Sans Culottes
20. La Perla Bar
21. Le Pick-Clops Bar Rest.

sprawling interior features elaborately decorated rooms reminiscent of the Roaring Twenties. Eating under the grand 1919 *coupole* is a memorable treat (as is using the "historic" 1919 WC downstairs). Check out the boys shucking and stacking seafood platters out front before you enter. Their €32 three-course *menu*, while not top cuisine, includes wine and is a good value. The kids' menu makes this restaurant family-friendly (open daily and nightly, 5 rue de la Bastille, don't be confused by the lesser "Petite" Bofinger across the street, tel. 01 42 72 87 82).

$$ Chez Janou, a Provençal bistro, tumbles out of its corner building and fills its broad sidewalk with happy eaters. At first glance, you know this is a find. Don't let the trendy and youthful crowd intimidate you—it's relaxed and charming, with helpful and patient service. While the curbside tables are inviting, I'd sit inside to immerse myself in the happy commotion. The style is French Mediterranean, with an emphasis on vegetables (€15 *plats du jour* that change with the season, open daily, 2 blocks beyond place des Vosges at 2 rue Roger Verlomme, tel. 01 42 72 28 41). They're proud of their 81 different varieties of *pastis* (licorice-flavored liqueur; €3.50 each, browse the list).

$$ L'Impasse, a relaxed bistro on a quiet alley, serves a simple three-course *menu* for €32. Fun-loving Françoise, a former dancer and artist, runs the place *con brio* (closed Sun, 4 impasse de Guéménée, tel. 01 42 72 08 45). Françoise promises anyone with this book a free glass of *byrrh*—it's pronounced "beer," but it's a French port-like drink. The restaurant is next to a self-serve launderette (open nightly until 21:30—clean your clothes while you dine).

$$ La Bastoche (Parisian slang for "the Bastille") is cozy and welcoming. Step down into an 18th-century building with exposed timbers and a great mural of the storming of the old prison, and choose from a nice selection of traditional French fare at good prices. Caring owners Sylvie and Lise work hard to please (€23 3-course *menu*, open daily, 7 rue St. Antoine, one block away from place de la Bastille, tel. 01 48 04 84 34).

$$ Vins des Pyrénées draws a young, lively crowd with its fun ambience, varying menus with lots of choices, and a reasonable wine list (€15–20 *plats*, open daily, 25 rue Beautreillis, tel. 01 42 72 64 94).

$ Au Temps des Cerises is a *très* local wine bar, with tight seating and wads of character. While they serve good, three-course, €15 lunch *menus*, it's also a fine choice for an early dinner or a pre-dinner glass of wine. "Dinner" is limited to bread, dry sausage, cheese, and wine served by goateed Yves and his wife, Michele. A small mixed plate of cheese (€4), meat (€4), and a carafe of good wine (€4–8) surrounded by the intimate and woody,

Old World ambience can be a good light meal (Mon–Fri until at least 20:00, closed Sat–Sun, at rue du Petit-Musc and rue de la Cerisaie).

Closer to Hôtel de Ville

These eateries, near the Pompidou Center, appear on the map on page 139. To reach them, use the Hôtel de Ville Métro stop.

$$$ Au Bourguignon du Marais is a small wine bar–bistro for Burgundian wine-lovers, where excellent wines blend with a selection of well-designed dishes (€35–45 plus wine, closed Sun–Mon, indoor and outdoor seating, 52 rue Francois Miron, tel. 01 48 87 15 40).

$ L'Ebouillanté, a romantically situated and breezy crêperie-café near the river, is ideal for an inexpensive and relaxing tea, snack, or lunch, or for dinner on a warm evening. Try a *brick*, the light-hearted chef's specialty (think beefy crêpe). The salads and desserts are also good (€13 *plats*, Tue–Sun 12:00–22:00, closed Mon, 6 rue des Barres, tel. 01 42 71 09 69).

$ Restaurante Sant Antonio is bustling and cheap, serving up €10 pizzas and salads on a fun Marais square (open daily, barely off rue de Rivoli on place du Bourg Tibourg).

$ BHV Department Store's fifth-floor cafeteria provides nice views, an escape from the busy streets below, and no-brainer, point-and-shoot cafeteria cuisine (Mon–Sat 11:30–18:00, closed Sun, at intersection of rue du Temple and rue de la Verrerie, one block from Hôtel de Ville).

In the Heart of the Marais

These are closest to the St. Paul Métro stop.

$$ On place du Marché Ste. Catherine: This small, romantic square, just off rue St. Antoine, is an international food festival cloaked in extremely Parisian, leafy-square ambience. On a balmy evening, this is clearly a neighborhood favorite, with a handful of restaurants offering €20–30 meals. Study the square, and you'll find a popular French bistro **(Le Marché)** and other inviting eateries serving a variety of international food. You'll eat under the trees, surrounded by a futuristic-in-1800 planned residential quarter.

$$ L'Enoteca is a high-spirited, half-timbered wine bar–restaurant serving affordable Italian cuisine (no pizza) with a tempting *antipasti* bar. It's a relaxed, open setting with busy, blue-aproned waiters serving two floors of local eaters (€15 pastas, €20 *plats*, €30 3-course *menu*, open daily, across from L'Excuse at rue St. Paul and rue Charles V, 25 rue Charles V, tel. 01 42 78 91 44).

$ Camille, a traditional corner brasserie, is a neighborhood favorite with great indoor and sidewalk seating. White-aproned waiters serve €10–13 salads and very French *plats du jour* (€16–20) from the chalkboard list to a down-to-earth but sophisticated clientele (open daily, 24 rue des Francs Bourgeois at corner of rue Elzévir, tel. 01 42 72 20 50).

$ Le Rouge Gorge's relaxed wine bar and bistro is six-table cozy. Come for a meal (€10 lunch *plats*, €16–20 dinner *plats*), a coffee, or a glass of wine. Friendly François, the owner, will send you downstairs to the *cave* (cellar) to choose your wine; there are different prices for take-away wine (closed Sun, 8 rue St. Paul, tel. 01 48 04 75 89).

$ Several hardworking **Asian fast-food eateries,** great for a €6 meal, line rue St. Antoine.

On Rue des Rosiers in the Jewish Quarter

To reach the Jewish Quarter, use the St. Paul Métro stop.

$ Chez Marianne, a neighborhood fixture, offers classic Jewish meals and Parisian ambience. Choose from several indoor zones with a cluttered wine shop/deli ambience, or sit outside. You'll select from two dozen "Zakouski" elements to assemble your €15 plate (great vegetarian options, eat cheap with a €6 falafel sandwich, or even cheaper with takeout, long hours daily, corner of rue des Rosiers and rue des Hospitalières St. Gervais, tel. 01 42 72 18 86). For takeout, pay inside first and get a ticket before you order outside.

$ L'As du Falafel rules the falafel scene in the Jewish quarter. Monsieur Isaac, the "Ace of Falafel" here since 1979, brags that he's got "the biggest pita on the street…and he fills it up." Apparently, it's Lenny Kravitz's favorite, too. Your inexpensive Jewish cuisine comes on plastic plates, with a bustling ambience that seems to prove he's earned his success. While the €6.50 "special falafel" is the big hit, many Americans enjoy his lighter chicken version *(poulet grillé)*. Their takeout service draws a constant crowd (day and night until late, closed Sat, 34 rue des Rosiers).

Picnicking in the Marais

Picnic at peaceful place des Vosges (closes at dusk) or on the Ile St. Louis *quais* (see below). Stretch your euros at the basement supermarket of the **Monoprix** department store (closed Sun, near place des Vosges on rue St. Antoine). You'll find a small **grocery** open until 23:00 near 48 rue St. Antoine).

Breakfast in the Marais

For an incredibly cheap breakfast, try **Hilaire boulangerie-pâtisserie,** where the hotels buy their croissants (coffee machine-€1, cheap baby quiches, 1 block off place de la Bastille, corner of rue St. Antoine and rue de Lesdiguières).

Nightlife in the Marais

The best scene for hard-core night owls is the dizzying array of wacky eateries, bars, and dance halls on **rue de Lappe.** This street is what the Latin Quarter aspires to be. Just east of the stately place de la Bastille, it's one of the wildest nightspots in Paris and not for everyone. Sitting amid the chaos like a van Gogh painting is the popular, old-time **Bistrot les Sans Culottes.**

Trendy cafés and bars—popular with gay men—also cluster on rue Vieille du Temple, rue des Archives, and rue Ste. Croix de la Bretonnerie (close at about 2:00 in the morning). You'll find a line of bars and cafés providing front-row seats for the buff parade on rue Vieille du Temple, a block north of rue de Rivoli. Nearby, rue des Rosiers bustles with youthful energy, but there are no cafés to observe from. **Vins des Pyrénées** is young and fun—find the small bar in the back (see above). **La Perla** is full of Parisian yuppies in search of the perfect margarita (26 rue François Miron).

$ Le Pick-Clops Bar Restaurant is a happy peanuts-and-lots-of-cocktails diner with bright neon, loud colors, and a garish local crowd. It's perfect for immersing yourself in today's Marais world—a little boisterous, a little edgy, a little gay, fun-loving, easygoing...and no tourists. Sit inside, on old-fashioned diner stools, or streetside to watch the constant Marais parade. The name means "Steal the Cigarettes"—but you'll pay €10 for your big salad (daily 7:00–24:00, 16 rue Vieille du Temple, tel. 01 40 29 02 18).

The most enjoyable peaceful evening may be simply donning your floppy "three musketeers" hat, and slowly strolling around the place des Vosges, window-shopping the art galleries.

Ile St. Louis

The Ile St. Louis is a romantic and peaceful neighborhood to window-shop for plenty of promising dinner possibilities. Cruise the island's main street for a variety of options, from cozy *crêperies* to Italian eateries (intimate pizzerias and upscale) to typical brasseries (a few with fine outdoor seating facing the bridge to Ile de la Cité). After dinner, sample Paris' best sorbet and stroll across to the Ile de la Cité to see an illuminated Notre-Dame, or enjoy a scenic drink on the deck of a floating café moored under the Notre-Dame's right transept. All of these listings line the island's main drag, the rue St. Louis-en-l'Ile (see map on page 119; to get here, use the Pont Marie Métro stop). Consider skipping dessert to enjoy a stroll while licking the best ice cream in Paris (described under "Ice-Cream Dessert," below).

$$$ Le Tastevin is an intimate, mother-and-son-run restaurant serving top-notch traditional French cuisine with white-tablecloth, candlelit, gourmet elegance under heavy wooden beams. The three-course *menus* start at about €36 and offer plenty of classic choices that change with the season to ensure freshness (open daily, good wine list, reserve for late-evening eating, 46 rue St. Louis-en-l'Ile, tel. 01 43 54 17 31; owner Madame Puisieux and waitress Laure speak just enough English).

$$$ *Medieval Theme Restaurants:* **Nos Ancêtres les Gaulois** on rue St. Louis-en-l'Ile is famous for its rowdy, medieval-cellar atmosphere. Ideal for barbarians—as the name ("Our Ancestors, the Gauls") implies—they serve all-you-can-eat buffets with straw baskets of raw veggies (cut whatever you like with your dagger), massive plates of pâté, a meat course, and all the wine you can stomach for €39. The food is just food; burping is encouraged. If you want to eat a lot, drink a lot of wine, be surrounded with tourists, and holler at your friends while receiving smart-aleck buccaneer service, this food fest can be fun (open daily from 19:00, at #39, tel. 01 46 33 66 07). **La Taverne du Sergeant Recruteur,** next door, serves up the same formula for €41 with a different historic twist: The "Sergeant Recruiter" used to get young Parisians drunk and stuffed here, then sign them into the army. You might swing by both and choose the…"ambience" is not quite the right word… that fits your mood (tel. 01 43 54 75 42).

$$ **La Brasserie de l'Ile St. Louis** is situated at the prow of the island's ship as it faces Ile de la Cité, offering purely Alsatian cuisine (try the *choucroute garni* for €18), served in Franco-Germanic ambience with no-nonsense brasserie service. This is a good balmy-evening perch for watching the Ile St. Louis promenade—or, if it's chilly, the interior is plenty characteristic for a memorable night out (closed Wed, no reservations, 55 quai de Bourbon, tel. 01 43 54 02 59).

$ **Café Med,** near Notre-Dame at #77, has inexpensive salads, crêpes, and a €20 *menu* served in a tight but cheery setting (open daily, limited wine list, tel. 01 43 29 73 17). Two similar *crêperies* are just across the street.

Riverside Picnic

On sunny lunchtimes and balmy evenings, the *quai* on the Left Bank side of Ile St. Louis is lined with locals who have more class than money, spreading out tablecloths and even lighting candles for elegant picnics. Otherwise, it's a great walk for people-watching.

Ice-Cream Dessert

Half the people strolling Ile St. Louis are licking an ice-cream cone, because this is the home of *les glaces Berthillon.* The original **Berthillon** shop, at 31 rue St. Louis-en-l'Ile, is marked by the line of salivating customers (closed Mon–Tue). Another Berthillon shop is across the street, and there's one more around the corner on rue Bellay. The three shops are so popular that the wealthy people who can afford to live on this fancy island complain about the congestion they cause. For a less famous but at-least-as-tasty treat, the homemade Italian gelato a block away at **Amorino Gelati** is giving Berthillon competition (no line, bigger portions, easier to see what you want, and they offer little tastes—Berthillon doesn't need to, 47 rue St. Louis-en-l'Ile, tel. 01 44 07 48 08). Having some of each is not a bad thing.

Luxembourg Neighborhood

Sleeping in the Luxembourg neighborhood puts you near many appealing dining and after-hours options. Because my hotels in this area cluster around the Panthéon and St. Sulpice Church (see page 122), I've organized restaurant listings the same way. Restaurants near the Panthéon tend to be calm, those around St. Sulpice more boisterous; it's a short walk from one area to the other. Anyone sleeping in this area is close to the inexpensive eateries that line the always-bustling rue Mouffetard.

Near the Panthéon

For locations, see the map on page 125.

These eateries are served by the Cluny-La Sorbonne Métro stop and the RER-B Luxembourg station.

$$ Restaurant Perraudin is a welcoming, family-run, red-checkered-tablecloth eatery understandably popular with tourists. Friendly Monsieur Correy serves classic *cuisine bourgeoise* with an emphasis on Burgundian dishes in air-conditioned comfort. The decor is vintage turn-of-the-20th-century, with big mirrors and old wood paneling (*bœuf bourguignon* is a specialty here, €18 lunch *menus*, €28 dinner *menus*, closed Sun, between the Panthéon and Luxembourg Garden at 157 rue St. Jacques, tel. 01 46 33 15 75).

$ Le Soufflot Café, between the Panthéon and Luxembourg Garden, is well-positioned for afternoon sun. It has a nifty, library-like interior, outdoor tables, and point-blank views of the Panthéon. The cuisine is café-classic: good €10 salads, omelets, and *plats du jour* (open daily, a block below the Panthéon on the right side of rue Soufflot as you walk toward Luxembourg Garden, tel. 01 43 26 57 56).

$ *Place de la Sorbonne:* This cobbled-and-leafy square, with a small fountain facing the Sorbonne University just a block from the Cluny Museum, offers several decent opportunities for a quick outdoor lunch or light dinner. At the tiny **Baker's Dozen,** you'll pay take-away prices for salads and sandwiches you can sit down to eat (daily €5 salad and quiche special, open daily until 17:00). **Café de l'Ecritoire** is a typical, lively brasserie with happy diners enjoying €11 salads, €13 *plats,* and fine square seating (open daily, tel. 01 43 54 60 02). **Patios,** with appealing decor inside and out, serves inexpensive Italian fare including pizza (open daily until late).

Near the Odéon Theater
To reach these, use the Odéon Métro stop.

$$ Brasserie Bouillon Racine takes you back to 1906 with an Art Nouveau carnival of carved wood, stained glass, and old-time lights reflected in beveled mirrors. The over-the-top décor, energetic waiters, and affordable menu combine to give it an inviting conviviality. Check upstairs before choosing a table (€18 *plats,* €29 *menu,* traditional French with lots of fish and meat, daily 12:00–2:00 & 7:00–23:00, 3 rue Racine, tel. 01 44 32 15 60).

$ Restaurant Polidor, a bare-bones neighborhood fixture since the 19th century, is much loved for its unpretentious quality cooking, fun old Paris ambience, and fair value. Their menu features *plats* from every corner of France, and their *menu fraîcheur* is designed for lighter summer eating (€20–30 3-course *menus,* €10–13 *plats,* daily 12:00–14:30 & 19:00–23:00, cash only, no reservations, 41 rue Monsieur-Le-Prince, tel. 01 43 26 95 34, Amelia).

On Rue Mouffetard
Lying several blocks behind the Panthéon, rue Mouffetard is a conveyer belt of comparison-shopping eaters with wall-to-wall budget options (fondue, crêpes, Italian, falafel, and Greek). Come here to join the fun parade of diners and eat a less-expensive meal (you get what you pay for). This street stays up late and likes to party (particularly place de la Contrescarpe). The gauntlet begins on top, at thriving place de la Contrescarpe, and ends below where rue Mouffetard ends at St. Médard Church. Both ends offer fun cafés where you can eat, drink, and watch the action. The upper end is pedestrian and touristic; the bottom end is purely Parisian. And anywhere between is no-man's-land for consistent quality. Still, strolling with so many fun-seekers is enjoyable, whether you eat here or not. To get here, use the Censier-Daubenton Métro stop.

$ Café Delmas, at the top of rue Mouffetard on picturesque place de la Contrescarpe, is *the* place to see and be seen. Come here for a before- or after-dinner drink on the broad outdoor terrace, or for typical café cuisine (€14 salads, €15–20 *plats,* great chocolate ice cream, open daily).

$ Le Mouffetard, a traditional café with a lively location in the heart of rue Mouffetard, is ideal for an inexpensive lunch or dinner (€13 lunches, €16 2-course *menus*, closed Mon, 16 rue Mouffetard, tel. 01 43 31 42 50).

$ Cave de Bourgogne is *très* local and serves reasonably priced café fare at the bottom of rue Mouffetard, with picture-perfect tables on a raised terrace, and a warm interior (€13–16 *plats*, specials listed on chalkboards, open daily, 144 rue Mouffetard).

Near St. Sulpice Church

Rue des Canettes and Rue Guisarde: For an entirely different experience, roam the streets between the St. Sulpice Church and boulevard St. Germain, abounding with restaurants, *crêperies,* wine bars, and jazz haunts (use Mo: St. Sulpice). Find rue des Canettes and rue Guisarde, and window-shop the many French and Italian eateries—most with similar prices, but each with a slightly different feel. For excellent crêpes, try **La Crêpe Rit du Clown** (Mon–Sat 12:00–23:00, closed Sun, 6 rue des Canettes, tel. 01 46 34 01 02). And for a bohemian pub lined with black-and-white photos of the artsy and revolutionary French '60s, have a drink at **Chez Georges.** Sit in a cool little streetside table nook, or venture downstairs to find a hazy, drippy-candle, traditionally French world in the Edith Piaf–style dance cellar (cheap drinks from old-fashioned menu, Tue–Sat 14:00–2:00 in the morning, closed Sun–Mon and in Aug, 11 rue des Canettes).

Near Canal St. Martin

Along the Canal, North of République

Escape the crowded tourist areas and enjoy a cool canalside experience. Take the Métro to place de la République and walk down rue Beaurepaire to Canal St. Martin. There you'll find two worthwhile cafés. They're both lively, with similarly reasonable prices; you decide: **$ Chez Prune** is the kind of place where revolutions are plotted. The ambience is Old-World-meets-hip-world inside and out, and the food is well-prepared (€10 salads, €15 *plats*, open daily, 71 quai de Valmy, tel. 01 42 41 30 47). **$ La Marine** is similarly chic, but less intense (open daily, 2 blocks to the right as you leave Chez Prune, 55 bis quai de Valmy, tel. 01 42 39 69 81).

In the summertime, most bars and cafés offer beer and wine to go (*à emporter*), so you can take it to the canal's edge and picnic there with the young locals.

Near Rue Oberkampf, South of République

$$ Le Grand Méricourt is a find. Grégory, the 22-year-old chef, inspires with his original flavor combinations and beautiful presentation. It's traditional French—but with a twist. Marie-Elizabeth (his mom) serves gently, while Greg's team of two cook everything fresh in a tiny kitchen. Don't come for a quick meal; this is a good place for special occasions and reservations are smart (*menus* from €29, 22 rue de la Folie Méricourt, tel. 01 43 38 94 04).

$$ Les Tables de la Fontaine, on a pleasant, leafy square, is a popular neighborhood place, with lots of windows and outdoor seating. Enjoy seafood specialties, salads, or traditional bistro fare (*menus* from €23, open daily, 33 rue Jean-Pierre Timbaud, tel. 01 43 57 26 00).

$ Au Trou Normand, near the recommended hotels on rue Malte, is a small, red-checkered-tablecloth eatery with reasonable prices (€12–16 *plats,* open daily, just off boulevard Voltaire at 9 rue Jean-Pierre Timbaud, tel. 01 48 05 80 23).

$ Chez Imogene is a tiny, brightly colored corner *crêperie,* with fresh products, friendly Michel and Emanuel in charge, and nothing but locals around you (3-course €15 dinner *menu,* closed Sun, 25 rue Jean-Pierre Timbaud, tel. 01 48 07 14 59).

Eating Elsewhere in Paris
Near the Louvre
$ Café le Nemours, a staunchly Parisian fixture serving pricey but good light lunches, is tucked into the corner of the Palais Royal adjacent to the Comédie Française. With elegant brass and Art Deco style, and outdoor tables under an arcade two minutes from the pyramid, its a great post-Louvre retreat (fun and filling €11 salads, open daily; leaving the Louvre, cross rue de Rivoli and veer left to 2 place Colette, located on Louvre map on page 70; Mo: Palais Royal, tel. 01 42 61 34 14).

Near Opéra Garnier
$ Bouillon Chartier is a noisy, old, classic eatery. It's named for the bouillon it served the neighborhood's poor workers back in 1896, when its calling was to provide an affordable warm meal for those folks. Workers used to eat *à la gamelle* (from a tin lunch-box). That same spirit—complete with surly waiters and a cheap menu—survives today. Among more than 300 simple seats and 15 frantic waiters, you can still see the restaurant's napkin drawers for its early regulars (€18 *menus,* open daily 11:30–15:00 & 18:00–22:00, east of the Opéra Garnier near boulevard Poissonniere, 7 rue de Faubourg-Montmartre, Mo: Grands Boulevards, tel. 01 47 70 86 29).

Montmartre
Montmartre is extremely touristy, with many mindless mobs following guides to cancan shows. But the ambience is undeniably fun, and an evening up here overlooking Paris is a quintessential experience in the City of Light. The steps in front of Sacré-Cœur

are perfect for a picnic with a view. Along the touristy main drag (near place du Tertre and just off it), several fun piano bars serve reasonable crêpes with great people-watching. To reach this area, use the Anvers Métro stop.

$$ Restaurant Chez Plumeau, just off jam-packed place du Tertre, is touristy yet moderately priced, with couldn't-care-less service but great seating on a tiny, characteristic square (elaborate €16 salads, €16–20 *plats,* closed Wed, place du Calvaire, tel. 01 46 06 26 29).

$ L'Eté en Pente Douce hides under generous branches below the crowds on a classic neighborhood corner. It features fine indoor and outdoor seating, €10 *plats du jour* and salads, vegetarian options, and good wines (open daily, 23 rue Muller, many steps below Sacré-Cœur to the left as you leave, down the stairs below the WC, tel. 01 42 64 02 67).

Dinner Cruises

The following companies all offer dinner cruises (reservations required). **Bateaux-Mouches** and **Bateaux Parisiens** have the best reputations and the highest prices. They offer multicourse meals and music in aircraft-carrier-size dining rooms with glass tops and good views. For both, proper dress is required—no denim, shorts, or sport shoes, and Bateaux-Mouches requires a jacket and tie for men. The main difference between these companies is the ambience: Bateaux-Mouches offers violin and piano to entertain you during your romantic evening, while Bateaux Parisiens boasts a lively atmosphere with a singer, band, and dance floor.

Bateaux Mouches, started in 1949, is hands-down the most famous. You can't miss its sparkling port on the north side of the river at pont de l'Alma. Board from 19:30–20:15, depart at 20:30, and return at 22:45 (€130/person, tel. 01 42 25 96 10, www .bateauxmouches.com).

Bateaux Parisiens leaves from Port de la Bourdonnais, just east from the bridge under the Eiffel Tower. Begin boarding at 19:45, leave at 20:30, and return at 23:00 (€95–140/person, 3 price tiers, depends on seating, tel. 08 25 62 75 13, www.bateauxparisiens.com). The middle level is best. Pay the few extra euros to get seats next to the windows—it's more romantic and private, with sensational views.

Le Capitaine Fracasse offers the blue-collar option (€50/person; tables are first-come, first-serve, so get there early; boarding times vary by season and day of week, usually at 19:45, 21:15 in summer, closed Mon, walk down stairs in the middle of Bir-Hakeim bridge near the Eiffel Tower to Iles aux Cygne, tel. 01 46 21 48 15, www.lecapitainefracasse.com).

TRANSPORTATION CONNECTIONS

Trains

Paris is Europe's rail hub, with six major train stations and one minor one, each serving different regions: Gare de l'Est (eastbound trains), Gare du Nord (northern France and Europe), Gare St. Lazare (northwestern France), Gare d'Austerlitz (southwestern France and Europe), Gare de Lyon (southeastern France and Italy), Gare Montparnasse (northwestern France and TGV service to France's southwest), and a smaller station, Gare de Bercy, the departure point for most night trains to Italy. Any train station has schedule information, can make reservations, and sell tickets for any destination. Unless you happen to pass a station in your sightseeing, buying tickets is handier from an SNCF neighborhood office (look for an *SNCF* sign in the window)—including those at the Louvre, Invalides, Orsay, Versailles, and airports—or at your neighborhood travel agency. It's worth the small fee.

All six main train stations have banks or change offices, ATMs, information desks, telephones, cafés, newsstands, and clever pickpockets. Because of security concerns, not all have baggage checks.

Each station offers two types of rail service: long distance to other cities, called *Grandes Lignes* (major lines); and suburban service to outlying areas, called *banlieue* or RER. Both *banlieue* and RER trains serve outlying areas and the airports; the only difference is that *banlieue* lines are operated by SNCF (France's train system, called Transilien) and RER lines are operated by RATP (Paris' Métro and bus system). You may also see ticket windows identified as *Ile de France*. This is for Transilien (SNCF) trains serving destinations outside Paris in the Ile de France region (usually no more than an hour from Paris).

Paris train stations can be intimidating, but if you slow down, avoid peak times, take a deep breath, and ask for help, you'll find them manageable and efficient. Bring a pad of paper for clear communication at ticket/info windows. All stations have helpful *accueil* (information) booths; the bigger stations have roving helpers, usually in red vests. They're capable of answering rail questions more quickly than the information or ticket windows.

To make your trip go more smoothly, be sure to review the many train tips in "Transportation," on page 791 in this book's appendix.

Station Overview

Here's an overview of Paris' major train stations. Métro and RER trains, as well as buses and taxis, are well-marked at every station.

Paris Train Stations

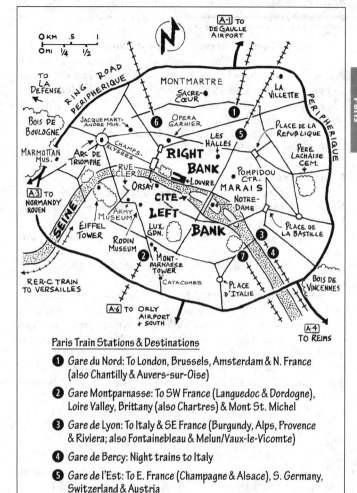

Paris Train Stations & Destinations

1 Gare du Nord: To London, Brussels, Amsterdam & N. France (also Chantilly & Auvers-sur-Oise)

2 Gare Montparnasse: To SW France (Languedoc & Dordogne), Loire Valley, Brittany (also Chartres) & Mont St. Michel

3 Gare de Lyon: To Italy & SE France (Burgundy, Alps, Provence & Riviera; also Fontainebleau & Melun/Vaux-le-Vicomte)

4 Gare de Bercy: Night trains to Italy

5 Gare de l'Est: To E. France (Champagne & Alsace), S. Germany, Switzerland & Austria

6 Gare St. Lazare: To Normandy (also Vernon/Giverny)

7 Gare d'Austerlitz: To SW France, Loire Valley & Spain

When arriving by Métro, follow signs for *Grandes Lignes–SNCF* to find the main tracks.

Gare du Nord

This vast station serves cities in northern France and international destinations north of Paris, including Copenhagen, Amsterdam, and the Eurostar to London. Arrive early to allow time to navigate this station. Monet-esque views over the trains and peaceful, air-conditioned cafés hide on the upper level, past the Eurostar ticket windows (find the cool view WCs down the steps in the café).

Key Destinations Served by Gare du Nord *Grandes Lignes:* **Brussels** (about 2/hr, 1.5 hrs), **Bruges** (about 2/hr, 2.5 hrs, change in Brussels), **Amsterdam** (nearly hourly, 4.5 hrs, change in Brussels), **Copenhagen** (7/day, 14–18 hrs, two night trains), **Koblenz** (9/day, 5 hrs, most change in Köln), and **London** via Eurostar Chunnel train (12–15/day, 2.5 hrs, tel. 08 36 35 35 39).

By *Banlieue/***RER Lines: Charles de Gaulle Airport** (5/hr, 30 min, runs 5:00–24:00, track 4).

Gare Montparnasse

This big and modern station covers three floors, serves lower Normandy and Brittany, and offers TGV service to the Loire Valley and southwestern France, as well as suburban service to Chartres. Air France buses to Orly and Charles de Gaulle airports stop in front of the station, down the escalators and outside. City buses are outside to the left (#28 connects conveniently to the rue Cler area).

Key Destinations Served by Gare Montparnasse: Chartres (10/day, 1 hr, *banlieue* lines), **Amboise** (12/day, 1.5 hrs, transfer in St. Pierre-des-Corps, requires TGV reservation; non-TGV trains leave from Gare d'Austerlitz), **Pontorson/Mont St. Michel** (7/day, 4–5.5 hrs, via Rennes or Lison, some with bus from Rennes), **Dinan** (6/day, 4 hrs, change in Rennes and Dol), **Bordeaux** (20/day, 3.5 hrs), **Sarlat** (7/day, 6 hrs, change in Bordeaux, Libourne, or Souillac), **Toulouse** (13/day, 5–7 hrs, most require change, usually in Bordeaux or Montpellier), **Albi** (6/day, 6–7.5 hrs, change in Toulouse, also night train), **Carcassonne** (14/day, 6.5 hrs, most require changes in Toulouse or Montpellier, direct trains take 8 hrs, night train also available), **Tours** (18/day, 1 hr), **Madrid** (3/day, 13–19 hrs, one overnight via Irun, more night trains from Gare d'Austerlitz), and **Lisbon** (1–2/day, 27 hrs via Irun or Madrid).

Gare de Lyon

This huge and bewildering station offers TGV and regular service to southeastern France, Italy, and other international destinations (for more trains to Italy, see "Gare de Bercy," below). Don't leave this station without relaxing in Le Train Bleu Restaurant lounge, up the stairs opposite track G.

Grande Ligne trains arrive and depart from one level, but are divided into two areas (tracks A–N in the blue area, and 5–23 in the yellow area). They are connected by the long platform along tracks A and 5, and by the hallway adjacent to track A and opposite track 9.

Air France buses to Montparnasse (easy transfer to Orly Airport) and direct to Charles de Gaulle Airport stop outside the station's main entrance (opposite tracks A–L, walk across the parking lot—the stop is opposite the Café Européen on the right; €12, 2/hr, normally at :15 and :45 after the hour).

Key Destinations Served by Gare de Lyon: Disneyland (RER line A-4 to Marne-la-Vallée-Chessy, at least 3/hr, 45 min), **Beaune** (nearly hourly, 2.5 hrs, most require change in Dijon), **Dijon** (nearly hourly, 1.5 hrs), **Chamonix** (8/day, 6–8 hrs, night train possible), **Annecy** (13/day, 4–5 hrs), **Lyon** (at least hourly, 2 hrs), **Avignon** (11/day in 2.5 hrs, 7/day in 3–4 hrs with change), **Arles** (17/day, 2 direct TGVs in 4 hrs, 15 with change in Marseille, Avignon, or Nîmes in 3.5–5 hrs), **Nice** (10/day, 5.5–7 hrs, many with change in Marseille, night train possible out of Gare d'Austerlitz), **Venice** (3/day, 4/night, 10–16 hrs, 1 direct overnight, important to reserve ahead), **Rome** (3/day, 13–16 hrs, plus several overnight options, important to reserve ahead), **Bern** (6/day, 5–7 hrs, most require changes, night train possible), **Interlaken** (9/day, 7 hrs, night train possible via Basel out of Gare de l'Est), and **Barcelona** (3/day, 9 hrs, 1–2 changes; night trains from Gare d'Austerlitz).

Gare de Bercy

This smaller station handles some night train service to Italy (Mo: Bercy, one stop east of Gare de Lyon on line 14).

Gare de l'Est

This single-floor station (with underground Métro), which serves eastern France and international destinations east of Paris, should be entirely renovated by 2008 to accommodate new TGV service east to Reims and Strasbourg. Once it's completed, train times to Strasbourg, Colmar, and points east will be cut by 2–3 hours. It should have the usual services (though baggage check is uncertain).

Key Destinations Served by Gare de l'Est: Colmar (12/day, 5.5 hrs, change in Strasbourg, , with TGV 3 hrs), **Strasbourg** (12/day with TGV 2.5 hrs), **Reims** (8/day, 2 hrs, with TGV 45 min), **Verdun** (2/day, 1.75 hrs with TGV and shuttle bus; non-TGV 7/day, 3–3.5 hrs, change in Metz or Chalon, 2/day with TGV and shuttle bus 95 min), **Munich** (7/day, 8–12 hrs, some require changes, night train possible), **Vienna** (2/day, 13–18 hrs, 1–7 changes, also 1 direct night train), **Zürich** (14/day, 7 hrs, most require changes, night train), and **Prague** (5/day, 14–18 hrs, night train possible via Frankfurt).

Gare St. Lazare

This relatively small station serves upper Normandy, including Rouen and Giverny. The station is undergoing renovation, so be prepared for the temporary displacement of shops and services. There is no baggage check.

Key Destinations Served by Gare St. Lazare: Giverny (train to Vernon, 6/day, get there in time to visit the gardens, 45 min—see schedule in "Giverny Day Trip" on page 180—then bus or taxi 15 min to Giverny), **Rouen** (20/day, 1–1.5 hrs), **Honfleur** (13/day, 2–3.5 hrs, via Lisieux, then bus), **Bayeux** (9/day, 2–2.5 hrs, some with change in Caen), **Caen** (14/day, 2 hrs), and **Pontorson/ Mont St. Michel** (2/day, 4–5.5 hrs, via Caen; more trains from Gare Montparnasse).

Gare d'Austerlitz

This small station provides non-TGV service to the Loire Valley, southwestern France, and Spain. To get to the Métro, you must walk outside and along either side of the station.

Key Destinations Served by Gare d'Austerlitz: Versailles (via RER line C, 4/hr, 40 min), **Amboise** (10/day direct in 2 hrs; faster TGV connection from Gare Montparnasse), **Cahors** (5/day, 5 hrs, also 1 direct night train; other slower trains from Gare Montparnasse), **Barcelona** (3/night, 12–14 hrs, 1 direct; day trains from Gare de Lyon), and **Madrid** (2/night, 13 hrs direct, 16 hrs via Irun; day trains from Gare Montparnasse).

To Brussels and Amsterdam by Thalys Train

The pricey Thalys train has the monopoly on the rail route between Paris and Brussels (for a cheaper option, try the Eurolines bus; see below). Without a railpass, you'll pay about €80–100 second class for the Paris–Amsterdam train (compared to €45 by bus) or about €60–80 second class for the Paris–Brussels train (compared to €25 by bus). Even with a railpass, you need to pay for train reservations (second class-about €14.50, first class-about €25). Book at least a day ahead, as seats are limited (www.thalys.com for tickets, but not for reservations with railpass). Or hop on the bus, Gus.

To London by Eurostar Train

The fastest and most convenient way to get from the Eiffel Tower to Big Ben is by rail. Eurostar is the speedy passenger train that zips you from downtown Paris to downtown London (12–15/day, 2.5 hrs).

Channel fares are reasonable but complicated. Prices vary depending on how early you reserve, whether you can live with restrictions, and whether you're eligible for any discounts (children, youth, seniors, round-trip travelers and railpass-holders all qualify). For specifics, visit www.ricksteves.com/rail/eurostar.htm.

Refund and exchange restrictions are serious, so don't reserve

Eurostar Routes

until you're sure of your plans (only the most expensive are fully refundable). You can check and book fares by phone or online in the US (order online at www.ricksteves.com/rail/eurostar.htm, prices listed in dollars; order by phone at US tel. 800-EUROSTAR) or in France (French tel. 08 92 35 35 39, www.eurostar.com, prices listed in euros).

If you buy from a US company, you'll pay for ticket delivery in the US; if you book with the European company, you'll pick up your ticket at the train station. In Europe, you can buy your Eurostar ticket at any major train station in any country, at neighborhood SNCF offices, or at any travel agency that handles train tickets (expect a booking fee). Passholder discount tickets can be purchased at Eurostar departure stations, online, or by phone, but may be harder to get at other train stations and travel agencies.

As with airfares, the most expensive and flexible option is a full-fare one-way ticket with no restrictions on refundability (figure about $380 in first class, $280 second class, comes with a meal but not worth the extra expense). Cheaper tickets (for second-class, one-way tickets, figure $90–200) come with more restrictions and are limited in number and sell out quickly. Those traveling with a railpass that covers France or Britain should look first at the passholder fare (as low as $77), a good value for one-way Eurostar trips.

Buses

The main bus station is the Gare Routière du Paris-Gallieni (28 avenue du Général de Gaulle, in suburb of Bagnolet, Mo: Gallieni, tel. 01 49 72 51 51). Buses provide cheaper—if less comfortable and more time-consuming—transportation to major European cities. The bus is also the cheapest way of crossing the English Channel; book at least two days in advance for the best fares. Eurolines' buses depart from here (tel. 08 36 69 52 52, www.eurolines.com). Look on their website for offices in central Paris.

Airports
Charles de Gaulle Airport

Expect some construction headaches as Paris' primary airport is undergoing a major renovation. The airport has two main terminals, T-1 and T-2, and one lesser terminal, T-3. Most flights from the US use T-1 or T-2. To see which terminal serves your airline, check your ticket, or contact the airport (tel. 3950, www .adp.fr). You can easily access all the terminals via a free shuttle bus *(navette)* or train (which should be completed by 2008). The RER (Paris suburban train, connecting to Métro) stops at T-2 and near T-1 and T-3, and the TGV (tay-zhay-vay, stands for *train à grande vitesse*—high-speed, long-distance train) station is at T-2. Baggage storage in T-1 is on the arrival level at doors labeled *12–14* (open daily, drop-off 10:00–16:00, pick up 8:30–19:30, tel. 01 48 16 34 90). Baggage storage in T-2 is at both 2A (door 3, daily 8:00–20:00, tel. 01 48 16 20 61) and 2F (arrival level, door 4, daily 7:00–19:00, tel. 01 48 16 20 64). Be especially aware of pickpockets on *navettes* between terminals, and on RER trains. Do not take an unauthorized taxi from the men greeting you on arrival; official taxi stands are well-signed.

Terminal 1 (T-1): This circular terminal has one main entry and covers three floors—arrival (*arrivées,* top floor), departure (*départs,* one floor down) and shops/boutiques (basement level). For information on getting to Paris, see "Transportation between Charles de Gaulle Airport and Paris," next page.

Arrival Level: You'll find a variety of services at the gates listed below. Expect changes during construction.

- Gate 36: Called "Meeting Point" (Point de Rencontre), this gate has an information counter with English-speaking staff, a café, and an ATM. Ask here for directions to Disneyland shuttle (every 45 min, daily 8:30–19:45, €14).
- Gate 34: Outside are Air France buses to Paris (see "Transportation Between Charles de Gaulle Airport and Paris," below) and Orly Airport (see "Connecting Paris' Airports," page 161).
- Gate 30: Outside are Roissy-Buses to Paris (buy tickets from driver) and hotel shuttle buses *(navettes hôtels).*
- Gates 24–30: Car-rental desks.
- Gate 18: Taxis outside.
- Gate 20: Shuttle buses *(navettes)* for Terminal 2 and the RER trains to Paris. Take the elevator down to level *(niveau)* 2, then walk outside (line 1 serves T-2 including the TGV station; line 2 goes directly to the RER station). A new intra-airport train should be in place by 2008 to shuttle riders between the various terminals in a snap.

Charles de Gaulle Airport

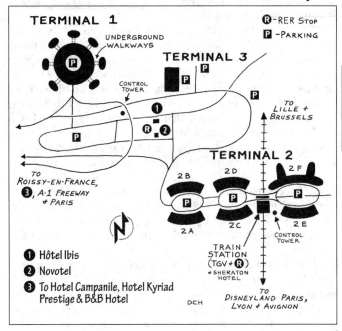

Departure Level (*niveau* 3): Flight check-in, restaurants, a PTT (post office), a pharmacy, boutiques, and a handy grocery store one floor below the ticketing desks (*niveau* 2 on the elevator).

Terminal 2 (T-2): This long, horseshoe-shaped terminal is dominated by Air France and is divided into six subterminals (or halls), each identified by a letter (A through F). You can walk from one hall to the other, or take the *navette* shuttle buses, which connect the halls with the RER, the TGV station, and T-1 every five minutes (line 5 runs to T-1). The RER and TGV stations are below the Sheraton Hotel (access by *navette* or on foot from some of the halls). Stops for *navettes*, Air France buses, and Roissy-Buses are all well-marked and near each hall (see "Transportation Between Charles de Gaulle Airport and Paris," below). ADP's orange information desks are located near Gate 5 in each hall. Car-rental offices, post offices, pharmacies, and ATMs *(point d'argent)* are also well-signed.

Transportation Between Charles de Gaulle Airport and Paris: Three efficient public-transportation routes, taxis, and airport shuttle vans link the airport's terminals with central Paris. All are well-marked, and stops are centrally located at all terminals. If you're carrying lots of baggage—or are just plain tired—taxis are well worth the extra cost (avoid the airport shuttle vans going in the airport-to-Paris direction).

To get to the rue Cler area, the Roissy-Bus to Opéra and transferring to Métro line 8 is the most convenient public-transport route. To reach the Marais, your best public-transport option is the Air France bus to the Gare de Lyon, with a quick trip on Métro line 1 to your hotel neighborhood. Both routes are described below. For the Luxembourg Garden area, take RER-B to the Luxembourg stop. For the Canal St. Martin area, take RER-B to Gare du Nord, then transfer to Métro line 5 (direction: Place d'Italie), and get off at République or Oberkampf. All your options into Paris are well-marked, but if you have trouble, ask any airport employee.

RER trains stop near T-1 and at T-2, cost €8, and run every 15 minutes with stops in central Paris at Gare du Nord, Châtelet–Les Halles, St. Michel, and Luxembourg (runs 5:00–24:00, 30 min to Gare du Nord). Buy tickets from the machines (requires €8 in coins) or at the often-crowded ticket windows (which take euro bills). To get out to the airport from the city, take RER line B, and make sure the sign over the platform shows *Roissy–Charles de Gaulle* as a stop served, since the line splits and not every train on this line serves the airport. If you're not clear, ask another rider "air-o-por sharl duh gaul?" Beware of pickpockets preying on jet-lagged tourists on these trains; wear your money belt. The other transportation options described below have far fewer theft problems.

Roissy-Buses run every 15–20 minutes to Paris' Opéra Garnier from 6:30–21:00 (€8.50, 40–60 min, buy ticket on bus, driver can change small bills). You'll arrive at a bus stop on rue Scribe on the left side of the Opéra building. To get to the Métro entrance, turn left out of the bus and walk counterclockwise around the Opéra to the front. The Métro station entrance is on the island in the middle of the square. For rue Cler hotels, take Métro line 8 (direction: Balard) to La Tour-Maubourg or Ecole Militaire. For hotels in the Marais neighborhood, take the same line 8 (direction: Créteil Préfecture) to the Bastille stop. You can also take a taxi (€12–15) to any of my listed hotels from behind the Opéra (the stand is in front of Galeries Lafayette department store).

Air France buses serve central Paris and continue to Orly Airport about every 15–30 minutes from 5:45 to 23:00 on three different routes. Allow 45 minutes to the Arc de Triomphe and Porte Maillot, 45 minutes to the Gare de Lyon train station, and 60 minutes to Montparnasse Tower/train station. To reach Marais hotels from the Gare de Lyon, take Métro line 1 (direction: La Défense) to the Bastille, St. Paul, or Hôtel de Ville stops. A ticket costs €12 one-way, €18 round-trip (pay driver).

Taxis with luggage run about €50 for up to three people, more if traffic is bad. Your hotel can call for a taxi to the airport. Usually 20 minutes ahead is enough time, unless your flight is very early (always ask ahead at your hotel). Specify that you want a real taxi *(un taxi normal)*, and not a limo service that costs €20 more. Remember, you pay a bit more on Sundays, before 7:00, and after 19:00. If you're happy with your driver, tip €2–3.

Airport shuttles also go straight to and from your hotel, but are not a good option to take from the airport to Paris; you have to book them in advance even though you don't know exactly when you'll arrive (getting baggage, going through customs). However, they are a good budget option to the airport (particularly for single travelers or families of four or more, as that's too many for a cab). If your hotel does not work with a shuttle service, reserve directly (book at least a day in advance—most hoteliers will make the call for you). Airport shuttles cost about €30 for one person, €40 for two, and €50 for three. Some offer deals if you do a round-trip, and most are more expensive at night (20:00–6:00 in the morning).

Golden Air is one of the many shuttles (from Paris to Charles de Gaulle: €27 for one person, €17 per person for two; from Charles de Gaulle to Paris: €35 for one person, €20 per person for two; these special prices possible only for readers of this book in 2008, tel. 01 34 10 12 92, fax 01 34 10 93 89, www.paris-airport-shuttle-limousine.com, goldenair@goldenair.net).

Sleeping at or near Charles de Gaulle Airport

Hôtel Ibis**, outside the Charles de Gaulle-1 RER stop, is huge and offers standard and predictable accommodations (Db-€95–120, near *navette* stop, free and fast shuttle bus to all terminals, tel. 01 49 19 19 19, fax 01 49 19 19 21, h1404@accor.com). **Novotel***** is next door and the next step up (weekend Db-€120–140, weekday Db-€150–170, tel. 01 49 19 27 27, fax 01 49 19 27 99, www.novotel.com, h1014@accor-hotels.com). Both have simple restaurants.

Orly Airport

This airport feels small. It's good for rental-car pickup and drop-off, as it's closer to Paris and far easier to navigate than Charles de Gaulle Airport.

Orly has two terminals: Ouest (west) and Sud (south). Air France flights arrive at Ouest, and all others use Sud. At the Sud terminal, you'll exit the baggage claim (near Gate H) and see signs directing you to city transportation, car rental, and so on. Turn left to enter the main terminal area, and you'll find exchange offices with bad rates, an American Express office, an ATM, the ADP counter (*Espace Tourisme*, a quasi-tourist office that offers free city maps and basic sightseeing information, open until 24:00), and an SNCF rail desk (next to ADP, daily 7:45–12:00 & 13:00–20:00, sells train tickets and even Eurailpasses). Downstairs is a sandwich bar, WCs, a bank (same bad rates), a newsstand (buy a phone card), and a post office. Car-rental offices are located in the parking lot in front of the terminal opposite Gate C. For flight info on any airline serving Orly, call 3950. For information on either of Paris' airports, visit www.adp.fr.

Transportation Between Orly Airport and Paris: Several efficient public-transportation routes, taxis, and a couple of airport shuttle services link Orly with central Paris. The gate locations listed below apply to Orly Sud, but the same transportation services are available from both terminals.

Air France buses (outside Gate K) run to Montparnasse train station (with many Métro lines) and to Invalides Métro stop (€8 one-way, €12 round-trip, 4/hr, 40 min to Invalides). These buses are handy for those staying in or near the rue Cler neighborhood (from Invalides bus stop, take the Métro to La Tour-Maubourg or Ecole Militaire to reach recommended hotels; see also "RER trains," below). Remember that to continue on the Métro, you'll need to buy a separate ticket (for ticket types and prices, see "Getting Around Paris," page 45).

Jetbus (outside Gate H, €5.50, 4/hr) is the quickest way to the Paris subway and a good way to the Marais and Luxembourg Garden neighborhoods. Take Jetbus to the Villejuif–Louis Aragon Métro stop. To reach the Marais neighborhood, take the Métro to the Sully-Morland stop. For the Luxembourg area, take the same train to the Censier-Daubenton or Place Monge stops. If taking the Jetbus from the Marais to the airport, make sure before you board the Métro that your train is going to Villejuif–Louis Aragon (not Mairie d'Ivry), as the route splits at the end of the line.

The **Orlybus** (outside Gate H, €6, 3/hr) takes you to the Denfert-Rochereau RER-B line and the Métro, offering Métro access to central Paris, including the Luxembourg Area and Notre-Dame Cathedral, as well as the Gare du Nord train station.

Shuttle Buses to Disneyland also depart from Gate H (€14, daily 8:30–19:45, confirm gate and schedule at ADP *Espace Toursime* office—described above).

These two routes provide access to Paris via **RER trains:** an ADP shuttle **(Orly Rail bus)** takes you to RER-C (Pont d'Orly stop), with connections to Gare d'Austerlitz, St. Michel/Notre-Dame, Musée d'Orsay, Invalides, and Pont de l'Alma stations and is handy for some rue Cler hotels (outside Gate G, 4/hr, €5.50). **Orlyval trains** take you to the Antony stop on RER-B (serving Luxembourg, Châtelet–Les Halles, St. Michel, and Gare du Nord stations in central Paris, €9, includes RER ticket).

Taxis are to the far right as you leave the terminal, at Gate M. Allow €25–35 with bags for a taxi into central Paris.

Airport shuttles are good for single travelers or families of four or more (too many for a taxi), if going from Paris to the airport (see page 159 for a company to contact; from Orly, figure about €23/1 person, €30/2 people, less per person for larger groups and kids).

Beauvais Airport

Budget airlines such as Ryanair use this airport, offering dirt-cheap airfares, but leaving you 50 miles north of Paris. Still, this small airport has direct buses to Paris (see below). It's ideal for drivers who want to rent a car here and head to Normandy or north to Belgium. The airport is basic (the terminal for departing passengers and baggage claim is under a tent, and waiting areas are crowded and have few services), but it's being improved as it deals with an increasing number of passengers (airport tel. 08 92 68 20 66, www.aeroportbeauvais.com; Ryanair tel. 08 92 68 20 73, www .ryanair.com).

Transportation Between Beauvais Airport and Paris: Buses depart from the airport about 20 minutes after flights arrive, and take 90 minutes to reach Paris. Buy your ticket at the little kiosk to the right as you exit the airport (€13). Buses wait nearby and depart once they are full (baggage goes underneath), and arrive at Porte Maillot on the west edge of Paris, which has a Métro and RER stop. The closest taxi stand is across the street at Hôtel Concorde La Fayette.

Buses depart Paris for Beauvais Airport three hours before scheduled flight departures (catch bus at Porte Maillot in parking lot on boulevard Pershing next to Hôtel Concorde La Fayette). Bus tickets must be booked 24 hours in advance; call Beauvais Airport for details or buy tickets on their website (see contact info above).

Trains connect Beauvais' city center and Paris' Gare du Nord (20/day, 80 min).

Taxis run from Beauvais Airport to Paris: €125 to central Paris, €11 to Beauvais' train station or city center.

Connecting Paris' Airports

Air France buses directly and conveniently link Charles de Gaulle and Orly airports (roughly every 30 minutes, 5:45–23:00, 80 min, €16).

RER line B also connects Charles de Gaulle and Orly, but requires a transfer to the Orlyval train, and isn't as easy as the Air France bus (5/hr, 90 min, €17). This line splits at both ends: Heading to Orly, take trains that serve the Antony stop (then tranfer to Orlyval train); heading to Charles de Gaulle, take trains that end at the airport ("Roissy–CDG"), not Mitry-Claye. Connect to and from the Beauvais Airport train at Gare du Nord (see "Beauvais Airport," above).

Taxis are easiest, but pricey (between Charles de Gaulle and Orly-€80, between Charles de Gaulle and Beauvais-€110, between Orly and Beauvais-€130).

NEAR PARIS

Versailles, Giverny, Chartres Cathedral, and Disneyland Paris

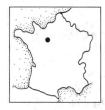

Efficient trains bring oodles of day trips within the grasp of temporary Parisians. Europe's best palace at Versailles; the flowery gardens at Giverny that inspired Monet; the awesome cathedral of Chartres; and a mouse-run amusement park await the traveler looking for a refreshing change from urban Paris.

Versailles

Every king's dream, Versailles was the residence of the French king and the cultural heartbeat of Europe for about 100 years—until the Revolution of 1789 ended the notion that God deputized some people to rule for him on Earth. Louis XIV spent half a year's income of Europe's richest country turning his dad's hunting lodge into a palace fit for a divine monarch. Louis XV and Louis XVI spent much of the 18th century gilding Louis XIV's lily. In 1837, about 50 years after the royal family was evicted, King Louis Philippe opened the palace as a museum. Europe's next-best palaces are Versailles wannabes.

Visiting Versailles can seem daunting because of its size and the hordes of visitors. Fortunately, new changes are making it easier. Before you go, read the "Orientation," below, to avoid wasting your time and money.

Versailles has two main areas with separate entries: the all-important Château (the main palace) and the less-important Domaine de Marie-Antoinette (the queen's estate). The entire complex is undergoing a complete renovation that may change entry points and exits. The information listed here is accurate as of

Near Paris

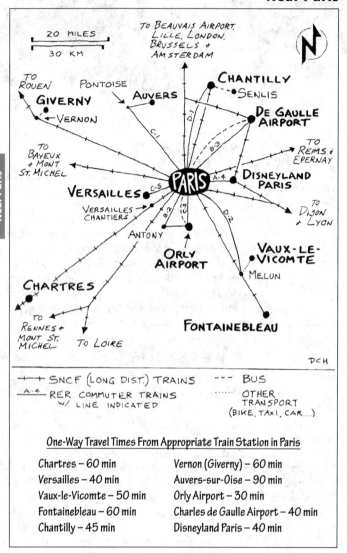

+++ SNCF (LONG DIST.) TRAINS   --- BUS

A-4 RER COMMUTER TRAINS   ...... OTHER
   W/ LINE INDICATED   TRANSPORT
                                         (BIKE, TAXI, CAR...)

One-Way Travel Times From Appropriate Train Station in Paris

Chartres – 60 min	Vernon (Giverny) – 60 min
Versailles – 40 min	Auvers-sur-Oise – 90 min
Vaux-le-Vicomte – 50 min	Orly Airport – 30 min
Fontainebleau – 60 min	Charles de Gaulle Airport – 40 min
Chantilly – 45 min	Disneyland Paris – 40 min

mid-2007, and most should still apply in 2008. Still, expect some changes in fees and entry points.

ORIENTATION

Cost: The **Château**—the main palace—costs €13.50 (€10 after 16:00, under 18 always free, covered by Paris Museum Pass and Le Passeport pass, see below). The Château contains the **Chapel** and **Opera House** (likely closed in 2008), the **King's and Queen's State Apartments** (with the famous Hall of Mirrors), the **French History Galleries** (rarely open), the **Dauphin's Apartments** (heirs to the throne), and the **Mesdames Apartments** (Louis XV's daughters, open weekends only); all are included with your Château ticket.

Entry to the **Domaine de Marie-Antoinette,** the estate of the queen, costs €9 from April through October (€5 after 17:00, under 18 always free; covered by Le Passeport, and the Paris Museum Pass). In winter, it costs €5 to enter the Petit Trianon (free for rest of Domaine grounds). Tickets are available at the entry to the Domaine or at the main Château ticket office. With this ticket, you'll see the queen's Hamlet, the Grand and Petit Trianons, and a smattering of other nearby buildings.

The **gardens** are free, except on April–Sept weekends, when the fountains blast and the price shoots up to €7 (see "Fountain Spectacles," page 174).

Passes: Smart travelers arrive at Versailles with one of these two passes.

The **Le Passeport** one-day pass is a good deal for most sightseers (April–Oct it's €20 Mon–Fri, €25 Sat–Sun; Nov–March it's €16 Tue–Sun). The pass covers your entrance to just about everything, as well as audioguides. (The pass is not a good value on Mon, when only the Domaine de Marie-Antoinette and gardens are open.) The pass gives you access to all open sections of the Château, the Domaine de Marie-Antoinette, and the fountain spectacles (that flow only on spring and summer weekends—hence the higher weekend pass prices). If you're coming by train from Paris, buy this pass before you leave the city—you'll pay €1.50 more, but it will cover your round-trip train ride (a €6 value). This buy-in-Paris option makes the pass an even better deal, as it saves you money and lets you avoid the palace's long ticket lines. Le Passeport passes are sold at RER stations that serve Versailles (listed under "Getting There," below), the Ile de France TI in the Louvre, the TI in Versailles, and the palace itself. The palace's website may also be selling the pass by the time you visit (see www.chateauversailles.fr).

The **Paris Museum Pass** works at Versailles, covering the Château and the Domaine de Marie-Antoinette but not the gardens (on fountain spectacle weekends) or audioguides. Since a visit to Versailles can take up an entire sightseeing day, you'll likely get better use out of the Museum Pass in Paris, where it's easy to visit several sights in a day.

Hours: The **Château** is open April–Oct Tue–Sun 9:00–18:30, Nov–March Tue–Sun 9:00–17:30, closed Mon. The **Domaine de Marie Antoinette** is open daily April–Oct 12:00–19:30; Nov–March 9:00–17:00. The **gardens** are open daily from 9:00 to sunset (17:30 to 21:30). Last entry to all of these areas is one hour before closing.

When to Go: From May through September, Versailles can be a zoo between 10:00 and 13:00, and all day Tue and Sun. For fewer crowds, go early or late: Arrive by 9:00 (when the palace opens—tour the palace first, then the gardens) or after 16:00 (you'll get a reduced-price ticket, but note that the last guided tours of the day generally depart by 15:00).

Pickpocket Alert: As you jostle through the crowded corridors of the palace, pickpockets will be working the tourist crowds.

Getting There: Take the RER-C **train** (every 15 min, €6 round-trip, or included in Le Passeport if you buy it in Paris—30–40 min one-way) from any of these RER stops: Gare d'Austerlitz, St. Michel, Musée d'Orsay, Invalides, Pont de l'Alma, or Champ de Mars. Any train whose name starts with a V (e.g., "Vick") goes to Versailles; don't board other trains. Get off at the last stop (Versailles R.G., or "Rive Gauche"), and exit through the turnstiles by inserting your ticket. To reach the château, turn right out of the train station, then left at the first boulevard. It's a 10-minute walk to the palace. If you want to visit Versailles and Chartres on the same day by using public transportation, see page 177.)

Your Eurailpass covers this inexpensive trip, but it uses up a valuable "flexi" day. To get free passage, show your railpass at an SCNF ticket window—for example, at the Invalides or Musée d'Orsay RER stop—and get a *contremarque de passage*. Keep this ticket to exit the system.

All trains leaving Versailles from the Rive Gauche station serve all downtown Paris RER stops on the C line.

Taxis for the 30-minute ride between Versailles and Paris cost about €50.

It's a 30-minute drive to reach Versailles from Paris by **car,** if the traffic's not bad. Get on the *périphérique* freeway that circles Paris, and take the toll-free A-13 autoroute toward Rouen. Follow signs into Versailles, then look for *château* signs and park in the huge pay lot (€4.50/2 hrs, €8/4 hrs, €12/8 hrs, free 19:00–8:30).

Versailles

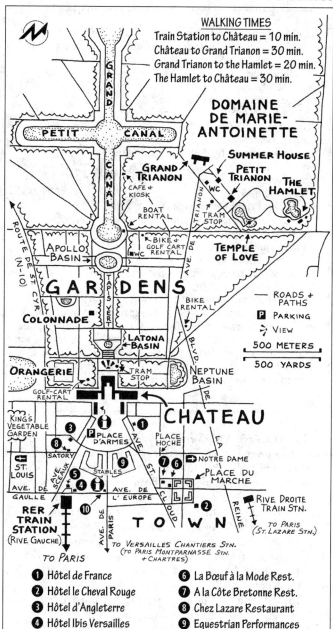

WALKING TIMES
Train Station to Château = 10 min.
Château to Grand Trianon = 30 min.
Grand Trianon to the Hamlet = 20 min.
The Hamlet to Château = 30 min.

DOMAINE DE MARIE-ANTOINETTE

SUMMER HOUSE

GRAND TRIANON

PETIT TRIANON

THE HAMLET

WC

CAFÉ + KIOSK

BOAT RENTAL

TRAM STOP

PETIT CANAL

GRAND CANAL

BIKE + GOLF CART RENTAL

WC

TEMPLE OF LOVE

APOLLO BASIN

ROUTE DE ST. CYR (N-10)

GARDENS

COLONNADE

TAPIS VERT

AVE. DE TRIANON

BIKE RENTAL

BLVD.

ROADS + PATHS

P PARKING

VIEW

500 METERS

500 YARDS

LATONA BASIN

ORANGERIE

TRAM STOP

NEPTUNE BASIN

DE

GOLF-CART RENTAL

KING'S VEGETABLE GARDEN

CHATEAU

PLACE D'ARMES

PLACE HOCHE

NOTRE DAME

PLACE DU MARCHE

SATORY

ST. LOUIS

AVE. DE SCEAUX

STABLES

AVE. DE GAULLE

AVE. DE L'EUROPE

AVE. DE PARIS

RER TRAIN STATION (RIVE GAUCHE)

TO PARIS

T O W N

REINE

ST. CLOUD

LA

RIVE DROITE TRAIN STN.

TO PARIS (ST. LAZARE STN.)

TO VERSAILLES CHANTIERS STN. (TO PARIS MONTPARNASSE STN. + CHARTRES)

1 Hôtel de France
2 Hôtel le Cheval Rouge
3 Hôtel d'Angleterre
4 Hôtel Ibis Versailles
5 Hôtel du Palais

6 La Bœuf à la Mode Rest.
7 A la Côte Bretonne Rest.
8 Chez Lazare Restaurant
9 Equestrian Performances
10 City of Versailles TI: Ticket Sales, Hotel Info, etc.

Planning Your Time at Versailles

While there seems to be a myriad of options for touring Versailles, your best plan for a first-time visit is easy to determine. Here is what I'd do and how I'd pay for it:

Before you head out, save yourself money and the hassle of a long wait in line by buying a Le Passeport (see "Passes" under "Orientation," near the beginning of this chapter).

Leave Paris by 8:00 and arrive at the palace just before opening. At 9:00 or so, follow my self-guided tour through the Chapel and Opera House (likely closed in 2008), the King's and Queen's State Apartments, and the Hall of Mirrors. Supplement the tour in this chapter with an audioguide (free with Le Passeport).

Consider the 15-minute walk to Versailles town center for lunch, or plan to buy lunch at the Château or in the gardens (see "Cuisine Art," below).

Spend your afternoon touring the gardens and the Domaine de Marie-Antoinette. On spring or summer weekends, you can catch the fountain show in the gardens (see "Fountain Spectacles" on page 174). You could stick around for dinner (see recommended Versailles restaurants on page 176), or head back to Paris. Keep your Le Passeport on you if you plan to use it for the return train ride.

Information: Visit Versailles' good website before you go: www.chateauversailles.fr. Versailles has two information offices: the town's official TI (helpful, less crowded), and one at the palace (books tours, but has long lines). Both sell palace tickets and Le Passeport passes. You'll go by the town TI on your walk from the main RER station to the palace—it's just past the Sofitel Hôtel (daily April–Sept 9:00–19:00, Oct–March 9:00–18:00, tel. 01 39 24 88 88). The palace's information office is on the left side of the Château courtyard (as you face the Château, tel. 01 30 83 78 00). The useful *Versailles Orientation Guide* brochure explains your sightseeing options.

Guided Tours: The primary guided tour of Versailles in English covers the Private Apartments of Louis XV and XVI and the Opera House (€7.50 not including palace admission—see above, 90 min, Opera House likely closed in 2008). To take a guided tour, make reservations upon arrival at the busy information office in the Château courtyard, as tours can sell out by 13:00 (first tours generally begin at 10:00; last tours usually depart by 15:00). The tours can be long, but those with an appetite for palace history will enjoy them (and effective remote audio-systems make it easy to hear the guide). It's smart to keep your ticket as proof that you've already paid for the palace entry—in case you decide to take a guided tour after you've wandered through Versailles by yourself.

Audioguide Tours: Audioguides are available at the entrances of the King's and Queen's State Apartments, the Dauphin's Apartments, and the Mesdames Apartments (all included in Le Passeport, also covered if you pay €13.50 Château admission; not included with the Paris Museum Pass). If you don't have Le Passeport, you'll pay €10 per audioguide on weekends and €6 on weekdays (note that the Mesdames Apartments are only open on weekends).

A free audioguide tour of the most important rooms of the State Apartments is available for users of iPods and MP3 players at www.ricksteves.com. You may also want to check out the podcasts at www.podibus.com/versailles.

Length of This Day Trip: Allow two to three hours for the Château and two for the Domaine de Marie-Antoinette and the gardens. Add another two hours to cover your round-trip transit and walking time, and it's a five- to ten-hour day trip from Paris.

Baggage Check: There's a free checkroom at the main entrance—use it to check forbidden items (food, big bags, baby carriages, and so on). Strollers are not allowed inside the Château, so today's a good day for parents to either hire a babysitter or carry their toddler in a backpack with a child seat.

WCs: Reminiscent of the days when dukes urinated behind the potted palm trees, WCs are few and far between, and come with long lines. Use the public WC just before the palace gates.

Cuisine Art: In the **palace,** the cafeteria and WCs are at the main entrance. There's a sandwich kiosk and a restaurant at the canal in the gardens.

In the **town,** you'll find restaurants on the street to the right of the parking lot (as you face the Château), though the best eateries line the lively market square, place du Marché, in the town center. A handy McDonald's is immediately across from the train station (WC without crowds, Internet café next door). An appealing assortment of affordable restaurants line rue de Satory between the station and the palace (see "Eating," page 176).

Photography: Allowed indoors without a flash.

Starring: Louis XIV, Marie-Antoinette, and the *ancien régime.*

Versailles' Entrances

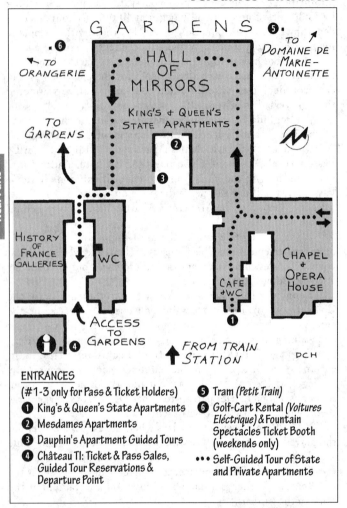

ENTRANCES
(#1-3 only for Pass & Ticket Holders)
❶ King's & Queen's State Apartments
❷ Mesdames Apartments
❸ Dauphin's Apartment Guided Tours
❹ Château TI: Ticket & Pass Sales, Guided Tour Reservations & Departure Point

❺ Tram *(Petit Train)*
❻ Golf-Cart Rental *(Voitures Eléctrique)* & Fountain Spectacles Ticket Booth (weekends only)
••• Self-Guided Tour of State and Private Apartments

Overview

Five routes through the Château are included in your entry fee:

Blue Itinerary: Chapel and Opera House
Red Itinerary: King's and Queen's State Apartments
Yellow Itinerary: History of France Gallery (rarely open)
Purple Itinerary: Mesdames Apartments (weekends only)
Green Itinerary: Dauphin's Apartments

Most first-time visitors will be more than satisfied following the Blue and Red itineraries.

Welcome to Versailles

This commentary, which leads you through the various attractions at Versailles, covers just the basics. For background, first read the "Kings and Queens and Guillotines" sidebar. If you don't have *Rick Steves' Paris* (buy in the US), the guidebook called *The Châteaux, the Gardens, and Trianon* gives a more detailed room-by-room run-down (sold at Versailles).

Stand in front of the palace, in the central courtyard, with two of the palace's wings on either side of you. If you don't have a ticket or if you want to book a tour, you must stand in the line to your left. If you already have a ticket or pass, read the section below, then go directly to the entry on your right.

The Château: Enter the palace and take a one-way walk through the State Apartments from the King's Wing, through the Hall of Mirrors, and out via the Queen's Wing. The **Hall of Mirrors** was the ultimate hall of the day—250 feet long, with 17 arched mirrors matching 17 windows with royal garden views, 24 gilded candelabra, eight busts of Roman emperors, and eight Classical-style statues (seven of them ancient). The ceiling is decorated with stories of Louis XIV's triumphs. Imagine this place filled with silk gowns and powdered wigs, lit by thousands of candles. The mirrors—a luxury at the time—were a reflection of an era when aristocrats felt good about their looks and their fortunes. In another age altogether, this was the room in which the Treaty of Versailles was signed, ending World War I.

Before going downstairs at the end, take a stroll clockwise around the **Hall of Battles,** the long room filled with murals depicting the great battles of France (rarely open, in the History of France Gallery).

Getting Around the Gardens: It's a 50-minute hike from the palace, down to the canal, past the two Trianon palaces to

the Hamlet—the heart of the Domaine de Marie-Antoinette. Renting a bike (€6/hr, near the Grand Canal) gives you the most freedom to explore the gardens effortlessly, freely, and economically. The fast-looking, slow-moving tram *(petit train)* leaves from behind the Château (north side) and serves the Grand Canal and the Domaine. You can hop on and off as you like (€6, 4/hr, three stops, commentary is nearly worthless). Another option is to rent a golf cart for a fun drive through the gardens (€28/hr, pick up at Orangerie side of palace, shuts off automatically if you diverge from prescribed route).

Kings and Queens and Guillotines

• *You could read this on the train ride to Versailles. Relax...the palace is the last stop.*

Come the Revolution, when they line us up and make us stick out our hands, will you have enough calluses to keep them from shooting you? A grim thought, but Versailles raises these kinds of questions. It's the symbol of the *ancien régime*, a time when society was divided into rulers and the ruled, when you were born to be rich or to be poor. To some, it's the pinnacle of civilization; to others, the sign of a civilization in decay. Either way, it remains one of Europe's most impressive sights.

Versailles was the residence of the king and seat of France's government for a hundred years. Louis XIV (r. 1643–1715) moved out of the Louvre in Paris, the previous royal residence, and built an elaborate palace in the forests and swamps of Versailles, 10 miles west. The reasons for the move were partly personal—Louis XIV loved the outdoors and disliked the sniping environs of stuffy Paris—and partly political.

Louis XIV was creating the first modern, centralized state. At Versailles, he consolidated Paris' scattered ministries so that he could personally control policy. More importantly, he invited France's nobles to Versailles in order to control them. Living a life of almost enforced idleness, the "domesticated" aristocracy couldn't interfere with the way Louis ran things. With 18 million people united under one king (England had only 5.5 million), a booming economy, and a powerful military, France was Europe's number-one power.

By about 1700, Versailles was the cultural capital of Europe, and French culture was at its zenith. Throughout Europe, when you said "the king," you were referring to the French king...Louis XIV. Every king wanted a palace like Versailles. Everyone learned French. French taste in clothes, hairstyles, table manners, theater, music, art, and kissing spread across the Continent. That cultural dominance continued, to some extent, right up to the 20th century.

Louis XIV

At the center of all this was Europe's greatest king. He was a true Renaissance man, a century after the Renaissance: athletic, good-looking, a musician, dancer, horseman, statesman, art-

lover, lover. For all his grandeur, he
was one of history's most polite and
approachable kings, a good listener
who could put even commoners at
ease in his presence.

Louis XIV called himself the
Sun King because he gave life and
warmth to all that he touched. He
was also thought of as Apollo, the
Greek god of the sun. Versailles
became the personal temple of this
god on earth, decorated with statues and symbols of Apollo, the sun,
and Louis XIV himself. The classical
themes throughout underlined the divine right of France's kings
and queens to rule without limit.

Louis XIV was a hands-on king who personally ran affairs
of state. All decisions were made by him. Nobles, who in other
countries were the center of power, became virtual slaves dependent on Louis XIV's generosity. For 70 years, he was the perfect
embodiment of the absolute monarch. He summed it up best
himself with his famous rhyme—*"L'état, c'est moi!"* (lay-tah say-
mwah): "The state, that's me!"

Another Louis or Two to Remember
Three kings lived in Versailles during its century of glory. Louis XIV
built it and established French dominance. Louis XV, his great-
grandson (Louis XIV reigned for 72 years), carried on the tradition and policies, but without the Sun King's flair. During Louis
XV's reign (1715–1774), France's power abroad was weakening, and
there were rumblings of rebellion from within.

France's monarchy was crumbling, and the time was ripe for
a strong leader to reestablish the old feudal order. They didn't get
one. Instead, they got Louis XVI (r. 1774–1792), a shy, meek book-
worm, the kind of guy who lost sleep over Revolutionary graffiti...
because it was misspelled. Louis XVI married a sweet girl from
the Austrian royal family, Marie-Antoinette, and together they
retreated into the idyllic gardens of Versailles while Revolutionary
fires smoldered.

Near Paris

Palace Gardens: The gardens offer a world of royal amusements. Outside the palace is the Orangerie. The warmth from the Sun King was so great that he could even grow orange trees in chilly France. Louis XIV had a thousand of these to amaze his visitors. In winter, they were kept in the greenhouses that surround the courtyard. On sunny days, they were wheeled

out in their silver planters and scattered around the grounds. A promenade leads from the palace to the Grand Canal, an artificial lake that, in Louis' day, was a mini-sea with nine ships, including a 32-cannon warship. France's royalty floated up and down the canal in Venetian gondolas.

Domaine de Marie-Antoinette (Marie-Antoinette's Estate): While Louis XIV cleverly used palace life at Versailles to "domesticate" his nobility, turning otherwise meddlesome nobles into groveling socialites, all this pomp and ceremony hampered the royal family as well. For an escape from the public life at Versailles, they built more intimate palaces as retreats in their garden. Later, his successors retreated still farther into the garden and built a fantasy world of simple pleasures, allowing them to ignore the real world that was crumbling all around them.

The beautifully restored **Grand Trianon Palace** is as sumptuous as the main palace, but much smaller. With its pastel-pink colonnade and more human scale, this is a place you'd like to call home. Nearby are the **French Pavilion** and the **Petit Trianon,** which has a fine Neoclassical exterior and an interior that can be skipped. It was Marie-Antoinette's favorite residence (and should remain open during the renovation planned for this year).

You can almost see princesses bobbing gaily in the branches as you walk through the enchanting forest, past the white marble **Temple of Love** to the queen's fake-peasant **Hamlet** (*le Hameau*). Palace life really got to Marie-Antoinette. Sort of a back-to-basics queen, she retreated further and further from her blue-blooded reality. Her happiest days were spent at the Hamlet, under a bonnet, tending her perfumed sheep and her manicured gardens in a thatch-happy wonderland.

ACTIVITIES

Fountain Spectacles—On spring and summer weekends, classical music fills the king's backyard, and the garden's fountains are in full squirt (April–Sept Sat–Sun 11:00–12:00 & 15:30–17:00, finale from 17:20–17:30). On these "spray days," the gardens cost €7 (pay at ticket booth near golf-cart rental in the gardens; covered by Le Passeport but not Paris Museum Pass). Pick up the helpful *Les Grandes Eaux Musicales* brochure at any information or ticket booth. Louis had his engineers literally reroute a river to fuel these fountains. Even by today's standards, they are impressive. Also ask about the various impressive evening spectacles (Sat in July–Aug).

Equestrian Performances—The Equestrian Performance Academy (Academie du Spectacle Equestre) has brought the art of horseback riding back to Versailles. You can watch its rigorous training sessions, including "equestrian fencing," performed to classical music inside Versailles' main arena (€9.50, 60-min shows at 10:30 and 11:15 only on Sat–Sun; musical shows-€21, Sat at 20:30 and Sun at 15:00). The stables (Grande Ecurie) are across the square from the Château, next to the post office. For information, call 01 39 02 07 14. For reservations, call 08 92 68 18 91 or visit www.acadequestre.fr.

Town of Versailles—After the palace closes and the tourists go, the prosperous, wholesome town of Versailles feels a long way from Paris. The central market thrives on place du Marché on Sunday, Tuesday, and Friday until 13:00 (leaving the RER station, turn right and walk 10 min). Consider the wisdom of picking up or dropping your rental car in Versailles rather than in Paris. In Versailles, the Hertz and Avis offices are at Gare des Chantiers (Versailles C.H., served by Paris' Montparnasse station).

SLEEPING

For a laid-back alternative to Paris within easy reach of the big city by RER train (4/hr, 40 min), Versailles, with easy, safe parking and reasonably priced hotels, can be a good overnight stop, especially for drivers. Park in the palace's main lot while looking for a hotel, or leave your car there overnight (€4.50/2 hrs, free 19:30–8:00). Get a map of Versailles at your hotel or at the TI.

$$$ **Hôtel de France*****, in an 18th-century townhouse, offers Old World class, with air-conditioned, appropriately royal rooms, a pleasant courtyard, elaborate public spaces, a bar, and a restaurant (Db-€141, Tb-€180, Qb-€240, Wi-Fi, just off parking lot across from Château at 5 rue Colbert, tel. 01 30 83 92 23, fax 01 30 83 92 24, www.hotelfrance-versailles.com, hotel-de-france-versailles @wanadoo.fr).

$$ **Hôtel le Cheval Rouge****, built in 1676 as Louis XIV's stables, now houses tourists. It's a block behind the place du Marché in a quaint corner of town on a large, quiet courtyard with free parking and crisp, sufficiently comfortable rooms, many with open beams (Sb-€68, Db with shower-€76, Db with tub-€89, Tb-€98–112, Qb-€110–120, 18 rue André Chénier, tel. 01 39 50 03 03, fax 01 39 50 61 27,

Sleep Code

(€1 = $1.30, country code: 33)
S = Single, **D** = Double/Twin, **T** = Triple, **Q** = Quad, **b** = bathroom,
s = shower only, ***** = French hotel rating system (0–4 stars).
Unless otherwise noted, credit cards are accepted and English
is spoken.

To help you sort easily through these listings, I've divided
the rooms into three categories based on the price for a standard double room with bath:

$$$ Higher Priced—Most rooms €100 or more.
$$ Moderately Priced—Most rooms between €75–100.
$ Lower Priced—Most rooms €75 or less.

www.chevalrouge.fr.st, chevalrouge@club-internet.fr).

$$ Hôtel d'Angleterre**, away from the frenzy, is a tranquil,
homey place with smiling, Polish-born Madame Kutyla in control.
Rooms are modest, comfortable, and spacious. Park in the nearby
Château lot (one D-€54, Db-€82–92, family Qb-€100–125, extra
bed-€15, Wi-Fi, just below palace to the right as you exit, 2 rue
de Fontenay, tel. 01 39 51 43 50, fax 01 39 51 45 63, www.hotel
-angleterre-versailles.com, hotel.angleterre.versailles@wanadoo.fr).

$ Hôtel Ibis Versailles** offers a great weekend value and
modern comfort, with 85 air-conditioned rooms but no character
(Db-€70 Fri–Sun, €105 Mon–Thu, extra bed-€10, parking-€10,
across from RER station, 4 avenue du Général de Gaulle, tel. 01 39
53 03 30, fax 01 39 50 06 31, h1409@accor.com).

$ Hôtel du Palais, facing the RER station, rents 24 clean,
basic rooms—the cheapest that I list in this area. Ask for a quiet
room off the street (Db-€60–68, piles of stairs, 6 place Lyautey,
tel. 01 39 50 39 29, fax 01 39 50 80 41, hotelpalais@ifrance.com).

EATING

Place du Marché Notre-Dame is lined with a thriving open market
(Sun, Tue, and Fri mornings until 13:00) and colorful and inex-
pensive eateries. I particularly like these two, which serve good
food and are open for lunch and dinner: **La Bœuf à la Mode,** right
on the square, is a bistro with traditional cuisine and a passion
for red meat (two-course lunch *menu*-€16–24, three-course din-
ner *menu*-€30, open daily, 4 rue au Pain, tel. 01 39 50 31 99). **A
la Côte Bretonne** is your best bet for crêpes in a friendly, cozy
setting (€4–10 crêpes from a fun and creative menu, fine indoor
and outdoor seating, Tue–Sun 12:00–14:30 & 19:00–22:30, closed

Mon, a few steps off the square on traffic-free rue des Deux Portes at #12, tel. 01 39 51 18 24). The pedestrian-friendly street of Rue Satory on the south side of the château is lined with a rich variety of restaurants, including **Chez Lazare,** at #18.

Chartres Cathedral

Chartres and its cathedral make a ▲▲▲ day trip.

In 1194, a terrible fire destroyed the church at Chartres that housed the much-venerated veil of Mary. With almost unbelievably good fortune, the monks found the veil miraculously pre-served in the ashes. Money poured in for the building of a bigger and better cathedral—decorated with 2,000 carved figures and some of France's best stained glass. The cathedral feels too large for the city because it was designed to accommodate huge crowds of pilgrims. One of those pilgrims, an impressed Napoleon, declared after a visit in 1811: "Chartres is no place for an atheist." Auguste Rodin called it the "Acropolis of France." Mary's veil is on display behind glass in the cathedral, while the crypt can be visited only with a French tour.

Cost: Church entry free; climbing the 300-step north tower costs €6.50 (free on first Sun of the month, and for those under 18). Skip the Chartres Pass sold at the TI.

Hours: Church—daily 8:30–19:30; Tower—May–Aug Mon–Sat 9:30–12:30 & 14:00–18:00, Sun 14:00–18:00, Sept–April closes at 16:30 (entrance inside church after bookstore on left); Mass—Mon–Fri at 11:45 and 18:15; Sat at 11:45 and 18:00; Sun at 9:15 (Gregorian), 11:00, and 18:00 (in crypt).

Getting There: Chartres is a one-hour train trip from Paris' Gare Montparnasse (about €12.70 one-way, 10/day; figure on a round-trip total of 3 hours from Paris to cathedral doorstep and back). Upon arrival in Chartres, jot down times when the train returns to Paris (last train generally departs Chartres at about 21:00). Leaving the train station, you'll see the cathedral dominat-ing the town, a five-minute walk uphill (TI at cathedral).

Combining with Versailles: TER trains link Versailles and Chartres frequently (up to 30/day), on the route from Paris to Le Mans. In Versailles, this train runs from the Chantiers sta-tion (that's "Versailles C.H.")—not the Versailles R.G., or Rive Gauche, station listed in this book's Versailles visit (see page 166).

Chartres

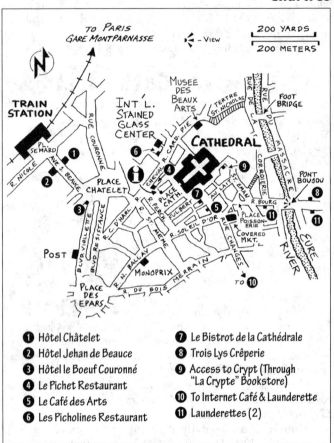

1. Hôtel Châtelet
2. Hôtel Jehan de Beauce
3. Hôtel le Boeuf Couronné
4. Le Pichet Restaurant
5. Le Café des Arts
6. Les Picholines Restaurant
7. Le Bistrot de la Cathédrale
8. Trois Lys Crêperie
9. Access to Crypt (Through "La Crypte" Bookstore)
10. To Internet Café & Launderette
11. Launderettes (2)

If you're going from Chartres to Versailles, it means a longer walk from the Versailles C.H. station to the Château (figure about 25 min; station agents have maps, but the walk is easy—just ask locals, "Château?").

Bring: Binoculars, if you got 'em.

Information: The TI offers a free map with basic information on the town and cathedral, as well as audioguides for the town only, described below (open April–Sept Mon–Sat 9:00–19:00, Sun 9:30–17:30; Oct–March Mon–Sat 10:00–18:00, Sun 10:00–13:00 & 14:30–16:30; located 100 yards in front of church, tel. 02 37 18 26 26, www.chartres-tourisme.com). The church has two bookstores: One—called Le Crypte—is outside near the south porch; the other, which is inside near the entrance, rents audioguides. Routes include the cathedral (€4.20, 45 min), the choir only (€3.20, 25 min), or both (€6.20, 70 min). Church tel. 02 37 21 59 08, www .diocese-chartres.com.

Cathedral Tours by Malcolm Miller: This fascinating English scholar, who moved here nearly 50 years ago, has dedicated his life to studying this cathedral—and sharing its wonder through his 75-minute guided lecture tours. No reservation is needed—just show up (€10, Mon–Sat at 12:00 and 14:45, no tours last half of Aug and Jan–Feb). Tours begin at the orange-and-purple *Cathedral Tours* sign, just outside the bookstore but inside the church. Consult this sign for changes or cancellations (it's rare, but Malcolm can fall ill). He also offers private tours (private tour info tel. 02 37 28 15 58, fax 02 37 28 33 03, millerchartres@aol.com). For a detailed look at Chartres' windows, sculpture, and history, pick up Malcolm Miller's two guidebooks (sold at cathedral).

SLEEPING

(€1 = $1.30, country code: 33)
The first two hotels face each other (200 yards straight out of train station, 300 yards below cathedral). All three add a mandated daily tax of €1/person.

$$ Hôtel Châtelet***, run by friendly Chantal, Marilou, Franck, and Nathalie, is comfortable, from its welcoming lobby to its spotless, spacious, well-furnished rooms. Choose between plush, modern, recently renovated "privilege" rooms with air-conditioning, or the cheaper "standing" rooms with Old World charm (Sb-€79–119, Db-€89–131, extra bed-€23, breakfast-€6, parking-€7.50, 6 avenue Jehan de Beauce, tel. 02 37 21 78 00, fax 02 37 36 23 01, www.hotelchatelet.com, reservation@hotelchatelet .com).

$ Hôtel Jehan de Beauce** is basic, clean (despite the shabby hallways), and quiet. Some of its rooms have tiny bathrooms (S-€38, Ss-€52–57, Sb-€59, D-€48, Ds-€57–63, Db-€67, Tb-€72, 19 avenue Jehan de Beauce, tel. 02 37 21 01 41, fax 02 37 21 59 10, jehandebeauce@club-internet.fr).

$ Hôtel le Bœuf Couronné** is warmly run by Madame Vinsot, with 21 clean but slightly worn rooms, and a handy location (S-€30, Sb-€47, D-€35, Db-€57–61, elevator, 15 place Châtelet, tel. 02 37 18 06 06, fax 02 37 21 72 13).

EATING

Le Pichet, run by friendly Marie-Sylvie and Xavier, is reasonable and homey, with good daily specials (€12–18 *plats*, €12–15 daily *menu*, closed Tue evening and all day Wed, 19 rue du Cheval Blanc, near TI, tel. 02 37 21 08 35).

Le Café des Arts is a sleek, modern place just a block from the cathedral. It's perfect for a quick, reasonably priced three-egg omelet or salad. Yvon, the owner, prides himself on the delicious €6–14 *tartines*—warm, open-faced sandwiches served with a small salad (€16–18.50 *menus*, 45–47 rue des Changes, tel. 02 37 21 07 05).

Les Picholines is a favorite for Mediterranean-inspired cuisine. Come here to get your fix of tapas and olives, or to feast on €11–14 pastas and salads (€14–19 lunch *menu*, €23–28 dinner *menu*, Mon–Sat lunch and dinner, Sun lunch only, rue du Cheval Blanc, tel. 02 37 36 85 84).

Le Bistrot de la Cathédrale is fine for salads and traditional bistro fare, but you'll pay for the view (*menus* from €20, open daily, south side of cathedral at 1 cloître Notre-Dame, tel. 02 37 36 59 60).

Trois Lys Crêperie makes good, cheap crêpes just across the river on pont Boujou (closed Mon, 3 rue de la Porte Guillaume, across from recommended launderette, tel. 02 37 28 42 02).

Near Paris

Giverny

Claude Monet spent 43 of his most creative years here (1883–1926). His gardens and home, a ▲ sight, are unfortunately split by a busy road and packed with tourists. Buy your ticket, explore the gardens, and take the underpass into Monet's famous lily-pad land. The path leads over the Japanese Bridge, under weeping willows, and past countless scenes that leave artists aching for an easel. Back on the other side, visit his more robust, structured garden and mildly interesting home.  The jammed gift shop at the exit is Monet's actual skylit studio.

Cost and Hours: €5.50, €4 for gardens only, April–Oct Tue–Sun 9:30–18:00, last entry 17:30, closed Mon and Nov–March, open some Mon holidays—check website, tel. 02 32 51 28 21, www .fondation-monet.com. While lines may be long and tour groups may trample the flowers, true fans still find magic in the gardens. Minimize crowds by arriving by 9:15 (get in line, it opens at 9:30), during lunchtime, or after 16:00.

Nearby Sights: The Museum of American Art (Musée d'Art Américain, turn left when leaving Monet's place and walk 100 yards) is devoted to American artists who followed Claude to Giverny (same price and hours as Monet's home). Monet and his garden had a great influence on American artists of his day.

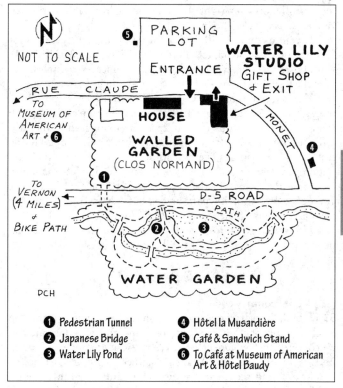

Giverny

N

NOT TO SCALE

RUE CLAUDE

TO
MUSEUM OF
AMERICAN
ART & ⑥

PARKING
LOT

ENTRANCE

⑤

WATER LILY
STUDIO
GIFT SHOP
& EXIT

HOUSE

WALLED
GARDEN
(CLOS NORMAND)

MONET

④

TO
VERNON
(4 MILES)
&
BIKE PATH

D-5 ROAD

① PATH

② ③

WATER GARDEN

DCH

❶ Pedestrian Tunnel
❷ Japanese Bridge
❸ Water Lily Pond
❹ Hôtel la Musardière
❺ Café & Sandwich Stand
❻ To Café at Museum of American
   Art & Hôtel Baudy

Near Paris

Getting There by Tour: Big tour companies do a Giverny day trip from Paris for about €60; ask at your hotel.

By Car: From Paris's Périphérique ring road, follow A-13 toward Rouen, get off at Vernon, follow *Centre-Ville* signs, then signs to Giverny.

By Train: Take the Rouen-bound train from Paris' Gare St. Lazare station to Vernon (6/day, more on Sat, about €22 round-trip, 45 min one-way, 4 miles from Giverny, no baggage check). From the Vernon train station to Monet's garden (4 miles one-way), you have four good options: by bus, taxi, bike, or on foot.

The Vernon–Giverny **bus** meets arriving trains for the 15-minute run to Giverny (no buses on Mon) and takes you back to meet the return train to Paris. If you miss the last bus, find others to share a taxi (see below). The stop to Giverny is in front of Vernon's train station, facing Café du Chemin de Fer (don't dally, the bus leaves soon after your train arrives). The ticket office at Monet's home in Giverny has bus schedules for the return trip. The bus stop for the return trip is in the bus parking lot on the opposite side of the main road, by the roundabout. The stop is the first one on your right. Look for the white #18 bus marked *Vernon–Giverny Car.*

If you take a **taxi,** allow €12 for up to three people, €13 for four (tel. 06 07 34 36 68, tel. 06 76 08 50 78, or tel. 02 32 21 31 31). With buses meeting every train, taxis are unnecessary (unless you miss the bus). Taxis wait in front of the station in Vernon.

You can rent a **bike** at Café du Chemin de Fer opposite the train station (€13, tel. 02 32 21 16 01), and follow a paved bike path *(piste cyclable)* that runs from near Vernon along an abandoned railroad right-of-way (figure about 30 min to Giverny). Get an easy-to-follow map to Giverny with your bike and leave the train station paralleling tracks to your right, take the first left and follow that to the river, cross the river, turn right, and meet the bike trail). There's a lovely riverside park on the left side of the bridge after crossing the Seine (where you turn right for the bike path).

Hikers can go on **foot** to Giverny, following the bike instructions above, and take a bus or taxi back.

SLEEPING AND EATING

(€1 = $1.30, country code: 33)
$$ Hôtel la Musardière** is nestled in the village of Giverny two blocks from Monet's home (exit home and go right). It's cute and welcoming (Sb-€59, Db-€62–94, 123 rue Claude Monet, tel. 02 32 21 03 18, fax 02 32 21 60 00, hotelmusardieregiverny@wanadoo.fr).

You'll find a **café and sandwich stand** near the entrance to Monet's home and a peaceful **garden café** at the Museum of American Art (surrounded by gardens that Monet would appreciate, but a little pricey). I also like **Hôtel Baudy**'s meals (*menus* from €16, popular with tour groups, closed Sun eve and Mon, 5-min walk past Museum of American Art at 81 rue Claude-Monet, tel. 02 32 21 10 03).

Disneyland Paris

Europe's Disneyland is a remake of California's, with most of the same rides and smiles. The main difference is that Mickey Mouse speaks French, and you can buy wine with your lunch. My kids went ducky. The latest buzz is the Buzz Lightyear ride, where kids can fire back at attacking aliens from their spaceship.

Disneyland is easy to get to, and worth a day, if Paris is handier than Florida or California. Saturday, Sunday, Wednesday, public holidays, and any day in July and August are the most crowded. After dinner, crowds are gone. Food is fun and not outrageously priced. (Still, many smuggle in a picnic.) The free FASTPASS system is a worthwhile time-saver (get FASTPASS card at entry, good for five of the most popular rides, at ride insert card in machine to get a window of time to enter—often within about 45 minutes). You'll also save time by buying your tickets

ahead (at airport TIs, more than 100 Métro stations, or along the Champs-Elysées at the TI, Disney Store, or Virgin Megastore). Disney brochures are in every Paris hotel. For Disneyland information and reservations, call 08 25 30 60 30 (€0.15/min) or try www.disneylandparis.com or www.mickey-mouse.com.

Walt Disney Studios: This zone, which opened in 2002 next to the original 10-year-old amusement park, has a Hollywood focus geared for an older crowd, with animation, special effects, and movie-magic "rides." The Aerosmith Rock 'n' Roller Coaster is nothing special. The highlight is the Stunt Show Spectacular, filling a huge back-lot stadium five times a day for 45 minutes of car chases and thriller filming tips. An actual movie sequence is filmed with stunt drivers, audience bit players, and brash MTV-style hosts.

Cost: Disneyland Paris and Walt Disney Studios charge the same. You can pay separately for each or buy a combo-ticket for both, called a "Hopper" ticket. A one-day pass to either park is about €48 for adults and €40 for kids aged 3–11. Kids under 3 are free. In the summer, save 25 percent by going after 17:00.

For entry to both parks, adults pay approximately €60 for one day, €100 for two days, and €115 for three days (less for kids). Regular prices are discounted about 25 percent Nov–March and promotions are offered occasionally (check www.disneylandparis.com).

Hours: Disneyland is open daily mid-July–Aug 10:00–23:00, Sept–mid-July 10:00–19:00, some weekends have longer hours—check website or ask at the ticket office. Walt Disney Studios is open summer daily 9:00–18:00; winter Mon–Fri 10:00–18:00, Sat–Sun 9:00–18:00.

Getting There: By **car,** Disneyland is about 40 minutes (20 miles) east of Paris on the A-4 autoroute (direction: Nancy/Metz, exit #14). Parking is €8 per day at the park.

By **RER,** the slick one-hour trip is the best way to Disneyland from downtown Paris. Take RER line A-4 to Marne-la-Vallée–Chessy (from Charles de Gaulle–Etoile, Auber, Châtelet–Les Halles, or Gare de Lyon stations, about €8 each way, hourly, drops you one hour later right in the park). The last train back to Paris leaves shortly after midnight. Be sure to get a ticket that is good on both the RER and Métro; when returning, remember to use your same RER ticket for your Métro connection in Paris.

Both of Paris' major airports have direct shuttle **buses** to Disneyland Paris (€14, daily 8:30–19:45, every 45 min).

Pricey **TGV** trains connect Disneyland directly with **Charles de Gaulle Airport** (10 min), the **Loire Valley** (1.5 hrs, Tours–St. Pierre-des-Corps station, 15 min from Amboise), **Avignon** (3 hrs, TGV station), **Lyon** (2 hrs, Part Dieu station), and **Nice** (6 hrs, main station).

SLEEPING

(€1 = $1.30, country code: 33)

Most are better off sleeping in reality (Paris), though with direct buses and freeways to both airports, Disneyland makes a convenient first- or last-night stop. Seven different Disney-owned hotels offer accommodations at or near the park in all price ranges. Prices are impossible to pin down, as they vary by season and by the "package deal" you choose (deals that include park entry are usually a better value). The cheapest is **Davy Crockett's Ranch,** but you'll need a car. **Hôtel Santa Fe**** offers the best midrange value, with shuttle service to the park every 12 minutes. The most expensive is **Disneyland Hotel******, right at the park entry, about twice the price of Hôtel Santa Fe. To reserve any Disneyland hotel, call 01 60 30 60 30, fax 01 60 30 60 65, or check www.disneylandparis .com. The prices you'll be quoted include entry to the park.

NORMANDY

Dramatic coastlines, half-timbered towns, and thatched roofs punctuate the green, rolling hills of Normandy. Parisians call Normandy "the 21st arrondissement." It's their escape—the nearest beach. The Brits also consider this area close enough for a weekend away (the BBC came through loud and clear on my car radio). Despite the peacefulness you feel in today's Normandy, the region's history is filled with war. It was founded by Viking Norsemen who invaded from the north, settled here in the ninth century, and gave Normandy its name. A couple hundred years later, William the Conqueror invaded England from Normandy. His victory is commemorated in a remarkable tapestry at Bayeux. A few hundred years after that, France's greatest cheerleader, Joan of Arc (Jeanne d'Arc), was convicted of heresy in Rouen, and burned at the stake by the English, against whom she rallied France during the Hundred Years' War. And in 1944, Normandy hosted a World War II battle that changed the course of history.

The rugged, rainy coast of Normandy harbors wartime bunkers and enchanting fishing villages such as little Honfleur. And, on the border of Brittany, the almost surreal island abbey of Mont St. Michel rises serene and majestic, oblivious to the tides of tourists.

Planning Your Time

Honfleur, the D-Day beaches, and Mont St. Michel each merit overnight visits. At a minimum, you'll want a full day for the D-Day beaches and a half-day each in Honfleur and on Mont St. Michel.

If you're driving between Paris and Honfleur, Giverny (see previous chapter) or Rouen (covered in this chapter) are worthwhile stops; by train, they're best as day trips from Paris. The WWII memorial museum in Caen works well as a stop between Honfleur and Bayeux (and the D-Day beaches). Mont St. Michel must be seen early or late to avoid the masses of midday tourists. Dinan, just 45 minutes by car from Mont St. Michel, offers a fine introduc-  tion to Brittany (see next chapter). Drivers can enjoy Mont St. Michel as a day trip from Dinan.

Getting Around Normandy

Trains from Paris serve Rouen, Caen, Bayeux, Mont St. Michel (via Pontorson or Rennes), and Dinan, though service between these sights can be frustrating. Plan ahead: For bus information in English, check http://normandy.angloinfo.com/information/3/busses.asp. Buses make Giverny, Honfleur, Arromanches, and Mont St. Michel accessible to train stations in nearby towns, though Sundays have little if any bus service. Mont St. Michel is a challenge by train, except from Paris.

This region is ideal with a car. If you're driving into Honfleur from the north, take the impressive but pricey Normandy Bridge (pont de Normandie, €5 toll). If you're driving between Mont St. Michel and Dinan, follow my recommended scenic route (see page 251).

Cuisine Scene in Normandy

Normandy is known as the land of the four Cs: Calvados, Camembert, cider, and *crème*. The region specializes in cream sauces, organ meats (sweetbreads, tripe, and kidneys—the "gizzard salads" are great), and seafood *(fruits de mer)*. Dairy products are big here. Local cheeses are Camembert (mild to very strong; see sidebar), Brillat-Savarin (buttery), Livarot (spicy and pungent), Pavé d'Auge (spicy and tangy), and Pont l'Evêque (earthy flavor). Normandy is famous for its powerful Calvados apple brandy, Benedictine brandy (made by local monks), and three kinds of alcoholic apple ciders (*cidre* can be *doux*—sweet; *brut*—dry; or *bouche*—sparkling, and the strongest). Try a *kir Normand* (crème de cassis and cider), and look also for *poiret*, a tasty pear cider.

Remember, restaurants serve only during lunch (11:30–14:00) and dinner (19:00–21:00, later in bigger cities); cafés serve food throughout the day.

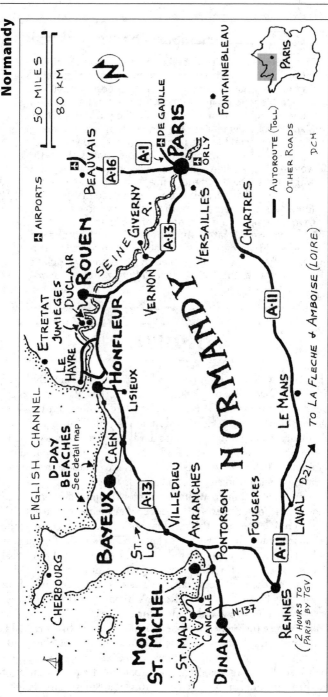

Normandy

50 MILES
80 KM

N

PARIS

✈ AIRPORTS

ENGLISH CHANNEL

D-DAY BEACHES
See detail map

ÉTRETAT
LE HAVRE
LES JUMIEGES
DUCLAIR
ROUEN
SEINE R.
GIVERNY
BEAUVAIS
✈ DE GAULLE
A·16
A·1
PARIS
✈ ORLY
FONTAINEBLEAU

CHERBOURG

BAYEUX
ST. LÔ
CAEN
HONFLEUR
LISIEUX
VERNON
A·13
A·13
VILLEDIEU
AVRANCHES
PONTORSON
FOUGERES
VERSAILLES
CHARTRES
LAVAL
D·21
LE MANS
A·11

MONT ST. MICHEL
ST. MALO
CANCALE
DINAN
N·137
RENNES
(2 HOURS TO
PARIS BY TGV)
A·11

NORMANDY

TO LA FLECHE & AMBOISE (LOIRE)

AUTOROUTE (TOLL)
OTHER ROADS

DCH

Normandy

Camembert Cheese

This cheap, soft, white, Brie-like cheese is sold all over France (and America) in distinctive, round, wooden containers. Camembert has been known for its cheese for 500 years, but local legend has it that today's cheese got its start in the French Revolution, when a priest on the run was taken in by Marie Harel, a Camembert farmer. He repaid the favor by giving her the secret formula from his own hometown—Brie.

From cow to customer, Camembert takes about three weeks to make. High-fat milk from Norman cows is curdled with rennet, ladled into round five-inch molds, sprinkled with *Penicillium camemberti* bacteria, and left to dry. In the first three days, the cheese goes from the cow's body temperature to room temperature to refrigerator cool (50 degrees).

Two weeks later, the ripened and aged cheese is wrapped in wooden bands and labeled for market. Like wines, Camembert cheese is controlled by government regulations and must bear the "A.O.C." *(Appellation d'Origine Contrôlée)* stamp of approval.

Rouen

This 2,000-year-old city mixes Gothic architecture, half-timbered houses, and contemporary bustle like no other place in France. Busy Rouen (roo-ohn) is France's fifth-largest port and Europe's biggest food exporter (mostly wheat and grain). While its cobbled old town is a delight to wander, it's hard to ignore Rouen's growing pains—homeless people ask for handouts near the monuments, and many of Rouen's great Gothic sights are in desperate need of cleaning. Rouen works best for me as a day trip.

Rouen is nothing new. It was a regional capital during Roman times, and France's second-largest city in medieval times (with 40,000 residents—only Paris had more). In the ninth century, the Normans made the town their capital. William the Conqueror called it home before moving to England. Rouen walked a political tightrope between England and France for centuries. An English base during the Hundred Years' War, it was the place where Joan of Arc was burned (in 1431). Rouen's historic wealth was based on its wool industry and trade—for centuries, it was the last bridge across the Seine River before the Atlantic. In April 1944, as America and Britain weakened German control of Normandy before the D-Day landings, Allied bombers destroyed 50 percent of Rouen. While the industrial suburbs were devastated, most of the historic core survived, keeping Rouen a pedestrian's delight.

And on summer evenings, a sound-and-light show transforms the facade of its Notre-Dame Cathedral into the changing colors of Monet's Impressionist canvas (mid-June–mid-Sept).

Planning Your Time

Rouen, with convenient connections to Paris (hourly, 1–1.5-hour trains from Gare St. Lazare), makes an easy day trip if you want a dose of a much smaller—yet lively—French city. Considering the easy Paris connection and Rouen's handy location in Normandy, drivers can save money and headaches by seeing Paris, then taking the train to Rouen to pick up a rental car (for car-rental companies, see "Helpful Hints," page 191).

ORIENTATION

While Paris embraces the Seine, Rouen ignores it. The area we're most interested in is bounded by the river to the south, the Museum of Fine Arts (esplanade Marcel Duchamp) to the north, rue de la République to the east, and the place du Vieux Marché to the west. It's a 20-minute walk from the train station to the river. Everything of interest is within a 10-minute walk from the Notre-Dame Cathedral.

Tourist Information

The TI faces the cathedral. Pick up their good English walking-tour flier (called *Into the Heart of Rouen's History*, €1), and a map with information on Rouen's museums. The TI also has audio-guide tours covering the cathedral and Rouen's historic center for €5, though my walking tour (below) is enough for most (May–Sept Mon–Sat 9:00–19:00, Sun 9:30–12:30 & 14:00–18:00; Oct–April Mon–Sat 9:00–18:00, Sun 10:00–13:00; tel. 02 32 08 32 40, www.rouentourisme.com). A small office in the TI changes money (closed during lunch year-round).

Arrival in Rouen

By Train: Rue Jeanne d'Arc cuts down from Rouen's train station (no baggage check) through the town center to the Seine River. Day-trippers should **walk** from the station down rue Jeanne d'Arc to rue du Gros Horloge. This street—a pedestrian mall in the medieval center—connects the open-air market and Joan of Arc Church (to your right) with the Notre-Dame Cathedral (to your left, starting point of my self-guided "Welcome to Rouen" walk, below).

Rouen's **subway** (Métrobus) whisks travelers from under the train station to the Palais de la Justice in one stop (€1.50, descend and buy tickets from machines one level underground, then validate ticket on subway two levels down). From the station, take a

Rouen

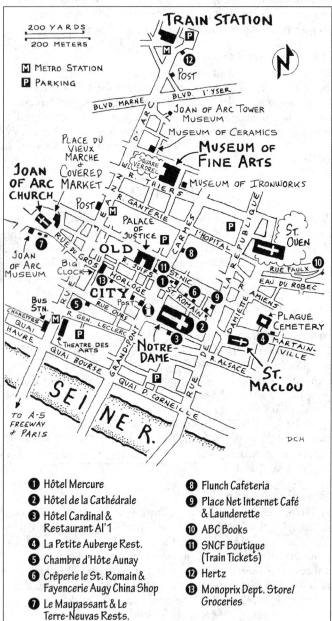

200 YARDS
200 METERS

M METRO STATION
P PARKING

TRAIN STATION

P

M

12

Post

BLVD. MARNE

BLVD. l'YSER

BLVD. MARNE

JOAN OF ARC TOWER
MUSEUM

MUSEUM OF CERAMICS

MUSEUM OF
FINE ARTS

PLACE DU
VIEUX
MARCHE
+
COVERED
MARKET

SQUARE
VERDREL

R. THIERS

MUSEUM OF IRONWORKS

JOAN
OF ARC
CHURCH

Post

R. GANTERIE

PALACE
OF
JUSTICE

P

T'HOPITAL

P

LA REPUBLIQUE

ST.
OUEN

RUE DU GROS

OLD

R. JUIFS

8

10

RUE FAULX

JOAN
OF ARC
MUSEUM

BIG
CLOCK

13

HORLOGE

11

ST.NIC.

1

6

9

EAU DU ROBEC

AMIENS

BUS
STN.

5

CITY

RUE OURS

Post

1

ST. ROMAIN

2

DANIELLE

PLAGUE
CEMETERY

CHARETTES
QUAI
HAVRE

M

R. GEN. LECLERC

P

THEATRE DES
ARTS

GRAND-PONT

NOTRE-
DAME

3

4

MARTAIN-
VILLE

QUAI BOURSE

QUAI P. CORNEILLE

P

R. ALSACE

ST.
MACLOU

SEINE R.

TO A-5
FREEWAY
+ PARIS

DCH

N

- **1** Hôtel Mercure
- **2** Hôtel de la Cathédrale
- **3** Hôtel Cardinal & Restaurant Al'1
- **4** La Petite Auberge Rest.
- **5** Chambre d'Hôte Aunay
- **6** Crêperie le St. Romain & Fayencerie Augy China Shop
- **7** Le Maupassant & Le Terre-Neuvas Rests.
- **8** Flunch Cafeteria
- **9** Place Net Internet Café & Launderette
- **10** ABC Books
- **11** SNCF Boutique (Train Tickets)
- **12** Hertz
- **13** Monoprix Dept. Store/ Groceries

Normandy

train headed to Technopole or Georges Braque. Returning to the station, take the direction Boulingrin and get off at *gare rue verte.*

Taxis (to the right as you exit station) will take you to any of my recommended hotels from the train station for about €7.

By Car: Assume you'll get lost—then found. Follow signs reading *Centre-Ville* and *Rive Droite* (right bank). Park near the cathedral. You can park free overnight along the river (metered until 19:00), or pay to park more securely in one of many well-signed underground lots. The La Haute Vieille Tour parking garage, just below the cathedral, is handy (€10/day). If you get turned around (likely because of the narrow, one-way streets), aim for the highest cathedral spires you spot.

Helpful Hints

Closed Days: Rouen's museums are closed on Tuesday, and many sights also close midday (12:00–14:00). The cathedral is closed Monday morning and during Mass (Tue–Sat at 8:00 and 10:00, Sun and holidays at 8:30, 10:30, and 12:00). The Joan of Arc Church is closed Fri and Sun mornings, and during Mass.

Market Days: The best open-air market is on place St. Marc, a few blocks east of St. Maclou Church (all day Tue, Fri, and Sat; on Sun until 13:30, it's filled with antiques and other good stuff). The next best is on place du Vieux Marché, by the Joan of Arc Church (Tue–Sun until 13:30, closed Mon).

Supermarket: It's inside the **Monoprix,** at the back of the store (Mon–Sat 8:30–21:00, closed Sun, on rue du Gros Horloge).

Internet Access: Place Net is just behind the cathedral (Mon–Sat 12:00–23:00, Sun 14:00–23:00, 37 rue de la République, tel. 02 32 78 02 22). Or surf with a view of the Joan of Arc Church at **Cybernet** (daily 10:00–21:00, sometimes until 22:00, has American keyboards, 47 place du Vieux Marché, tel. 02 35 07 73 02).

English Bookstore: ABC Books has nothing but English-language books—some American but mostly British (Tue–Sat 10:00–18:00, closed Sun–Mon, south of Eglise St. Ouen at 11 rue des Faulx, tel. 02 35 71 08 67).

Laundry: Try **Lav-pratic Laverie** (daily 7:00–21:00, no attendant and no English—completely coin-operated and automated from central control box, doors shut and lock automatically at 21:00, 43 rue de la République, near recommended hotels and next to Place Net Internet café).

Taxi: Call **Les Taxi Blancs,** tel. 02 35 61 20 50.

Car Rental: Hertz is across from the train station (Mon–Sat 8:00–12:00 & 14:00–19:00, closed Sun, 130 rue Jeanne d'Arc, tel. 02 35 70 70 71). **Europcar** has an office inside the station (Mon–Fri 8:00–12:30 & 13:30–19:00, Sat 8:30–12:00 & 14:00–19:00, closed Sun, tel. 02 35 88 21 20), as does **Avis** (tel. 02 35 88 60 94).

SNCF Boutique: Visit their office in town at the corner of rue aux Juifs and rue Eugène Boudin (Mon–Sat 10:00–19:00, closed Sun).

SELF-GUIDED WALK

Welcome to Rouen

On this one-hour walk, you'll see the essential historical Rouen sights. Remember that many sights are closed midday (12:00–14:00).

Start at the square in front of Notre-Dame Cathedral (which faces the TI), walk four blocks west to the plague cemetery, and return by walking six blocks east of the Notre-Dame Cathedral to the Joan of Arc Church, where you'll find several recommended restaurants.

Notre-Dame Cathedral (Cathédrale Notre-Dame): This cathedral is a landmark of art history, rated ▲▲. You're seeing essentially what Claude Monet saw as he painted 20 different studies of this cathedral's frilly Gothic facade at various times of day. Using the physical building only as a rack upon which to hang light, mist, dusk, and shadows, Monet was capturing "impressions." One of the paintings is in Rouen's Museum of Fine Arts, and four others are at the Orsay Museum in Paris. Find the plaque showing two of these paintings (in the corner of the square, about 30 paces to your right as you exit the TI).

Enter the cathedral (Tue–Sun 8:00–19:00, Mon 14:00–19:00; closed during Mass Tue–Sat at 8:00 and 10:00, Sun at 8:30, 10:30, and 12:00).

• *Stand at the back, and look down the **nave**.*

This is a classic Gothic nave—four stories of pointed-arch arcades, the top one filled with windows to help light the interior. Today, the interior is lighter than intended, because the original colored glass (destroyed mostly in World War II) was replaced by clear glass. Why such a big cathedral in a small town? Until the 1700s, Rouen was the second city of France—rich from its wool trade and its booming port.

• *Circle counterclockwise three-quarters of the way around the church along the ambulatory (the side aisle that leads behind the high altar) before exiting via the left transept.*

The side chapels and windows are described in English; they come from an assortment of centuries and styles—bold blues and reds are generally from the 13th century. Photos halfway

Welcome to Rouen Self-Guided Walk

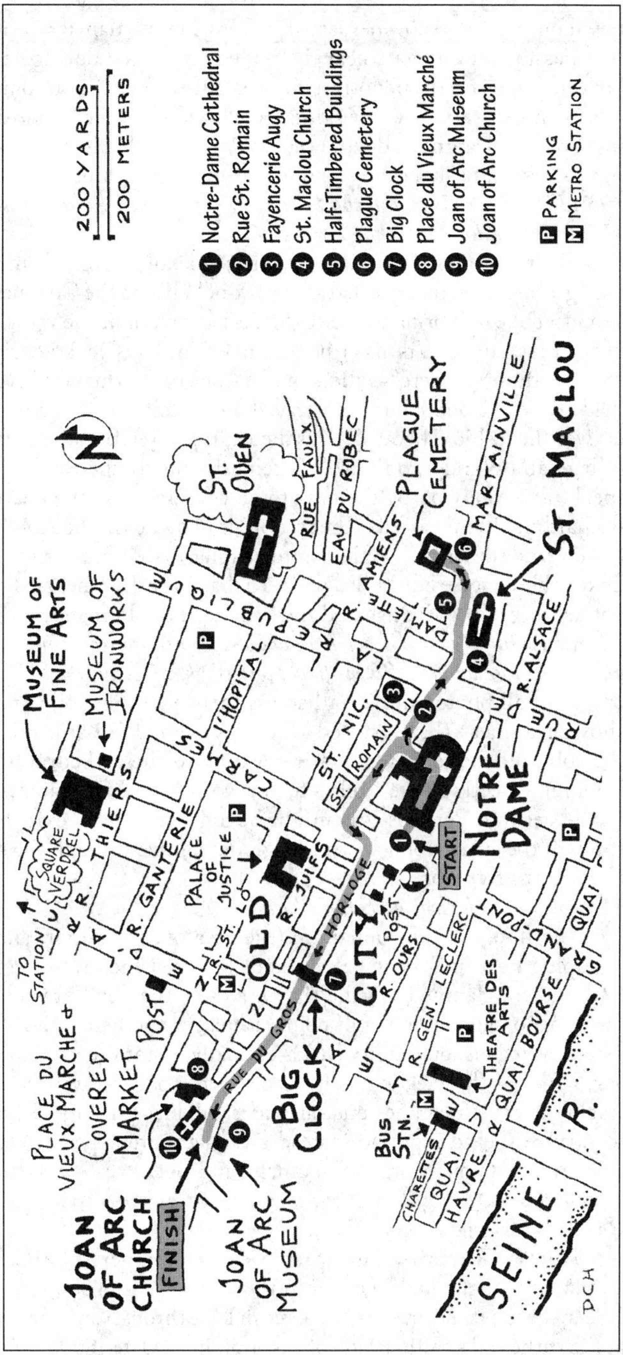

200 YARDS
200 METERS
1 Notre-Dame Cathedral
2 Rue St. Romain
3 Fayencerie Augy
4 St. Maclou Church
5 Half-Timbered Buildings
6 Plague Cemetery
7 Big Clock
8 Place du Vieux Marché
9 Joan of Arc Museum
10 Joan of Arc Church
P PARKING
M METRO STATION
JOAN OF ARC CHURCH
FINISH
JOAN OF ARC MUSEUM
PLACE DU VIEUX MARCHE & COVERED MARKET
TO STATION
SQUARE VERDREL
MUSEUM OF FINE ARTS
MUSEUM OF IRONWORKS
R. THIERS
R. GANTERIE
PALACE OF JUSTICE
R. ST. LO
R. JUIFS
OLD CITY
BIG CLOCK
RUE DU GROS HORLOGE
POST
R. OURS
R. GEN. LECLERC
THEATRE DES ARTS
BUS STN.
QUAI CHARETTES
QUAI HAVRE
QUAI BOURSE
SEINE R.
RUE DU GRAND PONT
START
NOTRE-DAME
ST. ROMAIN
ST. NIC.
R. DAMIETTE
R. AMIENS
EAU DU ROBEC
RUE FAULX
ST. OUEN
RUE DE L'HOPITAL
RUE DE LA REPUBLIQUE
PLAGUE CEMETERY
MARTAINVILLE
ST. MACLOU
R. ALSACE
DCH

down on the right show devastating WWII bomb damage.

Passing an iron gate near the high altar (closed during Mass, but often open on the opposite side even during Mass), you come to several **stone statues.** These saints were lifted from the facade during a recent cleaning and will eventually be installed in a museum. For us, it's a rare chance to stand toe-to-toe with a saint.

• *Find important Norman **tombs**, dating from when Rouen was the Norman capital.*

The first tomb is of Rollo—the first duke of Normandy in 933 (and great-great-great-great grandfather of William the Conqueror, seventh duke of Normandy, c. 1028). As the first duke, he was chief of the first gang of Vikings (the original "Normans") who decided to actually settle here. Called the "Father of Normandy," Rollo died at the age of 80, but is portrayed on his tomb as if he were 33 (as was the fashion, because Jesus died at that age). Because of later pillage and plunder, only Rollo's femur is inside the tomb. And speaking of body parts, the next tomb contains only the heart of Richard the Lionhearted. (The rest of his body lies in the Abbey of Fontevraud, described in the Loire chapter.) A descendant of the duke who conquered the English, Richard the Lionhearted was both a king of the English and the 12th duke of Normandy.

• *Circle behind the altar. Look back above the entry to see a rare black-and-white rose window (its medieval colored glass is long gone).*

A small photo on the wall across the nave from Rollo's tomb shows the mess that resulted when a violent 1999 storm blew the spire off the roof, sending it crashing to the cathedral floor. Looking directly above Rollo's femur, you can see the patchwork in the ceiling. Perhaps this might be a good time to exit. Pass through the small iron gate, turn right, and leave through the side door (north transept).

• *Stepping outside, look back at the **facade**.*

The fine, carved tympanum (the area over the door) shows a graphic Last Judgment. Jesus stands between the saved (on the left) and the damned (on the right). Notice the devil grasping a miser, who clutches a bag of coins. Look for the hellish hot tub, where even a bishop (pointy hat) is eternally in hot water.

Most of the facade has been cleaned—blasted with jets of water—but the fine limestone carving is still black. It's too delicate to survive the hosing, and instead awaits a more expensive laser cleaning (as do many other monuments in Rouen).

• *From this courtyard, a gate deposits you on a traffic-free street, rue St. Romain. Turn right and walk along...*

Rue St. Romain: This street has half-timbered buildings and lanes worth a look. Peek into the flowery pastel shop run by Rouen's last hatmaker. Nearby, you can look through an arch, back at the cathedral's spire. Made of cast iron in the late 1800s—about

---

The Hundred Years' War
(1336–1453)

It would take a hundred years to explain all the causes, battles, and political maneuverings of this century-plus of warfare between France and England, but here goes:

In 1300, before the era of the modern nation-state, the borders between France and England were fuzzy. French-speaking kings had ruled England, English kings owned the south of France, and English merchants dominated trade in the north. Dukes and lords in both countries were aligned more along family lines than by national identity. When the French king died without a male heir (1328), both France and England claimed the crown, and the battle was on.

England invaded the more populous country (1345) and—thanks to skilled archers using armor-penetrating longbows—won big battles at Crécy (1346) and Poitiers (1356). Despite a truce, roving bands of English mercenaries stayed behind and paid themselves by looting French villages. The French responded with guerrilla tactics.

In 1415, the English took still more territory, with Henry V's big victory at Agincourt. But rallied by the heavenly visions of young Joan of Arc, the French slowly drove the invaders out. Paris was liberated in 1436, and when Bordeaux fell to French forces (1453), the fighting ended without a treaty.

---

the same time Gustave Eiffel was building his tower in Paris—the spire is, at 490 feet, the tallest in France. You can also see the former location of the missing smaller (green) spire—downed in that 1999 storm.

• *Farther down the street, just past the Mormon church, a skinny and very picturesque half-timbered side lane (rue des Chanoines) leads left. Head beyond that, to a shop that shows off a traditional art form in action.*

Fayencerie Augy: Monsieur Augy (at #26, with the blue facade) welcomes potential shoppers to browse his studio/gallery/shop and see Rouen's clay "china" being made the traditional way. First, the clay is molded and fired. Then it's dipped in white enamel, dried, lovingly hand-painted, and fired a second time. Rouen was the first city in France to make faience, earthenware with colored glazes. In the 1700s, the town had 18 factories churning out the popular product (closed Sun, 26 rue St. Romain, VAT tax refunds nearly pay for the shipping, www.fayencerie-augy.com). For more faience, visit the local Museum of Ceramics (see "Sights," below).

• *Follow rue St. Romain, which leads to the very fancy...*

St. Maclou Church: This church's unique, bowed facade is textbook Flamboyant Gothic (sadly, its doorways are blackened by pollution). Notice the flame-like tracery decorating its gable. Since this was built at the very end of the Gothic age—and construction took many years—the doors are from the next age: the Renaissance (c. 1550). The interior is pretty, but skippable (Mon–Sat 10:00–17:00, Sun 10:30–17:30).

• *Leaving the church, turn right, and then take another right (giving the little boys on the corner wall a wide berth). Wander past a fine wall of half-timbered buildings fronting rue Martainville, to the end of St. Maclou Church.*

Half-Timbered Buildings: Because the local stone—a chalky limestone from the cliffs of the Seine River—was of poor quality (your thumbnail is stronger), and because local oak was plentiful, half-timbered buildings became a Rouen forte from the 14th through 19th centuries. Cantilevered floors were standard until the early 1500s. These top-heavy designs made sense: City land was limited, property taxes were based on ground-floor square footage, and the cantilevering minimized unsupported spans on upper floors. The oak beams provided the structural skeleton of the building, which was then filled in with a mix of clay, straw, pebbles...or whatever was available.

• *A block farther down, at 186 rue Martainville, a covered lane leads to the...*

Plague Cemetery (Aître St. Maclou): During the great plagues of the Middle Ages, as many as two-thirds of the people in this parish died. For the decimated community, dealing with the corpses was an overwhelming task. This half-timbered courtyard (c. 1520) was a mass grave, an ossuary where the bodies were "processed." Bodies would be dumped into the grave (where the well is now) and drenched in liquid lime to help speed decomposition. Later, the bones would be stacked in alcoves above the colonnades that line this courtyard. Notice the ghoulish carvings (c. 1560s) of gravediggers' tools, skulls, crossbones, and characters doing the "dance of death." In this *danse macabre,* Death, the great equalizer, grabs people of all social classes (free, daily mid-March–Oct 8:00–20:00, Nov–mid-March 8:00–19:00). The place is now an art school. Peek in on the young artists. As you leave, find the dried black cat (died c. 1520, in tiny glass case to the left of the door). To overcome evil, it was buried during the building's construction.

• *Farther down rue Martainville, at place St. Marc, a colorful market blooms Sunday until 12:30 and all day Tuesday, Friday, and Saturday. If it's not market day, turn right upon leaving the boneyard and hike back up to the Notre-Dame Cathedral. As rue du Gros Horloge—the town's main shopping street since Roman times—passes the cathedral, it leads to Rouen's...*

Joan of Arc
(1412–1431)

The cross-dressing teenager who rallied French soldiers to drive out English invaders was born the illiterate daughter of a humble farmer. One summer day, in her dad's garden, 13-year-old Joan heard a heavenly voice accompanied by bright light. It was the first of several saints (including Michael, Margaret, and Catherine) to talk to her during her short life.

In 1429, the young girl was instructed by the voices to save France from the English. Dressed in men's clothing, she traveled to see the king and predicted that the French armies would be defeated near Orléans—they were. King Charles VII equipped her with an ancient sword and a banner saying "Jesus, Maria," and sent her to rally the troops.

Soon, "the Maid" *(la Pucelle)* was bivouacking amid rough soldiers, riding with them into battle, and suffering an arrow to the chest, while liberating the town of Orléans. On July 17, 1429, she held her banner high in the cathedral of Reims as Charles was officially proclaimed king of a resurgent France.

Joan and company next tried to retake Paris (1429), but the English held out. She suffered a crossbow wound through the thigh, and her reputation of invincibility was tarnished. During a battle at Compiègne (1430), she was captured and turned over to the English for £10,000. In Rouen, they chained her by the neck inside an iron cage, while the local French authorities (allied with the English) plotted against her. The Inquisition—insisting that Joan's voices were "false and diabolical"—tried and sentenced her as a witch and heretic.

On May 30, 1431, Joan of Arc was tied to a stake on Rouen's old market square (place du Vieux Marché). She yelled, "Rouen! Rouen! Must I die here?" Then they lit the fire; she fixed her eyes on a crucifix and died chanting, "Jesus, Jesus, Jesus."

After her death, her place in history was slowly rehabilitated. French authorities proclaimed her trial illegal (1455), prominent writers and artists were inspired by her, and the Catholic Church finally beatified (1909) and canonized her (1920) as St. Joan of Arc.

Big Clock (Gros Horloge): The impressive Renaissance public clock, le Gros Horloge (groh oar-lohzh), from 1528, decorates the former city hall. In the 16th century, an hour hand offered ample precision; minute hands only became necessary in a later, faster-paced age. The lamb at the end of the hour hand is a reminder that wool rules, and is the source of Rouen's wealth. The town medallion features the sacrificial lamb, with both religious and business significance. But the artistic highlight fills the underside of the arch (walk under and stretch your back), with the good shepherd and lots of sheep. The tiny pub lodged in the clock tower reminds us how close we are to Britain.

• *Continue walking downhill, and cross the busy rue Jeanne d'Arc. Fifty yards past the medieval McDonald's is a chocolate shop, Les Larmes de Jeanne d'Arc de Rouen (at #163), which would love to tempt you with its chocolate-covered almond "tears (larmes) of Joan of Arc." While you must resist touching the chocolate fountain, you are welcome to taste a tear. The first one is free; a small bag costs about €7. The street continues to...*

Place du Vieux Marché: Surrounded by half-timbered buildings, this old market square has a covered produce market, a park commemorating Joan of Arc's burning, and a modern church in her name. The market leads to the garden, where a tall aluminum cross marks the spot where Rouen publicly punished and executed people. The pillories stood here, and during the Revolution, the town's guillotine made 800 people "a foot shorter at the top." In 1431, Joan of Arc—only 19 years old—was burned. As the flames engulfed her, an English soldier said, "Oh my God, we've killed a saint." (Nearly 500 years later, Joan was canonized, and the soldier was proved right.)

A waxy **Joan of Arc Museum** on the square tells the story of this inspirational teenager of supreme faith who, after hearing voices for several years, won the confidence of her countrymen, was given an army, and rallied the French against their English invaders. Those touched by her story will enjoy this humble museum (€5, English descriptions, daily mid-April–Sept 9:30–19:00, Oct–mid-April 10:00–12:00 & 14:00–18:30, 33 place du Vieux Marché, tel. 02 35 88 02 70, www.jeanne-darc.com). Between the museum and the church are ruins of a 15th-century church that once stood on this spot, and was destroyed during the French Revolution.

Joan of Arc Church (Eglise Jeanne d'Arc): This modern church, rated ▲▲, is a tribute to Joan of Arc, who was canonized in 1920 and later became the patron saint of France. The church, completed in 1979, feels Scandinavian inside and out—another reminder of Normandy's Nordic roots. Sumptuous 16th-century windows, salvaged from a church lost in World War II, were worked into the soft architectural lines. With a ship's-hull vaulting, the church is a delightful place, similar to churches designed by the architect Le Corbusier (free entry, €0.50 English pamphlet, Mon–Thu and Sat 10:00–12:15 & 14:00–18:00, Fri and Sun 14:00–18:00, closed Fri and Sun mornings and during Mass, public WC 30 yards from church doors).

Normandy

SIGHTS

In Rouen

These three museums are within a block of each other, closed on Tuesdays, never crowded, and can all be visited with the same €5.40 combo-ticket (www.rouen-musees.com).

▲**Museum of Fine Arts (Musée des Beaux-Arts)**—Paintings from many periods are beautifully displayed in this museum, including works by Caravaggio, Peter Paul Rubens, Paolo Veronese, Jan Steen, Théodore Géricault, Jean-Auguste-Dominique Ingres, Eugène Delacroix, and the Impressionists. Don't miss Monet's painting of Rouen's Notre-Dame Cathedral, and the room dedicated to Géricault. Pick up the museum map at the ticket desk. Important rooms have excellent English descriptions on small, portable boards, and even have clever foldaway stools. The €2.30 audioguide is good, but spotty in its coverage (€3, occasional temporary exhibitions cost extra, Wed–Mon 10:00–18:00, 15th–17th-century rooms closed 13:00–14:00, closed Tue, 3 blocks below train station at 26 bis rue Jean Lecanuet, tel. 02 35 71 28 40).

Museum of Ironworks (Musée le Secq des Tournelles, a.k.a. Musée de la Ferronnerie)—This deconsecrated church houses iron objects, many of them more than 1,500 years old. Locks, keys, tools, coffee grinders—virtually anything made of iron is on display. You can duck into the entry area for a glimpse of a medieval iron scene without passing through the turnstile (€2.30, no English explanations, Wed–Mon 10:00–13:00 & 14:00–18:00, closed Tue, behind Museum of Fine Arts, 2 rue Jacques Villon, tel. 02 35 88 42 92).

Museum of Ceramics—Rouen's famous faience (earthenware), which dates from the 16th to the 18th centuries, fills this fine old mansion. Unfortunately, there is not a word of English (same hours and cost as Museum of Ironworks, above; 1 rue Faucon, tel. 02 35 07 31 74).

Near Rouen

The Route of the Ancient Abbeys (La Route des Anciennes Abbayes)—This route—punctuated with abbeys, apples, and Seine River views—provides a pleasing detour for drivers connecting Rouen and destinations farther west (if you're traveling *sans* car, skip it). Follow D-982 west of Rouen to Jumièges (visit its abbey), then cross the Seine on the car ferry at Duclair (about €2).

Drivers can stop to admire the gleaming Romanesque church at the **Abbey of St. Georges de Boscherville** (but skip the abbey grounds). The romantically ruined **Abbey of Jumièges** is *the* sight to visit on this route. (Follow the river on D-65 from Duclair for a more scenic approach.) Founded in A.D. 654, it was destroyed by

Vikings and rebuilt by William the Conqueror, only to be torn down again by French Revolutionaries (€5, helpful English handout, more detailed booklet for €6, daily 9:30–13:00 & 14:30–18:30, open all day July–Aug, until 17:30 Sept–April, last entry 30 min before closing, tel. 02 35 37 24 02). Several decent lunch options lie across the street from the abbey.

SLEEPING

While I don't think Rouen merits an overnight, by staying here you can enjoy a mostly tourist-free Rouen after-hours (most hotels cater to business travelers). These hotels are perfectly central, within two blocks of Notre-Dame Cathedral.

$$$ Hôtel Mercure*, ideally situated a block north of the cathedral, is a sprawling business hotel with a professional staff, a vast lobby and bar, and 125 rooms loaded with modern comforts. Suites come with views of the cathedral, but are overpriced and not much bigger than a double (Sb-€145, Db-€155, view Db-€160, suite-€260, air-con, elevator, Internet access and Wi-Fi, parking garage-€10/day, 7 rue Croix de Fer, tel. 02 35 52 69 52, fax 02 35 89 41 46, www.mercure.com, h1301@accor.com).

$$ Hôtel de la Cathédrale** is run by friendly Nathalie and Alexandra, who welcome you with a flowery courtyard, a cozy, wood-beamed breakfast room, and frumpy but mostly country-French rooms. Some rooms have hardwood floors, and most have basic bathrooms and poor sound insulation (Sb-€56–76, Db-€66–93, Tb-€95, Qb-€115, extra bed-€15, elevator, Internet access and Wi-Fi, overnight parking-€5, 24-hour parking-€10, 12 rue St. Romain, a block from St. Maclou Church, tel. 02 35 71 57 95, fax 02 35 70 15 54, www.hotel-de-la-cathedrale.fr, contact@hotel-de -la-cathedrale.fr).

$$ Hôtel Cardinal** offers rooms facing the cathedral, without the street appeal of the Hôtel de la Cathédrale. It's run by English-speaking, born-and-raised-Rouennais Pascal and his wife Agnes. Nearly all of its 18 sufficiently comfortable rooms look right onto the cathedral, and a few are ideal for families. Rooms on the fourth floor are best, with small balconies and great cathedral views (Sb-€48–60, Db-€60–72, Tb-€68–82, Qb-€94, extra bed-€11, non-smoking rooms available, elevator, 1 place de la Cathédrale, tel. 02 35 70 24 42, fax 02 35 89 75 14, www.cardinal -hotel.fr, cardinalhotel.rouen@wanadoo.fr).

$ *Chambre d'Hôte:* Monsieur Philippe Aunay rents two rooms in his 17th-century half-timbered home. A cross between a museum and a rummage sale, it's like sleeping at your eccentric grandma's house. One room comes with a piano, bathtub, and shower. The other is a three-room mini-apartment, complete with

---

Sleep Code

(€1 = $1.30, country code: 33)
S = Single, **D** = Double/Twin, **T** = Triple, **Q** = Quad, **b** = bathroom,
s = shower only, ***** = French hotel rating system (0–4 stars).
Unless otherwise noted, credit cards are accepted and English
is spoken.

To help you easily sort through these listings, I've divided
the rooms into three categories based on the price for a standard double room with bath:

 $$$ **Higher Priced**—Most rooms €90 or more.
  $$ **Moderately Priced**—Most rooms between €60–90.
   $ **Lower Priced**—Most rooms €60 or less.

---

a small kitchen and two bathrooms (Sb-€40, Db-€58, Tb-€98,
Qb-€116, apartment for 5-€148, includes breakfast, cash only, 45
rue aux Ours, no sign, push buzzer, tel. 02 35 70 99 68, speaks
enough English).

EATING

Near the Cathedral

Restaurant Al'1, on a leafy square under the facade of the cathedral (next door to the Hôtel Cardinal), is *the* place for a hearty
salad—best when you can sit outside (enormous €11 salads—sorry,
no splitting, Mon–Fri 12:00–14:30 & 19:00–22:00, closed Sat–Sun,
3 place de la Cathédrale).

Crêperie le St. Romain, between the cathedral and St.
Maclou Church, is an excellent budget option. It's run by gentle
Mr. Pegis, who serves filling €8 crêpes with small salads in a
warm setting (lunch Tue–Sat, lunch and dinner Thu–Sat, closed
Sun–Mon, 52 rue St. Romain, tel. 02 35 88 90 36).

La Petite Auberge offers a local dining experience: simple,
cheap, and welcoming, with two rooms crammed with tables and
happy clients (*menus* from €15 on weeknights, €19 on weekends,
closed Mon, 164 rue Martainville, tel. 02 35 70 80 18).

At **Flunch,** you'll find family-friendly, cheap, point-and-shoot,
cafeteria-style meals in a fast-food setting (*menu* with salad bar, main
course, and drink for €9; good kids' *menu,* open daily until 22:00, a
block from cathedral at 66 rue des Carmes, tel. 02 35 71 81 81).

On Place du Vieux Marché

Two moderately priced restaurants that cater more to tourists than
locals face place du Vieux Marché, across from the Joan of Arc

Normandy

Church. **Le Maupassant** is a welcoming place, with an outdoor terrace and three lively floors filled with orange leather booths. It's famous for its duck dishes and *moelleux au chocolat* melted chocolate over ice cream and cake (regional *menus* from €18, daily, 39 place du Vieux Marché, tel. 02 35 07 56 90). **Le Terre-Neuvas** is best for seafood (*menus* from €18, daily, 3 place du Vieux Marché, tel. 02 35 71 58 21).

TRANSPORTATION CONNECTIONS

Rouen is well-served by trains from Paris, through Amiens to other points north, and through Caen to other destinations west and south.

From Rouen by Train to: Paris' Gare St. Lazare (20/day, 1–1.5 hrs), **Bayeux** (12/day, 3.5–4.5 hrs, change in Paris' Gare St. Lazare), **Pontorson–Mont St. Michel** (5/day, 4–7 hrs, most via Paris, 1 via Caen, change train stations from St. Lazare to Montparnasse, then TGV to Rennes, then 1.75-hr bus to Mont St. Michel).

By Train and Bus to: Honfleur (5/day Mon–Sat, 3/day Sun, 2 hrs via train and bus: train to Le Havre, then 30-min bus over Normandy Bridge to Honfleur; Le Havre's bus station is right next to the train station, making connections easy; or train to Paris' Gare St. Lazare and transfer to Caen, 13/day, 2–3.5 hrs; then take 1–2-hr bus to Honfleur—either take express bus, 2/day, 1 hr, about €16; or the longer, more scenic *par la côte*—along the coast, 8/day, 2 hrs, about €13).

Honfleur

Gazing at its cozy harbor lined with skinny, soaring houses, it's easy to overlook the historic importance of this port. For more than a thousand years, sailors have enjoyed Honfleur's (ohn-flur) ideal location, where the Seine River greets the English Channel. William the Conqueror received supplies shipped from Honfleur. Samuel de Champlain sailed from here in 1608 to North America, where he discovered the St. Lawrence River and  founded Quebec City. The town was also a favorite of 19th-century Impressionists: Eugène Boudin (boo-dan) lived and painted in Honfleur, attracting Monet and other creative types from Paris.

In some ways, modern art was born in the fine light of idyllic little Honfleur.

Honfleur escaped the bombs of World War II, and today offers a romantic port enclosed on three sides with sprawling outdoor cafés. Long eclipsed by the gargantuan port of Le Havre just across the Seine, Honfleur happily uses its past as a bar stool...and sits on it.

ORIENTATION

All of Honfleur's appealing streets and activities are within a short stroll of its old port (Vieux Bassin). The Seine River flows just east of the center, the hills of the Côte de Grâce form its western limit, and rue de la République slices north–south through the center to the port. Honfleur has one can't-miss sight (Ste. Catherine Church) and a handful of good, if second-rate sights...but really, the town itself is its best sight.

Tourist Information

The **TI** is in the flashy glass public library (Mediathéque) on quai le Paulmier, two blocks from Vieux Bassin toward Le Havre (July–Aug Mon–Sat 10:00–19:00, Sun 10:00–17:00; Sept–June Mon–Sat 10:00–12:30 & 14:00–18:00, Sun 10:00–17:00; free WCs inside, tel. 02 31 89 23 30, www.ot-honfleur.fr). Pick up the good town map, as well as tourist maps of Normandy and the Calvados region. If you're headed to the D-Day beaches, get information here. Skip the useless museum pass. Ask about concerts, special events, and guided visits of Honfleur (tours usually Wed at 15:00, €6, 1.5 hours, smart to reserve by calling TI).

Arrival in Honfleur

By Bus: Get off at the small bus station *(gare routière)* near the TI (English-speaking information counter, confirm your departure, see "Transportation Connections," page 251). To reach the TI and old town, turn right out of the station and walk five minutes up quai le Paulmier.

By Car: Follow *Centre-Ville* signs and park as close to the port (Vieux Bassin) as possible to unload your bags. Parking can be a headache in Honfleur, especially on summer and holiday weekends—but you can avoid this by parking a short walk from town. Follow signs to *Parking du Môle*, park for free there, and enjoy the 10–15-minute walk to most hotels (note that some hotels offer parking...for a price). The more central Parking du Bassin (across from the TI) is monitored (€1.75/hour, €12/day). Street parking, metered during the day, is free from 19:00 to 9:00.

Honfleur

P PARKING
B BOAT EXCURSIONS

100 YARDS
100 METERS

MAISONS SATIE
JARDIN PUBLIC
BLVD. CHAR.
To **P** Ste. Cath.
VIEW OF PONT NORMANDIE
B
P du Mole
AVANT PORT
BOUDIN MUSEUM
RUE HAUTE
RUE DE L'HOMME DE BOIS
PLACE HAMELIN
QUAI DES PASS
LIEUTENANCE
STE-CATHERINE
QUAI DE LA QUARANTAINE
B
RUE ALBERT 1er
QUAI DE LA VILLE
P du Bassin
RUE DES CAPUCINS
PLACE BERTH-ELOT
VIEUX BASSIN
QUAI ST-ETIENNE
MUSEUMS OF OLD HONFLEUR
QUAI DE LA TOUR
BUS STN
RUE BUCAILLE
RUE DU DOUBLET
RUE DU PUITS
WC
PRIS
COURS DES FOSSES
QUAI LE PAULMIER
PLACE DU PUITS
RUE BRULEE
RUE MONTPENSIER
R. DELACHAUSSEE
St. LEONARD
To COTE DE GRACE
EUGENE BOUDIN
RUE DES PRES
RUE DE LA REPUBLIQUE
RUE CACHIN
To **9**
DCH

● 1 Les Maisons de Lea
● 2 Hôtel le Cheval Blanc
● 3 L'Absinthe Hôtel & Le Bouilland Normand Rest.
● 4 La Maison de Lucie
● 5 Hôtel du Dauphin
● 6 Etap Hôtel
● 7 La Cour Ste. Catherine B&B
● 8 Odile & Jean-Luc's Rooms
● 9 To Madame Bellegarde's Rooms
● 10 P'tit Mareyeur Restaurant
● 11 La Terrasse et l'Assiette Rest.
● 12 La Cidrerie Bar & Crêperie
● 13 Le Bréard Restaurant
● 14 La Lipouille Restaurant
● 15 Le Perroquet Vert & L'Albatross Bars
● 16 Waterfront Crêpe Stand
● 17 Tourist Train Stop
● 18 Launderette
● 19 Produits Regionaux Gribouille
● 20 Internet Café
● 21 Casino Grocery
● 22 Champion Market

Normandy

Helpful Hints

Market Day: The area around Ste. Catherine Church becomes a colorful open-air market every Saturday morning (9:00–13:00). A smaller organic food–only market takes place here on Wednesday mornings.

Grocery Stores: The **Champion Market** is the biggest in town (Mon–Sat 8:30–12:20 & 14:00–19:00, Sun 9:00–13:00 July–Aug only, about a 10-min walk up rue de la République from Vieux Bassin, on place Sorel). There's also a good **Casino Grocery** near the TI (same hours as Champion Market, except open Sun mornings year-round, 16 quai le Paulmier).

Regional Products with Panache: Visit **Produits Regionaux Gribouille** for any Normand delicacy you can dream up. Say *bonjour* to Monsieur Gribouille (gree-boo-ee) and watch your head—his egg-beater collection hangs from above (open 364 days a year, 9:30–13:00 & 14:00–19:00, 16 rue de l'Homme de Bois).

Internet Access: Cyberpub has unpredictable hours but plenty of computers (at Hôtel de la Diligence, 55 rue de la République, tel. 02 31 89 95 83).

Laundry: Lavomatique is a block behind the TI and toward the port (daily 7:00–20:00, 4 rue Notre-Dame).

Taxi: Call 06 18 18 36 36 or 06 08 60 17 98.

Tourist Train: Honfleur's *petit train* toots you up the Côte de Grâce—the hill overlooking the town—and back in about 50 minutes (€6, daily 10:30–11:30 & 14:30–17:30, departs from across gray swivel bridge that leads to Parking du Môle).

SIGHTS AND ACTIVITIES

In Honfleur

Vieux Bassin—Stand facing Honfleur's square harbor, with the merry-go-round across the lock to your left. Survey the town. The word Honfleur is Scandinavian, meaning the shelter *(fleur)* of Hon (a Norse settler). Eventually, the harbor was fortified by a wall with two gatehouses (the one surviving gatehouse is on your right) and a narrow boat passage protected by a chain. Just in front of the old barrel-vaulted entry to the town (20 steps to your right), you can see a bronze bust of Samuel de Champlain—the explorer who sailed with an Honfleur crew to make his discoveries in Canada. The harbor, once crammed with fishing boats, is now home to local yachts. Turn around to see various tour and fishing boats and the Normandy Bridge (described below), a sleek suspension bridge, in the distance. Fisherfolk catch flatfish, scallops, and tiny shrimp.

On the left, you may see fishermen's wives selling *crevettes* (shrimp). You can buy them *cuites* (cooked) or *vivantes* (alive and wiggly). They are happy to let you sample one (rip off the cute little head and tail, and pop the middle into your mouth—*délicieuse!*) or buy a cupful to go (€1.50, daily in season).

You're also likely to see artists sitting at easels around the harbor, as Boudin and Monet did. Many consider Honfleur the birthplace of Impressionism. This was a time when people began to revere, not fear, the out-of-doors, and started to climb mountains "because they were there." Pretty towns like Honfleur and the nearby coast were ideal subjects to paint. Artists would set up easels on this side of the basin to catch the light playing on the line of buildings, slates, timbers, geraniums, clouds, and reflections in the water. Monet came here to visit the artist Boudin, a hometown boy, and the battle cry of the Impressionists—"Out of the studio and into the light! "—was born.

Early risers can watch what's left of Honfleur's fishing fleet prepare for the day, and will be treated to good light for photographing the harbor.

▲▲Ste. Catherine Church (Eglise Ste. Catherine)—The unusual wood-shingled exterior suggests that this church has a different story to tell than most. Walk inside. You'd swear that if it were turned over, it would float—the legacy of a community of sailors and fishermen, with plenty of boatbuilders and no cathedral architects. When the first nave was constructed in 1466, it was immediately apparent that more space was needed—so the second was built in 1497. Because it felt too much like a market hall, they added side aisles. Notice the oak pillars. Since each had to be the same thickness, and since trees come in different sizes, some are full-length and others are supported by stone bases. In the last months of World War II, a bomb fell through the roof—but didn't explode. The pipe organ is popular for concerts, and the modern pews are designed to flip so that you can face the music. Take a close look at the many medieval instruments carved into the railing below the organ—a 16th-century combo band in wood (free, daily July–Aug 9:00–18:30, Sept–June 9:00–12:00 & 14:00–18:00).

The church's bell tower is equally unusual. It was not built atop the church, but across the square—to lighten the load of the wooden church's roof and to minimize fire hazards. Peek inside, where you'll find a tiny museum with a few church artifacts (€2—not worth it, free with your ticket to the Eugène Boudin Museum; April–Sept Wed–Mon 10:00–12:00 & 14:00–18:00, closed Tue; Oct–March Wed–Mon 14:00–18:00 only, closed Tue).

▲Eugène Boudin Museum—This pleasing little museum has three interesting floors with many paintings of Honfleur and the surrounding countryside. The first floor up displays Norman folk costumes; the second floor up has the Boudin collection; and the third floor houses the Hambourg/Rachet collection and the Katia

Eugène Boudin
(1824–1898)

Born in Honfleur, Boudin was the son of a harbor pilot. As an amateur teenage artist, he found work in an art-supply store that catered to famous artists from Paris (such as Jean-Baptiste-Camille Corot and Jean-François Millet) who came to paint the seaside. Boudin studied art in Paris, but kept his hometown roots. Thanks to his Paris connections, Boudin's work was exhibited at the Paris salons.

At age 30, Boudin met the teenage Claude Monet. Monet had grown up in nearby Le Havre, and, like Boudin, sketched the world around him—beaches, boats, and small-town life. Boudin encouraged him to don a scarf, set up his easel outdoors, and paint the scene exactly as he saw it. Today, we say: "Well, duh!" But "open-air" painting was unorthodox for artists trained to thoroughly study their subjects in the perfect lighting of a controlled studio setting. Boudin didn't teach Monet as much as he gave him the courage to follow his artistic instincts.

In the 1860s and 1870s, Boudin spent summers at his farm (St. Siméon) on the outskirts of Honfleur, hosting Monet, Edouard Manet, and others. They taught Boudin the Impressionist techniques of using bright colors, and building a figure with many individual brushstrokes. Boudin adapted those "strokes" to build figures with "patches" of color. In 1874, Boudin joined the renegade Impressionists at their "revolutionary" exhibition in Paris.

Granoff room. Pick up a map at the ticket counter, tip your beret to Eugène Boudin, and climb the stairs (or take the elevator).

First Floor (Costumes): Monsieur and Madame Louveau (see their photo as you enter) gave Honfleur this quality collection of local traditional costumes. The hats, blouses, and shoes are supported by paintings that place them in an understandable historical and cultural context. Of special interest are the lace bonnets, typical of 19th-century Normandy. You could name a woman's village by her style of bonnet. The dolls are not toys for tots, but marketing tools for traveling clothing merchants—designed to show off the latest fashions.

Second Floor (Boudin Collection and More): A right off the stairs leads into a large room of appealing 20th-century paintings and sculpture, done by artists who produced most of their works while living in Honfleur. A left off the stairs leads through a temporary exhibition hall into a fine gallery of 19th-century paintings (in the room on the left). The artwork here is arranged chronologically, from Romanticism through Realism to Impressionism (the heart of this museum).

Upon showing their work in Paris, Normandy artists—such as Eugène Boudin—created enough of a stir that Normandy came into vogue; many Parisian artists (including Monet and other early Impressionists) traveled to Honfleur to tune in to the action. Boudin himself made a big impression on the father of Impressionism. This collection of his paintings—which he gave to his hometown—provides a good study of the evolution from realistic portrayals of subjects (outlines colored in, like a coloring book) to masses of colors catching light (Impressionism). Boudin's beach scenes, showing aristocrats taking a healthy saltwater dip, helped fuel that trend. His skies were good enough to earn him the nickname "King of Skies." (Find the glass display case titled *Précurseur de l'Impressionisme*, with little pastel drawings).

Third Floor (Hambourg/Rachet Collection): There are two access points to the third floor. First follow the steps that lead from the Boudin room to the small Hambourg/Rachet collection (and a smashing painting of Honfleur). In 1988, André Hambourg and his wife, Nicole Rachet, donated their art to this museum. The collection is enjoyably Impressionistic, but with artwork from the mid-20th century.

Third Floor (Salle Katia Granoff): Retrace your steps back to the main stairway to reach the other third-floor room, where you'll find a worthwhile collection of 20th-century art by artists who lived and learned in Honfleur. Check out the few paintings by Raoul Dufy (a French Fauvist painter) and compare his imaginative scenes of Honfleur with others you've seen. Don't miss the brilliant view of the Normandy Bridge through the windows.

Cost and Hours: €5.30, English audioguide-€2 (no English explanations—but none needed); April–Sept Wed–Mon 10:00–12:00 & 14:00–18:00, closed Tue; Oct–Dec and mid-Feb–March Mon and Wed–Fri 14:00–17:00, Sat–Sun 10:00–12:00 & 14:00–17:00, closed Tue; closed Jan–mid-Feb; elevator, no photos, rue de l'Homme de Bois, tel. 02 31 89 54 00.

▲**Maisons Satie**—This peaceful museum, housed in composer Erik Satie's birthplace, presents his music in a creative and enjoyable way. As you wander from room to room with your headset, infrared signals transmit bits of Satie's music, along with a first-person story. As if you're living as an artist in 1920s Paris, you'll drift past winged pears, strangers in the window, and small girls with green eyes. (If you like what you hear...don't move; the infrared transmission is sensitive, and the soundtrack switches every few feet.) The finale—performed by you—is the *Laboratory of Emotions*. For a relaxing sit, enjoy the 12-minute movie (4/hr) featuring modern dance springing from Satie's collaboration with Picasso types

(€5.30; May–Sept Wed–Mon 10:00–19:00, Oct–Dec and mid-Feb–April Wed–Mon 11:00–18:00, closed Tue and Jan–mid-Feb; last entry 1 hour before closing, free English audioguide, 5-min walk from harbor at 67 boulevard Charles V, tel. 02 31 89 11 11).

Museums of Old Honfleur—Two side-by-side museums combine to paint a picture of daily life in Honfleur since the Middle Ages. The curator creatively supports the artifacts with paintings, making the cultural context more clear.

The **Museum of the Navy** (Musée de la Marine) fills a small 15th-century church (facing Vieux Bassin) with an interesting collection of ship models and marine paraphernalia. The **Museum of Ethnography and Norman Popular Art** (Musée d'Ethnographie et d'Art Populaire), located in the old prison and courthouse, re-creates typical rooms from various eras and crams them with objects of daily life (€4.40 for both or €3.20 each; both open April–Sept Tue–Sun 10:00–13:00 & 14:00–18:30, March and Oct–mid-Nov Tue–Fri 14:00–18:00, Sat–Sun 10:00–12:00 & 14:00–18:00, closed Mon and mid-Nov–Feb; ask for English explanation pages).

Near Honfleur

Boat Excursions—Boat trips in and around Honfleur depart near Hôtel le Cheval Blanc (Easter–Nov usually about 11:00–17:00). The tour boat *Calypso* operates good 45-minute trips around Honfleur's harbor (€6, tel. 02 31 89 07 77). You'll also find several boats with cruises to the Normandy Bridge (see below) that unfortunately include two boring stops through the locks (about €8, 90 min, details at TI).

▲**Côte de Grâce Walk**—For good exercise and a bird's-eye view of Honfleur and the Normandy Bridge, take the steep, 20-minute walk up to the Côte de Grâce viewpoint—best in the early morning or at sunset. Drivers can follow rue du Puits, and then turn right on rue des Capucins, following *Côte de Grâce* signs. On foot, go past the hotel Les Maisons de Léa (across from Ste. Catherine Church) and up rue du Puits. Turn right (up the hill), following the *piétons* (pedestrians) sign, and climb la Rampe du Mont Joli to see the splendid view. Two hundred yards past the top, the **Chapel of Notre-Dame de Grâce** merits a visit. Built in the early 1600s by the mariners and people of Honfleur, the church oozes seafaring memories. Model boats hang from the ceiling, pictures of boats balance high on the walls, and what's left is decorated by stained-glass images of sailors praying to the Virgin Mary while at sea. Even the holy water basins to the left and right of the entrance are in the shape of seashells.

Just below the chapel, a second lookout point gives a sweeping view of the super-industrial Le Havre, with the Manche (channel) to your left and the Normandy Bridge to your right.

▲**Normandy Bridge (Pont de Normandie)**—The 1.25-mile-long pont de Normandie is the longest cable-stayed bridge in the Western world. This is a key piece of a super-expressway that links the Atlantic ports from Belgium to Spain (allow €5 each way). View the bridge from Honfleur (better from an excursion boat or above the town from the Côte de Grâce viewpoint—see above, and best at night, when bridge is floodlit) and consider visiting the free Exhibition Hall (under tollbooth on Le Havre side, daily 8:00–19:00). The Seine finishes its winding 500-mile journey here, dropping only 1,500 feet from its source. The river flows so slowly that in certain places, a stiff breeze can send it flowing upstream.

SLEEPING

(€1 = about $1.30, country code: 33)
Honfleur is busy on weekends, holidays, and in the summer. English is widely spoken. A few moderate accommodations remain, but most hotels are pretty pricey. Budget travelers should consider the *chambres d'hôte* listed below.

Hotels

$$$ Les Maisons de Léa*** just might charm your socks off with its designer's attention to detail—from country-French wood furnishings, to antiques, to a library room that may keep you inside even in good weather (light meals available). Its 30 rooms are adorable, with elaborate furnishings and Laura Ashley–style decor (small Db-€110, bigger Db-€145–180, suite-€250–290, cottage house for up to 4-€315, across from the church on place Ste. Catherine, tel. 02 31 14 49 49, fax 02 31 89 28 61, www.lesmaisonsdelea.com, contact@lesmaisonsdelea.com).

$$$ Hôtel le Cheval Blanc*** is a waterfront splurge in an old, half-timbered building with port views from all of the 32 unremarkable but pleasant enough rooms (many with queen-size beds and high-tech showers), plus a rare-in-this-town elevator (small Db-€80–115, Db with view-€135–160, bigger Db-€150–200, family rooms-€300–425, includes good buffet breakfast, must cancel by 16:00 the day before or forfeit deposit, 2 quai des Passagers, tel. 02 31 81 65 00, fax 02 31 89 52 80, www.hotel-honfleur.com, lecheval.blanc@wanadoo.fr).

$$$ L'Absinthe Hôtel*** hides seven cushy rooms in a tastefully restored hotel behind the restaurant Le Bistro du Port. Whirlpool tubs, wood-beamed decor, and a cozy lounge with a fireplace make this place worthwhile (Db-€110–140, Db suite-€230, extra bed-€25, 1 rue de la Ville, keys available at L'Absinthe restaurant across alley, tel. 02 31 89 23 23, fax 02 31 89 53 60, www.absinthe.fr, reservation@absinthe.fr).

$$$ **La Maison de Lucie*** offers 10 plush rooms in a quiet and flowery setting. From the serene courtyard to the spa in their underground vault, this is *the* place to relax in style in Honfleur (Db-€150–170, larger Db-€220, two-story cottage-€315, 44 rue des Capucins, tel. 02 31 14 40 40, www.lamaisondelucie.com, info@lamaisondelucie.com).

$$$ **Hôtel du Dauphin**** is Honfleur's best midrange value, with a homey lounge/breakfast room, many stairs, and an Escher-esque floor plan. The 30 rooms—some with open-beam ceilings, most with queen- or king-size beds—are all quite comfortable and well-maintained (Db-€70–95, Tb-€115–127, free Internet access and Wi-Fi, a stone's throw from Ste. Catherine Church at 10 place Pierre Berthelot, tel. 02 31 89 15 53, fax 02 31 89 92 06, www .hoteldudauphin.com, hotel.dudauphin@wanadoo.fr).

$ **Etap Hôtel** is modern, efficient, tight, and cheap, with antiseptically clean rooms (Db-€35–42, €6 for each extra person, reception is closed 11:00–17:00 & 21:00–6:00 but room-renting automat available 24 hours, elevator, across from bus station and main parking lot on rue des Vases, tel. 08 92 68 07 81, fax 02 31 89 77 88, www.etaphotel.com).

Chambres d'Hôte

The TI has a long list of Honfleur's many *chambres d'hôte* (rooms in private homes), but most are too far from the town center. These three are all fine values.

$$ **La Cour Ste. Catherine** is an enchanting bed-and-breakfast run by the gregarious Madame Giaglis ("call me Liliane"). Her six big, modern rooms—each with firm beds and a separate sitting area—surround a perfectly Norman courtyard with a small terrace and fine plantings. The rooms are as cheery as the owner (Db-€70, Tb-€85, Qb-90, includes breakfast, cash only, Internet access, free parking in 2008 with this book, 200 yards up rue du Puits from Ste. Catherine Church at 74 rue du Puits, tel. 02 31 89 42 40, www.giaglis.com, giaglis@wanadoo.fr).

$ **Odile and Jean-Luc**'s five good-value *chambres* are above the Atelier Cedric Eudeline art gallery (though the gallery isn't affiliated with the rooms). The rooms are big, comfortable, and fairly priced (Db-€55, big Tb-€75, Qb-€95, cash only, pick-up at Deauville train station possible if arranged in advance, behind Les Maisons de Léa at 8 rue du Puits, tel. 06 72 98 02 29, j.l.ferey @orange.fr). This place works closely with La Cour Ste. Catherine (above), where you are welcome to take breakfast for €5.

$ Gentle **Madame Bellegarde** offers two simple rooms in her traditional home (Db-€35–40, family-friendly Tb with great bathroom view-€60, cash only, 54 rue St. Léonard, 10-min uphill walk from TI, 3 blocks up from St. Léonard Church in untouristy part of Honfleur, look for small *chambres* sign in window, she'll try to hold a parking spot if you ask, tel. 02 31 89 06 52).

EATING

Eat seafood or cream sauces here. It's a tough choice between the hard-to-resist waterfront tables of the many look-alike places lining the harbor, and eateries with more solid reputations elsewhere in town. Tuesdays are tricky, as many restaurants are closed, though a few good options remain. Trust my dinner suggestions below and consider your hotelier's opinion, but if you want to dine at my first three places, have your hotel call ahead.

P'tit Mareyeur is warm, intimate, all about seafood, and a good value. Reservations are smart (€24 *menu*, try the bouillabaisse *honfleuraise*, closed Mon–Tue and Jan, 4 rue Haute, tel. 02 31 98 84 23, friendly owner Julie speaks some English).

La Terrasse et l'Assiette is a higher-end, dress-up affair with a romantic redbrick-and-timbered interior and outdoor tables facing the church. Locals love this place, so book ahead (€29–48 *menus*, closed Mon–Tue, faces Ste. Catherine Church's left transept, 8 place Ste. Catherine, tel. 02 31 89 31 33).

La Cidrerie is a purely Norman cider bar with award-winning crêpes made in the traditional style, Calvados apple brandy, and an inviting atmosphere for adults and kids, closed Tue–Wed, set back on cathedral side of place Hamelin at #26, tel. 02 31 89 59 85).

Le Bouilland Normand offers a true Norman experience at fair prices (€16–24 *menus*, closed Sun and Wed, outside tables are best, on a charming square next to the recommended L'Absinthe Hôtel on rue de l'Hôtel de Ville, tel. 02 31 89 02 41).

Le Bréard serves exquisite, modern French cuisine presented with care, style, and ingenuity. The chefs have returned to Honfleur after working many years in Paris' finer restaurants, bringing their considerable talents with them. Some will find this place a bit precious, but true foodies will feel right at home (€26–34 *menus*, tel. 02 31 89 53 40, 7 rue du Puits).

Along the Waterfront: If the weather cooperates, or you just need to see the water, slide down to the harbor and table-shop the joints that line the high side. Several places have effective propane heaters that keep outdoor diners happy when it's cool. **La Lipouille** has been the most reliable of the normal restaurants, with reasonable *menus* from €17 and good service (closed Mon–Tue, at #40, tel. 02 31 89 71 90).

Breakfast: If it's even close to sunny, skip your hotel breakfast and enjoy ambience for a cheaper price by eating on the port, where several cafés offer *petit déjeuner* for about €7–12, depending on the *menu* you select. Morning sun and views are best from the high side of the harbor.

Dessert: If you need a Ben & Jerry's fix or a scrumptious dessert crêpe, find the waterfront stand at the southeast corner of Vieux Bassin.

Nightlife: Nightlife in Honfleur centers on the old port. Two bar/cafés with different personalities sit 50 yards apart: **Le Perroquet Vert** entertains a somewhat higher-end crowd, while **L'Albatross** is more down and dirty.

TRANSPORTATION CONNECTIONS

Buses connect Honfleur with Le Havre, Caen, Deauville, and Lisieux (all with direct rail service to Paris), where you'll catch a train to other points. (Coming from Paris, the best train-to-bus transfers are usually in Lisieux or Deauville.) While train and bus service are usually coordinated, ask at Honfleur's bus station for the best connection for your trip (information desk open Mon–Fri 9:00–12:15 & 14:30–18:30, in summer Sat–Sun 9:15–12:15, tel. 02 31 89 28 41, www.busverts.fr). Railpass-holders will save money by connecting through Deauville, as bus fares increase with distance.

From Honfleur by Bus and/or Train to: Caen (express buses 2/day, 1 hr, about €16; more scenic *par la côte* 8/day, 2 hrs, about €13), **Bayeux** (5/day, 2–3 hrs via bus and train, 1-hr express bus to Caen, then 30-min train; or 2-hr bus via the coast to Caen, then 30-min train), **Rouen** (5/day Mon–Sat, 3/day Sun, 2 hrs via bus and train, bus over Normandy Bridge to Le Havre, then transfer to train to Rouen), **Paris'** Gare St. Lazare (13/day, 2–3.5 hrs; 1-hr bus to Lisieux, Deauville, or Le Havre, then 2-hr train to Paris; buses from Honfleur meet most Paris trains).

Bayeux

Only six miles from the D-Day beaches, Bayeux was the first city liberated after the landing. Incredibly, the town was spared the bombs of World War II. After a local convent chaplain made sure London knew that this was not a German headquarters and of no strategic importance, a scheduled bombing raid was canceled—making Bayeux the closest city to the D-Day landing site not destroyed. Even without its famous tapestry and proximity to the D-Day beaches, Bayeux would be worth a visit for its enjoyable town center and awe-inspiring cathedral, beautifully illuminated at night. Bayeux makes a good home base for visiting the area's sights, particularly if you lack a car.

ORIENTATION

Tourist Information

The TI is on a small bridge two blocks north of the cathedral—conveniently located on the pedestrian street that connects place St. Patrice (with its recommended hotels and a Saturday market) and the tapestry. Pick up a town map, the excellent *D-Day Landings and the Battle of Normandy* brochure, bus schedules to the beaches, and regional information (June–Aug Mon–Sat 9:00–19:00, Sun 9:00–13:00 & 14:00–18:00; April–May and Sept–Oct daily 9:30–12:30 & 14:00–18:00; Jan–March and Nov–Dec Mon–Sat 9:30–12:30 & 14:00–17:30; on pont St. Jean leading to rue St. Jean, tel. 02 31 51 28 28, www.bayeux-bessin-tourism.com).

For a **self-guided walking tour,** pick up the brochure at the TI called *Discover Old Bayeux.* Follow the bronze plates embedded in the sidewalk, and look for information plaques with English translations that correspond to the numbers on the map. English-language guided **tours** of old Bayeux are offered in July and August, and sometimes also off-season (€4, 1.5 hours, call for times, tel. 02 31 92 14 21).

Arrival in Bayeux

By Train: It's a 20-minute walk from the train station to the tapestry, and 15 minutes from the tapestry to place St. Patrice (and several recommended hotels). To reach the tapestry, the cathedral, and the hotels, cross the street in front of the station and follow rue Cremel, then make a left on rue Nesmond (follow the huge spire). Allow €7 for a taxi from the train station to any recommended hotel or sight in Bayeux (taxi tel. 02 31 22 10 50).

By Car: Look for the cathedral spires and follow signs reading *Centre-Ville,* and then signs for the *Tapisserie* (tapestry) or your hotel (individual hotels are well-signed from the ring road—wait for yours to appear).

Helpful Hints

Market Days: The Saturday open-air market on place St. Patrice is much larger than the Wednesday market on pedestrian rue St. Jean. Both end by 13:00.

Grocery Store: Marché Plus, at rue St. Jean 14, is next to the recommended Hôtel Churchill (Mon–Sat 7:00–21:00, Sun 8:30–12:00).

Internet Access: Ask at your hotel or the TI (last year's cybercafé is this year's poodle-pampering shop).

Laundry: There's a launderette a block behind the TI, on rue Maréchal Foch. Two launderettes are near place St. Patrice: One is at 4 rue St. Patrice and the other is at 69 rue des

Bayeux

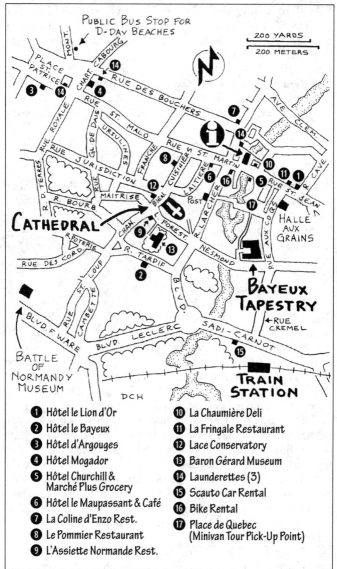

1. Hôtel le Lion d'Or
2. Hôtel le Bayeux
3. Hôtel d'Argouges
4. Hôtel Mogador
5. Hôtel Churchill & Marché Plus Grocery
6. Hôtel le Maupassant & Café
7. La Coline d'Enzo Rest.
8. Le Pommier Restaurant
9. L'Assiette Normande Rest.
10. La Chaumière Deli
11. La Fringale Restaurant
12. Lace Conservatory
13. Baron Gérard Museum
14. Launderettes (3)
15. Scauto Car Rental
16. Bike Rental
17. Place de Quebec (Minivan Tour Pick-Up Point)

Bouchers (both open daily 7:00–21:00).

Bike Rental: The deli **Le Verger de l'Aure,** across from the TI, has what you need (€10/half-day, €15/day, €5 picnic lunch, daily April–Oct 8:00–20:30, closes earlier off-season, 5 rue Larcher, tel. 02 31 92 89 16).

Taxi: Call 06 70 40 07 96.

Car Rental: Bayeux offers few choices. **Scauto** is handiest, just below the train station at the BP gas station (16 boulevard Sadi-Carnot, tel. 02 31 51 18 51, fax 02 31 51 18 30, www .scauto.fr).

SIGHTS

▲▲▲**Bayeux Tapestry (Tapisserie de Bayeux)**—Made of wool embroidered onto linen cloth, this precious-to-historians document is a 70-yard cartoon. The tapes-

try tells the story of William the Conqueror's rise from duke of Normandy to king of England, and shows his victory over Harold at the Battle of Hastings in 1066. Long and skinny, it was designed to hang in the nave of Bayeux's cathedral.

Your visit consists of separate parts, explaining the basic story of the battle three times—which was about right for me: First (after noting the time of the next movie showing at the top of the steps), you'll walk through a room full of mood-setting images into a room that contains a reproduction of the tapestry, with extensive explanations. Then you'll continue to a room showing Norman culture and the impact it ultimately had on England. Next, a 15-minute film in the cinema (up one flight) gives a relaxing, though not essential, dramatization of the battle. Finally, you'll see the real McCoy: the tapestry itself. Before entering, pick up the audioguide (worth the wait and included in the entry ticket), which gives a top-notch, fast-moving, 20-minute, scene-by-scene narration complete with period music. If you lose your place, you'll find subtitles in Latin.

Remember, this is Norman propaganda—the English (the bad guys, referred to as *les goddamns,* after a phrase the French kept hearing them say) are shown with mustaches and long hair; the French (*les* good guys) are clean-cut and clean-shaven—with even the backs of their heads shaved for a better helmet fit.

Cost and Hours: €8, includes audioguide for adults and a special kids' version, daily mid-March–Oct 9:00–18:30, Nov–mid-March 9:30–12:30 & 14:00–18:00, last entry 45 min before closing,

Bayeux History—The Battle of Hastings

Because of this pivotal battle, the most memorable date of the Middle Ages is 1066. England's king, Edward the Confessor, was about to die without an heir. The big question: Who would succeed him—Harold, an English nobleman and the king's brother-in-law, or William, duke of Normandy and the king's cousin? Edward chose William and sent Harold to Normandy to give William the news. On the journey, Harold was captured. To win his release, he promised he would be loyal to William and not contest the decision. To test his loyalty, William sent Harold to battle for him in Brittany. Harold was successful, and William knighted him. To further test his loyalty, William had Harold swear on the relics of the Bayeux cathedral that when Edward died, he would allow William to ascend the throne. Harold returned to England, Edward died... and Harold grabbed the throne.

William, known as William the Bastard, invaded England to claim the throne. Harold met him in southern England at the town of Hastings, where their forces fought a fierce 14-hour battle. Harold was killed, and his Saxon forces were routed. William—now "the Conqueror"—marched to London, claimed his throne, and became king of England as well as duke of Normandy.

The advent of a Norman king of England muddied the political waters and set in motion 400 years of conflict between England and France—not to be resolved until the end of the Hundred Years' War (about 1450). The Norman conquest of England brought that country into the European mainstream (but still no euros). The Normans established a strong central English government. Historians speculate that had William not succeeded, England would have remained on the fringe of Europe (like Scandinavia), and French culture (and language) would have prevailed in the New World. Hmmm.

Normandy

tel. 02 31 51 25 50. Arrive by 9:00 or late in the day to avoid crowds. When buying your ticket, find out the English film times if you want to see the 15-minute film. To minimize congestion in the actual tapestry hall, try to see the film first, exit the way you entered, and backtrack to see the reproduction before the original tapestry (cinemagoers pile into the original tapestry room after each film).

▲▲**Bayeux Cathedral**—This massive building dominates Bayeux. As you approach, notice its two towers—originally Romanesque, capped later with tall Gothic spires. The little rectangular stone house atop one tower was the watchman's home, from which he'd keep an eye out for incoming English troops during the Hundred

Years' War...and for Germans five centuries later (it didn't work—Germans took the town in 1940). Bayeux was liberated on D-Day plus one, June 7. About the only casualty was the German look-out—shot while doing just that from the window of this house. The west facade is structurally Romanesque, but with a decorative Gothic "curtain" added. There's an information board about the cathedral in the corner of the small square in front.

Walk inside. The view of the **nave** from the top of the steps shows a mix of Romanesque and Gothic. Historians believe the Bayeux tapestry originally hung here. Imagine it proudly circling the Norman congregation, draped around the nave from the arches. The nave's huge, round lower arches are Romanesque (11th century) and decorated with the same zigzag pattern that characterizes this "Norman" art in England. The nave is so brightly lit because of the huge windows above, in the Gothic half of the nave. The glass was originally richly colored (see the rare surviving 13th-century bits in the high central window above the altar). The finest example of 13th-century "Norman" Gothic is in the choir (the fancy area behind the central altar). Each of the columns is decorated with Romanesque carvings. But those carvings lie under a Gothic-style stone exterior (with characteristic tall, thin lines adding a graceful verticality to the overall feel of the interior).

For maximum 1066 atmosphere, step into the spooky crypt (below the central altar), which was used originally as a safe spot for the cathedral's relics. The crypt displays two interesting columns and capitals with fine Romanesque carving. During a reinforcement of the nave, these two columns were replaced. Workers removed the Gothic veneer and discovered their true inner Romanesque beauty. Orange angel-musicians add color to this somber room (free, daily July–Aug 8:30–19:00, Sept–June 8:30–18:00). The cathedral is beautifully illuminated after dark.

Lace Conservatory (Conservatoire de la Dentelle)—Notable for its carved 15th-century facade, the Adam and Eve house (find Adam, Eve, and the snake) offers a free chance to watch workers design and weave intricate lace, just as artisans did in the 1600s. You can also see examples of lace from the past (free, daily 10:00–12:30 & 14:00–18:00, across from cathedral entrance, tel. 02 31 92 73 80).

Baron Gérard Museum—The museum, housed in Hôtel du Doyen outside the cathedral's south transept, has a modest painting gallery and a collection of porcelain and lace (€2.60, or free with ticket to tapestry, daily 10:00–12:30 & 14:00–18:00, July–Aug until 19:00 with no midday closing).

▲Battle of Normandy Memorial Museum (Musée Memorial de la Bataille de Normandie)—Recently renovated, this museum provides a good overview of WWII's Battle of Normandy, with an enlightening 25-minute film, and some tanks, jeeps, and uniforms.

The museum's walls are covered in long and informative explanations in both French and English (those in a hurry should read the red signs and skim the rest). This museum is only worthwhile if you haven't visited the Caen Memorial Museum (€6.50, daily May–mid-Sept 9:30–18:30, mid-Sept–April 10:00–12:30 & 14:00–18:00, on Bayeux's ring road, 20 min on foot from center, tel. 02 31 51 46 90, www.normandiememoire.com). A **British War Cemetery,** the final resting place of 4,100 fallen soldiers, is located across the street.

SLEEPING

In Bayeux
(€1 = about $1.30, country code: 33)

Hotels are a good value here. Drivers should also see "Sleeping" under Arromanches, page 230.

Near the Tapestry

$$$ Hôtel Churchill***, on a traffic-free street across from the TI, could not be more central, and has 32 plush rooms with fine furnishings and tasteful art. The professional owners, the Heberts, were made for this business, and will take excellent care of you (Db-€105–120, Tb-€145, Qb-€160, easy parking, most central of my listings at 14 rue St. Jean, tel. 02 31 21 31 80, fax 02 31 21 41 66, www.hotel-churchill.fr, info@hotel-churchill.fr)

$$$ Hôtel le Lion d'Or*** is Bayeux's classy Old World hotel, with a palm-tree-lined courtyard, easy parking, professional service, comfy leather lounges, and an elegant restaurant (small Db-€95, bigger Db-€115, still bigger Db-€145, suite Tb-€215, extra bed-€30, no elevator, 71 rue St. Jean, tel. 02 31 92 06 90, fax 02 31 22 15 64, www.liondor-bayeux.fr, lion.d-or.bayeux@wanadoo.fr).

$$ Hôtel le Bayeux**, the closest hotel I list to the train station (600 yards), is a simple place run by chatty (French only) Madame Bajum (who will do your laundry for €5). It caters to student groups with long halls, bright colors, and 29 clean, unimaginative rooms at fair rates (Db-€50–63, Tb-€65–78, Qb-€80–93, some family rooms with bunk beds, easy parking, a block from cathedral's right transept at 9 rue Tardif, tel. 02 31 92 70 08, fax 02 31 21 15 74, www.lebayeux.net, lebayeux@wanadoo.fr).

Near Place St. Patrice

These two good hotels are just off the big place St. Patrice (easy parking), but a 10-minute walk up rue St. Martin from the TI (a 15-min walk to the tapestry).

$$$ Hôtel d'Argouges** (dar-goo-zhah) makes a good first impression as you enter...and doesn't let you down. Named for its builder, Lord d'Argouges, this tranquil retreat has a mini-château feel, with classy public spaces and a lovely private garden. The hotel is run by helpful and formal owners, Monsieur and Madame Ropartz (Sb-€52–84, Db-€68–102, fine family suites-€130–184, deluxe mega-suite for up to 6 good for two couples-€200–295, extra bed-€15, includes breakfast (except Nov–April when breakfast is optional and €8), parking-€2, just off huge place St. Patrice at 21 rue St. Patrice, tel. 02 31 92 88 86, fax 02 31 92 69 16, hotel .dargouges@orange.fr).

$ Hôtel Mogador** is a good two-star bet, with welcoming Monsieur Mencaroni at the helm. Choose between cozy, wood-beamed rooms on the busy square, or quiet, more colorful, more modern rooms off the street. There are no public areas beyond the small breakfast room (Sb-€44, Db-€49–54, Tb-€64, Qb-€74, good breakfast-€6, 20 rue Alain Chartier at place St. Patrice, tel. 02 31 92 24 58, fax 02 31 92 24 85, hotel.mogador @wanadoo.fr).

$ Hôtel le Maupassant is a no-star, no-frills place, but its few rooms above a central café are sufficiently comfortable. The bartender doubles as the receptionist (S-€29, Db-€40, 19 rue St. Martin, tel. 02 31 92 28 53, fax 02 31 92 35 40).

Near Bayeux

Drivers will pass scads of good-value *chambres d'hôte* on the way from Bayeux to Arromanches, and on the road from Arromanches to the American Cemetery. (See also "D-Day Beaches," page 227.)

$$ Château de Lignerolles is run by Roel (pronounced "rule") and his charming wife Pia, who have followed their bliss and moved from Holland to Normandy. Their lovely and isolated accommodations (outside tiny Planquery, between Bayeux and St. Lô) has modern decor, with wonderful beds and linens in four rooms, three with bathroom down the hall. There are no restaurants nearby—though Bayeux is just a 15-minute drive (D-€70–75, Db-€80, Tb-€105, 2-night minimum, cash only, includes great breakfast; from Bayeux, take D-572 toward St. Lô and turn left to Balleroy, then stay left on D-13, heading toward Tilly-sur-Seulles; tel. 02 31 51 98 14, mobile 06 76 50 94 27, www.victorytours.com, ch.de.lignerolles@wanadoo.fr). Roel's "hobby" for the last 20 years has been the history of D-Day and the Battle of Normandy. (His 15 yards of history books on the subject are proof of his dedication.) Roel leads tours of the D-Day beaches (see "Victory Tours" under "Getting Around the D-Day Beaches," page 226).

$$ La Ferme du Pressoir is a lovely, traditional B&B on a big working farm, immersed in Norman landscapes about 15 minutes south of Bayeux. The five rooms and kind owners (Jacques and Odile) are vintage French (Db-€80, Tb-€100, Qb-€120, includes good breakfast, tel. 02 41 53 04 96, Le Haut St. Louet, just off A-84, exit at Villers-Bocage, www.bandbnormandie.com, lafermedupressoir@bandbnormandie.com).

EATING

Drivers can also consider the short drive to Arromanches for seaside options (see page 230).

On or near Traffic-Free Rue St. Jean

This street is lined with cafés, *crêperies,* and inexpensive dining options.

La Chaumière is the best charcuterie (deli) in town; you'll find salads, quiches, and prepared dishes to go (closed 13:00–15:00, Sun afternoons, and Mon; otherwise open until 19:30, on rue St. Jean across from Hôtel Churchill). The grocery store across the street has what you need to complete your picnic.

La Fringale works for a simple, cheap meal on this pedestrian street (€9 salads, €15 *menu,* closed Wed, indoor and outdoor seating, 43 rue St. Jean, tel. 02 31 21 34 40).

Hôtel le Lion d'Or is where locals and Brits go for a special meal, in a big, elegant dining room (€29, €40, and €50 *menus,* small portions, 71 rue St. Jean; see "Sleeping—Near the Tapestry," page 219).

La Coline d'Enzo is where discerning diners should go for Norman nouvelle cuisine at fair prices. The dining room is an appealing blend of modern and traditional decor, with gracious owner Delfine in charge. A few tables line the side street outside (*menus* from €24, closed Sun–Mon, 2 rue des Bouchers, tel. 02 31 92 03 01).

Near the Cathedral

L'Assiette Normande is a fun and popular place where you'll dine well for a steal. It's kid-friendly and easygoing, and serves well-presented local dishes in rooms that sprawl over several levels (€16–30 *menus,* closed Mon, 3 rue des Chanoines, tel. 02 31 22 04 61).

Le Pommier is a fine place to sample regional products with clever twists in a relaxed yet refined atmosphere. Owner Thierry mixes old and new with his cuisine and decor. His *lotte* (whitefish) is excellent no matter how he prepares it, and his meat dishes are *très* tasty (*menus* from €22, open daily, 38 rue des Cuisiniers, tel. 02 31 21 52 10).

If you'd prefer *le pizza,* a few atmospheric **pizza places** can be found near the recommended Le Pommier on rue des Cuisiniers.

TRANSPORTATION CONNECTIONS

From Bayeux by Train to: Paris' Gare St. Lazare (11/day, 2.5 hrs, 3 require change in Caen), **Amboise** (12/day, 5–6 hrs, change in Caen and Tours, or Paris-Montparnasse and Tours' St. Pierre des Corps), **Rouen** (12/day, 3.5–4.5 hrs, change in Paris' Gare St. Lazare), **Caen** (10/day, 15 min), **Honfleur** (5/day, 2–3 hrs via train and bus; 30-min train to Caen, then 1 hr express bus to Honfleur or more scenic 2 hr bus via the coast; or 1 hr train to Lisieux then 1 hr bus to Honfleur; for bus information, call 02 31 89 28 41), **Pontorson–Mont St. Michel** (2–3/day, 2 hrs to Pontorson, then bus to Mont St. Michel).

By Bus to the D-Day Beaches: Bus Verts du Calvados offers minimal service to D-Day beaches with stops in Bayeux at place St. Patrice and at the train station (schedules at TI, tel. 08 10 21 42 14, www.busverts.fr). Line #74 runs to Arromanches (2/day, 20 min), and line #70 serves the American Cemetery and Vierville-sur-Mer (4/day in summer, 2/day off-season, 35 min to American Cemetery, 40 min to Vierville-sur-Mer). Bus Verts runs an all-day summer bus excursion to key D-Day sights (called "Le D-Day line," allow about €18; in 2007, departures were on Mon, Wed, and Sat only—from Bayeux station at 9:30 and place St. Patrice at 9:40, returning at about 17:30; confirm at the TI).

D-Day Beaches

The 75 miles of Atlantic coast north of Bayeux, stretching from Ste. Marie-du-Mont to Ouistreham, is littered with WWII museums, monuments, cemeteries, and battle remains left in tribute to the courage of the British, Canadian, and American armies who successfully carried out the largest military operation in history: D-Day (*Jour J* in French). It was on these serene beaches, at the crack of dawn on June 6, 1944, that the Allies finally gained a foothold in France, and Nazi Europe began to crumble.

> *"The first 24 hours of the invasion will be decisive....The fate of Germany depends on the outcome....For the Allies, as well as Germany, it will be the longest day."*
> —Field Marshal Erwin Rommel to his aide, April 22, 1944 (from the movie *The Longest Day*)

Planning Your Time
You'll probably want at least one full day to explore the D-Day beaches. If you only have one day, I'd spend it entirely on the beaches and—regretfully—miss the Caen Memorial Museum.

D-Day Beaches

ENGLISH CHANNEL

5 MILES
10 KM

ARROMANCHES

COURSEULLES + JUNO BEACH CENTER

SWORD BEACH

OUISTREHAM

TO CABOURG

JUNO BEACH

GOLD BEACH

D-514

TO HONFLEUR (VIA COAST)

TO HONFLEUR (VIA AUTOROUTE), ROUEN + PARIS

D-7

CAEN

RING FREEWAY

A-13

D-404

D-79

CANADIAN CEMETERY

CAEN MEMORIAL MUSEUM (EXIT #7)

US CEMETERY

POINTE DU HOC

VIERVILLE-SUR-MER

OMAHA BEACH

GUN BATTERY

LONGUES-SUR-MER

RYES + ❺

❸

N-13

D-12

D-6

D-516

TO MONT ST MICHEL

D-9

TILLY-SUR-SEULLES

D-514

ST. LAURENT

LA CAMBE

D-113

GERMAN CEMETERY

N-13

ISIGNY-SUR-MER

TO STE. MERE EGLISE

UTAH BEACH

D-514

BAYEUX

D-6

D-572

TO ST. LO

BALLEROY

❶

D-13

TO VILLERS-BOCAGE, A-84 + ❷

❹

AUTOROUTE (TOLL)

OTHER ROADS

❶ Château de Lignerolles B&B
❷ To La Ferme du Pressoir B&B
❸ Le Mas Normand B&B
❹ Hôtel du Casino
❺ André & Madeleine Sebire B&B

Normandy

Countdown to D-Day

1939 On September 1, Adolf Hitler invades Poland, sparking World War II.

1940 Germany's "Blitzkrieg" ("lightning war") quickly overwhelms France, Nazis goose-step down the avenue des Champs-Elysées, and the country is divided into Occupied France (the north) and Vichy France (the south, ruled by right-wing French). Just like that, virtually the entire Continent is fascist.

1941 The Allies (Britain, the Soviet Union, and others) peck away at the fringes of "fortress Europe." The Soviets repel Hitler's invasion at Moscow, while the Brits (with American aid) battle German U-boats for control of the seas. On December 7, Japan bombs the US naval base at Pearl Harbor, Hawaii. The US enters the war against Japan and its ally Germany.

1942 Three crucial battles—at Stalingrad, El-Alamein, and Guadalcanal—weaken the German forces and their ally, Japan. The victorious tank battle at El-Alamein in the deserts of North Africa soon gives the Allies a jumping-off point (Tunis) for the first assault on the Continent.

1943 150,000 Americans and Brits, under the command of George Patton and Bernard ("Monty") Montgomery, land in Sicily and begin working their way north through Italy. Meanwhile, Germany has to fend off tenacious Soviets on their eastern front.

1944 On June 6, 1944, the Allies launch "Operation Overlord," better known as D-Day. Three million Allies and six million tons of *matériel* had been amassed in England in preparation for the biggest fleet-led invasion in history—across the English Channel to France, then

(If you want to squeeze in the museum, visit it on your way to or from the beaches—but remember that the American Cemetery closes at 17:00.) I've listed the D-Day sights in the order of importance, with the most visit-worthy first. Naturally, most Americans prefer to focus on the American sector (west of Arromanches), rather than the British and Canadian sectors (east of Arromanches)—which have been overbuilt with resorts, making it harder to re-create the events of June 1944.

By Car: Begin on the cliffs above Arromanches and see the movie at the Arromanches 360° Theater to set your mood. Walk or drive a quarter-mile downhill to the town and visit Port Winston and the D-Day Landing Museum, then continue west to Longues-

eastward to Berlin. The Germans, hunkered down in northern France, knew an invasion was imminent, but the Allies kept it top secret. On the night of June 5, 150,000 soldiers board ships and planes, not knowing where they are headed until they're under way. Each one carries a note from General Dwight D. Eisenhower: "The tide has turned. The free men of the world are marching together to victory."

At 6:30 in the morning on June 6, 1944, Americans spill out of troop transports into the cold waters off a beach in Normandy, code-named Omaha. The weather is bad, seas are rough, and the prep bombing has failed. The soldiers, many seeing their first action, are dazed, confused, and weighed down by heavy packs. Nazi machine guns pin them against the sea. Slowly, they crawl up the beach on their stomachs. More than a thousand die. They hold on until the next wave of transports arrives.

All day long, Allied confusion does battle with German indecision—the Nazis never really counter-attack, thinking D-Day is just a ruse, not the main invasion. By day's end, the Allies have taken several beaches along the Normandy coast and begun building artificial harbors, providing a tiny port-of-entry for the reconquest of Europe. The stage is set for a quick and easy end to the war. Right.

1945 After liberating Paris (August 26, 1944), the Allied march on Berlin bogs down, hit by poor supply lines, bad weather, and the surprising German counterpunch at the Battle of the Bulge. Finally, in the spring, Soviet soldiers take Berlin, Hitler shoots himself, and—after five long years of war—Europe is free.

sur-Mer. Spend your afternoon visiting the American Cemetery, walking on the beach at Vierville-sur-Mer, and seeing the Pointe du Hoc Ranger Monument. Make a quick stop at the German Military Cemetery on your way back. Canadians may want to start at the Juno Beach Center and Canadian Cemetery (in Courseulles-sur-Mer, 10 min east of Arromanches), then pick up the itinerary described above.

Sans **Car:** It's easiest to take a minivan tour from Bayeux or combine a visit to the Caen Memorial Museum with their guided minivan tour of the beaches for an excellent full day. Public transport is available, though limited to certain sights; it does not work for the Canadian sights.

Getting Around the D-Day Beaches

On Your Own: Though the minivan excursions listed below offer superb history lessons—drawing Americans and Canadians out of their cars—**renting a car** is ideal, particularly for three or more people (see Bayeux's "Helpful Hints" for rental suggestions, page 216). Park in monitored locations at the sights, since break-ins have been a problem—particularly at the American Cemetery. Hardy souls can **bike** between the sights (though distances are enough to discourage most). Limited **bus service** links Bayeux, the coastal town of Arromanches, and the most impressive sights of D-Day (see Bus Verts du Calvados information under Bayeux's "Transportation Connections," page 222).

By Taxi: Taxi minivans shuttle up to seven people between the key sights at surprisingly fair rates. Approximate prices per taxi (not per person): €20 one-way from Bayeux to Arromanches, €35 round-trip with one hour of wait time; €30 one-way from Bayeux to the American Cemetery, €45 round-trip with one hour of wait time; and €65 round-trip for the American Cemetery and Pointe du Hoc with two hours of total wait time at the sights (other combinations possible, 50 percent surcharge after 19:00 and on Sun, taxi tel. 02 31 92 92 40).

By Minivan Tour: Several small companies offer excursions to the D-Day beaches from Bayeux or Caen for about €40–50 per person for a half-day, €80 per person for all day, and about €450 for groups of up to eight (all prices include entry fees, some levy a surcharge of about €15 for Caen pickup). Most companies give only all-day tours, and none (except the **Caen Memorial Museum**) offer half-day tours during busy periods. Some companies provide excellent commentary to these moving sights, while others are so-so. The following companies get rave reviews from my readers (book them ahead as they are all tiny operations):

British-owned **Battlebus** has top-notch guides, offers a full slate of tour options from Bayeux (including family-friendly tours), and gets the best reviews from historians (full-day tours only in peak season, tel. 02 31 22 28 82 or 06 72 02 50 74, www.battlebus.fr, tours@battlebus.fr).

Victory Tours is a one-man show run by friendly Dutchman Roel; he's informal but very informative, covering sights mostly in the American sector (departs from Bayeux only, www.victorytours.com; see Château de Lignerolles listing on page 220).

The **Caen Memorial Museum** offers well-done tours of the American and Canadian sectors in combination with a visit to their museum; it's handy for those who have limited time (see museum listing on page 236).

Overlordtours offers a French perspective but less content (based in Bayeux, tel. 06 70 21 43 42, www.overlordtour.com,

Normandy

achesnel@wanadoo.fr).

D-Day Battle Tours is for true enthusiasts. British owner and zealot Ellwood von Siebold has realized his dream by moving here and living out his fantasy: teaching about the D-Day invasion. He dresses in WWII army gear, drives a WWII Dodge Command Car (very cool), bought a home where an American paratrooper landed in the garden, and owns a café in Ste. Mère Eglise (C-47 Café) that has the rudder of a WWII-era C-47 plane as its centerpiece. His specialty is the American sector, particularly the Pointe du Hoc and Ste. Mère Eglise areas. He prefers guiding all-day tours, though he's happy to spend two hours explaining the invasion and the events at Ste. Mère Eglise—from his house across from the famous church (see description on page 234). Consider this option if you really want to learn about the invasion and have only a few hours to devote to a guide, but call ahead to reserve (4 rue Eisenhower, Ste. Mère Eglise, tel. 02 33 94 44 13, fax 02 33 94 13 42, www.ddaybattletours.com, ellwood@ddaybattletours.com).

SLEEPING

Along the D-Day Beaches
(€1 = about $1.30, country code: 33)
For more options, see "Sleeping" in the Arromanches section, page 230.

$$ Le Mas Normand, a few minutes east of Arromanches, is deservedly popular, with adorable rooms and an adorable owner (Mylène). It's an 18th-century, white stone home with a pretty yard and no smoking allowed (Db-€60–80, Tb-€100, Qb-€115, includes breakfast, Wi-Fi; book ahead for Christian's home-cooked, gourmet dinner including wine, cider, and coffee-€35; requires 4 people, kid menus available, well-signed in Ver-sur-Mer at 8 impasse de la Rivière, tel. & fax 02 31 21 97 75, www.ohotes .com/lemasnormand, lemasnormand@wanadoo.fr).

$$ Hôtel du Casino** is a good place to be one with the D-Day invasions and Omaha Beach. This average-looking hotel is surprisingly comfortable and sits alone overlooking the beach in Vierville-sur-Mer, between the American Cemetery and the Pointe du Hoc. Sleeping here comes with formal owners, sand, waves, seagulls, and your own thoughts. It's worth requesting one of the several rooms with good views (Db-€65–71, extra bed-€16, pebble walls in the halls, view restaurant with *menus* from €22, café bar on the beach below, tel. 02 31 22 41 02, fax 02 31 22 41 12, hotel-du-casino@orange.fr).

$ André and Madeleine Sebire run a working farmhouse, with four homey, cheap rooms and a pleasant garden. It's worth the effort to track it down in tiny Ryes (between Bayeux and

Arromanches) at Ferme du Clos Neuf (Sb-€30, Db-€35, Tb-€40, includes breakfast, tel. 02 31 22 32 34, emmanuelle.sebire @wanadoo.fr, no English spoken except when daughter Emmanuelle is there on the weekends). Try these directions from Arromanches: Take D-87, enter Ryes, and pass the church on the left; then, at the first junction, turn right onto rue de la Forge (look for the faded *Chambres* signs), and continue until you cross a tiny bridge. Turn right just after the bridge onto rue de la Tringale, and follow that road until you see a small sign on the right to *Le Clos Neuf*. Park near the tractors. If the Sebires prove too elusive, call from Ryes and they'll come get you.

Arromanches

This small town was ground zero for the D-Day invasion. Almost overnight, it sprouted the immense Port Winston, which gave the Allies a foothold in Normandy, allowing them to begin their victorious push to Berlin and end World War II. Today, you'll find a good museum, an evocative beach and bluff (with an interesting film), and a touristy but fun little town that offers a pleasant cocktail of war memories, cotton candy, and beachfront trinket shops. The population of tiny Arromanches finally reached 500 a few years ago...about the same as on June 5, 1944. Arromanches makes a good base for sightseeing (accommodations listed below).

ORIENTATION

Tourist Information
The TI is at the opposite end of the parking lot from the museum on avenue Maréchal Joffre. They have the well-done *D-Day Landings and the Battle of Normandy* brochure, bus schedules, a photo booklet of area hotels, and easy parking (daily 10:00–12:00 & 14:00–17:00, June–Aug 9:30–18:00, tel. 02 31 22 36 45, www .arromanches.com).

Arrival in Arromanches
The main parking lot, on the road toward Courseulles-sur-Mer, costs €2. If traffic seems bad, you can park at the Iveco market (across from Mountbatten Hôtel) and stroll three blocks down to the museum and town center (and save the €2 parking fee).

Helpful Hints
The main **post office** (PTT)—which has an **ATM**—is opposite the museum. There's a little **supermarket** a few blocks above the beach, just below the main post office. **Internet access** is possible

at the TI. To get a **taxi,** you'll need to call one based in Bayeux (tel. 02 31 92 92 40).

SIGHTS

Artificial Harbor—Start at the cliffs above the town. (Drive two minutes toward Courseulles-sur-Mer and pay €2 to park, hike 10 min uphill from Arromanches; or take the free white train from the museum to the top of the bluff, weekends and summers only.) Wander out to the cliffs and look to the sea.

Beyond Arromanches to the left is the American sector, with Omaha Beach and then Utah Beach (notice the cliffs); below and to the right lie the British, French, and Canadian sectors (with the more level terrain).

Look and ponder how, from the makeshift harbor below, the liberation of Europe commenced. On June 7, 1944, 17 old ships crossed the English Channel under their own steam, and were sunk by their crews from bow to stern, forming the first shelter. Then, 115 football-field-size cement blocks (called "Mulberries") were towed across the channel and sunk, creating a four-mile-long breakwater located a mile and a half offshore—a port the size of Dover, England. Finally, seven floating steel "pierheads" with extendable legs were set up; they were linked to shore by four mile-long floating roads made of concrete pontoons. Anti-aircraft guns were set up on the pontoons. Within just six days of operation, 54,000 vehicles, 326,000 troops, and 110,000 tons of goods had been delivered. An Allied toehold on Normandy was secure. Eleven months later, Hitler was dead and the war was over.

The **Arromanches 360° Theater** shows a moving film, *The Price of Freedom*, with D-Day footage that flashes back from quiet farmlands and beaches to June 1944. It's a noisy montage of videos on a 360-degree screen—stand as near to the center as you can (€4, Feb–Dec daily 10:00–18:00, closed Jan, 2 shows/hr at :10 and :40 past the hour, 20 min, tel. 02 31 22 30 30).

▲▲**Port Winston and the D-Day Landing Museum (Musée du Débarquement)**—The world's first prefab harbor was created by the British in Arromanches. Since it was Churchill's brainchild, it was named Port Winston. The D-Day Landing Museum, which faces the still-visible remains of the temporary harbor, provides an instructive hour-long visit. As you visit this little museum, imagine the remarkable undertaking that resulted in this harbor being built in just 12 days, while battles raged all around. Through models, maps, mementos, and two short videos, this low-tech exhibit tells the story of the port's creation. One video (8 min, ground floor) recalls D-Day. The other (15 min, upstairs) features the construction of the temporary port—ask for English times (€6.50, daily

May–Sept 9:00–18:30, Oct–Dec and Feb–April 9:30–12:30 & 13:30–17:30, closed Jan, pick up English flier at door, tel. 02 31 22 34 31, www.normandy1944.com).

The most thought-provoking experience in town is to wander the beach among the concrete and rusted litter of the battle, and be thankful that all you hear are birds and surf.

SLEEPING

(€1 = about $1.30, country code: 33)
Arromanches, with its pinwheels and seagulls, has a salty beach-town ambience that makes it a good overnight stop. For evening fun, try the cheery bar at **Hôtel d'Arromanches-Restaurant "Le Pappagall"** (see below), or, for more of a nightclub scene, have a drink at **Pub Marie Celeste,** around the corner on rue de la Poste.

$$ Hôtel de la Marine* has one of the best locations for D-Day enthusiasts, with point-blank views to the artificial harbor site from most of its 28 quite comfy, modern, non-smoking rooms (non-view Db-€62, view Db-€74–90, most are €90, Tb-€100–135, good family rooms for up to five-€146–176, elevator, fine restaurant, half-board encouraged in busy periods, quai du Canada, tel. 02 31 22 34 19, fax 02 31 22 98 80, www.hotel-de-la-marine.fr, hotel.de.la.marine@wanadoo.fr).

$$ Hôtel d'Arromanches-Restaurant "Le Pappagall"** is a reasonable value, with nine smartly appointed rooms, tight stairways and halls, and a cheery restaurant run by hardworking Alain and Rosa (Db-€69–76, Tb-€98, includes breakfast, 2 rue Colonel René Michel, tel. 02 31 22 36 26, fax 02 31 22 23 29, www.hoteldarromanches.fr, hoteldarromanche@ifrance.com).

$ Mountbatten Hôtel**, located a long block up from the water, is an eight-room, two-story, motel-esque place with generous-size, clean, and good-value rooms. Upstairs rooms have a little view over the sea (Db-€51–61, easy parking, short block below the main post office at 20 boulevard Gilbert Longuet, tel. 02 31 22 59 70, fax 02 31 22 50 30, www.hotelmountbatten.com, mountbattenhotel@wanadoo.fr).

EATING

You'll find cafés, *crêperies,* and a few shops selling sandwiches to go (ideal for beachfront picnics). The two restaurants below offer reliable dining.

Hôtel d'Arromanches-Restaurant "Le Pappagall" has great mussels, *"les* feesh and cheeps," salads, and a full menu at fair prices (€17–26 *menus,* family-friendly, may be closed on Thu, see hotel listing above).

Hôtel de la Marine allows you to dine or drink in style on the water. The cuisine is as refined as the views (*menus* from €22, nice bar, daily, see hotel listing above).

TRANSPORTATION CONNECTIONS

From Arromanches by Bus to Bayeux: Catch bus #74 (4/day summer, 2/day off-season, 20-min ride). The bus stop is across from the main post office, four long blocks above the sea.

American D-Day Sights West of Arromanches

▲**Longues-sur-Mer Gun Battery**—Four German bunkers with guns intact, left to guard against seaborne attacks on the city, stand a 10-minute drive west of Arromanches (follow signs reading *Port en Bessin*; once in Longues-sur-Mer, follow *Batterie* signs). The guns, 300 yards inland, were arranged in a semicircle to maximize the firing range east and west, and are the only original guns remaining in place in the D-Day region. They originally formed a critical link in Hitler's Atlantic Wall defense, which ran from Norway to the Pyrénées. The guns could fire up to 13 miles at great accuracy, and were a major obstacle to the landings at Omaha and Gold beaches. (American and British forces were pounded from this site.) The lone observation bunker (on the cliffs) directed the firing; field telephones were connected to the gun batteries by underground wires. Head to the bunker to appreciate the strategic view over the channel. From here, you can walk 15 minutes or drive down to the water by continuing on the small road past the parking lot (great coastal views, including the remains of Port Winston at Arromanches. The site is always open and free (€5 booklet helpful, skip the €6 tour).

▲▲▲**WWII Normandy American Cemetery and Memorial**—Crowning a bluff just above Omaha Beach and the eye of the D-Day storm, 9,387 brilliant white-marble crosses and Stars of David glow in memory of Americans who gave their lives to free Europe on the beaches below. You'll find this stirring sight in Colleville, near St. Laurent.

First, stop by the Visitors' Office to pick up an English information sheet. Read the 1956 letter from the French president (on the wall above the fireplace), which eloquently expresses the feeling of gratitude the French still have for the US. The attendant at the computer terminal has a database that can provide ready access to the story of any serviceman who died in Normandy.

Walk past the memorial and cemetery to the bluff that overlooks the piece of Normandy beach called "that embattled shore—portal of freedom." It's quiet and peaceful today, but imagine the horrific carnage of June 6, 1944. Steps lead down to the beautiful beach below. A walk on the beach is a powerful experience (also see below, under "Vierville-sur-Mer").

Walk back to the memorial, where you'll see giant reliefs of the Battle of Normandy and the Battle of Europe etched on the walls. Behind that is the semicircular Garden of the Missing, with the names of 1,557 soldiers who were never found. A small metal knob next to the name indicates one whose body was eventually found—there aren't many.

Finally, wander among the peaceful and poignant sea of headstones. Notice the names, home states, and dates of death inscribed on each. Immediately after the war, all the dead were buried in temporary cemeteries. In the mid-1950s, the families of the soldiers decided whether their loved ones should remain with their comrades or be brought home (61 percent opted for repatriation). Officers (including General Theodore Roosevelt, Jr.) were disproportionately left here. Their families knew they'd want to be buried alongside the men with whom they fought and died. Two of the Niland brothers, now famous from *Saving Private Ryan,* are buried here.

France has given the US permanent free use of this 172-acre site. It is immaculately maintained by the American Battle Monuments Commission (free, daily 9:00–17:00, park carefully as break-ins have been a problem, tel. 02 31 51 62 00, www.abmc.gov).

▲**Vierville-sur-Mer**—This worthwhile detour for drivers allows direct access onto Omaha Beach. From the American Cemetery, drive west along D-514 into St. Laurent, then follow *Vierville par la Côte* signs to the beach. A right turn leads to **Le Ruquet** (where the road ends), a good place to appreciate the Allied soldiers' challenge on D-Day. The small bunker and gun above the parking area protected this easiest access point inland from Omaha Beach. It was here that the Americans established their first road inland. Find your way out to the beach and stroll to the right, below the American Cemetery, to better understand the overwhelming assignment that American forces were handed on June 6. Imagine landing in a small flat-bottomed boat, cheek-to-jowl with other soldiers, all of you weighed down with wet, heavy packs and guns.

The boat door drops open, and you run for your life through water and sand onto this open beach while Germans fire on you at will from above. Twelve hundred American soldiers died on this beach the first day alone. As you walk, notice the scattered remains of rusted metal objects, and try to imagine their purpose. At least 150,000 tons of metal were taken from these beaches after WWII, and they still didn't get it all.

Take a left turn where the road from St. Laurent meets the beach, and head along the beach toward the Pointe de la Percé cliff, which, from here, looks very Pointe du Hoc–like (American Army Rangers mistook this cliff for Pointe du Hoc, costing them time and lives). Park near Hôtel Casino. It was here that the Americans tried to assemble a floating bridge and their own artificial harbor (à la Arromanches), but the weather and tides did not cooperate. Have a seaside drink or lunch at the Casino's café and consider a stroll along the beach toward the jutting Pointe de la Percé (best at lower tides). You may see tractors doing double duty pulling boats into and out of the sea.

As you leave Vierville-sur-Mer to the west, you'll pass the very pontoon bridge that was to be assembled at this beach. During the fighting, it was moved to Arromanches and used as a second off-loading ramp. It was discovered only a few years ago...in a junk-yard.

▲▲Pointe du Hoc Ranger Monument—This was the Germans' most heavily fortified position along the coast, thanks to its strategic location. For the American landings to succeed, the Allies determined that it was essential to take out this cliffside German battery, which could punish American forces attempting to land at Utah and Omaha beaches. For this task, 300 US Army Rangers were hand-picked to attempt a castle-style assault of the German-occupied cliffs, using grappling hooks and ladders borrowed from London fire departments. Try to imagine a fire-engine ladder extending from a bobbing boat in the water far below, and men climbing it to reach the top of the cliff in the heat of the battle. (I can't.) Only about a third of the Rangers survived the vertical assault. After finally succeeding in their task, the Rangers learned that the German guns they had come to neutralize had been moved. Still, the taking of this jutting cliff was important to securing the safe landing of American forces.

The large monument at the end of the bluff is the Ranger "Dagger," planted firmly in the ground. The German bunkers and the bombed-out landscape remain just as they were found. This position was the most heavily bombarded of all on D-Day, receiving more than 10,000 tons of bombs (that equals 1,000 tons of TNT)—the bombing was essential to the Rangers' ability to succeed in their mission. Picnicking is forbidden here—the bombed bunkers are considered gravesites. The new building at the parking lot was built for the 60th anniversary of the invasion, and serves no other purpose than to house WCs (free, daily 9:00–17:00, 20 min by car west of American Cemetery just past Vierville-sur-Mer, tel. 02 31 51 62 00). A museum dedicated to the Rangers is in nearby Grandcamp-Maisy.

▲**German Military Cemetery**—To ponder German losses, drop by this somber, thought-provoking resting place of 21,000 German soldiers. While the American Cemetery is the focus of American travelers, visitors here speak in hushed German. The site seems appropriately bleak, with two graves per simple marker and dark crosses in groups of five. It's just south of Pointe du Hoc (daily April–Oct 8:00–19:00, Nov–March until 17:30; right off N-13 in village of La Cambe, 3.5 miles west of Bayeux, follow signs reading *Cimetière Allemand*; tel. 02 31 22 70 76).

Ste. Mère Eglise—This celebrated village lies 30 minutes east of the Pointe du Hoc and was the first village to be liberated by the Allies. For *The Longest Day* movie buffs, this is a necessary pilgrimage. It was around Ste. Mère Eglise that many paratroopers landed off-target, most notably two Americans who dangled from the town's church while Germans took pot shots at them (a parachute has been reinstalled on the steeple where Captain John Steele's became snagged—though not in the correct corner). While many paratroopers were killed before landing, those who survived played a critical role in the successful invasion by landing behind the lines. Today, the village greets travelers with 1940s music from street speakers, flag-draped streets, and a museum dedicated to the paratroopers (Musée des Troupes Aéroportées, €5.50, daily 9:00–18:30, tel. 02 33 41 41 35). To make the events surrounding this village come alive, hire WWII enthusiast Ellwood von Siebold for a two-hour tour (€25 per person, look for C-47 Café on the main square; see "Getting Around the D-Day Beaches," page 227).

Canadian D-Day Sights East of Arromanches

You'll need a car or taxi to get to either of these places, because they're not served by buses or trains.

Juno Beach Center—Located on the beachfront in the Canadian sector, about 15 minutes east of Arromanches in Courseulles-sur-Mer, this center is dedicated to teaching travelers about the vital role Canadian forces played in the invasion, and about Canada in general (Canada declared war on Germany two years before the United States, a fact little recognized by most Americans today). After attending the 50th anniversary of the D-Day landings, Canadian veterans were saddened by the absence of information on their contribution (after the US and Britain, Canada contributed the largest number of troops—14,000), so they generated funds to build this center (the plaques in front honor key donors). Your visit includes a short film, then many thoughtful exhibits that bring to life Canada's unique ties with Britain, the US, and France, and explain how the war affected daily life in Canada. The center also has exhibits about Canada's geography, economy, and more. The one-hour guided tours of Juno Beach are worthwhile (June–Aug at 10:00, 11:00, 12:00, 14:00, 15:00, and 16:00; Sept–May at 11:00 and 15:00). Your charming guide will be one of four red-shirted young Canadians who each spend four months a year in France as a part of the center's plan to improve ties between France and Canada (€6.50, €9 with guided tour, daily April–Sept 9:30–19:00, Oct and March 10:00–18:00, Nov–Feb 10:00–13:00 & 14:00–17:00, tel. 02 31 37 32 17).

Canadian Cemetery—This small, touching cemetery hides a few miles above the Juno Beach Center and makes a modest statement when compared with other, more grand cemeteries in this area. To me, it perfectly captures the low-profile nature of Canadians. Surrounded by farmland with distant views to the beaches, graves are marked with the names of the soldiers, and all have live flowers planted in their honor. It's located between Courseulles-sur-Mer and Caen, just off D-79.

Caen

Though it was mostly destroyed by WWII bombs, today's Caen (pronounced "kahn," population 115,000) is a thriving, workaday city packed with students and a few tourists. The brilliant WWII museum and the vibrant old city are the targets for travelers, though these sights come wrapped in a big city with rough edges. Charming Bayeux makes the best base for most D-Day sights, though train travelers with limited time might find urban Caen more practical because of its buses to Honfleur and easy access to the Caen Memorial Museum.

The looming château, built by William the Conqueror in 1060, sits across the street from the TI. West of the TI, modern rue St. Pierre is a popular shopping area and pedestrian zone. To the east of the TI, the more historic Vagueux quarter has many restaurants and cafés in half-timbered buildings.

Tourist Information

The TI is on place St. Pierre, 10 blocks across the canal from the train station. Pick up a map and free visitor's guide filled with practical information (Mon–Sat 9:30–18:00, closed Sun, free bag check at Memorial Museum; from the station, head right, take a right on rue Ste. Jean, cross the Vaucelles bridge and continue on Rue Ste. Jean for 15 minutes—the TI is on your left across from the castle, drivers follow signs reading *Parking Château;* tel. 02 31 27 14 14, www.tourisme.caen.fr).

SIGHTS

▲▲▲**Caen Memorial Museum (Le Mémorial de Caen)**—Caen, the modern capital of lower Normandy, has the best and by far priciest WWII museum in France. Officially named the "The Caen Memorial: History to Understand the World" *(Le Mémorial de Caen: L'histoire pour comprendre le monde),* it effectively puts the Battle of Normandy in a broader context. You'll see two video presentations and numerous exhibits on the lead-up to World War II, the actual Battle of Normandy, the Cold War, and the ongoing fight for peace (Nobel Prize Gallery and Peace Gardens). Expect special events and exhibits in 2008 as the museum celebrates its 20th anniversary.

The museum is brilliant. Begin with a downward spiral stroll, tracing (almost psychoanalyzing) the path Europe followed from the end of World War I to the rise of fascism to World War II.

The lower level gives a thorough look at how World War II was fought—from General Charles de Gaulle's London radio broadcasts to Hitler's early missiles to wartime fashion to the D-Day landings.

You then see two powerful movies. *Jour J (D-Day)* is a 30-minute film that shows the build-up to D-Day itself and the successful campaign from there to Berlin (every 40 min from 10:00 to 19:00, works in any language, pick up schedule as you enter). While snippets come from the movie *The Longest Day,* most of the film consists of footage from actual battle scenes. The second movie, *Espérance (Hope),* is a thrilling sweep through the pains and triumphs of the 20th century (on the half-hour, 20 min, also good in all languages).

The Cold War wing sets the scene with audio testimonies and photos of European cities destroyed during World War II. It continues with a helpful overview of the bipolar world that followed the war, with fascinating insights into the psychological battle waged by the Soviet Union and the US for the hearts and minds of their people until the fall of communism. The next wing, titled "Worlds for Peace," has a white, space-age design to encourage contemplation of a different future. The museum is the only place outside the US that displays building remains from the 9/11 attacks (you can see them at the end of the building, through the glass windows). The British Gardens, inaugurated in 2004 by Prince Charles, are located east of the Hall for Peace building.

The next section of the museum celebrates the irrepressible human spirit in the Gallery of Nobel Peace Prizewinners. It honors the courageous and too-often-inconspicuous work of people like Andrei Sakharov, Elie Wiesel, and Desmond Tutu, who understand that peace is more than an absence of war.

The finale is a walk through the US Armed Forces Memorial Garden. I was bothered by the mindless laughing of lighthearted children unable to appreciate their blessings. Then I read on the pavement: "From the heart of our land flows the blood of our youth, given to you in the name of freedom." Then their laughter made me happy.

Cost and Hours: €16, free for all veterans and kids under 10 (ask about family rates); March–Oct daily 9:00–19:00 (mid-July–Aug until 20:00); Nov–Feb Tue–Sun 9:00–18:00, closed Mon; last entry 1.25 hours before closing, free bag storage, tel. 02 31 06 06 44—as in June 6, 1944, fax 02 31 06 06 70, www.memorial-caen.fr).

Allow a minimum of 2.5 hours for your visit, including an hour for the movies. You could easily spend all day here; in fact, tickets purchased after 13:00 are valid for 24 hours, so you can return the next day. There are no guided tours. Free supervised babysitting is offered for children under 10 (for whom exhibits may be too graphic). The museum has a large gift shop with plenty of books in English, an all-day cafeteria, and a restaurant with a garden-side terrace (lunch only, located in the Cold War wing). Picnicking in the gardens is also an option.

Tours: The museum offers well-devised minivan guided tours of the D-Day beaches, combined with entry to the Museum. The "D-Day Tour" package is designed for day-trippers, and includes pickup from the Caen train station (with frequent service from Paris), a four-hour tour in English of the major Anglo-Canadian beaches, lunch, and then an afternoon at the Memorial Museum. Your day ends with a drop-off at the Caen train station in time to catch a train back to Paris or elsewhere (€100, includes English information book, contact museum for details, reservations, and advance payment—see contact information above).

Getting to the Museum: Finding the memorial is quick and easy for drivers. It's just off the ring-road expressway *(périphérique nord)* in Caen *(sortie* #7, look for signs reading *le Mémorial)*.

By train, Caen is two hours from Paris (14/day) and 15 minutes from Bayeux (10/day). By bus, Caen is one hour from Honfleur by express bus (2/day), or two hours by the scenic coastal bus (8/day). At Caen's train station, take the tramway (line #A or #B) from in front of the station to the Eglise St. Pierre stop, buy tickets from the machine at the tram stop (€1.20) and validate them on board (good for 1 hour). Exit the tram and walk a block west to the bus stop (look for reader boards posting bus arrival times). Use the same ticket to take bus #2 (4/hr) to *le Mémorial,* which is the last stop on that line. Taxis cost about €12 one-way from the station.

SLEEPING

(€1 = about $1.30, country code: 33)
$ Hôtel Bernières* is a good-value, one-star, traditional place with helpful staff and a we-try-harder attitude. It's simple, clean, and a 20-minute walk from the station (Sb-€38–50, Db-€50, Tb-€55, Qb-€65, €6 buffet breakfast is a swinging deal, 50 rue de Bernières, tel. 02 31 86 01 26, fax 02 31 86 51 76, www.hotelberni-eres.com, hotelbernieres@wanadoo.fr). From Caen's train station, follow *Centre-Ville* signs (crossing pont Churchill and up avenue du 6 Juin) and keep walking straight for about 15 minutes, then turn left on rue Bernières. You can also take tram #A or #B right from the station and get off at rue Bernières.

Mont St. Michel

For more than a thousand years, the distant silhouette of this island abbey sent pilgrims' spirits soaring. Today, it does the same for tourists. Mont St. Michel, among the top four pilgrimage sites in Christendom through the ages, floats like a mirage on the horizon—though it does show up on film. Today, 3.5 million visitors—far more tourists than pilgrims—flood the single street of the tiny island each year.

ORIENTATION

Mont St. Michel is connected by a two-mile causeway to the mainland and is surrounded by a vast mudflat. Your visit features a one-street village that winds up to the fortified abbey. Between 10:00 and 16:00, tourists trample the dreamscape (as earnest pilgrims did 800 years ago). A ramble on the ramparts offers mudflat views and an escape from the tourist zone. While four tacky history-in-wax museums tempt visitors, the only worthwhile sight is the  abbey itself, at the summit of the island.

Daytime Mont St. Michel is a touristy gauntlet—worth a stop, but a short one will do. The tourist tide recedes late each afternoon. On nights from autumn through spring, the island stands serene, its floodlit abbey towering above a sleepy village.

Arrive late and depart early. The abbey interior should be open until 22:30 in July and August. To avoid the human traffic jam on the main drag, follow the detour path up or down the mount (see "The Village below the Abbey" under "Sights and Activities," on page 242).

Tourist Information

The overwhelmed yet helpful TI (and €0.40 WC) is to your left as you enter Mont St. Michel's gates. They have listings of *chambres d'hôte* (B&Bs) on the nearby mainland, English tour times for the abbey, tour times for walks outside the island, bus schedules, and the tide table *(Horaires des Marées),* which is essential if you plan to explore the mudflats outside Mont St. Michel (July–Aug daily 9:00–19:00; Sept–June Mon–Sat 9:00–12:30 & 14:00–18:30, Sun 9:00–12:30 & 14:00–17:00; tel. 02 33 60 14 30, www.ot-montsaintmichel.com). A post office (PTT) and ATM are 50 yards beyond the TI.

Arrival in Mont St. Michel

By Train: The nearest train station is in Pontorson (called Pontorson–Mont St. Michel), with an easy bus connection to Mont St. Michel (12/day July–Aug, 6/day Sept–June, 15 min). The few trains that stop here are met by a bus waiting to take passengers to Mont St. Michel. The bus stop should be on the main street in front of the Pontorson station, on the same side of the street as the station; verify as you leave the station. Winter evening trains may not have a bus connection (call Couriers Bretons for bus information in this region—tel. 02 99 19 70 70). The bus drives right up to the entry gate of Mont St. Michel. Taxis from Pontorson to Mont St. Michel (or vice versa) cost about €15 (€22 after 19:00 and weekends/holidays, try to share a cab; see phone numbers under "Helpful Hints," next page).

By Car: Drive in slowly on the causeway, watching out for fine views and crossing sheep. Park in the pay lot near the base of the island (€4, free after 19:00). If sleeping on the island, you can park much closer; tell the attendant and you'll be instructed where to go. Very high tides rise to the edge of the causeway, which leaves the causeway driveable...but any cars parked below it are left underwater. (You'll be instructed where to park under high-tide conditions.) There's plenty of parking, except midday in high season. Jot down your parking sector and plan on a 10-minute walk to the island. Don't leave any luggage visible in your car.

If you'll be driving into Brittany from Mont St. Michel, see a suggested route in "Transportation Connections" on page 251.

Helpful Hints

Tides: The tides here rise above 50 feet—the largest and most dangerous in Europe. High tides *(grandes marées)* lap against the TI door (where you'll find tide hours posted).

Internet/Laundry/Groceries/Bike Rental: The industrious **Hôtel Vert,** located at the beginning of the causeway on the right, has Internet access, a 24-hour self-service launderette, a grocery store, and bikes for rent (daily 8:00–20:00, see hotel listing under "Sleeping," on page 247).

Taxi: Call 02 33 60 26 89, 02 33 60 33 23, or 06 79 64 49 35.

Guided Walks: The TI has information on inexpensive guided walks across the bay (there's little commentary, so English-only speakers are fine). **La Traversée Traditionelle** traces the footsteps of pilgrims, starting across the bay at Le Bec d'Andaine and walking over the mudflat to Mont St. Michel (weekends only, May–Oct; €5.50, 4 miles—or 1.75 hours—each way, round-trip takes 4.5 hours, including 1 hour on Mont St. Michel; ask at TI or call 02 33 89 80 88, www .cheminsdelabaie.com). For a tour within the **abbey** itself, see my self-guided tour under "Sights and Activities," below.

Best Light: Since Mont St. Michel faces west, morning light from the causeway is eye-popping. Take a memorable walk before breakfast. And don't miss the illuminated island after dark (also best from the causeway).

SIGHTS AND ACTIVITIES

Mont St. Michel

These sights are listed in the order you approach them from the mainland.

The Bay of Mont St. Michel—The vast Bay of Mont St. Michel has long played a key role. Since the sixth century, hermit monks in search of solitude lived here. The word "hermit" comes from an ancient Greek word meaning "desert." The next best thing to a desert in this part of Europe was the sea. Imagine the desert this bay provided as the first monk climbed the rock to get close to God. Add to that the mythic tide, which sends the surf speeding eight miles in and out with each tide cycle. Long before the causeway was built, when Mont St. Michel was an island, pilgrims would approach across the mudflat, aware that the tide swept in "at the speed of a galloping horse" (well, maybe a trotting horse... 12 mph, or about 2 feet per second).

Mont St. Michel Area

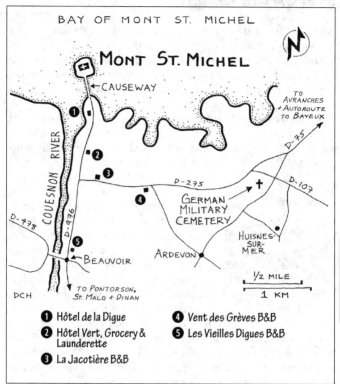

- ① Hôtel de la Digue
- ② Hôtel Vert, Grocery & Launderette
- ③ La Jacotière B&B
- ④ Vent des Grèves B&B
- ⑤ Les Vieilles Digues B&B

Quicksand was another peril. But the real danger for adventurers today is the thoroughly disorienting fog and the fact that the sea can encircle unwary hikers. (Bring a mobile phone.) Braving these devilish risks for centuries, pilgrims kept their eyes on the spire crowned by their protector, St. Michael, and eventually reached their spiritual goal.

The Causeway—In 1878 a causeway was built, letting pilgrims come and go without hip boots, regardless of the tide. While this increased the flow of visitors, it stopped the flow of water around the island. The result: Much of the bay has silted up, and Mont St. Michel is no longer an island. A new bridge and dam *(barrage)* on the Couesnon River will be built over the next few years, allowing the water to circulate—so Mont St. Michel will once again be an island (with a shuttle bus or train to zip visitors between the island and a 4,100-space parking lot, with modern hotels at the tip of the causeway). The gray door in the tower where the causeway meets Mont St. Michel is used in very high tides; otherwise, travelers enter on the wooden walkway to the left.

▲▲**Stroll Around Mont St. Michel**—To resurrect that Mont St. Michel dreamscape and evade all those tacky tourist stalls, you can walk out on the mudflats around the island. At low tide, it's reasonably dry and a great memory-maker. However, this can be hazardous, so be sure to double-check the tides or consider a tour (see "Guided Walks," page 240). Remember the scene from the Bayeux tapestry where Harold rescues Normans from the quicksand? It happened somewhere in this bay.

The Village Below the Abbey—Mont St. Michel's main street (rue Principale, or "Grande Rue"), lined with shops and hotels

leading to the abbey, is grotesquely touristy. It is some consolation to remember that, even in the Middle Ages, this was a commercial gauntlet, with stalls selling souvenir medallions, candles, and fast food. With only 30 full-time residents, the village lives solely for tourists. After visiting the TI, check the tide warnings posted on the wall and pass through the imposing doors. Before the drawbridge, on your left, peek through the door of Restaurant la Mère Poulard. The original Madame Poulard (the maid of an abbey architect who married the village baker) made quick and tasty omelets here. These were popular for pilgrims, who needed to beat the tide to get out in pre-causeway days and—even at the rip-off price of €30—they're still a hit with tourists today (and much cheaper elsewhere). Pop in for a minute, just to enjoy the show as old-time-costumed cooks beat eggs.

Pass through the old drawbridge, join the main street, and begin your trudge through the crowds uphill past several gimmicky museums to the abbey (all island hotel receptions are located on this street). Or, if the abbey's your goal, you can miss the crowds by climbing the first steps on your right after the drawbridge and following the ramparts in either direction up and up to the abbey (quieter if you go right). Public WCs are next to the TI at the town entry, partway up the main drag, and at the abbey entrance.

You can attend Mass at the tiny St. Pierre Church (Thu and Sun at 11:00, opposite Hôtel la Vieille Auberge).

▲▲**Abbey of Mont St. Michel**—Mont St. Michel has been an important pilgrimage center since A.D. 708, when the bishop of Avranches heard the voice of Archangel Michael saying, "Build here and build high." With brilliant foresight, Michael reassured the bishop, "If you build it...they will come." Today's abbey is built on the remains of a Romanesque church, which stands on the remains of a Carolingian church. St. Michael, whose gilded statue

Mont St. Michel

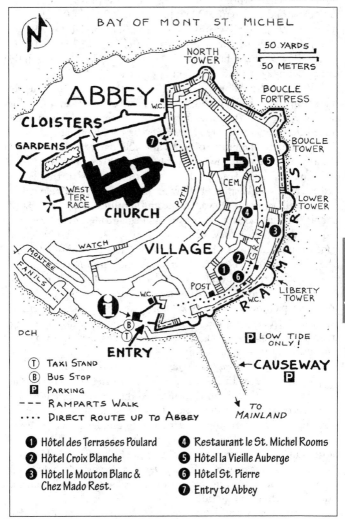

Map legend:

- (T) Taxi Stand
- (B) Bus Stop
- (P) Parking
- – – – Ramparts Walk
- ···· Direct Route up to Abbey

1. Hôtel des Terrasses Poulard
2. Hôtel Croix Blanche
3. Hôtel le Mouton Blanc & Chez Mado Rest.
4. Restaurant le St. Michel Rooms
5. Hôtel la Vieille Auberge
6. Hôtel St. Pierre
7. Entry to Abbey

decorates the top of the spire, was the patron saint of many French kings, making this a favored site for French royalty through the ages. St. Michael was particularly popular in Counter-Reformation times, as the Church employed his warlike image in the fight against Protestant heresy.

While this abbey has 1,200 years of history, much of its story was lost when its archives were taken to St. Lô for safety during World War II—only to be destroyed during the D-Day fighting. As you climb the stairs, imagine the centuries of pilgrims and monks who have worn down the edges of these same stone steps.

Cost and Hours: €9, May–June daily 9:00–19:00; July–Aug Mon–Sat 9:00–22:30, Sun 9:00–19:00; Sept–April daily 9:30–18:00; last entry 1 hour before closing (tel. 02 33 89 80 00). Buy your ticket to the abbey and keep climbing. Mass is held daily except Monday at 12:15 in the abbey church.

Visiting the Abbey: Allow 20 minutes to hike at a steady pace from the TI. If visiting in the morning, arrive by 10:00 for far fewer crowds. In summer evenings when the abbey is open until 22:30 and crowds are gone, visits come with music and mood lighting (nighttime program starts at 19:00; daytime tickets aren't valid for re-entry, but you can visit before 19:00 and stay on).

Tours: You'll find no English explanations in the abbey (except for a small leaflet). Follow my **self-guided tour,** below. For more detail, consider the well-done **audioguide** (€4/1 person, €6/2 people) or the 1.25-hour English-language **guided tour** (free, tip requested, 4–6 tours/day, first tour usually at 10:00, last at 16:00, confirm tour times at TI, meet at top terrace in front of church). The guided tours, which can be good, come with big crowds. You can start a tour, then decide if it works for you—I skip them.

◐ Self-Guided Tour: Tour the abbey by following a one-way route. Keep climbing to the ticket booths and turnstile, then climb some more. Pass a public WC (€0.40), a room with interesting models of the abbey through the ages, a guides' desk (posting the time of the next tour), and—finally—the terrace.

• *Walk to the round lookout at the far end and face the church.*

West Terrace: In 1776, a fire destroyed the west end of the church, leaving this grand view terrace. The original extent of the church is outlined with short walls (as well as the stonecutter numbers, generally not exposed like this—a reminder that they were paid by the piece). The buildings of Mont St. Michel are made of granite stones quarried from the Isles of Chausey (visible on a clear day, 20 miles away). Tidal power was ingeniously harnessed to load, unload, and even transport the stones, as barges hitched a ride with each incoming tide.

As you survey the Bay of Mont St. Michel, notice the polder land—farmland reclaimed by Normans in the 19th century with the help of Dutch engineers. The lines of trees mark strips of land used in the process. Today, this reclaimed land is covered by salt-loving plants and grazed by sheep whose salty meat is considered a local treat. You're standing 240 feet above sea level, at the summit of what was an island called "the big tomb." The small island just farther out is "the little tomb."

Survey the bay stretching from Normandy to Brittany. The river below marks the historic border between the two lands. Brittany and Normandy have long vied for Mont St. Michel. In fact, the river used to pass Mont St. Michel on the other side, making the abbey part of Brittany. Today, it's just barely—but thoroughly—on Normand soil. Construction on a new dam across this river will begin soon; it's the first phase of the project to return Mont St. Michel to being an island.

• *Now head back into the...*

Abbey Church: Sit on a pew near the front of the church, under the little statue of the Archangel Michael (with the spear to defeat dragons and evil, and the scales to evaluate your soul). Monks built the church on the tip of this rock in order to be as close to heaven as possible. The downside: There wasn't enough level ground to support a sizable abbey and church. The solution: Four immense crypts were built under the church to create a platform to support each of its wings. While most of the church is Romanesque (round arches, 11th century), the Gothic, light-filled apse behind the altar was built later. In 1421, the crypt that supported the apse collapsed, taking that end of the church with it. Almost none of the original windows survive (victims of fires, storms, lightning, and the Revolution).

• *Just outside the church, you'll find the...*

Cloisters: A standard feature of an abbey, this was the peaceful zone that connected various rooms where monks could meditate, read the Bible, and tend their gardens (growing food and herbs for medicine). The great view window is enjoyable today (what's the tide doing?), but it was of no use to the monks. The more secluded a monk could be, the closer he was to God. (A cloister, by definition, is an enclosed place.) Notice the carvings, which feature various plants and heighten the Garden-of-Eden ambience the cloister offered the monks. The statues of various saints, carved among some columns, were de-faced—literally—by French Revolutionary troops.

• *Continue on the tour to the...*

Refectory: This was the dining hall where the monks consumed both food and the word of God in silence—one monk read in a monotone from the Bible during meals (pulpit on the right near the far end). The monks gathered as a family here in one undivided space under one big arch (an impressive engineering feat in its day). The abbot ate at the head table; guests sat at the table in the middle. The clever columns are thin but very deep, allowing maximum light while offering solid support. From 966 until 2001, this was a Benedictine abbey. In 2001, the last three Benedictine monks checked out, and a new order of monks from Paris took over.

• *Stairs lead down to the...*

Guests' Hall: St. Benedict wrote that guests should be welcomed according to their status. That meant that when the king (or other VIPs) visited, they were wined and dined without a hint of monastic austerity. This room was once brilliantly painted, with gold stars on a blue sky across the ceiling. (The painting of this room was said to be the model for Sainte-Chapelle in Paris.) The floor was of glazed red-and-green tiles. The entire space was bathed in glorious sunlight, made divine as it passed through a filter of stained glass. The big double fireplace, kept out of sight by hanging tapestries, served as a kitchen.

• *Hike the stairs to the...*

Hall of the Grand Pillars: Perched on a pointy rock, the huge abbey had four sturdy crypts like this to prop it up. You're standing under the Gothic portion of the abbey church—this was the crypt that collapsed in 1421. Notice the immensity of the columns (15 feet around) in the new crypt, rebuilt with a determination not to let it fall again.

• *To see what kind of crypt collapsed, walk on to the...*

Crypt of St. Martin: This simple, 11th-century Romanesque vault has minimal openings, since the walls needed to be solid and fat to support the buildings above. As you leave, notice the thickness of the walls.

• *Next, you'll find the...*

Ossuary (identifiable by its big treadwheel): The monks celebrated death as well as life. This part of the abbey housed the hospital, morgue, and ossuary. Because the abbey graveyard was small, it was routinely emptied, and the bones were stacked here.

During the Revolution, monasticism was abolished. Church property was taken by the atheistic government, and from 1793 to 1863, Mont St. Michel was used as an Alcatraz-type prison. Its first inmates were 300 priests who refused to renounce their vows. (Victor Hugo complained that using such a place as a prison was like keeping a toad in a reliquary.) The big treadwheel—the kind that did heavy lifting for big building projects throughout the Middle Ages—is from the decades when the abbey was a prison. Teams of six prisoners marched two abreast in the wheel—hamster-style—powering two-ton loads of stone and supplies up Mont St. Michel. Spin the rollers of the sled next to the wheel. Look down the steep ramp (another sled hangs just below). While you're here, notice the parking lot and the crowds down there. When the tide is very high, careless drivers can become carless drivers. A few years ago, a Scottish bus driver (oblivious to the time and tide, and very busy in a hotel room) lost his bus...destroyed by a salty bath. Local police tethered it to the lot so it wouldn't float away.

Finish your visit by walking through the Promenade of the Monks, under more Gothic vaults, and through the **Scriptorium Hall,** where monks decorated illuminated manuscripts. You'll then spiral down to the gift shop, turn right, and follow signs to *Jardin*. The room after the shop holds temporary exhibitions about the history and future of Mont St. Michel.

• *Exit the room and walk out into the rear garden. From here, look up at the miracle of medieval engineering.*

The "Merveille": This was an immense building project—a marvel back in 1220. Three levels of buildings were created: the lower floor for the lower class, the middle floor for VIPs, and the top floor reserved for the clergy. It was a medieval skyscraper, built with the social strata in mind. (Remember looking out of those top windows earlier?) The vision was even grander—the place where you're standing was to be built up in similar fashion, to support a further expansion of the church. But the money ran out, and the project was abandoned.

• *Stairs lead from here back into the village. To avoid the crowds on your descent, veer to the right down the small lane past the Musée Historique or, at the same place, follow chemin des Ramparts to the left and hike down via the...*

Ramparts: Mont St. Michel is ringed by a fine example of 15th-century fortifications. They were built to defend against a new weapon: the cannon. They were low, rather than tall—to make a smaller target—and connected by protected passageways, which enabled soldiers to zip quickly to whichever zone was under attack. The five-sided Boucle Tower (1481) was crafted with no blind angles, so defenders could protect it and the nearby walls in all directions. While the English took all of Normandy, they never took this well-fortified island. Because of its stubborn success against the English in the Hundred Years' War, Mont St. Michel became a symbol of French national identity.

After dark, the island is magically floodlit. Views from the ramparts are sublime. For the best view, exit the island and walk out on the causeway a few hundred yards.

Near Mont St. Michel

German Military Cemetery (Cimetière Militaire Allemand)— Located three miles from Mont St. Michel, near tiny Huisnes-sur-Mer (drive east from Mont St. Michel on D-275, then follow signs), this somber but thoughtfully presented cemetery-mortuary houses the remains of 12,000 German soldiers. It offers insight into their lives, with letters they sent home (English translations). From the lookout, take in the sensational views over Mont St. Michel.

SLEEPING

(€1 = about $1.30, country code: 33)

Sleeping on the island—inside the walls—is without question the best way to experience Mont St. Michel. You'll need to carry your bags about 10 to 15 minutes (some of it uphill), so take only what you need for one night in a smaller bag. Leave no luggage visible in your car. Drivers can also consider the nearby and excellent-value *chambres d'hôte* listed below.

On the Island

There are eight small hotels on the island, two of which are family-run and more hospitable. While some pad their profits by requesting that guests buy dinner from their restaurant, *requiring* it is illegal. Several hotels are closed from November until Easter. Because most visitors only day-trip here, finding a room is generally no problem. If there's a price range for rooms, the higher-priced rooms generally have bay views. On arrival, remember to tell the parking attendant that you're staying at a hotel on the island, which allows you to park closer.

The following hotels are listed in order of altitude, with the first lowest on the island and closest to the parking.

$$$ Hôtel des Terrasses Poulard***, 50 yards after the TI, rents the lowest, most polished, and priciest rooms on the island (small Db-€60, standard Db with some view-€105, Db with better view Db-€195, most Db are €105, Tb suite-€280, tel. 02 33 89 02 02, fax 02 33 60 37 31, www.terrasses-poulard.fr, hoteltp @wanadoo.fr).

$$$ Hôtel St. Pierre*** and **Hôtel Croix Blanche***,** with the same owners and reception desks, sit side by side (reception at St. Pierre). Each has comfortable rooms, some with good views. St. Pierre is sharper and pricier, with several family loft rooms and Wi-Fi; Croix Blanche has an Internet terminal and restaurant (Db-€95–120, most are €95–105, Tb-€130–150, Qb-€140–160, tel. 02 33 60 14 03, fax 02 33 48 59 82, www.auberge-saint-pierre.fr, aubergesaintpierre@wanadoo.fr).

$$ Hôtel le Mouton Blanc** is a decent value but is poorly managed. The rooms need a fresh coat of paint and the carpets need to be tossed into the bay (both promised), and the thin walls should be thicker (not promised). Their 15 rooms are split between two buildings: the main building *(bâtiment principal)* is cozier, with wood beams in most rooms; the "annex" is brighter and more modern (Db-€75, Tb-€90, Qb-€105, tel. 02 33 60 14 08, fax 02 33 60 05 62, www.lemoutonblanc.com, contact@lemoutonblanc.fr).

$$ Restaurant le Saint Michel, across from Hôtel le Mouton Blanc, rents the island's six cheapest and most basic rooms in a nearby annex. It's run by lighthearted Patricia and Frédéric (Ds-€60, Db-€55–80, depends on view, extra person-€10, simple decor, no dinner requirements but a good restaurant, tel. & fax 02 33 60 14 37, www.lesaintmichelridel.com).

$$ Hôtel la Vieille Auberge** is family-run by entrepreneurial Nadine (who speaks English) and her Old World mother-in-law,

Normandy

Madame. Their 11 traditional rooms in two buildings require the longest walk, but are among the best for the price. The four rooms with large view terraces are exceptional if the weather cooperates (and if you don't mind regular chimes from the bell tower). Arrive by 17:00; call if you'll be late or lose your reservation (Db-€75–85, Db with view and terrace-€125, extra bed-€16, hotel is closed after 19:00, closed Wed Oct–April, tel. 02 33 60 14 34, fax 02 33 70 87 04, www.lavieilleauberge-montsaintmichel.com, lavieilleauberge -montsaintmichel@wanadoo.fr).

On the Mainland

Modern hotels gather at the mainland end of the causeway. These have soulless but cheaper rooms with easy parking and many tour groups. Hôtel Vert (see below) rents bikes, offering easy access to the island.

$$ Hôtel de la Digue***, popular with groups, is the best and most convenient place to stay on the mainland. Most rooms are spacious and well-equipped. Ask for one of the four rooms with private terrace on the river side: *une chambre avec petit balcon sur le Couesnon* (small Db-€68, spacious Db-€82, Db with terrace-€86, Tb-€90, Qb-€102, good breakfast, tel. 02 33 60 14 02, fax 02 33 60 37 59, www.ladigue.fr, hotel-de-la-digue@wanadoo.fr). From here, it's a wonderful 20-minute walk to Mont St. Michel. You can dine at their good-value restaurant with a partial view of Mont St. Michel (*menus* from €19).

$$ Hôtel Vert, which offers many services (see "Helpful Hints," page 240), is huge, with 112 rooms. But it's clean, close, and reasonable (Db-€64, Tb-€78, Qb-€90, tel. 02 33 60 09 33, fax 02 33 60 20 02). Their musty and basic annex, Motel Formule Vert, is across the road (rooms about €10 less).

Chambres d'Hôte

Simply great values, these converted farmhouses are near the village of Ardevon, a few minutes' drive from the island toward Avranches.

$ La Jacotière, charming Claudine Brault's stone farmhouse, is closest to Mont St. Michel and walkable to the causeway. She has six immaculate, three-star-quality rooms and views of the island from her side yard (Db-€46, studio with great view from private patio-€48, extra bed-€12, tel. 02 33 60 22 94, fax 02 33 60 20 48, www.bedbreak.com/lajacotiere, la.jacotiere@wanadoo.fr).

$ Vent des Grèves, Madame Audienne's stone farmhouse, is about a mile down D-275 from Mont St. Michel. There are two wings, each with five rooms. Like Mama, the older wing feels a wee bit tired, but has more character; and, like daughter Estelle (who speaks English), the modern wing is young and bright. Most rooms have good views of Mont St. Michel, but they're better from Estelle's wing (which also has spacious, tiled rooms and modern facilities). A good deck has tables to let you soak in the view (Sb-€32, Db-€42, Tb-€52, Qb-€62, includes breakfast, tel. & fax 02 33 48 28 89).

$ Les Vieilles Digues, with delightful Danielle to pamper you, is two miles toward Pontorson on the main road (on the left if you're coming from Mont St. Michel). There's a lovely garden and seven beautifully furnished, spotless, and homey rooms, all with showers and exterior entrances (but no views). Ground-floor rooms have patios on the garden (D-€50, Db-€50–60, Tb-€78, includes good breakfast, easy parking, 68 route du Mont St. Michel, tel. 02 33 58 55 30, fax 02 33 58 83 09, www.bnb-normandy.com, danielle.tchen@wanadoo.fr).

In Pontorson

Train travelers could sleep in dismal Pontorson, a 15-minute bus ride from Mont St. Michel.

$$ Hôtel de France et Vauban**, across from the train station, welcomes you with a pleasant terrace, and is quiet and comfortable (Db-€44–68, 50 boulevard Clémenceau, tel. 02 33 60 03 84, fax 02 33 60 35 48, www.hotel-france-vauban.fr, hotel-france-vauban @wanadoo.fr).

EATING

Puffy omelets *(omelette montoise)* are Mont St. Michel's specialty. Also look for mussels (best with crème fraîche) and seafood platters, locally raised lamb (a saltwater-grass diet gives the meat a unique taste), and Muscadet wine (dry, white, and cheap). Several restaurants have outdoor seating with views along the ramparts walk, ideal when it's sunny (usually lunch only).

Restaurant le St. Michel is lighthearted, reasonable, family-friendly, and run by helpful Patricia (decent omelets, mussels, and pasta, open daily, check out the stone toilet, across from Hôtel du Mouton Blanc, tel. 02 33 60 14 37).

Chez Mado is a stylish, three-story café-*crêperie*-restaurant one door up from the Hôtel Mouton Blanc. It's worth considering for its upstairs terrace with views up to the abbey and down over the bay (open daily).

Hôtel la Vieille Auberge is good for lunch; try the *moules* à la crème fraîche (mussels with cream), omelets, and seafood platter (closes at 19:00, no dinner service, listed under "Sleeping," page 248).

The **supermarket,** located on the mainland at the Hôtel Vert, has what you need for a romantic picnic (see "Helpful Hints," page

240). You can also buy sandwiches, salads, and drinks to go on the island. Picnic in the small park below the abbey, to the left as you look up at it.

TRANSPORTATION CONNECTIONS

By Train and Bus

Bus and train service to Mont St. Michel is a challenge. Unless you're coming from Paris, you're likely to find that you must arrive and depart early or late—leaving you too much or too little time on the island.

From Mont St. Michel to Paris: There are three ways to get to Paris. Most take the regional bus from Mont St. Michel to Rennes (€10, not covered by railpass) and connect directly to the TGV (4/day, 4 hrs total from Mont St. Michel to Paris). You can also take the quick bus ride to Pontorson (see below) and catch one of a very few trains from there (2/day, 5.5 hrs, transfer in Caen or Rennes). In summer, you can take the SNCF bus to Villedieu les Poêles, and transfer there to the train to Paris' Gare Montparnasse (4/day, 4 hrs total, bus and train covered by railpass).

From Mont St. Michel to Pontorson: The nearest train station to Mont St. Michel is five miles away, in Pontorson (called Pontorson–Mont St. Michel), connected by bus (12/day July–Aug, 6/day Sept–June, 15 min) or taxi (€15 by day, €22 at night and on weekends; see "Helpful Hints," page 240). For more information, see page 239.

From Pontorson by Train to: Bayeux (2–3/day, 2 hrs), **Rouen** (5/day, 4–7 hrs, most via Paris, 1 via Caen), **Dinan** (3/day, 2 hrs, transfer in Dol), **St. Malo** (2–3/day, 1–2 hrs, transfer in Dol), **Amboise** (2–3/day; 5.5–7.5 hrs via transfers in Caen and Tours, or via Rennes, Le Mans, and Tours).

Pontorson also has a **bus station** with buses to many regional destinations (turn left out of the train station and walk 100 yards).

From Mont St. Michel by Bus to: St. Malo (2–3/day, 2 hrs via Pontorson; connections work well: the 9:15 bus from Mont St. Michel usually connects with a bus in Pontorson that arrives in St. Malo at 11:00, from where later buses run to Dinan—TI has schedules, www.lescourriersbretons.fr), **Rennes** (4/day, 1.75 hrs).

By Car

From Mont St. Michel to Dinan, Brittany: For a scenic drive into Brittany, take the following route: Head to Pontorson, and then find D-797, which leads to D-155 and on to the oyster capital of Cancale. From Cancale, head to Pointe du Grouin. From here, follow D-201 west as it hugs the coast to St. Malo. From St. Malo, signs direct you to Dinan. This drive adds about 1.75 hours to the fastest path between Mont St. Michel and Dinan, but is well worth it. For more details, including ideas of where to stop along this route, see page 265.

From Mont St. Michel to Bayeux: Take the free and zippy A-84 and be ready to navigate if new signs to Bayeux are not yet in place (keep asking, "oo ay Bayeux?").

Normandy

BRITTANY

The broad peninsula of Brittany is windswept and rugged, with a forgotten interior, a well-discovered coast, strong Celtic ties, and a passion for crêpes and *cidre* (alcoholic apple cider served in bowls). This region of independent-minded locals is linguistically and culturally different from Normandy and, for that matter, the rest of France. The Couesnon River skirts the western edge of Mont St. Michel, and marks the border between Normandy and Brittany.

In 1491, the French King Charles VIII forced Brittany's 14-year-old Duchess Anne to marry him (at Château de Langeais in the Loire Valley). Their union made the independent, feisty Brittany a part of France. Brittany lost its freedom, but with Anne as queen gained certain rights, such as free roads. (Even today, 500 years later, Brittany's highways come with no tolls...unique in France.)

Locals take great pride in their distinct Breton culture. In Brittany, music stores sell more Celtic music than anything else. It's hard to imagine that this music was forbidden as recently as the 1980s. During a more repressive time, many of today's big pop stars were underground artists. And not long ago, a child would lose French citizenship if christened with a Celtic name.

But the freckled locals are now free to wave their flag, sing their songs, and speak their language (there's a Breton TV station and radio station). Like their Irish counterparts, Bretons—many with red hair—are chatty, their music is alive with struggles against an oppressor, and the sea forms an integral part of their identity. The coastal route between Mont St. Michel and Dinan—through the town of Cancale (famous for oysters; good lunch stop), Pointe du Grouin (fabulous ocean views), and the historic walled city of St. Malo—gives travelers with limited time a good look at this province.

Cuisine Scene in Brittany

While the endless coastline suggests otherwise, there is more than seafood in this rugged Celtic land. Crêpes are to Bretons what pasta is to Italians: a basic, reasonably priced, daily necessity. *Galettes* are savory buckwheat crêpes, commonly filled with ham, cheese, eggs, mushrooms, spinach, seafood, or a combination.

Oysters *(huîtres)* are the second food of Brittany, and are available all year. Mussels, clams, and scallops are often served as main courses. Look for crêpes with scallops and *moules marinières* (mussels steamed in white wine, parsley, and shallots). Farmers compete with fishermen for the hearts of locals by growing fresh vegetables, such as peas, beans, and cauliflower.

For dessert, look for *far breton,* a traditional custard often served with prunes. Dessert crêpes, made with white flour, are served with a variety of toppings.

Cider is the locally produced drink. Order *une bolée de cidre* (a traditional bowl of hard apple cider) with your crêpes.

Remember, restaurants serve only during lunch (11:30–14:00) and dinner (19:00–21:00, later in bigger cities); cafés serve food throughout the day.

Dinan

If you have time for only one stop in Brittany, do Dinan. Hefty ramparts corral its half-timbered and cobbled quaintness into Brittany's best medieval town center. While it has a touristic icing—plenty of *crêperies,* shops selling Brittany kitsch, and colorful flags—it's a workaday Breton town filled with people who appreciate the beautiful place they call home. This impeccably preserved ancient city (which escaped the bombs  of World War II) is peaceful and conveniently located (about a 45-minute drive from Mont St. Michel). For a great day, spend your morning exploring Dinan, and your afternoon walking, biking, or boating the Rance River below.

ORIENTATION

Dinan's old city, contained within its medieval ramparts, sits on a hill well above the Rance River. Cobbled lanes climb steeply from the river and Dinan's small port to the huge and central place du Guesclin (gek-lahn). There, you'll find lots of parking (see "Arrival in Dinan," below), Château de Dinan, and the TI. The bustling place des Merciers, just north of place du Guesclin, is the center of most shopping activities.

Tourist Information

Pick up a free map and bus and train schedules, and ask about boat trips on the Rance River (July–Aug Mon–Sat 9:00–19:00, Sun 9:00–12:30 & 14:30–18:00; Sept–June Mon–Sat 9:00–12:30 & 14:00–18:00, closed Sun; just off place du Guesclin near Château de Dinan on 9 rue du Château, tel. 02 96 87 69 76, www.dinan-tourisme.com).

Arrival in Dinan

By Train: To get to the town center from Dinan's Old World train station (no lockers or baggage check), either find a taxi (see "Helpful Hints," below) or walk 20 minutes. If walking, head left out of the train station, make a right at Hôtel de la Gare up rue Carnot, turn right on rue Thiers, and then go left across big place Duclos-Pinot; from here, to get to the old center, go to the left of Café de la Mairie. To reach the TI and place du Guesclin, go to the right of this café (on rue du Marchix).

By Bus: Dinan's main bus stop is in front of the post office on place Duclos-Pinot, 10 minutes above the train station and five minutes below place du Guesclin (cross the square passing to the left of Café de la Mairie for the historic core).

By Car: Dinan can be confusing for drivers; follow *Centre-Ville* signs and park on the massive place du Guesclin (free parking except July–Sept and on market days on Thu). If you enter Dinan by *la gare SNCF* (train station), drive the walking route described above and keep to the right of Café de la Mairie (see "By Train") to reach place du Guesclin. Check with your hotelier before leaving your car overnight on place du Guesclin; they will tow it before 8:00 on market or festival days.

Helpful Hints

Market Days: On Thursday, a big open-air market is held on place du Guesclin (8:00–13:00). In July and August, Wednesday is flea-market day on place St. Sauveur.

Supermarkets: Groceries are upstairs in the **Monoprix** (Mon–Sat 9:00–19:30, closed Sun, 7 rue du Marchix). On Sundays, try

Marché Plus, on place Duclos-Pinot (Mon–Sat 7:00–19:00, Sun 9:00–13:00).

Laundry: Pressing-Laverie's Madame Heurlin can usually do your laundry in a few hours (€8/wash and dry, Tue–Fri 8:30–12:00 & 14:00–19:00, Sat 8:30–18:00, closed Sun–Mon, a few blocks from place Duclos at 19 rue de Brest, tel. 02 96 39 71 35).

Bike Rental: Try **Cycles Yves Gauthier** (€15/day, Mon–Sat 9:00–12:00 & 14:00–19:00, closed Sun, near the train station at 15 rue Déroyer, tel. 02 96 85 07 60).

Taxi: Call 02 96 39 74 16 or 06 08 00 80 90 (8-seat minivans available).

Tourist Train: If the *petit train* is running (ask at the TI), it gets you down to the port easily (€5, daily 11:00–18:00, every 40 min, 40-min loop, departs from Théâtre des Jacobins; see self-guided walk of Dinan, below).

Picnic-Park: The small but flowery Jardin Anglais hides behind the Church of St. Sauveur.

SELF-GUIDED WALK

Welcome to Dinan

Frankly, I wouldn't go through a turnstile in Dinan. The attraction here is the town itself. Enjoy the old town center, ramble around the ramparts, and explore the old riverfront harbor. Here are some ideas, laced together as a relaxed one-hour walk (not including exploring the port), starting near the TI. As you wander, notice the pride locals take in their Breton culture.

• *Start behind the TI in front of Château de Dinan.*

Château de Dinan: The nearby walls and the 120-foot-high *donjon* (keep) are all that's left of Dinan's once-massive castle. This was the centerpiece of Dinan's two miles of ramparts that once encircled the city. The museum inside (some English) and the view from the top are both disappointing unless you love looms.

• *Walk to the center of place du Guesclin, and find the statue of the horseback rider.*

Place du Guesclin: This sprawling town square is named after Bertrand du Guesclin, a native 14th-century knight and hero (described as small in stature but big-hearted) who became a great French military leader, famous for his daring victories over England during the Hundred Years' War (like Joan of Arc, he played a major role in defeating the English). On this very square, he defeated Sir Thomas of Canterbury in a thrilling joust that locals still talk about to this day. The victory freed his brother, whom Thomas had taken prisoner in violation of a truce. For 700 years, merchants have filled this square to sell their produce and

Dinan

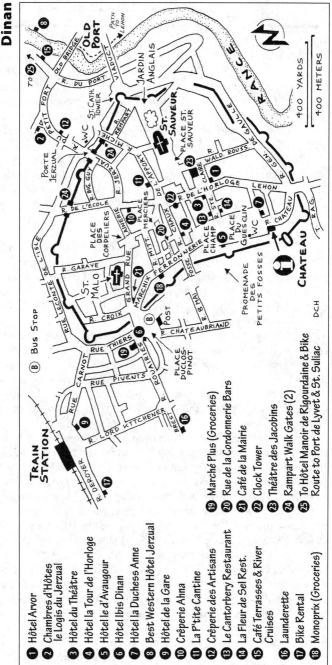

1 Hôtel Arvor
2 Chambres d'Hôtes
   le Logis du Jerzual
3 Hôtel du Théâtre
4 Hôtel la Tour de l'Horloge
5 Hôtel d'Avaugour
6 Hôtel Ibis Dinan
7 Hôtel la Duchess Anne
8 Best Western Hôtel Jerzual
9 Hôtel de la Gare
10 Crêperie Ahna
11 La P'tite Cantine
12 Crêperie des Artisans
13 Le Cantorbery Restaurant
14 La Fleur de Sel Rest.
15 Café Terrasses & River
   Cruises
16 Launderette
17 Bike Rental
18 Monoprix (Groceries)
19 Marché Plus (Groceries)
20 Rue de la Cordonnerie Bars
21 Café de la Mairie
22 Clock Tower
23 Théâtre des Jacobins
24 Rampart Walk Gates (2)
25 To Hôtel Manoir de Rigourdaine & Bike
   Route to Port de Lyvet & St. Suliac

crafts (in modern times, it's Thu 8:00–13:00).

• *With the statue of Guesclin behind you, follow rue Ste. Claire to the right, into the old town and to the...*

Théâtre des Jacobins: Fronting a pleasant little square, the theater was once one of the many convents that dominated the town. In fact, in medieval times, a third of Dinan consisted of convents. (They're not uncommon in Brittany, which remains the most Catholic part of France.)

• *Turn left and walk down rue de l'Horloge ("Clock Street") toward the clock tower, where on your left, you'll see...*

Nobody's Tombstone: The tombstone without a head is a town mascot. It's actually a prefab tombstone, made during the Hundred Years' War, when there was more death than money in France. A portrait bust would be attached to this generic body for a proper, yet economical, burial.

• *Continue to the...*

Clock Tower: The old town spins around this clock tower, which has long symbolized the power of the town's merchants. The tower comes with 160 steps (the last few on a ladder) to a fine city view. Warning: Plug your ears at the quarter hour, when the bells ring (€2.80, daily June–Aug 10:00–18:30, otherwise 14:00–18:00 only, closed Oct–March).

• *Past the tower, take the first left into Dinan's historic commercial center, the place des Merciers. Look for a bakery selling* ker-y-pom *(about €1.50), traditional Breton shortbread biscuits with butter, honey, and an apple-pie filling. When warm, they're the best-tasting treat in town. Now, find the stone bench near the restaurant La Mère Pourcel.*

Old Town Center: The arcaded, half-timbered buildings in front of you are Dinan's oldest. They date from the time when property taxes were based on the square footage of the ground floor. To provide shelter from both the taxes and the rain, buildings started with small ground floors, then expanded outward with their upper floors. Medieval shopkeepers sold goods in front of their homes under the shelter of leaning walls. Most streets are named for the key commerce that took place there. Picturesque rue de la Cordonnerie (literally, "Shoe Street," to the left of La Mère Pourcel) is a fine example of a medieval lane, with overhanging buildings whose roofs nearly touch. After a disastrous 18th-century fire, a law required that the traditional thatch be replaced by safer slate. At the end of place des Merciers, the building with the stone arched facade protecting an alley was a Franciscan monastery in the Middle Ages; today, it's a middle school—wrap your brain around that change.

• *Wander a short block up rue de la Cordonnerie, turn right, then double back on rue du Petit Pain, passing the unusual market-hall stalls.*

Continue around place des Merciers and turn right on rue de la Lainerie ("Street of Wool Shops"), staying on it as it turns into rue du Jerzual.

Rue du Jerzual: This spiraling road was the primary medieval link to the port, and ground zero for commercial activity in Dinan. The steep cobbled street (slippery when wet) was chock-a-block with potential customers making their way between the port and the upper city. Notice the waist-high stone and wooden shelves that front many of the buildings. Here, medieval merchants could display their products and tempt passersby. You can continue all the way down to the port (for more on the port, see below); it's a 10-minute walk down (remember, what goes down must come back up). If your knees disagree, follow the path described immediately below, to the ramparts.

• *For the best look at Dinan's impressive fortified wall, turn right after passing under the massive medieval gate (Porte du Jerzual) and work your way up the curving road. Turn right on rue Michel, then turn right again through the iron gate to walk along the...*

Ramparts: In the Middle Ages, this elevated walkway was connected with Château de Dinan (figure about a mile in either direction to the château from here). While the old port town was repeatedly destroyed, these ramparts were never taken by force (they *were* taken, however, by siege). If an attacker got by the *contrescarpe* (second outer wall) and through the (dry) moat, he could be pummeled by nasty things dropped through the holes lining the ramparts. Today, the ramparts seem to guard only the town's residential charm and immaculate gardens. Venture out on the huge Governor's Tower to see how the cannon slots enabled defenders to shoot in all directions. The St. Malo tower lies to your left, and the furthest visible tower to your right is our next stop.

• *Double back to rue Michel and turn right. Take the first left, onto rue du Rempart. Walk to the round tower (St. Catherine's Tower), in the corner of the park, for a...*

Territorial View: Standing on yet another tower from Dinan's original ramparts, you have a strategic view of the river valley and over the old port. The English gardens behind you are picnic-pleasant.

• *Walk around the church behind you, and dip into the...*

Church of St. Sauveur: Enter this asymmetrical church (typical in Brittany) to see striking, modern, stained-glass windows. Pick up the English explanation and learn the church's raison d'être. The church is a thousand years old—the wood balcony in the entry looks even older as it strains under the weight of the organ above. When built, the church sat isolated on this hill as activity remained focused on and around the port.

• *Your tour is over, and you are a block below the main rue de l'Horloge.*

SIGHTS

Dinan's Old Port

Following the self-guided walk outlined above, you can reach the modest little port by walking down rue du Jerzual (which becomes rue du Port). Notice the unusual wood-topped building just before the port on the left. This was a leather tannery. Those wooden shutters could open, allowing air flow to dry freshly tanned hides while the nearby river flushed the waste products (swimming was not in vogue at this time). The last business before the port is a memorable bakery highlighting local specialties. You deserve a break.

The port was the birthplace of Dinan a thousand years ago. For centuries, this is where people lived and worked. Once an important port, it was connected to the sea—15 miles away—by the Rance River. By taxing river traffic, the town grew prosperous. The tiny Vieux Pont (Old Bridge) dates to the 15th century. Because the port area was so exposed, the townsfolk retreated to the bluff behind its current fortifications. Notice the viaduct high above, built in 1850 to alleviate congestion and to send traffic around the town. Until then, the main road crossed the tiny Old Bridge, heading up rue du Jerzual to Dinan.

▲Rance River Valley

The best thing about Dinan's port is the access it provides to dreamy riverside paths, which meander along the gentle Rance River Valley. You can walk, bike, drive, or boat in either interesting direction.

On Foot: For a breath of fresh Brittany air, visit the village of Léhon. Cross the Old Bridge in Dinan's port, turn right, and walk the level river trail for 30 minutes. You'll come to pristine Léhon. Visitors are greeted by a proud ninth-century abbey and church (check out the cloisters), flowery cobbled lanes, a town-topping medieval castle, and **La Marmite de l'Abbaye** café/restaurant (wood fire–grilled meats for lunch and dinner, drinks in between, July–Aug open daily, Sept–June closed Mon and maybe Tue, tel. 02 96 87 39 39).

By Bike: For bike rental, see "Helpful Hints," above. Cyclists can follow the "On Foot" route (above), then cross Léhon's bridge and continue along the canal as far as they can pedal. You'll pass Breton cows, cute little lock houses, sublime scenery, and other nature-lovers. The villages of Evran and Treverien are both within reach (allow 45 min from Dinan to Evran, 25 min more to Treverien).

For another biking excursion, turn left rather than right at

Brittany

Dinan's port. Staying on the Dinan side of the river, bikers can join the parade of ocean-bound boats. It's a breezy and level 30-minute ride past rock faces, cornfields, and slate-roofed homes to the picturesque Port de Lyvet (cross small dam to reach village, trail ends a short distance beyond). **L'Effet Mer** café/restaurant is perfectly positioned in the village (open daily for lunch, dinner, or a refreshing drink, closed Wed off-season, tel. 02 96 83 21 10). Serious bikers should continue on to St. Suliac via La Vicomte and Modreuc (see "By Car," below).

By Boat: Boats depart from Dinan's port, at the bottom of rue du Jerzual, 50 feet to the left of the Old Bridge on the Dinan side (schedules depend on tides, get details at TI). The one-hour cruise on the *Jaman IV* boat comes with an English-speaking guide, plenty of scenery, and a chance to go through a lock (€9, runs April–Oct, 2–4/day, closed Mon except July–Aug, tel. 06 07 87 64 90). A longer cruise with **Compagnie Corsaire** goes to St. Malo (one-way–€22, runs April–Sept, 1/day, slow and scenic 2.5 hrs one-way, schedule changes with the tide, tel. 08 25 16 81 20 or ask at TI). Enjoy St. Malo (described below), then take the bus back (or vice versa), get bus schedule before leaving Dinan (5/day, 50 min, no buses Sun). You can also rent a small motorboat from **Danfleurenn Nautic** (€21–36/hour, €61–71/half-day, €116–131/day, prices depend on boat size, 21 rue du Quai, tel. 06 07 45 89 97, book ahead for a half or full day.)

By Car: Meandering the Rance River Valley by car requires a good map (the orange Michelin #309 worked for me) and good navigation skills. Drivers connecting Dinan and St. Malo can include this short Rance joyride detour. For a manageable loop trip from Dinan, drop down to the port, then follow D-12 with the river to your right toward Taden and Plouër-sur-Rance. Cross the Rance on the small dam at la Hisse to cute little Port de Lyvet. Head to La Vicomte, then stop in Modreuc for a fine view up the river. From here, find D-29 north and track your way to little **St. Suliac,** a pretty little port town with a handful of restaurants, a small grocery store, and a photogenic *boulangerie*. Stroll the ancient alleys, find a bench on the grassy waterfront, and consider lunch here. **La Ferme du Boucanier Bistrot** is a good bet (closed Tue–Wed, 2 rue de l'Hôpital, tel. 02 23 15 06 35). From here, continue on to St. Malo or return to Dinan.

SLEEPING

Dinan is popular. Weekends and summers are tight; book ahead if you can. Dinan likes its nightlife, so be careful of loud rooms over bars, particularly on lively weekends.

Sleep Code

(€1 = $1.30, country code: 33)
S = Single, **D** = Double/Twin, **T** = Triple, **Q** = Quad, **b** = bathroom,
s = shower only, * = French hotel rating system (0–4 stars).
Unless otherwise noted, credit cards are accepted and English
is spoken.

To help you sort easily through these listings, I've divided
the rooms into three categories based on the price for a standard double room with bath:

\$\$\$ Higher Priced—Most rooms €90 or more.
\$\$ Moderately Priced—Most rooms between €60–90.
\$ Lower Priced—Most rooms €60 or less.

In the Old Center

\$\$ Hôtel Arvor**, ideally located in the old city a block off place
du Guesclin, has 24 modern and sufficiently comfortable rooms
behind an old stone façade (standard Db-€50–65, Tb-€68–75,
larger rooms for up to 6 people-€105–165, elevator, 5 rue Pavie, tel.
02 96 39 21 22, fax 02 96 39 83 09, www.hotel-arvor-dinan.com,
hotel-arvor@wanadoo.fr).

\$\$ Chambres d'Hôtes le Logis du Jerzual is just about as
cozy as it gets. The ideal host, Sylive Ronserray, welcomes guests
with five warmly decorated rooms, period furnishings, and
thoughtful touches throughout. Enjoy the terraced yard in this
haven of calm so close to the action. It's just up from the port but a
long, steep walk below the main town (Db-€70–85, extra bed-€20,
includes breakfast, 25 rue du Petit Fort, tel. 02 96 85 46 54, fax 02
96 39 46 94, www.logis-du-jerzual.com, ronsseray@wanadoo.fr).
Drive up rue du Petit Fort from the port (it's well-signed) and drop
your bags. Parking is nearby.

\$\$ Hôtel la Tour de l'Horloge** is burrowed deep in the
center, with 12 rooms with little personality but fair-enough rates.
The place needs new carpeting and a fresh coat of paint, and
rooms fronting the bar-lined rue de la Chaux can be noisy (Sb-
€45–55, Db-€50–60, Tb-€66–70, Qb-€81, 5 rue de la Chaux, ring
doorbell to enter, tel. 02 96 39 96 92, fax 02 96 85 06 99, hiliotel
@wanadoo.fr).

\$ Hôtel du Théâtre is a budget traveler's dream, with seven
surprisingly good rooms (when you consider the price) above a
snappy café/bar, right across from Hôtel Arvor (S/D-€24, Db-
€29, Tb-€39, 2 rue Ste. Claire, tel. 02 96 39 06 91).

Brittany

On Place du Guesclin

These hotels offer the easiest, closest parking on place du Guesclin (except on Wed night, since Thu is market day).

$$$ Hôtel le d'Avaugour***, facing a busy street, is Dinan's reliable three-star hotel, with an efficient staff and a backyard garden oasis near the town's medieval wall. The wood-furnished rooms have great beds (all queen or king) and modern hotel amenities, including a TV sound system that works in the bathroom (street-side Db-€90–170, garden-side Db-€120–220, third person-€30, suites available, prices vary greatly by season, rooms over garden are best, elevator, bikes available, 1 place du Champ, tel. 02 96 39 07 49, fax 02 96 85 43 04, www.avaugourhotel.com, contact @avaugourhotel.com).

$$ Hôtel Ibis Dinan** stands a few minutes below place du Guesclin (on place Duclos), offering shiny, predictable comfort in cookie-cutter rooms. They may have rooms when others don't (Db-€46–86, Tb-€56–96, Qb-€87–140, 1 place Duclos, tel. 02 96 39 46 15, fax 02 96 85 44 03, www.ibishotel.com, h5977@accor .com).

$ Hôtel la Duchess Anne* has nine bright, simple, linoleum-floored rooms (one for families) and small bathrooms above a modest café/restaurant. The owners, les Gourgands, are Old World French, but will work with you (Sb-€39, Db-€46, Tb/Qb-€55–83, 10 place du Guesclin, tel. 02 96 39 59 76, fax 02 96 87 57 26).

At the Port

$$$ Best Western Hôtel Jerzual*** feels *très americain* with a spacious lobby, a pool, a sauna, a café/bar, a restaurant, and comfortable rooms with big beds. It's well below the old city of Dinan, on the port (standard Db-€89–120, bigger Db-€165–215, extra person-€22, 26 quai des Talard, tel. 02 96 87 02 02, fax 02 96 87 02 03, www.bestwestern.com, hotel-jerzual.dinan@wanadoo.fr).

Near the Train Station

$ Hôtel de la Gare* faces the station and offers the complete Breton experience, with *charmant* Laurence and Claude (who both love Americans), a local café hangout, and surprisingly quiet, clean, and comfy rooms for a bargain. Don't let the hallways scare you (D-€24, Ds-€37, Db/Tb/Qb-€45, place de la Gare, tel. 02 96 39 04 57, fax 02 96 39 02 29).

Near Dinan

$$ Hôtel Manoir de Rigourdaine** is *the* place to stay if you have a car and two nights, and want to experience Brittany. Overlooking a gorgeous scene of green meadows and turquoise water, this well-renovated farmhouse comes with beams, generous and cozy public spaces, immaculate grounds, Internet access, and three-star rooms (many with views) for two-star prices. Run by ever-so-helpful Patrick and Anne-France, you won't want to leave (perfectly fine Db-€68, roomier Db-€76–82, extra person-€15, I prefer the upstairs rooms, 15-min drive north of Dinan, tel. 02 96 86 89 96, fax 02 96 86 92 46, www.hotel-rigourdaine.fr, hotel.rigourdaine @wanadoo.fr). If coming from Dinan, drop down to the port and follow D-12 toward Taden, then drive along Plouër-sur-Rance toward Langrolay and look for signs. If coming from the St. Malo area, take N-137 toward Rennes, then N-176 toward Dinan, take the Rance Plouër exit, and follow Langrolay until you see signs.

EATING

Dinan has good restaurants for every budget. Since *galettes* (savory crêpes) are the specialty, *crêperies* are a good and inexpensive choice, available on every corner. Crêpes with ham can be salty. Be daring and try the crêpes with scallops and cream, or go for the egg-and-cheese crêpes.

Crêperie des Artisans is well worth the walk for connoisseurs of fine crêpes. Gentle, knowledgeable owner Patrick uses traditional local ingredients. Try the *lait ribot* (a frothy, slightly sour milk drink) or the extra dry cider from the wooden barrel in the corner (€9–14 *menus*, 6 rue du Petit Fort, halfway down to the port, tel. 02 96 39 44 10).

Crêperie Ahna, which has good street appeal, is perennially busy satisfying its loyal clientele with tasty crêpes and salads (closed Sun, 7 rue de la Poissonnerie, tel. 02 96 39 09 13).

La P'tite Cantine offers friendly greetings, fine salads, and meats grilled in the small fireplace (3 courses of crêpes-€12, closed Tue, 17 rue de l'Apport, tel. 02 96 87 56 75).

Le Cantorbery, a traditional restaurant, is a warm place (literally), where meats are grilled in the dining-room fireplace *à la tradition*. The seafood is *très* tasty (2-course *menu* from €12, 3-course *menu* from €25, open daily, just off place du Guesclin at 6 rue Ste. Claire, tel. 02 96 39 02 52).

La Fleur de Sel is named after sea salt, a prized local resource, and features well-prepared seafood and traditional fare served in an elegant setting (*menus* from €23–53, closed Mon and for dinner Sun and Wed, 7 rue Ste. Claire, tel. 02 96 85 15 14).

You'll find several cozy restaurants along the river in the old port. **Café Terrasses** sits right on the river, next to **L'Atelier Gourmand,** and offers views, pasta, and other basic dishes (come for the setting, not the cuisine). Consider a drink on its riverfront terrace (*menus* from €17, tel. 02 96 39 09 60).

Nightlife: So many lively bars line the narrow, pedestrian-friendly **rue de la Cordonnerie** that the street is nicknamed "rue de la Soif" (Street of Thirst). When the weather is good, you can sit outside at the long, wooden tables and strike up a conversation with a friendly Breton.

TRANSPORTATION CONNECTIONS

From Dinan by Train to: Paris' Gare Montparnasse (6/day, 4 hrs, change in Dol and Rennes; or take the €9 70-min bus to Rennes and transfer to the 2-hr TGV, 6/day), **Pontorson–Mont St. Michel** (3/day, 2 hrs, change in Dol, then bus or taxi from Pontorson, see "Transportation Connections" on page 251), **St. Malo** (5/day, 1 hr, change in Dol, bus is better, see below), **Amboise** (5/day, 5–6 hrs, via Rennes, then TGV to Paris with no station change needed in Paris; or cross-country via Rennes, Le Mans, and Tours—2/day, 5–6 hrs).

By Bus to: **St. Malo** (5/day, 50 min, faster and better than trains, as bus stops in both cities are more central), **Mont St. Michel** (2/day, 5 hrs, awkward connection in St. Malo).

More Sights near Dinan

▲▲ Scenic Drive Between Dinan and Mont St. Michel

Brittany

This lovely ride is worth ▲▲▲ if it's clear. Dinan is ideally situated for a quick taste-of-Brittany driving tour that samples a bit of the rugged peninsula's coast. If you're connecting Dinan and Mont St. Michel, link the two with this worthwhile little detour. These directions are from Dinan to Mont St. Michel, but it works well in reverse order (see page 251). Allow 2.5 hours for the drive between Mont St. Michel and St. Malo, including stops (the direct drive takes 45 min). On a weekend or in summer, the drive will take longer. Start early.

From St. Malo (a worthwhile stop described on page 267), take the scenic road hugging the coast east on D-201 to Pointe du Grouin, where the appropriately named Emerald Coast (Côte d'Emeraude) begins. Leave St. Malo, following Cancale and passing countless roundabouts, then look for signs to *Rothéneuf* where you'll access D-201, which skirts in and out of film-gobbling views. Many brown signs lead to short worthwhile detours to the coast, and these are my two favorite ones:

Ile Besnard and Dunes de Chevets: A five-minute detour off D-201 leads to this glorious, sandy beach arcing alongside a crescent bay. There's a nature trail above the beach, rocks rising from the water to scramble on, and a view restaurant by the campground

Near Dinan

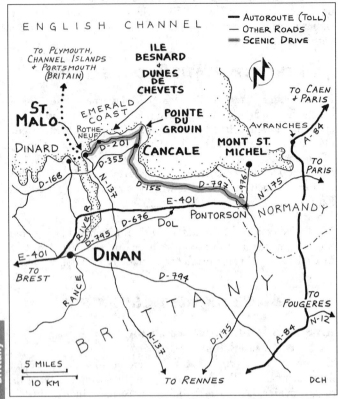

(Les Chevets Bar/Restaurant, closed Mon–Tue). From the hamlet of La Guimorais, a 10-minute drive above Rothéneuf, follow signs to *Ile Besnard* and *Dunes de Chevets* to the very end (past the campground), and park at the far end of the lot.

Pointe du Grouin: This striking rock outcrop yields views from easy trails in all directions. Park near Hôtel du Grouin (outdoor café with views), and continue on foot. Pass the *semaphore du grouin* (signal station), where paths lead everywhere. Breathe in the sea air. Can you spot Mont St. Michel in the distance? The big rock below is L'Ile des Landes, an island earmarked for a fort during the French Revolution. The fort was never built, and the island remains home to thousands of birds. What fool would build on an island in this bay?

Return to your car and leave Pointe du Grouin, following signs to *Cancale,* Brittany's appealing oyster capital. Its harbor *(le port)* is lined with restaurants, all offering oysters and mussels. Upon arrival in Cancale, follow *par la côte* signs to arrive on the port side, where you'll find plenty of restaurants to choose from. Slurp oysters here.

Cancale is a 45-minute drive from Mont St. Michel. Head out of Cancale toward Mont St. Michel on D-155, then D-797, and drive along *la Route de la Baie,* which skirts the bay and passes big-time oyster farming, windmills, flocks of sheep, and at low tide, grounded boats waiting for the sea to return. On a clear day, look for Mont St. Michel in the distance. On a foggy day, look harder.

▲St. Malo

Come here to experience *the* Breton beach resort. The old center (called Intra Muros) is your target, with powerful ramparts that encircle the entire town. It has an eerie, almost claustrophobic feeling, due to the concentration of tall, dark stone buildings hemmed in by the tall ramparts. The town feels better up top on the walls. It's a rewarding half-mile romp around the walls; stairs provide access at each door *(porte).* Drop down and walk on the beaches (if the tides allow), then find your way inside the walls to sample seafood. There's no shortage of restaurants here. St. Malo is a zoo best avoided in summer. But if you're game, it's an easy 45-minute drive—or a manageable bus or train ride—from Mont St. Michel or Dinan.

If you're arriving in St. Malo **by car,** follow *Centre-Ville* signs to the old center (signs lead to Intra-Muros), and park as close to the walls as you can. Parking is usually available on the port side of the walls (follow *Gare Maritime* signs) or near the TI, directly across from the entrance gate (Porte St. Vincent).

To turn this town into a ▲▲ sight (best by car), follow signs to *Centre-Ville,* then *Alet,* and park near the **Tour de Solidor.** The village of Alet is just a few minutes' drive past St. Malo's port (a 20-min walk to the old center), but feels a world apart. A splendid walking path above the tower leads (best clockwise) around this small point with splendid views of crashing waves, the city of Dinard, the open sea, and finally, St. Malo (allow 30 min at a relaxed pace). WWII bunkers cap the small hill with a memorial you can visit. You'll find several popular cafés facing the bay back near the Tour de Solidor.

St. Malo's **TI** is across from the main city gate on Esplanade St. Vincent (July–Aug Mon–Sat 9:00–19:30, Sun 10:00–18:00; Sept–June daily 9:00–12:30 & 13:30–18:00; tel. 08 25 13 52 00, www.saint-malo-tourisme.com). A ferry runs between St. Malo and Dinard (below).

The main **bus stops** are across from the TI (buses to Dinan: 5/day, 50 min; and to Mont St Michel: 2–3/day, 2 hrs via Pontorson).

Brittany

▲Dinard

This upscale old resort comes with a kid-friendly beach and plenty of old-time, Coney Island–style, beach-promenade ambience (2 buses/day from Dinan). The small passenger-only ferry to St. Malo provides the most scenic arrival (departs from below Promenade du Clair de Lune at Embarcadère).

The **TI,** between the casino and place de la République parking lot, is at 2 boulevard Féart (daily 9:30–12:30 & 14:00–18:00, July–Aug until 19:00, tel. 02 99 46 94 12, www.ot-dinard.com). To get to the TI from place de la République, walk toward the water, take your first right, and make another right onto boulevard Féart.

Dinard is a 10- to 20-minute drive from St. Malo. Leaving St. Malo, follow signs through the unappealing port reading *Barrage de la Rance;* in Dinard, follow *Centre-Ville* signs, and park on place de la République.

▲Fougères

This very Breton city is a handy stop for drivers traveling directly between the Loire châteaux and Mont St. Michel. Fougères has one of Europe's largest medieval castles, a fine old city center, and a panoramic park viewpoint. Drivers should follow *Centre-Ville* signs, then *Château,* and park at the free lot just past the château.

For a terrific leg-stretching introductory stroll, start from the parking lot by the château. Walk into Fougères with the water-filled moat on your left, then follow *Jardin Public* signs. Stop for a peek in the handsome church of St. Sulpice (English handout inside); the woodwork is exceptional, from the paneled walls and ceiling to the choir stalls and the carved altar. Then let the *Jardin Public* signs lead you through back streets, passing gingerbread-like Breton homes, up into the lush park. Walk up through mani-cured gardens to the base of St. Léonard Church and a gorgeous floral panorama. Double back most of the way you came, then veer right to the château and under the stone gate. There's no reason to enter the château unless you need more exercise or a town map (€4, daily 10:00–12:30 & 14:00–18:00). For a good view of the castle without the previous climb, walk a block above the castle (up rue de la Pinterie) and find the short ramparts across from the *crêperie* recommended below.

Try one of the cafés near the castle, such as the locally popular **Crêperie des Remparts,** one block uphill from the castle; you can't miss the orange windows (closed Wed, 102 rue de la Pinterie, tel. 02 99 94 53 53).

Brittany

THE LOIRE

The Loire River—which gives its name to this popular tourist region—glides gently east to west, officially separating northern from southern France. The strategic value of this river, and the valley's prime location in the center of the country (and near Paris) has made this an essential area to defend for more than a thousand years. And defended it was, as the Loire region is home to more than a thousand castles and palaces in all shapes and sizes. When a "valley address" became a must-have among 16th-century hunting-crazy royalty, rich Renaissance palaces replaced outdated medieval castles.

Hundreds of these castles and palaces are open to visitors, and they're the key reason to visit the Loire (you'll see better villages and cities elsewhere). Today's Loire Valley is carpeted with fertile fields, crisscrossed by rivers, and laced with rolling hills. It's one of France's most important agricultural regions, but it's also a burgeoning bedroom community of Paris, thanks to the TGV bullet trains that put France's capital within an hour of this pastoral area.

Choosing a Home Base

This is a big, unwieldy region for travelers, so I've divided it into two halves, each centered around a good, manageable town to use as a base: Amboise or Chinon. Châteaux-holics stay longer and sleep in both towns.

Amboise is the best home base for first-timers to this area, as it offers handy access to these important châteaux: Chenonceau, Blois, Chambord, Cheverny, Fougères-sur-Bièvre, Chaumont-sur-Loire, Loches, and Valençay.

The Loire

Chinon and its nearby châteaux feel less touristed and appeal to road-less-traveled types. The key sights in this area include the châteaux of Azay-le-Rideau, Langeais, Villandry, Chatonnière, Rivau, Ussé, and the Abbaye Royale de Fontevraud.

Loches and Azay-le-Rideau are two possible home-base options for drivers, who should also consider the tempting rural accommodations listed throughout this chapter.

Amboise is east of the big city of Tours, and Chinon lies to Tours' west. It's about a 90-minute drive from Amboise to Chinon. Visiting châteaux west of Tours while sleeping in or near Amboise leaves you with a three-hour round-trip drive (and vice versa from Chinon)—certainly doable, but not my idea of good travel. Do what you can to avoid crossing the traffic-laden city of Tours (trust me).

Planning Your Time

With convenient trains to Paris and Charles de Gaulle Airport, the Loire can be a good first or last stop on your French odyssey (22 trains/day between Paris and Amboise, 2 hrs; 5 trains/day connect Paris' Charles de Gaulle airport and Tours in one hour, easy car rental at Tours' station).

A day and a half is sufficient to sample the best châteaux. Don't go overboard. Two châteaux, possibly three (if you're a big person), make up the recommended daily dosage. Famous châteaux are least crowded early and late in the day. Most open at about 9:00 and close between 18:00 and 19:00. During the off-season, some close from 12:00 to 14:00 and at 17:00.

Drivers: For the single best day in the Loire, consider this plan: Sleep in or near Amboise and visit Chenonceau early (arrive by 9:00), when crowds are smaller; spend midday at Chambord (30-min drive from Chenonceau); enjoy Chaumont or Cheverny on the way back to your hotel (the hunting dogs are fed at 17:00 on most days at Cheverny—see page 300). Remember to allow time to visit Amboise. With a second full day, move to Chinon and visit Villandry and Langeais en route, then devote your afternoon to Chinon, and your evening to Azay-le-Rideau (sound-and-light show). The best map of the area is Michelin #518, covering all the sights described in this chapter (the TI's free map of Touraine, the area surrounding Tours, is also quite good).

Try to see one château on your drive in (for example, if arriving from the north, visit Chambord, Cheverny, or Blois; if coming from the west or the south, see Azay-le-Rideau, Chinon, Langeais, or Villandry). If you're coming from Burgundy, don't miss the remarkable Château de Guédelon (see page 672 in Burgundy chapter). If you're driving to the Dordogne from the Loire, the A-20 autoroute via Limoges (near Oradour-sur-Glane) is fastest and toll-free until Brive-la-Gaillarde.

Without Wheels: A limited visit to the Loire is doable as a day trip from Paris. Several minivan and bus tours make getting to the main châteaux a breeze (see "Getting Around the Loire Valley," below).

On a tight budget, catch the once-per-day bus (weekdays only) from Amboise to Chenonceaux (the town), tour Chenonceau (the château), then spend the afternoon enjoying Amboise, its château, and Leonardo's last stand at Clos-Lucé. With a second day, take the train to Blois, tour its castle and old town, then take the excursion bus from there to Chambord and Cheverny. For a little more money, you could take a minivan excursion to these châteaux directly from Amboise. (For more train and bus specifics, see "Transportation Connections" from Amboise, page 287.) Budget travelers based in Chinon can bike to Langeais, Ussé, and Villandry, and/or train via Tours to Azay-le-Rideau and Langeais.

The Loire

Getting Around the Loire Valley

In the Loire Valley, you can see most highlights via train, bus, or minivan tour. However, to get to the less famous châteaux without a car, you'll either need to arrange for a custom minivan excursion (affordable for small groups), or be up for a bike ride (gorgeous scenery, great option for those with enough time and stamina).

By Train

With easy access from Amboise and Chinon, the big city of Tours is the transport hub for travelers bent on using the train or buses to explore the Loire (but has little else to offer visitors). Tours has two important train stations and a major bus station (with service to several châteaux). The main train station is called Tours SNCF, and the smaller, suburban TGV station is St. Pierre-des-Corps. Check the schedules carefully, as service is sparse on some lines. The châteaux of Amboise, Blois, Chenonceau, Langeais, Chinon, and Azay-le-Rideau have some train and/or bus service from Tours' main station (although Chenonceau is better by bus or bike from Amboise). See under each sight for specifics, and seriously consider a minivan excursion (see below).

By Bus or Minivan Excursion

A variety of bus and minivan excursions offer painless transportation to the valley's châteaux. These organized itineraries make life far easier for those without a car. TIs in the region should have details on the options listed here, and on others offering similar services.

While the minivan companies listed below don't visit all the castles in this chapter, they organize custom excursions to more remote châteaux, and will pick up your small group in Amboise, Chinon, or Azay-le-Rideau (€20–35/person on half-day itineraries from Tours, €45–50 for all day; figure €200 for groups of up to seven for 4 hours, €380 for all day).

From Amboise to Châteaux East of Tours: This area's three big-name castles—Chenonceau, Chambord, Cheverny—are all reachable via bus; minivan tours offer visits to the same three, and quick glances of a few others.

By Bus: If you're on a budget and visiting in summer, the region's buses aren't a bad option. Two bus routes described below run from the Blois train station, which is an easy train ride from Amboise (14/day, 20 min).

On weekdays year-round, the #2 city bus runs from Blois to Chambord (1/day, about 30 min, leaves Blois train station at about noon, returns from Chambord at about 18:00, allow €3.50, no bus on Sun). Far better is the excursion bus that runs between Blois, Chambord, and Cheverny three times a day, allowing you to visit both châteaux with your pick of three return times. This service runs from mid-May to early September (departures from Blois train station are at 9:10, 11:10, and 13:40). You can stay at Chambord (the first stop) for two, five, or seven hours, then catch the next bus to Cheverny, or head back to Blois (€11.50 includes bus fare and good discounts on château entries, buy tickets and get schedule from TI or bus driver, look for bus marked *Chambord/Cheverny* in front of the restaurant at the Blois train station). When combined with a visit to the château in Blois, this makes a good, full day from Amboise. For details, call the Blois TI at 02 54 90 41 41 (also see Blois section on page 294).

By Minivan: **Touraine Evasion** offers daily excursions from Amboise to Chambord and Cheverny in a minibus with some commentary. You'll also enjoy drive-by views of the Chaumont and Blois châteaux (€31, runs March–Nov, leaves from Amboise TI at 14:00, returns at 18:30, also leaves from Tours train station, tel. 06 07 39 13 31, fax 02 47 44 31 10, www.tourevasion.com, ask for friendly Patrick).

Pascal Accolay runs **Acco-Dispo,** a small, personal minibus company with good all-day château tours from Amboise and Tours. Costs vary with the itinerary (€32/half-day, €50/day, daily, free hotel pickups, 18 rue des Vallées in Amboise, tel. 06 82 00 64 51, fax 02 47 57 67 13, www.accodispo-tours.com). English is the primary language. While on the road, you'll get a fun and enthusiastic running commentary covering each château's background, as well as the region's contemporary scene—but you're on your own at each château (and you pay the admission fee). All-day tours depart 8:30–10:30 (varies by itinerary); afternoon tours depart 13:20–13:50. Both return to Amboise at about 18:30. Several itineraries are available; most include Chenonceau, and some throw in a wine-tasting. Reserve two to three days ahead, if possible. Groups are small, ranging from two to eight château-hoppers. (Day-trippers from Paris find this service convenient; after a 1-hour TGV ride to Tours, you're met near the central station and returned there at day's end.) Acco-Dispo also runs multiday tours of the Loire and Brittany.

From Chinon to Châteaux West of Tours: A new **bus** service runs three times a day from Chinon to Langeais and Azay-le-Rideau; ask at the TI for schedules. **Minivan** excursions head to Azay-le-Rideau and Villandry from Tours, an easy train ride from Chinon (12 trains or SNCF buses/day, 1 hr). Try **Touraine Evasion, Acco-Dispo** (both described above), or **Quart de Tours** (tel. 06 85 72 16 22, fax 02 47 49 98 57, www.quartdetours.com, also offers excursions to châteaux near Amboise, but picks up only from Tours). For similar rates, these three companies offer minivan trips with regular departures on fixed itineraries from Tours' main train station (for example, Villandry and Azay-le-Rideau for about €20).

By Bike

Cycling options are endless in the Loire, where the elevation gain is generally manageable. (However, if you only have a day or two, rent a car or stick to the châteaux easily reached by buses and mini-vans.) Amboise, Blois, and Chinon—with easy rental options—

Hot-Air Balloon Rides

In France's most popular regions, you'll find hot-air balloon companies eager to take you for a ride (Burgundy, the Loire, Dordogne, and Provence are best suited for ballooning). It's not cheap, but it's unforgettable—a once-in-a-lifetime chance to sail serenely over châteaux, canals, vineyards, Romanesque churches, and villages. Balloons don't go above 3,000 feet, and usually fly much lower than this, so you get a bird's-eye view of France's sublime landscapes.

Most companies offer similar deals and work this way: Trips range from 45 to 90 minutes of air time, to which you must add an hour for preparation, champagne toast, and transport back to your starting point. Deluxe trips add a gourmet picnic, making it a three-hour event. Allow about €150 for a short tour, and about €260 for longer flights. Departures are, of course, weather dependent, and are usually scheduled first thing in the morning or in early evening. If you've booked ahead and the weather turns bad, you can reschedule your flight, but you can't get your money back. Most balloon companies charge about €20 more for a bad-weather refund guarantee; unless your itinerary's very loose, it's a good idea.

Flight season is from April through October. It's smart to bring a jacket for the breeze, though temperatures in the air won't differ too much from temperatures on the ground. Air sickness is usually not a problem, as the ride is typically slow and even. Baskets have no seating, so count on standing the entire trip. Group (and basket) size can vary from 4 to 16 passengers. Area TIs have brochures. France Montgolfières gets good reviews and offers flights in the areas that we recommend (tel. 08 10 60 01 53, or 02 54 32 20 48, fax 02 54 32 20 07, www.france-montgolfiere.com).

The Loire

make good biking bases. A network of nearly 200 miles of bike paths and well-signed small roads connect many châteaux between Chambord and Chaumont. Pick up the free bike-path map, *Le Pays des Châteaux à Vélo*, at any TI. (I also list several accommodations with easy access to these bike paths below.) Biking specifics are listed per town for Amboise, Blois, and Chinon.

Near Chinon, a 30-mile bike path runs along the Cher River, passing right by Villandry and Ussé and near Langeais, joining the Loire River at Tours and continuing along the Loire River from there. To follow this route, pick up the *La Loire à Vélo* brochure at any area TI.

Tours-based **Detours du Loire** can deliver rental bikes to most places in the Loire for reasonable rates (5 rue du Rempart, tel. 02 47 61 22 35, www.locationdevelos.com).

By Car

You can rent a car in most of the towns listed (see "Helpful Hints" for Amboise and for Chinon). I've listed specific driving instructions for each destination covered in this chapter.

Cuisine Scene in the Loire Valley

Here in "the garden of France," locally produced food is delicious. Loire Valley rivers yield fresh trout *(truite)*, salmon *(saumon)*, and smelt *(éperlau)*, which are often served fried *(friture)*. *Rillettes,* a stringy pile of cooked and whipped pork, makes for a cheap, mouthwatering sandwich spread (use lots of mustard and add a baby pickle, called a *cornichon*). The area's fine goat cheeses include Crottin de Chavignol (*crottin* means horse dung, which is what this cheese, when aged, resembles), Saint-Maure Fermier (soft and creamy), and Selles-sur-Cher (mild). For dessert, try a delicious *tarte tatin* (upside-down caramel-apple tart).

The best and most expensive white wines are the Sancerres, made on the less touristed, western edge of the Loire. Less expensive, but still tasty, are Touraine Sauvignons and the sweeter Vouvray, whose grapes are grown near Amboise. Vouvray is also famous for its light and refreshing sparkling wines (called *vins pétillants*)—locals will tell you the only proper way to begin any meal in this region is with a glass of it, and I can't disagree. The better reds come from Chinon and Bourgeuil.

Remember, restaurants serve only during lunch (11:30–14:00) and dinner (19:00–21:00, later in bigger cities); bigger cafés serve food throughout the day.

East of Tours

Amboise

Straddling the widest stretch of the Loire River, the town slumbers in the shadow of its hilltop château. A castle has overlooked

the Loire from Amboise since Roman times. Leonardo da Vinci retired here...just one more fine idea of his.

As the royal residence of François I (r. 1515–1547), Amboise wielded far more importance than you'd imagine from a lazy walk through its pleasant, pedestrian-only commercial zone. In fact, its 14,000 residents are quite conservative, giving the town an attitude—as if no one told them they're no longer the second capital of France. The locals keep their wealth to themselves; consequently, many fine mansions hide behind nondescript facades. There's even a Royalist element in Amboise (and the duke of Paris, the guy who'd be king if there was one, lives here).

The half-mile-long "Golden Island" is the only island in the Loire substantial enough to be flood-proof and to have permanent buildings (including a soccer stadium and a 13th-century church). It was important historically as the place where northern and southern France, divided by the longest river in the country, came together. Truces were made here. The Loire marked the farthest point north that the Moors conquered as they pushed through Europe from Morocco. (Loire means "impassable" in Arabic.) Today, this region still divides the country—for example, weather forecasters say, "north of the Loire...and south of the Loire..."

With or without a car, Amboise is an ideal small-town home base for exploring the best of château country.

ORIENTATION

Amboise (pop. 11,000) covers ground on both sides of the Loire, in addition to the "Golden Island" (l'Ile d'Or) in the middle. The train station is on the north side of the Loire, but nearly everything else is on the south (château) side, including the TI and steady traffic.

Pedestrian-friendly rue Nationale parallels the river a few blocks inland and leads from the base of Château d'Amboise through the town center and past the clock tower—once part of the town wall—to the striking Romanesque Church of St. Denis.

Tourist Information

The information-packed TI is in the round building on the riverbank, on quai du Général de Gaulle (May–Sept Mon–Sat 9:30–13:00 & 14:00–18:30, Sun 9:30–13:00 & 14:00–17:00; Oct–April Mon–Sat 10:00–13:00 & 14:00–18:00, Sun 10:00–13:00; tel. 02 47 57 09 28, www.amboise-valdeloire.com). Ask about sound-and-light shows in the region (generally summers only). The TI can reserve a room for you in a hotel or *chambre d'hôte* (for a €2.50 fee), but first peruse the photo album of regional *chambres d'hôte*. Their free English service, SOS Chambres d'Hôte, can tell you what rooms are still available when the TI is closed (call 02 47 23 27 42). Public WCs are behind the TI.

Arrival in Amboise

By Train: Amboise's train station, with a post office and taxi stand, is birds-chirping peaceful. Turn left out of the station, make a quick right, and walk down rue Jules Ferry five minutes to the bridge, which leads over the Loire River to the center city. Within three blocks of the station, you'll find some of my recommended accommodations (see "Sleeping," on page 282) and one of the bike-rental shops.

By Car: Drivers set their sights on the flag-festooned château that caps the hill. Most recommended accommodations and restaurants cluster just downriver (west). Warning: If driving through Amboise with the river on your left, be aware that some streets on your right have the right-of-way when merging.

Helpful Hints

Market Days: Open-air markets are held on Friday (smaller, food only) and Sunday (bigger) in the parking lot behind the TI on the river (both 8:30–13:00).

Supermarket: Marché Plus is across from the TI (Mon–Sat 7:00–21:00, Sun 9:00–13:00), though the shops on pedestrian-only rue Nationale are infinitely more pleasing.

Internet Access: Playconnect Cyber C@fe has good rates (Tue–Sat 10:00–22:00, Sun–Mon 15:00–22:00, 119 rue Nationale, tel. 02 47 57 18 04).

Bookstore: Maison de la Presse is a fine bookstore with a small selection of English novels and a big selection of maps and English guidebooks—such as Michelin's Green Guide *Châteaux of the Loire* (English version costs €15; bookstore open Mon 14:00–19:00, Tue–Sat 8:00–19:00, Sun 9:00–13:00, across from TI at 5 quai du Général de Gaulle).

Laundry: The handy coin-op **Lav'centre** is just across the street from the TI and up allée du Sergent Turpin at #9 (allow €7/load, daily 7:00–21:00, last wash at 20:00, English instructions). The door locks at closing time; leave beforehand, or you'll trigger the alarm.

Bike Rental: You can rent a bike (roughly €11/half-day, €14/day, leave your passport or a photocopy) at either of these reliable places: **Locacycle** (daily 9:00–12:30 & 14:00–19:00, full-day rentals can be returned the next morning, near TI at 2 rue Jean-Jacques Rousseau, tel. 02 47 57 00 28) or **Cycles Richard** (Tue–Sat 9:00–12:00 & 14:30–19:00, closed Sun–Mon, located on train-station side of river, just past bridge at 2 rue de Nazelles, tel. 02 47 57 01 79). The signed bike route to Chenonceaux leads past Leonardo's Clos-Lucé.

Taxi: Call 02 47 45 19 55 or 02 47 57 13 53 (allow €20 to Chenonceaux, €30 in the evening or on Sun). Taxis wait at the Avis car rental across from the TI (see below).

Car Rental: Garage Jourdain rents cars (about a mile downriver from the TI, roughly €45/day for a small car with 100

The Loire

kilometers/60 miles free, Mon–Fri 7:45–12:00 & 14:00–18:30, Sat 9:00–12:00, closed Sun, 105 avenue de Tours, tel. 02 47 57 17 92, fax 02 47 57 77 50). Pricier **Europcar** is just outside Amboise on route de Chenonceaux (€65/day for a small car, tel. 02 47 57 07 64, fax 02 47 23 25 14).

Chocolate Fantasy: An essential and historic stop for chocoholics is **Bigot Pâtisserie & Chocolatier** (daily, one block off the river, where place Michel Debré meets rue Nationale, tel. 02 47 57 04 46).

SIGHTS AND ACTIVITIES

In Amboise

▲Château du Clos-Lucé and Leonardo da Vinci Park—In 1516, Leonardo da Vinci packed his bags (and several of his favorite paintings, including the *Mona Lisa*) and left an imploding Rome for better wine and working conditions here, in the Loire Valley. He accepted the position of engineer, architect, and painter to the French king. This "House of Light" is the plush palace where he spent his last three years. (He died May 2, 1519.) France's Renaissance king, François I, set Leonardo up  here just so he could enjoy his intellectual company. François I was 22 when his 65-year-old mentor moved in.

Cost and Hours: The €12 entry price is steep, but worthwhile for Leonardo fans with two hours to take full advantage of this sight. It's open daily April–Oct 9:00–19:00, Nov–Dec and Feb–March 9:00–18:00, Jan 9:00–17:00, follow the helpful free English handout, tel. 02 47 57 00 73, www.vinci-closluce.com.

Getting There: It's a 10-minute walk uphill from Château d'Amboise, past troglodyte homes. (The parking lot at Clos-Lucé is unsafe; don't leave anything visible in the car.)

◗ Self-Guided Tour: Your visit begins with a tour of Leonardo's elegant yet livable Renaissance home. Find the touching sketch in Leonardo's bedroom of François I comforting his genius pal on his deathbed. The house was built in 1450—just within the protective walls of the town—as a guest house to the Château d'Amboise. Today it thoughtfully re-creates (with helpful English information) the everyday atmosphere Leonardo enjoyed as he lived here—pursuing his passions to the very end.

The basement floor is filled with sketches recording the storm patterns of Leonardo's brain and models of his remarkable

Amboise

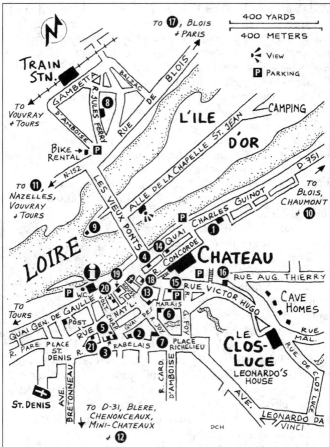

1 Le Manoir les Minimes

2 Hôtel le Clos d'Amboise

3 Le Vieux Manoir

4 Hôtel Belle-Vue

5 La Grange Chambres

6 L'Iris des Marais Chambres

7 Hôtel le Blason & L'Alliance Rest.

8 Hôtel la Brèche

9 L'Auberge de Jeunesse

10 To Château de Pray

11 To Château de Noizay, Château de Nazelles & Domaine des Bidaudieres Chambres

12 To Le Moulin du Fief Gentil & La Chevalerie

13 Le Pavillon des Lys Rest.

14 Le Lion d'Or

15 L'Epicerie & Le Parvis Restaurants

16 L'Amboiserie Restaurant

17 To L'Auberge de Launay Rest.

18 Bigot Pâtisserie & Chocolatier

19 Maison de la Presse Bookstore & Marché Plus Supermarket

20 Launderette

21 Internet Café

The Loire

inventions (inspired by nature and built according to his notes). It's hard to imagine that this Roman candle of creativity died nearly 500 years ago. In the model room, notice the entry to the long tunnel that connected this house with the château—created so the king could come and go as he pleased. The adjacent garden café is reasonable and appropriately meditative; above it is a French-only 25-minute video about Leonardo.

Your visit finishes with a stroll through the park grounds, which feature life-size models of his inventions (including some that function, such as a "revolving bridge"), "sound stations" (in English), and translucent replicas of some of his paintings. Here it's clear that everything that Leonardo observed and created was based on his intense study of nature.

▲**Château d'Amboise**—This historic royal residence was partially designed by Leonardo da Vinci. The king who did most of the building (Charles VIII) is famous for accidentally killing himself by walking into a doorjamb on his way to a tennis match (seriously). Later occupants were shorter—including his successor, Louis XII, who moved the royal court to Blois. François I brought the Renaissance here in 1516 (through Leonardo da Vinci). The good English handout gives a credible tour and provides a helpful historical perspective. While several rooms are well-decorated, no one room stands out as exceptionally furnished or compelling, and this place pales when compared to other area châteaux. Still, it's handy, and offers terrific views over Amboise that alone almost merit the entry fee.

Cost and Hours: €8.20, daily April–June 9:00–18:30, July–Aug 9:00–19:00, Sept–Oct and March 9:00–18:00, Nov–Jan 9:00–12:00 & 14:00–16:45, Feb 9:00–12:00 & 13:30–17:30, tel. 02 47 57 00 98, www.chateau-amboise.com.

❍ **Self-Guided Tour:** After climbing the flower-lined ramp, our first stop is the lacy, petite chapel where Leonardo da Vinci is supposedly buried. This flamboyant little Gothic chapel comes with two fireplaces "to comfort the king" and two plaques "evoking the final resting place" of Leonardo (one in French, the other in Italian). Where he's actually buried, no one seems to know. Look up at the ceiling to appreciate the lacy design.

Views of rooftops and the Loire River escort you to the castle entry. Inside, you'll find redbrick rooms lined with high-backed chairs and massive stone fireplaces. At stop #2 ("the Sentry Walk"), several plans show the château's original size. From here,

The Loire

the strategic value of this site is clear—the visibility is great and the river below provided a natural defense. The bulky horsemen's tower climbs 130 feet in five spirals—designed for a mounted soldier in a hurry. Before entering the tower ramp, take a sharp right and walk on the outside passage around the same tower; mind the gargoyles' big mouths above.

The top-floor rooms are well-furnished from the post-Revolutionary 1800s and demonstrate the continued interest in this château among French nobility. What a difference in comfort a few hundred years make.

After touring the interior, wander the gardens for good views of the château.

▲Château d'Amboise Sound-and-Light Show—If you're into S&L, this is considered one of the best shows of its kind in the area. While it's entirely in French, you can buy the English booklet for €5. Volunteer locals from toddlers to pensioners re-create the life of François I with costumes, juggling, impressive light displays, and fireworks. Dress warmly, and be prepared for a long show (€13–16, Wed and Sat late June–July 22:30–24:00, Aug 22:00–23:30, get details at TI or call 02 47 57 14 47, www.renaissance-amboise.com). The ticket window is on the ramp to the château and opens at 20:30. While you may feel locked in, you're welcome to leave at any time.

Mini-Châteaux—This five-acre park on the edge of Amboise (on the route to Chenonceaux) shows the major Loire châteaux in 1:25-scale models, forested with 2,000 bonsai trees and laced together by a model TGV train. For children, it's a great introduction to the real châteaux they'll be visiting. The English brochure is essential (adults-€12, kids-€8, daily June–Aug 10:00–19:00, Sept–Oct 10:00–18:00, April–May 10:30–19:00, closed Nov–March, last entry 1 hour before closing, tel. 02 47 23 44 44, www.mini-chateaux.com).

You'll find other kid-oriented attractions at Mini-Châteaux; skip the donkey show, but consider playing a round of mini-golf and feeding the fish in the moat (a great way to get rid of that old baguette).

Caveau des Vignerons—This small cave offers free tastings of cheeses and regional wines from 12 different vintners (mid-March–mid-Nov daily 10:00–19:00; under Château d'Amboise, across from recommended l'Epicerie restaurant—see "Eating," page 287; tel. 02 47 57 23 69).

Biking from Amboise—Allow an hour to Chenonceaux (about eight miles one-way), but be warned: The first two miles are uphill, and the entire ride is on a road with light traffic. White-and-green biking signs will guide you past Clos-Lucé to Chenonceaux. Serious bikers can ride to Chaumont (see page 301) in 90 minutes, connecting Amboise, Chenonceaux, and Chaumont in an all-day, 37-mile pedal (see "Recommended Bike Route" in the map on page 290).

Near Amboise

Wine-Tasting in Vouvray—In the nearby town of Vouvray, 10 miles toward Tours from Amboise, you'll find wall-to-wall opportunities for wine-tasting, including a convenient and top-quality winery, **Marc Brédif.** They have a good selection of Vouvray wines, as well as red wines from Chinon and Bourgueil (the most reputed reds in the Loire). Reserve ahead for their wine and cheese tastings, where five wines are paired with different cheeses. You can also take a €5 tour of their impressive 1.2 miles of cellars dug into the hillside (free tasting room open Mon–Fri 9:00–12:00 & 14:00–18:00, Sat 10:30–12:00 & 13:00–18:00, Sun 10:30–13:00, tel. 02 47 52 61 44). Coming from Amboise, you'll pass it on N-152 after Vouvray in the direction of Tours; it's on the right a few hundred yards after you enter Rochecorbon. (For tips on wine-tasting, see "French Wine-Tasting 101" on page 30.)

SLEEPING

Amboise is busy in the summer, but there are lots of reasonable hotels and *chambres d'hôte* in and around the city; the TI can help with reservations.

In the Center

$$$ Le Manoir les Minimes**** is a good place to experience the refined air of château life in a 17th-century mansion, with antique furniture and precious art objects in the public spaces. Its 15 rooms are large and modern, and it works for those seeking luxury (tall folks take note: top-floor attic rooms have low ceilings). Several rooms have views of Amboise's château (standard Db-€115–135, larger Db-€165–185, suite-€240–260, 3–4-person suites-€445, extra bed-€25, air-con, 3 blocks upriver from bridge at 34 quai Charles Guinot, tel. 02 47 30 40 40, fax 02 47 30 40 77, www.manoirlesminimes.com, reservation@manoirlesminimes.com).

$$$ Hôtel le Clos d'Amboise*** is a solid value if you want luxury without the financial pain. Amboise's best upper-range urban refuge, it's a combination of a central location, lovely gardens, and well-designed rooms that mix a touch of modern with a classic, traditional look (Db-€73–130—most are €120, Db suite-€140–170, Tb-€140, big buffet breakfast for €10, heated swimming pool, fitness room, sauna, 27 rue Rabelais, tel. 02 47 30 10 20, fax 02 47 57 33 43, www.leclosamboise.com, contact@leclosamboise.com).

Sleep Code

(€1 = about $1.30, country code: 33)
S = Single, **D** = Double/Twin, **T** = Triple, **Q** = Quad, **b** = bathroom,
s = shower only, ***** = French hotel rating system (0–4 stars).
Unless otherwise noted, credit cards are accepted and English
is spoken.

To help you easily sort through these listings, I've divided
the rooms into three categories based on the price for a standard double room with bath:

  $$$ **Higher Priced**—Most rooms €90 or more.
    $$ **Moderately Priced**—Most rooms between €60–90.
     $ **Lower Priced**—Most rooms €60 or less.

$$$ Le Vieux Manoir*** is an entirely different high-end
splurge. American expats Gloria and Bob Belknap have lovingly
restored this secluded but central one-time convent with an atten-
tion to detail that Martha Stewart could learn from. The gardens
are flawless, as is the atrium-like breakfast room; the public spaces
are oh-so-cozy; and the six bedrooms would make an antique col-
lector drool. Eager-to-help Gloria is a one-person tourist office
(Db-€135–180, cottages-€210–295 require 3-night minimum stay,
includes hearty breakfast, air-con, non-smoking, easy parking, 13
rue Rabelais, tel. & fax 02 47 30 41 27, www.le-vieux-manoir.com,
info@le-vieux-manoir.com).

$$ Hôtel Belle-Vue** is central, overlooking the river where
the bridge hits the town. This sprawling, traditional hotel offers
spacious public rooms, dark halls, and fair-value rooms, most
with modern furnishings and effective double-paned windows.
Half the rooms have views up to the château; four come with
huge shared terraces (Db-€66–72, Tb-€83–92, Qb-€110, elevator,
12 quai Charles Guinot, tel. 02 47 57 02 26, fax 02 47 30 51 23,
bellevuehotel.amboise@wanadoo.fr).

$$ La Grange Chambres welcomes you with a lovely court-
yard and four smashing, spacious rooms. The rooms have all been
tastefully restored, with modern conveniences and big beds. There's
also a common room with a fridge, couch, and tables for do-it-
yourself dinners (Db-€68, Tb-€75, Qb-€90, cash only, at 18 rue
Châptal—where rues Châptal and Rabelais meet, tel. 02 47 57 57
22, yvelinesavin-lagrange@wanadoo.fr). Adorable Yveline Savin
also rents a cool two-room apartment (€460–515/week).

$ At L'Iris des Marais, animated Katia Frain offers three
family-oriented *chambres* in a ramshackle building on a busy road.
The rooms are simple and a decent value, and her artsy garden will

The Loire

make you smile. The top-floor rooms provide basic comfort, but can be stuffy if it's hot. The garden room sleeps two more comfortably and is worth booking early (Db-€50–60, big Tb-€65, Qb-€80, Quint/b-€90, cash only, includes breakfast, 14 quai des Marais, tel. 02 47 30 46 51, www.irisdesmarais.com, vianney.frain @wanadoo.fr).

$ Hôtel le Blason** has 25 rooms in a 15th-century, half-timbered building five blocks from the river on a busy street. It's run by eager-to-please owners Agnes and Thomas, who speak beautiful English. The rooms are tight, bright, and well-maintained, with ship-cabin-like bathrooms, double-paned windows, and air-conditioning on the top floor (Sb-€48, Db-€58, Tb-€68, Qb-€78, quieter rooms in back and on top floor, free Internet access and parking, 11 place Richelieu, tel. 02 47 23 22 41, fax 02 47 57 56 18, www.leblason.fr, hotel@leblason.fr).

Near the Train Station

$$ Hôtel la Brèche*, a sleepy budget place near the station, has 14 modest rooms with thin walls and small bathrooms. Many rooms overlook a neglected garden; those on the street are generally larger and louder (S-€46, Sb-€56, D-€57, Db-€67, Tb-€79, Qb-€94, room for up to five-€105, includes breakfast, a few good family rooms, 15-min walk from city center and 2-min walk from station, 26 rue Jules Ferry, tel. 02 47 57 00 79, fax 02 47 57 65 49, www.labreche-amboise.com, info@labreche-amboise.com).

Hostel: **$ L'Auberge de Jeunesse** (Centre Charles Péguy) is ideally located on the western tip of the "Golden Island," a 10-minute walk from the train station. It's a friendly place and a great value, so book ahead (bunk in 4-bed room-€11, sheets-€3.50, breakfast-€3, first-night fee-€10, reception open daily 15:00–20:00, Ile d'Or, tel. 02 47 30 60 90, fax 02 47 30 60 91, www.mjcamboise .fr, cis@mjcamboise.fr).

Near Amboise

The area around Amboise is replete with good-value accommodations of every shape, size, and price range. This region offers drivers the best chance to experience château life at affordable rates—and my recommendations below justify the detour. You should also consider the accommodations in Chenonceaux and Hôtel du Grand St. Michel at Chambord (both listed later in this chapter).

$$$ Château de Pray**** is a 750-year-old fortified castle with hints of its medieval origins revealed beneath its Renaissance elegance. The 14 rooms provide all the comforts, with appropriately heavy furniture in the main château. A more recent annex offers four additional rooms (that sleep up to three each) with

lofts, terraces, and views of the castle. An overflowing pool and the restaurant's vegetable garden lie below the château (smaller Db in main building-€125–160, most are larger-€180, Db in annex-€100–120, family room-€230, extra bed-€32, no air-con; 3-min drive upriver from Amboise toward Chaumont on D-751, look for turnoff just after passing under bridge; tel. 02 47 57 23 67, fax 02 47 57 32 50, http://praycastel.online.fr, praycastel@online.fr). The dining room is as splendid as the chef is talented, and the service is tops—it's a relaxing place to splurge and feel good about it. Reservations are required—see contact info above (*menus* from €45, reasonable wine list).

$$$ Château de Noizay**** stands proudly over the village of Noizay. With 14 elegant rooms in a 16th-century castle and five rooms in a next-door annex, it's the most expensive place I list. You'll enter a world of polished but relaxed service, with aristocratic public spaces, a big pool, a library room, and a *très* elegant dining room (*menus* from €48). It's worth considering if Château de Pray (above) is full or if you prefer being closer to Vouvray and Tours (standard Db-€140–180, larger Db-€250–280, extra bed-€25, annex rooms have air-con, American breakfast-€25, halfway between Amboise and Vouvray in little Noizay, tel. 02 47 52 11 01, fax 02 47 52 04 64, www.chateaudenoizay.com, noizay @relaischateaux.com).

$$$ Château de Nazelles Chambres' friendly owners Veronique and Olivier Fructus have tastefully restored this five-room, 16th-century hillside manor house, once home to Chenonceau's original builder. You'll be treated to a cliff-sculpted pool, lush gardens with views over Amboise, and trails to the forest above. The three rooms in the main building are four-star quality, while the two rooms cut into the rock come with private terraces and rock-walled bathrooms (Db-€100, bigger Db-€120, includes breakfast, tel. & fax 02 47 30 53 79, www.chateau-nazelles.com, info@chateau-nazelles.com). From Amboise, take N-152 toward Tours, turn right on D-5, and then turn left in Nazelles-Négron on D-1. Quickly veer right above the post office (PTT) to 16 rue Tue-la-Soif. Look for the sign on your left, and enter through the archway on the right.

$$$ Domaine des Bidaudieres Chambres, just outside Vouvray, offers eight rooms in a gleaming 18th-century château overlooking a large pool, with a pond and the forest beyond.

The Loire

Welcoming owners Sylvie and Pascal will teach you the ins and outs of château life. This place is kid-friendly, rooms are big (and air-conditioned), the pool is bigger, and there's ping-pong, a Jacuzzi, and room to roam (Db-€125, Tb-€150, two-room troglodyte apartment that sleeps up to five-€170, small cottage ideal for four-€150, all prices include breakfast in a striking atrium room; off D-46 on the Amboise end of Vouvray—from N-152 at Vouvray, follow D-142, then D-46 toward Vernou; tel. 02 47 52 66 85, fax 02 47 52 62 17, www.bidaudieres.com, contact@bidaudieres.com).

$$ Le Moulin du Fief Gentil, a beautifully renovated 16th-century mill house, offers a lovely experience a 15-minute drive from Amboise and Chenonceaux. You get four acres, a backyard pond (fishing possible in summer, dinner picnics anytime), the possibility of home-cooked dinners (4-course dinner *menu* with wine-€26), and large, smartly decorated rooms (Db-€75, bigger Db-€95, 2-room apartment-€125, includes breakfast, cash only, tel. 02 47 30 32 51, mobile 06 64 82 37 18, www.fiefgentil.com, contact@fiefgentil.com). It's located on the edge of Bléré; from Bléré, follow signs toward Luzille, and it's on the right.

$ La Chevalerie owner Martine Aleksic rents four simple, bargain *chambres* that are family-friendly in every way. Here, you'll have a warm reception and total seclusion in a farm setting, with a swing set, tiny fishing pond, shared kitchens, and connecting rooms (Db-€43, Tb-€58, Qb-€73, includes breakfast with fresh eggs, cash only, in La Croix-en-Touraine, tel. 02 47 57 83 64, lyoubisa.aleksic@orange.fr). From Amboise, take D-31 toward Bléré, and look for the *Chambres d'Hôte* sign on your left at about three miles, then turn left onto C-105.

EATING

In Amboise

Amboise is filled with inexpensive and forgettable restaurants, but I have found a handful of places worthy of your attention. If you want to eat well and are willing to spend at least €18 for a *menu*, consider the first three listings. If ambience and price matter more than top quality, consider the last three suggestions. The focal point for most dining is across from the château entrance.

Le Pavillon des Lys is the talk of Amboise. It's where locals go for a dressy meal at reasonable prices in an intimate, elegant setting. Enjoy a drink on the terrace or in the candlelit lounge before sitting down to a special dinner (*menus* from €38, vegetarian *menu*-€26, closed Tue and late Nov–Jan, reserve ahead, 9 rue d'Orange, tel. 02 47 30 01 01, www.pavillondeslys.com).

Le Lion d'Or is also causing a stir around town, mixing traditional cuisine with good service and a comfortable setting (*menus* from €18.50, daily July–Aug, otherwise closed Wed, 17 quai Charles Guinot, tel. 02 47 57 00 23).

L'Epicerie, across from the château entry, attracts a local following and hungry tourists. It serves classic cuisine at fair prices outdoors facing the château, or beneath wood beams inside. The chef's specialty is the ducky *Tournedos de Canard* (*menus* from €23—I prefer the €25 *menu,* open daily, reserve ahead, 46 place Michel Debré, tel. 02 47 57 08 94).

L'Alliance is a sharp restaurant run by an engaging young couple (Pamela and Ludovica) trying to make their mark in Amboise. You'll dine well on creatively prepared regional specialties in a calming outdoors courtyard, almost outdoors in a glass "greenhouse," or in a lovely interior dining room (*menus* from €18, closed Wed, next to the Hôtel le Blason at 14 rue Joyeuse, tel. 02 47 30 52 13).

Le Parvis hides down a small alley opposite the château entry. Good eating energy surrounds a central grill, and budget diners are stashed on several levels inside and out (*menus* from €15, daily, 3 rue Mirabeau, tel. 02 47 57 50 07).

L'Amboiserie is a scenic budget option, with a large selection of basic dishes (crêpes, salads, meats) and a pleasant, umbrella-dotted upstairs terrace (daily July–Aug, otherwise closed Tue, Wed and Sun, 7 rue Victor Hugo, tel. 02 47 30 50 40).

Near Amboise

Drivers should consider making the three-minute drive to **Château de Pray** or **Château de Noizay** for a royal experience—but reserve first (see "Near Amboise" under "Sleeping," page 284). It's also worth a call to see if Laurent has tables available in nearby Chenonceaux, at the recommended **Hôtel la Roseraie** (15-min drive, tel. 02 47 23 90 09; see page 293).

L'Auberge de Launay gets rave reviews for its warm welcome, cozy ambience and delicious meals (*menus* from €24, daily June–Sept, otherwise closed Sun–Mon, 9 rue de la Rivière, in Limeray, about 4 miles from Amboise, across the river toward Blois, tel. 02 47 30 16 82). Owners Françoise and Helene Bail are natural hosts.

TRANSPORTATION CONNECTIONS

By Bus and Taxi

From Amboise to Nearby Châteaux: For easiest access to area châteaux, see "Getting Around the Loire Valley," page 271.

By Bus to: Chenonceaux (1–2/day, Mon–Fri only, none Sat–Sun, 15 min, one-way-€1.10; departs Amboise about 9:50, returns from Chenonceaux at about 12:25, allowing you about 80 min at the château; in summer, there's also an afternoon departure at about 14:50, with a return from Chenonceaux at about 17:10; the Amboise stop is on the post-office side of the street—look for the green-and-yellow sign at bus stop, confirm times with the TI; the Chenonceaux stop is across the street from the TI, tel. 02 47 05 30 49); **Tours** (8/day Mon–Sat, none on Sun, buses are cheaper than trains—about €2.30).

By Taxi: A cab from Amboise to Chenonceaux costs about €20, €30 on Sundays and after 19:00. (Other châteaux are too expensive by cab.) Your hotel can call one for you. The meter doesn't start until you do (see "Helpful Hints" for Amboise, on page 277).

By Train

Destinations Within the Loire

From Amboise by Train to: Blois (14/day, 20 min, bus excursions from there to Chambord and Cheverny—see "Getting Around the Loire Valley" on page 271), **Tours** (12/day, 25 min, allows connections to châteaux west of Tours), **Chinon** (9/day, 90 min, transfer in Tours).

Beyond the Loire

Twelve 15-minute trains link Amboise daily to the regional train hub of St. Pierre-des-Corps (suburban Tours). From there, you'll find reasonable connections to distant points (including the TGV to Paris' Gare Montparnasse). Transferring in Paris can be the fastest way to reach many French destinations, even in the south.

From Amboise by Train to: Paris (12/day in 1.5 hrs to Paris' Gare Montparnasse with change to TGV at Tours' St. Pierre-des-Corps, requires TGV reservation; and 10/day in 2 hrs direct to Paris's Gare d'Austerlitz, no reservation required), **Sarlat** (4/day, 5–6 hrs, several routes possible, best is to change at Tours' St. Pierre-des-Corps, then TGV to Libourne or Bordeaux–St. Jean, then train through Bordeaux vineyards to Sarlat; it's a bit slower on the route via Les Aubrais Orléans to Souillac then scenic SNCF bus to Sarlat), **Limoges** (near Oradour-sur-Glane, 9/day, 4 hrs, change at Tours' St. Pierre-des-Corps and Vierzon or at Les Aubrais–Orléans and Vierzon, then tricky bus connection from Limoges to Oradour-sur-Glane—see page 361), **Pontorson–Mont St. Michel** (2–3/day, 5.5–7.5 hrs, changes at Caen and Tours or Rennes, Le Mans, and Tours), **Bayeux** (12/day, 5–6 hrs, changes in Caen and Tours, or at Paris's Gare Montparnasse and Tours' St. Pierre-des-Corps), **Beaune** (8/day, 6 hrs, most with changes in Paris and in Dijon—arrive at Paris' Austerlitz station, then Métro to Gare de Lyon).

Chenonceaux

This one-road, sleepy village—with a knockout château—makes a good home base for drivers. Note that Chenonceaux is the name of the town, and Chenonceau (no "x") is the name of the château, but they're pronounced the same: shuh-nohn-soh.

ORIENTATION

Tourist Information

The small TI is on the main road from Amboise as you enter the village (Mon–Sat 10:00–12:30 & 14:00–18:30, closed Sun, tel. 02 47 23 94 45). Warning: Because this parking lot is not patrolled, don't leave any luggage visible in your car. The bus stops are at the TI (across the street to go to Amboise).

Helpful Hints

Money: There's an ATM near the château ticket office.

Internet Access: The town's entrepreneurial **Tabac,** a few doors east of the recommended Hostel du Roy (daily 7:00–13:00 & 13:30–19:00, on rue du Dr. Bretonneau) has one computer, €2/30 min. They also sell English-language newspapers.

Picnic Supplies: La Maison des Pages has some bakery items, cold drinks to go, and just enough groceries for a modest picnic (Thu–Tue 8:00–20:00, Wed 10:00–20:00, on the main drag between Hostel du Roy and Hôtel la Roseraie).

Bike Rental: The **Tabac** (see "Internet Access," above) has a few bikes, as does the recommended **Relais Chenonceaux** (May–Sept daily 9:00–19:00, see hotel listing, below).

SIGHTS

▲▲▲Château de Chenonceau

Chenonceau is the toast of the Loire. This 16th-century Renaissance palace arches gracefully over the Cher River and is impeccably

maintained, with fresh flower arrangements in the summer and roaring log fires in the winter. Understandably popular, Chenonceau is the third-most-visited château in France (after Versailles and Fontainebleau). Chenonceau's crowds are worth

planning around; to beat the crowds, arrive by 9:00 or after 17:00. Plan on a 15-minute walk from the parking lot to the château.

Châteaux near Amboise

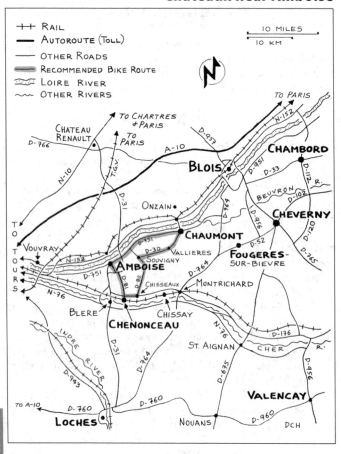

The Loire

While earlier châteaux were built for defensive purposes, Chenonceau was the first great pleasure palace. Nicknamed "the château of the ladies," it housed many famous women over the centuries. The original builder's wife oversaw the construction of the main part of the château. In 1547, King Henry II gave the château to his mistress, Diane de Poitiers. She added an arched bridge across the river to access the hunting grounds. She enjoyed her lovely retreat until Henry II died (pierced in a jousting tournament in Paris) and his vengeful wife, Catherine de Médicis, unceremoniously kicked her out (and into the château of Chaumont, described on page 301). Catherine added the three-story structure on Diane's bridge. She died before completing her vision of a matching château on the far side of the river, but not before turning Chenonceau into *the* place to see and be seen by local aristocracy. (Note that whenever you see a split coat of arms, it belongs to a woman—half her husband's and half her father's.)

Cost and Hours: Château-9.50; audioguide-€4; château, audioguide, and wax museum-€14.50 (described below); daily mid-March–mid-Sept 9:00–19:00, closes earlier off-season; tel. 02 47 23 90 07, www.chenonceau.com. Consider a moonlit **evening walk**—*"promenade nocturne"*—on the château grounds (€5, July–Aug daily 21:30–23:30, only Fri–Sun in June, none Sept–May).

Tours: The interior is fascinating—but only if you take full advantage of the free and excellent 20-page **booklet** (included with entry), or rent an audioguide. Two different **iPod video/audioguide tours** are available (45 and 90 min); the 45-minute tour is plenty. There's also a 45-minute audioguide for kids (€2 for any audioguide, leave ID as deposit). Pay for the audioguide when you're buying your ticket (before entering the château grounds), then pick up the iPod just inside the château's door.

Wax Museum (La Galerie des Dames–Musée de Cires): This museum—located in the château stables—puts a waxy face on the juicy history of the château (€3, tickets only available at the château ticket office). It's well-described in English, with a focus on period clothing, and provides a good introduction before you sightsee.

Cuisine Art: A reasonable cafeteria is next door to the wax museum. Fancy meals are served in the orangery behind the stables. There's a cheap *crêperie*/sandwich shop at the entrance gate.

Boat Trips: In summer, the château has rental **rowboats**—an idyllic way to savor graceful château views (€2/30 min, July–Aug daily 10:00–19:00, four people per boat).

◑ Self-Guided Tour: Saunter like an aristocrat down the tree-canopied path to the château. (There's a fun plant maze partway up on the left.) You'll cross three moats and two bridges and pass an old round tower, which predates the main building. Notice the tower's fine limestone veneer, added so the top would better fit the new château.

The main château's original oak door greets you with Fs (for François I, r. 1515–1547), his fire-breathing salamander emblem, and coats of arms. The knocker is high enough to be used by visitors on horseback. The smaller door within the larger one could be for two purposes: to slip in after curfew, and to enter during winter without letting out all the heat.

As you continue, read your pamphlet or listen to your audioguide, and also notice these details:

In the **guard room,** the original tiles survive best near the walls. While the tapestries kept the room cozy, they also functioned to tell news or recent history (to the king's liking, of course).

The superbly detailed **chapel** survived the vandalism of the Revolution because the fast-thinking lady of the palace filled it with firewood. Angry masses were supplied with mallets and instructions to smash everything royal or religious. While this room was both, all they saw was stacked wood. The hatch door provided a quick path to the kitchen and an escape boat downstairs. The windows, blown out during World War II, are replacements from the 1950s.

The centerpiece of the **bedroom of Diane de Poitiers** is a severe portrait of Catherine de Médicis at 40 years old. After the queen booted out the mistress, she placed her own portrait over the fireplace, but she never used this bedroom. The 16th-century tapestries are among the finest in France. Each one took an average of 60 worker-years to make. Study the complex compositions of the *Triumph of Charity* and the violent *Triumph of Force*.

The **gallery**, at 200 feet long, spanned the river with three stories. The upper stories house double-decker ballrooms and guest rooms. Notice how differently the slate and limestone of the checkered floor wear after 500 years. Imagine grand banquets here. Catherine, a contemporary of Queen Elizabeth I of England, wanted to rule with style. She threw wild parties and employed her ladies to circulate and soak up all the political gossip possible from the well-lubricated Kennedys and Rockefellers of her realm. Parties included grand fireworks displays and mock naval battles on the river.

For a quick walk outside (and more good palace views), cross the bridge, pick up a re-entry ticket, take your stroll (you're across the river from the château), then show your re-entry ticket when you return. The river you crossed marked the border between free and Nazi France in World War II. Back then, Chenonceau witnessed many prisoner swaps. During World War I, the Grand Gallery also served as a military hospital, where more than 2,200 soldiers were cared for—imagine hundreds of beds lining the gallery.

Back inside the gallery, the state-of-the-art (in the 16th century) **kitchen** is not to be missed. It was built near water (to fight the inevitable kitchen fires) and in the basement; since heat rises, the placement helped heat the palace. Beyond the fancy servants' dining room, there's a landing bay for goods to be ferried in and out.

The staircase leading **upstairs** wowed royal guests. It was the first non-spiral staircase they'd seen...quite a treat in the 16th century. The upper gallery usually contains a temporary modern-art exhibit. Small side rooms on the upper floor show fascinating old architectural sketches of the château. The walls, 20 feet thick, were honeycombed with the flues of 224 fireplaces and passages for servants to do their pleasure-providing work unseen. There was no need for plumbing. Servants fetched, carried, and dumped everything pipes do today. The balcony provides excellent views of the gardens—originally functional with vegetables and herbs. (Diane built the one to the right, Catherine the one to your left.) The estate is still full of wild boar and deer—the primary dishes of past centuries. The third floor is worth a peek for its black bedroom, designed by a widow whose husband was murdered by a monk.

SLEEPING

(€1 = about \$1.30, country code: 33)

Hotels are a good value in Chenonceaux.

\$\$ Hôtel la Roseraie*** is like an Impressionist painting you can enter. It has a flowery terrace and 17 warmly decorated,

French-country rooms. Laurent and Sophie try their best to spoil you in their entirely non-smoking hotel (standard Db-€62–80, bigger Db-€95–119, a few grand family rooms-€75–125, air-con, queen- or king-size beds, free parking, heated pool, pleasant gardens, across from Hôtel du Bon Laboreur at 7 rue du Dr. Bretonneau, closed mid-Nov–March, tel. 02 47 23 90 09, fax 02 47 23 91 59, www.charmingroseraie .com, sfiorito@wanadoo.fr). The classy dining room and charming terrace are ideal for an exceptional dinner, available for guests and non-guests alike, but be sure to reserve ahead (€25–43 *menus*, closed Mon).

\$\$ Relais Chenonceaux***, across from Hôtel la Roseraie, has a nice patio and unimaginative but wood-finished rooms at reasonable rates. The coziest—and warmest—rooms are on the top floor, but watch your head (Db-€53–62, Tb-€62–70, Qb-€90, tel. 02 47 23 98 11, fax 02 47 23 84 07, 10 rue du Dr. Bretonneau, www .chenonceaux.com, info@chenonceaux.com).

\$ Hostel du Roy** offers 32 simple rooms, some in a quiet garden courtyard, and a mediocre but inexpensive restaurant (Db-€40–56, Tb-€56, Qb-€62, 2 room Qb-€88, 9 rue du Dr. Bretonneau, tel. 02 47 23 90 17, fax 02 47 23 89 81, www.hostelduroy .com, hostelduroy@wanadoo.fr).

EATING

For a treat, reserve ahead for **Hôtel la Roseraie** (listed above, closed Mon). To eat crêpes, salads, and *plats* at fair prices, try the recommended **Relais Chenonceaux** (pleasant interior and exterior terrace, daily, see listing above).

The Loire

TRANSPORTATION CONNECTIONS

From Chenonceaux by Train to: Tours (3/day, 30 min).

By Bus to: Amboise (1–2/day, Mon–Fri only, none Sat–Sun, 15 min, one-way-€1.10, departs Chenonceaux at about 12:35, and in summer also at about 17:10, catch bus at the TI, tel. 02 47 05 30 49).

By Taxi to: Amboise (€20, €30 on Sun and after 19:00).

Blois

Bustling Blois is a good urban stop in this mostly rural region. Blois (pronounced "blah") boasts a rich history, dolled-up pedestrian areas, a handsome château, good train service to Paris and Amboise, and quick access to Chambord and Cheverny by excursion bus or car (see "Getting Around the Loire Valley," page 271).

Arrival in Blois

Train travelers can walk 10 minutes straight out of the station down avenue Jean Laigret to the TI and château (or take a taxi from in front of the station). Drivers follow signs reading *Centre-Ville* and *Château* (metered parking along avenue Jean Laigret or inside at Parking du Château—first 30 min free).

Tourist Information

The TI is just across from the château entrance (May–Sept Mon–Sat 9:00–19:00, Sun 10:00–19:00; Oct–April Mon–Sat 9:30–12:30 & 14:00–18:00, Sun 10:00–13:00; 23 place du Château, tel. 02 54 90 41 41). Save time as you explore the center of Blois by using the TI's handy walking-tour brochure (skip the €6 audioguide). The brown and purple routes are best.

Unlike most other châteaux, Château Royal is right in the city center, without a nearby forest, river, or lake. It's an easy walk from the train station, near ample underground parking, and just above the TI.

SIGHTS AND ACTIVITIES

▲▲**Château Royal**—This château, home to Louis XII and François I, is where Catherine de Médicis spent her last night (see page 290). At the castle's ticket office, pick up the helpful

English brochure, then read the well-presented English displays. Begin in the courtyard, where four different wings—ranging from Gothic to Neoclassical—underscore this château's importance over many centuries. (Find the model of the château to get your bearings.) Visit the interior counterclockwise. Begin immediately to the right—after entering the courtyard—in the dazzling Hall of the Estates-General; continue to a great display of gargoyles and models in a small lapidary museum; then go up through several richly tiled and decorated royal rooms (can you say busy?). Your visit ends with a walk through the ironworks room and a mini fine-arts museum, with a 16th-century who's-who portrait gallery where you can see what the château's inhabitants looked like (€7, €12 combo-ticket with House of Magic—described below, daily April–Sept 9:00–18:30, Oct–March 9:00–12:30 & 14:00–17:30, tel. 02 54 55 26 26).

The **sound-and-light show** is usually in French, but is still worthwhile (daily mid-April–Sept at about 22:00). An English version is planned for Wednesdays—confirm locally (€10, €11 combo-ticket also covers daytime château entry, €16 gets you both plus the House of Magic, below).

House of Magic—The home of Jean-Eugène Robert-Houdin, the illusionist whose name was adopted by Harry Houdini, offers an interesting but overpriced history of illusion and magic. Several daily shows have no words—so any language works (30 min, schedule posted at entry). Kids enjoy the gift shop (€8, €12 combo-ticket with château; July–Aug daily 10:00–12:30 & 14:00–18:00, Sept–June Tue–Sun 10:00–12:30 & 14:00–18:00, closed Mon; at the opposite end of the square from the château).

Biking from Blois—Cycling from Blois to Chambord is a level 75-minute, one-way ride, and allows connections to a good network of bike paths. Adding Cheverny makes a full-day, 30-mile round-trip (details available at TI, better at the bike shop). **Detours du Loire** rents bikes and is located in the town center near the river at 8 rue Henri Drussy (tel. 02 54 56 07 73, www.locationdevelos.com).

SLEEPING

(€1 = about $1.30, country code: 33)
If you need to bed down in Blois, do so at the warm and friendly **$ Hôtel Anne de Bretagne**** (Sb-€45, Db-€54–60, Tb-€74, Qb-€84, 150 yards uphill from Parking du Château, 5-min walk below the train station at 31 avenue Jean Laigret, tel. 02 54 78 05 38, fax 02 54 74 37 79, http://annedebretagne.free.fr, annedebretagne @free.fr).

EATING

If you're stopping in Blois around lunchtime, plan on eating at **Le Marignan,** located on a breezy, traffic-free square in front of the château (daily, good salads, fast service, 5 place du Château, tel. 02 54 74 73 15). At the top of the hour, you can watch the stately mansion opposite the château become "the dragon house," as monsters crane their long necks out its many windows.

TRANSPORTATION CONNECTIONS

From Blois by Train to: Amboise (14/day, 20 min), **Chinon** (9/day, 2 hrs, transfer in Tours), **Paris** (14/day, 1.5 hrs). The **excursion bus to Chambord and Cheverny** leaves from the train station in Blois as does the once-a-day bus #2 (see "Getting Around the Loire Valley," page 271).

Château de Chambord

With its huge scale and distinctive prickly silhouette, Château de Chambord is the granddaddy of all châteaux in the Loire. It's surrounded by Europe's largest enclosed forest park, a game preserve defined by a 20-mile-long wall and teeming with wild deer and boar. Chambord (shahn-bor), which began as a simple hunting lodge for bored Blois counts, became a monument to the royal sport and duty of hunting. (Apparently, hunting was considered important to keep the animal population under control and the vital forests healthy.)

The château, six times the size of most, has 440 rooms, and a fireplace for every day of the year. It consists of a keep in the shape of a Greek cross, with four towers and two wings surrounded by stables. It has four floors, with many stairs in between thanks to the high ceilings. The ground floor has reception rooms, the first floor up houses the royal apartments, the second floor up is mostly a hunting museum, and the rooftop offers a hunt-viewing terrace. Because hunting visibility is best after autumn leaves fall, Chambord was a winter palace (which helps explain the number of fireplaces). Only 80 of Chambord's rooms are open to the public—and that's plenty. This place would be great for hide-and-seek.

Cost and Hours: €8.50 Sept–June, €9.50 July–Aug; open daily

The Loire

April–Sept 9:00–18:15, Oct–March 9:00–17:15, last entry 30 min before closing (but you'll need more time there anyway), tel. 02 54 50 50 40, www.chambord.org. There are two ticket offices: one in the village in front of the château, and another inside the château. Horse-riding demonstrations take place daily in summer (€8.50; July–Aug daily at 11:45 and 16:30; May–June and Sept Tue–Fri at 11:45, Sat–Sun at 11:45 and 16:30, none on Mon; tel. 02 54 20 31 01, www.chambord-horse-show.fr). Call ahead or check the French-only website to verify hours, guided tour times, horse shows, and evening visits.

Getting There: On weekdays, one 40-minute bus connects Chambord with Blois' train station (leave Blois at about noon, return from Chambord at about 18:00, about €3.50). The Blois excursion bus is better (€11.50, three daily departures from Blois station mid-May–mid-Sept; for more info, see "Getting Around the Loire Valley," page 271).

Information: This château requires helpful information to make it come alive. All rooms except the hunting museum have good English explanations (the free brochure is useless). Overachievers can rent an **audioguide** (€4) for a thorough history of the château and its rooms.

Services: There's a fantastic bookshop in the château with a good selection of children's books. Among the collection of shops near the château, you'll find an ATM, WCs, local souvenirs, a wine-tasting room and cafés. Bikes, rowboats, and electric boats can be rented across the small road by the canal. The canal is small, so room for boating is limited.

Views: For the best views, cross the small river in front of the château and turn right toward the picnic perch. The Hôtel du Grand St. Michel has a broad view terrace, ideal for post-château refreshment (see "Sleeping," below).

☉ Self-Guided Tour: Starting in 1518, François I created this "weekend retreat," using 1,800 workmen over 15 years. (You'll see his signature salamander symbol everywhere.) François I was an absolute monarch—with an emphasis on absolute. In 32 years of rule (1515–1547), he never once called the Estates-General to session (a rudimentary Parliament in *ancien régime* France). This grand hunting palace was another way to show off his power. Charles V—the Holy Roman Emperor and most powerful man of the age—was invited here and was, like, totally wowed. Here are the highlights:

The ground-floor reception rooms offer little to see, except for the subtitled video with helpful information on the château's construction. Climb the monumental **double-spiral staircase,** which was likely inspired by Leonardo da Vinci, who died just as construction was starting. Allowing people to go up and down without passing each other (look up the center from the ground floor), it's a masterpiece of the French Renaissance. Peek at other visitors through the openings as you climb, and admire the ingenious design.

The first floor up offers the most interesting rooms: the very royal apartments in the **king's wing,** including François I's, Louis XIV's, and Maria Theresa's bedrooms. Gaze at their portraits to get to know the onetime occupants. I liked François' bedroom the best—because he was a traveling king, his furniture was designed to be easily disassembled and moved with him (you'd think the king could afford to buy new furniture). The rooms devoted to the **Count of Chambord,** the final owner of the château, are also interesting. This 19th-century count, last of the French Bourbons, was next in line to be the king when France decided it didn't need one. He was raring to rule. You'll see his coronation outfits and even souvenirs from the coronation that never happened. Notice his boyhood collection of little guns, including a working mini-cannon.

The second floor up, with its beautiful coffered ceilings (notice the "F" for you-know-who), holds a series of ballrooms that once hosted post-hunt parties. It's now a museum with finely crafted **hunting weapons and exhibits** on myths, legends, traditions, and techniques from the 16th, 17th, and 18th centuries—unfortunately, with little information in English.

To see what happens when you put 365 fireplaces in your house (used to heat the palace in winter even today), climb to the **rooftop.** Here, a pincushion of spires and chimneys decorate a viewing terrace where the ladies would enjoy the spectacle of their ego-pumping hunters. On hunt day, a line of beaters would fan out and work inward from the distant walls, flushing wild game to the center, where the king and his buddies waited. Notice the lantern tower of the tallest spire, which glowed with a nighttime torch when the king was in. From the rooftop, view the elegant king's wing—marked by *FRF (François Roi de France)* and bristling with fleurs-de-lis.

SLEEPING

Near Chambord and Cheverny
(€1 = about $1.30, country code: 33)
$$ Hôtel du Grand St. Michel** lets you wake up with Chambord outside your window. It's an Old World, hunting-lodge kind of place, with a trophy-festooned dining room (€21 and €28 *menus*). Sleep here, and you'll have a chance to roam the château grounds after the peasants have been run out (small Db-€55–66, standard Db-€65–75, Db with view of château-€75–90—worth the extra

cost, extra bed–€12, tel. 02 54 20 31 31, fax 02 54 20 36 40, on place Saint Louis, www.saintmichel-chambord.com, hotelsaintmichel @wanadoo.fr).

$ Chambres la Flânerie, sitting right on the bike route from Chambord to Cheverny, offers two ideal family rooms in an adorable home. It's riddled with flowers, crawling with ivy, and surrounded by wheat fields and forests. The gentle Delabarres speak enough English, and have bikes to loan their fortunate guests (Db–€55–62, Tb–€72–80, Qb–€90–96, 25 rue de Gallerie, tel. 02 54 79 86 28, mobile 06 75 72 28 41, www.laflanerie.com, laflanerie @laflanerie.com). Coming from Blois on D-765, it's before Cheverny in the hamlet of Les Fées, right after the antique shop on the left. Turn right at the wooden bus shelter, where you'll see a sign to *Eric Auge Menuiserie,* then follow *Flânerie* signs.

Cheverny

This stately hunting palace—a ▲▲ sight—is the most lavishly furnished of all the Loire châteaux. Those who complain that the

Loire châteaux have stark and barren interiors missed Cheverny (shuh-vehr-nee). Because the palace was built and decorated from 1604 to 1634, and is immaculately preserved, it offers a unique architectural harmony and unity of style. From the start, this château has been in the Hurault family, and Hurault pride shows in its flawless preservation and intimate feel. The viscount's family still lives on the third floor. (You'll see some family photos.) Cheverny was spared by the French Revolution; the owners were popular then, as today, even among the village farmers.

The château is flanked by a pleasant village, with a small grocery, cafés offering good lunch options, and a few hotels. The town is easy to reach from Blois or Amboise by bus or minivan tour (see "Getting Around the Loire Valley," page 271).

Cost and Hours: €7, daily July–Aug 9:15–18:45, April–June and Sept 9:15–18:15, Oct 9:45–17:30, Nov–March 9:45–17:00, tel. 02 54 79 96 29, www.chateau-cheverny.fr. Pick up the English self-guided-tour brochure—which describes the interior beautifully—inside the château, not where you buy your ticket.

⊘ Self-Guided Tour: Walking across the manicured grounds, you approach the gleaming château, with its row of Roman emperors, including Julius Caesar in the center. Inside, the private apartments upstairs were occupied until 1985 (the viscount's family now lives a floor above), and show the French art of living. In the **bedroom**—literally fit for a king—study the fun ceiling art, especially the "boys will be boys" cupids. You'll find a Raphael painting, a grandfather clock with a second hand

that's been ticking for 250 years, a family tree going back to 1490, and a letter of thanks from George Washington to this family for their help in booting out the English. The attic of the orangery out back was filled during World War II with treasures from the Louvre, including the *Mona Lisa*.

Barking dogs remind visitors that the viscount still loves to hunt. The **kennel** (200 yards in front of the château, look for *Chenil* signs) is especially interesting at dinnertime, when the 70 hounds are fed (April–mid-Sept daily at 17:00, mid-Sept–March Mon and Wed–Fri at 15:00). The dogs—half English foxhound and half French Poitou—are bred to have big feet and bigger stamina. They're fed once a day and the feeding *(la soupe des chiens)* is a fun spectacle that shows off their strict training. Before chow time, the hungry hounds fill the little kennel rooftop and watch the trainer bring in troughs stacked with delectable raw meat. He opens the gate, and they gather enthusiastically around the food and yelp hysterically. Only when the trainer says to eat can they dig in. You can see the dogs at any time, but the feeding show is fun to plan for. The adjacent trophy room is stuffed with more than a thousand antlers and the heads of five wild boar.

Fougères-sur-Bièvre

The feudal castle of Fougères-sur-Bièvre (foo-zher sewr bee-ehv) dominates its small village and is worth a stop, even if you don't go inside (though I would). Located a few minutes from Cheverny on the way to Chenonceaux and Amboise, Fougères-sur-Bièvre was constructed for defense, not hunting, and was built over the small river (to provide an unlimited water supply during sieges). Destroyed in the Hundred Years' War, then rebuilt in the 1500s, it has been completely restored. While there are no furnishings (there weren't many in the Middle Ages in any case), it offers a good look at how castles were built.

Follow the route with the helpful English handout (brief

English explanations are also provided in most rooms). You'll see models of castle-construction techniques, including good exhibits on the making of half-timbered walls (oak posts provide the structural skeleton, and the areas between were filled in with a mix of clay, straw, and pebbles...or whatever was available). Walk under medieval roof supports, gaze through loopholes, and stand over machicolations (holes for dropping rocks and scalding liquids on attackers) in the main tower. Seeing the main tower from within adds an entirely new appreciation of these structures' complexity, and the two medieval latrines demonstrate how little toilet technology has changed in 800 years.

Cost and Hours: €5; May–mid-Sept daily 9:30–12:30 & 14:00–18:30; mid-Sept–April Wed–Mon 10:00–12:30 & 14:00–17:00, closed Tue; last entry 30 min before closing, tel. 02 54 20 27 18, http://fougeres-sur-bievre.monuments-nationaux.fr).

Getting There: Fougères-sur-Bièvre has no easy public-transport link from Amboise...or anywhere else. If you're *sans* rental car or bike, arrange for a custom minivan tour—or skip it.

Chaumont-sur-Loire

A castle has been located on this spot since the 11th century. The current version is a ▲▲ sight. The first priority here was defense. You'll appreciate the strategic location on the long climb up from

the village below. (Drivers can avoid the uphill hike by driving up and around to park at the higher *Annex du Château* entrance—follow *Stade du Tennis* signs as you climb.) Gardeners will appreciate the extraordinary Festival of Gardens (every year from mid-May to October, described below). Anglophones will miss the better English information provided at other châteaux.

The Chaumont (show-mon) château you see today was built mostly in the 15th and 16th centuries. Catherine de Médicis forced Diane de Poitiers to swap Chenonceau for Chaumont; you'll see tidbits about both women inside. Louis XVI, Marie-Antoinette, Voltaire, and Benjamin Franklin all spent time here. Today's château offers a good look at the best defense design in 1500: on a cliff with a dry moat, big and small drawbridges with classic ramparts, loopholes for archers, and machicolations—hot oil anyone?

Cost and Hours: €6.50, includes stables, daily May–mid-Sept 9:30–18:30, April and late Sept 10:30–17:30, Oct–March

10:00–17:00, last entry 30 min before closing, stables close daily 12:00–14:00, ticket office sometimes closes during lunch off-season, English handout available, tel. 02 54 51 26 26.

Getting There: There is no public transport to Chaumont; bikes and chartered minivans are the only means for non-drivers to visit this château (see "Getting Around the Loire Valley," page 271).

Festival of Gardens: This annual exhibit, with 25 elaborate gardens arranged around a different theme each year, draws rave reviews from international gardeners (€9, not included in château admission, mid-May–Oct only, tel. 02 54 20 99 22, www .chaumont-jardin.com).

◆ Self-Guided Tour: Your walk through the palace—restored mostly in the 19th century—is poorly described in the flier you'll pick up as you enter. Here's some helpful information on what you'll see.

Start at the entry, littered with various coats of arms. As you walk in, take a close look at the two drawbridges. Inside, the heavy defensive feel is replaced with palatial luxury. Around 1700, a more stable age, the fourth wing was taken down to give the terrace a fine river-valley view. The 165-foot-deep well is fun for echoes. Study the entertaining spouts and decor on the courtyard walls.

A case contains **ceramic portrait busts** dating from 1770, when the lord of the house had a tradition of welcoming guests by having their portrait sketched, then giving them a ceramic bust made from this sketch when they departed. Find Ben Franklin's medallion.

The **dining room**'s fanciful limestone fireplace is exquisitely carved. Find the food (frog legs, snails, goats for cheese), the maid with the bellows, and even the sculptor with a hammer and chisel at the top (on the left).

The treasury box in the **guard room** upstairs is a fine example of 1600s-era locksmithing. The lord's wealth could be locked up here as safely as possible in those days, with a false keyhole, no handles, and even an extra box inside for diamonds.

The beautifully tiled **Salle de Conseil** has wall-to-wall tapestries, and fireplaces designed to keep this meeting room warm.

The **bedroom** has a private balcony that overlooks the chapel, handy when the lord wanted to go to church on a bad-hair day. The sentimental glass, from 1880, shows scenes from the castle's history. The tiny balcony window has an original etching of Catherine de Médicis' favorite nephew. Gaze at him and imagine the elegance of 16th-century court life. Catherine de Médicis, who missed her native Florence, brought a touch of Italy to all her châteaux. As you leave, appreciate the nifty central handrail on the spiral staircase.

The **stables** *(ecuries)* were entirely rebuilt in the 1880s. The medallion above the door reads *pour l'avenir* (for the future), which shows off a real commitment to horse technology. Inside, circle clockwise—you can almost hear the horses walking about. Notice the deluxe horse stalls, padded with bins and bowls for hay, oats, and water, and complete with a strategically placed drainage gutter. The horses were named for Greek gods and great châteaux. The Horse Kitchen (Cuisine des Chevaux) produced mash twice weekly for the horses. The horse gear was rigorously maintained for the safety of carriage passengers. The covered alcove is where the horse and carriage were prepared for the prince, and the round former kiln was redesigned to be a room for training the horses.

The estate is a **tree garden,** set off by a fine lawn. Trees were imported from throughout the Mediterranean world to be enjoyed—and to fend off any erosion on this strategic bluff. The annual **Festival of Gardens** (described on the opposite page) takes place behind the stables.

Loches and Valençay

The overlooked town of **Loches** (lohsh), located about 30 minutes south of Amboise, makes a good base for drivers wanting to visit sights east and west of Tours (in effect triangulating between Amboise and Chinon), but has no easy connections via train or bus. This pretty town sits on the region's loveliest river, the Indre, and offers an appealing mix of medieval monuments, stroll-worthy streets, and fewer tourists. Its château, which dominates the skyline, is worth a short visit. The Wednesday street market is small but lively. For an overnight stay, try **$$ Hôtel George Sand*****, located on the river, with a well-respected restaurant, idyllic terrace, and rustic, comfortable rooms (Db-€67, Tb-€74, Qb-€115, no elevator, 300 yards south of TI at 39 rue Quintefol, tel. 02 47 59 39 74, fax 02 47 91 55 75, www.hotelrestaurant-georgesand.com, contactGS@hotelrestaurant-georgesand.com).

The nearby Renaissance château of **Valençay** (vah-lahn-say) is a massive, luxuriously furnished structure with echoes of Talleyrand (Napoleon's prime minister), lovely gardens, and many kid-friendly summer events, such as fencing demonstrations (€9, ask about family rates, daily July–Aug 9:30–19:30, April–June and Sept–Nov 9:30–18:00, closed Dec–March, audioguide available, tel. 02 54 00 10 66).

The Loire

West of Tours

Chinon

This pleasing town straddles the Vienne River and hides its ancient cobbles under a historic castle. Today's Chinon (shee-nohn) is better known for its popular red wines. But for me, it makes the best home base for seeing the sights west of Tours: Azay-le-Rideau (sound-and-light show), Langeais, Villandry, Chatonnière, Rivau, Ussé, and the Abbaye Royale de Fontevraud. Each of these worthwhile sights is no more than a 20-minute drive away, and trains and minivan excursions provide a reasonable alternative for non-drivers (see "Getting Around the Loire Valley," page 271, and "Transportation Connections," page 309).

Chinon stretches out along the Vienne River, and everything of interest to travelers is between it and the hilltop château. Charming place du Général de Gaulle—ideal for café-lingering—is in the center of town. The famous Renaissance writer and satirist François Rabelais was born here in the late 1400s—you'll see many references to him in his proud town. His best-known works, *Gargantua* and *Pantagruel*, describe the amusing adventures of father-and-son giants.

Tourist Information

It's a 15-minute walk from the train station to the TI, where you'll find *chambre d'hôte* listings, wine-tasting details (wine-route maps available for the serious taster), bike-rental information, and an English-language, self-guided tour of the town (May–Sept daily 10:00–19:00; Oct–April Mon–Sat 10:00–12:00 & 14:00–18:00, closed Sun; in village center on place Hofheim, tel. 02 47 93 17 85, www.chinon.com). Free public WCs are around the back of the TI.

Helpful Hints

Market Days: On Thursday and Saturday mornings, a market takes place on place Jeanne d'Arc (western end of town). There's a smaller market on Sunday, around place du Général de Gaulle.

Groceries: Shopi is across from the Hôtel de Ville, on place du Général de Gaulle (closed for lunch 13:00–15:00 and on Sun afternoon).

Internet Access: Ask at the TI.

Laundry: Salon Lavoir is near the bridge at #7 quai Charles VII (daily 7:00–21:00).

The Loire

Chinon

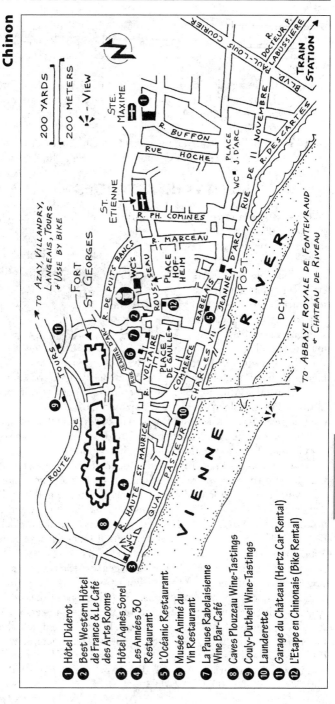

200 YARDS
200 METERS

☆ - View

1. Hôtel Diderot
2. Best Western Hôtel de France & Le Café des Arts Rooms
3. Hôtel Agnès Sorel
4. Les Années 30 Restaurant
5. L'Océanic Restaurant
6. Musée Animé du Vin Restaurant
7. La Pause Rabelaisienne Wine Bar-Café
8. Caves Plouzeau Wine-Tastings
9. Couly-Dutheil Wine-Tastings
10. Launderette
11. Garage du Château (Hertz Car Rental)
12. L'Etape en Chinonais (Bike Rental)

Bike Rental: Try **L'Etape en Chinonais,** a busy little café with
  bikes and picnic supplies (across from TI, €8/half-day, €15/
  day).

Taxi: Call 02 47 98 37 98.

Car Rental: Garage du Château, opposite the château parking lot,
  rents Hertz cars (about €65/day, includes 400 kilometers/250
  miles, Mon–Sat 8:00–19:00, closed Sun, rue du Tours, tel. 02
  47 93 04 65).

Best View: You'll find terrific views back to Chinon by crossing
  the bridge in the center of Chinon and turning right.

SIGHTS AND ACTIVITIES

▲**Château de Chinon**—Don't underestimate this crumbled castle,
especially if you're looking
for a stark medieval com-
parison to châteaux of the
lavish hunting-lodge variety. Note that a massive
renovation will be under
way through 2008; expect
some areas of the interior
to be roped off.

The château's history, and the views it offers, justify your visit.
Henry II, Eleanor of Aquitaine, and their son, Richard the Lionhearted all called this home at one time. Most importantly, it was
in this castle that Joan of Arc first implored Charles VII to take
the throne back from the nasty English. (Charles had taken refuge
in this well-fortified castle during the Hundred Years' War, making Chinon France's capital city during that period.)

It's a steep walk up from town, but the expansive vistas of
Chinon and the valleys are sensational. Start in the "exposition
tent" with a short, automated history of the château, complete with
a big model of what the restored castle will look like. Then wander
up and down and in and out of the various towers. End at the clock
tower, which houses a three-floor museum of knickknacks about
Joan of Arc—the top floor has terrific views.

What little remains of this 12th-century castle is well-
presented in English by tour-on-your-own pamphlets (plus
English plaques posted at key places). Try to join one of the excellent English-language tours (45 min, free with entry ticket, 5/day
in summer, 4/day off-season, call château for tour schedule). The
tours focus the big picture—why the castle was built here, how it
differed from others in the Loire, the importance of Joan's visit,
and how châteaux are rebuilt (€3, daily April–Sept 9:00–19:00,
Oct–March 9:30–17:00, tel. 02 47 93 13 45).

Touring the Old City—Chinon offers a tasty cocktail of cobbled lanes, historic buildings, and few tourists. Using the TI's self-guided tour and reading plaques at key buildings, you'll gain a good understanding of this city's historic importance. Stop for a drink on place du Général de Gaulle and cross the river for best views to the castle.

Wine-Tasting—Chinon wines are among the most respected in the Loire, and there are a variety of ways to sample them. The most convenient is at the café/wine bar **La Pause Rabelaisienne** on place du Général de Gaulle; serious owner Rainer Schmidt offers weekly selections of reds and at least one white for €3–6 per glass (daily 10:00 to about 19:00, tel. 02 47 93 35 25). **Caves Plouzeau,** at the eastern end of town, allows visits of their cellars under the château—and a tasting (April–Sept Tue–Sat 10:30–12:30 & 15:00–18:00, closed Sun–Mon and Oct–March, 94 rue Haute St-Maurice, tel. 02 47 93 16 34). **Couly-Dutheil** has a modern, user-friendly tasting room, called Caveau de l'Echo, across from the château entry at the top of Chinon's hill (€1.50/glass, free if you buy, most wines about €7–9/bottle, May–Oct daily 10:00–12:30 & 14:00–19:00, closed Nov–April, on route de Tours, tel. 02 47 81 20 86).

▲Biking from Chinon—Many good options are available from Chinon. Most bikers can do the pleasant bike ride from Chinon to Ussé—though you encounter a monumental hill when you're leaving Chinon. From there you can join the bike path along the Cher River that runs to Villandry and near Langeais. Connecting these three châteaux is a full-day, 40-mile, round-trip ride that only those in good condition will enjoy.

SLEEPING

(€1 = about $1.30, country code: 33)
If you stay overnight in Chinon, walk out to the river and cross the bridge for a floodlit view of the château walls. Hotels are a good value here; the first two I list are best.

$$ Hôtel Diderot** is a handsome 18th-century manor house on the western edge of town. (It's the closest hotel I list to the train station; drivers, look for signs from place Jeanne d'Arc.) It's a family affair, run by Laurent and his sisters, Françoise and Martine. The hotel is built around a courtyard (with easy parking), and has a full bar with a good selection of area wines. Rooms in the main building vary in size and decor, but all are well-maintained, with personal touches. Ground-floor rooms are a bit dark, but have private patios. The four good family rooms have connecting rooms, each with a private bathroom. Breakfast includes a rainbow of homemade jams (Sb-€43–53, Db-€53–75, extra bed-€12, limited parking-€6/day, 4 rue Buffon, tel. 02 47 93 18 87, fax 02 47 93 37 10, www.hoteldiderot.com, hoteldiderot@hoteldiderot.com).

$$ Best Western Hôtel de France* offers good comfort without the personal touches of the other hotels I list. Still, I like the location—at Chinon's best square—as well as the open patios inside the hotel (Db-€56–92, most are about €84, Tb/Qb-€120–134, several rooms have balconies over the square, 49 place du Général de Gaulle, tel. 02 47 93 33 91, fax 02 47 98 37 03, www.bestwestern.fr, elmachinon@aol.com).

$ Hôtel Agnès Sorel, at the eastern end of town, is right on the river and handy for drivers, but a 30-minute walk from the train station. Of its 10 sharp rooms, three have river views, two have balconies, five surround a small flowery courtyard, and a few are air-conditioned (Db-€48–72, most are €58, big Db suite-€100, T/Qb suite-€120, 4 quai Pasteur, tel. 02 47 93 04 37, fax 02 47 93 06 37, www.agnes-sorel.com, pierre.catin@orange.fr).

$ Le Café des Arts is ideal for budget travelers, with six simple, spotless rooms above Chinon's most atmospheric square (Db-€39–45, 4 rue Jean-Jacques Rousseau, tel. & fax 02 47 93 09 84, frederic.giessinger@wanadoo.fr).

EATING

In Chinon

For a low-stress meal with ambience, choose one of the cafés on the photogenic place du Général de Gaulle. If food matters more than sitting outside, try one of the first two places I list. But for something really different and fun, you must visit Dédé la Boulange at the "Wine and Barrel Museum" (see below).

Les Années 30 welcomes you with consistently good, classic French cuisine, attentive service (thanks to hostess Karine and chef Stephane), cozy interior rooms, and a small outdoor patio (*menus* from €26, closed Wed year-round and Tue–Wed in winter, in the eastern end of town at 78 rue Voltaire, tel. 02 47 93 37 18).

L'Océanic, in the thick of the pedestrian zone, is where locals go for seafood. It also offers the best wine list in town, and good indoor or outdoor seating (*menus* from €22, closed Sun–Mon, 13 rue Rabelais, tel. 02 47 93 44 55).

Musée Animé du Vin et de la Tonnellerie ("Wine and Barrel Museum") is a one-man show where mustachioed Dédé la Boulange dishes up all-you-can eat *fouées* (little pastry shells filled with a garlic paste, cheese, or a meat spread called *rillettes*) accompanied by a *mâche* salad (tossed with walnut oil), soft white beans stewed in goose fat, dessert *fouées,* wine, and coffee—all for €18. Watch Dédé slap the *fouées* in his rustic oven and let your hair down in this get-to-know-your-neighbor kind of place. There's no menu, because there's no need; sit down and let the food roll in (daily 10:00–22:00, 12 rue Voltaire, tel. 02 47 93 25 63).

In Villandry, near Chinon

Etape Gourmande at Domaine de la Giraudière offers a rustic but marvelous farmhouse dining experience a 25-minute drive away, in Villandry. Owner Beatrice provides great service and exquisite cuisine from her limited menu (ask her how she landed here). The *salade gourmande* makes a perfect lunch, or a hearty first course for dinner (consider splitting it as a first course). The *cochon au lait* (melt-in-your-mouth pork) weakened my defenses, and the nougat dessert finished me off (€15–28 *menus,* daily 12:00–15:00 & 19:30–21:00, closed mid-Nov–mid-March, a half-mile from Villandry's château toward Druye, tel. 02 47 50 08 60, fax 02 47 50 06 60). Domaine de la Giraudière works best for lunch, as it's between Villandry and Azay-le-Rideau. It also combines well with a visit to Azay-le-Rideau's sound-and-light show.

TRANSPORTATION CONNECTIONS

By Minivan

From Chinon to Loire Châteaux: Three companies, **Touraine Evasion, Acco-Dispo,** and **Quart de Tours,** offer fixed-itinerary minivan excursions from Tours. Take the train to Tours from Chinon, or get several travelers together to book your own van from Chinon (see "Getting Around the Loire Valley," page 273).

By Train

Twelve trains and SNCF buses link Chinon daily with the city of Tours (1 hr, connections to other châteaux and minibus excursions from Tours—see "Getting Around the Loire Valley," page 273), and to the regional rail hub of St. Pierre-des-Corps in suburban Tours (TGV trains to distant destinations, and the fastest way to Paris). Traveling by train to the nearby châteaux (except for Azay-le-Rideau) requires a transfer in Tours and healthy walks from the stations to the châteaux. Fewer trains run on weekends.

From Chinon to Loire Châteaux: Azay-le-Rideau (7/day, 20 min, direct), **Langeais** (5/day, 2 hrs, transfer in Tours), **Amboise** (9/day, 90 min, transfer in Tours), **Blois** (9/day, 2 hrs, transfer in Tours).

To Destinations Beyond the Loire: Paris' Gare Montparnasse (9/day, 2 hrs), **Sarlat** (4/day, 5–6 hrs, change at Tours' St. Pierre-des-Corps, then TGV to Libourne or Bordeaux–St. Jean, then train through Bordeaux vineyards to Sarlat), **Pontorson–Mont St. Michel** (3/day, 7 hrs, change at Tours main station and Caen, then bus from Pontorson; or via Paris TGV with changes at Tours' St.

Pierre-des-Corps and Paris' Gare Montparnasse, then bus from Rennes), **Bayeux** (9/day, 5–6 hrs, changes in Caen and Tours, or at Paris' Gare Montparnasse and Tours' St. Pierre-des-Corps).

By Bus

From Chinon to Langeais and Azay-le-Rideau: Ask at the TI about buses to these towns (this service recently started, with 3/day to each).

Azay-le-Rideau

30 minutes west of Tours, Azay-le-Rideau (ah-zay luh ree-doh) is a pleasant little town with a small but lively pedestrian zone and a château that gets all the attention. Azay-le-Rideau works as a base for touring sights west of Tours by car, bike, or train (though the train station is a half-mile walk from the town center), and tempts travelers to bed down here with a fun sound-and-light show at its château.

ORIENTATION

Tourist Information

Azay-le-Rideau's TI is just below place de la République, a block to the right of the post office (April–Oct Tue–Sat 9:00–13:00 & 14:00–18:00, Nov–March Tue–Sat 14:00–18:00, closed Sun–Mon year-round, 4 rue du Château, tel. 02 47 45 44 40). Pick up information on the sound-and-light show, and for biking near Azay.

Arrival in Azay-le-Rideau

It's just farther than a half-mile from the station to the town center (taxi tel. 06 98 72 17 10). Walk down from the station, turn left, and follow *Centre-Ville* signs. Drivers can head for the château and park there.

SIGHTS

▲▲Château d'Azay-le-Rideau

This handsome 16th-century château is made magnificent by the way it seems to float in a romantic reflecting pond. Come for the serene setting, and enjoy the well-furnished rooms. You'll see more elaborately furnished châteaux elsewhere, but this one has that water thing going on.

Azay-le-Rideau's builder—a government bureaucrat—wanted to design the most glorious castle of the time (not an unusual objective in this region 500 years ago). He came close enough to draw

Châteaux near Chinon

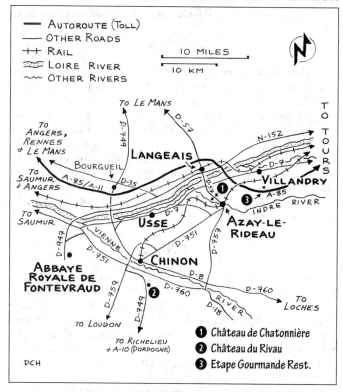

- **AUTOROUTE (TOLL)**
- **OTHER ROADS**
- **RAIL**
- **LOIRE RIVER**
- **OTHER RIVERS**

10 MILES
10 KM

TO LE MANS

TO ANGERS, RENNES & LE MANS

TO SAUMUR & ANGERS

TO SAUMUR

TO LOUDON

TO RICHELIEU & A-10 (DORDOGNE)

D-749
D-53
N-152
LANGEAIS
BOURGUEIL
A-85/A-11
D-35
VILLANDRY
A-85
INDRE RIVER
D-7
USSE
AZAY-LE-RIDEAU
D-751
D-757
VIENNE
D-947
ABBAYE ROYALE DE FONTEVRAUD
D-751
CHINON
D-8
D-760
D-760
TO LOCHES
D-759
D-749
D-18
RIVER

TO TOURS

DCH

❶ Château de Chatonnière
❷ Château du Rivau
❸ Etape Gourmande Rest.

the attention of the king (François I). This was what he wanted, but not what he needed—for the bureaucrat, who was France's treasurer, soon landed in jail for tax fraud.

Rooms are well-described in English, with a free handout and English plaques in most rooms. For the unabridged version, rent a €4 audioguide (€6 for two people). The château's manageable interior offers a collection of warmly furnished, I-could-live-here rooms. Try to recognize familiar faces among the portraits of those who stayed here. You'll see many bedchambers and antechambers, a dining room, a kitchen, and a not-to-be-missed, 19th-century billiard room with a nifty scoring board. The gardens are a big grassy area with good views from benches to the château.

Cost and Hours: €7.50, daily July–Aug 9:30–19:00, April–June and Sept–Oct 9:30–18:00, Nov–March 9:30–12:30 & 14:00–17:30, last entry 45 min before closing, tel. 02 47 45 42 04, http://azay-le-rideau.monuments-nationaux.fr/en.

Sound-and-Light Show: The château hosts a sound-and-light show Friday and Saturday nights in May, June, and September, and nightly in July and August. These shows allow you to stroll the grounds with interesting lighting and a musical background (€10).

SLEEPING

(€1 = about $1.30, country code: 33)
The town's appealing center may convince you to set up here (a good idea if you plan to see the sound-and-light show).

$ Hôtel Biencourt** is ideally located on a traffic-free street between place de la République (easy parking) and the château. Owned by helpful Emmanuelle and Cédric, this modest hotel is a restored convent. Rooms are homey and comfortable enough, and there are a few big family rooms (Db-€49–55, Tb-€58, Qb-€68, air-con in some rooms, open March–mid-Nov, 7 rue de Balzac, tel. 02 47 45 20 75, fax 02 47 45 91 73, www.hotelbiencourt.com, biencourt@infonie.fr).

EATING

For dining, consider **Ridelloise,** which is small, central, and budget-friendly (*menus* from €12, daily, 34–36 rue Nationale, tel. 02 47 45 46 53). For more serious, formal cuisine at fair prices, try **L'Aigle d'Or** (€27 for 4 courses, closed Wed and Sun, 10-min walk from place de la République toward Langeais, 10 avenue Adélaide-Riché, tel. 02 47 45 24 58). If you have a car, by all means take it 10 minutes to **La Domaine de la Giraudière** in Villandry (see the next page).

TRANSPORTATION CONNECTIONS

From Azay-le-Rideau by Bus to: Chinon and **Langeais** (this service recently started, 3/day, ask at TI).
By Train to: Tours (8/day, 30 min), **Chinon** (7/day, 20 min).

The Loire

Langeais

One of the most imposing fortresses of the Middle Ages, this sight—rated ▲▲—towers above its appealing little village. It comes with a moat, a drawbridge, lavish defenses, and turrets. It's a well-furnished place with just enough rooms to hold your interest, and basic English descriptions throughout.

This castle was built on the

ruins of a 10th-century fortress—you'll see the lone remnant in the garden as you enter. Langeais served a strategic role in the 1400s as a French outpost, facing the troublesome duchies of Anjou and Brittany. This castle's 15 minutes of fame came when it witnessed the secret marriage of King Charles VIII and 14-year-old Anne (the Duchess of Brittany), a union that brought independent Brittany into France's fold. You can witness the wedding in a large room outfitted with wax figures; a mini sound-and-light show explains the event (in French only, for now). The scene raises the obvious question: How could such a short person rule such a big country? Ponder that question as you walk along the parapet, and consider dropping something scalding on intruders below (€8, daily July–Aug 9:00–19:00, Feb–June and Sept–mid-Nov 9:30–18:30, mid-Nov–Jan 10:00–17:00, last entry 1 hour before closing, tel. 02 47 96 72 60, www.chateaulangeais.com).

Getting There: Nine trains a day link Langeais and Tours (20 min), with about five connections a day from there to **Chinon** (2 hrs total). A new bus service runs to Chinon and Azay-le-Rideau (likely 3/day—confirm and get schedules locally). Drivers should turn right at the foot of the castle and follow the road left (around the castle) to find the parking lot on the right.

Villandry

Villandry (vee-lahn-dree) has an unremarkable castle, but its grounds make it a ▲▲ sight (worth ▲▲▲ for gardeners). Built in 1536 as the home of the finance minister, this château has the Loire's best gardens, immaculately maintained and arranged in elaborate geometric patterns. Pick up the well-done English handout that describes the four garden types and suggests a good walking route. The viewpoint behind the château is terrific. The 10-acre, Italian Renaissance–style garden (designed c. 1530) is full of symbolism. Even the herb and vegetable sections are artistic—design mattered to the monks who first planted these gardens (only vegetables used in the 16th century are still grown). Paying extra for the château interior isn't worth it, but it does include a 15-minute *Four Seasons of Villandry* slide show (with period music) that offers a look at the gardens throughout the year. You can stay as late as you like in the gardens, though you must enter before the ticket office closes (€8, €5.50 for gardens only, daily April–Sept 9:00–19:00, March and Oct 9:00–18:00, Nov–Feb 9:00–17:00, tel. 02 47 50 02 09, www.chateauvillandry.com).

The pleasant little village of Villandry offers several cafés and restaurants, a small grocery store, and a bakery. Consider combining your visit with a meal at the nearby **Etape Gourmande at**

The Loire

Domaine de la Giraudière (follow signs to Druye from Villandry; see "Eating" in Chinon, page 312).

More Château Gardens

Gardeners will be tempted by these untouristy "lesser châteaux" because of their pleasing plantings.

Château de Chatonnière impresses with nine different garden themes (€5, daily mid-March–mid-Nov 10:00–19:00, château interior closed to visitors, between Langeais and Azay-le-Rideau just off D-57, tel. 02 47 45 40 29, www.lachatonniere.com).

Château du Rivau is well off the beaten path, a lovely 10-minute drive from Chinon. This gleaming-white château sits smack in the middle of wheat fields, with owners who are busily re-creating the fine gardens as they were 500 years ago (using medieval tapestries as models). Here you'll see vegetable and flower gardens and another castle interior—though you're here for the gardens (€8, July–Aug daily 10:00–19:00; June and Sept Wed–Mon 10:00–12:30 & 14:00–19:00, closed Tue; May and Oct Wed–Sun 14:00–19:00, closed Mon–Tue; closed Nov–April; in Lémeré on D-759—from Chinon follow *Richelieu* signs, then signs to the château; tel. 02 47 95 77 47, www.chateaudurivau.com).

Ussé

This château, famous as an inspiration for Charles Perrault's classic version of the Sleeping Beauty story, is worth a quick photo stop for its fairy-tale turrets and gardens, but don't bother touring the interior of this pricey pearl. The best view, with reflections and a golden-slipper picnic spot, is from just across the bridge (€12, daily July–Aug 9:30–19:00, mid-Feb–June and Sept–mid-Nov 10:00–18:00, closed mid-Nov–mid-Feb, tel. 02 47 95 54 05, www.chateaudusse.fr).

Abbaye Royale de Fontevraud

The Abbaye Royale de Fontevraud (fohn-tuh-vroh), a 15-minute drive west of Chinon, is worth ▲▲. This vast 12th-century abbey provides the best look you'll get at medieval monastic life in this area. Here you can commune with Richard the Lionhearted and Eleanor of Aquitaine, and get a better grip on the important role medieval abbeys played in pulling Europe out of the Dark Ages. Europe's largest abbey feels like the economic engine it was 900

years ago—you can almost hear the gears grinding as you tour this elaborate monastic complex.

Cost and Hours: €6.50, daily June–Sept 9:00–18:30, April–May and Oct 10:00–18:00, Nov–March 10:00–17:30, tel. 02 41 51 71 41, www.abbaye-fontevraud.com.

Tours: This abbey is unusually well-presented for English speakers. English-language **tours** depart four times a day from June to September (call for times in any season). If you miss the tour, the English leaflet and room-by-room explanations are quite informative. The best book on the abbey is *Fontevraud, Royal Abbey—Between Chinon and Saumur* by Francis Collombert (€12).

○ **Self-Guided Tour:** Your visit begins in the bright church (Eglise Abbatiale). Sit on the entry steps and take in the ethereal light, the cavernous setting, and gaze down the nave. Two-thirds of the way down, Eleanor of Aquitaine lies next to her second husband, England's Henry II. Next to them lies their son Richard, Coeur de Lion (Heart of the Lion).

Exit through the right transept into the Grand Moutier Cloister. This was the focus of the monastery, where monks read, exercised, checked email, and washed. From here, keep left and you'll find a chapter house (Salle Capitulaire), where the monks' meetings took place, as well as the Chauffoir—the only heated room in the abbey, where monks could copy manuscripts when it was cold. You'll also see an open-beam-ceilinged dormitory (where most monks slept with little or no padding) currently used for expositions, plus an elegant refectory and a maze of underground tunnels *(accès souterrain)*. As you tour the abbey, remember that monastic life was dirt-simple: Nothing but prayer, reading, and work. Daily rations were a loaf of bread and a quarter-liter of wine.

Your visit ends in the honeycombed 16th-century kitchen, with five chapel-chimneys, and many holes for smoke to escape.

SLEEPING AND EATING

(€1 = about $1.30, country code: 33)
$$$ Hôtel la Croix Blanche**, 10 steps from the abbey, welcomes travelers with open terraces and will have you sleeping and dining in comfort. This traditional restaurant-hotel combines a hunting-lodge feel with polished service, comfortable open spaces, and rooms with classic French decor (perfectly comfortable Db-€76–105, "privilege" Db-€100–135, Tb-€120–160, grand suite-€130–180, place Plantagenets, tel. 02 41 51 71 11, fax 02 41 38 15 38,

www.fontevraud.net, info@fontevraud.net). Their three restaurants meet every need: The elegant country restaurant has *menus* from €22, the brasserie has café fare, and the *crêperie* has...crêpes.

The **boulangerie** opposite the entrance to the abbey serves mouthwatering quiche and sandwiches at impossibly good prices. You'll also find a few *crêperies* and cafés near the abbey.

DORDOGNE AND NEARBY

The Dordogne River Valley is a splendid blend of natural and man-made beauty. Walnut orchards, tobacco plants, and cornfields carpet the valley, while stone fortresses patrol the cliffs above. During much of the on-again, off-again Hundred Years' War, this strategic river—so peaceful today—separated warring Britain and France. Today's Dordogne River carries more travelers than goods, as the region's economy relies heavily on tourism.

The joys of the Dordogne include rock-sculpted villages, fertile farms surrounding I-should-retire-here cottages, film-gobbling vistas, lazy canoe rides, and a local cuisine worth loosening your belt for. But its big draw is its concentration of prehistoric artifacts. Limestone caves—decorated with prehistoric artwork—litter the Dordogne region.

Planning Your Time

While tourists inundate the region in the summer, the Dordogne's charm is protected by its relative inaccessibility. Given the time it takes to get here, I'd allow a minimum of two nights and most of two days...or I'd skip it. Your sightseeing obligations, in order of priority, are: prehistoric cave art; the Dordogne River Valley, nearby villages, and castles; the town of Sarlat; and, if you have a bit more time, the less-traveled Lot River Valley (most efficiently done when heading to or from the south). Wine-lovers work in a pilgrimage to St. Emilion, two hours to the west.

If you're connecting the Dordogne with the Loire region by car, the fastest path is via the A-20 autoroute (exit at Souillac for Sarlat and nearby villages). Break up your trip from the north by stopping in Oradour-sur-Glane and/or Collonges-la-Rouge (see

"Oradour-sur-Glane and Nearby," page 360): Take autoroute A-20 to Limoges and follow *Angoulême* signs, then follow signs to *Oradour-sur-Glane*. If you need to spend the night in this area, consider tiny Mortemart (near Oradour-sur-Glane—see page 361). If you're connecting the Dordogne and Carcassonne, explore the Lot River Valley on your way south (see page 375). When heading west, take time to sample the Bordeaux wine region's prettiest town, St. Emilion (see page 362).

Those serious about visiting the Dordogne's best caves (especially with a relatively rare English-speaking tour) need to book well in advance (as explained on page 357).

The following three-day itinerary is designed to be done by car, but it's doable—if you're determined—via taxi rides, a canoe trip (the best way to see the Dordogne regardless of whether you've got a car or not), and an organized minivan tour.

Day 1: Enjoy a morning in Sarlat (ideally on a market day—Sat or Wed), then spend the afternoon on a canoe trip, with time at the day's end to explore Beynac and Castelnaud. If it's not market day in Sarlat, do the canoe trip, Beynac, and castle first, and enjoy the late afternoon and evening in Sarlat. (Since all of the town's essential sights are outdoors, my Sarlat self-guided walk works great in the evening, when many places are closed.) The sensational views from Castelnaud's castle and Domme are best in the morning; visit Beynac's castle or viewpoint late in the day for the best light. With sufficient lead time, canoe-rental companies can pick up non-drivers in Sarlat, and taxis are also reasonable between Sarlat and the river villages.

Day 2: Drivers can begin at Lascaux II (the best cave art intro in the area, even though it's a replica). Then, follow the scenic Vézere River toward Les Eyzies-de-Tayac, stopping for lunch in idyllic little St. Léon and then on to the caves at La Roque St. Christophe (no reservations needed; doesn't close for lunch, unlike other caves). In Les Eyzies-de-Tayac, visit the museum of prehistory, then see the real thing at the cave or caves of your choice (I prefer Grotte de Font-de-Gaume and Grotte de Rouffignac). If you lack a car, this day's activities are only possible by taxi or minivan tour.

Day 3: Head east and upriver to explore Rocamadour, Gouffre de Padirac, and storybook villages such as Carennac, Autoire, and Loubressac. While Rocamadour is accessible by train and a short taxi ride, the rest of these places are only feasible with your own wheels, by taxi, or on a minivan tour.

Choosing a Home Base

Sarlat is the only viable solution for train travelers, but those with a car should sleep riverside in La Roque-Gageac (a beautiful village with good hotels, see page 346) or Beynac (a spectacular and pho-togenic village with decent *chambres* and hotels, see page 346). For a grand château hotel experience that won't break the bank, sleep near the Lascaux caves, at Château de la Fleunie (30 min north of Sarlat, see page 356). And if you'd rather frolic on a real farm, sleep near Les Eyzies-de-Tayac at Auberge Veyret (see page 354). I recommend several other rural places that are good for drivers (see page 345). Note that in this traditionally French area, air-conditioning and Internet access are less common, and breakfasts are mostly continental.

Getting Around the Dordogne

This region is a joy with a car, but tough without one. Consider renting a car for a day, or take a minivan excursion (see below). If you're up for a splurge, consider a hot-air balloon ride (see sidebar on page 274).

By Bike or Moped: Cyclists find the Dordogne beautiful, but hilly, with too much traffic on key roads. Mopeds are an option. Rent bikes and mopeds in Sarlat (see "Helpful Hints" on page 325).

By Train: While it's possible to get into the region by train, connecting the Dordogne's sights by train once there is miserable. Trains run from Sarlat to the Grotte de Font-de-Gaume caves in Les Eyzies-de-Tayac (transfer in Le Buisson, 30-min walk from station to caves), but leave you in Les Eyzies-de-Tayac all day. Consider a taxi back (see below).

By Car: Roads are small, slow, and scenic. There is no auto-route near Sarlat, so you'll need more time than usual to get into, out of, and around this relatively remote region. Little Sarlat is routinely snarled in traffic, so passing through it can slow you down. You can rent a car in Sarlat (see "Helpful Hints" on page 325), though bigger cites, such as Bordeaux and Brive-la-Gaillarde, offer greater drop-off flexibility. You'll pay to park in most river-front lots between 10:00 and 19:00. Leave nothing in your car at night—thieves enjoy the Dordogne, too.

By Custom Taxi/Minivan Excursion: You have two good options. **Allô-Philippe Taxi** is run by amiable Philippe, who speaks English and has a comfortable minivan with raised seats for better viewing. Philippe will custom-design your tour, help you with cave reservations, and provide some commentary during your excursion. He can pick you up anywhere—including Bordeaux's airport (€265) and remote train stations (€31/hr for up to 7 people—but 6 is more comfortable, €46/hr on Sun, €74 round-trip to Lascaux II from Sarlat area, book early, tel. 05 53 59 39 65, mobile 06 08 57 30 10, http://allophilippetaxi.monsite.wanadoo.fr, allophilippetaxi@wanadoo.fr).

Dordogne

Decouverte et Loisirs is run by friendly Christine, who offers minivan tours for one to eight people. She is less flexible than Philippe, with several fixed itineraries in English (€29–50 per person, tel. 05 65 37 19 00, mobile 06 22 70 13 76, decouverte.loisirs@wanadoo.fr). While her fixed tours don't include Grotte de Font-de-Gaume, she can make a custom tour for you that does, and will make the necessary cave reservations for you if you book with her early enough.

By Taxi: For taxi service from Sarlat to Beynac or La Roque-Gageac, allow €19 (€25 at night and on Sun); from Sarlat to Les Eyzies-de-Tayac, allow €30 one-way (€45 at night and on Sun) or €60 round-trip. Philippe (see above) can often pick you up within a few minutes if you call. Corrine, who runs Beynac-based **Taxi Corrine**, is helpful, speaks a little English, and is eager to provide good service to tourists (tel. 05 53 29 42 07, mobile 06 72 76 03 32, corrine.broqui@wanadoo.fr).

By Boat: Renting a canoe is my favorite mode of transportation for exploring a slice of this region (see page 338 for rental information and suggested routes). For the same scenery with less work, you can also take a boat cruise from Beynac (see page 343) or La Roque-Gageac (page 340).

Cuisine Scene in the Dordogne

Gourmets flock to this area for its geese, ducks, and wild mushrooms. The geese produce (involuntarily) the region's famous foie gras. (They're force-fed, denied exercise, and slaughtered for their livers—see sidebar on page 344.) Foie gras tastes like butter and costs like gold. The duck specialty is *confit de canard* (duck meat preserved in its own fat— sounds terrible, but tastes great). *Pommes de terre sarladaises* are

mouthwatering, thinly sliced potatoes fried in duck fat and commonly served with *confit de canard*. Wild truffles are dirty black mushrooms that grow underground, generally on the roots of oak trees. Farmers traditionally locate them with sniffing pigs and then charge a fortune for their catch (roughly $250 per pound). Native cheeses are Cabécou (a silver-dollar-size, pungent, nutty-flavored goat cheese) and Echourgnac (made by local Trappist monks). You'll find walnuts *(noix)* in salads, cakes, liqueurs, and salad dressings (also see "Anything with Walnuts," under "Dordogne Markets," next page). Wines to sample are Bergerac (red and white), Pecharmant (red, must be at least four years old), Cahors (a full-bodied red), and Monbazillac (sweet dessert wine). The *vin de*

The Dordogne Region

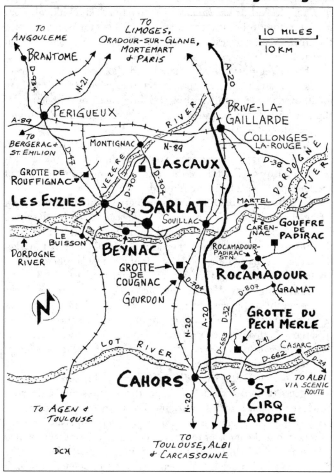

noix (sweet walnut liqueur) is delightful before dinner.

Remember, restaurants serve only during lunch (11:30–14:00) and dinner (19:00–21:00, later in bigger cities); bigger cafés serve food throughout the day.

Dordogne Markets

Markets are a big deal in rural France, and nowhere more so than in the Dordogne. I've listed good markets below for every day of the week, so there's no excuse for drivers not to experience a Dordogne market. Here's what to look for:

Strawberries *(fraises):* For the French, the Dordogne is the region famous for the very tastiest strawberries. Available from

April to November, they're gorgeous, and they smell even better than they look. Buy *une barquette* (small basket), and suddenly your two-star hotel room is a three-star. Look also for *fraises des bois*, the tiny, sweet, and less visually appealing strawberries found in nearby forests.

Fresh Veggies: Outdoor markets offer locals a chance to meet the farmer, and a chance to buy direct. (See what's fresh, and look for it on your menu this evening.) Subtly check out the hands of the person helping customers—if they're not gnarled and rough from working the fields, move on.

Cheeses *(fromages):* The region is famous for its Cabécou cheese (see above), though often you'll also find Auvergne cheeses (St. Nectaire and Cantal are the most common) from just east of the Dordogne (usually in big rounds).

Truffles *(truffes):* Only the bigger markets will have these ugly, jet-black mushrooms on display. Truffle season is our off-season (Nov–Feb), when you'll find them at every market. If you see truffles displayed at other times, they are sterilized. On Sarlat market days, there's usually a guy in the center of place de la Liberté with a photo of his grandfather and his truffle-hunting dog.

Anything with Walnuts *(aux noix): Pain aux noix* are thick-as-a-brick bread loaves chock-full of walnuts. *Moutarde de noix* is walnut mustard. *Confiture de noix* is a walnut spread for hors d'oeuvres. *Gâteaux de noix* are tasty cakes studded with walnuts. *Liqueur de noix* is a marvelous creamy liqueur, great over ice or blended with a local white wine.

Goose- or Duck-Liver Pâté (foie gras): This spread is made from geese (better) and ducks (still good), or from a mix of the two. You'll see two basic forms: *entier* and *bloc*. Both are 100 percent foie gras; *entier* is a piece cut right from the product, while *bloc* has been whipped to make it easier to spread. Foie gras is best accompanied by a sweet white wine (like the locally produced Monbazillac, or Sauterne from Bordeaux). You can bring the unopened tins back into the US, *pas de problème*. For more on foie gras, see the sidebar on page 344.

Confit de Canard: At butcher stands, look for hunks of duck smothered in white fat, just waiting for someone to take them home and cook them up.

Dried Sausages *(saucissons secs):* Long tables piled high with dried sausages covered in herbs or stuffed with local goodies are a common sight in French markets. You'll always be offered a mouthwatering sample. Some of the variations you'll see include *porc, canard* (duck), *fumé* (smoked), *à l'ail* (garlic), *cendré* (rolled in ashes), *aux myrtilles* (with blueberries), *sanglier* (wild boar), and even *âne* (donkey)—and, but of course, *aux noix* (with walnuts).

Olive Oil *(huile d'olive):* You'll find stylish bottles of oil flavored with walnuts, chestnuts *(châtaignes),* and hazelnuts *(noisettes)*—good for cooking, ideal on salads, and great as gifts.

Olives and Nuts *(olives et noix):* These interlopers from Provence find their way to every market in France.

Liqueurs: While they're not made in this region, Armagnac, Cognac, and other southwestern fruit-flavored liquors are often available from a seller or two. Try the liqueur de pomme verte, and sample Armagnac in the tiny plastic cups.

Dordogne Market Days

The best markets are in Sarlat (Sat and Wed, in that order), followed by the markets in Cahors on Saturday, St. Cyprien on Sunday, and Le Bugue on Tuesday. Markets usually shut down by 13:00.

Sunday: St. Cyprien (lively market, 10 min west of Beynac, difficult parking), Montignac (near Lascaux), and St. Genies (a tiny, intimate market with few tourists; halfway between Sarlat and Montignac)

Monday: Les Eyzies-de-Tayac (Grotte de Font-de-Gaume caves are here) and a tiny one in Beynac

Tuesday: Cénac (you can canoe from here—see "Dordogne Canoe Trips," page 337) and Le Bugue (great market 20 min west of Beynac)

Wednesday: Sarlat (big market)

Thursday: Domme

Friday: Souillac (transfer point to Cahors, Carcassonne)

Saturday: Sarlat and Cahors (both are excellent)

Sarlat

Sarlat (sar-lah) is a pedestrian-filled banquet of a town, serenely set amid forested hills. There are no blockbuster sights—the only thing worth going inside for is the cathedral (and that just barely). Still, Sarlat features a seductive tangle of traffic-free, golden cob-

blestone lanes peppered with beautiful buildings, lined with foie gras shops (geese hate Sarlat), and stuffed with tourists. The town is warmly lit at night, and ideal for after-dinner strolls. It's just the right size—large enough to have a theater with four screens, but small enough so that everything is an easy meander from the town center. While undeniably popular with tourists, it's the handiest home base for those without a car.

ORIENTATION

Rue de la République slices like an arrow through the circular old town. Sarlat's smaller half has few shops and many quiet lanes. The action lies east of rue de la République. Make it a point to wander.

Tourist Information

The TI, with English-speaking staff, is 50 yards to the right of the Cathedral of St. Sacerdos as you face the front entrance (Mon–Sat April–Oct 9:00–12:00 & 14:00–19:00, Sun 10:00–13:00 & 14:00–17:00, no midday closing in July–Aug, Nov–March closes at 18:00 and all day Sun, on rue Tourny, tel. 05 53 31 45 45, www.sarlat -tourisme.com). Ask for an English version of the free city map, and pick up brochures on most regional sights. Their *Guide Pratique* booklet is good for car-, bike-, and canoe-rental information. They also sell the well-done, laminated *City of Sarlat* walking-tour map for €5, and booklets on sights throughout the region. For €2, the TI can also reserve you a hotel room or a time slot for a prehistoric cave visit (for more on cave reservations, see page 357).

Arrival in Sarlat

By Train: The sleepy train station keeps a lonely vigil (without a shop, café, or hotel in sight). It's a mostly downhill, 20-minute walk to the town center (consider a taxi, about €8—see "Helpful Hints," below). To walk into town, turn left out of the station and follow the *Centre-Ville* sign down avenue de la Gare as it curves downhill, then turn right at the bottom on avenue Thiers. Some trains (such as those from Oradour and Cahors) arrive at nearby Souillac, which is connected to Sarlat's train station by an SNCF bus.

By Car: Sarlat's limited-access downtown funnels cars through narrow streets, creating long backups. Parking can be a headache, particularly on market days. Try parking along avenue Gambetta (at the north end of town), or in one of the signed lots on the ring road. Most parking is free.

Helpful Hints

Market Days: Sarlat has been an important market town since the Middle Ages. Outdoor markets thrive on Wednesday morning and all day Saturday (see "Dordogne Market Days," on page 323). Saturday's market, which seems to swallow the entire town, is best in the morning (produce and food vendors leave at noon). Come before 8:00 to watch them set up, and once the market is under way, plant yourself at a well-positioned café to observe the civilized scene. Don't miss the market action in the former Church of Ste. Marie.

Supermarket: There's a **Petite Casino** grocery at 32 rue de la République (Tue–Sat 8:30–12:30 & 14:00–19:00, Sun 8:30–12:30, closed Mon).

Internet Access: Easy Planet is open daily, but it's expensive (Tue–Thu 10:00–19:00, Fri–Sat 10:00–24:00, Sun 18:00–24:00, closed Mon, 17 avenue Gambetta, tel. 05 53 29 23 48).

Laundry: Madame Mazzocato runs a good launderette across from the recommended Hôtel la Couleuvrine (self-serve daily 6:00–22:00, drop-off/pickup Mon–Fri only 8:00–12:30 & 14:00–18:30, 10 place de la Bouquerie). There's another self-service laundry near the recommended Hôtel de Selves (open daily 7:00–21:00, 74 avenue de Selves).

Bike Rental: Friendly Englishman **Joel Caine** offers bike delivery and pickup (free for at least 4-day rental in Sarlat area), provides maps, and can help you plan your route. The Dordogne River Valley Scenic Loop (described on page 335) makes a good bike ride. You can also check Joel's website (listed below, click on "open source") for excellent bike itineraries with detailed directions (€20/day, €60/4 days, includes helmet, lock, and tire kit; daily 9:00–19:00, tel. 06 08 94 42 01, www.multitravel.co.uk, info@multitravel.co.uk).

Taxi: Call Philippe of **Allô-Philippe Taxi** (tel. 05 53 59 39 65, mobile 06 08 57 30 10—see page 319 for information about using Philippe for regional day trips) or **Taxi Sarlat** (tel. 05 53 59 02 43, mobile 06 80 08 65 05).

Car Rental: Try **Europcar** (Le Pontet, at south end of avenue Leclerc on roundabout, place du Maréchal de Lattre de Tassigny, tel. 05 53 30 30 40, fax 05 53 31 10 39).

Walking Tours: Passion Périgord is a two-man tour company run by passionate guides Jeff and Pierre, who offer €5 walks of Sarlat in English to small groups (even just two people). Call a few days ahead to book, or drop in to check their schedule. Their tiny office sits just above place de la Liberté (2 impasse Gaubert, tel. 05 53 30 42 55, passionperigord@yahoo.fr).

SELF-GUIDED WALK

Welcome to Sarlat

This short walk starts facing the Cathedral of St. Sacerdos (a few steps from the TI). While it's designed to do by day (when the cathedral is open), it works beautifully after dinner, when the gas-lit lanes and candlelit restaurants twinkle.

Place du Peyrou: An eighth-century Benedictine abbey once

Sarlat

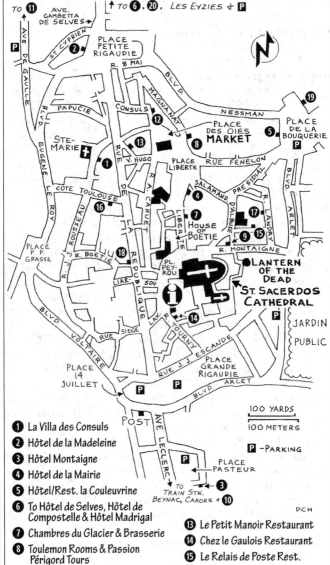

1. La Villa des Consuls
2. Hôtel de la Madeleine
3. Hôtel Montaigne
4. Hôtel de la Mairie
5. Hôtel/Rest. la Couleuvrine
6. To Hôtel de Selves, Hôtel de Compostelle & Hôtel Madrigal
7. Chambres du Glacier & Brasserie
8. Toulemon Rooms & Passion Périgord Tours
9. La Lanterne Rooms
10. To Hôtel le Relais de Moussidière & Europcar
11. To Hôtel la Verperie
12. La Mirondal Restaurant
13. Le Petit Manoir Restaurant
14. Chez le Gaulois Restaurant
15. Le Relais de Poste Rest.
16. Pizzeria Romane
17. Le Présidial Restaurant
18. Petite Casino Grocery
19. Launderette
20. To Internet Café

stood where the Cathedral of St. Sacerdos does today. It provided the stability for Sarlat to develop into an important trading city during the Middle Ages. The old Bishop's Palace, built right into the cathedral (on the right, with its top-floor Florentine-style loggia), recalls Sarlat's Italian connection. The Italian bishop was the boyfriend of Catherine de Médicis (queen of France)—a connection that got him this fine residence. After a short stint here, he split to Paris with lots of local money. While his departure scandalized the town, it left Sarlat with a heritage of Italian architecture. (Notice the fine Italianate house of Etienne de la Boëtie on the opposite side of the square, and the similar loggia to its right.)

Another reason for Sarlat's Italian-flavored architectural zenith was its loyalty to the king during wartime. Sarlat's glory century was from about 1450 to 1550, after the Hundred Years' War (see sidebar on page 195). Loyal to the French cause—through thick and thin and a century of war—Sarlat was rewarded by the French king, who gave lots of money to rebuild the town in stone. Sarlat's new nobility needed fancy houses, complete with ego-boosting features. Many of Sarlat's most impressive buildings date from this prosperous era, when the Renaissance style was in vogue, and everyone wanted an Italian architect.

• *Take a closer look (opposite the cathedral) at...*

The House of Étienne de la Boëtie: This house was a typical 16th-century merchant's home—family upstairs and open ground floor (its stone arch now filled in) with big, fat sills to display retail goods. Pan up, scanning the crude-but-still-Renaissance carved reliefs. It was a time when anything Italian was trendy (when yokels "stuck a feather in their cap and called it macaroni"). La Boëtie (lah bow-ess-ee), a 16th-century bleeding-heart liberal who spoke and wrote against the rule of tyrannical kings, remains a local favorite.

Notice how the house just to the left arches over the small street. This was a common practice to maximize buildable space in the Middle Ages. Sarlat enjoyed a population boom after the Hundred Years' War ended in 1468.

• *If you're doing this walk during the day, head into the cathedral now. If you're doing this walk in the evening or the little door is closed, skip ahead to the Lantern of the Dead (below): Facing the cathedral, walk around it to the left, up the lane, and through the little door in the wall to the rocket-shaped building on a bluff 30 yards behind the church.*

Cathedral of St. Sacerdos: While the cathedral's facade has a few well-worn 12th-century carvings, most of it dates from the 18th and 19th centuries.

Step inside the only historic Sarlat interior that merits a visit. The faithful believed that Mary delivered them from the great plague of 1348, so you'll find a full complement of Virgin Marys here and throughout the town. The Gothic interiors you'll see in this part of France are simple, with clean lines and nothing extravagant. The first chapel on the left is the baptistery. Locals gave these as thanks after they made the pilgrimage to Lourdes for healing and returned satisfied. A column on the right shows a long list of hometown boys who gave their lives for France in World War I.

• *Exit the cathedral from the right transept (through a padded, brown, and unmarked door) into what was once the abbey's cloisters. Snoop through two quiet courtyards and then turn left at the café, making your way uphill toward the rear of the cathedral, hooking left through a stony passage along the back of the church. Climb the steps (through the monks' graveyard) to a bluff 30 yards directly behind the church. You'll find a bullet-shaped building ready for some kind of medieval take-off, known as the...*

Lantern of the Dead (Lanterne des Morts): Dating from 1147, this is the oldest monument in town. In four horrible days, a quarter of Sarlat's population died in a plague (1,000 out of 4,000). People prayed to St. Bernard of Clairvaux for help. He blessed their bread—and instituted hygiene standards while he was at it, stopping the disease. This lantern was built in gratitude. If it feels a bit eastern or Moorish, it's likely because of Bernard's Crusades experience in the Holy Land.

• *From the Lantern of the Dead, exit downhill and to the right, past an adorable house. Cross one street, turn left on impasse de la Vieille Poste, make a quick right on rue d'Albusse and then take a left onto...*

Rue de la Salamandre: The salamander—unfazed by fire or water—was Sarlat's mascot. Befitting its favorite animal, Sarlat was also unfazed by fire (from war) and water (from floods). Walk 10 yards down this "Street of the Salamander" and find the Gothic-framed doorway just below on your right. Step back and notice the tower that housed the staircase. Staircase towers like this (Sarlat has about 20) date from about 1600 (after the wars of religion between the Catholics and Protestants), when the new nobility needed to show off.

• *Continue downhill, passing under the salamander-capped arch, and pause near (or better, sit down at) the café on the...*

Place de la Liberté: This has been Sarlat's main market square since the Middle Ages. Sarlat's patriotic town hall stands behind you (with a café perfectly situated for people-watching). Downhill (to your left) is the tall, tiled cathedral tower (with a salamander swinging happily from its spire). Top shops line the road between here and the cathedral. These tourist-pleasing stores are filled with the finest local products (truffles, liquors, foie gras, and so on).

You can't miss the dark **stone roofs** topping the buildings across the square. They're typical of this region: Called *lauzes* in French, the flat limestone rocks were originally gathered by farmers clearing their fields, then made into cheap, durable roofing material (today few people can afford them). The unusually steep pitch of the *lauzes* roofs—which last up to 300 years—helps distribute the weight of the roof over a greater area. Over time, most *lauzes* roofs have been replaced by more affordable roofing materials, but Sarlat retains a great number of stone-roofed homes. The small window is critical—it provides air circulation, allowing the lichen that coat the porous stone to grow, sealing gaps between the stones and effectively waterproofing the roof. Without that layer, the stone would crumble after repeated freeze-and-thaw cycles.

The tall building with the fine *lauzes* roof (located uphill and to the right) was the parish Church of Ste. Marie, which was converted into a gunpowder factory in 1789. Today, it's an indoor market (open daily 8:30–13:00). Marvel at its tall, strangely modern, seven-ton doors. Walk past the big doors and go up a few steps to meet the "boy of Sarlat"—marking the best view over place de la Liberté.

• *Turn left (behind the boy) and trickle like medieval rainwater down the ramp into a postcard-perfect square. Here, you'll find a little gaggle of geese.*

Place des Oies: Feathers fly when geese are traded on this "Square of the Geese" on market days (Saturdays Nov–March). The birds are serious business here, and have been since the Middle Ages. Trophy homes surround this cute little square on all sides. Check out the wealthy merchant's home front and center, with a tower built big enough to match his ego. Off the square, a few steps to the right (before the recommended restaurant Le Mirondal), a 14th-century vault leads to a fountain. For generations, this was the town's only source of water, protected by the Virgin Mary. Opposite the restaurant and fountain, enter the wooden doorway (open only July–Aug) and pass through one room to find the massive Renaissance stairway. These show-off stairways, which replaced more space-efficient spiral ones, required a big house and a bigger income. Impressive.

• *Follow the cobbled gutter left on rue des Consuls, and enter the straight-as-an-arrow...*

Rue de la République: This modern thoroughfare dates from the mid-1800s, when blasting big roads through medieval cities was the fashion. It wasn't until 1963 that Sarlat's other streets would become off-limits to cars, thanks to France's forward-thinking minister of culture, André Malraux. The law that bears his name has served to preserve and restore important monuments and neighborhoods throughout France. Eager to protect the country's architectural heritage, private investors, cities, and regions worked together to create traffic-free zones, rebuild crumbling buildings, and make sure no cables or ugly wiring messed up the ambience of towns like this. Without the Malraux Law, Sarlat might well have "efficient" roads like rue de la République slicing through what was once a charming old town center.

Your tour is done, but make sure you take time for a poetic ramble—ideally after dark—through this town. This is the only town in France illuminated by gas lamps, which cause the warm limestone to glow, turning up the romance of Sarlat even higher.

• *From here, you can cross rue de la République and wander through Sarlat's quiet, less commercial side, or find a café and raise a toast to Monsieur Malraux.*

SLEEPING

In Sarlat

Even with summer crowds, Sarlat is the train-traveler's best home base. Note that in July and August, some hotels require half-pension, and hotels in downtown Sarlat book up first. Parking can be a headache here—drivers will find rooms and parking more easily just outside of town (see "Near Sarlat," see page 333) or in the nearby villages and destinations described under "The Best of the Dordogne River Valley" (most a 15-minute drive away; see page 335).

Hotels in the Town Center

$$ La Villa des Consuls*, in an 18th-century mansion buried on Sarlat's quiet side, has 13 lovely and spacious rooms, several with a kitchen and a living room. Rooms surround a small courtyard, and come with wood floors, private decks, high ceilings, and no-expense-spared amenities such as Internet access, microwave ovens, and free washers and dryers. Helpful David helms the ship (Db-€80–90, Db/Tb/Qb-€116–139, big Db/Tb/Qb-€135–162, lower rates are for stays of two nights or longer, air-con, garage-€8/day, train station pickup-€6, 3 rue Jean-Jacques Rousseau, tel. 05 53 31 90 05, fax 05 53 31 90 06, www.villaconsuls.com, villadesconsuls @aol.com).

$$ Hôtel de la Madeleine* is a central three-star value with professional service, elegant lounges, 39 well-maintained and air-conditioned rooms, and lots of tour groups (Db-€70–105, Tb-€100–125, Qb-€115–140, higher prices listed are for larger rooms, usually with bathtubs; less-expensive rooms are on street side, with smaller bathrooms and showers rather than baths; elevator, Internet access and Wi-Fi, garage-€7/day, at north end of ring road at 1 place de la Petite Rigaudie, tel. 05 53 59 10 41, fax 05 53 31 03 62, www.hoteldelamadeleine-sarlat.com, hotel.madeleine @wanadoo.fr).

$ Hôtel Montaigne, a block south of the pedestrian zone, is sharper than its lackluster lobby lets on and well-run by the

Sleep Code

(€1= about \$1.30, country code: 33)
S = Single, **D** = Double/Twin, **T** = Triple, **Q** = Quad, **b** = bathroom,
s = shower only, ***** = French hotel rating system (0–4 stars).
Unless otherwise noted, credit cards are accepted and English
is spoken.

To help you sort easily through these listings, I've divided
the rooms into three categories based on the price for a standard double room with bath:

\$\$\$ Higher Priced—Most rooms €90 or more.
\$\$ Moderately Priced—Most rooms between €60–90.
\$ Lower Priced—Most rooms €60 or less.

hardworking Martinats. The rooms are spotless, spacious, and comfortable. Of the hotels I recommend, this one is nearest the train station (Db-€53–61, Tb-€62–72, easy parking, place Pasteur, tel. 05 53 31 93 88, fax 05 53 31 99 71, www.hotelmontaigne.fr, contact@hotelmontaigne.fr).

\$ Hôtel de la Mairie plays second fiddle to its café, which can keep hotel guests awake late. The hotel is young and basic, but well-located, with big rooms right on the main square (Ds-€50, Db-€58, Tb-€75, Qb-€90, rooms #3 and #6 have the best views, room #8 has the most character, best to reserve by phone, check in at café, place de la Liberté, tel. 05 53 59 05 71, fax 05 53 59 59 95, www.hotel-mairie-sarlat.com, contact@hotel-mairie-sarlat.com).

\$ Hôtel la Couleuvrine** is in a historic building with a good location, across from the launderette and near the park, with easy parking (for Sarlat). It offers medieval atmosphere in its simple (but mostly cozy) rooms. Families enjoy *les chambres familles*—#19 and #20 are in the tower. A few rooms have private terraces (Db-€52–65, Tb-€78, air-con in some rooms, elevator, on ring road at 1 place de la Bouquerie, tel. 05 53 59 27 80, fax 05 53 31 26 83, www.la-couleuvrine.com, lacouleuvrine@wanadoo.fr). Half-pension is encouraged during busy periods and in the summer—figure €50–58 per person for room, breakfast, and a good dinner in the classy restaurant. The hotel also has a jazzy stone-vaulted wine bar that serves light meals and good wine by the glass.

Hotels North of Town

The following hotels are a 10-minute walk north of the old town on avenue de Selves. All have easy parking.

\$\$ Hôtel de Selves***, with 40 well-equipped rooms in a modern shell, offers reliable comfort and amenities, including

Dordogne

Internet access, Wi-Fi, sauna, a swimming pool, and a grand piano (Db-€76, bigger Db-€96, Db with balcony-€120, extra bed-€25, all rooms non-smoking, air-con, elevator, garage-€10/day, 93 avenue de Selves, tel. 05 53 31 50 00, fax 05 53 31 23 52, www.selves-sarlat.com, hotel@selves-sarlat.com).

$$ Hôtel de Compostelle** features a sleek, open lobby, and bright, modern, mostly spacious rooms, including several big ones for families (Db-€70–84, Tb-€130, Qb-€148 for 4–6 people, air-con, Wi-Fi in lobby, elevator is one floor up, backyard terrace, 64 avenue de Selves, tel. 05 53 59 08 53, fax 05 53 30 31 65, www.hotel-compostelle-sarlat.com, info@hotel-compostelle-sarlat.com).

$ Hôtel Madrigal**, one block past Hôtel Compostelle, is a well-maintained 11-room hotel with air-conditioning, Wi-Fi, a weight room, and solid two-star rooms, all with queen-size beds and smallish bathrooms (Db-€60–73, Tb/Qb-€78–85, 50 avenue des Selves, tel. 05 53 59 21 98, fax 05 53 30 31 65, www.hotel-madrigal-sarlat.com, info@hotel-madrigal-sarlat.com).

Chambres d'Hôte

These *chambres d'hôte* are central, and compare well with the hotels listed above.

At **$ Chambres du Glacier,** gentle Monsieur Da Costa offers four cavernous and surprisingly elegant rooms above an outdoor café, in the thick of Sarlat's pedestrian zone (perfect for market days). Rooms come with café noise, sky-high ceilings, big windows over Sarlat's world, wood floors, and bathrooms you can get lost in (Db-€55, Tb-€65, Qb-€77, place de la Liberté, tel. 05 53 29 99 99, www.chambres-du-glacier-sarlat.com, carlos.da.costa.24@wanadoo.fr).

$ Friendly, English-speaking **Pierre-Henri Toulemon** and French-speaking Diane have three large rooms with a private entry in a 17th-century home. They're located a few steps from the main square (Db-€40–47, €8 per extra person up to five, cash only, no deposit required—simply call a day or two ahead to confirm your approximate arrival time, look for big steps from northeast corner of place de la Liberté, 4 rue Magnanat, tel. 05 53 31 26 60, mobile 06 08 67 76 90, www.toulemon.com, p-h.toulemon@wanadoo.fr). They also rent two cottages with living rooms and kitchens. One has one bedroom and sleeps four; the other cottage, just renovated, has three bedrooms (3-day minimum, easy parking).

$$ La Lanterne, named for the monument it faces, is home to Brits Terri and Roy Bowen, who have restored a 500-year-old building that could not be more central or more welcoming. Rooms are thoughtfully appointed, and the guest living room was made for lounging (Db-€75–105, Tb apartment-€140, breakfast-€7, cash only, Wi-Fi, 9 bis rue Montaigne, tel. 05 53 59 17 79, mobile 06 31 57 18 23, www.sarlat.biz, info@sarlat.biz).

Near Sarlat

Many golden stone hotels (with easy parking) surround Sarlat; these listings are good for drivers who prefer to be close to Sarlat, yet in a semi-rural location.

$$$ Hôtel le Relais de Moussidière***, a five-minute drive from Sarlat (on the way to Beynac), offers affordable luxury in a lush setting. This nontraditional hotel has a huge pool, private decks, and an almost tropical feel. Friendly husband-and-wife team Dominique and Dominique (no kidding) love Americans, and run the place with enthusiasm. Dominique (she) enjoys taking Americans on hikes and exploring little-known villages with them—just for the pleasure. Faye Dunaway stayed here for a month while filming *The Messenger: The Story of Joan of Arc* (fine standard Db-€112–122, bigger Db-€152, Tb-€144–174, includes buffet breakfast, most rooms have air-con; in Moussidière Basse: leave Sarlat to the south, direction Bergerac, watch for hotel sign on left just after Citroën garage; tel. 05 53 28 28 74, fax 05 53 28 25 11, www.hotel-moussidiere.com, contact@hotel-moussidiere.com).

$ Hôtel la Verperie** (Green Fields) is aptly named, since it sits barely above Sarlat, surrounded by a park-like setting. Ideal for budget-minded families, the hotel has 25 rooms, a pool, table tennis, swings, restaurant, affordable rates, and adequate comfort in the bungalow-like rooms, each with a simple terrace (Db-€60, Tb-€73, Qb-€94, half-pension requested in high season-€54–58 per adult per day, a 15-min walk just west of Sarlat, look for brown signs to *La Verperie* above the town's eastern side, tel. 05 53 59 00 20, fax 05 53 28 58 94, www.laverperie.com, hotellaverperie @wanadoo.fr).

EATING

Sarlat is slammed with restaurants that cater mostly to tourists. Even so, you can still dine well and cheaply. The first three places described below have been very reliable, while the last two are the most formal. If you have a car, consider driving to Beynac (page 341) or La Roque-Gageac (page 339) for a riverfront dining experience. Wherever you dine, sample a glass of sweet Monbazillac wine with your foie gras.

La Mirondal, a high-energy spot in a town of sleepy restaurants, satisfies local diners with several floors of jam-packed rooms. Those in the know come here for hearty, affordable regional cuisine, thanks to the owner's commitment to providing good food at fair prices. Cap your meal with a wander through their mysteriously lit *cave* (reasonable salads, *plats du jour*, terrific €13–29 *menus*, open daily, a block off rue de la République at 7 rue des Consuls, tel. 05 53 29 53 89).

Le Petit Manoir offers creative regional cuisine served in a quiet, elegant setting. Ambience is best in the lovely courtyard; prices are reasonable (*menus* at €19 and €24); and the desserts deserve your attention (open daily; just off rue de la République, near the western end of Sarlat, at 3 Passage Payen; tel. 05 53 29 82 14).

Chez le Gaulois is a welcome change from the predictable traditional Dordogne places. Olivier serves alpine cuisine: fondue, raclette, and *tartiflette*—roasted potatoes mixed with ham, cheese, and more. They have a few sidewalk tables, but the fun is inside. The ceiling is cluttered with ham hocks, the tablecloths are blue-and-white checked, and the soundtrack is jazz (good salads, daily April–Oct, Nov–March closed Sun–Mon, near the TI at 1 rue Tourny, tel. 05 53 59 50 64).

Le Relais de Poste serves good regional cuisine at fair prices in a welcoming setting (closed Tue–Wed, impasse de la Vieille Poste, tel. 05 53 59 63 13).

Brasserie le Glacier offers the best main square views from its outdoor tables and good, basic café fare at reasonable prices. Come here for friendly service, a big salad or *plat*, and a view of the lights warming the town buildings (open daily, same contact info as Chambres du Glacier—see Sleeping section).

Pizzeria Romane is a cheap, spacious, and family-friendly eatery where you can watch your pizza cook (closed Sun–Mon, on the quiet side of Sarlat at 3 côte de Toulouse, tel. 05 53 59 23 88).

Hôtel la Couleuvrine reeks of ambience, with heavy wood beams and white tablecloths. Choose between reliable regional cuisine in a fancy dining room, or less-expensive, simpler fare in the jazzy bistro (€19 and €25 *menus*, open daily; also listed under "Sleeping," on page 331).

Le Présidial is a venerable place in a historic mansion, with lovely gardens, high ceilings, and almost-stuffy service. With Sarlat's most romantic garden setting, it's best on a balmy evening (*menus* from €26, closed Sun, reservations smart, rue Landry, tel. 05 53 28 92 47).

TRANSPORTATION CONNECTIONS

Sarlat's TI has train schedules. Souillac and Périgueux are the train hubs for points within the greater region. For all destinations below, you can go west, via the Libourne/Bordeaux line (transferring in either city, depending on your connection); or east, via SNCF bus to Souillac (covered by railpass, bus leaves from Sarlat train station). I've listed the fastest path in each case. Sarlat train info: tel. 05 53 59 00 21.

From Sarlat by Train to: Paris (7/day, allow 6 hrs: 3/day with change in Libourne or Bordeaux–St. Jean, then TGV; and 4/day via bus to Souillac, then train with possible change in Brive-la-Gaillarde), **Amboise** (4/day, 5–6 hrs, via Libourne or Bordeaux–St. Jean, then TGV to St. Pierre-des-Corps, then local train to Amboise), **Limoges/Oradour-sur-Glane** (slow and difficult trip with lots of changes, 5/day, 3–4 hrs: 3/day via bus to Souillac and train to Limoges, then bus to Oradour-sur-Glane; and 2/day with change in Le Buisson and Périgueux), **Cahors** (5/day, 2–3 hrs, bus to Souillac, then train to Cahors), **Albi** and **Carcassonne** (2/day, 4.5 hrs with changes in Le Buisson, Agen, and Toulouse; or 3/day, 6–7 hrs via bus to Souillac, then train with changes possible in Brive-la-Gaillarde and Toulouse), **St. Emilion** (4/day, 2 hrs via Libourne, then bus or taxi).

To Beynac, La Roque-Gageac, Castelnaud, and Domme: These are accessible only by taxi (allow €19–23) or bike (best rented in Sarlat). See Sarlat's "Helpful Hints," page 325, for specifics.

Best of the Dordogne River Valley

The most scenic stretch of the Dordogne lies between Carsac and Beynac. Traveling by canoe (described below) is the best way to savor the highlights of the Dordogne River Valley, though several scenic sights lie off the river and require a car or bike. Following my "Dordogne River Valley Scenic Loop" directions, below, you can easily link Sarlat (described above) with La Roque-Gageac (see page 339), Beynac and its château (see page 341), and Castelnaud (see page 341) before returning to Sarlat.

Planning Your Time

Remember that Vitrac Port (near Sarlat) is the best place to park for a canoe ride down the river. Both La Roque-Gageac and Beynac have good restaurants for a riverside dinner (described below). There are several good places to witness the *gavage* (feeding of the geese and ducks to make foie gras—see sidebar on page 344) between Beynac and Sarlat (their dinner time is generally about 18:00).

SELF-GUIDED TOURS

▲▲Dordogne River Valley Scenic Loop

Following the directions below, you can see this area by car or bike (27 hilly miles) beginning and ending in Sarlat. Cyclists can cut 10 miles off this distance and see most of the highlights by aiming for La Roque-Gageac first (leave Sarlat to the south, then follow signs

Dordogne

to *La Roque-Gageac;* skip directions in the next three paragraphs below). For a longer bike trip that still avoids a busy road, skip Carsac and head first to Montfort (see map on the next page).

From Sarlat, drivers should follow signs along D-704 toward *Cahors* and *Carsac.* Cyclists heading to Montfort should start on the same route, then take the Montfort turn-off. On the way, note the old houses (and wealthy new ones) with the lemony local limestone. Even in homes made with modern construction, you'll see the same distinct local color; it comes from the stucco made of limestone sand. The cornfields are busy growing food for ducks and geese—locals are appalled that humans would eat the stuff.

Drivers shouldn't miss the little signposted exit on the right to the *Eglise de Carsac* (**Church of Carsac**), just before Carsac. Set peacefully among cornfields, with its WWI monument, bonsai-like plane trees, and simple Romanesque exterior, the church is part of a classic rural French scene.

From here drivers should continue on, following signs to *Montfort.* About a half-mile (1 kilometer) west of Carsac, pull over to enjoy the scenic viewpoint (overlooking a bend in the river known as Cingle de Montfort). Across the Dordogne River, fields of walnut trees stretch to distant castles, while the nearby hills are covered in oak trees. This region, Périgord, is nicknamed "black Périgord" for its thick blanket of oaks, which stay leafy throughout the winter. The fairy-tale castle on the right is **Montfort.** While it was once the medieval home of Simon de Montfort—who led the Cathar Crusades in the early 13th century—today it's considered mysterious by locals. (The hometown rumor is that the castle is now the home of a brother of the emir of Kuwait.)

Continue on, passing under Montfort's castle (not worth a stop). From here, follow the signs to **La Roque-Gageac,** then on to **Castelnaud,** and finally to **Beynac,** with its imposing castle (all three towns are described in this chapter). From Beynac, it's a quick run back to Sarlat.

If you're driving, the charming, very touristy *bastide* (fortified village) of **Domme** may be worth the side trip from La Roque-Gageac for its famous views. Follow signs up to *La Bastide de Domme,* and park at a pay lot in the town (parking meters are checked), then walk, following *Le Panorama* signs. To resume your tour, return to La Roque-Gageac and follow signs downriver to Castelnaud.

▲▲▲Dordogne Canoe Trip

For a refreshing break from the car or train, explore the riverside castles and villages of the Dordogne on a canoe (see my recommended canoe route, below).

You can rent canoes—which are hard, light, indestructible,

Dordogne Canoe Trips

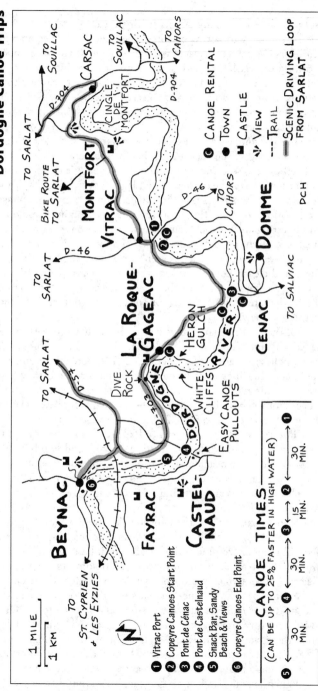

Legend:
- ⓒ CANOE RENTAL
- ● TOWN
- ♖ CASTLE
- ⚐ VIEW
- - - - TRAIL
- ▬▬ SCENIC DRIVING LOOP FROM SARLAT

DCH

Map labels:
TO SOUILLAC
CARSAC
TO SOUILLAC
D-704
CINGLE DE MONTFORT
TO CAHORS
D-704
TO SARLAT
BIKE ROUTE TO SARLAT
MONTFORT
VITRAC
D-46
TO CAHORS
❶
❷ ⓒ
LA ROQUE-GAGEAC
D-46
TO SARLAT
DOMME
❸ ⓒ
ⓒ
CENAC
TO SALVIAC
HERON GULCH
DORDOGNE RIVER
TO SARLAT
D-57
DIVE ROCK
WHITE CLIFFS
D-703
EASY CANOE PULLOUTS
❹
❺
CASTELNAUD
FAYRAC
BEYNAC
❻
TO ST. CYPRIEN & LES EYZIES

1 MILE
1 KM

N

Numbered points:
❶ Vitrac Port
❷ Copeyre Canoes Start Point
❸ Pont de Cénac
❹ Pont de Castelnaud
❺ Snack Bar, Sandy Beach & Views
❻ Copeyre Canoes End Point

CANOE TIMES
(CAN BE UP TO 25% FASTER IN HIGH WATER)

❶ →30 MIN.→ ❷ →15 MIN.→ ❸ →30 MIN.→ ❹ →30 MIN.→ ❺

Dordogne

and plastic—from many outfits in this area. Whether they're a one-person kayak or a two-person canoe, they're stable enough for beginners. Many rental places will pick you up at an agreed-upon spot (even in Sarlat, provided that your group is big enough, or that they aren't too busy). All companies let you put in anytime between from 9:30 and 16:00 (if you start at 16:00, they'll pick you up at about 18:00). They all charge about the same (€10–15 per person for two-person canoes, €15–20 for one-person kayaks). You'll get a life vest and, for a few extra euros, a watertight bucket to store your belongings. (The bucket is too big for a camera, watch, wallet, and cell phone, so bring a resealable plastic baggie or something similar for dry storage on the canoe.) If you get frustrated by wind or slow water, remember that the downstream current is often fastest near the shoreline. The trip is fun even in the rain (if you don't mind getting wet). Beach your boat wherever you want to take a break—it's light enough that you can simply drag it up high and dry to go explore. (The canoes aren't worth stealing, since they're cheap and clearly color-coded for their parent company.) It's OK if you're a complete novice—the only whitewater you'll encounter will be the rare wake of passing tour boats...and your travel partner frothing at the views.

Of the region's many canoe companies, only **Copeyre Canoes** has a pull-out arrangement in Beynac (handy for my suggested route, below). Readers of this book get a 10 percent discount in 2008, and they'll even pick you up in Sarlat for free if they have the time (this allows non-drivers a chance to explore the riverfront villages for the price of a canoe trip—tip the driver a few euros for this good service, tel. 05 53 28 23 82, www.canoe-copeyre.com).

The Nine-Mile, Two-Hour Paddle from Vitrac Port to Beynac: This is the most interesting, scenic, and handy trip if you're based in or near Sarlat. Vitrac Port, on the river close to Sarlat, is a handy starting point. And, with its impressive castle and pleasant hotels and restaurants, Beynac is a great place to end your journey.

Here's a rundown of the two-hour Vitrac–Beynac adventure: Leave Vitrac Port, paddling through lush, forested land. The fortified hill town of Domme will be dead ahead. Pass through Heron Gulch, and after about 45 minutes, you'll come to La Roque-Gageac (one of two easy and worthwhile stops before Beynac).

Paddle past La Roque-Gageac's wooden docks (where the tour boats normally tie up) to the stone ramp at the town. Do a 180-degree turn and beach thyself, dragging the boat high and dry. From there, you're in La Roque-Gageac's tiny town center, with a TI and plenty of restaurants nearby. Enjoy the town (described below) before heading back to your canoe and into the water.

When leaving La Roque-Gageac, turn around to enjoy the

village view. About 15 minutes farther downstream, you'll approach views of the feudal village and castle of Castelnaud. Look for the castle's huge model of a medieval catapult silhouetted menacingly against the sky (it's a steep but worthwhile climb to tour this castle, see page 341). Two grassy pullouts flank the bridge below the castle, and the bridge arches make terrific frames for castle views. Just past the grass there's a small market and charcuterie with all you need for a fine picnic, and a café/restaurant.

Another 15 minutes downstream brings views of Château de Fayrac on your left. The lords of Castlenaud built this to better spy on Beynac during the Hundred Years' War. Now on to your last stop: Beynac. The awesome Beynac castle—looming high above the town—gets better and better as you approach. Slow down and enjoy the ride (there's a snack stand with the same views at the bridge on the right). Head to the Copeyre canoe depot at the downstream end of town. You'll see the ramp just before the parking lot and wooden dock (where the tour boats generally tie up). Do another 180-degree turn, and beach yourself hard. The office is right there. Return your boat, and explore Beynac.

Other Canoe Options: All along the river you'll see companies, each with their color-coded plastic canoes stacked up. Depending on their location and relations with places to pull out, each one works best on a particular stretch of the river. All of them have essentially the same policies. Below Domme in Cénac, **Dordogne Randonées** has canoes and kayaks for the scenic two-hour stretch to a pullout near Beynac (to reach their office coming from Sarlat or Beynac, take the first left after crossing the bridge to Cénac, tel. 05 53 28 22 01, randodordogne@wanadoo.fr). In La Roque-Gageac, **Canoe-Dordogne** rents canoes for the appealing two-hour float to Château des Milandes, allowing canoers to stop in Beynac before the pullout (tel. 05 53 29 58 50). **Copeyre** also arranges a 14-mile trip from Carsac to Beynac, adding the gorgeous Montfort loop, called *Cingle de Montfort* (they also do a longer two-day trip, tel. 05 53 28 23 82, www.canoe-copeyre.com). For a lazier no-paddle alternative, try a river cruise from Beynac or La Roque-Gageac (€8, 50–60-minute trips great for landlubbers, see page 341 and below).

SIGHTS AND ACTIVITIES

▲▲▲La Roque-Gageac

Whether you're joyriding or paddling the Dordogne, La Roque-Gageac (lah rohk-gah-zhahk) is an essential stop—and a strong contender on all the "cutest towns in France" lists. Called by most simply "La Roque" ("The Rock"), it looks sculpted out of the rock between the river and the cliffs. While very touristy and packed with day-trippers, it's tranquil at night. At the upstream end of town, you'll find plenty of parking, the **TI** (Easter–Sept daily 10:00–12:00 & 14:00–18:00, closed off-season, tel. 05 53 29 17 01), a WC, swings and slides for kids, canoe rental, and *pétanque (boules)* courts, which are lively on summer evenings (17:00–21:00). A small market brightens La Roque-Gageac on Friday mornings.

La Roque-Gageac is a one-street town stretching along the river. Cars and strollers compete for the same riverfront space. Standing above the boat dock, survey the town: The highest stone work (on the far right) was home to the town's earliest inhabitants in the 10th century. The 12th-century cave-dwellers' village (to the left, high above the Hôtel Belle Etoile) was built during the era of Norman (Viking) river raids. Long after the Vikings were tamed, French soldiers used this lofty perch as a barracks while fighting against England in the Hundred Years' War.

Now locate the exotic foliage by the church on the right. Tropical gardens (bamboo, bananas, lemons, and so on) are a village forte, since limestone absorbs heat.

Every winter, La Roque-Gageac endures a flood that would leave you (standing where you are now) underwater. When there's a big rain in central France, La Roque-Gageac floods two days later. The first floors of all the riverfront buildings are vacated off-season. (A house about five buildings down from Hôtel Belle Etoile shows various high-water marks—*inondation* means "flood.")

Looking further downstream, notice the fanciful castle built in the 19th century by a British aristocrat (whose family still nurtures Joan of Arc dreams in its turrets). The old building just beyond that (downstream end of town) actually is historic—it's the quarantine house, where lepers and out-of-town visitors who dropped by in times of plague would be kept (after their boats were burned).

On the river are little tour boats. While modern, they're modeled after the boats that were originally built here to take prized oak barrels down to Bordeaux. Unable to return against the river current, those boats were routinely taken apart for their lumber. Today, tourists, rather than barrels, fill the boats as they make a scenic round-trip on one-hour cruises to Beynac (€8, 2/ hour, April–Nov daily, tel. 05 53 29 40 44). If you're experiencing a movie-based déjà vu, it's because these actual boats (dolled up, of course) were used by Johnny Depp, who delighted viewers and Juliette Binoche alike in the movie *Chocolat*.

Climb into the town by strolling up the cobbled lane to the right of the Hôtel Belle Etoile. The path ends where a right turn takes you to the exotic garden and viewpoint (in front of the simple church), and a left turn takes you to the privately owned and overpriced Fort Troglodyte (€5, daily 10:00–19:00). Fort

Troglodyte—with lots of steps, grand views, and piles of rocks in caves evoking medieval paranoia—is worth the money and energy only if you won't be visiting the similar but much better La Roque St. Christophe (see page 359).

▲▲Castelnaud

This crumbling castle looks less mighty than Château de Beynac (across the river), but this sight packs a fine medieval punch. Now a museum, the château has a story to tell in every room. Several rooms display weaponry and artifacts from the Hundred Years' War, and others have videos, interactive computers (in English), and castle models. From the armory to the kitchen, the whole experience is designed to teach you about daily castle life, from the battlefield to the dinner table. The upper courtyard has a 150-foot-deep well (drop a pebble). The rampart views are as unbeatable as the siege tools (located outside the walls) are formidable. Pick up the free and essential English explanations (€7.50, daily July–Aug 9:00–20:00, April–June and Sept 10:00–19:00, Oct and Feb–March 10:00–18:00, Nov–Jan 14:00–17:00, last entry 1 hour before closing; from the river, it's a steep 20-min hike through the village, or drive to the €2 parking lot at the castle gate; view café and daily demonstrations of medieval warfare mid-July–Aug, tel. 05 53 31 30 00, www.castelnaud.com).

You can stop at Castelnaud on your canoe trip, or hike an hour from Beynac along a riverside path (while it's tricky to follow in parts—it hugs the river as it passes through campgrounds and farms—determined walkers do fine).

▲▲▲Beynac

The other must-see, picture-perfect Dordogne village, located four miles downstream from La Roque-Gageac, is Beynac (bay-nak). It comes with a big, foreboding bonus: one of the most imposing castles in France.

The feudal village of Beynac tumbles down a steep hill from its majestic castle to the river far below. You'll have the Dordogne River at your doorstep and a perfectly preserved medieval village winding, like a sepia-tone film set, from the beach to the castle above. Except for the castle, there's nothing to "tour." The purely stone village—with steep streets that still have their Languedoc (old French) names—is just plain pretty. The floodlit village is always open for evening strollers.

Orientation: The **TI** is across from the recommended Hôtel du Château (daily 10:00–12:30 & 14:00–17:30, tel. 05 53 29 43 08). Pick up the *Plan de Beynac* in English for a simple self-guided walking tour, and get information on hiking and canoes. A few steps down from the TI is the post office (which has an ATM).

Dordogne

If you need a lift, call Beynac-based **Taxi Corrine** (see "Getting Around the Dordogne," page 320). There's a sweet little market on Monday mornings in the river parking lot. Drivers pay to park at different lots located on the river, way up at the castle (follow signs to *Château de Beynac*), or halfway between. The same parking ticket works up at the château if you decide against the climb. Take everything out of your car.

Hikes: A too-busy road separates Beynac from its river. The village climbs steeply uphill from there to the château—the farther you get from the road, the more medieval the village feels. (You can drive up via a long lane looping around the back of town.) A trail, which begins across from Hôtel Bonnet, follows the river toward Castelnaud, with great views back toward Beynac and—for able route-finders—a healthy one-hour hike to Castelnaud. Find time to walk at least a few hundred yards along this trail to enjoy the view to Beynac.

Château de Beynac: Beynac's brooding, cliff-clinging château—worth ▲▲—soars 500 feet above the Dordogne River. During the Hundred Years' War (see sidebar on page 195), the castle of Beynac housed the French, while the British set up camp across the river at Castelnaud. From the condition of the castles, it looks like France won. This sparsely furnished castle is most interesting for the valley views, but it still manages to evoke a powerful medieval feel. (These castles never had much furniture in any case.) Stone oil lamps light the way; swords, spears, and crossbows keep you honest; and the two stone WCs keep kids entertained. I like the soldiers' party room best—park your sword at the door and hang your crossbow on the hooks above, please. Notice the list across from the ticket window showing *Beynac et Ses Barons* (the barons of Beynac: *croisade* means Crusade, and *Coeur de Lion* means Lionheart—Richard the Lionhearted spent 10 years here). The current owner lives above the ticket booth. Authentic-looking wooden stockades were installed for the 1998 filming of the movie *The Messenger: The Story of Joan of Arc*. You're free to wander on your own, though after 17:00, you might be required to follow a tour. Pick up the English explanations (€0.15) or spring for the €5 well-done Château de Beynac pamphlet (€7, daily June–Sept 10:00–18:30, April–May and Oct closes at 18:00, Nov–March at 16:00 or 17:00—depending on weather and whim, last entry 45 min before closing, tel. 05 53 29 50 40).

Viewpoints: Even if you pass on the castle, hike or drive up to the town lookout for a commanding top-of-the-village view, which overlooks several castles and the river. Walk outside the village at the top (parking available), turn right (passing the little cemetery), and walk uphill until the view opens up. Castelnaud's castle hangs on the hill in the distance straight ahead; Château de Fayrac (owned by a Texan) is by the bridge just in front of Castelnaud, and was originally constructed by the lords of Castlenaud to keep a closer eye on the castle of Beynac. The Château de Marqueyssac is on a hill a bit to the left, which was built by the barons of Beynac to keep a closer eye on the boys at Castlenaud. More than a thousand such castles were erected in the Dordogne alone during the Hundred Years' War (1336–1453).

Two exceptional views of Beynac are nearby. The first lies on the river at the bridge halfway to Castlenaud (take the riverside path that's opposite Hôtel Bonnet, or drive about a half-mile toward La Roque-Gageac, and turn right at the Auberge du Château restaurant and follow to road to its end). But for the best (and easiest) village view, simply step up on the short wall between the parking lot and the river—just try fitting it all in your camera's viewfinder.

Boat Trips: Boats leave from Beynac's riverside parking lot for relaxing, 50-minute river cruises to La Roque-Gageac and back (€8, nearly hourly, departures Easter–Oct daily 10:00–12:30 & 14:00–18:00, more frequent trips July–Aug, written English explanations, tel. 05 53 28 51 15).

Foie Gras Farms

During the evenings, many farms in this area let you witness the force-feeding of geese for the "ultimate pleasure" of foie gras. Look for *Gavage* signs, but beware: It's hard for the squeamish to watch (read the sidebar on the next page for a description before you visit). Of the three places listed below, the first is by far the best, with the only real tour. The second is a short walk from the Beynac castle (and therefore very handy), while the last is tiny, homey, and the most flexible in its hours. For locations, see the map on page 349.

Elevage du Bouyssou, a big homey goose farm a short drive from Sarlat, is run by a couple who enjoy their work. Denis Mazet (the latest in a long line of goose farmers here) spends five hours a day feeding his gaggle of geese. His wife Nathalie—clearly in love with country life—speaks wonderful English and enthusiastically shows guests around their idyllic farm. Each evening, she leads a one-hour, kid-friendly tour. You'll meet the geese babies, do a little unforced feeding, and hear how every part of the goose (except heads and feet) is used—even feathers (for pillows). Nathalie explains why locals see the force-feeding as humane (the same as raising any other animal for human consumption) before you step into the dark barn where about a hundred geese await another dinner. The tour finishes in the little shop. They raise and slaughter a thousand geese annually, producing about 1,500 pounds of foie gras—most of which is sold directly to visitors on their happy farm at good prices. In July and August, Nathalie includes a tasting of

Dordogne

Foie Gras and Force-Feeding the Geese

The force-feeding of geese is designed to fatten the animals' livers in short order for the making of the Dordogne specialty, goose-liver pâté, or foie gras. The practice is as controversial among animal rights' activists as bullfighting (a topic of much debate in Spain). While some view these geese as tortured prisoners, here's the (politically incorrect) perspective of those who produce and consume such farm-raised animals:

French enthusiasts of *la gavage* (as the force-feeding process is called) say the animals are calm, in no pain, and are designed to take in food in this manner, because of their massive gullets and expandable livers (used to store lots of fat for their long migrations). Geese do not have a gag reflex, and the linings of their throats are tough (they swallow rocks to store in their gizzards for grinding the food they eat). They can eat lots of food easily, without choking. They live lives at least as comfy as the chickens, cows, and pigs that many people have no problem eating, and are slaughtered as humanely as any non-human can expect in this food-chain existence.

The quality of foie gras depends on a stress-free environment; geese do best with the same human feeder and a steady flow of good corn. These mostly free-range geese live six months (most of our battery chickens in the US live less than two months,

sweet wine on the tour (tours daily at 18:30 year-round, groups welcome, English tour on request at any time, tel. 05 53 31 12 31, elevagebouyssou@wanadoo.fr). To get to the farm, leave Sarlat on the Carsac-bound road (D-704), go about seven kilometers in the direction of Carsac, turn left at the cement plant, and follow *Bouyssou* signs until you reach the farm.

Madame Gauthier, a small farm where you can also observe the *gavage* and buy the product, is just down the road behind Château de Beynac. You can park there, or walk 10 minutes from the château through the parking lot and away from the river—you'll see signs (demonstrations 17:30–19:30, no tour, tel. 05 53 29 51 45).

La Ferme de l'Angle is a tiny goose farm in the scenic middle of nowhere, a short distance north of Sarlat. Christiane (who speaks English) and Cyril (who speaks goose) are retired, and enjoy playing host to the guests who drop by. In July and August,

and are plumped with hormones). Their "golden weeks" are the last three or four, when they go into the pen to have their livers fattened. With two or three feedings a day, their liver grows from about a quarter-pound to nearly two pounds. A goose with a fattened liver looks like he's waddling around with a full diaper under his feathers. (Signs and placards in the towns of the region show geese with this unique and, for foie gras lovers, mouth-watering shape.) The same process is applied to ducks to get the marginally less exquisite and less expensive duck-liver pâté.

The varieties of product you'll be tempted to buy (or order in restaurants) can be confusing. Here's a primer: first, *foie gras* means "fattened liver"; *foie gras d'oie* is from a goose, while *foie gras de canard* is from a duck (you'll also see a blend of the two). *Pâté de foie gras* is a "paste" of foie gras combined with other meats, fats, and seasonings (think of liverwurst). Most American consumers only get the chance to eat foie gras in the form of pâtés.

The *foie gras d'oie entier* (a solid chunk of pure goose liver) is the most expensive and prized version of foie gras, costing about €18 for 130 grams (about a tuna-can-size tin). The *bloc de foie gras d'oie* is made of chunks of pure goose liver that have been whipped to make them spreadable (figure €13 for 130 grams). The *medaillons de foie gras d'oie* must be at least 50 percent foie gras (the rest will be a pâté filler, about €7 for 130 grams). A small tin of blended duck-and-goose foie gras costs about €5.

After a week in the Dordogne, I leave feeling a strong need for foie gras detox.

they offer a small tasting *menu* in their yard. While there's no formal tour here and only a handful of geese, this is an easy way to see the *gavage* in action, since Cyril will demonstrate at just about any time (open daily, tel. 05 53 31 16 63). To get to the farm, located three miles from Sarlat, take D-704 (direction: Brive/Montignac), at Restaurant la Vieille Grange, take a left and follow signs.

SLEEPING AND EATING

Along the Dordogne River
(€1= about $1.30, country code: 33)

Those with a car can enjoy plush and tranquil rural accommodations at great prices. Here are a handful of exceptionally good-value places located within a 15-minute drive of Sarlat. I like them for their locations in charming villages, the comfort they provide, the views they offer, or for a combination of these qualities. Read about the villages they're in (listed above), then make your choice—you can't go wrong.

Sleeping and Eating in La Roque-Gageac

Along with Beynac (see below), this is one of the region's most beautiful villages. Park in the lot at the eastern end of town if you're staying in any of these hotels, and take everything out of your car to be safe.

$ Hôtel Belle Etoile**, located on the river in the center of La Roque-Gageac, is one of the best-run two-star hotel-restaurants in the region. Hostess Danielle and chef Régis (ray-geez)—who greets every diner—make the ideal team, with a loyal staff. Rooms are comfy and well-maintained; most have river views. The hotel is closed from November through March (non-riverview Db-€50, riverview Db-€66, or €76 for better view—I like the €66 rooms, reserve private parking ahead, tel. 05 53 29 51 44, fax 05 53 29 45 63, hotel.belle-etoile@wanadoo.fr). The hotel's **restaurant** is how I discovered this place—it's where locals go for a fine meal. They serve a memorable dinner of classic French cuisine in a romantic setting. The serving sizes are not great, but the quality is (*menus* from €24, closed for lunch Wed and all day Mon).

$ Auberge des Platanes** has 13 rooms above a sprawling café and restaurant across from the TI and parking lot. Service is less personal than at Hôtel Belle Etoile, as hotel guests take a back seat to café clients, but rooms are traditional, comfortable, and a good value (Sb-€35, Db-€45–50, Tb-€55–65, tel. 05 53 29 51 58, fax 05 53 31 19 32, www.aubergedesplatanes.com, contact @aubergedesplatanes.com).

Sleeping in Beynac

My favorite village on the river comes with some traffic noise and the region's greatest castle. Pay to park at the riverside lot during the day, or park for free 300 yards up the road toward the castle. All parking is free overnight (19:00–10:00) and appealing to thieves.

$ Hôtel du Château**, on the river at Beynac's only intersection, is run by an enterprising couple who are busily transforming this hotel. There's a full café/bar, a good restaurant, free Internet access, Wi-Fi, and a swimming pool. It's run by eager-to-please Sarissa and Christoph, a French-Dutch couple with toddler Timon (tee-mohn) and dog Max. The 16 rooms, most with queen-size beds, are bright and pleasant. Some have street noise, though air-conditioning (available in most rooms) solves that. Other rooms have terraces facing the river; four rooms can sleep up to four people and one has a full kitchen. Their half-pension is a good value (Sb-€45–65, Db-€50–70, price range is from mid- to high-season, tel.

05 53 29 19 20, fax 05 53 28 55 56, www.hotelduchateau-dordogne. com, info@hotelduchateau-dordogne.com).

$ Le Café de la Rivière, a few doors down from Hôtel du Château, is where affable John welcomes guests with three airy and pleasant rooms. The rooms are above a garden café, two have river views and some road noise, and one quieter room is in the back, with village views (Db-€50–65, 2-night minimum, air-con, tel. 05 53 28 35 49, mobile 06 32 91 36 05, www.cafedelariviere .com, info@cafedelariviere.com).

$ Chambres Residence Versailles does its name justice, with five immaculate and spacious rooms that Louis himself would have appreciated. They have laundry facilities, a quiet terrace and garden, and—best of all—the welcoming Fleurys, Jean-Claude and Françoise, who speak just enough English (Db-€60, three rooms have fine views, all have big beds, includes large English breakfast, cash only, no smoking anywhere, reserve ahead for a terrific home-cooked dinner, route du Château, tel. & fax 05 53 29 35 06, www.lepetitversailles.fr, info@lepetitversailles.fr). With the river on your right, take the small road—wedged between the hill and Hôtel Bonnet—for a half-mile, turn right when you see the sign that points left to *le Château,* and continue 100 yards, then take a right down a steep driveway.

Eating in Beynac

Beynac has a handful of worthwhile restaurants and a bakery with handy picnic-ready lunch items (across from the TI). Have a drink up high at the café opposite the castle entry, or down below at the café that hides right on the river (walk down the steps across from Hôtel du Château), and stay for dinner if the spirit moves you.

Hôtel du Château offers cozy dining in air-conditioned comfort, generous servings and reasonable prices (€15 lunchtime salad/ pasta bar, dinner *menus* from €18, daily, see hotel listing above).

Taverne/Café des Remparts, Beynac's scenic eatery, faces the castle at the top of the town and serves copious salads (try the *Paysanne* or *Gourmande*), good omelets, *plats*—or just a drink. I can't imagine leaving Beynac without relaxing at their view-perfect café for at least a drink; it's best at night, but call ahead to be sure they're open (July–Aug daily for lunch and dinner, otherwise open daily for lunch and Fri–Mon for dinner, across from castle, tel. 05 53 29 57 76).

La Petite Tonnelle is an endearing little place serving reliable cuisine at fair prices. It's a block up from Hôtel du Château, with a good terrace and appealing interior seating (€16/28 *menus,* closed Tue–Wed except in summer, on the road to the castle, tel. 05 53 29 95 18).

Sleeping near Castelnaud

This village is ideally situated, between La Roque-Gageac and Beynac.

$$ La Tour de Cause is where California refugees Albert and Caitlin have found their heaven, amid their renovated farmhouse with five top-quality rooms, a well-tended garden, a big pool, Internet access, and, best of all, a *pétanque (boules)* court. Albert restores homes in California, and has taken his considerable talent to France (Sb-€70, Db-€85, includes breakfast, cash only, 2-night minimum mid-July–Aug, closed Nov–April, tel. 05 53 30 30 51, US tel. Nov–March 707/527-5051, www.latourdecause.com, info @latourdecause.com). From the Dordogne River, cross the bridge to Castelnaud, follow signs toward *Daglan*, and turn right in the hamlet of Pont de Cause; park at the blue gate.

$$ Château Nineyrol is a relaxed, welcoming place run by British expats Anne and and Phil Penfold; they're as excited about this region as you are. They have five guest rooms with personality: two big rooms (each sleeps up to four) and three smallish doubles; all the rooms have en-suite bathrooms. Enjoy the large pool and terrace with views of Castelnaud castle. Anne cooks a nice dinner—€25 for the works, including wine (Db-€65–75, Tb-€78–98, Qb-€86–136, laundry service available, bikes for rent, guided tours, tel. 05 53 30 46 01, mobile 06 33 61 34 63, www.nineyrol.com, nineyrol@wanadoo.fr). From Beynac it's on the road to La Roque-Gageac, 100 yards past the turnoff for Castelnaud, on your left.

Sleeping in Montfort

There's more to this castle-topped village than meets the eye—leave most tourists behind and find a few cafés, a pizzeria, and a handful of *chambres d'hôte,* including this recommended listing.

$$ Chambres la Barde is where Steve (he's British) and Bronwen (she's Welsh) offer five sumptuous rooms in their modern and warm stone home. They have a swimming pool, cozy lounge, big grass yard, *pétanque,* a game room, and views to Montfort castle from each room's terrace (Db-€62–82, €15 per extra person, one room sleeps five, includes breakfast, cash only, tel. 05 53 28 24 34, mobile 06 21 96 51 90, www.perigord-dordogne-sarlat.com, steve.houghton@wanadoo.fr).

Cro-Magnon Caves

The towns and sights of the Dordogne region—including Les Eyzies-de-Tayac, Grotte de Font-de-Gaume, Abri du Cap Blanc, Grotte de Rouffignac, Lascaux II, and Grotte de Cougnac—have a rich history of prehistoric cave art. The paintings you'll see here are

Cro-Magnon Caves near Sarlat

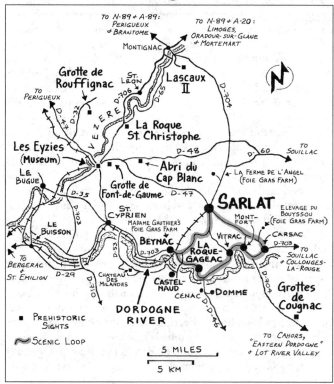

famous throughout the world for their remarkably modern-looking technique, beauty, and mystery. To fully appreciate them, take time to read the following information, written by Gene Openshaw, on the purpose of the art and the Cro-Magnon style of painting.

Cave Art 101

From 18,000 to 10,000 B.C., long before Stonehenge, before the pyramids, before metalworking, farming, and domesticated dogs, back when mammoths and saber-toothed cats still roamed the earth, prehistoric people painted deep inside limestone caverns in southern France and northern Spain. These are not crude doodles with a charcoal-tipped stick. They're sophisticated, costly, and time-consuming engineering projects planned and executed by dedicated artists supported by a unified and stable culture—the Magdalenians.

The Magdalenians (c. 18,000–10,000 B.C.): These hunter-gatherers of the Upper Paleolithic period (40,000–10,000 B.C.) were driven south by the Second Ice Age. (Historians named them after the Madeline archaeological site.) The Magdalenians flourished in southern France and northern Spain for eight millennia—long enough to chronicle the evolution and extinction of several animal species. (Think: Egypt lasted a mere 3,000 years; Rome lasted 1,000; America fewer than 250 so far.)

Physically, the people were Cro-Magnons. Unlike hulking, beetle-browed Neanderthals, Cro-Magnons were fully developed *Homo sapiens* who could blend in to our modern population. We know these people by the possessions found in their settlements: stone axes, flint arrowheads, bone needles for making clothes, musical instruments, grease lamps (without their juniper wicks), and cave paintings and sculpture. Many objects are beautifully decorated.

The Magdalenians did not live in the deep limestone caverns they painted (which are cold and inaccessible). Many did live in the shallow cliffside caves that you'll see throughout your Dordogne travels, which were continuously inhabited from prehistoric times until the Middle Ages.

The Paintings: Though there are dozens of caves painted over a span of more than 8,000 years, they're all surprisingly similar. These Stone Age hunters painted the animals they hunted—bison or bulls (especially at Lascaux and Grotte de Font-de-Gaume, both listed below), horses, deer, reindeer, ibex (mountain goats), wolves, bears, and cats, plus animals that are now extinct—mammoths (the engravings at Grotte de Rouffignac, see below), woolly rhinoceros (at Grotte de Font-de-Gaume, also below), and wild oxen.

Besides animals, you'll see geometric and abstract designs, such as circles, squiggles, and hash marks. There's scarcely a *Homo sapiens* in sight (except the famous "fallen hunter" at Lascaux), but there are human handprints traced on the wall by blowing paint through a hollow bone tube around the hand. The hunter-gatherers painted the animals they hunted...but none of the plants they gathered.

Style: The animals stand in profile, with unnaturally big bodies and small limbs and heads. Black, red, and yellow dominate (with some white, brown, and violet). The thick black outlines are often wavy, suggesting the animal in motion. Except for a few friezes showing a conga line of animals running across the cave wall, there is no apparent order or composition. Some paintings are simply superimposed atop others. The artists had clearly mastered the animals' anatomy, but they chose to simplify the outlines and distort the heads and limbs for effect, always painting in the distinct Magdalenian style.

Many of the cave paintings are on a Sistine Chapel–size scale. The "canvas" was huge: Lascaux's main caverns are more than a football field long; Grotte de Font-de-Gaume is 430 feet long; and Grotte de Rouffignac meanders six miles deep. The figures are monumental (bulls at Lascaux are 16 feet high). All are painted high up on walls and ceilings, like the woolly rhinoceros of Grotte de Font-de-Gaume.

Techniques: Besides painting the animals, these early artists also engraved them on the wall by laboriously scratching outlines into the rock with a flint blade, many following the rock's natural contour. A typical animal might be made using several techniques—an engraved outline that follows the natural contour, reinforced with thick outline paint, then colored in.

The paints were mixed from natural pigments dissolved in cave water and oil (animal or vegetable). At Lascaux, archaeologists have found more than 150 different minerals on hand to mix paints. Even basic black might be a mix of manganese dioxide, ground quartz, and a calcium phosphate that had to be made by heating bone to 700 degrees Fahrenheit, then grinding it.

No paintbrushes have been found, so artists probably used a sponge-like material made from animal skin and fat. They may have used moss or hair, or maybe even finger-painted with globs of pure pigment. Once they'd drawn the outlines, they filled everything in with spray paint—either spit out from the mouth or blown through tubes made of hollow bone.

Imagine the engineering problems of painting one of these caves, and you can appreciate how sophisticated these "primitive" people were. First, you'd have to haul all your materials into a cold, pitch-black, not-easily-accessible place. Assistants erected scaffolding to reach ceilings and high walls, ground up minerals with a mortar and pestle, mixed paints, tended the torches and oil lamps, prepared the "paintbrushes," laid out major outlines with a connect-the-dots series of points...then stepped aside for Magdalenian Michelangelos to ascend the scaffolding and create.

Dating: Determining exactly how old this art is—and even if it's authentic—is tricky. As different caves feature different animals, prehistorians can derive which caves are relatively older and younger, since climate changes caused various animal species to come and go. (Since much of the actual paint is mineral-based with no organic material, carbon-dating techniques are often ineffective.) In several cases, experts confirmed the authenticity of a painting because the portrayals of the animals showed anatomical details not previously known—until they were discovered by modern technology. (For instance, in Grotte de Rouffignac, the mammoths are shown with a strange skin flap over their anus, which was only discovered during the 20th century in a Siberian glacier.) They can also estimate dates by checking the amount of calcium glaze formed over the paint, which can sometimes only be seen by infrared photography.

Why? No one knows the purpose of the cave paintings. Interestingly, the sites the artists chose were deliberately awe-inspiring, out of the way, and special. They knew their work here would last for untold generations, as had the paintings that came before theirs. Here are some theories of what this first human art might mean:

It's no mystery that hunters would paint animals, the source of their existence. The first scholar to study the caves, Abbé Henri Breuil, thought the painted animals were magic symbols made by hunters to increase the supply of game. Or perhaps hunters thought that if you could "master" an animal by painting it, you could later master it in battle. Some scholars think the paintings teach the art of hunting, but there's very little apparent hunting technique shown. Did they worship animals? The paintings definitely depict an animal-centered (rather than a human-centered) universe.

The paintings may have a religious purpose, and some of the caverns are large and special enough that rituals and ceremonies could have been held there. But the paintings show no priests, sacrifices, rituals, or ceremonies. Scholars writing on primitive art in other parts of the world speculate that art was made by shamans in a religious or drug-induced trance, but France's paintings are very methodical.

The order of paintings on the walls seems random. Could it be that the caves are a painted collage of the history of the Magdalenians, with each successive generation adding their distinct animal or symbol to the collage, putting it in just the right spot that established their place in history?

The fact that styles and subject matter changed so little over the millennia might imply that the artists purposely chose timeless images to relate their generation with those before and after. Or they simply lived in a stable culture that did not value innovation. Or these people were too primitive to invent new techniques and topics.

Maybe the paintings are simply the result of the universal human drive to create, and these caverns were Europe's first art galleries, bringing the first tourists.

Very likely, there is no single meaning that applies to all the paintings in all the caves. Prehistoric art may be as varied in meaning as current art.

Picture how a Magdalenian would have viewed these paintings: You'd be guided by someone into a cold, echoing, and otherworldly chamber. In the darkness, someone would light torches and lamps, and suddenly the animals would flicker to life, appearing to run around the cave, like a prehistoric movie. In front of you, a bull would appear, behind you a mammoth (which you'd never seen in the flesh), and overhead a symbol that might have tied the whole experience together. You'd be amazed that an artist could capture the real world and reproduce it on a wall. Whatever the purpose—religious, aesthetic, or just plain fun—there's no doubt the effect was (and is) thrilling.

Today, you can visit the caves and share a common experience with a caveman. Feel a bond with these long-gone people... or stand in awe at how different they were from us. Ultimately, the paintings are as mysterious as the human species.

SIGHTS

All of the prehistoric caves listed here are within a short drive of Sarlat. Considering the scarcity of public transit, if you don't have a car, you're a caveman without a spear (see page 319 for guided tours that connect some of these sights). July, August, and holiday weekends are busiest, so book as far ahead as you can during these times. Saturdays are generally quiet. Three caves take reservations (by phone, fax or email): Grotte de Font-de-Gaume, Abri du Cap Blanc, and Grotte du Pech Merle (all described in this section). The rest are first-come, first-served. Remember that Sarlat's TI and some hotels can reserve cave visits for you (and are likely to be more effective in landing a reservation).

A Few General Tips: Read "Cave Art 101" (page 349) to gain a better understanding of what you'll see. Dress warmly, even if it's hot outside. Tours can last up to an hour, and the caves are

all a steady, chilly 55 degrees Fahrenheit, with 98 or 99 percent humidity. While on tour, lag behind the group to have the paintings to yourself for a few moments. Photos, day packs, big purses, and strollers are not allowed. (You can take your camera—without using it—and check the rest on site.)

Les Eyzies-de-Tayac

This single-street town is the touristy hub of a cluster of Cro-Magnon caves, castles, and rivers, and merits a stop only for its National Museum of Prehistory (see below) and the Grotte de Font-de-Gaume cave (a 10-minute walk outside of town, described below).

Les Eyzies-de-Tayac is famous because it's where Monsieur Magnon first discovered the original Cro-Magnon man in 1870. That breakthrough set of bones was found just behind the hotel of Monsieur Magnon—Hôtel le Cro-Magnon, which is in business to this day on the main street in Les Eyzies. The name "Cro-Magnon" translates as "Mr. Magnon's Hole."

Les Eyzies-de-Tayac's **TI** rents bikes (July–Aug Mon–Sat 9:00–19:00, Sept–June Mon–Sat 10:00–12:00 & 14:00–18:00, open Sun June–Sept only 10:00–12:00 & 14:00–17:00; tel. 05 53 06 97 05, fax 05 53 06 90 79, www.leseyzies.com). The train station is a level 500 yards from the town center (turn right out of the station to get into town).

Sleeping in and near Les Eyzies-de-Tayac: Train travelers wanting to see the museum and famous cave will find Les Eyzies-de-Tayac a practical place to sleep, as will drivers interested in a fun farm experience. **$$$ Auberge Veyret,** a 15-minute drive from Les Eyzies-de-Tayac, is as real a farm experience as it gets, with beefy cows and plump pigs. Mama greets you with a huge smile and nary a word of English, her son cooks, and her daughter (Laurence) and husband (Patrick) do everything else. The rooms are spotless and furnished like Grandma's, but with modern conveniences. You'll be expected to dine here—and you'd be a fool not to, since dinner includes everything from apéritif to *digestif,* with five courses in between and wine throughout (Db-€52 per person, lower rates for kids, includes breakfast and dinner, cash only, large pool, en route to Abri du Cap Blanc—look for any sign that says *Veyret,* tel. 05 53 29 68 44, fax 05 53 31 58 28, www.auberge-veyret.com, contact @auberge-veyret.com).

$ Madame Bauchet (call her "Nanou") owns the closest rooms to the train station, and they're a good clean value (Db-€36–40, Tb/Qb-€53, cash only, 200 yards from the station at 40 avenue de la Préhistoire—look for the brown *Chambres* sign, tel. 05 53 06 97 71, bauchetgerard@wanadoo.fr). Madame Bauchet does not speak English, but she's a creative communicator.

▲▲National Museum of Prehistory (Musée National de Préhistoire)

This modern museum houses more than 18,000 bones, stones, and crude little doodads that were uncovered locally. It takes you through prehistory, starting 400,000 years ago. With English info sheets provided along the way, it's a good first stop for learning about the age. While the museum does an excellent job presenting its exhibits, you have to be engaged and determined to learn to follow the museum's complex and serious teaching style.

Appropriately located on a cliff that's been inhabited by humans for 35,000 years (above Les Eyzies-de-Tayac's TI), the museum has a sleek design intended to help it blend in to the surrounding rock. Videos demonstrate scratching designs, painting techniques, and how spearheads were made. Full-size models of

Dordogne

Cro-Magnon people and animals stare at racks of countless arrow-heads. The first floor sets the stage, describing human evolution and the importance of tools. The second (and better) floor highlights prehistoric artifacts found in France. The most interesting things you'll see are in this order: a handheld arrow launcher, a 5,000-year-old flat-bottomed boat made from oak (pirogue), prehistoric fire pits, amazing cavewoman jewelry (including a necklace made of 70 stag teeth—pretty impressive, given that stags only have two teeth each—do the math), engravings on stone (don't miss the unflattering yet impressively realistic female figure), a handheld lamp used to light cave interiors *(lampe de Lascaux)*, and beautiful rock sculptures of horses (much like the paintings at the cave of Abri du Cap Blanc). Your visit ends on the cliff edge, with a Fred Flintstone–style photo op on a porch that some of our ancient ancestors once called home (€5; July–Aug daily 9:30–18:30; Sept–June Wed–Mon 9:30–12:00 & 14:00–17:30, closed Tue; www.leseyzies.com/musee-prehistoire).

▲▲Lascaux II

The region's—and the world's—most famous cave paintings are at Lascaux, 14 miles north of Sarlat and Les Eyzies. The Lascaux caves were discovered accidentally in 1940 by four kids and their dog. From 1948 through 1963, more than a million people climbed through this prehistoric wonderland. But these visitors tracked in fungus on their shoes and changed the temperature and humidity with their heavy breathing. In just 15 years, the precious art deteriorated more than during the 15,000 years before that. The original caves were closed. A copy cave—accurate to within one centimeter, reproducing the best 40-yard-long stretch, and showing 90 percent of the paintings found in Lascaux—was opened next to the original in 1983. Guides assure that the original is every bit as crisp and has just as much contrast as the facsimile you'll see.

At impressive Lascaux II, the reindeer, horses, and bulls of Lascaux I are painstakingly reproduced by top artists using the same dyes, tools, and techniques their predecessors did 15,000 years ago. Of course, seeing the real thing at the other caves is important, but come here first (taking one of the scheduled English-language tours) for a great introduction to the region's cave art. While it feels a bit rushed—40 people per tour are hustled through the two-room cave reproductions—the guides are committed to teaching, the paintings are astonishing, and the experience is mystifying. (Forget that they're copies, and enjoy being swept away by the prehistoric majesty of it all.)

Cost and Hours: €9; July–Aug daily 9:00–19:00; April–June and Sept daily 9:30–18:30; Oct–Dec and Feb–March Tue–Sun 10:00–12:00 & 14:00–17:30, closed Mon; closed Jan.

Dordogne

Touring the Replica Cave: You'll see Lascaux II with a 40-minute English tour (4–6/day May–Sept, usually at about 11:50 and 14:20, about 2/day off-season, call 05 53 51 96 23 for ticket availability and English tour times, but no reservations except in July–Aug). Unless you're visiting in winter (Oct–March), you must buy your ticket before coming to Lascaux; the ticket office is next to the TI in Montignac, five minutes away by car. Deep-blue signs direct drivers to *La Billeterie* in Montignac (follow signs for *Centre-Ville*, then look for *La Billeterie*, and don't double-park); Lascaux is well-signed from there. In July and August, tours are usually sold out by 13:00, so book ahead. It's always 56 degrees in the cave, so dress warmly. Pleasant Montignac is worth a wander if you have time to kill.

Sleeping near Lascaux: **$$$ Château de la Fleunie***** offers regal 15th-century château accommodations surrounded by pastures and mountain goats, the biggest private pool I've seen in France, tennis courts, and a restaurant with *beaucoup d'ambiance* (Db in modern annex with terrace–€85–100, Db in château–€75–115, most are about €100, tower room for two–€145, €20 per extra person, prices rise an additional €20 July–Aug, *menus* from €30, half-pension required July–Aug–€80–90 per person, 10-min drive north of Montignac on road to Brive-la-Gaillarde, in Condat-sur-Vézère, tel. 05 53 51 32 74, fax 05 53 50 58 98, www.lafleunie.com, lafleunie@free.fr).

▲▲▲Grotte de Font-de-Gaume

Even if you're not a connoisseur of Cro-Magnon art, you'll dig this cave. It's the last cave in Europe with prehistoric multicolored (polychrome) painting still open to the public. (Lascaux—just down the road—and Spain's Altamira are closed, with copy caves for visitors instead.) The cave, made millions of years ago—not by a river, but by the geological activity that created the Pyrénées mountains—is entirely natural. It contains 15,000-year-old paintings of 230 animals, 82 of which are bison.

On a carefully guided and controlled 100-yard walk, you'll see about 20 red-and-black bison—often in elegant motion—painted with a moving sensitivity. When two animals face each other, one is black, and the other is red. Your guide, with a laser pointer and great reverence, will trace the faded outline of the bison and explain how, 15,000 years ago, cave dwellers used local minerals and the rock's natural contour to give the paintings dimension. Some locals knew about the cave long ago, when there was little interest in prehistory, but the paintings were officially discovered in 1901 by the village schoolteacher.

Cost, Hours, Information: €6.50, mid-May–mid-Sept Sun–Fri 9:30–17:30, mid-Sept–mid-May Sun–Fri 9:30–12:30 &

14:00–17:30, closed Sat, last departure 90 min before closing, no photography or large bags, tel. 05 53 06 86 00, fax 05 53 35 26 18, fontdegaume@monuments-nationaux.fr. Those planning to visit Abri du Cap Blanc can reserve and buy tickets here (see below).

Getting a Ticket: For the health of the precious and fragile art, the number of daily visitors allowable is strictly regulated (180 people per day, in groups of 12). Of the 180 spots available, 130 tickets are allotted to visitors who call to make advance reservations, and 50 are kept open for those wanting to enter badly enough to come early and wait for a ticket. In July and August (when spots get booked up months in advance), you'll need to reserve ahead by phone or email, or arrive by 8:00; the rest of the year, you should be OK if you pop in by 9:00. Sundays are always first-come, first-served, with no reservations taken. You can call the site at certain times (10:30–12:00 and 14:30–16:00) to see if spots happen to be open (they often are) before doing the early-morning bit. You must check in 15 minutes before your tour, or you'll lose your place to the sightseeing vultures waiting to snatch up the spots of late arrivals. You can join this flock, and try to snag a seat given to standbys 15 minutes before the tour time (many don't show).

Tours: Since English tours are limited to two per day (usually at 11:30 and 15:30, May–Sept only), you'll likely make the visit with a French guide. While the English-info flier is useless, the actual tour is little more than pointing out legs, eyes, heads, and bellies of the bison, so don't fret if you're not on an English tour. Pierre Fanlac Editeur's *The Font-de-Gaume Cave* guidebook, sold for €6 in the shop, is an excellent substitute.

Getting There: The caves are a 10-minute walk from Les Eyzies-de-Tayac (toward Sarlat). From the ticket house, walk 400 yards on an uphill path to the cave entrance (where there's a free and safe bag check and a WC). There's easy parking on site, but drivers who can't get a ticket here (or who want to see completely different caves) should try the caves at Grotte de Rouffignac (see next page), or aim for the more remote Grotte du Pech Merle, about 30 minutes east of Cahors (see page 377).

▲Abri du Cap Blanc

In this prehistoric cave (a 10-minute drive from Grotte de Font-de-Gaume), early artists used the rock's natural contours to add dimension to their sculpture. The small museum (with English explanations) will prepare you, and the useful English handout will guide you. Look for places where the artists smoothed or roughened the surfaces to add depth. In this single stone room, your French-speaking guide will spend 30 minutes explaining 14,000-year-old carvings. Impressive as these are, their subtle majesty is lost on some people. Free 45-minute tours leave on the

Dordogne

half-hour (€6.50, hours in flux so call to verify, mid-May–mid-Sept Sun–Fri 9:30–17:30, mid-Sept–Oct and April–mid-May Sun–Fri 9:30–12:30 & 14:00–17:30, closed Sat and Nov–March, no photos, walk 200 yards down from parking lot, tel. 05 53 59 21 74). Tickets and reservations are available at Font-de-Gaume cave, or at the site. Abri du Cap Blanc is well-signed, located two miles after Grotte de Font-de-Gaume (see above) on the road to Sarlat.

▲▲Grotte de Rouffignac

Rouffignac provides a different experience from other prehistoric caves in this area. Here, you'll ride a clunky little train down a giant subterranean riverbed, exploring about half a mile of this six-mile-long gallery. The cave was known to locals for decades—hence the oblivious graffiti (with dates going back to the 18th century) that litters the ceiling—but the 13,000-year-old paintings were discovered only in 1956.

Cost, Hours, Information: €6.50, daily July–Aug 9:00–11:30 & 14:00–18:00, April–June and Sept–Nov 10:00–11:30 & 14:00–17:00, closed Dec–March, tours 2/hr, no reservations, tel. 05 53 05 41 71, www.grottederouffignac.fr. Dress warmly; the visit lasts 60 minutes. It's really crowded only from mid-July through August—especially in the afternoons. Weekends tend to be quietest.

Getting There: Grotte de Rouffignac is well-signed from the route between Les Eyzies-de-Tayac and Périgueux; allow 25 minutes from Les Eyzies-de-Tayac.

⟲ Self-Guided Tour: Your tour will likely be in French (guides may answer questions in English), but here's the gist of what they're saying on the stops of your train ride:

The cave was created by the underground river. It's entirely natural, but it was much shallower before the train-track bed was excavated. As you travel, imagine the motivation and determination of the painters who crawled so deep into this dark and mysterious cave. They left behind their art...and the wonder of people who crawled in centuries later to see it all.

All along the way, you'll see crater-like burrows made by hibernating bears long before the first humans painted here. There are hundreds of them—not because there were so many bears, but because year after year, a few of them would return, preferring to make their own private place to sleep (rather than using some other bear's den). After a long winter nap, bears would have one thing on their mind: Cut those toenails. The walls are scarred with the scratching of bears in need of clippers (look to the right as you ride).

Stop 1: The images of woolly mammoths etched into the walls can only be seen when lit from the side (as your guide will demonstrate). As the rock is very soft here, these were simply gouged out by the artists' fingers.

Stop 2: Look for images of finely detailed rhinoceroses in black paintings. The rock is harder here, so nothing is engraved.

Stop 3: On the left, you'll see woolly mammoths and horses engraved with tools in the harder rock. On the right is the biggest composition of the cave: a herd of peaceful mammoths. A mysterious calcite problem threatens to cover the paintings in ugly white splotches.

Off the Train: When you get off the train, notice how high the original floor was (the bear-crater level), and remember to imagine both the prehistoric makers and viewers of this art crawling back here with pretty lousy flashlight-substitutes. Here, the ceiling is covered with a remarkable gathering of animals. You'll see a fine 16-foot-long horse, a group of mountain goats, and a grandpa mammoth. There was even art that decorated the walls far down the big, scary hole. When the group chuckles, it's because the guide is explaining how the mammoth with the fine detail (showing a flap of skin over its anus) helped authenticate the paintings—these paintings couldn't be fakes, because no one knew about this anatomical detail until the remains of an actual mammoth were found in a Siberian ice field in modern times. (The discovery explained the skin flap that had long puzzled French prehistorians.)

▲La Roque St. Christophe

Five fascinating terraces carved by the Vézère River have provided shelter to people here for 50,000 years. While the terraces were inhabited in prehistoric times, there's no prehistoric art on display—the exhibit (except for one small cave) is entirely medieval. The official recorded history goes back to 976 A.D., when people settled here to steer clear of the Viking raiders who'd routinely sail up the river. (Back then in this part of Europe, the standard closing of a prayer wasn't "amen," but, "and deliver us from the Norseman, amen.")

A clever relay of river watchtowers kept an eye out for raiders. When they came, cave-dwellers gathered their kids, hauled up their animals (see the big, re-created winch), and pulled up the ladders. While there's absolutely nothing old here except for the carved-out rock (with holes for beams, carved out of the soft limestone), it's easy to imagine the entire village—complete with butcher, baker, and even candlestick-maker—in this family-friendly exhibit. This place is a dream for kids of any age who hold fond tree-house memories.

It's simple to visit: There's a free parking lot across the stream, with picnic tables, a WC, and—adjacent to the babbling brook—a pondside café (providing good salads, omelettes, and drinks—the nearby and pretty village of St. Léon provides more lunch choices). Borrow the English guide booklet (or buy it for €2) at the turnstile; stop to take in the picture showing its medieval buildings; and climb through the one-way circuit, which is slippery when damp (€7, daily April–Sept 10:00–18:30, March and Oct 10:00–18:00, Nov–Feb 11:00–17:00, last entry 45 min before closing, lots of steps, 5 miles north of Les Eyzies-de-Tayac, follow signs to *Montignac*, tel. 05 53 50 70 45). When planning your day, note that this is one of the rare sights that stays open through lunch.

▲Grottes de Cougnac

Located 19 miles south of Sarlat (and three well-signed miles north of Gourdon on D-704), this cave holds the oldest (14,000–25,000-year-old) paintings open to the public and fascinating rock formations. Less touristy than others, it provides a more intimate look at cave art, since guides have more time to explain the paintings (allow an hour for the visit). You'll get some explanations in English (unless it's high season), and see about 10 drawings of ibex and deer (with rust or black outlines) as well as a few representations of humans (€6.50, these hours correspond to first/last tour times: daily July–Aug 10:00–18:00, May–June and Sept 10:00–11:30 & 14:30–17:00, April and Oct 14:30–17:00, closed Nov–March, English book available, 70-min tours, some in English—call ahead, tel. 05 65 41 47 54, www.grottesdecougnac.com).

Oradour-sur-Glane and Nearby

▲▲▲Oradour-sur-Glane

Located two hours north of Sarlat and 15 miles west of Limoges, this is one of the most powerful sights in France. French school-children know this town well—most make a pilgrimage here. *Village des Martyrs*, as it is known, was machine-gunned and burned on June 10, 1944, by Nazi troops. The Nazis were either seeking revenge for the killing of one of their officers (by French Resistance fighters in a neighboring village) or simply terrorizing the populace in preparation for the upcoming Allied invasion (this was four days after D-Day). With cool attention to detail, the Nazis methodically rounded up the entire population of 642 townspeople. The women and children were herded into the town church, where they

were tear-gassed and machine-gunned. Plaques mark the place where the town's men were grouped and executed. The town was then set on fire, its victims left under a blanket of ashes. Today, the ghost town, left untouched for more than 60 years, greets every pilgrim who enters with only one English word: Remember.

Follow *Village des Martyrs* signs and start at the rust-colored **underground museum** (Centre de la Mémoire), which provides a good social and political context for the event (with English explanations and audioguide), including home movies of locals before the attack and disturbing footage of similar events (don't miss the 12-minute film with English audioguide translations). Then, with hushed visitors, walk the length of Oradour's main street, past gutted, charred buildings in the shade of lush trees, to the underground memorial on the market square (rusted toys, broken crucifixes, town mementos under glass). The plaques on the buildings tell us the names and occupations of the people who lived there (*laine* means wool; a *sabotier* is a maker of wooden shoes; a *quincaillerie* is a hardware store; *cordonnier* means shoe repair; a *menuisier* is a carpenter; and *tissus* means fabrics). Visit the cemetery where most lives ended on June 10, 1944, and finish at the church, with its bullet-pocked altar.

Cost, Hours, Information: Entering the village is free, while the museum costs €7 (includes audioguide). Both are open daily mid-May–mid-Sept 9:00–19:00, closes at 17:00 or 18:00 off-season, last visit 1 hour before closing, tel. 05 55 43 04 30, www.oradour .org.

Getting There: Public transport here is a challenge. Four daily buses connect Limoges with Oradour in 20 minutes (10-min walk from Limoges train station to bus stop on place Winston Churchill). Consider a taxi. Limoges is a stop on an alternative train route between Amboise and Sarlat.

Sleeping and Eating in Oradour-sur-Glane: **$ Hôtel La Glane**** is the best hotel in the modern town, with the most respected restaurant. Both are cheap and good (Db-€45, *menus* from €10, next to Hôtel de Ville on place de la Mairie, tel. 05 55 03 10 43, fax 05 55 03 15 42).

Mortemart

With a car and extra time, visit this bucolic village (15-min drive northwest of Oradour-sur-Glane on D-675). You'll find a medieval market hall, a smattering of appealing buildings, one café, and a sweet château (good picnic benches behind).

Sleeping in Mortemart: **$ Hôtel Relais**** offers a tempting overnight stop. Located on the main road, it has five small but quite comfortable rooms over a fine restaurant. Formal Madame Pradeau speaks no English, but she'll work with you (Db-€42,

Dordogne

Tb-€65, *menus* from €18, kids' *menu*-€10, restaurant closed Tue–Wed, tel. & fax 05 55 68 12 09).

▲Collonges-la-Rouge

Connoisseurs of beautiful villages need to visit this deep-red sandstone and slate-roofed village that curls down a friendly hill. Collonges-la-Rouge is a scenic 15-minute drive east of the A-20 autoroute (exit at Noailles), just south of Brive-la-Gaillarde and about a 50-minute drive from Sarlat. The **TI** has a brochure with English explanations and information on other nearby worth-a-wander villages (TI located near the top of town, tel. 05 55 25 32 25). Don't miss the church's Moorish entry, wavy floor, and holy dome. Like all adorable villages, Collonges-la-Rouge has plenty of shops and is busy at midday from June through September.

St. Emilion and Bordeaux Wine Country

Two hours due west of Sarlat and just 40 minutes from Bordeaux, St. Emilion is another pretty face just waiting to flirt with you. Unlike other French lookers, this one flirts in English—the historic presence of British interest in the wine industry has given the town an almost bilingual feel. It's a relaxing place for Americans.

Carved like an amphitheater in the bowl of a limestone hill, St. Emilion's manicured streets connect a few picture-perfect squares with heavy cobbles and scads of well-stocked wine shops. There's little to do in this town of well-heeled and well-wined residents other than enjoy the setting, and, of course, sample the local sauce. (*Bien sûr*, St. Emilion's primary sightseeing is for your palate.) Wine has been good to St. Emilion, though it accounts for barely 5 percent of Bordeaux's famous red-wine production (about 60 percent of the grapes you see are Merlot). Also try a tasty homemade macaroon, sold at many shops here. Sunday is market day in St. Emilion.

ORIENTATION

Tourist Information

The TI is a critical stop, at the top of the town on place des Créneaux, across from the high church bell tower. It's located in a one-time abbey and connected to pretty cloisters (that go ignored by most tourists—find the door in the rear of the TI and enter a peaceful place). The TI is well-armed with good information in English about anything you need. Check the bulletin board for

English visits of the city, wine-tasting classes, vineyard tours, and more. Ask about bike rental (and recommended bike routes), information on St. Emilion's few sights, and a helpful booklet on *chambres d'hôte* (daily mid-June–mid-Sept 9:30–19:00, mid-Sept–mid-June 9:30–12:30 & 13:45–18:30, Nov–March closes at 18:00, place Pioceau, tel. 05 57 55 28 28, fax 05 57 55 28 29, www .saint-emilion-tourisme.com, st-emilion.tourisme@wanadoo.fr). There's also a TI annex planned for the Tour du Donjon viewpoint (see below, under "Activities").

Arrival in St. Emilion

By Train: While there is a train station near St. Emilion, it's a 20-minute walk from town, with no taxis and scant trains. Get off in Libourne (five miles away, with good train service and easy car rental near the station). From here, you can catch a cab (€15, see "Taxi and Local Guide," below) or take an infrequent bus to St. Emilion (2/day) from the bus station *(gare routière)* next to the train station.

By Car: If coming from Sarlat, take the autoroute from Périgueux and save 40 minutes over the local roads. You'll find parking (generally €1/hour) in lots at the upper end of the town, or along the wall.

Helpful Hints

Taxi and Local Guide: Robert Faustin, who drives a minivan taxi, can arrange visits to wineries (tel. & fax 05 57 25 17 59, mobile 06 77 75 36 64, www.taxi-st-emilion.com, robert.faustin @wanadoo.fr).

Tourist Train: A *petit train* toots you from St. Emilion through vineyards and back in 30 minutes (€6, 2/hr, stop is behind TI by vineyards).

ACTIVITIES

Wine-Tasting—A fair starting point for oenophiles is the **Maison du Vin,** located next to the TI, where you can get a good introduction to wine, beginning with an hour-long video (played on the hour, English subtitles). In a small room, you'll read a description of the winemaking process and sniff cool glass cylinders that let you smell elements in the wines before you taste them (free, daily 9:30–12:30 & 14:00–18:30, tel. 05 57 55 50 55, www.vins-saint -emilion.com).

While the TI offers various €10 "tasting initiations," including a guided bus excursion to the vineyards (in English and French, includes a tasting, usually departs TI at 14:30 or 15:30 mid-May–Sept), the many **wine shops** offer the best and easiest

Dordogne

way to sample the array of local wines (see "French Wine-Tasting 101" on page 30). Small shops greet visitors with a central tasting table, maps of the vineyards, and several open bottles (most shops open daily 10:00–19:00, until 20:00 in summer). And while it's hard to distinguish these classy wine stores from each other, you'll be pleasantly surprised at the welcoming attitude that the passionate shopkeepers show for their wines. (Remember, everyone here speaks English.) Americans may represent only about 15 percent of the visitors, but we buy 40 percent of their wine. While the owners hope that you'll buy a bottle (particularly if you taste many wines) and shipping is easy (except to California and Texas), there's no pressure or fee for the tastings. Start at **Cercle des Oenophiles** and ask to visit the nearby cellars that have more than 400,000 stored bottles of wine (daily 10:00–19:00, at 12 rue Guadat, tel. 05 57 74 45 55).

Views over St. Emilion—You can climb the **bell tower** in front of the TI for a fine view (€1, give ID at TI in exchange for the key, daily 9:30–12:30 & 13:45–18:30, no midday closure in summer, closes at 18:00 Oct–March). But the view is best from the **Tour du Donjon** several blocks below (€1, daily 9:30–12:30 & 13:45–21:00, TI annex planned here for 2008).

Underground Tours of St. Emilion—The TI offers frequent and marginally interesting 45-minute tours with three stops: the catacombs (sorry, no bones); the underground monolithic church, which literally rocks; and Trinity Chapel. Learn who St. Emilion was, and be impressed that it took dedicated Benedictine monks 300 years to dig this monolithic church out of one big rock (9th–12th centuries). You'll also learn that there are about 125 miles of underground tunnels in the St. Emilion area originally dug as quarries. Today, they're ideal for wine storage. The tour is mandatory if you want to see these sights (€6, some tours are in English, though the English handout given on French tours is thorough). If time's limited and you can't get an English tour, I'd skip this sight.

SLEEPING

(€1 = about $1.30, country code: 33)
There are no cheap hotels in St. Emilion. (Those that exist are fine, but they're more costly than elsewhere in France.) Instead, consider staying at a *chambre d'hôte* (listed below). Hotel prices skyrocket during the VinExpo festival at the end of June, and during harvest time (the end of Sept).

Hotels
The first two places are a few doors apart, at the upper end of the city.

$$$ Au Logis des Remparts*** offers ample comfort, with mod rooms, a pool, and a relaxing garden with vineyards to touch (standard Db-€100, nicer Db with bathtubs and garden views-€125–150, most about €130, suites-€180, Wi-Fi, easy on-site parking, tel. 05 57 24 70 43, fax 05 57 74 47 44, www.logisdesremparts .com, contact@logisdesremparts.com).

$$ L'Auberge de la Commanderie** welcomes visitors with a neon entry and modern touches in its two buildings—a main hotel and an annex. Run by amiable owner Henri, the hotel's 16 rooms are well-maintained, with ceiling fans and contemporary decor. Rooms in the main building come with loud paintings, while annex rooms have more subtle stone walls and more space (small Db-€70, standard Db-€85, bigger Db-€100–115, Tb-€120, two-room apartment for up to four-€140, closed Jan–Feb, Internet access and Wi-Fi, free parking, tel. 05 57 24 70 19, fax 05 57 74 44 53, www.aubergedelacommanderie.com, contact @aubergedelacommanderie.com).

$$ Le Logis de la Tourelle rents five spacious rooms at the lower end of town for fair rates (Db-€65–75; check in at La Côte Braisée restaurant at 3 rue du Tertre de la Tente, and they'll escort you to rooms, which are several blocks away; tel. 05 57 24 79 65, fax 05 57 74 05 51, lacotebraisee@wanadoo.fr).

Chambres d'Hôte

The vineyards that surround St. Emilion hide many good-value *chambres d'hôte*. Places below the town are scattered among the villages and are hard to find—get good directions before you go. You can meander the villages just outside St. Emilion's upper entry point, and pick the place you prefer (the village of Montagne has many good *chambres d'hôte*). Or stop by the TI for a long list with small photos (no room booking fee).

$$ Moulin la Grangère, run by charming Marie-Annick and Alain Noel, has three rooms in a 19th-century mill. It's a few miles below St. Emilion, in Saint-Laurent-des-Combes on route de St. Christophe des Bardes (Db-€70, includes breakfast, cash only, tel. 05 57 24 72 51, www.moulin-la-grangere.com, alain-noel@moulin -la-grangere.com).

$ Château Meylet is where Madame Favard rents four traditional rooms in her workaday wine *domaine*. The château is within a quarter-mile of St. Emilion's doorstep (Db-€53–60, Tb-€72, includes breakfast, cash only, shared kitchen, washer/dryer and bikes available; from the top of St. Emilion, follow D-243 toward Libourne, at 1.5 kilometers turn left at signs to *Château Meylet;* tel. 05 57 24 68 85, http://chateau.meylet.free.fr, chateaumeylet @free.fr).

Dordogne

EATING

Skip the cafés lining the street by the TI and find the cafés on the melt-in-your-chair square, place du Marché.

Amelia-Canta is *the* happening spot on place du Marché for lunch or dinner on a warm evening. It has café fare, salads, and veggie options (€15–38 *menus,* open daily March–Nov, tel. 05 57 74 48 03).

L'Envers du Décor is the coolest place to dine inside (a few outdoor tables sit in a quiet garden). This wine bar–bistro is about fun, food, and wine. (If none of these matter to you, go elsewhere.) The restaurant's tabletops are wooden wine crates, and the floor is a cool blue-and-brown tile. The feel of this place is perfect for this wine-happy town (lunch *menus* from €15, dinner *menus* from €25, open daily, a few doors from the TI at 11 rue du Clocher, tel. 05 57 74 48 31).

Logis de la Cadène, sitting just above place du Marché, has romantic tables inside a manor home or outside on a lovely patio (*menus* from €28, closed Sun–Mon, reserve ahead, tel. 05 57 24 71 40).

Rocamadour

An hour east of Sarlat, this historic pilgrimage town with its dramatic rock-face setting is a ▲▲ sight after dark. While once one of Europe's top pilgrimage sites (see next sidebar), today it feels more tacky than spiritual. Still, if you can get into the medieval mindset, its peaceful and dramatic setting—combined with the memory of the countless thousands of faithful who trekked from all over Europe to worship here—overwhelms the kitschy tourism, and it becomes a fine (short) stop.

Those who arrive late and spend the night enjoy fewer crowds and a floodlit spectacle. Those who visit only during the day might wonder why they did, as there's little to do here except to climb the pilgrims' steps (with people who aren't pilgrims) to a few churches, and then stare at the view.

ORIENTATION

Rocamadour has three basic levels, connected by steps or elevators. The bottom level (Cité Medievale or Cité Pietonne) is a single pedestrian street lined with shops and restaurants (see "Sights— The Town," page 370). The sanctuary level (Cité Religieuse) is up 223 holy steps whose centerpiece is a church, with its seven chapels gathered around its small square. A switchback trail, the Way of the Cross (with 14 Stations of the Cross), leads to the top level and château (closed to the public) that crowns the cliff, and offers a fine view and free parking. For most, the goal is the sanctuary at midlevel.

Tourist Information

There are two TIs in Rocamadour: the glassy TI that drivers come to first, in the village of **l'Hospitalet** above Rocamadour (daily July–Aug 9:30–18:00, April–June and Sept–Oct 10:00–12:30 & 14:00–18:00, Nov–March until 17:00); and another on the level pedestrian street in **La Cité Medievale** (roughly same hours, tel. 05 65 33 22 00). Also on the pedestrian street in La Cité Medievale is an ATM, located next to the post office (PTT).

Arrival in Rocamadour

By Train: Five daily trains (transfer in Brive-la-Gaillarde) leave you 2.5 miles from the village at an unstaffed station. It's a €10 taxi ride to Rocamadour (see "Helpful Hints—Taxi," below). Start at the Cité Medievale (lower level), and visit from there.

By Car: Drivers have two options: You can park at the bottom of town (follow signs to *Cité Pietonne*), and walk to the end of the long pedestrian street (in Cité Medievale), then climb to the chapels. Or, for less walking, park above the town (from l'Hospitalet, follow *Château* signs) to a free lot and hike down.

By Elevator: With fewer pilgrims climbing steps on their knees, this very vertical town has added two handy yet pricey elevators. *Ascenseur Cité* (€2 one-way, €3 round-trip) connects the town with the church, but you skip the holy stairs. *Ascenseur Incliné* (€2.50 one-way, €4 round-trip) connects the church with the château and parking lot at the top, but you skip the zigzag Stations of the Cross. Each is run like any other elevator: on demand. Managed by two different companies, they're connected within 50 yards at the church level.

Helpful Hints

Views After Dark: If you're staying overnight, don't miss the views of a floodlit Rocamadour from the opposite side of the valley (doable by car, on foot, or by tourist train; see below). It's best as a half-hour (round-trip) stroll. From the town's southeast end, follow the quiet road down, cross the bridge, and head up the far side of the gorge opposite the town. Leave before it gets dark, as the floodlighting is best at twilight. Wear light-colored or reflective clothing, or take a flashlight—it's a dark road with no shoulder. Within the town, climb the steps to just below the sanctuary, and consider a drink with a view at the Hôtel Sainte Marie.

Rocamadour's Religious History

Rocamadour was once one of Europe's top pilgrimage sights. Today, tourists replace the pilgrims, enjoying a dramatically situated one-street town under a pretty forgettable church—all because of a crude little thousand-year-old black statue of the Virgin Mary.

Of France's roughly 200 "Black Virgins," this was perhaps the most venerated. Black Virgins began at the end of the pagan era—when Europe was being forcefully Christianized. In Europe's pagan religions, black typically symbolized fertility and motherhood. For newly converted (and still reluctant) pagans, it was easier to embrace the Virgin if she was black.

Y2K was just a high-tech rerun of Y1K. A thousand years ago, many Europeans also expected the world to end, and pilgrimages became immensely popular. About that time, the first pilgrims came here—to a little cave in a cliff over a gorge created by the Alzou River—to pray to a crude statue of a Black Virgin. Then, in 1166, a remarkably intact body was found beneath the threshold of the troglodyte chapel. People assumed this could only be a hermit (certainly a saintly hermit) who had lived in this cave. He was given the name Amadour (servant of Mary) and the place was named Rocamadour (the rock of the servant of Mary).

Suddenly, this humble site was on the map. The Benedictines moved in to develop the spot, building a church over the cave. Like Mont St. Michel, a single-street town sprouted at its base to

Tourist Train: You can take the cheesy but convenient *petit train* to enjoy the view, complete with 50 other travelers, a bad speaker blaring a worthless commentary in four languages, a flashing yellow light, and a rooftop crimping your view (€5, round-trip in 30 min, 2 trips/evening, departures starting at twilight—the first one is by far the best, check at the TI or call 05 65 33 67 84). You can walk its route in 30 minutes (see above), and take much better photos.

Grocery Store: It's on place de l'Europe, in the upper city (daily 8:00–20:00).

Taxi: Call 06 81 60 14 60 or 05 65 50 14 82.

SIGHTS

In Rocamadour

L'Hospitalet—Your first view of Rocamadour is the same one medieval pilgrims first saw—at the top of the gorge from the hamlet of l'Hospitalet, named for the hospitality it gave pilgrims. Stop here for the grand views (and its glassy TI). Imagine the impact

handle the needs of its growing pilgrim hordes. During Europe's great age of pilgrimages (12th and 13th centuries), the greatest of pilgrims (St. Louis, St. Dominique, Richard the Lionhearted, and so on) all trekked to this spot to pray. Rocamadour became a powerful symbol of faith and hope.

During the 14th-century Golden Age of Rocamadour, up to 8,000 people lived here, earning their living off of the pilgrims—who arrived in numbers of up to 20,000 a day. But with the 16th-century wars of religion and the Age of Enlightenment (in the 18th century), pilgrimages declined...and so did Rocamadour.

During the Romantic Age of the 19th century, pilgrimages were again in vogue, and Rocamadour rebounded. Local bishops rebuilt the château above the sanctuary, making it a pilgrims' reception center, and connecting it to the church with the Way of the Cross. (Most of the current buildings in the Sanctuary of Our Lady of Rocamadour date from the 19th century.) But there hasn't been a bona fide miracle here for eight centuries...and that hurts the pilgrimage business. Since the mid-20th-century, Rocamadour has become more of a tourist attraction, and today, Rocamadour's 650 inhabitants earn a living off its million visitors a year. The vast majority of those who climb the holy steps to the sanctuary are tourists—more interested in burning calories than incense.

of this sight in the 13th century, as awestruck pilgrims first gazed on the sanctuary cut out of the limestone cliffs. It was through l'Hospitalet's fortified gate that medieval pilgrims gained access to the "Holy Way," which led from l'Hospitalet to Rocamadour.

Château—Dating from the 14th century, the "château" fortified a bluff that was an easy base for bandits to attack the wealthy church below. Today's structure is a 19th-century private house that was transformed to be a reception spot for pilgrims. It's *privé* unless you are a pilgrim (in which case you can sleep here). For tourists, all it offers is a short rampart walk for a grand view (probably not worth the €2.50 fee).

The zigzag **Way of the Cross** (a path marked with Stations of the Cross, with a chapel for each station at each corner) gives religious purpose to the 15-minute hike between the sanctuary and the château.

▲▲**The Sanctuary of Our Lady of Rocamadour**—While it seems more like a tourist attraction, Rocamadour's church remains a sacred place of worship. At the entrance, a sign reads: "To admire, to contemplate, to pray. You're welcome to respectfully visit." (Free,

Dordogne

open daily about 8:00–19:00.)

Crammed onto a ledge on a cliff, this church couldn't follow the standard floor plan. So rather than surround the church, its seven chapels surround the square (called the *parvis*). There's also a small museum and a shop selling various pilgrimage mementos, including modern versions of the medallions that pilgrims prized centuries ago as proof of their visit.

While the buildings originated much earlier, most of what you see was redone in the 19th century. From the square, a flight of steps leads up to a landing immediately under the cliff, where (between the two most historic chapels) a tomb is cut into the rock. This is where the miraculously preserved body of St. Amadour was found in 1166.

Places of pilgrimage do better with multiple miracles. So, along with its Black Virgin and the miracle of St. Amadour's body (see sidebar), Rocamadour has the **sword of Roland.** The rusty sword of Charlemagne's nephew sticks in the cliffside, 10 yards above Amadour's tomb. According to medieval sources, when Roland was about to die in battle, the great warrior didn't want his sword to fall into enemy hands. He hurled it from the far south of France, and it landed here—stuck miraculously into the Rocamadour cliffs just above the Black Virgin. (The sword is clearly from the 18th century, but never mind.)

As you face the tomb, **St. Michael's Chapel** (open only to pilgrims, with little to see inside) is built around the original cave. To your right, the **Chapel of the Virgin** is the focal point of pilgrims. Step inside. High above the altar is the much-venerated Black Virgin, a 12th-century statue (covered with a thin plating of blackened silver) that depicts Mary presenting Jesus to the world. The oldest thing in the sanctuary—from the ninth century—is a simple rusted bell hanging from the ceiling.

The adjacent **St. Savior's Church** is the sanctuary's main place of worship. Next to the altar, a copy of the Black Virgin is displayed to give visitors a closer look. The double wooden balcony (newly rebuilt) was for the monks. Imagine attending a Mass here in centuries past, when the church was filled with pilgrims and the monks lined the balconies.

The Town—Rocamadour's town is basically one long street traversing the cliff below the sanctuary. For eight centuries, it has housed, fed, and sold souvenirs to the site's countless visitors. There's precious little here other than tacky trinket shops, but I enjoyed popping into the Galerie le Vieux Pressoir (named for its 13th-century walnut millstone). It fills a simple medieval vaulted room with the fine art of a talented couple: Richard Begyn and Veronique Guinard.

Seven of Rocamadour's 11 original gates survive. These were

designed to control the pilgrim crowds. In the 14th century, as many as 20,000 would converge on this spot from all over Europe on a single day. From the end of town, 223 steps lead to church. Traditionally, pilgrims kneel on each and pray an "Ave Maria" to Our Lady.

Grottes Préhistorique des Merveilles—This cave, located next to the upper TI, has the usual geological formations and a handful of small, blurred cave paintings. It's of no interest if you have seen or will see other prehistoric caves—its sole advantages are that it requires little effort to visit (with only about 10 steps down), and the guide can answer questions in English on the 40-minute tour (€6, daily July–Aug 9:30–19:00, April–June and Sept 10:00–12:00 & 14:00–18:00, Oct–March until 17:00, decent handout available, tel. 05 65 33 67 92, www.grotte-des-merveilles.com).

Near Rocamadour

▲**Gouffre de Padirac**—Twenty minutes from Rocamadour is the huge sinkhole of Padirac, with its underground river and miles of stalagmites and stalactites (but no cave art). While it's an impressive cave, if you've seen caves already, it's slow, with an insufficient payoff (lots of climbing and not a word of English). While there's no attempt to help English-speakers, the mechanics of the visit are easy, and there's not much to communicate anyway. Here's the drill: After paying, hike the stairs (with big views of the sinkhole—a round shaft about 100 yards wide and deep), or ride the elevator to the river level. Line up and wait for your boat. Pack into the boat with about a dozen others for the slow row past a fantasy world of hanging cave formations. Get out and hike a big circle with your group and guide, enjoying lots of caverns, underground lakes, and mighty stalagmites and stalactites. Get back on the boat and retrace your course. Two elevators zip you back to the sunlight. The visit takes 90 minutes (crowds make it take longer in summer, when I'd skip it). Dress warmly (€9, daily July–Aug 9:00–18:00, April–June and Sept 9:00–12:00 & 14:00–18:00, Oct–March 9:00–12:00 & 14:00–17:00, long lines at 14:00, tel. 05 65 33 64 56, www.gouffre -de-padirac.com). For knickknack Padirac, don't miss the shop.

SLEEPING

In Rocamadour

(€1= about $1.30, country code: 33)

Hotels are a deal here. You have two locations to choose from: the upper city, La Cité Religieuse (near l'Hospitalet), which has views down to Rocamadour; or below, within the medieval city, called La Cité Medievale. Parking is easier up top, but the spirit of St. Amadour is more present below. (I prefer the lower medieval city.)

Every hotel—including the ones I recommend—has a restaurant where they'd like you to dine.

In La Cité Medievale

$ Hôtel-Restaurant le Terminus des Pèlerins**, at the western end of the pedestrian street in La Cité Medievale, has immaculate, comfortable rooms with wood furnishings; the best have balconies and face the valley. Helpful owner Geneviève was born in this hotel (Db-€50, Db with view and balcony-€65, Tb-€72, tel. 05 65 33 62 14, fax 05 65 33 72 10, www.terminus-des-pelerins.com, hotelterm.pelerinsroc@wanadoo.fr).

In La Cité Religieuse

$ Hôtel Belvédère** has 18 well-maintained, modern, and appealing rooms, 12 of which have views over Rocamadour—some better than others (Db with no view-€52–55, Db with view-€65–72, tel. 05 65 33 63 25, fax 05 65 33 69 25, www.lebelvedere-rocamadour.com, lebelvere@wanadoo.fr).

Near Rocamadour

$$ Moulin de Fresquet is a dreamy *chambre d'hôte* five miles east of Rocamadour. Gracious Gérard and his wife Claude have lovingly restored an ancient mill in a lush, park-like setting. The four antique-furnished rooms come with wood beams and oodles of character. You're free to enjoy the outdoor terraces, chaise lounges, and duck pond—with ducks for pets, not for dinner. If you're really on vacation, stay here, and if Claude is cooking, eat here (dinner-€21, daily except Thu). Book as far ahead as possible, since this place is popular for a reason (Db-€57–89, Tb-€91, Qb-€97, includes breakfast, cash only, closed Nov–March, in Gramat, tel. 05 65 38 70 60, mobile 06 08 85 09 21, fax 05 65 33 60 13, www.moulindefresquet.com, info@moulindefresquet.com). Go to Gramat, then follow signs through town to *Figeac*; the *chambre d'hôte* is well-signed at the east end of Gramat.

EATING

In Rocamadour

Hôtel Belvédère, in the upper town, has the best interior view from its modern dining room. Book a window-side table ahead, ideally for a meal just before sunset (*menus* from €16, open daily, tel. 05 65 33 63 25; also listed under "Sleeping," above).

The **Bar l'Esplanade** hunkers cliffside below Hôtel Belvédère, and owns the best outside views from the tables in its garden café. They're open for lunch, dinner, drinks, and snacks (daily, tel. 05 65 33 18 45).

Dordogne

Near Rocamadour:
The Overlooked Eastern Dordogne

Many find this remote, less-visited section of the Dordogne (Quercy *département*) even more beautiful than the area around Sarlat, and all find it less visited. For a pleasant introduction to this area, follow this self-guided driving tour.

SELF-GUIDED DRIVING TOUR

Welcome to the Eastern Dordogne

Follow the Dordogne heading east, driving about an hour upriver from Souillac, to connect these worthwhile stops: Martel, Carennac, Château de Castelnau-Bretenoux, Loubressac, and Autoire. Rocamadour lies just beyond this area, as do the Tom Sawyer–like Gouffre de Padirac caves (both described above).

• *From Souillac, take D-803 east. In about 30 minutes, you'll land in...*

Martel: A well-preserved medieval town of 1,500 souls and seven towers, this peaceful place has a fine pedestrian area with many shops (good chance to stock up on picnic items). Neither on a river nor crowning a hilltop, it's largely overlooked by tourists. The town is named for Charles Martel (Charlemagne's grandfather and role model), who made his name by stopping the Moors as they marched into northern France in 732. A good walking tour of Martel starts at its fine main square (place des Consul, with a medieval covered market), and connects the seven towers.

• *From Martel, continue east on D-803 to Vayrac and Bétraille, then cross the Dordogne on D-20 to find...*

Carennac: This riverside town demands to be photographed. Park along the river, by the fortified Prieuré St-Pierre. Explore the evocative church and examine its exquisitely carved tympanum. It was built as an outpost of the Cluny Abbey in the 10th century, then fortified in the 1500s during the wars of religion. For a memorable meal inside or out, head to **Le Prieuré Crêperie,** with a cozy interior, fine salads, and beefy crêpes (closed Mon, lunch served all day, across from the church, tel. 05 65 39 76 75). Cross the small bridge behind the *crêperie* for a postcard-perfect scene.

• *From here, head east on D-30, tracking the Dordogne River. Turn left, following signs to...*

Château de Castelnau-Bretenoux: A splendidly situated and once-powerful military castle, this château has fine views in all directions and several well-furnished rooms. It's worth ▲. The reddish-golden stone and massive 12th-century walls make an

Near Rocamadour

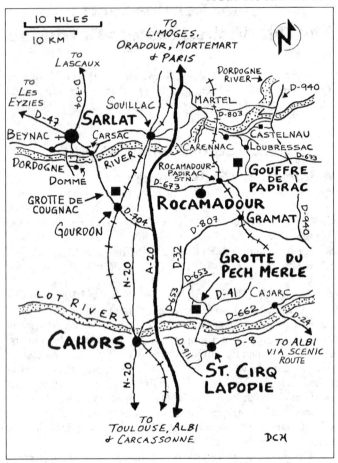

impression, as does its height—almost 800 feet. Cross the moat to the castle courtyard, and climb the round military tower for sensational views, then join a 30-minute, mercifully brief French-only tour (meager English handout) to view the seven furnished rooms (€6.50, €2 to park, or park for free at the restaurant/café lot if you plan to have a snack or lunch, daily July–Aug 9:30–19:00, Sept–June 9:30–12:00 & 14:00–18:00, last entry 1 hour before closing, tel. 05 65 10 98 00).

• *Return to D-30, cross it, and continue straight up D-14. You'll come to...*

Loubressac: Arguably the most beautiful village in France, Loubressac hangs atop a massive ridge, with outlandish views and a gaggle of adorable homes at its eastern end. You'll find an Old World café and modern hotel-restaurant, **$$$ Le Relais de Castelnau*****, with a view terrace and pool (Db €80–110, tel. 05 65 10 80 90, fax 05 65 38 22 02, www.relaisdecastelnau.com).

• *From here, it's a short hop on D–118 to lovely little…*

Autoire: Arguably the *other* most beautiful village in France, this one lies a few minutes beyond Loubressac. Visit and decide which village is fairest of them all.

Lot River Valley

Ninety minutes south of the Dordogne, the overlooked Lot River meanders under stubborn cliffs, past tempting villages, and through a strikingly beautiful valley. The fortified bridge at Cahors, the prehistoric cave paintings at Grotte du Pech Merle, and the breathtaking town of St. Cirq Lapopie are remarkable sights in this valley—each within a half-hour of the others. These sights can be combined to make a terrific day for travelers willing to invest the time (doable as a long day trip from the Sarlat area). They also work well as a day trip from Rocamadour, and are worthwhile for drivers connecting the Dordogne with Albi (see page 411) or Carcassonne (see page 424). (If you're going to or coming from the south, you can scenically connect this area with Albi via Villefranche-de-Rouergue and Cordes-sur-Ciel.) With extra time, spend a night in St. Cirq Lapopie, since it makes a good base for visiting the area.

St. Cirq Lapopie

This spectacularly situated village is a ▲▲ sight, clinging to a ledge sailing above the Lot River. It knows only two directions—straight up and way down. In St. Cirq Lapopie, there's little to do but wander the rambling footpaths, inspect the flowers and stones, and thrill over the vistas. You'll find picnic perches, a few galleries, a handful of restaurants, and views from the bottom and top of the village that justify the pain.

St. Cirq Lapopie is 30 minutes east of Cahors (well-signed), an hour south of Rocamadour, and just 20 minutes from the cave paintings of Grotte du Pech Merle (see page 377).

Dordogne

ORIENTATION

While you need to be careful of weekend and high-season (July–Aug) crowds, St. Cirq Lapopie has not been blemished by too many boutiques. It remains pin-drop peaceful after hours in any season. Arrive later in the day and spend the night to best appreciate where you are—your first views of St. Cirq Lapopie are eye-popping enough to convince you to stay.

Tourist Information

The TI is located across from the recommended Auberge du Sombral (May–Sept daily 10:00–13:00 & 14:00–18:00, Oct–April closes at 17:00 and on Sun, tel. 05 65 31 29 06). Pick up the visitor's guide in English, with brief descriptions of 22 historic buildings, and ask for information on hikes in the area. There's a beautiful riverside path (Chemin de Halage) that you can reach by walking way down from the village (remember: easier going down)—get details at the TI.

Arrival in St. Cirq Lapopie

By Car: Arriving by car from the west, you'll pass the town across the Lot River, then cross a narrow bridge and climb. You have three parking options: There's a small, free, dirt parking lot partway up, leaving you with a hefty uphill walk; a much closer pay lot at village level (€2, exact change required); and a third lot that lies at the top (€2, great views from here). Pull over for photo stops as you climb.

SLEEPING

(€1= about $1.30, country code: 33)

The village has all of 18 rooms, none of which is open off-season (mid-Nov–March).

$$ At Hôtel de la Pélissaria***, serene Marie-Françoise takes good care of her guests. Ten tastefully appointed rooms are built into the hillside, so they're a bit dark (but cool when it's hot). The terraced gardens are just so, the pool is just tiny, and the views to the main village are just incredible. The hotel is at the lower end of the village, so be ready to earn your dinner (standard Db-€78, bigger Db-€95, superior Db-€124, tel. 05 65 31 25 14, fax 05 65 30 25 52, http://perso.wanadoo.fr/hoteldelapelissaria, hoteldelapelissaria @wanadoo.fr).

$$ Auberge du Sombral**, run with panache by Madame Haldeveled, is in the town center. She'll welcome you with an oh-so-cozy lobby area and eight very comfortable rooms above in various sizes (Sb-€50, Db with shower-€70, Db with tub-€77, tel. 05 65 31 26 08, fax 05 65 30 26 37).

EATING

Dinner is tricky here; reliable help seems to be a problem, leaving restaurants understaffed at busy times. But this town was made for picnics; consider picking up dinner fixings in the hamlet of La Tour de Faure. (There's a small grocery store just west of the bridge to St. Cirq Lapopie, and a bakery a short way east of the bridge.)

As restaurants go, **Lou Boulat Brasserie** works for me. It serves low-risk lighter meals (salads, crêpes, and *plats*) in a low-stress setting, with good views from the side terrace (closed Wed, located at the upper end of town, off the main road by the post office/PTT, tel. 05 65 30 29 04).

L'Oustal has been the most reliable traditional restaurant in town (€16 and €32 *menus*, €15 *plats du jour*, closed Mon, below the towering church, tel. 05 65 31 20 17).

More Sights in the Lot River Valley

Cahors and the Pont Valentré—One of Europe's finest medieval monuments, this fortified bridge was built in 1308 to keep the English out of Cahors. It worked. Learn the story of the devil on the center tower. The steep trail on the non-city side leads to great views (views are actually better partway up, but be careful if the trail is wet) and was once part of the pilgrimage route to Santiago de Compostela in northwest Spain. Imagine that cars were allowed to cross this bridge until recently. Just past the city-side end of the bridge is **Le Cèdre,** a wine shop/café/souvenir stand with delightful owners; say *bonjour* to Marie-Danielle and Jean-Claude, and ask to sample Cahors' black wine and foie gras.

If you need an urban fix, stroll the pedestrian-friendly alleys between Cahors' cathedral and the river, a thriving place filled with good lunch options. To find this area by car, follow *Centre-Ville* and *St. Urcisse Eglise* signs, and park where you can.

▲▲Grotte du Pech Merle—This cave, about 30 minutes east of Cahors, has prehistoric paintings of mammoths, bison, and horses—rivaling the better-known cave art at Grotte de Font-de-Gaume. Grotte du Pech Merle is easier to view, as more people per day are allowed in (700), but that also makes the cave a bit less special. Still, it has brilliant cave art and interesting stalactite and stalagmite formations. I like the mud-preserved Cro-Magnon footprint. Call to reserve a time (English spoken) or book on their website at least one week ahead, and ask about rare English tours. Start at the museum with a 20-minute film subtitled in English, then descend to the caves. If you can't join an English tour, ask for the English-translation booklet. In summer, arrive by 9:30 or call

Dordogne

to reserve a spot four to five days in advance. It's best to call before you arrive in any season, as private groups can fill the cave's quota (€7.50, Easter–Oct daily 9:30–12:00 & 13:30–17:00, closes earlier off-season, tel. 05 65 31 27 05, fax 05 65 31 20 47, www.pechmerle .com). Before you visit, read "Cave Art 101" on page 349.

BASQUE COUNTRY

Le Pays Basque—Euskadi

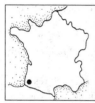

Two hours southwest of Bordeaux and far off most Americans' radar screens lies an ancient, free-spirited corner of Europe. In Basque country, bright white chalet-style homes with deep-red-and-green shutters scatter across lush rolling hills, the Pyrénées mountains soar high above the Atlantic, and surfers and sardines share the waves. Insulated from mainstream Europe for centuries, this plucky region has maintained its spirit while split between Spain and France. An easily crossed border separates the French Pays Basque from the Spanish País Vasco, thus allowing you to sample both sides from a single base. Central, cozy, and manageable St. Jean-de-Luz makes the ideal place for exploring the best of the French region, and fun-loving San Sebastián offers a great taste of the Spanish Basque lands.

The French and Spanish Basque regions share a common language (Euskara), flag (like a Union Jack, but white, red, and green), and cuisine. But they have taken different routes since the French Revolution. The Revolution "tamed" French Basque ideas of independence 130 years before Spain's Generalissimo Franco did the same to his separatist-minded Basques. As a result, while Euskara is still spoken and signs are printed in both languages, there is no doubt about what country you're in when you're on the French side.

Language is one important key to this unique culture; locals say that Euskara, which is unrelated to any other language, dates back to Neolithic times. Euskara, with its seemingly impossible-to-pronounce words filled with k's, tx's, and z's (rest rooms in Basque are *gizonak* for men and *emakumeak* for women), suddenly makes speaking French seem easy. Look for Euskara street signs, menus, and signs in shops. Proud of their language and culture, many locals can switch effortlessly from Euskara to Spanish or French.

Today, the Basque lands are undergoing a 21st-century renaissance, with striking revitalization occurring in long-ignored cities such as Bayonne, dazzling architecture replacing rusted industries in Bilbao, and enthusiastic visitors rejuvenating the resorts of San Sebastián and Biarritz.

The Basque terrorist organization, ETA (which stands for the Euskara phrase *Euskadi Ta Askatasuna*, or "Basque Country and Freedom"), is primarily active on the Spanish side of the border, and is supported by a tiny minority of the population. The ETA tends to focus their anger on political targets and goes largely unnoticed by tourists.

Planning Your Time

Allow two full days to sample French and Spanish Basque country (or spend three days for a leisurely pace). Most of your sightseeing will be cultural and scenic, as only two sights merit the entry fee (the Museum of Basque Culture in Bayonne and the Guggenheim modern art museum in Bilbao).

On the French side, plan time for the easygoing beach resort of St. Jean-de-Luz, the striking capital city of Bayonne, and the villages that curl up in the protective arms of the Pyrénées foothills, such as Aïnhoa, Sare, Espelette, and St. Jean-Pied-de-Port. If the weather is clear, consider the cogwheel train trip up to La Rhune, the region's highest peak, with sweeping views (mid-March–Oct only).

On the Spanish side, across the border, is the glittering resort of San Sebastián, and an hour beyond that, Bilbao.

Getting Around the Basque Country

Just 80 miles separates the two Basque capitals, Spanish Bilbao and French Bayonne. Freeways, trains, and buses provide convenient connections between Bayonne, St. Jean-de-Luz, San Sebastián, and, to a lesser extent, Bilbao.

By Bus and Train: Trains link St. Jean-de-Luz with Bayonne (hourly, 25 min), St. Jean-Pied-de-Port (7/day, 80 min, transfer in Bayonne), San Sebastián (2/hour, 60 min, transfer in Hendaye; faster but less frequent by bus: 2/day direct, 45 min). Excursion tours provide the easiest public-transport access to the Guggenheim modern art museum in Bilbao (see page 401).

By Car: From St. Jean-de-Luz, drivers can zoom on the autoroute to San Sebastián (45 min) and Bilbao (90 min). For a good sampling of traditional Basque villages, connect St. Jean-de-Luz to Sare, Aïnhoa, Espelette, and St. Jean-Pied-de-Port.

Basque Country

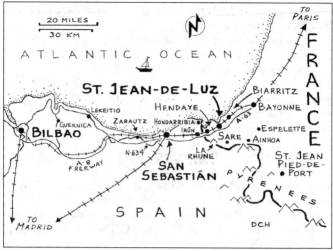

Cuisine Scene in Basque Country

Mixing influences from the mountains, sea, Spain, and France, Basque food is reason enough to visit the region. The local cuisine—dominated by seafood, tomatoes, and red peppers—offers some spicy dishes, unusual in France. The red peppers (called *piments*) hanging from homes in small villages end up in *piperade,* a dish that combines peppers, tomatoes, garlic, ham, and eggs. Don't leave without trying *ttoro* (tchoo-roh), a seafood stew that is Basque country's answer to bouillabaisse and cioppino. Look for anything *basquaise* (cooked with tomato, eggplant, red pepper, and garlic), such as *thon* (tuna) or *poulet* (chicken). *Marmitako* is a hearty tuna stew. Local cheeses come from Pyrenean sheep's milk *(pur brebis),* and the local ham *(jambon de Bayonne)* is famous throughout France. To satisfy your sweet tooth, look for *gâteau basque,* a local tart filled with cream or jams, or chocolates from Bayonne. Hard apple cider is the locally made beverage, but the region's wine, Irouleguy, isn't worth its price.

St. Jean-de-Luz

St. Jean-de-Luz (san zhahn-duh-looz; "Donibane Lohizune" in Euskara) sits happily off the beaten path, cradled between its small port and gentle bay. Pastry shops serve Basque specialties, and store windows proudly display berets. Ice-cream lickers meet traffic-free streets, while soft, sandy beaches tempt travelers to toss their itineraries into the bay. The knobby little mountain La

Rhune towers above the festive scene. Locals like to say that if it's clear enough to see La Rhune's peak, it's going to rain, but if you can't see it, it's raining already.

The town has precious little of sightseeing importance. But it's a fine base for exploring the Basque country, and a relaxing beach and port town that provides the most enjoyable dose of Basque culture in France. In July and August, the town fills with French tourists from the north—especially the first two weeks of August, when it's practically impossible to find a room without a reservation made long in advance.

ORIENTATION

St. Jean-de-Luz's old city lies between the train tracks, the Nivelle River, and the Atlantic. The main traffic-free street, rue Gambetta, channels walkers through the center, halfway between the train tracks and the ocean. The small town of Ciboure, across the river, holds nothing of interest to us.

The only sight worth entering in St. Jean-de-Luz is the church where Louis XIV and Marie-Thérèse tied the royal knot (Eglise St. Jean-Baptiste, described below). St. Jean-de-Luz is best appreciated along its pedestrian streets, lively squares, and golden, sandy beaches. The park at the far eastern end of the beachfront promenade at Pointe Ste. Barbe makes a good walking destination, with views and walking trails.

Tourist Information

The helpful TI is in a small, red-roofed building on place du Maréchal Foch, a block off the port and three blocks from the train station and bus stops (July–Aug Mon–Sat 9:00–19:30, Sun 10:00–13:00 & 15:00–19:00; Sept–June Mon–Sat 9:00–12:30 & 14:30–18:30, Sun 10:00–13:00—except Jan–March, when it's closed Sun; tel. 05 59 26 03 16, www.saint-jean-de-luz.com).

Arrival in St. Jean-de-Luz

By Train or Bus: From the station, take the pedestrian underpass, then walk left along the busy street. Stay straight around the traffic circle and carry on along avenue de Verdun to the TI, just across the second traffic circle.

By Car: Follow signs for *Centre-Ville*, then *Gare* and *Office de Tourisme*. Parking (except on some peak summer days) is relatively easy. Hotels or the TI can advise you.

By Plane: The nearest airport is in Biarritz, 10 miles to the northeast. The tiny airport is easy to navigate, with a useful TI desk (airport tel. 05 59 43 83 83, www.biarritz.aeroport.fr). The 20-minute taxi ride into St. Jean-de-Luz runs about €30. The bus costs only €3, but the bus stop is a 300-yard walk from the terminal (8/day, fewer on Sun, 30 min, tel. 05 59 26 06 99 for schedule).

Helpful Hints

Market Days: Tuesday and Friday mornings (and summer Saturdays), the farmers' stands spill through the streets from the Les Halles covered market, and seem to give everyone a whiff of "life is good" flavor.

Supermarkets: There's a **Petit Casino** grocery on rue Gambetta, just before boulevard Thiers (Tue–Sat 8:00–12:30 & 15:30–19:30, Sun 8:00–12:30 only, closed Mon, tel. 05 59 26 00 41). Or try the **Les Halles** market (above).

Internet Access: Run by friendly Irish ex-pats Margaret and Peter, **Internet World** is best (July–Aug Mon–Sat 9:00–24:00, Sun 10:00–18:00; Sept–June Mon–Sat 10:00–18:00, closed Sun; 7 rue Tourasse, tel. 05 59 26 86 92, www.friendsinfrance.com).

Laundry: Laverie du Port is across from the TI at 5 place du Maréchal Foch (daily 7:00–21:00, self-serve and full-service, €8 per full-service load).

Car Rental: Avis, at the train station, is handiest (Mon–Fri 8:00–12:00 & 14:00–18:00, Sat opens at 9:00, closed Sun, tel. 05 59 26 76 66, fax 05 55 26 19 42).

SELF-GUIDED WALK

Welcome to St. Jean-de-Luz

To get a feel for the town, take this self-guided, two-mile walk. You'll start at the port and make your way to the historic church. Allow about one hour.

Port: From the TI, inspect the little working port (pleasure craft are in the next port over). While fishing boats used to catch lots of whales, now they take in cod, sardines, tuna, and anchovies, and take out tourists (two boats advertise today's and tomorrow's mini-Atlantic cruises and fishing excursions, summer only). St. Jean-de-Luz feels cute and non-threatening now, but in the 17th century, it was home to the Basque Corsairs. With the French government's blessing, these pirates, who worked the sea—and enriched the town—moored here.

• *After walking the length of the port, to the left find...*

Place Louis XIV: The town's main square, named for the king who was married here, is a hub of action. During the summer, the bandstand features traditional Basque music at 21:00 (almost nightly July–Aug, otherwise Sun and Wed). Facing the square is the City Hall (Herriko Etxea) and the "House of Louis XIV" (in which he lived for 40 festive days in 1660). A visit to this house is worthwhile only if you like period furniture (€4.60, open

Basque Country

St. Jean-de-Luz

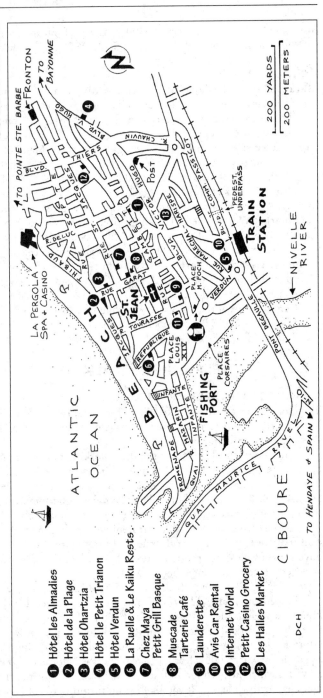

1. Hôtel les Almadies
2. Hôtel de la Plage
3. Hôtel Ohartzia
4. Hôtel le Petit Trianon
5. Hôtel Verdun
6. La Ruelle & Le Kaiku Rests.
7. Chez Maya
   Petit Grill Basque
8. Muscade
   Tarterie Café
9. Launderette
10. Avis Car Rental
11. Internet World
12. Petit Casino Grocery
13. Les Halles Market

DCH

June–Sept, mandatory guided tours at 11:00, 15:00, & 16:00, closed Oct–May—when the privately owned mansion is occupied by the same family who've had it for over three centuries, tel. 05 59 26 01 56). The king's visit is memorialized by a small black equestrian statue at the entrance of the City Hall (a miniature of the huge one that marks the center of the Versailles courtyard).

• *Opposite the port on the far side of the square is...*

Rue de la République: From place Louis XIV, this historic lane—lined with mostly edible temptations—leads to the beach. Facing the square, the shop Macarons Adam still bakes (according to the family recipe) the macaroons Louis XIV enjoyed during his visit. You can try one (€0.90), or sample a less historic but just as tasty *gâteau basque*, a baked tart with a cream or jam filling (€2). Farther down rue de la République, you'll find the Pierre Oteiza shop, stacked with rustic Basque cheeses and meats from mountain villages (with a few samples generally out for the tasting). You'll likely eat on this lane tonight. Kaiku, the town's top restaurant, fills the oldest building in St. Jean-de-Luz (with its characteristic stone lookout tower), dating from the 1500s.

• *Continue to the...*

Beach: A high embankment protects the town from storm waters, but generally the Grande Plage—which is lovingly groomed daily—is the peaceful haunt of sun-seekers and happy children. Walk the elevated promenade (to the right). Various tableaux tell history in French. Storms (including a particularly disastrous one in 1749) routinely knocked down buildings until Napoleon III built the three breakwaters in the 1800s.

• *Stroll past the late Art Deco–style La Pergola, which houses a casino and the Hélianthal spa center (entrance around back), and overlooks the beach. Anyone in a white robe strolling the beach is from the spa. Beyond La Pergola is the neo-Romantic Grand Hôtel (c. 1900), with an inviting terrace for a coffee break. From here, dive back into town until you reach the bustling...*

Rue Gambetta: Turn right and circle back to your starting point, following the town's lively pedestrian shopping street. You'll notice many stores selling the renowned *linge Basque*—cotton linens such as tablecloths, napkins, and dishcloths, in the characteristic Basque red, white, and green.

• *Just before place Louis XIV, you'll see the town's main church...*

Eglise St. Jean-Baptiste: The marriage of Louis XIV and Marie-Thérèse put St. Jean-de-Luz on the map, and this church is where it all took place. The ultimate in political marriages, the knot tied between Louis XIV and Marie-Thérèse in 1660 also cinched a reconciliation deal between Europe's two most powerful countries. The king of Spain, Philip IV—who lived in El Escorial Palace—gave his daughter in marriage to the king of France, who

Pelota

In the traditional Basque game of *pelota* or *cesta punta* (which Americans know as jai alai), players in white pants and red scarves or shirts use a long, hook-shaped racket (called a *txistera*) to whip a ball (smaller and far bouncier than a baseball) back and forth off walls at more than 150 miles per hour. This men's-only game can also be played bare-handed (ouch) or with a glove, and with a wall at one or both ends of the court. You'll also see outdoor *fronton* courts, which resemble handball courts, in every town, and indoor versions signed as *trinquet*. These players are not professional, but betting on them is common.

The TI in St. Jean-de-Luz sells tickets and has a schedule of matches throughout the area; you're more likely to find a match in summer (21:00, almost daily July–mid-Sept, afternoon matches sometimes on Sat–Sun). The professional *cesta punta* matches on Tuesdays and Fridays often come with Basque folkloric halftime shows.

lived in Versailles. This marriage united Europe's two largest palaces, which helped end a hundred years of hostility and forged an alliance that enabled both to focus attention on other matters (like England). Little St. Jean-de-Luz was selected for its 15 minutes of fame because it was roughly halfway between Madrid and Paris, and virtually on the France–Spain border. The wedding cleared out both Versailles and El Escorial palaces, as anyone who was anyone attended this glamorous event.

The church, centered on the pedestrian street rue Gambetta, seems modest enough from the exterior...but step inside (daily 8:00–12:00 & 14:00–18:00). The local expertise was in shipbuilding, so the ceiling resembles the hull of a ship turned upside down. The dark wood balconies running along the nave segregated the men from the women and children (men went upstairs until the 1960s), and were typical of Basque churches. The number of levels depended on the importance of the church, and this church, with three levels, is the largest Basque church in France. The three-foot-long paddle-wheel ship hanging in the center was a gift from Napoleon III's wife, Eugènie. It's a model of a ship she had been on that had almost sunk just offshore. The 1670 Baroque altar feels Franco-Spanish, and features 20 French saints. Locals call it the finest in Basque country. Drop €1 in the box to see it light up. The place has great acoustics, and the 17th-century organ is still used for concerts (€10, Thu at 21:00 in summer, buy tickets at TI). As you leave the church, turn left to find the bricked-up doorway—the church's original entrance. It was sealed after the royal marriage (shown on the wall to the right in a photo of a painting) to symbolize a permanent closing of the door on troubles between France and Spain.

SLEEPING

Hotels are a good value here. The higher prices are for peak season (generally June–Sept). In winter, some prices drop below those I've listed. Most hoteliers speak English. Breakfast costs extra, except for my first listing. Those wanting to eat and sleep for less will do better just over the border, in San Sebastián.

$$$ Hôtel de la Plage*** has the best location, right on the ocean. Its 22 rooms, 16 with ocean views, have a lively, yellow-and-blue, modern nautical decor (Db-€88–108, ocean view Db-€112–144, family rooms, includes breakfast, air-con, elevator, garage-€10, 33 rue Garat, tel. 05 59 51 03 44, fax 05 59 51 03 48, www.hoteldelaplage.com, reservation@hoteldelaplage.com, run by friendly Pierre and Yanik).

$$$ Hôtel les Almadies***, on the main pedestrian street, is a bright boutique hotel with seven flawless rooms, comfy public spaces with clever modern touches, a pleasant breakfast terrace, and an owner who cares (Sb-€75–105, Db with shower-€90–115, Db with tub-€115–125, child's bed-€20, buffet breakfast-€10, parking-€9, Wi-Fi, 58 rue Gambetta, tel. 05 59 85 34 48, fax 05 59 26 12 42, www.hotel-les-almadies.com, hotel.lesalmadies @wanadoo.fr, Monsieur and Madame Hargous will charm you with their Franglish).

$$ Hôtel Ohartzia**, one block off the beach, is comfortable, clean, peaceful, and characteristic, with the most charming facade I've seen. It comes with 17 simple but well-cared-for rooms,

---

Sleep Code

(€1 = about $1.30, country code: 33)
S = Single, **D** = Double/Twin, **T** = Triple, **Q** = Quad, **b** = bathroom,
s = shower only, ***** = French hotel rating system (0–4 stars).
Unless otherwise noted, credit cards are accepted and English is spoken.

To help you sort easily through these listings, I've divided the rooms into three categories based on the price for a standard double room with bath:

$$$ **Higher Priced**—Most rooms €90 or more.
  $$ **Moderately Priced**—Most rooms between €60–90.
    $ **Lower Priced**—Most rooms €60 or less.

and generous, homey public spaces. The highlight for me is the bird-chirping, flower-petaled garden in the back—try for one of the four rooms with views over this little Eden (July–Sept Sb/Db-€77–85, April–June Sb/Db-€68–72, Oct–March Sb/Db-€60–68, extra bed-€15, rooms with showers generally less than those with tubs, 28 rue Garat, tel. 05 59 26 00 06, fax 05 59 26 74 75, www.hotel-ohartzia.com, hotel.ohartzia@wanadoo.fr). Their desk is technically open only 8:00–20:00, but it's usually staffed longer in peak season; owners Madame and Monsieur Audibert live in the building.

$ Hôtel le Petit Trianon**, on a major street, is simple and traditional, with 25 worn but nicely appointed rooms and accommodating staff (Sb/Db-€49–72, air-con, Wi-Fi, garage-€10, 56 boulevard Victor Hugo, tel. 05 59 26 11 90, fax 05 59 26 14 10, www.hotel-lepetittrianon.com, lepetittrianon@wanadoo.fr). To get a room over the quieter courtyard, ask for *côté cours* (coat-ay coor).

$ Hôtel Verdun, a bleak little 11-room place above a dreary restaurant, faces the train station and offers the cheapest beds in town (D-€28–40, Ds-€33–45, Db/Tb-€35–60, €5 breakfast at downstairs café, 13 avenue de Verdun, tel. 05 59 26 02 55, Henri). It's often full off-season, when it houses seasonal laborers.

EATING

St. Jean-de-Luz restaurants are known for offering good-value, high-quality cuisine. You can find a wide variety of eateries in the old center. For forgettable food with unforgettable views, choose from several places overlooking the beach. Most places serve from 12:15 to 14:00, and from 19:15 on.

The traffic-free rue de la République, which runs from place Louis XIV to the ocean promenade, is lined with hardworking restaurants (two of which are recommended below). Places are empty at 19:30, but packed at 20:30. Making a reservation, especially on weekends or in summer, is wise. Consider a fun night of bar-hopping for dinner in San Sebastián instead (an hour away in Spain, described later in this chapter).

La Ruelle serves good, traditionally Basque cuisine—mostly seafood—in two tight little rooms jam-packed with tables, happy eaters, and kitschy Basque decor. André and his playful staff obviously enjoy their work, which gives this popular spot a relaxed and fun ambience. Portions are huge; their €17 *ttoro* (seafood stew) easily feeds two (*menus* from €18, closed Tue–Wed Oct–May, 19 rue de la République, tel. 05 59 26 37 80).

Le Kaiku is *the* gastronomic experience in town, with a chef who studied with Alain Ducasse (famous for his restaurants in

Paris and Monaco). They serve modern cuisine, specializing in "wild" (rather than farmed) seafood. The place is dressy, but offers a good time (*menus* from €30, closed Tue–Wed, 17 rue de la République, tel. 05 59 26 13 20).

Chez Maya Petit Grill Basque serves good traditional Basque cuisine. Their *ttoro* was a highlight of my day. They have €19 and €27 *menus*, but à la carte is more interesting (closed Wed, 2 rue St. Jacques, tel. 05 59 26 80 76).

Fast and Cheap: Try the take-away crêpe stands on rue Gambetta. For a sit-down salad or a tart—either sweet or savory—consider **Muscade Tarterie** (€5–10 per slice, daily July–Aug, closed Mon Sept–June, 20 rue Garat, tel. 05 59 26 96 73).

TRANSPORTATION CONNECTIONS

The train station in St. Jean-de-Luz is called St. Jean-de-Luz-Ciboure. Its clever departure board displays lights next to any trains leaving that day. Buses leave from the green building across the street. There is reduced bus and rail service on Sundays and off-season.

From St. Jean-de-Luz by Train to: Bayonne (hourly, 25 min), **St. Jean-Pied-de-Port** (7/day, 80 min, transfer in Bayonne), **Paris** (4 direct/day, 5.5 hrs), **Bordeaux** (11/day, 2 hrs), **Sarlat** (4/day, 4 hrs, transfer in Bordeaux), **Carcassonne** (5/day, 6 hrs, transfers likely in Bayonne and Toulouse).

By Train to San Sebastián: First, take the 10-minute train to the French border town of Hendaye (Gare SNCF stop; about 10/day, €4.60). Or get to Hendaye by bus (3/day, 35 min); check the schedule to see which leaves first.

Leave the Hendaye station to the right, and look for the light-blue EuskoTren building, where you'll catch the commuter train into San Sebastián (2/hour, generally at :03 and :33 after the hour 7:00–22:00, 60-min trip—faster by bus, €1.40). This milk-run train is known as the Topo train, since it goes underground part of the time (*topo* means mole).

By Bus to: San Sebastián (2/day direct, 45 min, info in Spain tel. 902-101-210).

By Taxi to: San Sebastián will cost you about €70 for up to four people, but it's convenient (tel. 05 59 26 10 11).

By Excursion Bus: The TI has information and sells tickets for popular day-trip excursions, including **Guggenheim Bilbao** (€30 round-trip, includes €10 museum admission, Wed only, departs 11:00 from bus terminal next to train station, returns 19:30). Other day trips are available (Aïnhoa, Lourdes, and St. Jean-Pied-de-Port) on different days of the week.

Villages in the French Basque Country

Traditional villages among the green hills, with buildings colored like the Basque flag, offer the best glimpse at Basque culture. Cheese, hard cider, and *pelota* players are the primary products of these villages, which attract few foreigners but many French summer visitors. Most of these villages have welcomed pilgrims bound for Santiago de Compostela since the Middle Ages. Today's hikers lace together local villages or head into the Pyrénées. The most appealing villages lie in the foothills of the Pyrénées, spared from beach-scene development.

SIGHTS

Use St. Jean-de-Luz as your base to visit the Basque sights described below.

Sare, which sits at the base of the towering mountain La Rhune, is among the most picturesque villages—and the most touristed. It's easily reached from St. Jean-de-Luz by bus or car. The small TI is on the main square (Mon–Fri 9:30–12:30 & 14:00–18:00, Sat 9:30–12:30, closed Sun, tel. 05 59 54 20 14). Don't miss the interior of the church.

Between the villages of Sare and Ascain, near the border with Spain, a small cogwheel train takes tourists to the top of **La Rhune,** the region's highest peak (2,969 feet). You'll putt-putt up the hillside for 30 minutes in an open-air train car to reach panoramic views of land and sea (runs mid-March–Oct, departures weather-dependent—so the trip is worthless if it's not clear, departures every 35 min when busiest in July–Aug, tel. 05 59 54 20 26, www.rhune.com).

Aïnhoa, farther up, is a one-street town that sees fewer tourists. Its chunks of fortified walls and gates mingle with red-and-white half-timbered buildings. The 14th-century church, with a beautiful golden retable (shelf) behind the altar, and the *fronton* court share center stage. For a great village view, drive five minutes (or walk 90 sweaty minutes) up the steep, dirt road to the Chapelle de Notre-Dame d'Aranazau ("d'Aubepine" in French). Go downhill to the parking lot directly across the main street from the church, then head straight uphill from there. Follow signs for *oratoire*, then count the giant white crosses to the top.

Espelette won't let you forget that it's the capital of the region's AOC red peppers *(piments d'Espelette)*, with strands of them dangling like good-luck charms from many houses and storefronts. After strolling the charming, cobbled center, wander downhill to find the town church and the well-restored château and medieval tower, which now houses the town hall (TI tel. 05 59 93 95 02). For a good regional meal, consider the **$ Hôtel Euzkadi** restaurant (*menus* from €25, daily 12:30–14:00 & 19:30–21:00, closed Mon–Sun off-season, 285 Karrika Nagusia, tel. 05 59 93 91 88). The hotel has 32 rooms and a swimming pool (Db-€52-60, www .hotel-restaurant-euzkadi.com).

St. Jean-Pied-de-Port is the most popular village of all, but the farthest inland (60 min from Bayonne by scenic train, 70 min by car from St. Jean-de-Luz, and just 10 min to Spain; TI tel. 05 59 37 03 57). This walled town is famous as the final stopover in France for Santiago-bound pilgrims, who gathered here to cross the Pyrénées together and continue their march through Spain. Scallop shells—the symbol of St. Jacques (French for "James")—are etched on walls throughout the town. This place is packed in the summer (so come early or late). Find the main drag, rue de la Citadelle, with its pastel-pink buildings, and stroll it as pilgrims have for more than 1,000 years. Climb to la Citadelle for views, but skip the €3 Bishop's Prison (Prison des Evêques).

Bayonne (Baiona)

To feel the urban pulse of French Basque country, visit Bayonne. This workaday capital of the French Basque lands has been modestly but honestly nicknamed "your anchor in the Basque Country" by its tourist board. With frequent, fast train connections with St. Jean-de-Luz (hourly, 25 min), Bayonne makes an easy, half-day side-trip.

Come here to browse through Bayonne's atmospheric and well-worn yet lively Old Town, and to admire its impressive Museum of Basque Culture. Known for establishing Europe's first whaling industry and for inventing the bayonet, Bayonne is more famous today for its ham *(jambon de Bayonne)* and chocolate.

Bayonne's two rivers, Adour and Nive, divide the city into three parts: St. Esprit, with the train station; and the more interesting Grand Bayonne and Petit Bayonne, which together make up the Old Town.

In pretty Grand Bayonne, tall, slender buildings climb above cobbled streets, decorated in Basque fashion with green-and-red shutters. Make sure to stroll the streets around the cathedral and along the banks of the smaller Nive River, where you'll find the market (Les Halles).

ORIENTATION

Tourist Information

The TI is in a modern parking lot a block off the mighty Adour River, on the northeastern edge of Grand Bayonne (Mon–Fri 9:00–18:30, Sat 10:00–18:00, closed Sun except 10:00–13:00 in July–Aug, place des Basques, tel. 05 59 46 01 46). They have very little in English other than a map.

Arrival in Bayonne

By Train: The TI and Grand Bayonne are a 10-minute walk from the train station: Walk straight out of the station, cross the traffic circle, and then cross the imposing bridge (pont St. Esprit). Once past the big Adour River, continue across a smaller bridge (pont Mayou), which spans the smaller Nive River. Stop on pont Mayou to orient yourself: You just left Petit Bayonne (left side of Nive River). Ahead of you is Grand Bayonne (spires of cathedral straight ahead, TI a few blocks to the right). The Museum of Basque Culture is in Petit Bayonne, facing the next bridge up the Nive River.

By Car: Drivers follow signs for the Office de Tourisme and park there. In high season, use one of the lots just outside the center (follow signs to Glain or Porte d'Espagne as you arrive in town), then catch the little orange *navette* (shuttle bus) to get into the center (free, find route maps posted at stops in town, Mon–Sat 7:30–19:30, closed Sun).

SIGHTS

Museum of Basque Culture (Musée Basque)—This superb museum (in Petit Bayonne, facing the Nive River at pont Marengo) explains French Basque culture from cradle to grave—in French, Euskara, and Spanish. The only English you'll read is "do not touch" (unless you buy their English booklet for €5). Videos take you into traditional Basque villages and sit you in the front row of time-honored festivals (€5.50, May–Oct Tue–Sun 10:00–18:30, closed Mon except July–Aug, July–Aug also open and free Wed 18:30–21:30; Nov–April Tue–Sun 10:00–12:30 & 14:00–18:00, closed Mon; last entry 1 hour before closing, 37 quai des Corsaires, tel. 05 59 46 61 90, www.musee-basque.com).

Cathédrale Ste. Marie—Bankrolled by the whaling community, this cathedral sits dead-center in Grand Bayonne and is worth a peek (Mon–Sat 10:00–11:45 & 15:00–17:45, Sun 15:30–17:45). Find the unique keystones on the ceiling along the nave, then circle the church to find the peaceful 13th-century cloisters (free, daily 9:00–12:30 & 14:00–17:00).

Ventas Shops

Dancing between France and Spain and along the foothills of the Pyrénées, you'll see many signs for *ventas* (from the Spanish *vender*, "to sell"). Follow one of these signs to a cultural detour. Originally used as contraband outposts, *ventas* shops operate as a café, bar, restaurant, grocery store, gas station, cheap boutique, and more. Most are lost in the hills and hard to find, and many still don't have signs—locals just know where they are. Today, they are legal in a borderless Europe, and still offer inexpensive products—customers are mostly the French Basque, who cause traffic jams on weekends driving to the border to do cheap shopping or fill the gas tank. In most *ventas*, gas is cheaper by 25 percent, cigarettes and alcohol leave by the case, and the Spanish, French, and Euskara languages mingle as locals enjoy a coffee or beer among hanging garlands of cheap hams.

Sweets Shops—With no more whales to catch, Bayonne turned to producing mouthwatering chocolates and marzipan; look for shops on the arcaded **rue du port Neuf** (running between the cathedral and the Adour River).

Ramparts—While open for walking, and great for picnicking, the ramparts do not allow access to either of Bayonne's castles—both are closed to the public.

EATING

Le Bayonnais serves traditional Basque specialties à la carte (also €15 *menu* on weekdays, closed Sun–Mon, a block from the Museum of Basque Culture at quai des Corsaires 38, tel. 05 59 25 61 19). On the other side of the river and to the left, **La Cidrerie Txotx** (pronounced "choch") has a Spanish ambience (€7–10 Basque tapas or €12–16 *plats,* daily, tel. 05 59 59 16 80). Both restaurants have outdoor seating on the river. If the weather is good, consider gathering a **picnic** from the pedestrian streets and head for the park around the ramparts below the *Jardin Botanique* (benches galore).

Day Trip to Spanish Basque Country (País Vasco)

A short dash into Spain is now a breeze, thanks to the euro currency and lack of border checks.

    Phones: Spain's telephone country code is 34. Remember that

Basque Country

French phone cards and stamps will not work in Spain.

Hours: Most Spanish sights and stores close from about 13:00 to 16:00, and dinner doesn't begin until 21:00 (though tapas appetizers are always available).

San Sebastián

Shimmering above the breathtaking bay of La Concha, elegant and prosperous San Sebastián ("Donostia" in Euskara) has a favored location with golden beaches, capped by twin peaks at either end, with a cute little island in the center. A delightful beachfront promenade runs the length of the bay, with an intriguing Old Town at one end and a smart shopping district in the center. It has 180,000 residents and almost that many tourists in high season (July–Sept). With a romantic setting, a soaring statue of Christ gazing over the city, and a late-night lively Old Town, San Sebastián has a Rio de Janeiro aura. While there's no compelling museum to visit, the scenic city provides a pleasant introduction to Spain's Basque country.

In 1845, Queen Isabel II's doctor recommended she treat her skin problems by bathing here in the sea. Her visit mobilized Spain's aristocracy, and soon the city was on the map as a seaside resort. By the turn of the 20th century, Donostia was the toast of the belle époque, and a leading resort for Europe's beautiful people. Before World War I, Queen María Cristina summered here and held court in her Miramar Palace overlooking the crescent beach. Hotels, casinos, and theaters flourished. Even Franco enjoyed 35 summers in a place that he was sure to call San Sebastián, not Donostia.

Planning Your Time

San Sebastián is worth a day. Stroll the two-mile-long promenade and scout the place you'll grab to work on a tan. The promenade leads to a funicular that lifts you up to the Monte Igueldo viewpoint (described below). After exploring the Old Town and port, walk up to the hill of Monte Urgull. A big part of any visit to San Sebastián is enjoying tapas in the Old Town bars.

Key Spanish Phrases

English	Spanish	Pronounced
Good day.	*Buenos días.*	**bway**-nohs **dee**-ahs
Mr./Mrs.	*Señor/Señora*	sayn-**yor**/ sayn-**yor**-ah
Please.	*Por favor.*	por fah-**bor**
Thank you.	*Muchas gracias.*	**moo**-chahs **grah**-thee-ahs
coffee with milk	*café con leche*	kah-**feh** kohn **lay**-chay
sandwich	*bocadillo*	boh-kah-**dee**-yoh
Where is...?	*¿Donde está...?*	**dohn**-day ay-**stah**
tourist office	*turismo*	too-**rees**-moh
city center	*centro ciudad*	**thehn**-troh thee-oo-**dahd**
Do you speak English?	*¿Habla usted inglés?*	**ah**-blah oo-**stehd** een-**glays**

ORIENTATION

The San Sebastián we're interested in surrounds Concha Bay (Bahía de la Concha), and can be divided into three areas: Playa de la Concha (best beaches), the shopping district (called Centro Romántico), and the skinny streets of the grid-planned Old Town (called Parte Vieja, to the north of the shopping district). The Centro Romántico, just east of Playa de la Concha, has beautiful turn-of-the-20th-century architecture, but no real sights.

It's all bookended by mini-mountains: Monte Urgull to the north and east, Monte Igueldo to the south and west. The river (Río Urumea) divides central San Sebastián from the district called Gros (which has a lively night scene and surfing beach).

Tourist Information

San Sebastián's TI, a block from the river on the boulevard that separates the Centro Romántico from the Old Town, has information on city and regional sights, as well as bus and train schedules. Pick up the excellent town booklet, which has English descriptions of the three walking tours—the Old Quarter/Monte Urgull walk is best (TI open July–Sept Mon–Sat 9:00–20:00, Sun 10:00–14:00 & 15:30–19:00; Oct–June Mon–Sat 9:00–13:30 & 15:30–19:00, Sun 10:00–14:00; just off Zurriola bridge at Calle Reina Regente 3, tel. 943-481-166, www.sansebastianturismo.com). Skip the **San**

San Sebastián

GROS

KURSAAL CONFERENCE CENTER

BOULEVARD

R. PLAYA ZURRIOLA

SURF

RENFE TRAIN STATION (NAT'L + INT'L TRAINS)

URUMEA RIVER

To PLAZA PÍO XII + AMARA BUS STN.

PLAZA DE GIPUZKOA

LEGAZPI

DEL

CENTRO ROMÁNTICO

SAN MARTÍN

SAN CALLE

R. LOYOLA

R. URBIETA

WC. CONCHA

PLAZA EASO

EASO

EUSKOTREN STATION (TOPO TRAINS TO HENDAYE)

(TOPO TRAINS TO HENDAYE)

MUSEUM OF SAN TELMO

OLD TOWN

ALAMEDA

CITY HALL

MONTE URGULL

CASTILLO DE LA MOTA

TICKETS FOR ISLAND BOATS

NAVAL MUSEUM

AQUARIUM

CONCHA BAY

LA CONCHA

PLAYA DE

BEACHES

SWIM

PASEO DE LA CONCHA

SANTA CLARA ISLAND

R. PLAYA DE ONDARRETA

AV. SATRUSTEGUI

DCH

MONTE IGUELDO

FUNICULAR

P

300 YARDS

300 METERS

N

P PARKING

VIEW

1 Hotel Niza
2 La Perla Spa
3 Miramar Palace
4 Launderette

Sebastián Card unless you plan to use the bus a lot (€10 for 3 days of free bus transport plus minor sightseeing discounts).

English-language **walking tours** of the Parte Vieja, Old Quarter/Monte Urgull, and the Centro Romántico cost €5 (most routes July–Aug only, time and meeting places vary—confirm with TI). The TI also rents **audioguides** (€10/2 hrs).

Arrival in San Sebastián

By Train: If you're coming on a regional Topo train from Hendaye ("Hendaia" in Euskara) on the French border, get off at the EuskoTren station (end of the line, called Amara). Nearby Continental Auto provides luggage storage (€2/day, Mon–Sat 7:00–13:00 & 15:00–20:30, Sun 7:00–12:00 & 15:00–20:30, tel. 943-469-074). It's a level 15-minute walk to the center; exit the station and walk across the long plaza, then walk eight blocks down Calle Easo to the beach. The Old Town will be ahead on your right, with Playa de la Concha to your left. To speed things up, catch bus #26 or #28 along Calle Easo and take it to the Boulevard stop, near the TI at the bottom of the Old Town.

If you're arriving by train from elsewhere in Spain (or from France with a transfer in Irún), you'll get off at the main RENFE station (luggage lockers available, €3/day, daily 7:00–22:00). It's just across the bridge (Puente María Cristina) from the Centro Romántico shopping district. To reach the Old Town and most recommended hotels, cross the fancy, dragon-decorated María Cristina bridge (across and left when exiting station), turn left on Paseo de los Fueros and follow the Urumea River until the last bridge.

By Bus: If you're arriving by bus from Hondarribia, hop off at pretty Plaza de Gipuzkoa (first stop after crossing the river, in shopping area, near TI). To reach the TI, walk down Legazpi, cross Alameda del Boulevard, and turn right.

By Car: Take the Amara freeway exit, follow *Centro Ciudad* signs into the city center, and park in a pay lot (many are well-signed). If you're picking up or returning a rental car, "The Big Autorental"—which includes Hertz (Zubieta 5, tel. 943-461-084) and Avis (Triunfo 2, tel. 943-461-527)—is near Hotel Niza, and Europcar is at the RENFE train station (tel. 943-322-304).

Helpful Hints

Useful Telephone Numbers: For the police, dial 943-538-920. For flight information, call San Sebastián's airport (in Hondarribia, 12 miles away) at tel. 943-668-500.

Internet Access: There are many places in the Old Town; the handiest is **Donosti-NET** (daily 9:00–23:00, Calle Narrika 3 Bajo, tel. 943-429-497). They also sell cheap phone cards for calling home, offer expensive luggage storage, and can arrange car rentals with Avis or National. Also try **Navi.net,** located on the main tapas drag in the Old Town (Mon–Fri 10:00–24:00, Sat–Sun 11:00–24:00, Calle Fermín Calbetón 15).

Bookstore: Bilintx, near several recommended restaurants in the Old Town, has a wide selection, including some guidebooks in English (daily, closed 14:00–16:00, Calle Fermín Calbetón 21, tel. 943-420-080).

Laundry: Wash & Dry is in the Gros neighborhood, across the river behind the train station (self-service daily 8:00–20:00, drop-off service Mon–Fri 9:30–13:00 & 16:00–20:00, Iparragirre 6, tel. 943-293-150). Unfortunately, there are no launderettes in the Old Town.

Bike and Scooter Rental: Try **Bicicletas Alai,** behind the Amara bus station (Avenida de Madrid 24, tel. 943-470-001), or **Bici Rent Donosti** (Avenida de Zurriola 22, 3 blocks across the river from the TI, tel. 943-290-854).

Local Guides and Activities: The **Just Follow Me** company offers guide services and excursions in the Basque region by foot, bike, or minivan (tel. 685-757-601, www.justfollowme.com). **Enjoy SS** offers activities ranging from tapas tours to hikes, surfing lessons, and boat parties (€20 and up, tel. 943-005-060, www.enjoyss.com).

Getting Around San Sebastián

By Bus: At Alameda del Boulevard, along the bottom edge of the Old Town, you'll find a line of public buses ready to take you anywhere in town; give any driver your destination and he'll tell you the number of the bus to catch (€1.10, pay driver).

Some handy bus routes: #26 and #28 connect the bus and EuskoTren stations to the TI (get off at the "Boulevard" stop); #16 begins at the Boulevard/TI stop, goes along Playa de la Concha and through residential areas, and eventually arrives at the base of the Monte Igueldo funicular. The TI has an excellent bus-route map, if you want to see exactly where you're going (www.ctss.es).

By Taxi: Taxis start at €3, then charge €0.50 per kilometer. You'll do better calling one or finding a taxi stand (such as along Alameda del Boulevard, described above) rather than trying to hail one (tel. 943-464-646 or 943-404-040).

By Tourist Train or Bus: Two options are available, but they're not necessary in this walkable city: the **"txu-txu"** tourist train (€4.40, daily July–Aug 11:00–19:00, Sept–June 11:00–13:00 & 16:00–19:00, 40-min round-trip, tel. 943-422-973) and the **Donosti** hop-on, hop-off bus tour (€10, 60 min, ticket good for 24 hours, leaves from theater across from TI, tel. 696-429-847). Both do similar routes with minimal commentary along the Playa de La Concha, toward Monte Igueldo, and back through Centro

Romántico—but only the bus tour goes up Monte Igueldo and also crosses the river into the Gros neighborhood (neither tour goes into the mainly pedestrian Old Town).

SIGHTS AND ACTIVITIES

The Beach

▲▲**La Concha Beach and Promenade**—The shell-shaped Playa de La Concha, the pride of San Sebastián, has one of Europe's

loveliest stretches of sand. Lined with a two-mile-long promenade, it allows even backpackers to feel aristocratic. While pretty empty off-season, in summer, sunbathers pack its shores. But year-round, it's surprisingly devoid of eateries and money-grubbing businesses. There are free showers, and *cabinas* provide lockers, showers, and shade for a fee. The Miramar palace and park, which divides the crescent in the middle, was where Queen María Cristina held court when she summered here. Her royal changing rooms are used today as inviting cafés, restaurants, and a fancy spa (La Perla, described below). For a century, the lovingly painted wrought-iron balustrade that stretches the length of the promenade has been a symbol of the city; it shows up on everything from jewelry to headboards.

La Perla Spa—The spa attracts a less royal crowd today and appeals mostly to visitors interested in sampling "the curative properties of the sea." You can enjoy its Talaso Fitness Circuit, featuring a hydrotherapy pool, relaxation pool, panoramic Jacuzzi, cold-water pools, seawater steam sauna, dry sauna, and a relaxation area. For those seriously into spas, they offer additional services, from Dead Sea mud wraps to massages to daylong "personalized programs" (€19 for 2.5-hr fitness circuit, €24.50 for 3-hr circuit, daily 8:00–22:00, caps sold and towels rented, bring or buy a swimsuit, on the beach at the center of the crescent, Paseo de La Concha, tel. 943-458-856, www.la-perla.net).

▲▲Old Town (Parte Vieja)

Huddled in the shadow of its once-protective Monte Urgull, the Old Town is where San Sebastián was born about 1,000 years ago. The grid plan of streets hides heavy Baroque and Gothic churches, surprise plazas, and fun little shops, including venerable pastry stores, rugged produce markets, Basque-independence souvenir shops, and seafood-to-go delis. "THC shops" offer the latest from the decriminalized marijuana scene in Spain—adults are allowed to grow two plants. Be sure to wander out to the port to see the fishing industry in action. The Old Town's main square, Plaza de la Constitución (where bullfights used to be held—notice the seat numbering on the balconies) features inviting café tables spilling from all corners. The highlight of the Old Town is its incredibly lively tapas bars—though here, these snacks are called *pintxos* (PEEN-chohs; see "Eating," page 405).

Museum of San Telmo—This humble museum displays exhibits and paintings in rooms arranged around the peaceful cloister of a former Dominican monastery. There are a few exhibits on Basque folk life, and a small collection of 19th- and 20th-century paintings by Basque artists that offer an interesting peek into the spirit, faces, and natural beauty of this fiercely independent region (free, other featured artists include El Greco and Peter Paul Rubens, minimal English information, Tue–Sat 10:30–13:30 & 16:00–19:30, Sun 10:30–14:00, closed Mon, Plaza Zuloaga 1, tel. 943-481-580).

The Port

At the west end of the Old Town, protected by Monte Urgull, is the port. To reach the first three sights, take the passage through the wall at the appropriately named Calle Puerto, and jog right along the level, portside Paseo del Muelle. You'll pass fishing boats unloading the catch of the day (while hungry locals look on), salty sailors' pubs, and fisherfolk mending nets. The trails to Monte Urgull are just above this scene, near Santa María Church (or climb up the stairs next to the aquarium).

Cruise—Small boats cruise from the Old Town's port to the island in the bay (Isla Santa Clara), where you can hike the trails and have lunch at the lone café, or pack a picnic before setting sail (€7.50 round-trip; departures hourly on the hour from 12:00–13:00 & 16:00–20:00, no boats Oct–May).

▲Aquarium—San Sebastián's impressive aquarium exhibits include a history of the sea, fascinating models showing various drift-netting techniques, a petting tank filled with nervous fish, a huge whale skeleton, and a 45-foot-long tunnel that allows you to look up at floppy rays and menacing sharks (€10, €6 for kids under 13, May–Sept 8:00–21:00, Oct–April 8:00–19:00, ongoing renovations may close some exhibits, Paseo del Muelle 34, tel. 943-440-099, www.aquariumss.com).

Naval Museum (Museo Naval)—Located at the port, this museum's two floors of exhibits describe the seafaring city's history, revealing the intimate link between the Basque culture and the sea (€1.20, free on Thu, borrow the English translation booklet, Tue–Sat 10:00–13:30 & 16:00–19:30, Sun 11:00–14:00, closed Mon, just before aquarium at Paseo del Muelle 24, tel. 943-430-051).

▲**Monte Urgull**—The once-mighty castle (Castillo de la Mota) atop the hill deterred most attackers, allowing the city to prosper in the Middle Ages. The museum located within the castle features San Sebastián history and is mildly interesting. The best views from the hill are not from the statue of Christ, but from the ramparts on the left side (as you face the hill), just above the port's aquarium. Café El Polvorín, nestled in the park, is a friendly place with salads, sandwiches, and good sangria. A new walkway allows you to stroll the mountain's entire perimeter near sea level. This route is continuous from Hotel Parma to the aquarium. Paths are technically open only from sunrise to sunset (generally daily May–Sept 8:00–21:00, Oct–April 8:00–19:00). Why are some of the directional signs defaced? Because you're in the land of Euskadi, not in Spain—and to remind you, some proud Basque has spray-painted over the Spanish.

Monte Igueldo

For commanding city views (if you ignore the tacky amusements on top), ride the funicular up Monte Igueldo, a mirror image of Monte Urgull. The views over San Sebastián, along the coast, and into the distant green mountains are sensational day or night. The entrance to the funicular is on the road behind the tennis club on the far western end of Playa de Ondarreta, which extends from Playa de la Concha to the west (funicular-€2 round-trip; July–mid-Sept daily 10:00–22:00; April–June and mid-Sept–Oct daily 11:00–20:00; Nov–March Mon–Fri 11:00–18:00, Sat–Sun 11:00–20:00, closed Wed). If you drive to the top, you'll pay €1.50 to enter. The #16 bus takes you here from the Old Town in about 10 minutes, stopping at the funicular station.

Near San Sebastián

If you want to venture farther into Spain, visit the exciting modern-art museum in nearby Bilbao (see "Transportation Connections," page 407).

▲▲▲**Guggenheim Bilbao**—While the collection of art in this museum is no better than anything in Europe's other great modern-art museums, the building itself—designed by Frank Gehry and opened in 1997—is the reason why so many travelers eagerly splice Bilbao into their itineraries.

Gehry's triumph offers a fascinating look at 21st-century

architecture. Using cutting-edge technologies, unusual materials, and daring forms, he created a piece of sculpture that smoothly integrates with its environment and serves as the perfect stage for some of today's best art.

This limestone and titanium-tile-clad building looks like a huge, silvery fish, and connects the city with its river. The building's skin—shiny, metallic, fish-like scales—is made of thin titanium, carefully created to give just the desired color and reflective quality.

As you enter, pick up the English brochure explaining the architecture and the monthly bulletin detailing the art currently on display. Because this museum is part of the Guggenheim "family" of museums, the collection perpetually rotates among the sister Guggenheim galleries in New York, Venice, and Berlin. The best approach to your visit is simply to immerse yourself in a modern-art happening, rather than to count on seeing a particular piece or a specific artist's works.

Cost, Hours, Information: €12.50; July–Aug daily 10:00–20:00; Sept–June Tue–Sun 10:00–20:00, closed Mon (café, no photos allowed inside, you can leave for lunch and return if you get a sticker on your way out, tram stop: Guggenheim, Metro stop: Moyua, Avenida Abandoibarra 2, tel. 944-359-080, www.guggenheim-bilbao.es). The museum offers excellent free audio-guides, which give descriptions of current exhibits and fascinating information about the building's architecture, and guided tours in English (call 944-359-090 for the schedule).

SLEEPING

In San Sebastián

$$$ Hotel Niza, set in the middle of Playa de la Concha, is understandably often booked well in advance. Half of its 40 rooms (some with balconies) overlook the bay. From its chandeliered and plush lounge, a classic elevator takes you to its comfortable, pastel rooms with wedding-cake molding (Db-€118–140, view rooms cost the same—requests with reservation considered...but no promises, extra bed-€20, only streetside rooms have air-con, great buffet breakfast-€10, Internet access and free Wi-Fi, parking-€13.50/day—must reserve in advance, Zubieta 56, tel. 943-426-663, fax 943-441-251, www.hotelniza.com, niza@hotelniza.com). The breakfast room has a sea view and doubles as a bar with light snacks throughout the day (Bar Biarritz, daily 7:30–24:00, food

---

Sleep Code

(€1 = about $1.30, country code: 34)
S = Single, **D** = Double/Twin, **T** = Triple, **Q** = Quad, **b** = bathroom,
s = shower only. You can assume these places accept credit
cards and speak English unless otherwise noted. Breakfast is
generally not included (unless noted), but you have plenty of
churrerías and cafeterias to choose from in the Old Town.

To help you sort easily through these listings, I've divided
the rooms into three categories based on the price for a standard double room with bath in peak season:

$$$ **Higher Priced**—Most rooms €90 or more.
 $$ **Moderately Priced**—Most rooms between €60–90.
  $ **Lower Priced**—Most rooms €60 or less.

---

service ends at 22:30). The cheap and cheery restaurant downstairs,
called La Pasta Gansa, serves good pizzas and salads (Wed–Mon
13:30–15:30 & 20:30–24:00, closed Tue).

$$$ Hotel Parma is a business-class place with 27 fine
rooms and family-run attention to detail and service. It stands on
the edge of the Old Town, away from the bar-scene noise, and
overlooks the river and a surfing beach (Sb-€58–78, windowless
interior Db-€85–118, view Db-€104–130, air-con, modern lounge,
Paseo de Salamanca 10, tel. 943-428-893, fax 943-424-082, www
.hotelparma.com, hotelparma@hotelparma.com; Iñaki, Arantxa,
Quique, and Ibon).

$$ Pensión Edorta elegantly mixes wood, brick, and color into
12 modern, stylish rooms (S-€35–50, D-€40–60, Sb/Db-€60–80,
extra bed-€20–25, elevator, Calle Puerto 15, tel. 943-423-773, fax
943-433-570, www.pensionedorta.com, info@pensionedorta.com).

$$ Pensión Anne is a tiny, well-run place on a relatively quiet
lane in the Old Town, with six rooms sharing three bathrooms. Its
simple rooms are bright and clean but have no sinks (S-€38–46,
D-€49, Db-€64, Esterlines 15, tel. 943-421-438, www.pensionanne
.com, pensionanne@yahoo.com, Anne).

$ Pensión Amaiur Ostatua is a popular hangout with the
Let's Go backpacker crowd, but don't let that scare you. It's a flowery
and inviting place buried deep in the Old Town, with great-value
rooms. Kind Virginia gives the place a homey warmth, and the
colorful pension is absolutely spotless. Her 13 rooms share seven
bathrooms (S-€24–37, exterior D-€38–55, quiet interior D-€33–
47, T-€51–75, Q-€63–90, family room, kitchen facilities, Internet
access, next to Santa María Church at Calle 31 de Agosto 44, tel.
943-429-654, www.pensionamaiur.com, no direct email—can

San Sebastián's Old Town

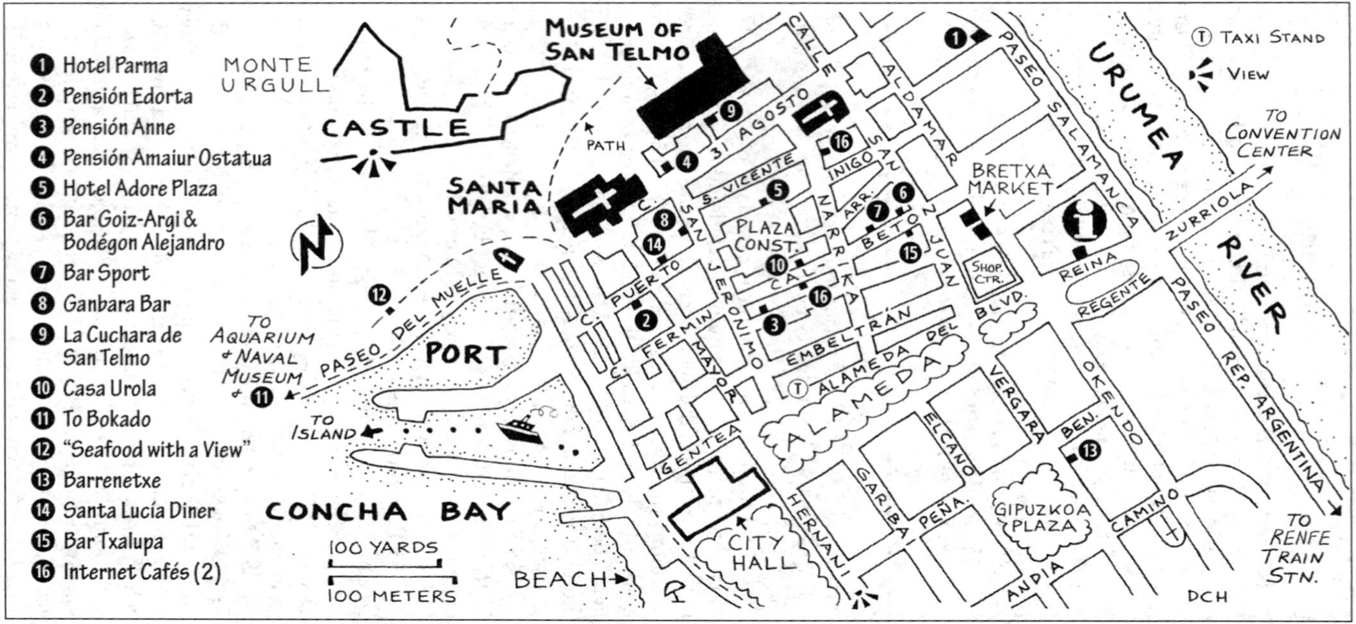

1 Hotel Parma
2 Pensión Edorta
3 Pensión Anne
4 Pensión Amaiur Ostatua
5 Hotel Adore Plaza
6 Bar Goiz-Argi & Bodegón Alejandro
7 Bar Sport
8 Ganbara Bar
9 La Cuchara de San Telmo
10 Casa Urola
11 To Bokado
12 "Seafood with a View"
13 Barrenetxe
14 Santa Lucía Diner
15 Bar Txalupa
16 Internet Cafés (2)

reserve online by completing form on their website).

$ Adore Plaza, run by young and energetic Santi, offers bright and good-value rooms overlooking the Old Town's centerpiece, Plaza de la Constitución. If Santi isn't around, his parents offer a warm, friendly welcome. Seven rooms—four with balconies and views of the plaza, and three interior rooms with less noise—share four bathrooms (D-€50–60, one Db-€75, beds in 4-bed room with lockers-€20–25/person, Plaza de la Constitución 6, tel. & fax 943-422-270, mobile 610-521-092 or 610-521-532, www.adoreplaza.com, adoreplaza@yahoo.es).

EATING

On menus, you'll see *bacalao* (salted cod), best when cooked *a la bizkaina* (with tomatoes, onions, and roasted peppers); *merluza* (hake, a light whitefish prepared in a variety of ways); and *chipirones en su tinta* (squid served in their own black ink). Carnivores will find plenty of lamb (try *chuletas,* massive lamb chops). Local brews include *sidra* (hard apple cider), Txakolí (cha-koh-LEE, a local, light, sparkling white wine—often theatrically poured from high above the glass for aeration), and *izarra* (herbal-flavored brandy). Spanish wine is generally served by the glass; red *crianza* spends one year in oak kegs and is *con cuerpo* (full-bodied). If you ask for *una copa de tinto*, they'll likely give you the local wine, bottled without a label. Surprisingly, *rosados* (rosés) have become very popular lately, as Spanish wineries have increased their production.

Bar-Hopping

Txiquiteo (chih-kee-TAY-oh) is the word for hopping from bar to bar, enjoying characteristically small sandwiches and tiny snacks *(pintxos,* PEEN-chohs) and glasses of wine. Local competition drives small bars to lay out the most appealing array of *pintxos*, and the selection is amazing. Later in the evening, the best spreads get picked over (20:30 is prime time). As the night progresses, bars get more crowded and bartenders bounce around. If you can't get the bartender's attention to serve you a particular *pintxo*, don't be shy—just grab it and a napkin, and munch away. If it comes with a toothpick, don't throw it on the ground (it's how they keep track of how many tasty tapas you've had). Bars with restaurants often have the Euskara word *jatetxea* on their sign outside. Even if you only see *pintxos* from the street, inquire about the restaurant. It usually has an entrance from the bar area.

Do the *Txiquiteo* Tango: San Sebastián's Old Town provides the ideal backdrop for tapas-hopping; just wander the streets and sidle up to the bar in the liveliest spot. Calle Fermín Calbetón has about the best concentration of bars (don't miss Bar Goiz Argi, described below); the streets San Jerónimo and 31 de Agosto are also good.

Bar Goiz-Argi serves its tiny dishes with pride and attitude. Advertising *pintxos calientes*, they cook each treat for you, allowing you a montage of petite gourmet snacks; try their *tartaleta de txangurro* (spider-crab spread on bread). Wash it all down with a glass of whichever wine you like—open bottles are clearly priced and displayed on the shelf. You stand at the bar since there are no chairs (closed Mon–Tue, Calle Fermín Calbetón 4, tel. 943-425-204).

Hop across the street to continue the evening at **Bar Txalupa**. While their meatballs are tasty, look for the more inventive *pintxos*, such as a crowded mix of duck breast, raspberries, bleu cheese, and dates topping a baguette slice. While service is barely acceptable, the food and ample seating compensate (closed Mon, Calle Fermín Calbetón 3, tel. 943-425-204).

Next, make your way down to the nearby **Bar Sport** for more action. They may offer to *calentar* (heat up) some of your selections, such as the toothpick-towering *jamón* and mushroom *pintxo*. They have a few tables, but don't expect service. Order at the bar and take it to your table...if you're lucky enough to get one (closed Mon, Calle Fermín Calbetón 10, tel. 943-426-888).

For top-end tapas, seek out these two bars—each packed with locals rather than tourists: **Ganbara Bar** serves the typical little sandwich *pintxos*, but also heaps piles of peppers and mushrooms—whatever's in season—on its bar, and sautées tasty *raciones* for a steep price (see the dry-erase board, closed Mon, San Jerónimo 21, tel. 943-422-575). **La Cuchara de San Telmo**—with cooks taught by a big-name Basque chef—is a cramped place that devotes as much space to its thriving kitchen as its bar. It has nothing precooked and set on the bar—you order your mini-gourmet plates with a spirit of adventure from the constantly changing blackboard (€3 *pintxos*, closed Mon, tucked away on a lonely alley behind Museo San Telmo at 31 de Agosto 28, tel. 943-420-840).

Restaurants, Picnics, and Churros

Bodégon Alejandro is a good spot for modern Basque cuisine in a dark and traditional setting (3-course *menu*—€32, from 13:00 and 21:00, closed Mon, no dinner Sun and Tue, in the thick of the Old Town, Calle Fermín Calbetón 4, tel. 943-427-158). **Casa Urola,** a block away, is *the* place in the Old Town for a good, traditional, sit-down Basque meal (more expensive, €18 entrées, reservations smart from 13:00 and 20:00, Calle Fermín Calbetón 20, tel. 943-423-424).

For **seafood** with a salty sailor's view, check out the half-dozen hardworking, local-feeling restaurants that line the harbor on the way to the aquarium. For a fancy splurge, try **Bokado,** halfway up Monte Urgull at the aquarium entrance. The black-box exterior hides a bright white dining room that elegantly mixes Asian and Spanish cuisines. Reservations are smart (daily 13:30–16:00 & 21:00–23:00, €44 sampling *menu*, €23 entrées, Plaza Jacques Cousteau 1, tel. 943-431-842). If you don't have the extra cash, consider an unforgettable sunset drink on their **rooftop terrace** (daily 11:00–22:00, €2 tapas, €8 *raciones*).

For **picnics,** drop by one of the countless tiny grocery stores or the Bretxa public market at Plaza Sarriegi (down the modern escalator) near the TI. Then head for the beach or up Monte Urgull. Upscale picnic-goers can tempt their tastebuds at **Barrenetxe** for an amazing array of breads, prepared foods, and some of the best desserts in town. In business since 1699, the somewhat formal service is justified (open daily, hours vary but always closed Sun afternoon, Plaza de Guipúzcoa 9, tel. 943-424-482).

Santa Lucía, a '50s-style Basque diner, is ideal for a cheap Old Town breakfast or *churros* break (*churros* are like deep-fried, sweet French fries that can be dipped in pudding-like hot chocolate). Photos of 20 different breakfasts decorate the walls, and plates of fresh *churros* with sugar keep patrons happy (daily 8:00–22:00, Calle Puerto 6, tel. 943-425-019). Grease is liberally applied to the grill...from a squeeze bottle. To counteract this place's heart-attack potential, get a glass of O.J., fresh-squeezed by the clever machine.

TRANSPORTATION CONNECTIONS

From San Sebastián by Train: Remember that San Sebastián has two train stations: RENFE and EuskoTren (described in "Arrival in San Sebastián," page 397). The station you use depends on your destination. The RENFE station handles long-distance destinations within Spain, including **Barcelona** (2/day, 8.5 hrs; 1 at night except Sat, 10 hrs), **Madrid** (3/day, 6–8.5 hrs, or 10.5 hr night train), and **Santiago de Compostela** (1/day, 11–14 hrs, final destination A Coruña). Note that all trains to Barcelona, Madrid, and Paris require reservations.

If you're going into France, it's best to take the regional Topo train (which leaves from the EuskoTren station) over the French border into **Hendaye** (2/hr, 30 min, departs EuskoTren station at :15 and :45 after the hour 7:15–21:45). From Hendaye, connect to France's SNCF network, including **Paris** (from Hendaye: 4/day, 5.5 hrs, or 8.5-hr night train). Unfortunately, San Sebastian's EuskoTren station doesn't have info concerning Paris-bound trains from Hendaye. Don't preplan too much—EuskoTren tickets to Hendaye can only be purchased two hours in advance (after which they expire). Also from San Sebastián's EuskoTren station, slow regional trains depart to other destinations in Spain's Basque region, including **Bilbao** (hourly, roundtrip €10.50 ticket saves you €2, some are 2.25 hrs direct but most are 2.75 hrs—the bus is much better, described below; EuskoTren info: tel. 902-543-210, www.euskotren.es).

By Bus: There is no real bus station in San Sebastián—it's more a congregation of bus parking spots, called Amara, at Plaza Pío XII (on the river, four blocks south of EuskoTren station). Some schedules are posted at various stops, but confirm departure times and buy your tickets in advance at any of the bus companies with offices along Avenida de Sancho El Sabio. Pesa, which serves St. Jean-de-Luz and Bilbao, is located same side as the "station," along Avenida de Sancho el Sabio (www.pesa.net).

From San Sebastián, buses go to Madrid (8/day, 6 hrs direct otherwise 7 hrs), **Bilbao** (2/hr, hourly on weekends, 6:30–22:00, 1.25 hrs, get €9.15 ticket from office, departs from Amara, bus tel. 902-101-210; once in Bilbao, buses leave you at Termibús stop with easy tram connections to the Guggenheim modern art museum), and **St. Jean-de-Luz,** France (2/day direct, at 9:00 and 14:30, 45 min, €4.15 one-way, €7.50 round-trip, runs only 1/week off-season, departs from Amara, tel. 902-101-210).

LANGUEDOC

From the 10th to the 13th centuries, this mighty and independent region controlled most of southern France. The ultimate in mean-spirited crusades against the Cathars (or Albigensians) began here in 1208, igniting Languedoc's meltdown and eventual incorporation into the state of France.

The name *languedoc* comes from the *langue* (language) that its people spoke: *Langue d'oc* ("language of Oc," *Oc* for the way they said "yes") was the dialect of southern France; *langue d'oïl* was the dialect of northern France (where *oïl*, later to become *oui*, was the way of saying "yes"). Languedoc's language faded with its power.

The Moors, Charlemagne, and the Spanish have all called this area home. The Spanish influence remains in this region, particularly in the south, where restaurants offer paella, and the siesta is still respected.

While sharing many of the same attributes as Provence (climate, wind, grapes, and sea), this sunny, intoxicating, southwesternmost region of France is allocated little time by most travelers. Lacking Provence's cachet and sophistication, Languedoc feels more real. Pay homage to Henri de Toulouse-Lautrec in Albi; spend a night in Europe's greatest fortress city, Carcassonne; scamper up to a remote Cathar castle; and sift through sand in Collioure. That wind you feel is called *la tramontane* (trah-mohn-tahn-yuh), Languedoc's version of Provence's mistral wind.

Planning Your Time

Albi makes a good day or overnight stop between the Dordogne region and Carcassonne (figure about 2.5 hours from Albi to either place). Plan your arrival in Carcassonne carefully: If you arrive

Languedoc

late in the afternoon, spend the night, and leave by noon the next day, you'll miss the day-trippers. Collioure lies a few hours from Carcassonne and is your Mediterranean beach-town vacation from your vacation, where you'll want two nights and a full day. To find the Cathar castle ruins and the village of Minerve, you'll need wheels of your own and a good map. If you're driving, the most exciting Cathar castles—Peyrepertuse and Quéribus—work well as day stops between Carcassonne and Collioure. And if nature beckons, the Gorges du Tarn makes an idyllic joyride a few hours east of Albi. No matter what kind of transportation you use, Languedoc is a logical stop between the Dordogne and Provence, or on the way to Barcelona, which is just over the border.

Getting Around Languedoc

Albi, Carcassonne, and Collioure are all accessible by train, but a car is essential for seeing the remote sights. Pick up your rental car in Albi or Carcassonne, and buy the Michelin Local maps #344 and #338. Roads can be pencil-thin, and traffic slow.

For a one-hour-detour scenic route connecting Albi and points north (such as the Dordogne), take D-964 between Caussade (30 min south of Cahors), Bruniquel, Gaillac, and Albi. With a bit more time, link Caussade, Saint-Antonin-Noble-Val (D-926), Bruniquel, Castelnau-de-Montmiral, Gaillac, and Albi (using D-115 and D-964; see "Route of the Bastides," page 421). If you really want to joyride, take a half-day drive through the glorious Lot River Valley via Villefranche-de-Rouergue, Cajarc, and St. Cirq Lapopie (covered in the Dordogne and Nearby chapter—see page 375). If speed is of the essence, connect the Dordogne with Albi via the autoroute to Montauban.

Cuisine Scene in Languedoc

Hearty peasant cooking and full-bodied red wines are Languedoc's tasty trademarks. Be adventurous. Cassoulet, an old Roman concoction of goose, duck, pork, mutton, sausage, and white beans, is the main-course specialty. You'll also see *cargolade*, a satisfying stew of snail, lamb, and sausage. Local cheeses are Roquefort and Pelardon (a nutty-tasting goat cheese). Corbières, Minervois, and Côtes du Roussillon are the area's good-value red wines. The locals distill a fine brandy, Armagnac, which tastes just like cognac and costs less.

Remember, restaurants serve only during lunch (11:30–14:00) and dinner (19:00–21:00, later in bigger cities); some cafés serve food throughout the day.

Albi

Albi, an enjoyable river town of sienna-tone bricks and half-timbered buildings, is worth a stop for its two world-class sights: its towering cathedral and the Toulouse-Lautrec Museum. Lost in the Dordogne-to-Carcassonne shuffle and overshadowed by its big brother Toulouse, unpretentious Albi rewards the stray tourist well.

ORIENTATION

Albi's cathedral is home base. For our purposes, all sights, pedestrian streets, and hotels fan out from here, and are less than a five-minute walk away. The Tarn River hides below and behind the cathedral. The best city view is from the 22 Août 1944 bridge. Albi is dead quiet on Sundays and Monday mornings.

Tourist Information

The helpful TI is on the square in front of the cathedral, next to the Toulouse-Lautrec Museum (July–Aug Mon–Sat 9:00–19:30, Sun 10:30–12:30 & 14:00–18:30; Sept–June Mon–Sat 9:00–12:30 & 14:00–18:00, Sun 10:30–12:30 & 14:00–18:30; tel. 05 63 49 48 80, www.albi-tourisme.fr). Ask about concerts, pick up a map of the city center with the walking-tour brochure, and get the map of *La Route des Bastides Albigeoises* (hill towns near Albi).

Arrival in Albi

By Train: There are two stations in Albi; you want Albi-Ville (no baggage check—but you can check bags for the day at the Toulouse-Lautrec Museum). It's a level, 15-minute walk to the town center. Take the second left out of the station onto avenue Maréchal Joffre, and then take another left on avenue du Général de Gaulle. Go straight across place Lapérouse and find the traffic-free street to the left that leads into the city center. This turns into rue Ste. Cécile, which takes you to my recommended hotels and the cathedral.

By Car: Follow *Centre-Ville* and *Cathédrale* signs (if you lose your way, follow the tall church tower). There's a big, free lot on avenue du Général de Gaulle, just before place Lapérouse. Metered parking (free 19:00–8:00 and all day Sun) is close to the old city along boulevard Général Sibille (also near place Lapérouse).

Helpful Hints

Market Day: The town's outdoor market is held on Saturday morning on place Lapérouse (until 12:30) and every day except Monday in the market hall. (The Art Nouveau market hall should reopen in 2008 following restoration.)

Groceries: The store **8 à Huit** is across from the recommended Hôtel Lapérouse (Tue–Sat 8:00–20:00, plus Sun mornings and Mon afternoons, 14 place Lapérouse).

Wine Shop: Au Roussillon has a fine selection of this area's surprisingly tasty wines; try a wine from Gaillac (Tue–Sat 10:00–12:00 & 14:00–18:00, closed Sun–Mon, 2 rue de Saunal).

Internet Access: Ludi.com is at 62 rue Séré de Rivières (Mon–Sat 11:00–24:00, closed Sun, tel. 05 63 43 34 24).

Albi

Languedoc

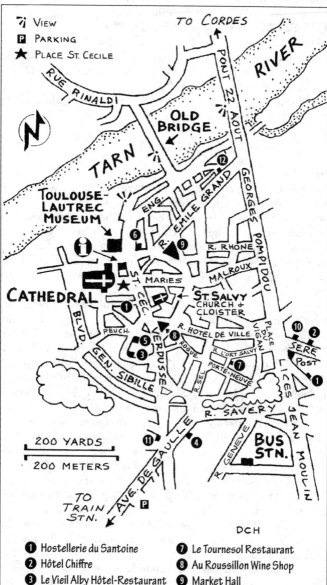

KEY

- 7 View
- P Parking
- ★ Place St. Cecile

TO CORDES

RIVER

RUE RINALDI

OLD BRIDGE

PONT 22 AOUT

TARN

GEORGES POMPIDOU

TOULOUSE-LAUTREC MUSEUM

ENG.

EMILE GRAND

R.

⑫

⑥

⑨

R. RHONE

MALROUX

CATHEDRAL

ST. CEC.

MARIES

★

St. SALVY CHURCH & CLOISTER

BLVD.

PEUCH.

VERPUSSE

① ⑤ ⑧ R. HOTEL DE VILLE

③

ROQUE.

R. L'ORT SALVY

PLACE DU VIGAN

R. SEL

PORTE-NEUVE

⑦

SERE POST

⑩ ②

①

GEN. SIBILLE

R. SAVERY

LICES JEAN MOULIN

200 YARDS

200 METERS

⑪

④

GENEVE

R.

BUS STN.

AVE. DE GAULLE

P

TO TRAIN STN.

DCH

- ① Hostellerie du Santoine
- ② Hôtel Chiffre
- ③ Le Vieil Alby Hôtel-Restaurant
- ④ Hôtel Lapérouse
- ⑤ La Viguière & Le Papillon Restaurants
- ⑥ La Tartine Restaurant
- ⑦ Le Tournesol Restaurant
- ⑧ Au Roussillon Wine Shop
- ⑨ Market Hall
- ⑩ Internet Café
- ⑪ 8 à Huit Grocery
- ⑫ Launderette

Laundry: Do your washing at **Lavotop,** above the river at 10 rue Emile Grand (daily 7:00–21:00).

Taxi: Call **Albi Taxi Radio** at 05 63 54 85 03.

Car Rental: Europcar is closest to the train station (24 avenue François Verdier, walk 1 long block down avenue Général Leclerc from the station and turn right, tel. 05 63 48 88 33). All others require a taxi ride.

Local Guide: Philippe Bos is both good and cute and lives in Toulouse (bos.philippe@wanadoo.fr).

SIGHTS

In Albi

Everything of sightseeing interest is within a few blocks of the towering cathedral. Get oriented on the main square.

▲▲▲**Place Ste. Cécile**—Grab a bench on the far side of place Ste. Cécile and face the church. With the church directly in front of you, the bishop's palace (with the Toulouse-Lautrec Museum, river view, and TI) is a bit to the right. The market is a block behind you on your right. And the sleepy St. Salvy cloister is a block behind on your left.

Why the big church? Albi was the administrative center for 465 churches at its peak. Back when tithes were essentially legally required taxes, everyone gave their 10 percent, or "*dime*" (dee-may), to the church. The local bishop was filthy rich, and with all those *dimes*, he had money to build a dandy church. In medieval times, there was no interest in making a space so people could step back and get a perspective on such a fine building. A clutter of houses snuggled right up to the church's stout walls, and only in the 19th century were things cleared away. Just in the last few years were the cars cleared out (another triumph for the European pedestrian).

Why so many bricks? Because there were no stone quarries nearby. Albi is part of a swath of redbrick towns from here to Toulouse (nicknamed "the pink city" for the way its bricks dominate that townscape). Notice on this square the buffed brick addresses next to the sluggish stucco ones. As late as the 1960s, the town's brickwork was considered low-class, and was covered by stucco. Today, the stucco is being peeled away, and Albi has that brick pride again.

▲▲▲**St. Cécile Cathedral (Cathédrale Ste. Cécile)**—When the heretical Cathars were defeated in the 13th century, this massive cathedral was the final nail in their coffin. Big and bold, it made clear who was in charge. The imposing exterior and the stunning interior drive home the message of the Catholic (read: "universal") Church in a way that would have stuck with any medieval worshipper. This place oozes power—get on board, or get run over.

The Cathars

The Cathars were a heretical group of Christians who grew in numbers from the 11th through the 13th centuries under tolerant rule in Languedoc. They saw life as a battle between good (the spiritual) and bad (the material), and they considered material things evil and of the devil. While others called them "Cathars" (from the Greek word for "pure") or "Albigensians" (for their main city, Albi), they called themselves simply "friends of God." Cathars focused on the teachings of St. John, and recognized only baptism as a sacrament. Because they believed in reincarnation, they were vegetarians.

Travelers encounter traces of the Cathars in their Languedoc sightseeing because of the Albigensian Crusades (1209–1240s). The king of France wanted to consolidate his grip on southern France. The pope needed to make a strong point that the only acceptable Christianity was Roman-style. Both found self-serving reasons to wage a genocidal war against the Cathars, who never amounted to more than 10 percent of the local population and coexisted happily with their non-Cathar neighbors. After a terrible generation of torture and mass burnings, the Cathars were wiped out. There were many thousands of victims in this tragedy (Cathar and others). The last Cathar was burned in 1321.

Today, tourists find haunting castle ruins (once Cathar strongholds) high in the Pyrénées, and eat hearty *salade Cathar.*

Cost and Hours: Free entry, open daily June–Sept 9:00–18:30, Oct–May 9:00–12:00 & 14:00–18:30. Once inside, you'll pay an additional €1 to enter the choir (worthwhile). The treasury (a single room of reliquaries and church art) is not worth the €3 or the climb.

Organ Concerts: The cathedral hosts frequent concerts (the TI has a schedule); free organ concerts are usually offered in July and August (Sundays at 16:00 and Wednesdays at 17:00).

❷ Self-Guided Tour: Visit the cathedral using the following self-guided commentary. Begin facing the...

Exterior: The cathedral looks less like a church and more like a fortress. In fact, it was a central feature of the town's defensive walls. Notice how high the windows are (out of stone-tossing range). The simple Gothic style was typical of this region—designed to be sensitive to the anti-materialistic tastes of the local Cathars.

The top (from the gargoyles and newer, brighter bricks upward) is a fanciful, 19th-century, Romantic-era renovation. The church was originally as plain and austere as the bishop's palace (the similar, bold brick building to the right, now housing the Toulouse-Lautrec Museum). Imagine the church with a rooftop more like that of the bishop's palace.

• *Climb up to the extravagant Flamboyant Gothic entry porch.*

Entry and Interior: The entry was built about two centuries after the original plain church (1494), when concerns about Cathar sensitivities were long gone. Originally colorfully painted, it provided one fancy entry.

The interior, also far from plain, looks essentially as it did in 1500. The highlights are the vast *Last Judgment* painting (west wall, under the organ) and the ornate choir (east end).

• *Walk to the front of the altar and face the...*

Last Judgment: The oldest art in the church (1474), this is also the biggest Last Judgment painting from the Middle Ages. The dead come out of the ground, then line up (above) with a printed accounting of their good and bad deeds displayed in ledgers on their chests. Judgment, here we come. Those on the left (God's right) look confident and comfortable. Those on the right—the hedonists—look pretty nervous. Get closer. Below on both sides of the arch are seven frames illustrating a wonderland of gruesome punishments sinners could suffer through while attempting to earn a second chance at salvation. Those who fail, end up in the black clouds of Hell (upper right). But where's Jesus—the key figure in any Judgment Day painting? The missing arch in the middle (cut out in late-Renaissance times to open the way to a new chapel) once featured Christ overseeing all the action. (While no one knows for sure, a good guess at how this painting would have looked is on a small stand near the last pew back where you entered.) The assembly above (on the left) shows the heavenly hierarchy: The pope and bishops sit closest to (the missing) Jesus, then more bishops and priests—before kings—followed by monks, and then, finally, commoners like you and me.

The **altar** is the newest art in the church. But this is not the front of the church at all—you're facing west. Turn 180 degrees and head east, for Jerusalem (where medieval churches almost always point).

• *Stop first at the choir—a fancy, more intimate room within the finely carved stone "screen."*

The Choir: In the Middle Ages, nearly all cathedrals had ornate Gothic choir screens like this one. These highly decorated walls divided the church into a private place for clergy and a general zone for the common rabble. The screen enclosed the altar and added mystery to the Mass. In the 16th century, with the success of the Protestant movement and the Catholic Church's Counter-Reformation, choir screens were removed. (In the 20th century, the Church took things one step further, and priests actually turned and faced their parishioners.) Later, French Revolutionary athe-ists destroyed most of the choir screens that remained—Albi's is a rare survivor. Pay €1 to stroll around it. You'll see Old Testament figures in the Dark Ages exterior, and New Testament figures in the enlightened interior. Stepping inside, marvel at the fine lime-stone carving. Scan each of the 72 unique little angels. Check out the brilliant ceiling, which hasn't been touched or restored in 500 years. A bishop, impressed by the fresco technique of the Italian Renaissance, invited seven Florentine artists to do the work. Good call.

• *Exit through the side door, next to where you paid for the choir. You'll pass a WC on your way to the...*

▲▲Toulouse-Lautrec Museum (Musée Toulouse-Lautrec)—

The Palais de la Berbie (once the fortified home of Albi's arch-bishop) has the world's largest collection of Henri de Toulouse-Lautrec's paintings, posters, and sketches.

Cost and Hours: €5, audioguide-€3; April–May daily 10:00–12:00 & 14:00–18:00; June and Sept daily 9:00–12:00 & 14:00–18:00; July–Aug daily 9:00–18:00; Oct and March Wed–Mon 10:00–12:00 & 14:00–17:30, closed Tue; Nov–Feb Wed–Mon 10:00–12:00 & 14:00–17:00, closed Tue; tel. 05 63 49 48 70, www.musee-toulouse-lautrec.com.

Background: Henri de Toulouse-Lautrec, born here in 1864, was crippled from youth. After he broke both legs, the lower half of his body never grew correctly. His father, once very engaged in parenting, lost interest in his son. Because of this, Henri was on the fringe of society, and therefore had an affinity for people who didn't quite fit in. He later made his mark painting the dregs of the Parisian underclass with an intimacy only made possible by a man with his life experience.

◗ Self-Guided Tour: The museum displays Toulouse-Lautrec's work chronologically. As you tour, use the dates of the paintings (always indicated) to tie Henri's evolution as an artist to his work.

1870s: First, you'll see the works of his youth *(jeunesse)* in a glass case—the impressive doodles of an 11-year-old.

1880: During his later, yet still pre-Paris years, Henri lived far from any artistic action (in Albi) and could only be inspired by magazines. This was his Impressionistic stage.

1882: Henri moved to the big city to pursue his passion. In his early Paris works, we see his trademark shocking colors and down-and-dirty, street-life scenes emerge. Compare his art-school work and his street work: Henri augmented his classical training with vivid life experience. His subjects were from bars, brothels, and cabarets...we're not in Albi anymore. Henri was particularly fascinated by cancan dancers (whose legs moved with an agility he'd never experience), and captured them expertly.

1880–1889: These were his exploratory years—dabbling in any style he encountered.

1890s: Henri started making some money by illustrating for magazines and newspapers. Back then, the daily happy hour included brothel visits—1892 to 1894 was his prostitution period. He respected the ladies, feeling both fascination and empathy toward them. The prostitutes accepted him the way he was and let him into their world...and he sketched great portraits.

Notice the big *Au Salon de la Rue des Moulins* (1894). There are two versions: the quick sketch, then the finished studio version. With this piece, Toulouse-Lautrec arrived. No more sampling; the artist has established his unique style: colors—garish; subject matter—hidden worlds; moralism—none, oblivious to society's norms. Henri's trademark use of cardboard was simply his quick, snapshot way of working: He'd capture these slice-of-life impressions on the fly on cheap, disposable material, intending to convert them to finer canvas paintings later, in his studio. But the cardboard quickies survive as Toulouse-Lautrec masterpieces.

Toulouse-Lautrec's bread and butter were his advertising posters, and the room of these posters is the museum's highlight. He was an innovative advertiser, creating simple, bold, and powerful lithographic images for printing posters. Displays show his original lithograph blocks (simply prepare the stone with a backwards image, then apply ink—which sticks chemically to the black points—and print posters). Four-color posters required creating four different blocks. The Moulin Rouge poster established his business reputation in Paris—strong symbols, bold and simple: just what, where, and when.

Toulouse-Lautrec's cane (in a glass case) gives additional insight into this tortured artistic genius. To protect him from his self-destructive lifestyle, loved ones had him locked up in a psychiatric hospital. But, with the help of this clever hollow cane, he still got his booze. Friends would drop by with hallucinogenic absinthe, his (now-illegal) drink of choice—also popular among many other artists of the time. With these special deliveries, he'd restock his cane, which even came equipped with a fancy little glass.

In 1901, at age 37, alcoholic, paranoid, depressed, and syphilitic, Henri de Toulouse-Lautrec returned to his mother—the only woman who ever really loved him—and died in her arms. The art world didn't mourn. Obituaries, speaking for the art establishment, basically said good riddance to Toulouse-Lautrec and his ugly art. Although no one in the art world wanted Henri's art, thankfully his mother and best friend recognized his genius and saved his work. They first offered it to the Louvre, which refused.

Finally, in 1922, the mayor of Albi accepted the collection and hung Toulouse-Lautrec's work here in what, for more than a century, had been a boring museum of archeology. There are more than a thousand works in this collection, and a huge expansion is expected to open in 2008 (see below).

• *Facing the Toulouse-Lautrec Museum, go left, leaving the courtyard and rounding the building for a good city view over the Tarn River.*

▲**Albi Town View**—Albi was situated here because of its river access to Bordeaux (which gave it access to the rest of the trading world). In medieval times, the fastest and most economical way to transport goods was down rivers like this. The lower, older bridge (pont Vieux) was first built in 1020. Before the bridge, the weir (which you can see just beyond this first bridge) provided a series of stepping stones that enabled people to cross the river. Notice the bishop's palace. The garden below dates from the 17th century (when the palace at Versailles was inspiring people all over France to create fancy gardens). The palace itself grew from the 13th century until 1789, when the French Revolution ended the power of the bishops and the state confiscated the building. Since 1905, it's been a museum.

St. Salvy Church and Cloister (Eglise St. Salvi et Cloître)— While this church (the oldest in town) is nothing special, the cloister creates a delightful space. Delicate arches surround an enclosed courtyard (open all day), providing a peaceful interlude from the shoppers that fill the pedestrian streets. Notice the church wall from the courtyard. It was the only stone building in Albi in the 11th century; the taller parts, added later, are made of brick. This is just one of many appealing little courtyards hiding throughout town. In the rough and tumble Middle Ages, many buildings faced inward. If doors are open, you're welcome to pop into courtyards. The Hôtel Décazes (8 rue Toulouse-Lautrec, across from La Viguière restaurant) is another good example.

Market Hall (Marché Couvert)—Albi's quiet Art Nouveau market should reopen in 2008 following a renovation. It's good for picnic-gathering and people-watching (Tue–Sun until 13:00, closed Mon, 2 blocks from cathedral).

SLEEPING

$$$ Hostellerie du Santoine*** is Albi's oldest hotel (established in 1784), and the most comfortable and traditional place I list. Guests enter an inviting and spacious lobby which opens onto an enclosed garden. Rooms are Old World cozy with all the comforts (Db-€125, big Db-€165, suites-€185, a block above big place du Vigan at 17 rue Santoine, tel. 05 63 54 04 04, fax 05 63 47 10 47, www.saint-antoine-albi.com, hotel@saint-antoine-albi.com).

Sleep Code

(€1 = about $1.30, country code: 33)
S = Single, **D** = Double/Twin, **T** = Triple, **Q** = Quad, **b** = bathroom,
s = shower only, * = French hotel rating system (0–4 stars).
Unless otherwise noted, credit cards are accepted and English
is spoken.

To help you sort easily through these listings, I've divided
the rooms into three categories based on the price for a standard double room with bath:

$$$ Higher Priced—Most rooms €90 or more.
 $$ Moderately Priced—Most rooms between €60–90.
  $ Lower Priced—Most rooms €60 or less.

$$ Hôtel Chiffre* is a safe bet, with 38 comfortable and well-appointed rooms (Db-€86-107, some with queen-size beds, air-con, elevator, garage-€8/day, traditional restaurant, near place du Vigan at 50 rue Séré de Rivières, tel. 05 63 48 58 48, fax 05 63 47 20 61, www.hotelchiffre.com, hotel.chiffre@yahoo.fr).

$ Le Vieil Alby Hôtel-Restaurant**, in the heart of Albi's pedestrian area, has modern, well-maintained, non-smoking rooms, run by helpful Monsieur Sicard (Db-€47–63, Tb-€68, garage-€7/day, 25 rue Toulouse-Lautrec, tel. 05 63 54 14 69, fax 05 63 54 96 75, levieilalby@wanadoo.fr).

$ Hôtel Lapérouse** is a work in progress, one block from the old city and a 10-minute walk to the train station. The hotel offers simple rooms; some are renovated and cheery, though I'd skip the rooms on the busy street. There's easy parking, a quiet garden, a big pool, and *très* friendly owners. Spring for a room with a balcony over the garden and pool (Sb/Db on street-€42, Sb/Db on garden-€52, Sb/Db on garden with deck-€60, Internet access and Wi-Fi, 21 place Lapérouse, tel. 05 63 54 69 22, fax 05 63 38 03 69, www.hotel-laperouse.com, hotel.laperouse@wanadoo.fr).

EATING

Albi is filled with reasonable restaurants that serve a rich local cuisine. Be warned: "Going local" here is likely to get you *tripe* (cow intestines), *andouillette* (sausages made from pig intestines), *foie de veau* (calf liver), and *tête de veau* (calf's head). Choose a restaurant or select one of the many cafés on the lively place du Vigan. For a choice of traditional restaurants, survey the places along rue Toulouse-Lautrec (2 blocks from Hôtel St. Clair).

La Viguière is *the* place to go for a fine meal, served in a nice interior or in a pleasant courtyard. The cuisine is classic French with a dash of local specialties tossed in. Sitting in the courtyard is best, where a wall of windows allows you to watch owner/chef Thierry and his charming wife Evelynne prepare your meal (€18, €24, and €39 *menus*; closed Wed off-season, 7 rue Toulouse-Lautrec, tel. 05 63 54 76 44).

Le Papillon Restaurant, a jazzy, six-table, Cathar-cool eatery under medieval stones and timbers, fuses Californian and French cuisines. It's the dream come true of two Californians—while Michael Gabel cooks, his partner, Rick Perry, serves. Seafood is their forte, there are good vegetarian options, and the salads are tops. Reserve for both lunch and dinner (€10–15 evening *plats*, closed Sun–Mon, 1 bis rue Toulouse-Lautrec, tel. 05 63 43 10 77).

La Tartine restaurant-bar, across from the TI, offers salads and simple fare for €9, *menus* at €14 and €24, and a large terrace. From its outdoor tables, you can marvel at the mountain of bricks that is the cathedral. The view and their extensive ice-cream menu make dessert here a good option (daily, tel. 05 63 54 50 60).

Le Tournesol is a good lunch option for vegetarians, as this is all they do. The food is delicious, the setting is bright with many windows, and the service is friendly (open for lunch only Tue–Thu and Sat, Fri for lunch and dinner, closed Sun–Mon, 11 rue de l'Ort en Salvy, tel. 05 63 38 38 14).

TRANSPORTATION CONNECTIONS

You'll connect to just about any destination through Toulouse.

From Albi by Train to: Toulouse (11/day, 70 min), **Carcassonne** (9/day, 2.5 hrs, change in Toulouse), **Sarlat** (2/day in 4.5 hrs with changes in Toulouse, Agen, and Le Buisson; or 3/day in 6–7 hrs via Souillac with changes possible in Brive-la-Gaillarde and Toulouse, then bus from Souillac), **Paris** (6/day, 6–7.5 hrs, change in Toulouse, also night train).

Near Albi

West of Albi

▲**Route of the Bastides**—The hilly terrain north of Albi was tailor-made for medieval villages to organize around for defensive purposes. Here, scores of fortified villages *(bastides)* spill over hilltops, above rivers, and between wheatfields, creating a worthwhile detour for drivers. These planned communities were the medieval product of community efforts organized by local religious or military leaders. Most *bastides* were built during the Hundred Years' War (see sidebar on page 195) to establish a foothold for French or

Near Albi

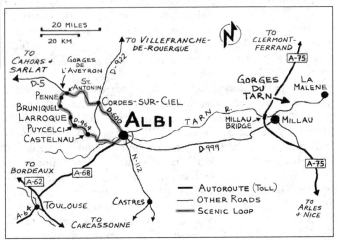

British rule in this hotly contested region. Unlike other French hill towns, *bastides* were not the product of a safe haven provided by a castle. Instead, they were a premeditated effort by a community to collectively construct houses as a planned defensive unit, *sans* castle.

Connect these *bastides* as a day trip from Albi, or as you drive between Albi and the Dordogne. For a good loop route from Albi, cross the 22 Août 1944 bridge and follow signs to *Cordes-sur-Ciel* (allow 30 min). The view of Cordes as you approach is memorable, but that's as close as I'd get (see listing below). From Cordes, follow signs to *Saint-Antonin-Noble-Val*, an appealing, flat "hill town" on the river, with few tourists. Then pass vertical little Penne, Bruniquel (signed from Saint-Antonin-Noble-Val), Larroque, Puycelci (my favorite—see below), and finally, Castelnau-de-Montmiral (with a fine main square), before returning to Albi. Each of these places is worth exploring if you have the time.

For a scenic route north to the Dordogne that includes many of the same *bastides*, leave Albi on N-88 to Gaillac, then follow D-964 to Castelnau-de-Montmiral, Puycelci, and on to Bruniquel. Then either head directly to Caussade (tricky turnoff shortly after leaving Bruniquel) and Cahors, or continue scenically north on D-115 to Saint-Antonin-Noble-Val through the Gorges de l'Aveyron. From Saint-Antonin, follow D-5 and D-926 to Caussade, then take N-20 to Cahors.

▲**Puycelci**—This town crowns a bluff surrounded only by green (15 minutes north of Gaillac). Drive to the top, where you'll find easy parking and an unspoiled and level village with a couple of cafés, one "serious" restaurant, a small grocery, a few *chambres d'hôte*, and one sharp little hotel. The park-like ramparts come with picnic benches and grand vistas—a good place to listen to the birds and the wind. As you wander, consider the recent history of an ancient town like this. In 1900, 2,000 people lived here with neither running water nor electricity. Then things changed radically. Half of all French men were casualties of World War I, and Puycelci didn't escape—as the monument (by the car park) attests. In 1968, when the village was down to three families, running water replaced the venerable cisterns, and things started looking up. Today, while still with almost no commercial activity, the town has a stable population of 100, all marveling at how the value of their land has skyrocketed.

Stroll through the village, starting at the parking lot. Enter the village, passing the recommended Puycelci Roc Café. At the opposite side of town, a rampart walk circles you counterclockwise back to the parking lot, where an orientation table explains what's in the distance. As you stroll this sleepy little place, look for photos of the town at the turn of the 20th century.

Eating and Sleeping in Puycelci: **Puycelci Roc Café,** at the parking lot, has good café fare, a warm interior, and pleasant outdoor tables (daily for dinner, Sat–Wed for lunch, tel. 05 63 33 13 67).

A night in Puycelci is my idea of a vacation. **$$ L'Ancienne Auberge** is the place to eat and sleep, with eight surprisingly smart and comfortable rooms, a country-elegant restaurant, a cozy *bistrot* with a fireplace you could walk into, and two outdoor patios (*plats* from €13, *menus* from €24). Owner/chef Dorothy moved here from New Jersey 18 years ago and is eager to share her cuisine and her passion for this region (Db-€70–95, air-con, place de l'Eglise, tel. 05 63 33 65 90, fax 05 63 33 21 12, www.ancienne-auberge.com, caddack@aol.com).

Bruniquel—This *très* photogenic but less-tended village will test your thighs as you climb the lanes upward to the château (€2.50, April–Sept daily 10:00–12:30 & 14:00–18:00, closed Oct–March). Good food and three rooms (Db-€50) can be found at the mellow **$ L'Etape du Château** (salads for €10, €12–15 *plats*, *menus* from €17, tel. 05 63 67 25 00).

Cordes-sur-Ciel—It's hard to resist this brilliantly situated hill town just 15 miles north of Albi, but I would. Enjoy the fantastic view on the road from Albi, but go no closer. Cordes, once an important Cathar base, has slipped over the boutique-filled edge to the point where it's hard to find the medieval town, and it's jammed on weekends and in the summer.

East of Albi

Two hours east of Albi lies a hauntingly beautiful region unknown to most Americans. Mountains, rivers, and lost villages conspire to give the adventurous nature lover a true experience of *la France profonde.*

Gorges du Tarn—Adventure-lovers can canoe, hike, or drive the stunning Tarn River Gorge by heading east from Albi to Millau, then following the gorge all the way to St. Enimie. Roads are slow but spectacular.

The best base for canoeing is from tiny La Malène (on the way to St. Enimie, 25 miles northeast of Millau). In La Malène, **Company Canoë 2000** rents what you need to run the mellow river (down the path to the right of bridge, tel. 04 66 48 57 71); the 8- or 11-kilometer trips (about 5 or 7 miles, €28–35) have the best views. Take your lunch and picnic along the way. If you'd rather not paddle a canoe, you can take a Batelier boat (leaves from bridge, seats 5–6 people, ask for a boatman who speaks a leetle English).

Sleeping in La Malène: Stay at the simple but comfortable **$ Auberge de l'Embarcadère** (Db-€45, Tb-€52, tel. 04 66 48 51 03, fax 04 66 48 58 94) or in the country-luxurious **$$$ Manoir de Montesquiou,** run entirely by one family: Dad runs the hotel, Mom is the head chef, the three sisters serve your meals, and son-in-law Greg runs the bar (Db-€68–106, suites fit for a queen-€131–139, extra bed-€16, you'll be expected to dine at its great restaurant, *menus* from €24, tel. 04 66 48 51 12, fax 04 66 48 50 47, www.manoir-montesquiou.com).

Millau Bridge (Viaduc de Millau)—Completed in 2005, the sleek and futuristic 1.5-mile-long suspension bridge, which shoots across the Tarn River Valley, is the world's highest at 885 feet. A modern-day Pont du Gard (see page 494), the Millau Bridge was built as a critical link in the A-75 autoroute, which connects Paris with the Mediterranean and Barcelona. A quarter-million tons of concrete were used to set the supporting pillars, with the tallest rising 1,125 feet—taller than the Eiffel Tower. It was built by the same construction company that built the Eiffel Tower in 1889. The bridge's British architect, Lord Norman Foster, also designed London's egg-shaped City Hall, as well as Berlin's equally glassy Reichstag Parliament dome (bridge always open; current car toll about €5.50, or €7 in July–Aug; bridge is 70 miles northeast of Albi on A-75).

Carcassonne

Medieval Carcassonne is a 13th-century world of towers, turrets, and cobblestone alleys. It's Europe's ultimate walled fortress city—packed with too many tourists. At 10:00, the salespeople stand at the doors of their main-street shops, their gauntlet of tacky

temptations poised and ready for their daily ration of customers. But early, late, or off-season, a quieter Carcassonne is an evocative playground for any medievalist. Forget midday...spend the night.

Locals like to believe that Carcassonne got its name this way: 1,200 years ago, Charlemagne and his troops besieged this fortress-town (then called La Cité) for several years. A cunning townsperson named Madame Carcas saved the town. Just as food was running out, she fed the last bits of grain to the last pig and tossed him over the wall. Splat. Charlemagne's bored and frustrated forces, amazed that the town still had enough food to throw fat party pigs over the wall, decided they would never succeed in starving the people out. They ended the siege, and the city was saved. Madame Carcas *sonne*-d (sounded) the long-awaited victory bells, and La Cité had a new name: Carcas-sonne. It's a cute story... but historians suspect that Carcassonne is a Frenchified version of the town's original name (Carcas).

As a teenager on my first visit to Carcassonne, I wrote this in my journal: "Before me lies Carcassonne, the perfect medieval city. Like a fish that everyone thought was extinct, somehow Europe's greatest Romanesque fortress city has survived the centuries. I was supposed to be gone yesterday, but here I sit imprisoned by choice—curled in a cranny on top of the wall. The wind blows away the sounds of today, and my imagination 'medievals' me. The moat is one foot over and 100 feet down. Small plants and moss upholster my throne." Let this place make you a kid on a rampart.

ORIENTATION

Contemporary Carcassonne is neatly divided into two cities: The magnificent La Cité (the fortified old city, with 200 full-time residents taking care of lots more tourists) and the lively Ville Basse (modern lower city). Two bridges, the busy pont Neuf and the traffic-free pont Vieux, both with great views, connect the two parts.

Tourist Information

Carcassonne's TI has three locations. The main TI, in **Ville Basse**, is useful only if you're walking to La Cité (28 rue de Verdun, tel. 04 68 10 24 30). A far more convenient branch is in **La Cité**, to your right as you enter the main gate (Narbonne Gate—or porte Narbonnaise, tel. 04 68 10 25 35). Both TIs have the same hours (daily April–Oct 9:00–18:00, until 19:00 July–Aug, until 17:00 Nov–March). The tower across from La Cité's TI has informa-

tion on walking tours of the walls, a good book selection, and a fine wooden model of La Cité (notice that no house rises above the fortified walls). If you're arriving by train, the most convenient TI is the small kiosk across the canal from the **train station**—though its opening times are limited and vary off-season (generally daily July–Aug 9:00–19:00, April–June and Sept–Oct 14:00–18:00, closed Nov–March, tel. 04 68 25 94 81).

At any of these TI locations, pick up the map of La Cité and the one-page history in English, and ask about festivals (www .carcassonne-tourisme.com).

From mid-June through mid-September, the TI offers a few **excursion vans or buses** to some of the Cathar castles (see "Near Carcassonne," page 438 (usually €35–50 per person, check with TI for dates and times).

Arrival in Carcassonne

By Train: The train station (which has no baggage storage) is located in the Ville Basse, a 30-minute walk from La Cité. You have three options for reaching La Cité: by taxi, by shuttle bus, or on foot.

Taxis charge €8 for the short but worthwhile trip to La Cité, but cannot enter the city walls (taxis wait in front of the train station, or find the taxi stand one block across the canal).

A **shuttle bus** (*navette*) whisks you from boulevard Omer Sarraut (a block in front of the train station) to La Cité (€1.50, 4/hr, June–mid-Oct daily 9:30–19:30, no bus off-season, ticket good for round-trip—so hang onto it).

The 40-minute **walk** to La Cité is pleasant (but uphill at the end), crossing Carcassonne's appealing lower city via traffic-free streets and passing the lively place Carnot (good cafés, busy market on Tue, Thu, and Sat). Walk straight out of the station, cross the canal, then the busy ring road, and keep straight on rue Clémenceau for about seven blocks. After place Carnot, turn left

Carcassonne Overview

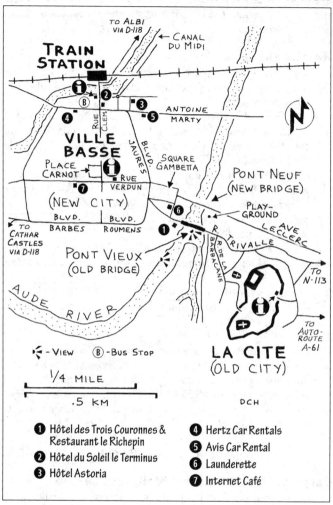

TO ALBI
VIA D-118

CANAL
DU MIDI

**TRAIN
STATION**

ANTOINE
MARTY

**VILLE
BASSE**

RUE
CLEM.

BLVD.
JAURES

SQUARE
GAMBETTA

PLACE
CARNOT

RUE
VERDUN

PONT NEUF
(NEW BRIDGE)

PLAY-
GROUND

(NEW CITY)

BLVD.
BARBES

BLVD.
ROUMENS

AVE.
LECLERC

R. TRIVALLE

RD DE LA
BARBACANE

TO
CATHAR
CASTLES
VIA D-118

PONT VIEUX
(OLD BRIDGE)

TO
N-113

AUDE
RIVER

TO
AUTO-
ROUTE
A-61

- VIEW   Ⓑ - BUS STOP

LA CITE
(OLD CITY)

1/4 MILE

.5 KM

DCH

❶ Hôtel des Trois Couronnes &
Restaurant le Richepin

❷ Hôtel du Soleil le Terminus

❸ Hôtel Astoria

❹ Hertz Car Rentals

❺ Avis Car Rental

❻ Launderette

❼ Internet Café

on rue de Verdun, walk three blocks, and turn right on the big square Gambetta. Angle across the square and turn right after Hôtel Ibis, then cross pont Vieux (great views). Signs will guide you up rue Trivalle and rue Nadaud to La Cité.

By Car: Use the *Carcassonne Est* exit from the autoroute, then carefully track signs to *La Cité*. You'll come to a large parking lot (first 30 min/free, 3–6 hrs/€4.50, 24 hrs/€9) and a drawbridge at the Narbonne Gate, at the walled city's entrance. If staying inside the walls, you can park for free in the castle moat (facing the Narbonne Gate, turn left, then right after the small cemetery). You must show your reservation (verbal assurances won't do). You are allowed to drive into the city after 18:00. Theft is common—leave nothing in your car at night.

Helpful Hints

Market Days: Pleasing place Carnot in Ville Basse hosts a non-touristy open market (Tue, Thu, and Sat mornings until 13:00; Sat is the biggest).

Summer Festivals: Carcassonne becomes colorfully medieval during many special events each July and August. Highlights are the *spectacle équestre* (jousting matches) and July 14 (Bastille Day) fireworks. The TI has details.

Internet Access: Most hotels in La Cité have Internet access; you'll also find several places in the Ville Basse. **Alerte Rouge** is best, with lots of computers, free Wi-Fi, and a small bar (€3/hour, Mon–Sat 10:00–23:00, closed Sun, 73 rue de Verdun, tel. 04 68 25 20 39).

Laundry: Try **Laverie Express** (daily 8:00–22:00, 5 square Gambetta at Hôtel Ibis; from La Cité, cross pont Vieux and turn right).

Bike Rental: **Evasion 2 Roues** has bikes to go (85 allée d'Iéna, tel. 04 68 11 90 40). Canalfront rides are a fun and level way to spin your wheels.

Taxi: Call 04 68 71 50 50 or 04 68 71 36 36.

Car Rental: The **Avis** agency is at 52 rue A. Martyet (from train station, cross canal, then turn left on boulevard Omer Sarraut), but with a prior reservation, you can pick up your car at the train station (tel. 04 68 25 05 84). **Hertz** is two blocks straight out of the station (turn right on boulevard Omer Sarraut; Hertz is at #33, tel. 04 68 25 41 26, closed 12:00–14:00).

SELF-GUIDED WALK

Carcassonne's Medieval Walls and La Cité

While the tourists shuffle up the main street, this walk, rated ▲▲▲, introduces you to the city with history and wonder, rather than tour groups and plastic swords. We'll sneak into the town on the other side of the wall...through the back door.

Start outside La Cité's main entrance, the Narbonne Gate (porte Narbonnaise). You're welcomed by a contemporary-looking bust of Madame Carcas—which is actually modeled after a 16th-century original of the town's legendary first lady (for her story, see page 425).

• *Cross the bridge toward the...*

Narbonne Gate: Pause at the drawbridge and survey this immense fortification. When forces from northern France finally

Carcassonne's La Cité

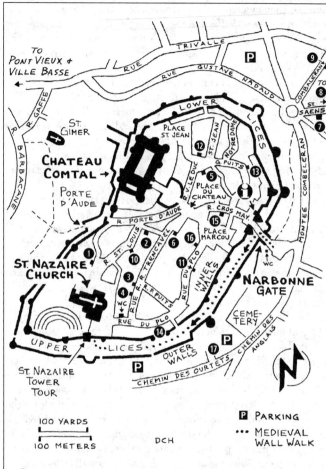

100 YARDS
100 METERS

DCH

🅿 PARKING

••• MEDIEVAL
WALL WALK

❶ Hôtel de la Cité & Barbacane
Restaurant

❷ Best Western Hôtel le Donjon

❸ Chambres l'Echappée Belle

❹ Auberge des Lices Rooms & Rest.

❺ Chambres le Grand Puits

❻ Auberge de Jeunesse &
Comptoir des Vins et Terroirs

❼ Hôtels du Château &
le Montmorency

❽ To Hôtel Mercure

❾ Hôtel Espace Cité

❿ Au Comte Roger Restaurant

⓫ Le Tour DaveJean Restaurant

⓬ L'Auberge du Grand Puits Rest.

⓭ Restaurant des Musées

⓮ Le Bar à Vins Café & Jazz Bar

⓯ Grocery

⓰ Gérard Sion Galerie (Photos)

⓱ Hotel Parking Entrance
(Daytime Only)

conquered Carcassonne, it was a strategic prize. Not taking any chances, they evicted the residents, whom they allowed to settle in the lower town (Ville Basse)—as long as they stayed across the river. (While called "new," this lower town actually dates from the 13th century.) La Cité remained a French military garrison until the 18th century.

The drawbridge was made crooked to slow any attackers' rush to the main gate. (It's just as effective today with tourists.) After crossing the drawbridge, lose the crowds and follow the cobbled path to the left and uphill, between the walls. (The only reason to continue straight is to visit the TI—just inside the next gate to the right, with fine Gothic vaulting and a medieval cistern.)

• At the first short set of stairs, climb to the outer-wall walkway and linger while facing the inner walls.

Wall View: These massive walls—nearly two miles around, with 52 towers—defended an important site near the intersection of the north–south and east–west trade routes. People have occupied this spot since Neolithic times. The Romans built Carcassonne's first wall, upon which the bigger medieval wall was constructed. Identify the ancient Roman bits by finding the smaller rocks mixed with narrow stripes of red bricks (and no arrow slits). The outer wall was not built until the 1300s.

Look over the wall and down at the moat below. Like most medieval moats, it was never filled with water (or even alligators). A ditch like this—which was originally even deeper—effectively stopped attacking forces from rolling up against the wall in their mobile towers and spilling into the city. Another enemy tactic was to "undermine" (tunnel underneath) the wall, causing a section to cave in. Notice the small, square holes at foot level along the ramparts. Wooden extensions of the rampart walkways (which we'll see later at the castle) once plugged into these holes, so that townsfolk could drop nasty and sticky things on anyone tunneling in. In peacetime, the area between the two walls was used for medieval tournaments, jousting practice, and markets.

During La Cité's Golden Age, the 1100s, independent rulers with open minds allowed Jews and Cathars to live and prosper within the walls, while troubadours wrote poems of ideal love. This liberal attitude made for a rich intellectual life, but also proved to be La Cité's downfall. The Crusades aimed to rid France of the dangerous Cathar movement (and their liberal sympathizers), which led to Carcassonne's defeat and eventual incorporation into the kingdom of France.

The walls of this majestic fortress were partially reconstructed in 1855 as part of a program to restore France's important monuments. The tidy crenellations and the pointy tower roofs are generally 19th-century. As you continue your wall walk to higher elevations, the lack of guardrails is striking. This would never happen in the United States; in France, if you fall, it's your own fault (so be careful). Also, notice the lights embedded in the walls. This fortress, like most important French monuments, is beautifully illuminated every night (for directions to a good nighttime view, see "Night Wall Walk to Pont Vieux," page 432).

• *You could keep working your way around the walls, and finish with the five Roman towers just before you return to the starting point. Walking the entire circle between the inner and outer gate is a terrific 20–30 minute stroll (and fantastic after dark).*

But for this tour, we'll enter La Cité at the first entrance possible, the...

Inner Wall Gate: The wall has the same four gates it had in Roman times. Before entering, notice the squat tower on the outer wall—this was a "barbican" (placed opposite each inner gate for extra protection). Barbicans were always semicircular—open on the inside to expose anyone who breached the outer defenses. Invading today is far easier than in the good old days. As you leave the square gate room to finally enter the town, look up, and you'll see various slots and holes (used for dumping things on intruders), a slot for the portcullis (the big iron grate), the frame for a heavy wooden door, and more of the same.

Once safely inside, look back up at the inner wall tower. If it's open, climb it. It's the only section of the inner wall you can climb without a tour, and the tower-top bookstore is good.

• *Opposite the tower is...*

St. Nazaire Church (Basilique St. Nazaire): This was a cathedral until the 18th century, when the bishop moved to the lower town. Today, due to the depopulation of the basically dead-except-for-tourism Cité, it's not even a functioning parish church. Notice the Romanesque arches of the nave and the delicately vaulted Gothic arches over the altar and transepts. After its successful conquest of this region in the 13th-century Albigensian Crusades, France set out to destroy all the Romanesque churches and replace them with Gothic ones—symbolically asserting its northern rule with this more northern style of church. With the start of the Hundred Years' War in 1317, the expensive demolition was abandoned. Today, the Romanesque remainder survives, and the destroyed section has been rebuilt Gothic, which makes it one of the best examples of Gothic architecture in southern France. When the lights are off (as they often are), the interior—lit only by candles and 14th-century stained glass—is evocatively medieval (daily 9:00–11:45 & 14:00–18:30, until 17:00 in winter).

Hôtel de la Cité: Located across from St. Nazaire Church, this beyond-posh hotel sits where the Bishop's Palace did 700 years ago. Today, it's a worthwhile detour to see how the privileged few travel. You're free to wander, so find the library-cozy bar, then the rear garden, and turn right for super wall views that you can't see from anywhere else.

• *From here, follow the main road (rue St. Louis) several blocks to a small castle-view terrace on your left.*

Château Comtal: Carcassonne's third layer of defense, while originally built in 1125, was completely redesigned in later reconstructions. From this fine viewpoint, you can see the wooden rampart extensions that once encircled the entire city wall. (Notice the empty peg holes to the left of the bridge.) When *Robin Hood: Prince of Thieves*, starring Kevin Costner, was filmed here in 1990, the entire city was turned into a film set. Locals enjoyed playing bit parts and seeing their château labeled "Nottingham Castle" in the fanciful film.

The castle is open to the public and provides a predictable medieval interior, a modest museum, and a romp on the inner wall and up a tower (€7.50, daily April–Sept 10:00–18:30, Oct–March 9:30–17:00, last entry 45 min before closing, audioguide for two-€6, tel. 04 68 11 75 87).

• *Fifty yards away, opposite the entrance to the castle, is...*

Place du Château: This busy little square sports a modest statue remembering the man who saved the city from deterioration and neglect in the 19th century. The bronze model circling the base of the statue shows Carcassonne's walls as they looked before the 1855 reconstruction by Eugène Viollet-le-Duc. Just uphill is the town's lively restaurant square (place Marcou), and straight down the tiny main drag is the Narbonne Gate, where you began this walk.

SIGHTS AND ACTIVITIES

▲▲▲**Night Wall Walk to Pont Vieux**—Save post-dinner energy for a don't-miss walk around the same walls you visited today (great dinner picnic sites as well). The effect at night is mesmerizing: The embedded lights become torches and unfamiliar voices the enemy. End at the pont Vieux for a floodlit fantasy, and you can do no better. The best route is a partial circumnavigation clockwise between the walls. Start at the Narbonne Gate, following my self-guided walk (above), and continue until the Inner Wall Gate. Don't enter through this gate, but continue your walk between the walls around La Cité. In about five minutes, you'll pass through a narrow passage behind Château Comtal, and come to a ramp leading down; look for a hard left at the bottom of a cobbled decline where the path rises back up. This ramp leads all the way down to rue de la Barbacanne, where you'll turn right to reach the pont Vieux and exceptional views of floodlit Carcassonne. Return from the pont

Vieux the same way you came, then complete your clockwise walk between the walls back to the Narbonne Gate. For an easier return climb, cross the bridge and continue straight on rue Trivalle, then veer right up rue Nadaud and track the walls.

Comptoir des Vins et Terroirs—Slip into this attractive wine bar to sample a good selection of local wines, tapas, and hors d'oeuvres. Christiane—who represents the small vintners of the Languedoc, does a fine job introducing you to this up-and-coming wine region and can arrange shipping. Prices are reasonable; besides, you'll need something to sip on the ramparts tonight (hours vary, generally about 10:00–13:00 & 14:00–21:00, often later in summer, across from Auberge de Jeunesse hostel at 3 rue du Comte Roger, tel. 04 68 26 44 76).

Gérard Sion Galerie—Duck into this impressive photo gallery before selecting which Cathar castles you want to visit (brilliant shots of many monuments in Languedoc, generally open daily 10:00–19:00, just up from place Marcou at 27 rue du Plô).

Canal du Midi—Completed in 1681, this sleepy, 155-mile canal connects France's Mediterranean and Atlantic coasts and runs right by the train station in Carcassonne. Before railways, Canal du Midi was clogged with commercial traffic—today, it entertains only pleasure craft. Look for the slow-moving hotel barges strewn with tanned and well-fed vacationers. The TI has information on half-day rides in modern boats from Carcassonne (€10/2.5 hours). A better way to experience the canal is on a relaxed bike ride along the canal's level towpath (for bike rental, see "Bike Rental," page 428).

SLEEPING

(€1 = about $1.30, country code: 33)

In Carcassonne's La Cité

Sleep in or near the old walls. Two pricey hotels, two good B&Bs, and an excellent youth hostel offer a full range of rooms inside the walls. Hôtel du Terminus and Hôtel Astoria have lodgings near the train station. In the summer, when La Cité is jammed with tourists, think of sleeping in quieter Caunes-Minervois (see "Near Carcassonne, in Caunes-Minervois," page 436). Top prices listed are for July and August, when the place is packed. At other times of the year, prices drop and there are generally plenty of rooms.

$$$ Hôtel de la Cité**** offers 61 rooms with deluxe everything in a beautiful building next to St. Nazaire Church. Peaceful gardens, a swimming pool, royal public spaces, an elegant restaurant, and reliable luxury are yours—for a price (Db-€400–550, suites-€550–1,300, extra adult-€55, breakfast-€26, 20 percent winter discount, air-con, garage-€20/day, place de l'Eglise, tel. 04 68

71 98 71, fax 04 68 71 50 15, www.hoteldelacite.com, reservations @hoteldelacite.com).

$$$ Best Western Hôtel le Donjon*** offers 75 overpriced and smallish—but well-appointed—rooms, a polished lobby, and a great location inside the walls. Rooms are located in three different buildings in La Cité. Most prefer the main building (standard Sb/Db-€130–160, Db suite-€145–200, standard Tb-€145–185, Tb suite-€165–220, Qb-€185–240, air-con, Wi-Fi, elevator, private parking-€10, 2 rue Comte Roger, tel. 04 68 11 23 00, fax 04 68 25 06 60, www.hotel-donjon.fr, hotel.donjon.best.western@wanadoo.fr).

$$ Chambres l'Echappée Belle is an oasis of peace in the center of La Cité, with four traditional, comfy rooms with wood floors and queen-size beds and a peaceful garden—but no air-conditioning (Db-€75–105, €10 per extra person up to four, includes breakfast and accepts credit cards, a few blocks past the youth hostel at 5 rue Raymond Roger Trencavel, tel. 04 68 25 33 40 or 06 21 70 17 67, www.lechappeebelle.co.uk, info@lechappeebelle .co.uk). Sincere owners Bruce and Johanna Lace sold their B&B in Scotland and moved here for a change of pace...this ought to do it.

$$ Auberge des Lices hides two lovely rooms above its restaurant with tile floors, high ceilings, exposed beams and stone walls (Db-€80, larger Db-€140, €20 per extra person up to five; 3 rue Raymond Roger Trencavel, tel. 04 68 72 34 07, fax 04 68 72 61 55, www .blasco.fr, leslices@blasco.fr).

$ Chambres le Grand Puits, across from Hôtel des Remparts, is a splendid value, with one cute double room and two cavernous apartment-like rooms that could sleep five, with kitchenette, private terrace, and nice personal touches. Inquire in the small boutique, and say *bonjour* to happy-go-lucky Nicole (Sb/Db-€45–60, Tb-€62–67, Qb-€72–82, includes self-serve breakfast, cash only, 8 place du Grand Puits, tel. & fax 04 68 25 16 67, http://legrandpuits.free.fr).

$ The Auberge de Jeunesse (youth hostel) is big, clean, and well-run, with an outdoor garden courtyard, self-service kitchen, TV room, bar, washer/dryer, Internet access, and a welcoming ambience that begins with jolly Michele at the reception. If you ever wanted to bunk down in a hostel, do it here—all ages are welcome. Only summer is tight; reserve ahead. Nonmembers pay €3 extra per night (bunk in 4- to 6-bed dorm-€17, includes sheets and breakfast, open all day, rue du Vicomte Trencavel, tel. 04 68 25 23 16, fax 04 68 71 14 84, www.fuaj.org or www.hihostels.com, carcassonne@fuaj.org).

Just Outside La Cité

Sleeping just outside La Cité offers the best of both worlds: quick access to the ramparts, less claustrophobic surroundings, and easy parking.

At **$$$ Hôtel du Château***** and **$$ Hôtel le Montmorency****, Cécile, Stéphane, Nicole, dog Opus, and lazy cat Minet are perfect hosts and offer the best hotel value in Carcassonne, with comfortable rooms knocking at the door of La Cité's drawbridge. The two hotels are separated by a small street and have different personalities, but share a reception lobby, stylish swimming pool with views to the ramparts (heated all year), whirlpool tub, airy terrace tables, free parking, and free Internet access. The *très* smart **Hôtel du Château** occupies the main building, selling four-star comfort at three-star prices, with 15 gorgeous rooms boasting marble floors, flat-screen TVs, CD players, and you name it (standard Db-€130, Db with view–€150, Db with terrace on pool-€180, €20 less in winter, 2 rue Camille Saint-Saëns, tel. 04 68 11 38 38, fax 04 68 11 38 39, www.hotelduchateau.net, contact @hotelduchateau.net). The **Hôtel le Montmorency** annex, behind Hôtel du Château, is no slouch, with 20 tight but well-designed rooms, warm colors, firm beds, and air-conditioning (Db-€65–75, Tb-€95, 2 rue Camille Saint-Saëns, tel. 04 68 11 96 70, fax 04 68 11 96 79, www.lemontmorency.com, le.montmorency@wanadoo.fr).

$$$ Hôtel Mercure*** hides behind the Hôtel le Montmorency and is a five-minute walk to La Cité. It has 61 snug-but-comfy, air-conditioned rooms, a refreshing garden, a good-sized pool, big elevators, a bar-lounge, a restaurant, and free parking. A few rooms have views of La Cité (small Db-€110, moderate Db-€130, big Db-€175, Tb-€190, 18 rue Camille Saint-Saëns, tel. 04 68 11 92 82, fax 04 68 71 11 45, h1622@accor-hotels.com).

$$$ Hôtel des Trois Couronnes*** offers 40 good rooms with terrific views up to La Cité (and 40 non-view rooms that you don't want), all trapped in an ugly concrete shell. It's a 20-minute walk below La Cité, and 20 minutes on foot from the train station (Db with view-€107, air-con, Wi-Fi, elevator, indoor pool with views, garage-€8, 2 rue des Trois Couronnes, tel. 04 68 25 36 10, fax 04 68 25 92 92, www.hotel-destroiscouronnes.com, hotel3couronnes @wanadoo.fr). The reasonably priced restaurant also has good views.

$$ Hôtel Espace Cité**, two blocks downhill from Hôtel le Montmorency, is sterile and shiny, with small rooms, but it's handy for drivers (Db-€60–75, Tb-€75–90, Qb-€90–105, air-con, Internet access and Wi-Fi, 132 rue Trivalle, tel. 04 68 25 24 24, fax 04 68 25 17 17, www.hotelespacecite.fr, infos@hotelespacecite.fr).

At the Train Station

$$$ Hôtel du Soleil le Terminus***, just across from the train station, is turn-of-the-century faded-grand. The lobby reminds me of a train-station waiting hall. Rooms are big and comfortable, with high ceilings (standard Db-€92–122, superior Db-€122–140, air-con, elevator, Wi-Fi, lots of groups, 2 avenue Maréchal Joffre, tel. 04 68 25 25 00, fax 04 68 72 53 09, www.hotels-du-soleil.com, reservation@hotels-du-soleil.com). They have six bikes to rent to guests.

$ Hôtel Astoria* offers the cheapest hotel beds that I list. The tiled rooms are basic, modern, clean, and perfectly sleepable, and the owners are helpful. Call ahead—it's popular. From the train station, walk across the canal, turn left, and go two blocks (D-€28, Ds-€34, Db-€42–50, Tb/Qb-€54–64, 18 rue Tourtel, tel. 04 68 25 31 38, fax 04 68 71 34 14, www.astoriacarcassonne.com, hotel-astoria@wanadoo.fr).

Near Carcassonne, in Caunes-Minervois

To experience unspoiled, tranquil Languedoc, sleep surrounded by vineyards a 25-minute drive from Carcassonne, in the authentic-feeling village of Caunes-Minervois. Comfortably nestled in the foothills of the Montagne Noire, Caunes-Minervois offers an eighth-century abbey (complete with Internet access), two cafés, a good pizzeria, a few wineries, and very few tourists. My two recommendations sit side-by-side in the heart of the village, and their owners are eager to help you explore their region.

$$ Hôtel d'Alibert**, in a 15th-century home with ambience galore, has a mix of nicely renovated and good ol' traditional rooms. It's managed with a relaxed *je ne sais quoi* by Frédéric "call me Fredo" Dalibert (small Db-€52, standard Db-€72, huge Db-€82, extra person-€10, place de la Mairie, tel. 04 68 78 00 54, frederic.dalibert@wanadoo.fr). Eat lunch or dinner in his terrific restaurant (closed Sun–Mon).

$ L'Ancienne Boulangerie is a simple, relaxed place with thoughtfully appointed rooms and a breakfast terrace that will slow your pulse. Retired Irishmen Garreth and Roy run the place while their wives teach back home (Sb-€50, Db-€65, lofty family room-€70 per couple, €10 per child, includes breakfast, rue St. Genes, tel. 04 68 78 01 32, www.caunes-minervois .com/ancienboul.htm, ancienne.boulangerie@free.fr).

EATING

In La Cité

For a social dinner, take your pick from a food circus of basic eateries on a leafy courtyard—often with strolling musicians in the summer—on lively **place Marcou** (just inside the front gate and up to the left). While cassoulet (described under "Cuisine Scene" on page 411) is the traditional must, gourmet salads can provide a light yet rich alternative.

Hôtel de la Cité's **Barbacane Restaurant** owns Carcassonne's only Michelin star (€75 *menus*, see Hôtel de la Cité under "Sleeping—In Carcassonne's La Cité," page 433).

Au Comte Roger's quiet elegance seems out of place in this touristy town. For half the price of the Barbacane, you can celebrate a special occasion memorably. Chef Roger specializes in fresh products and Mediterranean cuisine. Ask for a table in the courtyard or dine inside with modern art, but book ahead (€30–40 *menus*, closed Sun–Mon, 14 rue St. Louis, tel. 04 68 11 93 40). Don't confuse this place with a part of the Hôtel du Donjon, called Le Comte Roger.

L'Auberge des Lices, a shy place hidden down a quiet lane, has a feminine interior, a peaceful courtyard, fine dishes, and the best balance of price and quality for traditional cuisine I found (€17 and €24 *menus*, closed Tue–Wed, 3 rue Raymond Roger Trencavel, tel. 04 68 72 34 07).

Le Tour DaveJean is a soft, intimate place where diners climb one level to enjoy a good meal at fair prices without sacrificing ambience (*menus* from €14, closed Tue–Wed, 32 rue du Plô, tel. 04 68 71 60 63).

At inexpensive **L'Auberge du Grand Puits,** you'll sit (best outside) in a flimsy chair to eat a copious meal served by a mellow Jerome (many choices, €16 *menu* is enough for two, open daily, great music, 1 place des Grands Puits, tel. 04 68 71 27 88).

Restaurant des Musées is as cheap and relaxed as it gets, with eager young servers hustling meals to diners as fast as they can with varying degrees of success. The terrace is far more appealing than the interior rooms (*menus* from €8.50, open daily; does not serve alcohol—but you can buy wine from nearby shop and bring it in; on the right as you enter La Cité on rue des Grands Puits.)

Restaurant le Richepin, in Hôtel des Trois Couronnes (described under "Sleeping—In Carcassonne's La Cité," page 433), gives you a panorama of Carcassonne—from the top floor of a concrete hotel (*menus* from €22, open daily, 2 rue des Trois Couronnes).

Le Bar à Vins is tucked away in a pleasant garden just inside the wall, but away from the crowds. It serves an enticing selection of open wines and €12 tapas—open-faced sandwiches, along with a meal-sized variety plate of ham, cheese, fish, and chorizo (€2 per glass of wine, mid-June–mid-Sept daily 10:00–2:00 in the morning, closes earlier off-season, 6 rue du Plô, tel. 04 68 47 38 38).

Picnics: Supplies can be gathered at the small *magasin d'alimentation* (grocery) on the main drag (generally open until at least 19:30). For your beggar's banquet, picnic on the city walls. For fast, cheap, hot food, look for places on the main drag that have quiche and pizza to go.

NIGHTLIFE

For relief from all the medieval kitsch, savor a drink in four-star library-meets-bar ambience at the **Hôtel de la Cité** bar (€8 for a glass of wine or beer). To enjoy the liveliest square with lots of tourists and strolling musicians, sip a drink or nibble a dessert on place Marcou. To be a medieval poet, share a bottle of wine in your own private niche somewhere remote on the ramparts. **Le Bar à Vins** offers jazz, good wines by the glass (€2), and a young crowd enjoying a garden in the moonshadow of the wall... without any tourists (described above, daily, 6 rue du Plô, tel. 04 68 47 38 38).

TRANSPORTATION CONNECTIONS

From Carcassonne by Train to: Sarlat (2/day in 4.5 hrs, with changes in Toulouse, Agen, and Le Buisson; or 3/day in 6–7 hrs via Souillac, with changes possible in Brive-la-Gaillarde and Toulouse, then bus from Souillac), **Arles** (6/day, 3 hrs, 3 require changes in Narbonne and Nîmes or Avignon), **Nice** (6/day, 6–9 hrs, fastest via change in Marseille), **Paris**' Gare Montparnasse (14/day, 6.5 hrs, most require changes in Toulouse or Montpellier, direct trains take 8 hrs, night train also available), **Toulouse** (hourly, 1 hr), **Barcelona** (3/day, 5–7 hrs, change in Narbonne and Port Bou, the border town).

Near Carcassonne

The land around Carcassonne is carpeted with vineyards and littered with romantically ruined castles, lost abbeys, and photogenic hill towns. The castle remains of Peyrepertuse and Quéribus make good stops between Carcassonne and Collioure (allow 2 hours from Carcassonne on narrow, winding roads). The gorge-village of Minerve works well for Provence-bound travelers.

Getting There: While public transportation is hopeless, taxis capable of seating six cost €150–200 for a day-long excursion (taxi tel. 04 68 71 50 50). The Carcassonne TI provides occasional excursion buses to these places (call for dates and times, usually €30–50 per person, tel. 04 68 10 25 35 or 04 68 10 24 30).

▲▲▲**Châteaux of Hautes Corbières**—Two hours south of Carcassonne, in the scenic foothills of the Pyrénées, lie a series of surreal, mountain-capping castle ruins. Like a Maginot Line of the 13th century, these sky-high castles were strategically located between France and the Spanish kingdom of Roussillon. As you can see by flipping through the picture books in Carcassonne

Near Carcassonne

20 MILES

20 KM

TO ALBI

TO BORDEAUX — A-68

TO ARLES & NICE

A-62

TOULOUSE

CASTRES

CAUNES-MINERVOIS

BARDOU

N-112

MONS ST. PONS

CASTEL-NAUDARY

MAZAMET

N-112

MINERVE

A-9

TO LOURDES

CANAL DU MIDI

LASTOURS

D-118

AZILLANET

BEZIERS

D-11

D-610

OLONZAC

NARBONNE

CARCASSONNE

A-61

N-20

D-119

LIMOUX

CORBIERES

D-613

M E D.

FOIX

D-118

SEA

QUILLAN

CUBIERES

D-117

PEYREPERTUSE

ST. PAUL

MAURY

QUERIBUS

P Y R E N E E S

ANDORRA

PERPIGNAN

N-114

ARGELES-SUR-MER

CERET

A-9

COLLIOURE

BANYULS

CERBERE

PORT BOU

DCH

FIGUERES

CADAQUES

S P A I N

TO BARCELONA

— AUTOROUTE (TOLL)
— OTHER ROADS
◪ CASTLES

tourist shops, these castles' crumbled ruins are an impressive contrast to the restored walls of La Cité. Bring a good map (lots of
tiny roads) and sturdy walking shoes—prepare for a climb, and be
wary of slick stones.

The most spectacular is the château of **Peyrepertuse,** where
the ruins seem to grow right out from the narrow splinter of cliff.
The views are sensational—you can almost reach out and touch
Spain. Let your imagination soar, but watch your step as you try
to reconstruct this eagle's nest (€5, daily July–Aug 9:00–20:30,
April–June and Sept 10:00–19:00, Oct 10:00–18:00, Nov–March
10:00–17:00, tel. 04 68 45 40 55 or 06 71 58 63 36, www.chateau
-peyrepertuse.com). Canyon-lovers will enjoy the detour to the
nearby and narrow **Gorges de Galamus,** just north of St. Paul de
Fenouillet. Closer to D-117, impressive **Quéribus** towers above the
road and requires a steep hike. It's famous as the last Cathar castle
to fall and was left useless after 1659, when the border between
France and Spain was moved farther south into the high Pyrénées
(same cost and hours as Peyrepertuse).

The next two Cathar sights tie in well with a visit to Caunes-Minervois (described under "Near Carcassonne, in Caunes-Minervois," page 436), and provide an easy excursion from Carcassonne, offering you a taste of this area's appealing countryside.

Châteaux of Lastours—Ten miles north of Carcassonne, these four ruined castles cap a barren hilltop and give drivers a handy (if less dramatic) look at the region's Cathar castles. From Carcassonne, follow signs to *Mazamet,* then *Conques-sur-Orbiel,* then *Lastours.* In Lastours, you can hike to the castle or drive to a viewpoint.

Hikers park at the lot as they enter the village, walk 10 minutes upriver to the glass entry (look for *Accueil* signs), then walk 20 minutes uphill to the castles (allow at least an hour for a reasonable tour). The castles surrounded a fortified village and date from the 11th century. The village welcomed Cathars (becoming a bishop's seat at one point) but paid for this "tolerance" with destruction by French troops in 1227. Everyone should make the short drive to the belvedere for a smashing panorama over the castles (€5—access to castles and belvedere viewpoint, €2—belvedere viewpoint only, July–Aug daily 9:00–20:00, April–Sept daily 10:00–18:00, Oct daily 10:00–17:00, Nov–Mar Sat–Sun 10:00–17:00 only. An idyllic lunch awaits near the lower entry at **Le Moulin,** where a small bakery has arranged a few tables serenely overlooking the river (good quiche, sandwiches, drinks, closed Thu).

▲Minerve—A one-time Cathar hideout, the spectacular village of Minerve is sculpted out of a deep canyon that provided a natural defense. Strong as it was, it couldn't keep out the Pope's armies, and the village was razed during the vicious Albigensian Crusades. The view from the small parking lot alone (€2) justifies the detour. Cross the bridge on foot, then wander into the village to its upper end and a ruined tower. A worthwhile path leads across from the tower, around the village, and  down to the river (watch your step as you descend); you can re-enter the village from the riverbed at its lower end.

Minerve has two pleasant cafés, one hotel, a nifty little bookshop, a few wine shops, and a smattering of art galleries. You'll also find two intriguing museums: a little prehistory museum, and the compact **Hurepel de Minerve** with models from the Cathar era that describe this terrible time (€2.50, excellent English explanations, interesting for kids, daily April–Oct 10:00–12:45 & 14:00–18:00).

Sleeping and Eating in Minerve: Stay here and melt into southern France (almost literally, if it's summer). **$ Relais Chantovent's** simple but spotless rooms are designed for those who came to get away from it all—no phones and no TV but lots of quiet (Db-€41–53, tel. 04 68 91 14 18, fax 04 68 91 81 99, www.relais.chantovent.fr). Its sharp restaurant deserves your business and is popular, so reserve ahead (*menus* from €26, closed Sun–Mon). The **Café de la Place** provides the perfect break and has a pool for anyone's use (€3, tel. 05 68 91 22 94).

Getting There: Minerve is between Carcassonne and Béziers, nine miles northeast of Olonzac and 40 minutes by car from Carcassonne. It's a good stop between Provence and Carcassonne.

Wine-Tasting: In the mood to sample some wine? Stop at **Domaine de Pech d'André** and visit my friends Monsieur and Madame Remaury. They offer a good selection and an exquisite setting in which to sample the local product (coming from Minerve, it's just past Azillanet, look for *Domaine* signs on your left, tel. 04 68 91 22 66, a leetle English spoken).

Collioure

Surrounded by less-appealing resorts, lovely Collioure is blessed with a privileged climate and a romantic setting. By Mediterranean standards, this seaside village should be overrun—it has everything. Like an ice-cream shop, Collioure offers 31 flavors of pastel houses and six petite, scooped-out, pebbled beaches sprinkled with visitors. This sweet scene, capped by a winking lighthouse, sits under a once-mighty castle in the shade of the Pyrénées. Evenings are best in Collioure—as the sky darkens, yellow lamps reflect warm pastels and deep blues.

Just 15 miles from the Spanish border, Collioure (Cotlliure in Catalan) shares a common history and independent attitude with its Catalan siblings on the other side of the border. Happily French yet proudly Catalan, it sports the yellow-and-red flag of Catalunya, street names in both French and Catalan, and business names with *el* and *las*, rather than *le* and *les*. Sixty years ago, most villagers spoke Catalan, and today the language is enjoying a resurgence as Collioure rediscovers its roots.

Come here to unwind and regroup. Even with its crowds of vacationers in peak season (July and August are jammed),

Collioure is what many look for when they head to the Riviera—a sunny, relaxing splash in the Mediterranean.

Planning Your Time

Check your ambition at the station. Enjoy a slow coffee on *le Med*, lose yourself in the old town's streets, compare the *gelati* shops on rue Vauban, and snuggle into a pebble-sand beach (waterproof shoes are helpful). And if you have a car, don't miss a drive into the hills above Collioure (described below).

ORIENTATION

Most of Collioure's shopping, sights, and hotels are in the old town, across the drainage channel from Château Royal. There are good views of the old town from across the bay near the recommended Hôtel Boramar, and brilliant views from the hills above.

Tourist Information

The TI hides behind the main beachfront cafés at 5 place du 18 Juin (July–Aug Mon–Sat 9:00–20:00, Sun 10:00–18:00; April–June and Sept Mon–Sat 9:00–12:00 & 14:00–19:00, closed Sun; Oct–March Tue–Sat 9:00–12:00 & 14:00–19:00, closed Sun–Mon; tel. 04 68 82 15 47, www.collioure.com).

Arrival in Collioure

By Train: Walk out of the station (which has no baggage check), turn right, and follow the road downhill for 10 minutes until you see Hôtel Fregate (hotels are listed from this reference point). The station ticket office has irregular hours; if they're open, pick up a schedule for any Spain side-trips or for your next destination.

    By Car: Collioure is 16 miles south of Perpignan. Take the *Perpignan-Sud Sortie* exit from the autoroute and follow signs to *Argelès-sur-Mer* (also called simply *Argelès*), then *Collioure*. Parking is tricky, and almost impossible in summer—arrive early or late. Follow *Collioure Centre-Ville* signs, turn left onto rue de la République when you see the *Garage Renault* sign, and look for any available spots. There's a big pay lot (Parking Glacis) off rue de la République (stay right at the bottom of rue de la République and pass through a metered lot, about €1.40/hour, €9/24 hours). Ask your hotelier for parking suggestions, and take everything of value out of the car.

Helpful Hints

Market Days: Markets are held on Wednesday and Sunday mornings on place Maréchal Leclerc, across from Hôtel Fregate.

Collioure

TO
AUTOROUTE &
CARCASSONNE

100 YARDS

100 METERS

P – PARKING

TRAIN STN.

TO
OVERFLOW
PARKING

ROUTE ARGELES

AVE. MAILLOL

PLACE LECLERC

AVE. MIRADOU

❶ Hôtel Casa Pairal
❷ Hôtel les Templiers
❸ Hôtel Princes de Catalogne
❹ Peroneille's Chambres
❺ Hôtel Boramar
❻ Hôtel les Caranques
❼ Le Tremail Restaurant
❽ La Marinade Restaurant
❾ Café Copacabana

❿ La Neptune Restaurant
⓫ Brasserie au Casot
⓬ Les Caves du Roussillon Wine Shop
⓭ Launderettes (2)
⓮ Promenade sur Mer Cruises
⓯ Garage Renault (Car Rental)
⓰ Café Sola (Internet)
⓱ Espace Fauve

RUE REPUBLIQUE
AVE. DE GAULLE
ONE WAY
Parking Glacis
ONE WAY
POST
WC

CHATEAU ROYAL
WC

KIDS' PLAY AREA
TRAIL TO WINDMILL & ST. ELME
BOULES
PORT D'AVALL BEACH (SANDY)

RUE DEMOCRATIE

RUE JEAN BART
MUSEUM

LA BALETTE BEACH (QUIET)

TO BANYULS & SPAIN

RUE PELLETAN
JAUBAN
BLVD BORAMAR
AVE. PASTEUR ARAGO
FERRY
AVE. BIRADOU

NORD BEACH (ROCKY)

BORAMAR BEACH (ROCKY)

NOTRE-DAME DES ANGES

ST. VINCENT BEACH (SANDY)

CHAPELLE ST. VINCENT

MEDITERRANEAN SEA

DCH

Internet Access: Try the lighthearted **Café Sola,** next to the recommended Hôtel Casa Pairal (daily, about 7:00–21:00 or later, free Wi-Fi if you buy a drink, or use their computers, 2 avenue de la République, tel. 04 68 82 55 02).

Laundry: Laverie 3L will do your laundry while you do your relaxing (daily July–Aug 9:00–19:00, otherwise 9:00–12:00 & 15:00–18:00, at roundabout at 28 rue de la République, tel. 04 68 98 04 17; the sign tells you to drop laundry next door at Immosud). There's also a **self-serve launderette** a block away (daily 7:00–21:00, across from bike shop, near 10 rue de Gaulle).

Taxi: Call 04 68 82 27 80 or 04 68 82 09 30.

Car Rental: National is located in Garage Renault, opposite the launderette on rue de la République (tel. 04 68 82 08 34).

SIGHTS

There's no important sight here except what lies on the beach and the views over Collioure. Indulge in a long seaside lunch, inspect the colorful art galleries, catch up on your postcards, and maybe take a hike. Don't be surprised to see French Marines playing commando in their rafts; Collioure's bay caters to more than just sun-loving tourists.

View from the Beach—Walk out to the jetty's end, past the church and past the little chapel with the Matisse poster, and find a seat above the beach. Collioure has been a popular place since long before your visit. For more than 2,500 years, people have fought to control its enviable position on the Mediterranean at the foot of the Pyrénées. The mountains that rise behind Collioure provide a natural defense, while its port gives it a commercial edge. This combination made Collioure an irresistible target. A string of forts defended Collioure's landlocked side. To the left, you can see the still-standing Fort St. Elme (built by powerful Spanish king Charles V, the same guy who built El Escorial near Madrid). The 2,100-foot-high observation tower of Madeloc rises high above, front and center, and scattered ruins crown several other hilltops. To the far right, the 18th-century *citadelle*, Fort Mirador, is now home to a French Marine base. Back to the left, that ancient windmill (1344) was originally used for grain; today it grinds out olive oil.

Collioure's medieval town gathers between its church and royal château, sandwiched defensively and spiritually between the two. The town was batted back and forth between the French and Spanish for centuries. Locals just wanted to be left alone—as Catalans—and most still do (notice the yellow-and-red Catalan flag flying above the château). It was Spanish for nearly 400 years before becoming definitively French in 1659 (*merci* to Louis XIV). After years of neglect, Collioure was rediscovered by artists drawn to its pastel houses and lovely setting. Henri Matisse, André Derain, Pablo Picasso, Georges Braque, Raoul Dufy, and Marc Chagall all parked their brushes here at one time or another. In fact, you're likely to recognize Collioure in paintings in many museums in Europe.

Château Royal (Royal Castle)—The 800-year-old castle, built over Roman ruins, served as home over the years to Majorcan kings, Crusaders, Dominican monks, and Louis XIV (who had the final say on the appearance we see now). Today, it serves tourists, offering great rampart walks, views, and mildly interesting local history exhibits (€4, daily June–Sept 10:00–18:00, Oct–May 9:00–17:00, last entry 45 min before closing, tel. 04 68 82 06 43).

Notre-Dame des Anges (Our Lady of the Angels Church)—This waterfront church is worth a gander—after all, how many times can you hear waves crashing when you're inside a church? Supporting a guiding light (in more than one way), its foundations are built into the sea, and its one-of-a-kind lighthouse–bell tower helped sailors return home safely. The highlight is its over-the-top golden altar, unusual in France but typical of Catalan churches across the border. Drop €1 in the box to the left of the altar: lights, cameras, reaction—wow! (Daily 9:00–12:00 & 14:00–18:00.)

Path of Fauvism (Chemin du Fauvisme)—As you stroll Collioure's lanes, notice occasional prints hanging on the walls. You're on the "Chemin du Fauvisme," where you'll find 20 copies of Derain's and Matisse's works, inspired by their stays in Collioure in 1905. The **Espace Fauve** office, across from the château at the foot of the footbridge, sells well-done booklets that feature postcard-size images of the works and identify where the copies are mounted in Collioure (June–Sept daily 9:30–12:00 & 15:00–19:00, Oct–May closed Mon and weekend mornings, quai de l'Amirauté, tel. 04 68 98 07 16). As with Arles and Vincent van Gogh, there are no original paintings by Derain or Matisse here for the public to enjoy. However, the museum in Céret has a good collection (page 447), as does the recommended Hôtel les Templiers (page 448).

Beaches (Plages)—You'll usually find the best sand-to-stone ratio at plage St. Vincent and at plage de Port d'Avall (sporadically open paddleboat/kayak rental-€11/hr). The tiny plage de la Balette is quietest, with views of Collioure.

Wine-Tasting—Collioure and the surrounding area produce well-respected wines, and many shops offer informal tastings of the sweet Banyuls and Collioure reds and rosés. Try **Les Caves du Roussillon,** with a good selection from many wineries and good prices (daily 10:00–13:00 & 15:00–20:00, next to Hôtel Fregate at 6 place Maréchal Leclerc).

Cruise—Mildly interesting **Promenades sur Mer** boat excursions provide views of Collioure from the Mediterranean as they cruise toward Spain and back (€8, 60-min tour, 3–5/day Easter–Sept weather permitting, leaves from breakwater near château, commentary in French only, tel. 04 68 81 43 88).

Hikes

The three views described below offer different perspectives of this beautiful area.

Stone Windmill—Stone steps lead 10 minutes up behind Collioure's museum to a 13th-century windmill with magnificent views that are positively peachy at sunset. Find the museum behind Hôtel Triton, walk through its stony backyard, and follow the paved path marked with yellow dashes. Bring your own beverage.

▲**Hike to Fort St. Elme**—This vertical hike (one hour each way) is best done early or late (no shade) and is worth the sweat, even if you don't make it to the top (trail starts from windmill described above). You can't miss the square castle lurking high above Collioure. The view from the top is sensational, though the privately owned castle is not open to the public.

Cheaters can do it by car. Drive to Port Vendres, then find the small sign marked *Fort St. Elme* on your right just before leaving the port (the road also leads to a supermarket). Continue on the small road that leads up from behind the train station.

▲▲▲**Drive/Hike Through Vineyards to Madeloc Tower (Tour de Madeloc)**—Check your vertigo at the hotel, fasten your seatbelt, and take this drive-and-hike combination high above Collioure. The narrow road, hairpin turns, and absence of guardrails only add to the experience, as Collioure shrinks to Lego-size and the clouds become your neighbors. Leave Collioure and head toward Perpignan, and look for signs reading *Tour de Madeloc* at the roundabout above the town. Climb through impossibly steep and rocky terraced vineyards, following *Tour* and *Balcon de Madeloc* signs. After about 20 minutes, you'll come to a fork in the road with a paved path (and a *Do Not Enter* sign that applies to cars) and a road leading downhill (the sign identifies it as *La Route des Vignobles*—The Route of the Vineyards). Park at the fork in the road, and walk 10–15 minutes up the paved path to the first ruined structure (the *Balcon*). The views everywhere are magnificent—the Pyrénées on one side, and the beach towns of Port Vendres and Collioure on the other (scenic picnic tables provided). While this satisfies most, you can continue hiking up and up the tiny road to *la Tour* (the Tower) and commune with the gods. Allow an hour at a slow yet steady pace along the splintered ridgetop, and you'll reach the eagle's-nest setting of this ancient tower, now fitted with communication devices. There's no shade, so do this hike early or late in the day. Once you're back down among mortals, you can return to Collioure following *La Route des Vignobles* to Banyuls-sur-Mer, then take coastal N-114 to Collioure and your hotel.

Near Collioure

Day Trip to Spain—The 15-mile, 40-minute coastal drive via the Col de Banyuls into Spain is beautiful and well worth the countless curves, even if you don't venture past the border.

Train travelers can day-trip to Spain, either to **Barcelona** (3 hrs one-way, 4/day) or, closer, to **Figueres** (1.5 hrs) and its Salvador Dalí museum (June daily 9:30–18:30; July–Sept daily 9:00–20:00; March and Oct Tue–Sun 9:30–18:30 closed Mon; Nov–Feb Tue–Sun 10:30–18:00, closed Mon; last entry 45 min before closing, Spanish tel. 972-677-500, www.salvador-dali.org). Get train schedules at the station. Since Figueres is just off the autoroute, it works well for drivers, too.

Céret—To see the art that Collioure inspired, you'll have to drive 25 windy miles inland to this pleasant town, featuring fountains and mountains at its doorstep. Céret's claim to fame is its modern-art museum with works by some of Collioure's more famous visitors, including Picasso, Joan Miró, Chagall, and Matisse (€5.50, daily mid-June–mid-Sept 10:00–19:00, otherwise 10:00–18:00, tel. 04 68 87 27 76). This makes a good day trip from Collioure (allow 40 min to Céret by car, or take a train to nearby Perpignan and a bus from there—get details at TI).

SLEEPING

(€1 = about $1.30, country code: 33)

Collioure has a fair range of hotels at favorable rates. You have two good choices for your hotel's location: central, in the old town (closer to train station); or across the bay, with views of the old town (10-min walk from the central zone, with easier parking).

In the Old Town

Directions to the following places are given from the big Hôtel Fregate, at the edge of the old town, a five-minute walk down from the train station. Price ranges reflect low versus high season.

$$$ Hôtel Casa Pairal***, opposite Hôtel Fregate and hiding down a short alley (behind Café Sola), is Mediterranean-elegant and Collioure's best splurge. Enter to the sounds of a fountain gurgling in the flowery courtyard. Reclining lounges await in the garden and by the pool. The rooms are quiet, comfortable, and tastefully designed. "Medium" rooms, on the first floor, have high ceilings and small balconies over a courtyard (small Db-€85–95, medium Db-€115–155, big Db suite with terrace-€168–188, extra bed-€24, air-con, parking-€8, impasse des Palmiers, tel. 04 68 82 05 81, fax 04 68 82 52 10, www.hotel-casa-pairal.com, contact @hotel-casa-pairal.com, reserve ahead for room and parking).

$$ Hôtel les Templiers, in the thick of things in the old town, has wall-to-wall paintings squeezed in every available space, a perennially popular café-bar, and good-value rooms. The paintings were payments in kind and thank-yous from artists who have stayed here—find the black-and-white photo in the bar of the hotel's owner with Picasso. The rooms—some of which have views—are either new and modern, or older and characteristic (standard Db-€60–70, bigger Db-€72–86, ask about connecting family rooms, pass on their annex rooms unless they're next to main hotel block, air-con, a block toward beach from Hôtel Fregate along drainage canal at 12 quai de l'Amirauté, tel. 04 68 98 31 10, fax 04 68 98 01 24, www.hotel-templiers.com, info @hotel-templiers.com).

$$ Hôtel Princes de Catalogne* offers 29 comfortable, spacious, American-style rooms (Db-€66–73, extra person-€12, air-con, next to Casa Pairal, rue des Palmiers, tel. 04 68 98 30 00, fax 04 68 98 30 31, www.hotel-princescatalogne.com, contact @hotel-princescatalogne.com). Get a room on the quieter mountain side—*côté montagne* (coat-ay mon-tan-yah).

$ Monsieur and Madame Peroneille's Chambres, on the pedestrian street two blocks past Hôtel Fregate, are the cheapest rooms in the old town. The rooms are simple, clean, and mostly spacious. The more serious Monsieur (who speaks Catalan) and bubbly Madame are both in their late 80s and have rented these rooms for more than 30 years without learning a word of English—so don't hold your breath (Sb-€32, D-€40, Db-€45, Tb-€65, Qb-€70, cash only, 20 rue Pasteur, tel. 04 68 82 15 31, fax 04 68 82 35 94). The rooms in the main building *(la maison principale)* are better than the cheaper rooms in the annex, but both are acceptable. Ask to see the rooftop terrace.

Across the Bay

$$ Hôtel les Caranques, a few curves toward Spain from Collioure's center, tumbles down the cliffs and showcases million-dollar sea views from each of its small, spotless, modestly decorated rooms (most with balconies beyond sliding glass doors). Enjoy the view terraces with mod plastic furniture, and the four-star breakfast-room panorama. This idyllic place, run by gentle Monsieur and Madame Sarrazin, is a steal (D-€45, Db-€70–82, most are €72, route de Port Vendres, 30-min walk from train station, tel. 04 68 82 06 68, fax 04 68 82 00 92, www.les-caranques.com, contact @les-caranques.com). To scenically walk to Collioure's center, follow the sidewalk, then turn right down the steps just after the *Relais des Trois Mas* sign.

$ Hôtel Boramar**, which faces Collioure's center across the bay, is understated and modest, but well-maintained. Get a room with a terrace facing the sea and smile...or sleep elsewhere (Db without view-€59, Db with view-€69, Tb with view-€72, rue Jean Bart, tel. 04 68 82 07 06, www.hotel-boramar.com).

EATING

Try the local wine and eat anything Catalan, including the fish and anchovies (hand-filleted, as no machine has ever been able to accomplish this precise task).

All of my recommended restaurants have indoor and outdoor tables, and most are in the old town (the first three are within 50 yards of each other). Your task is to decide whether you want to eat well or with a view. Several delicious *gelati* shops and a Grand Marnier crêpe stand next to the Café Copacabana fuel after-dinner strollers with the perfect last course. If you're traveling off-season, call ahead, since many restaurants here are closed December through February.

Café Copacabana, on the main beach (Boramar), offers big salads and a few seafood dishes in its sandy café. Skip their sidewalk-bound restaurant (which has a bigger selection but smaller view) and find a red sway-back chair beachside. The quality is good enough, considering the view, and it's family-friendly—kids can play on the beach while you dine (daily mid-March–mid-Dec, plage Boramar, tel. 04 68 82 06 74, best at sunset).

Le Tremail is *the* place to go for contemporary seafood and Catalan specialties served outside or in. It's a small, popular place one block from the bay, where rue Arago and rue Mailly meet. Reserve ahead if you can (€22–34 *menus*, open daily, 16 bis rue Mailly, tel. 04 68 82 16 10).

La Marinade, across from the TI, is a consistently good bet for seafood served in a lively outdoor setting (*menus* from €20, 14 place du 18 Juin, tel. 04 68 82 09 76).

Brasserie au Casot owns the best setting away from the crowds, past the church on plage St. Vincent, and serves salads and *plats* with views for a fair price. Matisse would dig the decor (daily June–Sept 11:00–20:00 weather permitting, lunch only Oct and May, closed on Thu in winter, plage St. Vincent, tel. 04 68 22 42 46).

La Neptune, across the bay, dishes up top seafood and views of Collioure to discerning diners. Dress up a bit, cross the bay, and ask for a table with a view (*menus* from €40, closed Tue–Wed, 9 route de Port Vendres, tel. 04 68 82 02 27).

Small places sell a variety of meals to go (*à emporter;* ah em-pohr-tay) for budget-minded romantics wanting to dine on the bay.

For post-dinner fun, head to one of the bayfront cafés on plage Boramar, or try the recommended **Hôtel les Templiers** and get down with the locals (daily, 12 quai de l'Amirauté, tel. 04 68 98 31 10).

TRANSPORTATION CONNECTIONS

From Collioure by Train to: Carcassonne (9/day, 2 hrs, most require change in Narbonne), **Paris** (5/day, 6 hrs, changes in Perpignan or Montpellier and Lyon, then TGV to Gare Montparnasse, one direct train to Gare d'Austerlitz in 10 hrs, plus a handy night train), **Barcelona** (6/day, 3–4 hrs, change in Cerbère), **Figueres,** Spain (2/day, 1.5 hrs, transfer in Cerbère), **Avignon/Arles** (7/day, 3.5 hrs, many transfer points possible). Consider handy night trains to Paris, key Italy destinations, and Geneva, Switzerland. The train station's ticket office closes at 17:45 (tel. 04 68 82 05 89).

PROVENCE

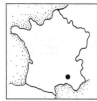

This magnificent region is shaped like a giant wedge of quiche. From its sunburned crust, fanning out along the Mediterranean coast from Nîmes to Nice, it stretches north along the Rhône River Valley to Orange. The Romans were here in force and left many ruins—some of the best anywhere. Seven popes; great artists such as van Gogh, Cézanne, and Picasso; and author Peter Mayle all enjoyed their years in Provence. The region offers a splendid recipe of arid climate (except for occasional vicious winds, known as the mistral), captivating cities, exciting hill towns, dramatic scenery, and oceans of vineyards.

Explore the ghost town that is ancient Les Baux and see France's greatest Roman ruin, the Pont du Gard. Spend your starry, starry nights where van Gogh did, in Arles. Uncover its Roman past, then find the linger-longer squares and café corners that inspired Vincent. Youthful but classy Avignon bustles in the shadow of its brooding pope's palace. It's a short hop from Arles or Avignon into the splendid scenery and villages of the Côtes du Rhône and Luberon regions that make Provence so popular today.

Planning Your Time

Make Arles or Avignon your sightseeing base, particularly if you have no car. Arles has a blue-collar quality and good-value hotels, while Avignon (three times larger than Arles) feels sophisticated and offers more nightlife and shopping. Italophiles prefer smaller Arles, while poodles pick urban Avignon.

To measure the pulse of Provence, spend at least one night in a smaller town. Vaison la Romaine is ideal for those heading to/ from the north, and Isle-sur-la-Sorgue is centrally located between

Avignon and the Luberon. Most destinations are accessible by public transit, though bus service can be sketchy.

You'll want a full day for sightseeing in Arles (best on Wed or Sat, when the morning market rages), a half-day for Avignon, and a day or two for the villages and sights in the countryside.

Getting Around Provence

By Car: The Michelin map #528 is good for drivers and covers the Riviera as well as Provence (map #332 also works, but covers only Provence). Avignon (pop. 100,000) is a headache for drivers; Arles (pop. 35,000) is easier, though it still requires go-cart driving skills. Park only in well-watched spaces, and leave nothing in your car. If you're heading north from Provence, consider a three-hour detour through the spectacular Ardèche Gorges (see page 519).

By Train or Bus: Travelers relying on public transportation might find their choices limited. Public transit is good between cities and decent to some towns, but marginal at best to the villages.

Frequent trains link Avignon and Arles (about 20 min between each). Orange is easy from Avignon by train. Buses connect smaller towns (including Les Baux in July–Aug, which otherwise can be reached only by taxi or tour).

Isle-sur-la-Sorgue offers the most accessible small-town experience (an easy hop by train or bus from Avignon). The Pont du Gard—and, to a lesser extent, Vaison la Romaine and some Côtes du Rhône villages—are also connected by bus from Avignon.

Tours of Provence

Wine Safari—Dutchman Mike Rijken runs a one-man show, taking travelers through the region he adopted 20 years ago. Mike came to France to train as a chef, later became a wine steward, and has now found his calling as a driver/guide. His English is fluent, and while his focus is wine and wine villages, Mike knows the region thoroughly and is a good teacher of its history (€45/half-day, €90/day, priced per person; tel. 04 90 35 59 21, mobile 06 19 29 50 81, www.winesafari.net, mikeswinesafari@wanadoo.fr).

Taxi des Oliviers—Friendly Frenchman Roland Vanove offers tours with English commentary. His air-conditioned minivan has room for up to eight people (the same price regardless of the number of passengers). He'll take you wherever you like in his native Provence, or to the Riviera (no preset itineraries). Roland's services are a boon for carless visitors wanting to explore the Luberon and the Côtes du Rhône villages near Vaison la Romaine. He'll happily shuttle bikers to or from their destination, allowing rides to areas farther afield (€280/day, ask about shuttle-trip rates, best to contact by phone, tel. 06 80 75 40 90, taxidesoliviers@wanadoo.fr).

Provence

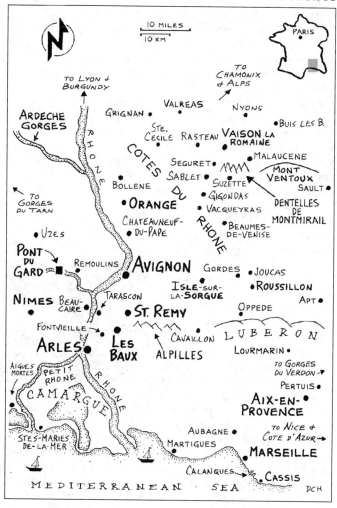

Visit Provence—This tour company, based in Avignon, offers a good variety of guided tours to most destinations covered in this book. They have eight-seat minivans and English commentary (about €50/half-day, €100/day; they'll pick you up at your hotel in Avignon). Their Hop On/Off tour is a clever service, with a bus circulating between Avignon, the Pont du Gard, Les Baux, and St. Rémy several times a day, allowing travelers to linger at a sight—and catch the next bus—if they prefer (€60, valid for two days, June–Sept). Other day-trip destinations vary, but may include Aix-en-Provence, Cassis, and Marseille (last tour of the day allows a drop-off at the TGV station in Marseille, saving money and time if you're headed to the Riviera next). Not all tours include entry fees for sights, but reservations are required for all. Ask about their cheaper big-bus excursions, or consider hiring a van and driver for your own private use (plan on €210/half-day, €400/day, tel. 04 90 14 70 00, check website for current destinations, www.provence -reservation.com).

Lieutaud—This company operates cheap, unguided big-bus excursions from Avignon to many hard-to-reach places at a fraction of the price you'd pay for a taxi (admission fees not included). Different itineraries are available each day, and these can change with the season. Trips often include the Pont du Gard (€20/half-day, 3/week) and Les Baux and the Alpilles Mountains (€22/half-day, 2/week, tel. 04 90 86 36 75, www.cars-lieutaud.fr).

Cuisine Scene in Provence

The almost extravagant use of garlic, olive oil, herbs, and tomatoes makes Provence's cuisine France's liveliest. To sample it, order anything *à la provençale*.

Among the area's spicy specialties are ratatouille (a thick mixture of vegetables in an herb-flavored tomato sauce), *brandade* (a salt cod, garlic, and cream mousse), aioli (a garlicky mayonnaise, often served atop fresh vegetables, potatoes, fish, or whatever), tapenade (a paste of pureed olives, capers, anchovies, herbs, and sometimes tuna), *soupe au pistou* (vegetable soup with basil, garlic, and cheese), and *soupe à l'ail* (garlic soup). Look also for *riz camarguaise* (rice from the Camargue) and *taureau* (bull meat). Banon (wrapped in chestnut leaves) and Picodon (nutty taste) are the native cheeses. The region's sheep's milk cheese, Brousse, is creamy and fresh. Provence also produces some of France's great wines at relatively reasonable prices. Look for Gigondas, Sablet, Côtes du Rhône, and Côte de Provence. If you like rosé, try the Tavel. This is the place to splurge for a bottle of Châteauneuf-du-Pape.

Remember, restaurants serve only during lunch (11:30–14:00) and dinner (19:00–21:00, later in bigger cities), but some cafés serve food throughout the day.

Provence Market Days

Provençal market days offer France's most colorful and tantalizing outdoor shopping. The best markets are on Monday in Cavaillon, Tuesday in Vaison la Romaine, Wednesday in St. Rémy, Thursday

Le Mistral

Provence lives with its vicious mistral winds, which blow 30–60 miles per hour, about 100 days out of the year. Locals say it blows in multiples of threes: three, six, or nine days in a row. *Le mistral* clears people off the streets and turns lively cities into virtual ghost towns. You'll likely spend a few hours taking refuge—or searching for cover. The winds are strongest between 12:00 and 15:00.

When *le mistral* blows, it's everywhere, and you can't escape. Author Peter Mayle said it could blow the ears off a donkey. Locals say it ruins crops, shutters, and roofs (look for the stones holding tiles in place on many homes). They'll also tell you that this pernicious wind has driven many crazy (including young Vincent van Gogh). A weak version of the wind is called a *mistralet.*

The mistral starts above the Alps and Massif Central mountains and gathers steam as it heads south, gaining momentum as it screams over the Rhône River Valley (which acts like a funnel between the Alps and Pyrénées) before exhausting itself as it hits the Mediterranean. While this wind rattles shutters throughout the Riviera and Provence, it's strongest over the Rhône River Valley...so Avignon, Arles, and the Côtes du Rhône villages bear its brunt. While wiping the dust from your eyes, remember the good news: The mistral brings clear skies.

in Nyons, Friday in Lourmarin, Saturday in Arles, Uzès, and Apt, and, best of all, Sunday in Isle-sur-la-Sorgue. Crowds and parking problems abound at these popular events—arrive by 9:00, or, even better, sleep in the town the night before.

Monday:	Cavaillon, Bedoin (between Vaison la Romaine and Mont Ventoux)
Tuesday:	Vaison la Romaine, Tarascon, Gordes, and Lacoste
Wednesday:	St. Rémy, Arles, Uzès, and Malaucène (near Vaison la Romaine)
Thursday:	Nyons, Beaucaire, Vacqueyras, Roussillon, and Isle-sur-la-Sorgue
Friday:	Lourmarin, Remoulins (near the Pont du Gard), Bonnieux, and Châteauneuf-du-Pape
Saturday:	Arles, Uzès, Apt, and Valréas (north of Vaison la Romaine)
Sunday:	Isle-sur-la-Sorgue, Coustellet, Mausanne (near Les Baux), and Beaucaire

Arles

By helping Julius Caesar defeat Marseille, Arles (pronounced "arl") earned the imperial nod and was made an important port city. With the first bridge over the Rhône River, Arles was a key stop on the Roman road from Italy to Spain, the Via Domitia. After reigning as the seat of an important archbishop and a trading center for centuries, the city became a sleepy backwater of little importance in the 1700s. Vincent van Gogh settled here a hundred years ago, but left only a chunk of his ear (now gone). American bombers destroyed much of Arles in World War II as the townsfolk hid out in its underground Roman galleries. But today, Arles thrives again, with its evocative Roman ruins, an eclectic assortment of museums, made-for-ice-cream pedestrian zones, and squares that play hide-and-seek with visitors. It's an understandably popular home base from which to explore Provence.

ORIENTATION

Arles faces the Mediterranean and turns its back on Paris. While the town is built along the Rhône, it completely ignores the river (it was the part of Arles most damaged by Allied bombers in World War II, and therefore the least appealing today).

Landmarks hide in Arles' medieval tangle of narrow, winding streets. Virtually everything is close—but first-time visitors can walk forever to get there. Hotels have good, free city maps, and Arles provides helpful street-corner signs that point you toward sights and hotels. Racing cars enjoy Arles' medieval lanes, turning sidewalks into tightropes and pedestrians into leaping targets.

Tourist Information

The **main TI** is on the ring road, boulevard des Lices, at esplanade Charles de Gaulle (April–Sept daily 9:00–18:45; Oct–March Mon–Sat 9:00–16:45, Sun 10:00–13:00; tel. 04 90 18 41 20, www.arlestourisme.com). There's also a **train station TI** (Mon–Fri 9:00–13:00 & 14:00–16:45, closed Sat–Sun). Pick up the city map with current museum prices and hours, note the bus schedules (in books), and get English information on nearby destinations such as the Camargue wildlife area (described in the next chapter). Ask about bullgames (Provence's more humane version of bullfights— see "Sights and Activities" in Arles, page 467) and walking tours of Arles. If you're a van Gogh fan, buy the €1 Arles Walking Tours brochure locating his "easels," explained on page 464). Both TIs charge €1 to reserve hotel rooms (you'll pay a small fraction of the room price here, and the rest at the hotel).

Arrival in Arles

By Train: The train station is on the river, a 10-minute walk from the town center (baggage storage nearby, see "Helpful Hints," below). Before heading into town, get what you need at the train station TI (see previous page).

To reach the town center, turn left out of the train station, or take bus #3 from the shelter directly across from the station (2/hr, €0.80, buy ticket from driver). Taxis generally wait out front; if not, call the numbers posted (rates are fixed, allow about €9 to any of my recommended hotels).

By Bus: The Centre-Ville bus station is in the city center, a few blocks below the main TI on the ring road (16–24 boulevard Georges Clemenceau).

By Car: Most hotels have nearby parking—ask for detailed directions. Arles' only parking structure is Parking des Lices, near the TI on boulevard des Lices (€7/24 hours). Otherwise, follow signs marked *Centre-Ville*, then *Gare SNCF* (train station). You'll come to a big roundabout (place Lamartine) with a Monoprix department store to the right. You can park along the city wall or in nearby lots; pay attention to *No Parking* signs on Wednesday and Saturday until 13:00 (violators will be towed to make way for Arles' huge outdoor produce markets). Theft is a big problem; leave nothing in your car, and trust your hotelier's advice on where to park. From place Lamartine, walk into the city between the two stumpy towers. From here, the hotels I list are no more than a 10-minute walk away.

Helpful Hints

Market Days: The big markets are on Wednesdays and Saturdays. For all the details, see page 466.

Internet Access: Arles has no reliable Internet cafés—ask at the TI.

Baggage Storage and Bike Rental: Helpful Patrick will store your bags for €2 each at **Arles VAE,** located across from the train station (Easter–Oct Mon–Sat 9:00–19:00, closed Sun except July–Aug; Feb–Easter and Nov–Dec Tue–Sat 9:00–18:00; closed Sun–Mon; closed Jan, tel. 04 90 43 33 14, www.arles-vae.com). Patrick also rents bikes for cheap (€5/4 hrs, €10/day). Ask about his electric bikes—handy on windy days. From Arles, you can ride to Les Baux (20 miles round-trip, very steep climb) or into the Camargue (40 miles round-trip, forget it in the wind)—provided you're in great shape.

Laundry: There's a launderette at 12 rue Portagnel (daily 7:00–21:00, you can stay later to finish if you're already inside, English instructions).

Car Rental: Avis is at the train station (tel. 04 90 96 82 42), and

Europcar and **Hertz** are downtown (both at 2 bis avenue Victor Hugo, Europcar tel. 04 90 93 23 24, Hertz tel. 04 90 96 75 23).

Local Guide: Charming Jacqueline Neujean, an excellent guide, knows Arles and nearby sights intimately, and loves her work (€90/2 hrs, tel. 04 90 98 47 51).

Language and Cooking Courses: Food- or language-lovers enjoy classes offered by outgoing American (and Arles resident) Madeleine Vedel and her French husband, Eric. In addition to renting out rooms (see Maison d'Hôtes en Provence under "Sleeping" in Arles, page 471), they present a wide range of cooking and language-learning experiences (www .cuisineprovencale.com).

Public Pools: Arles has three public pools (indoor and outdoor). Ask at the TI or your hotel.

Boules: The local "*boul*ing alley" is by the river on place Lamartine. After their afternoon naps, the old boys congregate here for a game of *pétanque (boules)*—it's fun to watch (see page 771 for details on this popular local pastime).

Getting Around Arles

In this flat city, everything's within walking distance. Only the Ancient History Museum requires a long walk (take a taxi for €9, or a public bus for €0.80—details in listing on the next page). The elevated riverside promenade provides Rhône views and a direct route to the Ancient History Museum (to the southwest) and the train and bus stations (to the northeast). Keep your head up for *Starry Night* memories, but eyes down for decorations by dogs with poorly trained owners.

Arles' **taxis** charge a set fee of about €9, but nothing except the Ancient History Museum is worth a taxi ride. To call a cab, dial 04 90 96 90 03.

SIGHTS AND ACTIVITIES

The worthwhile **Monument Pass** *(le pass monuments)* covers almost all of Arles' sights (adults-€13.50, under 18-€12, sold at each sight except the Arlaten Folk Museum; Fondation Van Gogh discounted, but not fully covered). The less-tempting €9 *Circuit Romain* ticket covers Arles' four Roman sights, but not the Ancient History Museum. With no pass, you'll pay €3–5.50 per sight. While any sight is worth a few minutes, many aren't worth the individual admission.

Start at the Ancient History Museum for a helpful overview (drivers should try to do this museum on their way into Arles), then dive into the city-center sights. Remember, many sights stop selling tickets 30–60 minutes before closing (both before lunch and at the end of the day).

▲▲Ancient History Museum (Musée de l'Arles et de la Provence Antiques)

Begin your Arles tour here—it's Roman Arles 101. On the site of the Roman chariot racecourse (the arc of which is built into the parking lot), this air-conditioned, all-on-one-floor museum is just west of central Arles along the river. Models and original sculptures (with almost no English translations) re-create the Roman city, making workaday life and culture easier to imagine.

You're greeted by an impressive row of pagan and early-Christian sarcophagi (from the second to fifth centuries). These would have lined the Via Aurelia outside the town wall. In the early days of the Church, Jesus was often portrayed beardless and as the good shepherd, with a lamb over his shoulder (see relief at end of ramp, #41).

Next, you'll find models of every Roman structure in (and near) Arles. These are the high-light for me, as they breathe a little life into buildings as they looked 2,000 years ago. Find the Forum (still the center of town, though only two columns survive today); the pontoon bridge (over the widest, and therefore slowest, part of the river); the Arena (with its moveable stadium cover, which sheltered spectators from sun or rain); and the Circus, or chariot racecourse (while long gone, it must have been like Rome's Circus Maximus in its day—its obelisk is now the centerpiece of Arles' place de la République).

The model of the Roman city shows that an emphasis on sports—with the Arena and huge stadium—is not unique to modern America. It also illustrates how little Arles seems to have changed over two millennia—with warehouses still on the opposite side of the river and houses clustered around the city center.

All of the museum's statues are original, except for the greatest—the *Venus of Arles*, which Louis XIV took a liking to and had moved to Versailles. It's now in the Louvre (and, as locals say, "When it's in Paris...bye-bye"). Jewelry, fine metal and glass artifacts, and well-crafted mosaic floors make it clear that Roman Arles was a city of art and culture.

Cost, Hours, Location: €5.50, covered by Monument Pass, daily April–Oct 9:00–19:00, Nov–March 10:00–17:00, presqu'île du Cirque Romain.

Arles

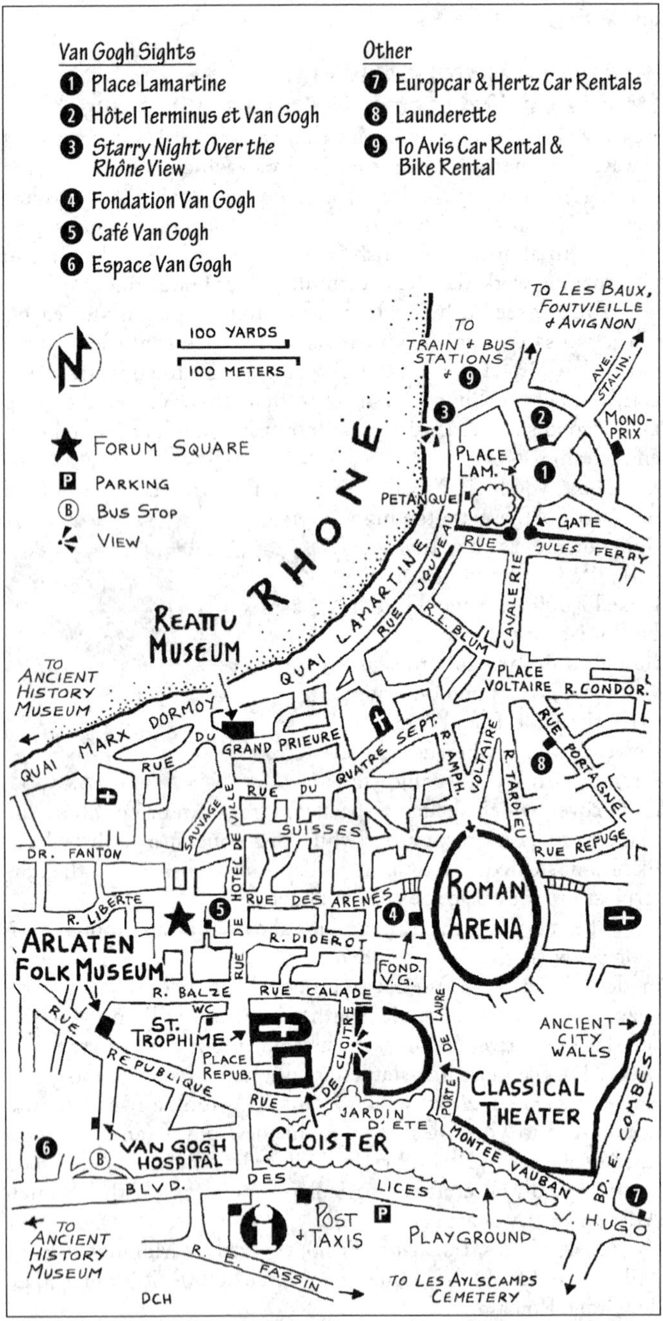

Van Gogh Sights
1 Place Lamartine
2 Hôtel Terminus et Van Gogh
3 Starry Night Over the Rhône View
4 Fondation Van Gogh
5 Café Van Gogh
6 Espace Van Gogh
Other
7 Europcar & Hertz Car Rentals
8 Launderette
9 To Avis Car Rental & Bike Rental
100 YARDS
100 METERS
Forum Square
Parking
Bus Stop
View
To Les Baux, Fontvieille & Avignon
To Train + Bus Stations + 9
Ave. Stalin.
Mono-prix
Place Lam.
Petanque
Gate
Rue Jules Ferry
Rhone
Rue Jouve au
Quai Lamartine
Rue R.L. Blum
Cavalerie
Reattu Museum
To Ancient History Museum
Quai Marx Dormoy
Place Voltaire
R. Condor.
Rue du Grand Prieure
Rue Quatre Sept.
R. Amph.
Voltaire
R. Tardieu
Rue Portagnel
Rue du Suisses
Sauvage
Hotel de Ville
Rue de Hotel de Ville
Dr. Fanton
Rue Refuge
Roman Arena
Rue des Arenes
R. Liberte
Arlaten Folk Museum
R. Diderot
Fond. V.G.
R. Balze
Rue Calade
WC
St. Trophime
Place Repub.
Rue de Cloitre
Rue de Laure
Ancient City Walls
Rue Republique
Classical Theater
Porte
Jardin d'Ete
Cloister
Van Gogh Hospital
Montee Vauban
Bd. E. Combes
Blvd. des Lices
V. Hugo
Post + Taxis
Playground
To Ancient History Museum
R. E. Fassin
To Les Aylscamps Cemetery
DCH

Information: Request the English booklet, which provides some background on the collection, and ask if there are any free English tours (usually daily July–Sept at 17:00, 90 min). Tel. 04 90 18 88 88, www.arles-antique.cg13.fr.

Getting There: To reach the museum by **foot** from the city center (a 25-min walk), turn left at the river and take the riverside path to the big, modern building just past the new bridge. The **taxi** ride costs €9 (museum can call a taxi for your return). **Bus #1** gets you within a five-minute walk (€0.80, 3/hr, daily except Sun). Catch the bus in Arles on boulevard des Lices, then get off at the Musée de l'Arles Antique stop and follow the signs (to your left as you step off the bus).

In Central Arles

Ideally, visit these sights in the order listed below. I've included some walking directions to connect the dots.

▲▲**Forum Square (Place du Forum)**—Named for the Roman forum that once stood here, this was the political and religious center of Roman Arles. Still lively, this café-crammed square is a local watering hole and popular for a *pastis* (see "Eating" in Arles, page 472). The bistros on the square, while no place for a fine dinner, can put together a good-enough salad or *plat du jour*—and when you sprinkle on the ambience, that's €10 well spent.

At the corner of Grand Hôtel Nord-Pinus, a plaque shows how the Romans built a foundation of galleries to make the main square level. The two columns are all that survive of a temple. Steps leading to the entrance are buried (the Roman street level was about 20 feet below you).

The statue on the square is of **Frédéric Mistral** (1830–1914). This popular poet, who wrote in the local dialect rather than French, was a champion of Provençal culture. After receiving the Nobel Prize in Literature in 1904, Mistral used his prize money to preserve and display the folk identity of Provence. He founded the regional folk museum (see "Arlaten Folk Museum," page 466) at a time when France was rapidly centralizing. (The local mistral wind—literally, "master"—has nothing to do with his name.)

The **bright yellow café**—called Café Van Gogh today, but previously named Café la Nuit—is famous as the subject of one of Vincent van Gogh's most famous works in Arles. While his painting showed the café in a brilliant yellow from the glow of gas lamps, the facade was bare limestone, just like the other cafés on this square. The café's current owners have painted it to match van Gogh's version...and to cash in on the Vincent-crazed hordes who pay too much to eat or drink here.

• *Walk a block to rue du Hôtel de Ville, turn right, and you'll find the big...*

Republic Square (Place de la République)—This square used to be called "place Royale"...until the French Revolution. The obelisk was the centerpiece of Arles' Roman Circus. The lions at its base are the symbol of the city, whose slogan is (roughly) "the gentle lion." Find a seat and watch the peasants—pilgrims, locals, and street musicians. There's nothing new about this scene.

• *Overlooking this square is...*

▲▲**St. Trophime Church**—Named after a third-century bishop of Arles and located on a large square, this church sports the finest Romanesque main entrance (west portal) that I've seen anywhere.

Like a Roman triumphal arch, the church facade trumpets the promise of Judgment Day. The tympanum (the semicircular area above the door) is filled with Christian symbolism. Christ sits in majesty, surrounded by symbols of the four evangelists: Matthew (the winged man), Mark (the winged lion), Luke (the ox), and John (the eagle). The 12 apostles are lined up below Jesus. It's Judgment Day...some are saved and others aren't. Notice the condemned (on the right)—a chain gang doing a sad bunny-hop over the fires of hell. For them, the tune trumpeted by the three angels above Christ is not a happy one. Below the chain gang, St. Stephen is being stoned to death, with his soul leaving through his mouth and instantly being welcomed by angels. Ride the exquisite detail back to a simpler age. In an illiterate medieval world, long before the vivid images of our Technicolor time, this was a neon billboard over the town square.

There's no charge to enter the church (daily April–Sept 9:00–12:00 & 14:00–18:30, Oct–March 9:00–12:00 & 14:00–17:00). A handy chart just inside the door on the right locates the interior highlights and helps explain the carvings you just saw on the tympanum. The tall, 12th-century Romanesque nave is decorated by a set of 17th-century tapestries showing scenes from the life of Mary. This church is a stop on the ancient pilgrimage route to Santiago de Compostela in northwest Spain. For 800 years, pilgrims on their way to Santiago have paused here...and they still do today. Look for the modern-day pilgrimages advertised on the far right near the church's entry.

• *Leaving the church, turn left, then left again through a courtyard to enter the cloisters.*

The adjacent **cloisters** are interesting, with many small columns that were scavenged from the ancient Roman theater. Enjoy the sculpted capitals, the rounded 12th-century Romanesque arches, and the pointed 14th-century Gothic ones. On the second floor, you'll walk an angled rooftop designed to catch rainwater—notice the slanted gutter that channeled the water into a cistern (€3.50, daily May–Sept 9:00–18:00, March–April and Oct 9:00–13:00 & 14:00–17:30, Nov–Feb 10:00–11:30 & 14:00–16:30).

• *To get to the next sight (the Classical Theater), face the church, walk left, then take the first right on rue de la Calade.*

Classical Theater (Théâtre Antique)—This first-century B.C. Roman theater once seated 10,000. In the Middle Ages, it served as a convenient town quarry—precious little of the original theater survives (though considerable effort is ongoing to rebuild sections of the seating area).

Walk to a center aisle and pull up a stone seat. To appreciate its original size, look to the upper-left side of the tower and find the protrusion that supported the highest of three seating levels. Today, 3,000 can attend events here. Two lonely Corinthian columns look out from the stage over the audience. The orchestra section is defined by a semicircular pattern in the stone. Stepping up onto the left side of the stage, look down to the slender channel that allowed the curtain to disappear below, like magic. Go backstage and browse through broken bits of Rome, and loop back to the entry behind the grass (€3, covered by Monument Pass, daily May–Sept 9:00–18:00, March–April and Oct 9:00–13:00 & 14:00–17:30, Nov–Feb 10:00–11:30 & 14:00–16:30). For more on Roman theaters, see page 505 of the Orange section. Budget travelers can peek over the fence from rue du Cloître, and see just about everything for free.

• *A block uphill is the...*

▲▲▲Roman Arena (Amphithéâtre)—Nearly 2,000 years ago, gladiators fought wild animals here to the delight of 20,000 scream-

ing fans. Today, local daredevils still fight wild animals here—bull-game posters around the Arena advertise upcoming spectacles (see "Bullgames," page 467). A lengthy restoration process is well underway, giving the amphitheater an almost bleached-teeth whiteness.

In Roman times, games were free (sponsored by city bigwigs) and fans were seated by social class. The many exits allowed for rapid dispersal after the games—fights would break out among frenzied fans if they couldn't leave quickly. Through medieval times and until the early 1800s, the arches were bricked up and the stadium became a fortified town—with 200 humble homes crammed within its circular defenses. Three of the medieval towers survive (the one above the ticket booth is open

Van Gogh in Arles

The whole future of art is to be found in the south of France.
—Vincent van Gogh, 1888

Vincent was 35 years old when he came to Arles in 1888, and it was here that he discovered the light that would forever change him.

Coming from the gray skies and flat-lands of the Netherlands and Paris, he was bowled over by everything Provençal—jagged peaks, gnarled olive trees, brilliant sunflowers, and the furious wind. Van Gogh worked in a flurry in Arles, producing more paintings than at any other period in his too-brief career—more than 200 in just a few months. (The fact that locals pronounced his name "vahn-saw van gog" had nothing to do with his psychological struggles here.)

Sadly, none of van Gogh's paintings remain in Arles—but you can still visit the places that inspired him. Around down-town Arles, you'll find 17 steel-and-concrete van Gogh **"easels"** that mark places Vincent painted, including the *Café at Night* on Forum Square. Each comes with a photo of the actual painting (see photo at left) and provides fans with a fun opportunity to compare the scene then and now. The TI has a €1 brochure that locates all the easels. Small stone markers with yellow accents embedded in the pavement lead to the easels. Here is a quick summary of the places that inspired a few of his most famous paintings.

Vincent arrived in Arles on February 20, 1888, to a foot of snow. He rented a small house on the north side of **place Lamartine.** The house was destroyed in 1944 by an errant, bridge-seeking bomb, but the four-story building behind it—next to the defunct Hôtel Terminus et Van Gogh—still stands

and rewards those who climb it with a good view). To see two still-sealed arches—complete with cute medieval window frames—turn right as you leave, walk to the Andaluz restaurant, and look back to the second floor (€5.50, covered by Monument Pass, daily May–Sept 9:00–18:00, March–April and Oct 9:00–17:30, Nov–Feb 10:00–16:30, tel. 08 91 70 03 70, www.arenes-arles.com).

• *Turn left out of the Arena and walk uphill to find the...*

▲▲**Fondation Van Gogh**—A refreshing stop for any art-lover and especially interesting to van Gogh fans, this small gal-lery features works by contemporary artists who pay homage

(find it in the painting).

From place Lamartine, walk to the river, then look toward the town to find where Vincent set his easel for this **Starry Night over the Rhône** painting, where stars boil above the skyline of Arles. Riverfront cafés that once stood here were destroyed by bridge-seeking bombs in World War II, as was the bridge whose remains you see on your right. (Note: This painting is not the *Starry Night* you're thinking of, which van Gogh painted at a hospital in nearby St. Rémy.)

Vincent—who dreamed of making Arles a magnet for fellow artists—persuaded his friend Paul Gauguin to come. At first, the two got along well. They spent days side-by-side, rendering the same subject in their two distinct styles. At night, they hit the bars and brothels. Van Gogh's well-known *Café at Night* captures the glow of an absinthe buzz at the Café du Terrace (now Café Van Gogh) on **place du Forum.**

After two months together, the two artists clashed over art and personality differences. One December night, they were drinking absinthe at the café when Vincent suddenly went ballistic. He threw his glass at Gauguin. Gauguin left. Walking through place Victor Hugo, Gauguin heard footsteps behind him and turned to see Vincent coming at him, brandishing a razor. Gauguin quickly fled town. Later that night, van Gogh sliced off his own earlobe and gave it to a prostitute.

Vincent was checked into the local hospital, today's **Espace Van Gogh** cultural center. It surrounds a garden that the artist loved (and the only flower garden that I've seen in Arles). Only the courtyard is open to the public; find the "easel" to see what Vincent painted here (free, near the Arlaten Museum on rue President Wilson).

In the spring of 1890, Vincent left Provence to be cared for by a doctor in Auvers-sur-Oise, north of Paris. On July 27, he wandered into a field and shot himself. He died two days later.

to Vincent through thought-provoking interpretations of his works. Many pieces are explained in English by the artists. The black-and-white photographs (both art and shots of places Vincent painted) complement the paintings. Unfortunately, this collection is often on the road July through September, when non–van Gogh material is shown (€7, €5 with Monument Pass, great collection of van Gogh souvenirs, prints, and postcards for sale in free entry area; April–June daily 10:00–18:00; July–Sept daily 10:00–19:00; Oct–March Tue–Sun 11:00–17:00, closed Mon; facing Arena at 24 bis rond-point des Arènes, tel. 04 90 49 94 04, www.fondationvangogh-arles.org). For more on Vincent, see the "Van Gogh in Arles" sidebar, on page 464.

• *The next two sights are back across town. The Arlaten Folk Museum is close to place du Forum, and the Réattu Museum is near the river.*

▲Arlaten Folk Museum (Musée Arlaten/Museon Arlaten)— Built on the remains of the Roman Forum (first century A.D., see the courtyard), this museum houses the treasures of daily Provençal life and offers an enjoyable audioguide (€2). A one-way route takes you through 30 rooms and past guards in traditional dress. The first few rooms display folk costumes chronologically until about 1900, when the traditional garb was replaced by the modern, nondescript norm. The second floor covers local history, and a large room shows the lifestyles of residents of the marshy Camargue region. A fascinating case shows antique bullfighting memorabilia, including this region's unique hooks and ribbons used in *courses camarguaises* (see the next page). The last rooms display two dioramas, the museum's pride and joy. In one, a wealthy mom is shown with her newborn. Her friends visit with gifts representing four physical and moral qualities hoped for in a new baby—good as bread, full as an egg, wise as salt, and straight as a match (€4, covered by Monument Pass, free first Sun and last Wed of the month; open June–Aug daily 9:00–13:00 & 14:00–18:30; Sept–May Tue–Sun 9:00–12:00 & 14:00–17:30, closed Mon; last entry 1 hour before closing, enjoyable audioguide-€2, 29 rue de la République, tel. 04 90 96 08 23, www.cg13.fr).

Réattu Museum (Musée Réattu)—Housed in a beautiful 15th-century mansion, this mildly interesting, mostly modern art collection includes 57 Picasso drawings (some two-sided and all done in a flurry of creativity—I liked the bullfights best), a room of Henri Rousseau's Camargue watercolors, and an unfinished painting by the Neoclassical artist Jacques Réattu...but none with English explanations (€4, covered by Monument Pass, €2 extra for special exhibits, daily July–Aug 10:00–19:00, March–June and Sept–Nov 10:00–12:30 & 14:00–18:30, Dec–Feb 13:00–18:00, last entry 30 min before closing for lunch or at end of day, 10 rue du Grand Prieuré, tel. 04 90 96 37 68).

▲▲Wednesday and Saturday Markets—Twice a week in the morning, Arles' ring road erupts into an open-air market of fish, flowers, produce, and you-name-it. The Wednesday market runs along boulevard Emile Combes, between place Lamartine and avenue Victor Hugo; the segment nearest place Lamartine is all about food, and the upper half is about clothing, tablecloths, purses, and so on. On the first Wednesday of the month, it's a flea market, with less produce. The Saturday market is along boulevard des Lices near the TI. Join in, buy flowers, try the olives, sample some wine, and swat a pickpocket. Both markets are open until 12:00.

▲▲Bullgames (Courses Camarguaises)—Occupy the same seats fans have used for nearly 2,000 years, and take in Arles' most memorable experience—the *courses camarguaises* in the ancient Arena. These nonviolent "bullgames" are more sporting than bloody Spanish bullfights. The bulls of Arles (who, locals stress, "die of old age") are promoted in posters even more boldly than their human foes. In the bullgame, a ribbon *(cocarde)* is laced between the bull's horns. The *razeteur*, with a special hook,

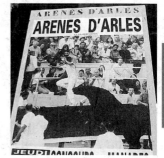

has 15 minutes to snare the ribbon. Local businessmen encourage a *razeteur* (dressed in white with a red cummerbund) by shouting out how much money they'll pay for the *cocarde*. If the bull pulls a good stunt, the band plays the famous "Toreador" song from *Carmen*. The following day, newspapers report on the games, including how many *Carmens* the bull earned.

Three classes of bullgames—determined by the experience of the *razeteurs*—are advertised in posters: The *course de protection* is for rookies. The *trophée de l'Avenir* comes with more experience. And the *trophée des As* features top professionals. During Easter and the fall rice harvest festival (Féria du Riz), the Arena hosts actual Spanish bullfights (look for *corrida*) with outfits, swords, spikes, and the whole gory shebang. Bullgame tickets run €5–15, while bloody bullfights *(corrida)* are pricier (€12–80). Schedules change every year—ask at the TI or check online at www .arenes-arles.com (usually bullgames are every Wed at 17:00 in June–Aug, but confirm).

Don't pass on a chance to see *Toro Piscine,* a silly spectacle for warm summer evenings where the bull ends up in a swimming pool (uh-huh...get more details at TI). Nearby villages stage *courses camarguaises* in small wooden bullrings nearly every weekend; the TI has the latest schedule.

Near Arles

The Camargue—Knocking on Arles' doorstep, this is one of the few truly "wild" areas of France, where pink flamingos, wild bulls, and the famous white horses wander freely amid rice fields, lagoons, and mosquitoes. It's a ▲▲▲ sight for nature-lovers, but boring for others. The D-37 has some of the best views, follow this road from Arles toward Salin de Giraud and Le Sambuc as it skirts the Etang de Vaccarès lagoon; turn right onto the tiny road at Villeneuve and find La Capelière and Fielouse, then drive to Le Paradis and see how far you can get on the road that heads

Near Arles

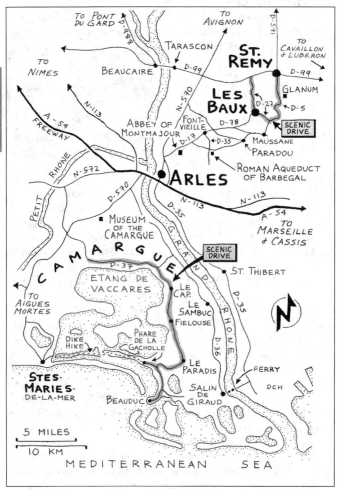

to the right. A slow dirt road ultimately leads to Beauduc (the end of the Camargue's world). Head back east to find Salin de Giraud, cross the Grande Rhône River by ferry, then return to Arles on D-35. For public transportation options, see "Transportation Connections" for Arles, page 474.

Stes-Maries-de-la-Mer—At the western end of the Camargue lies this whitewashed, Spanish-feeling seafront town with flamingos, bulls, and miles of horses at its doorstep. The place feels like a French Coney Island and is so popular that it's best avoided on weekends and during holidays. The town has little to offer except its beachfront promenade, bullring, and towering, five-belled, fortified church. Most tourists come to take a horse, jeep, or bike into the Camargue—and there's no lack of outfits ready to take you for a ride. The TIs in Arles (see page 456) and Stes-Maries-de-la-Mer have long lists (Stes-Maries-de-la-Mer TI open daily April–Sept 9:00–19:00, until 20:00 in summer, Oct–March 9:00–17:00, tel. 04 90 97 82 55, www.saintesmaries.com).

SLEEPING

In Arles

Hotels are a great value here; many are air-conditioned, though few have elevators. The Calendal, Musée, and Régence hotels offer exceptional value.

$$$ Hôtel le Calendal*,** located between the Arena and Classical Theater, is Provençal chic and does everything right. Its comfortable rooms, in all shapes and sizes, surround a large, palm-shaded courtyard. Enjoy the great €9 buffet breakfast, the €15 salad-and-pasta-bar lunch buffet, the children's play area, and the seductive ambience. They even have my Provence video on DVD in the lobby (smallest Db-€51, standard Db-€74–90, Db with balcony-€92–108, price depends on room size, air-con, Wi-Fi and four free laptops for guests, reserve ahead for parking-€10, just above Arena at 5 rue Porte de Laure, tel. 04 90 96 11 89, fax 04 90 96 05 84, www.lecalendal.com, contact@lecalendal.com).

$$$ Hôtel d'Arlatan*,** built over the site of a Roman basilica, is classy in every sense of the word. It has sumptuous public spaces, a tranquil terrace, a designer pool, a turtle pond, and antique-filled rooms, most with high, wood-beamed ceilings and stone walls. In the lobby of this 15th-century building, a glass floor looks down into Roman ruins (smallest Db-€90, standard

---

Sleep Code

(€1 = about $1.30, country code: 33)
S = Single, **D** = Double/Twin, **T** = Triple, **Q** = Quad, **b** = bathroom, **s** = shower only, ***** = French hotel rating system (0–4 stars). Unless otherwise noted, credit cards are accepted and English is spoken.

To help you sort easily through these listings, I've divided the rooms into three categories based on the price for a standard double room with bath:

  $$$ **Higher Priced**—Most rooms €80 or more.
   $$ **Moderately Priced**—Most rooms between €55–80.
    $ **Lower Priced**—Most rooms €55 or less.

Arles Hotels and Restaurants

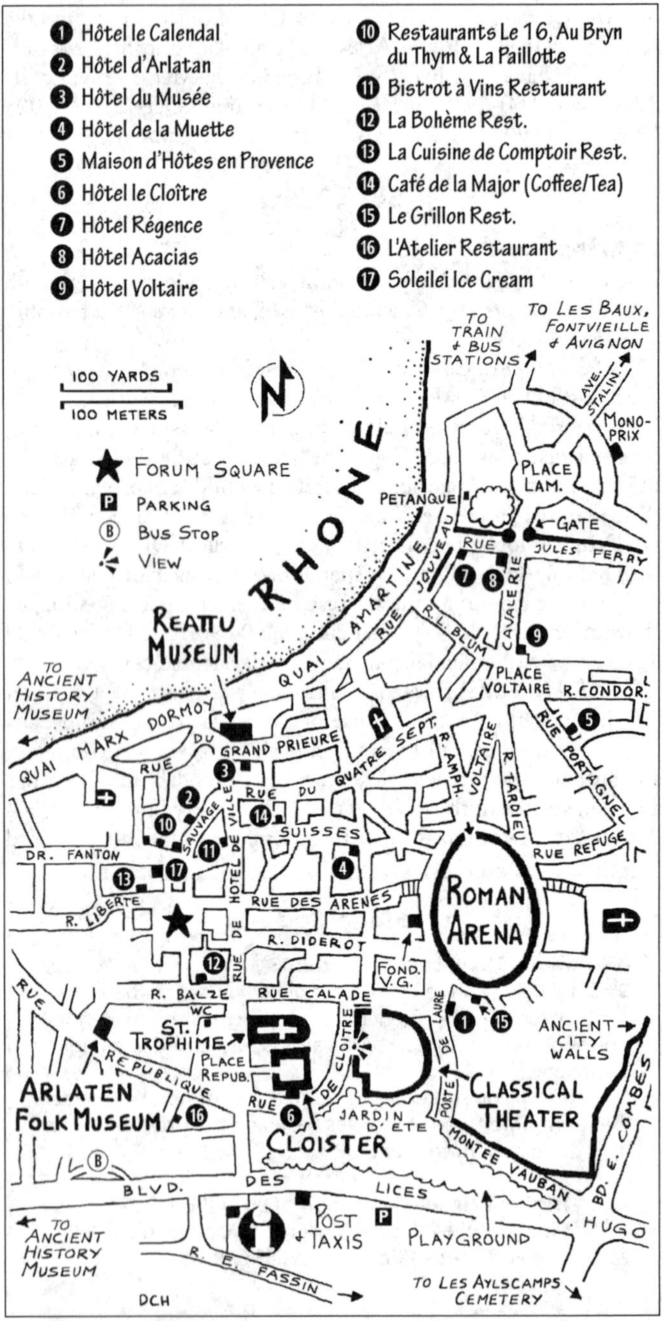

1. Hôtel le Calendal
2. Hôtel d'Arlatan
3. Hôtel du Musée
4. Hôtel de la Muette
5. Maison d'Hôtes en Provence
6. Hôtel le Cloître
7. Hôtel Régence
8. Hôtel Acacias
9. Hôtel Voltaire
10. Restaurants Le 16, Au Bryn du Thym & La Paillotte
11. Bistrot à Vins Restaurant
12. La Bohème Rest.
13. La Cuisine de Comptoir Rest.
14. Café de la Major (Coffee/Tea)
15. Le Grillon Rest.
16. L'Atelier Restaurant
17. Soleilei Ice Cream

Provence

Db-€105–120, bigger Db-€120–155, Db/Qb suites-€180–250, excellent buffet breakfast-€11, air-con, bathrobes, ice machines, elevator, Wi-Fi, parking-€13–16, 1 block below place du Forum at 26 rue Sauvage, tel. 04 90 93 56 66, fax 04 90 49 68 45, www .hotel-arlatan.fr, contact@hotel-arlatan.fr).

$$ Hôtel du Musée** is a quiet and affordable manor-home hideaway tucked deep in Arles. This delightful refuge comes with 28 air-conditioned rooms, a flowery two-tiered courtyard, and a snazzy art-gallery lounge. The rooms in the new section are worth the few extra euros and steps. Claude and English-speaking Laurence, the gracious owners, are eager to help (Sb-€45–50, Db-€55–70, Tb-€70–80, Qb-€85, higher prices are for new section, Wi-Fi and a laptop available for guests, parking-€8, follow signs for *Réattu Museum* to 11 rue du Grand Prieuré, tel. 04 90 93 88 88, fax 04 90 49 98 15, www.hoteldumusee.com, contact @hoteldumusee.com).

$$ Hôtel de la Muette**, with reserved owners Brigitte and Alain, is a good choice. Located in a quiet corner of Arles, this low-key, traditional hotel is well-kept, with stone walls, wood beams, mini-fridges, and air-conditioning (Db-€48–65, Tb-€65–70, Qb-€80, buffet breakfast with eggs-€8, Internet access and Wi-Fi, parking-€7, 15 rue des Suisses, tel. 04 90 96 15 39, fax 04 90 49 73 16, www.hotel-muette.com, hotel.muette@wanadoo.fr).

$$ Maison d'Hôtes en Provence, run by engaging American Madeleine and her soft-spoken French husband Eric, combines an interesting B&B experience—four spacious and funky-but-comfy rooms—with optional Provençal cooking workshops. Foodies should check out their website for its affordable range of gourmet classes (Db-€65, extra person-€15; good family room, across from launderette at 11 rue Portagnel, tel. & fax 04 90 49 69 20, www .cuisineprovencale.com, actvedel@wanadoo.fr).

$$ Hôtel le Cloître** was originally the cloister provost's residence. Caring owners Jean-François and Agnes run a warm, ramshackle place with 30 simple but character-filled rooms with so-so beds. The best rooms are on the first floor; cheaper rooms are on the second floor (Ss/Ds-€44, Sb/Db-€49, bigger Db-€60–65, Tb-€70, Qb-€80, no air-con, no elevator, parking-€5, closed Nov–mid-March, 16 rue du Cloître, tel. 04 90 96 29 50, fax 04 90 96 02 88, www.hotelcloitre.com, hotel_cloitre@hotmail.com).

$ Hôtel Régence**, about the best deal in Arles, has a riverfront location, immaculate and comfortable Provençal rooms, good beds, safe parking, and easy access to the train station (Db-€40–50, Tb-€50–60, Qb-€60–70, good buffet breakfast-€6, choose river view or quieter courtyard rooms, most rooms have showers, air-con, no elevator but only 2 floors, Internet access and Wi-Fi, from place Lamartine turn right immediately after passing between towers to reach 5 rue Marius Jouveau, tel. 04 90 96 39 85, fax 04 90 96 67 64, www.hotel-regence.com, contact@hotel-regence.com). The gentle Nouvions speak some English.

$ Hôtel Acacias**, just off place Lamartine and inside the old city walls, is a modern, pastel paradise. Its smallish, well-maintained, reasonably priced rooms have all the comforts (Sb/Db-€46–55, larger Db-€62–71, extra bed-€15, air-con, elevator, 1 rue Marius Jouveau, tel. 04 90 96 37 88, fax 04 90 96 32 51, www.hotel-acacias.com, contact@hotel-acacias.com).

$ Hôtel Voltaire* rents 12 small and spartan rooms with ceiling fans and nifty balconies overlooking a caffeine-stained square. A block below the Arena, it's perfect for starving artists. Smiling owner Mr. Ferran (fur-ran) loves the States (his dream is to travel there), and hopes you'll add to his postcard collection (D-€28, Ds-€32, Db-€38, 1 place Voltaire, tel. 04 90 96 49 18, fax 04 90 96 45 49, levoltaire@aol.com). They also serve lunch and dinner (see "Eating" in "Arles," below).

Near Arles, in Fontvieille

Many drivers, particularly those with families, prefer staying in the peaceful countryside with easy access to the area's sights. Just 10 minutes from Arles and Les Baux, and 20 minutes from Avignon, little Fontvieille slumbers in the shadows of its big-city cousins (though it has its share of restaurants and boutiques). See also "Sleeping—In or near Les Baux" on page 502.

$$$ Le Peiriero*** is a pooped parent's dream come true, with a grassy garden, massive pool, table tennis, badminton, massage parlor, indoor children's play area, and even a few miniature golf holes. The spacious family loft rooms, capable of sleeping up to five, have full bathrooms on both levels. This complete retreat also comes with a terrace café and a well-respected restaurant (streetside Sb or Db-€90–98, garden-side Db-€108–120, Db with terrace-€125–135, loft-€170–210, dinner *menu*-€29, €34 for breakfast and dinner, air-con, Wi-Fi, free parking, just east of Fontvieille on road to Les Baux, 34 avenue des Baux, tel. 04 90 54 76 10, fax 04 90 54 62 60, www.hotel-peiriero.com, info@hotel-peiriero.com).

EATING

You can dine well in Arles on a modest budget—in fact, it's hard to blow a lot on dinner here (most of my listings have *menus* for €22 or less). The bad news is that restaurants here change regularly, so double-check my suggestions. All restaurants I list (except Bistrot à Vins and La Bohème) have outdoor seating. Before dinner, go local on place du Forum and enjoy a *pastis*. This anise-based apéritif is served straight in a glass with ice, plus a carafe of water—dilute to taste.

For **picnics,** a big, handy Monoprix supermarket/department store is on place Lamartine (Mon–Sat 8:30–19:25, closed Sun).

On or near Place du Forum

Great atmosphere and mediocre food at fair prices await you on place du Forum. By all accounts, the garish, yellow Café Van Gogh is worth avoiding. A half-block below the Forum, on rue du Dr. Fanton, lies a lineup of more tempting restaurants (including the first three listed below).

Le 16, with warm ambience inside and out, is an affordable place to enjoy a fresh salad (€8, bright and creative) or a one-course dinner (their "bull and red rice" is popular). They also offer a daily *plat du jour,* a two-course €14 *formule,* and a seasonal *menu* (closed Sat–Sun, 16 rue du Dr. Fanton, tel. 04 90 93 77 36).

La Paillotte, a few doors down, features soft tablecloths under wood-beamed comfort inside, a nice terrace outside, and fine regional cuisine at affordable prices. It's quite popular with tourists (€18–30 *menus,* closed Wed, 28 rue du Dr. Fanton, tel. 04 90 96 33 15).

Au Bryn du Thym, almost next door, has long been reliable and specializes in traditional Provençal cuisine. Arrive early for an outdoor table (€19 *menu,* closed Tue, 22 rue du Dr. Fanton, tel. 04 90 49 95 96).

Bistrot à Vins is for wine addicts who love matching food and wine. This comfortable *bistrot* is run by affable Ariane. She speaks English and offers simple, tasty dishes designed to highlight her reasonably priced wines—many available by the glass (closed Mon, 2 rue du Dr. Fanton, tel. 04 90 52 00 65).

La Bohème seems lost a block above the Forum. Here you'll be greeted by gentle Nicholas and dine under a long, vaulted ceiling with good budget options (€15 vegetarian *menu,* €20 Provençal *menu,* closed Sun–Mon, 6 rue Balze, tel. 04 90 18 58 92). The occasional tour group usually leaves by 19:30.

At **La Cuisine de Comptoir,** locals leave behind Provençal décor and pretend they're urbanites in Paris. This cool little bistro serves light €9 *tartine* dinners—a cross between pizza and bruschetta served with soup or salad (closed Sun, just off place du Forum's lower end at 10 rue de la Liberté, tel. 04 90 96 86 28).

Recharge at **Café de la Major** with some serious coffee or tea (closed Sun, 7 bis rue Réattu, tel. 04 90 96 14 15).

Near the Roman Arena

For about the same price as on place du Forum, you can enjoy regional cuisine with a point-blank view of the Arena. It's hard to distinguish between the handful of mostly outdoor eateries overlooking the Arena, as they change regularly.

Le Grillon, with good salads, crêpes, and *plats du jour* for €9–12, has been the most reliable (closed Wed, at the top of the Arena on rond-point des Arènes, tel. 04 90 96 70 97).

The recommended **Hôtel le Calendal** (see "Sleeping," page 469) hosts an all-you-can-eat salad-and-pasta bar (€15, daily 12:00–15:00); the selection is as good as the quality. Retreat from the city and enjoy a healthy lunch in the hotel's palm-shaded garden (just above the Arena at 5 rue Porte de Laure, tel. 04 90 96 11 89).

The recommended **Hôtel Voltaire** (see "Sleeping," page 472) serves a nothing-fancy three-course dinner (or lunch) for €11 and hearty salads for €8–10—try the *salade fermière* (open daily, 1 place Voltaire, tel. 04 90 96 49 18).

A Gastronomic Dining Experience

L'Atelier is so intriguing that people travel great distances just for the experience of dining here. Diners fork over €55 (lunchers spoon out €38) and trust Chef Jean-Luc Rabanel to create a memorable evening (which he does). There is no menu, just an onslaught of about 20 delicious taste sensations served on artsy dishes. Don't plan on a quick dinner and don't come for the setting—it's a contemporary shoebox-shaped dining room with a get-to-know-your-neighbor atmosphere where you can't help but join the party; several outdoor tables are also available (closed Mon–Tue, best to book ahead, friendly servers will hold your hand through this palate-widening experience, 50 yards downhill from place de la République at 7 rue des Carmes, tel. 04 90 91 07 69, www.rabanel.com).

And for Dessert...

Soleilei has Arles' best ice cream, with all-natural ingredients and unusual flavors such as *fadoli*—olive oil (open daily, across from recommended Le 16 restaurant at 9 rue du Dr. Fanton).

TRANSPORTATION CONNECTIONS

From Arles by Train to: Paris (17/day, 2 direct TGVs in 4 hrs, 15 with transfer in Avignon in 5 hrs), **Avignon Centre-Ville** (11/day, 20 min, less frequent in the afternoon), **Nîmes** (9/day, 30 min), **Orange** (4/day direct, 35 min, more frequently with transfer in Avignon), **Aix-en-Provence Centre-Ville** (10/day, 2 hrs, requires at least 1 transfer in Marseille), **Marseille** (20/day, 1–2 hrs), **Cassis** (7/day, 2 hrs), **Carcassonne** (8/day, 2.5–4 hrs, 5 with transfer in Nîmes or Narbonne), **Beaune** (10/day, 4.5 hrs, 9 with transfer in Nîmes or Avignon and Lyon), **Nice** (11/day, 3.75–4.5 hrs, most require transfer in Marseille), **Barcelona** (2/day, 6 hrs, transfer in Montpellier), **Italy** (3/day, transfer in Marseille and Nice; from Arles, it's 4.5 hrs to Ventimiglia on the border, 8 hrs to Milan, 9.5 hrs to Cinque Terre, 11 hrs to Florence, and 13 hrs to Venice or Rome).

By Bus to: Avignon TGV (11/day, 1 hr, by SNCF bus—take the faster train from the Centre-Ville station instead), **Nîmes** (6/day, 1 hr), **St. Rémy** (3/day Mon–Sat only, 50 min), **Fontvieille** (6/day, 10 min), **Camargue/Stes-Maries-de-la-Mer** (6/day Mon–Sat, 3/day Sun, 1 hr). The bus stop in Arles' Centre-Ville is at 16–24 boulevard Georges Clemenceau (2 blocks below main TI, next to Café le Wilson). Bus info: tel. 04 90 49 38 01 (unlikely to speak English).

Les Baux can be tricky to reach by bus out of peak season (usually July–Aug only, 6/day, 35 min, €4 one-way). For other ideas, see "Getting to Les Baux" on page 503. In a pinch, a taxi to Les Baux costs €32 each way (€40 after 19:00; tel. 04 90 96 90 03).

Avignon

Famous for its nursery rhyme, medieval bridge, and brooding Palace of the Popes, contemporary Avignon (ah-veen-yohn) bustles and prospers behind its mighty walls. During the 68 years (1309–1377) that Avignon starred as the *Franco Vaticano*, it grew from a quiet village into the thriving city it remains today. With its large student population and fashionable shops, today's Avignon is an intriguing blend of youthful energy and urban sophistication. Street performers entertain the international crowds who fill Avignon's ubiquitous cafés and trendy boutiques. If you're here in July, be prepared for the rollicking theater festival. (Reserve your hotel months in advance.) Clean,

sharp, and popular with tourists, Avignon is more impressive for its outdoor ambience than for its museums and monuments. See the Palace of the Popes, and then explore the city's thriving streets and beautiful vistas from the parc des Rochers des Doms.

ORIENTATION

The cours Jean Jaurès, which turns into rue de la République, runs straight from the Centre-Ville train station to place de l'Horloge and the Palace of the Popes, splitting Avignon in two. The larger eastern half is where the action is. Climb to the parc des Rochers des Doms for a fine view, enjoy the people scene on place de l'Horloge, meander the back streets (see my self-guided walk, page 479), and lose yourself in a quiet square. Avignon's shopping district fills the traffic-free streets where rue de la République meets place de l'Horloge.

Tourist Information

The main TI is between the Centre-Ville train station and the old town, at 41 cours Jean Jaurès (April–Oct Mon–Sat 9:00–18:00, until 19:00 in July, Sun 9:00–17:00; Nov–March Mon–Fri 9:00–18:00, Sat 9:00–17:00, Sun 10:00–12:00; tel. 04 32 74 32 74, www.avignon-tourisme.com). From April through mid-October, a branch TI office, called Espace Ferruce, is usually open at the St. Bénezet Bridge (but it's slow, with just one person working).

At either TI, get the good tear-off map and pick up the free and handy *Guide Pratique* (info on car and bike rental, hotels, and museums). Also pick up the free **Avignon Passion Pass** (valid 15 days, for up to five people). Get the pass stamped when you pay full price at your first sight, and then receive reductions at the others; for example, €2 less at the Palace of the Popes and €3 less at Petit Palais. The pass comes with the Avignon "Passion" map and guide, which includes several good (but tricky-to-follow) walking tours.

The TI offers informative, two-hour English **walking tours** of Avignon (€10–15, €8 with Avignon Passion Pass; April–Oct daily at 10:00, Nov–March on Sat only; depart from main TI, Sun departures from ticket room at Palace of the Popes; themes vary daily). The TI also offers information and bookings for bus excursions to popular regional sights, including the wine route, the Luberon, and the Camargue (see "Tours of Provence," on page 452).

Arrival in Avignon

By Train: Avignon has two train stations, the TGV and Centre-Ville (connected by frequent shuttle bus—see details below, under "Arrival at the TGV Station").

Arrival at the TGV Station (Gare TGV): There is no baggage check here, though you can check your bags at the Centre-Ville Station (see below). You'll find a tourist information booth across from the shuttle bus stop described below. For the city shuttle bus *(navette)*, go out the north exit *(sortie nord)*, down the stairs, and to the left. Look for the shuttle bus or the stop marked *Navette/*

Avignon

Provence

❶ Best View of Bridge & Stairs to Ramparts	❼ Webzone Internet Café
❷ More Views & Orientation Table	❽ Provence Bike Rental
❸ TGV Shuttle Stop	❾ Shopi Grocery
❹ Launderette	❿ City Hall
❺ To Shakespeare Bookshop	⓫ Tourist Train Stop
❻ Chez W@M Internet Café	⓬ Shuttle Boat Stops (2)

Avignon Centre (€1.10, 3/hr, 15 min, buy tickets at info booth or from the driver). It drops you in front of the post office on cours Président Kennedy, across from the Centre-Ville station and just inside the city walls where cours Jean Jaurès begins, three blocks down from the TI.

A taxi ride between the TGV station and downtown Avignon costs about €13. For car rentals, take the south exit *(sortie sud)* to find the *location de voitures.*

Arrival at Centre-Ville Station (Gare Avignon Centre-Ville): All non-TGV trains serve the central station. You can check bags here (exit the station to the left, look for *consignes* sign, daily May–Sept 6:00–22:00, Oct–April 7:00–19:00). The bus station *(gare routière)* is 100 yards to the right of the Centre-Ville station as you leave (beyond and below Ibis Hôtel). To reach the town center, walk out of the train station and through the city walls onto cours Jean Jaurès. The TI is three blocks down, at #41.

If you're renting a car at the TGV station and heading off to Arles, St. Rémy, Les Baux, or the Luberon, start by leaving the TGV station and following signs reading *Avignon Sud*, then *La Rocade.* You'll soon see exits to Arles (best for St Rémy and Les Baux as well), and Cavaillon (for Luberon villages).

By Bus: The dingy bus station is located just east of the Centre-Ville train station; to get to Avignon's sights, follow the walking directions given for train station, above.

By Car: Drivers entering Avignon should follow *Centre-Ville* and *Gare SNCF* (train station) signs. Park in the parking structure next to the Centre-Ville train station (€10/half-day, €11.50/day). Free parking is available near the city walls (on boulevard Saint-Roch near Porte de la République), though a new parking garage is under construction that will eliminate some of this free parking. To park in an underground garage at the Palace of the Popes, follow the signs from the riverside road (boulevard St. Lazare) just past the St. Bénezet Bridge. Leave nothing in your car. Hotels have advice for smart overnight parking.

Helpful Hints

Book Ahead for July: During the July theater festival, rooms are rare—reserve very early or stay in Arles (see page 456) or St. Rémy (page 502).

Internet Access: Consider **Webzone** (Mon–Sat 10:00–23:00, Sun 12:00–22:00, 3 rue St. Jean le Vieux on place Pie, tel. 04 32 76 29 47) or **Chez W@M** (Mon–Thu 8:00–20:00, Fri–Sat 8:00–23:00, Sun 8:00–18:00, 34 rue Bonneterie, tel. 04 90 86 19 03), or ask your hotelier for the nearest Internet café.

English Bookstore: Try **Shakespeare Bookshop** (Tue–Sat 9:30–12:00 & 14:00–18:30, closed Sun–Mon, 155 rue Carreterie, in

Provence

Avignon's northeast corner, tel. 04 90 27 38 50).

Baggage Storage: You can leave your bags at the Centre-Ville train station (see "Arrival at Centre-Ville Station," page 478).

Laundry: The launderette at 66 place des Corps-Saints, where rue Agricol Perdiguier ends, has English instructions and is handy to most hotels (daily 7:00–20:00).

Grocery Store: Shopi is central and has long hours (Mon-Sat 7:00–21:00, Sun 9:00–12:00, 2 blocks from the TI, toward place de l'Horloge on rue de la République).

Bike Rental: You can rent a bike or a scooter near the bus station at **Provence Bike** (52 boulevard Saint-Roch, tel. 04 90 27 92 61). You'll enjoy riding on the Ile de la Barthelasse, but bike riding is better in Isle-sur-la-Sorgue (page 523) and Vaison la Romaine (page 512).

Car Rental: The TGV station has the car-rental agencies (open long hours daily).

Tourist Trains: Two little trains, designed for tired tourists, leave regularly from the Palace of the Popes (mid-March–mid-Oct daily 10:00–19:00, tel. 06 11 35 06 66, www.petittrainavignon .com). One does a town tour (€7, 3/hr, 45 min, English commentary) and the other choo-choos you sweat-free to the top of the park, high above the river (€1 one-way, schedule depends on demand, no commentary).

Shuttle Boat: A free shuttle boat plies back and forth across the river (as it did in the days when the town had no functioning bridge) from near St. Bénezet Bridge (daily July–Aug 11:00–21:00, Sept–June roughly 11:00–18:00, 3/hr). It drops you on the peaceful Ile de la Barthelasse, with its riverside restaurant (see page 492), grassy walks, and bike rides with city views. If you stay on the island for dinner, check the schedule for the last return boat—or be prepared for a pleasant 25-minute walk back to town.

Commanding City Views: Walk or drive across Daladier Bridge (pont Daladier) for a great view of Avignon and the Rhône River (there's a good walking path across the bridge, along the river). You can enjoy other impressive vistas from the top of parc des Rochers des Doms, the tower cafeteria in the Palace of the Popes, and from the end of the famous, broken St. Bénezet Bridge.

SELF-GUIDED WALK

▲▲Welcome to Avignon

This walk connects Avignon's best sights.

• *Start your tour where the Romans did, on place de l'Horloge, and find a seat on a stone bench in front of City Hall (Hôtel de Ville).*

Provence

Place de l'Horloge

This café square was the town forum during Roman times and the market square through the Middle Ages. (Restaurants here come with ambience, but marginal-quality meals.) Named for a medieval clock tower that the City Hall now hides, this square's present popularity arrived with the trains in 1854.

• *Walk past the merry-go-round (public WCs behind), veer right, and continue into...*

Palace Square (Place du Palais)

This grand square is surrounded by the forbidding Palace of the Popes, the Petit Palais, and the cathedral. In the 1300s, the Vatican moved the headquarters of the Catholic Church to Avignon. The Church bought Avignon and gave it a complete makeover. Along with clearing out vast spaces like this square and building this three-acre palace, the Church erected more than three miles of protective wall, with 39 towers, "appropriate" housing for cardinals (read: mansions), and residences for the entire Vatican bureaucracy. The city was Europe's largest construction zone. Avignon's population grew from 6,000 to 25,000 in short order. (Today, 13,000 people live within the walls.) The limits of pre-pope Avignon are outlined on city maps: Rues Joseph Vernet, Henri Fabre, des Lices, and Philonarde all follow the route of the city's earlier defensive wall.

The Petit Palais (Little Palace) seals the uphill end of the square and was built for a cardinal; today, it houses medieval paintings (museum described on opposite page). The church just to the left of the Palace of the Popes is Avignon's cathedral. It predates the Church's purchase of Avignon by 200 years. Its small size reflects Avignon's modest, pre-pope population. The gilded Mary was added in 1854, when the Vatican established the doctrine of her Immaculate Conception. Mary is purposefully taller than the Palace of the Popes. The Vatican never accepted what it called the "Babylonian Captivity," and had a bad attitude about Avignon long after the pope was definitively back in Rome.

Directly across the square from the palace's main entry stands a cardinal's residence built in 1619. Its fancy Baroque facade was a visual counterpoint to the stripped-down Huguenot aesthetic of the age. During this time, Provence was a hotbed of Protestantism—but, buried within this region, Avignon was a Catholic stronghold.

Notice the stumps in front of the Conservatoire National de Musique. Nicknamed *bites*, slang for the male anatomy, they effectively keep cars from double-parking in areas designed for people. Many of the metal ones slide up and down by remote control to let privileged cars come and go.

• *You can visit the massive Palace of the Popes (described on page 483) now, but it works better to visit that palace at the end of this walk. But now is a good time to take in the...*

Petit Palace Museum (Musée du Petit Palais)

This palace displays the Church's collection of mostly medieval Italian painting (including one delightful Botticelli) and sculpture. All 350 paintings deal with Christian themes. A visit here before going to the Palace of the Popes helps furnish and populate that otherwise barren building (€6, €3 with Avignon Passion Pass; June–Sept Wed–Mon 10:00–13:00 & 14:00–18:00, closed Tue; Oct–May Wed–Mon 9:30–13:00 & 14:00–17:30, closed Tue; at north end of Palace Square, tel. 04 90 86 44 58).

• *From Palace Square, we'll head up to the rocky hilltop where Avignon was first settled, then down to the river. With this short loop, you can enjoy a park, hike to a grand river view, walk a bit of the wall, and visit Avignon's beloved broken bridge—an experience worth ▲▲. Begin by hiking (or taking the tourist train—see "Helpful Hints" for Avignon, page 479) up to the...*

Parc des Rochers des Doms: While the park itself is a delight (with public WCs and a sweet little café), don't miss the climax—a panoramic view of the Rhône River Valley and the broken bridge. You'll find a huge terrace on the north side of the park with an orientation table and information plaques, but inferior views to the smaller viewpoint described next.

For the best views (and the spot where teenage lovers hang out), find the small terrace past the park café and behind the odd zodiac display. An orientation table explains the view. On a clear day, the tallest peak you see, with its white limestone cap, is Mont Ventoux (literally, "Windy Mountain"). St. André Fortress (across the river) was built by the French in 1360, shortly after the pope moved to Avignon, to counter the papal incursion into this part of Europe. The castle was in the kingdom of France. Avignon's famous bridge was a key border crossing, with towers on either end—one French and one Vatican.

• *From this viewpoint, take the stairs (closed at night) down to the tower. As the stairs spiral down, just before the St. Bénezet Bridge, catch a glimpse of the...*

Ramparts: The only bit of the rampart you can walk on is just beyond the tower (access from St. Bénezet Bridge). When the pope came in the 1360s, small Avignon had no town wall...so he built one. What you see today was restored in the 19th century.

• *When you come out of the tower on street level, exit outside the walls and walk left to find the bridge's entrance (it's outside the walls on boulevard du Rhône).*

St. Bénezet Bridge (Pont St. Bénezet)

This bridge, whose construction and location were inspired by a shepherd's religious vision, is the "pont d'Avignon" of nursery-rhyme fame. The ditty (which you've probably been humming all day) dates back to the 15th century: *Sur le pont d'Avignon, on y danse, on y danse, sur le pont d'Avignon, on y danse tous en rond* ("On the bridge of Avignon, we will dance, we will dance, on the bridge of Avignon, we will dance all in a circle").

But the bridge was a big deal even outside of its kiddie-tune fame. Built between 1171 and 1185, it was the only bridge crossing the mighty Rhône in the Middle Ages. It was damaged several times by floods and subsequently rebuilt, until 1668, when most of it was knocked down by a disastrous icy flood. The townsfolk decided not to rebuild this time, and for more than a century, Avignon had no bridge

across the Rhône. While only four arches survive today, the original bridge was huge: Imagine a 22-arch, 3,000-foot-long bridge extending from Vatican territory to the lonely Tower of Philip the Fair, which marked the beginning of France. A Romanesque chapel on the bridge is dedicated to St. Bénezet. While there's not much to see on the bridge, the audioguide included with your ticket tells a good story. It's also fun to be in the breezy middle of the river with a fine city view.

Cost and Hours: €4, €3.30 with Avignon Passion Pass, €12 combo-ticket includes Palace of the Popes, daily mid-March–Oct 9:00–19:00, until 20:00 July and Sept, until 21:00 in Aug, Nov–mid-March 9:30–17:45, last entry 1 hour before closing, tel. 04 90 27 51 16). The ticket booth is housed in what was a medieval hospital for the poor (funded by bridge tolls). Admission includes a small museum about the song of Avignon's bridge *(Musée de la Chanson d'Avignon)* and your only chance to walk a bit of the ramparts (both keep same hours as bridge and are entered from the tower).

• *Step off the bridge and turn left out of the tower to walk on the rampart wall (called* chemin de ronde*). To cross the river on the free shuttle boat (a good restaurant on the opposite side is described on page 492), look for the small boat near the base of the bridge. To get to the Palace of the Popes from here, exit left, turn left again back into the walls (following signs marked* Palais des Papes*), then go right onto rue Ferruce. After a block, look for the brown signs leading you left under the passageway, and up the stairs to Palace Square and the Palace of the Popes.*

SIGHTS

Palace of the Popes (Palais des Papes)

In 1309, a French pope was elected (Pope Clement V). At the urging of the French king, His Holiness decided he'd had enough of unholy (and dangerous) Italy. So he loaded up his carts and moved to Avignon for a secure rule under a supportive king. The Catholic Church literally bought Avignon (then a two-bit town), and popes resided here until 1403. From 1378 on, there were twin popes, one in Rome and one in Avignon, causing a schism in the Catholic Church that wasn't fully resolved until 1417.

The mighty yet barren papal palace visit—worth ▲▲—comes with an audioguide that leads you along a one-way route and does a credible job of overcoming the lack of furnishings. It teaches the basic history while allowing you to tour at your own pace.

As you wander, ponder that this palace—the biggest surviving Gothic palace in Europe—was built to accommodate 500 people as the administrative center of the Vatican and home of the pope. This was the most fortified palace of the age (remember, the pope left Rome to be more secure). You'll walk through the pope's personal quarters (frescoed with happy hunting scenes), see models of how the various popes added to the building, and learn about its state-of-the-art plumbing. The rooms are huge. The "pope's chapel" is twice the size of the adjacent Avignon cathedral.

While the last pope checked out in 1417, the Vatican owned Avignon until the French Revolution in 1789. During this interim period, the pope's "legate" (official representative...normally a nephew) ruled Avignon from this palace. Avignon residents spoke Italian for a century after the pope left, making it a linguistic island within France. In the Napoleonic age, the palace was a barracks, housing 1,800 soldiers. Climb the tower (Tour de la Gâche) for a grand view and windswept café.

A room at the end of the tour is dedicated to the region's wines, of which they claim the pope was a fan. Sniff "Le Nez du Vin"—a black box with 54 tiny bottles designed to develop your "nose." (Blind-test your travel partner.) The nearby village of Châteauneuf-du-Pape is where the pope summered in the 1320s. Its famous wine is a direct descendant of his wine. You're welcome to taste here (€6 for three fine wines and souvenir tasting cup).

Cost and Hours: €9.50, €7.50 with Avignon Passion Pass, €12 combo-ticket includes St. Bénezet Bridge, daily, same hours as **St. Bénezet Bridge** (page 482), last entry 1 hour before closing, tel. 04 90 27 50 74, www.palais-des-papes.com).

• *After you finish, you'll exit at the rear of the palace. To return to Palace Square, make two rights after exiting the palace.*

More Sights

Avignon's Synagogue—Jews first arrived in Avignon with the Diaspora (exile) of the first century. Avignon's Jews were nick-named "the Pope's Jews" because of the protection that the Pope offered to Jews expelled from France. While this synagogue dates from the 1220s, in the mid-19th century it was completely rebuilt in a Neoclassical Greek-temple style by a non-Jewish architect. This is the only synagogue under a rotunda that you'll see anywhere. The ark holding the Torah is in the east—next to a list of Jews deported from here to Auschwitz in 1942, after Vichy France was overtaken by the Nazis. To visit the synagogue, press the buzzer and friendly Rabbi Moshe Amar will be your guide (Mon–Fri 10:00–12:00 & 15:00–17:00, closed Sat–Sun, 2 place Jerusalem).

Rue des Teinturiers—This "Street of the Dyers" is Avignon's hipster headquarters. You'll pass the Grey Penitents chapel. The facade shows the GPs, who dressed up in robes and pointy hoods to do their anonymous good deeds back in the 13th century (long before the KKK dressed this way).

As you stroll, you'll see the work of amateur sculptors, who have carved whimsical car barriers out of limestone. Earthy cafés, galleries, and a small stream (a branch of the Sorgue River) with waterwheels line this tie-dyed street. This was the cloth industry's dyeing and textile center in the 1800s. Those stylish Provençal fabrics and patterns you see for sale everywhere started here, after a pattern imported from India.

For trendy restaurants on this atmospheric street, see page 491.

• *Farther down rue des Teinturiers, you'll come to the...*

Waterwheel—Standing here, imagine the Sorgue River—which hits the mighty Rhône in Avignon—being broken into several canals in order to turn 23 such wheels. Around 1800, waterwheels powered the town's industries. The little cogwheel above the big one could be shoved into place, kicking another machine into gear behind the wall. (For more on the Sorgue River and its waterwheels, see under "Wandering Isle-sur-la-Sorgue, page 522.) Across from the wheel at

#41 is **La Cave Breysse,** offering regional wines by the glass and good lunch fare (see page 491).

Fondation Anglados-Dubrujeaud—Visiting this museum is like being invited into the elegant home of a rich and passionate art collector. It mixes a small but enjoyable collection of art from Post-Impressionists (including Paul Cézanne, Vincent van Gogh, Honoré Daumier, Edgar Degas, and Pablo Picasso) with re-created art studios and furnishings from many periods. It's a quiet place with a few superb paintings (€6, €4 with Avignon Passion Pass; May–Nov Tue–Sun 13:00–18:00, closed Mon; Dec–April Wed–Sun 13:00–18:00, closed Mon–Tue; 5 rue Laboureur, tel. 04 90 82 29 03, www.angladon.com).

Calvet Museum (Musée Calvet)—This fine-arts museum impressively displays its good collection without a word of English explanation (€6, €3 with Avignon Passion Pass, Wed–Mon 10:00–13:00 & 14:00–18:00, closed Tue, in quieter western half of town at 65 rue Joseph Vernet, its antiquities collection is a few blocks away at 27 rue de la République—same hours and ticket, tel. 04 90 86 33 84).

Near Avignon, in Villeneuve-lès-Avignon
▲**Tower of Philip the Fair (Tour Philippe-le-Bel)**—Built to protect access to St. Bénezet Bridge in 1307, this bulky tower offers the finest view over Avignon and the Rhône basin. It's best late in the day (€2, €1 with Avignon Passion Pass, April–Sept daily 10:00–12:30 & 14:00–18:30; March and Oct–Nov Tue–Sun 10:00–12:00 & 14:00–17:00, closed Mon and Dec–Feb; tel. 04 32 70 08 57). To reach the tower from Avignon, you can drive (5 min, cross Daladier Bridge, follow signs to *Villeneuve-lès-Avignon*); take a boat (Bateau-Bus departs from Mireio Embarcadère near Daladier Bridge); or take bus #11 (2/hr, catch bus across from Centre-Ville train station, in front of post office, on cours Président Kennedy).

SLEEPING

Hotel values are better in Arles. Avignon is particularly popular during its July festival, when you must book ahead (expect inflated prices). Also note that only a few hotels have elevators—specifically, the first three listed near place de l'Horloge.

Near Avignon's Centre-Ville Station
The first three listings are a 10-minute walk from the main train station; turn right off cours Jean Jaurès on rue Agricol Perdiguier.

$$ Hôtel Colbert** is a good midrange bet with a variety of rooms in many sizes and a sweet little patio. Your efficient hosts—Patrice, Annie, and *le chien* Brittany—care for this restored

Avignon Hotels

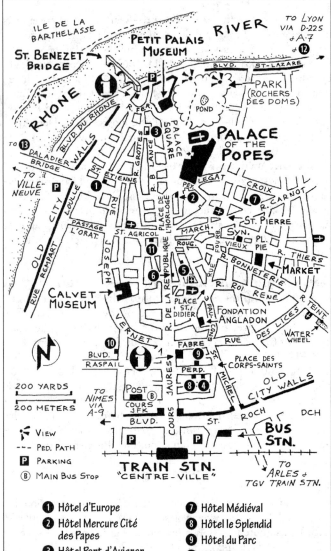

1. Hôtel d'Europe
2. Hôtel Mercure Cité des Papes
3. Hôtel Pont d'Avignon
4. Hôtel Colbert
5. Hôtel de Blauvac
6. Hôtel Danieli
7. Hôtel Médiéval
8. Hôtel le Splendid
9. Hôtel du Parc
10. Hôtel Boquier
11. Villa Agapè B&B
12. To Le Clos du Rempart Rooms
13. To Auberge Bagatelle

manor house and its cozy public spaces (Sb-€45–60, Db-€60–75, Tb-€83–90, air-con, Wi-Fi, parking-€9, 7 rue Agricol Perdiguier, tel. 04 90 86 20 20, fax 04 90 85 97 00, www.lecolbert-hotel.com, contact@avignon-hotel-colbert.com).

$ Hôtel du Parc* is a spotless value with white walls, tiny bathrooms, and stone accents. It's scrupulously managed by entertaining Avignon native Madame Rous, who bakes her own bread and pastries for breakfast—and even made the bedspreads by hand (S-€28, Ss-€38, D-€39, Ds-€47–54, Ts-€65, no TVs or phones, tel. 04 90 82 71 55, fax 04 90 85 64 86, hotel.parc@modulonet.fr). This place is cheaper and sharper than Hôtel le Splendid, across the street.

$ Hôtel le Splendid* rents 17 small, musty-but-cheery rooms with good beds, ceiling fans, and small bathrooms. Your room comes with a smile from Madame Prel-Lemoine (Sb-€43–46, Db-€55–65, bigger Db with air-con-€61–71, three Db apartments with kitchenettes-€80, extra person-€10, 17 rue Agricol Perdiguier, tel. 04 90 86 14 46, fax 04 90 85 38 55, www.avignon-splendid-hotel.com).

$ Hôtel Boquier** offers 12 quiet, modest rooms under wood beams at fair prices, though a major renovation is planned that should change this information (Db-€50–60, Tb-€72, Qb-€90, extra bed-€10, parking-€7, near the TI at 6 rue du portail Boquier, tel. 04 90 82 34 43, fax 04 90 86 14 07, www.hotel-boquier.com, contact@hotel-boquier.com).

In the Center, near Place de l'Horloge

$$$ Hôtel d'Europe*****, with Avignon's most prestigious address, lets peasants sleep royally—if you get one of the 15 surprisingly reasonable "standard rooms." Enter a fountain-filled courtyard, linger in the lounges, and enjoy every comfort. The hotel is located on the handsome place Crillon near the river (classic Db-€169, superior Db-€340, prestige Db-€475, breakfast-€17, elevator, Internet access, garage-€16, near Daladier Bridge at 12 place Crillon, tel. 04 90 14 76 76, fax 04 90 14 76 71, www.heurope.com, reservations@heurope.com). The hotel's restaurant is Michelin-rated (one star) and serves an upscale €50 *menu* in its formal dining room or front courtyard.

$$$ Hôtel Mercure Cité des Papes**** is a modern chain hotel within spitting distance of the Palace of the Popes. It has 89 smartly designed, smallish rooms, air-conditioning, elevators, and all the comforts (Sb-€108, Db-€118, up to €138 during holiday weekends and the July festival, many rooms have views over place de l'Horloge, 1 rue Jean Vilar, tel. 04 90 80 93 00, fax 04 90 80 93 01, www.mercure.com, h1952@accor.com).

$$$ Hôtel Pont d'Avignon****, just inside the walls near St. Bénezet Bridge, is part of the same chain as the Hôtel Mercure Cité des Papes, with the same prices for its 87 rooms (direct access to a garage makes parking easier than at the other Mercure hotel, elevator, on rue Ferruce, tel. 04 90 80 93 93, fax 04 90 80 93 94, www.mercure.com, h0549@accor.com).

$$ At Hôtel de Blauvac**, friendly owner Veronica offers 16 mostly spacious, high-ceilinged rooms (many with an additional upstairs loft), a sky-high atrium and Internet access for a fee). It's a faded old manor home near the pedestrian zone with reliable noise at night (Sb-€67–77, Db-€72–82, Tb-€87–97, Qb-€102, €10 less off-season, 1 block off rue de la République at 11 rue de la Bancasse, tel. 04 90 86 34 11, fax 04 90 86 27 41, www.hotel-blauvac.com, blauvac@aol.com).

$$ Hôtel Danieli** is a *Hello Dolly* fluffball of a place that rents 29 colorful and simple rooms on the main drag to lots of tour groups (Sb-€70, Db-€80, Tb-€90, Qb-€100, 17 rue de la République, tel. 04 90 86 46 82, fax 04 90 27 09 24, www.hotel-danieli-avignon.com, hoteldanieli@wanadoo.fr, kind owner Madame Shogol).

$$ Hôtel Médiéval** is burrowed deep a few blocks from the Church of St. Pierre. Built as a cardinal's home, this massive stone mansion has a small garden, friendly managers, and 35 wood-paneled, mostly air-conditioned, unimaginative rooms (Sb-€47, Db-€57–72, larger Db-€81–88, Tb-€88, kitchenettes available but require 3-night minimum stay, Wi-Fi, 5 blocks east of place de l'Horloge, behind Church of St. Pierre at 15 rue Petite Saunerie, tel. 04 90 86 11 06, fax 04 90 82 08 64, www.hotelmedieval.com, hotel.medieval@wanadoo.fr, Mike).

Chambres d'Hôte

$$$ Villa Agapè, just off busy place de l'Horloge right in the center of town, is an oasis of calm and good taste. Run by friendly Madame de La Pommeraye, the villa has three handsomely decorated rooms, a peaceful courtyard, lovely public spaces, and a soaking pool to boot (Db-€100–150, extra person-€30, includes breakfast, 2-night minimum, Internet access and Wi-Fi; from place de l'Horloge it's one block down on left above the pharmacy at 13 rue St. Agricol—ring buzzer; tel. & fax 04 90 85 21 92, mobile 06 07 98 71 30, www.villa-agape.com, michele@villa-agape.com). For a weeklong stay, ask about renting her entire house, where you get Madame's room, study, and kitchen (€2,500–3,300).

$$$ Le Clos du Rempart, while less central, is still within the walls and worth considering. Madame Assad, another Parisian refugee, rents two rooms and one apartment on a pleasant courtyard decorated in a Middle Eastern theme, complete with a hammock (Db-€90–120 depending on season and room size, 2-bedroom apartment for 4 with kitchen-€150–230, apartment cheaper by the week, includes breakfast, air-con, 1 parking spot in garage, a

20-min walk from the Centre-Ville station at 35–37 rue Crémade, call for directions, tel. & fax 04 90 86 39 14, www.closdurempart .com, aida@closderempart.com).

Sleeping Cheaply near Avignon

$ Auberge Bagatelle's hostel offers dirt-cheap beds, a lively atmosphere, café, grocery store, launderette, great views of Avignon, and campers for neighbors (D–€38, dorm bed–€16, across Daladier Bridge on l'Ile de la Barthelasse, bus #10 from main post office, tel. 04 90 86 71 31, fax 04 90 27 16 23, www.aubergebagatelle.fr, auberge.bagatelle@wanadoo.fr).

EATING

Skip the overpriced places on place de l'Horloge (Les Domaines and La Civette near the carousel are the least of the evils here) and find a more intimate location for your dinner. Avignon has many delightful squares filled with tables ready to seat you.

Near the Church of St. Pierre

The church has enclosed squares on both sides, offering outdoor yet intimate ambience.

L'Epicerie, located on a small, unpretentious square, serves the highest-quality and highest-priced cuisine around the Church of St. Pierre (€20–25 *plats,* closed Sun, cozy interior good in bad weather, 10 place St. Pierre, tel. 04 90 82 74 22).

Pass under the arch by L'Epicerie restaurant and enter enchanting place des Châtaignes, a tasty commotion of tables from four restaurants: **Crêperie du Cloître** (big salad and main-course crêpe for about €14, closed Sun–Mon); **Restaurant Nem,** tucked in the corner (Vietnamese, family-run, *menus* from €12); and **Pause Gourmande** (lunch only, €9 *plats du jour,* always a veggie option, closed Sun). Just through the arch past the Pause Gourmande is **La Goulette** (Tunisian specialities such as *tagine* or couscous for €19, closed Mon).

Place Crillon

This large and trendy open square just off the river provides more atmosphere than quality. Several cafés offer inexpensive bistro fare with *menus* from €16, *plats* from €12, and many tables to choose from. **Restaurant les Artistes** is most popular (daily until 22:30, 21 place Crillon, tel. 04 90 82 23 54).

Avignon Restaurants

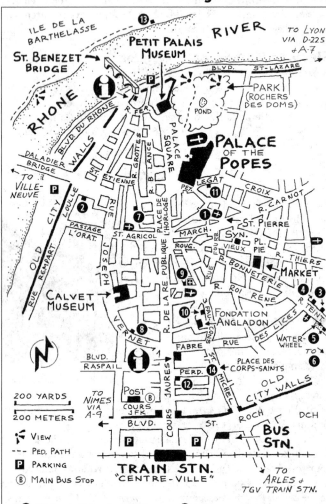

1 L'Epicerie, Crêperie du Cloître, La Goulette Rest., Rest. Nem, & Pause Gourmande

2 Restaurant les Artistes & Other Place Crillon Eateries

3 La Cave Breysse Wine Bar

4 Restaurant l'Empreinte

5 Woolloomooloo Restaurant

6 To Restaurant Numéro 75

7 L'Isle Sonnante Restaurant

8 La Compagnie des Comptoirs Restaurant

9 La Crêperie du Figuier

10 Le Caveau du Théâtre Rest.

11 Hôtel la Mirande Restaurant

12 Bakery Eric Convert

13 Le Bercail Restaurant

14 Cuisine et Comptoire Rest. & Other Place des Corps - Saints Eateries

Rue des Teinturiers

While a bit of a walk from the center, this street has a wonderful concentration of eateries that are popular with the natives. It's a youthful and trendy area, recently spiffed up with a canalside ambience and little hint of tourism. I'd survey the four eateries listed here before choosing.

La Cave Breysse is a fun and colorful stop for a lunch salad, or a good pause before dinner. Midday or evening, Christine and Tim would love to serve you a fragrant €2.50 glass of regional wine. Choose from the blackboard by the bar that lists all the bottles open today. You're welcome to take yours out and sit by the canal. In the evening, this place is a hit with the young local crowd for its wine (flexible hours, usually Tue–Sat 12:00–14:30 & 18:00–22:30, closed Sun–Mon, no food in evening; across from waterwheel at 41 rue des Teinturiers).

L'Empreinte is good for North African cuisine. Choose a table in its tent-like interior, or sit canalside on the cobbles (copious couscous for €11–20, take-out and veggie options available, open daily, 33 rue des Teinturiers, tel. 04 32 76 31 84).

Woolloomooloo was named, Dada-style, for the aboriginal term for "little black kangaroo." It's a funky and young-spirited eatery...think van Gogh drunk on rum-and-fruit punch. The food—while slopped together from a precooked buffet—is hearty, creative, and a good value. You'll mix and match from a very fun menu (€18/1 course and a drink, €21/2 courses, €28/3 courses, open daily, frequent jazz evenings, 16 rue des Teinturiers, tel. 04 90 85 28 44).

Restaurant Numéro 75 is worth the walk, filling the Pernod mansion (of *pastis* liquor fame) and a large, romantic courtyard with outdoor tables. The menu is limited to Mediterranean cuisine, but everything's *très* tasty. It's best to go with the options offered by your young, black-shirted server (three entrées, plus a fish and a meat main course; 2-course lunch *menu* with wine and coffee-€20; dinner *menus:* €25/first course and dessert, €27/appetizer and main course, €33/three courses; Mon–Sat 12:00–14:00 and 20:00–22:00, closed Sun, 75 rue Guillaume Puy, tel. 04 90 27 16 00).

Elsewhere in Avignon

At **L'Isle Sonnante,** join chef Boris and his wife Anne to dine intimately in their charming one-room *bistrot.* You'll choose from a small menu offering only fresh products and be served by owners who care (*menus* from €27, closed Sun–Mon, 100 yards from the carousel on place de l'Horloge at 7 rue Racine, tel. 04 90 82 56 01, best to book ahead).

La Compagnie des Comptoirs is the brainchild of famous twin-brother chefs who established a following in southern France with their inventive cuisine. Enter a Mediterranean world of cool bars, smart interiors, and a dazzling courtyard. This is where young Avignon professionals enjoy foods from the Mediterranean basin (allow €45 for dinner with wine, 83 rue Joseph Vernet, tel. 04 90 85 99 04).

La Crêperie du Figuier has good crêpes and salads that won't break the bank (dinner crêpe or salad for €11, open daily July–Aug, otherwise closed Sun–Mon, 3 rue du Figuier, tel. 04 90 82 60 67).

Le Caveau du Théâtre invites relaxed diners to share a glass of wine or dinner at one of a few sidewalk tables. Its wild posters decorate a carefree interior (€13 *plats*, €19 *menus*, fun ambience for free, closed Sun, 16 rue des Trois Faucons, tel. 04 90 82 60 91).

Hôtel la Mirande is the ultimate Avignon splurge. Reserve ahead here for understated elegance and Avignon's top cuisine (€35 lunch *menu*, €105 dinner tasting *menu*, closed Tue–Wed, behind Palace of the Popes, 4 place de la Mirande, tel. 04 90 86 93 93, fax 04 90 86 26 85).

On **Place des Corps Saints,** a pleasing square, you'll find several relaxed and reasonable eateries with tables sprawling under big plane trees (such as **Cuisine et Comptoire,** closed Sun, 04 90 82 18 39).

Bakery Eric Convert has excellent bread and sandwiches for lunch. Here you'll find a great selection of breads, including olive, Roquefort, orange chocolate, and dark Russian, and all varieties of baguettes and mouthwatering pastries (closed Sun, 45 cours Jean Jaurès, tel. 04 90 85 80 62).

Across the River

Le Bercail offers a fun opportunity to get out of town (barely) and take in *le fresh air* with a terrific river-front view of Avignon, all while enjoying inexpensive Provençal cooking served in big portions. Book ahead, as this restaurant is popular (*menus* from €16, serves late, daily April–Oct, tel. 04 90 82 20 22). To get here, take the small shuttle boat (located near St. Bénezet Bridge) to the Ile de la Barthelasse, turn right, and walk five minutes. As the boat usually stops running at about 18:00 (except in July–Aug, when it runs until 21:00), you can either taxi home or walk 25 minutes along the pleasant riverside path and over Daladier Bridge.

TRANSPORTATION CONNECTIONS

Trains

Remember, there are two train stations in Avignon: the suburban TGV station and the Centre-Ville station in the city center (€1.10 shuttle buses connect to both stations, 3/hr, 15 min). Only the Centre-Ville station has baggage check (see "Arrival in Avignon," page 476). Car rental is available at the TGV station. Some cities are served both by slower local trains from the Centre-Ville station and by faster TGV trains from the TGV station; I've listed the most convenient stations for each trip.

From Avignon's Centre-Ville Station by Train to: Arles (11/day, 20 min, less frequent in the afternoon), **Orange** (10/day, 15 min), **Nîmes** (14/day, 30 min), **Isle-sur-la-Sorgue** (10/day on weekdays, 5/day on weekends, 30 min), **Lyon** (10/day, 2 hrs, also from TGV station—see below), **Carcassonne** (8/day, 7 with transfer in Narbonne, 3 hrs), **Barcelona** (2/day, 6 hrs, transfer in Montpellier).

From Avignon's TGV Station to: Arles (11/day, 1 hr, by SNCF bus—take the faster train from the Centre-Ville station instead), **Nice** (20/day, 13 of which are via TGV, 4 hrs, most require transfer in Marseille), **Marseille** (10/day, 1 hr), **Aix-en-Provence TGV** (10/day, 25 min), **Lyon** (12/day, 1.5 hrs, also from Centre-Ville station—see above), **Paris'** Gare de Lyon (9/day in 2.5 hrs, 6/day in 3-4 hrs with change), **Paris'** Charles de Gaulle airport (7/day, 3 hrs).

Buses

The bus station *(gare routière)* is just past and below the Ibis Hôtel, to the right as you exit the train station (information desk open Mon–Fri 10:15–13:00 & 14:00–18:00, Sat 8:00–12:00, closed Sun, tel. 04 90 82 07 35). Nearly all buses leave from this station. The biggest exception is the SNCF bus service from the Avignon TGV station to Arles (11/day, 1 hr—the train is a much better option). The Avignon TI has schedules. Service is reduced or nonexistent on Sundays and holidays. Check your departure time beforehand and make sure to verify your destination with the driver.

From Avignon by Bus to: Pont du Gard: Buses leave regularly for Pont du Gard (4/day, 50 min; more with inconvenient transfer), but the schedule doesn't work well for day-trippers from Avignon—the way the return buses are timed, you get either far too little time there (20 min) or a bit too much (5 hrs). See page 494 under the Pont du Gard for transportation strategies).

By Bus to Other Regional Destinations: Uzès (4/day Mon–Sat, none Sun, 1 hr), **St. Rémy** (6/day, 50 min, handy way to visit its Wed market); **Orange** (hourly, 55 min), **Isle-sur-la-Sorgue** (6/day Mon–Sat, fewer on Sun, 45 min); **Vaison la Romaine, Nyons, Sablet,** and **Séguret** (2–3/day during school year, called *période scolaire*, 1/day otherwise and 1/day from TGV station, 75–90 min); **Gordes** (via Cavaillon, 1/day, not on Wed or Sun, 2 hrs, spend the night or taxi back to Cavaillon); **Lourmarin** (3/day, 90 min).

Pont du Gard, Les Baux, and Orange

The countryside around Arles and Avignon is littered with world-class sightseeing opportunities. Below I've described key sights and a half-day excursion into the countryside ("Côtes du Rhône Scenic Loop," page 516). Les Baux works well by car from Avignon or Arles, and by bus from Arles in July and August. The town of Orange ties in tidily with a trip to the Côtes du Rhône villages. The Pont du Gard is a short hop west of Avignon and on the way to/from Languedoc for drivers. Travelers relying on public transportation will find their choices very limited. Isle-sur-la-Sorgue in the Luberon (page 521) is the most accessible small town.

Pont du Gard

Throughout the ancient world, aqueducts were like flags of stone that heralded the greatness of Rome. A visit to this sight still

works to proclaim the wonders of that age. This perfectly preserved Roman aqueduct was built as the critical link of a 30-mile canal that, by dropping one inch for every 350 feet, supplied nine million gallons of water per day (about 100 gallons per second) to Nîmes—one of ancient Europe's largest cities. Though most of the aqueduct is on or below the ground, at the Pont du Gard it spans a canyon on a massive bridge—one of the most remarkable surviving Roman ruins anywhere.

Getting to the Pont du Gard

The famous aqueduct is between Remoulins and Vers-Pont du Gard on D-981, 17 miles from Nîmes and 13 miles from Avignon.

By Car: The Pont du Gard is an easy 25-minute drive due west of Avignon on N-100 and D-981 (follow signs to *Nîmes*, then *Pont du Gard*) and 45 minutes northwest of Arles (via Tarascon). The handy Rive Gauche parking is off D-981 (the road from Remoulins to Uzès). (Parking is also available on the Rive Droite side, but it's farther away from the museum.) If going to Arles from the Pont du Gard, follow signs to *Nîmes* (not *Avignon*), then follow D-986.

By Bus: Buses run to the Pont du Gard (on the Rive Gauche side) from Avignon, Nîmes, and Uzès, but schedules are not well-coordinated. Consider this plan: Take the 12:05 bus from Avignon, arriving at the Pont du Gard at 12:50, then take the 14:45 bus from there to Nîmes where you can take the train back to Avignon (14/day, 30 min).

In high season, most buses from Avignon enter the Pont du Gard site and stop at the parking ticket booth. Other buses stop at the traffic roundabout 300 yards from the Pont du Gard. The stop from Avignon and to Nîmes is on the far side of the roundabout from the Pont du Gard; the stop from Nîmes and to Avignon is on the same side as the Pont du Gard, to the left as you enter the traffic circle from the Pont du Gard. Make sure you're waiting for the bus on the correct side of the traffic circle. You have to signal the bus to get the driver to stop. When you get on, verify that the bus is going to your destination, then buy your ticket.

ORIENTATION

There are two riversides to the Pont du Gard: the left bank (Rive Gauche) and right bank (Rive Droite). Park on the Rive Gauche, where you'll find the museums, ticket booth, ATM, cafeteria, WCs, and shops—all built into a modern plaza. You'll see the aqueduct in two parts: first, the fine museum complex, then the actual river gorge spanned by the ancient bridge.

Cost: While it's free to see the aqueduct, the various optional activities each have a cost: parking (€5), museum (€7), corny film (€4), and a kids' space called *Ludo* (€5, scratch-and-sniff experience in English of various aspects of Roman life and the importance of water). The extensive outdoor *garrigue* natural area, featuring historic crops and landscapes of the Mediterranean, is free (though €4 buys you a helpful English booklet). During summer months, a nighttime sound-and-light show plays against the Pont du Gard. All these attractions are designed to give the sight more meaning—and they do—but for most visitors, only the museum is worth paying for. The **€12 combo-ticket**—which covers all sights and parking—is a no-brainer for drivers, and the best bet for most visitors. Families save even more money with the €24 family ticket (covers two parents and up to four kids). If you get a combo-ticket, check the movie schedule; the romancing-the-aqueduct 25-minute film is silly, but it offers good information in a flirtatious French-Mediterranean style...and a cool, entertaining, and cushy break.

Hours: The museum is open May–Sept Tue–Sun 9:30–19:00, Mon 13:00–19:00; Oct–April closes at 17:00; closed two weeks in Jan. The aqueduct itself is free and open until 1:00 in the morning, as is the parking lot.

Information: Tel. 08 20 90 33 30, www.pontdugard.fr.

Pont du Gard

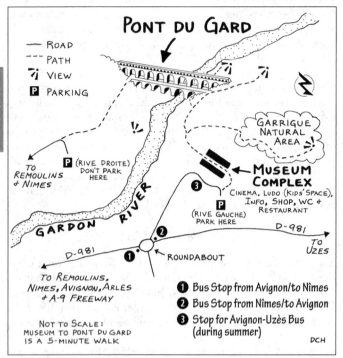

PONT DU GARD

—— ROAD
--- PATH
↗ VIEW
P PARKING

GARRIGUE NATURAL AREA

MUSEUM COMPLEX
CINEMA, LUDO (KIDS' SPACE), INFO, SHOP, WC & RESTAURANT

TO REMOULINS & NÎMES

P (RIVE DROITE) DON'T PARK HERE

P (RIVE GAUCHE) PARK HERE

GARDON RIVER

D-981

TO UZÈS

D-981

ROUNDABOUT

TO REMOULINS, NÎMES, AVIGNON, ARLES & A-9 FREEWAY

NOT TO SCALE: MUSEUM TO PONT DU GARD IS A 5-MINUTE WALK

❶ Bus Stop from Avignon/to Nîmes
❷ Bus Stop from Nîmes/to Avignon
❸ Stop for Avignon-Uzès Bus (during summer)

DCH

Canoe Rental: Consider seeing the Pont du Gard by canoe. Collias Canoes will pick you up at the Pont du Gard (or elsewhere, if prearranged) and shuttle you to the town of Collias. You'll float down the river to the nearby town of Remoulins, where they'll pick you up and take you back to the Pont du Gard (€18 per person, €9 for kids under 12, usually 2 hours, though you can take as long as you like, good idea to reserve the day before in July–Aug, tel. 04 66 22 85 54).

SIGHTS

▲**Museum**—The state-of-the-art museum's multimedia approach (well-presented in English) shows how water was an essential part of the Roman "art of living." You'll see examples of lead pipes, faucets, and siphons; walk through a rock quarry; and learn how they moved those huge rocks into place and how those massive arches were made. While actual artifacts from the aqueduct are few, the exhibit shows the immensity of the undertaking as well as the payoff. Imagine the excitement as this extravagant supply of water finally tumbled into Nîmes. A relaxing highlight is the scenic video helicopter ride along the entire 30-mile course of the structure, from its start at Uzès all the way to Nîmes.

▲▲▲Viewing the Aqueduct—A park-like path leads to the aqueduct. Until a few years ago, this was an actual road—adjacent to the aqueduct—that had spanned the river since 1743. Before you cross the bridge, pass under it and hike about 300 feet along the riverbank for a grand viewpoint from which to study the second-highest standing Roman structure. (Rome's Colosseum is only six feet taller.)

This was the biggest bridge in the whole 30-mile-long aqueduct. It seems exceptional because it is: The arches are twice the width of standard aqueducts, and the main arch is the largest the Romans ever built—80 feet (so it wouldn't get its feet wet). The bridge is about 160 feet high, and was originally about 1,100 feet long. Today, 12 arches are missing, reducing the length to 790 feet.

While the distance from the source (in Uzès) to Nîmes was only 12 miles as the eagle flew, engineers chose the most economical route, winding and zigzagging 30 miles. The water made the trip in 24 hours with a drop of only 40 feet. Ninety percent of the aqueduct is on or under the ground, but a few river canyons like this required bridges. A stone lid hides a four-foot-wide, six-foot-tall chamber lined with waterproof mortar that carried a stream for more than 400 years. For 150 years, this system provided Nîmes with good drinking water.

The appearance of the entire gorge changed in 2002, when a huge flood flushed lots of greenery downstream. Those floodwaters put Roman provisions to the test. Notice the triangular-shaped buttresses at the lower level—designed to split and divert the force of any flood *around* the feet of the arches rather than *into* them. The 2002 floodwaters reached the top of those buttresses. Anxious park rangers winced at the sounds of trees crashing onto the ancient stones...but the arches stood strong.

The stones that jut out—giving the aqueduct a rough, unfinished appearance—supported the original scaffolding. The protuberances were left, rather than cut off, in anticipation of future repair needs. The lips under the arches supported wooden templates that allowed the stones in the round arches to rest on something until the all-important keystone was dropped into place. Each stone weighs four to six tons. The structure stands with no mortar—taking full advantage of the innovative Roman arch, made strong by gravity.

Hike over the bridge for a closer look. Across the river, a high trail (marked *panorama*) leads upstream and offers commanding views. On the exhibit side of the structure, a trail marked *Accès l'Aqueduc* leads up to surviving stretches of the aqueduct. For a peaceful walk alongside the top of the aqueduct (where it's on land and no longer a bridge), follow the red-and-yellow markings. Remains of this part are scant because of medieval cannibalization—frugal builders couldn't resist the precut stones as they constructed local churches. The ancient quarry (about a third of a mile downstream on the exhibit side) may be opened by 2008.

Les Baux

Crowning the rugged Alpilles (ahl-pee) Mountains, this rock-capping castle town evokes a tumultuous medieval history. Even with the crowds of tourists, you can imagine the struggles of a strong community that lived a rugged life—thankful more for their top-notch fortifications than for their dramatic views. While mobbed with tourists most of the day, Les Baux rewards those arriving by 9:00 or after 17:00 with serenity. (While the hilltop citadel's entry closes at the end of the day, once inside you're welcome to live out your fondest medieval fantasies all night long.) Sunsets are dramatic, the castle is brilliantly illuminated after dark, and nights in Les Baux are pin-drop peaceful.

ORIENTATION

Les Baux is actually two visits in one: castle ruins on an almost lunar landscape and, below, a medieval town packed with shops, cafés, and tourist knickknacks. See the castle, then savor or blitz the lower town on your way out.

A cobbled lane leads up through the town to the castle (20-min uphill walk from the parking area). The TI is on the main drag into town (daily 9:30–12:30 & 14:00–17:30, tel. 04 90 54 34 39, www.lesbauxdeprovence.com). Ask about ticket combo deals (like the castle ruins and Cathédrale d'Image). If you'll be doing a lot of sightseeing, consider the €13.50 "Les Baux Jours" pass, which covers the castle ruins, the Yves Brayer Museum, and the Cathédrale d'Images (saves €5.50 if you visit all three; available at TI).

SIGHTS

The Castle Ruins (The "Dead City")

The sun-bleached ruins of the "dead city" of Les Baux are carved into, out of, and on top of a rock 650 feet above the valley floor.

Provence

Les Baux

❶ Hostellerie de la Reine Jeanne

❷ Le Mas d'Aigret

❸ Le Mas de l'Esparou B&B

❹ To Le Mazet des Alpilles B&B

❺ Renaissance Window

❻ City Hall

NOT TO SCALE

TO ST REMY VIA MOST SCENIC ROUTE

CAVES DE SARRAGAN

CATHEDRALE D'IMAGES

MUSEUM OF SANTONS

CHAPEL OF PENITENTS

EYGUIERES GATE

TO ARLES & FONTVIEILLE

CEM.

ST. VINCENT

WC

YVES BRAYER MUSEUM

RUE DE LA CALADE

PLACE LOUIS JOU

R. PORTE MAGE

WC

T O W N

RUE DES

R. NEUVE

GRAND RUE F. MISTRAL

UPHILL!

CASTLE RUINS

CHAPEL

RUE TRENCAT

TICKETS & ENTRY TO "DEAD CITY"

RUE DU CHATEAU

RUE DU FOURS

R. DE LORME

C L I F F S

TO ST REMY

P - PARKING

View - VIEW

DCH

TO MAUSSANE, PARADOU, ABBEY DE MONTMAJOUR, ARLES, ❹ & BARBEGAL

Many of the ancient walls of the striking castle still stand as a testament to the proud past of this once-feisty village.

Cost and Hours: €7.50, includes good audioguide, daily July–Aug 9:00–20:00, Easter–June and Sept–Oct 9:00–19:00, Nov–Easter 9:30–17:00. Those inside the castle when the entry closes can stay as long as they like. From mid-July through late August, the mountaintop is enlivened by medieval pageantry and tournaments.

History: Imagine the importance of this citadel in the Middle Ages, when the Lords of Baux were notorious warriors. (How many feudal lords could trace their lineage back to one of the "three kings" of Christmas-carol fame, Balthazar?) In the 11th century,

Les Baux was a powerhouse in southern France, controlling about 80 towns. The Lords of Baux fought the counts of Barcelona for control of Provence...and eventually lost. But while in power, these guys were mean. One ruler enjoyed forcing unransomed prisoners to jump off his castle walls.

In 1426, Les Baux was incorporated into Provence and France. Not accustomed to subservience, Les Baux struggled with the French king, who responded by destroying the fortress in 1483. Later, Les Baux regained some importance and emerged as a center of Protestantism. Arguing with Rome was a high-stakes game in the 17th century, and Les Baux's association with the Huguenots brought destruction again in 1632 when Richelieu (under King Louis XIII) demolished the castle. Louis rubbed salt in the wound by billing Les Baux's residents for his demolition expenses. The once-powerful town of 4,000 was forever crushed.

In the old olive mill where you buy your ticket, study the models of the town before its 17th-century destruction. Take full advantage of the included audioguide—it narrates 30 stops while you wander as you like, keying in the number for any sight that interests you.

As you wander out on the windblown field, past kid-thrilling medieval siege weaponry, try to imagine 4,000 people living up here. Notice the water catchment system (a slanted field that caught rainwater and drained it into a cistern—necessary during a siege). In the little chapel across from the entry, the slide show *(Van Gogh, Gauguin, and Cézanne: Painting in the Land of the Olive Trees)* provides a relaxing 10-minute interlude (plays constantly; no words—just images and music).

For the most sensational views, climb to the blustery top of the citadel. Hang on. The mistral wind just might blow you away.

Lower Town

After your castle visit, you can shop and eat your way back through the new town. Or you can escape the crowds by taking the first left as you leave the castle, continuing downhill, and checking out these minor but worthwhile sights as you descend:

Yves Brayer Museum (Musée Yves Brayer)—This enjoyable museum lets you peruse three floors of paintings (van Gogh–like Expressionism, without the tumult) by Yves Brayer (1907–1990), who spent his final years here in Les Baux. Like Van Gogh, Brayer was inspired by all that surrounded him (€4, daily 10:00–12:30 & 14:00–18:30, tel. 04 90 54 36 99). Pick up the descriptive English sheet at the entry.

• *Next door is the...*

St. Vincent Church—This 12th-century Romanesque church was built short and wide to fit the terrain. The center chapel on the right (partially carved out of the rock) houses the town's traditional Provençal processional chariot. Each Christmas Eve, a ram pulled this cart—holding a lamb, symbolizing Jesus, and surrounded by candles—through town to the church.

• *A few steps away is the...*

Chapel of Penitents—Notice the nativity scene painted by Yves Brayer, illustrating the local legend that says Jesus was born in Les Baux. Leaving the church, turn left. Wash your shirt in the old-town "laundry"—with a pig-snout faucet and 14th-century stone washing surface designed for short women.

• *Head downhill. After passing a free (and curiously evangelical) "museum of aromas and perfumes" you hit the awe-inspiring...*

Museum of Santons—This free museum displays a collection of *santons*, popular folk figurines that decorate local Christmas mangers. Notice how the nativity scene "proves" once again that Jesus was born in Les Baux. These painted clay dolls show off local dress and traditions. Find the old couple leaning heroically into *le mistral*.

• *If you choose to visit the main drag through town (grand rue Frédéric Mistral), you'll find the following sights. The first is halfway up to the castle entry.*

Manville Mansion City Hall—The 15th-century city hall flies the red-and-white flag of Monaco, a reminder that the Grimaldi family (who have long ruled the tiny principality of Monaco) owned Les Baux until the French Revolution (1789). In fact, in 1982, Princess Grace Kelly and her royal husband, Prince Rainier Grimaldi, came to Les Baux to receive the key to the city.

Across the street and 20 yards farther up, the fine 1571 **Renaissance window**—marking the site of a future Calvinist museum—stands as a reminder of this town's Protestant history. This was probably a place of Huguenot worship—the words carved into the lintel, *Post tenebras lux*, were a popular Calvinist slogan: "After the shadow comes the light."

Near Les Baux

A half-mile beyond Les Baux, D-27 leads to dramatic views of the hill town, with pull-outs and walking trails at the pass, and two sights that fill cool, cavernous caves in former limestone quarries dating back to the Middle Ages. (The limestone is easy to cut, but gets hard and nicely polished when exposed to the weather.) Speaking of quarries, in 1821 the rocks and soil of this area were discovered to contain an important mineral for the making of aluminum. It was named after the town: bauxite.

Caves de Sarragan—The best views of Les Baux are from this parking lot, occupied by the Sarragan Winery (which invites you in for a taste). While this place looks like it's designed for groups, the friendly, English-speaking staff welcomes individuals (free, daily April–Sept 10:00–12:00 & 14:00–19:00, Oct–March until 18:00, tel. 04 90 54 33 58).

Cathédrale d'Images—This similar cave nearby offers a mesmerizing sound-and-slide show. Its 48 projectors flash countless images set to music on the quarry walls as visitors wander around (€7.50, daily March–Dec 10:00–18:00, closed Jan–Feb, tel. 04 90 54 42 65). Dress warmly as the cave is cool.

SLEEPING

In or near Les Baux

$$$ Le Mas d'Aigret***, on the road to St. Rémy-de-Provence, is a well-run, lovely refuge that crouches just past Les Baux. Lie on your back and stare up at the castle walls rising beyond the swimming pool or enjoy sensational valley views from the groomed terraces (Db with no view-€95, larger Db with balcony and view-€145, Tb/Qb-€200–230, two cool troglodyte rooms-€190–230, half-pension option with big breakfast and good dinner-€39, air-con, rooms have some daytime road noise, tel. 04 90 54 20 00, fax 04 90 54 44 00, www.masdaigret.com, contact@masdaigret.com, Dutch Marieke and French Eric).

$$ Le Mas de l'Esparou *chambre d'hôte*, a few minutes below Les Baux toward Paradou, is welcoming and kid-friendly, with three spacious rooms, a big swimming pool, table tennis, and distant views of Les Baux. Sweet Jacqueline loves her job, and her lack of English only makes her more animated (Db-€62, extra bed-about €16, includes breakfast, cash only, between Les Baux and Maussane les Alpilles on D-5, look for white sign with green lettering, tel. & fax 04 90 54 41 32).

$$ Hostellerie de la Reine Jeanne**, an exceptional value, is a good place to watch the sun rise and set from Les Baux. Run by Gaelle and Marc, this place offers a handful of comfy rooms above a busy (and good value) restaurant (standard Ds-€50, standard Db-€56, Db with view deck-€65, cavernous family suite-€100, air-con in most rooms, ask for *chambre avec terrasse*, good *menus* from €16, 150 feet to your right after entry to the village of Les Baux, tel. 04 90 54 32 06, fax 04 90 54 32 33, www.la-reinejeanne.com, reine .jeanne@wanadoo.fr).

$ Le Mazet des Alpilles is a small home with three tidy, air-conditioned rooms just outside the unspoiled village of Paradou, five minutes below Les Baux. It may have space when others don't (Db-€55, ask for largest room, includes breakfast, cash only, air-con, child's bed available, pleasant garden, follow brown signs from D-17, in Paradou look for route de Brunelly, tel. 04 90 54 45 89, www.alpilles.com/mazet.htm, lemazet@wanadoo.fr). Sweet Annick speaks just enough English.

Getting to Les Baux

By Car: Les Baux is a 20-minute drive from Arles: Follow signs for *Avignon*, then *Les Baux*. Parking costs €4. As you enter, take a ticket, then drive as close to the top of the parking lot as you can. Pay at the machine just below the town entry.

By Bus: From Arles, the direct bus service to Les Baux runs only during July and August (6/day, 35 min, €4 one-way, via Abbey of Montmajour, Fontvieille, and Paradou). To go directly to Les Baux (not including St. Rémy-de-Provence) from Arles at other times of the year, take the bus to Maussane (6/day Mon–Sat, none on Sun, 20 min, €4 one-way), and taxi from Maussane to Les Baux (allow €10 one-way).

You can also combine Les Baux and St. Rémy into a worthwhile day trip from Arles or Avignon. From either city, take the bus to St. Rémy (50 min, €4 one-way, from Arles: 3/day Mon–Sat April–Oct, none Sun or Nov–March; from Avignon: 6/day Mon–Sat, none Sun); then take a taxi to Les Baux from there (figure €15 one-way).

By Taxi: Figure €32 for a taxi one-way from Arles (€40 after 19:00, tel. 06 80 27 60 92).

By Minivan Tour: The best option for many is an excursion tour, which can be both efficient and economical (see page 453).

Orange

Orange is notable for its Roman arch and grand theater. Orange was an important city in ancient times—strategically situated on the Via Agrippa, connecting Lyon and Arles. It was actually founded as a comfortable place for Roman army officers to enjoy their retirement. Even in Roman times, career military men retired after only 20 years. Does the emperor want thousands of well-trained, relatively young guys hanging around Rome? No way. What to do? "How about a nice place in the south of France...?"

ORIENTATION

Tourist Information

The unnecessary TI is located next to the fountain and parking area at 5 cours Aristide Briand (April–Sept Mon–Sat 9:30–19:00, Sun 10:00–13:00 & 14:00–18:30; Oct–March Mon–Sat 10:00–13:00 & 14:00–17:30, closed Sun; tel. 04 90 34 70 88).

Arrival in Orange

By Train: Orange's **train station** is a level 15-minute walk from the Roman Theater (or an €8 taxi ride, tel. 06 09 51 32 25). The

Orange

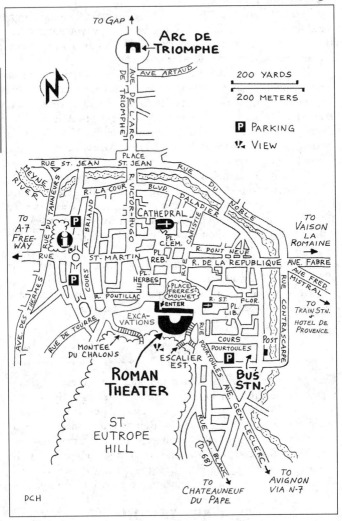

recommended Hotel de Provence across from the station will keep your bags (see below). To walk into town from the train station, head straight out of the station (down avenue Frédéric Mistral), merge left onto Orange's main shopping street (rue de la République), then turn left on rue Caristie; you'll run into the Roman Theater's massive stage wall.

By Bus: Buses drop you at place Pourtoules, two blocks from the Roman Theater (walk to the hill and turn right to reach the theater).

By Car: Drivers follow *Centre-Ville* signs, then *Théâtre Antique* signs, and park as close to the Roman Theater's huge wall as possible. Parking Théâtre Antique (by the fountain and the TI) is easiest. Those coming from the autoroute will land here by following *Centre-Ville* signs; others should follow *Centre-Ville* signs then *Tourist Information* signs to find this parking. To reach the theater, walk to the hill and turn left.

SIGHTS

▲▲▲**Roman Theater (Théâtre Antique)**—Orange's ancient theater is the best-preserved in existence, and the only one in Europe with its acoustic wall still standing. (Two others in Asia Minor also survive.)

After you enter (to the right of the actual theater), you'll see a huge dig—the site of the Temple to the Cult of the Emperor.

Climb the steep stairs to the top of the theater to appreciate the acoustics (eavesdrop on people by the stage) and contemplate the idea that, 2,000 years ago, Orange residents enjoyed grand spectacles with high-tech sound and lighting effects—such as simulated thunder, lightning, and rain. The glass and iron stage roof is new and was designed to protect the stage wall and improve acoustics. It was built by the Eiffel Engineering Company (yes, the same folks who built that tower).

This is the standard Roman theater design: a semicircular orchestra, a half-circle of theater seats, and a small stage with a high back wall—originally covered with a marble veneer and colorfully painted. A huge awning could be unfurled from the 130-foot-tall stage wall to provide shade. Wow.

A grandiose Caesar overlooks everything. The horn has blown. It's time to find your seat: row two, number 30. Sitting down, you're comforted by the "EQ GIII" carved into the seat (Equitas Gradus #3...three rows for the Equestrian order). The theater is filled with 10,000 people. Thankfully, you mix only with your class, the nouveau riche—merchants, tradesmen, and city big shots. The people above you are the working-class, and way up in the "chicken roost" section is the scum of the earth—slaves, beggars, prostitutes, and youth hostellers. Scanning the orchestra section (where the super-rich sit on real chairs), you notice the town dignitaries hosting some visiting VIPs.

Okay, time to worship. They're parading a bust of the emperor from its sacred home in the adjacent temple around the stage. Next is the ritual animal sacrifice called *la pompa* (so fancy, future generations will use that word for anything full of such...pomp). Finally, you settle in for an all-day series of spectacles and dramatic entertainment. All eyes are on the big stage door in the middle—where the Julia Roberts and Tom Hanks of the day will appear. (Lesser actors come out of the side doors.)

With an audience of 10,000 and no amplification, acoustics were very important. At the top of the side walls, a slanted line of stones marks the position of a long-gone roof—not to protect from the weather, but to project the voices of the actors into the crowd. For further help, actors wore masks with leather caricature mouths that functioned as megaphones.

The Roman Theater was all part of the "give them bread and circuses" approach to winning the support of the masses (not unlike today's philosophy of "give them tax cuts and Fox News"). The spectacle grew from 65 days of games per year when the theater was first built (and when Rome was at its height) to about 180 days each year by the time Rome finally fell.

Cost and Hours: Theater entry-€8, April–Sept daily 9:00–18:00, until 19:00 in summer, until 17:00 Oct–March, tel. 04 90 51 17 60.

Information: Your ticket includes a worthwhile audioguide, a 13-minute film (English subtitles), and entrance to the small museum across the street (Musée d'Art et d'Histoire). Pop in to see a few theater details and a rare grid used as the official property-ownership registry—each square represented a 120-acre plot of land. Vagabonds wanting to see the theater for free can hike up nearby stairs (*escalier est* off rue Pourtoules is closest) to view it from the bluff high above.

Cafés: A shaded café-filled square hides a block across from the theater up rue Ségond Weber.

▲**Roman "Arc de Triomphe"**—Technically the only real Roman arches of triumph are in Rome's Forum, built to commemorate various emperors' victories. The great Roman arch of Orange is actually a municipal arch erected (about A.D. 19) to commemorate a general, named Germanicus, who protected the town. The 60-foot-tall arch is on a noisy traffic circle (north of city center, on avenue Arc de Triomphe).

SLEEPING

$$ Hotel de Provence**, at the train station, is pleasant, air-conditioned, and affordable (Db-€60, restaurant and café, 60 avenue Frédéric Mistral, tel. 04 90 34 00 23, fax 04 90 34 91 72, www .hoteldeprovence84.com, hoteldeprovence84@wanadoo.fr).

TRANSPORTATION CONNECTIONS

From Orange by Train to: Avignon (10/day, 15 min), **Arles** (4/day direct, 35 min, more with transfer in Avignon), **Lyon** (16/day, 2 hrs).

By Bus to: Vaison la Romaine (2–3/day, 45 min), **Avignon** (hourly, 55 min). Buses to Vaison la Romaine and other wine villages depart from the big square, place Pourtoules (turn right out of the Roman Theater and right again on rue Pourtoules).

Villages of the Côtes du Rhône

The sunny Côtes du Rhône wine road—one of France's best—starts at Avignon's doorstep and winds north through an appealingly rugged, mountainous landscape carpeted with vines, peppered with warm stone villages, and presided over by the Vesuvius-like Mont Ventoux. The wines of the Côtes du Rhône (grown on the *côtes,* or hillsides, of the Rhône River Valley) are easy on the palate and on your budget. But this hospitable place offers more than famous wine—its hill-capping villages inspire travel posters, and its vistas are unforgettable. Yes, there are good opportunities for enjoyable wine-tasting, but there is also a soul to this area...if you take the time to look.

Planning Your Time

Vaison la Romaine is the small hub of this region, offering limited bus connections with Avignon and Orange, bike rental, and a mini-Pompeii in the town center. Nearby, you can visit the impressive Roman Theater in Orange (described above), drive to the top of Mont Ventoux, follow my "Côtes du Rhône Scenic Loop," page 516, through villages and wineries, and pedal to nearby villages for a breath of fresh air. The Dentelles de Montmirail mountains are laced with a variety of exciting trails, ideal for hikers.

Two nights make a good start for exploring this area. Drivers should head for the hills. Those without wheels find that Vaison la Romaine makes an easier home base.

Getting Around the Côtes du Rhône

By Car: Pick up the Michelin Local maps #332 or #528 to navigate your way around the Côtes du Rhône. (Landmarks like Dentelles de Montmirail and Mont Ventoux make it easier to get your bearings.) I've described my favorite driving route on page 516. If your plan is to connect the Côtes du Rhône with the Luberon, do it scenically via Mont Ventoux (follow signs to *Malaucène*, then to *Mont Ventoux*, allowing 2 hours to Roussillon). This route is one of the most spectacular in Provence. If continuing north toward Lyon, consider the worthwhile detour via the Ardèche Gorges (described on page 519).

By Bus: Buses run to the Côtes du Rhône from Orange and Avignon (2–3/day, 45 min from Orange, 90 min from Avignon) and connect wine villages (including Gigondas, Sablet, and Beaumes-de-Venise) with Vaison la Romaine and Nyons to the north. Another line runs from Vaison la Romaine to Carpentras, serving Le Crestet, Malaucène, and Le Barroux (2/day, tel. 04 90 36 09 90). Both routes provide scenic rides through this area.

By Train: Trains get you as far as Orange (from Avignon: 10/day, 15 min), where buses make the 45-minute trip to Vaison la Romaine (see above).

By Tour: Two companies—**Wine Safari** and **Taxi des Oliviers**—can expertly guide you through this tricky-without-a-car region. **Lieutaud** offers big-bus excursions from Arles and Avignon to Vaison la Romaine and Orange. For details on these companies, see "Tours of Provence," on page 452.

Vaison la Romaine

With quick access to vineyards, villages, and Mont Ventoux, this lively little town of 6,000 makes a great base for exploring the Côtes du Rhône region by car or by bike. You get two villages for the price of one: Vaison la Romaine's "modern" lower city is like a mini-Arles, with worthwhile Roman ruins, a lone pedestrian street, and too many cars. The car-free medieval hill town looms above, with meandering cobbled lanes, a dash of art galleries and cafés, and a ruined castle with a good view from its base.

ORIENTATION

The city is split in two by the Ouvèze River. The Roman Bridge connects the more modern lower town (Ville-Basse) with the hill-capping medieval upper town (Ville-Haute).

Tourist Information
The superb TI is in the lower city, between the two Roman ruin sites, at place du Chanoine Sautel (Mon–Sat 9:00–12:00 & 14:00–17:45, Sun 9:00–12:00, closed Sun Oct–April, tel. 04 90 36 02 11, www.vaison-la-romaine.com). Say *bonjour* to *charmante* and ever-so-patient Valerie—get bus schedules, ask about festivals and evening programs, and pick up information on walks and bike

rides from Vaison la Romaine. The TI sells a helpful €5 guide to biking, *Parcours Cyclo Touristiques,* with detailed maps for several bike tours ranging from easy half-day trips to all-day pedals.

Arrival in Vaison la Romaine

By Bus: The unmarked bus stop to Orange and Avignon is in front of the Cave la Romaine winery. Buses from Orange or Avignon drop you across the street (2–3/day, 45 min from Orange, 90 min from Avignon). Tell the driver you want the stop for the Office de Tourisme. When you get off the bus, walk five minutes down avenue Général de Gaulle to reach the TI and recommended hotels.

By Car: Follow signs to *Centre-Ville,* then *Office de Tourisme;* park free across from the TI. Most parking is free in Vaison la Romaine.

Helpful Hints

Market Day: Sleep in Vaison la Romaine on Monday night, and you'll wake to an amazing Tuesday market. But be warned: Mondays are quiet, and the town's two best restaurants are closed. If you do spend a Monday night, avoid parking at market sites or you won't find your car where you left it.

Internet Access: Find **Brasserie du Siècle** near the recommended Hôtel Burrhus on place Montfort (daily 7:00–1:00 in the morning, tel. 04 90 36 00 19).

Laundry: The self-service **Laverie la Lavandière** is on cours Taulignan, near avenue Victor Hugo (daily 8:00–22:00). The friendly owners (who work next door at the dry cleaners) will do your laundry while you sightsee—when you pick up your laundry, thank them with a small tip (dry cleaners open Mon–Sat 9:00–12:00 & 15:00–19:00, closed Sun).

Bike Rental: Try **Mag 2 Roues,** in the lower town on cours Taulignan (tel. 04 90 28 80 46).

Taxi: To call a taxi, dial 04 90 46 81 36 or 06 22 28 24 49.

Car Rental: **Wallgreen** has a few cars for rent at Vaison Pneus (avenue Marcel Pagnol, tel. 04 90 28 73 54).

SIGHTS AND ACTIVITIES

Roman Ruins—Ancient Vaison la Romaine had a treaty that gave it the preferred "federated" relationship with Rome (rather than simply being a colony). This, along with a healthy farming economy (olives and vineyards), made it a most prosperous place... as a close look at its sprawling ruins demonstrates. About 6,000 people called Vaison la Romaine home 2,000 years ago. When the barbarians arrived, the Romans were forced out, and the towns-people fled into the hills. Here's a mind-boggling thought: The

Vaison la Romaine

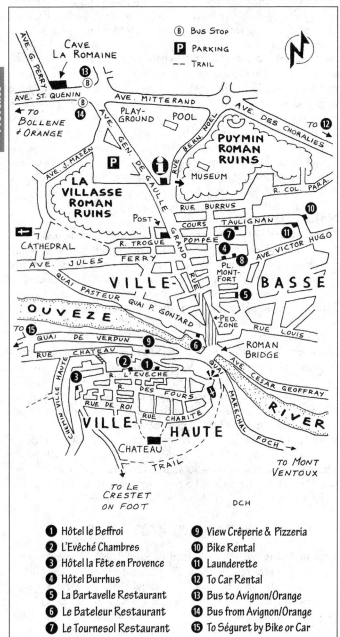

Ⓑ Bus Stop
Ⓟ Parking
-- Trail

1 Hôtel le Beffroi
2 L'Evêché Chambres
3 Hôtel la Fête en Provence
4 Hôtel Burrhus
5 La Bartavelle Restaurant
6 Le Bateleur Restaurant
7 Le Tournesol Restaurant
8 Brasserie du Siècle

9 View Crêperie & Pizzeria
10 Bike Rental
11 Launderette
12 To Car Rental
13 Bus to Avignon/Orange
14 Bus from Avignon/Orange
15 To Séguret by Bike or Car

town has only recently reached the same population as during its Roman era.

Vaison la Romaine's Roman ruins are split by a modern road

into two sites: Puymin and La Villasse. Each is well-presented, offering a good picture of life during the Roman Empire. Visit **Puymin** first. Inside the site, climb the hill to the museum (exhibits explained in English loaner booklet). Behind the museum is a 6,000-seat theater (just enough seats for the number of residents). Nearest the entry are the scant but impressive remains of a sprawling mansion. Back across the modern road in **La Villasse,** you'll explore a "street of shops" and the foundations of more houses.

Cost and Hours: €8 Roman ruins combo-ticket includes both ruins, a helpful audioguide, and the cloister at the Notre-Dame de Nazareth cathedral (see below), daily March–May 10:00–18:00, June–Sept 9:30–18:00, Oct–Feb 10:00–12:00 & 14:00–17:00.

Lower Town (Ville-Basse)—Vaison la Romaine's nondescript modern town stretches from its car-littered main square, place Montfort. A few blocks away, the stout **Notre-Dame de Nazareth** cathedral—with an evocative cloister—is a good example of Provençal Romanesque (cloister entry-€1.50, covered by €8 Roman ruins combo-ticket—see above). The pedestrian-only Grand Rue is a lively shopping street leading to the small river gorge and the Roman Bridge (see below).

Roman Bridge—Two thousand years ago, the Romans cut this sturdy, no-nonsense vault into the canyon rock, and it has survived ever since. Until the 20th century, this was the only way to cross the Ouvèze River. The metal plaque on the wall *(Crue du 22-09-92)* shows the high-water mark of the record flood that killed 30 people and washed away the valley's other bridges. The flood swept away the modern top of this bridge...but couldn't budge the 55-foot Roman arch.

Upper Town (Ville-Haute)—While there's nothing of particular importance to see in the fortified medieval old town atop the hill, the cobbled lanes and charming fountains make you want to break out a sketchpad. Vaison la Romaine had a prince-bishop since the fourth century. He came under attack by the Count of Toulouse in the 12th century. Anticipating a struggle, the prince-bishop abandoned the lower town and built a château on this rocky outcrop (about 1195). Over time, the rest of the townspeople followed, vacating the lower town and building their homes at the base of the château behind the upper town's fortified wall.

▲Market Day—In the 16th century, the pope gave Vaison la Romaine market-town status. Each Tuesday since then, the town has hosted a farmers' market. Today, merchants gather with gusto, turning the entire place into a festival of produce and Provençal products. This Tuesday-morning market is one of France's best, but it can challenge those who suffer from claustrophobia. Be warned that parking is a real headache unless you arrive early (see "Helpful Hints," page 509; and "Provence Market Days" on page 454).

Wine-Tasting—Cave la Romaine, a five-minute walk up avenue Général de Gaulle from the TI, offers a variety of great-value wines from nearby villages in a pleasant, well-organized tasting room (daily 8:30–13:00 & 14:00–19:00, avenue St. Quenin, tel. 04 90 36 55 90).

Hiking—The TI has good information on easy hikes into the hills above Vaison la Romaine. It's about 90 minutes to the tiny hill town of Le Crestet, though great views begin immediately. To find this trail, drive or walk up past the upper town (with the castle just on your left), find the *chemin des Fontaines*, and stay the course as far as you like. Cars are not allowed on the road after about a mile. Consider taking the bus (2/day, 5 min) or a taxi to Le Crestet, and walking back.

Biking—This area is not particularly flat, and it's often hot and windy, making bike-riding a dicey option. But if it's calm, the five-mile ride to cute little Villedieu is a delight (the bike route is signed along small roads). With a little more energy, you can pedal beyond Villedieu on the lovely road to Mirabel (ask in Villedieu for directions). Or get a good map and connect the following villages for an enjoyable 11-mile loop ride: Vaison la Romaine, St. Romain-en-Viennois, Puyméras, Faucon, and St. Marcellin-lès-Vaison. The TI has ample information on nearby mountain-biking trails.

SLEEPING

In Vaison la Romaine

Hotels in Vaison la Romaine are a good value. Those in the medieval upper town (Ville-Haute) are quieter, cozier, cooler, and a 15-minute walk uphill from the parking lot next to the TI. If you have a car, consider staying in one of the charming Côtes du Rhône villages near Vaison la Romaine (see page 516). If staying at one of the first three places, follow signs to *Cité Médiévale* and park just outside the upper village entry (driving into the Cité Médiévale itself is a challenge, with tiny lanes and nearly impossible parking).

$$$ Hôtel le Beffroi*** hides deep in the upper town, just above a demonstrative bell tower (you'll hear what I mean). It's a 16th-century, red-tile-and-wood-beamed-cozy place with nary a level surface. The rooms—split between two buildings a few doors apart—are Old World comfy, and some have views. You'll also find classy public spaces, a garden with view tables (light meals available in the summer), a small pool with more views, and animated Nathalie at reception (standard Db-€85–105, superior Db-€135, Tb-€160, rue de l'Evêché, tel. 04 90 36 04 71, fax 04 90 36 24 78, www.le-beffroi.com, info@le-beffroi.com). The hotel's restaurant offers *menus* from €30.

$$ L'Evêché Chambres, almost next door to le Beffroi in the upper town (look for the ivy), is a five-room, melt-in-your-chair B&B. The owners (the Verdiers) own the art boutique across the street, have an exquisite sense of interior design, and are passionate about books, making this place feel like a cross between a library and an art gallery (Sb-€70–80, standard Db-€80–90, Db suite-€105–130, the *solanum* suite is worth every euro, Tb-€110–150, Internet access and Wi-Fi, rue de l'Evêché, tel. 04 90 36 13 46, fax 04 90 36 32 43, http://eveche.free.fr, eveche@aol.com).

$$ Hotel La Fête en Provence, conveniently located for drivers at the upper entry to the medieval upper town, offers a variety of room shapes and sizes. All the rooms are chiffon-comfortable, and several have small kitchenettes. Rooms are located around a calming courtyard, and there's a pool and Jacuzzi next door (standard Db-€68, bigger Db with king-size bed and bath-€98, extra person-€15, cash only, Cité Médiévale, tel. & fax 04 90 36 36 43, www.hotellafete-provence.com, fete-en-provence@wanadoo.fr). Their apartment (€110) sleeps up to six people, and comes with a kitchenette and sitting area.

$ Hôtel Burrhus** is part art gallery, part funky hotel—and the best value in the lower town. It's a central, laid-back, go-with-the-flow-place, with a broad terrace over the raucous place Montfort (for maximum quiet, request a back room). Its floor plan will confound even the ablest navigator. The bigger, newer rooms come with cool colors and contemporary decor and are worth the extra euros (Db-€47–54, new Db-€58–70, extra bed-€15, air-con in some rooms, free Internet access and Wi-Fi, 1 place Montfort, tel. 04 90 36 00 11, fax 04 90 36 39 05, www.burrhus.com, info @burrhus.com).

Near Vaison la Romaine

These four accommodations are within a 10-minute drive of Vaison la Romaine.

$$$ Domaine de Cabasse*** is a lovely spread flanked by vineyards at the foot of Séguret (with a walking path to the village). Winemaking is their primary business (tastings possible), though the hotel is well-run by its relaxed staff. The 13 rooms have retained a simple Old World feel. All the rooms have decks, and a big pool and bikes are at your disposal. From the entry gate—which opens automatically...and slowly—the place appears more formal than it is (Db-€110–150, Tb/Qb-€120–155, on D-23 between Sablet and Séguret, tel. 04 90 46 91 12, fax 04 90 46 94 01, www.domaine -de-cabasse.fr, info@domaine-de-cabasse.fr). The restaurant offers a mouthwatering, though limited, dinner *menu* (€32) served inside or out. (Hotel guests start with an apéritif.)

$$$ Hôtel les Florets**, a half-mile above Gigondas, is surrounded by pine trees at the foothills of the Dentelles de Montmirail. It comes with a huge terrace that van Gogh would have loved, thoughtfully designed rooms, and an exceptional restaurant (Db-€98–113, Tb-€115–135, annex rooms are best, Gigondas, tel. 04 90 65 85 01, fax 04 90 65 83 80, www.hotel -lesflorets.com, accueil@hotel-lesflorets.com). For more details about the hotel's restaurant, see the next page.

$$$ Domaine de Tilleuls***, 10 minutes from Vaison la Romaine in workaday Malaucène, is a splendid, moderately priced refuge, and the most family-friendly place I list. (Welcoming owners Arnaud and Dominique have three kids.) Its 20 country-modern rooms fill an old farmhouse, overlooking lovely grounds with namesake linden trees *(tilleuls)*, a sandbox, toys, and a large pool. If you missed market day in Vaison la Romaine, sleep here Tuesday night and wake to a bustling market (Db-€78–88, Tb/Qb-€115, well-signed in Malaucène on the route to Mont Ventoux, tel. 04 90 65 22 31, fax 04 90 65 16 77, www.hotel-domainedestilleuls .com, info@hotel-domainedestilleuls.com). An Internet café is close by.

$$ L'Ecole Buissonnière Chambres are run by an engaging Anglo-French team, Monique and John, who share their peace and quiet 10 minutes from Vaison la Romaine. This creatively restored farmhouse has three character-filled, half-timbered rooms, and convivial public spaces. Getting to know John, who has lived all over the south of France and even worked as a *gardian* (cowboy) in the Camargue, is worth the price of the room—he's also generous with his knowledge of the area. The outdoor kitchen allows guests to picnic in high fashion in the tranquil garden (Db-€54–60, Tb-€68–75, Qb-€84–90, includes breakfast, cash only, between Villedieu and Buisson on D-75, tel. 04 90 28 95 19, ecole.buissonniere@wanadoo.fr).

EATING

In Vaison la Romaine

Vaison la Romaine is a small town with a handful of good, popular places—arrive by 19:30 or reserve a day ahead, particularly on weekends. You can eat very well on a moderate budget in the lower town, or go for medieval ambience rather than memorable food in the atmospheric upper town (which has a view *crêperie* and an air-conditioned pizzeria, open daily and with fair prices). And if it's summer, a light dinner in the **Hôtel le Beffroi** garden is just right (recommended under "Sleeping," earlier in this chapter). With a car, it's well worth venturing to nearby Côtes du Rhône villages to eat (see page 516). Wherever you dine, begin with a fresh glass of Muscat from the nearby village of Beaumes-de-Venise.

La Bartavelle is a fine place to savor traditional French cuisine in the lower town. Owner Berangère (bear-ahn-zher), has put together a tourist-friendly mix-and-match menu of local options. You get access to the top-end selections even on the €20 bottom-end *menu*—just fewer courses (closed Mon, small terrace outside, air-con and pleasant interior, reserve ahead, 12 place de Sus Auze, tel. 04 90 36 02 16).

Le Bateleur, almost on the river, serves fine Provençal cuisine in a more formal setting. English-speaking owners Jean-François and his wife Fabienne are popular hosts; reserve ahead if you can (€16 lunch *menu,* €28 and €38 dinner *menus,* closed Mon year-round and Thu Oct–May, air-con, near Roman Bridge at 1 place Théodore Aubanel, tel. 04 90 36 28 04).

Le Tournesol offers the best €18 dinner value in town, with mostly Provençal dishes and friendly service. I love the *aubergine feuilleté* (eggplant puff pastry) and lamb with cheese. Show this book in 2008 to get a free *kir* (daily June–Oct, Nov–May closed Tue–Wed, 30 cours Taulignan, tel. 04 90 36 09 18, owner Patrick speaks a little English).

Near Vaison la Romaine

Drivers enjoy a wealth of country-Provençal dining opportunities in rustic settings, handy to many of the rural accommodations. Most are within a five-minute drive of Vaison la Romaine.

La Girocedre is an enchanting place to eat lunch or dinner if you have a car and it's nice outside. Just three picturesque miles from Vaison la Romaine in adorable Puyméras, this place offers a complete country-Provençal package: outdoor tables placed just so in a lush garden, warm interior decor, and mouthwatering, Provencal cuisine (*menus* from €24, closed Mon, tel. 04 90 46 50 67).

Hôtel les Florets, in Gigondas, is a traditional, family-run place that's worth the drive. Dinners are a sumptuous blend of classic French cuisine and Provençal accents, served with class by English-speaking Thierry. The marvelous terrace makes your meal even more memorable (*menus* from €26, restaurant closed Wed; see hotel listing, previous page).

La Maison Bleue, on Villedieu's adorable little square, is a pizza-and-salad place with great outdoor ambience. Skip it if the weather forces you inside (open for lunch and dinner, closed Wed, tel. 04 90 28 97 02).

TRANSPORTATION CONNECTIONS

The most central bus stop is at Cave Vinicole.

From Vaison la Romaine by Bus to: Avignon (2–3/day, 90 min), **Orange** (2–3/day, 45 min), **Nyons** (2–3/day, 45 min), **Le Crestet** (2/day, 5 min), **Carpentras** (2/day, 45 min). Bus info: tel. 04 90 36 05 22.

Côtes du Rhône Sights Near Vaison la Romaine

▲▲▲Côtes du Rhône Scenic Loop

With a car or minivan tour and a half-day, you can experience this glorious loop clockwise around the Dentelles de Montmirail, visiting the mountaintop village of Le Crestet, adorable little Suzette, and the famous wine villages of Beaumes-de-Venise, Gigondas, and Séguret. I've listed a few wineries *(domaines)* along the way. This easy loop is a shame to miss even if wine isn't your thing.

Leave Vaison la Romaine following signs toward Carpentras on D-938, detour up to Le Crestet, then return to D-938 and turn right onto D-90 just before entering Malaucene. Follow D-90 to Beaumes de Venise (passing Suzette and later, a turnoff to Domaine de Durban), then find D-8 and then D-7, which will take you back to Vaison la Romaine passing Gigondas, Sablet, and Séguret.

Here are the key stops on this route:

❶ Le Crestet

This hilltop village—founded after the fall of the Roman Empire, when laws were lost and people gathered in high places like this for protection from marauding barbarians—followed the usual hill town evolution. The outer walls of the village did double duty as ramparts and house walls. The castle above (dating about A.D. 850, closed to the public) provided a final safe haven if attacked. With about 500 residents in 1200, Le Crestet was a very important town in this region. The village reached its zenith in the mid-1500s, when 660 people called Le Crestet home. The village began its gradual decline in the 1600s, though the population remained fairly stable until WWII. Today, about 35 people live within the walls year-round (about 55 during the summer). The village's only business, café-restaurant **Le Panoramic,** has an upstairs terrace

Côtes du Rhône Scenic Loop

❶ Le Crestet ❹ Gigondas
❷ Suzette ❺ Séguret
❸ Domaine de Durban Winery

with a view that justifies the name...even if the food is overpriced (open daily for lunch and dinner, tel. 04 90 28 76 42).

❷ Suzette

Tiny Suzette floats on its hilltop (midway along D-90), with a small 12th-century chapel, one café, a handful of residents, and the gaggle of houses where they live. Find the big orientation board above the lot and find the broad shoulders of Mont Ventoux. At 6,000 feet, it always seems to have some clouds hanging around.

The top looks like it's snow-covered; if you drive up there, you'll see it's actually white stone (see page 519). Suzette's homes once huddled in the shadow of an imposing castle, destroyed during the religious wars of the mid-1500s. **Les Coquelicots** café makes a perfect lunch or drink stop. Try the *omelette au chèvre* for lunch (€10), or splurge for a more elaborate *plat* (€18–20, usually closed Tue–Wed May–Sept, then open weekends only Oct–April; tel. 04 90 65 06 94). Back across the road from the orientation table is a tasting room for Château Redortier wines (English brochure and well-explained list of wines provided; skip their white, but try the good rosé and two reds).

❸ Domaine de Durban

In this stunning setting, equally *charmante* Nathalie or Sylvie will take your taste buds on a tour. This *domaine* produces appealing whites, reds, and Muscats. Start with the 100 percent Viognier, then try their Viognier-Chardonnay blend. Their rosé is light and refreshing (and less than €4 a bottle). Next, their two reds are very different from each other: One is fruity, and the other—aged in oak—is tannic (both could use another year before drinking, but seemed fine to me). Finish with their popular Muscat de Venise (wines cost €4–10 per bottle, Mon–Sat 9:00–12:00 & 14:00–18:30, closed Sun, tel. 04 90 62 94 26). Picnics are not allowed, though strolling amid the gorgeous vineyards is. To find the winery, drive into Beaumes de Venise on D-90 and keep right at the first *Centre-Ville* sign as the road bends left, then carefully track signs for three incredibly scenic miles.

❹ Gigondas

This town produces some of the region's best red wines and is ideally situated for hiking, mountain biking, and driving into the mountains. The info-packed **TI** has a list of welcoming wineries, *chambres d'hôte,* and good hikes or drives (Mon–Sat 10:00–12:00 & 14:00–18:00, closed Sun, place du Portail, tel. 04 90 65 85 46). Take a walk up through the town (best after wine-tasting)—the church is an easy destination with good views over the heart of the Côtes du Rhône vineyards. Several good tasting opportunities sit side-by-side on the main square. **Caveau de Gigondas** is best, where Sandra and Barbara await your visit with a large and free selection of tiny bottles for sampling filled directly from the barrel (daily 10:00–12:00 & 14:00–18:30, 2 doors down from TI, tel. 04 90 65 82 29). Here you can compare wines from a variety of private producers in an intimate, low-key setting. There's a small grocery store and several eating options in the village. Across from the Caveau de Gigondas, find the shaded red tables of **Du Verre à l'Assiette** with terrific ambience outside and inside (€10 salads, €13 *plats,* €15 mixed plate of meats and salad, closed Mon, place du Village, tel. 04 90 12 36 64). To eat very well or to sleep nearby, consider **Hôtel les Florets,** a half-mile above town, surrounded by pine trees at the foothills of the Dentelles de Montmirail (see "Sleeping—Near Vaison la Romaine," page 514; restaurant closed Wed).

❺ Séguret
Blending into the hillside with a smattering of shops, two cafés, made-to-stroll lanes, and a natural spring, this village is understandably popular. Try to visit early or late in the day (Séguret works well for a breakfast stop or a pre-dinner stroll). The bulky entry arch just above the parking area came with a massive gate, which kept bad guys out for centuries. To appreciate how the homes' outer walls provided security in those days, stroll down the main drag, keep right, then take one of the tunnel exits to the right. These exit passages, or *poternes*, were needed in periods of peace to allow the town to expand below. Find Séguret's open washbasin—a hotbed of social activity and gossip over the ages—and the community bread oven *(four banal)*, used for festivals and celebrations. At Christmas, this entire village transforms itself into one big crèche scene (a Provençal tradition that has long since died out in other villages).

▲Ardèche Gorges (Gorges de l'Ardèche)
These gorges, which wow visitors with abrupt chalky-white cliffs, follow the Ardèche River through immense canyons and thick forests. This drive is scenic way to go north (to Lyon, for example). To reach the gorges from Vaison la Romaine, drive west 45 minutes, passing through Bollène and Pont Saint-Esprit to Vallon Pont d'Arc (the touristic hub of the Ardèche Gorges). From Vallon Pont d'Arc, you can canoe along the peaceful river through some of the canyon's most spectacular scenery and under the rock arch of Pont d'Arc (half-day, all-day, and 2-day trips possible), and learn about hiking trails that get you above it all (**TI** tel. 04 75 88 04 01, www.vallon-pont-darc.com). If continuing north toward Lyon, connect Privas and Aubenas, then head back via the autoroute. Endearing little Balazuc—a village north of the gorges, with narrow lanes, flowers, views, and a smattering of cafés and shops—makes a fine stop.

Hill Towns of the Luberon

The Luberon region, stretching 30 miles along a ridge of rugged hills east of Avignon, hides some of France's most appealing hill towns and sensuous landscapes. Those intrigued by Peter Mayle's

books love joyriding through the region, connecting I-could-live-here villages, crumbled castles, and meditative abbeys. Mayle's bestselling *A Year in Provence* describes the ruddy local culture from an Englishman's perspective as he buys a stone farmhouse, fixes it up, and adopts the region as his new home. His book is a great read while you're here.

The Luberon terrain in general (much of which is a French regional natural park) is as appealing as its villages. Gnarled vineyards and wind-sculpted trees separate tidy stone structures from abandoned buildings—little more than rock piles—that seem to challenge city slickers to fix them up. White rock slabs bend along high ridges, while colorful hot-air balloons survey the sun-drenched scene from above.

Getting Around the Luberon

By Car: Luberon roads are scenic and narrow. With no big landmarks, it's easy to get lost in this area—but getting lost is the point. Pick up the Michelin Local map #332 to navigate. If connecting this region with the Côtes du Rhône, consider doing so via Mont Ventoux—one of Provence's most spectacular routes (see page 519).

By Bus: Isle-sur-la-Sorgue is easy by bus from Avignon, with several daily trips and a central stop at the post office in Isle-sur-la-Sorgue (6/day Mon–Sat, fewer on Sun, 45 min). Without a car or minivan tour, I'd skip the hill towns of the Luberon.

By Train: Trains get you as far as Isle-sur-la-Sorgue (station called "L'Isle–Fontaine de Vaucluse") from Avignon (10/day on weekdays, 5/day on weekends, 30 min) or from Marseille (8/day, 1–2 hours). If you're day-tripping by train, check return times before leaving the station.

By Minivan Tour: Friendly Roland Vanove—and his **Taxi des Oliviers** tour service—offers half- or full-day English tours of his native Luberon. Just-as-friendly Dutchman Mike Rijken, who runs **Wine Safari,** offers similar services (see "Tours of Provence" on page 452).

By Bike: Hardy bikers can ride from Isle-sur-la-Sorgue to Gordes, then to Roussillon, connecting other villages in a full-day loop ride; it's 30 miles round-trip to Roussillon and back—with lots of hills. Other appealing villages are closer to Isle-sur-la-Sorgue and offer easier biking options (see "Bike Rental," page 522).

Isle-sur-la-Sorgue

This sturdy market town—literally, "Island on the Sorgue River"— sits within a split in its crisp, happy little river. After the arid cities and villages elsewhere in Provence, the presence of water at every turn is a welcome change. In Isle-sur-la-Sorgue—called the "Venice of Provence"—the Sorgue River's extraordinarily clear and shallow flow divides like cells, producing water, water everywhere. Today, every other shop seems to sell some kind of antique.

ORIENTATION

While Isle-sur-la-Sorgue is renowned for its market days, it's otherwise a pleasantly average town with no important sights and a steady trickle of tourism. It's calm at night and downright dead on Mondays.

Tourist Information

The TI has information on hiking and biking, and a line on rooms in private homes, all of which are outside the town (Mon–Sat 9:00–13:00 & 14:30–18:00, Sun 9:00–13:00, in town center next to church, tel. 04 90 38 04 78, www.ot-islesurlasorgue.fr, office-tourisme.islesur-sorgue@wanadoo.fr).

Arrival in Isle-sur-la-Sorgue

Traffic is a mess and parking is a headache on market days, (all day Sunday and Thursday mornings). Circle the ring road and look for parking signs, or give up and find the pay lot behind the post office (PTT).

Isle-sur-la-Sorgue's train station is called "L'Isle–Fontaine de Vaucluse." The bus from Avignon drops you at the post office, a block from the recommended Hôtel les Névons.

Helpful Hints

Internet Access: Try **Internet Station,** across from the church and TI and a block down rue Danton at #3 (tel. 04 90 20 03 28).

Laundry: It's just off the pedestrian street rue de la République, at 23 impasse de l'Hôtel de Palerme (daily 8:00–20:30).

Supermarket: A well-stocked **Spar** market is on the main ring road, near the Peugeot Car shop and the train station (Mon–Sat 9:00–12:00 & 15:00–19:00, Sun 15:00–19:00). A smaller **Casino** market is more central on pedestrian rue de la République (Tue–Sun 7:30–12:30 & 15:30–19:30).

Bike Rental: Isles 2 Roues, by the train station, rents bikes (€14/day, must show your passport, 10 avenue de la Gare, tel. 04 90 38 19 12).

Taxi: Call tel. 06 09 06 92 06 or 06 08 09 19 49.

Public WC: There's a good WC in the parking lot between the post office (PTT) and Hôtel les Névons.

Hiking: The TI has good information on area hikes; most trails are accessible by short drives, and you can use a taxi to get there.

Wandering Isle-sur-la-Sorgue

The town has crystal-clear water babbling under pedestrian bridges stuffed with flower boxes, and its old-time carousel is always spinning. Navigate by the town's splintered streams and nine mossy waterwheels, which, while still turning, power only memories of the town's wool and silk industries. Here are key sights along the way.

The Sorgue River: With its source (a spring) a mere five miles away, the Sorgue River never floods and has a constant flow and temperature in all seasons. Isle-sur-la-Sorgue prospered in the Middle Ages in spite of its exposed location, thanks to the natural protection this river provided. Walls with big moats once ran along the river, but they were destroyed during the French Revolution. Find Le Bassin, where the Sorgue River enters the town and separates into many branches (carefully placed lights make this a beautiful sight after dark). Fishing provided Isle-sur-la-Sorgue's economic base until the waterwheels took over. Fishermen trapped fish in nets or speared them while standing on skinny, flat-bottomed boats.

The clumsy looking **waterwheels** that you'll see at various points on the river have been in business since the 1200s, when they were used for grinding flour. Paper, textile, silk, and woolen mills would later find their power from this river. At its peak, the town had 70 waterwheels and in the 1800s, Isle-sur-la-Sorgue competed with Avignon as Provence's cloth-dyeing and textile center. Those stylish Provençal fabrics and patterns you see for sale everywhere were made possible by this river.

Notre-Dame des Anges: This 12th-century church has a festive Baroque interior and seems overgrown for today's town. Walk in. The curls and swirls and gilded statues date from an era that was all about Louis XIV, the Sun King. This is propagandist architecture, designed to wow the faithful into compliance.

▲▲**Market Days**—The town erupts into a carnival-like market frenzy each Sunday and Thursday, with hardy crafts and local produce. The Sunday market is astounding and famous for its antiques; the Thursday market is more intimate (see market tips on page 454). Find a table at the Café de France and enjoy the scene.

Antique Toy and Doll Museum (Musée du Jouet et de la Poupée Ancienne)—The town's lone fee sight is a fun and funky toy museum with more than 300 dolls displayed in three small rooms (€3.50, kids-€1.50; June–Sept Mon–Fri 13:00–17:30, Sat–Sun 11:00–17:00; Oct–May Sat–Sun 11:00–17:00, closed Mon–Fri; 26 rue Carnot).

Biking—These towns make easy biking destinations from Isle-sur-la-Sorgue: Velleron (5 miles north, flat, a tiny version of Isle-sur-la-Sorgue with waterwheels, fountains, and an evening farmer's market Mon–Sat 18:00–20:00); Lagnes (3 miles east, mostly flat, a pretty and well-restored hill town with views from its ruined château); and Fontaine-de-Vaucluse (5 miles northeast, gently uphill). Allow 30 miles and many hills for the round-trip ride to Roussillon. (see "Bike Rental," on previous page.)

SLEEPING

In and near Isle-sur-la-Sorgue

$$ Hôtel les Névons**, two blocks from the center (behind the post office), is concrete motel–modern outside. Inside, however, it does everything right, with eager-to-please staff, and two wings to choose from: the new wing, with cavernous and cushy rooms, or the old wing, with puce halls and more modest, cheaper (but good enough) rooms. There are several family suites and a roof deck with 360-degree views around a small pool (old wing—Db-€56–62; new wing—huge Db-€64–74, Tb-€75–84, Qb-€85–95; air-con, Internet access, easy parking, 205 chemin des Névons, tel. 04 90 20 72 00, fax 04 90 20 56 20, www.hotel-les-nevons.com, info@hotel-les-nevons.com).

$$$ Chambres Sous l'Olivier, located five minutes east of Isle-sur-la-Sorgue, is well-situated for exploring the hill towns of the Luberon and Isle-sur-la-Sorgue. Its six lovely, comfortable rooms are housed in a massive, 150-year-old farmhouse with lounges that you and your entire soccer team could spread out in. Julien and Carole take care of your every need, and they'll cook you a full-blown dinner with wine for €27 per person (Db-€80–130, 3-room suite-€180, cash only, pool, route d'Apt, tel. 04 90 20 23 54 or 04 90 20 33 90, www.chambresdhotesprovence.com, souslolivier@wanadoo.fr). It's below Isle-sur-la-Sorgue, about 40 minutes from Avignon toward Apt on D-22, look for signs 200 yards after the big sign to *le Mas du Grand Jonquier* on the right.

EATING

In Isle-sur-la-Sorgue

Inexpensive restaurants are easy to find in Isle-sur-la-Sorgue, but consistent quality is another story. Dining on the river is a unique experience in this arid land famous for its hill towns, and shopping for the perfect table is half the fun. Also consider a riverside picnic (the Fromenterie bakery across from the PTT stocks mouthwatering quiche and more).

Begin your dinner with a glass of wine at the cozy **Le Caveau de la Tour de l'Isle** (part wine bar, part wine-and-cheese shop, open Tue–Sat until about 20:00, closed Sun–Mon, 12 rue de la République, tel. 04 90 20 70 25).

Of the places lining the river, **Le Bistrot de l'Industrie** is less central, but is one of the better values for basic café fare (closed Mon–Tue, near the train station on quai de la Charité, tel. 04 90 38 00 40).

L'Ousteau de l'Isle, located in a Provençal farmhouse a mile from the town center, has a modern interior and lovely seating outside (request a table *sur la terrasse*). Serving regional cuisine with a modern twist, it draws a loyal clientele (dinner *menus* from €27, lunch *menu* for €17, closed Tue–Wed, 147 chemin de Bosquet, tel. 04 90 20 81 36). From Isle-sur-la-Sorgue's center, follow signs toward *Apt*, and turn right at Pain d'Antin Boulangerie; or walk 20 minutes along the river and cross the small bridge to chemin de Bosquet.

Roussillon

With all the trendy charm of Santa Fe on a hilltop, Roussillon will cost you at least a roll of film (and €2 for parking). Roussillon sits atop Mont Rouge (Red Mountain) at about 1,000 feet above sea level. The village curls around this hospitable mountain, and has been protected since 1943 (so there is almost no modern development).  An enormous deposit of ochre gives the earth and buildings that distinctive red color, and provided this village with its economic base until shortly after World War II. This place is popular; it's best to visit early or late in the day.

Tourist Information

The little TI is in the center, between the two parking lots and across from the David restaurant. Leaf through their informative binders that describe area hotels and *chambres d'hôte*. Walkers should get info on trails from Roussillon to nearby villages (April–Oct Mon–Sat 10:00–12:00 & 14:00–17:30, closed Sun except in summer; Nov–March Mon–Sat 14:00–17:30, closed Sun; tel. 04 90 05 60 25). There's an ATM next to the TI, and Internet access is available at the bookshop *(librairie)* on the main square (daily 10:00–18:00). The two best parking lots are Parking Sablons, on the northern edge (by the recommended Hôtel Rêves d'Ocres) and Parking Pasquier on its southern flank, closer to the ochre cliffs. Thursday morning is Roussillon's market day, when there is no parking at Pasquier.

The Village

Climb to the village top and find the orientation plaque and the dramatic viewpoint, often complete with a howling mistral. During the Middle Ages, a castle stood where you are, on the top of Mont Rouge. While nothing remains of the castle today, the strategic advantage of this site is clear: You can see forever. Notice how little sprawl is in the valley below. Because the Luberon is a natural reserve (Parc Naturel Régional du Luberon), development is strictly controlled.

A short stroll down leads to the church. Duck into the pretty 11th-century Church of St. Michel, and appreciate the well-worn center aisle and the propane heaters—winters can be frigid in this area. The white interior tells us that the stone came from elsewhere.

Examine the different hues of yellow and orange in the village. These lime-finished exteriors, called *chaux* (limes), need to be redone about every 10 years. Locals choose their exact color...but in this town of ochre, it's never white. The church tower you walk under marked the entrance to the fortified town.

See how local (or artsy) you can look in what must be the most scenic village square in Provence (place de la Mairie) and watch the river of shoppers. Is anyone playing *boules* at the opposite end? You could paint the entire town without ever leaving the red-and-orange corner of your palette. Many do. While Roussillon receives its share of day-trippers, evenings are romantically peaceful on this square.

Ochre Cliffs

Roussillon was Europe's capital for ochre production until World War II. A stroll to the south end of town, beyond the upper parking lot, will show you why: Roussillon sits on the world's largest

Provence

Roussillon

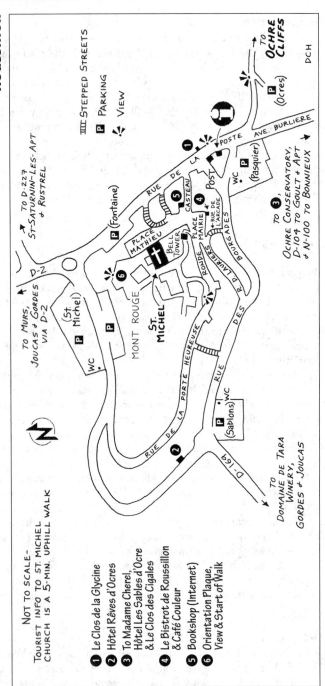

NOT TO SCALE—
TOURIST INFO TO ST. MICHEL
CHURCH IS A 5-MIN. UPHILL WALK

IIII STEPPED STREETS

P PARKING

🔆 VIEW

① Le Clos de la Glycine
② Hôtel Rêves d'Ocres
③ To Madame Cherel,
   Hôtel Les Sables d'Ocre
   & Le Clos des Cigales
④ Le Bistrot de Roussillon
   & Café Couleur
⑤ Bookshop (Internet)
⑥ Orientation Plaque,
   View & Start of Walk

known ochre deposit. A brilliant orange path leads through the richly colored ochre canyon, explaining the hue of this village (€2, ask about combo-tickets with Ochre Conservatory; daily 9:00–17:30, until 19:00 in summer; beware—light-colored clothing and orange powder don't mix).

The value of Roussillon's ochre cliffs was known in Roman times. Once excavated, the clay ochre was rinsed with water to separate it from sand, and bricks of the stuff were dried and baked for deeper hues. The procedure for extracting the ochre did not change much over 2,000 years, until ochre mining became industrialized in the late 1700s. Used primarily for wallpaper and linoleum, ochre use reached its zenith just before World War II. After that, cheaper substitutes took over.

SLEEPING

(€1 = about $1.30, country code: 33)

In Roussillon

The TI posts a list of hotels and *chambres d'hôte.* Parking is free in Roussillon—if you sleep in a hotel here, ask your hotelier where to park. The village offers three good-value accommodations—conveniently, one for each price range.

$$$ Le Clos de la Glycine**** provides Roussillon's four-star accommodations, with nine gorgeous rooms located dead-center in the village (Db-€124–155, big Db-€175, loft suite with deck and view-€260, Wi-Fi, located at the restaurant David, across from the TI on place de la Poste, tel. 04 90 05 60 13, fax 04 90 05 75 80, www.luberon-hotel.com, le.clos.de.la.glycine@wanadoo.fr).

$$ Hôtel Rêves d'Ocres**, the first building you pass coming from Gordes and Joucas, is a solid value run by eager-to-help Sandrine and Yvan. It's ochre-colored, warm, and comfortable, with 16 mostly spacious rooms (eight have view terraces) and a lounge where you can stretch out (Sb-€56, Db without balcony-€76, Db with balcony-€82, Tb-€95, air-con, route de Gordes, tel. 04 90 05 60 50, fax 04 90 05 79 74, www.hotel-revesdocres.com, hotelrevesdocres@wanadoo.fr).

$ Madame Cherel rents rooms that are just this side of a youth hostel. A common view terrace and good reading materials are available, and the beds have firm mattresses (D-€42–46, includes breakfast, cash only, 3 blocks from upper parking lot, between the gas station and school, La Burlière, tel. 04 90 05 71 71, mulhanc @hotmail.com). Chatty and sincere Cherel speaks English, is a wealth of regional travel tips, and rents mountain bikes to guests (€15/day).

Near Roussillon, in or near Joucas

The tiny village of Joucas lies a few minutes below Roussillon and hides a handful of good-value accommodations. Each of the three hotels listed below comes with a good restaurant.

$$$ La Ferme de la Huppe*** has a Gordes address, but it's closer physically and spiritually to Joucas. This small, farmhouse-elegant hacienda is an excellent mini-splurge if food matters. Sincere owners Gerald and Charlotte will make you feel at home. Ten low-slung rooms gather on two levels behind the stylish pool. The decor is understated and rustic, and the service can be *laissez-faire*—the owners devote most of their attention to the restaurant (which is a good thing). Dinners poolside or in the cozy dining room are memorable (small Db-€85, bigger Db-€105–125, much bigger Db-€145–165, includes breakfast, €45 dinner *menu* changes daily, restaurant closed Wed–Thu, air-con, Wi-Fi; between Joucas and Gordes on D-156 road to Goult, just off D-2; tel. 04 90 72 12 25, fax 04 90 72 01 83, www.lafermedelahuppe.com, charlotte.gerald@lafermedelahuppe.com).

$$$ Le Mas du Loriot is another worthwhile, almost-in-Joucas value. Charming owners Alain and Christine have carved the ideal escape out of an olive grove, with eight soothing rooms, private terraces, a generous pool, and home-cooked dinners—all at fair prices and with a view to remember (Db-€100–130, extra bed-€20, €28 four-course dinners available three nights each week, Internet access, on D-102 between Joucas and Murs, tel. 04 90 72 62 62, fax 04 90 72 62 54, www.masduloriot.com, hotel@masduloriot.com).

$$ Hostellerie des Commandeurs,** run by soft Sophie, has modern, comfortable, and clean rooms in a great Joucas location. It's kid-friendly, with a big pool and a sports field/play area next door. The relaxed restaurant offers tasty cuisine at very fair prices (*menus* from €18). Ask for a south-facing room (*côté sud*) for the best views (Db-€55–58, extra bed-€16, above park at village entrance, tel. 04 90 05 78 01, fax 04 90 05 74 47, www.lescommandeurs.com, hostellerie@lescommandeurs.com).

EATING

In Roussillon

Choose ambience over cuisine if dining in Roussillon, and enjoy any of the eateries on the main square. It's a festive place, where children dance while parents dine, and dogs and cats look longingly for leftovers. Restaurants change with the mistral here—what's good one year disappoints the next. Consider my suggestions and go with what looks best. One of the two places listed below is always open.

Le Bistrot de Roussillon is easily the most consistent value on the square, with excellent salads (try the *salad du bistrot*) and *plats* for the right price, a breezy terrace in back, and helpful David and Yann in charge (daily, tel. 04 90 05 74 45).

Café Couleur sits next door, offering similar atmosphere and prices, but less-steady quality (daily, tel. 04 90 05 62 11).

More Luberon Hill Towns

Le Lubéron is packed with appealing villages and beautiful scenery, but it has only a handful of must-see sights. If you don't have a car, skip this area. If you do, pick up an in-depth local map (Michelin Local map #332 works fine) and explore. And remember, getting lost in the Luberon is half the fun.

Gordes—For the last 40 years, Gordes has been the most touristy and trendy town in the Luberon—creating gridlock and parking headaches (come early). In the 1960s, Gordes was a virtual ghost town of derelict buildings. But now it's thoroughly renovated and filled with people who live in a world without calluses. Many Parisian big shots and wealthy foreigners have purchased and restored older homes here, putting property values out of sight for locals. As you approach Gordes, make a hard right at the impressive view of the village (you'll find some parking along the small road). Beyond here, the village has little of interest, except its many boutiques and its Tuesday market (which ends at 13:00). The town's 11th-century castle houses a mildly interesting collection of contemporary art. The more interesting Abbey Notre-Dame de Sénanque (see below) is nearby and well-marked from Gordes.

Abbey Notre-Dame de Sénanque—This still-functioning and beautifully situated Cistercian abbey, just 10 minutes from Gordes, was built in 1148 as a back-to-basics reaction to the excesses of Benedictine abbeys. The Cistercians strove to be separate from the world, and to recapture the simplicity, solitude, and poverty of the early Church. To succeed required industrious self-sufficiency—a skill that these monks had. Their movement spread and colonized Europe with a new form of Christianity. By 1200, there were more than 500 such monasteries and abbeys in Europe.

The abbey is best appreciated from the outside, and is worth the trip for its splendid and remote setting alone. Come early or late, stop at a pullout for a bird's-eye view as you descend, then wander the abbey's perimeter with few tourists. In late June through much of July, the lavender fields that surround the abbey make a breathtaking picture.

The abbey interior is only open for attending Mass (Sun at 10:00, Mon at 8:30, Tue–Sat at 12:00) and for tours (€4.60 admission includes tour in French only, about 6/day Mon–Sat, 1 hour, limited to 50 people so call ahead or check their website, good bookshop open Mon–Sat 10:00–12:00 & 13:30–18:00, Sun 14:00–18:00, tel. 04 90 72 05 72, www.senanque.fr).

Museum of Lavender (Musée de la Lavande)—Located halfway between Gordes and Isle-sur-la-Sorgue in Coustellet, this surprisingly interesting museum does a fine job of explaining the process of lavender production with interesting exhibits and good English information (via an audioguide, a film, and posted explanations at the exhibits). It's popular with tour groups, smells great inside, and offers the ultimate "if they make it with lavender, we sell it" gift shop (€5, daily 10:00–12:00 & 14:00–18:00, in Coustellet just off N-100 toward Gordes, tel. 04 90 76 91 23).

The next three listings are all located just below N-100, near the hill town of Bonnieux.

St. Julien Bridge (Pont St. Julien)—This small, three-arched bridge survives as a testimony to Roman engineers—and to the importance of this rural area 2,000 years ago. It's the only surviving bridge on what was once the main road from northern Italy to Provence. This 215-foot-long bridge was built from 27 B.C. to A.D. 14. Mortar had not been invented, so (as with the Pont du Gard) stones were carefully set in place. Amazingly, the bridge survives today, having outlived Roman marches, hundreds of floods, and decades of automobile traffic. A new bridge finally rerouted traffic from this beautiful structure in 2005.

Bonnieux—Spectacular from a distance, this town disappoints up close. It lacks a pedestrian center, though the Friday-morning market briefly creates one. The one reason I visit Bonnieux is to eat at **Le Fournil,** where creative Provençal specialties are served in a splendid outdoor setting (€20 lunch *menu,* €40 dinner *menus,* closed Mon, eat outside by the fountain or skip it, next to TI at 5 place Carnot, tel. 04 90 75 83 62).

Lacoste—Little Lacoste slumbers across the valley from Bonnieux in the shadow of its looming castle. Climb through this photogenic village of arches and stone paths, passing American art students (from the Savannah College of Art and Design) showing their work. Support an American artist, learn about their art, then keep climbing and climbing to the ruined castle base. The view of Bonnieux from the base of Lacoste's castle is as good is it gets.

The Marquis de Sade (1740–1814) lived in this castle for more than 30 years. Author of pornographic novels, he was notorious for hosting orgies behind these walls, and for kidnapping peasants for scandalous purposes. He was eventually arrested and imprisoned, and thanks to him, we have a word to describe his favorite hobby—sadism.

For the perfect lunch café complete with killer views, walk to the other end of Lacoste and find the **Bar/Restaurant de France**'s outdoor tables overlooking Bonnieux (daily, lunch only, tel. 04 90 75 82 25).

Provence

THE FRENCH RIVIERA

A hundred years ago, celebrities from London to Moscow flocked here to socialize, gamble, and escape the dreary weather at home. Belle époque resorts now also cater to budget vacationers at France's most sought-after, fun-in-the-sun destination. This scenic strip is speckled with intriguing museums and countless sun-worshippers.

Some of the Continent's most stunning scenery and intriguing museums lie along this strip of land—as do millions of heat-seeking tourists. Nice has world-class museums, a grand beachfront promenade, a seductive old town, and all the drawbacks of a major city (traffic, crime, pollution, etc.). But the day trips possible from Nice are easy and varied: Monte Carlo welcomes everyone, with cash registers open; Antibes has a romantic port and silky-sandy beaches; and the hill towns present a breezy and photogenic alternative to the beach scene. Evenings on the Riviera, a.k.a. the Côte d'Azur, were made for a promenade and outdoor dining.

Choosing a Home Base

My favorite home bases are Nice, Antibes, and Villefranche-sur-Mer.

Nice is the region's capital and France's fifth-largest city. With convenient train and bus connections to most regional sights, this is the most practical base for train travelers. Urban Nice also has a full palette of museums, a beach scene that rocks, the best selection of hotels in all price ranges, and good nightlife options. A car is a headache in Nice, though it's easily stored at one of the many pricey parking garages.

Nearby **Antibes** is smaller, with a bustling center, terrific nightlife, great sandy beaches, grand vistas, and good walking trails. (Its much-admired Picasso Museum should reopen in the spring of 2008 after renovation.) Antibes has frequent train service to Nice and Monaco, and it's easy for drivers.

Villefranche-sur-Mer is the romantic's choice, with a serene setting and small-town warmth. It has finely ground pebble beaches, quick public transportation to Nice and Monaco, easy parking, and hotels in most price ranges.

Planning Your Time

Most should plan a full day for Nice, a full day for Monaco and the Corniche route that connects it with Nice, and a half-day for Villefranche-sur-Mer or Antibes. Monaco and Villefranche-sur-Mer have good energy at night (sights are closed, but crowds are few; consider dinner there), and Antibes is good day or night (good beaches and hiking, plus lively nightlife). Hill-town- and nature-lovers should allow a day to explore the hill-capping hamlets near Vence (but for most, these are a lower priority).

Helpful Hints

Medical Help: Riviera Medical Services has a list of English-speaking physicians for anywhere along the Riviera. They can help you make an appointment or call an ambulance (tel. 04 93 26 12 70, www.rivieramedical.com).

Sightseeing Schedules: On Monday, the Modern and Contemporary Art Museum, Fine Arts Museum, and cours Saleya market in Nice, along with Antibes' Marché Provençal, are closed; on Tuesday, the Chagall, Matisse, and Archaeological museums in Nice are closed.

Events: The Riviera is famous for staging major events. Unless you're actually taking part in the festivities, these events give you only room shortages and traffic jams. Here are the three biggies in 2008: Nice Carnival (Feb 16–March 2), Grand Prix of Monaco (May 22–25), and the Festival de Cannes, better known as the Cannes Film Festival (May 14–25).

Getting Around the Riviera

Nice is well-located for exploring the Riviera by public transport. Eze-le-Village, Villefranche-sur-Mer, Antibes, and St-Paul-de-Vence are all within a 50-minute bus or train ride of Nice (details are provided under each destination). Boats go from Nice to Monaco and St-Tropez.

By Bus and Train: Many key Riviera destinations are

connected by direct service from Nice. As the fare for any bus ride is just €1.30, the pricier train is only a better choice when it saves you time. You make the call—both modes of transportation work well.

Destination	Bus from Nice	Train from Nice
Villefranche	4/hr, 20 min	2/hr, 10 min, €1.80
Monaco	4/hr, 45 min	2/hr, 20 min, €3.40
Menton	4/hr, 60 min	2/hr, 25 min, €3.60
Antibes	3/hr, 60 min	2/hr, 15–30 min, €3.90
Cannes	3/hr, 75 min	2/hr, 30–40 min, €6
St-Paul	every 40 min, 45 min	none
Vence	every 40 min, 50 min	none
Eze-le-Village	16/day, 25 min	none
La Turbie	4/day, 45 min	none

Buses also run from Monaco to Eze-le-Village, allowing travelers to triangulate Nice, Monaco, and Eze-le-Village (then back to Nice) for a good all-day excursion (see page 585 for details).

By Minivan Excursion: Local TIs and most hotels have information on minivan excursions from Nice (€50–60/half-day, €80–110/day). **Med-Tour** is one of many (tel. 04 93 82 92 58 or mobile 06 73 82 04 10, www.med-tour.com); **Tour Azur** is a bit pricier (tel. 04 93 44 88 77 or 06 71 90 76 70, www.tourazur.com); and **Revelation Tours** specializes in English tours (tel. 04 93 53 69 85, www.revelation-tours.com). All companies also offer private tours by the day or half-day (check with them for their outrageous prices, about €90/hr).

By Boat: From June to mid-September, Trans Côte d'Azur offers scenic trips from Nice to Monaco and to St-Tropez. Boats leave in the morning and return in the evening, giving you all day to explore your destination. Drinks and WCs are available on board. Boats to **Monaco** depart at 9:30 and return at 18:00 (€28 round-trip, 50 min each way; July–Aug daily; May, June, and Sept Tue, Thu, and Sat only). Boats to **St-Tropez** depart at 9:00 and return at 19:00 (€55 round-trip, 2.5 hrs each way; July–Aug Tue–Sun, no boats Mon; late June and early Sept Tue, Thu, and Sun only). Tickets for St-Tropez boats often sell out—book a few days ahead (tel. 04 92 00 42 30, fax 04 92 00 42 31, www.trans-cote-azur.com). The boats leave from Nice's port, bassin des Amiraux, just below Castle Hill, with a blue ticket booth *(billeterie)* on quai de Lunel (see map on page 538). The same company also runs one-hour round-trip cruises along the coast to Cap Ferrat (see "Tours" on page 541).

The French Riviera

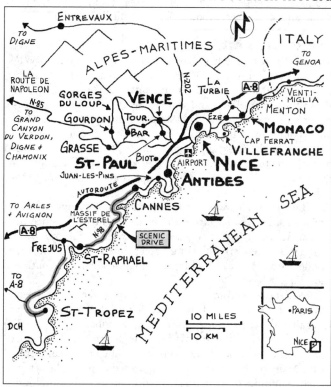

Cuisine Scene in the Riviera

The Riviera adds a Mediterranean flair to the food of Provence. While many of the same dishes served in Provence are available throughout the Riviera (see "Cuisine Scene in Provence," page 454), you can celebrate the differences by looking for anything Italian or from the sea.

Local specialties are bouillabaisse (the spicy seafood stew that seems worth the cost only for those with a seafood fetish), *bourride* (a creamy fish soup thickened with aioli, a garlic sauce), and *salade niçoise* (nee-swaz; a tomato, potato, olive, anchovy, and tuna salad). You'll also find these tasty bread treats: *pissaladière* (bread dough topped with onions, olives, and anchovies), *fougasse* (a spindly, lacelike bread), *socca* (a thin chickpea crêpe), and *pan bagnat* (like a *salade niçoise* stuffed into a huge hamburger bun). Italian cuisine is native (ravioli was first made in Nice), easy to find, and generally a good value (*pâtes fraîches* means "fresh pasta"). White and rosé Bellet and the rich reds and rosés of Bandol are the local wines.

Remember, restaurants serve only during lunch (11:30–14:00)

and dinner (19:00–21:00, later in bigger cities); cafés—except for the smaller ones—serve food throughout the day.

The Riviera's Art Scene

The list of artists who have painted the Riviera reads like a Who's Who of 20th-century art. Pierre-Auguste Renoir, Henri Matisse, Marc Chagall, Georges Braque, Raoul Dufy, Fernand Léger, and Pablo Picasso all lived and worked here—and raved about the region's wonderful light. Their simple, semi-abstract, and—most importantly—colorful works reflect the Riviera. You'll experience the same landscapes they painted in this bright, sun-drenched region, punctuated with views of the "azure sea." Try to imagine the Riviera with a fraction of the people and development you see today.

But the artists were mostly drawn to the uncomplicated life-style of fishermen and farmers that has reigned here since time began. As the artists grew older, they retired in the sun, turned their backs on modern art's "isms," and painted with the wide-eyed wonder of children, using bright primary colors, basic outlines, and simple subjects.

Well-organized modern-art museums (such as the Picasso Museum in Antibes—likely closed for most of 2007—and the Chagall and Matisse museums in Nice, described in this chapter) litter the Riviera, allowing art-lovers to appreciate these artists' works while immersed in the same sun and culture that inspired them. Many of the museums were designed to blend the art with the surrounding views, gardens, and fountains, thus highlighting that modern art is not only stimulating, but sometimes simply beautiful.

Nice

Nice (sounds like "niece"), with its spectacular Alps-to-Mediterranean surroundings, eternally entertaining seafront promenade, and intriguing museums, is an enjoyable big-city highlight of the Riviera. In its traffic-free old city, Italian and French flavors mix to create a spicy Mediterranean dressing. Nice may be nice, but it's hot and jammed in July and August—reserve ahead and get a room with air-conditioning *(une chambre avec climatisation)*. Everything you'll want to see in Nice is walkable or a short bus or taxi ride away.

ORIENTATION

Most recommended sights and hotels are between the train station and the beach, near avenue Jean Médecin or boulevard Victor Hugo. It's a 20-minute walk (or a €10 taxi ride) from the train station to the beach, and a 20-minute walk along the promenade from the fancy Hôtel Negresco to the heart of Old Nice.

The first of three new tramway lines should be running in time for your visit in 2008.

Tourist Information

Nice's helpful TI has three locations: at the **airport** (daily 8:00–21:00), next to the **train station** (usually busy, Mon–Sat 8:00–19:00, Sun 10:00–17:00, 1 hour later in summer), and facing the **beach** at 5 promenade des Anglais (often fairly quiet, daily 9:00–18:00, until 20:00 July–Aug, tel. 08 92 70 74 07 costs €0.34/min, www .nicetourisme.com). Pick up the thorough *Practical Guide to Nice*, information on day trips (such as city maps and details on boat excursions), and a free Nice map (or find a better one at your hotel).

Only art-lovers should consider buying the seven-day, Nice-only **museum pass,** called Carte Passe-Musées 7 Jours (€7, does not include Chagall Museum). A second museum pass, the Riviera Carte Musée, may be brought back for 2008—ask about it at any TI (this pass was discontinued in 2006, when many museums were undergoing extensive renovation, but most will be open again in 2008).

Arrival in Nice

By Train: All trains stop at Nice's main station, Nice-Ville (baggage check at the far right with your back to the tracks, lockers open daily 7:00–21:45, left luggage desk Mon–Sat 8:45–12:00 & 14:00–15:45, closed Sun). This is one busy station, and theft is a problem, so never leave your bags unattended.

Turn left out of the station to find a branch of the **TI** a few steps away. Continue a few more blocks for the **tram** to place Masséna, the **old city,** and **bus station** (board the tram on the near side of the street, going to the right down avenue Jean Médecin). Many of my recommended **hotels** are within walking distance down the same street (figure 15 minutes from the station; see "Sleeping—Between Nice Etoile and Old Nice" on page 555).

To find **car-rental** offices, turn right out of the station. For more recommended **hotels,** cross avenue Thiers, then walk down the steps by Hôtel Interlaken (see "Sleeping—Between the Train Station and Nice Etoile," page 553). Continue past these hotels if you'd rather head straight to the beach—keep walking down avenue Durante as it turns into rue des Congrès to find yourself in

Nice

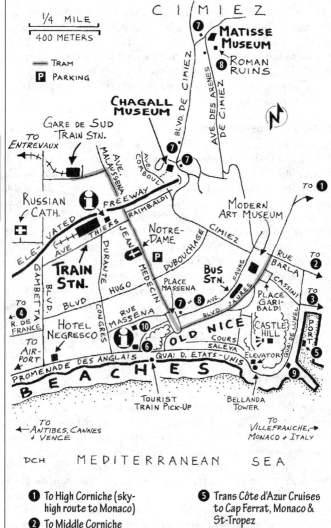

1/4 MILE
400 METERS

— TRAM
P PARKING

C I M I E Z

MATISSE MUSEUM

ROMAN RUINS

CHAGALL MUSEUM

BLVD. DE CIMIEZ

AVE. DES ARÈNES DE CIMIEZ

GARE DE SUD TRAIN STN.

TO ENTREVAUX

AVE. MALAUSSÉNA

AVE. COMBOUL

FREEWAY

RUSSIAN CATH.

MODERN ART MUSEUM

TO ①

RAIMBALDI

ELE-VATED

AVE. THIERS

AVE. DURANTE

NOTRE-DAME

CIMIEZ

RUE BARLA

TO ②

TRAIN STN.

JEAN MEDECIN

DUBOUCHAGE

BUS STN.

FAURE

CASSINI

TO ③

GAMBETTA

BLVD.

HUGO

BLVD.

CONGRES

PLACE MASSÉNA

JAURES

BLVD.

PLACE GARI-BALDI

TO ④
R. DE FRANCE

RUE MASSÉNA

HOTEL NEGRESCO

OLD NICE

CASTLE HILL

PORT

TO AIR-PORT

PROMENADE DES ANGLAIS

COURS SALEYA

ELEVATOR

QUAI DE LUNEL

⑤

B E A C H E S

QUAI D. ETATS-UNIS

⑨

TOURIST TRAIN PICK-UP

BELLANDA TOWER

TO ANTIBES, CANNES & VENCE

TO VILLEFRANCHE, MONACO & ITALY

DCH   M E D I T E R R A N E A N   S E A

① To High Corniche (sky-high route to Monaco)

② To Middle Corniche (middle route, best for Monaco & Eze-le-Village)

③ To Low Corniche (low route to Villefranche-sur-Mer)

④ To Fine Arts Museum

⑤ Trans Côte d'Azur Cruises to Cap Ferrat, Monaco & St-Tropez

⑥ Le Grand Tour Bus Departure Point

⑦ Bus #15 Stops

⑧ Bus #17 Stops

⑨ War Memorial

⑩ US Embassy

French Riviera

the heart of Nice's beachfront promenade.

By Bus: Nice's bus station *(gare routière)* is sandwiched between boulevard Jean Jaurès and avenue Félix Faure, next to the old city. The station has no bag check. Cross boulevard Jean Jaurès and enter teeming Old Nice, or cross avenue Félix Faure to get to my recommended hotels near Nice Etoile.

By Car: Driving into Nice on the autoroute from the west, take the first Nice exit (for the airport—called Côte d'Azur, Central) and follow signs reading *Nice Centre* and *Promenade des Anglais.* (Be ready to cross three left lanes of traffic right after getting off the autoroute.) Try to avoid arriving at rush hour, when promenade des Anglais grinds to a halt (usually Mon–Fri 8:00–9:30 & 17:00–19:30). Hoteliers know where to park (allow €14–20/day). The parking garage at the Nice Etoile shopping center on avenue Jean Médecin is pricey but near many of my recommended hotels (ticket booth on third floor, about €20/day, €10–12 from 20:00–8:00). All on-street parking is metered 9:00–18:00 or 19:00, but usually free all day on Sunday.

By Plane: For information on Nice's handy airport, see "Transportation Connections," page 563.

Helpful Hints

Theft Alert: Nice has more than its share of pickpockets. Have nothing important on or around your waist, unless it's in a money belt tucked out of sight (thieves target fanny packs); don't leave anything visible in your car; be wary of scooters when standing at intersections; don't leave things unattended on the beach while swimming; and stick to main streets in Old Nice after dark.

US Consulate: You'll find it at 7 avenue Gustave V (tel. 04 93 88 89 55, fax 04 93 87 07 38).

Canadian Consulate: It's at 10 rue Lamartine (tel. 04 93 92 93 22, fax 04 93 92 55 51).

Medical Help: Riviera Medical Services has a list of English-speaking physicians. They can help you make an appointment or call an ambulance (tel. 04 93 26 12 70, www.rivieramedical.com).

Museums: Some Nice museums (Chagall, Matisse, Archae-ological) are closed Tuesdays, while others (Modern and Contemporary Art, Fine Arts) close on Mondays. Most are free (and crowded) the first and third Sundays of the month. For information on Nice's museum pass, see "Tourist Information," above.

Internet Access: Places to get online are everywhere in Nice. Ask at your hotel, or just look up as you walk (keep your eye out for the "@" symbol).

English Bookstore: The Cat's Whiskers has an eclectic selection of novels and regional travel books, including mine. Say *bonjour* to mellow owner Linda (Mon–Sat 9:30–12:00 & 14:00–19:00, closed Sun, 26–30 rue Lamartine, near recommended Hôtel du Petit Louvre, tel. 04 93 80 02 66).

Laundry: You'll find launderettes everywhere in Nice—ask your hotelier for the nearest one. The self-service Point Laverie at the corner of rue Alberti and rue Pastorelli, next to Hôtel Vendôme, is central (daily 8:00–20:00).

Grocery Store: The big **Monoprix** on avenue Jean Médecin and rue Biscarra has a wide selection and cold drinks (closed Sun). You'll also find many small grocery stores (some open Sun and/or until late hours) near my recommended hotels.

Renting a Bike (and Other Wheels): Roller Station rents bikes (*vélos,* €5/hr, €10/half-day, €15/day), rollerblades (*rollers,* €6/day), Razor-type scooters (*trotinettes,* €6/half-day, €9/day), and skateboards (€6/half-day, €9/day). You'll need to leave your ID as a deposit (daily 9:30–19:00, next to yellow awnings of Pailin's Asian restaurant at 49 quai des Etats-Unis—see map on page 557, another location at 10 rue Cassini near place Garibaldi, tel. 04 93 62 99 05).

Car Rental: Renting a car is easiest at Nice's airport, which has offices for all the major companies. You'll also find most companies represented at Nice's train station.

English Radio: Tune into Riviera-Radio at FM 106.5.

Views: For panoramic views, climb Castle Hill (see page 546), or take a one-hour boat trip (see the next page).

Rocky Beaches: To make life tolerable on the rocks, swimmers should buy a pair of the cheap plastic beach shoes sold at many shops (flip-flops fall off in the water). **Go Sport** at 13 place Masséna has them for cheap (daily 10:00–19:00).

Getting Around Nice

While you can easily walk to most attractions in Nice, you'll want to ride the **bus** to the Chagall and Matisse museums and maybe to the Russian Cathedral. A single ride costs €1.30 (ticket good for 74 min in one direction—can't be used for a round-trip or for express buses to airport). An all-day pass is €4 (not valid on TAM buses). Make sure to validate your ticket in the machine just behind the driver—watch to see how locals do it.

The same ticket is valid on the inaugural line of the brand-new **tramway** runs along avenue Jean Médecin and boulevard Jean Jaurès. This handy tram connects the main train station, bus station, Old Nice, place Masséna (a few blocks from the sea), the Modern and Contemporary Art Museum, and comes within a few blocks of the Gare du Sud station (where the scenic Chemins de

Fer de Provence trains depart from; see page 549).

Taxis are even handier for getting to Nice's outlying sights, and worth it if you're nowhere near a bus stop (figure €10–12 from promenade des Anglais). They normally only pick up at taxi stands *(tête de station),* or you can call 04 93 13 78 78.

The hokey **tourist train** gets you up Castle Hill (see "Tours," below).

Tours

Bus Tour—Le Grand Tour Bus provides a hop-on, hop-off option on an open-deck bus with headphone commentary. The full route (about 90 min) includes promenade des Anglais, old port, Cap de Nice, and the Chagall and Matisse museums on Cimiez Hill (€19/1-day pass, €22/2-day pass, cheaper for seniors and students, €10 for last tour of the day at about 18:45, departures 2/hr, buy tickets on bus, main stop is near where promenade des Anglais and quai des Etats-Unis meet, across from plage Beau Rivage—look for signs, tel. 04 92 29 17 00). This tour is a pricey way to get to the Chagall and Matisse museums, but it's a good option if you also want a city overview tour.

Tourist Train—For €6.50, you can spend 40 embarrassing minutes on the tourist train tooting along the promenade, through the old city, and up to Castle Hill. This is a sweat-free way to get to Castle Hill...but so is the elevator, which is much cheaper (every 30 min, recorded English commentary, meet train near Le Grand Tour Bus stop on quai des Etats-Unis, tel. 04 93 62 85 48).

▲Boat Cruise—Here's your chance to join the boat parade and see Nice from the water. On this one-hour, star-studded tour you'll cruise in a comfortable, yacht-size vessel to Cap Ferrat and past Villefranche-sur-Mer, then return to Nice with a run along promenade des Anglais. It's a scenic trip, worthwhile if you won't be hiking along the Cap Ferrat trails that provide similar views. French (and sometimes English-speaking) guides play Robin Leach, pointing out mansions owned by some pretty famous people, including Elton John (just as you leave Nice, soft-yellow square-shaped place right on the water), Sean Connery (on the hill above Elton, with rounded arches and tower), Microsoft mogul Paul Allen (in saddle of Cap Ferrat hill, above yellow-umbrella beach with sloping red-tile roof), and Mick Jagger (between Cap Ferrat and Villefranche-sur-Mer, pink place hidden by trees). I wonder if this gang ever hangs out together... The best views are from the seats on top (€13, June–Oct 2/day, fewer departures in off-season, arrive 30 min early to get best seats, drinks and WCs available). For directions to the dock and contact information, see "Getting Around the Riviera—By Boat," page 536.

Walking Tours—The TI on promenade des Anglais organizes weekly walking tours of Old Nice (€12, May–Oct only, usually Sat morning, 2.5 hours, reservations necessary, depart from TI, tel. 08 92 70 74 07).

Nice's cultural association (Centre du Patrimoine) offers €3 on-demand walks on varying themes in English that are a great value. Call 04 92 00 41 90 a day ahead to make a reservation. Most tours start at their office at 75 quai des Etats-Unis; look for the red plaque next to Musée des Ponchettes.

Les Petits Farcis Cooking Tour and Classes—Canadian food-journalist-turned-Francophile Rosa Jackson is making a Mediterranean splash with her one-day or four-day cooking classes in Old Nice. Her single-day classes include a morning trip to the open-air market, where you'll pick up ingredients, and an afternoon learning what to do with your purchases. Her four-day courses focus exclusively on the art of cooking (1 day–€200, 4 days–€480, tel. 06 81 67 41 22, www.petitsfarcis.com).

SELF-GUIDED WALK

A Scratch-and-Sniff Walk Through Old Nice

• See the map on page 557, and start at Nice's main market square, the...

Cours Saleya (koor sah-lay-yuh): Named for its broad exposure to the sun *(soleil)*, this commotion of color, sights, smells, and people has been Nice's main market square since the Middle Ages (produce market held Tue–Sun until 13:00—on Mon, an antique market takes center stage). Amazingly, part of this square was a parking lot until 1980, when the mayor of Nice had an underground garage built.

Stroll down the center of the cours. The first section is devoted to the plants and flowers that seem to grow effortlessly and everywhere in this ideal climate. Carnations, roses, and jasmine are local favorites in what has been the Riviera's biggest flower market since the 19th century. The boisterous produce section trumpets the season with mushrooms, strawberries, white asparagus, zucchini flowers—whatever's fresh gets top billing.

Place Pierre Gautier (also called Plassa dou Gouvernou—bilingual street signs include the old Niçoise language, an Italian dialect) is where the actual farmers set up stalls to sell their produce and herbs directly.

Continue down the center of cours Saleya, stopping when you see La Cambuse restaurant on your left. In front, hovering over the black barrel fire with the paella-like pan on top, is the self-proclaimed Queen of the Market, Thérèse (tehr-ehz). When she's not looking for a husband, Thérèse is cooking *socca*, Nice's chickpea crêpe specialty. Spend €2 for a wad of *socca* (careful—it's hot, but good). If she doesn't have a pan out, that means it's on its way (watch for the frequent scooter deliveries). Wait in line...or else it'll be all gone when you return.

• *Continue down cours Saleya. The fine golden building at the end is where Henri Matisse lived for 17 years. Turn left at the Café des Ponchettes, and head down...*

Rue de la Poissonnerie: Look up at the first building on your right. Adam and Eve are squaring off, each holding a zucchini-like gourd. This scene (post-apple) represents the annual rapprochement in Nice to make up for the sins of a too-much-fun Carnival (Mardi Gras). Nice residents have partied hard during Carnival for more than 700 years. A few doors down, on the left, find the small church dedicated to St. Rita, the patron saint of desperate causes. She holds a special place in locals' hearts, and this church is the most popular in Nice.

• *Turn right on the next street where you'll pass Old Nice's most happening café/bar (**Distilleries Ideales**), with a lively happy hour (18:00–20:00) and a* Pirates of the Caribbean–*style interior. Now turn left on "Right" Street (rue Droite), and enter an area that feels like a Little Naples.*

Rue Droite: In the Middle Ages, this straight, skinny street provided the most direct route from wall to wall, or river to sea. Stop at Esipuno's bakery (at place du Jésus) and say *bonjour* to the friendly folks. This baker was once voted the best in France, and his son now runs the place. Notice the firewood stacked by the oven and his trophies (earned for best breads). Farther along, at #28, Thérèse (whom you met earlier) cooks her *socca* in the wood-fired oven before she carts it to her barrel on cours Saleya. The balconies of the mansion in the next block mark the Palais Lascaris (1647), a rare souvenir from one of Nice's most prestigious families (free, Wed–Mon 10:00–18:00, closed Tue, worth touring for a peek at 1700s Baroque Italian high life, look up and make faces back at the guys under the balconies).

• *Turn left on the rue de la Loge, then left again on rue Centrale, to reach...*

Place Rossetti: The most Italian of Nice's piazzas, place Rossetti feels more like Rome than Nice. This square comes alive after dark. Fenocchio is popular for its many gelato flavors. Walk to the fountain and stare back at the church. This is the Cathedral of St. Réparate—an unassuming building for a major city's cathedral. The cathedral was relocated here in the 1500s, when Castle Hill was temporarily converted to military-only use. The name comes from Nice's patron saint, a teenage virgin named Réparate whose martyred body floated to Nice in the fourth century, accompanied by angels. The interior gushes Baroque. Remember that Baroque was a response to the Protestant Reformation. With the Catholic Church's "Counter-Reformation," the theatrical energy of churches was cranked up—with reenergized, high-powered saints and eye-popping decor.

• *Our walk is over. Castle Hill is straight up the stepped lane opposite the cathedral (see page 546).*

ACTIVITIES

▲**Wheeling the Promenade**—Get a bike and ride along the coast in both directions along Nice's waterfront boulevard (described below). Allow 30 minutes each

way. Roller Station rents bikes, in-line skates, and mini-scooters (see "Helpful Hints" near the beginning of this chapter). Both of the following paths start along promenade des Anglais.

The path to the west stops just before the airport at perhaps the most scenic *boules* courts in France. Stop and watch the old-timers while away their afternoon tossing those shiny metal balls (see page 771).

Heading east, you'll round the hill—passing a scenic cape and the town's memorial to both World Wars—to the harbor of Nice, with a chance to survey some fancy yachts. Pedal around the harbor and follow the coast past the Corsica ferry terminal (you'll need to carry your bike up a flight of steps). From there, the path leads to an appealing tree-lined residential district.

Relaxing at the Beaches—Nice is where the masses relax on the rocks. After settling into the smooth pebbles, you can play beach volleyball, table tennis, or *boules*; rent paddleboats, personal watercraft, or windsurfing equipment; explore ways to use your zoom lens as a telescope; or snooze on comfy beach beds with end tables. To rent a spot on the beach, compare rates, as prices vary—beaches on the east end of the bay are usually cheaper (mattress and chaise lounge-€12–18, umbrella-€5, towel-€3). Many hotels have special deals with certain beaches for discounted rental (check with your

hotel for details). Consider lunch in your bathing suit (€10–12 salads and pizzas in bars and restaurants all along the beach). Several beach bars offer drinks with a view (ideal before dinner). *Plage Publique* signs explain the 15 beach no-nos (translated in English).

While Nice's beaches are traditionally rocky, a few years ago a small sandy area appeared toward the Italy end of the bay.

SIGHTS

Along Promenade des Anglais

There's something for everyone along this four-mile-long seafront circus, worth ▲▲▲. Watch the Europeans at play, admire the azure Mediterranean, anchor yourself on a blue bench, and prop your feet up on the made-to-order guardrail. Later in the day, come back to join the evening parade of tans along the promenade.

The broad sidewalks of promenade des Anglais ("walkway of the English") were financed by wealthy English tourists who wanted a safe place to stroll and admire the view. In 1822, the walk was paved in marble for aristocrats who didn't want to dirty their shoes or smell the fishy gravel. For now, stroll like the belle époque English aristocrats for whom the promenade was built.

Start at the pink-domed Hôtel Negresco, then cross to the sea and end your promenade at Castle Hill. The following sights are listed in the order you'll pass them. This walk is ideally done at sunset (as a predinner stroll).

Hôtel Negresco—Nice's finest hotel (also a historic monument) offers the city's most expensive beds (€460 minimum for a sea view, see "Sleeping—Between Boulevard Victor Hugo and Promenade des Anglais"), and a free "museum" interior (always open—provided you're dressed decently, absolutely no beach attire). March straight through the lobby (as if you're staying there) into the exquisite Salon Royal. The chandelier hanging from the Eiffel-built dome is made of 16,000 pieces of crystal. It was built in France for the Russian czar's Moscow palace...but because of the Bolshevik Revolution in 1917, he couldn't take delivery. Read the explanation of the dome and saunter around counterclockwise: The bucolic scene, painted in 1913 for the hotel, sets the tone. Nip into the toilets for either a turn-of-the-century powder room or a Battle of Waterloo experience. The chairs nearby were typical of the age (cones of silence for an afternoon nap sitting up).

Bay of Angels (Baie des Anges)—Grab a blue chair and face the sea. The body of Nice's patron saint, Réparate, was supposedly escorted into this bay by angels in the fourth century. To your right is where you might have been escorted into France—Nice's airport, built on a massive landfill. On that tip of land way beyond the runway is Cap d'Antibes. Until 1860, Antibes and Nice were in different countries—Antibes was French, but Nice was a protectorate of the Italian kingdom of Savoy-Piedmont, a.k.a. the Kingdom of Sardinia. (During that period, the Var River—just west of Nice—was the geographic border between these two peoples.) In 1850, locals spoke Italian and ate pasta. As Italy was uniting, the region was given a choice: Join the new country of Italy or join France (which was enjoying good times under the rule of Napoleon III). The vast majority voted in 1860 to go French...and voilà!

The green hill to your left is Castle Hill. Further left lies Villefranche-sur-Mer (marked by the tower at land's end, and home to lots of millionaires), then Monaco (which you can't see, with more millionaires), then Italy (with lots of pasta). Behind you are the foothills of the Alps (Alpes Maritimes), which gather threatening clouds, ensuring that the Côte d'Azur enjoys sunshine more than 300 days each year. While half a million people live here, pollution is carefully treated—the water is routinely tested and very clean. Stroll the promenade with the sea starboard, and read about "Relaxing at the Beaches" (under "Activities," page 544).

Albert I Park—The park was named for the Belgian king who enjoyed wintering here. While the English came first, the Belgians and Russians were also huge fans of 19th-century Nice. The 1960 statue in the park commemorates Nice's being part of France for 100 years. If you detour from the promenade into the park and continue down the center of the grassy strip, you'll be walking over Nice's river, the Paillon (covered since the 1800s). For centuries, this river was Nice's natural defense to the north and west (the sea protected the south, and Castle Hill defended the east). Imagine the fortified wall ran along its length from the hills behind you to the sea. With the arrival of tourism in the 1800s, Nice expanded over and beyond the river.

Castle Hill (Colline du Château)—The hill, in an otherwise flat city center, offers sensational views over Nice, the port (to the east), the foothills of the Alps, and the Mediterranean. The views are best early or at sunset, or whenever it's really clear (park closes at 20:00 in summer, earlier off-season). You can get to the top by foot, by elevator (€0.70 one-way, €1.10 round-trip, runs daily 10:00–19:00, until 20:00 in summer, next to beachfront Hôtel Suisse), or by tourist train (described under "Tours" on page 541). Up top, you'll find cafés and an extensive play area for kids.

The city of Nice was first settled here by Greeks circa 400 B.C. In the Middle Ages, a massive castle stood there, with turrets, high walls, and soldiers at the ready. With the river guarding one side and the sea the other, this mountain fortress seemed strong—until Louis XIV leveled it in 1706. Nice's medieval seawall ran along the lineup of two-story buildings below. Today, you'll find a waterfall, a playground, two cafés (fair prices), and a cemetery—but no castle—on Castle Hill. Nice's port, where you'll find Trans Côte d'Azur's boat cruises (described on page 541), is just below on the east edge of Castle Hill.

Museums

Remember that many Nice museums are free (and more crowded) the first and third Sundays of the month. The first two museums (Chagall and Matisse) are northeast of Nice's city center. Because they're both relatively difficult to reach and on the same bus line (in the same direction), it only makes sense to visit them at the same time. The Chagall Museum is much closer to the center, while the Matisse Museum is a 30-minute walk (or quick bus ride) farther out.

▲▲▲**Chagall Museum (Musée National Marc Chagall)**—Even if you're suspicious of modern art, this museum—with the largest collection of Chagall's work in captivity anywhere—is a delight. After World War II, Chagall returned from the US to settle in nearby Vence. Between 1954 and 1967, he painted a cycle of 17 large murals designed for, and donated to, this museum. These paintings, inspired by the biblical books of Genesis, Exodus, and the Song of Songs, make up the "nave," or core, of what Chagall called the "House of Brotherhood."

Each painting is a lighter-than-air collage of images that draw from Chagall's Russian-folk-village youth, his Jewish heritage, biblical themes, and his feeling that he existed somewhere between heaven and earth. He believed that the Bible was a synonym for nature, and that color and biblical themes were key ingredients for understanding God's love for his creation. Chagall's brilliant blues and reds celebrate nature, as do his spiritual and folk themes.

On your way out, be sure to visit the three Chagall stained-glass windows in the auditorium (depicting God's creation of the universe). An idyllic garden café with fair prices awaits by the entrance to the museum grounds. A spick-and-span WC is to the far left in the garden as you face the museum (there's one inside, too).

Cost, Hours, Location: €6.70, free first Sunday of the month, can cost a little more during special exhibits, Oct–June Wed–Mon 10:00–17:00, July–Sept until 18:00, closed Tue year-round, avenue Docteur Ménard, tel. 04 93 53 87 20, www.musee-chagall.fr.

Getting to the Chagall Museum: You can reach the museum by bus or on foot. **Bus #15** serves the Chagall Museum from place Masséna (stop faces eastbound on rue Gioffredo, a block east of Galeries Lafayette; 5/hr Mon–Sat, 3/hr Sun, €1.30). The museum's bus stop (called Musée Chagall, shown on the bus shelter) is on boulevard de Cimiez (walk uphill from the stop to find the museum). To **walk** from central Nice to the Chagall Museum, go to the train-station end of avenue Jean Médecin and turn right onto

Chagall's Style

Chagall uses a deceptively simple, almost childlike style to paint a world that's hidden to the eye—the magical, mystical world below the surface. Here are some of his techniques:

- **Deep, radiant colors,** inspired by Expressionism and Fauvism (an art movement pioneered by Matisse and other French painters).
- **Personal imagery,** particularly from his childhood in Russia—smiling barnyard animals, fiddlers on the roof, flower bouquets, huts, and blissful sweethearts.
- **A Hasidic Jewish perspective,** the idea that God is everywhere, appearing in everyday things like nature, animals, and humdrum activities.
- **A fragmented Cubist style**, multifaceted and multidimensional, a perfect style to capture the multifaceted and multidimensional complexity of God's creation.
- **Overlapping images,** like double-exposure photography, with faint imagery that bleeds through, suggesting there's more to life under the surface.
- **Stained-glass-esque technique** of dark, deep, earthy, "potent" colors, and simplified, iconic, symbolic figures.
- **Gravity-defying compositions,** with lovers, animals, and angels twirling blissfully in mid-air.
- **Happy, not tragic mood,** that despite the violence and turmoil of world wars and revolution, he painted a world of personal joy.
- **Childlike simplicity,** drawn with simple, heavy outlines, filled in with Crayola colors that often spill over the lines. Major characters in a scene are bigger than the lesser characters. The grinning barnyard animals, the bright colors, the magical events presented as literal truth… Was Chagall a lightweight? Or a lighter-than-air-weight?

boulevard Raimbaldi. Walk four long blocks along the elevated road, then turn left onto avenue Raymond Comboul and follow *Musée Chagall* signs.

Leaving the Museum: Taxis usually wait outside the museum. To take bus #15 back to downtown Nice, turn right out of the museum, then make a left up boulevard de Cimiez, and catch the bus on that side of the street. To continue on to the Matisse Museum, catch bus #15 using the uphill stop, located across the street.

To walk to the train station from the museum, turn left out of the museum, turn left on the street behind it, and then look for the staircase on your left (leading down). Cross under the freeway, then turn right to reach the station.

▲**Matisse Museum (Musée Matisse)**—This museum, worth ▲▲▲ for his fans, contains the world's largest collection of Henri Matisse paintings. It offers a painless introduction to the artist, whose style was shaped by Mediterranean light and by fellow Côte d'Azur artists Pablo Picasso and Pierre-Auguste Renoir. The collection is scattered through several rooms with a few worthwhile works, though it lacks a certain *je ne sais quoi* when compared to the Chagall Museum.

Henri Matisse, the master of leaving things out, could suggest a woman's body with a single curvy line—leaving it to the viewer's mind to fill in the rest. Ignoring traditional 3-D perspective, he used simple dark outlines saturated with bright blocks of color to create recognizable but simplified scenes, all composed into a decorative pattern to express nature's serene beauty. You don't look "through" a Matisse canvas, like a window; you look "at" it, like wallpaper.

Matisse understood how colors and shapes affect us emotionally. He could create either shocking, clashing works (Fauvism) or geometrical, balanced, harmonious ones (later works). While other modern artists reveled in purely abstract design, Matisse (almost) always kept the subject matter at least vaguely recognizable. He used unreal colors and distorted lines not just to portray what an object looks like, but to express the object's inner nature (even inanimate objects). Meditating on his paintings helps you connect with nature—or so Matisse hoped.

Cost, Hours, Location: €4, Wed–Mon 10:00–18:00, closed Tue, tel. 04 93 81 08 08, www.musee-matisse-nice.org. The museum, at 164 avenue des Arènes de Cimiez, is set in an olive grove amid the ruins of the Roman city of Cemenelum.

Getting to the Matisse Museum: It's a long uphill walk from the city center. Take the bus (details below) or a cab (about €12 from promenade des Anglais). Once here, walk into the park to find the pink villa.

Buses #15 and **#17** provide frequent service to the Matisse Museum from just off place Masséna on rue Gioffredo, a block east of the Galeries Lafayette department store (€1.30). The bus stop for the museum is called Arènes–Matisse. When leaving the museum, find the stop for bus #15 (with the most frequent service downtown, stopping en route at the Chagall Museum) by exiting the park and crossing boulevard de Cimiez, where the two roads meet (the stop is on boulevard de Cimiez, not avenue des Arènes de Cimiez; see map on page 538). The stop for bus #17 (less frequent, no Chagall stop) also faces downhill, but it's on avenue des Arènes de Cimiez. Confusing, I know.

Modern and Contemporary Art Museum (Musée d'Art Moderne et d'Art Contemporain)—This ultramodern museum features an explosively colorful, far-out, yet manageable permanent collection (on the second floor) of mostly American and European art from the 1960s and 1970s. The exhibits include a few works by Andy Warhol, Roy Lichtenstein, and Jean Tinguely, and small models of Christo's famous wrappings. Several of Niki de Saint Phalle's works are almost huggable. The temporary exhibits can be as appealing to modern-art-lovers as the permanent collection—ask the TI what's playing.

Cost, Hours, Location: €4, Tue–Sun 10:00–18:00, closed Mon, about a 15-minute walk from place Masséna, near bus station on promenade des Arts, tel. 04 93 62 61 62, www.mamac-nice.org.

Molinard Perfume Museum—The Molinard family has been making perfume in Grasse (about an hour's drive or train ride from Nice) since 1849. Their Nice store has a small museum in the back illustrating the story of their industry. Back when people believed water spread the plague (Louis XIV supposedly bathed less than once a year), doctors advised people to rub fragrances into their skin and then powder their body. Back then, perfume was a necessity of everyday life.

Room 1 shows photos of the local flowers used in perfume production. Room 2 shows the earliest (18th-century) production method. Petals would be laid on a bed of animal fat. After baking in the sun, the fat would absorb the essence of the flowers. Petals would be replaced daily for two months until the fat was saturated. Models and old photos show the later distillation process (660 pounds of lavender would produce only a quarter-gallon of essence). Perfume is "distilled like cognac and then aged like wine." Room 3 shows the desk of a "nose" (top perfume creator). Of the 150 real "noses" in the world, more than 100 are French. You are welcome to enjoy the testing bottles before heading into the shop.

Cost, Hours, Location: Free, daily 10:00–19:00, sometimes closed Mon off-season, just between beach and place Masséna at 20 rue St. François de Paule, tel. 04 93 62 90 50, www.molinard .com.

Other Nice Museums—These museums are acceptable rainy-day options.

The **Fine Arts Museum** (Musée des Beaux-Arts), located in a sumptuous villa with lovely gardens, houses 6,000 works from the 17th to 20th centuries, and will satisfy your need for a fine-arts fix (€4, Tue–Sun 10:00–18:00, closed Mon, 3 avenue des Baumettes, western end of Nice, take bus #38 from the bus station, tel. 04 92 15 28 28).

The **Archaeological Museum** (Musée Archeologique) displays various objects from the Romans' occupation of this region. It's convenient—just below the Matisse Museum—but has little of interest to anyone but Ancient Rome aficionados. You also get access to the Roman bath ruins...which are, sadly, overgrown with weeds (€4, very limited information in English, Wed–Mon 10:00–18:00, closed Tue, near Matisse Museum at 160 avenue des Arènes de Cimiez, tel. 04 93 81 59 57).

Nice's city history museum, **Masséna Museum** (Musée Masséna), is closed, likely through 2008 (but may re-open earlier than expected—check with the TI for the latest).

▲Russian Cathedral

Nice's Russian Orthodox church—claimed to be the finest outside Russia—is worth a visit. Five hundred rich Russian families

wintered in Nice in the late 19th century. Since they couldn't pray in a Catholic church, the community needed a worthy Orthodox house of worship. Czar Nicholas I's widow provided the land (which required tearing down her house), and Czar Nicholas II gave this church to the Russian community in 1912. (A few years later, Russian comrades—who didn't winter on the Riviera—assassinated him.) Here in the land of olives and anchovies, these proud onion domes seem odd. But, I imagine, so did those old Russians.

Step inside (pick up English info sheet). The one-room interior is filled with icons and candles, and the old Russian music adds to the ambience. The wall of icons (iconostasis) divides things between the spiritual world and the temporal world of the worshippers. Only the priest can walk between the two worlds, by using the "Royal Door." Take a close look at items lining the front (starting in the left corner). The angel with red boots and wings—the protector of the Romanov family—stands over a symbolic tomb of Christ. The tall, black, hammered-copper cross commemorates the massacre of Nicholas II and his family in 1918. Notice the Jesus icon to the right of the Royal Door. According to a priest here, as the worshipper meditates, staring deep into the eyes of Jesus, he enters a lake where he finds his soul. Surrounded by incense, chanting, and your entire community...it could happen. Farther to the right, the icon of the unhappy-looking Virgin and Child is decorated with semiprecious stones from the Ural Mountains. Artists worked a triangle into each iconic face—symbolic of the Trinity.

Cost, Hours, Location: €3, daily 9:00–12:00 & 14:30–18:00, until 17:00 off-season, chanted services Sat at 17:30 or 18:00, Sun at 10:00, no tourist visits during services, no short shorts, tel. 04 93 96 88 02. The park around the church stays open at lunch and makes a fine setting for picnics.

Getting to the Russian Cathedral: It's a 10-minute walk from the train station to the cathedral; exit the station to the right onto avenue Thiers, turn right on avenue Gambetta, and follow signs to the cathedral. Or, from the station, take any bus heading west on avenue Thiers and get off at avenue Gambetta (a few stops away). The cathedral is at 17 boulevard du Tzarewitch.

NIGHTLIFE

Promenade des Anglais, cours Saleya, and rue Masséna are all worth an evening walk. Nice's bars play host to one of the Riviera's most happening late-night scenes, full of jazz, rock, and heat-seeking singles. Most activity focuses on Old Nice, near place Rossetti and along rue Droite. *Distilleries Ideales* is a fine place to start or end your evening, with a lively, international crowd and a fun interior (where rues de la Poissonnerie and Barillerie meet, happy hour 18:00–20:00).

Plan on a cover charge or expensive drinks when music is involved. If you're out very late, avoid walking alone. The plush bar at Hôtel Negresco is fancy-cigar old English. Nice is well-known for its lively after-dark action; for more relaxed and accessible nightlife, consider nearby Antibes (page 585).

SLEEPING

Don't look for charm in Nice. Go for modern and clean, with a central location and, in summer, air-conditioning. Reserve early for summer visits. The rates listed here are for April through October. Prices generally drop €10–20 from November through March, but go sky-high during the Nice Carnival (Feb 16–March 2 in 2008), Monaco's Grand Prix (May 22–25 in 2008), and the Cannes film festival (May 14–25 in 2008). June is convention month, and Nice is one of Europe's top convention cities—so book ahead and be ready for higher prices at some hotels. For parking, ask your hotelier (several have limited private parking), or see "Arrival in Nice—By Car" page 539.

I've divided my sleeping recommendations into three areas: between the train station and Nice Etoile shopping center (with easy access to the train station and a 15-min walk to Old Nice, or a 20-min walk to promenade des Anglais); between Nice Etoile and Old Nice (east of avenue Jean Médecin, with better access to Old Nice and the sea at quai des Etats-Unis); and between boulevard Victor Hugo and promenade des Anglais (a somewhat classier

---

Sleep Code

(€1 = about $1.30, country code: 33)
S = Single, **D** = Double/Twin, **T** = Triple, **Q** = Quad, **b** = bathroom, **s** = shower only, ***** = French hotel rating (0–4 stars). Hotels speak English, have elevators, and accept credit cards unless otherwise noted.

To help you sort easily through these listings, I've divided the rooms into three categories based on the price for a standard double room with bath:

$$$ **Higher Priced**—Most rooms €100 or more.
 $$ **Moderately Priced**—Most rooms between €70–100.
  $ **Lower Priced**—Most rooms €70 or less.

---

area, offering better access to the promenade but longer walks to the train station and Old Nice). I've also listed a hotel near the airport.

Every hotel I list has Wi-Fi and nearly all have Internet access.

Between the Train Station and Nice Etoile

Most hotels near the station ghetto are overrun, overpriced, and loud. These are the pleasant exceptions (most are near avenue Jean Médecin).

$$$ Hôtel Excelsior***, one block below the station, is an elegant place with turn-of-the-century decor, a pleasing garden courtyard, and 40 top-notch rooms. Rooms on the garden are best in the summer; streetside rooms have balconies and get winter sun (standard Db-€140, bigger Db-€160, Tb-€160–190, Qb with kitchenettes on the garden-€200–250, air-con, 19 avenue Durante, tel. 04 93 88 18 05, fax 04 93 88 38 69, www.excelsiornice.com, excelsior@wanadoo.fr).

$$ Hôtel le Laurier Blanc***, clean and homey, is run with pride by the hardworking owners, the Marets. The quite comfortable rooms come with real quilts and ceiling fans, but no air-conditioning (Db-€70–90, fine 2-room Tb-€95–150, on a quiet dead-end street, 18 avenue Durante, tel. 04 93 88 89 45, fax 04 93 88 16 11, www.hotel-laurier-blanc.fr, reservation@hotel-laurier-blanc.fr).

$$ Hôtel Durante**, run by smiling Nathalie, feels like a Mediterranean villa, with its way-orange facade, spacious central courtyard, and cool bathroom tiles. Rooms are good enough, and the price is right (Db-€71–79, bigger Db-€130–150, Tb-€130–150, air-con, 16 avenue Durante, tel. 04 93 88 84 40, fax 04 93 87 77 76,

Nice Hotels

French Riviera

1. Hôtels Excelsior & la Belle Meunière
2. Hôtels le Laurier Blanc & Durante
3. Hôtels Clemenceau & St. Georges
4. Hôtel du Petit Louvre
5. Hôtel Masséna
6. Hôtel Suisse
7. Hôtel Mercure
8. Hôtel Lafayette
9. Hôtel de la Mer
10. Hôtel Negresco
11. Hôtel le Royal
12. Hôtel Windsor
13. Hôtels les Cigales
14. Hôtels Splendid & Gounod
15. Hôtel Villa Victoria
16. To Hôtel Ibis
17. Hôtel Vendôme & Launderette
18. Cat's Whiskers Bookstore
19. Bus #98 to Airport
20. Bus #15 to Chagall Museum & Bus #17 to Matisse Museum
21. Buses #99 & 23 to Airport

www.hotel-durante.com, info@hotel-durante.com).

$$ Hôtel St. Georges** is big and bright, with a backyard garden, reasonably clean and comfortable high-ceilinged rooms, orange tones, blue halls, fair rates, and happy Jacques at reception (Sb-€76, Db-€90, Tb with 3 separate beds-€106, extra bed-€19, air-con, 7 avenue Georges Clemenceau, tel. 04 93 88 79 21, fax 04 93 16 22 85, www.hotelsaintgeorges.fr, contact@hotelsaintgeorges.fr).

$ Hôtel Clemenceau****, run by the La Serre family, is an exceptional budget value with a humble, comfy feel. Rooms—some with balconies, some without closets, all air-conditioned—are mostly spacious, simple, and traditional (S-€31, Sb-€43, D-€46, Db-€58, Tb-€69, Qb-€84, kitchenette-€8 extra and only for stays of at least 3 nights, no elevator, 3 avenue Georges Clemenceau, 1 block west of avenue Jean Médecin, tel. 04 93 88 61 19, fax 04 93 16 88 96, hotel-clemenceau@wanadoo.fr, Marianne and Cedric speak English, Mama and Papa no speak).

$ Hôtel la Belle Meunière, in a fine old mansion built for Napoleon III's mistress, has cheap beds and private rooms just a block below the train station. Lively and hostel-esque, this place attracts budget-minded travelers of all ages with basic-but-adequate, decent-value rooms and charismatic Madame Marie-Pierre presiding. Tables in the front yard greet guests and provide opportunities to meet other travelers (bed in 4-person dorm with private bathroom-€23, €18 *sans* private shower, Db-€60, includes breakfast, 21 avenue Durante, tel. 04 93 88 66 15, fax 04 93 82 51 76, www.bellemeuniere.com, hotel.belle.meuniere@cegetel.net).

$ Hôtel du Petit Louvre* offers an interesting concept at a good price, with clean, small rooms—all recently renovated with kitchenettes and air-conditioning—and beds that convert to couches to allow more space during the day (Db-€58, Tb-€68, no breakfast, 10 rue Emma Tiranty, tel. 04 93 80 15 54, fax 04 93 62 45 08, www.hotelgoodprice.com, petilouvr@wanadoo.com).

Between Nice Etoile and Old Nice

$$$ Hôtel Masséna******, in a classy building a few blocks from place Masséna, is a stylish business hotel showcasing 100 rooms with every amenity at almost-reasonable rates (small Db-€130, larger Db-€165, still larger Db-€240, extra bed-€30, some non-smoking rooms, reserve parking ahead-€20/day, 58 rue Gioffredo, tel. 04 92 47 88 88, fax 04 92 47 88 89, www.hotel-massena-nice.com, info@hotel-massena-nice.com).

$$$ Hôtel Suisse*****, below Castle Hill, has Nice's best ocean and city views for the money, and is surprisingly quiet given the busy street below. Rooms are quite comfortable and decorated with class. There's no reason to sleep here if you don't land a view, so I've listed prices only for view rooms—many of which have balconies (Db-€150–190, extra bed-€36, breakfast-€15, 15 quai Rauba Capeu, tel. 04 92 17 39 00, fax 04 93 85 30 70, www .hotels-ocre-azur.com, hotel.suisse@hotels-ocre-azur.com).

$$$ **Hôtel Mercure***, a chain hotel ideally situated across from the sea and behind cours Saleya, offers smallish yet tastefully designed rooms (some with beds in a loft). The rates are decent, considering the sensational location (Sb-€105–125, Db-€115–130, Tb-€145–160, sea view-€30 extra, air-con, 91 quai des Etats-Unis, tel. 04 93 85 74 19, fax 04 93 13 90 94, h0962@accor.com).

$$$ **Hôtel Vendôme*** gives you a whiff of the belle époque, with pink pastels, high ceilings, and grand staircases in a mansion set off the street with limited parking (book ahead, €11/day). That whiff could be sharper (many tour groups stay here and the rooms seem a tad tired), but the location is good, prices are almost fair, and rooms are modern and come in all sizes. The best have balconies—request *une chambre avec balcon* (Sb-€95–110, Db-€144, Tb-€160, air-con, 26 rue Pastorelli, tel. 04 93 62 00 77, fax 04 93 13 40 78, www.vendome -hotel-nice.com, contact@vendome-hotel-nice.com).

$$ **Hôtel Lafayette***, well-located a block behind the Galeries Lafayette department store, looks average from the outside. But inside it's homey and a good value, with 18 well-designed, mostly spacious rooms, all one floor up from the street. Sweet Sandrine and Christine take darned good care of you (standard Db-€90–110, spacious Db-€95–120, extra bed-€22, central air-con, no elevator, 32 rue de l'Hôtel des Postes, tel. 04 93 85 17 84, fax 04 93 80 47 56, www.hotellafayettenice.com, info@hotellafayettenice.com).

$$ **Hôtel de la Mer*** sits in an enviable location between place Masséna and Old Nice. It's one of my closest listings to Old Nice and is a small, modest place run by gracious Madame Ferry (Db-€65–95, Tb-€78–120, air-con, 4 place Masséna, tel. 04 93 92 09 10, fax 04 93 85 00 64, www.hoteldelamernice.com, hotel.mer @wanadoo.fr).

Between Boulevard Victor Hugo and Promenade des Anglais

$$$$ **Hôtel Negresco**** owns Nice's most prestigious address on promenade des Anglais and knows it. Still, it's the kind of place that, if you were to splurge just once in your life.... Rooms are opulent (see page 545 for further description), and tips are expected (viewless Db-€360, Db with sea view-€460–580, view suite-€770–1,900, breakfast-€35, cool bar, 37 promenade des Anglais, tel. 04 93 16 64 00, fax 04 93 88 35 68, www.hotel-negresco-nice.com, reservation@hotel-negresco.com).

$$$ **Hôtel le Royal*** stands shoulder-to-shoulder on promenade des Anglais with the big boys (the Negresco, Concorde, and Westminster hotels). With 140 rooms, big lounges, and hallways

Old Nice Hotels and Restaurants

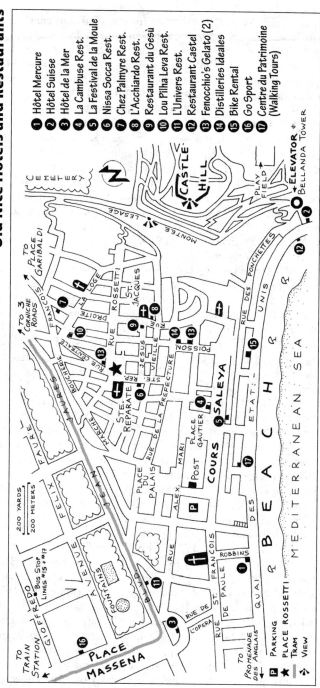

1. Hôtel Mercure
2. Hôtel Suisse
3. Hôtel de la Mer
4. La Cambuse Rest.
5. La Festival de la Moule
6. Nissa Socca Rest.
7. Chez Palmyre Rest.
8. L'Acchiardo Rest.
9. Restaurant du Gesù
10. Lou Pilha Leva Rest.
11. L'Univers Rest.
12. Restaurant Castel
13. Fenocchio's Gelato (2)
14. Distilleries Ideales
15. Bike Rental
16. Go Sport
17. Centre du Patrimoine (Walking Tours)

MEDITERRANEAN SEA

CASTLE HILL

PLACE MASSENA

COURS SALEYA

ELEVATOR + BELLANDA TOWER

200 YARDS
200 METERS

P PARKING
★ PLACE ROSSETTI
Tram
View

that stretch forever, it feels a bit institutional. But considering the solid, air-conditioned comfort and terrific location, this is a good value—and they sometimes have rooms when others don't (viewless Db-€110, Db with sea view-€150–170, bigger view room-€180 and worth the extra euros, extra person-€25, 23 promenade des Anglais, tel. 04 93 16 43 00, fax 04 93 16 43 02, www.hotel-royal-nice.cote.azur.fr, royal@vacancesbleues.com).

$$$ Hôtel Windsor*** is a snazzy garden retreat that feels like a cross between a modern-art museum and a health spa. The contemporary rooms include some designed by modern artists that defy explanation. It has a full-service bar, a swimming pool and gym (both free for guests), an €11 sauna, €55 massages, and light, full meal service in the garden (standard Db-€120, bigger Db-€150, big Db with balcony-€175, extra bed-€20, rooms over garden worth the higher price, air-con, Internet access, 11 rue Dalpozzo, tel. 04 93 88 59 35, fax 04 93 88 94 57, www.hotelwindsornice.com, reservation@hotelwindsornice.com).

$$$ Hôtel les Cigales*** is a smart little pastel place with tasteful decor, 19 plush rooms (most with tub-showers), air-conditioning, and a nifty upstairs terrace, all well-managed by friendly Mr. Valentino with Veronique and Elaine. Book directly through the hotel and show this book for a surprise treat on arrival (standard Db-€90–120, big Db-€115–140, Tb-€150, €30 more during major events, extra bed-€20, 16 rue Dalpozzo, tel. 04 97 03 10 70, fax 04 97 03 10 71, www.hotel-lescigales.com, info @hotel-lescigales.com).

$$$ Hôtel Splendid***** is a worthwhile splurge if you miss your Marriott. The panoramic rooftop pool, Jacuzzi, bar, restaurant, and breakfast room alone almost justify the cost...but throw in good rooms (4 of 6 floors are non-smoking), a free gym, and air-conditioning, and you're as good as home. Check their website for deals (Db-€225, deluxe Db with terrace-€250, suites-€335–360, free breakfast if you stay at least 3 nights, 10 percent off for weeklong stays, parking-€20/day, 50 boulevard Victor Hugo, tel. 04 93 16 41 00, fax 04 93 16 42 70, www.splendid-nice.com, info @splendid-nice.com).

$$$ Hôtel Gounod*** is behind Hôtel Splendid and shares the same owners, who allow its clients free access to Hôtel Splendid's pool, Jacuzzi, and other amenities. Don't let the lackluster lobby fool you. Most rooms are richly decorated, with high ceilings and air-conditioning—though quality can vary (Db-€145, palatial 4-person suites-€225, parking-€14/day, 3 rue Gounod, tel. 04 93 16 42 00, fax 04 93 88 23 84, www.gounod-nice.com, info @gounod-nice.com).

$$$ Hôtel Villa Victoria*** is well-managed by cheery Marlena, who welcomes travelers in a classy old building with a green awning and an attractive lobby, which overlooks a generous garden. Rooms are traditional and well-kept, with space to stretch out (Db-€115–140, Tb-€128–153, suites-€160–180, pricier rooms face the garden, breakfast-€15, air-con, parking-€10–15, 33 boulevard Victor Hugo, tel. 04 93 88 39 60, fax 04 93 88 07 98, www .villa-victoria.com).

Closer to the Airport

$$ Hôtel Ibis** offers a handy port-in-the-storm outlet for those with early flights or single nights (Db-€80-120, 359 promenade des Anglais, tel. 04 89 88 30 30, fax 04 93 21 19 43, reception@ibisnice .com).

EATING

Remember, you're in a resort...go for ambience and fun, and lower your palate's standards. Italian is a low-risk and local cuisine. My recommended restaurants are concentrated in neighborhoods close to my favorite hotels, though you should focus your dining energy on Old Nice. Promenade des Anglais is ideal for picnic dinners on warm, languid evenings. Old Nice has the best and busiest dining atmosphere, while the Nice Etoile area is more convenient and offers a good range of choices. To eat cheaply, eat on rue Droite in Old Nice, or explore the area around the train station. For a more peaceful meal, dine in nearby Villefranche-sur-Mer (see page 570). For terribly touristy trolling, wander the wall-to-wall places lining rue Masséna. Yuck.

In Old Nice

Nice's dinner scene converges on cours Saleya—entertaining enough in itself to make its restaurants' generally mediocre food a good value. It's a fun, festive place to compare tans and mussels. Even if you're eating elsewhere, wander through here in the evening. For locations, see the map on page 557.

La Cambuse, a small island of refinement for those who want to dine on cours Saleya, is the one place along here that doesn't try to reel in passersby. Owner Gregory is swimming upstream in his effort to provide quality cuisine with attentive service in this touristy area. Split a starter like the filling *petits farcis niçois* (stuffed vegetables), then order your own *plat* (€13 starters, €18–24 *plats*, open daily, 5 cours Saleya, tel. 04 93 80 82 40).

La Festival de la Moule is a fun place where it's all about the mussels. For just €11, you get all-you-can-eat mussels and fries (across the square from la Cambuse, 20 cours Saleya, tel. 04 93 62 02 12).

Nissa Socca offers good, cheap Italian cuisine and a lively atmosphere in a small room a few blocks from cours Saleya. Inside

Nice Restaurants

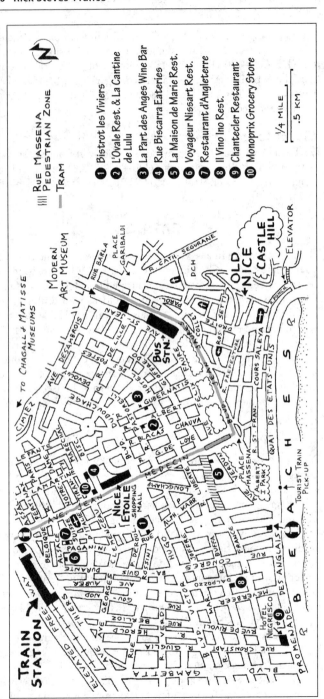

1 Bistrot les Viviers
2 L'Ovale Rest. & La Cantine de Lulu
3 La Part des Anges Wine Bar
4 Rue Biscarra Eateries
5 La Maison de Marie Rest.
6 Voyageur Nissart Rest.
7 Restaurant d'Angleterre
8 Il Vino Ino Rest.
9 Chantecler Restaurant
10 Monoprix Grocery Store

||||| RUE MASSENA PEDESTRIAN ZONE
— TRAM

¼ MILE
.5 KM

tables are usually steamy—arrive early to land a table outside (€9 pizza, €10 pastas, €15 *menus*, Mon–Sat from 19:00, closed Sun, a block off place Rossetti on rue Ste. Réparate, tel. 04 93 80 18 35).

L'Univers, a block off place Masséna, earned a Michelin star while maintaining a warm ambience. This elegant place is as relaxed as a "top" restaurant can be, from its casual decor to the tasteful dinnerware. When the artfully presented food arrives, you know this is high cuisine (*menus* from €42, closed Sun, 53 boulevard Jean Jaurès, tel. 04 93 62 32 22, plumailunivers@aol.com).

Restaurant Castel is your best eat-on-the-beach option. Eating here, you almost expect Don Ho to grab a mic. You're right on the beach below Castle Hill, perfectly positioned to watch evening swimmers get in their last laps as the sky turns pink and city lights flicker on. The views are unforgettable; you can even have lunch at your beach chair if you've rented one. Dinner here is best, so arrive before sunset and linger long enough to merit the few extra euros the place charges (open daily, €13–15 salads and pastas, €20–24 main courses, 8 quai des Etats-Unis, tel. 04 93 85 22 66).

Dining Cheap *à la Niçoise*

Try at least one of these four places—not just because they're terrific budget options, but primarily because they offer authentic *niçoise* cuisine.

Chez Palmyre is as real as it gets, where your hostess Madame Palmyre shuffles between her small kitchen and the seven-table dining room. The four-course *menu* is only €13, and the cuisine could not be more homemade (closed Sun, cash only, 5 rue Droite, tel. 04 93 85 72 32).

L'Acchiardo, in the heart of Old Nice, does a good job of mixing a loyal local and tourist clientele. Its simple, hearty, *niçoise* cuisine is served for fair prices in a homey setting overseen by gentle Monsieur Acchiardo (€13 dinner *plats*, cash only, closed Sat–Sun, 38 rue Droite, tel. 04 93 85 51 16).

Restaurant du Gesù, a happy-go-lucky budget eatery, squeezes plastic tables into a slanting square deep in the old city (sailors accustomed to dining at an angle will feel right at home). Arrive early or join the mobs waiting for an outside table, or, better, have fun in the soccer banner–draped interior (€8 pizzas, €10 pastas, closed Sun, 1 place du Jésus, tel. 04 93 62 26 46).

Lou Pilha Leva offers a fun, *très* cheap dinner option with *niçoise* specialties and outdoor-only benches. Order your food from one side and drinks from the other (open daily, located where rues de la Loge and Centrale meet in Old Nice).

And for Dessert...

Gelato-lovers should save room for the tempting ice cream stands in Old Nice—such as **Fenocchio,** which serves up 86 flavors, from tomato to lavender (daily until 23:30, 2 locations in Old Nice: on place Rossetti and on rue de la Poissonnerie).

Eating near Nice Etoile

On Rue Biscarra: Laid-back cafés line up along the broad sidewalk on rue Biscarra (just east of avenue Jean Médecin behind Nice Etoile, all closed Sun). **L'Authentic, Le Vin sur Vin, Marre'n,** and **Le Cenac** are all reasonable enough. **Le Vin sur Vin** seems most popular, though **L'Authentic** is also good, with memorable owners (burly Philippe and sleek Laurent), daily specials, €19 *menus,* and reasonable pasta dishes (closed Sun, 18 bis rue Biscarra, tel. 04 93 62 48 88).

Bistrot les Viviers appeals to those who require attentive service, silver warming covers, and authentic *niçoise* cuisine. At this cozy splurge, allow €65 per person for wine and three courses. It has two different settings: a formal restaurant and a more relaxed *bistrot* next door. Reserve for the atmospheric *bistrot*; the prices are the same. Fish is the chef's forte (closed Sun, 22 rue Alphonse Karr, 5-min walk west of avenue Jean Médecin, tel. 04 93 16 00 48).

L'Ovale is a find. How this ever-so-local and rugby-loving café survives in a tourist mecca, I'll never know. It's run by Nice's nicest couple, Jean-Marc and Jacqueline, who serve quality food at good prices. Join the lively local crowd and dine inside on big *plats* for €11. Consider their specialty, cassoulet (€36 for two people), or enjoy *la planche de charcuterie* as a meaty, filling first course (excellent €15 3-course *menu,* closed Sun, air-con, 29 rue Pastorelli, tel. 04 93 80 31 65).

La Maison de Marie is a surprisingly high-quality refuge off touristy rue Masséna, where most other places serve mediocre food to tired tourists. Enter through a deep-red arch to a bougainvillea-draped courtyard, and enjoy the fair prices and good food that draw locals and travelers alike. The interior tables are as appealing as those in the courtyard (*menus* from €20, open daily, look for the square red flag at 5 rue Masséna, tel. 04 93 82 15 93).

La Cantine de Lulu is small, charming, and Czech-owned, with homemade recipes from Nice and Prague (closed Sat–Mon, 26 rue Alberti, tel. 04 93 62 15 33).

La Part des Anges, an atmospheric wine shop with a few tables in the back, serves a limited, good menu with a large selection of wines (open daily for lunch, Fri–Sat only for dinner, reserve ahead, 17 rue Gubernatis, tel. 04 93 62 69 80).

Near Promenade des Anglais

Il Vino Ino, near several recommended hotels a block from promenade des Anglais, has street appeal. This lively, reasonably priced eatery serves only Italian food amid cheery decor inside or out (closed Sun, 33 rue de la Buffa, tel. 04 93 87 94 25).

Chantecler has Nice's most prestigious address—inside the Hôtel Negresco. This is everything a luxury restaurant should be: elegant, soft, and top-quality. If your trip is ending in Nice, call or email for reservations—you've earned this splurge (*menus* from €90, open daily, 37 promenade des Anglais, tel. 04 93 16 64 00, chantecler@hotel-negresco.com).

Near the Train Station

These two places are hardly undiscovered—they're listed in many other guidebooks—but they deserve their acclaim.

Restaurant d'Angleterre is ideal for hungry travelers on a tight budget. For €15 you get a filling three-course dinner with tasty choices and great service (indoor and outdoor tables, closed Sun–Mon, 25 rue d'Angleterre, tel. 04 03 88 64 48).

Voyageur Nissart blends budget cuisine with cool Mediterranean ambience and friendly service (€17 *menus*, closed Mon, 19 rue d'Alsace-Lorraine, tel. 04 93 82 19 60).

TRANSPORTATION CONNECTIONS

For train, bus, and boat schedules from Nice to nearby towns, see "Getting Around the Riviera" on page 533. Note that most long-distance train connections to other French cities require a change in Marseille.

From Nice by Train to: Arles (11/day, 3.75–4.5 hrs, most change in Marseille or Avignon), **Avignon** (20/day, 13 of which are by TGV, 4 hrs, a few direct, most require transfer in Marseille), **Marseille** (18/day, 2.5 hrs), **Paris'** Gare de Lyon (10/day, 6 hrs, may require change; 11-hr night train goes to Paris' Gare d'Austerlitz), **Aix-en-Provence** TGV station (10/day, 3.5 hrs, may require transfer in Marseille or Toulon), **Chamonix** (4/day, 10 hrs, 3 transfers), **Beaune** (7/day, 7 hrs, 1–2 changes), **Munich** (4/day, 12–13 hrs with 2–4 transfers, night trains possible via Italy), **Interlaken** (6/day, 9–11 hrs, 2–5 transfers), **Florence** (6/day, 7–9 hrs, 1–3 transfers), **Milan** (7/day, 5–5.5 hrs, 4 with transfers), **Venice** (5/day, 2/night, 8–9 hrs, all require transfers except one direct night train), **Barcelona** (2/day, 11–12 hrs; 1 decent night train via Port Bou, 13 hrs).

Nice's Airport

Nice's easy-to-navigate airport (Aéroport de Nice Côte d'Azur) is on the Mediterranean, a 20–30-minute drive west of the city center. Planes leave about hourly to Paris (1-hour flight, about the same price as a train ticket). The two terminals (Terminal 1 and Terminal 2) are connected by frequent shuttle buses. Both terminals have TIs, banks, ATMs, taxis, and buses to Nice (www .nice.aeroport.fr, tel. 08 20 42 33 33 or 04 89 88 98 28).

Taxis into the center are expensive, charging €30 to Nice hotels and €50 to Villefranche-sur-Mer (10 percent more at night—that's 19:00–7:00—and all day Sunday). Taxis stop outside door *(Porte)* A-1 at Terminal 1 and outside *Porte* A-3 at Terminal 2. Nice taxis are not always so nice—and are notorious for overcharging. If your fare for a ride into Nice is much higher than €30 (or €33 at night or on Sun), refuse to pay more. If this doesn't work, tell the cabbie to call a *gendarme* (police officer).

Airport shuttle vans work with some of my recommended hotels. These only make sense when going *to* the airport, not when arriving. Unlike taxis, shuttle vans offer a fixed price that doesn't rise on Sundays, early mornings, or evenings. Prices are best for groups (figure €25 for one person, and only a little more for additional people—ask at your hotel).

Three bus lines connect the airport with the city center, offering good alternatives to high-priced taxis and shuttles. **Bus #99** runs from both terminals to Nice's main train station (€4, 2/hr, 8:00–21:00, 30 min, drops you within a 10-min walk of many recommended hotels). To take this bus *to* the airport, catch it right in front of the train station (departs on the half-hour). If you're sleeping within walking distance of the station, this bus is a €4 breeze. The **yellow "NICE" bus #98** serves both terminals, and runs along promenade des Anglais to Nice's main bus station *(gare routière)*, near Old Nice (€4, 3/hr, 30 min). The slower, cheaper local **bus #23** serves only Terminal 1, and makes every stop between the airport and train station (€1.30, 4/hr, 40 min, direction: St. Maurice). Buy tickets in the bus information office just outside either terminal, or from the driver. To reach the bus information office and bus stops at Terminal 1, turn left after passing customs and exit the doors at the far end. Buses serving Terminal 2 stop across the street from the exit. If you take bus #98 or #99, keep your ticket, which is good all day on any public bus in Nice, and for Ligne d'Azur buses between Nice and nearby towns (see page 533 for details).

To get to **Villefranche-sur-Mer** from the airport, take the yellow "NICE" bus #98 to Nice's bus station *(gare routière)*, then transfer to the Villefranche-sur-Mer bus (bus #100, use same ticket).

To reach **Antibes** and **Cannes,** take line #200 from either terminal (€1.30, 2–3/hr, 45–70 min to Antibes depending on traffic, an additional 30 min to Cannes). Express buses (line #110) run directly to **Monaco** from the airport (€15, hourly, 50 min).

Villefranche-sur-Mer

Located halfway between the world-famous resorts of Nice and Monaco, Villefranche-sur-Mer offers travelers an easygoing slice of small-town Mediterranean life. In just 15 minutes, you can be gambling in style in Monaco or sauntering the promenade des Anglais in Nice. This town feels Italian—with soft-orange buildings, steep, narrow streets spilling into the sea, and pasta *con* pesto. Luxury sailing yachts glisten in the bay, an inspiration to those lazing along the harborfront to start saving when their trips are over. Sand-pebble beaches and a handful of interesting sights keep visitors just busy enough.

ORIENTATION

Tourist Information

The TI is in the park named Jardin François Binon, below the main bus stop labeled *Octroi* (July–Aug daily 9:00–19:00; Sept–June Mon–Sat 9:00–12:00 & 14:00–18:00, closed Sun; a 20-min walk or €10 taxi from train station, tel. 04 93 01 73 68, www .villefranche-sur-mer.org). Pick up the brochure detailing a self-guided walking tour of Villefranche-sur-Mer and information on boat rides (usually mid-June–Sept).

Arrival in Villefranche-sur-Mer

By Bus: Buses from Nice and Monaco drop you next to Jardin François Binon, at the bus stop labeled *Octroi* just above the TI.

The old town and most hotels are downhill. The stop for buses going back to Nice is across the street from where you were left off (buses run every 10–15 min).

By Train: Villefranche-sur-Mer's train station is a level 15-minute walk along the water from the old town and many of my listed hotels. Taxis to my recommended hotels cost €10, but they don't wait here and prefer longer rides; call instead, and pray the phone is working (tel. 06 09 33 36 12 or 06 39 32 54 09).

By Car: From Nice's port, follow signs for *Menton, Monaco,* and *Basse Corniche.* In Villefranche-sur-Mer, turn right at the TI (first signal after Hôtel la Flore) for parking and hotels. For a quick visit to the TI, park at the nearby pay lot. You'll find free parking within the boundaries of the citadel, a bit farther down—better for longer visits and well-signed from main road *(Parking Fossés)*. There's a safer pay lot on the water across from the recommended Hôtel Welcome, and some hotels also have parking.

Helpful Hints

Market Day: An antiques market enlivens Villefranche-sur-Mer on Sundays (on place Amélie Pollonnais by Hôtel le Welcome and in Jardin François Binon by the TI). On Saturday mornings, a small food market sets up near the TI (only in Jardin François Binon).

Internet Access: Chez Net, an "Australian International Sports Bar Internet Café," is a fun place to get a late-night drink or check your e-mail (open daily, place du Marché).

Laundry: The town has two launderettes—both just below the main road on avenue Sadi Carnot. The upper *laverie* does your wash for you (next to Hôtel Riviera, Tue–Sun 8:00–12:00 & 14:00–18:30, closes Sat at 17:00, closed Mon, tel. 04 93 01 73 71), while the lower *laverie* is self-service (daily 7:00–20:00, opposite 6 avenue Sadi Carnot).

Taxi: Beware of taxi drivers who overcharge—the normal weekday daytime rate to central Nice is about €35; to the airport, figure €50; to Eze-le-Village, about €30; and the five-minute trip up to the main street level (to bus stops on Low Corniche) from the waterfront should be under €10 (tel. 06 09 33 36 12 or 06 39 32 54 09).

Minibus: Little electric bus #80 will save you the sweat from the harbor up the hill, but it only runs once per hour (€1.30). It runs from the port to the top of the hill, stopping near my recommended hotel, La Fiancée du Pirate, before going over the hill to the outlying, suburban Nice Riquier train station (only convenient if you're already on minibus, must transfer to train to downtown Nice).

Sports Fans: Lively *boules* action takes place each evening just below the TI and the huge soccer field (see page 771).

SIGHTS

The Harbor—Browse Villefranche-sur-Mer's minuscule harbor. Only eight families still fish to make money. Gaze out to sea and marvel at the beautiful sailing yachts that call this bay home. (You might see well-coiffed captains being ferried in by dutiful mates to pick up their statuesque call girls.) Local guides keep a

Villefranche-sur-Mer

1. Hôtel Welcome & Souris Gourmande Rest.
2. Hôtel Villa Vauban
3. Hôtel la Flore
4. To Hôtel la Fiancée du Pirate & Minibus Stop
5. Hôtel le Provençal
6. Hôtel de la Darse
7. Les Palmiers, Michel's & Le Cosmo Rest.
8. La Mère Germaine Rest.
9. Le Roxy Rest.
10. La Grignotière Rest.
11. Casino Grocery
12. Chez Net Bar & Internet
13. Boat Rides
14. Launderette
15. Octroi Bus Stop (from Nice; to Monaco & Cap Ferrat)
16. Octroi Bus Stop (to Nice; from Monaco & Cap Ferrat)

French Riviera

TO EZE & MONACO VIA LOW CORNICHE ROAD

TRAIN STATION

BLVD NAPOLEON

PONCHARD

BEACH

TO CAP FERRAT ON FOOT

TO 4

N

P PARKING
T TAXI STAND
STEPPED STREETS

AVE. ALBERT 1er

AVE. GALLIENI

AVE. GEORGES CLEMENCEAU

QUAI AM. COURBET

R. VOLTI

R. BARON

R. DE POILU

RUE OBSCURE

RUE DU POILU

OLD TOWN

Post

SADI

CARNOT

AVE. CH. JEUN.

AVE. JOFFRE

AVE. VERDUN

ALLEE DUVAL

i

9 16

14

10 11 8

12

1 13

7

T +ATM

CHAPEL OF ST. PIERRE

5

15

P

PLAY AREA

2

CITADEL

SCENIC WALKWAY

AVE. FOCH

3

AVENUE DE GAULLE

6

TO NICE

PLAY AREA

QUAI CORDERIE

PORT DE LA DARSE

200 YARDS
200 METERS

MEDITERRANEAN SEA

DCH

list of the world's 100 biggest yachts and talk about some of them like they're part of the neighborhood.

Parallel to the beach and about a block inland, you can walk the mysterious rue Obscura—a covered lane running 400 feet along the medieval rampart.

Chapel of St. Pierre (Chapelle Cocteau)—This chapel, decorated by artist, poet, and filmmaker Jean Cocteau, is the town's cultural highlight. A brooding fisherwoman collects a €2 donation for the fishermen's charity, and then sets you free to enjoy the chapel's small but intriguing interior. In 1955, Jean Cocteau covered the barrel-vaulted chapel with heavy black lines and pastels. Each of the Cocteau scenes—the Roma (Gypsies) of Stes-Maries-de-la-Mer who dance and sing to honor the Virgin, girls wearing traditional outfits, and three scenes from the life of St. Peter—are explained in English. Is that Villefranche-sur-Mer's citadel in the scene above the altar? (€2, Tue–Sun 9:30–12:00 & 15:00–19:00, closed Mon and when fisherwoman is tired, below Hôtel Welcome.)

Citadel—The town's immense castle was built in the 1500s by the Duke of Savoy to defend against the French. When the region joined France in 1860, it became just a barracks. In the 20th century, with no military use, the city started using the citadel to house its police station, City Hall, and two art galleries.

Church—The town church features a fine crucifix—carved, they say, from a fig tree by a galley slave in the 1600s.

Boat Rides (Promenades en Mer)—These little cruises, with English handouts, are offered two to three days a week (€16 for 2-hour cruise as far as Monaco—but doesn't stop there, €11 for 1-hour cruise around Cap Ferrat, boats depart from the harbor across from Hôtel Welcome, 4/day July–Aug, 2/day late June and Sept, tel. 04 93 76 65 65).

Beachwalk—A seaside walkway leads under the citadel and connects the old town with the yacht harbor, where you'll find one hotel and a few cafés. This scenic walk turns downright romantic after dark. Even if you're sleeping elsewhere, consider an ice-cream-licking stroll here. You can also saunter Villefranche-sur-Mer's waterfront going the other direction, and continue beyond the train station for postcard-perfect views back to Villefranche-sur-Mer (ideal in the morning—go before breakfast). You'll come to a quieter beach with good picnic benches.

SLEEPING

(€1 = about $1.30, country code: 33)
You have a handful of good hotels to choose from in Villefranche-sur-Mer. The ones I list have sea views from at least half of their rooms—well worth paying extra for.

$$$ Hôtel Welcome*, with easily the best location in Villefranche-sur-Mer, is anchored right on the water in the old town, with all 32 balconied rooms overlooking the harbor. You'll pay top price for all the comforts in this smart hotel. Skip the claustrophobic sixth-floor rooms ("comfort" Db-€188, bigger "superior" Db-€218, suites-€324–366, extra bed-€35, air-con, no Wi-Fi, elevator, parking garage-€20/day, 1 quai Amiral Courbet, tel. 04 93 76 27 62, fax 04 93 76 27 66, www.welcomehotel.com, resa@welcomehotel.com).

$$$ Hôtel Villa Vauban*, an intimate villa two blocks below the TI, has nine freshly painted, handsome rooms—many with balconies and sea views, and most with Old World bathrooms. Amiable British expat Alan Powers adds a personal touch that's rare in this area (Db with small view-€90–120, Db with big sea view-€125–165, Db suite with sea view-€135–175, air-con, Wi-Fi, 11 avenue Général de Gaulle, tel. & fax 04 93 55 94 51, www.hotelvillavauban.com, info@hotelvillavauban.eu).

$$$ Hôtel la Flore*** is good if your idea of sightseeing is to enjoy the view from your spacious bedroom deck, or the pool. Most rooms have decks, there's a swimming pool, and the free parking couldn't be easier, but the staff is a tad formal and it's a 10-minute uphill walk from the old town (Db with no view-€85–125, Db with view and deck-€120–140, bigger Db that sleeps up to five and has a better view and bigger deck-€165–210, Db mini-suite-€220, Qb loft with huge terrace-€240, extra bed-€34, 10–15 percent cheaper Oct–March, air-con, elevator, restaurant open evenings only, just off main road high above harbor—near the bus stop to Nice and Monaco, 5 boulevard Princesse Grace de Monaco, 2 blocks from TI toward Nice, tel. 04 93 76 30 30, fax 04 93 76 99 99, www.hotel-la-flore.fr, hotel-la-flore@wanadoo.fr).

$$ Hôtel la Fiancée du Pirate is only for drivers, as it's high up in Villefranche-sur-Mer on the Middle Corniche (parking is no problem). Don't let the streetside appearance deter you. Friendly Eric and Laurence offer 15 bright and comfortable rooms with a pool, Jacuzzi, lush garden, roomy lounge area, and breakfast terrace with partial views of Cap Ferrat and the sea. Choose between rooms in the main building (Db-€88–108, Tb/Qb-€130–165), or view rooms on the garden patio (standard Db-€75–95, Tb/Qb-€100–125). From June to September, they require a three-night minimum stay and offer lunch, salads, and snacks by the pool (air-con, Wi-Fi, 8 boulevard de la Corne d'Or, Moyenne Corniche N7, tel. 04 93 76 67 40, fax 04 93 76 91 04, www.fianceedupirate.com, info@fianceedupirate.com).

$$ Hôtel le Provençal** is a well-situated, bare-bones place crying out for an owner who cares. The uninspired yet sleepable-for-some rooms are affordable, and some come with fine views and balconies (Db-€66–115, most about €90, Tb-€90–125, extra bed-€10, forget the cheaper non-view rooms, air-con, right below the main road, a block from TI at 4 avenue Maréchal Joffre, tel. 04 93 76 53 53, fax 04 93 76 96 00, www.hotelprovencal.com, provencal @riviera.fr).

$$ Hôtel de la Darse**, a shy and unassuming little hotel burrowed in the shadow of its highbrow neighbors, offers a good-value, low-profile alternative right on the water at Villefranche-sur-Mer's old port (a 10-min walk to the harbor). The sufficiently comfortable rooms facing the sea have million-dollar-view balconies and are worth the extra euros (view Db-€80, view Tb-€93, most with air-con, no elevator, some noise on weekend nights, quieter garden view Db-€65, extra bed-€10, no elevator, from TI walk or drive down avenue Général de Gaulle to the old Port de la Darse, parking usually available nearby, tel. 04 93 01 72 54, fax 04 93 01 84 37, www.hoteldeladarse.com, hoteldeladarse@ wanadoo.fr).

EATING

Comparison-shopping is half the fun of dining in Villefranche-sur-Mer. Make an event out of a predinner stroll through the old city. Check what looks good on the lively place Amélie Pollonnais (next to the Hôtel Welcome), saunter the string of candlelit places lining the waterfront, and consider the smaller, cheaper eateries embedded in the old city's walking streets. I prefer eating on place Amélie Pollonnais, where the whole village seems to converge at night.

Les Palmiers is a beachy place buzzing with cheery diners (€11–14 hearty salads and pizza, open daily, on place Amélie Pollonnais, tel. 04 93 01 71 63).

Le Cosmo Restaurant is next door. It's sharper, with great tables overlooking the harbor and the Cocteau chapel's facade (after some wine, Cocteau pops). It serves nicely presented and tasty meals. Ask for the daily suggestions and consider the €10 *omelet niçoise* (€10–14 fine salads and pastas, €13–21 *plats*, great Bandol red wine, open daily, place Amélie Pollonnais, tel. 04 93 01 84 05).

Michel's, on the other side of the fountain, is more romantic and stylish and is the most reliable splurge restaurant in Villefranche-sur-Mer (allow €35 per person, closed Tue and in Nov, tel. 04 93 76 73 24).

La Mère Germaine, right on the harborfront, is the only place in town classy enough to lure a yachter ashore. It's dressy, with fine service and a harborside setting. The name comes from when the current owner's grandmother fed hungry GIs in World

War II. Try the bouillabaisse, served with panache (€68 per person with 2-person minimum, ask about the less expensive but ample mini-version, €39 *menu,* open daily, reserve harborfront table, tel. 04 93 01 71 39).

Le Roxy, on the main road just above the TI, is a *très* local, friendly, and cheap diner with hardworking Monique and chef-hubbie Bebert. They make good pizza (€8.50), salad, and a killer *soup de poisson* that makes a meal for €11. Ask for seconds (closed Mon–Tue, 2 avenue de Grande Bretagne, tel. 04 93 76 71 80).

Disappear into Villefranche-sur-Mer's walking streets and find cute little **La Grignotière,** serving a €31 *gourmet menu,* an €18 couscous, and plenty of pizza and pasta options (May–Oct open daily, Nov–April closed Wed, cozy in bad weather, 3 rue Poilu, tel. 04 93 76 79 83).

Souris Gourmande ("Gourmet Mouse") is handy for a sandwich, either to take away or to eat there (daily 11:30–19:30, closed Fri in winter, at base of steps behind Hôtel Welcome, €5 made-to-order sandwiches...be patient and get to know your chef, Albert). Sandwich in hand, you'll find plenty of great places to enjoy a harborside sit.

There's a handy **Casino market/grocery store** a few blocks above the Hôtel Welcome at 12 rue Poilu (Thu–Tue 7:30–13:00 & 15:00–19:30, Wed 7:30–13:00 only).

For Drivers: If you have a car and are staying a few nights, consider the short drive up to Eze-le-Village, or better still, La Turbie (restaurant recommendations listed under each destination below).

If it's summer (June–Sept) and you have a car, live the consummate Mediterranean experience by driving 10 minutes to Cap Ferrat and lunch or dine beachside at the **Restaurant de la Plage Passable,** located across the bay from Villefranche-sur-Mer. Enjoy sensational views, and a surprisingly elegant dining experience to the sounds of children still at play on the beach. Watch as darkness descends and lights flicker over Villefranche-sur-Mer's heavenly setting. Follow signs to *Cap Ferrat* and *Villa Ephrussi,* then look for signs pointing down to *Plage de Passable* (€15 starters, €18–25 *plats,* open daily late June–Sept only; until 20:00 in good weather April–May and Oct, tel. 04 93 76 06 17).

TRANSPORTATION CONNECTIONS

The last bus leaves Nice for Villefranche-sur-Mer at about 19:45; the last bus from Villefranche-sur-Mer to Nice leaves at about 20:50; and one train runs later (24:00).

From Villefranche-sur-Mer by Train to: Monaco (2/hr, 10 min), **Nice** (2/hr, 10 min), **Antibes** (2/hr, 40 min).

By Bus to: Monaco (#100, 25 min), **Nice** (#100, 20 min). Bus #100 leaves every 15 minutes; all rides cost €1.30. All buses use stops on the main drag, just above the TI (labeled *Octroi*).

The Three Corniches: Villefranche to Monaco

Nice, Villefranche-sur-Mer, and Monaco are linked with three coastal routes: the Low, Middle, and High Corniches. The roads are nicknamed for the decorative frieze that runs along the top of a building (cornice). Each Corniche offers sensational views and a different perspective on this exotic slice of real estate. You can find the three routes from Nice by driving up boulevard Jean Jaurès past the bus station *(gare routière)*. For the Low Corniche, follow signs to N-98 *(Monaco par la Basse Corniche)*, which leads right past Nice's port. Shortly after the turnoff to the Low Corniche, you'll see signs for N-7 *(Moyenne Corniche)* leading to the Middle Corniche. Signs for the Grande (High) Corniche appear a bit after that; follow D-2564 to Col des 4 Chemins and the Grande Corniche.

Low Corniche: The Basse Corniche (also called "Corniche Inférieure") strings ports, beaches, and villages together for a traffic-filled ground-floor view. It was built in the 1860s (along with the train line) to bring people to the casino in Monte Carlo. When this Low Corniche was finished, many hill-town villagers came down and started the communities that line the sea today. Before 1860, the population of the coast between Villefranche-sur-Mer and Monte Carlo was zero. Think about that as you make the trip today.

Middle Corniche: The Moyenne Corniche is higher, quieter, and far more impressive. It runs through Eze-le-Village (described below) and provides breathtaking views over the Mediterranean, with several scenic pullouts. (The one above Villefranche-sur-Mer is particularly stunning.)

High Corniche: Napoleon's crowning road-construction achievement, the Grande Corniche caps the cliffs with staggering views from almost 1,600 feet above the sea. It is actually built atop the Via Aurelia, used by Romans to conquer the West.

Villas: Driving from Villefranche-sur-Mer to Monaco, you'll come upon impressive villas. A particularly grand entry leads to the sprawling estate built by King Leopold II of Belgium in the 1920s. Those driving up to the Middle Corniche from Villefranche-sur-Mer will look down on this yellow mansion that fills an entire hilltop with a lush garden. This estate was later owned by the Agnelli

Villefranche, Monaco, and the Corniches

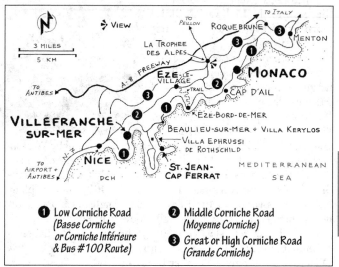

1 Low Corniche Road
(Basse Corniche
or Corniche Inférieure
& Bus #100 Route)

2 Middle Corniche Road
(Moyenne Corniche)

3 Great or High Corniche Road
(Grande Corniche)

French Riviera

family (of Fiat fame and fortune), and then by the Safra family (American bankers).

The Best Route: For a ▲▲▲ route, **drivers** should take the Middle Corniche from Nice or Villefranche-sur-Mer to Eze-le-Village; from there, follow signs to the *Grande Corniche* and *La Turbie*, then finish by dropping down into Monaco. **Buses** travel each route; the higher the Corniche, the less frequent the buses (roughly 5–6/day on Middle and High, 4/hr on Low; get details at Nice's bus station). There are no buses between Eze-le-Village and La Turbie, though buses do connect Nice and Monaco with La Turbie.

SIGHTS

The following two sights, Eze-le-Village and La Trophée des Alpes monument, are listed in the order you'll reach them, traveling from Villefranche-sur-Mer to Monaco.

▲Eze-le-Village

Floating high above the sea, flowery and flawless Eze-le-Village (don't confuse it with the seafront town of Eze-Bord-de-Mer) is entirely consumed by tourism. This *village d'art et de gastronomie* (as it calls itself) mixes perfume outlets, upscale boutiques, steep cobbled lanes, and magnificent views. Touristy as this place certainly Eze, its stony state of preservation and magnificent hilltop setting over the Mediterranean justify a visit.

Bus stops and parking lots weld the town to the highway (Middle Corniche) that passes under its lowest wall. The helpful TI is in the far corner of the car park below the town; ask them about English-language tours of the village and gardens (May–Oct daily 9:00–18:00; Nov–April Mon–Sat 9:00–17:00, closed Sun; place Charles de

Gaulle, tel. 04 93 41 26 00, www.eze-riviera.com). Public WCs are located just behind the TI and in the village behind the church.

At the **Jardins d'Eze,** you'll find a prickly festival of cactus. Since 1949, these ruins have been home to 400 different plants 1,300 feet above the sea (well-described in English, €5, open daily, hours change frequently but usually May–Sept 9:00–19:00, Oct–April until dusk, tel. 04 93 41 10 30). At the top, you'll be treated to a commanding 360-degree view, with a helpful *table d'orientation.* On a really clear day, you can see Corsica.

The **Perfume Factory Fragonard,** 350 feet below Eze-le-Village, is designed for tour groups—it cranks them through all day long. Drop in for a free 20–40 minute tour (daily 8:30–18:00 but best Mon–Fri 9:00–11:00 & 14:00–15:30, when the "factory" actually has people working, tel. 04 93 41 05 05). You'll see how the perfume and scented soaps are made and bottled before you're herded into the gift shop. For a more personal and intimate look at perfume, cross the main road in Eze-le-Village to visit the **Gallimard** shop.

Eating in Eze-le-Village: To enjoy the village in relative peace, visit at sunset and stay for dinner. You'll dine well at the stone-cozy **Le Troubador** (€33 *menu,* closed Sun–Mon, 4 rue du Brec, tel. 04 93 41 19 03), or for less, at the basic **Nid de l'Aigle** ("Eagle's Nest," open daily in summer, otherwise closed Wed, tel. 04 93 41 19 08).

Getting to Eze-le-Village: There are two Ezes: Eze-le-Village (the spectacular hill town, your destination) and Eze-Bord-de-Mer (a modern beach resort far below Eze-le-Village). Eze-le-Village is about 20 minutes east of Villefranche-sur-Mer on the Middle Corniche. Two bus lines (#82 and #112, €1.30/ticket) provide 16 buses per day from Nice to Eze-le-Village (eight on Sun), and one less-frequent bus runs directly from Monaco to Eze-le-Village. You can also take the train or Nice–Monaco bus to Eze-Bord-de-Mer. From there, take the shuttle bus (#83, also €1.30) straight up to Eze-le-Village from the Gare SNCF stop (daily 9:30–18:30, 8/day). There are no direct buses from Villefranche-sur-Mer to Eze-le-Village or between La Turbie and Eze-le-Village.

You can also take a taxi between the two Ezes (allow €22 one-way, tel. 06 09 84 17 84).

▲▲La Trophée des Alpes (in La Turbie)

High above Monaco, on the Grande (High) Corniche in the over-looked village of La Turbie, lies one of this region's most evocative historic sights (with dramatic views over the entire country of Monaco as a bonus). This massive Roman monument commemorates Augustus Caesar's conquest of the Alps and its 44 hostile tribes. It's exciting to think that, in a way, La Trophée des Alpes celebrates a victory that kicked off the Pax Romana—joining Gaul and Germania, freeing up the main artery of the Roman Empire, and lacing together Spain and Italy.

Walk around the monument and notice how the Romans built a fine, quarried-stone exterior, filled in with rubble and coarse concrete. Flanked by the vanquished in chains, the towering inscription tells the story: It was erected "by the senate and the people to honor the emperor." The monument was restored in the 1930s and 1940s with money from the Tuck family of New Hampshire.

The one-room museum shows a reconstruction and translation of the dramatic inscription, which lists all the feisty alpine tribes that put up such a fight (€5; mid-May–mid-Sept Tue–Sun 9:30–13:00 & 14:30–18:30, mid-Sept–mid-May Tue–Sun 10:00–13:30 & 14:30–17:00, closed Mon year-round; tel. 04 93 41 20 84). Escorts from the museum take people up to the monument, but it's not worth waiting for.

The sweet old village of **La Turbie** sees almost no tourists, but it has plenty of cafés and restaurants at its doorstep. To stroll the old village, park in the main lot on place Neuve (follow *Monaco* signs one block from the main road), then walk behind the post office and find brick footpaths—they lead through a village with nary a shop. To eat very well and in the Riviera's most welcoming restaurant (I'm not kidding), try **La Terrasse,** where tables gather under sun shades, the sea lies miles below, and clients seem oblivious to the incredible setting. Let Helen and Jacques tempt you to return for dinner at sunset, and book ahead for a table with a view (closed Tue evening and all day Wed, near the PTT/post office at the main parking lot, 17 place Neuve, tel. 04 93 41 21 84).

Getting to and from La Trophée des Alpes (in La Turbie): By **car,** take the High Corniche to La Turbie, ideally from Eze-le-Village (La Turbie is 10 min east of, and above, Eze-le-Village), then look for signs to *La Trophée des Alpes.* Once in la Turbie, you can park in the lot in the center of town (place Neuve, follow *Monaco* signs for a short block) and walk from there (walk 5 min around the old village, with the village on your right); or drive to the site by turning right in front of La Régence Café. Those coming from farther afield can take the efficient A-8 to the La Turbie exit. To reach Eze-le-Village from La Turbie, follow signs to *Nice*, and then look for signs to *Eze-le-Village*.

You can also get here by **bus** from Nice (4/day, 45 min, €1.30; last bus returns to Nice at about 18:00) or Monaco (6/day, 20 min, €1.30). The bus stop is across from the PTT/post office on place Neuve (the 5-min walk to La Trophée des Alpes is described earlier in this chapter).

Monaco

French Riviera

Despite overdevelopment, high prices, and wall-to-wall daytime tourists, Monaco is a Riviera must. Monaco is on the go. Since 1929, cars have raced around the port and in front of the casino in one of the world's most famous auto races, the Grand Prix de Monaco (May 22–25 in 2008). The new breakwater—constructed elsewhere and towed in by sea—enables big cruise ships to dock here. The district of  Fontvieille, reclaimed from the sea, bristles with luxury high-rise condos. But don't look for anything too deep in this glittering tax haven. Two-thirds of its 30,000 residents live here because there's no income tax—leaving fewer than 10,000 true Monegasques.

This minuscule principality (0.75 square mile) borders only France and the Mediterranean. The country has always been tiny, but it used to be...less tiny. In an 1860 plebiscite, Monaco lost two-thirds of its territory when the region of Menton voted to join France. To compensate, France suggested that Monaco build a fancy casino and promised to connect it to the world with a road (the Low Corniche) and a train line. This started a high-class tourist boom that has yet to let up.

While "independent," Monaco is run as a piece of France. A French civil servant appointed by the French president—with the blessing of Monaco's prince—serves as state minister and manages the place. Monaco's phone system, electricity, water, and so on, are all French.

The death of Prince Rainier in 2005 ended a 56-year career of enlightened rule. Today, Monaco is ruled by Prince Rainier's unassuming son, Prince Albert Alexandre Louis Pierre Grimaldi, Marquis of Baux. Prince Albert II is 47, and considered Europe's most eligible bachelor—though he has admitted to fathering two children out of wedlock. He's a bobsled enthusiast and avid

Monaco

❶ Hôtel de France

❷ Rue Basse (Boulangerie at #8 & Notari Cyberspace Internet Café at #3 bis)

❸ Huit et Demi Restaurant & English Bookstore

❹ Jardin Exotique

❺ Local Bus Stop & Barclays Bank

❻ Bus #100 to Nice: Place d'Armes Stop

❼ Bus #100 from Nice: Place d'Armes Stop

❽ Bus #100 to/from Nice: Stade Nautique Stop

❾ Bus #100 to Nice: Casino Stop

❿ Bus #100 from Nice: Casino Stop

⓫ Bus #112 to Eze-le-Village & #114 to La Turbie

environmentalist who seems determined to clean up Monaco's tarnished, tax-haven, money-laundering image.

Monaco is big business, and Prince Albert is its CEO. While its famous casino provides only 5 percent of the state's revenue, its 43 banks—which offer an attractive way to hide your money—are hugely profitable. The prince also makes money with a value-added tax (19.6 percent, the same as in France), plus real estate and corporate taxes.

The glamorous romance and marriage of the American actress Grace Kelly to Prince Rainier added to Monaco's fairy-tale mystique. Grace Kelly (Prince Albert's mother) first came to Monaco to star in the 1955 Hitchcock film *To Catch a Thief*, in which she was filmed racing along the Corniches. Later, she married her prince and adopted the country. Tragically, Monaco's much-loved Princess Grace died in a car wreck on that same Corniche in 1982.

It's a special place...there are more people in Monaco's philharmonic orchestra (about 100) than in its army (about 80 guards). The princedom is well-guarded, with police and cameras on every corner. (They say you could win a million dollars at the casino and walk through the wee hours to the train station without a worry.) Stamps are so few, they increase in value almost as soon as they're printed. And collectors snapped up the rare Monaco versions of euro coins (with Prince Rainier's portrait) so quickly that many locals have never even seen one.

ORIENTATION

The principality of Monaco consists of three distinct tourist areas: Monaco-Ville, Monte Carlo, and La Condamine. Monaco-Ville fills the rock high above everything else and is referred to by locals as Le Rocher ("The Rock"). This is the oldest section, home to the Prince's palace and all the sights except the casino. Monte Carlo is the area around the casino; La Condamine is the port (which divides Monaco-Ville and Monte Carlo). You'll look down over a fourth, less-interesting area, Fontvieille, reclaimed from the sea by Prince Rainier in the 1970s.

The port is the center of Monaco. From here it's a 15-minute walk up to the Prince's Palace or to the casino (40 min from palace to casino). Local buses shave time off this commute (see "Getting Around Monaco," page 580).

Tourist Information

The main TI is near the casino (Mon–Sat 9:00–19:00, Sun 10:00–12:00, 2 boulevard des Moulins). You'll run across TI annexes in other parts of Monaco, including one at the train station (Mon–Sat 9:00–19:00, Sun 10:00–12:00, tel. 00-377/92 16 61 16 or 00-377/92

French Riviera

16 61 66, www.visitmonaco.com). From June to September, you might find information kiosks in the Monaco-Ville parking garage and on the port.

Arrival in Monaco

By Bus from Nice and Villefranche-sur-Mer: Bus riders need to pay attention, since stops are not announced. Cap d'Ail is the town before Monaco, so be on the lookout after this. You'll enter Monaco by passing the modern high-rises of the Fontvieille district. When you see the rocky outcrop of old Monaco, be ready to get off.

There are three stops in Monaco. Listed in order from Nice, they are: "Place d'Armes" (in front of a tunnel at the base of Monaco-Ville's rock), "Stade Nautique" (on the port, though this stop may change in 2008), and "Casino" (below the casino, on avenue d'Ostende). The Place d'Armes stop is the best starting point. From there, you can walk up to Monaco-Ville and the palace (10 min straight up), or catch a local bus (line #1 or #2, details below). To reach the bus stop and steps up to Monaco-Ville, cross the street right in front of the tunnel and walk with the rock on your right for about 200 feet. If you prefer starting at the casino, turn left off the bus at the casino stop, then turn right and walk past Häagen-Dazs to find the Casino.

For directions on returning to Nice by bus, see "Transportation Connections" on page 585.

By Train from Nice: This loooooong underground train station is in central Monaco, about a 15-minute walk to the casino in Monte Carlo or to the port, and about 25 minutes to the palace in Monaco-Ville.

The TI and ticket windows are up the escalator at the Italy end of the station. There are three exits: two from the train platform level (one at each end) and one from above the platforms (up the escalator, past the TI). To walk to the casino, use this upper exit (go past the TI, then up the elevator, then up escalator, exit station, turn left on boulevard de la Princesse Charlotte, and turn right after about 5 blocks when you see the pedestrian *Casino* sign; allow 10 min).

To reach Monaco-Ville and the palace from the station, take one of the two platform-level exits. The exit near the Italy end of the platform leads to the port and right to the bus stop for city buses #1 and #2, serving Monaco-Ville and the casino (follow *Sortie la Condamine aign* and go down 2 escalators, then go left following *Accès Port* signs). The port is across the street from this exit, from which you can walk another 25 minutes to the palace (to your right) or to the casino in 15 minutes (up the road to your left).

The other platform-level exit is at the Nice end of the tracks (signed *Sortie Fontvieille/Monaco-Ville*), which takes you through a long tunnel (TI annex at end) to the foot of Monaco-Ville; turn left at the end of the walkway and walk 15 minutes up to the palace, or take the bus (#1 or #2).

By Car: Follow *Centre-Ville* signs into Monaco, then follow the red-letter signs to parking garages at *Le Casino* (for Monte Carlo) or *Le Palais* (for Monaco-Ville). The first hour of parking is free (€4 next hour, €7/3 hours).

Helpful Hints

Telephone Tip: To call Monaco from France, dial 00, then 377 (Monaco's country code) and the eight-digit number. Within Monaco, simply dial the eight-digit number.

Internet Access: Notari Cyberspace is just a block off Palace Square in Monaco-Ville (daily 10:00–19:00, 3 bis rue Basse).

English Bookstore: Scruples Bookstore has plenty of English offerings (Mon–Fri 10:00–12:30 & 14:30–19:00, Sat 10:00–12:30 & 14:30–18:30, closed Sun, at 7 rue de la Princesse Caroline, just below the recommended Huit et Demi restaurant).

Minivan Tours from Nice: Several companies offer day and night-time tours of Monaco, allowing you freedom to gamble without worrying about the last train or bus home (see "Getting Around the Riviera," page 534).

Loop Trip: From Nice or Villefranche-sur-Mer you can visit Monaco by bus, then return via Eze-le-Village or La Turbie (no Sun bus). See "Transportation Connections" on page 585 for details.

Getting Around Monaco

By Local Bus: Buses #1 and #2 link all areas (single ticket-€1, 10 tickets-€6, pay the driver, 10/hr, buses run until 21:00, less on Sun). You can split a 10-ride ticket with your travel partners. For most, two rides in Monaco does it.

By Tourist Train: "Monaco Tour" tourist trains begin at the aquarium and pass by the port, casino, and palace (€7, 2/hr, 10:30-18:00 in summer, 11:00–17:00 in winter depending on weather, 30 min, recorded English commentary).

By Taxi: If you've lost track of time at the casino, you can call the 24-hour taxi service (tel. 08 20 20 98 98 or 00-377/93 50 56 28)... provided you still have enough money to pay for the cab home.

SELF-GUIDED WALK

Welcome to Monaco-Ville

Most of Monaco's sights (except the casino) are in Monaco-Ville, packed within a few Disney-esque blocks. This walk makes a tidy loop around Monaco-Ville.

• *To get from anywhere in Monaco to the palace square (place du Palais, Monaco-Ville's sightseeing center, home of the palace and the Napoleon Collection), take bus #1 or #2 to place de la Visitation. Turn right as you step off the bus and walk straight for five minutes, passing a fountain and continuing down either street. If you're walking up from the port, the well-marked lane leads directly to the Palais.*

Palace Square (Place du Palais): This square is the best place to get oriented to Monaco. Facing the palace, go to the right and

look out over the city (err...principality). This rock gave birth to the little pastel Hong Kong look-alike in 1215, and it's managed to remain an independent country for most of its nearly 800 years. Looking beyond the glitzy port, notice the faded green roof above and to the right: the casino that put Monaco on the map. The famous Grand Prix runs along the port, and then up the ramp to the casino. Just beyond the casino is France again—you could walk one way from France to France, passing through Monaco in about 50 minutes.

The curious statue of a woman with a fishing net is dedicated to Prince Albert I's glorious reign (1889–1922). Albert possessed a Jacques Cousteau–like fascination with the sea (and built Monaco's famous aquarium), and he was a determined pacifist who made many attempts to dissuade Germany's Kaiser Wilhelm II from becoming involved in World War I.

• *Now walk to the statue of the monk grasping a sword near the palace.*

Meet **François Grimaldi,** a renegade Italian dressed as a monk, who captured Monaco in 1297 and began the dynasty that still rules the principality. Prince Albert II is his great-great-great...grandson, which makes Monaco's royal family Europe's longest-lasting dynasty.

• *Make your way to the...*

Prince's Palace (Palais Princier): A medieval castle sat where Monaco's palace is today. Its strategic setting has had a lot to do with Monaco's ability to resist attackers. Today, Prince Albert II lives in the palace; princesses Stephanie and Caroline live just down the main street. The palace guards protect the prince 24/7 and still stage a Changing of the Guard ceremony with all the pageantry of an important nation (daily at 11:55, fun to watch but jam-packed). Audioguided tours take you through part of the prince's lavish palace in 30 minutes. The rooms are well-furnished and impressive, but interesting only if you haven't seen a château lately (€7 includes audioguide, €9 with Napoleon Collection, daily

French Riviera

May–Sept 9:30–18:30, April and Oct 10:30–17:30, closed Nov–March, tel. 00-377/93 25 18 31).

• *Next to the palace entry is the...*

Napoleon Collection: Napoleon occupied Monaco after the French Revolution. This is the prince's private collection of what Napoleon left behind: military medals, swords, guns, letters, and, most interesting, his hat. I found this collection more appealing than the palace (€4 includes audioguide; €9 with Prince's Palace, daily May–Sept 9:30–18:30, April and Oct 10:00–17:00, closed Nov–March).

• *With your back to the palace, leave the square through the arch to the right and you'll find the...*

French Riviera

Cathedral of Monaco (Cathédrale de Monaco): The somber cathedral, rebuilt in 1878 to show that Monaco cared for more than just its new casino, is where centuries of Grimaldis are buried. Circle slowly behind the altar (counterclockwise). The second-to-last tomb—inscribed *"Gratia Patricia, MCMLXXXII"*—is where Princess Grace was buried in 1982. The last tomb is Prince Rainier's (daily 8:30–18:45, until 18:00 in winter).

• *As you leave the cathedral, step across the street and look down on the newly reclaimed Fontvieille district, with fancy condos that contribute to the incredible population density of this minuscule country. Walk left through the immaculately maintained Jardin Botanique, with more fine views and good places to picnic. Find the...*

Cousteau Aquarium (Musée Océanographique): Prince Albert I built this impressive cliff-hanging aquarium in 1910 as a monument to his enthusiasm for things from the sea. One wing features Mediterranean fish; tropical species swim around in the other (all well-described in English). Overall, the aquarium has 2,000 different specimens and 250 species. Jacques Cousteau directed the aquarium for 17 years. The fancy Albert I Hall upstairs houses the museum (included in entry, little English information), featuring models of Albert and his beachcombers hard at work (€12.50, kids-€7, daily April–Sept 9:30–19:30, Oct–March 10:00–18:00; at opposite end of Monaco-Ville from palace, down the steps from Monaco-Ville bus stop; tel. 00-377/93 15 36 00, www.oceano.mc). Don't miss the rooftop terrace (with WCs and a café).

• *The redbrick steps across from the aquarium lead up to buses #1 and #2, both of which run to the port, the casino, and the train station. To walk back to the palace and through the old city, turn left at the top of the brick steps. For a brief movie break, take the escalator to the right of the aquarium; as you leave it into the parking garage, you'll find the...*

Monte Carlo Story: This informative 35-minute film gives a helpful account of Monaco's history and offers a comfortable, soft-chair break from all that walking (€7, headphone commentary in English, usually shows on the hour, daily 10:00–17:00, July–Aug until 18:00, closed Nov–Dec, you can join frequent extra showings for groups on summer mornings, tel. 00-377/93 25 32 33).

SIGHTS

Above Monaco-Ville

Jardin Exotique—This cliffside municipal garden, located above Monaco-Ville, has eye-popping views from France to Italy. It's a fascinating home to more than a thousand species of cacti (some giant) and other succulent plants, but probably worth the entry only for view-loving botanists (some posted English explanations provided). Your ticket includes entry to a skippable natural cave and an anthropological museum, as well as a not-to-be-missed view snack bar/café (€7, daily mid-May–mid-Sept 9:00–19:00, mid-Sept–mid-May 9:00–18:00 or dusk, tel. 00-377/93 15 29 80). Bus #2 runs here from any stop in Monaco and makes a worthwhile €1 mini-tour of Monaco even if you don't visit the gardens—you can get a similar views over Monaco for free from behind the souvenir stand at the garden bus stop, or cross the street and hike toward La Turbie for even grander views).

In Monte Carlo

▲**Casino**—Monte Carlo, which means "Charles' Hill" in Spanish, is named for the local prince who presided over Monaco's 19th-cen-

tury makeover. Begin your visit to Europe's most famous casino in the park above the traffic circle. In the mid-1800s, olive groves stood here. Then, with the construction of this casino, spas, and easy road and train access, one of Europe's poorest countries was on the Grand Tour map—*the* place for the vacationing aristocracy to play. Today, Monaco has the world's highest per-capita income.

The casino is designed to make the wealthy feel comfortable while losing money. Charles Garnier designed this casino (with an opera house inside) in 1878, in part to thank the prince for his financial help in completing Paris' Opéra Garnier (which Garnier also designed). The central doors provide access to slot machines, private gaming rooms, and the opera house. The private gaming rooms occupy the left wing of the building.

Anyone over 21 (even in shorts, if before 20:00) can get as far as the one-armed bandits (push button on slot machines to claim your winnings), though you'll need decent attire to go any further.

After 20:00, shorts are off-limits anywhere. The scene is great at night—and downright James Bond–like in the private rooms.

If paying an entrance fee to lose money is not your idea of fun, access to all games in the new, plebeian, American-style Loews Casino, adjacent to the old casino, is free.

Cost and Hours: The slot machines and the first gaming rooms *(salons européens)* open at Mon–Fri at 14:00 and Sat–Sun at 12:00. Slots are free, buy you'll pay €10 to enter *les salons européens*. These glamorous private game rooms—where you can rub elbows with high rollers—open at Mon–Fri at 16:00 and Sat–Sun at 15:00, others not until 21:00–22:00, and cost an additional €10 (you must be 18 and have your passport). Men can rent a tie and jacket (necessary in the evening) at the bag check for €30, plus a €40 deposit. Dress standards for women are far more relaxed (only tennis shoes are a definite no-no, tel. 00-377/92 16 20 00, www .casino-monte-carlo.com).

Take the Money and Run: The return bus stop to Nice is at the top of the park, above the casino on avenue de la Costa (under the arcade to the left). To return to the train station from the casino, walk up the parkway in front of the casino, turn left on boulevard des Moulins, turn right on impasse de la Fontaine, climb the steps, and turn left on boulevard de la Princesse Charlotte (the entrance to the train station is next to Parking de la Gare; look for *Gare SNCF* sign).

SLEEPING AND EATING

(€1 = about $1.30, country code: 377)
For many, Monaco is best after dark.

Hôtel de France** is a perfectly pleasant, central, spotless, and reasonable place, run by friendly Sylvie (Sb-€84, Db-€103, Tb-€135, includes breakfast, no air-con, Wi-Fi, 6 rue de la Turbie, near west exit from train station, tel. 00-377/93 30 24 64, fax 00-377/92 16 13 34, www.monte-carlo.mc/france, hotel-france @monte-carlo.mc).

Several cafés serve basic, inexpensive fare (day and night) on the port. I prefer the places that line the flowery and traffic-free rue de la Princesse Caroline, which runs between rue Grimaldi and the port. The best on this street is **Huit et Demi,** with most of its tables outside. It has a white-tablecloth-meets-director's-chair ambience, and cuisine worth returning for (€11–13 salads, €12–15 pizzas, €18–24 *plats*, closed Sat for lunch and all day Sun, rue de la Princesse Caroline, tel. 00-377/93 50 97 02). In Monaco-Ville, you'll find incredible *pan bagnat*, quiche, and sandwiches at the *boulangerie* at 8 rue Basse, a block off Palace Square.

TRANSPORTATION CONNECTIONS

From Monaco by Train to: Nice (2/hr, 20 min, €3.30), **Villefranche-sur-Mer** (2/hr, 10 min), **Antibes** (2/hr, 45–60 min).

By Bus to: Nice (#100, 4/hr, 45 min, €1.30), **Nice Airport** (line #110 express on the freeway, hourly, 50 min, €15), **Villefranche-sur-Mer** (#100, 4/hr, 25 min, €1.30), **La Turbie** (#114, 6/day, Mon–Fri, 3/day Sat morning only, none on Sun, 20 min), Eze-le-Village (#112, 3/day Mon–Sat, none on Sun, 15 min).

The Monaco-to-Nice bus (#100) is not identified at every stop—verify with a local by asking *"Direction Nice?"* One stop is across from the Place d'Armes stop in front of the Brasserie Monte Carlo. Another is a few blocks above the casino, under the arcade to the left of Barclays Bank.

Bus #112 departs Monaco for Eze-le-Village and La Turbie from place de la Cremaillière, one block above main TI and casino park. Walk up rue Iris with Barclays Bank to your left, curve right and find the bus shelter across the street by the Costa à la Cremaillière café. Bus numbers for these routes are not posted, but this is the stop.

The last bus leaves Monaco for Villefranche-sur-Mer and Nice at about 20:00; the last train leaves Monaco for Villefranche-sur-Mer and Nice at about 23:30.

Antibes

Antibes has a down-to-earth, easygoing ambience (rare in this area). Its old town is a maze of narrow streets and red-tile roofs

rising above the blue Mediterranean, watched over by twin medieval lookout towers and wrapped in extensive ramparts. Visitors making the short trip from Nice browse Europe's biggest yacht harbor, snooze on a sandy beach, loiter through an enjoyable old town, and hike along a seaswept trail. The town's cultural claim to fame, the Picasso Museum, will likely reopen in the spring of 2008 after renovation.

Though it's much smaller than Nice, Antibes has a history that goes back just as far. Both towns were founded by Greek traders in the fifth century B.C. To the Greeks, Antibes was "Antipolis"—the town *(polis)* opposite *(anti)* Nice. For the next several centuries, Antibes remained in the shadow of its neighbor. By the turn of the 20th century, the town was a military base—so the rich and famous partied elsewhere. But when the army checked out after World War I, Antibes was "discovered" and enjoyed a particularly roaring '20s—with the help of party animals like Rudolph Valentino and the rowdy-yet-very-silent Charlie Chaplin. Fun-seekers even invented waterskiing right here in the 1920s.

ORIENTATION

Antibes' old town lies between the port and boulevard Albert 1er and avenue Robert Soleau. Place Nationale is the old town's hub of activity. The restaurant-lined rue Aubernon connects the port and the old town. Stroll along the sea between the old port and place Albert 1er (where boulevard Albert 1er meets the water). The best beaches lie just beyond place Albert 1er, and the path is beautiful. Good play areas for children are on place des Martyrs de la Résistance (close to recommended Hôtel Relais du Postillon).

Tourist Information

Antibes has two TIs. The most convenient is in the old town, just inside the walls at 21 boulevard d'Aguillon (Mon–Sat 10:00–12:00 & 13:30–18:00, closed Sun, tel. 04 93 34 65 65, www.antibes-ville .com). The *Maison de Tourisme* is in the newer city, where the fountains squirt at 11 place Général de Gaulle (where boulevard Albert 1er and rue de la République meet, July–Aug daily 9:00–18:00; Sept–June Mon–Sat 9:00–12:30 & 13:30–18:00, closed Sun; tel. 04 92 90 53 00, www.antibesjuanlespins.com). At either TI, pick up the excellent city map and the *Strolling Through the Heart of Old Antibes* brochure, and get details on the hikes described below. The Nice TI has Antibes maps; plan ahead.

Arrival in Antibes

By Train: To get to the port and the old town (10-min walk), cross the street in front of the station, skirting left of the Piranha Café, and follow avenue de la Libération downhill. As you come to the end of the street, the port will be on the left and the old town to the right. To reach the main TI in the modern city (10-min walk), exit right from the station on avenue Robert Soleau; follow *Maison du Tourisme* signs to place Général de Gaulle. Or hop on the free minibus (see "Getting Around Antibes," later in this chapter; exit station to the right and cross the street to the park). The last train back to Nice leaves at about 21:00.

By Bus: Bus #200 from Nice and to Cannes stops on avenue Dugommier, around the corner from the main TI; buses going to Nice and coming from Cannes stop on Aristide Briand (a block below the stop on avenue Dugommier, also near the TI). Buses from other destinations use the bus station at the edge of the old town on place Guynemer, a block below the old town TI (info desk open Mon–Sat 8:30–12:00 & 14:30–17:30, closed Sun).

By Car: Day-trippers should follow signs marked *Centre-Ville,* then *Vieux Port,* and park near the old town walls (first 30 min free, then about €2/hr). Enter the old town through the last arch on the right. If you're sleeping here, hotels are signed; get advice from your hotelier on where to park.

Helpful Hints

Internet Access: Get online at **Exlankaa Cyber Café,** near the main TI (24 avenue Gambetta, tel. 04 93 74 70 40), or **The Office,** in the old town (Galerie du Port, 8 boulevard d'Aguillon, tel. 04 93 34 09 96). The TI keeps an updated list of Internet cafés.

English Bookstore: **Heidi's English Bookshop** has a great selection of new and used books (daily 10:00–19:00, 24 rue Aubernon).

Laundry: Smiling Madame Hallepau will do your laundry while you swim. Her launderette is near the market hall on rue de la Pompe (Mon–Fri 8:30–12:00 & 15:00–19:00, closed Sat–Sun).

Grocery Store: Picnickers will appreciate **Epicerie de la Place** (daily until 22:00 in summer, until 21:00 off-season, where rue Sade meets place Nationale).

Taxi: Call 08 25 56 07 07 or 04 93 67 67 67.

Car Rental: The big-name agencies have offices in Antibes—**Avis** (32 avenue Albert 1er, tel. 04 93 34 65 15), **Europcar** (26 boulevard Foch, tel. 08 25 35 83 58), or **Hertz** (129 boulevard Wilson, tel. 04 93 61 18 15).

Airport Bus: Bus #200 runs from avenue Dugommier, near the main TI (at the second shelter when coming from the TI), to Nice's airport (2–3/hr, 45–70 min depending on traffic).

Getting Around Antibes

Antibes' most appealing hotels require a car to reach. Luckily, Antibes works well for drivers and most hotels have free parking. Compared to Nice, it's a breeze to navigate and a convenient springboard for the Inland Riviera. Pay parking is usually available at Antibes' train station, so drivers can ditch their cars and day-trip by train.

Several free **minibuses** (*Navettes Gratuites*) circle Antibes serving the train station, the beaches and Juan-les-Pins (Mon–Sat 7:30–19:30, not on Sun). There are four different circuits making it hopelessly confusing for tourists—just look for *Envisbus* signs and ask if they are going near your destination (stops are tricky to find—look for bus stop signs around town, the TI has a small map).

A **tourist train** offers several circuits around old Antibes, the port, the ramparts, and to Juan-les-Pins (€7, departs from place de la Poste, tel. 06 03 35 61 35).

Antibes

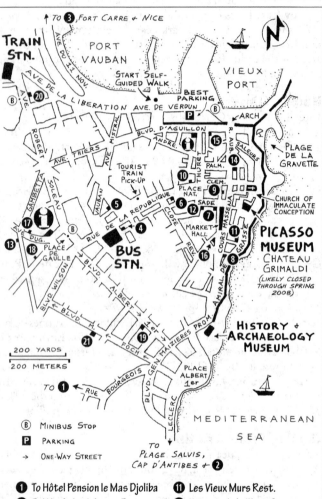

Legend:
- **B** Minibus Stop
- **P** Parking
- → One-Way Street

1. To Hôtel Pension le Mas Djoliba
2. To Hôtels La Jabotte, Beau Site & Beach-Front Dining
3. Bastide de la Brague
4. Modern Hôtel
5. Hôtel Relais du Postillon
6. Hôtel le Cameo
7. Le Jardin Restaurant
8. Le Comptoir de la Tourraque
9. Le Brulot & Le Brulot Pasta
10. Auberge Provençale
11. Les Vieux Murs Rest.
12. Epicerie de la Place Grocery
13. Exlankaa Cyber Café
14. Heidi's English Bookshop
15. The Office Internet Café
16. Launderette
17. Bus to Nice Airport
18. Bus from Nice & to Cannes
19. Avis Car Rental
20. Hertz Car Rental
21. Europcar Car Rental

SELF-GUIDED WALK

Welcome to Antibes

This 40-minute amble will help you get your bearings, and works well day or night. Begin at the old port (Vieux Port) along avenue  de Verdun (below the train station—parking right there). This is among the oldest of Europe's yachting harbors and was the model for many to come. Locals claim that this is Europe's first and biggest pleasure-boat harbor, with 1,600 stalls. That four-pointed structure crowning the opposite end of the port is **Fort Carré**—it protected Antibes from foreigners for more than 500 years. At the end of the yachts, opposite the arch that leads into the old town, you'll see the pathetic remains of a once-hearty fishing fleet. The Mediterranean is pretty much fished out. Most of the seafood you'll eat here comes from fish farms or the Atlantic. Pass the sad fleet and keep walking along the harbor, then find the entry—through the wall on your right—to the shell-shaped **plage de la Gravette,** a quiet public beach tucked right in the middle of old Antibes. Wander up the ramp to the round lookout to better appreciate the scale of the ramparts that protected this town. Because Antibes was the last fort before the Italian border, the French king made sure the ramparts were strong and well-defended.

Backtrack and enter Antibes' **old town** through the arch under the rampart. Today, the town is the haunt of a large community of English, Irish, and Aussie boaters who help crew the giant yachts of the rich and famous. (That helps explain the Irish pubs and English bookstores.)

Continue straight and uphill and you'll arrive at Antibes' **market hall** (Tue–Sun until 13:00, closed Mon except June–Aug). Like many other places in Antibes, this hall does double duty...it's filled with café tables at night.

If you take a left where the market starts, you'll find Antibes' pretty pastel **Church of Immaculate Conception,** built on the site of a Greek temple (worth a peek inside). The little church served as the area's cathedral until the mid-1200s.

Looming above the church on prime real estate is the whitestone **Château Grimaldi,** home to the **Picasso Museum** (should reopen in the spring of 2008 and is described below). This site has been home to the acropolis of the Greek city of Antipolis, a Roman fort, and a medieval bishop's palace (once connected to the cathedral below). The château was the home of the Grimaldi family (who still rule Monaco). Its proximity to the cathedral symbolized the sometimes too-cozy relationship between society's two dominant landowning classes: the Church and the nobility. (In 1789, the French Revolution changed all that.)

Find your way to the water and, heading right, follow the ramparts and views to the **History and Archaeology Museum.** From the terrace above the museum, you'll get a clear view of the forested **Cap d'Antibes**, crowned by its lighthouse and studded with mansions (see "Cap d'Antibes Hike," later in this chapter). The Cap was long the refuge of Antibes' rich and famous, and a favorite haunt of F. Scott Fitzgerald and Ernest Hemingway. After a quick tour of the museum (described below), continue hugging the coast past place Albert 1er until you see the terrific views back to old Antibes. Benches and soft sand await. You're on your own from here—strong walkers can continue to the fantastic view from the Phare de la Garoupe (see below); others can return to old Antibes and poke around in its peaceful back lanes.

SIGHTS AND ACTIVITIES

▲▲**Picasso Museum (Musée Picasso)**—Sitting serenely where the old town meets the sea, this small, three-floor museum will offer a remarkable collection of Picasso's paintings, sketches, and ceramics when it re-opens (with luck, by the spring of 2008). Picasso lived in the castle for four months in 1946, when he cranked out an amazing amount of art. The resulting collection (donated by Picasso) put Antibes on the tourist map. You'll see many of his ceramics: plates with faces, bird-shaped vases, woman-shaped bottles, bull-shaped statues, and colorful tiles. But the highlight is his lively, frolicking *La Joie de Vivre* painting. This large (4 feet by 8 feet) Greek bacchanal sums up the newfound freedom in a newly liberated France (1946) and sets the tone for the rest of the collection. You'll also see several Cubist-style nudes *(nus couchés)*, plus the *Antipolis Suite*—a series of 25 (mostly reclining) nudes, very simplified and stripped-down in style, and works that demonstrate his cartoonist and caricaturist skills (details not available at press time, but possibly €5, probably open Tue–Sun 10:00–18:00, maybe until 20:00 some evenings in summer, likely closed 12:00–14:00 off-season and Mon year-round; confirm these details—and be sure the museum is open—at Antibes' TI).

History and Archaeology Museum (Musée d'Histoire et d'Archéologie)—More than 2,000 years ago, Antibes was the center of a thriving maritime culture. It was also an important Roman city, featuring many of the hallmarks of Roman civilization—aqueducts, theaters, baths, and so on. This museum displays

Greek, Roman, and Etruscan odds and ends in two easy-to-visit rooms (no English descriptions). Your visit starts at an 1894 model of Antibes and continues past displays of Roman coins, cups, plates, and scads of amphorae (€3, daily 10:00–18:00, on the water between Picasso Museum and place Albert 1er).

▲**Market Hall (Marché Provençal)**—The daily market bustles under a 19th-century canopy, with flowers, produce, Provençal products, and beach accessories (in old town behind Picasso Museum on cours Masséna). The market wears many appealing hats: produce daily until 13:00, handicrafts Thursday through Sunday in the afternoon, and fun outdoor dining in the evenings (market closed Mon Sept–May).

Other Markets—Antibes' lively antique/flea market fills place Nationale and place Audiberti (next to the port) on Saturdays (7:00–18:00). Its clothing market winds through the streets around the post office (rue Lacan) on Thursdays (9:00–18:00).

Fort Carré—This impressively situated citadel, dating from 1487, was the last fort inside France. It protected Antibes from Nice, which until 1860 was part of Italy. You can tour this unusual four-pointed fort, but there's little to see inside. People visit for the fantastic views (€3, includes tour, daily June–Sept 10:00–18:00, Oct–May until 16:30).

Beaches *(Plages)*—The best beaches stretch between Antibes' port and Cap d'Antibes, and the very best (plage de la Salis and plage du Ponteil) are just south of place Albert 1er. All are groomed and beautifully sandy. Plage de la Salis is busy but man-ageable in summer and on weekends, with snack stands  and views of the old town. The closest beach to the old town is at the port (plage de la Gravette), which seems calm in any season.

Walks and Hikes

From place Albert 1er (where boulevard Albert 1er meets the beach), you get a good view of plage de la Salis and Cap d'Antibes. That tower on the hill is your destination for the first walk described below. The longer "Cap d'Antibes Hike" begins on the next beach, just over that hill.

▲▲**Chapelle et Phare de la Garoupe**—The territorial views—good at sunset, best at sunrise, skippable if hazy—from this view-point more than make up for the 25-minute uphill climb from the plage de la Salis (a few blocks after Maupassant Apartments, follow the rough, cobbled chemin du Calvaire up to lighthouse tower). An orientation table explains that you can see from Nice to Cannes and up to the Alps. By car, follow signs reading *Cap d'Antibes*, then look for *Chapelle et Phare de la Garoupe* signs.

▲Cap d'Antibes Hike (Sentier Touristique Piétonnier de Tirepoil)—At the end of the mattress-ridden plage de la Garoupe (over the hill from lighthouse) is a well-maintained trail around Cap d'Antibes. The beautiful path follows a rocky coastline below exclusive mansions for about two miles, then heads inland along small streets, ending at the recommended Hôtel Beau-Site (and bus stop). You can walk as far as you'd like and then double back, or do the whole loop (allow 2 hours, use the TI Antibes map).

To get to the trail from Antibes, take **bus #2** from the bus station (almost hourly Mon–Sat, 8/day Sun) for about 15 minutes to the La Fontaine stop at the Hôtel Beau-Site (almost hourly Mon–Sat, 8/day Sun, return stop is 50 yards down on opposite side, get return times at station). Walk 10 minutes down to plage de la Garoupe and start from there. By **car**, follow signs to *Cap d'Antibes*, then *plage de la Garoupe*, and park there. The trail begins at the far-right end of plage de la Garoupe.

Near Antibes

Juan-les-Pins—This village, across the Cap d'Antibes isthmus from Antibes, is where the action is in the evenings. It's a modern beach resort with good beaches, plenty of lively bars and restaurants, and a popular jazz festival in July. Buses, trains, and even a tourist train (see "Getting Around Antibes," page 587) make the 10-minute trip to and from Antibes constantly.

SLEEPING

My favorite Antibes hotels require a car or taxi—central pickings are slim in this city, where many hoteliers seem more interested in their restaurants.

Outside the Town Center

$$$ Hôtel Pension le Mas Djoliba*** is a good splurge, best for drivers (since it's a 15–20-min walk from the beach and old Antibes, and a 25-min walk from the train station). Reserve early for this tranquil, bird-chirping, flower-filled manor house where no two rooms are the same. From May to September, they definitely prefer (but won't insist) that you dine here. It's hard to pass up once you see the setting—after a busy day of sightseeing, dinner by the pool is a treat. The bigger rooms are well worth the small additional cost (Db with breakfast and dinner

€85–100 per person, Db only €80-125, several excellent family rooms-€162–190, big suite-€240, breakfast-€11, air-con, Wi-Fi, cool *boules* court and loaner balls, 29 avenue de Provence; from boulevard Albert 1er, look for blue signs and turn right up avenue Gaston Bourgeois; tel. 04 93 34 02 48, fax 04 93 34 05 81, www .hotel-djoliba.com, hotel.djoliba@wanadoo.fr).

$$$ Hôtel La Jabotte** defies the rules. Hiding down an ignored alley just a block from the famous beaches and a 20-minute walk from the old town, this small, cozy place is run by owners who care. Yves, Claude, and dog Tommy have turned a small beach villa into a boutique hotel with personality: The colors are rich, the decor shows a personal touch, and most rooms have individual terraces that face a small, central garden (Db-€105–115, includes good breakfast and a few parking spots, no air-con, 13 avenue Max Maurey, take the third right after passing the big Hôtel Josse, tel. 04 93 61 45 89, fax 04 93 61 07 04, www .jabotte.com, info@jabotte.com).

$$ Hôtel Beau-Site*** is my only listing on Cap d'Antibes, a 10-minute drive from the old town. It's a terrific value if you want to get away...but not *too* far away. This place is a sanctuary, with delightful owners (sweet Nathalie and papa Jean-Louis), a pool, a comfy patio garden, and easy parking. Eleven rooms have balconies (standard Db-€82–90, bigger Db-€100–115, even bigger Db-€134–148, family rooms-€160–210, extra bed-€25; incredible boaty breakfast-€11.50, continental breakfast-€6.50, air-con, Wi-Fi, bikes available, 141 boulevard Kennedy, tel. 04 93 61 53 43, fax 04 93 67 78 16, www.hotelbeausite.net, hbeausit@club-internet.fr). From the hotel, it's a 10-minute walk down to the crowded plage de la Garoupe and a nearby hiking trail (see "Walks and Hikes," page 591).

$$ Bastide de la Brague is a six-room bed-and-breakfast hacienda in a no-man's land, up a dirt road above Marineland (10-min drive east of Antibes). But the place is a find, as it's central to Riviera sights and run by Antibes' sweetest family (*les* Sanchis: wife Isabelle, hubby Frank, and Mama). Rooms are new, quite comfortable, air-conditioned, and affordable; several are made for families. Request the €20 home-cooked dinner and you'll get the works—from apéritif to coffee and everything in between (costs less for kids). There's more than enough space to stretch out, and they love families (Db-€70–90, Tb/Qb-€90–110, includes breakfast, 55 avenue No. 6, tel. 04 93 65 73 78, www.bbchambreantibes .com, bb06@wanadoo.fr). From Antibes, drive toward *Nice par Bord de la Mer,* turn left at Marineland, then right at the roundabout (to Groules) and follow signs.

In the Town Center

$$ Modern Hôtel**, in the pedestrian zone near the bus station, is modest and spick-and-span. The 17 standard-size rooms, each with air-conditioning and bright decor, are an excellent value (Sb-€58–69, Db-€65–84, 1 rue Fourmillière, tel. 04 92 90 59 05, fax 04 92 90 59 06, www.modernhotel06.com, modern-hotel @wanadoo.fr, helpful Laurence).

$$ Hôtel Relais du Postillon**, on a thriving square, offers 15 mostly small but well-designed rooms. Each room has a name instead of a number, and they could all use a little TLC... which is promised for 2008 (Db-€46–84, price depends on size and whether you're facing courtyard or park, tight bathrooms, 8 rue Championnet, tel. 04 93 34 20 77, fax 04 93 34 61 24, www .relaisdupostillon.com, disponibilite@relaisdupostillon.com). Owner Yves-Jean speaks flawless English.

$ Hôtel le Cameo** is a rambling old place above a bustling bar (where you'll find what little reception there is). The public areas are dark, and the nine simple, linoleum-lined rooms are almost cute. All open onto the boisterous place Nationale, which means you don't sleep until the restaurant sleeps (Ds-€55, Db-€66, Tb-€74, Qb-€82, 5 place Nationale, tel. 04 93 34 24 17, fax 04 93 34 35 80, no English spoken).

EATING

Antibes is a fun place to dine out. You can eat on a budget, enjoy a fine meal at an acceptable price, or join the party just inside the walls on boulevard d'Aguillon, in the festive Marché Provençal, or on place Nationale (all filled with tables and tourists—I prefer the Marché Provençal). The options are endless. Take a walk and judge for yourself, and be tempted by these good suggestions. Romantics should picnic at the beach. Everyone should stroll along the ramparts after dinner.

Le Jardin is reliable and reasonable, with tables filling a pretty and peaceful garden courtyard. Arrive early to secure a table outside and enjoy good regional cooking (€19–27 *menus* and good €17 *plats*, closed Tue, 5 rue Sade, tel. 04 93 34 64 74).

Le Comptoir de la Tourraque bucks Antibes' showy trend. It has an intimate interior, caring service, fair prices, and top-notch cuisine mixing traditional French and Italian flavors and served at fair prices (€34 *menu*, closed Mon, 1 rue de la Tourraque, tel. 04 93 95 24 86).

Le Brulot runs two restaurants—Le Brulot and Le Brulot Pasta—that sit almost side-by-side a short block below Marché Provençal on rue Frédéric Isnard. Join locals at the very popular and inexpensive **Le Brulot,** known for its Provençal cuisine and open-fire-cooked meats. It's a small place, overflowing onto the street, with a few outside tables and a dining room below. Try the aioli (€15 *menus*, €12 *plats*, closed Sun, at #2, tel. 04 93 34 17 76). **Le Brulot Pasta** is family-friendly and goes Italian with excellent pizza (the €11 Printanière is tasty and huge) and big portions of pasta, served in air-conditioned comfort under stone arches (open daily, at #3, tel. 04 93 34 19 19).

Auberge Provençale entertains discerning diners in a vine-covered courtyard. This is where the locals go for seafood special-ties (*menus* from €34, open daily, 61 place Nationale, tel. 04 93 34 13 24).

Les Vieux Murs is *the* place to splurge in Antibes for regional specialties. Its candlelit, red-tone, *très romantique* interior overlooks the sea, and the outside tables are worth your booking ahead—pass on the upstairs room (€43 *menu*, open daily June–mid-Sept, closed Tue off-season, valet parking available, along ramparts beyond Picasso Museum at 25 promenade Amiral de Grasse, tel. 04 93 34 06 73).

Beach-Front Dining: You'll find two restaurants on pretty plage de la Garoupe, below the recommended Hôtel Beau Site. **Le César/Plage Keller** makes for an elegant seaside meal (same owner as Les Vieux Murs above, allow €60 per person with wine, open daily, tel. 04 93 61 33 74). **Plage Joseph Restaurant** next door features basic fare at lower prices with the same view (open daily).

TRANSPORTATION CONNECTIONS

TGV and local trains serve Antibes' little station.

From Antibes by Train to: Cannes (2/hr, 15 min), **Nice** (2/hr, 15–30 min, €3.90), **Villefranche-sur-Mer** (2/hr, 40 min), **Monaco** (2/hr, 45–60 min), **Marseille** (16/day, 2.5 hrs).

By Bus to: Cannes (2–3/hr, 25 min), **Nice Airport** (bus #200, 2–3/hr, 40–70 min depending on traffic).

Inland Riviera

For a verdant, rocky, fresh escape from the beaches, head inland and upwards. Some of France's most perfectly perched hill towns and splendid scenery are overlooked in this region more famous for beaches and bikinis. Driving is the easiest way to get around, though the bus gets you to many of the places described. Vence and St-Paul-de-Vence are well-served by bus from Nice every 30 minutes (see "Getting Around the Riviera," page 534).

Vence

Vence is a well-discovered yet appealing town set high above the Riviera. While growth has sprawled well beyond Vence's old walls, and cars jam its roundabouts, the mountains are front and center, and the breeze is fresh in this engaging town that bubbles with workaday life and ample tourist activity. Vence is peaceful at night, and makes a handy base for travelers wanting the best of both worlds: a hill-town refuge near the sea.

ORIENTATION

Tourist Information

Vence's fully loaded and eager-to-help TI faces the main square at 8 place du Grand Jardin. It has bus schedules, brochures on the cathedral, and a city map with a well-devised self-guided walking tour (25 stops, incorporates informative wall plaques). It also publishes a list of Vence art galleries with English descriptions of the collections. To properly engage you in French culture, the TI also has information on French language classes, and—even better—*pétanque* instruction with loaner *boules* (TI open June–Sept Mon–Sat 9:00–19:00, Sun 10:00–17:00; Oct–May Mon–Sat 9:00–18:00, closed Sun; tel. 04 93 58 06 38, www.ville-vence.fr).

Market day in the Cité Historique is on Tuesday and Friday mornings on place Clemenceau. There's a big, all-day antique market on place du Grand Jardin every Wednesday.

Arrival in Vence

By Bus: The bus stop is on place du Grand Jardin, next to the TI (schedules are posted in the window).

By Car: Follow signs to *cité historique,* and park where you can. A central pay lot is under place du Grand Jardin, across from the TI. Park here if you're spending the night somewhere other than Hôtel Miramar (which has its own parking).

SIGHTS

Stroll the narrow lanes of the old town *(cité historique)* using the TI's self-guided tour map. Connect the picturesque streets, enjoy a drink on a quiet square, inspect an art gallery, and find the small, 11th-century cathedral with its colorful Chagall mosaic of Moses (for background, see the Chagall Museum description on page 547). If you're here later in the day, enjoy the *boules* action across from the TI (and ask at the TI to borrow a set).

Château de Villeneuve—This 17th-century mansion, adjoining an imposing 12th-century watchtower, bills itself as "one of the Riviera's high temples of modern art," with a rotating collection. Check with the TI to see what's playing in the temple (€5, Tue–Sun 10:00–12:30 & 14:00–18:00, closed Mon, tel. 04 93 58 15 78).

▲**Chapel of the Rosary (Chapelle du Rosaire)**—The chapel, a 20-minute walk from town, was designed by an ailing Henri

Matisse in thanks to the Dominican sister who had taken care of him (he was 81 when the chapel was completed). The modest chapel is a simple collection of white walls, laced with yellow, green, and blue stained-glass windows and charcoal black-on-white tile sketches. The experience may underwhelm all but his fans, for whom this is the ultimate pilgrimage

(€2.80, Mon, Wed, and Sat 14:00–17:30, Tue and Thu 10:00–11:30 & 14:00–17:30, Sun only open for Mass at 10:00 followed by tour of chapel, closed Fri and Nov, tel. 04 93 58 03 26). To reach the chapel from the Vence TI, turn right out of the TI and walk down avenue Henri Isnard, then right on avenue de Provence, following signs to *St. Jeannet*. Or take the little white train that runs to the chapel from in front of the TI (1/hr).

SLEEPING

(€1 = about $1.30, country code: 33)

$$$ Hôtel Miramar*** is a fine refuge about a 10-minute walk from the old center. Friendly owner Daniel welcomes you into his 18-room Mediterranean villa, perched on a ledge with grand panoramas. The place is filled with personal touches, and every soothing room feels well cared for. The pool and view terrace could make you late for dinner, or seduce you into skipping it altogether—picnics are allowed (Sb-€80–92, standard Db-€90–105, Db with balcony-€100–135, Db with great view and balcony-€148, family suite-€130–185, some rooms have air-con, most don't need it, bar, table tennis, parking, turn left out of the TI and follow the brown signs to 167 avenue Bougearel, tel. 04 93 58 01 32, fax 04 93 58 20 22, www.hotel-miramar-vence.com, resa@hotel-miramar-vence.com).

$$$ **La Maison du Frêne** is an art-packed B&B with four sumptuous rooms located behind the TI. Energetic Thierry combines his passion for contemporary art and hosting travelers in his lovingly restored manor house (Db-€140, includes breakfast, air-con, 1 place du Frêne, tel. 04 93 24 37 83, www.lamaisondufrene.com, lamaisondufrene@wanadoo.fr).

$$**L'Auberge des Seigneurs**** is an overlooked throwback just inside the old town. Its six character-filled rooms—above a cozy restaurant—have wood furnishings, red-tile floors, and good-enough bathrooms (spacious Sb-€65, Db-€85–95, place du Frêne, tel. 04 93 58 04 24, fax 04 93 24 08 01). It's a short walk from the TI, next to the Château de Villeneuve: Turn right out of the TI, then right again, then left.

EATING

Tempting outdoor eateries litter Vence's old town; they all look good to me.

On Place Clemenceau: These two restaurants serve delectable Provençale cuisine a few doors apart on the charming place Clemenceau: **La Cassolette,** at #10, is an intimate place with reasonable prices and a pleasant terrace across from the floodlit church (€16 and €25 *menus,* daily, tel. 04 93 58 84 15). **Le P'tit Provençal,** at #4, is the romantic's choice, with a lovely upstairs dining room (€24 and €30 *menus,* closed Mon all year, also closed Tue off-season, tel. 04 93 58 50 64).

At nearby **La Peyra,** enjoy an elegant dinner salad or pasta dish outdoors to the sound of the town's main fountain (closed Tue–Wed, 13 place du Peyra, tel. 04 93 58 67 63).

L'Auberge des Seigneurs is good for a cooler day, when you can sit by the fire and watch your meat being cooked (*menus* from €35, closed Sun–Mon; also recommended under "Sleeping," page 597).

Near Vence

St-Paul-de-Vence

The most famous of the Riviera hill towns, and the most-visited village in France, feels that way—like an overrun and over-restored artist-shopping-mall. Its attraction is understandable, as every cobble and flower seems *just-so,* and the setting is remarkable.

Still, wall-to-wall galleries and ice cream shops, and hordes of day-trippers strangle the appeal for many. Avoid visiting between 11:00 and 18:00, particularly on weekends. If you must go, arrive early and have *café et croissant* (a.k.a. breakfast) at the picture-

perfect **Café de la Place.** The **TI,** just through the gate into the old city on rue Grande, has maps with minimal explanations of key buildings (daily 10:00–18:00, tel. 04 93 32 86 95, www.saint-pauldevence.com). If the entrance to the old city is jammed, take the road that veers left just before the entrance, and enter the town through its side door. Meander deep into St-Paul-de-Vence's quieter streets to find the panoramic views.

SIGHTS

▲**Fondation Maeght**—This inviting, pricey, far-out private museum is situated a steep walk or short drive above St-Paul-de-Vence. Fondation Maeght (fohn-dah-shown mahg) offers an

excellent introduction to modern Mediterranean art by gathering many of the Riviera's most famous artists under one roof. The founder, Aimé Maeght, long envisioned the perfect exhibition space for the artists he supported and befriended as an art dealer. He purchased a dry piece of hilltop land, planted more than 35,000 plants, and hired an architect (Josep Lluís Sert) with the same vision.

A sweeping lawn laced with amusing sculptures and bending pine trees greets visitors. On the right, a chapel designed by Georges Braque—in memory of the Maeghts' young son, who died of leukemia—features a moving, purple stained-glass work over the altar. The unusual museum building is purposefully low-profile, to let its world-class modern-art collection take center stage. Works by Fernand Léger, Joan Miró, Alexander Calder, Georges Braque, and Marc Chagall are thoughtfully arranged in well-lit rooms. The backyard of the museum has views, a Gaudí-esque sculpture labyrinth by Miró, and a courtyard filled with wispy works by Alberto Giacometti. The only permanent collection in the museum consists of the sculptures, though the museum tries to keep a good selection of paintings by famous artists here year-round. For a review of modern art, see "The Riviera's Art Scene" on page 536. There's also a great gift shop and cafeteria.

Cost and Hours: €11, €2.50 to take photos, daily July–Sept

10:00–19:00, Oct–June 10:00–12:30 & 14:30–18:00, tel. 04 93 32 81 63, www.fondation-maeght.com.

Getting There: The museum is a steep, uphill-but-doable, 20-minute walk from St-Paul-de-Vence and the bus stop. Blue signs indicate the way (parking is available at the top, though the lot can be full).

La Route Napoléon: North to the Alps

After getting bored in his toy Elba empire, Napoleon gathered his entourage, landed on the Riviera, bared his breast, and told his fellow Frenchmen, "Strike me down or follow me." France followed. But just in case, he took the high road, returning to Paris along the route known today as La Route Napoléon. (Waterloo followed shortly afterward.)

By Car: The route between the Riviera and the Alps is beautiful (from south to north, follow signs: Digne, Sisteron, and Grenoble). An assortment of pleasant villages with inexpensive hotels lies along this route, making an overnight easy. Little Entrevaux feels forgotten and still stuck in its medieval shell. Cross the bridge, meet someone friendly, and consider the steep hike up to the citadel (€2). Sisteron's Romanesque church and view from the citadel above make this town worth a quick leg-stretch.

By Narrow-Gauge Train (Chemins de Fer de Provence): Leave the tourists behind and take your kids on the scenic train-bus-train combination that runs between Nice and Digne through canyons, along whitewater rivers, between snow-capped peaks, and through many tempting villages (Nice to Digne: 4/day, 3 hrs, about €18, 25 percent discount with railpass, departs Nice from the South Station—Gare du Sud—about 10 blocks behind the city's main train station, 4 rue Alfred Binet, tel. 04 97 03 80 80, www.trainprovence.com).

Start with an 8:50 departure and go as far as you want. **Entrevaux** is an easy destination (about 2 scenic hours from Nice, €9 one way). Climb high to the citadel for great views.

The narrow-gauge train ends in **Digne-les-Bains,** where you can catch a main-line train (covered by railpasses) to other destinations—or better, continue scenically to **Annecy** following this plan (assuming you've taken the 8:50 train from Nice): take the bus (quick transfer, free with railpass) to **Veynes** (4/day, 90 min), then catch the most scenic two-car train to **Grenoble** (5/day, 2 hrs, easy transfer from Veynes bus). From there, you can catch a train to **Annecy** (16/day, 90 min), arriving at about 18:50.

To do the entire trip from Nice to Annecy in one day, you must start with the 8:50 departure from Nice, but I'd rather spend the night in one of the tiny villages en route. **Clelles** has a decent hotel: **Hôtel Ferrat**,** a basic, family-run mountain hacienda at the base of Mont Aiguille (after which Gibraltar was modeled), is a good place to break this train trip. Enjoy your own *boules* court, the swimming pool, and a good restaurant (Sb-€38, Db-€53, tel. 04 76 34 42 70, fax 04 76 34 47 47, hotel.ferrat@wanadoo.fr).

THE FRENCH ALPS

Alpes-Savoie

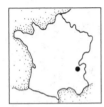

Savoie grows Europe's highest mountains and is the top floor of the French Alps (the lower Alpes-Dauphiné lie to the south). More than just a pretty-peaked face, stubborn Savoie maintained its independence from France until 1860, when mountains became targets, rather than obstacles, for travelers. Its borders once extended south to the Riviera and far west across the Rhône River Valley. Home to skier Jean-Claude Killy and the first winter Olympics (1924 in Chamonix), today's Savoie is France's mountain-sports capital, featuring 15,771-foot Mont Blanc as its centerpiece. With wood chalets overflowing with geraniums and cheese fondue in every restaurant, Savoie feels more Swiss than French.

The scenery is drop-dead spectacular. Serenely self-confident Annecy is a postcard-perfect blend of natural and man-made beauty. In Chamonix, it's just you and Madame Nature—there's not a museum or important building in sight. If the weather's right, take Europe's ultimate cable-car ride to the 12,600-foot Aiguille du Midi in Chamonix.

Planning Your Time

Hemmed in by mountains, lakefront Annecy has boats, bikes, and hikes for all tastes and abilities. Its trademark arcaded walking streets and good transportation connections (most trains to Chamonix pass through Annecy) make it a convenient stopover. But if

The French Alps

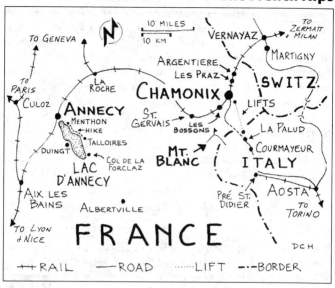

you're pressed for time and antsy for Alps, get thee to Chamonix. There you can skip along alpine ridges, glide over mountain meadows, zip down the mountain on a luge (wheeled bobsled), or meander along riverside paths on a mountain bike. Plan a minimum of two nights and one day in Chamonix, and try to work in a night in Annecy. Since weather is everything in this area, get the forecast by calling Chamonix's TI (tel. 04 50 53 00 24) or the weather-report line (in English, dial from anywhere in France, tel. 08 92 68 02 74). If it looks good, make haste to Chamonix; if it's gloomy, Annecy offers more distraction. Both Chamonix and Annecy are mobbed with tourists in summer. (If you're driving or taking the train from here to the Riviera, see "La Route Napoléon" tips at the end of the previous chapter.)

Getting Around the Alps

Annecy and Chamonix are well-connected by trains. Buses run from Chamonix to nearby villages, and the Aiguille du Midi lift takes travelers from Chamonix to Italy over Europe's most scenic border crossing.

Cuisine Scene in Savoie

Savoie cuisine is mountain-hearty. Its Swiss-similar specialties include *fondue savoyarde* (melted Beaufort and Comté cheeses and local white wine, sometimes with a dash of Cognac), raclette (chunks of semi-melted cheese served with potatoes, pickles, sausage, and bread), *tartiflettes* (hearty scalloped potatoes with melted cheese), *poulet de Bresse* (the best chicken in France), *Morteau* (smoked pork sausage), *gratin savoyard* (a potato dish with cream, cheese, and garlic), and fresh fish. Local cheeses are Morbier (look for a charcoal streak down the middle), Comté (like Gruyère), Beaufort (aged for two years, hard and strong), Reblochon (mild and creamy), and Tomme de Savoie (mild and semi-hard). Evian water comes from Savoie, as does Chartreuse liqueur. Apremont and Crépy are two of the area's surprisingly good white wines. The local beer, Baton de Feu, is more robust than other French beers.

Remember, restaurants serve only during lunch (11:30–14:00) and dinner (19:00–21:00, later in bigger cities); some cafés serve food throughout the day.

Annecy

There's something for everyone in this lakefront city that knows how to be popular: mountain views, flowery lanes, romantic canals, a hovering château, and swimming in—or boating on, or biking around—the translucent lake. Sophisticated yet outdoors-oriented and bike-crazy Annecy (ahn-see) is France's answer to Switzerland's Luzern, and, while you may not have glaciers knocking at your door as in nearby Chamonix, the distant peaks paint a darn pretty picture

with Annecy's lakefront setting. Annecy has a few museums, but don't kid yourself—you're here for its lovely setting and strollable streets.

ORIENTATION

Modern Annecy (pop. 50,000) sprawls for miles, but we're interested only in its compact old town, hunkered on the southwest corner of the lake. The old town is split by the Thiou River and bounded by the château to the south, the TI and rue Royale to the north, rue de la Gare to the west, and the lake to the east.

Tourist Information

The TI is a few blocks from the old town, across from the big grass field in the brown-and-glass Bonlieu shopping center (daily mid-May–mid-Sept 9:00–18:30, mid-Sept–mid-May 9:00–12:30 & 13:45–18:00, closed Sun Nov–March, 1 rue Jean Jaurès,

Annecy

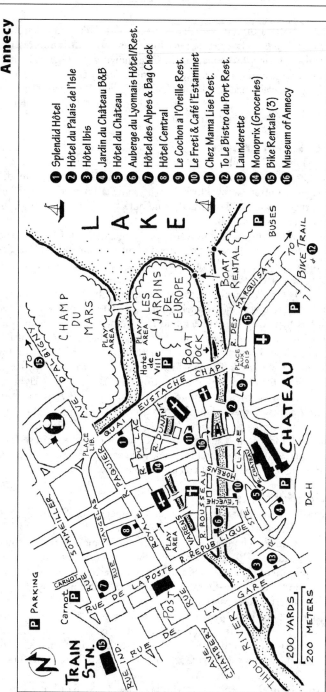

1. Splendid Hôtel
2. Hôtel du Palais de l'Isle
3. Hôtel Ibis
4. Jardin du Château B&B
5. Hôtel du Château
6. Auberge du Lyonnais Hôtel/Rest.
7. Hôtel des Alpes & Bag Check
8. Hôtel Central
9. Le Cochon a l'Oreille Rest.
10. Le Freti & Café l'Estaminet
11. Chez Mama Lise Rest.
12. To Le Bistro du Port Rest.
13. Launderette
14. Monoprix (Groceries)
15. Bike Rentals (3)
16. Museum of Annecy

tel. 04 50 45 00 33, www.lac-annecy.com). Get a city map, the *Town Walks* walking-tour brochure (several mildly interesting walks described), the map of the lake showing the bike trail, and, if you're spending a few days, the helpful *Annecy Guide*, with everything a traveler needs to know. Ask about walking tours in English (€6, July–Aug only, normally Tue and Fri at 16:00). You'll also find TIs in most villages on the lake.

Arrival in Annecy

By Train: To reach the old town and TI, leave the station, veer left at street level, and cross the big road to the pinkish Hôtel des Alpes. Continue a few blocks down rue de la Poste, then turn left on rue Royale for the TI and some hotels, or continue straight to more recommended hotels.

While the train station has no baggage-check facilities, you can store your bags across the street at the recommended Hôtel des Alpes (see "Sleeping," page 609; €2/bag, reception open 24 hours, ring bell after 23:00).

By Car: Annecy is a traffic mess; in high season (July–Aug), try to arrive very early, during lunch, or late. Avoid most of the snarls by taking the Annecy Sud exit from the autoroute and following *Albertville* signs. Upon entering Annecy, turn left at the roundabout below the hospital for the city center. (Don't follow signs for *Annecy-le-Vieux*, which is another town entirely.) Refer to my map to find these pay parking lots: You can park right on the lake with the buses opposite the boat dock at *Parking Stade Nautique* (few spaces for cars, but this might be your lucky day), or follow signs to the new *Parking Hôpital-Clinique* where you should find a spot. There are also handy lots near the train station. If you're staying at a hotel in town, you can park overnight for free at a public lot, but only if you ask at your hotel.

Helpful Hints

Market Days: The biggest market in Annecy is on Saturday, with food, clothes, and crafts (until 12:30, around boulevard Taine). A thriving outdoor food market occupies most of the old town center on Tuesday, Friday, and Sunday mornings.

Department Store: The **Monoprix** is at the corner of rue du Lac and rue Notre-Dame (Mon–Sat 8:30–19:50, closed Sun, supermarket upstairs).

Internet Access: Most hotels have Internet access; otherwise Annecy is an Internet desert for travelers. Ask at the TI.

Laundry: The launderette is at the western edge of the old town near where rue de la Gare meets rue Ste. Claire (daily 7:00–21:00, 6 rue de la Gare).

Bike Rental: Across from the lake steamers, **Roul' ma Poule**

The French Alps

rents bikes (€8/half-day, €12/day, includes helmet and basket, leave ID as deposit, mid-May–mid-Oct daily 9:00–12:00 & 13:30–19:00, closed mid-Oct–mid-May, 4 rue Marquisats, tel. & fax 04 50 27 86 83, www.annecy-location-velo.com, helpful owner Stefan). **Localoisirs** will deliver and pick up a bike at your hotel for free (€14/day, 47 avenue du Petit Port, tel. 06 08 86 81 59). You can also rent a bike at **Vélonecy,** at the train station (€6/half-day, €10/day, includes helmet and basket, requires credit-card deposit; Mon–Sat 9:00–12:00 & 13:00–19:30, closed Sun; tel. 04 50 51 38 90).

Bad Weather: If it's raining, consider a day trip to Lyon (7 trains/day, 2 hours; see Lyon chapter). The last train to Annecy usually leaves Lyon at about 20:00, allowing a full day in the big city.

SIGHTS AND ACTIVITIES

Strolling—Most of the old city is wonderfully traffic-free. The river, canals, and arcaded streets are made for ambling. The TI's *Town Walks* brochure describes Annecy with basic historical information. Get lost—the water is your boundary. Surrender to the luscious ice cream shops and waterfront cafés.

Museum of Annecy (Palais de l'Isle)—This serenely situated 13th-century building cuts like the prow of a ship through the heart of the Thiou river. Once a prison, now a boring museum, it held French Resistance fighters during World War II (€3.40, June–Sept Wed–Mon 10:30–18:00, Oct–May Wed–Mon 10:00–12:00 & 14:00–18:00, closed Tue).

Château Museum (Musée-Château d'Annecy)—The castle was built in the late 1100s by aristocrats from nearby Geneva. Today, it houses a modestly interesting museum that mixes local folklore, anthropology, natural history, and modern and fine art with great views over the lake and city. The only compelling reason to enter the château is for the view (€5, same hours as Museum of Annecy).

▲Boating—To tool around the lake, rent a paddleboat (*pédalos,* some equipped with a slide, about €10/30 min, €14/hour) or a motorboat (*hors-bord,* no license needed, for 2 people about €26/30 min, €42/hour, each extra person about €1, up to 7 people, several companies all have the same rates). This is one of Europe's cleanest, clearest lakes, and the water is warmer than you'd think.

Compagnie des Bateaux du Lac d'Annecy offers worthwhile lake cruises. The one-hour cruise makes no stops but has frequent departures (€12, 12/day May–Aug, 6–8/day April and Sept). The two-hour cruises, called *Circuit Omnibus,* make stops at several villages around the lake (€14, 3/day); these are ideal for hikers and bikers (see below). The elaborate dinner (€45–70 *menu*) and danc-ing cruises look like fun. Get schedules and prices for all boat trips at the TI or on the lake behind Hôtel de Ville (tel. 04 50 51 08 40, www.annecy-croisieres.com).

Boat and Hike—For a scenic workout and a rewarding full-day excursion, take the 10:30 boat to **Menthon–St. Bernard** (€4.60), hike 2.5 hours to lovely **Talloires,** then catch the boat back to Annecy (€8). From the boat dock in Menthon–St. Bernard, walk to the right along the shore toward the large palace and follow the signposts for Roc de Chère. The path leads up and over the Roc, passing the Golf de Talloires. The last stretch into Talloires drops steeply—wear good shoes. Cross Talloires to the port and beach (swim and lunch there), then catch the 15:00 boat back to Annecy to arrive at about 16:15 (the last boat for Annecy from Talloires leaves at 17:30).

▲**Biking**—Annecy was made for biking; it's an ain't-it-great-to-be-alive way to poke around the lake and test waterfront cafés and parks. A popular bike trail *(piste cyclable)* runs along the west side of the lake (some sections of the trail are on a roadway); it's smart to wear sunglasses and bring water. The small village of Duingt is seven level miles away and makes a good destination. Steady bikers make it in 45 minutes, and smell-the-roses cyclists need at least an hour. You can ride to Duingt and take the *Omnibus* boat back to Annecy (€6, 3 departures per day from Duingt, normally at 11:45, 15:30, and 18:00, verify at boat dock or TI, bikes allowed).

To get to Duingt, leave Annecy on the main road (N-508) with the lake on your left and join the bike trail after about a mile. Once the painted bike lane ends in Sévrier, you'll see a sign for the trail *(piste cyclable)* to the left. Follow it to Duingt (exit the trail just before the tunnel for Duingt, ride down to main road and turn right, then find the small, green boat-dock shelter just after the castle). The trail beyond Duingt is beautiful, as the lake narrows—hardy cyclists can make it all the way around the lake in about three hours (no bike path on opposite side of lake, just narrow roads, with one good hill).

This route also works well in reverse: Take the *Omnibus* boat to Duingt and pedal back (turn right when you get off the boat and join the bike trail behind Duingt's tall church).

Driving—For the best car-accessible views overlooking Annecy, drive 12 miles to Col de la Forclaz (3,600 feet, restaurants with view terraces). Take D-508 south along the lake past Duingt and turn left on D-42 a few minutes after leaving the lake (allow 45 min one-way with traffic). This also ties in easily with the scenic route to Chamonix via N-508.

SLEEPING

Annecy is popular—particularly on weekends and during the summer. Hotel rates drop from about mid-October through late April and generally increase in summer. Most hotels can help you find free overnight parking (in lots, after 18:00 until 9:00). Unless otherwise noted, these hotels do not have elevators.

Hôtel du Château and Jardin du Château Bed & Breakfast are at the foot of the château, a steep five-minute walk up from the old town on rampe du Château. The rest of my listings are in the pedestrian-friendly town center and tend to be noisier (ask about parking deals). If a hotel does not have a website listed below, try the site for Annecy's TI: www.lac-annecy.com.

$$$ Splendid Hôtel*** makes a striking impression with its grand facade and flags. This business hotel, with every comfort (including elevators, bar, terrace, free Internet access and Wi-Fi), sits on Annecy's busiest street across from the park and the TI. Rooms are handsome with parquet floors (Sb-€100–110, Db-€112–122, Tb-€158, Qb-€173, breakfast buffet-€14, air-con, big beds, 4 quai Eustache Chappuis, tel. 04 50 45 20 00, fax 04 50 45 52 23, www.splendidhotel.fr).

$$$ Hôtel du Palais de l'Isle*** offers a romantic canalside location in the thick of the old town and 33 stylish, contemporary rooms—several with canal or rooftop views—but uninterested management (Sb-€80–105, Db-€87–115, deluxe Db-€145, grand suites-€190–250, air-con, elevator, pricey Internet access, 13 rue Perrière, tel. 04 50 45 86 87, fax 04 50 51 87 15, www .hoteldupalaisdelisle.com, palisle@wanadoo.fr).

Sleep Code

(€1 = about $1.30, country code: 33)
S = Single, **D** = Double/Twin, **T** = Triple, **Q** = Quad, **b** = bathroom, **s** = shower only, ***** = French hotel rating system (0–4 stars). Unless otherwise noted, credit cards are accepted and English is spoken.

To help you sort easily through these listings, I've divided the rooms into three categories based on the price for a standard double room with bath:

  $$$ Higher Priced—Most rooms €85 or more.
   $$ Moderately Priced—Most rooms between €65–85.
    $ Lower Priced—Most rooms €65 or less.

$$ Hôtel Ibis** is a cheery place and a decent chain-hotel option, with narrow rooms, a canalside breakfast room and lounge, and easy underground parking. It's well-situated on a modern courtyard on the edge of the old town, a few blocks from the train station (Sb/Db-€80, extra bed-€10, buffet breakfast-€7, air-con, elevator, 12 rue de la Gare, tel. 04 50 45 43 21, fax 04 50 52 81 08, www.ibishotel.com,H0538@accor.com).

At **$$$ Jardin du Château Bed & Breakfast,** welcoming Anne-Marie and Jean-Paul have created Annecy's highest urban refuge (near the château entry). Their chalet *chambre d'hôte* comes with a small garden and eight modern yet comfy rooms, all with kitchenettes and some with views and balconies. Jean-Paul doubles as a mountain guide and offers a wealth of information (small Db-€66, bigger Db-€88–122, most are about €88, good family rooms-€82–122, includes breakfast except Nov–March when rooms are cheaper, cash only, bike rental, 1 place du Château, tel. & fax 04 50 45 72 28, jardinduchateau@wanadoo.fr).

$$ Hôtel du Château** is just below the château and comes with a great view terrace and 15 simple, bright, and spotless rooms; about half have views, and all have updated bathrooms with showers. It's first-come, first-get for the precious few free parking spots (Db-€60–68, Tb-€73, Qb-€83, free Internet access and Wi-Fi, 16 rampe du Château, tel. 04 50 45 27 66, fax 04 50 52 75 26, www .annecy-hotel.com, hotelduchateau@noos.fr).

$$ Auberge du Lyonnais** has 10 good-value, alpine-decorated rooms above a bustling restaurant (recommended under "Eating," below). It's as central as you can get with adequately comfortable rooms; the rooms on the canal are worth the few extra euros (Db-€60–70, 9 rue de la République, walk through the restaurant to the small reception, tel. 04 50 51 26 10, fax 04 50 51 05 04).

$ Hôtel des Alpes**, an excellent budget option, has 32 immaculate, comfortable, bright rooms at a busy intersection just across from the train station. Rooms on the courtyard are quieter but darker; those on the street have effective double panes (Sb-€48–52, Db-€53–60, Tb-€65–76, Qb-€72–87, €7 more for a bathtub, free Wi-Fi, 12 rue de la Poste, tel. 04 50 45 04 56, fax 04 50 45 12 38, www.hotelannecy.com, info@hotelannecy.com).

$ Hôtel Central* is just that. This modest and homey place, behind an ivy-covered courtyard off a big pedestrian street, is just this side of a youth hostel (Ds-€40, Db-€46, extra person-€8, 6 bis rue Royale, tel. 04 50 45 05 37, fax 04 50 51 80 19, www .hotelcentralannecy.com, stefanpicollet@hotmail.com, informal owners Stefan and mama Parel).

EATING

While the touristy old city is well-stocked with forgettable restaurants, I've found a few worthy places. And while you'll pay more to eat with views of the river or canal, the experience is uniquely Annecy. The ubiquitous and sumptuous *gelati* shops remind us how close Italy is. If it's sunny, assemble a gourmet picnic at the arcaded stores and dine lakeside. Wherever you eat, don't miss an ice-cream-licking stroll along the lake after dark.

Le Cochon à l'Oreille ("The Pig's Ear") is a meat-lover's nirvana. Just off the Thiou canal, it welcomes with a leafy courtyard, red-and-white checkered tablecloths, and a warm interior. Amicable owners "Fred" and Jean speak English and are serious about their cooking. The accent is on fresh products and meat dishes, not on melted cheese (€18 *menu* that changes weekly, daily for lunch and dinner, quai du Perrière, tel. 04 50 45 92 51).

Le Freti, with a light-hearted waitstaff, is the most reliable restaurant for local cuisine I've found in Annecy. It's the place to go for mouthwatering fondue, raclette, or anything with cheese. Each booth comes with its own outlet for melting raclette (fondue-€12, good salads and onion soup and cheap wine, open daily; walk through door at 12 rue Ste. Claire, it's upstairs; tel. 04 50 51 29 52).

If Le Freti sounds cheesy, go next door to **Café l'Estaminet** for a Belgian welcome. You'll get salads, omelets, pasta, mussels, fries, and more for fair prices and a sliver of a backyard deck hanging over the river (open daily in summer, closed Sun off-season, 8 rue Ste. Claire, tel. 04 50 45 88 83).

Chez Mama Lise is like eating in an alpine folk museum, with stuffed mountain animals, rusted tools, tourists, and knick-knacks everywhere. The cuisine—fondue, raclette, and other cheese dishes—is as alpine as the decor (open daily, 11 rue Grenette, tel. 04 50 45 41 18).

Auberge du Lyonnais is a well-respected and classy eatery that specializes in seafood with a sweet setting on the river (indoor and outdoor seating). The outgoing owners love Americans; ask Dominique about his many trips to the States, and about his Ford pickup (*menus* from €30, open daily, 9 rue de la République, tel. 04 50 51 26 10).

Near Annecy

Many cafés and restaurants ring Annecy's postcard-perfect lake. If you have a car and need views, prowl the many lakefront villages. **Le Bistro du Port,** a nautical place with blue deck chairs, is beautifully situated at the boat dock in Sévrier (€10 salads, €15–20 main courses, €26 *menus*, open daily in summer, closed Sun–Mon off-season, Port de Sévrier, tel. 04 50 52 45 00).

TRANSPORTATION CONNECTIONS

From Annecy by Train to: Chamonix (8/day, 2.5 hrs, change in St. Gervais), **Lyon** (7/day, 2 hrs, most change in Aix-les-Bains, some by bus), **Beaune** (7/day, 5–6 hrs, change in Lyon), **Nice** (8/day, 7–9 hrs, at least 3 changes), **Paris'** Gare de Lyon (13/day, 4–5 hrs, many with change in Lyon, night train also available).

Chamonix

Bullied by snow-dipped peaks, churning with mountain lifts, and littered with hiking trails, the resort of Chamonix (shah-moh-nee) is France's best base for alpine exploration. Officially called Chamonix–Mont Blanc, it's the largest of five villages at the base of Mont Blanc with about 10,000 residents. Chamonix's purpose in life has always been to accommodate visitors with some of Europe's top alpine thrills—it's slammed

from mid-July through mid-August and on winter holidays, but it's *très* peaceful at other times. Chamonix's sister city is Aspen, Colorado.

Planning Your Time

Ride the lifts early (crowds and clouds roll in later in the morning) and save your afternoons for lower altitudes. If you have one sunny day, spend it this way: Start with the Aiguille du Midi lift (go early, reservations possible and recommended July–Aug), take it all the way to Helbronner (linger around the rock needle longer if you can't get to Helbronner), double back to Plan de l'Aiguille, hike to Montenvers and the Mer de Glace (only with good shoes and snow level permitting), and take the train down from there. End your day with a well-deserved drink at a view café in Chamonix. If the weather disappoints or the snow line's too low, hike the Petit Balcon Sud or Arve River trails.

ORIENTATION

Eternally white Mont Blanc is Chamonix's southeastern limit; the Aiguilles Rouges mountains form the northwestern border. The frothy Arve River splits Chamonix in two. The thriving pedestrian zone, just west of the river along rues du Docteur Paccard

Chamonix Valley Overview

MT. BLANC
15,771

ITALY

"Wow!"

LE BREVENT
8,284

PANORAMIC DU MONT BLANC

AIGUILLE DU MIDI
12,605

GARE HELBRONNER
11,371

GLACIER DU GEANT

PLAN DE L'AIGUILLE
7,556

PLAN PRAZ
6,562

LES GRANDS MONTETS
10,745

MER DE GLACE

LUGE

MONTENVERS
6,276

CHAMONIX TOWN
3,399

LA FLEGERE
6,158

LAC BLANC

LES PRAZ
4,108

N

ARGENTIERE

ELEVATIONS IN FEET

❶ Grand Balcon Nord Hike
(2-3 Hrs One-Way, Moderate)

❷ Grand Balcon Sud Hike
(2-3 Hrs One-Way, Moderate)

❸ La Flégère to Lac Blanc Hike
(3 Hrs Round-Trip, Difficult)

❹ Petit Balcon Sud Hike
(2 Hrs One-Way, Easy-Moderate)

❺ Arve Riverbank Stroll
(1-2 Hr Loop, Easy)

The French Alps

and Joseph Vallot, is Chamonix's core. The TI is just above the pedestrian zone, and the train station is east of the river.

Tourist Information

Visit the TI to prepare your attack. Get the weather forecast, pick up the free town and valley map and the "panorama" map of all the valley lifts, and consider the €4 hiking map called *Carte des Sentiers* (see "Chamonix Area Hikes," page 623). Ask about hours of lifts (important), the *Multipass* lift pass (described under "Getting Around and Up and Down the Valley," page 615), biking information, and help with hotel reservations. Their helpful website has updated sightseeing info, weather forecasts, and more (July–Aug daily 8:30–19:00; Sept–June Mon–Sat 9:00–12:30 & 14:00–18:30, Sun 9:00–12:00; hours may vary—call ahead, free 24-hour Wi-Fi outside the TI, tel. 04 50 53 00 24, fax 04 50 53 58 90, www .chamonix.com).

Chamonix Quick History

1786 Jacques Balmat and Michel-Gabriel Paccard are the first to climb Mont Blanc (find the statue in Chamonix's pedestrian zone).

1818 First ascent of Aiguille du Midi.

1860 The Savoy region (including Chamonix) becomes part of France. After a visit by Napoleon III, the trickle of nature-loving visitors to Chamonix turns to a gush.

1901 Train service reaches Chamonix, unleashing its tourist appeal forever.

1908 The cogwheel train to Montenvers is completed.

1924 First Winter Olympics held in Chamonix.

1930 Le Brévent *téléphérique* (gondola lift) opens to tourists.

1955 Aiguille du Midi *téléphérique* opens to tourists.

2008 You visit Chamonix.

Grab a beachy sling chair outside the TI and plan a hike or check your email. Also outside is a huge map of the area's lifts—lights indicate which ones are operating. Check the Compagnie du Mont Blanc's website (www.compagniedumontblanc.com) for current lift information and to book the Aiguille du Midi lift.

For a quick mountain overview, leave the TI and walk between the church and the Office de la Haute Montagne. Climb the stone steps that lead over a road, then up more steps to a small park-like area (good picnic spot). Mont Dru, the dominant peak to the left, sits alone and towers above the Mer de Glace glacier. Burly, rounded Mont Blanc stands high to the right. The menacing glacier below seems to threaten Chamonix—but is actually in quick retreat.

Arrival in Chamonix

By Train: Walk straight out of the station (no baggage check available) and up avenue Michel Croz. In three blocks, you'll reach the town center; turn left at the big clock, then right for the TI.

By Bus: The long-distance bus station is at the train station (see "Transportation Connections," page 633).

By Car: For most of my recommended hotels and the TI, take the Chamonix Nord turnoff (second exit coming from Annecy). Most parking is metered and well-signed, though your hotel can direct you to free parking.

The Mont Blanc tunnel (7.2 miles long, about a 12-min drive) allows quick access between Chamonix and Italy (one-way-€32, round-trip-€40 with return valid for 1 week, €360 if you're driving a truck, www.tunnelmb.com).

By Plane: The nearest international airports are in Lyon (linked by 10 trains/day, 4 hrs; 3 hrs by car) and in Geneva, Switzerland (hourly trains, 3.5 hrs; 1.5 hrs by car).

Helpful Hints

Beat the Crowds: In high season, take the first lift to beat the crowds and afternoon clouds. Consider breakfast at "*le* top."

Be Prepared: Snow surrounds the high lifts, making the glare unbearable, so bring your sunglasses, along with plenty of batteries for those perfect alpine shots. For Chamonix's weather, check at the TI or at www.chamonix.com. For a five-day weather forecast in English, call 08 92 68 02 74 from anywhere in France for a small charge per minute.

Supermarkets: Little **Casino** markets are omnipresent in Chamonix, though the **Super U** market is big and central (Mon–Sat 8:15–19:30, Sun 8:30–12:00, rue Joseph Vallot).

Internet Access: The TI has free Wi-Fi and a good list of Internet cafés. **Le Bure@u** has American keyboards and is open long hours (daily 10:00–22:00, 7–13 quai du Vieux Moulin).

Laundry: Laverie Alpina (look for *Pressing* sign) is in the rear of Galerie Alpina shopping center. Marie-Paule will do your laundry for the cost of the washer and dryer (allow €9 for a load, leave a small tip, and fold your clothes yourself, Mon–Sat 8:00–18:00, no midday closing and open until 19:00 in summer, closed Sun, tel. 04 50 53 30 67). Another *laverie* is one block up from the Aiguille du Midi lift at 174 avenue de l'Aiguille du Midi (daily 9:00–20:00, instructions in English).

Car Rental: Avis and **Europcar** are both at the train station (Avis tel. 04 50 47 82 92, Europcar tel. 04 50 53 63 40).

Getting Around and Up and Down the Valley

Note that lifts and cogwheel trains are named for their highest destination (e.g., Aiguille du Midi, Montenvers, and Le Brévent).

By Lift: Gondolas *(téléphériques)* climb mountains all along the valley, but the best one leaves from Chamonix (see "Sights and Activities," next page). While sightseeing is optimal from the Aiguille du Midi gondola, there are more hiking options from the Le Brévent gondola.

The lift to Aiguille du Midi is open summer and winter (closures possible in May and late Oct–early Dec). The *télécabines* on the Panoramic Mont Blanc lift to Helbronner (Italy) run only from May to late September, and even then only in good weather (call the TI to confirm). Other area lifts are open from January to mid-April and from mid-June to late September.

If you're spending two or more days in the Chamonix valley, a *Multipass* saves time and money. It allows unlimited access to all the lifts and trains (except the Helbronner gondola to Italy), and includes all reservation fees (both Aiguille du Midi and Montenvers) and the elevator at the top of Aiguille du Midi. Best of all, it allows you to bypass lift-ticket lines after your first purchase (1 day-€46, 2 days-€62, 3 days-€71.50, 5 days-€87.50, available for up to 21 days; days are consecutive, though you can also buy a pass for nonconsecutive days; kids age 12–15 and adults over 60 pay about 15 percent less, kids age 4–11 pay 30 percent less, kids under 4 usually not allowed, www.compagniedumontblanc.com).

Families can benefit from reduced fares by asking for family tickets (2 adults and 2 children under 15).

By Foot: See "Chamonix Area Hikes" on page 623.

By Bike: The TI has a brochure showing bike-rental shops and the best biking routes. The peaceful river valley trail is ideal for bikes and pedestrians.

By Bus or Train: One road and one scenic rail line lace together the towns and lifts of the valley. Local buses run hourly off-season, and twice an hour in summer to valley villages (main stop is 200 yards to the right when you leave the TI, past Hôtel Mont Blanc, look for the bus shelters). Direction "Le Tour" takes you toward Les Praz (for Hike #2) and Switzerland; direction "Les Houches" takes you the opposite direction.

To help reduce traffic pollution in the valley, hotels distribute free Chamonix Guest Cards providing free travel on all Chamonix area buses (except the night bus) and the valley train between Serves and Vallorcine for the duration of your hotel stay. This is a great value for those with time to explore the valley. The train ride toward Martigny in Switzerland is gorgeous, and villages such as Les Praz and Tines (10 min by bus) offer quiet village escapes from busy Chamonix.

SIGHTS AND ACTIVITIES

▲▲▲**Aiguille du Midi**—This is easily the valley's (and arguably, Europe's) most spectacular and popular lift. If the weather's clear, the price doesn't matter. Pile into the *téléphérique* (gondola) and soar to the tip of a rock needle 12,600 feet above sea level. Chamonix shrinks as trees fly by, soon replaced by whizzing rocks, ice, and snow until you reach the top. No matter how sunny it is, it's cold. The air is thin. People are giddy. Fun things can happen at Aiguille du Midi (ay-gwee doo mee-dee) if you're not too winded to join the locals in the halfway-to-heaven tango.

Over the Alps—France to Italy

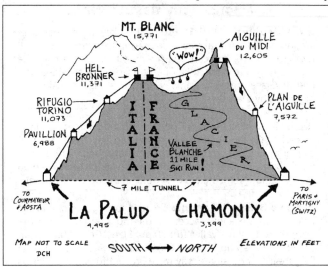

From the top of the lift station, you have several options. Follow *ascenseur* signs through a tunnel, then ride the elevator through the rock to the summit of this pinnacle (€3 in high season, free off-season). Missing the elevator is a kind of Alpus-Interruptus I'd rather not experience. The Alps spread out before you. In the distance and behind a broader mountain, you can see the bent little Matterhorn—the tall, shady pyramid listed in French on the observation table as "Cervin—4,505 meters" (14,775 feet). And looming just over there is **Mont Blanc,** the Alps' highest point at 4,810 meters (15,771 feet). Use the telescopes to spot mountain climbers; more than 2,000 scale this mountain each year. That rusty tin-can needle above you serves as a communication tower. Check the temperature next to the elevator. Plan on 32 degrees Fahrenheit, even on a sunny day. Sunglasses are essential.

Back down, explore Europe's tallest lift station. More than 150 yards of tunnels lead to a cafeteria (fair prices—have lunch or coffee with a view), toilets, gift shop, and an icicle-covered gateway to the glacial world. Follow *la Vallée Blanche* signs to an "ice tunnel" where skiers and mountain climbers make their exit. The views are sensational, and just observing is exhilarating. Peek down the icy cliff and ponder the value of an ice ax. Skiers make the 11-mile run from here to the Mer de Glace (described below) in about half a day (in winter they can ski 13 miles all the way back to the valley at Argentière).

Next, for your own private glacial dream world, get into the little red *télécabine* (called Panoramic Mont Blanc) and sail south

Chamonix Activities at a Glance

▲▲▲**Aiguille du Midi Gondola** The valley's most spectacular and popular lift takes you to magnificent views at 12,600 feet. From here, you can ride the cute télécabines over the Alps to Italy and back, take Chamonix's greatest hike to the Mer de Glace (from the halfway-up stop at Plan de l'Aiguille), or just enjoy the views.

▲▲**Train to Montenvers** Cogwheel train to la Mer de Glace, an eight-mile long glacier where you can walk inside the glacier, admire jagged mountain peaks, have lunch with a view (or sleep) at the Montenvers hotel, and hike to the Aiguille du Midi lift (though the hike is best done in the other direction).

▲▲▲**Le Brévent Gondola** Second most spectacular lift from Chamonix allows access to the mountain range on the opposite side of the valley from Mont Blanc. Get off halfway at the Plan Praz station for the Grand Balcon Sud hike to the La Flégère lift, or go all the way to Le Brévent for sky-high views and a restaurant.

▲▲▲**La Flégère Lift** Starting point for hikes to Lac Blanc and to the Grand Balcon Sud trail back to Plan Praz (on the Le Brévent Gondola). Refuge-Hôtel La Flégère is at the station, and offers drinks, snacks, and accommodations, all with a view.

Arve River Valley Stroll Several trails allow a level walk or bike ride in the woods between Chamonix and Les Praz. See paragliders make dramatic landings and enjoy mountain views outside Chamonix to the sound of the Arve River.

The French Alps

to **Helbronner Point,** the Italian border station. This line stretches three miles with no solid pylon. (It's propped by a "suspended pylon," a line stretched between two peaks 1,300 feet from the Italian end.) In a gondola for four, you'll dangle silently for 40 minutes as you glide over the glacier to Italy. Hang your head out the window; explore every corner of your view. From Helbronner Point, you can continue down into Italy (see "Day Trips—A Little Italy," page 627), but there's really no point unless you're traveling that way.

From Aiguille du Midi, you can ride all the way back to Chamonix, or better (if you like to hike and are wearing good shoes, or just want a break), get off halfway down at **Plan de l'Aiguille.** You'll find a small bar with outdoor tables at the lift station; paragliders jumping off cliffs; and a 15-minute walk below, the Plan de l'Aiguille refuge (snacks, drinks and views, see page 631). But the best reason to get off here is to follow the trail to the Mer de Glace. From Plan de l'Aiguille, walk 15 minutes down to the refuge, go right, and hike the spectacularly scenic, undulating, and at times quite strenuous two- to three-hour trail to Montenvers (overlooking the Mer de Glace glacier—described later). From here, you'll catch the train back into Chamonix (for all the hike details, see "Chamonix Area Hikes—Hike #1," on page 623). Don't hike all the way down to Chamonix from Plan de l'Aiguille or Montenvers–Mer de Glace; it's a long, steep walk through thick forests with few views.

Hours: Lift hours are weather- and crowd-dependent, but generally run daily July–Aug 6:00–16:30, late May–June and Sept 8:00–16:30, and Oct–late May 8:00–15:30. The last return from the Aiguille du Midi lift is generally one hour after the last ascent. The last *télécabine* departure to Helbronner Point is about 14:00–15:00, and the last train down from Montenvers is about 17:00–18:00.

Strategy: To beat the hordes and clouds, ride the Aiguille du Midi lift (up and down) as early as you can. To beat major delays in summer, leave no later than 7:00 or reserve ahead (first lift departs at about 6:00). If the weather has been bad and turns good, expect big crowds in any season (even worse on weekends). If it's clear, don't dillydally.

In peak season, smart travelers reserve the Aiguille du Midi lift in advance (€2 fee). You can reserve at the information booth next to the lift (open mid-June–mid-Sept), online at www .compagniedumontblanc.com, or by telephone (year-round, tel. 04 50 53 22 75, automated reservations in English). Reservations are taken up to 10 days in advance (six days in winter); pick them up at the lift station at least 30 minutes before departure. Reservations are free with a *Multipass* (see "Getting Around and Up and Down the Valley," above), and are not possible for the *télécabines* to Helbronner.

Costs: The following prices are for ages 16 and over; kids age 4–11 are 30 percent less and kids age 12–15 and adults over 60 are 15 percent less (family rates for 2 adults and 2 children under 15 are also available). From Chamonix to: Plan de l'Aiguille—round-trip-€19 (one-way-€17); Aiguille du Midi—round-trip-€38 (one-way-€35, not including parachute); the Panoramic Mont Blanc *télécabine* to Helbronner—round-trip-€54 (one-way-€45). If you are planning to stop at Plan de l'Aiguille on the way back down and hike to Montenvers, ask about a *"spécial randonée"* ticket for about €35.

Tickets just for the stretch from Aiguille du Midi to Helbronner are sold at both base and summit lift stations with no difference in price (round-trip-€18, one-way-€12). It's €25 to drop into Italy (sold at Helbronner, other currencies also accepted). *Oui* and *si,* you can bring your luggage.

Time to Allow: Chamonix to Aiguille du Midi—20 minutes one-way, two hours round-trip, three to four hours in peak season; Chamonix to Helbronner—90 minutes one-way, three to four hours round-trip, longer in peak season. On busy days, minimize delays by making a reservation for your return lift time upon arrival at the top. (For information on Aiguille du Midi, call 04 50 53 30 80.)

▲▲**Mer de Glace (Montenvers)**—From Gare de Montenvers (the little station over the tracks from Chamonix's main train station), the cute cogwheel Train du Montenvers toots you up to tiny Montenvers (mohn-tuh-vehr). There you'll see a dirty, rapidly receding glacier called the Mer de Glace (mayr duh glahs, "Sea of Ice"), and fantastic views up the white valley (Vallée Blanche) of splintered, snow-capped peaks (2–3/hr, 20 min, round-trip-€20, one-way-€17, family rates available, prices include gondola and ice caves entry, daily 8:30–17:00, July–Aug 8:00–18:00, confirm times with TI or call 04 50 53 12 54).

France's largest **glacier,** at eight miles long, is impressive from both above and below. Walk to the view deck. The glacier extends under the dirt about a half-mile downhill to the left. Imagine that it recently rose as high as the vegetation below (note the mounds of dirt—moraines—left in its retreat). In 1860, this glacier stretched all the way down to the valley floor. They say this fast-moving glacier is just doing its cycle thing, growing and shrinking—a thousand years ago, cows grazed on grassy fields here. Al Gore thinks differently.

Now look up to the peaks (find the orientation charts). Monsieur Dru's powerful spire dominates your view at about 11,700 feet. It was first scaled in 1860 (long before the train you took here was built) and was recently free-climbed (no ropes, belays, etc.); see the colored lines indicating different routes taken—one by an *Américain.* Those guys are nuts. The smooth snow field to the left of Dru's spire (Les Grands Montets) is the top of Chamonix's most challenging ski run, with a vertical drop of about 6,500 feet. The glacier's **ice caves** are below (take the small gondola down and prepare to walk 280 steps each way). If you've already seen a glacier up close, you might skip this one, though I found it a relevant trip given the attention being paid to global warming (*le rechauffement climatique*)—the speed of melting is impressive. This is also where skiers end their run from the Aiguille du Midi (you might recognize someone if you rode that lift earlier).

Walking left to **Hôtel le Montenvers** leads to a full-service restaurant, view tables (fair prices, limited selection), and a cozy interior (for information on sleeping here, see page 631). The hotel was built in 1880, when "tourists" arrived on foot or by mule. The three-hour trail to Plan de l'Aiguille begins from above the hotel. For terrific views, hike toward Plan de l'Aiguille—via the trail that veers left—even just a short distance. The views get better the higher you climb (follow signs on the stone building opposite the hotel; you want *sentier gauche* to *Signal Montenvers*). Bring a picnic and join the locals.

▲**Luge (Luge d'Eté)**—Here's something for thrill-seekers—ride a chairlift up the mountain and then scream down a twisty, banked, concrete slalom course on a wheeled sled. Chamonix has two roughly parallel luge courses. While each course is just longer than a half mile and about the same speed, one is marked for slower sledders and the other for speed demons. Young or old, hare or tortoise, any fit person can manage a luge. *Freinez* signs tell you when to brake. Don't take your hands off your stick; the course is fast and slippery. The luge courses are set in a grassy park with kids' play areas—see under "Kid Activities," below (1 hour of "unlimited" runs—figure you'll get three-€12.50, 1.5 hours-€15, 1 ride-€5, 6 rides-€25, 12 rides-€42, rides can be split with companions and tickets are good for a month; daily early July–late Aug 10:00–19:30, Thu until 22:00; daily mid-June–early July and late Aug–mid-Sept 13:30–18:00; otherwise weekend and holiday afternoons only, call for spring and fall hours, covered with snow in winter, 15-min walk from town center over the tracks from train station, follow signs to Planards, tel. 04 50 53 08 97).

▲▲▲**Paragliding (Parapente)**—When it's sunny and clear, the skies above Chamonix sparkle with colorful parachute-like sails that circle the valley like birds of prey. For €90, launch yourself off a mountain in a tandem paraglider with a trained, experienced pilot and fly like a bird for about 20 minutes. Try **Summits Parapente** (smart to reserve a day ahead, open year-round, tel. 04 50 53 50 14, mobile 06 84 01 26 00, fax 04 50 55 94 16, across from Galerie Alpina at 27 allée du Savoy, www.summits.fr/parapente_chamonix).

For a sneak preview, walk to the main landing area and watch paragliders perfect their landings (see "Chamonix Area Hikes—Hike #5," below).

▲▲▲**Gondola Lifts (Téléphériques) to Le Brévent and La Flégère**—While Aiguille du Midi gives a more spectacular ride, the Le Brévent and La Flégère lifts offer different hiking and viewing options with unobstructed panoramas across to the Mont Blanc range. Le Brévent (luh bray-vahn) lift is in Chamonix; La Flégère (lah flay-zhair) lift is in nearby Les Praz (lay prah). The lifts are connected by a scenic hike or by bus along the valley floor (free with Chamonix Guest Card, see "Chamonix Area Hikes—Hike

Kid Activities

Chamonix provides a wealth of fun opportunities for kids—consider these options.

Parc de Loisirs des Planards Chamonix's most ambitious activities for kids of all ages, including a luge (summer only—see preceding page), and a Parc d'Aventure with tree courses, Tarzan swings, trampolines, electric motorbikes, jet skis, and more (Parc d'Aventure-€23, under 18-€19, daily mid-June–mid-Sept, 13:30–18:00, early July–Aug 10:00–19:30, May–mid-June and mid-Sept–Oct generally weekends only, 13:30–18:00; 15-min walk from town center, over the tracks from train station and past Montenvers train station, tel. 04 50 53 08 97, www.planards.com).

Le Paradis des Praz Pleasant activity park ideal for 4–10 year olds with pony rides, zip-wire rides, and more. It's in the small village of Les Praz, by the lift to Flégère (daily mid-June–mid-Sept, otherwise Wed and weekend afternoons, www.paradis-des-praz.com). Rent a bike in Chamonix and ride along the level Arve River trail to reach this park, or take the free bus (see "Getting Around and Up and Down the Valley," page 616).

Parc de Merlet Animal sanctuary with trails that let you discover mountain animals (marmots, mountain goats, llamas, deer, and more). It's located in Coupeau above Les Houches, and offers exceptional views. You can get there by car or a two-hour hike (€5, ages 4–12-€3, daily May–Sept 10:00–18:00, July–Aug until 19:30, tel. 04 50 53 47 89, www.parcdemerlet.com).

Maison de la Montagne Daily or weekly outdoor programs for kids (rafting, hiking, mountain biking, etc.) allow parents time alone in the mountains (ages 8–12-€67/day, ages 13–17-€90/day, tel. 04 50 53 00 88 or 04 50 53 55 70).

#2," page 625); both have sensational view cafés for nonhikers.

Le Brévent lift is a steep, 10-minute walk up the road above Chamonix's TI. This *téléphérique* stops halfway up at Planpraz station (round-trip-about €12, one-way-€10, nice restaurant, great views and hiking) and continues to Le Brévent station at the top with more views and hikes, though Planpraz offers plenty for me (round-trip-€22, one-way from Chamonix-€17, daily 9:00–16:00, July–Aug 8:00–17:00, last return from Planpraz 1 hour after last ascent, closed late April–mid-June and Oct, tel. 04 50 53 13 18).

La Flégère lift runs from the neighboring village of Les Praz, with just one stop at La Flégère station (round-trip-€12, one-way-€10, daily 8:40–16:00, summer 7:40–17:00, last return from La Flégère 50 min after last ascent, closed late April–mid-June and mid-Sept–Oct, tel. 04 50 53 18 58). Hikes to Planpraz and Lac Blanc leave from the top of this station (see below).

Chamonix Area Hikes

Your first stop should be at the full-service **Maison de la Montagne,** across from the TI. On the third floor, the **Office of the High Mountain** (Office de Haute-Montagne) can help you plan your hikes and tell you about trail and snow conditions (daily 9:00–12:00 & 15:00–18:00, tel. 04 50 53 22 08, www.ohm -chamonix.com). The staff speaks enough English, has vital weather reports and maps, and some English hiking guidebooks (you can photocopy key pages). Ask to look at the trail guidebook (sold in many stores, includes the extremely helpful €4 *Carte des Sentiers,* the region's hiking map—also sold at the TI). You can also use the handy restroom here on the second floor.

At **Compagnie des Guides de Chamonix** on the ground floor, you can hire a guide to take you hiking for the day (€290), help you scale Mont Blanc, or hike to the Matterhorn and Zermatt (€780 for the 2-day climb up Mont Blanc, daily 9:00–12:00 & 15:30–19:00, closed Sun–Mon off-season, tel. 04 50 53 00 88, fax 04 50 53 48 04, www.chamonix-guides.com).

I've described three big hikes (Hikes #1, #2, and #3) and two easier walks (Hikes #4 and #5) below; see the map on page 624. These hikes give nature-lovers of any ability good options for enjoying the valley in most seasons. Start early, when the weather's generally best. This is critical in summer; if you don't get to the lifts by 8:30, you'll meet a conveyor belt of hikers. If starting later or walking longer, confirm lift closing hours, or prepare for a long, steep hike down.

For your hike, pack sunglasses, sunscreen, rain gear, water, and snacks. Wear warm clothes and good shoes. Trails are rocky and uneven. Take your time, watch your footing, don't take short-cuts, and say *"Bonjour!"* to your fellow hikers.

▲▲▲**Hike #1: Plan de l'Aiguille to Montenvers–Mer de Glace (Grand Balcon Nord)**—This is the most efficient way to incorporate a two- to three-hour high-country hike into your ride down from the valley's greatest lift, and check out a big-league glacier to boot. The well-used trail rises but mostly falls (dropping 1,500 feet from **Plan de l'Aiguille to Montenvers–Mer de Glace**) and is moderately difficult, provided the snow is melted (generally covered by snow until June; get trail details at the Office of the High Mountain, above). Some stretches are steep and strenuous, with uneven footing and slippery rocks. From the Aiguille du Midi lift, get off halfway down at Plan de l'Aiguille and follow signs to the unmarked wooden refuge (reasonable food and drinks, closed off-season). From there, take a right and follow *Montenvers*

Chamonix Area Hikes and Lifts

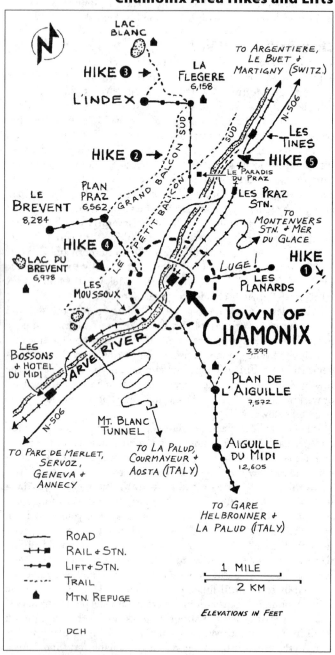

LAC BLANC

TO ARGENTIERE, LE BUET + MARTIGNY (SWITZ.)

HIKE ❸

LA FLEGERE 6,158

L'INDEX

N-506

LES TINES

HIKE ❷

HIKE ❺

GRAND BALCON SUD

BALCON SUD

Le PARADIS DU PRAZ

PLAN PRAZ 6,562

LES PRAZ STN.

LE BREVENT 8,284

PETIT BALCON

TO MONTENVERS STN. + MER DU GLACE

HIKE ❹

LAC DU BREVENT 6,978

LUGE!

HIKE ❶

LES MOUSSOUX

LES PLANARDS

TOWN OF CHAMONIX 3,399

LES BOSSONS + HOTEL DU MIDI

ARVE RIVER

N-506

PLAN DE L'AIGUILLE 7,572

MT. BLANC TUNNEL

TO PARC DE MERLET, SERVOZ, GENEVA + ANNECY

TO LA PALUD, COURMAYEUR + AOSTA (ITALY)

AIGUILLE DU MIDI 12,605

TO GARE HELBRONNER + LA PALUD (ITALY)

ROAD

RAIL + STN.

LIFT + STN.

TRAIL

MTN. REFUGE

1 MILE

2 KM

ELEVATIONS IN FEET

DCH

signs for about an hour. If you don't see signs, ask for the way to Montenvers: *"Quelle direction pour Montenvers?"* (kell dee-reck-shown poor mohn-ton-vare). When the trail splits, follow signs up the steep trail to Signal Montenvers (more scenic and easier), rather than to the left toward Montenvers (it may look easier at first, but it becomes difficult). At this point, you'll grind it out up and up to the best views of the trail. It's a long, steep, and memorable drop to Montenvers and the Mer de Glace (described on page 620). In Montenvers, take the train back to Chamonix. Don't walk the rest of the trail down from Montenvers (long, steep, disappointing views).

▲▲Hike #2: La Flégère to Planpraz (Grand Balcon Sud)—This glorious hike undulates above Chamonix Valley with staggering views of Mont Blanc and countless other peaks, glaciers, and wild-flowers. There's just 370 feet of difference in elevation between La Flégère and Planpraz lift stations—so this hike, while not without its ups and downs, is relatively easy, but still requires serious stamina. You can do it in either direction, but I prefer starting at La Flégère, which is how I've described the hike.

From Chamonix, drive five minutes, walk 40 minutes along the Arve River (see Hike #5, below), or take the Chamonix bus (every 30–60 min, 10-min ride, free with Chamonix Guest Card) to the tiny village of Les Praz and its La Flégère lift station. Ride the lift up to La Flégère (€10) and walk down to the Refuge-Hôtel La Flégère. Find the signs to *Planpraz* (you don't want Les Praz–Chamonix—that's straight down), then hike the rolling Grand Balcon Sud to Planpraz station, the midway stop on the Le Brévent lift line (allow 2.5 hours). Take the Planpraz lift down to Chamonix (€10) and skip the steep hike down. Ask for the round-trip rate allowed with La Flégère and Planpraz (Le Brévent) lifts, available at either lift (saves €6).

▲▲Hike #3: La Flégère to Lac Blanc—This is the most demanding hiking trail of those I list; it climbs steeply and steadily over a rough, boulder-strewn trail for 90 minutes to snowy Lac Blanc (pronounced "lock blah"). Some footing is tricky and good shoes or boots are essential. I like this trail, as it gets you away from the valley edge and opens views to peaks you don't see from other hikes. The destination is a frigid, snow-white lake surrounded by peaks and a nifty chalet-refuge offering good lunches (and dinners with accommodations). The views on the return trip are breathtaking. Check for snow conditions on the trail and go early (particularly in summer), as there is no shade and this trail is popular. Follow directions from Hike #2 to La Flégère station (above), then walk out the station's rear door past the orientation table and view area, and follow signs to *Lac Blanc*. The trail is well-signed and improves in surface quality as you climb. While you can eliminate a good portion of the uphill hiking by riding the lift up to L'Index from La Flégère, beware: the trail from L'Index can require serious skill and equipment because of snow; ask before you go on.

▲**Hike #4: Petit Balcon Sud**—This trail runs above the valley on the Brévent side from the village of Servoz to Argentiere, passing Chamonix about halfway, and is handy when snow or poor weather make other hikes problematic. No lifts are required—just firm thighs to climb up to and down from the trail. Access paths link villages below. Once you're up, the trail rises and falls with some steep segments and uneven footing, but is generally easy to walk. To reach the trail from Chamonix, walk up to Le Brévent lift station, then follow the asphalt road to the left of the lift leading uphill; it turns into a dirt road that signs mark as the *Petit Balcon Sud* trail. After about 20 minutes on the dirt road, a sign for the *Petit Balcon Sud* points left and up a smaller trail. This segment of the hike doubles back above Chamonix, taking you toward Servoz (keep following *Petit Balcon Sud*). Go as far as you like, taking any trail down (signed to the village below). For an easier hike to **Les Praz** (where you can take the Arve River trail back to Chamonix), bypass this Petit Balcon turnoff and stay on the dirt road. After about 30 minutes, follow *la Floria* signs right and join the Petit Balcon Sud trail, then find *Les Praz* signs to get down the hill (a worthwhile 20-min round-trip detour leads to **La Floria chalet,** which has drinks, snacks, tables, flowers and views, open mid-June–late Sept; at about the same junction, you'll see a shortcut back to Chamonix through the woods). Continuing to Les Praz, when you reach the asphalt road below, turn left to explore the village and to connect with the river trail back to Chamonix (turn right immediately after the bridge), or turn right for the bus stop back to Chamonix (figure it takes the bus 20 min to reach Les Praz from the time point posted in Le Tour).

Hike #5: Arve Riverbank Stroll and Paragliding Landing Field—For a level, forested-valley stroll, follow the Arve River toward Les Praz. Find Chamonix's Hôtel Alpina, then follow the path upstream past red-clay tennis courts and find the green arrow to *Les Praz*. Cross two bridges to the left and turn right along the rushing Arve River, and then follow Promenade des Econtres. Several trails loop through these woods; if you continue walking straight, you'll reach Les Praz—a pleasant destination with several cafés and a pleasing village green. If you keep right after the tennis courts (passing the piles of river sediment excavated to keep the river from flooding), you'll come to a grassy landing field, signed *Parapente*, where paragliders hope to touch down. Walk to the top of the little grassy hill for fine Mont Blanc views and a great picnic spot. The recommended Micro Brasserie de Chamonix is nearby (see "Eating," page 633).

The French Alps

Rainy Day Activities

If the weather disagrees with your plans, stay cool and check out the options below, which are both included in one €5 ticket. Although neither offers a word of English, the exhibits are fairly straightforward.

Alpine Museum (Musée Alpin)—Situated in one of Chamonix's oldest "palaces," this place has good exhibits about Chamonix's evolution from a farming area to one focused on skiing. The museum shows off Chamonix's mountaineering, skiing, and mineralogical history (explanations in French only) and has exhibits on the first Winter Olympics held right here (€5, includes Espace Tairraz, daily, 15:00–19:00, 89 avenue Michel Croz).

Espace Tairraz—This fascinating collection features crystals from the region in every color, shape, and size (€5, includes Alpine Museum, daily 14:00–19:00).

DAY TRIPS

A Day in French-Speaking Switzerland—Plenty of tempting alpine and cultural thrills await just an hour or two away in Switzerland. A road-and-train line sneaks you scenically from Chamonix to the Swiss town of Martigny. While train travelers cross without formalities, drivers are charged a one-time fee of 40 Swiss francs (€30) for a permit to use Swiss autobahns (valid for one calendar year).

A Little Italy—The remote Valle d'Aosta and its historic capital city of Aosta are a spectacular gondola ride over the Mont Blanc range. The side-trip is worthwhile if you'd like to taste Italy (spaghetti, gelato, and cappuccino), enjoy the town's great evening ambience, or view the ancient ruins in Aosta (often called the "Rome of the North").

Take the spectacular lift (Aiguille du Midi–Helbronner) to Italy, described on page 617. From Helbronner, catch the lift down to La Palud and take the bus to Aosta (hourly, change in Courmayeur). Aosta's train station has connections to anywhere in Italy (usually on slow trains via Turin, about every 2 hours).

For a more down-to-earth experience, you can take the bus from Chamonix to Aosta (about €10, reservation required, 5/day July–mid-Sept, 2/day mid-Sept–June). Get schedules at Chamonix's bus station (located at train station, tel. 04 50 53 01 15). For buses using the Mont Blanc tunnel, it's a two-hour trip to Aosta (otherwise it's three hours via Martigny). Drivers can simply drive through the Mont Blanc tunnel (round-trip-€40, one-way-€32, www.tunnelmb.com).

SLEEPING

(€1 = about $1.30, country code: 33)

Reasonable hotels and dorm-like chalets abound in Chamonix with easy parking and quick access from the train station. With the helpful TI, you can find budget accommodations anytime. Outside winter, mid-July to mid-August is most difficult, when some hotels have five-day minimum-stay requirements. Prices tumble off-season (outside July–Aug and Dec–Jan). Many hotels and restaurants are closed in April, June, and November, but you'll still find a room and a meal. If you want a view of Mont Blanc, ask for *côté Mont Blanc* (coat-ay mohn blah). Summertime travelers should seriously consider a night high above in a refuge-hotel.

All hoteliers speak English. Price ranges usually reflect low-to-high season rates. Ask at your hotel about the Chamonix Guest Card, which provides free use of most buses and trains during your stay (see "Getting Around and Up and Down the Valley," page 616). The TI can help you book a room—either in person or by email (reservation@chamonix.com).

Hotels in the City Center

$$$ Hôtel Gourmets et Italy*** is run by quiet Erique and effer-vescent Christine, and is a sharp, 40-room place with cozy public spaces, a cool riverfront terrace, balcony views from many of its appealing rooms, and a small pool (standard Db with shower-€75–95, larger Db with bath and Mont Blanc view-€90–120, extra person-€16, closed late April–early June, 2 blocks from casino on Mont Blanc side of river, 96 rue du Lyret, tel. 04 50 53 01 38, fax 04 50 53 46 74, www.hotelgourmets-chamonix.com, hgicham @aol.com).

$$$ Hôtel Richemond** is a grand place with a retirement-home feel in its faded-alpine-elegant public spaces. The same family has run this hotel since it was built in 1914, and the rooms are traditional, comfortable, and generally spacious, with period furniture. There's also an outdoor terrace and a game room with a pool table, "flipper" (pinball), and table tennis (Sb-€60–68, Db-€90–106, Tb-€110–135, Qb-€127–150, includes good buffet break-fast, free parking, 228 rue du Docteur Paccard, tel. 04 50 53 08 85, fax 04 50 55 91 69, www.richemond.fr, richemond@wanadoo.fr, Claire and brother Bruno love meeting Americans).

$$$ Hôtel l'Oustalet*** is a modern chalet hotel that makes me feel like I'm in Austria. It's warmly run by two sisters who understand the importance of good service. The place is family friendly with lots of grass, a pool, and six family suites. All rooms are sharp with wood paneling, views, and balconies (Sb-€75–114, Db-€105–120, Qb family rooms-€150–195, easy parking, near

Chamonix Town

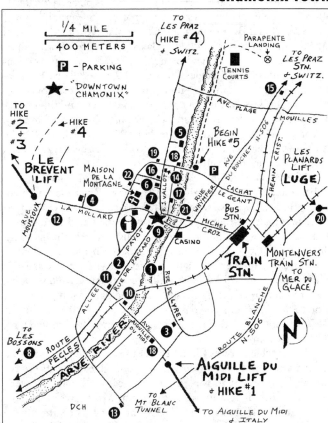

1. Hôtel Gourmets et Italy
2. Hôtel Richemond
3. Hôtel l'Oustalet
4. Chalet Beauregard
5. Hôtel de l'Arve
6. Hôtel les Crêtes Blanches
7. Hôtel le Chamonix
8. To Hôtel l'Aiguille du Midi
9. La Calèche & Midnight Express Rest.
10. Le Boccalatte Brasserie
11. Le Bivouac & Le Panier des 4 Saisons
12. La Cabolée Restaurant
13. L'Impossible Restaurant
14. Café des Sports
15. Micro Brasserie de Chamonix (MBC)
16. Super U Grocery
17. Internet Café
18. Launderettes (2)
19. Summits Parapente (Paragliding)
20. Parc de Loisirs des Planards
21. Alpine Museum
22. Espace Tairraz (Crystals)

Aiguille du Midi lift at 330 rue du Lyret, tel. 04 50 55 54 99, fax 04 50 55 54 98, www.hotel-oustalet.com, infos@hotel-oustalet.com).

$$$ **Chalet Beauregard,** an upscale *chambre d'hôte*, is a short but steep walk above the TI. It's relaxed and peaceful, with a private garden, table tennis, and swings. Five of its seven cushy rooms have balconies with great views (Sb-€49–89, Db-€69–99, Tb-€89–129, ask about amazing top-floor suite-€135–195, cash only—or personal checks in US dollars, may require 4-night minimum stay in summer, includes breakfast, free parking, often closed in May, on road to Le Brévent lift, 182 rue de La Mollard, tel. 04 50 55 86 30, www.chalet-beauregard.com, infos@chalet-beauregard.com, friendly Manuel and Laurence).

$$ **Hôtel de l'Arve**** has a contemporary alpine feel, with 37 comfortable rooms, some right on the Arve River looking up at Mont Blanc. Owners Isabelle and Beatrice, wood accents, fireplace lounge, pool room, pleasant garden, sauna, climbing wall, and easy parking add to the appeal. When available, the half-pension option is a good value at €20 extra per person for a buffet breakfast and simple four-course dinner; let them know ahead if you want it (standard Db-€58–85, larger or view Db-€66–99, big view room-€76–118, extra person-€13, free parking, behind huge Hôtel Alpina, 60 impasse des Anémones, tel. 04 50 53 02 31, fax 04 50 53 56 92, www.hotelarve-chamonix.com, contact@hotelarve-chamonix.com).

$$ **Hôtel les Crêtes Blanches**** is a sweet little place wrapped around a peaceful courtyard (with outdoor tables) just off the rue Joseph Vallot (next to the Super U grocery). Rooms are well-designed with appealing wood paneling. Most have small balconies and all come with views of Mont Blanc. A ceramic wood stove and soft couches anchor the comfy lounge area (Db-€53–85, Tb-€74–110, Qb-€86–130, 16 impasse du Génépy, tel. 04 50 53 05 62, fax 04 50 53 67 25, www.cretes-blanches.com, cretes-blanches@wanadoo.fr).

$$ **Hôtel le Chamonix****, centrally located across from the TI and above a café, offers red carpets and wood paneling with 16 good-value rooms, but no elevator. The rooms facing Mont Blanc have great views are larger and brighter, and have little balconies... but also attracts noise from *le café* below, which closes at 20:00 (standard Db-€52–76, standard Db with Mont Blanc view-€58–86, Tb-€72–96, Qb-€86–110, no elevator, 11 rue de l'Hôtel de Ville, tel. 04 50 53 11 07, fax 04 50 53 64 78, www.hotel-le-chamonix.com, hotel-le-chamonix@wanadoo.fr).

Near Chamonix

If Chamonix overwhelms you, spend the night in one of the valley's overlooked, lower-profile villages.

$$ Hôtel l'Aiguille du Midi** lies in the village of Les Bossons, about two miles from Chamonix toward Annecy. Self-assured English-speaking Martine Farini runs this mountain retreat in a park-like setting, with a swimming pool, tennis court, whirlpool tub, table tennis, and a laundry room to boot. The alpine-comfortable rooms aren't big...and you won't care. The pricey, classy restaurant offers good à la carte options, and a required half-pension in summer (Db-€70–82, Tb-€99, Qb-€118, elevator, €20–45 *menu* or à la carte, easy by train, get off at Les Bossons, tel. 04 50 53 00 65, fax 04 50 55 93 69, www.hotel-aiguilledumidi.com, hotel-aiguille-du-midi@wanadoo.fr).

Refuges and Refuge-Hotels near Chamonix

Chamonix has the answer for hikers who want to sleep high above, but aren't into packing it all in: refuge-hotels (generally open mid-June to mid- or late September, depending on snow levels). Refuge-hotels usually have some private rooms (and dorm rooms), hot showers down the hall, and restaurants. Reserve in advance (a few days are generally enough), then pack your small bag for a memorable night among new international friends. The **Office of the High Mountain** in Chamonix can explain your options (see "Chamonix Area Hikes," page 623).

$$ Refuge-Hôtel Montenvers, Chamonix's oldest refuge, is a cool experience at the Montenvers train stop. It was built in 1880 as a climbing base for mountain guides before the train went there, so materials had to be gathered from nearby. The five simple wood-cozy rooms and dining room feel as though they haven't been modified since then (half-pension in a double room about €50 per person, €38 per person in dorm room, good showers down the hall, tel. 04 50 53 87 70, fax 04 50 55 38 55, restauration.montenvers @compagniedumontblanc.fr). For directions, see "Chamonix Area Hikes—Hike #1," page 623.

$ Refuge-Hôtel La Flégère hangs on the edge and is also at the lift station. It's simple, but ideally located for hiking to Lac Blanc or Planpraz (3 private rooms with 5 beds, many dorm beds, half-pension-€40 per person, fireplace, cozy bar-café, right at La Flégère lift, tel. 06 03 58 28 14). For directions, see "Chamonix Area Hikes—Hike #2," page 625.

EATING

You have two basic dining options in Chamonix—cozy, traditional *savoyarde* restaurants serving fondue, raclette, and the like, or big cafés in central locations serving a wide variety of dishes (including regional specialties) that allow you to watch rivers of hikers return from a full day in the mountains. Prices are roughly the same—you choose. If it's a beautiful day, take an outdoor table at a central café; if you're dining inside, go local and consider these places (most are closed between lunch and dinner).

In the Town Center

La Calèche presents delectable regional dishes in a warm, hyper-decorated alpine setting. You'll dine amid antique dolls, cuckoo clocks, copper pots, animal trophies, and more. Servers sport traditional outfits to complete the picture. It's centrally located just off place Balmat (€23 *menu*, the €28 *menu* is much better, open daily, 18 rue du Docteur Paccard, tel. 04 50 55 94 68). Don't leave without a visit to the WCs.

Le Boccalatte Brasserie serves a simple but good-value lunch or dinner with a pleasing atmosphere, a few blocks above the Aiguille du Midi lift. The place is family-friendly with a playful waitstaff. Choose the €14 or €17 *menus* or from a large selection of local specialties, large €9 salads, and 20 kinds of beer. It's run by English-speaking Thierry, a friendly Alsatian (daily 12:00–22:00, 59 avenue de l'Aiguille du Midi, tel. 04 50 53 52 14).

Le Bivouac is an unassuming, shoebox-size place where you'll eat cheaply and well in an informal setting. It's a family affair run by gregarious owner-chef Jean-Guy (who should sing opera), along with son Chris and sweet Cloé. Salads are a meal in themselves, and the *plats* are tasty—ask *le chef*'s opinion—he likes his souvlaki and *roulée savoyarde* (266 rue Docteur Paccard, tel. 04 50 53 34 08).

Le Panier des 4 Saisons is where locals go for traditional French (not local) cuisine like Grand-mère used to make. The place is charmingly elegant, and deserves its good reputation (*menus* from €24, closed Wed, in Galerie Blanc Neige at 266 rue Docteur Paccard, tel. & fax 04 50 53 98 77).

Sandwiches: **Midnight Express** serves fine sandwiches until late and has a few outside tables across from the recommended La Calèche restaurant. Try a *pain rond-rustique* (round-bread rustic sandwich), served hot *(chaud)* or cold *(froid).*

Away from the Pedestrian Center

These eateries, each a 10-minute walk from Chamonix's center, merit the detour if they strike your fancy.

La Cabolée, next to La Brévent station, is a small, hip eatery with great omelets and a wonderful view from its outdoor tables. This is a Slow Food place—everything is cooked fresh—so be patient if the restaurant is full and the service feels slow (daily 10:00–14:00 & 18:00–22:00, may be closed mid-May–mid-June and Nov, tel. 04 50 55 97 28).

L'Impossible, housed in a beautiful 150-year-old farmhouse, mixes alpine coziness with soft elegance, and is a fine bet for traditional alpine cuisine (*menus* from €22, €18 gourmet fondue, open daily, 5-min walk from Aiguille du Midi lift on route des Pélerins, tel. 04 50 53 20 36).

Aprés Hike: The **Café des Sports** is where locals hang their ice picks after a hard day in the mountains. Drinks are cheap, the crowd is loud, and the ambience works (daily until late, 176 rue Joseph Vallot). **Micro Brasserie de Chamonix,** a knock-off of the microbrew pubs back home, is a cool place to hang out after a day of paragliding or rappelling. It's not central, across from the *parapente* landing strip (see "Chamonix Area Hikes—Hike #5," page 626), but it's reasonable and lively. Come here for a homemade brew, a glass of wine, or a pub dinner, and expect crowds of twenty- and thirtysomethings (daily 16:00–1:00 in the morning, 350 route du Bouchet, look for *MBC* sign, tel. 04 50 53 61 59).

TRANSPORTATION CONNECTIONS

Bus and train service to Chamonix is surprisingly good. You'll find helpful bus and train information desks at the train station. Some train routes pass through Switzerland to reach Chamonix (such as from Paris and Colmar) and require a supplement if you have a France-only railpass. You can avoid passing through Switzerland if you plan ahead.

From Chamonix by Train to: Annecy (8/day, 2.5 hrs, change in St. Gervais), **Beaune** and **Dijon** (7/day, 6–7 hrs, changes in St. Gervais and Lyon), **Nice** (4/day, 10 hrs, change in St. Gervais and Lyon), **Arles** (5/day, 7–8 hrs, change in St. Gervais and Lyon), **Paris'** Gare de Lyon (8/day, 6–8 hrs, some change in Switzerland, handy night train with one change in nearby St. Gervais), **Martigny, Switzerland** (nearly hourly, 2 hrs, scenic trip), **Geneva, Switzerland** and its airport (roughly hourly, 3–4 hrs, two changes).

From Chamonix by Bus to: Geneva, Switzerland city center and airport (3/day, 2 hrs), **Courmayeur** via Mont Blanc tunnel with connections to Aosta and Milan (2/day, 45 min). Long-distance buses depart from the train station, not from local bus stops. Get information at the TI or at the bus station (tel. 04 50 78 05 33).

To Italy: See "Day Trips—A Little Italy," page 627.

BURGUNDY

The rolling hills of Burgundy gave birth to superior wine, fine cuisine, and a sublime countryside. This deceptively peaceful region witnessed Julius Caesar's defeat of the Gauls, then saw the Abbey of Cluny rise from the ashes of the Roman Empire to vie with Rome for religious influence in the 12th century. Burgundy's last hurrah came in the 15th century, when its powerful dukes controlled an immense area stretching north to Holland. Today, bucolic Burgundy runs from about Auxerre in the north to near Lyon in the south, and it's crisscrossed with canals and dotted with quiet farming villages. It's also the transportation funnel for eastern France and makes a convenient stopover for travelers (car or train), with quick access north to Paris or Alsace, east to the Alps, and south to Provence.

Only a small part of Burgundy is covered by vineyards, but grapes are what they do best. The white cows you see everywhere are Charolais. France's best beef ends up in *bœuf bourguignon*.

Planning Your Time

With limited time, stay in or near Beaune. It's conveniently located for touring; plan on a half-day in Beaune and a half-day for the vineyards and countryside. With a full day, spend the morning in Beaune and the afternoon exploring the surrounding vineyards and wine villages (good by bike, car, or minibus tour). If you have a car (cheap rentals are available), or strong legs and a bike, the best way to spend your afternoon is by following my scenic vineyard drive to La Rochepot (see page 657).

To explore off-the-beaten-path Burgundy, visit unspoiled Semur-en-Auxois and France's best-preserved medieval abbey complex at Fontenay (they're on the way to Paris, or doable as a long day trip from Beaune). The magnificent church at Vézelay is harder to reach, and is best done as a day-trip from Semur-en-Auxois, or en route to Paris or the Loire Valley. If you're connecting Burgundy with the Loire, don't miss the medieval castle construction at Guédelon. And if you're driving between Beaune and Lyon (see next chapter), take the detour to adorable Brancion and once-powerful Cluny.

Getting Around Burgundy

Trains link Beaune with Dijon to the north and Lyon to the south. Ten buses per day cruise between vineyards on N-74, linking Dijon, Beaune, and Chalon-sur-Saône (the bus detours into some wine villages, and serves others from N-74—see page 655). Bikes, minibus tours, and short taxi rides get nondrivers from Beaune into the countryside. Buses connect Semur-en-Auxois with the Dijon and Montbard train stations.

Cuisine Scene in Burgundy

Arrive hungry. Considered by many to be France's best, Burgundian cuisine is peasant cooking elevated to an art, and entire lives are spent debating the best restaurants and bistros.

Several classic dishes were born in Burgundy: *escargots bourguignon* (snails served sizzling hot in garlic butter), *bœuf bourguignon* (beef simmered for hours in red wine with onions and mushrooms), *coq au vin* (chicken stewed in red wine), and *œufs en meurette* (poached eggs on a large crouton in red wine), as well as the famous Dijon mustards. Look also for *jambon persillé* (cold ham layered in a garlic-parsley gelatin), *pain d'épices* (spice bread), and *gougère* (light, puffy cheese pastries). Native cheeses are Époisses and Langres (both mushy and great) and my favorite, Montrachet (a tasty goat cheese). *Crème de cassis* (black currant liqueur) is another Burgundian specialty; look for it in desserts and snazzy drinks (try a *kir*).

Remember, restaurants serve only during lunch (11:30–14:00) and dinner (19:00–21:00, later in bigger cities); some cafés serve food throughout the day.

Burgundy's Wines

Along with Bordeaux, Burgundy is why France is famous for wine. From Chablis to Beaujolais, you'll find it all here: great fruity reds, dry whites, and crisp rosés. The three key grapes are Chardonnay

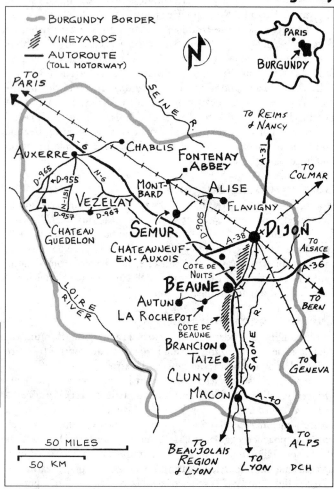

Burgundy

- BURGUNDY BORDER
- VINEYARDS
- AUTOROUTE (TOLL MOTORWAY)

PARIS
BURGUNDY

N

TO PARIS

SEINE R.

TO REIMS & NANCY

A-6

CHABLIS

FONTENAY ABBEY

AUXERRE

D-965 ←D-955 N-6

N-151

VEZELAY

D-957 D-967

CHATEAU GUEDELON

MONT-BARD

ALISE

FLAVIGNY

D-905

SEMUR

CHATEAUNEUF-EN-AUXOIS

COTE DE NUITS

A-38

DIJON

TO COLMAR

A-31

TO ALSACE

A-36

LOIRE RIVER

BEAUNE

AUTUN

LA ROCHEPOT

COTE DE BEAUNE

BRANCION

TAIZE

CLUNY

MACON

SAONE R.

TO BERN

TO GENEVA

A-40

TO ALPS

50 MILES

50 KM

TO BEAUJOLAIS REGION & LYON

TO LYON

DCH

Burgundy

(dry white wines), Pinot Noir (medium-bodied red wines), and Gamay (light, fruity red wines, such as Beaujolais). Every village produces its own distinctive wine, from Chablis to Meursault to Chassagne-Montrachet. Road maps read like fine-wine lists. If the wine village has a hyphenated name, the latter half of its name often comes from the town's most important vineyard (e.g., Gevrey-Chambertin, Ladoix-Serrigny). Look for *Dégustation Gratuite* (free tasting) signs, and prepare for serious wine-tasting—and steep prices, if you're not careful. For a more relaxed tasting, head for the hills: The less prestigious Hautes-Côtes (upper slopes) produce some terrific, inexpensive, and overlooked wines. Look for village cooperatives (usually called *Caveau des Vignerons*), or try my suggestions for Beaune tastings. The least expensive (but still tasty) wines are Bourgogne Ordinaire and Passetoutgrain (both red), and whites from the Mâcon and Chalon areas. If you like rosé, try Marsannay, considered one of France's best. For tips on tasting, see "French Wine-Tasting 101" on page 30.

Beaune

You'll feel comfortable right away in this prosperous and popular little wine capital, where life centers on the production and consumption of the prestigious, expensive Côte d'Or wines. *Côte d'Or* means "golden hillside," and such hillsides are a spectacle to enjoy in late October as the leaves turn.

Medieval monks and powerful dukes of Burgundy laid the groundwork that established this town's prosperity. The monks cultivated wine...and the dukes cultivated wealth. Today, one of the world's most important wine auctions takes place here during the third week of November.

ORIENTATION

Beaune is a compact place (pop. 25,000) with a handful of interesting monuments and vineyards on its doorstep. Limit your Beaune ramblings to the town center, lassoed within its medieval walls and circled by a one-way ring road, and leave time to stroll into the vineyards. All roads and activities converge on the perfectly French square, place Carnot (as do Wednesday and Saturday markets). Beaune is quiet on Sundays and Monday mornings.

Tourist Information
The TI is located across from the post office on the ring road's southeastern corner (look for *Porte Marie de Bourgogne* on the red banner, daily 9:00–12:30 & 13:30–18:00). From June through August, the TI is open all day (no lunch break) and closes an hour later than usual. The TI has extensive information on wine-tasting in and near Beaune; a room-finding service; a list of *chambres d'hôte*; and bus schedules. Ask about guided English walking tours (€7, daily July–mid-Sept, call to verify), but pass on the museum pass.

Arrival in Beaune
By Train: To reach the city center from the train station (no bag check), walk straight out of the station up avenue du 8 Septembre, cross the busy ring road, and continue up rue du Château. Follow

it as it angles left and pass the mural, veering right onto rue des Tonneliers. A left on rue de l'Enfants leads to Beaune's pedestrian zone and place Carnot.

By Bus: Beaune has no bus station—only several stops in the town center. Ask the driver for *le Centre-Ville*. The Jules Ferry (zhul fair-ee) stop is central and closest to the train station; the Clemenceau stop is best for visiting Château de la Rochepot (see page 659). Bus #44 connects Beaune with other wine villages along the famous Route du Vin (about 7/day, bus info: tel. 03 80 42 11 00).

By Car: Follow *Centre-Ville* signs to the ring road. Once on the ring road, turn right at the first signal after the modern post office (rue d'Alsace), and park for free a block away in place Madeleine. If the lot is full—which it often is on market days—look for spaces on surrounding streets or along the ring road.

Helpful Hints

Market Days: Beaune hosts a smashing Saturday market and a small Wednesday market on its main squares (both until 12:30). The Saturday market animates the entire town and is worth planning ahead for (for more on market days, see the sidebar on page 26). Locals watch the action from the Baltard Café on place de la Halle, then have lunch at an outdoor café (many good choices—see my "Eating" listings, on page 652, for ideas—but sit down by 12:30 or forget it).

Supermarket: Supermarché Casino has a great selection, a deli, and fair prices (Mon–Sat 8:30–20:00, closed Sun, through the arch off place Madeleine).

Internet Access: The **Baltard Café,** across from the main TI at 14 place de la Halle, has Wi-Fi and computers upstairs (tel. 03 80 24 21 86).

Laundry: Beaune's two launderettes are both open daily 7:00–21:00. One is in the town center at 65 rue Lorraine; the other is between the train station and place Madeleine at 17–19 rue du Faubourg St. Jean.

Bike Rental: See "Getting Around the Beaune Region," on page 655, for information.

Taxi: Call Gerard Rebillard for Beaune's friendliest taxi (cabbies speak English, tel. 06 11 83 06 10, allo-beaune.taxi @libertysurf.fr). For other taxis, call 06 09 42 36 80 or 06 09 36 06 44.

Tourist Train: A TGV-esque little train will show you Beaune and nearby vineyards (€5, almost hourly departures from near Hôtel Dieu, runs April–Oct 11:00–17:00, no morning trips on Wed and Sat market days, 40 min).

Beaune's Best Wine and Food Stores

Beaune overflows with wine boutiques eager to convince you that their wines are best. Here are a few to look for.

The wine shop **Denis Perret** has a good selection in all price ranges and a helpful, English-speaking staff managed by friendly owner Alain (they can chill a white for your picnic). If you've tasted a wine elsewhere that you like, they can usually find a less costly bottle with similar qualities (Mon–Sat 9:00–12:00 & 14:00–19:00, closed Sun, 40 place Carnot, tel. 03 80 22 35 47, www.denisperret.fr).

I also like the wines and helpful staff at **Doudet Naudin** (fine wines at good prices from a well-respected producer Mon–Sat 9:00–12:00 & 14:00–19:00, Sun 9:00–12:00, 14 rue du Faubourg Madeleine, tel. 03 80 24 23 52).

The cool wine hardware store, **Comptoir Viticole**, is good for wine paraphernalia (Mon–Sat 8:00–12:45 & 13:45–19:00, closed Sun, where rue d'Alsace runs into place Carnot).

For food, **Alain Hess** beautifully displays fine cheeses, mustards, and other gourmet food products (7 place Carnot). A few doors down, welcoming **Mulet Pain d'Epices** shows off exquisite packages of this tasty and local spice bread, also handy as gifts (1 place Carnot).

Car Rental: ADA is cheap and closest to the train station (allow €50/day for a small car with 100 kilometers/62 miles free, Mon–Sat 8:00–12:00 & 14:00–18:00, closed Sun, 26 avenue 8 Septembre, tel. 03 80 22 72 90). **Avis** is five blocks away on the ring road, near place Madeleine (Mon–Sat 8:30–12:00 & 14:00–17:30, closed Sun, 48 bis Jules Ferry, tel. 03 80 24 96 46).

Local Guide: Colette Barbier, a professor of gastronomy and wines at the University of Dijon, is an engaging guide and fluent in English. She knows Burgundy like a local—because she is one (her family has lived in the region for 250 years). Book well in advance, though last-minute requests sometimes work out (€195/half-day, €350/day, tel. & fax 03 80 23 94 34, mobile 06 80 57 47 40, www.burgundy-guide.com, cobatour@aol.com).

Best Souvenir Shopping: The **Athenaeum** has a great variety of souvenirs, including wine and cooking books in English, with a great children's section upstairs (daily 10:00–19:00, across from Hôtel Dieu at 7 rue de l'Hôtel Dieu). And you won't find a bookstore with a better wine bar.

SIGHTS

▲▲▲Hôtel Dieu

This medieval charity hospital is now a museum. The Hundred Years' War and the plague called the Black Death devastated Beaune, leaving three-quarters of its population destitute. Nicholas Rolin, chancellor of Burgundy (enriched, in part, by his power to collect taxes), had to do something for "his people" (or, more likely, was getting old and wanted to close out his life on a philanthropic, rather than a greedy, note). So, in 1443, Rolin paid to build this hospital. It was completed in just eight years.

Cost, Hours, Location: €6, daily April–mid-Nov 9:00–18:30, mid-Nov–March 9:00–11:30 & 14:00–17:30, last ticket sold one hour before closing. It's right in the center of Beaune, dominating place de la Halle (across from the TI).

◆ Self-Guided Tour: While the English flier and English descriptions throughout are helpful, this self-guided tour gives your visit more meaning. Tour the rooms, which circle the court-yard in a clockwise direction, starting from near the turnstile.

Courtyard of Honor: Honor meant power, and this was all about showing off. While the exterior of the hospital and the town side of the courtyard are less ostentatious (because there was no point in attracting the pesky 15th-century brigands who looted whatever looked most rewarding), the inner rooftop is dazzling. The colorful glazed tile roof established what became a style rec-ognized as typically "Burgundian." The tiles, which last 300 years, are fired three times: once to harden, then to burn in the color, and finally for the glaze. They were redone in 1902. The building is lacy Flamboyant Gothic with lots of decor—and more weathervanes than any other building in France.

Paupers' Ward: This grandest room of the hospital was the ward for the poorest patients. The vault, typical of big medieval rooms, was constructed like the hull of a ship. The screen separates the ward from the chapel. Every three hours, the door was opened, and patients could experience Mass from their beds. Study the ceiling. Crossbeams are held by the mouths of creatively carved monsters—each mouth is stretched realistically, and each face has individual characteristics. Between the crossbars are busts of real 15th-century townsfolk—leading citizens, with animals humor-ously indicating their foibles (e.g., a round-faced glutton next to a pig). This room housed patients until 1949 (see painting, middle left). During epidemics, there were two to a bed.

The carved wooden statue over the door shows a bound Christ—demonstrating graphically to patients that their savior suffered and was able to empathize with their ordeal. Its realism shows that Gothic art had moved beyond the stiff formality of

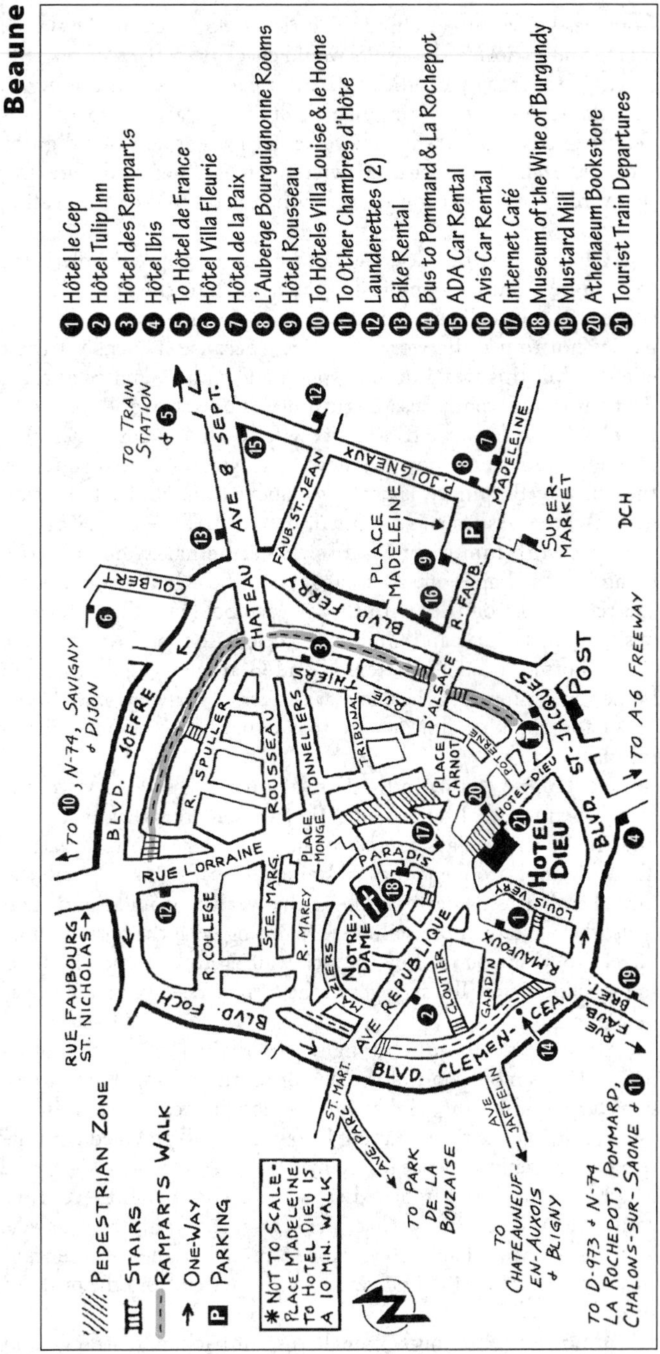

Beaune
1 Hôtel le Cep
2 Hôtel Tulip Inn
3 Hôtel des Remparts
4 Hôtel Ibis
5 To Hôtel de France
6 Hôtel Villa Fleurie
7 Hôtel de la Paix
8 L'Auberge Bourguignonne Rooms
9 Hôtel Rousseau
10 To Hôtels Villa Louise & le Home
11 To Other Chambres d'Hôte
12 Launderettes (2)
13 Bike Rental
14 Bus to Pommard & La Rochepot
15 ADA Car Rental
16 Avis Car Rental
17 Internet Café
18 Museum of the Wine of Burgundy
19 Mustard Mill
20 Athenaeum Bookstore
21 Tourist Train Departures
PEDESTRIAN ZONE
STAIRS
RAMPARTS WALK
ONE-WAY
PARKING
* NOT TO SCALE - PLACE MADELEINE TO HOTEL DIEU IS A 10 MIN. WALK
TO D-973 + N-74 LA ROCHEPOT, POMMARD, CHALONS-SUR-SAONE + 11
TO CHATEAUNEUF-EN-AUXOIS + BLIGNY
TO PARK DE LA BOUZAISE
RUE FAUBOURG ST. NICHOLAS
TO 10, N-74, SAVIGNY + DIJON
TO TRAIN STATION + 5
TO A-6 FREEWAY
BLVD. FOCH
BLVD. JOFFRE
BLVD. CLEMENCEAU
BLVD. ST. JACQUES
BLVD. FERRY
AVE 8 SEPT.
AVE REPUBLIQUE
AVE PARC
AVE JAFFELIN
ST. MART.
RUE LORRAINE
R. COLLEGE
STE. MARG.
R. MAREY
R. SPULLER
ROUSSEAU
TONNELIERS
TRIBUNAL
RUE THIERS
CHATEAU
COLBERT
FAUB. ST. JEAN
R. JOIGNEAUX
R. FAUB. MADELEINE
PLACE MADELEINE
PLACE MONGE
PLACE CARNOT
PARADIS
NOTRE-DAME
MAIZIERS
CLOUTIER
GARDIN
R. MAUFOUX
LOUIS VERY
HOTEL DIEU
POTERNE
D'ALSACE
RUE FAUB. BRET.
SUPER-MARKET
POST
DCH

Burgundy

Romanesque carving. Behind the little window, next to the statue, was the nuns' dorm. The sisters would check on patients from here. Notice the scrawny candleholder; if a patient died in the night, the candle would be extinguished. Study the glass display cases near the beds. Rolin, who believed every patient deserved dignity, provided each patient with a pewter jug, mug, bowl, and plate. But the ward didn't get heat until the 19th century (notice the heating grates on the floor).

Chapel: The hospice was not a place of hope. People came here to die. Care was more for the soul than the body. (Local guides are routinely instructed in writing by American tour companies not to use the word "hospice," because it turns off their clients. But this was a hospice, plain and simple, and back then, death was apparently less disturbing.) The stained glass shows Nicolas Rolin (lower left) and his wife, Guigone (lower right)—dressed as a nun to show her devotion. Nicolas' feudal superior, the Duke of Burgundy, is portrayed above him. Notice the action on Golgotha. As Jesus is crucified, the souls of the two criminals crucified with him (portrayed as miniature naked humans) are being snatched up—one by an angel and the other by a red devil. You're standing on tiles with the love symbol (or "gallant device") designed by Nicolas and Guigone to celebrate their love (as noble couples often did). The letters N and G are entwined in an oak branch, meaning that their love was strong. The word *seule* ("only one") and the lone star declare that Guigone is the only star in Nicolas' cosmos.

St. Hugue Ward: In the 17th century, this smaller ward was established for wealthy patients. They were more likely to survive, and the decor displays themes of hope, rather than resignation: The series of Baroque paintings lining the walls show the biblical miracles that Jesus performed. As the wealthy would lie in their beds, they'd stare at the ceiling—a painting with the bottom of an angel's foot, surrounded by the sick waiting to be healed by Jesus in his scarlet robe. The syringes in the display case are as delicate as caulking guns.

St. Nicolas Room: Originally part of the kitchen, this room now exhibits more tools of the doctoring trade (amputation saws, pans for blood-letting, and so on). Notice the nearby hatch in the floor, showing the river running below; the hole provided a primitive but convenient disposal system.

Kitchen: The kitchen display here shows a 16th-century rotisserie. When fully wound, the cute robot would crank away, and the spit would spin slowly for 45 minutes. The 19th-century stove provided running hot water, which spewed from the beaks of swans.

Pharmacy: The nuns grew herbs out back, and strange and

wondrous concoctions were stored in pottery jars. The biggest jar (by the window) was for *theriaca* ("panacea"). The most commonly used medicine back then, it was a syrup of herbs, wine, and opium.

St. Louis Ward: A maternity ward until 1969, this room is lined with fine 16th- and 17th-century tapestries illustrating mostly Old Testament stories. Dukes traveled with tapestries to cozy up the humble places they stayed in while on the road. The 16th-century pieces have better colors, but inferior perspective. (The most precious tapestries here are from the 15th century and are displayed in the next room, where everyone is enthralled by the great van der Weyden painting.)

Roger van der Weyden's *Last Judgment:* This exquisite painting, the treasure of the Hôtel Dieu, was commissioned by Rolin in 1450 for the altar of the Paupers' Ward. He spared no cost, hiring the leading Flemish artist of his time. The entire altarpiece survives. The back side (on right wall) was sliced off so everything could be viewed at the same time. The painting is full of symbolism. Christ presides over Judgment Day. The lily is mercy, the sword is judgment, the rainbow promises salvation, and the jeweled globe at Jesus' feet symbolizes the universality of Christianity's message. As four angels blow their trumpets, St. Michael the archangel—very much in control—determines which souls are heavy with sin. Mary and the apostles pray for the souls of the dead as they emerge from their graves. But notice how both Michael and Jesus are expressionless—at this point, the cries of the damned and their loved ones are useless. In the back row are real people of the day.

The intricate detail, painted with a three-haired brush, is typical of Flemish art. While Renaissance artists employed mathematical tricks of perspective, these artists captured a sense of reality by painting minute detail upon detail. Stare at Michael's robe and wings. Check out John's delicate feet and hands. Study the faces of the damned; you can almost hear the gnashing of teeth. The feet of the damned show the pull of a terrible force. On the far left, notice those happily entering the pearly gates. On the far right—it's the flames of hell (no, this has nothing to do with politics).

Except for Sundays and holidays, the painting was kept closed and people saw only the panels that now hang on the right wall: Nicolas and Guigone piously at the feet of St. Sebastian—invoked to fight the plague—and St. Anthony, whom patients called upon for help in combating burning skin diseases.

Collégiale Notre-Dame—Built in the 12th and 13th centuries, Beaune's cathedral was a "daughter of Cluny" (built in the style of the Cluny Abbey; page 676). Except for the 14th-century Gothic front porch addition, it's a fine example of Cluny-style

Romanesque architecture. Enter to see the 15th-century tapestries (behind the altar), a variety of stained glass, and what's left of frescoes depicting the life of Lazarus (tapestry open daily 9:30–12:30 & 14:00–19:00).

To get to the Museum of Wine (listed below) from here, walk 30 steps straight out of the cathedral, turn left down a cobbled alley (rue d'Enfer, or "Hell Street"—named for the fires of the Duke's kitchens once located on this street), keep left, and enter the courtyard of Hôtel des Ducs.

Museum of the Wine of Burgundy (Musée du Vin de Bourgogne)—From this folk-wine museum, which fills the old residence of the Dukes of Burgundy, it's clear that the history and culture of Burgundy and its wine were fermented in the same bottle. Wander into the free courtyard for a look at the striking palace, antique wine presses (in the *cuverie,* or vatting shed; good English explanations), and a concrete model of Beaune's 15th-century street plan (a good chance to understand the town's impressive fortified wall). Inside the museum, you'll see a model of the region, with tools, costumes, and scenes of Burgundian wine history—but no tasting. English explanations are in each room (€5.40; April–Nov daily 9:30–18:00; Dec–March Wed–Mon 9:30–17:00, closed Tue, tel. 03 80 22 08 19).

The Mustard Mill (La Moutarderie Fallot)—The last of the independent mustard mills in Burgundy opens its doors for guided tours in French only (one section has an English audioguide). At the end, visitors get to mix their own mustard, then taste-test their concoctions (€7, open Mon–Sat with tours at 10:00 and 11:30, extra afternoon tours probable July–Aug, closed Sun, call TI to confirm and reserve, across ring road in the appropriately yellow building at 31 rue du Faubourg Bretonniere, www.fallot.com).

Ramparts Walk, Parc de la Bouzaise, and Vineyards—Stroll above Beaune along its 13th-century wall to get a sense of its once-commanding medieval defenses, then wander into nearby vineyards. Most of the rampart is accessible from inside the town, but much has melted into peaceful residential lanes. Walk out rue Maufoux and find the ramp leading to the ramparts (Remparts des Dames) on the right. Wander north along the fortification to the next street (avenue de la République), drop down and turn left, and cross the ring road and leave town, following the same stream that runs under the Hôtel Dieu for three blocks to the park. The vineyards are behind the park, with small roads, paths, and great early-morning and sunset views (walkers need 15 min from Beaune's center to reach the vineyards; drivers need only about 2 min).

WINE-TASTING

In Beaune

Countless opportunities exist for you to learn the fine points of Burgundy's wines. Shops everywhere offer free, informal, and informative tastings (with the expectation that you'll buy at least one bottle). For tips on wine-tasting, see "French Wine-Tasting 101," page 30.

A few large cellars *(caves)* charge an entry fee, allowing you to taste a variety of wines (with less expectation that you'll buy). Most of these *caves* offer some form of introduction or self-guided tour (see also "Minibus Tours of Vineyards near Beaune," under "Outside of Beaune," page 646). Don't mind the mossy ceilings. Many cellars have spent centuries growing this "angel's hair"—the result of humidity created by the evaporation of the wines stored there.

The following two places (a block apart and close to the TI) charge an entry fee, but then allow you to sample a variety of wines (15 wines for €10, or 7 wines for €7) in atmospheric cellars.

Caves des Cordeliers—Compared to the Marché aux Vins (listed below), this cellar is smaller (with just four, rather than 15, wines to taste), but it's just as atmospheric, more historic, and it comes with more personalized help. You enter via a cloister that survives from the original 13th-century Convent des Cordeliers. (The cells upstairs house retired nuns to this day.) After paying, tour the historical exhibit upstairs, then descend into cellars where monks stored their wine for centuries. The "cellar master" (in the coat and tie) is happy to teach you about the wine in English. Your last stop: a classy wine-lovers' boutique where you'll be offered four wines to sample (€7, Fri–Tue 9:30–12:00 & 14:00–17:30, closed Wed–Thu, 6 rue de l'Hôtel Dieu, 1 block toward ring road from Marché aux Vins, tel. 03 80 25 08 85).

Marché aux Vins—Across the street from the Hôtel Dieu, this is Beaune's wine smorgasbord and a fun way to sample its wines (though quality is variable). Pay €10 for a wine-tasting cup (yours to keep) and scorecard (no cheating), then plunge into the labyrinth of candlelit *caves* dotted with 15 barrels, each offering a new tasting experience (3 Chardonnays, 12 Pinot Noirs). In Burgundy, most whites are Chardonnays, and most reds are Pinot Noirs. You're on your own. Tip: The better reds are upstairs in the chapel, at the end of the tasting. While you technically have 45 minutes in the cellars, this is rarely enforced—especially if you look like a serious buyer. Discreetly bring some crackers to cleanse your palate and help you really taste the differences (daily July–Aug 9:30–17:30, Sept–June 9:30–11:15 & 14:00–17:30, arrive more than 45 min before closing or your time will be limited, 2 rue Nicolas Rolin, tel. 03 80 25 08 20).

Burgundy

Burgundian Wine Quality, 1999–2006

1999 This is an outstanding vintage, especially for reds, which are supple and easy to drink now, and for the next several years.

2000 This year is a less impressive vintage than the previous two years; reds should be consumed soon, as they lack concentration for aging purposes. Whites are much better.

2001 A difficult growing season, with rain and a late frost, producing reds that are thinner, less consistent, and more tannic than in previous years. Whites fared much better.

2002 Called the "vintage of the decade" by some, the reds have recently been released. The whites are excellent, with good structure, balance, and pure, clean fruit flavors.

2003 A most unusual year due to the extreme summer heat. The harvest was a month early, so the grapes were small, with thick skins, and produced only about half the usual yield. The reds are deeper in color and taste very different from usual Pinot Noirs. All wines need to be drunk sooner—the average time you can keep this year's vintage is about half the normal (10 years at most for reds; whites should be consumed right away).

Burgundy

Outside of Beaune

The TI has a long list of area vintners. The famous Route des Grands Crus that connects Burgundy's most prestigious wine villages is disappointing north of Aloxe-Corton, as you're forced onto unappealing N-74. Consider instead the beautiful routes connecting villages between Beaune and La Rochepot and south to Santenay (for example, Monthelie, Nantoux, St. Romain, and St. Aubin are all off the famous path and offer ample tastings).

I've listed a few favorites below. For directions to the first three places, see "Bike (or Drive) the Vineyards," page 655. Taxis are a practical way to sample village life and prowl the vineyards. (La Cave de Pommard, just two miles from Beaune, is the closest place that I describe.) Transco bus #44 serves Pommard (4/day, 5 min) and Puligny Montrachet (4/day, 20 min) from Beaune (Beaune TI has schedules, only afternoon buses work). Note that at free tastings, you're expected to buy a bottle or two, unless you're with a group tour.

Caveau de Montrachet—This wine bar–like tasting room, 10 minutes south of Beaune in Puligny Montrachet (pool-ee-nee mohnt-

2004 A lousy summer (rain, hail, and wind) but a brilliant September (three weeks of bright sunshine). The good *domaines* produced reds that are very fruity, clean, supple, and "flattering" (according to my friend). They can be drunk and appreciated early, though they will last a long time. The whites are excellent, with a precise acidity giving them the freshness and pure fruitiness of a great vintage.

2005 Has the makings of a great vintage: The harvest was healthy and balanced, with great natural sugar. A local magazine called 2005 "the vintage of dreams." The reds are superb—rich, plain, concentrated, full-bodied, and intense. They will age magnificently. The whites may be a little less impressive, but are still good.

2006 Challenged even the most experienced wine-makers with capricious weather that didn't allow an idle moment in the vineyards or the cellar. The whites look to be of high quality with good consistency from Chablis to Mâcon. Supple and fresh, they are already fruity with considerable richness. The reds are excellent across the board, with beautiful and intense color. Some are delicate and elegant, while others are robust and full-bodied. Their aromas vary from red fruits to cherry, spices, and cocoa.

rah-shay) on the scenic route to Château de la Rochepot, represents many local white-wine vintners. They offer a great selection from this area that's known as *the* king of white wines (these kings are pricey but worth it). Knowledgeable Julien is happy to answer your every question, and if he's out, Papa will smile his way through the tasting with nary a word of English (€7 for 4 wines, free if you buy 6 bottles; March–Oct daily 9:30–12:00 & 14:00–19:00; Nov–Feb Tue–Sat 10:00–12:00 & 15:00–18:00, closed Mon; tel. 03 80 21 96 78). Transco bus #44 from Beaune stops near the *cave*.

Caveau des Proprietaires in Aloxe-Corton—Here you can sample from eight makers of the famous Aloxe-Corton; prices are very affordable, and easygoing Philippe speaks just enough English (€1–6 per wine, free if you buy, Thu–Mon 10:00–13:00 & 15:00–19:00, usually closed Tue–Wed, tel. 03 80 26 49 85). You'll find the *caveau* a few steps from the church on the little square.

La Cave de Pommard—A short drive or level two-mile bike ride from Beaune leads to this unusually good cellar in Pommard (on the way to or from Château de la Rochepot). British Stephanie, a graduate from Beaune's prestigious wine school, is ready to demystify Burgundy's wines. She has wines from all of Burgandy's famous villages. The ambience is good, tastings are free, and prices are reasonable (bottles from €5–65, most €15–20). From Beaune's ring road, follow signs for *Chalon-sur-Saône*, then *Autun*, to reach Pommard. The cellars are on the right, just after the Château de Pommard's long wall; park in the village and walk back (free, daily 10:00–19:00, ask to visit the small *caves* below, 3 route de Beaune, tel. 03 80 24 99 00, www.cavedepommard.com).

Minibus Tours of Vineyards near Beaune—Wine Safari offers minibus tours of the villages and vineyards around Beaune in three two-hour itineraries, usually with one wine-tasting (€34–40, tour #2 is best for beginners, tours depart from TI generally at 12:00, 14:30 & 17:00, tel. 03 80 24 79 12, www.burgundy-tourism -safaritours.com, or call TI to reserve). These English-speaking tours are relaxed, friendly, and get you into the countryside and smaller wineries, though you won't do much tasting. **Transco** buses also run from Beaune through or near many of the great wine villages (see "Getting Around the Beaune Region," page 655).

SLEEPING

In the Center

$$$ Hôtel le Cep**** is the place to stay in Beaune if you have the means. Buried in the town center, this historic building comes with exquisite public spaces, 62 gorgeous wood-beamed and traditionally decorated rooms, and a restaurant that has long been the talk of the town (standard Sb-€130, standard Db-€165, deluxe Db-€205, suites-€245–340, family duplexes-€500, continental breakfast-€18, air-con, king-size beds, Wi-Fi, fitness center, parking-€13/day, 27 rue Maufoux, tel. 03 80 22 35 48, fax 03 80 22 76 80, www.hotel-cep-beaune.com, resa@hotel-cep-beaune.com).

$$$ Hôtel Tulip Inn*** charges top euro for its central location a block from the cathedral, and mixes modern comfort with a touch of old Beaune (small Db-€98, *superieure* Db-€116, deluxe Db-€150, extra bed-€18, some rooms with air-con, Wi-Fi, elevator, skip overpriced breakfast, garage-€9/day but a long walk away, 9 avenue de la République, tel. 03 80 24 09 20, fax 03 80 24 09 15, www.athanor-hotel-bourgogne.com, hotel.athanor@wanadoo.fr).

$$$ Hôtel des Remparts***, a peaceful oasis in a manor house, features rustic-classy, affordable rooms with beamed ceilings, period furniture, a quiet courtyard, and a few great family suites (Db-€78–108—pricier rooms are bigger with elaborate bathrooms, Db suite-€116–135, Tb-€89–118, Qb-€148, cozy attic rooms, Internet access and Wi-Fi, laundry service, bike rental, garage-€9/day, just inside ring road between train station and main

Burgundy

Sleep Code

(€1 = about $1.30, country code: 33)
S = Single, **D** = Double/Twin, **T** = Triple, **Q** = Quad, **b** = bathroom,
s = shower only, ***** = French hotel rating system (0–4 stars).
Unless otherwise noted, credit cards are accepted and English
is spoken.

To help you easily sort through these listings, I've divided
the rooms into three categories based on the price for a standard double room with bath:

$$$ **Higher Priced**—Most rooms €90 or more.
$$ **Moderately Priced**—Most rooms between €60–90.
$ **Lower Priced**—Most rooms €60 or less.

square at 48 rue Thiers, tel. 03 80 24 94 94, fax 03 80 24 97 08,
www.hotel-remparts-beaune.com, hotel.des.remparts@wanadoo
.fr, run by the formal Epaillys and friendly Chantal).

$$ Hôtel Ibis**, modern with 73 efficient rooms, is an acceptable last resort for most, but a good first resort if you have kids
and want a pool. The bigger "Club" rooms are worth the extra
euros (standard Db-€80, "Club" Db-€88, extra person-€10, nonsmoking floor, air-con, free parking, you'll pass it as you enter
Beaune from the autoroute, tel. 03 80 22 75 67, fax 03 80 22 77 17,
www.hotelibis.com, h1363@accor.com). There's another, cheaper
Ibis Hôtel—along with a gaggle of Motel 6–type places—closer to
the autoroute.

$$ Hôtel de France** is a well-run place and easy for train
travelers and drivers (parking across from the train station). It
comes with clean rooms, Internet access, and outgoing owners Tita
and Eric. Half-board is required on Saturday (Sb-€50–77, Db-
€57–77, most are about €67, Tb-€67–77, air-con, Wi-Fi, garage-
€9/day, 35 avenue du 8 Septembre, tel. 03 80 24 10 34, fax 03 80
24 96 78, www.hoteldefrance-beaune.com, hoteldefrance.beaune
@wanadoo.fr).

$$ Hôtel Villa Fleurie***, an adorable 10-room refuge, is run
by affable Madame Chartier on a plain street a few blocks outside
the ring road (15-min walk from the center). Most rooms are woodfloored, plush, and *très* traditional, and come with big bathrooms
and air-conditioning (small Db-€70, bigger Db-€80, nifty Tb/Qb
loft-€120, Wi-Fi, easy and free parking, 19 place Colbert, tel. 03 80
22 66 00, fax 03 80 22 45 46, www.lavillafleurie.fr, la.villa.fleurie
@wanadoo.fr). From Beaune's ring road, turn right in front of the
Bichot winery.

Place Madeleine

These hotels are a few blocks from the city center and train station, with easy parking.

$$ Hôtel de la Paix*,** a few steps off place Madeleine, is intimate and welcoming, with 14 plush and well-appointed rooms, four good family rooms, Internet access, and a snazzy bar with a pool table (Sb-€56, Db-€72–80, loft Tb-€97, Qb-€118–130, air-con, 45 rue du Faubourg Madeleine, tel. 03 80 24 78 08, fax 03 80 24 10 18, www.hotelpaix.com, contact@hotelpaix.com).

$ L'Auberge Bourguignonne's restaurant hides a handful of comfortable enough, well-priced rooms (Db-€57, Tb-€72, a few rooms with air-con, 4 place Madeleine, tel. 03 80 22 23 53, fax 03 80 22 51 64, contact@aubergebourguignonne.fr).

$ Hôtel Rousseau is a good-value, no-frills, frumpy manor house that turns its back on Beaune's sophistication. Cheerful, quirky, and hard-to-find owner Madame Rousseau, her pet birds, and the quiet garden will make you smile, and the tranquility will help you sleep. The cheapest rooms are simple, nearly clean, and a godsend for budget travelers. The rooms with showers are like Grandma's, with enough comfort (S-€29, D-€35, D with toilet-€44, Db-€54, T with toilet-€54, Tb-€63, Q-€56, Qb-€68–80, showers down the hall-€3, reservations preferred by email, cash only, free parking, 11 place Madeleine, tel. 03 80 22 13 59). Check-ins after 19:00 and morning departures before 7:30 need to be arranged in advance.

Near Beaune

You'll find some exceptional and family-friendly values within a short drive of Beaune. Hotels in famous wine villages are generally pricey and overrated.

Hotels

$$$ Hôtel Villa Louise* is a romantic place burrowed in the prestigious wine hamlet of Aloxe-Corton, five minutes north of Beaune. Many of its 13 *très* cozy and tastefully decorated rooms overlook the backyard vineyards, a small covered pool, and a large, grassy garden made for sipping wine. The winemaking owners—the Perrins—are happy to show you their vaulted cellars (Db-€110–152, most are about €110–130, Db suite-€195, buffet breakfast-€15, Internet access and Wi-Fi, sauna, next to the château at 21420 Aloxe-Corton, tel. 03 80 26 46 70, fax 03 80 26 47 16, www.hotel-villa-louise.fr, hotel-villa-louise@wanadoo.fr).

$$ Hôtel le Home,** just off busy N-74 a half-mile north of Beaune, is a good value, with comfy rooms in an old mansion. Engaging owner Mathilde (mah-teel-dah) has recently returned from life in Los Angeles and is eager to introduce you to her region.

Burgundy

(She has two children, so there's a small play area and kids are welcome.) The rooms in the main building are Laura Ashley–soft (Db-€66–73, Tb-€70–78, Qb-€86, top-floor rooms have the most character). Rooms on the parking courtyard (only Db-€66) come with stone floors, small terraces, and bright colors, but can be dark (free parking, 138 route de Dijon, tel. 03 80 22 16 43, fax 03 80 24 90 74, www.lehome.fr, info@lehome.fr).

Chambres d'Hôte

The Côte d'Or has scads of *chambres d'hôte;* get a list at the TI and reserve ahead in the summer. The cliff-dwelling villages of Baubigny, Orches, and Evelles, just under La Rochepot, are my favorite non-Beaune bases, with several *chambres d'hôte* (well-signed in the villages). You'll need a car to get to any of these. Families should make a beeline for Isabelle Raby's place.

$$ Château de Melin, run by friendly Hélène, is a semi-restored château that offers comfort, though no interior public spaces. Four huge rooms play second fiddle to their winery (don't expect prompt service). Outside you can enjoy a small pond, vineyards (tastings available), and gardens to stretch out in (Db-€86–100, Tb-€115, Qb-€130, includes good breakfast, cash only, 10 min from Beaune toward La Rochepot, between villages of Auxey-Duresses and La Rochepot, tel. 03 80 21 21 19, fax 03 80 21 21 72, www.chateaudemelin.com, chateaumelin@free.fr).

$$ Domaine du Moulin aux Moines is an old-stone winery just five minutes from Beaune, with a privileged location between Meursault and Auxey-Duresses. This place faces away from the road and embraces a divine hillside of vines and a small stream. The rooms are traditional and quite comfortable, and garden tables await your dinner picnic (Db-€86, huge apartment-€128, on south side of the road from Pommard to La Rochepot, 36 terrasse St. Pierre, tel. & fax 03 80 21 60 79, www.laterrasse.fr, contact @laterrasse.fr).

$$ La Domaine de Corgette is hunkered below a hillside in lovely little St. Romain. Welcoming Véronique has restored an old vintner's home with style. A stay-a-while terrace, private parking, cozy common rooms, and wine-tastings are at your disposal (Db-€60–90, cash only, follow signs from Auxey-Duresses, on rue de la Perrière, tel. & fax 03 80 21 68 08, www.domainecorgette.com, maisondhotescorgette@yahoo.fr).

$ Isabelle Raby rents three good rooms at very fair rates a half-mile above Baubigny in rocky little Orches. She offers the best set up for families, including a pretty pool, table tennis, swings, and fine views from her manicured backyard. Reserve ahead for a homemade dinner for €25 (Db-€60, Tb-€70, Qb-€80, Quint-€90, includes big breakfast, cash only, tel. 03 80 21 78 45).

EATING

For a small town, Beaune offers a wide range of reasonably priced restaurants. Review my suggestions below carefully before setting out, and reserve ahead to avoid frustrations (especially on weekends).

In the Center of Beaune

Bistrot Bourguignon is a relaxed wine bar–bistro with a lengthy wine list and 15 wines available by the glass (order by number from display behind bar). The bon vivant owner, Jean-Jacques, offers the same affordable prices at either bar or table. Come for a glass of wine or to enjoy a light dinner. Dine at the counter, the tables, or in the living room out back (€8 starters, €15 *plats*, closed Sun–Mon, on a pedestrian-only street at 8 rue Monge, tel. 03 80 22 23 24).

La Ciboulette—friendly, intimate, and family-run—offers fine cuisine, mixing traditional Burgundian flavors with creative dishes; it's worth the longer walk (€20 and €25 *menus*, closed Mon–Tue; from place Carnot, walk out rue Carnot and keep on going until you reach 69 rue Lorraine, tel. 03 80 24 70 72).

Brasserie le Carnot is Beaune's vintage café, with good interior and great exterior seating in the pedestrian zone. It serves excellent pizza and the usual café fare (open daily, where rue Carnot and rue Monge meet).

Palais des Gourmets' Salon de Thé provides the best-value outdoor lunch on place Carnot, with delicious quiche, salads, crêpes, and memorable desserts (open daily for lunch only, next to The Athenaeum's back door entrance at 14 place Carnot, tel. 03 80 22 13 39).

Le Jardin des Remparts is a fine Burgundian splurge. This dressy stone manor house is elegant inside and out (leafy terrace dining in summer), yet the service is relaxed and helpful. The excellent nouvelle cuisine proudly works with regional products (€35–60 *menus*, eight-course "discovery *menu*" for €90, closed Sun–Mon, always reserve ahead, just past Hôtel Dieu on ring road at 10 rue de l'Hôtel Dieu, tel. 03 80 24 79 41, lejardin@club -internet.fr).

On Place Madeleine

Le Piquebœuf, on the busy ring road, feels like an upscale café, with fair-priced dishes served in a pleasant setting (€10 salads and pizza, €10–14 *plats du jour*, closed Tue–Wed, air-con, family-friendly seating upstairs, 2 rue de la Madeleine, tel. 03 80 24 07 52).

Les Caves Madeleine is a wine shop that keeps its cozy little dining room busy. Diners are surrounded by shelves of this week's

Beaune Restaurants and Wine Cellars

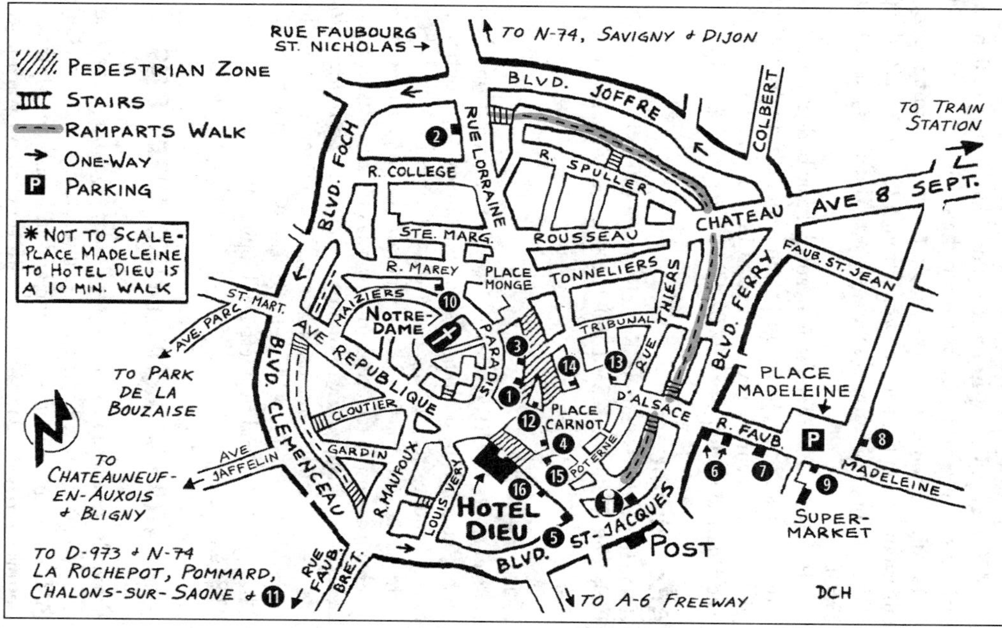

1. Bistrot Bourguignon
2. La Ciboulette Restaurant
3. Brasserie le Carnot
4. Palais des Gourmets' Salon de Thé
5. Le Jardin des Remparts Rest.
6. Le Piqueboeuf Café & Les Caves Madeleine Restaurant
7. Le Comptoir des Tontons & Doudet Naudin Wine Shop
8. L'Auberge Bourguignonne Rest.
9. Relais de la Madeleine Restaurant
10. Pickwicks Pub
11. To Le Relais de la Diligence Rest.
12. Denis Perret Wine Shop
13. Comptoir Viticole Wine Hardware
14. Alain Hess Deli & Mulet Pain d'Epices
15. Marché aux Vins Wine-Tasting
16. Caves des Cordeliers Wine-Tasting

wines with prices chalked onto bottles. Choose a private table, or join the convivial communal table, where good food and wine kindle conversation, then lubricate new friendships. The owners are wine merchants who pass their savings on to you. (As you choose a bottle at store prices and add €5 to drink here, top-end wines become affordable.) This small place is family-run by "Lo-lo," who enjoys sharing his love of wine (good wines by the glass, €14 and €24 *menus*, closed Thu and Sun, 8 rue du Faubourg Madeleine, tel. 03 80 22 93 30).

Le Comptoir des Tontons is a welcoming place with 10 tables, organic foods, and creative *menus* featuring foods from the region (€23 *menu*, 22 rue du Faubourg Madeleine, tel. 03 80 24 19 64).

L'Auberge Bourguignonne is decidedly Burgundian, with serious service and proudly displayed awards. Choose from the dressy dining room; the folksy, more traditional dining room; or tables outside on the square (*menus* from €20, some seafood, open daily, air-con, reservations smart, 4 place Madeleine, tel. 03 80 22 23 53).

Relais de la Madeleine is Beaune's basic budget diner—with little emphasis on ambience or presentation. It's run by the entertaining "Monsieur Neaux-Problem" (€12.50 *menu*, closed Wed, 44 place Madeleine, tel. 03 80 22 07 47).

After Dinner

If you're tired of speaking French, pop into the late-night-lively **Pickwicks Pub** (Mon–Sat 17:00–05:00, closed Sun, behind church at 2 rue Notre-Dame).

Near Beaune

Le Relais de la Diligence, a five-minute drive from Beaune, serves budget Burgundian cuisine, with many *menu* options. The dressy (smoke-free) dining room with sliding-glass walls has you feeling like you're sitting in the vineyard. Or, on a balmy evening, you can eat on the terrace. Either way, as the sun sets, you'll enjoy views of rural Burgundy (*menus* from €18, the €2.50 *Menu Tutu* for dogs—I'm serious—includes ground hamburger and pâté, June–Sept open daily, Oct–May closed Tue–Wed, take N-74 toward Chagny/Chalon and turn left at L'Hôpital Meursault on D-23, tel. 03 80 21 21 32).

TRANSPORTATION CONNECTIONS

From Beaune by Train to: Dijon (14/day, 25 min), **Paris'** Gare de Lyon (nearly hourly, 2.5 hrs, most require change in Dijon), **Colmar** (6/day, 4–5 hrs, changes in Dijon and in Besançon, Mulhouse, or Belfort), **Arles** (10/day, 4.5 hrs, 9 with transfer in Lyon and Nîmes or Avignon), **Chamonix** (7/day, 6–7 hrs, change in Lyon and St. Gervais, some require additional changes), **Annecy** (7/day, 5–6 hrs, change in Lyon), **Amboise** (8/day, 6 hrs, most with changes in Dijon and in Paris, arrive at Paris' Gare de Lyon, then Métro to Austerlitz or Montparnasse stations).

The Beaune Region

Getting Around the Beaune Region

By Bus: Transco bus #44 runs from Beaune through the vineyards and villages south to Chalon-sur-Saône, west to La Rochepot, and north to Dijon. About seven buses per day link Beaune and Dijon via several famous wine villages; ask at the TI for schedules and stops, or call for information (tel. 03 80 42 11 00).

By Bike: Well-organized, English-speaking Florent at Bourgogne Randonnées has good bikes, bike racks, maps, and detailed itineraries (his advice inspired the trips described below). Ask about his favorite routes that follow only small roads and dedicated bike paths. I like his *Discovering the Chardonnay Kingdom* tour. It departs from Beaune's parc de la Bouzaise and connects the wine villages of Pommard, Meursault, and Volnay in a scenic, mostly level, 14-mile loop ride (can be extended to Puligny Montrachet for a level 22-mile loop). Florent can deliver your bike to your hotel anywhere in France (bikes–€3/hr, €15/day, Mon–Sat 9:00–12:00 & 13:30–19:00, Sun 10:00–12:00 & 14:00–17:00, near train station at 7 avenue du 8 Septembre, tel. 03 80 22 06 03, fax 03 80 22 15 58, www.bourgogne-randonnees.com, info@bourgogne-randonnees.com).

SIGHTS

▲Bike (or Drive) the Vineyards

Hop on a bike in Beaune, and in minutes, you can be immersed in the lush countryside and immaculate vineyards of the Côte d'Or. The bike lane that circles Beaune's ring road, and the many little-traveled roads (and friendly bike-rental place in Beaune—described above) make this area good for biking. For an easy and very rewarding roll through wine paradise, follow this relatively level 10-mile half-day loop from Beaune. It laces together three renowned wine villages—Aloxe-Corton, Pernand

The Beaune Region

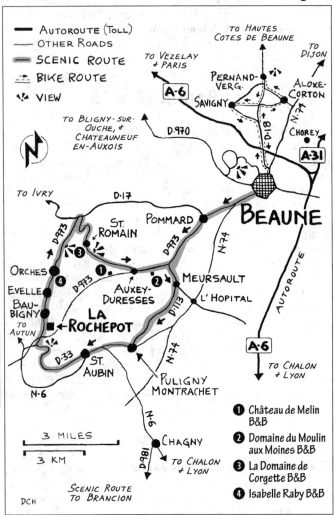

- AUTOROUTE (TOLL)
- OTHER ROADS
- SCENIC ROUTE
- BIKE ROUTE
- VIEW

TO HAUTES
COTES DE BEAUNE

TO VEZELAY
+ PARIS

TO DIJON

PERNAND-
VERG.

ALOXE-
CORTON

SAVIGNY

CHOREY

TO BLIGNY-SUR-
OUCHE, +
CHATEAUNEUF
EN-AUXOIS

D.970

D.18

N.74

A-6

A-31

N

TO IVRY

D·17

POMMARD

BEAUNE

ST.
ROMAIN

D·973

❸

ORCHES

❹

D.973

❶

AUXEY-
DURESSES

❷

MEURSAULT

L'HOPITAL

AUTOROUTE

EVELLE

BAU-
BIGNY

TO
AUTUN

LA
ROCHEPOT

D.113

A-6

N.74

TO CHALON
+ LYON

D.33

ST.
AUBIN

N-6

PULIGNY
MONTRACHET

3 MILES

3 KM

N-6

CHAGNY

D.981

TO CHALON
+ LYON

DCH

SCENIC ROUTE
TO BRANCION

❶ Château de Melin
B&B

❷ Domaine du Moulin
aux Moines B&B

❸ La Domaine de
Corgette B&B

❹ Isabelle Raby B&B

Burgundy

Vergelesses, and Savigny-les-Beaune—connecting you with the best of Burgundian nature and village wine culture. (Bikers needn't be shy about tasting like a professional—spitting rather than swallowing.) Bring water and snacks, as there is precious little available until the end of this route. Your tour concludes in Savigny-les-Beaune, where you'll find several attractions, including a recommended café-restaurant, wine-tasting, a small grocery, and a unique château. This route, while best by bike, also works well by car.

➋ **Self-Guided Tour:** From Beaune's ring road bike lane, take N-74 north toward Dijon; soon after, take a left to Savigny-les-Beaune. Cross over the freeway, then follow signs to *Pernand Vergelesses* on D-18 (at the roundabout). Turn right at signs to *Aloxe-Corton,* and coast down to **Aloxe-Corton** (keep following its church spire in the distance to your left). This tiny town, with a world-class reputation among wine enthusiasts, has many tasting opportunities (but no cafés). Within a few steps of the church is the main square (like a small parking lot). The easygoing **Caveau des Propriétaires** offers tastings (see page 647).

Back on your bike, leave Aloxe's little square and head up the hill to Pernand Vergelesses. There's no compelling reason to stop at this quiet village (though drivers, or bikers in need of a challenge, can climb above the village to the panorama: Turn right into Pernand Vergelesses and go up and up past the church until you see small *Panorama* signs).

Most will turn left on the road back to Beaune, then veer right into the vineyards on the first lane. Make a quick left and follow this vineyard service road, keeping right for about 1.5 miles until you see a *5T* sign. Turn left before the sign, then right, and right again, and ride into **Savigny-les-Beaune.**

You'll come to a three-way intersection. The left fork leads back to Beaune. The middle fork leads to *Centre-Ville,* where you'll find the good **New Rock Café** on a pleasant little square (good salads and beef, outdoor tables, closed Mon, tel. 03 80 21 50 00); a grocery shop a few blocks past the café (closed 12:30–15:00); and a four-towered collectors' château, **Le Château de Savigny** (with 80 fighter jets parked in the side yard, 2,000 models of planes inside, Abarth antique cars, and 300 motorcycles to boot; €8, daily April–Oct 9:00–18:30, Nov–March 9:00–12:00 & 14:00–17:30, last entry 1.5 hours before closing, tel. 03 80 21 55 03). The leftmost road leads back to Beaune.

For a more scenic and very rigorous all-day ride, consider biking the route below (ideal by car). Bikers can shortcut this ride by following Florent's *Chardonnay Kingdom* itinerary (see "By Bike," page 655).

▲▲Scenic Vineyard Drive to/from La Rochepot

Take this pretty, peaceful detour for the best approach to La Rochepot's romantic castle, and to glide through several of Burgundy's most reputed vineyards. Bikers may prefer doubling back to Beaune after visiting Puligny Montrachet.

➋ **Self-Guided Tour:** Leave Beaune's ring road following signs for *Chalon-sur-Saône,* then follow signs to *Pommard,* where you'll find an user-friendly winery (**La Cave de Pommard,** see page 647; visit now or at the end of the loop). South of Pommard, the road climbs gradually through gorgeous views. From here, follow signs to *Meursault*, then work your way through this world-famous wine town by following small signs to *Centre-Ville* (not N-74). When you reach the main square, stay right and find the bike-route signs (to the right of the Casino store), and track signs to *Puligny Montrachet*.

You'll pass through low-slung vineyards deserving a snail's pace to enjoy, then come to a roundabout in the center of Puligny Montrachet with a cool bronze sculpture of vineyard workers. Across from the sculpture, the **Caveau de Montrachet** offers a chance to sample the world's best whites (see page 646). Signs from here lead through more manicured vineyards to St. Aubin. A hard right takes you on N-6 for a short distance; find *La Rochepot* signs as you bypass St. Aubin. Follow signs for *La Rochepot* (D-33) over hills and through the vineyards of the Hautes-Côtes (upper slopes), and you'll come to a drop-dead view of the castle (stop mandatory). Turn right when you reach La Rochepot, and follow *Le Château* signs to the castle (described below).

After visiting the castle, turn right out of its parking lot and mosey through Baubigny, Evelles, and rock-solid Orches. After Orches, climb to the top of Burgundy's world—keeping straight, you'll pass several exceptional lookouts (the village of St. Romain swirls below, and if it's really clear, look for Mont Blanc), then follow signs down to *Pommard* and *Beaune* (you'll pass Burgundy's most important wine-barrel-maker, François Frères, in St. Romain; notice the wood slats used for barrel-making).

▲Château de la Rochepot

This very Burgundian castle rises above the trees and its village, eight miles from Beaune. It's accessible by car, bike (hilly), or infrequent bus. Cross the drawbridge under the Pot family coat of arms and knock three times with the ancient knocker to enter. If no one comes, knock harder, or find a log and ram the gate. This pint-size castle is splendid inside and out. Tour half on your own and the other half with a French guide (get the English handout, some tours in English—call ahead, most guides speak some English and can answer questions). This castle's construction began during the end of the Middle Ages (when castles were built to defend) and was completed during the Renaissance (when castles were transformed into luxury homes). So it's neither a purely defensive structure (as in the Dordogne) nor a palace (as in the Loire)—it's a little of both.

The furnishings are surprisingly elaborate given the military look of the exterior. I could sleep like a baby in the Captain's Room, surrounded by nine-foot-thick walls. Don't miss the 15th-century alarmed safe. Notice the colorful doorjamb. These same colors were used to paint many buildings (including castles and churches) and remind us that medieval life went beyond beige and stone. The kitchen will bowl you over; the dining room sports a 15th-century walnut high-chair. Climb the tower and see the Chinese room, sing chants in the resonant chapel, and make ripples in the 240-foot-deep well. (Can you spit a bull's-eye?) Paths outside lead around the castle and make a worthwhile walk. Don't leave without driving, walking, or pedaling up D-33 a few hundred yards toward St. Aubin (behind Hôtel Relais du Château) for a romantic view.

Cost and Hours: €6, €8.50 if you add tour of exterior offered Sundays at 11:30, private tours in English-€55, call to confirm times; July–Aug Wed–Mon 10:00–18:00, closed Tue; April–June and Sept Wed–Mon 10:00–11:30 & 14:00–17:30, closed Tue; Oct Wed–Mon 10:00–11:30 & 14:00–16:30, closed Tue; closed Nov–March; tel. 03 80 21 71 37, www.larochepot.com.

Getting There: To reach the château from Beaune, follow signs for *Chalon-sur-Saône* from Beaune's ring road, then follow signs to *Autun* along a lovely 15-minute drive to La Rochepot. Once in the town, turn right a block before the Relais du Château Hôtel to reach the castle.

Between Beaune and Paris

North of Beaune, you'll find a handful of appealing places that string together well for a full-day excursion: towering Châteauneuf-en-Auxois, sleepy Semur-en-Auxois, remote Fontenay abbey, pretty little Flavigny-sur-Ozerain, and Julius Caesar's victorious Alise Ste. Reine.

Self-Guided Driving Tour

This all-day loop links Châteauneuf-en-Auxois, Semur-en-Auxois, Fontenay, Flavigny, and Alise Ste. Reine. The trip includes vineyards, pastoral landscapes, the Burgundy canal, a Cistercian abbey, Gallic-Roman history, and two medieval villages. (If you're heading to/from Paris, this scenic tour can be done en route or as an overnight stop; accommodations are listed.) It requires a car, Michelin Local map #520, and navigational patience.

○ **Self-Guided Tour:** Here's your itinerary for a full day in Back Door Burgundy. Leave Beaune, following signs for *Auxerre* and *Bligny-sur-Ouche;* from Bligny-sur-Ouche, take D-33 to Pont d'Ouche (following signs to *Pont du Pany* and *Dijon*), where you'll turn left along the canal, following signs to *Château de Châteauneuf.* In five minutes, you'll see Châteauneuf-en-Auxois castle looming above (described below). From Châteauneuf, drop back down to the canal to Vandenesse (nice picnic spot on its "port," with good views of Châteauneuf), then follow signs for *Pouilly-en-Auxois,* then *Semur-en-Auxois* (described below) on D-970. From Semur, follow *Montbard,* then *Fontenay* signs to reach the abbey. The abbey is your goal today; allow at least an hour here. With no stops, this one-way drive from Beaune to Fontenay should take about 75 minutes.

Return to Beaune along D-905, following signs for *Venary les Laumes,* and contemplate short detours to Alise Ste. Reine (the "Alésia" battlefield where Caesar defeated the Gauls) and lovely little Flavigny (of *Chocolat* film fame). If you're doing this trip on your way to or from Paris, visit Flavigny and Alise Ste. Reine between Semur-en-Auxois and Fontenay, or skip them. Better yet, sleep in Semur-en-Auxois or Châteauneuf-en-Auxois, and do it all at a sane pace (see below).

Nondrivers can get as far as Semur-en-Auxois by bus (3/day from Montbard or Dijon—early morning, noon, and evening; rail-pass gets you a free ticket, get ticket at station or at TI in Semur). There are no trains to Semur.

Châteauneuf-en-Auxois

This purely medieval castle monitored passage between Burgundy and Paris, with hawk's-eye views from its 2,000-foot setting. *Châteauneuf* means "new castle," so you'll see many in France. This one is in the Auxois area, so it's Châteauneuf-en-Auxois (not to be confused with the famous Châteauneuf-du-Pape in Provence). The living hill town hunkers in the shadow of its pit-bull château and merits exploring. Park at the lot in the upper end of the village; don't miss the panoramic viewpoint nearby. The military value of this site is powerfully clear from here. Find the Burgundy Canal and the three reservoirs that have maintained the canal's flow for more than 300 years. The small village below is Châteauneuf's port, Vandenesse-en-Auxois—you'll be there shortly. If not for phylloxera—the vine-loving insect that ravaged France in the early 1900s, killing all of its vineyards—you'd see more vineyards than wheat fields.

Saunter into the village, where every building feels historic and stocky farmers live side-by-side with slim artists. Walk into the courtyard, but skip the château's interior (€5, Tue–Sun 10:00–12:00 & 14:00–19:00, closed Mon, get English handout). You'll get better moat views and see the more important castle entry by walking below the Hostellerie du Château, and then turning right, following *Eglise* signs. If you're hungry, Châteauneuf has several affordable cafés and restaurants along its main drag.

SLEEPING

In or near Châteauneuf-en-Auxois

$$ Lady A Barge, in the canalside village of Vandenesse-en-Auxois, has tight but sufficiently comfortable rooms on a handsome hotel barge at two-star prices, with views of Châteauneuf's castle. Catherine entertains, while Sami cooks an elaborate dinner upon request for €25, including some wine (Sb-€60, Db-€65, one-night stay-€10 extra, includes breakfast, book way ahead in summer, open all year, cash only, bikes available, Lady A, Bord du Canal, tel. 03 80 49 26 96, fax 03 80 49 27 00, www.peniche-lady-a .com, ladyabarge@yahoo.fr). From the freeway exit in Pouilly-en-Auxois, take D-18 to Vandenesse-en-Auxois to find the canal.

$ Hostellerie du Château** is a simple but cozy place for a good night's sleep in Châteauneuf. It houses an enticing budget vacation ensemble: nine homey, inexpensive rooms with a kid-friendly garden overlooking a brooding castle, and a sharp restaurant serving traditional fare (Db-€47–72 depending on size, plumbing, and view—showers cheaper than baths; extra bed-€10, *menus* from €24, closed Nov–Feb, tel. 03 80 49 22 00, fax 03 80 49 21 27, www.hostellerie-chateauneuf.com, hdc@hostellerie -chateauneuf.com, family-run by Scottish Catherine and French husband Eric). Their "Residence" nearby has bigger rooms, but with less character.

Semur-en-Auxois

This happy town feels real. There are few tourists and no important sights to digest—just a pleasing jumble of Burgundian alleys

perched above the meandering Armançon River and behind the town's four massive towers, all beautifully illuminated after dark.

Semur-en-Auxois (suh-moor-ahn-ohx-wah) works well as a base to visit the sights described in this day trip, or as a handy lunch or dinner stop. Semur is also about 45 minutes from the famous church in Vézelay (see page 668) and two hours from Paris, making it an easy first- or last-night stop on your trip. Don't miss the smashing panorama of Semur (best at night) from the viewpoint by the Citroën shop where D-980 and D-954 intersect (see "View over Semur-en-Auxois" under "Sights," page 663).

Tourist Information

The TI is across from Hôtel Côte d'Or, at Semur's medieval entry (June–Sept Mon–Sat 9:30–13:00 & 13:45–18:00, Sun 10:00–12:00; Oct–May Mon 13:45–17:00, Tue–Sat 9:30–13:00 & 13:45–17:00, closed Sun; 2 place Gaveau, tel. 03 80 97 05 96, www.ville-semur-en -auxois.fr). Pick up their city-walking brochure, information on the regional sights, and bike-rental information and suggested routes (hilly terrain). There's an SNCF rail office in the TI where railpass users can get free tickets for the bus to Montbard.

SIGHTS

You can connect the following sights (and see everything of importance in Semur) with a short stroll. Begin at the TI, then stop under the Sauvigny gate.

Sauvigny and Guiller Gates—These two impressive gates provided safe entry to Semur in the Middle Ages. Look up at the Sauvigny gate and see the indentations for posts that held a drawbridge in place. The Guiller gate, 100 years older, marked the town's limit in the 1300s.

• *From here, enter charming rue Buffon, Semur's oldest commercial street. At the end of this street is the...*

Church of Notre-Dame—The town's main sight, the 13th-century church that dominates its small square, is worth a quick look. Walk counterclockwise around the ambulatory behind the altar. The first chapel on the right is dedicated to St. Eloi and has unusual stained-glass windows honoring Semur's WWI soldiers. Then notice the rich colors in the next chapel. Gothic churches were usually brightly painted, not as you see them today—somber and gray. The bits of stained glass around Mary's statue date from the 13th century and are the only originals left. Before leaving the church, glance at the second-to-last chapel on your right, with a large plaque honoring American soldiers who lost their lives in World War I (Mon–Sat 9:00–12:00 & 14:00–18:30, Sun 14:00–18:30, decent English handout).

• *Leave with the church to your back and walk down the square, then turn left at the bottom on rue du Rempart and see...*

Semur's Towers—You'll pass three of Semur's four burly towers. In the Middle Ages, 18 towers were connected by defensive ramparts to encircle the center city. Caught in a crossfire between the powerful Dukes of Burgundy and the king of France, Semur's defenses were first destroyed by Louis XI in 1478, then finished off during the wars of religion in 1602.

• *Keep straight for several blocks, and find the park where Semur's outer defenses once stood. Walk down the road that drops below the walls, turn left at the bottom, and follow the road for views up to Semur. Just after*

the medieval bridge, look for steps up to your left (rue du Fourneau) to
return to the town center. For even better vistas, consider the classic...

▲▲**View over Semur-en-Auxois**—Drive or hike downhill from
the TI, cross the river, then head uphill and turn left at the top
roundabout. Just after the Citroën dealership, there's a lookout
with an orientation table and a memorable view of the red roofs,
spires, and towers—especially striking at night. Walkers don't
need to go the distance; views are great well before this viewpoint.

SLEEPING AND EATING

If Semur-en-Auxois seduces you into spending a night, try
$$ Hôtel les Cymaises,** where you get three-star comfort for
the price of two, with comfortable rooms and big beds in a manor
house with a quiet courtyard (Db-€64, Tb-€75, 2-room Qb-€93,
private parking, 7 rue du Renaudot, tel. 03 80 97 21 44, fax 03 80
97 18 23, www.hotelcymaises.com, hotel.cymaises@libertysurf.fr).

L'Entracte is where everybody goes for pizza, pasta, salads,
and more in a relaxed atmosphere (daily, below the church on 4
rue Fevret). The historic **charcuterie** (delicatessen) across from the
church can supply your picnic needs.

Abbey of Fontenay

The entire ensemble of buildings making up this isolated Cistercian
abbey, rated ▲▲, has survived, giv-
ing visitors perhaps the best picture
of medieval abbey life in France. In
the Middle Ages it was written, "To
fully grasp the meaning of Fontenay
and the power of its beauty, you
must approach it trudging through
the forest footpaths...through the
brambles and bogs...in an October
rain." But even if you use the park-
ing lot, Fontenay's secluded setting,
blanketed in birdsong with a garden
lovingly used "as a stage set," is truly
magical.

Cost and Hours: €9, daily 10:00–18:00, tel. 03 80 92 15 00.

Getting There: The abbey is a 20-minute drive from Semur by
way of Montbard. There's no bus service—allow about €20 round-
trip for a taxi from Montbard's train station (taxi tel. 06 08 26 61
55 or 06 08 99 21 13, Montbard TI tel. 03 80 92 53 81).

History: This abbey—one of the oldest Cistercian abbeys in

France—was founded in 1118 by St. Bernard as a back-to-basics reaction to the excesses of Benedictine abbeys, such as Cluny. The Cistercians worked to recapture the simplicity, solitude, and poverty of the early Church. Bernard created "a horrible vast solitude" in the forest, where his monks could live like the desert fathers of the Old Testament. They chose marshland ("Cistercian" is derived from "marshy bogs") and strove to be separate from the world (which required the industrious self-sufficiency these abbeys were so adept at). The movement spread, essentially colonizing Europe religiously. In 1200, there were more than 500 such monasteries and abbeys in Europe.

Like the Cistercian movement in general, Fontenay flourished through the 13th to 15th centuries. A 14th-century proverb said, "Wherever the wind blows, to Fontenay money flows." Fontenay thrived as a prosperous "mini-city" for nearly 700 years, until the French Revolution, when it became property of the nation and was eventually sold.

◐ Self-Guided Tour: Like visitors centuries ago, you'll enter through the abbey's **gatehouse.** The main difference: Anyone with a ticket gets in, and there's no watchdog barking angrily at you (through the small hole on the right). Pick up the English self-guided tour flier with your ticket. Your visit follows the route below (generally clockwise). Arrows keep you on course, and signs tell you which sections of the abbey are private (as its owners still live here).

The **abbey church** is pure Romanesque and built to St. Bernard's specs: Latin cross plan, no fancy stained glass, unadorned columns, nothing to distract from prayer. The lone statue is the 13th-century *Virgin of Fontenay*, a reminder that the church was dedicated to St. Mary. Enjoy the ethereal light. You can almost hear the brothers chanting.

Stairs lead from the front of the church to a vast, 16th-century, oak-beamed **dormitory** where the monks slept—together, fully dressed, on thin mats. Monastic life was pretty simple: prayer, reading, work, seven services a day, one meal in the winter, two in the summer. Daily rations: a loaf of bread and a quarter-liter of wine.

Back down the stairs, enter the **cloister,** beautiful in its starkness. This was the heart of the community, where monks read, exercised, washed, did small projects—and, I imagine, gave each other those silly haircuts. The shallow alcove (next to the church door) once stored prayer books; notice the slots for shelves. Next to that, the chapter room was where the abbot led discussions and community business was discussed. The adjacent monks' hall was a general-purpose room, likely busy with monks hunched over tables copying sacred texts (a major work of abbeys). The dining hall, or refectory, also faced the cloister (closed to the public).

Across the garden stands the huge abbey **forge.** In the 13th century, the monks at Fontenay ran what many consider Europe's first metalworking plant. Iron ore was melted down in ovens with big bellows. Tools were made and sold for a profit. The hydraulic hammer—which became the basis of industrial manufacturing of iron throughout Europe—was first used here. Leaving the building, walk left around the back to see the stream, which was diverted to power the wheels that operated the forge. Water was vital to abbey life. The pond—originally practical, rather than decorative—was a fish farm (some whoppers survive to this day). Leave through the gift shop, which was the public chapel in the days when visitors were not allowed inside the abbey grounds.

Flavigny-sur-Ozerain

Ten minutes from Semur and five minutes from Alise Ste. Reine, little Flavigny-sur-Ozerain (flah-veen-yee-sur-oh-zuh-rain) had its 15 minutes of fame in 2000 when the movie *Chocolat* was filmed here. Taking its *chocolat*-covered image in stride, this unassuming and serenely situated village feels permanently stuck in the past, with one café, one *crêperie*, and two boutiques.

There's little to do here other than appreciate the setting (best from the grassy ramparts) and try the little *anis* (anise) candies. Pick up a map at the **TI** (May–Sept daily 10:00–12:30 & 13:00–18:30; April and Oct Tue–Sat 10:30–12:30 & 13:00–18:00, closed Sun–Mon; closed Nov–March; down rue de l'Église in front of church).

Chocolat-lovers will have to be satisfied with a few of the building facades featured in the film; there are no souvenirs or posters to be found, and nary a chocolate shop (locals, who prefer their homemade *anis* candies, weren't thrilled with the movie). There are four buildings that fans might recognize. Most significant is the one used as the *chocolaterie* (chocolate shop); it's across the square from the church entry, just past La Grange restaurant on rue du Four (look for the arched window). The Count's home is today's *mairie* (city hall), also opposite the church entry, but to the left as you leave the church. The *coiffure* (hair dresser) is one door down from the TI—look for the white shutters. And what was the Café de la République is three doors up from the TI, with an austere facade. Johnny Depp never visited Flavigny (his loss), and there is no river here (the river scene was filmed in the Dordogne, near Beynac).

Elsewhere in Flavigny, you can buy the locally produced *anis* candies in pretty tins. They make great souvenirs (see them being made 9:00–11:00 Mon–Fri in the Abbey of St. Pierre). You can also visit the ancient Church of St. Genest (daily 14:00–17:45; if it's closed, ask the town hall next door to open it). The grassy ramparts are worth a stroll for the view (behind the church, down rue de la Poterne, and out the gate).

SLEEPING AND EATING

(€1 = about $1.30, country code: 33)
$$ L'Ange Souriant Chambre d'Hôte is comfortable and intimate (Sb-€50, Db-€60, Tb/Qb-€94, on rue Voltaire, tel. & fax 03 80 96 24 93, www.ange-souriant.com, a.souriant@wanadoo.fr).

$ Le Relais de Flavigny, next door, is an appealing little restaurant with seven basic, bargain rental rooms above (S/D-€28, Ss/Ds-€33, *menus* from €16, €10 hearty summertime lunch salads, daily, at bottom of rue de l'Église from church, tel. 03 80 96 27 77, www.le-relais.fr, relais-de-flavigny@wanadoo.fr).

La Grange ("The Barn") serves farm-fresh fare, including luscious quiche, salad, fresh cheeses, pâtés, and fruit pies (July–mid-Sept Tue–Sun 12:30–18:00, closed Mon; April–June and mid-Sept–Nov open only on Sun, closed Dec–March; across from church, look for brown doors and listen for lunchtime dining, tel. 03 80 35 81 78).

TRANSPORTATION CONNECTIONS

To reach Flavigny, leave Semur following *Venary les Laumes* signs, and look for the turnoff to Flavigny (at the village of Pouillenay). The approach to Flavigny from Pouillenay via D-9 is picture-perfect. Park at the gate or in the lot just below. From this lot, signs lead to *Alise Ste. Reine*, described below (great views back to Flavigny as you leave).

Alise Ste. Reine

A united Gaul forming a single nation animated by the same spirit could defy the universe.
—Julius Caesar, *The Gallic Wars*

A five-minute drive from Venary les Laumes, above the vertical little village of Alise Ste. Reine, is where historians think Julius Caesar defeated the Gallic leader Vercingétorix in 52 B.C., thus winning

Burgundy

Gaul for the Roman Empire and forever changing France's destiny.

Follow the *Statue de Vercingétorix* signs leading up through Alise Ste. Reine to the park with the huge statue of the Gallic warrior overlooking his Waterloo. Stand as he did, imagine yourself trapped on this hilltop, and read about...

The Dying Gauls

In 52 B.C., General Julius Caesar and his 60,000 soldiers surrounded Alésia (today's Alise Ste. Reine), hoping to finally end the uprising of free Gaul and establish Roman civilization in France. Holed up inside the hilltop fortress were 80,000 die-hard (long-haired, tattooed) Gauls under their rebel chief, Vercingétorix (pronounced something like "verse in Genesis"). Having harassed Caesar for months with guerrilla-war attacks, they now called on their fellow Gauls to converge on Alésia to wipe out the Romans.

Rather than attack the fierce-fighting Gauls, Caesar's soldiers patiently camped at the base of the hill and began building a wall. In six weeks, they completed a 12-foot-tall stone wall all the way around Alésia (11 miles around), and then a second larger one (13 miles around), trapping the rebel leaders and hoping to starve them out. If the Gauls tried to escape, not only would they have to breach the two walls, they'd first have to cross a steep no-man's-land dotted with a ditch, a moat, and booby traps (like sharp stakes in pits and buried iron spikes).

The starving Gauls inside Alésia sent their women and children out to beg mercy from the Romans. The Romans (with little food themselves) refused. For days, the women and children wandered the unoccupied land, in full view of both armies, until they starved to death.

After months of siege, Vercingétorix's reinforcements finally came riding to save him. With 90,000 screaming Gallic warriors (Caesar says 250,000) converging on Alésia, and 80,000 more atop the hill, Caesar ordered his men to move between the two walls to fight a two-front battle. The Battle of Alésia raged for five days—a classic struggle between the methodical Romans and the impetuous "barbarians." When it became clear the Romans would not budge, the Gauls retreated.

Vercingétorix surrendered, and Gallic culture was finished in France. During the three-year rebellion, one in five Gauls had been killed, enslaved, or driven out. Roman rule was established for the next 500 years, strangling the Gallic/Celtic heritage. Vercingétorix spent his last years as a prisoner, paraded around as a war trophy. In 46 B.C., he was brought to Rome for Caesar's triumphal ascension to power, where he was strangled to death in a public ritual.

Between Burgundy and the Loire

These two sights—Vézelay and its Romanesque Basilica of Ste. Madeleine, and the under-construction Château de Guédelon—make good stops for drivers connecting Burgundy and the Loire Valley, or linking Burgundy and Paris, though you'll want to leave by 9:00 to fit in both. (Allow a total of six hours of driving, plus time to visit each sight.)

Vézelay and the Basilica of Ste. Madeleine

For over eight centuries, travelers have hoofed it up through this pretty little town to get to the famous hilltop church, the Basilica of Ste. Madeleine. In its 12th-century prime, Vézelay welcomed the medieval masses. Cultists of Mary Magdalene came to file past her (supposed) body. Pilgrims rendezvoused here to march to Spain to venerate St. James' (supposed) relics in Santiago de Compostela. Three Crusades were launched from this hill: the Second Crusade (1146), announced by Bernard of Clairveaux, the Cluny abbot with pope-like powers; the Third Crusade (1190), under Richard the Lionheart and King Philippe Auguste; and the Seventh Crusade (1248), by King (and Saint) Louis IX. Today, tourists flock to Vézelay's basilica, famous for its place in history, its soul-stirring Romanesque architecture—reproduced in countless art books—and for the relics of Mary Magdalene.

Tourist Information: Vézelay's TI, which has Internet access, is at the lower end of the village (on rue St. Etienne, which turns into rue St. Pierre; June–Oct daily 10:00–13:00 & 14:00–18:00; Nov–May Fri–Wed 10:00–13:00 & 14:00–18:00, closed Thu; tel. 03 86 33 23 69).

SIGHTS

▲Basilica of Ste. Madeleine

To accommodate the growing crowds of medieval pilgrims, the abbots of Vézelay enlarged their original church (1104), then rebuilt it after a disastrous 1120 fire. The building we see today—one of the largest and best-preserved Romanesque churches—was done in stages: nave (1120–1140), narthex (1132–1145), and choir (1215). The construction spanned the century-long transition from the

Romanesque style (round barrel arches like the ancient Romans', thick walls, small windows) to Gothic (pointed arches, flying buttresses, high nave, lots of stained glass). Vézelay blends elements of both styles.

Cost and Hours: Free entry, daily 8:00–19:30.

Tours and Information: Eager volunteers offer one-hour English guided tours that depart from inside the narthex (no tours 12:00–14:00, donation requested, call to get times or to arrange a private tour, tel. 03 86 33 39 50). For extra credit, buy the €5 guidebook as you enter. The view from the park behind the church is sublime.

⊘ Self-Guided Tour: The **facade**—with one tower missing its original steeple, another that's unfinished altogether, and an inauthentic tympanum—isn't why you came. Step inside.

The **narthex,** or entrance hall, served several functions. Religiously, it was a place to cross from the profane to the sacred. Practically, it gave shelter to overflow pilgrim crowds (even overnight, if necessary) as they shuffled through one of the three doorways. And aesthetically, the dark narthex prepares the visitor for the radiant nave.

The tympanum (carved relief) over the central doorway is one of Romanesque's signature pieces. It shows the risen Christ, ascending to heaven in an almond-shaped cloud, shooting Holy Ghost rays at his apostles and telling them to preach the Good News to the ends of the Earth. The whole diversity of humanity (appropriate, considering Vézelay's function as a gathering place) appears beneath: hunters, fishermen, farmers, pygmies, and men with long ears, feathers, and dog heads. The signs of the zodiac arch over the scene.

Gaze through the central doorway into the **nave** at the rows and rows of arches that seem to recede into a luminous infinity—the effect is mesmerizing. The nave is long, high, and narrow (200' x 60' x 35'), creating a tunnel effect formed by 10 columns-and-arches on each side. Overhead is the church's most famous feature—barrel vaults (wide arches) built of stones alternating between creamy-white and pink-brown. The side aisles have low ceilings, while the nave rises up between them, lined with slender, floor-to-ceiling columns that unite both stories. The interior glows with an even light from the unstained glass of the clerestory windows. The absence of distractions or bright colors makes this simple church perfect for meditation.

The capitals of the nave's columns are carved masterpieces by several sculptors of saints and Bible scenes. All are worth studying (the guidebook sold at the entry identifies each scene, starting in the narthex), but some you might easily recognize are David and Goliath (fourth column on left), Moses and the Golden Calf (sixth

Mary Magdalene

France has a special affection for Mary Magdalene (La Madeleine), and Vézelay is one of several churches dedicated to her—a rarity in Europe, where most churches honor Jesus' mother, the Virgin Mary.

The Bible says that Mary Magdalene, one of Jesus' followers, was exorcised of seven demons (Luke 8:2), witnessed the Crucifixion (Matthew 27:56), and was the first mortal to see the resurrected Jesus (Mark 16:9–11)—the other disciples didn't believe her.

Some theologians have fleshed out Mary's reputation by associating her with biblical passages that don't specifically name her: e.g., the sinner who washed Jesus' feet with her hair (Luke 7:36–50), the forgiven adulteress (John 8), or the woman with the alabaster jar who anointed Jesus (Matthew 26:7–13).

In medieval times, legends appeared (especially in France) that, after the Crucifixion, Mary Magdalene fled to southern France, lived devoutly in a cave, converted locals, performed miracles, and died in Provence. Renaissance artists portrayed her as a fanciful blend of Bible and legend: a red-headed, long-haired prostitute who was rescued by Jesus, symbolizing the sin of those who love too much.

In recent times, feminists have claimed Mary Magdalene a victim of male-dominated Catholic suppression. Bible scholars cite passages in two ancient (but non-canonical) gospels that cryptically allude to Mary as Jesus' special "companion." The Da Vinci Code—a popular if unhistorical novel—seizes on this, slathers it with medieval legend, and asserts that Mary Magdalene was actually Jesus' wife who bore him descendants, and that her relics lie not in Vézelay but in a shopping mall in Paris.

column), Adam and Eve (ninth column), Peter Freed from Prison (10th and final column on the left), and the well-known "Mystical Mill" (fourth column on right), showing Old Testament Moses and New Testament Paul working together to fill sacks with grain (and, metaphorically, the Bible with words).

The light at the end of the tunnel-like nave is the **choir** (altar area), radiating a brighter, blue-gray light. Constructed when Gothic was the rage, the choir has pointed arches and improved engineering, but the feel is monotone and sterile.

In the right transept stands a statue of the woman this church was dedicated to—not the Virgin Mary (Jesus' mother) but one of Jesus' disciples, Mary Magdalene. She cradles an alabaster jar of ointment she used (according to some Bible interpretations) to anoint Jesus.

Drop into the **crypt** for the ultimate medieval experience in one of Europe's greatest medieval churches. You're entering the foundations of the earlier, ninth-century church that monks built here on the hilltop after Vikings had twice pillaged their church at the base of the hill.

File past the small container with the **relics of Mary Magdalene.** In medieval times, Vézelay claimed to possess Mary's entire body, but the relics were later damaged and scattered by anti-Catholic Huguenots (16th century) and Revolutionaries (18th century), leaving only a few pieces.

Are they really her mortal remains? We only have legends—many different versions—that first appeared in the historical record around A.D. 1000. The most popular legends say that Mary Magdalene traveled to Provence where she died, and that her bones were brought from there by a monk to save them from Muslim pirates. In the 11th century, the abbots of Vézelay heavily marketed the notion that these were Mary's relics, and when the pope authenticated it in 1058, tourism boomed.

Vézelay prospered until the mid-13th century, when King Charles of Anjou announced that Mary's body was not in Vézelay, but had been found in another town. Vézelay's relics suddenly looked bogus, and pilgrims stopped coming. For the next five centuries, the church fell into disrepair and then was vandalized by secularists in the Revolution. The church was restored (1840–1860) by a young architect named Eugène Viollet-le-Duc, who would later revamp Notre-Dame in Paris.

After visiting the chapter house and cloisters (out the right transept), make sure you catch the view from behind the church of the Cure river valley.

SLEEPING AND EATING

(€1 = about $1.30, country code: 33)
You'll find pleasant cafés with reasonable food all along the street leading to the church.

$$ Hôtel de la Poste et du Lion d'Or has the best moderate, country-classy rooms in Vézelay (good Db-€70–76, bigger Db-€90, easy parking, at the foot of the village, place du Champ-de-Foire, tel. 03 86 33 21 23, fax 03 86 32 30 92, www.laposte-liondor.com, contact@laposte-liondor.com).

La Dent Creuse has the best terrace tables at the lower end of the village (left side), with salads, pizza, and more (daily until 21:30, place du Champ-de-Foire, tel. 03 86 33 36 33).

Auberge de la Coquille is a cozy place to eat inside and out, with reasonable prices (daily until 21:30, halfway up to the church at 81 rue St. Pierre, tel. 03 86 33 35 57).

TRANSPORTATION CONNECTIONS

Vézelay is about 45 minutes northwest of Semur-en-Auxois (20 min off the autoroute to Paris). Train travelers go to Sermizelles (by way of Auxerre or Avallon, 5/day) and taxi from there (6 miles, allow €17 one-way, taxi tel. 03 86 32 31 88 or 06 85 77 89 36).

Château de Guédelon

▲▲A historian's dream (and worth ▲▲▲ for kids), this medieval castle is being built by 35 enthusiasts using only the tools, techniques, and materials available in the 13th century. The project is the dream of two individuals and is based on plans drafted in 1250. When complete, it will include four towers surrounding a central courtyard with a drawbridge and a moat. The goal of this exciting project is to give visitors a better appreciation of medieval construction, and for the builders to learn about medieval techniques as they work. Ground was broken in 1998, but the castle won't be complete for another 18 years (the castle is currently about 10–20 feet tall). When the castle is done, the ambitious owners plan to build a medieval abbey.

Enter the project to the sound of chisels chipping rock and the sight of people dressed as if it were 800 years ago. A human-powered hamster wheel hoists carefully dressed stone up tower walls (the largest tower will reach six stories when completed). Carpenters whack away at massive beams, creating supports for stone arches, while weavers make the cloth worn by the builders (a sheep's pen provides the raw material). Thirteen workstations help visitors learn about castle construction, from medieval rope-making to blacksmithing. Feel free to ask the workers questions, since some speak English.

Kids can't get enough of Guédelon—it was my son's favorite place in France. It's a favorite for local school field trips, so expect lots of kids. And if it's been raining, expect a muddy mess—you are, after all, in a construction site.

Cost and Hours: €9, excellent English handout, picnic area and lunch café inside; castle open July–Aug daily 10:00–19:00; mid-March–June Thu–Tue 10:00–18:00, Sun until 19:00, closed Wed; Sept Thu–Tue 10:00–17:30, Sat–Sun until 18:00, closed Wed; Oct Thu–Tue 10:00–17:30, closed Wed; closed Nov–mid-March; tel. 03 86 45 66 66, www.guedelon.fr.

Guided Tours: To make the most of this sight—easily worth it if you have kids—contact Guédelon expert and American expat Julie Sonveau (€100, 90 min, tel. 03 86 74 64 75 or 06 63 54 86 88, julie.son@hotmail.com).

Getting There: Guédelon is an hour west of Vézelay on D-955, between St. Amand-en-Puisaye and St. Saveur-en-Puisaye.

Sleeping near Guédelon: Guédelon is remote. If you need to sleep nearby, try **Hôtel Les Grands Chênes**, where British Rachael and French Alain have restored a pretty manor home among trees, lakes, and waves of grass (Db-€72, Tb-€72–87, Qb-€110, on D-18 between St. Fargeau and St. Amand-en-Puisaye, tel. 03 86 74 04 05, fax 03 86 74 11 41, www.hotel-de-puisaye.com, contact@hotel -de-puisaye.com).

Between Burgundy and Lyon

Drivers traveling south from Beaune should think about detouring into the lovely and unspoiled Mâconnais countryside. Brancion, Chapaize, Cluny, and Taizé gather a few minutes from each other, about 25 minutes west of the autoroute between Mâcon and Tournus. Those day-tripping from Beaune should allow most of a day. To connect these towns scenically from Beaune, follow N-74 south to Chagny (Burgundy's ugliest town), find nearby Remigny (just east of Chagny), and follow D-109 to Aluze. Then follow D-978 east and D-981 south through Givry, Buxy, and on to Chapaize. Michelin map #520 is helpful.

Brancion and Chapaize

An hour south of Beaune by car (12 miles west of Tournus on D-14) are two tiny villages, each with "daughters of Cluny"—churches that owe their existence and architectural design to the nearby and once-powerful Cluny Abbey. Between the villages you'll pass a Stonehenge-era menhir (standing stone) with a cross added on top at a later point—evidence that this was sacred ground long before Christianity (from Brancion, it's on the right just after passing the bulky Château de Nobles).

Brancion

This is a classic feudal village. Back when there were no nations in Europe, control of land was delegated from lord to vassal. The Duke of Burgundy ruled here through his vassal, the Lord of Brancion. His vast domain—much of south Burgundy—was administered from this tiny fortified town.

Within its walls, the feudal lord had a castle, church, and all the necessary administrative buildings to provide justice, collect taxes, and so on. Strategically perched on a hill between two river valleys, he enjoyed a complete view of his domain. Brancion's population peaked centuries ago at 60. Today, it's home to only four full-time residents.

The castle, part of a network of 17 castles in the region, was destroyed in 1576 by Protestant Huguenots. After the French Revolution, it was sold to be used as a quarry and spent most of the 19th century being picked apart. While the flier gives a brief tour, the small castle is most enjoyable for its evocative angles and the lush views from the top of its keep (€4, daily 9:00–18:00).

Wandering from the castle to the church, you'll pass the town's lone business, a 15th-century market hall demonstrating France's boundless love affair with the market day (used by farmers from the surrounding countryside until 1900), plus several other buildings from that period.

The 12th-century warm-stone church (with faint paintings surviving from 1330) is the town's highlight. Circumnavigate the small building—this is Romanesque at its pure, unadulterated, fortress-of-God best (thick walls, small windows, once colorfully painted interior, no-frills exterior). Notice the stone roof; inside, find the English explanations of the paintings. From its front door, enjoy a lord's view over one glorious Burgundian estate.

Sleeping and Eating in or near Brancion: You have two good choices. In the center of the village, **$ L'Auberge du Vieux Brancion** serves traditional Burgundian fare (€14 lunch *menu*, €22 dinner *menu*) and also offers a perfectly tranquil place to spend the night (very simple and frumpy rooms, Ds-€37, Db-€50–56, family rooms-€55–72, tel. & fax 03 85 51 03 83, www.brancion.fr, josserand@brancion.fr).

For a much more upscale experience, including the best Burgundian view rooms that I've found, drive a mile south of the village, following the sign to **$$$ Hôtel la Montagne de Brancion*****. A vine-covered paradise awaits...for a price. Every one of the 19 sharp, deck-equipped rooms faces a territorial view over vineyards, hills, and pastures. The garden comes with sway-back view chairs, and a pool lies below. The owners pride themselves on their "gourmet restaurant" and expect you to dine there (Db-€138–162, Tb-170, suites-€215, breakfast-€15, *menus* from €45 or à la carte, tel. 03 85 51 12 40, fax 03 85 51 18 64, www.brancion .com, lamontagnedebrancion@wanadoo.fr).

Chapaize

This hamlet, a few miles closer to Beaune, grew up around its Benedictine monastery—only its 11th-century church survives. It's a pristine place (cars park at the edge of town), peppered with flowers and rustic decay, and surrounded by grassy fields. A ghost-town café faces the village's classic Romanesque church—study the fine stonework by Lombard masons. (Its lean seems designed to challenge the faith of parishioners.) The WWI monument near the entry—with so many names from such a tiny hamlet—is a reminder that half of all young French men were casualties in the war that *didn't* end all wars. Wander around the back for a view of the belfry, and then ponder Chapaize across the street while sipping a café au lait.

Cluny

People come from great distances to admire Cluny's great abbey that is no more. This mother of all abbeys once vied with the Vatican as the most important power center in Christendom (Cluny's abbot often served as mediator between Europe's kings and the pope). The building was destroyed during the French Revolution, and there's precious little to see today. Still, the abbey makes a worthwhile visit for history buffs looking to get some idea of the scale of this vast complex.

The pleasant little town that grew up around the abbey maintains its street plan, with plenty of original buildings, and even the same population it had in its 12th-century heyday (4,500). As you wander the town, which claims to be the finest surviving Romanesque town in France, enjoy the architectural details on everyday buildings. Much of the town's fortified walls, gates, and towers survive.

ORIENTATION

Everything of interest is within a few minutes' walk of the **TI** (daily June–Sept 10:00–12:30 & 14:30–18:45, May and Oct closes at 18:00, Nov–April closes at 17:00, pick up the "helpful practical guide," 6 rue Mercière, tel. 03 85 59 05 34).

The TI is at the base of the **"Cheese Tower,"** so named because it was used to age cheese (or perhaps for the way tourists smell after climbing to the top). The tower offers a fine city view (€1.25, same hours as TI).

A **farmers' market** animates the old town each Saturday.

Arrival in Cluny

Drivers will park at designated lots and follow *Centre-Ville* signs on foot. Bus connections are meager (3–4/day from Chalon-sur-Saône, 75 min; 6/day from Mâcon, 50 min), and there's no train station.

History of Cluny and its (Scant) Abbey

In 1964, St. Benedict (480–547), founder of the first monastery (Montecassino, south of Rome) from which a great monastic movement sprang, was named the patron saint of Europe. Christians and non-Christians alike recognize the impact that monasteries had in establishing a European civilization out of the dark chaos that followed the fall of Rome.

The Abbey of Cluny was the ruling center of the first great international franchise, or chain, of monasteries in Europe. It was the heart of an upsurge in monasticism, of church reform, and an evangelical revival that spread throughout Europe—a phenomenon historians call the Age of Faith (11th and 12th centuries). From this springboard came a vast network of abbeys, priories, and other monastic orders that kindled the establishment of modern Europe.

In 910, 12 monks founded a house of prayer at Cluny, vowing to follow the rules of St. Benedict. The cult of saints and relics was enthusiastically promoted. The order was independent and powerful. From the start, the Abbot of Cluny answered only to the pope (not to the local bishop or secular leader). The abbots of the other Cluniac monasteries were answerable only to the Abbot of Cluny (not to their local bishop or prince). This made the Abbot of Cluny arguably the most powerful person in Europe.

Guides at Cluny attribute the abbey's success to several factors. Most importantly, Cluny was blessed by a series of wise and long-lived abbots who managed to keep out of the costly Crusades that seduced so much of Europe into exciting but futile adventures in the Holy Land. (They believed that, by praising God in a glorious monastic setting, they could reach a "celestial Jerusalem" without even leaving home.) These Benedictines managed to get Europe's warrior class to respect the life and property of noncombatants (monks and clergy). They convinced Europe's noble class—its great landowners—to will their estates to the order in return for perpetual prayers for the benefit of their needy and frightened souls.

From all this grew the greatest monastic movement of the High Middle Ages. A huge church was built at Cluny, where in 1100, it was the headquarters of 10,000 monks who ran nearly a thousand monasteries and priories across Europe. Cluny peaked in the 12th century, then faded in influence (though monasteries continued to increase in numbers and remain a force until 1789).

SIGHTS

Cluny has two sights—a museum and the abbey—but most visitors will be satisfied without paying to enter either. The museum's highlight (a big model of medieval Cluny) is free to view from the entry, and the abbey itself is easily viewed from outside (€6.50 ticket covers both museum and abbey entrance, both open daily May–Aug 9:30–18:30, Sept–April 9:30–12:00 & 13:30–17:00, tel. 03 85 59 15 93). Historians should invest in the €7 *The Abbey of Cluny* guidebook, sold in the museum.

Museum of Art and Archaeology (Musée Ochier)—The small abbey museum fills the Palace of the Abbot with bits from medieval Cluny and a very helpful model of the abbey complex (visit this before you explore the ruins). I like seeing the stone carvings eye-to-eye, though the museum holds little else of interest.

Site of Cluny Abbey—Much of today's old town stands on the site of what was the largest church in Christendom. It was 555 feet long, and soared high with five naves. The whole complex (church plus monastery) covered 25 acres. Revolutionaries destroyed it in 1790. Today, only the tower and part of the transept still stand. The visitor's challenge: Visualize it. Get a sense of its grandeur. The National Stud Farm and a big school obliterate much of the floor plan of the abbey.

The best point from which to appreciate the abbey's awesome dimensions is atop the steps across from the museum. Look out to the remaining tower (there used to be three). You're standing above the end of the nave that stretched all the way to those towers. Down the steps, a marble table shows the original floor plan (*vous êtes ici* means "you are here"). Walk past the nubs that remain of the once-massive columns.

You can use the English flier to tour what little of the abbey still stands (entrance between the Hôtel Bourgogne—see below—and the cool Café du Nord). Along the way, you'll find helpful English information posted. Still, there's not much to see. The best reason to enter the site is to watch the 10-minute 3-D film. It's in French only, but still worthwhile, offering a virtual tour of the 1,000-year-old church that helps you grasp the tragedy of its destruction. If you tour the abbey, you'll exit at the flour mill (Tour de Farine), where you can loop back along the town's pleasing main drag, rue de Mercière (cafés, shops, and the TI line this pedestrian-friendly street).

National Stud Farm (Les Haras Nationaux)—Napoleon (who needed *beaucoup de* horses for his army of 600,000) established this horse farm in 1806. Today, 50 thoroughbred stallions kill time in their stables. If the stalls are empty, they're out doing their current studly duty...creating fine racehorses. The gate is next to Hôtel

Bourgogne (€5, visits only by guided tour, usually in the afternoon, guides speak some English, get schedule from TI).

SLEEPING

(€1 = about $1.30, country code: 33)
If you're spending the night, bed down at the cushy and traditional **$$ Hôtel Bourgogne*****, which is built into the wall of the abbey's right transept and is as central as can be for enjoying the town (standard Db-€82–98, bigger Db-€125, place de l'Abbaye, tel. 03 85 59 00 58, fax 03 85 59 03 73, www.hotel-cluny.com, contact @hotel-cluny.com). It also has a fine restaurant (*menus* from €24).

Taizé

To experience the latest in European monasticism, drop by the booming Christian community of Taizé (teh-zay), a few miles north of Cluny on the road to Brancion. The normal, un-cultlike ambience of this place—with thousands of mostly young, European pilgrims asking each other, "How's your soul today?"—is remarkable. Even if this sounds a tad airy, you might find the 30 minutes it takes to stroll from one end of the compound to the other—amid ancient abbeys and noble Romanesque churches—a worthwhile detour. A visit to Taizé can be a thought-provoking experience, particularly after a visit to Cluny. A thousand years ago, Cluny had a similar power to draw the faithful in search of direction and meaning in life.

The Taizé community welcomes visitors who'd like to spend a few days getting close to God through meditation, singing, and simple living. While designed primarily for youthful pilgrims in meditative retreat (there are about 5,000 here in a typical week), people of any age are welcome to pop in for a meal or church service.

Taizé is an ecumenical movement—prayer, silence, simplicity—welcoming Protestant as well as Catholic Christians. While it feels Catholic, it isn't. (But, as some of the brothers are actually Catholic priests, Catholics may take the Eucharist.) The Taizé style of worship is well-known among American Christians for its hauntingly beautiful chants—songbooks and CDs are the most popular souvenirs from here.

Three times a day, the bells ring and worshippers file into the long, low, simple, and modern Church of Reconciliation. It's dim—candlelit with glowing icons—as the white-robed brothers enter. The service features responsive singing of chants (from well-worn songbooks that list lyrics in 19 languages), reading of biblical passages, and silence, as worshippers on crude kneelers stare into icons. The aim: "Entering together into the mystery of God's presence." (Secondary aim: Helping Lutherans get over their fear of icons.)

Getting There: Drivers follow *La Communauté* signs and park in a dirt lot. Buses serve Taizé from Chalon-sur-Saône to the north and from Mâcon to the south (3/day, 60 min from each).

Orientation: At the southern (Cluny) end, the Welcome Office provides an orientation and daily schedule, and makes a good first stop (pick a copy of the bimonthly *Letter from Taizé* and the single-page information leaflet, *The Taizé Community*). Time your visit for a church service (Mon–Sat 8:15, 12:20, and 20:30; Sun 10:00 and 20:30, Catholic and Protestant communion available daily). The Exposition (next to the church) is the thriving community shop, with books, CDs, sheet music, handicrafts, and other souvenirs. The Oyak (near the parking lot) is where those in a less monastic mood can get a beer or burger.

Staying at Taizé: Those on retreat fill their days with worship services; workshops; simple, relaxed meals; and hanging out in an international festival of people searching for meaning in their lives. Visitors are welcomed free. The cost for a real stay is €10–20 per day (based on a sliding scale; those under 18 stay for less) for monastic-style room and board. Adults (over age 30) are accommodated in a more comfortable zone, but count on simple dorms. Call or email first if you plan to stay overnight (reception open Mon–Fri 10:00–12:00 & 18:00–19:00, tel. 03 85 50 30 02). The Taizé community website explains everything—in 29 languages (www.taize.fr).

LYON AND THE RHONE VALLEY

Rhône-Alpes

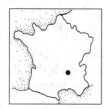

The Rhône Valley links Provence and Burgundy and is the gateway to the high Alps. The region is bordered to the west by the soft hills of the Massif Central and by the rolling foothills of the Alps just to the east. The mighty Rhône River rumbles through the valley from its origin in Lake Geneva to its final resting place 500 miles away in the Mediterranean near Arles.

Vineyards blanket the western side of the Rhône Valley, from those of the Beaujolais just north of Lyon, to the steep slopes of Tain-Hermitage below Lyon. On the eastern side of the river and closer to Avignon are the vineyards of the famous Côtes du Rhône.

The Rhône Valley has always provided the path of least resistance for access from the Mediterranean to northern Europe, and today Roman ruins litter the valley between Lyon and Orange.

This overlooked region is dominated by the energetic metropolis of Lyon, a center of industry and culture. Just 70 minutes south of Beaune, two hours north of Avignon, and 90 minutes west of Annecy, Lyon is France's best-kept urban secret, and deserves at least one night and a full day.

Cuisine Scene in Lyon

For the people of Lyon, eating out is a passion. It's all the buzz—a favorite conversation topic likely to generate heated debate. Here, great chefs are more famous than professional soccer players. (Paul Bocuse is the most famous chef.) Restaurants seem to outnumber cars, and all are busy. With an abundance of cozy, excellent restaurants in every price range, it's hard to go wrong—unless you order *tripes* (cow intestines, also known as *tablier de sapeur*), *foie de veau* (calf's liver), or *tête de veau* (calf's head). Beware: These questionable dishes are very common in small bistros *(bouchons)* and can be the only choices on cheaper *menus*. Look instead for these classics: St. Marcellin cheese, *salade lyonnaise* (croutons, ham, and a poached egg on a bed of lettuce), green lentils *(lentilles)* served on a salad or with sausages, *quenelles de brochet* (fish dumplings in a creamy sauce), and *filet de sandre* (local whitefish).

Lyon

Straddling the Rhône and Saône rivers between Burgundy and Provence, Lyon has been among France's leading cities since Roman times. Today, overlooked Lyon is one of France's big-city surprises. In spite of its workaday, business-first facade, Lyon is France's most historic and culturally important city after Paris. You'll experience two different-as-night-and-day cities: the Old World cobbled alleys, Renaissance mansions, and colorful facades of Vieux Lyon; and the more staid but classy, Parisian-feeling shopping streets of Presqu'île. Once you're settled, this big city feels small, welcoming, and surprisingly untouristy. It seems everyone's enjoying the place—and they're all French.

Planning Your Time

Lyon makes a handy day visit for train travelers, as many trains pass through Lyon and both stations have baggage check and easy connections to the city center. But those who spend the night can experience the most renowned cuisine in France at appetizing prices, and enjoy one of Europe's most beautifully floodlit cities.

For a full day of sightseeing, start on Fourvière Hill (to get here, take the funicular near St. Jean Cathedral in Vieux Lyon), visit the Notre-Dame Basilica, and tour the Roman Theaters and Gallo-Roman Museum. Then catch the funicular back down to Vieux Lyon and have lunch, then explore the old town and its hidden passageways. Finish your day touring the Museum of Fine Arts, Resistance Center, or Lumière Museum (on early films). Many of Lyon's important sights are closed on Mondays, Tuesdays, or both. Dine well in the evening and cap your day enjoying a stroll through the best-lit city in France.

Drivers connecting Lyon with southern destinations should consider the scenic detour via the Ardèche Gorges (see Lyon's "Transportation Connections," page 702), and those connecting to Burgundy should consider taking the Beaujolais Wine Route, then visiting Brancion and Cluny (see page 702).

ORIENTATION

Despite being France's third-largest metropolitan area (after Paris and Marseille), Lyon is peaceful and manageable. Traffic noise is

replaced by pedestrian friendliness in the old center—listen to how quiet this big city is. Notice the emphasis on environmentally friendly transport: Electric buses have replaced many diesel buses, and pedal taxis (called *"cyclopolitains,"* seek-loh-poh-lee-tan) are used instead of traditional taxis for short trips for a cost of just €1 per kilometer. A network of more than 1,000 city-owned bikes is available for locals' use (you'll see these black-and-red bikes everywhere—unfortunately, they require a French credit card to use).

Lyon provides the organized traveler with a full day of activities. Sightseeing can be done on foot from any of the recommended hotels, though it's handy to make use of the funiculars and Métro. Most of the town's attractions can be conveniently linked in an easy walking-tour route. Lyon's sights are concentrated in three areas: Fourvière Hill, with its white Notre-Dame Basilica glimmering over the city; historic Vieux Lyon, which lies below on the bank of the Saône River; and the Presqu'île (home to my recommended hotels), lassoed by the Saône and Rhone rivers. Huge place Bellecour lies in the middle of the Presqu'île, and always seems to be hosting an event.

Tourist Information

The well-equipped TI is generous with helpful, free information, and can reserve a hotel for you at no charge (daily mid-April–mid-Sept 9:30–18:30, mid-Sept–mid-April 10:00–17:30, tel. 04 72 77 69 69, www.lyon-france.com, corner of place Bellecour, free public WCs behind the TI building). Pick up the English version of the city map (with museum information, good enlargements of central Lyon and Vieux Lyon, and all public parking lots); an event schedule (ask about concerts in the Roman Theaters during *Les Nuits de Fourvière*—early June–early Aug—and events at the Opera House); and the *Enjoy Lyon City Guide* (with a directory of shopping and eateries, as well as articles on special aspects of the city).

The TI sells a useful **Lyon City Card** for serious sightseers (1 day-€19, 2 consecutive days-€29, 3 consecutive days-€39, under 18 half-price). This pass includes all Lyon museums, free use of the Métro/bus system, a walking tour of Lyon with a live guide or audioguide (see "Tours," below), and a river cruise. If you visit the Gallo-Roman Museum and the Resistance and Deportation History Center, plus take a guided walking tour, the one-day pass pays for itself. Consider getting the *World Heritage Excursions* **guidebook** (€6, see "Tours," page 685).

Arrival in Lyon

By Train: Lyon has two train stations—Lyon-Perrache and Part-Dieu. Many trains stop at both, and through-trains connect the two stations every 10 minutes. Both have baggage-check services (daily 6:00–23:00) and are well-served by Métro, bus, airport shuttle, and taxi.

The **Perrache station** is more central and within a 20-minute walk of place Bellecour (follow *Porte/Place Carnot* signs, then cross place Carnot and walk straight up pedestrian rue Victor Hugo). Or take the Métro (direction: Laurent Bonnevay) two stops to Bellecour and follow *sortie rue République* signs.

The **Part-Dieu station** is a bit smaller, but has the same services as Perrache. To get to the city center, follow *sortie Vivier Merle* signs outside the station to the Métro. Take the Métro toward Stade de Gerland, transfer at Saxe-Gambetta to the Gare de Vaise route, get off at Bellecour, and follow signs reading *sortie rue République* (see "Getting Around Lyon," below, for Métro help).

Figure about €12 for a **taxi** from either train station to the hotels listed near place Bellecour.

By Car: The city center has good signage and is relatively easy to navigate, though you'll encounter traffic on the surrounding freeways. To get from the freeways to the center, follow *Centre-Ville* and *Presqu'île* signs, and then follow *place Bellecour* signs. Park in the lots under place Bellecour or place des Célestins (yellow *P* means "parking lot") or get advice from your hotel. The TI's map identifies all public car parks. Overnight parking (generally 19:00–8:00) is only €3.50, but day rates are nearly €2 per hour.

By Plane: Lyon's sleek little airport, Saint-Exupéry—only 15 miles from the city center—is a breeze to navigate (ATMs, English information booths, tel. 08 26 80 08 26, www.lyon.aeroport.fr). It has connections to most major European cities, including two flights per hour to Paris' Charles de Gaulle Airport, and has its own TGV station (9 trains/day from downtown Paris, 2 hours). Car rental is a snap. Three shuttles *(navettes)* per hour make the 40-minute trip from the airport to both Lyon train stations for €9 (tel. 04 72 68 72 17, www.satobus.com). Allow €45 for a taxi.

Helpful Hints

Consulates: The **US Consulate** is near the Rhône River, east of the Cordeliers Métro stop at 1 quai Jules Courmant (tel. 04 78 38 36 88), and the **Canadian Consulate** is at 17 rue Bourgelat (tel. 04 72 77 64 07).

Market Days: A small market stretches along the Saône River between pont Bonaparte and passerelle du Palais de Justice (daily until 12:30). Tuesday through Saturday, it's produce; Sunday morning, it's crafts and contemporary art on the other side of the bridge near the Court of Justice; and Monday, it's textiles.

Supermarket: The little **Casino** below the recommended Hôtel Célestins is handy to most of my hotels (Mon–Fri 8:00–12:30 & 15:00–19:30, Sat 15:00–19:30, closed Sun).

Internet Access: Nearly all hotels I list have Internet access. **Raconte Moi La Terre** is a way cool travel bookstore with Internet access near the Cordelier Métro stop (where rues Grolée and Thomassin meet, tel. 04 78 92 60 62).

Laundry: A launderette is at 7 rue Mercière on the Presqu'île near the Alphonse Juin bridge (daily 6:00–21:00); another is between place Bellecour and Perrache station, a few steps off rue Victor Hugo (daily 7:30–20:30, 19 rue Ste. Helene).

SNCF Train Office: The **SNCF Boutique,** at 2 place Bellecour, is handy for train info, reservations, and tickets (Mon–Sat 9:00–18:00, closed Sun).

Children's Activities: The Parc de la Tête d'Or is vast, with rental rowboats, a miniature golf course, and ponies to ride (across Rhône River from La Croix-Rousse neighborhood, Métro: Masséna, tel. 04 72 69 47 60).

Getting Around Lyon

Lyon has a user-friendly public transit system, with two sleek streetcar lines (tramways T-1 and T-2), four underground Métro lines (A, B, C, and D), an extensive bus system, and two funiculars (there are two directions heading uphill: *Fourvière* for the basilica and *Saint-Just* for the Roman Theaters). The subway is similar to Paris' Métro in many ways (e.g., routes are signed by *direction* for the last stop on the line) but is more automated (you buy tickets at coin-op machines), cleaner, and less crowded. You can transfer between Métro and tramway lines with the same ticket (€1.50/1 hour, €2.20/2 hours, €4.40/1 day, €12.50/10 rides, all tickets include funicular, or buy the €2.20 ticket for funicular round-trip only). The €4.40 one-day ticket is a great deal if you use the funicular, and visit either the Resistance Center or the Lumière Museum. Use the black roller to *selectionner* your ticket, firmly push the top button twice to *confirmer* your request, and then insert coins. Change the display language to English by choosing the British flag option. If you're using the Métro, insert your ticket in the turnstile, then reclaim it. If the stop has no turnstile, you must validate your ticket by punching it in a nearby chrome machine (tramway users always validate on the trams). Study the wall maps to be sure of your *direction;* ask a local if you're not certain. Yellow signs are directional, and green signs lead to exits.

TOURS

The TI's handy **audioguide** (€8/half-day) offers good, self-guided walking tours of Vieux Lyon.

Live **guided walks** of Vieux Lyon are offered most days at 14:30 (€9, 2 hours, in French, in English if demand justifies, depart from the TI, no need to reserve—just show up, generally 5 days a week in summer, verify days and times with TI). Other, less-frequent English-language walks include tours of the Opera House, La Croix-Rousse district, and silk workshops.

The well-done *World Heritage Excursions* **guidebook,** sold for €6 at the TI, describes interesting self-guided walking tours (Vieux Lyon and Presqu'île North walks are best) and works well with my walking tour (below).

SELF-GUIDED WALKING TOUR

Bonaparte Bridge (Pont Bonaparte)

This central bridge, just a block from place Bellecour, is made-to-order for a spin-tour.

• *Stand on the bridge and face the golden statue of the Virgin Mary marking the Notre-Dame Basilica on Fourvière Hill. (It's actually capping the smaller chapel, which predates the church by 500 years.) The basilica is named for the Roman Forum (Fourvière) upon which it sits. Now begin to look clockwise.*

The Metallic Tower (called La Tour Métallique—not La Tour Eiffel), like the basilica, was finished just before World War I. It was originally an observation tower but today functions only as a TV tower. The husky church on the riverbank below (St. Jean Cathedral) marks the center of the old town. Upstream, the Neoclassical columns are part of the Court of Justice (where Klaus Barbie, head of the local Gestapo—a.k.a. "the Butcher of Lyon"—was sentenced to life in prison in the 1980s). Farther upstream, the hill covered with tall, pastel-colored houses is the La Croix-Rousse district, former home of the city's huge silk industry. With the invention of the "Jacquard looms," which required 12-foot-tall ceilings, new factory buildings were needed and the new weaving center grew up on this hill. In 1850, it was thriving with 30,000 looms.

The place Bellecour side of the river is the district of Presqu'île (*presqu'île* means "peninsula" in French, or literally "almost-an-island"). This strip of land created where the Saône and Rhône

Lyon at a Glance

Notre-Dame Basilica Lyon's ornate version of Paris' Sacré-Cœur. **Hours:** Daily 8:00–19:00, Sun Mass usually at 7:00, 9:30, 11:00, and 17:00.

▲▲**Roman Theaters and Gallo-Roman Museum** Terrific museum covering Roman Lyon. **Hours:** Tue–Sun 10:00–18:00, closed Mon.

St. Jean Cathedral Has 700-year-old astronomical clock. **Hours:** Mon–Fri 8:00–12:00 & 14:00–19:30, Sat–Sun 14:00–17:00.

Traboules Cool covered passageways in Vieux Lyon. **Hours:** Daily 8:00–20:00.

Atelier de la Soierie Workshop demonstrating handmade silk printing and screen painting. **Hours:** Mon–Sat 9:00–12:00 & 14:00–19:00, closed Sun.

▲**Museum of Fine Arts** France's second-most important fine-arts museum (after the Louvre). **Hours:** Wed–Thu and Sat–Mon 10:00–18:00, Fri 10:30–18:00, closed Tue.

Museums of Fabrics and Decorative Arts Museum of Fabrics tracing development of textile weaving over 2,000 years; Museum of Decorative Arts featuring 18th-century decor in a mansion. **Hours:** Tue–Sun 10:00–17:30, closed Mon, Museum of Decorative Arts closes 12:00–14:00.

▲▲**Resistance and Deportation History Center** Displays and videos telling the inspirational story of the French Resistance. **Hours:** Wed–Fri 9:00–17:30, Sat–Sun 9:00–18:00, closed Mon–Tue.

▲**Lumière Museum** Museum of film, dedicated to the Lumière brothers' pivotal contribution. **Hours:** Tue–Sun 11:00–18:30, closed Mon.

Lyon

rivers come together is home to Lyon's Opera House, City Hall, theater, top-end shopping, banks, and all of my recommended hotels. A morning market sets up daily under the trees (just beyond the red bridge), and the riverfront café **(La Buvette du Pont Bonaparte)** to your right is ideal for a drink with a view (best at night).

Speaking of bridges, all of Lyon's bridges—including the one you're standing on—were destroyed by the Nazis as they checked out in 1944. Looking downstream, you can see the stately mansions of Lyon's well-established families. Across the river again, the neo-Gothic St. Georges church marks the neighborhood of the first silk weavers. The ridge behind St. Georges is dominated by a big building—once a seminary for priests, now a state high school—and leads us back to Mary.

• *Walk across the bridge and continue toward the hill two blocks to find the funicular station, where you can ride up Fourvière Hill to the basilica (catch the train marked* Fourvière, *not* St. Just; *sit up front and admire the funicular's funky old technology). From there, you can tour the basilica, enjoy the city view, and visit the Roman Theaters and Gallo-Roman Museum, then catch another funicular back down and explore the old town (Vieux Lyon). Otherwise, it's a short walk back over the river to place des Terreaux (City Hall and Museum of Fine Arts). I've listed the following sights in this order.*

SIGHTS

Fourvière Hill
Notre-Dame Basilica (Basilique Notre-Dame de Fourvière)—
Bam, this ornate church is right in your face as your exit the funicular. About the year 1870, the bishop of Lyon vowed to build a magnificent tribute to the Virgin Mary if the Prussians spared his city. (Similar deal-making led to the construction of the basilica of Sacré-Cœur in Paris.) Building began in 1872, and the church was ready for worship by World War I (free entry, open daily 8:00–19:00, Sun Mass usually at 7:00, 9:30, 11:00, and 17:00).

 ❂ **Self-Guided Tour:** Before entering, step back to view the fancy facade, the older chapel on the right (supporting the statue of Mary; open daily 7:00–19:00), and the top of the Eiffel-like TV tower on the left.

You won't find a more Mary-centered church. Inside, everything—floor, walls, ceiling—is covered with fine **mosaics.** Scenes glittering on the walls tell stories of the Virgin (in Church history on the left, and in French history on the right). Amble down the center aisle at an escargot's pace and examine some of these scenes:

First scene on the left: In 431, the Council of Ephesus declared Mary to be the "Mother of God."

Across the nave, first on the right: The artist imagines Lugdunum (Lyon)—the biggest city in Roman Gaul, with 50,000 inhabitants—as the first Christian missionaries arrive. The first Christian martyrs in France (killed in A.D. 177) dance across heaven with palm branches.

Next left: In 1571, at the pivotal sea battle of Lepanto, Mary

Lyon

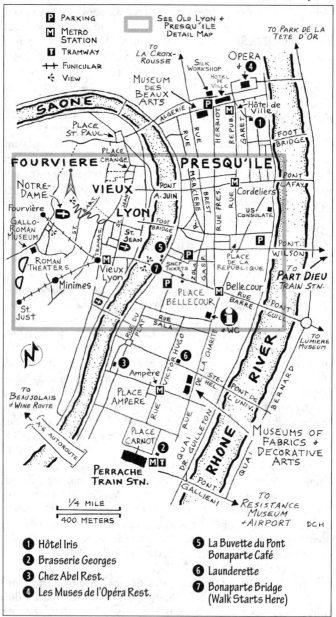

Legend:
- **P** Parking
- **M** Metro Station
- **T** Tramway
- **+++** Funicular
- **⋅⋅⋅** View

SEE OLD LYON & PRESQU'ILE DETAIL MAP

TO PARK DE LA TETE D'OR

TO LA CROIX-ROUSSE

OPERA

SILK WORKSHOP

HOTEL DE VILLE

MUSEUM DES BEAUX ARTS

Hôtel de Ville

SAONE

PLACE ST. PAUL

ALGERIE

RUE HERRIOT

RUE REPUB.

GARET

FOOT BRIDGE

FOURVIERE

PLACE CHANGE

PRESQU'ILE

NOTRE-DAME

VIEUX LYON

PONT A. JUIN

RUE MERCIERE

RUE DU BREST

RUE PRES.

PONT LAFAY.

Cordeliers

Fourvière

GALLO-ROMAN MUSEUM

ST. JEAN

Foot Bridge

US CONSULATE

PONT WILSON

ROMAN THEATERS

Vieux Lyon

SNCF TICKETS

RUE ZOLA

RUE GASP.

PLACE DE LA REPUBLIQUE

TO PART DIEU TRAIN STN.

Minimes

St. Just

PLACE BELLECOUR

Bellecour

RUE BARRE

PONT GUILL.

TO LUMIERE MUSEUM

WC

N

RUE DU PLAT

RUE SALA

RUE DE LA CHARITE

VICTOR HUGO

RHONE RIVER

TO BEAUJOLAIS & WINE ROUTE

A-6 AUTOROUTE

Ampère

PLACE AMPERE

RUE ST.-HEL.

PONT DE L'UNIV.

BERNARD

PLACE CARNOT

QUAI DR. GUILLETON

QUAI

MUSEUMS OF FABRICS & DECORATIVE ARTS

PERRACHE TRAIN STN.

PONT GALLIENI

TO RESISTANCE MUSEUM & AIRPORT

DCH

¼ MILE

400 METERS

Lyon (side tab)

① Hôtel Iris
② Brasserie Georges
③ Chez Abel Rest.
④ Les Muses de l'Opéra Rest.
⑤ La Buvette du Pont Bonaparte Café
⑥ Launderette
⑦ Bonaparte Bridge (Walk Starts Here)

Illuminated Lyon

The golden statue of Mary above Notre-Dame Basilica was placed atop a 16th-century chapel on December 8, 1852. Spontaneously, the entire city welcomed her with candles in their windows. Each December 8 ever since, the city glows softly with countless candles.

This tradition has spawned an actual industry. Lyon is famous as a model of state-of-the-art floodlighting, and the city hosts conventions on the topic. Each night, more than 200 buildings, sites, and public spaces are gloriously floodlit. Go for an after-dinner stroll and enjoy the view from Bonaparte Bridge after dark. Paris calls itself the City of Light—but actually it's Lyon.

---

provides the necessary miracle as the outnumbered Christian forces beat those nasty Turks.

Opposite (from right to left): Joan of Arc hears messages from Mary, rallies the French against the English at the Siege of Orléans in 1429 (find the Orléans coat of arms above), and is ultimately burned at the stake in Rouen at age 19 (1431).

On the left: In 1854, Pope Pius I proclaims the dogma of the Immaculate Conception in St. Peter's Square (establishing the belief among Catholics that Mary was born without the "Original Sin" of apple-eating Adam and Eve). To the left of the Pope, angels carry the tower of Fourvière Church; and to the right is the image of the Virgin of Lourdes (who miraculously appeared in 1858).

Finally, on the right: Louis XIII offers the crown of France to the Virgin Mary. (The empty cradle hints that while he had her on the line, he asked, "Could I please have a son?" Louis XIV was born shortly thereafter.) Above marches a parade of pious French kings, from Clovis and Charlemagne to Napoleon (on the far right—with the white cross and red coat). Below are the great Marian churches of France (left to right)—Chartres, Paris' Sacré-Cœur and Notre-Dame, Reims (where most royalty was crowned), and this church. These six scenes in mosaic all lead to the altar where Mary reigns as Queen of Heaven.

Exit under Joan of Arc and descend to the **lower church,** dedicated to Mary's earthly husband, Joseph. Priorities here are painfully clear, as money ran out for Joseph's church. Today, it's used as a concert venue (notice the spongy-yellow acoustic material covering the vaulting). Return on the same stairs to the humble 16th-century chapel to the Virgin; outside, look up to see the glorious statue of Mary that overlooks Lyon.

Just around this chapel (past the church museum and the recommended Panoramique Restaurant—described under "Eating," below) is a commanding **view** of Lyon. You can see from La Croix-Rousse district to the Bonaparte Bridge, with greater Lyon (pop. 1.3 million) spread out before you in the distance. The black barrel-vaulted structure to the left is the Opera House, and the rose-colored skyscraper in the distance is appropriately called "Le Crayon" (the pencil). On a clear afternoon, you'll get a glimpse of Mont Blanc (the highest point in Europe, just left of the pencil-shaped skyscraper), looking as *blanc* as can be.

• *To get to the Roman Theaters and the Gallo-Roman Museum, walk back toward the funicular station and turn left down rue Roger Radisson. The museum hides down the steps where rue Roger Radisson meets rue Cléberg. Before entering the museum, get the best overview of the ancient site by taking a short left on the road leading downhill (rue Cléberg). Then find the ramp that leads to the museum's rooftop (open the gate). A red banner marks the museum entry.*

▲▲**Roman Theaters and Gallo-Roman Museum (Musée de la Civilisation Gallo-Romaine)**—Constructed in the hillside with views of the two Roman Theaters, this museum makes clear Lyon's importance in Roman times. Lyon (founded in A.D. 43) was an important transportation hub for the administration of Roman Gaul (and much of modern-day France). Emperors Claudius and Caracalla were both born in Lugdunum (Roman Lyon).

The fascinating **Gallo-Roman Museum** is wonderfully explained in English, and takes you on a chronological stroll through ancient Lyon. All the artifacts are local ("Gallo-Roman"). The fine bronze chariot dates from the seventh century B.C. The model of Roman Lyon shows a town of 50,000 in its second-century A.D. glory days. (The forum stands where the basilica does today.) Curved stones in an arena were actual seats—inscribed with the names of big shots who sat there. A speech by Emperor Claudius carved into a big, black-bronze tablet recalls how, in A.D. 48, he worked to integrate Gauls into the empire by declaring that they were eligible to sit in the Roman Senate (English translation on the wall). A mosaic shows a *Ben Hur*–type chariot race and, with the push of a button, you can see the mechanics of a Roman theater stage curtain in action...raised instead of lowered (€4, €6 if special exhibits, free on Thu, open Tue–Sun 10:00–18:00, closed Mon, tel. 04 72 38 49 30, www.musees-gallo-romains.com).

• *Exit the museum into the theaters...*

The **big theater** (which originally held 10,000) today seats 3,000 for concerts. The **smaller theater,** an "odeon" (from the Greek "ode" for song), was acoustically designed for speeches and songs. The ground is peppered with gravestones and sarcophagi (free, open daily until 19:00). From early June through early August, the theaters host *Les Nuits de Fourvière*, an open-air festival of concerts, theater, dance, and film. Check programs and buy tickets at the TI, here at the theaters (box office at gate exit toward the Minimes funicular station, described below, Mon–Sat 11:00–18:00, closed Sun), or online at www.nuitsdefourviere.org.

• *The ancient road between the Roman Theaters leads down and out, where you'll find the Minimes funicular station (to the right as you leave the theaters). Take the funicular to Vieux Lyon (go to the side of the tracks labeled* Vieux Lyon, *not* St. Just*), where it will deposit you only a few steps from St. Jean Cathedral.*

Vieux Lyon (Old Lyon)

St. Jean Cathedral—Stand back in the square for the best view. This mostly Gothic cathedral took 200 years to build. It doesn't soar as high as its northern French counterparts. Influenced by their Italian neighbors, churches in southern France are typically less vertical than those in the north. This cathedral, while unremarkable inside (except for its 700-year-old astronomical clock that performs several times a day), is the "primate cathedral of Gaul," serving what's considered the oldest Christian city in France (Mon–Fri 8:00–12:00 & 14:00–19:30, Sat–Sun 14:00–17:00).

Outside (turn right around the back as you leave) are the ruins of a mostly 11th-century church, which was destroyed during the French Revolution (the cathedral was turned into a "temple of reason"). What's left of a baptistery from an early Christian church (c. A.D. 400) is under glass.

▲Old Lyon and Covered Passageways *(Traboules)*—Lyon offers the best concentration of well-preserved Renaissance buildings in the country. The city grew rich from its trade fairs and banking, and was the king of Europe's silk industry from the 16th to 19th centuries, humming with some 30,000 looms. The fine buildings of the old center were inspired by Italy and financed by the silk industry.

Rue St. Jean, leading from the cathedral to place du Change, is the main drag, flanked by parallel pedestrian streets. (The rue de Bœuf is quieter and more appealing than touristy rue St. Jean.) The city's trademark serpentine passageways *(traboules)* were essentially shortcuts linking the old town's three main streets. These hidden paths give visitors a hide-and-seek opportunity to discover pastel courtyards, lovely loggias, and delicate arches. Spiral staircases were often shared by several houses. The *traboules* provided shelter when silk was being moved from one stage to the next.

Take a break from walking along rue St. Jean and detour a few steps left up rue de la Bombarde. You'll find a well-restored Renaissance building (La Basoche) that gives you a good idea of what hides behind many facades in old Lyon (note the black-and-white

Old Lyon

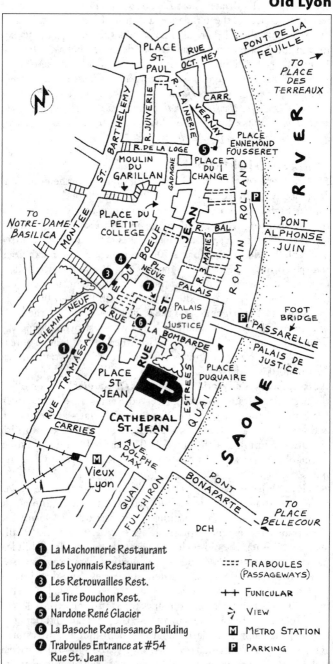

1. La Machonnerie Restaurant
2. Les Lyonnais Restaurant
3. Les Retrouvailles Rest.
4. Le Tire Bouchon Rest.
5. Nardone René Glacier
6. La Basoche Renaissance Building
7. Traboules Entrance at #54 Rue St. Jean

```
::::  TRABOULES
      (PASSAGEWAYS)
++    FUNICULAR
⇗     VIEW
M     METRO STATION
P     PARKING
```

photos showing this structure before its 1968 renovation). As you stroll along rue St. Jean, notice the heavy doors leading to the *traboules*. The longest is #54, which links to rue du Bœuf. When a doorway is open, you can wander in and explore inner courtyards. Only a few of Lyon's 315 *traboules* are open to the public, and some of those are open mornings only (press top button next to street-front door to release door when entering, push lit buttons to illuminate dark walkways, and slide door-handle levers when leaving). You're welcome to explore from 8:00 until 20:00 if you are quiet, respectful of the residents, and don't go up any stairs.

As you wander Vieux Lyon, look for door plaques giving a history of each building and *traboule*. After walking through a few *traboules*, you'll understand why Lyon's old town was an ideal center for the Resistance fighters to slip in and out of as they confounded the Nazis.

The place du Change, at the north end of rue St. Jean, was the banking center of medieval Lyon. This money scene developed after the city was allowed to host trade fairs in 1420. Its centerpiece is France's first stock exchange.

• *From here it's a short walk across the river to place des Terreaux and the Museum of Fine Arts (cross pont la Feuillée and continue straight four blocks). Ice-cream connoisseurs must stop at* **Nardone René Glacier** *before crossing the river (daily 10:00–24:00, on river near place du Change, 3 place Ennemond Fousseret).*

Presqu'île

This bit of land (French for "peninsula," and literally meaning "almost-an-island") between the two rivers is Lyon's shopping spine, with thriving pedestrian streets. The neighborhood's northern focal point is...

Place des Terreaux—This grand square hosts the City Hall (Hôtel de Ville), the Museum of Fine Arts, and a grand fountain by Frédéric-Auguste Bartholdi (the French sculptor who designed America's Statue of Liberty). Its most important function for locals is allowing the last rays of sun to penetrate the café tables near the City Hall. Join the crowd for an afternoon sip.

The fountain features Marianne (the Lady of the Republic) riding a four-horse-powered chariot. The square itself is pretty wet, with 69 fountains spurting playfully in a vast grid.

Atelier de la Soierie—This silk workshop, just off place des Terreaux (behind Café le Moulin Joli, (Resistance hangout during World War II), welcomes the public to drop in to see silk printing and screen painting by hand. Keep in mind that this is a lost art that today has mostly been replaced by machines. One hand-painted scarf can take up to four months to complete, with prices starting at €250 (free entry, Mon–Sat 9:00–12:00 &

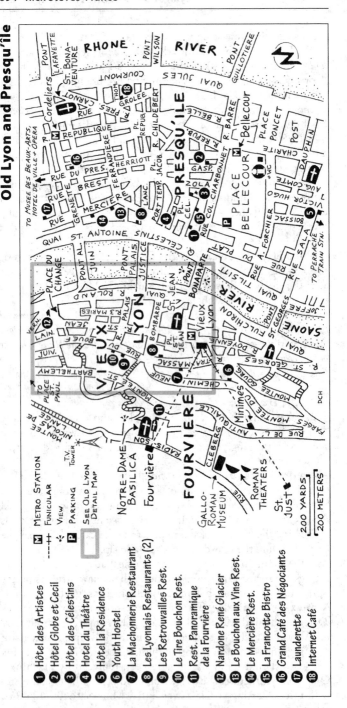

Old Lyon and Presqu'île

KEY

- METRO STATION
- FUNICULAR
- VIEW
- PARKING
- SEE OLD LYON DETAIL MAP

1. Hôtel des Artistes
2. Hôtel Globe et Cecil
3. Hôtel des Célestins
4. Hotel du Théâtre
5. Hôtel la Residence
6. Youth Hostel
7. La Machonnerie Restaurant
8. Les Lyonnais Restaurants (2)
9. Les Retrouvailles Rest.
10. Le Tire Bouchon Rest.
11. Rest. Panoramique de la Fourvière
12. Nardone René Glacier
13. Le Bouchon aux Vins Rest.
14. Le Mercière Rest.
15. La Francotte Bistro
16. Grand Café des Négociants
17. Launderette
18. Internet Café

14:00–19:00, closed Sun).

La Croix-Rousse—Hilly, untouristy, and Soho-esque, this neighborhood was home to 30,000 silk looms in the 1800s. You can explore its spine by climbing the steep but rewarding Montée de la Grande Côte pedestrian street that leaves from the west end of place Terreaux (follow rue Ste. Marie des Terreaux and wind your way up and up). Smarter types take the Métro to La Croix-Rousse stop, and stroll down the rue des Pierres Plantées to the long and winding Montée de la Grande to place Terreaux, stopping for views and cafés. Try to go in the morning and enjoy Lyon's best neighborhood market by La Croix-Rousse Métro station (closed Mon).

▲Museum of Fine Arts (Musée des Beaux-Arts)—Located in a former abbey, which was secularized by Napoleon in 1803 and made into a public museum, this fine-arts museum has an impressive collection, ranging from Egyptian antiquities to Impressionist paintings.

The first floor offers a stroll through a fine collection of ancient (especially Egyptian) art, medieval art, and Art Nouveau (furniture). The adjacent chapel is a dreamy Orsay-like display of 19th- and 20th-century statues (including work by Auguste Rodin and Bartholdi).

The second floor displays a pretty selection of paintings from many ages and countries (with no famous works, but a fine Impressionist collection). The highlight is a series of pre-Raphaelite-type works called *Le Poème de l'Ame* ("The Poem of the Soul") by Louis Janmot. This cycle of 18 paintings and 16 charcoal drawings traces the story of the souls of a boy and a girl as they journey through childhood, adolescence, and into adulthood. They struggle with fears and secular temptations before gaining spiritual enlightenment on the way to heaven. The boy loses his faith and enjoys a short but delicious hedonistic fling that leads to misery in hell. But a mother's prayers intercede, and he reunites with the girl to enjoy heavenly redemption.

Cost and Hours: €6, Wed–Thu and Sat–Mon 10:00–18:00, Fri 10:30–18:00, closed Tue, first floor closes 11:55–13:05, second floor closes 13:05–14:15, pick up museum map on entering, picnic-perfect courtyard, 20 place des Terreaux, Métro: Hôtel de Ville, tel. 04 72 10 30 30, www.mairie-lyon.fr. A bar/café with calming terrace seating is on the first floor, next to the bookstore.

Enjoying Presqu'île—There's more to this "almost-an-island" than just place des Terreaux. Join the treadmill of shoppers on sprawling rue de la République (north of place Bellecour) and the teeming rue Victor Hugo pedestrian mall (south of place Bellecour). Peruse the *bouchons* (characteristic bistros—especially characteristic in the evening) of rue Mercière.

Grand Café des Négociants is ideal for a break. This *grand café*, which has been in business since 1864, feels like it hasn't changed since then, with its soft leather chairs, painted ceilings, and glass chandeliers (daily, 1 place Francisque Régaud, near Cordeliers Métro stop, tel. 04 78 42 50 05).

South of Place Bellecour

Museums of Fabrics and Decorative Arts (Musées des Tissus et des Arts Décoratifs)—These museums fill two buildings (sharing a courtyard and connected with an interior hallway). While filled with exquisite exhibits, they provide little information in English (descriptive sheets upstairs in the Museum of Fabrics, nothing in Museum of Decorative Arts). The Museum of Fabrics traces the development of textile weaving over 2,000 years and shows off some breathtaking silk work. The Museum of Decorative Arts, billed as "an ambience museum," is a luxurious mansion decorated to the hilt with 18th-century furniture, textiles, and tapestries in a plush domestic setting (€5 covers both museums, Tue–Sun 10:00–17:30, closed Mon, Museum of Decorative Arts closes 12:00–14:00, 34 rue de la Charité, Métro: Bellecour, tel. 04 78 38 42 00, www.musee-des-tissus.com).

Away from the Center

▲▲Resistance and Deportation History Center (Centre d'Histoire de la Résistance et de la Déportation)—Located near Vichy (capital of the French puppet state) and neutral Switzerland, Lyon was the center of the French Resistance from 1942 to 1945. These ordinary heroes fought the Nazis—they were the "underground," or Resistance. Bakers hid radios inside loaves of bread to secretly contact London. Barmaids passed along tips from tipsy Nazis. Communists in black berets cut telephone lines. Farmers hid downed airmen in haystacks. Housewives spread news from the front with their gossip. Printers countered Nazi propaganda with anonymous pamphlets.

This well-done museum, which once served as a Nazi torture chamber, uses audioguides, videos, and easy-to-follow English descriptions to tell the inspirational story of the French Resistance (€4, Wed–Fri 9:00–17:30, Sat–Sun 9:00–18:00, closed Mon–Tue, 14 avenue Berthelot; 15-min walk from Perrache station across pont Gallieni, then 3 blocks to 14 avenue Berthelot; or, easier, take T-2 tramway from below Perrache station to Centre Berthelot; or ride the Métro to Jean Macé, exit toward the elevated train line, turn right on avenue Berthelot, and walk back 5 blocks).

▲Lumière Museum (Musée Lumière)—Antoine Lumière and his two sons Louis and Auguste—the Eastman-Kodaks of France—ran a huge factory with 200 workers in the 1880s, producing four million glass photographic plates a day. Then, in 1895, they made the first *cinématographe*, or movie. In 1903, they pioneered the "autochrome" process of painting frames to make "color photos." This museum tells their story.

The highlights are the many screens playing the earliest "movies." The first film reels held about 950 frames, which played at 19 per second, so these first movies were only 50 seconds long. About 1,500 Lumière films are catalogued between 1895 and 1907. (Notice that each movie is tagged with its "Catalog Lumière" number.) The very first movie ever made features workers piling out of the Lumière factory at the end of a work day.

The museum fills the Villa Lumière, the family's belle époque mansion, built in 1902. The ground floor shows movies and the earliest cameras and projectors. Upstairs are exhibits on still photography and the Lumière living quarters (furnished c. 1900). Across the park from the mansion is a shrine at what's left of the warehouse where the first movie was actually shot. In a wonderful coincidence, *lumière* is the French word for "light."

En route to the museum, enjoy your ride on the futuristic (and driverless) Métro D. Sit in the front and command your own underground starship (€6.50, Tue–Sun 11:00–18:30, closed Mon, half a block from the Monplaisir-Lumière Métro stop at 25 rue du Premier-Film, tel. 04 78 78 18 95, www.institut-lumiere.org).

NIGHTLIFE

Lyon has France's second-largest cultural budget after Paris, so there are always plenty of theatrical productions and concerts to attend. The TI has the latest information and schedules. From mid-June through mid-September, the Opera House terrace hosts an outdoor jazz café with three free concerts almost every evening (Mon–Sat, www.opera-lyon.com).

After dinner, a stroll through Lyon's old town and a walk along the river affords a chance to savor the city's famous illuminations (see sidebar on page 689). For a lively bar and people-watching scene, prowl rue de la Monnaie (angles off "restaurant row," rue Mercière to the south) and the streets between place des Terreaux and the Opera House.

SLEEPING

Hotels in Lyon are a steal compared to those in Paris. Weekends are generally discounted in this city that lives off business travelers (some hotels even offer 2-for-1 deals if booked ahead—ask about *le Bon Weekend* packages). Be aware that prices rise and rooms disappear when trade fairs are in town (which is not uncommon), so it's

Lyon

Sleep Code

(€1 = about $1.30, country code: 33)
S = Single, **D** = Double/Twin, **T** = Triple, **Q** = Quad, **b** = bathroom,
s = shower only, * = French hotel rating system (0–4 stars).
Unless otherwise noted, credit cards are accepted and English
is spoken.

To help you sort easily through these listings, I've divided
the rooms into three categories based on the price for a standard double room with bath:

$$$ **Higher Priced**—Most rooms €90 or more.
$$ **Moderately Priced**—Most rooms between €65–90.
$ **Lower Priced**—Most rooms €65 or less.

---

smart to reserve your room in advance. If you have trouble, the TI
can help for free in person or by email (resa@lyon-france.com).
All hotels listed below are on the Presqu'île. Hotels have elevators
unless otherwise noted, and air-conditioning is a godsend when
it's hot.

On or near Place des Célestins

It's well worth booking ahead to sleep in this classy yet unpretentious neighborhood (Métro: Bellecour). Just a block off the central
place Bellecour and a block to the Saône River, travelers have easy
access to Lyon's sights, can join shoppers perusing the upscale boutiques, or can watch children playing in the small square fronting
the Théâtre des Célestins. Warning: Weekend nights can be noisy
if you score a room facing place des Célestins.

$$$ Hôtel des Artistes*,** ideally located on place des
Célestins, is red-velvet plush, comfortable, professional, and the
best value in its price range (Sb-€80–90, standard Db-€95–100,
larger Db-€110–125, standard rooms are plenty comfortable, air-
con, Internet access and Wi-Fi, 8 rue Gaspard-André, tel. 04 78
42 04 88, fax 04 78 42 93 76, www.hoteldesartistes.fr, hartiste
@club-internet.fr).

$$$ Hôtel Globe et Cecil*,** the most elegant of my listings,
offers refined comfort on a refined street with traditionally deco-
rated and generously sized rooms. The lounge areas are spacious
(Sb-€125, Db-€155, includes breakfast, air-con, Internet access
and Wi-Fi, 21 rue Gasparin, tel. 04 78 42 58 95, fax 04 72 41 99 06,
www.globeetcecilhotel.com, accueil@globeetcecilhotel.com).

$$ Hôtel des Célestins,** just off place des Célestins, is
warmly run by Stephanie and Cornell-grad Laurent. Its cheery,
immaculate rooms are filled with thoughtful touches. Streetside

rooms have more light and weekend noise (Sb-€62-90, Db-€68-90, five large rooms-€100 and worth the extra euros, Tb-€95–125, apartments-€100–135, good buffet breakfast served 7:00–12:00, air-con, free Internet access, 4 rue des Archers, tel. 04 72 56 08 98, fax 04 72 56 08 65, www.hotelcelestins.com).

$$ Hotel du Théâtre** requires a tromp up two flights of stairs to reach the lobby and does not have air-conditioning, but it's well-located on place des Célestins (enter from the hotel's rear). It comes with firm beds, mostly spacious rooms, and simple but thoughtful touches (S-€45, Sb-€58, Db-€59–70, Tb-€86, place des Célestins, tel. 04 78 42 33 32, fax 04 72 40 00 61, www.hotel-du -theatre.fr, contact@hotel-du-theatre.fr).

South of Place Bellecour

This hotel is my closest listing to the Perrache train station.

$$ Hôtel la Residence*** feels big and institutional, but its 67 rooms are air-conditioned, well cared for, and a fine value. Most are spacious, with high ceilings (Db-€75, Tb-€90, Qb-€100, most rooms have bathtubs, Internet access, 18 Victor Hugo, tel. 04 78 42 63 28, fax 04 78 42 85 76, www.hotel-la-residence.com, hotel-la -residence@wanadoo.fr).

Near the Opera House

$ Hôtel Iris**, tucked away near the Opera House, is the best budget deal I found in Lyon. It's run by hardworking and friendly Cédric, a former bread baker who is creatively transforming this historic building (with a striking 16th-century inner courtyard stairway) into a snappy little 14-room hotel. Rooms are basic but comfortable, with brown tones and an African motif (D-€39, Db-€47–56, 36 rue de l'Arbre Sec, Métro: Hôtel de Ville, tel. 04 78 39 93 80, fax 04 72 00 89 91, www.hoteliris.freesurf.fr). Make your reservation only by phone; Cédric wants to hear your voice.

$ Vieux Lyon Youth Hostel is impressively situated a 10-minute walk above Vieux Lyon. Open 24 hours daily, it has a lively common area with kitchen access and cheap meals (bed in 4- to 6-bed room-€17, includes sheets and breakfast, small safes available, 45 Montée du Chemin, Métro: Hôtel de Ville, tel. 04 78 15 05 50, fax 04 78 15 05 51, www.fuaj.org, lyon@fuaj.org). Book only by email. Take the funicular to Minimes, exit the station and make a left U-turn, and follow the station wall downhill to Montée du Chemin.

EATING

Dining is a ▲▲▲ attraction in Lyon, and it comes at a bearable price. Half the fun is joining the procession of window-shoppers mulling over where they'll *diner ce soir*. At dinner, the city's population seems to double as locals emerge to stretch their stomachs.

Lyon's characteristic *bouchons* are small bistros that evolved from the days when Mama would feed the silk workers after a long day. True *bouchons* are simple places with limited selection and seating (just like Mama's), serving only traditional fare and special 46-centiliter *pot* (pronounced "poh") wine pitchers. The lively pedestrian streets of Vieux Lyon and rue Mercière on the Presqu'île are *bouchon* bazaars, worth strolling even if you dine elsewhere. While food quality may be better away from these popular restaurant rows, you can't beat the atmosphere. Many of Lyon's restaurants close on Sunday and Monday, except along rue Mercière. If you plan to dine somewhere special, book ahead.

Vieux Lyon

Come to Old Lyon for maximum ambience. For the epicenter of restaurant activity, go to place Neuve St. Jean, and survey the scene and menus before sitting down.

La Machonnerie, a block opposite the cathedral, serves traditional cuisine that draws in the locals—try to reserve in advance. Expect to be greeted by gregarious owner-chef Félix (*menus* from €22, closed Sun, air-con, 36 rue Tramassac, tel. 04 78 42 24 62).

Les Lyonnais, a block north, is lighthearted with rich colors, wood tables, and a photo gallery of loyal customers lining the walls (€18 and 22 *menus*, closed Sun, 1 rue Tramassac, tel. 04 78 37 64 82).

Les Retrouvailles serves tasty, but less traditional, Lyonnais cuisine in a charming setting under wood-beam ceilings. Here your dining experience is carefully managed by friendly owners Pierre *(le chef)* and Odile (€20 and €27 *menus,* closed Sun, 38 rue du Bœuf, tel. 04 78 42 68 84).

Le Tire-Bouchon ("The Corkscrew") is a tiny, simple, and fun *bouchon*, with low ceilings, ample wallpaper, and flowers (*menus* from €18, closed Sun–Mon, 2 floors, 16 rue de Bœuf, tel. 04 78 37 69 95).

Restaurant Panoramique de la Fourvière, atop Fourvière Hill with a spectacular view overlooking Lyon, serves traditional cuisine in a superb setting, but service can be slow. Choose from the non-smoking interior or the leafy terrace, both with views (*menus* from €24, lunch *plat du jour*-€12, daily until 22:00, 9 place de Fourvière, near Notre-Dame Basilica, tel. 04 78 25 21 15).

Nardone René Glacier, on the river near place du Change, serves up Lyon's best ice cream with pleasant outdoor seating (daily 10:00–24:00, 3 place Ennemond Fousseret).

On the Presqu'île

The pedestrian rue Mercière is the epicenter of *bouchons* on the Presqu'île. Along this street, an entertaining cancan of restaurants stretches four blocks from place des Jacobins to rue Grenette. Enjoy surveying the scene and choose whichever eatery appeals.

On or near rue Mercière

Le Bouchon aux Vins bustles with authentic Lyonnais atmosphere, plus good meals at fair prices. It must be famed chef-owner Jean-Paul Lacombe's least expensive establishment (*menus* from €25, open daily, 62 rue Mercière, tel. 04 78 38 47 40).

Le Mercière, at #56, fills two shoebox-size rooms and the *passage* between them with down and dirty, get-to-know-your-neighbor *bouchon* character (*menus* from €22, open daily, 56 rue Mercière).

Les Lyonnais (recommended above) has a second location facing the Saône River, with a generous terrace and stellar views up to the basilica—particularly at night (closed Sun–Mon, 1 quai des Célestins, tel. 04 78 37 41 80).

On Place des Célestins

La Francotte, an open and appealing zinc-bar bistro, is good for a relaxing drink or a meal (*menus* from €20, closed Sun, near many recommended hotels at 8 place des Célestins, tel. 04 78 37 38 64).

Worth a Detour

Brasserie Georges, next to Perrache station and almost as big, offers a forest of tables, dozens of frantic, aproned waiters, and decor from another time. It's been a Lyon institution since 1836, and makes a lively place to celebrate (*menus* from €22, *plats* from €15, good French onion soup, daily 8:00 until late, 30 cours de Verdon, tel. 04 72 56 54 54).

Chez Abel is the ultimate local *bouchon*, far away from restaurant rows and tourists, and catering to one kind of client only: local residents. It has a warm, chalet-like interior and a welcoming red-cheeked owner. Servings are generous; the *quenelle de brochet* is downright massive. Consider a *plat du jour* and maybe a salad. Reserve ahead (*menus* from €25, closed Sat–Sun and in Aug, about a 15-min walk south of place Bellecour, Métro: Ampère, a short block from Saône River, 25 rue Guynemer, tel. 04 78 37 46 18).

Les Muses de l'Opéra is an intriguing option for lunch or dinner (after 20:00) with a great view (and average quality). Ride the elevator to the seventh floor of the Opera House (€29 dinner *menu*, closed Sun, tel. 04 72 00 45 58).

TRANSPORTATION CONNECTIONS

After Paris, Lyon is France's most important rail hub. Train travelers find this gateway to the Alps, Provence, the Riviera, and Burgundy an easy stopover. Two main train stations serve Lyon: Part-Dieu and Perrache. Most trains officially depart from Part-Dieu, though many also stop at Perrache, and trains run between the stations every 10 minutes. Double-check which station your train departs from.

From Lyon by Train to: Paris (at least hourly, 2 hrs), **Annecy** (7/day, 2 hrs, most change in Aix-les-Bains, some by bus), **Chamonix** (10/day, 4 hrs), **Strasbourg** (5/day, 5 hrs), **Dijon** (12/day, 2 hrs), **Beaune** (10/day, 2 hrs, many change in Mâcon), **Avignon** (22/day, 12 to TGV station in 1.5 hrs, 10 to main station in 2 hrs), **Arles** (14/day, 2.5 hrs, most change in Avignon, Marseille, or Nîmes), **Nice** (6/day, 5 hrs), **Carcassonne** (6/day, 4 hrs), **Venice** (6/day, 11–13 hrs, most change in Geneva and Milan, night train), **Rome** (4/day, 10–12 hrs, at least one change in Milan, night train), **Florence** (3/day, 10 hrs), **Geneva** (8/day, 2 hrs), **Barcelona** (1 day train, 7 hrs, change in Perpignan; 2 night trains).

Route Tips for Drivers: En route to Provence, consider a three-hour detour through the spectacular Ardèche Gorges: Exit the A-6 autoroute at Privas and follow the villages of Aubenas, Vallon Pont d'Arc (offers kayak trips), and Pont Saint-Esprit (for more on this route, see page 519). En route to Burgundy, consider a Beaujolais detour (see below).

Beaujolais Wine Route

Just south of Cluny and north of Lyon, the beautiful vineyards and villages of the Beaujolais region (relaxed wine-tastings) make for an appealing detour. The most scenic and interesting section lies between Mâcon and Villefranche-sur-Saône, a few minutes west of A-6 on N-6. The route runs from the Mâconnais wine region and the famous village of Pouilly-Fuissé south through Beaujolais' most important villages: Chiroubles, Fleurie, and Juliénas. Look for *Route de Beaujolais* signs, and expect to get lost a few times. Trains running between Lyon and Macon stop at several wine villages, including Romanèche-Thorins (described below; 6 trains/day from Lyon).

For a pricey but thorough introduction to this region's wines, visit **Le Hameau du Vin** in Romanèche-Thorins. The king of Beaujolais, Georges DuBœuf, has constructed a Disneyesque introduction to wine at his wine museum, which immerses you into the life of a winemaker and features impressive models, exhibits, films, and videos. You'll be escorted from the beginning of the vine to present-day winemaking, with a focus on Beaujolais wines (several visits possible, best is €16 and includes a small tasting and free English headphones, daily April–Oct 9:00–18:00, Nov–March 10:00–17:00; in Romanèche-Thorins, look for signs labeled *Le Hameau du Vin* from N-6, then *La Gare* signs, and look for the old train-station-turned-winery; tel. 03 85 35 22 22, www .plaisirsenbeaujolais.com).

ALSACE AND NORTHERN FRANCE

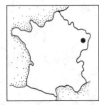

The province of Alsace stands like a flower-child referee between Germany and France. Bounded by the Rhine River on the east and the Vosges Mountains on the west, this is a green region of Hansel-and-Gretel villages, ambitious vineyards, and engaging cities. Food and wine are the primary industry, topic of conversation, and perfect excuse for countless festivals.

Alsace has changed hands several times between Germany and France because of its location, natural wealth, naked vulnerability—and the fact that Germany considered the mountains as the natural border, while the French felt the Rhine was the dividing line.

Having been a political pawn for 1,000 years, Alsace has a hybrid culture: Locals who swear do so bilingually, and the local cuisine features sauerkraut with fine wine sauces. If you're traveling in December, come here for France's most celebrated Christmas markets and festivals.

Colmar is one of Europe's most enchanting cities—with a small-town warmth and world-class art. Strasbourg is a big-city version of Colmar, worth a stop for its remarkable cathedral and to feel its high-powered and trendy bustle. The humbling WWI battlefields of Verdun and the bubbly vigor of Reims in northern France are closer to Paris than Alsace, and they follow logically only if your next destination is Paris.

Planning Your Time

Set up for two nights in or near Colmar. Allow one day for Colmar and another for Strasbourg and the Route du Vin (Wine Road). If you have only one day, spend your morning in Colmar and your

From Alsace to Champagne

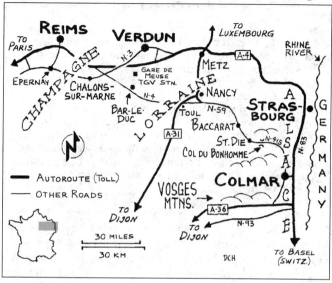

afternoon along the Route du Vin. Urban Strasbourg, with its soaring cathedral and vibrant center, is a headache for drivers but a quick 30-minute train ride from Colmar—do it by train as a day trip from Colmar (see below). Reims and Verdun are doable by car as stops between Paris and Colmar—if you're speedy.

The newest high-speed TGV-Est train links Paris with Reims, Verdun, Strasbourg, Colmar, and destinations farther east, allowing train travelers to easily reach Reims or Verdun en route from Paris to Alsace, or even as day trips from Paris (Paris to Reims-45 min, Paris to Verdun-65 min).

Getting Around Alsace

Frequent trains make the trip between Colmar and Strasbourg a snap (2/hr, 35 min). Buses and minivan excursions radiate from Colmar to villages along the Route du Vin, and you can rent bikes in Colmar and Turckheim if you prefer to pedal (for details on all of these options, see "Route du Vin," page 722).

Cuisine Scene in Alsace

Alsatian cuisine is a major tourist attraction in itself. The German influence is obvious: sausages, potatoes, onions, and sauerkraut. Look for *choucroute garnie* (sauerkraut and sausage—although it seems a shame to eat it in a fancy restaurant), the more traditionally Alsatian *baeckeoffe* (potato, meat, and onion stew), *rösti* (an oven-baked potato-and-cheese dish), fresh trout, and foie gras.

Early Crockpots

For old-school Alsatian comfort food, order the ubiquitous *baeckeoffe,* which is still served at your table in traditional pottery. The dish derives its name from where it was cooked—in the baker's oven. For centuries, Alsatian women would combine the week's leftover pork, beef, and veal with potatoes, onions, and leeks in a covered clay pot, then add white wine. Carrying the pot on their way to church on Sunday, the women would pass by the baker's and put their pot in one of the large stone ovens, still warm from baking the morning bread. During the three-hour Mass, the meat would simmer, and be perfectly stewed in time for lunch. The pottery, which is still produced and sold locally, remains an integral part of every Alsatian household.

At lunch, or for a lighter dinner, try a *tarte à l'oignon* (like an onion quiche, but better) or *tarte flambée* (like a thin-crust pizza with onion and bacon bits). If you're picnicking, buy some stinky Munster cheese. Dessert specialties are *tarte alsacienne* (fruit tart) and *glace kugelhopf* (a light cake mixed with raisins, almonds, dried fruit, and cherry liqueur).

Remember, restaurants serve only during lunch (11:30–14:00) and dinner (19:00–21:00, later in bigger cities), but some cafés serve food throughout the day.

Alsatian Wines

Alsatian wines are named for their grapes—unlike in Burgundy or Provence, where wines are commonly named after villages, or in Bordeaux, where wines are often named after châteaux. White wines dominate in the Alsace. The following wines are made entirely of their namesake grape variety: Sylvaner (fairly light, fruity, and inexpensive), Riesling (more robust than Sylvaner, but drier than the German style you're probably used to), Gewürztraminer (spicy, with a powerful bouquet; good with pâtés and local cheeses), Muscat (very dry, with a distinctive bouquet and taste; best as a before-dinner wine), Tokay Pinot Gris (more full-bodied than Riesling, but fine with many local main courses), Pinot Noir (the local red is overpriced; very light and fruity, generally served chilled), and the tasty Crémant d'Alsace (the region's good and inexpensive sparkling wine). You'll also see *eaux-de-vie,* powerful fruit-flavored brandies; try the *framboise* (raspberry) flavor.

Colmar

Colmar is a well-pickled old place of 70,000 residents, offering a few heavyweight sights in a comfortable, midsize-town package.

Historic beauty was usually a poor excuse for being spared the ravages of World War II, but it worked for Colmar. The American and British military were careful not to bomb the half-timbered old burghers' houses, characteristic red- and green-tiled roofs, and cobbled lanes of Alsace's most beautiful city. The town's distinctly French shutters combined with the ye-olde German half-timbering give Colmar an intriguing ambience.

Today, Colmar is alive with its colorful buildings, impressive art treasures, and German tourists. Schoolgirls park their rickety horse carriages in front of City Hall and are ready to give visitors a clip-clop tour of the old town. Antique shops welcome browsers, and hoteliers hurry down the sleepy streets to pick up fresh croissants in time for breakfast.

ORIENTATION

Assume you will get lost, as there isn't a straight street in Colmar. Thankfully, most streets are pedestrian-only, and it's a lovely town to be lost in. Navigate by the high church steeples and the helpful signs that seem to pop up whenever you need them (directing visitors to the various sights). For tourists, the town center is place Unterlinden (a 15-min walk from the train station), where you'll find the TI, Colmar's most important museum, and a huge Monoprix supermarket/department store. Every city bus starts or finishes on place Unterlinden.

Colmar is most crowded from May through September and during its festive Christmas season (www.noel-colmar.com). Weekends are busiest (reserve ahead). The impressive music festival fills hotels the first two weeks of July (www.festival-colmar .com), and the local wine festival rages for 10 days in early August. Open-air markets bustle next to the Dominican Church and St. Martin Cathedral on Thursdays and Saturdays.

Tourist Information

The TI, next to the Unterlinden Museum on place Unterlinden, is generous with printed material (April–Oct Mon–Sat 9:00–18:00, until 19:00 July–Aug, Sun 10:00–13:00; Nov–March Mon–Sat 9:00–12:00 & 14:00–18:00, Sun 10:00–13:00; tel. 03 89 20 68 92, (www.ot-colmar.fr). Pick up the excellent city map (describing a good town walk), a map of the Route du Vin (Wine Road), information on bike rental, and *Colmar Actualités*, a booklet with bus schedules. Get information about concerts and festivals in Colmar and in nearby villages, and ask about Colmar's Folklore Tuesdays (with folk dancing at 20:30 every Tue mid-May–mid-Sept on place de l'Ancienne Douane). Drivers exploring the Route du Vin can buy the *Blay Foldex Alsace* map (1:175,000, €6). Bikers can pay €5.50 for a map of the bike routes (*Le Haut-Rhin à Vélo*, suggests routes with estimated times), or get a good map for free with bike rental (see below). The TI also reserves hotel rooms and has *chambre d'hôte* listings for Colmar and the region. A public WC is 20 yards left of the TI.

Arrival in Colmar

By Train: Colmar's old train station and the new TGV station have been fused into a large single station, with separate entrances connected by an underground passageway. Because both TGV and non-TGV trains depart from the same station now, make sure you're boarding the right train (the trains have different access points).

The old train station was built during Prussian rule with the same plans for the station in Danzig (now Gdańsk, Poland). Check out the charming 1991 window that shows two local maidens about to be run over by a train and rescued by an artist. Opposite, he's shown painting their portraits.

To reach the town center from either station (15-min walk, baggage check should be available), walk straight out past Hôtel Bristol (keeping the hotel on your left), turn left on avenue de la République, and keep walking. Buses #1, #2, and #3 (to the left outside of the old station) all go to the TI (€1.10, pay driver). Buses to Route du Vin villages leave from the stop to the right as you leave the old station. Allow €8 for a taxi to any hotel in central Colmar (the taxi stand is on the left as you leave the station).

By Car: Follow signs reading *Centre-Ville,* then *place Rapp.* There's a 900-spot pay-parking garage under place Rapp, and free lots at Parking du Musée d'Unterlinden (across from Hôtel Primo) and off the ring road near Hôtel St. Martin (follow signs from ring road to *Parking de la Vieille Ville*). Several hotels have private parking, and those that don't can advise you where to park. When entering or leaving on the Strasbourg side of town, look for the big Statue of Liberty replica erected on July 4, 2004, to commemorate the 100th anniversary of the death of the sculptor Frédéric-Auguste Bartholdi.

Helpful Hints

Market Days: Markets take place Thursdays on place de l'Ancienne Douane, and Saturdays on place St. Joseph (both mornings only). Textiles are on sale Thursdays on place de la Cathédrale (all day) and Saturdays on place des Dominicains (afternoons only), and fish and produce are featured in the old market hall in the Tanners' Quarter on Thursday mornings. There's also a flea market every Friday from June to August on place des Dominicains.

Department Store: The big **Monoprix,** with a supermarket, is across from the TI and Unterlinden Museum (Mon–Sat 8:00–19:45, closed Sun).

Internet Access: Try **Infr@reseau,** near the TI at 12 rue du Rempart (Mon–Sat 10:00–21:00, Sun 14:00–20:00, tel. 03 89 23 98 45), or **Cyber Didim,** across the street at 9 rue du Rempart (above snack shop, daily 9:30–24:00, tel. 03 89 29 01 41).

Laundry: The city's lone launderette is near the recommended Maison Jund *chambre d'hôte* at 1 rue Ruest, just off the pedestrian street rue Vauban (usually open daily 7:00–21:00).

Bike Rental: Kiosque Colmarvélo is the cheapest around, with the most extensive hours and helpful, free route maps (€3/half-day, €5/day; bikes have 5 speeds, medium-width tires, basket, and lock; baby seats and helmets on request, €50 cash deposit and passport required, April–Oct daily 8:30–12:00 & 14:00–19:00, closed Nov–March, in orange-and-green kiosk at 4 avenue de la République on place Rapp, near the carousel, tel. 03 89 41 37 90).

Taxis: At the train station, call 03 89 41 40 19; otherwise, call 03 89 27 08 31 or 06 09 42 60 75.

Car Rental: The least expensive is **ADA** (Mon–Fri 8:00–12:00 & 14:00–18:30, Sat 8:00–12:00, closed Sun, 22 rue Stanislas, tel. 03 89 23 90 30, www.ada.fr). **Avis** is at the old train station (Mon–Fri 8:00–12:00 & 14:00–19:00, Sat until 17:00, closed Sun, tel. 03 89 23 21 82). The TI has a long list of other options.

Poodle Care: To give your poodle a shampoo and a haircut (or just watch the action), drop by **Quatt Pattes** (near Hôtel Rapp at 8 rue Berthe Molly).

TOURS

There are no city tours in English, but private English-speaking guides are available through the TI (about €120/3 hours). Tourist trains depart from the TI (€6, 30-min tours, recorded commentary). In the summer, horse-drawn carriages do the same (€6, 30-min tours).

For minivan tours of the Route du Vin, see "Getting Around the Route du Vin," page 724.

SELF-GUIDED WALK

Welcome to Colmar's Old Town

This walk—good by day or by night—is a handy way to link the city's three worthwhile sights. Supplement this information by reading the sidewalk information plaques that describe every point of interest in town.

The importance of 15th- to 17th-century Colmar is clear as you wander its pedestrian-friendly old center. It's decorated with 45 buildings classified as historic monuments. In the Middle Ages, most of Europe was fragmented into chaotic little princedoms and dukedoms. Merchant-dominated cities, natural proponents of the formation of large nation-states (a.k.a. globalization), banded together to form "trading leagues" (the World Trade Organizations of their day). The Hanseatic League was the super-league of northern Europe. Prosperous Colmar was the leading member of a smaller league of 10 Alsatian cities, called the Decapolis (founded 1354). The names of the streets you'll walk along bear witness to the merchants' historic importance to Colmar.

• *Start your tour at the old...*

Customs House (Koïfhus): Here, delegates of the Decapolis would meet to sort out trade issues, much like the European Union does in nearby Strasbourg today. Walk under its archway to place de l'Ancienne Douane and face the Frédéric-Auguste Bartholdi statue—arm raised, à la Statue of Liberty—and do a 360-degree spin to appreciate a gaggle of gables. This was the center of business activity in Colmar, with trade routes radiating to several major European cities. All goods that entered the city were taxed here. Today, it's the festive site of outdoor wine-tastings on many summer evenings.

• *The half-timbered commotion of higgledy-piggledy rooftops on the downhill side of the fountain marks the...*

Tanners' Quarter: These vertical 17th- and 18th-century rooftops competed for space in the sun to dry their freshly tanned hides, while the nearby river channel flushed the waste products. This neighborhood, restored in about 1970, was a pioneer in the government-funded renovation of old quarters. Residents had to play along or move out. Follow the statue's left elbow and walk down *petite* rue des Tanneurs (not "rue des Tanneurs"). Turn right at the end of the street (walking along the city's first wall—c. 1230, now built into the row of houses), then take the first left along the stream. On your right is the old market hall (fish, produce, and other products were brought here by flat-bottom boat). Today, it's

Colmar

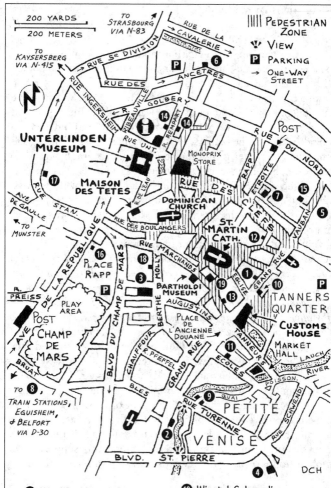

1. Hôtel St. Martin
2. Hostellerie le Maréchal
3. Hôtel/Restaurant le Rapp
4. Hôtel Turenne
5. Hôtel Ibis
6. Hôtel Primo
7. Maison Jund Rooms
8. To Grand Hôtel Bristol & B&B Chez Leslie
9. La Krutenau & Wistub "La Petite Venise"
10. Winstub Schwendi
11. La Maison Rouge Restaurant
12. Wistub Flory
13. Chez Hansi
14. Internet Cafés (2)
15. Launderette
16. Bike Rental
17. ADA Car Rental
18. Quatt Pattes Dog Grooming
19. Maison Pfister

Colmar's main market hall, where locals buy produce, meat, and fish on Thursday mornings.

• *Cross the canal and turn right on quai de la Poissonnerie (Wharf of the Fish Market), and you'll enter the...*

Petite Venise: This neighborhood, a collection of Colmar's most colorful houses lining the small canal, is almost too popular with tourists during the day. But at night it's romantic, with a fraction of the crowds. It lies between the town's first wall (built to defend against arrows) and its later wall (built in the age of gunpowder). The local river was canalized for medieval industry—to provide water for the tanners, to allow farmers to barge their goods into town, to power mills, and so on. Walk several blocks along the flower-box-lined canal to the end of rue de la Poissonnerie. Turn right, walk to the center of the bridge, and enjoy the view. To the right, you'll see examples of the flat-bottom gondolas used to transport goods on the small river. Today, they give tourists sleepy and scenic 30-minute, €5.50 canal tours (departure on demand, buy tickets at the bar/restaurant La Krutenau—see page 721).

• *Cross the bridge, take the second right on Grande Rue, and stroll several blocks back to the Customs House (green-tiled roof). Turn left and, with your back to the Customs House, walk uphill along rue des Marchands (Merchants' Street)—one of the most scenic stretches in town. (The ruler of Malaysia was so charmed by this street that he had it re-created in Kuala Lumpur.) In two blocks you come face-to-face with the...*

Maison Pfister (Pfister House): The richly decorated merchant's house from 1537, with its external spiral-staircase turret and painted walls, illustrates the city folks' taste for Renaissance humanism (a fine little wine shop fills the ground floor). The man carved into the side of the building the next door up (at #9) was a drape maker; he's shown holding a bar, Colmar's measure of about one meter. (In the Middle Ages, it was common for cities to have their own units of length; one reason merchants supported the "globalization" of their time was to get rid of different measuring systems.)

• *Look closely at the architecture.*

Half-Timbered Houses: House #9 (with the guy holding the bar) shows off the classic half-timbered design—the beams (upright, cross, angular supports) are grouped in what's called (and looks like) "a man." Typical houses are built with a man in the middle flanked by two "half men." While houses of the rich were made of stone, anyone on a budget built half-timbered structures (though all homes here sit on a stone base to prevent them from sinking into the marshy ground). Originally, proud townsfolk would plaster over their cheap half-timbered walls to create the illusion of a stone house. Then, in the 20th century, half-timbered became charming, so they peeled away the plaster to reveal the old beams. You can identify true stone homes by their window-sills: Wooden sills means they're half-timbered, while stone sills indicate the entire building is built of stone. As you explore the town, notice how upper floors are cantilevered out. This was both a structural trick and a tax dodge. A single supporting wall could support more if it rested in from the upper floor's edge. And real-estate taxes were based on the square footage of the ground floor.

If you wander at night, you'll notice that Colmar is not only beautifully pedestrianized, but also wonderfully floodlit. Countless small floodlights set in amid the cobbles illuminate the town after dark. They can be changed to give different intensities and colors, keeping Colmar fresh and inviting after dark.

One more block along on the left is the **Bartholdi Museum** (described under "More Sights," page 717). Next door (#28) is Au Pain Dorée, with its charming Art Nouveau facade and interior. Art Nouveau was rare in Colmar. During the style's heyday in the early 20th century—which was also just after this region was taken from France by Germany—Art Nouveau was considered an anti-German statement, and therefore controversial.

• *A passage to the right leads to...*

St. Martin Cathedral: The city's golden cathedral (erected in 1235), with its lone tower (two were planned) and gleaming tiles, was inspired by the Hôtel Dieu in Beaune. Walk left around the cathedral. Notice that the relief over the main door depicts not your typical Last Judgment scene, but the Three Kings who visited Baby Jesus. The Magi, whose remains are in the Rhine city of Köln, Germany, are popular in this region. Just past the cathedral, head left up the pedestrian-only rue des Serruriers (Locksmiths' Street) to the **Dominican Church** (worth entering; described under "More Sights," page 716). Compare the impressive St. Martin Cathedral with this low-slung, sober structure that perfectly symbolizes Dominican austerity. These two very different houses of worship were built at the same time.

• *Continue past the Dominican Church (rue des Serruriers becomes rue des Boulangers—Bakers' Street). Then make a right on rue des Têtes (notice the beautiful swan sign over the* pharmacie *at the corner). Walk a block to the fancy old house with all the heads (on the right).*

Maison des Têtes (House of Heads): Colmar's other famous merchant's house, built in 1609 by a big-shot winemaker, is playfully decorated with 105 faces and masks (on the ground floor, the guy in the center has pig's feet).

Four houses to the right, a 1947 bakery sign (look above the big pretzel) shows the *boulangerie* basics in Alsace: croissant, *kugelhopf,* and baguette. Across the street, study the fine early-20th-century store sign trumpeting the wonders of a butcher (including pork and foie gras—with the traditional maiden chasing a goose about to be force-fed), all hung on the beak of a chicken.

• *Angle down rue de l'Eau (Water Street) opposite Maison des Têtes for a shortcut to the TI and the Unterlinden Museum, with its namesake linden trees lining the front yard (popular locally for making the calming "Tilleul" tea).*

SIGHTS

▲▲▲Unterlinden Museum

Colmar's touristic claim to fame is one of my favorite museums in Europe. Its extensive yet manageable collection ranges from Roman Colmar to medieval winemaking exhibits, and from traditional wedding dresses to paintings that give vivid insight into the High Middle Ages. Plan on spending extra time in this museum, as its collection is so unique and varied, and the excellent audio-guide (included with your admission) makes the curator your best friend. The museum is one of the most visited in all of France for its devastatingly beautiful *Isenheim Altarpiece*, so it can be crowded and loud. (The best time to visit is about 12:00–14:00—when most are lunching—or at the end of the day.)

Cost, Hours, Location: €7, €6 for seniors, price includes indispensable audioguide; May–Oct daily 9:00–18:00; Nov–April Wed–Mon 9:00–12:00 & 14:00–17:00, closed Tue; 1 rue d'Unterlinden, tel. 03 89 20 15 58, www.musee-unterlinden.com.

⊙ Self-Guided Tour: Use this commentary to supplement the information provided by the included audioguide.

Gothic Statues (Room 1): Room 1 features 14th-century Gothic statues from St. Martin Cathedral's facade. Study the faces. Even though they endured the elements outdoors for more than 500 years, it's still clear that they were sculpted carefully. Take a close look at the 15th-century stained glass; fine details are painted into the glass that no one would see. The glass is essentially a jigsaw puzzle connected by lead. Around here, glass this old is rare—most of it was destroyed by rampaging Protestants in the Reformation wars.

Cloister: Step into the soothing cloister (the largest 13th-century cloister in Alsace) and walk right, passing the WCs in the corner. This was a Dominican convent founded for noblewomen in 1230. It functioned until the French Revolution, when the building became a garrison. Rooms with museum exhibits branch off from here. Don't miss the wine room (next corner) with its 17th-century oak presses and finely decorated casks. Wine revenue was used to care for Colmar's poor. The nuns owned many of the best vineyards around, and as this is a sun belt (with less rain than other parts of southern France), production was excellent. So was consumption. Notice (on the first cask on left) the Bacchus with the distended tummy straddling a keg. The quote from 1781 reads: "My belly's full of juice. It makes me strong. But drink too much and you lose dignity and health."

Painting Gallery: Left of the wine-press room, enter the painting gallery marked *art médiéval*. Stop first by the spinning case of engravings by Martin Schongauer, Albrecht Dürer's master. Throughout the museum, you'll see small photos of engravings illustrating how painters were influenced by other artists' engravings. Most German painters of the time were also engravers (that's how they made money—making lots of copies for sale). The following rooms are filled with paintings that are wonderfully described by the audioguide. As you enjoy the art, remember that Alsace was historically German and part of the upper Rhine River Valley. (This museum boasts France's only painting by Lucas Cranach.) Remember those Three Kings (of Bethlehem fame) from St. Martin Cathedral? They're prominently featured throughout this region, because their heads ended up as relics in Köln's cathedral (on the Rhine).

These rooms lead to the...

Isenheim Altarpiece: The highlight of the museum (and, for me, the city) is Matthias Grünewald's gripping *Isenheim Altarpiece*

(c. 1515), actually a series of three different paintings on hinges that pivot like shutters (study the little model on the wall, explained in English). Designed to help people in a medieval hospital endure horrible skin diseases (such as St. Anthony's Fire, later called rye ergotism)—long before the age of painkillers—it's one of the most powerful paintings ever produced. Germans know this painting like Americans know the *Mona Lisa*.

Stand as if you were a medieval peasant in front of the centerpiece and let the agony and suffering of the Crucifixion drag its fingers down your face. It's an intimate drama. The point—Jesus' suffering—is drilled home: the weight of his body bends the crossbar (unrealistically, creating to some eyes an almost crossbow effect). His elbows are pulled from their sockets by the weight of his dead body. People who are crucified die of asphyxiation, as Jesus' chest implies. His mangled feet are swollen with blood. The grief on Mary's face is agonizing. In hopes that the intended viewers (the hospital's patients) would know that Jesus understood their suffering, Jesus himself was even painted to appear as if he had a skin disease. Study the faces and the Christian symbolism. Mary is wrapped in the shroud that will cover Jesus. The sorrowful composition on the left is powerful. On the far left stands St.

Alsace

Sebastian (called upon by those with the plague) and on the right is St. Anthony (the Red Adair of rotten rye). Walk to the back of this panel.

The Resurrection scene is unique in art history (Grünewald had no master and no students). Jesus rockets out of the tomb as man is transformed into God. As if proclaiming once again, "I am the Light," he is radiant. His shroud is the color of light: Roy G. Biv. Around the rainbow is the "resurrection of the flesh." Jesus' pink and perfect flesh would appeal to the patients who meditated on the scene. The right half of this panel depicts the Annunciation.

In the nativity scene on the next panel—set in the Rhineland—much-adored Mary is tender and loving, true to the Dominican belief that she was the intercessor for all in heaven. The three scenes of the painting changed with the church calendar. The happy ending—a psychedelic explosion of Resurrection joy—is the spiritual equivalent of jumping from the dentist's chair directly into a whirlpool tub. The last two panels show the Temptation of St. Anthony and his visit to St. Paul the hermit. The final scene, carved in wood by Nikolaus Hagenauer, is St. Anthony on his throne.

The Rest of the Museum: Downstairs, you'll find a modern-art section, and Roman and prehistoric artifacts. The upstairs rooms contain local and folk history, with everything from 19th-century Romantic paintings, old armoires, and medieval armor to old-time toys.

More Sights

▲▲▲**Dominican Church (Eglise des Dominicains)**—Here's another medieval mindblower. In this church, you'll find Martin Schongauer's angelically beautiful *Virgin in the Rosebush* holding court, dating from 1473 but looking as if it were painted yesterday. Here, graceful Mary is shown as a welcoming mother. Jesus clings to her, reminding the viewer of the warmth of his relationship with Mary. The Latin on her halo reads: "Pick me also for your child, O very Holy Virgin." Rather than telling a particular Bible story, this is a general scene, designed to meet the personal devotional needs of any worshipper. Here, nature is not a backdrop; Mary and Jesus are encircled by it. Schongauer's robins, sparrows, and goldfinches bring extra life to an already impressively natural rosebush. The white rose anticipates Jesus' crucifixion. The frame, with its angelic orchestra, dates only from 1900. The contrast provided by the simple Dominican setting heightens the flamboyance of this Gothic masterpiece. Dominican churches were intentionally austere, symbolic of their zeal to purify their faith and compete with the growing popularity of 13th-century heretical movements, such as Catharism, which preached a simpler faith (€1.50, mid-March–Dec daily 10:00–13:00 & 15:00–18:00, last entry 15 min before closing, closed Jan–mid-March, no photos).

▲**Bartholdi Museum**—This little museum recalls the life and work of the local boy who gained fame by sculpting America's much-loved Statue of Liberty. Frédéric-Auguste Bartholdi (1834–1904) was a dynamic painter/photographer/sculptor with a passion for the defense of liberty and freedom. Because Prussia took Alsace in 1871, he spent most of his career in Paris, unable to move back to his home of Colmar without becoming a German. He devoted years of his life to realizing the vision of a statue of liberty for America that would stand in New York City's harbor. Closer to home, several Bartholdi statues grace Colmar's squares.

Cost, Hours, Location: €4.50, March–Dec Wed–Mon 10:00–12:00 & 14:00–18:00, closed Tue and Jan–Feb, pick up English flier, in heart of old town at 30 rue des Marchands, tel. 03 89 41 90 60, www.musee-bartholdi.com.

❷ **Self-Guided Tour:** Curiously, there is no English in this museum. The following commentary will help make things meaningful.

Behind the ticket desk, study Bartholdi's photo (actually six photos in a line) of New York City's harbor in 1876. The first piling of the Brooklyn Bridge is up. Bartholdi added the tiny Statue of Liberty on the far left (along with the boats).

The main floor hosts mostly temporary exhibits of Alsatian works. Upstairs to the left, rooms re-create Bartholdi's high-society flat in Paris. The dining room is lined with portraits of his aristocratic family. In the next room hangs a fine portrait of the sculptor, facing his mother (on a red chair). He was very close to his mom, writing her daily letters. Many see her features in the Statue of Liberty. Find the gloomy painting of the Statue of Liberty at the top of the stairs.

The rest of this first floor shows off Bartholdi's French work. Notice how his patriotic works tend to have one arm raised—*Vive la France*, God bless America, *Deutschland über alles*...you can fill in the flag-waving blank.

Bartholdi's most famous French work, the *Lion of Belfort*, celebrates the Alsatian town that fought so fiercely in 1871 that it was never annexed into Germany. Photos show the red sandstone lion sitting regally below the mighty Vauban fortress of Belfort—a symbol of French spirit standing strong against Germany.

The second floor up (top floor) is dedicated to Bartholdi's American works—the paintings, photos, and statues that Bartholdi made during his many travels to the States. You'll see statues of Columbus and Lafayette (who was only 19 years old when he came to America's aid) with George Washington. Then the exhibit traces the evolution and completion of the dream of a Statue of Liberty. Fascinating photos show the Eiffel-designed core, the frame being covered with plaster, and then the hand-hammered copper plating, which was ultimately riveted to the frame. The statue was assembled in Paris, then un-riveted and shipped to New York, in 1886...10 years late. The big ear is half-size.

While the statue was a gift from France, the US had to come up with the cash to build a pedestal. This was a tough sell, but Bartholdi was determined to see his statue erected. On 10 trips to the US, he worked to raise funds and lobbied for construction, bringing with him this painting and a full-size model of the torch—which the statue would ultimately hold. (Lucky for Bartholdi and his cause, his cousin was the French ambassador to the US.) Eventually, the project came together—the pedestal was built, and the Statue of Liberty has welcomed waves of immigrants into New York ever since.

SLEEPING

Hotels are busy on weekends in May, June, September, and October, and every day in July and August. But there are always rooms—somewhere. Should you have trouble finding a bed, ask the TI for help, or look in a nearby village, where small hotels and bed-and-breakfasts are plentiful (see my recommendations in nearby Eguisheim, page 730).

In the Center

$$$ **Hôtel St. Martin***, near the old Customs House, is a family-run place that began as a coaching inn (since 1361). Its 40 traditional yet well-equipped rooms, with air-conditioning and big beds, are woven into its antique frame. The hotel has three sections (young, middle-aged, and elderly) joined by a peaceful courtyard. All rooms offer good comfort and character, though the best rooms are in the new (young) wing, with traditional furnishings and stone walls (Db-€90–109). The cheapest rooms are the oldest, with showers instead of tubs and no elevator (Sb-€79, standard Db-€89–99, bigger Db-€109, still bigger Db-€149, Tb/Qb-€129, air-con in some rooms, free Internet access and Wi-Fi, free public parking nearby at Parking de la Vieille Ville, 38 Grand Rue, tel. 03 89 24 11 51, fax 03 89 23 47 78, www.hotel-saint-martin.com).

At $$$ **Hostellerie le Maréchal****, you'll pay top euro for Colmar's most famous and characteristic digs in the heart of La Petite Venise. While rooms are small for the price, the setting is romantic and the service is ever so professional (standard Db-€105–140, Db with whirlpool tub-€140–225, suite Db-€255, parking-€14, 4 place des Six Montagnes Noires, tel. 03 89 41 60 32,

Alsace

Sleep Code

(€1 = about $1.30, country code: 33)
S = Single, **D** = Double/Twin, **T** = Triple, **Q** = Quad, **b** = bathroom,
s = shower only, ***** = French hotel rating system (0–4 stars).
Unless otherwise noted, credit cards are accepted and English
is spoken.

    To help you sort easily through these listings, I've divided
the rooms into three categories based on the price for a standard double room with bath:

  $$$ **Higher Priced**—Most rooms €90 or more.
   $$ **Moderately Priced**—Most rooms between €50–90.
    $ **Lower Priced**—Most rooms €50 or less.

---

fax 03 89 24 59 40, www.le-marechal.com). Their well-respected
restaurant will melt a romantic's heart, and they'll encourage you
to dine here (€35–75 *menus*, reserve ahead).

    $$ Hôtel le Rapp***, ideally located off place Rapp, offers a
variety of rooms for many budgets. The cheapest rooms are small
but adequate; the larger rooms are tastefully designed, with queen-
size beds. There's also a small basement pool, sauna, Turkish bath,
and an indoor/outdoor bar-café. It's well-run and family-friendly,
with a big park one block away and lazy Pastaga, the hotel hound
(Sb-€75, standard Db-€87, bigger Db-€100, junior suite for 2–4
people-€135, good buffet breakfast-€9.50, air-con, elevator, free
Internet access and Wi-Fi, 1 rue Berthe Molly, tel. 03 89 41 62 10,
fax 03 89 24 13 58, www.hotel-rapp-colmar.com, rapp-hot@calixo
.net). Its restaurant serves a classy Alsatian *menu* with impeccable
service (closed Thu–Fri).

    $$ Hôtel Turenne** is a good though less-central value, with
83 rooms. The hotel capitalizes on its charming historic facade,
though most rooms are in a modern wing. It's a 10-minute walk
from the city center, a 15-minute walk from the train station, and
is located on a busy street with easy parking underneath. Rooms
vary in size and some have tight bathrooms. Half the rooms are
non-smoking (Sb-€47–68, Db-€60–68, Tb-€68, family-friendly
studios-€110, parking-€7, air-con, elevator for most rooms, cozy
bar and breakfast room, Internet access and free Wi-Fi, 10 rue
de Bâle; from train station walk straight out to avenue Raymond
Poincaré, then turn left on rue des Americains; tel. 03 89 21 58 58,
fax 03 89 41 27 64, www.turenne.com).

    $$ Hôtel Ibis**, on the ring road, sells hospital-white, efficient
comfort with tiny bathrooms (Sb-€50–60, Db-€66–78, bigger Db-
€75–85, Tb-€90, air-con, inside parking-€7, outside parking-€5, 10

rue St. Eloi, tel. 03 89 41 30 14, fax 03 89 24 51 49, www.ibishotel
.com, h1377@accor.com).

$$ Hôtel Primo**, near the Unterlinden Museum, is an effi-
cient, bright, nothing-but-the-plastic-and-concrete-basics place
to sleep for those who consider ambience a four-letter word. The
friendly staff will hold a room for you until 18:00 if you call. Rooms
facing the big square *(grand place)* are far quieter (S/D/T-€29, Sb-
€39–55, Db-€49–59, Tb/Qb-€69, small discount for Rick Steves
readers in 2008, foam mattresses, Internet access, free parking in
big square in front, 5 rue des Ancêtres, tel. 03 89 24 22 24, fax 03
89 24 55 96, www.villes-et-vignoble.com, hotel-primo@villes-et
-vignoble.com). Half the beds have footboards—a problem if
you're more than six feet tall.

$ Maison Jund holds my favorite budget beds in Colmar.
This ramshackle yet magnificent half-timbered house, the home
of a likeable winemaker and his wife (André and Myriam), feels
like a medieval tree house soaked in wine and filled with flow-
ers. The rooms are simple but adequately comfortable, spacious,
and equipped with kitchenettes. Most rooms are available only
April to mid-September, though four rooms are rented year-round
(D-€30, Db/Tb-€42–50, huge family apartment with steep stair-
case sleeps up to six—Db-€90, then €5 per person, no breakfast,
free Internet access, 12 rue de l'Ange, tel. 03 89 41 58 72, fax 03
89 23 15 83, www.martinjund.com, martinjund@hotmail.com).
Leave your car at the lot across from Hôtel Primo. Train travel-
ers can take bus #1, #2, or #3 from the station to the TI, walk
from Unterlinden Museum past Monoprix, and veer left on rue des
Clefs, left on rue Etroite, and right on rue de l'Ange. This is not a
hotel, so there is no real reception—though good-natured Myriam
seems to be around, somewhere, most of the time (call if you plan
to arrive after 22:00).

Near the Train Station

$$$ Grand Hôtel Bristol*** couldn't be closer to the station and,
in spite of its Best Western plaque and its popularity with groups,
it retains some character, with pleasant public spaces and 91
good, if pricey, rooms (Sb-€90, standard Db-€110, big Db-€146,
7 place de la Gare, tel. 03 89 23 59 59, fax 03 89 23 92 26, www
.grand-hotel-bristol.com).

$$ Bed-and-Breakfast Chez Leslie is a vintage B&B in a
residential neighborhood (a five-minute walk from the station,
20-minute walk from the city center). The rooms are bright and
whimsically decorated, and the garden makes for a refreshingly
flowery place to relax. San Franciscan Leslie Collins loves host-
ing visitors in her home (Sb-€52, Db-€72, family room €84–99,
includes breakfast, ask about apartment rental in town, 31 rue

de Mulhouse, tel. 03 89 79 98 99, mobile 06 82 58 91 98, www .chezleslie.com, info@chezleslie.com). From the train platform, exit down the stairs into the underground passageway toward rue du Tir (away from station), walk up the stairs at the end, go left down the street, and turn right at the first corner (rue de Soultz). Continue up to the square and turn left on rue de Mulhouse.

EATING

Colmar is full of good restaurants offering traditional Alsatian *menus* for €17–25, and expensive places with lighter fare. (Also see "Eating" in nearby Eguisheim, page 731.)

In Petite Venise

For dining with a canalside view, head into Petite Venise and make your way to the photo-perfect bridge on rue Turenne, where you'll find several picturesque places.

La Krutenau's wood tables sprawl along the canal, offering many desserts and only *tartes flambées*. Come for a light meal with ambience (inside or out), a dessert, or a drink on a warm evening (closed Sun–Mon, 1 rue de la Poissonnerie, tel. 03 89 41 18 80).

Wistub "La Petite Venise," buried in the middle of all the canal cuteness, serves well-presented creative dishes with a dash of Vosges Mountain inspiration in what feels like a well-polished mountain chalet. Walter and Christel work hard in their small eight-table place (among old-time family photos) and are accommodating—they explain their fun chalkboard menus and split desserts with a smile (€12–15 *plats*, Thu–Sat only, reservations smart, 4 rue de la Poissonnerie, tel. 03 89 41 72 59).

In the Old City Center

Winstub Schwendi has the lively feel of a German pub inside (with 10 beers on tap) and a nice terrace outside. Choose from a dozen different robust Swiss *rösti* plates or the *tarte flambées;* I like the *strasbourgoise* (€8–14 main dishes, daily 10:00–24:00, very popular on weekends, facing old Customs House at 3 Grand Rue, tel. 03 89 23 66 26).

La Maison Rouge has a folk-museum interior and noisy sidewalk seating with good, reasonably priced, traditional Alsatian cuisine and all-day service. You'll be greeted by the *jambon à l'os*—ham cooking on the bone (€17–35 *menus*, try the endive salad and *tarte flambée forestière*, closed Sun, 9 rue des Ecoles, tel. 03 89 23 53 22).

Winstub Flory, hiding in a small alley, is known for its large portions and reliable Alsatian specialties. There's some outdoor seating and a warm, half-timbered interior (€15–23 *plats*, €22 *menus*, daily in summer 18:30–21:45, closed Tue–Wed off-season, 1 rue Mangold, tel. 03 89 41 78 80).

Hôtel-Restaurant le Rapp is a traditional place to savor a slow, elegant meal served with grace and fine Alsatian wine by Laurent and his team. While *menus* start at €24, if you want to order high on the menu, this is a fine place to do it (great *baecke-offe* for €16 that makes a whole meal, good salads, they take their vegetarian options seriously, closed Thu–Fri, air-con, 1 rue Berthe Molly, tel. 03 89 41 62 10).

Chez Hansi, next to the customs house, is a popular place with something for every appetite. Try local specialties (such as chicken in Riesling sauce) or medieval "pub grub" like *choucroute garnie* (€13–25 main dishes, €18–44 *menus,* daily 11:45–14:00, Fri–Tue 18:45–21:30, closed for dinner Wed–Thu, 23 rue des Marchands, tel. 03 89 41 37 84).

TRANSPORTATION CONNECTIONS

From Colmar by Train to: Strasbourg (2/hr, 35 min), **Reims** (via TGV: 8/day, 2 hrs, most change in Strasbourg; via non-TGV train: 4/day, 5–7 hrs, 1–3 changes), **Beaune** (6/day, 4–5 hrs, changes in Besançon, Mulhouse, or Belfort and Dijon), **Paris'** Gare de l'Est (via TGV: 15/day, 3 direct, others change in Strasbourg, 3 hrs; via non-TGV train: 8/day, 5.5 hrs, change in Strasbourg, Dijon, or Mulhouse), **Amboise** (via TGV: 8/day, 5 hrs, most with transfer in Strasbourg and Paris; via non-TGV train: 8/day, 9 hrs, via Paris), **Basel, Switzerland** (13/day, 1 hr), **Karlsruhe, Germany** (10/day, 2.5 hrs, best with change in Strasbourg; from Karlsruhe, it's 90 min to Frankfurt, 3 hrs to Munich).

Route du Vin (Wine Road)

Alsace's Route du Vin is an asphalt ribbon that ties 90 miles of vineyards, villages, and feudal fortresses into an understandably popular tourist package. This is a sun belt that gets less rain than other parts of southern France. The generally dry climate has made for good wine and happy tourists since Roman days. Colmar and Eguisheim are ideally located for exploring the 30,000 acres of vineyards blanketing the hills from Marlenheim to Thann.

If you have only a day, focus on towns within easy striking range of Colmar. Top stops are Eguisheim, Kaysersberg, Hunawihr, Ribeauvillé, and the too-popular Riquewihr. Be careful not to overdose on all the half-timbered cuteness. Two, maybe three villages meet the needs of most. As you tour this region, you'll see storks' nests on many church spires and city halls, thanks to a campaign to reintroduce the birds to this area. (Nests can weigh as much as 1,000 pounds.)

Get a map of the Route du Vin from any TI. Review "French Wine-Tasting 101" (page 30) and information on half-timbered architecture (page 712).

Most towns have wineries that give tours (some charge a fee), and many small producers open their courtyards with free tastings. The modern cooperatives at Eguisheim, Bennwihr, Hunawihr, and Ribeauvillé, created after the destruction of World War II, provide a good look at modern and efficient methods of production.

Learn to recognize the basic grapes: Riesling is the king of Alsatian grapes. The name comes from the German word that describes its slightly smoky, gasoline smell. Gewürztraminer is "the lady's wine"—its bouquet is like a rosebush, its taste is fruity, and its aftertaste is spicy. In fact, it's named for the German word for "spicy." Crémant d'Alsace, the Alsatian sparkling wine, is very good—and much cheaper. The French term for headache, if you really get "Alsauced," is *mal à la tête*.

Towns are most alive during their weekly morning (until noon) farmers' markets (Monday: Kaysersberg; Tuesday: Munster; Friday: Turckheim; Saturday: Ribeauvillé and Colmar—behind station near St. Joseph's Church). Riquewihr and Eguisheim have no market days.

Getting Around the Route du Vin

If you're driving, buy a good regional map (1:200,000 or better) before heading out.

By Bus: Several companies run buses connecting Colmar's train station with most villages along the Route du Vin (except on Sundays, when there are none). Kaysersberg has good weekday service and makes an easy day trip from Colmar; Riquewihr, Hunawihr, and Ribeauvillé have decent service, but service to Eguisheim is minimal (Mon–Sat schedules from Colmar to Eguisheim: 3/day, usually at 12:00, 16:00, and 17:00, 20 min; to Kaysersberg: almost hourly, 25–40 min; to Riquewihr, Bennwihr, Hunawihr, Turckheim, and Ribeauvillé: 6/day, 30–45 min). Allow €1.50–3.50 one-way to these villages. Most schedules are posted where buses stop. Pick up schedules and get help deciphering them at the TI. Buy tickets from the driver.

By Taxi: Allow €15 from Colmar to Eguisheim, €25–30 from

Colmar or Eguisheim to Kaysersberg (call friendly William at 06 14 47 21 80, or another taxi at 03 89 80 71 71).

By Minivan Tour: Cheerful Jean-Claude Werner leads **Les Circuits d'Alsace** day trips in a comfortable seven-person mini-van (small groups: 2-person minimum, larger groups possible, in English and/or Japanese, great sound system on comfy air-con minibus). His informative tours include a few enjoyable, very short vineyard walks. Jean-Claude's enthusiasm and personal touches add to the experience. Wine-tastings and gourmet excursions can be arranged on request. Half-day tours for €49 visit three towns, generally Kaysersberg, Turckheim, and Eguisheim. Full-day tours for €93 add a couple more towns and the Haut-Kœnigsbourg Castle (5 percent discount with this book in 2008, reserve directly with Jean-Claude, pickup at your hotel, tel. 03 89 41 90 88, mobile 06 72 37 17 11, www.alsace-travel.com, werner@alsace-travel.com).

Regioscope is another good option, with full- and half-day tours in a 15-seat, air-conditioned minivan led by Frédéric Albert (departures from Colmar and Strasbourg possible). Morning departures leave Colmar at 9:15; afternoon departures leave at 13:45. Trips return by 12:15 or 18:30. On Tuesday, Thursday, Friday, and Sunday mornings, they go to Ribeauvillé and Kaysersberg (€44); then in the afternoon, they head to Haut-Kœnigsbourg and Riquewihr (€52 includes wine-tasting, €92 for both morning and afternoon tours). On Wednesday and Saturday, morning tours visit Eguisheim and Turckheim (€44), and afternoon tours go to Titisee in Germany's Black Forest (€63, or €103 for both tours). Prices include entrance fees and guided tours of the castles. In December, ask about Christmas Market excursions (tel. 06 88 21 27 15, www .regioscope.com, info@regioscope.com).

By Bike: The Route du Vin's more-or-less-level terrain and abundance of bike trails make biking a reasonable option, par-ticularly once you get to the villages (see "Helpful Hints," page 709, for bike rental in Colmar). To save yourself the ride out of Colmar, rent a bike in Turckheim (84 Grand Rue, tel. & fax 03 89 27 06 36). While there is no bike rental in Eguisheim, the Auberge Alsacienne has bikes for guests (see page 730). Colmar to Eguisheim to Turckheim and back makes a manageable 15-mile, half-day circuit; add Kaysersberg for a full day's outing, but beware—the road to Kaysersberg is busy. Most key roads leaving Colmar have a painted bike lane. One of those lanes leads to Eguisheim and is a level snap, though it's entirely on busy city streets (biking to Eguisheim is a practical means of visiting this village, given the poor bus service and easy bike access). From Eguisheim you can pedal along small vineyard roads. Figure on pedaling steadily for 60 minutes on mostly busy roads to Kaysersberg from Colmar (bike lane on the main road from Colmar, *route du Colmar*). Get advice

Alsace

Alsace's Route de Vin

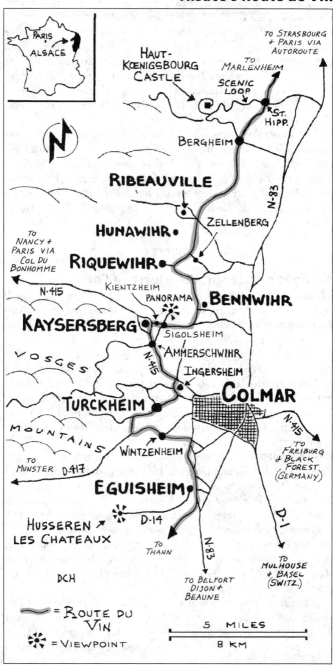

To Strasbourg & Paris via Autoroute

HAUT-KŒNIGSBOURG CASTLE

To Marlenheim

SCENIC LOOP

R. ST. HIPP.

Paris
Alsace

BERGHEIM

RIBEAUVILLE

N·83

HUNAWIHR

ZELLENBERG

To Nancy & Paris via Col du Bonhomme

RIQUEWIHR

N·415

KIENTZHEIM

PANORAMA

BENNWIHR

KAYSERSBERG

SIGOLSHEIM

AMMERSCHWIHR

VOSGES

N·415

INGERSHEIM

COLMAR

MOUNTAINS

TURCKHEIM

N·415

To Freiburg & Black Forest (Germany)

To Munster

D·417

WINTZENHEIM

EGUISHEIM

D·1

HUSSEREN LES CHATEAUX

D·14

To Thann

N·83

To Mulhouse & Basel (Switz.)

To Belfort Dijon & Beaune

DCH

= ROUTE DU VIN

= VIEWPOINT

5 MILES

8 KM

Alsace

and a good map from a bike shop and avoid major roads—except for those you use to leave Colmar (see below).

By Car: To reach the Route du Vin north of Colmar, leave Colmar's train station following signs to *Epinal*. In Wintzenheim, follow signs to *Turckheim*, then find D-10 (Route du Vin) to Ingersheim (Kaysersberg is a short detour from here), Riquewihr, Hunawihr, Ribeauvillé, and Château du Haut-Kœnigsbourg. Look for *Route du Vin* signs. For Eguisheim, leave Colmar on N-83 toward Belfort.

By Foot: Well-signed walking trails *(sentiers viticoles)* connect Route du Vin villages through the vineyards (get info at local TIs and see our walking trails in "Sights," below); hikers can climb high to the ruined castles of the Vosges mountains (Eguisheim and Ribeauvillé are good bases). The *sentier viticole* connecting Kaysersberg and Riquewihr is a good two-hour walk that works well with buses from Colmar (see page 732).

SIGHTS

Along the Route du Vin, North of Colmar

These sights are listed from south to north, in the order you'll encounter them if you're heading north out of Colmar.

Eguisheim—This is the most charming village of the region (described on page 728).

Turckheim—With a fine square and garden-filled moat, this pleasant town is refreshingly untouristy, just enough off the beaten path to be overlooked. WWII buffs appreciate its "Colmar Pocket" museum chronicling the American push to take Alsace from the Nazis. Turckheim is ideal for renting a bike and pedaling along the virtually traffic-free paved trail to Munster (Munster's market day is Tue).

Kaysersberg—This town has WWII sights, Dr. Albert Schweitzer's house, and plenty of hiking opportunities (described on page 732).

Riquewihr—This little village is so picturesque today because it was so rich centuries ago; you can recognize its old wealth because it has the most stone houses of any place in Alsace. The walled village is crammed with tourist shops, cafés, galleries, cobblestones, and flowers. Sharpen your elbows if you arrive with the many groups in the afternoon (**TI** tel. 03 89 47 80 80, www.ribeauville-riquewihr .com).

You'll enter at the lower end under the Hôtel de Ville (City Hall). Within a few yards, you'll see the tourist train (€6, next departure time posted, 30 min, recorded tour through vineyards). Try the excellent and free wine-tasting at Caves Dopff et Irion (uphill from Hôtel de Ville, daily 10:00–19:00, tel. 03 89 47 92 51). The wonderful "air-conditioning" is completely natural—you're in a cave.

Shop and browse—sampling fresh local baked goods given free to tourists—to the top of town, where you'll find one of the best bell towers in the region (1291). The Dolden Museum (at the tower) shows off farm and winemaking tools. Check out the engraving of 13th-century Riquewihr by the fountain. Walks both inside and outside the ramparts begin from here. (The best walk is to the left, or south.)

Zellenberg—This town has an impressive setting and is worth a quick stop for the views from either side of its narrow perch.

Hunawihr—This bit of wine-soaked Alsatian cuteness is far less visited than its more famous neighbors, and features a 16th-century fortified church that today is shared by Catholics and Protestants (the Catholics are buried next to the church; the Protestants are buried outside the church wall). Park below in the village at the sheltered picnic tables and follow the trail up to the church, then loop back through the village. Kids enjoy Hunawihr's small stork park, Parc des Cigognes (April–Sept daily 10:00–12:00 & 14:00–18:00, no midday closing June–Aug, closes at 17:00 March and Oct–Nov, closed Dec–Feb, other animals take part in the afternoon shows, tel. 03 89 73 72 62, www .cigogne-loutre.com). Eat well at **Winstub Suzel** near the church (€16–22 *menus*, serves lunch and dinner, closed Wed, 2 rue de l'Eglise, tel. 03 89 73 30 85).

Ribeauvillé—Come here to hike. Two brooding castles hang above this pleasant town seldom visited by Americans. The steep castle trail leaves from the top of the town (at Hôtel Trois Châteaux, park in city lot here). Allow 45 minutes one-way, or just climb 10 minutes for a view over the town (www.ribeauville -riquewihr.com).

Château de Haut-Kœnigsbourg—This granddaddy of Alsatian castles, strategically situated on a rocky spur high above the flat Rhine plain, protected the passage between Alsace and Lorraine for centuries. Its pink stones were quarried from the Vosges Mountains. Rebuilt in the early 20th century, the well-furnished castle highlights Germanic influence in Alsatian history with decorations that illustrate castle life from the 15th through 17th centuries. There's little English, so you'll want the informative 60-minute audioguide—press 3 for English (€7.50, under 18 free, audioguide-€4, daily June–Aug 9:30–18:30, April–May and Sept 9:30–17:30, March and Oct 9:45–17:00, Nov–Feb 9:45–12:00 & 13:00–16:30, last entry 30 min before closing, about 15 min north of Ribeauvillé above St. Hippolyte, tel. 03 88 82 50 60).

Alsace

Vieil-Armand WWI Memorial—This powerful memorial evokes the slaughter of the Western Front in World War I, when Germany and France bashed heads for years in a War of Attrition. It's up a windy road above Cernay (20 miles south of Colmar). From the parking lot, walk 10 minutes to the vast cemetery, and walk 30 more minutes through trenches to a hilltop with a grand Alsatian view. Here you'll find a stirring memorial statue of French soldiers storming the trenches in 1915–1916, facing near-certain death.

Eguisheim

Just a few miles south of Colmar's suburbs, this circular, flower-festooned little wine town (pop. 1,600) is pretty darn cute. It's ideal for a relaxing lunch and vineyard walks, and makes a good small-town base for exploring Alsace. It's a cinch by car (easy parking) and by bike, but barely accessible by bus. Consider taking the bus one-way and taxi the other to Colmar or other villages (bus schedules available at TIs and posted at key stops. Eguisheim's stop is at the lower end of the village by the PTT.

Tourist Information: The TI has information on accommodations, festivals, vineyard walks, and Vosges mountain hikes (Mon–Fri 9:30–12:00 & 14:00–18:00, Sat 9:30–12:00 & 13:30–17:30, closed Sun, 22 Grand Rue, tel. 03 89 23 40 33, www.ot-eguisheim.fr). They're happy to call a taxi for you.

Internet Access: Le Café has Internet access, lattes, and delicious baked goodies (daily 10:00–19:00, impasse Allmend, behind 2C rue du Rempart Nord, tel. 03 89 41 14 30).

SELF-GUIDED WALK

Welcome to Eguisheim

While Eguisheim's wall is gone, the rue des Remparts (Nord and Sud) survives, scenically circling the village. The main drag, Grand Rue, bisects the circle leading to a town square that's as darling as a Grimms' fairy tale.

Start your visit at the bottom of town (TI) and circle the ramparts clockwise (walking up rue du Rempart Sud). The most enchanting and higgledy-piggledy view in town is right at the start of the loop (at the tight Y in the road; go left and uphill). Rue du Rempart Sud is more picturesque than rue du Rempart Nord, but I'd walk the entire circle. After going about a quarter of the circle, when you see a church on your right, you may want to cut into the town center to enjoy the little square, place de l'Eglise.

Back on the rue des Remparts, you'll see that what was once

the moat is now lined with 13th- to 17th-century houses—a cancan of half-timbered charm. You're actually walking a lane between the back of fine homes (on the left) and their barns (on the right). Look for emblems of daily life, religious and magical symbols, dates on lintel stones, and so on. (The government pays 15 percent of the cost of any work locals do on their exteriors.) For more on half-timbered architecture, see page 712.

Once you've finished the loop, walk up Grand Rue to Eguisheim's main square, **place du Château St. Léon,** and lose all sense of discipline sampling the shops, cafés, and fruits of the local vine. This square, lined with fine Renaissance houses, marks the heart of the old town. The castle is privately owned and closed to the public. Surviving bits of its 13th-century, eight-sided wall circle the chapel, built in neo-Romanesque style on the site of the castle's keep in 1895. While it is of little historic importance, it's worth a peek to see how a Romanesque chapel may have been painted (drop any coin into the €0.50 box for light). The 19th-century fountain sports a statue of St. Leo IX (1048–1054), the only Alsatian pope. Equisheim's most famous son was a saint, to boot.

Exploring the town, you may come upon some of its 20 "tithe courtyards." Farmers who worked on land owned by the church used to come to these courtyards to pay their tithes (10 percent of their production). With so many of these courtyards, it's safe to conclude that the farming around here was excellent.

Don't leave without visiting one of Eguisheim's countless cozy **wineries** or the big and modern **Wine Cooperative** (Wolfberger, Cave Vinicole d'Eguisheim, Mon–Sat 8:00–12:00 & 14:00–18:00, Sun from 10:00, 6 Grand Rue, tel. 03 89 22 20 20).

SIGHTS

Views over Eguisheim—If you have a car, follow signs up to *Husseren Les Cinq Châteaux*, then walk 20 minutes to the ruined castle towers for a good view of the Vosges Mountains above and vineyards below.

By mountain bike or on foot, find any path through vineyards above Eguisheim for nice views (the TI has a free map, *Canton de Wintzenheim en Balade*). For a bracing and scenic 90-minute round-trip hike, walk uphill on Grande Rue, cross the ring road leaving Eguisheim's town center, and turn left at the *Camping* arrow. Pass the campground, then follow *Sentier Viticole* signs past the little Stork Park and keep straight. The five châteaux of Husseren float above on your right. *Sentier Viticole* signs will lead you on a loop trip through the vineyards to the village of Husseren at the base of those castles, then back to Eguisheim.

SLEEPING

(€1 = about $1.30, country code: 33)

Hotels

$$$ **Hôtel St. Hubert***** offers 15 rooms with polished and modern German hotel-esque comfort (and strict management to match), and an indoor pool and sauna (€7). The 10-minute walk from the town center is rewarded with vineyards out your window (big Db-€111, family suite for four-€182, extra bed-€16, four rooms have patios, free pickup at Colmar's train station if reserved a day in advance, reception open 8:00–12:00 & 15:00–22:00, 6 rue des Trois Pierres, tel. 03 89 41 40 50, fax 03 89 41 46 88, www.hotel-st-hubert.com, reservation@hotel-st-hubert.com).

$$$ **Hostellerie du Château***,** part art gallery, part hotel, provides stylish, contemporary luxury on the pleasant main square (Db-€81–99, Db with "view" over square-€95–114 and worth the splurge, suite with whirlpool tub-€135–155, extra bed-€16, Wi-Fi, garage €9/day, 2 place du Château St. Léon IX, tel. 03 89 23 72 00, fax 03 89 41 63 93, www.hostellerieduchateau.com, info@hostellerieduchateau.com).

$$ **Auberge Alsacienne***** is conveniently located near the bus stop, with small, tastefully designed rooms in a picturesque building and rental bikes for guests (Db-€55–65, Tb-€80, 12 Grand Rue, tel. 03 89 41 50 20, fax 03 89 23 89 32, www.auberge-alsacienne.net, auberge-alsacienne@wanadoo.fr).

$$ **Auberge du Rempart** is atmospheric, with white, bright, and airy rooms above a lively café/restaurant deep inside the town (standard Db-€51, bigger Db-€70, great family suite-€119, 3 rue du Rempart Sud, near TI, tel. 03 89 41 16 87, fax 03 89 41 06 50, www.auberge-du-rempart.com, auberge-du-rempart@wanadoo.fr).

Chambres d'Hôte

While none of these owners speak English, they're creative at communicating. Please remember to cancel if you reserve a room and can't use it.

$$ **Madame Hertz-Meyers,** your Alsatian grandmother who wishes you spoke French so she could chat with you, offers mostly big rooms in a mansion surrounded by vineyards, only 200 feet from the village. Rooms in the main house are great for families and better than her two modern apartments (Sb-€50, Db-€55–60, Tb-€75, includes breakfast, cash only, 3 rue du Riesling; look for sign *Albert-Hertz, Dégustation-Vente*, walk into courtyard and ring bell at *Chambres* sign; check-in after 18:00 unless otherwise pre-

arranged by fax, tel. & fax 03 89 23 67 74).

$ Monique Freudenreich rents spacious, light, and decent rooms at a good price. Charming Monique loves America and is learning English, but still relies on her son Alexandre to translate. She has four rooms in the village center and two more modern rooms in another building up in the vineyards. They will pick you up in Colmar if you book ahead (Db-€42, includes breakfast, cash only, take 2 rights out of the TI to 4 cour Unterlinden, tel. & fax 03 89 23 16 44, maisonhotes@aol.com).

$ Madame Dirringer has a formal place with four comfortable rooms facing a traditional courtyard (Db-€32–35, good family room, breakfast-€6, cash only, 11 rue du Riesling, tel. 03 89 41 71 87).

$ Madame Bombenger has a modern, graceful home that sits just above Eguisheim with three rooms, nice views into the vineyards and over Eguisheim, and sweet Madame Bombenger—who speaks some English—to welcome you (Sb-€34, Db-€44, €2 less for more than one night, includes breakfast, 3 rue des Trois Pierres, tel. & fax 03 89 23 71 19, mobile 06 61 94 31 09, bombenger.marie-therese @wanadoo.fr).

EATING

The **charcuterie** on place du Château has killer quiche to go and everything you need for a fine picnic (daily until 19:00, Mon–Fri closes 12:30–14:00). You can picnic on the wooden benches by the fountain, or listen to the trickling of the square's fountain at their adjacent restaurant and order directly from the menu (daily, €8–12 *tartes flambées* and quiche).

For a sit-down meal, **Auberge de Trois Châteaux** is very Alsatian, with cozy ambience and traditional cuisine (€16–22 *menus* and affordable *plats du jour*, closed Tue–Wed, 26 Grand Rue, tel. 03 89 23 70 61).

Auberge Alsacienne offers fine regional cuisine in a more refined setting (€21-two courses, €27-three courses, closed Sun eve and Mon, 12 Grand Rue, tel. 03 89 41 50 20).

Auberge du Rempart is best for outdoor dining in a pleasant courtyard around a fountain. Come here for less expensive and lighter meals and good *tartes flambées* (€8–17 *plats*, closed Mon, closed Sun and sometimes Thu evenings Sept–June, 3 rue du Remparts Sud, near TI, tel. 03 89 41 16 87).

Au Vieux Porche is a wood-beamed, white-tableclothed affair, ideal for a leisurely meal or a special occasion (€13–23 *plats*, closed Mon–Tue, upper end of town at 16 rue des Trois Châteaux, tel. 03 89 24 01 90).

Kaysersberg

Philosopher-physician Albert Schweitzer's hometown offers a cute jumble of 15th-century homes under a romantically ruined castle with easy vineyard trails at its doorstep, and plenty of tourists. Frequent buses from Colmar make Kaysersberg an easy day trip. Catch buses back to Colmar across the road from the bus shelter where riders are dropped coming from Colmar (a block from post office).

The **TI** is inside Hôtel de Ville (City Hall) near the town's main entry (June–Sept Mon–Sat 9:30–12:00 & 14:00–17:30, Sun 10:00–12:30; Oct–May Mon–Sat 9:30–12:00 & 14:00–17:30, closed Sun; tel. 03 89 78 22 78, www.kaysersberg.com, WCs out the door to left under arch). Walkers can pick up the free *Sentier Viticole* map for hiking between wine villages, and check bus schedules (from their destination back to Colmar). Serious walkers can buy the trail map (see "Walking Trails from Kaysersberg," below). The TI also has information on bike rental.

Strolling through Kaysersberg is a treat. Walking up the main drag through the town, you'll see **St. Croix Church** (daily 9:00–16:00, sometimes open later, unique crucifix in front of a fine 1518 altarpiece—push button for light); colorful shops (pop into the Moulin des Arts—a touristy shopping mall with waterwheels); the humble town museum (€2, Wed–Mon 14:00–18:00, closed Tue); and its 16th-century bridge. As the Nazis were preparing to evacuate, they planned to destroy the bridge. Locals reasoned with the commander, agreeing to dig an anti-tank ditch just beyond the bridge—and the symbol of the town was saved. At the top end of town, you'll come to **Dr. Albert Schweitzer's house,** a small and disappointing museum. It has two rooms of scattered photos and artifacts from his time in Africa, without a word of English (€2, Easter–Oct daily 9:00–12:00 & 14:00–18:00, closed Nov–Easter, 126 rue du Général de Gaulle). The square across the street hosts a thriving market each Monday until noon.

Walking Trails from Kaysersberg: Well-marked trails depart from just outside the TI (walk under the arch next to TI and find trail signs). Turn left on the trail to hike up to the **castle** (free, fine views and benches, 113 steps up a dark stairway to the tower). Hikers can continue past the castle for more views and walks on vineyard roads. This also leads to the well-signed, longer route to Riquewihr (2.5 hours).

For an easier hike to Riquewihr, turn right (rather than left) on the same trail back down by the TI. You'll start on a bike path *(piste cyclable)* to Kientzheim, then join the trail (marked *Sentier Viticole*) to Riquewihr (where buses can take you back to Colmar).

WWII Sights: The hill just north of Kaysersberg is soaked in WWII blood. Towns around it have gray- rather than red-tiled roofs (indicating they were entirely destroyed and rebuilt). **Kientzheim** has an American-made tank parked in its front yard (and a wine museum in its castle grounds). In 2004, the refreshing network of tiny streams trickling down its streets (standard before World War II) was restored. Both Sigolsheim (scene of fierce fighting—note its sterile rebuilt Romanesque church) and Bennwihr are modern, as they were taken and lost a dozen times by the Allies and Nazis, and entirely destroyed. The hill above is still called "Bloody Hill," as it was nicknamed by German troops. Between its cemeteries, you'll find some of the best vines on the Route du Vin.

A **WWII Monument** stands atop Bloody Hill. The spectacular setting, best at sunset, houses a monument to the American divisions that helped liberate Alsace in World War II (find the American flag). Up the lane, a beautiful cemetery is the final resting place of 1,600 men who fought in the French army (many gravestones are Muslim, for soldiers from France's North African colonies—Morocco, Algeria, and Tunisia). From this brilliant viewpoint, you can survey the entire southern section of the Route du Vin and into Germany. The road to the memorial leaves from the center of Sigolsheim (follow *Necropole* and *Cimitière* signs turning at Pierre Sparr winery, then keep straight and climb into the vineyards).

Sleeping in Kaysersberg: **$$ Hôtel à L'Arbre Vert**** gives you three-star comfort at two-star prices (Db-€67–75, across from Albert Schweitzer's house at top end of town, 1 rue Haute du Rempart, tel. 03 89 47 11 51, fax 03 89 78 13 40, http://perso.wanadoo.fr/arbrevertbellepromenade).

Strasbourg

Strasbourg is urban Alsace at its best—it feels like a giant Colmar with water and streetcars. It's a progressive, livable city, with generous space devoted to pedestrians, scads of bikes, mod trams,

meandering waterways, and a young, lively mix of university students, Eurocrats, and street people. This place has an Amsterdam-like feel. Situated just west of the Rhine River, Strasbourg provides the ultimate blend of Franco-Germanic culture, architecture, and ambience. A living symbol of the perpetual peace between France and Germany, Strasbourg was selected as home to the European Parliament, the European Council (sharing administrative responsibilities for the European Union with Brussels, Belgium), and the European Court of Human Rights.

Planning Your Time

Strasbourg makes a good day trip from Colmar. And, thanks to new high-speed TGV-train service, it also makes a handy stop for train travelers en route to or from Paris (baggage check available). None of its museums are essential (though the Alsatian Museum is worthwhile)—you're here to see the cathedral, wander the waterways, and take a bite out of the big city. Plan on three hours to hit the highlights, starting at Strasbourg's dazzling cathedral (try to be here by 12:15 for the clock's best performance—see "Sights and Activities," page 737) and ending with the district called La Petite France (ideally for lunch).

ORIENTATION

Tourist Information

Strasbourg's busy TI faces the cathedral (daily 9:00–19:00, 17 place de la Cathédrale, tel. 03 88 52 28 28, www.ot-strasbourg .fr). A second TI might be added at the newly renovated train station—ask. Buy the €1 city map (which describes a decent walking tour in English) or pay €6 (€3 with Strasbourg Pass, see below) for a cassette tour that covers the cathedral and old city in more detail than most need (available only at the main TI, includes a cute little map of the route, allow 90 min). The TI also has bike maps for the city and surrounding areas.

The €11 **Strasbourg Pass,** valid three days, is a good value for most travelers. It includes one museum free and half-off coupons for others, along with a free bike for a day, the boat cruise, 50 percent off the cassette tour, and free entry for the cathedral narthex view and the astrological clock tour.

Arrival in Strasbourg

By Train: TGV trains now serve Strasbourg's train station (which is getting a facelift—renovation still may be going on when you visit). The station has baggage check (daily 7:45–20:30, €4–8.50, depends on locker size, coins only, airport-type security screening so allow time, WCs nearby-€0.50). A TI may be located at the station in 2008.

To **walk** to the cathedral in 15 urban minutes, go straight out of the station, cross the big square (place de la Gare), and walk past Hôtel Vendôme and up rue du Maire Kuss. Cross the river, and

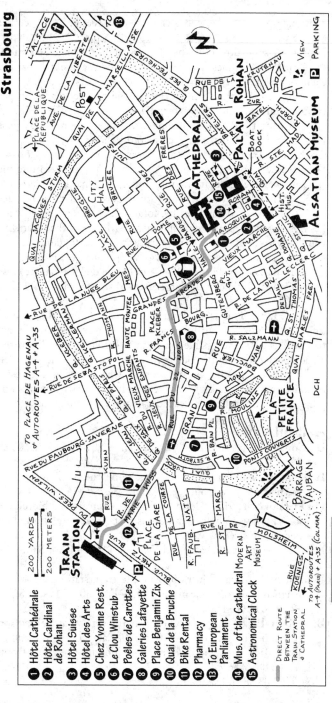

Strasbourg

1 Hôtel Cathédrale
2 Hôtel Cardinal de Rohan
3 Hôtel Suisse
4 Hôtel des Arts
5 Chez Yvonne Rest.
6 Le Clou Winstub
7 Poêles de Carottes
8 Galeries Lafayette
9 Place Benjamin Zix
10 Quai de la Bruche
11 Bike Rental
12 Pharmacy
13 To European Parliament
14 Mus. of the Cathedral
15 Astronomical Clock

DIRECT ROUTE BETWEEN THE TRAIN STATION & CATHEDRAL

200 YARDS
200 METERS

VIEW
P PARKING

continue up serpentine, pedestrian-friendly rue du 22 November all the way to place Kleber. Cross bustling place Kleber, maintaining the same direction, then turn right on the huge pedestrian street (rue des Grandes Arcades). Turn left on rue des Hallebardes, then follow that spire.

To get from the train station to the city center by **public transportation,** catch the caterpillar-like tram that leaves from under the station (buy €1.30 one-way ticket or €2.50 day pass from machines on platforms, coins only, then validate in skinny machines). Take Tram #A (direction: Illkirch) three stops to Grande Rue, two blocks from the cathedral. (You can return to the station, Gare Centrale, from same stop, direction: Hautepierre.)

By Car: The train station's lot is closed during construction (see above). To park nearby, follow *Gare Centrale* signs, then *Parking Aurélie* signs (it's on boulevard de Metz—to the right with your back to the station). To park closer to the center (and encounter more traffic), follow *Centre-Ville/Cathédrale* signs. Parking lots are well-marked—place Gutenberg and place du Château are close to the cathedral, though the larger Austerlitz lot works fine. Pay to park safely in Strasbourg.

By Plane: The user-friendly Strasbourg-Entzheim airport (tel. 03 88 64 67 67), with frequent and often inexpensive flights to Paris, is easily accessible via tram and shuttle bus: From the airport, catch the shuttle bus (*navette*, about €5.50 one-way, €10 round-trip, 2/hr) to the Baggersee stop, where Tram #A (transfer included in *navette* ticket) runs frequently to the city center, stopping at the train station and cathedral (allow 40 min total).

Helpful Hints

US Consulate: It's at 15 rue d'Alsace (tel. 03 88 34 06 95, fax 03 88 23 07 17).

Internet Access: Several cybercafés lie on the main street into town from the station, rue du Maire Kuss.

Quiet Transportation: Beware of quiet streetcars and bicycles—look both ways before crossing streets. Bikes are allowed on pedestrian streets.

Post Office: It's at the cathedral (Mon–Fri 8:00–18:30, Sat 8:00–17:00).

Pharmacy: It's located just opposite the train station; ask for an English-speaking pharmacist (Mon–Fri 8:30–19:15, Sat 8:30–12:30 & 14:00–17:00).

Bike Rental: You can rent bikes near the station at **Vélocation** (€5/half–day, Mon–Fri 9:30–19:00, Sat–Sun 9:30–12:00 & 14:00–19:00, 4 rue du Maire Kuss, look for the green front, tel. 03 88 23 56 75).

Taxi: Call 03 88 36 13 13.

SIGHTS AND ACTIVITIES

▲▲Strasbourg Cathedral (Cathédrale de Notre-Dame)

Stand in front of Hôtel de la Cathédrale and crane your neck up. If this church, with its cloud-piercing spire and pink sandstone color, wows you today, imagine its impact on medieval tourists. The delicate Gothic style of the cathedral (begun in 1176, not finished until 1429) is another Franco-German mixture that somehow survived the French Revolution, the Franco-Prussian War, World War I, and World War II. The square in front of the cathedral makes the ideal stage for street performers—it's like a medieval fair.

Before entering the cathedral, survey the scene. This square was Roman 2,000 years ago. Then, as now, it was the center of activity. The dark half-timbered building to your left, next to the TI, was the home of a wealthy merchant in the 16th century, and symbolizes the virtues of capitalism that Strasbourg has long revered. Goods were sold under the ground-floor arches; owners lived above. Strasbourg made its medieval mark as a trading center, taking advantage of its position at the crossroads of Europe and its access to the important Rhine River to charge tolls for the movement of goods. Its strong economy allowed for the construction of this remarkable cathedral. Strasbourg's location also made it susceptible to new ideas. Martin Luther's theses were posted on its main doors, and after the wars of religion, this cathedral was Protestant for more than 100 years. (Louis XIV returned it to Catholicism in 1621.)

As you enter the cathedral (free, daily 7:00–11:40 & 12:45–19:00), notice the sculpture over the left portal (complacent, spear-toting Virtues getting revenge on those nasty Vices). Enter and walk down the center. The stained glass on the lower left shows various rulers of Strasbourg, while the stained glass on your right depicts Bible stories. An ornate, gold-leafed organ hangs above the second pillars. Walk to the choir and stare at the stained-glass image of Mary; find the European Union flag at the top.

In the right transept is a high-tech, 15th-century **astronomical clock** (restored in 1883) that gives a ho-hum performance every 15 minutes (keep your eye on the little angel about 15 feet up, slightly left of center), better on the half-hour (angel on the right), and best at 12:30 (everybody gets in the act, including a rooster and 12 apostles—for the 12 hours). Arrive by 12:00 outside the right transept, buy your €1 ticket, then enter and hear an explanation of the clock's workings—and beware of pickpockets.

For €4.40, you can climb 332 steps to the **top of the narthex** for an amazing view (free first Sun of the month, access on right side of cathedral, daily April–Sept 9:00–19:30, June–Aug Fri–Sat nights sometimes until 22:00, Oct–March 10:00–17:30).

Alsace

Before leaving this area, investigate the network of small pedestrian streets that connect the cathedral with the huge place Kleber (home to various outdoor markets depending on the day of the week). Each street is named for the primary trade that took place there.

Museums near the Cathedral

These museums lie outside the cathedral's right transept and are interesting only for aficionados with particular interests or a full day in Strasbourg. They're all free on the first Sunday of the month (www.musees-strasbourg.org).

Palais Rohan—This stately palace houses three museums: the **Museum of Decorative Arts** (big rooms with red velvet chairs), the **Museum of Fine Arts** (a small, well-displayed collection of paintings from Middle Ages to Baroque, some by artists you would recognize), and the **Archaeological Museum,** the best of the three, with a stellar presentation of Alsatian civilization through the millennia and English explanations (€4 each, under 18 free, Wed–Mon 10:00–18:00, closed Tue, 2 place du Château, tel. 03 88 52 50 00).

Museum of the Cathedral (Musée de l'Oeuvre Notre-Dame)— This well-organized museum has plenty of artifacts from the cathedral (€4, includes English audioguide, under 18 free, Tue–Sun 10:00–18:00, closed Mon, 3 place du Château, tel. 03 88 32 88 17).

Alsatian Museum—One of Strasbourg's oldest and most characteristic homes hosts this extensive, well-presented collection of Alsatian folk art. You'll see scenes from daily life, traditional home interiors (including a close-up look at half-timbered construction), lots of tools, and a good overview of the life of a winemaker. Ask for the English handout (€4, Wed–Mon 12:00–18:00, Sun from 10:00, closed Tue, across the river and down 1 block to the right from the boat dock at 23 quai St. Nicholas, tel. 03 88 52 50 01).

Boat Ride on the Ill River

To see the cityscape from the water, take a loop cruise around Strasbourg. The glass-topped boats are air-conditioned and sufficiently comfortable—both sides have fine views. You'll pass through two locks as you circle the old city clockwise. The highlight for me was cruising by the European Parliament buildings and the European Court of Human Rights (adults-€8, under 18-half-price, 70 min, good English commentary with live guide or audioguide, 2 boats/hour, daily April–Oct 9:30–21:00, May–Sept until 22:00; boats depart only at 10:30, 13:00, 14:30, and 16:00 Nov–March; dock is 2 blocks outside cathedral's right transept, where rue Rohan meets the river, tel. 03 88 84 13 13, www.strasbourg.port.fr).

Alsace

▲La Petite France

Historic home to Strasbourg's tanners, millers, and fishermen, this awfully charming area is laced with canals, crowned with magnificent half-timbered homes, carpeted with cobblestones, and filled with tourists.

From the cathedral, walk down rue des Hallebardes to the merry-go-round, then continue straight following rue Gutenberg. Cross big rue des Francs Bourgeois and keep straight (now on Grande Rue). Turn left on the third little street (rue du Bouclier, street signs are posted behind you), and make your way to the middle of the bridge (pont St. Martin). Gaze at the various locks and the channels that meet here. Find your way down to the river and follow the walkway over the lock deep into La Petite France. Make friends with a leafy café table on place Benjamin Zix, or find the siesta-perfect parks between the canals across the bridge at rue des Moulins. Climb the once-fortified grassy wall (Barrage Vauban) for an okay view—the glass structure behind you is the new modern-art museum (interesting more for its architecture than its collection).

La Petite France's coziest cafés line the canal on quai de la Bruche near the barrage. From here, it's a 10-minute walk back to the station: With the river on your left, walk along quai de Turckheim, cross the third bridge, and find rue du Maire Kuss.

SLEEPING

(€1 = about $1.30, country code: 33)
You'll find a handy **launderette** on rue des Veaux, near the listed hotels.

$$$ Hôtel Cathédrale*** is comfortable and contemporary, with a Jack-and-the-beanstalk spiral stairway (elevator begins one floor up) and a hopelessly confusing floor plan. This modern yet atmospheric place lets you stare at the cathedral point-blank from your room. Skip the cheaper rooms *sans* view (small Db with no view-€85–110, medium Db with no view-€120, larger Db with view-€150, prices sometimes lower on weekends, includes good buffet breakfast, air-con, laundry service, free Wi-Fi, free bicycles can be reserved for up to 2 hours, book ahead for one of 5 parking spaces, 12–13 place de la Cathédrale, tel. 03 88 22 12 12, toll-free in France 08 00 00 00 84, fax 03 88 23 28 00, www.hotel-cathedrale.fr, reserv@hotel-cathedrale.fr).

$$ Hôtel Cardinal de Rohan*** is a classy place in the pedestrian zone just steps from the cathedral, with royal public spaces and 36 well-appointed rooms (standard Db-€75, bigger Db-€130–145, Tb-€140–155, air-con, free Internet access and Wi-Fi, book ahead for one of 6 parking spaces-€16, 17 rue du Maroquin, tel. 03 88 32 85 11, fax 03 88 75 65 37, www.hotel-rohan.com, info @hotel-rohan.com).

$$ Hôtel Suisse, across from the cathedral's right transept and off place du Château, is a low-profile, dark, central, serious, and solid two-star value (Sb-€55–74, Db-€69–89, prices €10 less in Jan–Feb and July–Aug—when parliament isn't in session, extra person-€10, elevator, free Wi-Fi, 2 place de la Râpe, tel. 03 88 35 22 11, fax 03 88 25 74 23, www.hotel-suisse.com, info@hotel-suisse .com).

$$ Hôtel des Arts, above a busy café, is a family-run, simple, bare-bones place with microscopic bathrooms and air-conditioning. Rooms overlooking the square in front are fun but noisy (Sb/ Db-€58–62, Tb-€68, entirely non-smoking, 10 place du Marché aux Cochons de Lait, tel. 03 88 37 98 37, fax 03 88 37 98 97, www .hotel-arts.com, info@hotel-arts.fr).

EATING

Atmospheric *winstubs* (wine bars) serving affordable salads and *tarte flambée* are a snap to find. If the weather is nice, head for **La Petite France** and choose ambience over cuisine—dine outside at any café/*winstub* that appeals to you. Alternatively, stock up on picnic supplies at the terrific grocery store on the main floor of the Galeries Lafayette department store (Mon–Sat 9:00–20:00, closed Sun, place Kleber).

For a real meal, skip the touristy restaurants on the cathedral square and along rue de Maroquin. Consider these nearby places instead; both are one block behind the TI (go left out of the TI, then take the first left through the passageway and keep walking): **Chez Yvonne** (marked *S'Burjerstuewel* above windows) has a tradition of good food, pleasant staff, and affordable prices (allow €25–30, reservations smart on weekends and holidays, open daily until late, 10 rue du Sanglier, tel. 03 88 32 84 15). Half a block left down rue du Chaudron at #3 lies **Le Clou Winstub,** with €12 salads and €14 *plats du jour*. This place often looks closed from the outside, but don't be shy (closed Wed lunch and all day Sun, tel. 03 88 32 11 67).

Vegetarians find respite from porky Alsatian cuisine at **Poêles de Carottes** (big €10 salads and stir fries, closed Sun–Mon, 2 place de Meuniers, tel. 03 88 32 33 23).

TRANSPORTATION CONNECTIONS

Strasbourg makes a good side-trip from Colmar or a stop on the way to or from Paris.

From Strasbourg by Train to: Colmar (2/hr, 35 min), **Reims**

(via TGV: 8/day, 1.5 hrs; via non-TGV train: 6/day, 4–6 hrs), **Paris'** Gare de l'Est (via TGV: 12/day, 2.5 hrs; via non-TGV train: 10/day, 4 hrs), **Karlsruhe, Germany** (via TGV: 4/day, 40 min; via non-TGV train: 12/day, 1–1.5 hrs, most with change in Appenweier or Wissembourg), **Basel, Switzerland** (via TGV: 4/day, 70 min; via non-TGV train: hourly, 2 hrs).

Verdun

Few traces of World War I remain in Europe today, but the battlefields of Verdun provide an appropriately hard-hitting tribute to the 700,000 lives lost here in the horrific war of 1914–1918. The lunar landscape left by World War I battles is today buried under thick forests. Millions of live bombs are scattered in vast cordoned-off areas—it's not unusual for French farmers or hikers to be injured by unexploded mines. Drive or ride through the eerie moguls surrounding Verdun, stopping at melted-sugar-cube forts and plaques marking where towns once existed. With three hours and a car, a tour (operated by the TI), or easy taxi rides, you can see the most important sights and appreciate the horrific scale of the battles. The town of Verdun is not your destination, but a starting point for your visit into the nearby battlefields.

Tourist Information

The TI is just across the river (cross pont Chausée) east of Verdun's city center on place de la Nation (May–Sept Mon–Sat 8:30–18:30, Sun 10:00–17:00; Oct–April Mon–Sat 9:00–12:00 & 14:00–17:00, Sun 10:00–13:00; tel. 03 29 86 14 18, www.verdun-tourisme.com, verduntourisme@wanadoo.fr). They have books in English, maps of the city center with English descriptions of key monuments, and maps of the battlefields. Most importantly for non-drivers, this is where tours to the battlefields depart (see next page; drivers don't need to stop here). The pleasant park across the street provides a good picnic setting and a more cheerful break from the heavy sights.

Arrival in Verdun

By Train: The new TGV train serves the new **Gare Meuse TGV station,** 30 minutes by shuttle bus from Verdun. This high-speed service puts the city of Verdun within 95 minutes of Paris and within 30 minutes of Reims. However, with only three high-speed trips a day, it's critical to confirm the schedule in advance (see "Transportation Connections" on page 747).

Non-TGV trains run to Verdun's **central station,** 15 minutes by foot from the TI. Walk straight out of the station (no baggage check), cross the parking lot and the roundabout and keep straight down avenue Garibaldi, then follow to *Centre-Ville* signs on rue St. Paul. (You'll pass a grocery store and a recommended car-rental agency soon after leaving the station.) Turn left on the first traffic-free street in the old center (rue Chausée, good lunch options) and walk past the towers and across the river to the TI.

By Car: Drivers can bypass the town center and TI and drive straight for the battlefields. Follow signs reading *Verdun Centre-Ville*, then signs toward *Longwy*, then find signs to *Douaumont* and *Champs de Bataille* (battlefields) on D-112, then D-913. By following signs to *Fort de Douaumont* and *Ossuaire*, you'll pass Mémorial–Musée de Fleury, your first stop. To reach the TI, follow signs to *Centre-Ville*, then *Office du Tourisme* (you'll pass the TI just before crossing the river).

Getting Around the Verdun Battlefield

The battlefield remains are situated on both sides of the Meuse River; the *rive droite* (right bank)—where we'll go—has more sights.

Verdun has sparse train service—plan your arrival and departure carefully. Once there, you have three choices for touring the battlefields:

By Car: Dirt-cheap car rental is available a block from the train station at **AS Location** (about €44/day with 100 km/80 miles included—easily enough to do the battlefields, Mon–Sat 7:45–11:45 & 14:00–18:00, closed Sun, 22 rue Louis Maury, tel. & fax 03 29 86 58 58). Book ahead if possible, though they normally have cars available.

By Tour: Verdun's TI offers four-hour tours of the battle sites described below. Though the tour is in French, the guides usually speak some English, and English handouts are provided (€26, includes entry fees, reserve ahead, May–mid-Sept daily departures at 14:00).

By Taxi: For about €40 round-trip, taxis can drop a carload at one sight and pick up at another (walk between sights). Ask to be dropped off at the Mémorial–Musée de Fleury and picked up at the Fort de Douaumont four hours later (visiting l'Ossuaire in between); it's about two miles from one sight to the other, so expect to walk a minimum of four miles for this plan. For less walking, ask to be dropped off at l'Ossuaire and picked up at either Fort de Douaumont or Mémorial–Musée de Fleury. Taxis normally meet trains at the station; otherwise they park at the TI (taxi tel. 06 07 02 24 16 or 03 29 86 05 22). It's easiest to arrange this through the TI (and with their help).

SELF-GUIDED TOUR

▲▲ The Battlefields of Verdun

Verdun's battlefields are littered with monuments and ruined forts. For most travelers, a half-day is enough, though historians could spend days here. We'll concentrate on the three most important sights: Mémorial–Musée de Fleury, l'Ossuaire de Douaumont, and Fort de Douaumont. Each offers a different perspective on the war.

Information: All sights are adequately described in English. If you want more, the TI and all sights sell a variety of helpful books in English describing the Battle of Verdun. The simple but adequate €5 booklet *Verdun: Images of War* provides helpful details (in three languages) and black-and-white photos. More readable is *The Battle of Verdun* by Yves Buffetaut (€12). The best is Alistair Horne's *The Price of Glory,* which sorts through the complex issues surrounding Verdun and offers perspectives from both sides of the conflict—if you can, read it ahead of your visit (€14).

Background: After the annexation of Alsace and Lorraine following the German victory in the Franco-Prussian War in 1871, Verdun found itself just 25 miles from the German border. This was too close for comfort for the French, who invested mightily in the fortification of Verdun, hoping to discourage German thoughts of invasion. The plan failed. World War I erupted in August of 1914, and after a lengthy stalemate, the Germans decided to strike a powerful knockout punch at the heart of the French defense to demoralize them and force a quick surrender. They chose Verdun as their target. By defeating the best of the French defenses, the Germans would cripple the French military and morale. The French chose to fight to the bitter end. Three hundred days of non-stop trench warfare ensued.

Soft, forested lands hide the memories of the vicious battles that raged here in 1916. Thirteen villages were caught in the middle and obliterated, never to be resurrected (signed as *Villages Détruits*). Only small monuments remind us that they ever existed. It's difficult to imagine today's lush terrain as it was generations ago...a gray, treeless, crater-filled landscape, smothered in mud and shattered in stone.

➲ Self-Guided Tour: Drivers (and cabbies) leave Verdun on N-3, then take a left on D-112. Take the first turnoff possible (see map on page 744) into the...

Alsace

Verdun

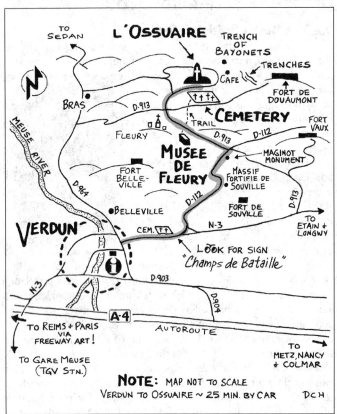

TO
SEDAN

L'OSSUAIRE

TRENCH
OF
BAYONETS

TRENCHES

CAFE

FORT DE
DOUAUMONT

BRAS

D.913

††††

CEMETERY

TRAIL

FORT
VAUX

D-112

FLEURY

D.913

D-112

**MUSÉE
DE
FLEURY**

MAGINOT
MONUMENT

FORT
BELLE-
VILLE

MASSIF
FORTIFIÉ DE
SOUVILLE

D-112

D.913

MEUSE RIVER

D.964

•BELLEVILLE

FORT DE
SOUVILLE

TO
ETAIN +
LONGWY

VERDUN

CEM.††

N-3

N-3

LOOK FOR SIGN
"Champs de Bataille"

D.903

D.904

A-4

AUTOROUTE

TO REIMS + PARIS
VIA
FREEWAY ART!

TO
METZ, NANCY
+ COLMAR

TO GARE MEUSE
(TGV STN.)

NOTE: MAP NOT TO SCALE
VERDUN TO OSSUAIRE ~ 25 MIN. BY CAR   DCH

Massif Fortifié de Souville: At this parking and picnic area, find a curving trench and craters that mark so much of the land here. A few communication trenches like this remain (see below), though all fortified trenches were destroyed during the battles or have since been filled in. After leaving the parking area, you'll soon pass a monument to André Maginot, the creator of the Maginot Line of forts that were to defend France against all future attacks from the east. He was wounded during the battle of Verdun.

• *Continue following signs to* Ossuaire *and* Douaumont.

Mémorial–Musée de Fleury: This museum makes a good first visit. It's built on the site of a village (Fleury) destroyed during the fighting. This museum provides a helpful visual presentation of this war that would see the potential of mankind's destructive creativity—machine guns, flamethrowers, poisonous gas, airplanes, and observation balloons were all first used in World War I. The museum houses a manageable number of displays of weapons, uniforms (note the French colonies' contributions), models, and photos. Its centerpiece is the re-creation of a battle-field (built by veterans of the battle), and a faded-but-worthwhile 15-minute movie narrated in English (request English version or read English subtitles; less important if you see the better film at l'Ossuaire—see below). Look for the model of the unblemished Fort de Douaumont, and remember this when you visit the fort. While basic information is posted in English, the €2 guide to the museum is informative and easy to follow for much of the museum (€7, daily March–mid-Sept 9:00–18:00, mid-Sept–mid-Dec and Feb 9:00–12:00 & 14:00–18:00, closed mid-Dec–Jan).

• *Continue to the next sight. For walkers, a trail leads from across the street and through the woods to that tall, missile-like building...*

L'Ossuaire de Douaumont: This is the tomb of 130,000 French and Germans whose last homes were the muddy trenches of Verdun. The artillery shell–shaped tower and cross design of this building symbolizes war and peace. Drivers can park at the rear and look through the low windows for a bony memorial to those whose political and military leaders asked them to make the "ultimate sacrifice" for their countries. Enter down the steps and start with the thought-provoking 20-minute film that seems particularly relevant today (€3, ask for English headphones—you can adjust volume). The little picture boxes in the gift shop are worth a look if you don't visit Mémorial–Musée de Fleury. Climb upstairs and experience a humbling and moving tribute to the soldiers who were convinced that this war would end all wars and that their children would grow up in a world at peace. The red lettering on the walls lists a soldier's name, rank ("Lt" is lieuten-ant, "Cal" is corporal, "St" is sergeant), regiment, and dates of birth and death. Skip the 204 steps up the tower (daily May–Aug 9:00–18:30, April and Sept 9:00–12:00 & 14:00–18:30, mid-Feb–March and Oct 9:00–12:00 & 14:00–17:30, Nov 9:00–12:00 & 14:00–17:00, Dec 14:00–17:00 only, closed Jan–mid-Feb, tel. 03 29 84 54 81).

Walk out to the cemetery and listen for the eerie buzz of silence and peace. Reflect on a war that ruined an entire genera-tion, leaving half of all Frenchmen aged 15 to 30 dead or wounded. Rows of 15,000 Christian crosses and Muslim headstones (oriented toward Mecca), all with roses, decorate the cemetery. Moroccan soldiers were instrumental in France's ultimate victory at Verdun, a fact often overlooked by right-wing politicians in France.

Looking over the cemetery from above, the road on the lower left leads 1.5 miles to Fort de Douaumont (see below). Also to the left, but behind you, a road leads to a good little café, **Abri des Pelerins** (salads, omelets, €13 *menu*, March–Nov daily until 18:00, tel. 03 29 85 50 58). While it's too far for walkers and there's not much to see there now, those interested can continue down the road to **Tranchée des Baïonnettes** (Trench of Bayonets). Here, an entire company of soldiers was buried alive in their trench (the soldiers' bayonets remained aboveground for decades). The bulky concrete monument to this sad event was donated by the US.

• *Now head for...*

Fort de Douaumont: This was the most important stronghold in the network of forts built to protect Verdun after the annexation of Alsace and Lorraine to Germany in 1871. Built into the hillside, it served as a strategic command center for both sides at various times. Inside, there's little to see except two miles of cold, damp hallways. Experiencing these corridors will add to your sympathy for the soldiers who were forced to live like moles (€3, ask for English descriptions, daily April–Aug 10:00–18:30, Sept–March 10:00–12:00 & 14:00–17:30, until 17:00 Nov–Dec and Feb, closed Jan). Climb to the bombed-out top of the fort and check out the round, iron-gun emplacements that could rise and revolve.

Between l'Ossuaire and Fort de Douaumont, on either side of the road, you'll pass what remains of the **London Communication Trench.** This served as a means of communication and resupply for the Fort de Douaumont. Notice the concrete-reinforced sides. You'll see the ruins of several *abri* (shelters) on the hillside above the trench—these provided safe haven for the trench's soldiers.

SIGHTS

In Verdun

Unless you're arriving by train and have some time to spare, there's no reason to visit central Verdun's sights. The severe **Victory Monument** (Monument à la Victoire) is a block from the river overlooking the pedestrian zone. Seventy-three steps follow a watery path to a crypt storing records of the soldiers who fought here (both French and German). The **Citadelle Souterraine** offers a disappointing walk through the tunnels of the French Command. While it tries to re-create the Battle of Verdun scene, it's not worth your time or money (€6, daily April–Sept 9:00–18:00, Oct–Dec and Feb–March 10:00–12:00 & 14:00–17:00, closed Jan).

SLEEPING AND EATING

Hotels in Verdun are cheap. A good bet is Monsieur Poirot's friendly, easygoing **$ Hôtel Montaulbain**** (Ss-€28, Sb-€32, Ds-€35, Db-€40, Tb-€48, near the Victory Monument, 10-min walk from the station at 4 rue de la Vieille Prison, tel. 03 29 86 00 47, fax 03 29 84 75 70). You'll find several inexpensive restaurants in the pedestrian zone and along the river. On rue Chausée, find the great take-away **Charcuterie Artisanale**. There's also a good café near l'Ossuaire in the battlefields, **Abri des Pelerins** (see page 745).

TRANSPORTATION CONNECTIONS

New high-speed TGV trains serve the Verdun area from the Gare Meuse TGV station, 30 minutes south of Verdun, while non-TGV trains continue to use Verdun's central station. For TGV connections listed below, allow an additional 30 minutes to reach Verdun's city center by shuttle bus.

From Verdun by Train to: Colmar (via TGV: 3/day, 2 hrs, possible change in Strasbourg; via non-TGV train: 3/day, 4–6 hrs, best with changes in Metz and Strasbourg), **Reims** (via TGV to nearby Gare Champagne–Ardenne: 1/day, 30 min; via non-TGV train: 3/day, 2–5 hrs, most change in Chalon), **Paris'** Gare de l'Est (via TGV: 2/day, 65 min; via non-TGV train: 4/day, 3–3.5 hrs, change in Metz or Chalon).

Reims

Deservedly famous for its cathedral and its Champagne, contemporary Reims (pronounced "rance," which rhymes with France) is a prosperous modern city. Reims has a turbulent history: This is where 26 French kings were coronated, where Champagne first bubbled, where WWI devastation met miraculous reconstruction, and where the Armistice of World War II was signed.

Flashy new bullet trains bring Reims within an hour of Paris and 90 minutes of Strasbourg, making it a convenient day trip or stopover en route to other destinations.

Planning Your Time

For most, a half day in Reims for visiting the cathedral and a champagne cellar is about right. It's also a smart place to rent a car for trips starting or ending in eastern France (this lets you avoid navigating Paris). To best experience contemporary Reims, explore the busy shopping streets between the cathedral and the train station; rue de Vesle, rue Condorcet, and place Drouet d'Erlon are most interesting.

ORIENTATION

Reims' hard-to-miss cathedral marks the city center and makes an easy orientation landmark. Most sights of interest (including champagne *caves*, or cellars, and the train station) are within a

20-minute walk of the cathedral. The city has been ambitiously renovating its downtown, installing a new streetcar along the streets around place Drouet d'Erlon and converting the square and streets around the cathedral into a pedestrian zone. While this work should be completed before your visit, be ready for some residual construction chaos from this project.

Tourist Information

At the TI outside the cathedral's left transept, pick up a free map of the town center and a map of the champagne *caves* (Easter–mid-Oct Mon–Sat 9:00–19:00, Sun 10:00–18:00; mid-Oct–Easter Mon–Sat 9:00–17:00, Sun 11:00–16:00; public WCs across street, tel. 03 26 77 45 00, www.reims-tourisme.com). Skip the costly audioguide tour (covers the city and cathedral).

Arrival in Reims

By Train: Reims is served by two stations: the new Champagne–Ardenne TGV station (3 miles from the city center), and the older Reims-Centre station. If you arrive at Champagne–Ardenne, take one of the frequent *navette* trains to Reims-Centre. From the Centre station (no baggage check), you can reach the cathedral by foot in 15 minutes: Walk straight out of the station and through the park, cross the huge boulevards Joffre and Foch, and stroll up the pedestrian place Drouet d'Erlon. Turn left on rue Condorcet, then right on rue de Talleyrand. You can also take the time-saving bus from the station (see "Getting Around Reims," next page).

By Car: Follow *Centre-Ville* and *Cathédrale* signs and park on the street approaching the cathedral (rue Libergier) or in the well-signed Parking Cathédrale structure (€1.30/hour).

Helpful Hints

Internet Access: You can surf and snack at **Clique et Croque** near the Grand Théâtre (€4/hr, Mon–Sat 10:00–24:00, Sun 14:00–20:00, 27 rue de Vesle, passage du Commerce, tel. 03 26 86 93 92).

Laundry: Laverie Chanzy, a few blocks in front of the cathedral, has long hours (daily 7:00–21:30, 59 rue Chanzy).

Taxi: Call 03 26 47 05 05. A taxi from the train station to the farthest champagne *cave* will cost about €8.

Car Rental: Avis is at the train station (cours de la Gare, tel. 03 26 47 10 08); **Europcar** is at 76 boulevard Lundy (tel. 03 26 88 38 38); and **Hertz** is at 26 boulevard Joffre (tel. 03 26 47 98 78; all three usually open Mon–Sat 8:00–12:00 & 14:00–19:00, closed Sun).

Alsace

Getting Around Reims

By Bus: While most sights are walkable, you can save time by taking the bus (saves a 35-minute walk between the station and champagne *caves* Martel, Taittinger, and Piper Heidsieck). Two lines, called Citadines, serve the historic center and cellars, with circular routes starting and ending at the Reims-Centre train station (5/hr, none on Sun). From in front of the station, Citadine #1 runs to the cathedral and TI (stop: Cathédrale), to Piper Heidsieck (stop: Pasteur), or to Taittinger and Martel (stop: St. Timothée). To return, board the same bus (and continue the loop back to the station), or for a more direct trip, catch Citadine #2 in the opposite direction to the cathedral (stop: Royale). Bus line #K also runs from the station (catch it just across the street from Hertz car rental, direction Béthany), getting you close to Mumm (stop: Justice). Buy a ticket from the driver; one ride is €0.90, which is good for one transfer within one hour in one direction (it can't be used for your return trip). Day passes cost €2.70.

SIGHTS

▲▲▲Reims Cathedral

The cathedral of Reims, which turned 1000 in 2007, is a glorious example of Gothic architecture, and one of Europe's greatest churches. Clovis, the first king of the Franks, was baptized at a church on this site in A.D. 496, establishing France's Christian roots that hold firm today. Since Clovis' baptism, Reims' cathedral has served as *the* place for the coronation of 26 French kings and queens—allowing it to play a more important role in France's political history than Paris' Notre-Dame cathedral. A self-assured Joan of Arc led a less-assured Charles VII to be crowned here in 1429. The French rallied around their new king to  push the English out of France and to finally end the Hundred Years' War. During the French Revolution, the cathedral was converted to a temple of reason (as was Notre-Dame in Paris), and during World War I, it was devastated by severe bombing (then completely restored, thanks in large part to John D. Rockefeller... just in time for the start of World War II).

Stand on the square in front of the cathedral and admire the best west portal anywhere (inside and outside), with more than 2,000 statues festooning its facade. (Since medieval churches always face east, toward the Holy Land, you usually enter through

Reims

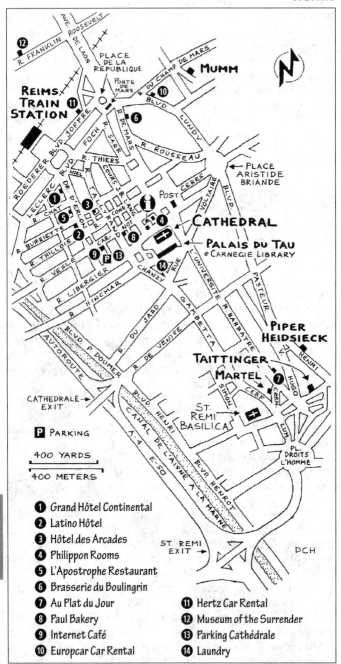

1. Grand Hôtel Continental
2. Latino Hôtel
3. Hôtel des Arcades
4. Philippon Rooms
5. L'Apostrophe Restaurant
6. Brasserie du Boulingrin
7. Au Plat du Jour
8. Paul Bakery
9. Internet Café
10. Europcar Car Rental
11. Hertz Car Rental
12. Museum of the Surrender
13. Parking Cathédrale
14. Laundry

the west portal.) Like the cathedrals in Paris and in Chartres, this church is dedicated to "Our Lady" (Notre-Dame). For eight centuries, Catholics have prayed to the "Mother of God" to ask her to intervene with God on their behalf. In 1429, Joan of Arc received messages from Mary encouraging her to rally French troops against the English at the Siege of Orléans.

Notice the flying buttresses soaring from the sides of the church. These massive "beams" are critical to supporting this structure. The pointed arches inside the church push the weight of the roof outward, rather than downward. The "flying" buttresses support the roof by pushing back inward, creating a delicate balance between the two forces. Gothic architects learned by trial and error—many church roofs caved in as they tested their theories and strove to build ever higher. Work on this cathedral began decades after the Notre-Dame cathedrals in Paris and Chartres, allowing architects to build on what they'd learned from those magnificent earlier structures.

Contemplate the lives of the people who built this huge building, starting in 1211. Construction on a scale like this required a wholesale community effort—all hands on deck. Most townsfolk who participated donated their money or their labor knowing that neither they, nor their children, nor their children's children, would ever see it completed—such was their pride, dedication, and faith. Imagine the effort it took to raise the funds and manage the workforce. Master masons supervised, while the average Jean did much of the sweat work. Labor was something even the poorest medieval peasant could donate generously.

Walk inside (daily 7:30–19:30). The weight of the roof is supported by a few towering columns that seem to sprout crisscrossing pointed arches. This technique allowed the church to grow higher, and liberated the walls to become window frames. Now, look back at the entry wall with its 120 statutes hiding in niches. The rose windows on this wall contain the best original stained glass in the church. The cathedral has many treasures, including a luminous set of Marc Chagall stained-glass windows from 1974, which somehow fit this ancient stone structure (behind the altar on the east end). Informative English explanations along the right aisle offer historical detail (including information about the Chagall windows) that's sufficient for most travelers.

More Sights

Palais du Tau—This former Archbishop's Palace houses artifacts from the cathedral (mostly tapestries and stone statues) in impressive rooms—these guys lived well. Sadly, there's little English information, and while I enjoyed seeing eye-to-eye with the original statues from the cathedral's facade—particularly the huge Goliath that hangs above the entry's rose window—this museum isn't worth the time for most (€6.50; May–Aug Tue–Sun 9:30–18:30, closed Mon; Sept–April Tue–Sun 9:30–12:30 & 14:00–17:30, closed Mon; tel. 03 26 47 81 79).

Museum of the Surrender (Musée de la Reddition)—World War II buffs can visit the room (slated to reopen in February 2008 after renovation) where the Armistice was signed by British, American, French, German, and Soviet leaders. General Eisenhower, head-quartered in Reims, received the unconditional surrender of all German forces in the early morning of May 7, 1945. The surrender was announced the next day, turning May 8 into Victory in Europe (V-E), or Armistice, Day. The museum's lone room was opened to the public in 1995 to celebrate the 50th anniversary of the Armistice. This is a modest sight—the 13 chairs of the signatories provide most of the furnishings. You'll also see plenty of photos and a short English-language film (€1.80, Wed–Mon 10:00–12:00 & 14:00–18:00, closed Tue, 12 rue Franklin Roosevelt, tel. 03 26 47 84 19).

Porte de Mars—The last vestige of Reim's ancient Roman heri-tage—an entry gate—is just a 10-minute walk from the central train station. The Porte de Mars, built in the second century A.D., was one of four principal entrances into the ancient Gallo-Roman town and the only one still in existence. Inspired by triumphal arches that Rome built to herald war victories, this one was con-structed to celebrate peace and stability. Unlike most of the rest of town, the Porte was undamaged in World War I but bears the marks of other eras, such as its integration into the medieval ramparts. Find the ruts under the arcade which guided chariots, and look for the depiction of the legend of Romulus and Remus, complete with suckling she-wolf, from which Reims gets its name (free, always open, place du Boulingrin).

Carnegie Library (Bibliothèque Carnegie)—The legacy of the Carnegie Library network, funded generously by the 19th-century American millionaire Andrew Carnegie and his steel fortune (notice the American flag above the main entrance on the left), extends even to Reims. Built in the flurry of inter-war reconstruc-tion, this beautiful Art Deco building still houses the city's public library. Since entrance is free and it's just behind the cathedral, it's worth a quick look. Visitors are welcome to admire the mosa-ics, onyx-laden entrance hall, and Jacque Simon chandelier, but are asked not to enter the reading room (there are some who come here to study). However, peer through the door to admire the stained-glass windows. The gorgeous wood-paneled card-catalogue room will take you back to 1928, the library's inaugural year (free, Tue–Sat 10:00–13:00 & 14:00–19:00, closed Thu morn-ing and Sun–Mon, place Carnegie).

EXPERIENCES

▲▲Champagne Tours

Reims is the capital of the Champagne region. While the bubbly stuff's birthplace is closer to Epernay, you can tour a Champagne *cave* right in Reims. All charge for tastings and are open daily; the last tours usually depart about an hour before midday and afternoon closings—the hours listed below reflect the hours of the last visit. All but the four listed below must be reserved in advance to visit. Remember to bring a sweater, even in summer, as the *caves* are cool.

Mumm is closest to the train station and offers three kinds of worthwhile visits. The "traditional visit" (€7.50, 1 hour) includes a good 10-minute video explaining the history of Mumm and the Champagne-making process, a tour of the cellars where 25 million bottles are stored, and a small museum of old Champagne-making contraptions. The tour ends with a glass of Cordon Rouge. The "enological visit" offers all that, plus a "guided" tasting at the end (€13 for 2 tastes, €18 for 3, 90 min). You can also add a "vineyard visit" by minivan (€25, 3 hours), but only by reservation in advance (March–Oct daily 9:00–11:00 & 14:00–17:00, Nov–Feb weekend afternoons and weekdays by reservation, tel. 03 26 49 59 70, www .mumm.com). Mumm is four blocks left out of the train station, on the other side of place de la République at 34 rue du Champ de Mars (also accessible by bus line #K from the train station). Don't go in #29 on the left-hand side of the street (as shown on the city map)—visits begin in the building on the right, #34, at the end of the courtyard. Follow *Visites des Caves* signs.

The next three places cluster near each other, about 20 minutes by foot southeast of the cathedral (from behind the cathedral's right transept, walk down rue de l'Université, then rue du Barbâtre; figure €8 for a one-way taxi from the train station, easier by Citadine bus—see "Getting Around Reims," page 749). **Taittinger,** one of the biggest, most elegant, and most famous, has a formal and informative tour that makes a valiant effort to convince you they're the best. After seeing their movie (in comfortable theater seats), follow your guide down into some of the three miles of chilly chalk *caves,* many dug by ancient Romans. Popping corks signal when the tour's done and the tasting's begun (€7, includes tasting, 1 hour, mid-March–mid-Nov daily 9:30–12:00 & 14:00–16:30, closed weekends in off-season, 9 place St. Nicaise, tel. 03 26 85 84 33, www.taittinger.com) **Piper Heidsieck** offers glitz over substance with a short, cheesy, Disney-esque train-ride tour and tasting (€7.50 for 1 sample, €13 for 3 samples, daily 9:30–11:45 & 14:00–17:00, closed Jan–Feb, one block beyond Taittinger up boulevard Victor Hugo to 51 boulevard Henri Vasnier, tel. 03 26 84 43 44, www.piper-heidsieck.com). Nearby **Martel** is smaller, less formal, and *sans* doubt the best deal in town, with a we-try-harder attitude. With only 20 percent of their product exported (and most of that within Europe), you won't find much of their Champagne in the US. Their €6, one-hour visit focuses on the basics and includes an informative 20-minute film, a tour of their cellars, and a tasting of three different champagnes in a casual living-room atmosphere (open through lunch, daily 10:00–17:45, 17 rue des Créneaux, tel. 03 26 82 70 67, www.champagnemartel.com).

Champagne Sights near Reims

Epernay—Champagne purists may want to visit Epernay (16 miles away, well-connected to Paris and Reims), where the granddaddy of Champagne houses, **Moët et Chandon,** offers tours with three tasting possibilities (€8 for single tasting, €17 for 2 tastes, €21 for 3, no reservation needed, daily mid-March–mid-Nov 9:30–11:30 & 14:00–16:30, closed weekends in off-season, tel. 03 26 51 20 20, www.moet.com). From the train station, walk five minutes straight up rue Gambetta to place de la République, and take a left on avenue de Champagne (how fitting). According to the story, it was near here in about 1700 that the monk Dom Perignon, after much fiddling with double fermentation, stumbled onto this bubbly treat. On that happy day, he ran through the abbey shouting, "Brothers, come quickly...I'm drinking stars!"

Route de la Champagne—Drivers can joyride through the scenic and prestigious vineyards just south of Reims (the TI has maps). Follow D-9 south to Cormontreuil, then Louvois, then Bouzy, to see the chalky soil and vines that produce Champagne's costly wines. Many of the villages have small hotels if you'd like to sleep surrounded by vineyards.

SLEEPING

(€1 = about $1.30, country code: 33)
It's hard to differentiate between the scads of hotels lining the vast pedestrian place Drouet d'Erlon.

$$ Grand Hôtel Continental*** is a business hotel with 50 rooms that offers reasonable three-star comfort, pleasant public spaces, nice staff, and frequent specials (standard Db-€58–71, "junior suites" Db-€85–105, "superior suites" with air-con Db-€155, apartments for 3–8 people-€135–356, suites cheaper in summer when the hotel isn't full, some non-smoking rooms, elevator, laundry service, free Wi-Fi, parking-€6, 93 place Drouet d'Erlon, tel. 03 26 40 39 35, fax 03 26 47 51 12, www.grandhotelcontinental.com, grand-hotel-continental@wanadoo.fr, friendly owner Philippe).

$$ Latino Hôtel, right on place Drouet d'Erlon, is part of the rejuvenation of Reims' pedestrian core. Although its effort to be trendy results at best in "budget boutique," its 11 brand-new rooms are freshly funky and a decent value. It's above a bar so it can be noisy on weekends. The rooms facing the back are quieter but smaller and face the adjacent building (Db-€54–74, ring door-bell next to restaurant for reception, 33 place Drouet d'Erlon, tel. 03 26 47 48 89, fax 03 26 86 92 67, www.latinocafe.fr, latinocafe @latinocafe.fr).

$$ Hôtel des Arcades** feels closer to a hostel than a hotel. It's modern, basic, and a fair deal (Sb-€50, Db-€60, Tb-€70, elevator, parking-€6, 16 passage Subé, off rue Condorcet in mall opposite merry-go-round, tel. 03 26 88 63 74, fax 03 26 40 66 56, hotel.des .arcades@wanadoo.fr).

$ Delightful **Bénédicte et Claude Philippon** offers Reims' best lodging value with two comfortable, homey, and centrally located rooms on place du Chapitre (#21), just behind the cathedral and TI–look for the yellow *Chambres d'Hôte* sign (S-€40, D-€50, T-€65, shared bathroom, includes French breakfast, fourth floor with elevator, parking on square, tel. 03 26 91 06 22, mobile 06 77 76 20 13, claude.philippon@tele2.fr).

EATING

Find good people-watching opportunities—if not high cuisine— with the scads of average restaurants on place Drouet d'Erlon.

L'Apostrophe wins the snazziness contest, with a library-like interior and a lively bar scene in the rear (€11–23 *plats*, €26 *menu*, look for their specials, daily, 59 place Drouet d'Erlon, tel. 03 26 79 19 89).

Brasserie du Boulingrin is the oldest brasserie in town, with an Art Nouveau style. While no secret, it is a dependable Reims institution for traditional French fare (€15–18 *plats*, €18–25 *menus*, closed Sun; 10-min walk north of the TI or central train station at 49 rue de Mars, or take the bus—Citadine #2, stop Boulingrin; tel. 03 26 40 96 22).

Au Plat du Jour, close to the cluster of *caves*, is a good post-Champagne-tasting option. Casually elegant, with old posters and Champagne labels adorning the walls, this is the place to enjoy hearty, classic French cuisine (€14–19 *plats*, €16–21 *menus*, closed Sun, 219 rue Barbatre, tel. 03 26 85 27 60).

Paul bakery, on place du Grand Théâtre, is good for a budget lunch. You can order good take-away sandwiches and pastries, and still use the tables and chairs out front (open daily).

Alsace

TRANSPORTATION CONNECTIONS

There are two train stations in Reims (Gare Champagne–Ardenne and Reims-Centre). TGV trains run to the Gare Champagne–Ardenne (3 miles from the center of Reims) with frequent shuttle-train connections to Reims-Centre station, which serves non-TGV trains.

From Reims by Train to: Epernay (12/day, 30 min, non-TGV), **Verdun** (via TGV to nearby Gare Meuse: 1/day, 30 min, plus 30-min shuttle bus from Gare Meuse to Verdun's city center; via non-TGV train: 3/day, 2–5 hrs, most with change in Chalon), **Paris'** Gare de l'Est (via TGV: 8/day, 45 min; via non-TGV train: 12/day, 2 hrs), **Strasbourg** (via TGV: 8/day, 1.5 hrs; via non-TGV train: 6/day, 4-6 hrs), **Colmar** (via TGV: 8/day, 2 hrs, most change in Strasbourg; via non-TGV train: 4/day, 5–7 hrs, several changes).

FRENCH HISTORY
AND CONTEMPORARY POLITICS

"La Marseillaise"

There's a movement in France to soften the lyrics of their national anthem. Sing it now...before it's too late.

Allons enfants de la Patrie, (Let's go, children of the motherland,)
Le jour de gloire est arrivé. (The day of glory has arrived.)
Contre nous de la tyrannie (The blood-covered flag of tyranny)
L'étendard sanglant est levé. (Is raised against us.)
L'étendard sanglant est levé. (Is raised against us.)
Entendez-vous dans les campagnes (Do you hear these ferocious soldiers)
    diers)
Mugir ces féroces soldats? (Howling in the countryside?)
Qui viennent jusque dans nos bras (They're nearly in our grasp)
Egorger vos fils et vos compagnes. (To slit the throats of your sons and your women.)
Aux armes citoyens, (Grab your weapons, citizens,)
Formez vos bataillons, (Form your battalions,)
Marchons, marchons, (March on, march on,)
Qu'un sang impur (So that their impure blood)
Abreuve nos sillons. (Will fill our trenches.)

French History in an Escargot Shell

About the time of Christ, Romans "Latinized" the land of the Gauls. With the fifth-century fall of Rome, the barbarian Franks and Burgundians invaded. Today's France evolved from this unique mix of Latin and Celtic cultures.

While France wallowed with the rest of Europe in medieval darkness, it got a head start in its development as a nation-state. In 507, Clovis established Paris as the capital of his Christian Merovingian dynasty. Clovis and the Franks would eventually become Louis and the French. Charles Martel stopped the spread

Top French Notables in History

Madame and Monsieur Cro-Magnon: Prehistoric hunter-gatherers who moved to France (c. 30,000 B.C.), painted cave walls at Lascaux and Font-de-Gaume, and eventually settled down as farmers (c. 10,000 B.C.).

Vercingétorix (72–46 B.C.): This long-haired warrior rallied the Gauls against Julius Caesar's invading Roman legions (52 B.C.). Defeated by Caesar, France fell under Roman domination, enduring 500 years of peace, prosperity, the establishment of cities, building of roads, education in Latin, and conversion to Christianity.

Charlemagne (A.D. 742–814): For Christmas in A.D. 800, the pope gave King Charlemagne the title of Emperor, thus uniting much of Europe under the leadership of the Franks ("France"). Charlemagne stabilized France amid centuries of barbarian invasions. After his death, the empire was split, carving the outlines of modern France and Germany.

Eleanor of Aquitaine (c. 1122–1204): The beautiful, sophisticated ex-wife of the King of France married the King of England, creating an uneasy union between the two countries. During her lifetime, French culture was spread across Europe by roving troubadours, theological scholars, and skilled architects pioneering "the French style"—Gothic.

Joan of Arc (1412–1431): When France and England fought the Hundred Years' War to settle who would rule (1337–1453), teenage Joan of Arc—guided by voices in her head—rallied the French troops. Though Joan was captured and burned as a heretic, the French eventually drove England out of France for good, establishing the current borders. Over the centuries, the church upgraded Joan's status from heretic to saint (canonized 1920).

François I (1494–1547): This Renaissance king ruled a united, modern nation, making it a cultural center that hosted the Italian Leonardo da Vinci. François set the tone for future absolute monarchs, punctuating his commands with the phrase, "for such is our pleasure."

Louis XIV (1638–1715): Charismatic and cunning, the "Sun King" ruled Europe's richest, most populous, most powerful nation-state. Educated Europeans spoke French, dressed in Louis-style leotards and powdered wigs, and built Versailles-like palaces. Though Louis ruled as an absolute monarch (distracting the nobility with courtly games), his reign also fostered the arts and philosophy, sowing the seeds of democracy and revolution.

Marie-Antoinette (1755–1793): As the wife of Louis XVI, she came to symbolize (probably unfairly) the decadence of France's ruling class. When Revolution broke out (1789), she was arrested, imprisoned, and executed—one of thousands who were guillotined on Paris' place de la Concorde as an enemy of the people.

Napoleon Bonaparte (1769–1821):  This daring young military man became a hero during the Revolution fighting Europe's royalty. He went on to conquer much of Europe, became leader of France, and eventually ruled as a dictator with the title of Emperor. In 1815, an allied Europe defeated and exiled Napoleon, reinstating the French monarchy—though future kings (including Napoleon's nephew, who ruled as Napoleon III) were subject to democratic constraints.

Claude Monet (1840–1926): Monet's Impressionist paintings capture the soft-focus beauty of the belle époque—middle-class men and women enjoying drinks in cafés, walks in gardens, and picnics along the Seine. At the turn of the 20th century, French culture reigned supreme while its economic and political clout was fading, soon to be shattered by the violence of World War I.

Charles de Gaulle (1890–1970): A career military man, de Gaulle helped France survive occupation by Nazi Germany during World War II with his rousing radio broadcasts and unbending faith in France. As president, he led the country through its postwar rebuilding, through divisive wars in Vietnam and Algeria (trying to preserve France's colonial empire), and through turbulent student riots in the 1960s.

Contemporary French: Which recent French people will history remember? President François Mitterand (1916–1996), the driving force behind La Grande Arche and Opéra Bastille? Marcel Marceau (b. 1923), white-faced mime? Chef Paul Bocuse (b. 1926), inventor of nouvelle cuisine? Or Brigitte Bardot (b. 1934), film actress, crusader for animal rights, and popularizer of the bikini?

French History

of Islam by beating the Spanish Moors at the Battle of Poitiers. And Charlemagne ("Charles the Great"), the most important of the "Dark Age" Frankish kings, was crowned Holy Roman Emperor by the pope in 800. Charlemagne presided over the "Carolingian Renaissance" and effectively ruled a vast-for-the-time empire.

The Treaty of Verdun (843), which divided Charlemagne's empire among his grandsons, marks what could be considered the birth of Europe. For the first time, a treaty was signed in vernacular languages (French and German), rather than in Latin. This split established a Franco-Germanic divide, and heralded an age of fragmentation. While petty princes took the reigns, the Frankish king ruled only Ile de France, a small region around Paris.

Vikings, or Norsemen, settled in what became Normandy. Later, in 1066, these "Normans" invaded England. The Norman king, William the Conqueror, consolidated his English domain, accelerating the formation of modern England. But his rule also muddied the political waters between England and France, kicking off a centuries-long struggle between the two nations.

In the 12th century, Eleanor of Aquitaine (a separate country in southwest France) married Louis VII, king of France, bringing Aquitaine under French rule. They divorced, and she married Henry of Normandy, soon-to-be Henry II of England. This marital union gave England control of a huge swath of land from the English Channel to the Pyrénées. For 300 years, France and England would struggle over control of Aquitaine. Any enemy of the French king would find a natural ally in the English king.

In 1328, a French king (Charles IV) died without a son. The English king (Edward III) was his nephew and interested in the throne, but the French resisted. This quandary pitted France, the biggest and richest country in Europe, against England, which had the biggest army. They fought from 1337 to 1453 in what was modestly called the Hundred Years' War.

Regional powers from within France actually sided with England. Burgundy took Paris, captured the royal family, and recognized the English king as heir to the French throne. England controlled France from the Loire north, and things looked bleak for the French king.

Enter Joan of Arc, a 16-year-old peasant girl driven by religious voices. France's national heroine left home to support Charles VII, the dauphin (boy prince, heir to the throne but too young to rule). Joan rallied the French, ultimately inspiring them to throw out the English. In 1430, Joan was captured by the Burgundians, who sold her to the English, who convicted her of heresy and burned her at the stake in Rouen. But the inspiration of Joan of Arc lived on, and by 1453, English holdings on the Continent had dwindled to the port of Calais.

By 1500, a strong, centralized France had emerged, with borders similar to today's. Its kings (from the Renaissance François I through the Henrys and all those Louises) were model divine monarchs, setting the standards for absolute rule in Europe.

Outrage over the power plays and spending sprees of the kings, coupled with the modern thinking of the Enlightenment—whose leaders were the French *philosophes*—led to the French Revolution (1789). In France, it was the end of the *ancien régime*, as well as its notion that some are born to rule, while others are born to be ruled.

The excesses of the Revolution in turn led to the rise of Napoleon, who ruled the French empire as a dictator. Eventually, *his* excesses ushered him into a South Atlantic exile, and the French settled on a compromise role for their leader. The modern French king was himself ruled by a constitution. Rather than dress in leotards and powdered wigs, he went to work in a suit with a briefcase.

The 20th century spelled the end of France's reign as a military and political superpower. Devastating wars with Germany in 1870, 1914, and 1940—and the loss of her colonial holdings—left France with not quite enough land, people, or production to be a top player on a global scale. But the 21st century may see France rise again: Paris is again the cultural capital of Europe, and France—under the EU banner—is a key player in integrating Europe as one unified economic power. And when Europe is a superpower, Paris may yet be its capital.

Contemporary Politics

The five key political issues in France today are high unemployment (about 10 percent), high taxes (about 44 percent of the gross domestic product), a steadily increasing percentage of ethnic minorities (almost 10 percent of France's population is Muslim), what to do about the European Union (the EU), and the balancing act between maintaining cushy workers' benefits with the need to compete in a global marketplace. The nation's challenge is to address these issues while maintaining the social benefits that the French expect from their government.

The unification of Europe has been powered by France and Germany. The EU's constitution—still in limbo—was negotiated by former French president Valéry Giscard d'Estaing, and represents a serious step in European unification. The constitution was designed to simplify decision-making and provide a more consistent and coordinated foreign policy for member states. The 25-member EU was well on its way to becoming a "United States of Europe" (having successfully dissolved borders and implemented a single currency, the euro)—until French citizens voted resoundingly against ratification in 2005. While France's major political parties supported the treaty, voters felt it gave too many concessions to other countries (such as Britain), and would ultimately result in a loss of job security and social benefits (a huge issue in France). Because of France's important role in establishing the EU, progress on the constitution and further unification has stalled.

French national politics are complex but fascinating. While only two parties dominate American politics, France has seven major parties and several smaller ones. From left to right, the major parties include: the Ligue Communiste Révolutionnaire (LCR), which is as far left as you get in France; the more moderate reformed Communists (PCF, or Parti Communiste Français); the environmental party (Les Verts, a.k.a. "The Greens"); the middle-of-the-road Socialists (PS, or Parti Socialiste); the aristocratically conservative UDF (Union pour la Démocratie Française); the center right UMP (Union pour la Majorité Présidentielle); and the racist, isolationist Front National party. In general, the UDF and UMP split the conservative middle ground, and the Socialists dominate the liberal middle ground. But in France, unlike in the US, informal coalitions are generally necessary for any party to "rule."

You've likely read about the Front National party, led by Jean-Marie Le Pen. His infamous "France for the French" platform calls for the expulsion of ethnic minorities and broader police powers. The situation was especially tense in fall 2005, when Muslim youths rioted in Parisian suburbs, protesting discrimination. Although the Front National has a staunch voter base of about 15 percent, the recent rise in unemployment and globalization worries have increased its following, allowing Le Pen to nudge the political agenda to the right. On the far left, the once powerful Communists (PCF) draw only about 5 percent of the popular vote, forcing them to work more flexibly with the less radical Socialists and the environmental party (Les Verts). The left end of the political spectrum in France has seen its fortunes rise when the economy is strong, and fall when it's weak.

In 2006, Parisian students took to the streets to protest threats to job security. Guaranteed "tenure" for life is important to French workers, and makes it extremely difficult for businesses to fire employees. Any changes that could weaken job security do not sit well with the public.

While the French president is elected by popular vote every five years, he is more of a figurehead than his American counterpart. The more-powerful prime minister is chosen by the president, then confirmed by the parliament (Assemblée Nationale). With five major parties, a single majority is rare, so it takes a coalition to elect a prime minister. Over the past 10 to 12 years, the right has been more successful in marshaling its supporters than the left. Previous President Jacques Chirac and current President Nicolas Sarkozy (elected in 2007) are both conservatives.

Sarkozy is pro-US (though he doesn't speak English) and pro-EU. To address a sluggish economy, he proposes a tough-love, carrot-and-stick approach—limiting the power of unions and cutting workers' benefits while offering tax incentives to workers who put in overtime (above the current 35–39-hour work week). Sarkozy is tough on crime and on unchecked immigration. It remains to be seen how his hard-line approach will play to France's feisty workers and disenfranchised immigrants. As the French say: *On verra* (we'll see).

APPENDIX

CONTENTS

RESOURCES

Tourist Offices

In the US

France has a national tourist information office (abbreviated **TI** in this book) that is a wealth of information. Before you go, you can contact the TI to briefly describe your trip and request any information (such as city maps and schedules of upcoming festivals).

To ask questions and request tourist materials, call 514/288-1904 or email info.us@franceguide.com. One brochure and the *France Guide* magazine are free; additional brochures are $0.50 each, with a handling fee of $2 per order. Orders will arrive in 2–3 weeks; rush delivery is an extra $4. You can download many brochures free of charge at www.franceguide.com.

Tourist Offices in France

Except in Paris, where they aren't very helpful, the local TI is your best first stop in any new city, offering useful maps, special events information, English-language tour information, lists of inexpensive bed-and-breakfasts, and more. If you're arriving in town after the office closes, consider calling ahead or picking up a map in a neighboring town. To call any TI in France, dial 3265 and say the city with your best French accent. Theoretically, you'll be connected (€0.34/min).

Throughout France, you'll find TIs are usually well-organized and have English-speaking staff. Most will help you find a room by calling hotels (for a small fee) or by giving you a complete listing of available bed-and-breakfasts. Towns with a lot of tourism generally have English-speaking guides available for private hire (about $100 for a 2-hour guided town walk).

The French call TIs by different names. *Office de Tourisme* and *Bureau de Tourisme* are used in cities, while *Syndicat d'Initiative* or *Information Touristique* are used in small towns. Also look for *Accueil* signs in airports and at popular sights. These are information booths staffed with seasonal helpers who provide tourists with limited, though generally sufficient, information. Smaller TIs are often closed from 12:00 to 14:00.

More Resources from Rick Steves

Guidebooks and Online Updates

This book is updated every year in person. The telephone numbers and hours of sights listed in this book are accurate as of mid-2007—but even with annual updates, things change. For the very latest, visit www.ricksteves.com/update. Also at my website, you'll find a valuable list of reports and experiences—good and bad—from fellow travelers (www.ricksteves.com/feedback).

This book is one of more than 30 titles in my series on European travel, which includes country guidebooks, city and regional guidebooks (including Paris, and Provence and the French Riviera), and my budget-travel skills handbook, *Rick Steves' Europe Through the Back Door*. My phrase books—for French, Italian, German, Spanish, and Portuguese—are practical and budget-oriented. My other books are *Europe 101* (a crash course on art and history, newly expanded and in full color), *European Christmas* (on traditional and modern-day celebrations), and *Postcards from Europe* (a fun

Begin Your Trip at www.ricksteves.com

At our travel website, you'll find a wealth of free information on European destinations, including fresh monthly news and

helpful tips from thousands of fellow travelers.

Our **online Travel Store** offers travel bags and accessories specially designed by Rick Steves to help you travel smarter and lighter. These include Rick's popular carry-on bags (wheeled and rucksack versions), money belts, totes, toiletries kits, adapters, other accessories, and a wide selection of guidebooks, planning maps, and DVDs.

Choosing the right **railpass** for your trip—amidst hundreds of options—can drive you nutty. We'll help you choose the best pass for your needs, plus give you a bunch of free extras.

Rick Steves' Europe Through the Back Door travel company offers **tours** with more than two dozen itineraries and 450 departures reaching the best destinations in this book... and beyond. Our France tours include Paris and the South of France in 15 days, Paris and the Heart of France in 11 days (focusing on the best of the north; a kid-friendly version of this tour is also available), the Best of Paris and London in eight days, and the one-week Paris city tour. You'll enjoy great guides, a fun bunch of travel partners (with small groups of generally about 25), and plenty of room to spread out in a big, comfy bus. You'll find European adventures to fit every vacation length. For all the details, and to get our Tour Catalog and a free Rick Steves Tour Experience DVD (filmed on location during an actual tour), visit www.ricksteves.com or call the Tour Department at 425-608-4217.

memoir of my travels over 25 years, offering an insight into French culture that you won't find in guidebooks). For a complete list of my books, see the inside of the last page of this book.

Public Television and Radio Shows

My TV series, *Rick Steves' Europe,* covers European destinations in 70 shows, with six episodes on France. My weekly public radio show, *Travel with Rick Steves,* features interviews with travel experts from around the world, including several hours on France and French culture. All the TV scripts and radio shows (which

are easy and free to download to an MP3 player) are at www
.ricksteves.com.

Free Audiotours

Rick Steves and Gene Openshaw (the co-author of seven books in
the Rick Steves series) have produced free, self-guided audiotours
of Paris—for the Louvre, Musée d'Orsay,
Versailles, and Historic Paris—as well as for
major sights in Florence, Rome, and Venice.
Created for users of iPods and other MP3
players, the tours allow you to focus on what
you're seeing rather than what you're reading.

The Paris tours are available through
iTunes and at www.ricksteves.com (Italy tours
available after January 2008). Simply down-
load them onto your computer and transfer them to your iPod or
MP3 player. (Remember to bring a Y-jack and extra set of ear buds
for your travel partner.)

Maps

The black-and-white maps in this book, drawn by Dave Hoerlein,
are concise and simple. Dave, who is well-traveled in France,
designed the maps to help you locate recommended places and
reach TIs, where you'll find more in-depth (and often free) maps
of cities or regions. Better maps are sold at newsstands—take a
look before you buy to be sure the map has the level of detail you
want.

Michelin maps are available throughout France at bookstores,
newsstands, and gas stations (about €5 each, half the US price).
The Michelin #528 map (1:1,000,000 scale) covers this book's
destinations with good detail for drivers. Train travelers do fine
with Michelin's #721 map. Drivers should consider the soft-cover
Michelin France atlas (the entire country at 1:200,000, well-
organized in a €20 book with an index and maps of major cities).
Spend a few minutes learning the Michelin key to get the most
sightseeing value out of these maps.

Other Guidebooks

If you're like most travelers, this book is all you need. But if you're
heading beyond my recommended destinations, you might want
some supplemental information. Considering the improvements
they'll make in your $3,000 vacation, $30 for extra maps and books
is money well spent.

I like Cadogan guides for their well-presented background
information and coverage of cultural issues. Their recommendations suit upscale travelers but are not updated annually. Lonely

Planet's *France* is well-researched, with good maps and hotel recommendations for low- to moderate-budget travelers. But because it tries to cover every city in France, you'll likely find too little information on the most important places and too much information on the minor places you don't care about. The highly opinionated *Let's Go: France* (St. Martin's Press) is ideal for students and vagabonds traveling by train and staying in hostels. The popular, skinny, green Michelin guides are dry but informative, especially for drivers. They're known for their city and sightseeing maps, and for their succinct, helpful information on all major sights. English editions, covering most of the regions you'll want to visit, are sold in France for about €14 (or $20 in the US).

Recommended Books and Movies

For information on France past and present, consider reading some of these books or seeing these films:

Non-Fiction

For a good introduction to the French culture and people, read *Sixty Million Frenchmen Can't Be Wrong* (Jean-Benoit Nadeau and Julie Barlow), *Culture Shock: France* (Sally Adamson Taylor) and/or *French or Foe* (Polly Platt).

For a readable history of the country, try *The Course of French History* (Pierre Goubert). *Portraits of France* (Robert Daley) is an interesting travelogue that roams from Paris to the Pyrénées. A mix of writers explore French culture in *Travelers Tales: France* (edited by James O'Reilly, Larry Habegger, and Sean O'Reilly).

Many great memoirs take place in Paris. Consider reading Ernest Hemingway's *A Moveable Feast*, Art Buchwald's *I'll Always Have Paris*, and/or *Paris to the Moon*, by *New Yorker* writer Adam Gopnik, who takes his young son for a carousel ride in the Luxembourg Garden.

If you'll be visiting Provence, pick up Peter Mayle's memoirs, *A Year in Provence* and *Toujours Provence*. Ina Caro's *The Road from the Past* is filled with enjoyable essays on her travels through France, with an accent on history. *The Da Vinci Code* fans will enjoy reading the book that inspired that book—*Holy Blood, Holy Grail* (Michael Baigent, Richard Leigh, and Henry Lincoln)—which takes place mostly in southern France.

War buffs may want to read these classics before visiting the D-Day Beaches: *The Longest Day* (Cornelius Ryan) and *Wine & War: The French, the Nazis, and the Battle for France's Greatest Treasure* (Donald and Petie Kladstrup). *Is Paris Burning?*, set in the post-WWII years, tells the story of Paris during its recovery from the Occupation (Larry Collins).

If you'll be enjoying an extended stay in France, consider

reading *Living Abroad in France* (Terry Link). Gourmands appreciate the *Marling Menu-Master for France* (William E. Marling).

Fiction

"It was the best of times, it was the worst of times," begins Charles Dickens' gripping tale of the French Revolution, *A Tale of Two Cities*. In *Les Misérables* (Victor Hugo), a Frenchman tries to escape his criminal past, fleeing from a determined police captain and becoming wrapped up in the Revolutionary battles between the rich and the starving. Another recommended book set during this time is *City of Darkness, City of Light*, by Marge Piercy.

Ernest Hemingway was a fan of Georges Simenon, a Belgian who wrote mysteries based in Paris, including *The Hotel Majestic*. Other mysteries using Paris as the backdrop are *Murder in Montparnasse* (Howard Engel), *Murder in the Marais* (Cara Black), and *Sandman* (J. Robert Janes).

A Very Long Engagement (Sebastien Japrisot) is a love story set during the bleak years when World War I raged. Using a similar timeframe, *Birdsong* (Sebastian Faulks) follows a 20-year-old Englishman into France, and into the romance that follows.

Chocolat (Joanne Harris)—a book and a 2000 movie with Johnny Depp and Juliette Binoche—charms readers with its story of magic and romance.

Films

In *The Grand Illusion* (1937, directed by Jean Renoir), WWI prisoners of war hatch an escape plan. Considered a masterpiece of French film, the movie was later banned by the Nazis for its anti-fascism message.

Stanley Kubrick's *Paths of Glory* (1957) is a WWI story about the futility and irony of war. François Truffaut, a filmmaker of the French New Wave school, shows the Parisian streets in *Jules and Jim* (1962). Wander the streets of Paris with a small boy as he chases *The Red Balloon* (1956).

Jean de Florette (1986), a marvelous tale of greed and intolerance, follows a hunchback as he fights for the property he inherited. *Blue/White/Red* (1990s) is a stylish trilogy of films by Krzystof Kieslowski, based on France's national motto—"Liberty, Equality, and Fraternity."

Cyrano de Bergerac (1990) is about a homely, romantic poet who woos his love with the help of another, better-looking man. Fans of crime films—and Robert De Niro—will like *Ronin* (1998), with multiple scenes shot in France. *Saving Private Ryan* (1998) is Steven Spielberg's intense and brilliant story of the D-Day landings.

The Gleaners & I (2000)—a quiet, meditative film by Agnès Varda—follows a few working-class men and women as they

The Rules of Boules

Throughout France, you'll see citizens playing *boules* (also known as *pétanque*). Each player starts with three iron balls, with the object of getting them close to the target, a small wooden ball called a *cochonnet*. The first player tosses the *cochonnet* about 30 feet, then throws the first of his iron balls near the target. The next player takes a turn. As soon as a player's ball is closest, it's the other guy's turn. Once all balls have been thrown, the score is tallied—the player with the closest ball gets one point for each ball closer to the target than his opponent's. The loser gets zero. Games are generally to 15 points.

A regulation *boules* field is 10 feet by 43 feet, but the game is played everywhere—just scratch a throwing circle in the sand, toss the *cochonnet*, and you're off. Strategists can try to knock the opponent's balls out of position, knock the *cochonnet* itself out of position, or guard their best ball with the other two.

gather sustenance from what's been thrown away. In *Amélie* (2001), a charming young waitress in Paris searches for love. If you'll be heading to Versailles, consider seeing *Marie Antoinette* (2006), which stars Kirsten Dunst as the infamous French queen (with a California accent).

MONEY MATTERS

Damage Control for Lost Cards

If you lose your credit, debit, or ATM card, you can stop people from using it by reporting the loss immediately to the respective global customer-assistance centers. Call these 24-hour US numbers collect: Visa (410/581-9994), MasterCard (636/722-7111), and American Express (623/492-8427). For another option (with the same results), you can call these toll-free numbers in France: Visa (08 00 90 11 79), MasterCard (08 00 90 13 87), and American Express (08 00 89 00 11). Diners Club has offices in the US (702/797-5532, call collect) and Britain (from France, dial 00-44-1695-53760).

At a minimum, you'll need to know the name of the financial institution that issued you the card, along with the type of card (classic, platinum, or whatever). Providing the following information will allow for a quicker cancellation of your missing card: full card number, whether you are the primary or secondary cardholder, the cardholder's name exactly as printed on the card, billing address, home phone number, circumstances of the loss or theft, and identification verification (your birth date, your mother's maiden name, or your Social Security number—memorize this, don't carry a copy). If you are the secondary cardholder, you'll also need to provide the primary cardholder's identification-verification details. You can generally receive a temporary card within two or three business days in Europe.

If you promptly report your card lost or stolen, you typically won't be responsible for any unauthorized transactions on your account, although many banks charge a liability fee of $50.

Tipping

Tipping *(donner un pourboire)* in France isn't as automatic and generous as it is in the US, but for special service, tips are appreciated, if not expected. As in the US, the proper amount depends on your resources, tipping philosophy, and the circumstances, but some general guidelines apply.

Restaurants: At cafés and restaurants, a 15 percent service charge *(service compris)* is generally included in the bill, though it's customary to tip 5 percent extra for good service. When you hand your payment plus a tip to your waiter, you can say, *"C'est bon"* (say bohn), meaning, "It's good" (and you don't want any change back). If you order a meal at a counter, don't tip.

Taxis: To tip the cabbie, round up. For a typical ride, round up to the next euro on the fare (to pay a €13 fare, give €14); for a long ride, round to the nearest €10 (for a €75 fare, give €80). If the cabbie hauls your bags and zips you to the airport to help you catch your flight, you might want to toss in a little more. But if you feel like you're being driven in circles or otherwise ripped off, skip the tip.

Special Services: It's thoughtful to tip a couple of euros to someone who shows you a special sight and who is paid in no other way. Tour guides at public sites sometimes hold out their hands for tips after they give their spiel; if I've already paid for the tour, I don't tip extra, though some tourists do give a euro or two, particularly for a job well done. I don't tip at hotels, but if you do, give the porter a euro for carrying bags and leave a couple of euros in your room at the end of your stay for the maid if the room was kept clean. In general, if someone in the service industry does a super job for you, a tip of a couple of euros is appropriate...but not required.

When in doubt, ask. If you're not sure whether (or how much) to tip for a service, ask your hotelier or the tourist information office; they'll fill you in on how it's done on their turf.

Clothing Size Comparisons for Shoppers

When shopping for clothing, use these US-to-France comparisons as general guidelines (but note that no conversion is perfect).

- Women's dresses and blouses: Add 30 (US women's size 10 is about French size 40)
- Men's suits and jackets: Add 10 (US men's size 40 regular is about French size 50)
- Men's shirts: Multiply by 2 and add about 8 (US men's size 15 collar is close to French size 38)
- Women's shoes: Add about 31 (US women's size 8 is about French size 39)
- Men's shoes: Add 32–34 (US men's size 9 US is about French size 43; US size 11 is French size 45)

Getting a VAT Refund

As is the case throughout the European Union, wrapped into the purchase price of your French souvenirs is a Value Added Tax (VAT) of about 19.6 percent. If you purchase more than €175 (about $225) worth of goods at a store that participates in the VAT-refund scheme, you're entitled to get most of that tax back. Getting your refund is usually straightforward and, if you buy a substantial amount of souvenirs, well worth the hassle. If you're lucky, the merchant will subtract the tax when you make your purchase. (This is more likely to occur if the store ships the goods to your home.) Otherwise, you'll need to:

Get the paperwork. Have the merchant completely fill out the necessary refund document, *Bordereau de Vente à l'Exportation*, also called a "cheque." You'll have to present your passport at the store.

Get your stamp at the border or airport. Process your cheque(s) at your last stop in the EU (e.g., at the airport) with the customs agent who deals with VAT refunds. It's best to keep your purchases in your carry-on for viewing, but if they're too large or dangerous (such as knives) to carry on, track down the proper customs agent to inspect them before you check your bag. You're not supposed to use your purchased goods before you leave. If you show up at customs wearing your chic new French ensemble, officials might look the other way—or deny you a refund.

Collect your refund. You'll need to return your stamped document to the retailer or its representative. Many merchants work with a service, such as Global Refund (www.globalrefund.com) or Premier Tax Free (www.premiertaxfree.com), which have offices at major airports, ports, or border crossings. These services, which extract a 4 percent fee, can refund your money immediately in your currency of choice or credit your card (within two billing cycles). If the retailer handles VAT refunds directly, it's up to you to contact the merchant for your refund. You can mail the documents from home, or quicker, from your point of departure (using a stamped, addressed envelope you've prepared or one that's been provided by the merchant)—and then wait. It could take months.

Customs for American Shoppers

You are allowed to take home $800 worth of items per person duty-free, once every 30 days. The next $1,000 is taxed at a flat 3 percent. After that, you pay the individual item's duty rate. You can also bring in duty-free a liter of alcohol (slightly more than a standard-size bottle of wine; you must be at least 21), 200 cigarettes, and up to 100 non-Cuban cigars. Food in cans or sealed jars is permissible as long as no meat is included. Some, but not all, types of cheese are allowed. Fresh fruits and vegetables are prohibited. Note that you'll need to carefully pack any bottles of wine and other liquid-containing items (jars of olives, etc.) in your checked luggage, due to the three-ounce limit on liquids in carry-on baggage. To check customs rules and duty rates before you go, visit www.cbp.gov, and click on "Travel," then "Know Before You Go."

TELEPHONES, EMAIL, AND MAIL

Telephones

Smart travelers learn the phone system and use it daily to reserve or reconfirm rooms, get tourist information, reserve restaurants, confirm tour times, or phone home. When spelling out your name on the phone, you'll find that some letters are pronounced differently in French: *a* is pronounced "ah," *e* is pronounced "eh," and *i* is pronounced "ee." To avoid confusion, say "*a*, Anne," "*e*, euro," and "*i*, Isabelle."

Types of Phones

You'll encounter various kinds of phones on your trip:

Card-operated phones—where you insert a locally bought phone card into a public pay phone—are common in Europe.

Coin-operated phones, the original kind of pay phone, are rare in France. You might see them at gas stations and in big hotel lobbies.

Hotel room phones are sometimes cheap for local calls (confirm at the front desk first), but can be a rip-off for long-distance calls unless you use an international phone card (described on next page). But incoming calls are free, making this a cheap way for friends and family to stay in touch, provided they have a good long-distance plan for calls to Europe.

American mobile phones work in Europe if they're GSM-enabled, tri-band or quad-band, and on a calling plan that includes international calls. They're convenient, but pricey. For example, with a T-Mobile phone, you'll pay $1 per minute for calls.

European mobile phones run about $75 (for the most basic models) and come without contracts. These phones are loaded with prepaid calling time that you can recharge as you use up the

minutes. As long as you're
not "roaming" outside the
phone's home country,
incoming calls are free. If
traveling to multiple countries within Europe, make
sure the phone is electroni-
cally "unlocked," so that you
can swap out its SIM card (a

fingernail-size chip that holds the phone's information, pictured
here) for a new one in other countries.

Using Phone Cards

Get a phone card for your calls. Prepaid phone cards come in two
types: international and insertable (both described below). Look
for these cards at any post office and most newsstands and tobacco
shops *(tabacs)*, which you'll find everywhere, including at train stations and airports.

Either type of phone card works only in France. While traveling in France, you can share either type of card with your companions (and, in the case of an international phone card, your buddy
doesn't even need the actual card—just the numbers on it). If you
have time left on a card when you leave the country (as you likely
will), simply give it to another traveler—anyone can use it.

For international calls, you'll get the best deal with an **international phone card,** called *carte à code* (cart ah code). It comes
with a dial-up code that can be used from nearly any phone, including the one in your hotel room (if it's set on "pulse," switch it to
"tone"). Cards are marked as national (for France) or international.
All cards work for domestic or international calls, but you get better rates if you use the card for the purpose it was intended—so if
you plan to use your card mostly for calls home, ask for an international card (denominations in €7 and €15 amounts). They're all
good values—my €15 international card lasted for four weeks of
regular calls home (about 5 cents a minute). These *carte à code* cards
all work the same way and are simple to use (English instructions
provided). Scratch to get your code (begins with 08). Dial the free
number. A voice (in French, but sometimes followed by English)
tells you to enter your code. After entering your code, you may
need to press (or "*touche*," pronounced toosh) either the pound key
(#, *dièse*, dee-ehz) or the star key (*, *étoile*, eh-twahl). At the next
message, dial the number you're calling, again followed by pound
or star (you don't have to listen through the entire sales pitch).

An **insertable phone card,** called a *télécarte* (tay-lay-kart),
can only be used at pay phones. While per-minute rates are much
cheaper with an international phone card than with an insertable

phone card, the international cards are slower to use (more numbers to dial). Use a *télécarte* for quick local calls from a phone booth. There are two denominations: *une petite* costs about €7.50; *une grande* about €15. While you can use a *télécarte* to call anywhere in the world, it's only a good deal for making local calls.

Using Hotel-Room Phones, VoIP, or US Calling Cards

The best way to call home is using an international phone card, but here are some other alternatives.

The phone in your **hotel room** is convenient...but expensive. While incoming calls (made by folks back home) can be an affordable way to keep in touch, charges for *outgoing* calls can be a very unpleasant surprise. Make sure you understand all the charges and fees associated with outgoing calls before you pick up that receiver.

Dialing direct from your hotel room—without using an international phone card (described above)—is usually quite expensive for international calls. Always ask first how much you'll be charged, even for local and (supposedly) toll-free calls.

If your family has an inexpensive way to call Europe, either through a long-distance plan or prepaid calling card, have them call you in your hotel room. Give them a list of your hotels' phone numbers before you go. Then, as you travel, send them an email or make a quick pay-phone call to set up a time for them to give you a ring.

If you're traveling with a laptop, consider trying **VoIP (Voice over Internet Protocol).** With VoIP, two computers act as the phones, allowing for a free Internet-based call. The major providers are Skype (www.skype.com) and Google Talk (www.google.com/talk).

US Calling Cards (such as the ones offered by AT&T, MCI, or Sprint) are the worst option. You'll nearly always save a lot of money by paying with a phone card (see above).

How to Dial

Calling from the US to Europe, or vice versa, is simple—once you break the code. The European calling chart on page 778 will walk you through it.

Dialing Within France

France has a direct-dial 10-digit phone system (no area codes). To call anywhere within France, just dial the number. For example, the number of one of my recommended hotels in Arles is 04 90 96 11 89. That's the number you dial whether you're calling it from the Arles train station or from Paris.

France's toll-free numbers start with 0800 (like US 800 numbers, though in France you don't dial a 1 first). In France, these

0800 numbers—called *numéro vert* (green number)—can be dialed free from any phone without using a phone card. Note that you can't call France's toll-free numbers from America, nor can you count on reaching America's toll-free numbers from France.

Note that any 08 number that does not have a 00 directly following is a toll call, generally costing €0.10 to €0.50 per minute. Many private companies and public services are changing to 08 numbers—expect some changes in telephone numbers.

Dialing Internationally

If you want to make an international call, follow these three steps:

1) Dial the international access code (00 if you're calling from Europe, 011 from the US or Canada).

2) Dial the country code of the country you're calling (33 for France, or 1 for the US or Canada).

3) Drop the initial zero of the 10-digit local number and dial the remaining nine digits.

For example, to call the recommended Arles hotel from the US, dial 011 (the US international access code), 33 (France's country code), then 4 90 96 11 89.

To call my office in Edmonds, Washington, from France, I dial 00 (Europe's international access code), 1 (the US country code), 425 (Edmonds' area code), and 771-8303.

Useful Phone Numbers

Consulates and Embassies

US Consulate in Nice: tel. 04 93 88 89 55, fax 04 93 87 07 38 (7 avenue Gustave V, does *not* provide visa services—Paris is the nearest office for these services)

Canadian Consulate in Nice: tel. 04 93 92 93 22, fax 04 93 92 55 51 (10 rue Lamartine)

US Consulate in Marseille: tel. 04 91 54 92 00, fax 04 91 55 09 47 (place Varian Fry)

US Consulate in Paris: tel. 01 43 12 22 22, passport services open Mon–Fri 9:00–12:00, closed Sat–Sun (2 rue St. Florentin, Mo: Concorde, www.amb-usa.fr)

US Embassy in Paris: tel. 01 43 12 22 22 (2 avenue Gabriel, to the left as you face Hôtel Crillon, Mo: Concorde)

Canadian Consulate and Embassy in Paris: tel. 01 44 43 29 02, open Mon–Fri 14:30–16:30, closed Sat–Sun (35 avenue Montaigne, Mo: Franklin D. Roosevelt, www.amb-canada.fr)

Australian Consulate in Paris: tel. 01 40 59 33 00, open Mon–Fri 9:00–16:00, closed Sat–Sun (4 rue Jean Ray, Mo: Bir-Hakeim, www.france.embassy.gov.au)

US Consulate in Strasbourg: tel. 03 88 35 31 04, fax 03 88 23 07 17 (15 rue d'Alsace)

European Calling Chart

Just smile and dial, using this key:
AC = Area Code, LN = Local Number.

European Country	Calling long distance within ...	Calling from the US or Canada to ...	Calling from a European country to ...
Austria	AC + LN	011 + 43 + AC (without the initial zero) + LN	00 + 43 + AC (without the initial zero) + LN
Belgium	LN	011 + 32 + LN (without initial zero)	00 + 32 + LN (without initial zero)
Bosnia-Herzegovina	AC + LN	011 + 387 + AC (without initial zero) + LN	00 + 387 + AC (without initial zero) + LN
Britain	AC + LN	011 + 44 + AC (without initial zero) + LN	00 + 44 + AC (without initial zero) + LN
Croatia	AC + LN	011 + 385 + AC (without initial zero) + LN	00 + 385 + AC (without initial zero) + LN
Czech Republic	LN	011 + 420 + LN	00 + 420 + LN
Denmark	LN	011 + 45 + LN	00 + 45 + LN
Estonia	LN	011 + 372 + LN	00 + 372 + LN
Finland	AC + LN	011 + 358 + AC (without initial zero) + LN	999 + 358 + AC (without initial zero) + LN
France	LN	011 + 33 + LN (without initial zero)	00 + 33 + LN (without initial zero)
Germany	AC + LN	011 + 49 + AC (without initial zero) + LN	00 + 49 + AC (without initial zero) + LN
Greece	LN	011 + 30 + LN	00 + 30 + LN
Hungary	06 + AC + LN	011 + 36 + AC + LN	00 + 36 + AC + LN
Ireland	AC + LN	011 + 353 + AC (without initial zero) + LN	00 + 353 + AC (without initial zero) + LN

European Country	Calling long distance within ...	Calling from the US or Canada to ...	Calling from a European country to ...
Italy	LN	011 + 39 + LN	00 + 39 + LN
Montenegro	AC + LN	011 + 382 + AC (without initial zero) + LN	00 + 382 + AC (without initial zero) + LN
Netherlands	AC + LN	011 + 31 + AC (without initial zero) + LN	00 + 31 + AC (without initial zero) + LN
Norway	LN	011 + 47 + LN	00 + 47 + LN
Poland	LN	011 + 48 + LN (without initial zero)	00 + 48 + LN (without initial zero)
Portugal	LN	011 + 351 + LN	00 + 351 + LN
Slovakia	AC + LN	011 + 421 + AC (without initial zero) + LN	00 + 421 + AC (without initial zero) + LN
Slovenia	AC + LN	011 + 386 + AC (without initial zero) + LN	00 + 386 + AC (without initial zero) + LN
Spain	LN	011 + 34 + LN	00 + 34 + LN
Sweden	AC + LN	011 + 46 + AC (without initial zero) + LN	00 + 46 + AC (without initial zero) + LN
Switzerland	LN	011 + 41 + LN (without initial zero)	00 + 41 + LN (without initial zero)
Turkey	AC (if no initial zero is included, add one) + LN	011 + 90 + AC (without initial zero) + LN	00 + 90 + AC (without initial zero) + LN

- The instructions above apply whether you're calling a land line or mobile phone.
- The international access codes (the first numbers you dial when making an international call) are 011 if you're calling from the US or Canada, or 00 if you're calling from virtually anywhere in Europe (except Finland, where it's 999).
- To call the US or Canada from Europe, dial 00, then 1 (the country code for the US and Canada), then the area code and number. In short, 00 + 1 + AC + LN = Hi, Mom!

US Consulate in Lyon: tel. 04 78 38 36 88 (1 quai Jules Courmant)
Canadian Consulate in Lyon: tel. 04 72 77 64 07 (21 rue Bourgelat)

Emergency/Medical Needs
Police: tel. 17
Emergency Medical Assistance: tel. 15

Travel Advisories
US Department of State: tel. 202/647-5225, www.travel.state.gov
Canadian Department of Foreign Affairs: Canadian tel. 800-267-6788, www.dfait-maeci.gc.ca
US Centers for Disease Control and Prevention: tel. 877-FYI-TRIP, www.cdc.gov/travel

Directory Assistance
Directory Assistance for France (some English spoken): tel. 12
Tourist Information Offices: To call any TI in France, dial 3265 and say the name of the city in your best French accent (€0.34/min)
Collect Calls to the US: tel. 00 00 11

Paris Information
Tourist Information: tel. 08 92 68 30 00 (recorded info with long menu, €0.34/min), www.parisinfo.com
American Church: tel. 01 40 62 05 00, www.acparis.org
American Hospital: tel. 01 46 41 25 25, www.american-hospital.org

Trains
Train (SNCF) Reservations and Information: tel. 3635

Airports
Nice: Aéroport de Nice—tel. 04 93 21 30 30, www.nice.aeroport.fr
Marseille: Aéroport Marseille–Provence—tel. 04 42 14 14 14, www.marseille.aeroport.fr
Paris: Aéroports Charles de Gaulle and Orly share the same numbers—tel. 3950 (€.39/min), www.adp.fr
Lyon: Saint-Exupéry Airport—€0.15/min toll tel. 08 26 80 08 26, www.lyon.aeroport.fr

Airlines
The following 08 numbers are toll calls; the per-minute fee generally ranges from €0.10 to €0.50.

Aer Lingus: tel. 08 21 23 02 67
Air Canada: tel. 08 25 88 08 81
Air France: tel. 08 20 82 08 20 or 08 20 82 36 54
Alitalia: tel. 08 02 31 53 15
American Airlines: tel. 08 10 87 28 72
Austrian Airlines: tel. 08 02 81 68 16
BMI British Midlands: tel. 01 41 91 87 04
British Airways: tel. 08 25 82 54 00
Continental: tel. 01 71 23 03 35
Delta: tel. 08 11 64 00 05
EasyJet: tel. 08 99 70 00 41
Iberia: tel. 08 25 80 09 65
Icelandair: tel. 01 44 51 60 51
KLM: tel. 08 90 71 07 10
Lufthansa: tel. 08 26 10 33 34
Northwest: tel. 08 90 71 07 10
Olympic: tel. 01 44 94 58 58
Royal Air Maroc: tel. 08 20 82 18 21
SAS: tel. 08 25 32 53 35
Swiss: tel. 08 20 04 05 06
United: tel. 08 10 72 72 72
US Airways: tel. 08 10 63 22 22

Car Leasing in France
Europe by Car: US tel. 800-223-1516, www.europebycar.com
Auto France: US tel. 800-572-9655, US fax 201/729-1917, www
.autofrance.net

Hotel Chains
Huge Chain of Hotels: www.accorhotels.com (handles Ibis,
Mercure, and Novotel hotels); US tel. 800-515-5679
Ibis Hotels: www.ibishotel.com, tel. 08 92 68 66 86; from US dial
011 33 8 92 68 66 86
Formule 1 Hotels: www.hotelformule1.com, tel. 08 92 68 56 85
(€0.34/min)
Mercure Hotels: www.mercure.com, tel. 08 25 88 33 33, US tel.
800-221-4542
Kyriad Hotels: www.kyriad.com, tel. 08 25 00 30 03; from US
dial 011 33 1 64 62 46 46
Best Western Hotels: www.bestwestern.com, tel. 08 00 90 44 90,
US tel. 800-428-2627
Château Hotels: www.chateaucountry.com
Country Home Rental: www.gites-de-france.fr/eng or www.gite
.com

The Language Barrier and that French Attitude

You've no doubt heard that the French are "mean and cold and refuse to speak English." This is an out-of-date preconception left over from the days of Charles de Gaulle. Be reasonable in your expectations: Waiters are paid to be efficient, not chatty. And postal clerks are every bit as speedy, cheery, and multilingual as ours are back home.

The biggest mistake most Americans make when traveling to France is trying to do too much with limited time. This approach is a mistake in the bustling north, and a virtual sin in the relaxed south. Hurried, impatient travelers who miss the subtle pleasures of people-watching from a sun-dappled café often misinterpret French attitudes. By slowing your pace and making an effort to understand French culture by living it, you're much more likely to have a richer experience. With the five weeks of paid vacation and 35-hour work week that many French workers get as non-negotiable rights, your hosts can't comprehend why anyone would rush through their vacation.

The French take great pride in their customs, clinging to their belief in cultural superiority despite the fact that they're no longer a world superpower. Let's face it: It's tough to keep on smiling when you've been crushed by a Big Mac, Mickey Moused by Disney, and drowned in instant coffee. Your hosts are cold only if you decide to see them that way. Polite and formal, the French respect the fine points of culture and tradition. Here, strolling

Youth Hostels

Hostelling International, US Office: www.hiayh.org
Hostelling International, Canada Office: www.hostellingintl.ca

Email and Mail

Email: Many travelers set up a free email account with Yahoo, Microsoft (Hotmail), or Google (Gmail). Email use among European hoteliers is quite common.

In France's key cities—such as Paris, Nice, Lyon, and Avignon—you'll find plenty of coffee shops offering wireless connections (Wi-Fi, pronounced "wee-fee" by the French) to travelers with laptop computers. Little hole-in-the-wall Internet-access shops, while common in the rest of Europe, are not prevalent in France. Post offices are a good solution in smaller towns offering Internet access (*cyberposte*); buy a chip-card (about same prices as phone cards, rechargeable for €4 per hour) and you're in business.

More and more hotels now offer their guests Internet access in their lobbies from a terminal (which may be free or operated

down the street with a big grin on your face and saying hello to strangers is a sign of senility, not friendliness (seriously). They think that Americans, while friendly, are hesitant to pursue more serious friendships. Recognize sincerity and look for kindness. Give them the benefit of the doubt.

French communication difficulties are exaggerated. To hurdle the language barrier, bring a small English/French dictionary, a phrase book (look for mine, which contains a dictionary and menu decoder), a menu reader (if you're a gourmet eater), and a good supply of patience. In transactions, a small notepad and pen minimize misunderstandings about prices; have vendors write the price down. If you learn only five phrases, learn and use these: *bonjour* (good day), *pardon* (pardon me), *s'il vous plaît* (please), *merci* (thank you), and *au revoir* (goodbye). The French place great importance on politeness. Begin every encounter with *"Bonjour (or S'il vous plaît), madame/monsieur"* and end every encounter with *"Au revoir, madame/monsieur."*

The French are language perfectionists—they take their language (and other languages) seriously. Often they speak more English than they let on. This isn't a tourist-baiting tactic, but timidity on their part about speaking another language less than fluently. Start any conversation with, *"Bonjour, madame/monsieur. Parlez-vous anglais?"* and hope they speak more English than you speak French.

with coins or a telephone card); the access is usually slow, though you'll probably be slow, too, getting used to a French keyboard. Every year, more hotels offer Wi-Fi (sometimes free, sometimes for a charge). And some even have laptop loaners. Ask if your hotel has access. If it doesn't, your hotelier will direct you to the nearest place to get online.

Mail: French post offices are sometimes called PTT, for "Post, Telegraph, and Telephone"—look for *La Poste* signs. Hours vary, though most are open weekdays 8:00–19:00 and Saturday morning 8:00–12:00. Stamps and phone cards are also sold at *tabac* (tobacco) shops. It costs about €0.90 to mail a postcard to the US. While you can arrange for mail delivery to your hotel (allow 10 days for a letter to arrive), phoning and emailing are so easy that I've dispensed with mail stops altogether. Federal Express makes pricey two-day deliveries.

One convenient, if pricey, way to send packages home is by using the PTT's Colissimo XL postage-paid mailing box. It costs about €33 for the International version, which allows you to send home all the goodies you can stuff into an 18" × 12" × 8" box (no weight limit).

TRANSPORTATION

By Car or Train?

Cars are best for three or more traveling together (especially families with small kids), those packing heavy, and those scouring the countryside. Trains and buses are best for solo travelers, blitz tourists, and city-to-city travelers. Train stations are usually centrally located in cities, which makes hotel-hunting and sightseeing easy. But in France, many of your destinations are likely to be small, remote places, such as Honfleur, Mont St. Michel, D-Day beaches, Loire châteaux, Dordogne caves, and villages in Provence and Burgundy. In such places, trains and buses can require great patience, planning, and time. If relying on public transportation, seriously consider the value of the minivan excursion tours listed throughout this book and focus more time on fewer key destinations. You won't regret it.

Trains

France's rail system (SNCF) sets the pace in Europe. Its super TGV (tay zhay vay; *train à grande vitesse*) system has inspired bullet trains throughout the world. The TGV runs at 170 to 220 mph. Its rails are fused into one long, continuous track for a faster and smoother ride. The TGV has changed commuting patterns in much of France by putting most of the country within day-trip distance of Paris. New in 2007, the TGV Est to Strasbourg and beyond is just the latest link in the grand European train system of the 21st century.

At any train station, you can get schedule information, make reservations, and buy tickets for any destination.

Schedules

Schedules change by season, weekday, and weekend. Verify train times shown in this book—on the Web, check http://bahn.hafas .de/bin/query.exe/en. You can also book and print tickets and reservations online at www.sncf.com (click on British flag for English)—where you may also find some cheaper tickets.

Bigger stations have helpful information agents (often wearing red vests) roaming the station and at *Accueil* offices or booths. They can answer rail questions more quickly than the information or ticket windows. Make use of these people; don't stand in a ticket line if all you need is a train schedule.

The nationwide information phone line for train schedules, reservations, and even purchasing tickets is 3635. Dial this four-

France Train Terms and Abbreviations

SNCF *(Société Nationale Chemins de Fer):* This is the Amtrak of France, operating all national train lines that link cities and towns.

TGV *(Train à Grande Vitesse):* SNCF's network of high-speed trains (twice as fast as regular trains) that connect major cities in France. These trains always require a reservation.

CORAIL: These trains are next best compared to the TGV in terms of speed and comfort.

TER *(Trains Express Régionale):* These trains serve smaller stops within a region. For example, you'll find trains called TER de Bourgogne (trains operating only in Burgundy) and TER Provence (Provence-only trains).

Paris Region Only

For more on Paris transit, see "Getting Around Paris," page 44.

RATP *(Réseau Autonome de Transport Parisienne):* This organization operates subways and buses within Paris.

Le Métro: This network of subway lines serves central Paris.

RER *(Réseau Express Régional):* This commuter rail and subway system links central Paris with suburban destinations.

Transilien: It's similar to the RER system, but travels farther afield, serving the Ile de France region around Paris. Railpasses cover these lines.

digit number, then press 3, then press 1 (trust me) for reservations or ticket purchase (you may be sent to a French-only phone tree as SNCF tries to automate its services; if so, hang up and ask your hotelier for help). Press 321 for Eurostar (London via Chunnel) information, or 322 for Thalys (high-speed trains to Brussels and Amsterdam). This incredibly helpful, time-saving service costs €0.34 per minute from anywhere in France. Ask for an English-speaking agent and hope for the best (allow 5 min per call). The time and energy you save easily justifies the telephone torture, particularly when making seat reservations (note that phoned-in reservations must be picked up at the station at least 30 minutes prior to departure).

Railpasses

Long-distance travelers can save big money with a France Railpass, sold only outside Europe (through travel agents or Europe Through the Back Door; see railpass sidebar on page 788). For roughly the cost of a Paris–Avignon–Paris ticket, the France Railpass offers

Whirlwind Three-Week Tour of France by Train and Bus

This itinerary is designed for train travelers. To do this trip by train and bus, make liberal use of minivan tours and taxis. A France Flexipass with nine train days—buying tickets in France for days 5, 7 and 14 (short and cheap trips)—works fine. A France Rail and Drive Pass is another good option. A car is especially handy for exploring Normandy, the Dordogne, and Provence. If you only have two weeks, end your tour in Nice and skip Honfleur. *Bonne route* and *bon courage!*

Day	Plan
1	Fly into Paris.
2	Sightsee Paris.
3	More time in Paris.
4	Train and bus to Mont St. Michel via Rennes (4 hrs, arrive on Mont St. Michel about 13:00). Afternoon and night on Mont St Michel.
5	Train to Bayeux (2 hrs, arrive about 11:45) Afternoon for visiting Bayeux. Sleep in Bayeux.
6	All day for D-Day beaches by minivan, taxi, bike, bus, or a combination of these. Sleep in Bayeux.
7	Train to Caen, then bus to Honfleur (2 hrs). Sleep in Honfleur.
8	Bus to Lisieux or Deauville then train to Paris. Transfer to Gare d'Austerlitz and take the train to Amboise (7 hrs total). Sleep in Amboise.
9	All day for touring Loire châteaux (good options by bus, bike or minivan tour). Sleep in Amboise.

three days of travel (within a month) anywhere in France. You can add up to six additional days for the cost of a two-hour ride each. Save money by getting the second-class instead of the first-class version and/or travel with a companion (the Flexi Saverpass gives 2 people traveling together a 20 percent discount). Each day of use allows you to take as many trips as you want on one calendar day (you could go from Paris to Beaune in Burgundy, enjoy wine-tasting, then continue to Avignon, stay a few hours, and end in Nice—though I wouldn't recommend it). Buy second-class tickets in France for shorter trips. Note that if you're connecting the French Alps with Alsace, you might travel through Switzerland, requiring France railpass holders to buy a ticket for that segment (about €50).

If traveling *sans* railpass, inquire about the many point-to-point discount fares possible (for youths, those over 60, married couples,

10 Train to Sarlat (5 hrs, arrive about 15:00). Afternoon and evening in Sarlat. Sleep in Sarlat.

11 All day for caves and canoes by bike or minivan/taxi tour. Sleep in Sarlat.

12 Train to Carcassonne (5.5 hrs, leaving about noon is best, though earlier trips are possible). Dinner and evening wall walk. Sleep in Carcassonne.

13 Morning wall walk, then train to Arles (2.5 hrs). Afternoon in Arles.

14 Train to Nîmes, then bus to Pont du Gard. Tour the Pont du Gard, then bus to Avignon and spend your afternoon/evening there (consider dinner). Train back to Arles. Sleep in Arles.

15 Morning in Arles or Les Baux (by taxi or tour), afternoon train to Nice (4 hrs), set up in Nice. Sleep in Nice.

16 All day for Nice and Monaco. Sleep in Nice.

17 Morning train to Lyon (4 hrs). Afternoon and night in Lyon.

18 Train to Chamonix (4 hrs, consider a halfway stopover in Annecy—easy bag check). Sleep in Chamonix.

19 With clear weather, take the mountain lifts up to Aiguille du Midi and beyond. Sleep in Chamonix.

20 Early train to Paris (arrive about 13:30). Last afternoon and night in Paris. (Or make it a 23-day tour with a scenic, 6.5-hr train through Switzerland to Colmar, spend two nights there, then take the TGV back to Paris.)

21 Fly home.

families, travel during off-peak hours, and more). Remember that second-class tickets provide the same transportation for up to 33 percent less (and many regional trains to less-trafficked places often have only second-class cars).

Families should ask about cheap Discovery fares. Travelers of any age can choose first or second class with the France Railpass. (But travelers who want a Eurailpass—and are 26 or older—must buy a first-class pass.) You can buy tickets on the train for a €4 surcharge, but you must find the conductor immediately on boarding, otherwise it's a €35 minimum charge.

Reservations

Reservations, while generally unnecessary for non-TGV trains, are advisable during busy times (e.g., Fri and Sun afternoons, weekday rush hours, and particularly holiday weekends; see "Major

Cost of Railpasses

Prices listed are for 2008 and are subject to change. For the latest prices, details, and train schedules (and easy online ordering), see my comprehensive *Guide to Eurail Passes* at www.ricksteves.com/rail.

"Saver" prices are per person for two or more people traveling together. "Youth" means under age 26. The fare for children 4–11 is half the adult individual fare or Saver fare. Kids under age 4 travel free.

FRANCE PASS

	Adult 1st Class	Adult 2nd Class	Senior 1st Class	Youth 1st Class	Youth 2nd Class
3 days in 1 month	$304	$258	$278	$225	$191
Extra rail days (max 6)	44	37	39	31	28

Senior = 60 and up.

FRANCE SAVERPASS

	1st Class	2nd Class
3 days in 1 month	$259	$222
Extra rail days (max 6)	37	31

FRANCE RAIL & DRIVE PASS

Any 2 rail days and 2 car days in 1 month.

Car Category	1st Class	Extra Car Day
Economy	$271	$55
Compact	286	70
Intermediate	293	77
Full-size	335	119
Premium Automatic	363	147
Minivan	396	180

Prices are per person, two traveling together. Solo travelers pay about $100 extra; third and fourth adults pay $207 per person. Extra rail days (3 max) cost $36 per day. To order a Rail & Drive pass, call your travel agent or Rail Europe at 800-438-7245. *This pass is not sold by Europe Through the Back Door.*

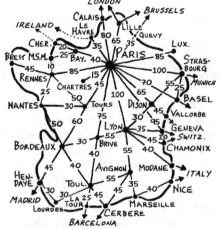

Map key:
Approximate point-to-point one-way second-class rail fares in US dollars. First class costs 50 percent more. Add up fares for your itinerary to see if a railpass will save you money.

SELECTPASS

This pass covers travel in three adjacent countries. For four- and five-country options, please visit **www.ricksteves.com/rail**.

	Individual 1st Class	Saver 1st Class	Youth 2nd Class
5 days in 2 months	$473	$402	$307
6 days in 2 months	522	445	342
8 days in 2 months	619	529	402
10 days in 2 months	717	607	464

FRANCE–SWITZERLAND PASS

	Individual 1st Class	Saver 1st Class	Youth 2nd Class
4 days in 2 months	$400	$340	$281
Extra rail days (max 6)	45	39	31

FRANCE–ITALY PASS

	Individual 1st Class	Individual 2nd Class	Saver 1st Class	Saver 2nd Class	Youth 2nd Class
4 days in 2 months	$381	$332	$332	$293	$250
Extra rail days (max 6)	44	38	38	33	30

Be aware of your route. Many daytime connections from Paris to Italy pass through Switzerland (an additional $60 in second class or $90 in first class if not covered by your pass). Routes via Nice, Torino, or Modane will bypass Switzerland. Paris–Italy trains are covered by the pass, regardless of their route.

FRANCE–SPAIN PASS

	Individual 1st Class	Individual 2nd Class	Saver 1st Class	Saver 2nd Class	Youth 2nd Class
4 days in 2 months	$381	$332	$332	$293	$250
Extra rail days (max 6)	44	38	38	33	30

If you're only dipping into a bit of Spain, you may not need the France–Spain pass. For instance, a ticket from the French border at Cerbère to Barcelona costs only $25. From the border at Hendaye to Madrid costs $50, but if you cover this ground via the fancy Paris–Madrid "Elipsos" night train, the same passholder fares ($70 and up) apply whether your pass covers one or both countries.

FRANCE–GERMANY PASS

	Individual 1st Class	Individual 2nd Class	Saver 1st Class	Saver 2nd Class	Youth 2nd Class
4 days in 2 months	$410	$370	$370	$334	$286
5 days in 2 months	454	407	407	365	318
6 days in 2 months	497	447	447	396	349
8 days in 2 months	583	524	524	457	410
10 days in 2 months	668	600	600	520	473

FRANCE–BENELUX PASS

	Individual 1st Class	Individual 2nd Class	Saver 1st Class	Saver 2nd Class	Youth 2nd Class
4 days in 2 months	$367	$323	$313	$276	$239
5 days in 2 months	403	360	342	307	269
6 days in 2 months	442	396	375	337	300
8 days in 2 months	515	471	438	402	360
10 days in 2 months	590	546	501	464	419

The French Rail System

Holidays and Weekends," page 5). Reservations are required for any TGV train (usually €3, more during peak periods), for selected other routes, and for *couchettes* (berths, €15) on night trains. Even railpass-holders need reservations for the TGV trains, and only a limited number of reservations are available for passholders. To avoid the more expensive fares, avoid traveling at peak times; ask at the station. You are required to validate (*composter*, kohm-poh-stay) all train tickets and reservations. Before boarding any SNCF train, look for a machine nearby to stamp your ticket or reservation. (Do not *composte* your railpass, but do validate it at a ticket window before the first time you use it.) Watch others and imitate.

Baggage check *(consigne)* is available only at the biggest train stations (about €4–8 per bag depending on size), and is noted where available in this book (depends on security concerns, so be prepared to keep your bag). For security reasons, all luggage must carry a tag with the traveler's first and last name and current address. This applies to hand luggage as well as bigger bags that are stowed. Free tags are available at all trains stations in France.

For mixing train and bike travel, ask at stations for informa-tion booklets *(Train + Vélo).*

Automatic Train Ticket Machines

The ticket machines available at most stations are great time-savers when ticket window lines are long (but your American credit card won't work so you'll need euro coins). Some have English instruc-tions, but for those that don't, here is what you are prompted to do. (The default is usually what you want; turn the dial or move the cursor to your choice, and press *"Validez"* to agree to each step.)

1. *Quelle est votre destination?* (What's your destination?)
2. *Billet Plein Tarif* (Full-fare ticket—yes for most.)
3. *1ère ou 2ème* (First or second class; normally second is fine.)
4. *Aller simple ou aller-retour?* (One-way or round-trip?)
5. *Prix en Euro* (The price should be shown if you get this far.)

Train Tips

- Arrive at the station with plenty of time before your departure to find the right platform, confirm connections, and so on. In small towns, your train may depart before the station opens; if so, go directly to the tracks and find the overhead sign that confirms your train stops at that track.
- Larger stations have platforms with monitors showing each car's layout (numbered forward or backward) so you can fig-ure out where your *voiture* will stop on the long platform and where to board each car. Notice the low baggage area placed every two cars—people use it to avoid hoisting their suitcases to the high overhead rack.
- Check schedules in advance. Upon arrival at a station, learn your departure possibilities. Large stations have a separate information window or office; at small stations, the ticket office gives information.
- If you have a rail flexipass, write the date on your "flexi" rail-pass each day you travel (before you board your first train).
- Validate tickets (not passes) and reservations in yellow machines before boarding. If you're traveling with a pass and have a reservation for a certain trip, you must validate the res-ervation.
- Reservations for all TGV trains are required and often sell out. You can reserve any train at any station, by telephone (dial 3635), or through SNCF Boutiques (small offices in city centers). A limited number of reservations are allocated for

railpass users during peak times—reserve as far ahead as you can for Friday and Sunday afternoons and Saturday mornings.

- Before getting on a train, confirm that it's going where you think it is. For example, if you want to go to Bayeux, ask the conductor or any local passenger, *"A Bayeux?"* (ah bah-yuh; meaning, "To Bayeux?").
- Some trains split cars en route. Make sure your train car is continuing to your destination by asking, for example, *"Cette voiture va à Bayeux?"* (set vwah-toor vah ah bah-yuh; meaning, "This car goes to Bayeux?").
- If a non-TGV train seat is reserved, it will usually be labeled *réservé*, with the cities to and from which it is reserved.
- Verify with the conductor all of the transfers you must make: *"Correspondance à?";* meaning, "Transfer to where?".
- To guard against theft, it's best to keep your bags right overhead. If you store them at the end of the car, make sure you can see them from your seat (they're most vulnerable to theft when the train stops).
- Note your arrival time, so you'll be ready to get off.
- Use the trains' free WCs before you get off (but not while the train is stopped).

Buses

Regional bus service takes over where the trains stop. You can get nearly anywhere in France by rail and bus...if you're well-organized, patient, and allow enough time. Review my bus schedule information and always verify times at the local tourist office or bus station; call ahead when possible. A handful of bus lines are run by SNCF (France's rail system) and are included with your railpass (show railpass at station to get free bus ticket), but most bus lines are independent of the rail system and are not covered by railpasses. Train stations often have bus information where train-to-bus connections are important—and vice versa for bus companies. On Sunday, regional bus service virtually disappears.

Bus Tips

- Read the train tips above, and use those that apply.
- TIs often have regional bus schedules and can help plan your trip.
- Remember that service is sparse or even nonexistent on Sunday. Wednesday bus schedules are often different during the school year, since school is out this day.
- Be at stops at least five minutes early.
- On schedules, *en semaine* means Monday through Saturday, *dimanche* is Sunday, and *jours fériés* are holidays.

Key Travel Phrases

Bonjour, monsieur/madame, parlez-vous anglais?
Pron: bohn-zhoor, muhs-yur/mah-dahm, par-lay-voo ahn-glay?
Meaning: Hello, sir/madam, do you speak English?

Je voudrais un départ pour (destination), **pour le** (date), **vers** (general time of day), **la plus direct possible.**
Pron: zhuh voo-dray uhn day-par poor (destination), poor luh (date), vehr (time), lah ploo dee-rehk poh-see-bluh.
Meaning/Example: I would like a departure for Avignon, on 23 May, about 9:00, the most direct way possible.

Regional Minivan Excursions

Worthwhile day tours are generally available in regions where bus and train service is sparse. For the D-Day beaches, châteaux of the Loire Valley, Dordogne Valley villages and caves, Provence's villages and vineyards, the Route du Vin (Wine Road) in Alsace, and wine-tasting in Burgundy, I list reliable companies that provide this helpful service at reasonable rates. Some of these minivan excursions offer just transportation between the sights; others add a running commentary and information on regional history.

Renting a Car

To rent a car in France, you must be at least 18 years old and have held your license for one year. Although an International Driving Permit is not required if your driver's license has been renewed within the last year, play it safe and get one anyway ($15 through AAA, plus two passport photos, www.aaa.com).

Drivers under the age of 25 may incur a young-driver surcharge, and some rental companies do not rent to anyone 75 and over. If you're considered too young or old, look into leasing, which has less-stringent age restrictions (see "Leasing," page 795).

Research car rentals before you go. It's cheaper to arrange most car rentals from the US. Call several companies and look online to compare rates, or arrange a rental through your hometown travel agent. Two reputable companies among many are Auto Europe (www.autoeurope.com) and Europe by Car (www.europebycar .com). Rent by the week with unlimited mileage. I normally rent the smallest, least-expensive model with a stick-shift (cheaper than an automatic). For a three-week rental, allow $800 per person (based on two people sharing a car), including insurance, tolls, gas, and parking. For long trips, consider leasing (see below); you'll save money on insurance and taxes. Compare pick-up costs (downtown can be cheaper than the airport) and explore drop-off options. Returning a car at a big-city train station can be tricky; get precise details on the car drop-off location and hours.

When picking up the car, check it thoroughly and make sure any damage is noted on your rental agreement. Find out how your car's lights, turn signals, wipers, and gas cap function. When you return the car, make sure the agent verifies its condition with you.

If you want a car for only a day or two (e.g., for the D-Day beaches or Loire châteaux), you'll likely find it cheaper to rent it in France—most US-arranged rentals make financial sense only for three days or more. You can rent a car on the spot just about anywhere in France. In many cases, this is a worthwhile splurge. All you need is your American driver's license and a major credit card (figure €65–80/day, including 100 kilometers, or 60 miles, per day).

A **rail-and-drive pass** (such as a EurailDrive, Selectpass Drive, or France Rail and Drive) allows you to mix car and train travel economically (sold only outside France, from your travel agent). Generally big-city connections are best done by train, and rural regions are best done by car. With a rail-and-drive pass, you can take advantage of the speed and comfort of the TGV trains for longer trips, and rent a car for as little as one day at a time for day trips that can't be done without one (such as the Loire, the Dordogne, and Provence).

The basic France Rail and Drive Pass comes with two days of car rental and three days of rail in two months. You can pick up a car in one city and drop it off in another. Though you're only required to reserve the first car day, it's safer to reserve all days, as cars are not always available on short notice.

Car Insurance Options

When you rent a car, you are liable for a very high deductible, sometimes equal to the entire value of the car. There are various ways you can limit your financial risk in case of an accident. For France, you have three options: buy Collision Damage Waiver (CDW) coverage from the car-rental company (figure roughly 25 percent extra), a travel insurance company, or get coverage through your credit card (free, if your card automatically includes zero-deductible coverage).

CDW includes a very high deductible (typically $1,000–1,500). When you pick up the car, you'll be offered the chance to "buy down" the deductible to zero (for $10–30/day; this is often called "super CDW").

If you opt for credit-card coverage, there's a catch. You'll technically have to decline all coverage offered by the car-rental company, which means they can place a hold on your card for the full deductible amount. In case of damage, it can be time-consuming to resolve the charges with your credit-card company. Before you decide on this option, quiz your credit-card company about how it works and ask them to explain the worst-case scenario.

Buying CDW insurance (plus "super CDW") is the easier but pricier option. Using the coverage that comes with your credit card saves money, but can involve more hassle. For longer trips, leasing—which includes taxes and insurance—is worthwhile.

Finally, you can buy CDW insurance from Travel Guard ($9/day plus a one-time $3 service fee covers you up to $35,000, $250 deductible, tel. 800-826-4919, www.travelguard.com). It's valid throughout Europe, but some car-rental companies refuse to honor it (especially in Italy and the Republic of Ireland). Oddly, residents of Washington state aren't allowed to buy this coverage.

For more fine print about car-rental insurance, see www.ricksteves.com/cdw.

Leasing

For trips of two and a half weeks or more, leasing (which automatically includes CDW-like insurance) is the best way to go. By technically buying and then selling back the car, you save lots of money on tax and insurance. Leasing provides you a brand-new car with unlimited mileage and a 24-hour emergency assistance program. You can lease for little as 17 days to as long as 6 months. Car leases must be arranged from the US. Two reliable companies offering 17-day lease packages from about $950 for a small car ($1,300 for a midsize) are Auto France (US tel. 800-572-9655, fax 201/729-1917, www.autofrance.net) and Europe by Car (US tel. 800-223-1516, www.europebycar.com). Anyone age 18 or over with a driver's license is eligible, and you can pick up and/or drop off at several cities in France and throughout Europe. This is very appealing for those whose age excludes them from standard car rental.

Driving

An International Driving Permit is not necessary in France, though I recommend one (see "Renting a Car," page 793). Seat belts are mandatory for all, and children under age 10 must be in the back seat. Almost all rentals are manual by default, so if you need an automatic, you must request one in advance.

Gas *(essence)* is expensive—about $6 per gallon. Diesel *(gazole)* is less—about $5 per gallon—so rent a diesel car if you can. Gas is most expensive on autoroutes and cheapest at big supermarkets (closed at night and on Sun). Many gas stations close on Sunday.

Four hours on the autoroute costs about €25 in tolls, but the alternative to these super "feeways" usually means being marooned in countryside traffic. Autoroutes save enough time, gas, and

Whirlwind (Kamikaze) Three-Week Trip Through France for Drivers

Day Plan

1 Fly into Paris, pick up your car, visit Giverny and Honfleur, and overnight in Honfleur (1 night). Save Paris sightseeing for the end of your trip.

2 Spend today at D-Day sights: Arromanches, American Cemetery, and Pointe du Hoc (and Caen Memorial Museum, if time allows). Dinner and overnight in Bayeux (1 night).

3 Bayeux Tapestry and church, Mont St. Michel, sleep on Mont St. Michel (1 night).

4 Spend your morning on Mont St. Michel, then head for châteaux country in the Loire Valley. Tour Chambord, then stay in Amboise (2 nights).

5 Do a day trip, touring Chenonceaux and Cheverny or Chaumont. Save time at the end of the day for Amboise and its sights.

6 Head south to the Dordogne region, stopping at Oradour-sur-Glane en route. End in a Dordogne village—your choice of the handful I recommend (2 nights).

7 Browse the town and market of Sarlat and tour Font-de-Gaume cave.

8 Head to the Languedoc region, lunch in Puycelci or Albi, and spend the evening in Carcassonne (1 night).

9 Morning in Carcassonne, then on to Provence with a stop at the Pont du Gard aqueduct. Stay in Arles (2 nights).

10 All day for Arles and Les Baux.

11 Visit Avignon or a Provençal hilltown such as Roussillon, then depart for the Riviera, staying in Nice or Villefranche-sur-Mer (2 nights).

12 Sightsee in Nice and Monaco.

13 Make the long drive north to the Alps, and sleep in Chamonix (2 nights).

14 With clear weather, take the mountain lifts up to Aiguille du Midi and beyond.

15 A half-day for the Alps (in Chamonix or Annecy) Then head for Burgundy, ending in Beaune for a wine-tasting. Sleep in Beaune (1 night).

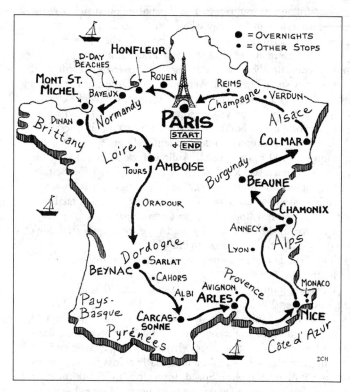

16 Spend the morning in Beaune, then move on to Colmar (2 nights).

17 Enjoy Colmar and the Route du Vin villages.

18 Return to Paris, visiting Verdun or Reims en route. Collapse in Paris hotel (4 nights).

19 Sightsee Paris.

20 More time in Paris.

21 Finish up your sightseeing in Paris, and consider side-tripping to Versailles.

nausea to justify the splurge. Mix high-speed "autorouting" with scenic country-road rambling. You'll usually take a ticket when entering an autoroute and pay when you leave. Shorter autoroute sections have periodic unmanned toll booths, where you can pay by dropping coins into a basket (change given, but keep a good supply of coins handy to avoid waiting) or by inserting a credit card (for even very small amounts). Autoroute gas stations usually come with well-stocked mini-marts, clean restrooms, sandwiches, maps, local products, and cheap vending-machine coffee (€1). Many have small cafés or more elaborate cafeterias with reasonable prices.

Roads are classified into departmental (D), national (N), and autoroutes (A). D routes (usually yellow lines on maps) are slow and often the most scenic. N routes (usually red lines) are the fastest after autoroutes (orange lines). Green road signs are for national routes; blue are for autoroutes. There are plenty of good facilities, gas stations, and rest stops along most French roads.

Because speed limits are by road type, they typically aren't posted, so it's best to memorize them:
- Two-lane D and N routes outside cities and towns: 90 km/hour
- Divided highways outside cities and towns: 110 km/hour
- Autoroutes: 130 km/hour

If it's raining, subtract 10 km/hour on D and N routes and 20 km/hour on divided highways and autoroutes. Speed limit signs are a red circle around a number; when you see that same number again in gray with a broken line diagonally across it, this means that limit no longer applies. Speed limits drop to 30–50 km/hour in villages (always posted) and must be respected. France has a new system of photo ticketing, where moveable cameras are carefully placed to trap the unsuspecting driver. They seem most common in 30–50 km/hour zones and will bust you even for going a few kilometers over the limit (believe me).

Parking is a headache in larger cities, and theft is a problem. Ask your hotelier for ideas, and pay to park at well-patrolled lots (blue *P* signs direct you to parking lots in French cities). Parking structures often require that you take a ticket with you and prepay at a machine (called a *caisse*, credit cards usually accepted) on your way back to the car. Overnight parking (usually 19:00–8:00) is generally very reasonable (except in Paris and Nice). Curbside metered parking also works (usually free 12:00–14:00 & 19:00–9:00, and all day and night in Aug). Look for a small machine selling time (called *horadateur*, usually one per block), plug in a few coins (€1.50 buys about an hour, though this varies by city), push the green button, get a receipt showing the amount of time you have, and display it inside your windshield.

Road Signs and Driving Tips

Instructional Signs that You Must Obey

Cédez le Passage	Yield
Priorité à Droite	Right-of-way is for cars coming from the right
Vous n'avez pas la priorité	You don't have the right of way (when merging)
Rappel	Remember to obey the sign
Déviation	Detour
Allumez vos feux	Turn on your lights
Doublage Interdit	No passing
Parking Interdit/ Stationnement Interdit	No parking

Signs for Your Information

Route Barrée	Road blocked
Sortie des Camions	Work truck exit
Centre Commercial	Grouping of large, suburban stores (not city center)
Centre-Ville	City center
Feux	Traffic signal
Horadateur	Remote parking meter, usually at the end of the block
Parc de Stationnement	Parking lot
Rue Piétonne	Pedestrian-only street
Sauf Riverains	Local access only

Signs Unique to Autoroutes

Aire	Rest stop with WCs, telephones, and sometimes gas stations
Bouchon	Traffic jam ahead
Fluide	No slowing ahead (fluid conditions)
Péage	Toll
Télépéage	Toll booths—automatic toll payment only
Toutes Directions	All directions (leaving city)
Autres Directions	Other directions (leaving city)
Par temps de Pluie	When raining (modifies speed limit signs)

Driving Tips

- Be aware that in city and town centers, traffic merging from the right normally has the right-of-way *(priorité à droite)*, even when merging on to a major road. In contrast, cars entering the many suburban roundabouts must yield *(cédez le passage)*.

- Be ready for many roundabouts—navigating them is an art. The key is to know your direction and be ready for your turnoff. If you miss it, just do another lap.

- When navigating through cities, approach intersections cautiously, stow the map, and follow the signs to *Centre-Ville* (city center). From there, head to the TI *(Office de Tourisme)*.

STOP AND LEARN THESE ROAD SIGNS

50 Speed Limit (km/hr)	**50** Speed Limit No Longer Applies
No Passing	End of No Passing Zone
SENS UNIQUE One Way	Intersection
Main Road	Freeway
Danger	No Entry
No Entry for Cars	All Vehicles Prohibited
P Parking	No Parking
DOUANE Customs	Yield

- When leaving or just passing through cities, follow the signs for *Toutes Directions* or *Autres Directions* (meaning "anywhere else") until you see a sign for your specific destination.

- Driving on any roads but autoroutes will take longer than you anticipated, so allow yourself plenty of time for slower traffic and deciphering hard-to-follow signs. First-timers should estimate how long they think a drive will take...then double it. I pretend that kilometers are miles (for distances) and base my time estimates accordingly. While locals are eating lunch (12:00–14:00), many sights (and gas stations) are closed, so you can make great time driving—but keep it slow when passing through villages.

- U-turns are illegal throughout France, and you cannot turn right on red lights.

- Be very careful when driving on smaller roads—many are narrow, flanked by little ditches that are easy to slide into. I've met several readers who "ditched" their cars (and were successfully pulled out by local farmers).

- On autoroutes, keep to the right lanes to let fast drivers by, and be careful when merging into a left lane, as cars can be coming at very high speeds. Cars and trucks commonly keep

Driving in France: Distance and Time

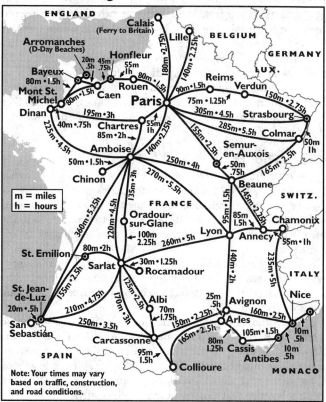

their left blinker on while in a passing lane, indicating that they plan to get back over to the right.

- Motorcycles will scream between cars in traffic. Be ready—they expect you to keep to the right in your lane to let them pass.
- Gas can be tricky to find in rural areas on Sunday, so fill up on Saturday. Autoroute filling stations are always open.
- Keep a stash of coins in your ashtray for parking and small autoroute tolls.

Biking

Throughout France, you'll find areas where public transportation is limited and bicycle touring might be a good idea. For many, biking is a romantic notion whose novelty wears off after the first hill or headwind—realistically evaluate your physical condition and be clear on the limitations bikes present. Start with an easy pedal to a nearby village or through the vineyards, then decide how ambitious you feel. Most find that two hours on a narrow, hard seat is enough. I've listed bike-rental shops where appropriate and suggested a few of my favorite rides. Local TIs always have addresses for bike-rental places. For a good touring bike, figure about €10 for a half-day and €16 for a full day. You'll pay more for better equipment; generally the best is available through bike shops, not at train stations or other outlets. French bikers often do not wear helmets, though most rental outfits have them (for a small fee).

Cheap Flights

If you're visiting one or more French cities on a longer European trip—or linking up far-flung French cities (such as Paris and Nice)—you might want to look into the affordable intra-European airlines. While trains are still the best way to connect places that are close together, a flight can save both time and money on long journeys.

One of the best websites for comparing inexpensive flights is www.skyscanner.net. Other comparison search engines include www.kayak.com, www.mobissimo.com, www.sidestep.com, and www.wegolo.com.

Well-known cheapo airlines include easyJet (www.easyjet .com) and Ryanair (www.ryanair.com). Be aware of the potential drawbacks of flying on the cheap: nonrefundable and nonchangeable tickets, rigid baggage restrictions (and fees if you have more than what's officially allowed), use of airports far outside town, tight schedules that can mean more delays, little in the way of customer assistance if problems arise, and, of course, no frills. To avoid unpleasant surprises, read the small print—especially baggage policies—before you book.

HOLIDAYS AND FESTIVALS

This list includes major festivals, plus national holidays observed throughout France. Many sights close down on national holidays, and weekends around those holidays are often wildly crowded with vacationers (book your hotel room for the entire holiday weekend well in advance). Note that this isn't a complete list; holidays often strike without warning. For more information, contact the France TI (listed at the beginning of the appendix).

Jan 1:	New Year's Day
Jan 6:	Epiphany
Feb 16–March 2:	Nice Carnival (Mardi Gras, parades, fireworks, www.nicecarnaval.com)

Appendix

2008

JANUARY
S	M	T	W	T	F	S
		1	2	3	4	5
6	7	8	9	10	11	12
13	14	15	16	17	18	19
20	21	22	23	24	25	26
27	28	29	30	31		

FEBRUARY
S	M	T	W	T	F	S
					1	2
3	4	5	6	7	8	9
10	11	12	13	14	15	16
17	18	19	20	21	22	23
24	25	26	27	28	29	

MARCH
S	M	T	W	T	F	S
						1
2	3	4	5	6	7	8
9	10	11	12	13	14	15
16	17	18	19	20	21	22
23/30	24/31	25	26	27	28	29

APRIL
S	M	T	W	T	F	S
		1	2	3	4	5
6	7	8	9	10	11	12
13	14	15	16	17	18	19
20	21	22	23	24	25	26
27	28	29	30			

MAY
S	M	T	W	T	F	S
				1	2	3
4	5	6	7	8	9	10
11	12	13	14	15	16	17
18	19	20	21	22	23	24
25	26	27	28	29	30	31

JUNE
S	M	T	W	T	F	S
1	2	3	4	5	6	7
8	9	10	11	12	13	14
15	16	17	18	19	20	21
22	23	24	25	26	27	28
29	30					

JULY
S	M	T	W	T	F	S
		1	2	3	4	5
6	7	8	9	10	11	12
13	14	15	16	17	18	19
20	21	22	23	24	25	26
27	28	29	30	31		

AUGUST
S	M	T	W	T	F	S
					1	2
3	4	5	6	7	8	9
10	11	12	13	14	15	16
17	18	19	20	21	22	23
24/31	25	26	27	28	29	30

SEPTEMBER
S	M	T	W	T	F	S
	1	2	3	4	5	6
7	8	9	10	11	12	13
14	15	16	17	18	19	20
21	22	23	24	25	26	27
28	29	30				

OCTOBER
S	M	T	W	T	F	S
			1	2	3	4
5	6	7	8	9	10	11
12	13	14	15	16	17	18
19	20	21	22	23	24	25
26	27	28	29	30	31	

NOVEMBER
S	M	T	W	T	F	S
						1
2	3	4	5	6	7	8
9	10	11	12	13	14	15
16	17	18	19	20	21	22
23/30	24	25	26	27	28	29

DECEMBER
S	M	T	W	T	F	S
	1	2	3	4	5	6
7	8	9	10	11	12	13
14	15	16	17	18	19	20
21	22	23	24	25	26	27
28	29	30	31			

March:	Grenoble Jazz Festival, near Lyon (www.jazzgrenoble.com)
March 23:	Easter Sunday
Late April–Mid-Oct:	Festival of Gardens, Chaumont-sur-Loire (www.chaumont-jardin.com)
May:	Versailles Festival (arts), Versailles; Festival Jeanne d'Arc (pageants), Rouen
May 1:	Labor Day and Ascension
May 8:	VE Day
May 11:	Pentecost
May 14–25:	Cannes Film Festival, Cannes (www.festival-cannes.fr)
May 22–25:	Monaco Grand Prix (auto race), Monaco
June 6:	Anniversary of the D-Day Landing, Normandy

June: Marais Festival (arts), Paris

Mid-June: Le Mans Auto Race, Le Mans—near Loire Valley (www.lemans.org)

June 21: Music Festival (Fête de la Musique), concerts and dancing in the streets throughout France (www.fetedelamusique.culture.fr)

July: Nice Jazz Festival (www.nicejazzfest.com); Avignon Festival (theater, dance, music, www.festival-avignon.com); Beaune International Music Festival; Music and Opera Festival, Orange (performed in Roman theater, www.choregies.asso.fr); "Jazz at Juan" International Jazz Festival, Antibes/Juan-les-Pins; Classical Music Festival, Cannes; Jousting matches and medieval festivities, Carcassonne; Nights of Fourvière, Lyon (theater and music in a Roman theater, www.nuits-de-fourviere.org); Colmar International Music Festival, www.festival-colmar.com); Aix-en-Provence International Music and Opera Festival, (www.festival-aix.com)

July 5–27: Tour de France, the national bicycle race (www.letour.fr)

July 14: Bastille Day (fireworks, dancing, and revelry all over France)

Aug: International Fireworks Festival, Cannes

Aug 15: Assumption of Mary

Late Aug: Jazz at La Villette Festival, Paris (www.villette.com)

Sept: Fall Arts Festival (Fête d'Automne), Paris; Wine harvest festivals in many towns

Early Oct: Grape Harvest Festival in Montmartre, Paris (www.commanderiemont.com)

Nov 1: All Saints' Day

Early Nov: Dijon International and Gastronomic Fair, Dijon, Burgundy

Nov 11: Armistice Day

Nov 15–18: Wine Auction and Festival (Les Trois Glorieuses), Beaune

Late Nov–Dec 24: Christmas Markets, Strasbourg

Dec 8: Festival of Lights (celebration of Virgin Mary, candlelit windows), Lyon

Dec 20–Jan 4: Winter holidays

Dec 25: Christmas Day

CONVERSIONS AND CLIMATE

Numbers and Stumblers

- Europeans write a few of their numbers differently than we do. 1 = $\mathcal{1}$, 4 = $\mathcal{4}$, 7 = $\mathcal{7}$.
- In Europe, dates appear as day/month/year, so Christmas is 25/12/08.
- Commas are decimal points and decimals commas. A dollar and a half is 1,50, and there are 5.280 feet in a mile.
- When pointing, use your whole hand, palm down.
- When counting with fingers, start with your thumb. If you hold up your first finger to request one item, you'll probably get two.
- What Americans call the second floor of a building is the first floor in Europe.
- On escalators and moving sidewalks, Europeans keep the left "lane" open for passing. Keep to the right.

Metric Conversions (approximate)

1 foot = 0.3 meter	1 square yard = 0.8 square meter
1 yard = 0.9 meter	1 square mile = 2.6 square kilometers
1 mile = 1.6 kilometers	1 ounce = 28 grams
1 centimeter = 0.4 inch	1 quart = 0.95 liter
1 meter = 39.4 inches	1 kilogram = 2.2 pounds
1 kilometer = 0.62 mile	32°F = 0°C

Climate

First line, average daily high temperature; second line, average daily low; third line, days without rain.

	J	F	M	A	M	J	J	A	S	O	N	D
Paris												
	43°	45°	54°	60°	68°	73°	76°	75°	70°	60°	50°	44°
	34°	34°	39°	43°	49°	55°	58°	58°	53°	46°	40°	36°
	14	14	19	17	19	18	19	18	17	18	15	15
Nice												
	50°	53°	59°	64°	71°	79°	84°	83°	77°	68°	58°	52°
	35°	36°	41°	46°	52°	58°	63°	63°	58°	51°	43°	37°
	23	22	24	23	23	26	29	26	24	23	21	21

Temperature Conversion: Fahrenheit and Celsius

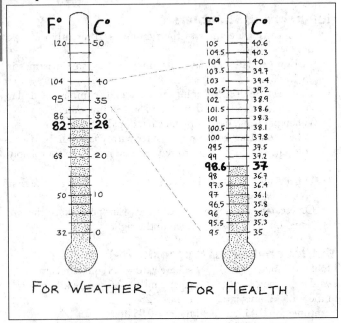

Europe takes its temperature using the Celsius scale, while we opt for Fahrenheit. For a rough conversion from Celsius to Fahrenheit, double the number and add 30. For weather, remember that 28°C is 82°F—perfect. For health, 37°C is just right.

Essential Packing Checklist

Whether you're traveling for five days or five weeks, here's
what you'll need to bring. Remember to pack light to enjoy
the sweet freedom of true mobility. Happy travels!

- ❏ 5 shirts
- ❏ 1 sweater or lightweight fleece jacket
- ❏ 2 pairs pants
- ❏ 1 pair shorts
- ❏ 1 swimsuit (women only—men can use shorts)
- ❏ 5 pairs underwear and socks
- ❏ 1 pair shoes
- ❏ 1 rainproof jacket
- ❏ Tie or scarf
- ❏ Money belt
- ❏ Money—your mix of:
    - ❏ Debit card for ATM withdrawals
    - ❏ Credit card
    - ❏ Hard cash in US dollars
- ❏ Documents (and backup photocopies)
- ❏ Passport
- ❏ Airplane ticket
- ❏ Driver's license
- ❏ Student ID and hostel card
- ❏ Railpass/car-rental voucher
- ❏ Insurance details
- ❏ Daypack
- ❏ Sealable plastic baggies
- ❏ Camera and related gear
- ❏ Empty water bottle
- ❏ Wristwatch and alarm clock
- ❏ Earplugs
- ❏ First-aid kit
- ❏ Medicine (labeled)
- ❏ Extra glasses/contacts and prescriptions
- ❏ Sunscreen and sunglasses
- ❏ Toiletries kit
- ❏ Soap
- ❏ Laundry soap (if liquid and carry-on, limit to 3 oz.)
- ❏ Clothesline
- ❏ Small towel
- ❏ Sewing kit
- ❏ Travel information
- ❏ Necessary map(s)
- ❏ Address list (email and mailing addresses)
- ❏ Postcards and photos from home
- ❏ Notepad and pen
- ❏ Journal

Hotel Reservation

To: _____   _____
                hotel   **email or fax**

From:_____   _____
                name   **email or fax**

Today's date: _____ /_____ /_____
                       day   month   year

Dear Hotel _____ ,
Please make this reservation for me:

Name: _____

Total # of people: _____   # of rooms: _____   # of nights: _____

Arriving: _____ /_____ /_____   My time of arrival (24-hr clock): _____
              day   month   year   (I will telephone if I will be late)

Departing: ____ /____ /____
                day   month   year

Room(s): Single____   Double ___   Twin ____   Triple ____   Quad____

With: Toilet ____   Shower____   Bath ____   Sink only____

Special needs: View___   Quiet___   Cheapest ___   Ground Floor___

Please email or fax confirmation of my reservation, along with the type of room reserved and the price. Please also inform me of your cancellation policy. After I hear from you, I will quickly send my credit-card information as a deposit to hold the room. Thank you.

_____
Name

_____
Address

_____
City   **State**   **Zip Code**   **Country**

Before hoteliers can make your reservation, they want to know the information listed above. You can use this form as the basis for your email, or you can photocopy this page, fill in the information, and send it as a fax (also available online at www.ricksteves.com/reservation).

Pronunciation Guide for Place Names

When using the phonetics: Try to nasalize the n sound (let the sound come through your nose). Note that the "ahn" combination uses the "ah" sound in "father," but the "an" combination uses the "a" sound in "sack." Pronounce the "ī" as the long "i" in "light." If your best attempt at pronunciation meets with a puzzled look, just point to the place name on the list.

In Paris

Arc de Triomphe ark duh tree-oh<u>n</u>f

arrondissement ah-rohn-dees-mohn

Bateaux-Mouches bah-toh moosh

Bon Marché boh<u>n</u> mar-shay

Carnavalet kar-nah-vah-lay

Champ de Mars shah<u>n</u> duh mar

Champs-Elysées shah<u>n</u>-zay-lee-zay

Conciergerie kon-see-ehr-zhuh-ree

Ecole Militaire eh-kohl mee-lee-tehr

Egouts ay-goo

Fauchon foh-shoh<u>n</u>

Galeries Lafayette gah-luh-ree lah-fay-yet

gare gar

Gare d'Austerlitz gar doh-stehr-leets

Gare de l'Est gar duh less

Gare de Lyon gar duh lee-oh<u>n</u>

Gare du Nord gar dew nor

Gare St. Lazare gar sa<u>n</u> lah-zar

Garnier gar-nee-ay

Grand Palais grah<u>n</u> pah-lay

Grande Arche de la Défense grah<u>n</u>d arsh duh lah day-fah<u>n</u>s

Ile de la Cité eel duh lah see-tay

Ile St. Louis eel sa<u>n</u> loo-ee

Jacquemart-André zhahk-mar-ah<u>n</u>-dray

Jardin des Plantes zhar-da<u>n</u> day plah<u>n</u>t

Jeu de Paume juh duh pohm

La Madeleine lah mah-duh-lehn

Le Hameau luh ah-moh

Les Halles lay ahl

Les Invalides lay-za<u>n</u>-vah-leed

Orangerie oh-rah<u>n</u>-zhuh-ree

Louvre loov-ruh

Marais mah-ray

marché aux puces mar-shay oh poos

Marmottan mar-moh-tah<u>n</u>

Métro may-troh

Monge moh<u>n</u>zh

Montmartre moh<u>n</u>-mart

Montparnasse moh<u>n</u>-par-nahs

Moulin Rouge moo-la<u>n</u> roozh

Musée de l'Armée mew-zay duh lar-may

Musée d'Orsay mew-zay dor-say

Notre-Dame noh-truh-dahm

Orsay or-say

palais pah-lay

Palais de Justice pah-lay duh zhew-stees

Palais Garnier pah-lay gar-nee-ay

Palais Royal pah-lay roh-yahl

Parc de la Villette park duh la vee-leht

Parc Monceau park mohn-soh
Père Lachaise pehr lah-shehz
Petit Palais puh-tee pah-lay
Pigalle pee-gahl
Place Dauphine plahs doh-feen
Place de la Bastille plahs duh lah bah-steel
Place de la Concorde plahs duh lah kohn-kord
Place de la République plahs duh lah ray-poo-bleek
Place des Vosges plahs day vohzh
Place du Tertre plahs dew tehr-truh
Place St. André-des-Arts plahs san tahn-dray day-zart
Place Vendôme plahs vahn-dohm
Pompidou pohn-pee-doo
Pont Alexandre III pohn ah-leks-ahn-druh twah
Pont Neuf pohn nuhf
Promenade Plantée proh-mehn-ahd plahn-tay
quai kay
Rive Droite reeve dwaht
Rive Gauche reeve gohsh

Rodin roh-dan
rue rew
Rue Cler rew klehr
Rue Daguerre rew dah-gehr
Rue des Rosiers rew day roz-ee-ay
Rue Montorgueil rew mohn-tor-goy
Rue Mouffetard rew moof-tar
Rue de Rivoli rew duh ree-voh-lee
Sacré-Cœur sah-kray-koor
Sainte-Chapelle sant-shah-pehl
Seine sehn
Sèvres-Babylone seh-vruh-bah-bee-lohn
Sorbonne sor-buhn
St. Germain-des-Prés san zhehr-man-day-pray
St. Julien-le-Pauvre san zhew-lee-ehn-luh-poh-vruh
St. Séverin sahn say-vuh-ran
St. Sulpice sahn sool-pees
Tour Eiffel toor ee-fehl
Trianon tree-ahn-ohn
Trocadéro troh-kah-day-roh
Tuileries twee-lay-ree
Venus de Milo vuh-news duh mee-loh

Outside of Paris

Abbey Notre-Dame de Sénanque ah-bay noh-truh-dahm duh say-nahnk
Abri du Cap Blanc ah-bree dew cah blahn
Aiguille du Midi ah-gwee dew mee-dee
Aïnhoa an-oh-ah
Albi ahl-bee
Alet ah-lay
Alise Ste. Reine ah-leez sant rehn

Aloxe-Corton ah-lohx kor-tohn
Alsace ahl-sahs
Amboise ahm-bwahz
Annecy ahn-see
Antibes ahn-teeb
Aosta (Italy) ay-oh-stah
Apt ahp
Aquitaine ah-kee-tehn
Arles arl
Arromanches ah-roh-mahnsh
Autoire oh-twahr

Auvergne oh-vehrn
Avignon ah-veen-yoh<u>n</u>
Azay-le-Rideau ah-zay luh
  ree-doh
Balazuc bah-lah-zook
Bayeux bī-yuh
Bayonne bī-yuhn
Beaucaire boh-kehr
Beaujolais boh-zhoh-lay
Beaune bohn
Bedoin buh-dwa<u>n</u>
Bennwihr behn-veer
Beynac bay-nak
Biarritz bee-ah-reetz
Blois blah
Bonnieux bohn-yuh
Bordeaux bor-doh
Brancion brahn-see-oh<u>n</u>
Brittany bree-tah-nee
Bruniquel brew-nee-kehl
Caen kah<u>n</u>
Cahors kah-or
Cajarc kah-zhark
Calais kah-lay
Camargue kah-marg
Cambord kah<u>n</u>-bor
Cancale kah<u>n</u>-kahl
Carcassonne kar-kah-suhn
Carennac kah-rehn-ahk
Carsac kar-sahk
Castelnaud kah-stehl-noh
Castelnau-de-Montmiral
  kah-stehl-noh-duh-
  moh<u>n</u>-mee-rahl
Caussade koh-sahd
Cavaillon kah-vī-oh<u>n</u>
Cénac say-nahk
Céret say-ray
Chambord shah<u>n</u>-bor
Chamonix shah-moh-nee
Champagne shah<u>n</u>-pahn-
  yuh
Chapaize shah-pehz
Chartres shart
Château de Chatonnière
  shah-toh duh shah-
  tuhn-yehr
Château de Rivau shah-toh

duh ree-voh
**Château du Haut-
  Kœnigsbourg**
  shah-toh dew oh-koh-
  neegs-boorg
Châteauneuf-du-Pape
  shah-toh-nuhf-dew-
  pahp
Châteauneuf-en-Auxois
  shah-toh-nuhf-eh<u>n</u>-
  ohx-wah
Chaumont-sur-Loire shoh-
  moh<u>n</u>-sewr-lwahr
Chenonceau shuh-noh<u>n</u>-
  soh
Chenonceaux shuh-noh<u>n</u>-
  soh
Cherbourg shehr-boor
Cheverny shuh-vehr-nee
Chinon shee-noh<u>n</u>
Cluny klew-nee
Colleville kohl-veel
Collioure kohl-yoor
Collonges-la-Rouge koh-
  lohnzh-lah-roozh
Colmar kohl-mar
Cordes-sur-Ciel kord-sewr-
  see-yehl
Côte d'Azur koht dah-zewr
Cougnac koon-yahk
Courseulles-sur-Mer koor-
  suhl-sewr-mehr
Coustellet koo-stuh-lay
Digne deen-yuh
Dijon dee-zhoh<u>n</u>
Dinan dee-nah<u>n</u>
Dinard dee-nar
Domme dohm
Dordogne dor-dohn-yuh
Eguisheim eh-geh-shīm
Entrevaux ah<u>n</u>-truh-voh
Epernay ay-pehr-nay
Espelette eh-speh-leht
Eze-Bord-de-Mer ehz-bor-
  duh-mehr
Eze-le-Village ehz-luh-vee-
  lahzh
Faucon foh-koh<u>n</u>

Flavigny-sur-Ozerain
flah-veen-yee-sewr-oh-
zuh-ra<u>n</u>

Font-de-Gaume fohn-duh-
gohm

Fontenay foh<u>n</u>-tuh-nay

Fontevraud foh<u>n</u>-tuh-vroh

Fontvieille foh<u>n</u>-vee-yeh-
ee

Fougères foo-zher

Fougères-sur-Bièvre foo-
zher-sewr-bee-ehv

Gaillac gī-yahk

Gigondas zhee-goh<u>n</u>-dahs

Giverny zhee-vehr-nee

Gordes gord

Gorges de l'Ardèche gorzh
duh lar-dehsh

Grenoble gruh-noh-bluh

Grouin groo-a<u>n</u>

Guédelon gway-duh-loh<u>n</u>

Hautes Corbières oht
kor-bee-yehr

Hendaye ehn-dī

Honfleur oh<u>n</u>-flur

Huisnes-sur-Mer ween-
sewr-mehr

Hunawihr uhn-ah-veer

Ile Besnard eel bay-nar

Isle-sur-la-Sorgue eel-
sewr-lah-sorg

Juan-les-Pins zhwa<u>n</u>-lay-
pa<u>n</u>

Kaysersberg kī-zehrs-behrg

Kientzheim keentz-īm

La Charente lah shah-rah<u>n</u>t

La Rhune lah rewn

La Rochepot lah rohsh-poh

La Roque St. Christophe
lah rohk sa<u>n</u> kree-stohf

La Roque-Gageac lah rohk-
gah-zhahk

La Trophée des Alpes lah
troh-fay dayz ahlp

La Turbie lah tewr-bee

Lacoste lah-kohst

Langeais lah<u>n</u>-zhay

Languedoc long-dohk

Lascaux lah-skoh

Lastours lahs-toor

Le Bugue luh bewg

Le Crestet luh kruh-stay

Le Havre luh hah-vruh

Le Ruquet luh rew-kay

Lémeré lay-muh-ray

Les Baux lay boh

Les Eyzies-de-Tayac lay
zay-zee-duh-tī-yahk

Les Praz lay prah

Les Vosges lay vohzh

Limoges lee-mohzh

Loches lohsh

Loire lwahr

Longues-sur-Mer long-
sewr-mehr

Loubressac loo-bruh-sahk

Lourmarin loo-mah-ra<u>n</u>

Luberon lew-beh-roh<u>n</u>

Lyon lee-oh<u>n</u>

Malaucène mah-loh-sehn

Marne-la-Vallée-Chessy
marn-lah-vah-lay-shuh-
see

Marseille mar-say

Martel mar-tehl

Mausanne moh-sahn

Ménerbes may-nehrb

Millau mee-yoh

Minerve mee-nerv

Mirabel mee-rah-behl

Modreuc mohd-rewk

Mont Blanc moh<u>n</u> blah<u>n</u>

Mont St. Michel moh<u>n</u> sa<u>n</u>
mee-shehl

Mont Ventoux moh<u>n</u>
vehn-too

Montenvers moh<u>n</u>-tuh-
vehr

Montfort moh<u>n</u>-for

Montignac moh<u>n</u>-teen-
yahk

Mortemart mort-mar

Munster mewn-stehr

Nantes nah<u>n</u>t

Nice nees
Normandy nor-mahn-dee
Nyons nee-yoh<u>ns</u>
Oradour-sur-Glane oh-rah-door-sewr-glahn
Orange oh-rah<u>nz</u>h
Padirac pah-dee-rahk
Paris pah-ree
Pech Merle pehsh mehrl
Peyrepertuse pay-ruh-per-tewz
Pointe du Hoc pwa<u>nt</u> dew ohk
Pont du Gard poh<u>n</u> dew gahr
Pontorson poh<u>n</u>-tor-soh<u>n</u>
Provence proh-vah<u>ns</u>
Puycelci pew-suhl-cee
Puyméras pwee-may-rahs
Queribus kehr-ee-bews
Reims ra<u>ns</u> (rhymes with France)
Remoulins ruh-moo-la<u>n</u>
Rennes rehn
Ribeauvillé ree-boh-vee-yay
Riquewihr reek-veer
Rocamadour roh-kah-mah-door
Rouen roo-ah<u>n</u>
Rouffignac roo-feen-yahk
Roussillon roo-see-yoh<u>n</u>
Route du Vin root dew va<u>n</u>
Sablet sah-blay
Sare sahr
Sarlat sar-lah
Savigny-les-Beaune sah-veen-yee-lay-bohn
Savoie sah-vwah
Séguret say-goo-ray
Semur-en-Auxois suh-moor-eh<u>n</u>-ohx-wah
Sigolsheim see-gohl-shīm
Souillac soo-ee-yahk
St. Suliac sa<u>n</u> soo-lee-ahk
St. Cirq Lapopie sa<u>n</u> seerk lah-poh-pee

St. Cyprien sa<u>n</u> seep-ree-eh<u>n</u>
St. Emilion sa<u>n</u> tay-meel-yoh<u>n</u>
St. Geniès sa<u>n</u> zhuh-nyehs
St. Jean-de-Luz sa<u>n</u> zhahn-duh-looz
St. Jean-Pied-de-Port sa<u>n</u> zhahn-pee-yay-duh-por
St. Malo sa<u>n</u> mah-loh
St. Marcellin-lès-Vaison sa<u>n</u> mar-suh-la<u>n</u>-lay-vay-zoh<u>n</u>
St. Rémy sa<u>n</u> ray-mee
St. Romain-en-Viennois sa<u>n</u> roh-ma<u>n</u>-eh<u>n</u>-vee-eh<u>n</u>-nwah
St-Paul-de-Vence sa<u>n</u>-pohl-duh-vah<u>ns</u>
Ste. Mère Eglise sa<u>nt</u> mehr ay-gleez
Stes-Maries-de-la-Mer sa<u>nt</u>-mah-ree-duh-lah-mehr
Strasbourg strahs-boorg
Suzette soo-zeht
Taizé teh-zay
Tarascon tah-rah-skoh<u>n</u>
Tours toor
Turckheim tewrk-hīm
Ussé oo-say
Uzès oo-zehs
Vacqueyras vah-kee-rahs
Vaison la Romaine vay-zoh<u>n</u> lah roh-mehn
Valançay vah-lah<u>n</u>-say
Valréas vahl-ray-ahs
Vence vah<u>ns</u>
Verdun vehr-duhn
Versailles vehr-sī
Veynes vay-nuh
Vézelay vay-zuh-lay
Vierville-sur-Mer vee-yehr-veel-sewr-mehr
Villandry vee-lahn-dry
Villefranche-de-Rouergue veel-frah<u>n</u>sh-duh-roo-ehrg

Villefranche-sur-Mer veel-frah<u>n</u>sh-sewr-mehr
Villeneuve-lès-Avignon veel-nuhv-lay-zah-veeh-yoh<u>n</u>

Vitrac vee-trahk
Vouvray voo-vray
Villedieu vee-luh-dyuh

French Survival Phrases

When using the phonetics, try to nasalize the <u>n</u> sound.

Good day.	**Bonjour.**	boh<u>n</u>-zhoor
Mrs. / Mr.	**Madame / Monsieur**	mah-dahm / muhs-yur
Do you speak English?	**Parlez-vous anglais?**	par-lay-voo ah<u>n</u>-glay
Yes. / No.	**Oui. / Non.**	wee / noh<u>n</u>
I understand.	**Je comprends.**	zhuh koh<u>n</u>-prah<u>n</u>
I don't understand.	**Je ne comprends pas.**	zhuh nuh koh<u>n</u>-prah<u>n</u> pah
Please.	**S'il vous plaît.**	see voo play
Thank you.	**Merci.**	mehr-see
I'm sorry.	**Désolé.**	day-zoh-lay
Excuse me.	**Pardon.**	par-doh<u>n</u>
(No) problem.	**(Pas de) problème.**	(pah duh) proh-blehm
It's good.	**C'est bon.**	say boh<u>n</u>
Goodbye.	**Au revoir.**	oh vwahr
one / two	**un / deux**	uh<u>n</u> / duh
three / four	**trois / quatre**	twah / kah-truh
five / six	**cinq / six**	sa<u>n</u>k / sees
seven / eight	**sept / huit**	seht / weet
nine / ten	**neuf / dix**	nuhf / dees
How much is it?	**Combien?**	koh<u>n</u>-bee-a<u>n</u>
Write it?	**Ecrivez?**	ay-kree-vay
Is it free?	**C'est gratuit?**	say grah-twee
Included?	**Inclus?**	a<u>n</u>-klew
Where can I buy / find...?	**Où puis-je acheter / trouver...?**	oo pwee-zhuh ah-shuh-tay / troo-vay
I'd like / We'd like...	**Je voudrais / Nous voudrions...**	zhuh voo-dray / noo voo-dree-oh<u>n</u>
...a room.	**...une chambre.**	ewn shah<u>n</u>-bruh
...a ticket to ___.	**...un billet pour ___.**	uh<u>n</u> bee-yay poor
Is it possible?	**C'est possible?**	say poh-see-bluh
Where is...?	**Où est...?**	oo ay
...the train station	**...la gare**	lah gar
...the bus station	**...la gare routière**	lah gar root-yehr
...tourist information	**...l'office du tourisme**	loh-fees dew too-reez-muh
Where are the toilets?	**Où sont les toilettes?**	oo soh<u>n</u> lay twah-leht
men	**hommes**	ohm
women	**dames**	dahm
left / right	**à gauche / à droite**	ah gohsh / ah dwaht
straight	**tout droit**	too dwah
When does this open / close?	**Ça ouvre / ferme à quelle heure?**	sah oo-vruh / fehrm ah kehl ur
At what time?	**À quelle heure?**	ah kehl ur
Just a moment.	**Un moment.**	uh<u>n</u> moh-mah<u>n</u>
now / soon / later	**maintenant / bientôt / plus tard**	ma<u>n</u>-tuh-nah<u>n</u> / bee-a<u>n</u>-toh / plew tar
today / tomorrow	**aujourd'hui / demain**	oh-zhoor-dwee / duh-ma<u>n</u>

In the Restaurant

I'd like / We'd like...	**Je voudrais / Nous voudrions...**	zhuh voo-dray / noo voo-dree-ohn
...to reserve...	**...réserver...**	ray-zehr-vay
...a table for one / two.	**...une table pour un / deux.**	ewn tah-bluh poor uhn / duh
Non-smoking.	**Non fumeur.**	nohn few-mur
Is this seat free?	**C'est libre?**	say lee-bruh
The menu (in English), please.	**La carte (en anglais), s'il vous plaît.**	lah kart (ahn ahn-glay) see voo play
service (not) included	**service (non) compris**	sehr-vees (nohn) kohn-pree
to go	**à emporter**	ah ahn-por-tay
with / without	**avec / sans**	ah-vehk / sahn
and / or	**et / ou**	ay / oo
special of the day	**plat du jour**	plah dew zhoor
specialty of the house	**spécialité de la maison**	spay-see-ah-lee-tay duh lah may-zohn
appetizers	**hors-d'oeuvre**	or-duh-vruh
first course (soup, salad)	**entrée**	ahn-tray
main course (meat, fish)	**plat principal**	plah pran-see-pahl
bread	**pain**	pan
cheese	**fromage**	froh-mahzh
sandwich	**sandwich**	sahnd-weech
soup	**soupe**	soop
salad	**salade**	sah-lahd
meat	**viande**	vee-ahnd
chicken	**poulet**	poo-lay
fish	**poisson**	pwah-sohn
seafood	**fruits de mer**	frwee duh mehr
fruit	**fruit**	frwee
vegetables	**légumes**	lay-gewm
dessert	**dessert**	duh-sehr
mineral water	**eau minérale**	oh mee-nay-rahl
tap water	**l'eau du robinet**	loh dew roh-bee-nay
milk	**lait**	lay
(orange) juice	**jus (d'orange)**	zhew (doh-rahnzh)
coffee	**café**	kah-fay
tea	**thé**	tay
wine	**vin**	van
red / white	**rouge / blanc**	roozh / blahn
glass / bottle	**verre / bouteille**	vehr / boo-teh-ee
beer	**bière**	bee-ehr
Cheers!	**Santé!**	sahn-tay
More. / Another.	**Plus. / Un autre.**	plew / uhn oh-truh
The same.	**La même chose.**	lah mehm shohz
The bill, please.	**L'addition, s'il vous plaît.**	lah-dee-see-ohn see voo play
tip	**pourboire**	poor-bwar
Delicious!	**Délicieux!**	day-lee-see-uh

For more user-friendly French phrases, check out *Rick Steves' French Phrase Book and Dictionary* or *Rick Steves' French, Italian & German Phrase Book*.

INDEX

Travel smart...carry on!

The latest generation of Rick Steves' carry-on travel bags is easily the best—benefiting from two decades of on-the-road attention to what really matters: maximum quality and strength; practical, flexible features; and no unnecessary frills. You won't find a better value anywhere!

Rick Steves' Convertible Carry-On $99.⁹⁵

Our roomy, versatile 9" x 21" x 14" carry-on has a large 2600 cubic-inch main compartment, plus four outside pockets (small, medium and huge) that are perfect for often-used items. Wish you had even more room to bring home souvenirs? Pull open the full-perimeter expando-zipper and its capacity jumps from 2600 to 3000 cubic inches. When you want to use it as a suitcase or check it as luggage (required when "expanded"), the straps and belt hide away in a zippered compartment in the back. It weighs just 3 lbs.

Rick Steves' Classic Back Door Bag $79.⁹⁵

This ultra-light (1½ lbs.) version of our Convertible Carry-On features the same 9" x 21" x 14" dimensions and hideaway straps, but does not include a waistbelt or expandability. This is the bag that Rick lives out of for three months a year!

Rick Steves' 21" Roll-Aboard $139.⁹⁵

Our sturdy 21" Roll-Aboard is rucksack-soft in front, but the rest is lined with a hard ABS-lexan shell to give maximum protection to your belongings. We've spared no expense on moving parts, splurging on an extra-long button-release handle and big, tough inline skate wheels for easy rolling on rough surfaces. It features the same 9" x 21" x 14" carry-on dimensions, pocket configuration and expandability as our Convertible Carry-On—and at 7 lbs. it's the lightest roll-aboard in its class.

Prices and features are subject to change.

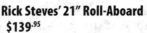

FREE-SPIRITED TOURS FROM

Rick Steves

Small Groups
Great Guides
No Grumps

Best of Europe ■ **Family Europe**
Italy ■ **Village Italy** ■ **South Italy**
Sicily ■ **France** ■ **Eastern Europe**
Adriatic ■ **Prague** ■ **Scotland**
Britain ■ **Ireland** ■ **Scandinavia**
Germany-Austria-Switzerland ■ **Spain** ■ **Turkey** ■ **Greece**
London-Paris ■ **Paris** ■ **Rome** ■ **Venice-Florence-Rome…and more!**

Looking for a one, two, or three-week tour that's run in the Rick Steves style?
Check out Rick Steves' educational, experiential tours of Europe.

Rick's tours are an excellent value compared to "mainstream" tours. Here's a taste
of what you'll get…

- **Small groups:** With just 24-28 travelers, you'll go where typical groups of
  40-50 can only dream.

- **Big buses:** You'll travel in a full-size 40-50 seat bus, with plenty of empty
  seats for you to spread out and be comfortable.

- **Great guides:** Our guides are hand-picked by Rick Steves for their wealth of
  knowledge and giddy enthusiasm for Europe.

- **No tips or kickbacks:** To keep your guide and driver 100% focused on giving
  you the best travel experience, we pay them well—and prohibit them from
  accepting tips and merchant kickbacks.

- **All sightseeing:** Your tour price includes all group sightseeing, with no
  hidden extra charges.

- **Central hotels:** You'll stay in Rick's favorite small, characteristic, locally-run
  hotels in the center of each city, within walking distance of the sights you
  came to see.

- **Visit www.ricksteves.com:** You'll find all our latest itineraries, dates and
  prices, be able to reserve online, and request a free copy of our Rick Steves Tour
  Experience DVD!

Rick Steves' Europe Through the Back Door, Inc.
130 Fourth Avenue North, PO Box 2009, Edmonds, WA 98020 USA
Phone: (425) 771-8303 ■ Fax: (425) 771-0833 ■ www.ricksteves.com

Start your trip at
www.ricksteves.com

Rick Steves' website is packed with over 3,000 pages of timely travel information. It's also your gateway to getting FREE monthly travel news from Rick—and more!

Free Monthly Travel News

Fresh articles on Europe's most interesting destinations and happenings. Rick will even send you an email every month (often direct from Europe) with his latest discoveries!

Timely Travel Tips

Rick Steves' best money-and-stress-saving tips on trip planning, packing, transportation, hotels, health, safety, finances, hurdling the language barrier…and more.

Travelers' Graffiti Wall

Candid advice and opinions from thousands of travelers on everything listed above, plus whatever topics are hot at the moment (discount flights, politics, nude beaches, scams…you name it).

Rick's Guide to Eurail Passes

The clearest, most comprehensive guide to the confusing array of railpass options out there, and how to choo-choose the railpass that best fits your itinerary and budget.

Great Gear at Our Travel Store

In the past year alone, more than 50,000 travelers have enjoyed great online deals on Rick's guidebooks, maps, DVDs—and his custom-designed carry-on bags, day packs, and light-packing accessories.

Rick Steves Tours

This year, 12,000 lucky travelers will explore Europe on a Rick Steves tour. Learn about our 28 different one- to three-week itineraries, read uncensored feedback from our tour alums, and get our free Tour Experience DVD.

Rick on TV, Radio and Podcasts

Read the scripts from the popular Rick Steves' Europe TV series, and listen to or download your choice of over 100 hours of our Travel with Rick Steves radio show.

Respect for Your Privacy

Whether you buy something from us or subscribe to Rick's monthly Travel News emails, we'll never share your name or email address with anyone else. You won't be spammed!

Have fun raising your Travel I.Q. at
www.ricksteves.com

Rick Steves

More *Savvy.* More *Surprising.* More *Fun.*

COUNTRY GUIDES

Croatia & Slovenia
England
France
Germany & Austria
Great Britain
Ireland
Italy
Portugal
Scandinavia
Spain
Switzerland

CITY GUIDES

Amsterdam, Bruges & Brussels
Florence & Tuscany
Istanbul
London
Paris
Prague & The Czech Republic
Provence & The French Riviera
Rome
Venice

BEST OF GUIDES

Best of Eastern Europe
Best of Europe

As the #1 authority on European travel, Rick gives you inside information on what to visit, where to stay, and how to get there—economically and hassle-free.

www.ricksteves.com

PHRASE BOOKS & DICTIONARIES

French
French, Italian & German
German
Italian
Portuguese
Spanish

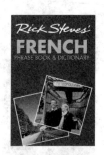

MORE EUROPE FROM RICK STEVES

Europe 101
Europe Through the Back Door
Postcards from Europe

RICK STEVES' EUROPE DVDs

All 70 Shows 2000–2007
Britain
Eastern Europe
France & Benelux
Germany, The Swiss Alps & Travel Skills
Ireland
Italy
Spain & Portugal

PLANNING MAPS

Britain & Ireland
Europe
France
Germany, Austria & Switzerland
Italy
Spain & Portugal

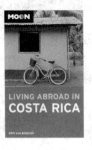

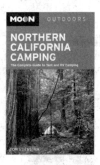
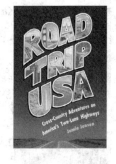

CREDITS

Researchers

In addition to Rick Steves and Steve Smith, the following researchers helped update this book:

Mary Bouron

Mary caught the travel bug as a child living in London, and later, as an exchange student in France. Fluent in French, Mary works in Rick Steves' tour department, lives in Seattle, and enjoys arguing with her French husband about how to best roast a chicken.

Karoline Vass

Raised in Germany by a Hungarian father and American mother whose only common language was French, Karoline has an affinity for all things *français*. When not researching guidebooks and leading tours for Rick Steves, Karoline can be seen in Paris pedaling to orchestra rehearsals with her viola on her back.

Daniela Williams

Born and educated in Munich, Daniela majored in Art History. She now makes her home in Avignon with her American husband. When not leading tours for Rick Steves, Daniela enjoys the Provençal life: bike-touring, playing basketball, and relaxing with family, friends, and a good glass of wine.

Robert Wright

Robert was raised in Memphis, but now lives a bit farther south—Buenos Aires, Argentina. A long-time Europhile, Robert spends his free time searching for the best *ttoro* (seafood stew) and hard apple cider in the French Basque Country.

Contributor

Gene Openshaw
Gene is the co-author of seven Rick Steves books. For this book, he wrote material on Europe's art, history, and contemporary culture. When not traveling, Gene enjoys composing music, recovering from his 1973 trip to Europe with Rick, and living everyday life with his wife and daughter.

IMAGES

Location	Photographer
Title Page: Villefranche-sur-Mer	Steve Smith
Full-Page Color: Burgundy	Steve Smith
Paris: Louvre	Rick Steves
Near Paris: Versailles	Rick Steves
Normandy: Mont St. Michel	Rick Steves
Brittany: Dinan	Dominic Bonuccelli
The Loire: Château d'Amboise	Rick Steves
Dordogne: Dordogne River Valley	David C. Hoerlein
Basque Country: St. Jean-de-Luz	Cameron Hewitt
Languedoc: Carcassonne	Dominic Bonuccelli
Provence: Pont du Gard Aqueduct	Rick Steves
The French Riviera: Cannes	Steve Smith
The French Alps: Chamonix Valley	David C. Hoerlein
Burgundy: Château de la Rochepot	Steve Smith
Lyon and the Rhône Valley: Saône River and Bonaparte Bridge	Steve Smith
Alsace and Northern France: Eguisheim	Rick Steves

Rick Steves' Guidebook Series

Country Guides

Rick Steves' Best of Europe
Rick Steves' Croatia & Slovenia
Rick Steves' Eastern Europe
Rick Steves' England
Rick Steves' France
Rick Steves' Germany & Austria
Rick Steves' Great Britain
Rick Steves' Ireland
Rick Steves' Italy
Rick Steves' Portugal
Rick Steves' Scandinavia
Rick Steves' Spain
Rick Steves' Switzerland

City and Regional Guides

Rick Steves' Amsterdam, Bruges & Brussels
Rick Steves' Florence & Tuscany
Rick Steves' Istanbul
Rick Steves' London
Rick Steves' Paris
Rick Steves' Prague & the Czech Republic
Rick Steves' Provence & the French Riviera
Rick Steves' Rome
Rick Steves' Venice

Rick Steves' Phrase Books

French
German
Italian
Spanish
Portuguese
French/Italian/German

Other Books

Rick Steves' Europe Through the Back Door
Rick Steves' Europe 101: History and Art for the Traveler
Rick Steves' Postcards from Europe
Rick Steves' European Christmas

(Avalon Travel Publishing)

Avalon Travel Publishing
a member of Perseus Books Group
1700 Fourth Street
Berkeley, CA 94710

Printed in the USA by Worzalla. Second printing February 2008.

Thanks to Steve's wife, Karen Lewis Smith, for her assistance covering French cuisine; and
to Steve's children, Travis and Maria, for help with children's activities.

For the latest on Rick's lectures, guidebooks, tours, public radio show, and public television
series, contact Europe Through the Back Door, Box 2009, Edmonds, WA 98020, 425/771-
8303, fax 425/771-0833, rick@ricksteves.com, www.ricksteves.com.

ISBN (10) 1-56691-855-3
ISBN (13) 978-1-56691-855-8
ISSN 1084-4406

Europe Through the Back Door Managing Editor: Risa Laib
ETBD Editors: Jennifer Madison Davis, Cathy McDonald, Gretchen Strauch, Jennifer
   Hauseman (Senior Editor)
Avalon Travel Publishing Senior Editor and Series Manager: Madhu Prasher
Avalon Travel Publishing Project Editor: Kelly Lydick
Research Assistance: Mary Bouron, Karoline Vass, Daniela Williams, Robert Wright
Copy Editor: Matthew Reed Baker
Proofreader: Rebecca Freed
Indexer: Stephen Callahan
Production & Typesetting: McGuire Barber Design
Cover Design: Kari Gim, Laura Mazer
Cover Art Manager: Laura VanDeventer
Maps & Graphics: David C. Hoerlein, Laura VanDeventer, Lauren Mills, Barb Geisler,
   Mike Morgenfeld
Front cover photos: Front image: View of Eiffel Tower from place du Trocadéro © Carol
   Ries; Back image: Carcassonne in the Languedoc © Dominic Bonuccelli
Front matter color photos: p. i, Villefranche-sur-Mer © Steve Smith; p. viii, Burgundy ©
   Steve Smith